American Comparative Law

American Comparative Law

A History

DAVID S. CLARK

OXFORD
UNIVERSITY PRESS

Oxford University Press is a department of the University of Oxford. It furthers the University's objective of excellence in research, scholarship, and education by publishing worldwide. Oxford is a registered trade mark of Oxford University Press in the UK and certain other countries.

Published in the United States of America by Oxford University Press
198 Madison Avenue, New York, NY 10016, United States of America.

© Oxford University Press 2022

All rights reserved. No part of this publication may be reproduced, stored in a retrieval system, or transmitted, in any form or by any means, without the prior permission in writing of Oxford University Press, or as expressly permitted by law, by license, or under terms agreed with the appropriate reproduction rights organization. Inquiries concerning reproduction outside the scope of the above should be sent to the Rights Department, Oxford University Press, at the address above.

You must not circulate this work in any other form
and you must impose this same condition on any acquirer.

Library of Congress Cataloging-in-Publication Data
Names: Clark, David Scott, 1944– author.
Title: American comparative law : a history / David S. Clark.
Description: New York, NY : Oxford University Press, [2022] |
Includes index.
Identifiers: LCCN 2022005984 (print) | LCCN 2022005985 (ebook) |
ISBN 9780195369922 (hardback) | ISBN 9780197653500 (epub) |
ISBN 9780199708550 (updf) | ISBN 9780197653517 (online)
Subjects: LCSH: Law—United States—Foreign influences. | Comparative law—Study and teaching—United States.
Classification: LCC KF358 .C43 2021 (print) | LCC KF358 (ebook) |
DDC 349.73—dc23/eng/20220606
LC record available at https://lccn.loc.gov/2022005984
LC ebook record available at https://lccn.loc.gov/2022005985

DOI: 10.1093/oso/9780195369922.001.0001

1 3 5 7 9 8 6 4 2

Printed by Integrated Books International, United States of America

Note to Readers

This publication is designed to provide accurate and authoritative information in regard to the subject matter covered. It is based upon sources believed to be accurate and reliable and is intended to be current as of the time it was written. It is sold with the understanding that the publisher is not engaged in rendering legal, accounting, or other professional services. If legal advice or other expert assistance is required, the services of a competent professional person should be sought. Also, to confirm that the information has not been affected or changed by recent developments, traditional legal research techniques should be used, including checking primary sources where appropriate.

(Based on the Declaration of Principles jointly adopted by a Committee of the American Bar Association and a Committee of Publishers and Associations.)

You may order this or any other Oxford University Press publication
by visiting the Oxford University Press website at www.oup.com.

To Marilee and Lee, Susanna, Eliina, Liisa, and David;
For the future—to Sienna, Ileana, Levi, Anika, Vida, Cai, and Piers.

Contents

Preface	xiii
Abbreviations	xvii

1. Legal History and Comparative Law	1
A. Introduction	1
1. Historical Comparative Law and Comparative Legal History	1
2. Methodological Issues	3
3. Scope of the Book	7
B. Historiography: 1771 to 1900	12
1. Establishing an American System of Legal Rules	12
2. The Codification Debate and Historical Jurisprudence	16
C. Historiography: 1900 to 1950	22
1. James Carter	23
2. Roscoe Pound	24
3. Max Radin	27
4. The Dominance of Intellectual Legal History	28
D. Historiography: 1950 to 2000	29
1. Perry Miller, Intellectual Legal History, and Its Decline	29
2. Willard Hurst and the Emergence of Social Legal History	31
3. Lawrence Friedman and a Comprehensive American Social History of Law	33
4. The Rise of American Legal History as a Distinct Discipline	36
E. Historiography: The Twenty-First Century	40
1. Eclecticism, Culture, and Thick Description: The Return of Intellectual Legal History	40
2. Legal History Meets Comparative Law	41
2. British Colonization in North America	45
A. Prelude: Comparative Law in England	45
1. Legal Education and Literature	45
2. Roman and Canon Law Influence in England	47
B. Roman and Civil Law in Colonial British America	49
1. Natural Law, the Law of Nations, and Moral Philosophy	49
2. Self-Study and Legal Apprenticeship	51
C. Social Factors Affecting Law	53
D. Lawyers and Courts	57
E. Religious and Cultural Variation	60
1. Religious Establishment and Attempts at Tolerance	60

	2.	Regional and Intraregional Religious Differences	63
	3.	The Anglicization Thesis	64
	4.	Eighteenth-Century Immigrants: The Germans and Scots	66
	5.	Regionalism and Legal Diversity	71
F.	John Adams: An American Comparatist		72
	1.	Study of the Civil Law	72
	2.	Law and Politics in Writing and Practice	74
	3.	The Boston Declaration of 1772	78
	4.	The *Novanglus* Letters of 1775	79
	5.	The Advantage of a Comparative Perspective	81

3. Legal Foundation for the New Republic: 1776 to 1791 — 85
  A. Inventing a New Nation: A Golden Age of Comparative Law — 85
  B. Learning Foreign Law and Political Theory: George Wythe — 88
  C. Thomas Jefferson, Natural Law, and Independence — 94
  D. A Republican Form of Government — 101
    1. The Roman Republic and Early Principate — 101
    2. Republican Images — 103
    3. The Debate about Republics and Democracies — 104
    4. Baron de Montesquieu — 105
    5. Diverse Influences — 107
  E. The Sacred Fire of Liberty — 109
  F. John Adams — 111
  G. James Wilson — 115
  H. *Publius*: The Federalist — 121
    1. James Madison — 122
    2. Alexander Hamilton — 129
    3. John Jay — 131
  I. The Bill of Rights — 133
  J. Classical Legal Models — 143

4. The Formative Era: 1791–1865 — 145
  A. The Shift from Public to Private Law — 145
  B. Territorial Expansion: Jefferson and the Louisiana Purchase — 147
  C. Resistance to English Law and the Beginning of American Legal Science — 156
  D. Legal Education and Law Books — 161
    1. Training American Lawyers — 161
    2. William Blackstone and the American Institutionalist Literature: St. George Tucker and James Kent — 166
    3. American Legal Treatises: Joseph Story — 171
    4. David Hoffman's Plan for Legal Education — 174
  E. Other Legal Literature Depicting Roman and Civil Law — 176
    1. Periodicals with Legal Content — 176
    2. Other American Translations — 183
    3. Law Libraries — 186

F.	Other Legal Comparatists	187
	1. Boston: Luther Cushing	187
	2. New Orleans: Samuel Livermore and Gustavus Schmidt	189
	3. Charleston and Columbia: Francis Lieber, Hugh Legaré, and James Walker	190
G.	Penal Reform: Law and Punishment	197
H.	Codification: Edward Livingston to David Dudley Field	204
I.	Slavery	214

5. Historical Jurisprudence and Learned Law: 1865–1900 — 223
    A. Science and Romanticism: German Historical Jurisprudence — 223
    B. German Legal Science — 227
    C. Making Legal Education Scientific: Harvard Law School — 228
        1. Americans Pursue Post-Secondary Education in Germany — 229
        2. Harvard Law School and the Development of Graduate Education: Charles Eliot and Christopher Langdell — 231
        3. The American Bar Association — 234
        4. Other Law Schools Adopt the Harvard Model — 238
        5. Refining Legal Science: Emulating Germany's Law Curriculum — 240
        6. Law Libraries — 244
    D. Historical Jurisprudence against Codification: James Carter and David Dudley Field — 245
    E. Other Uses of Roman and Civil Law — 251
        1. Teaching Roman Law: A Substitute for Academic Comparative Law — 251
        2. Law Journal Literature on Comparative Law — 254
        3. William Hammond — 256
        4. William Wirt Howe — 258
        5. Sociological Jurisprudence in Germany — 259
        6. Oliver Wendell Holmes, Jr. — 260
        7. Christopher G. Tiedeman — 263
    F. Comparative Law Emerges as a Discipline — 264
        1. Germany and France — 264
        2. Social Science Associations and Comparative Law — 265
        3. The 1900 International Congress of Comparative Law — 269

6. The Modern Development: 1900–1945 — 273
    A. Transition into a New Century — 273
        1. Woodrow Wilson — 274
        2. Early Attempts to Transplant American Law Abroad — 277
        3. A Timeline through Two World Wars — 284
    B. The 1904 Universal Congress of Lawyers and Jurists — 287
    C. The Comparative Law Bureau — 290
    D. The Persistence of Roman Law Interest — 294

- E. American Comparatists Look Abroad and Institutionalize at Home ... 297
  - 1. The International Academy of Comparative Law ... 298
  - 2. The American Foreign Law Association ... 302
  - 3. Social Science and the Johns Hopkins Institute of Law ... 303
  - 4. The American Law Institute and Unification of Law ... 306
  - 5. Tulane University College of Law ... 310
  - 6. The Law Library of Congress and Other Law Libraries ... 312
- F. Roscoe Pound and John Wigmore ... 320
  - 1. Roscoe Pound ... 321
  - 2. John Wigmore ... 323
- G. Two Sides of German-American Relations: The Nazis, Anti-Semitism, and Natural Law ... 326
  - 1. The Nazis and Anti-Semitism at American Universities ... 326
  - 2. Émigré Legal Scholars and U.S. Law Schools ... 331
  - 3. Natural Law ... 333
- H. The 1930s and 1940s: Achievement during a Difficult Period ... 339
  - 1. The ABA Section of International and Comparative Law ... 339
  - 2. The 1932 and 1937 International Congress of Comparative Law ... 340
  - 3. Domestic American Comparative Law Activities ... 343

7. Postwar Legal Transplants and Growth of the Academic Discipline: 1945–1990 ... 349
  - A. Government Supervision of American Legal Exports ... 349
    - 1. The Early Postwar Period ... 349
    - 2. New Constitutions in Germany, Japan, and Korea ... 354
    - 3. Other U.S. Government-Sponsored Legal Reforms in Germany, Japan, and Korea ... 364
    - 4. Federalism and Antitrust Reform for Western Europe ... 373
  - B. Re-establishing Comparative Law as an Academic Discipline ... 379
    - 1. The ABA Section of International and Comparative Law ... 380
    - 2. UNESCO, the AFLA, and the AALS ... 382
  - C. The American Association for the Comparative Study of Law ... 384
    - 1. Structure and Membership of the Organization ... 384
    - 2. The American Journal of Comparative Law ... 392
    - 3. Participation in International Congresses ... 396
  - D. Developments in American Law Schools ... 402
    - 1. Comparative Law Courses and Institutes ... 402
    - 2. General Comparative Law Coursebooks ... 404
    - 3. Specialized Comparative Law Coursebooks ... 408
    - 4. Comparative Law Journals and Projects ... 415
    - 5. Degree Programs for Foreign Students ... 417

	E. The Role of American Governmental and Nongovernmental Organizations in Legal Transplants	418
	1. Origins and Progression up to 1960	418
	2. The 1960s: Decade of Development	421
	3. Assessment and the Emergence of Human Rights Law	425
	F. Themes in Comparative Law Research	428
	1. Comparative Law Libraries and Projects to Facilitate Research	428
	2. Unification of Law	432
	3. Private International Law	437
	4. Comparative Legal Sociology and Law and Development	441
	5. Other Landmark Comparative Law Books	447
8.	Between Globalization and Nationalism: A History of the Future after 1990	451
	A. The 1990s as a Decade of Opportunities	452
	1. The Triumph of Globalization?	452
	2. Initial Comparative Law Reaction to Accelerated Globalization	456
	3. The Tenacity of Traditions, Cultures, and Legal Pluralism	461
	B. The American Society of Comparative Law	467
	C. Globalization of American Legal Institutions	479
	1. Global Law Schools and Law Firms	479
	2. Academic Law and Development Programs	484
	3. Constitutional and Judicial Globalization	489
	D. Rule of Law Programs: Governments, the ABA, and NGOs	494
	1. Conceptualization and Timeline from 1990 to 2020	494
	2. Specific Programs and Activities	498
	3. The Emergence of Legal Indicators	504
	E. Challenges in the Twenty-First Century	508
	1. Reassessment of Globalization and the Return to Nationalism	508
	2. Resistance from Islam	511
	3. The Importance of China	515
	F. An Interdisciplinary Empirical Comparative Law	518

Index   527

E. The Role of American Governmental and Nongovernmental
   Suggestions in Legal Transplants 416
   1. Origins and Progression up to 1960 418
   2. The 1980s: Decade of Desacrópeza 421
   a. Assertion and the Emergence of Human Rights Law 425
   b. Progress in Comparative Law Research 428
   1. Comparative Law, Liberalism, and Evolutionary Discourse ... 429
   2. Unification of Law 432
   3. Private International Law 436
   F. Comparative Legal Sociology, Law and Development 441
   5. Other Transactional Comparative Law Topics 447

8. Between Globalization and Nationalism: A History of the Future
   after 1990 451
   A. The 1990s as a Decade of Opportunities 452
   1. The Turn to Globalization 454
   a. Initial Comparative Law Reactions to a Federal Globalization .. 456
   b. The Emergency of Transactions, Cultures, and Legal Pluralism ... 461
   B. The American Society of Comparative Law 464
   C. Globalization in American Legal Institutions 469
   D. Global Law Schools and Law Firms 474
   1. Academic Law and Development Programs 484
   2. Constitutive Law and Judicial Globalization 490
   E. Roles of Law Programs, Governments, the ABA, and NGOs 494
   1. Conceptualization and Transactions from 1990 to 2020 494
   2. Specific Programs and Actions 498
   3. The Emergence of Legal Education 501
   F. Challenges in the Twenty-First Century 506
   1. Reassessment of Globalization and the Future of Legal Pluralism .. 508
   2. Resistance from China 513
   3. The Implications of China 515
   F. An Interdisciplinary Future of Comparative Law 519

index 523

Preface

> We shall not cease from exploration
> And the end of all our exploring
> Will be to arrive where we started
> And know the place for the first time.
>
> T.S. Eliot[1]

Comparative law is the science or practice of identifying, explaining, or using the similarities and differences between two or more legal systems or their constituent parts. The objectives or aims of comparative law include those that are practical or professional, scientific, and cultural. Its scientific aspirations can be looser, in the sense of accumulating or applying systematic knowledge (*Wissenschaft*); tighter, such as empirically testing general explanatory propositions; or some intermediate endeavor. These activities involve many distinct methods, such as functionalism or transplants (exporting or importing). Legal systems can be international, national, or subnational. They contain a complex mixture of distinctive legal norms, institutions, processes, actors, and cultures.

Comparatists confront many challenges in carrying out their objectives. First, they must select a legal element for study, such as a contract rule, the standard of proof in criminal procedure, the expected or actual role for prosecutors, civil discovery, legal education, the relationship among government structures, or people's attitudes toward mediation as a form of dispute resolution. Second, they should identify the aim of their inquiry—whether it is professional, scientific, or cultural. Third, they must choose at least two legal systems, which typically are their home system and that of a foreign nation. This one often does implicitly. The investigator may state that she is only interested in a foreign example, such as the presence of rule of law in Indonesia, but she must begin somewhere in her conceptual organization. That somewhere is usually the relevant element in the researcher's own legal system. The two systems need not be contemporary; one may be historical or idealized. It is here that one can see overlap with legal history or legal philosophy (jurisprudence). Fourth, comparatists must select a method or methods to use in making their comparison. These methods may

---

[1] T.S. Eliot, *Little Gidding*, in Four Quartets 31, 39, verse 5 (1943).

have developed within other disciplines, such as economics, sociology, or anthropology, which can make the activity interdisciplinary.

There is further discretion in determining the nature and extent of the similarities or differences the investigator will emphasize. Some comparatists prefer identifying similarities in what they find while others accentuate differences. This will often vary depending on the use or objective that the comparatist has.

Some comparative law utilizes a level of generality above the nation-state. The classification of the world's national and subnational legal systems into families or traditions is an effort to simplify the universe by focusing on the similarities of selected components within a legal tradition and then often pointing out the differences between that tradition and others. For instance, legal scholars commonly speak of the civil law tradition or the Islamic law tradition. Further analysis may lead to the recognition of mixed jurisdictions that reflect legal pluralism within a single legal system, such as Louisiana or Scotland.

From this portrayal, one can see that comparative law is not a discipline with fixed boundaries, either by subject or by method, and certainly, it does not need to be doctrinal. Over the course of American history, many legal scholars and lawyers who worked on issues related to law that involved a foreign element did not think of themselves as comparatists. This was true during the colonial period and at the beginning of the American republic. The term "comparative law" first appeared in an American law journal in 1839.[2] Prior to that time, common reference in the United States to foreign law other than that of Great Britain was to the civil law or Roman law, or more generally to natural law. Comparative law did not emerge as a discipline with journals and organizations in Europe until the middle to late nineteenth century. In the United States, scholars and lawyers only organized themselves to promote comparative law aims in the early twentieth century.

The accepted methods of comparative law have multiplied from the eighteenth century until the present. Thus, for much of the discussion of comparative law through the nineteenth century, I will use contemporary ideas sent back in time to analyze events that today we would call comparative law activities. The challenge is to understand how law-trained persons in colonial British America and the early United States thought about using foreign law examples to develop solutions to problems that ranged from maintaining social order, resolving disputes, constitution making and institution building, rule orderliness or

---

[2] L.S. C[ushing], *Civil and Criminal Laws of Modern States*, 21 AM. JURIST & L. MAG. 56 (1839).
[T]he advantages of such a collection of modern law, in the study of what may be called the science of comparative law, are chiefly . . . of a more practical nature, resulting from the absolute necessity of knowing the laws of foreign states, as so many positive and living institutions, operating directly upon the rights and obligations of the citizen in the daily business of life. *Id.*

simplicity, to doctrinal detail.[3] The experience from the centuries, from diverse lands, was available to them and they drew from those examples to understand, create, and reform law and to strive toward the promised more perfect union.

Finally, there is the matter of the law of Great Britain, today the United Kingdom. Modern American comparative law as it has evolved does not pay much attention to common law jurisdictions. There is no solid theoretical reason for this. One explanation might be the American tradition among lawyers to refer to the Anglo-American tradition as if there were dominant, seemingly inevitable, similarities between the United States and England.[4] Of course, there are important similarities, shared also by other common law jurisdictions. Above all, the legal language is English, whether the common law country is in Asia or Africa, which facilitates the study and use of foreign examples within that legal tradition. Many traditional private law rules in contracts, torts, and property are related. There are also important structural and procedural similarities such as the role for judges in court procedures, the doctrine of precedent, equitable remedies, and resistance to rule codification.

This emphasis on continuity with England has been the traditional approach to legal history in the United States, although the past half century has seen the rise of a vibrant American legal history that emphasizes the uniqueness of the legal system of the United States. Even though the two fields of legal history and comparative law have substantial overlap, this book's focus will exclude most efforts to emphasize the common Anglo-American legal heritage. Those efforts toward commonality have yielded many useful insights into American law. In fact, most American lawyers today readily accept those insights as standard wisdom.

However, the United Kingdom and the United States have distinct histories, cultures, and political and social structures that have resulted in singular legal systems that deserve more attention from comparatists. This focus on difference seems even more obvious in comparisons between the United States and other common law countries such as Australia, India, or Nigeria. Consequently, I disagree with the implication that because English has been the dominant language

---

[3] I am aware of the risks associated with "Whig history." Although I will use the anachronism of comparative law as shorthand for law-trained persons who used Roman and civil law examples to sharpen their thinking about a legal problem in eighteenth- and nineteenth-century America (before comparative law developed an organizational base), I attempt to refrain from characterizing the march of history as progress or to make moral assessments about people or circumstances of the past beyond what they themselves made. See Michael E. Parrish, *Friedman's Law*, 112 YALE L.J. 925, 954–59 (2003) (book review). See generally Herbert Butterfield, THE WHIG INTERPRETATION OF HISTORY (1931, reprinted 1978).

[4] For recent examples, *see, e.g.*, DANIEL R. COQUILLETTE, THE ANGLO-AMERICAN LEGAL HERITAGE: INTRODUCTORY MATERIALS (2d ed. 2004); JOHN H. LANGBEIN, RENÉE LETTOW LERNER, & BRUCE P. SMITH, HISTORY OF THE COMMON LAW: THE DEVELOPMENT OF ANGLO-AMERICAN LEGAL INSTITUTIONS (2009).

in the United States, English legal institutions and rules flowed easily, almost inevitably, into the American legal system.[5] Certainly, it is wrong to imagine that somehow the colonists, especially the large number of Germans, Scots, and later other European settlers in the first decades of the republic "carried" English law with them.[6] There were simply too many differences. In truth, it may be that the concept of a transnational common law legal tradition impedes our understanding of the reality of the American legal system.

I divide this book by era to treat the history of comparative law activities in British North America and then in the United States. Recent research suggests that the civil and Roman law have had a greater impact on American law, even during the colonial period, than commonly acknowledged. This book's challenge is to look beyond the common history with Great Britain and to discover the many other sources of ideas about law that have influenced the legal system of the United States. It is no longer adequate to say, "Not known, because not looked for."[7] Furthermore, the dominant approach to American legal history today emphasizes social history rather than the traditional intellectual history and its attention to change and adaptation of legal rules and doctrine. However, comparatists continue to use both approaches, and one's preference will affect her choice of method.

I am grateful to Mathias Reimann for many useful suggestions associated with Chapter 2, an earlier version of which appeared in the *American Journal of Comparative Law*.[8] I also am indebted to Justin Simard, who read and critiqued the first chapter, which improved the clarity and accuracy of the text. I thank Galin Brown, access services manager at Willamette University College of Law Library, for helpful interlibrary loan assistance. Finally, for their continuing support and encouragement, I recognize Lawrence Friedman and the late John Henry Merryman, two teachers who made a difference.

---

[5] LAWRENCE M. FRIEDMAN, A HISTORY OF AMERICAN LAW xii–xiii, 66 (3d ed. 2005).
[6] KERMIT L. HALL & PETER KARSTEN, THE MAGIC MIRROR: LAW IN AMERICAN HISTORY 10, 23, 36 (2d ed. 2009).
[7] Eliot, *supra* note 1, at 39, verse 5.
[8] David S. Clark, *Comparative Law in Colonial British America*, 59 AM. J. COMP. L. 637–74 (2011).

Abbreviations

AACSL	American Association for the Comparative Study of Law
AALL	American Association of Law Libraries
AALS	Association of American Law Schools
AASS	American Anti-Slavery Society
ABA	American Bar Association
ACC	Allied Control Council (Germany)
ACLS	American Council of Learned Societies
ACLU	American Civil Liberties Union
AFLA	American Foreign Law Association
ALAA	African Law Association in America
ALI	American Law Institute
AMG	American Military Governor or Government (Germany)
AMGK	Army Military Government in Korea
ASCL	American Society of Comparative Law
ASIL	American Society of International Law
ASSA	American Social Science Association
BCE	Before the Common Era
BIE	Bureau International des Expositions
BYU	Brigham Young University
CCP	Chinese Communist Party
CCP	Comparative Constitutions Project
CE	Common Era
CEELI	Central and East European Law Initiative
CEO	chief executive officer
CFR	Council on Foreign Relations
CIA	Central Intelligence Agency
CISG	(Convention on) Contracts for the International Sale of Goods
CLB	Civil Liberties Bureau (Japan)
CRS	Congressional Research Service
DAAD	Deutscher Akademischer Austauschdienst
D.C.	District of Columbia
D.C.L.	Legis Civilis Doctor or Doctor of Civil Law
ECA	Economic Cooperation Administration
ECSC	European Coal and Steel Community
EEC	European Economic Community
E.U.	European Union
FEA	Federal Economic Administration

GDP	gross domestic product
GHQ	General Headquarters or SCAP
HEC	École des Hautes Études Commerciales de Paris
IACL	International Academy of Comparative Law
IALL	International Association of Law Libraries
IALS	International Association of Legal Science
IBM	International Business Machines Corporation
IBRD	International Bank for Reconstruction and Development
ICCL	International Committee for Comparative Law
ICJ	International Commission of Jurists
IDA	International Development Association
ILC	International Legal Center
IMF	International Monetary Fund
ISIS	Islamic State (of Iraq and Syria)
JCLU	Japan Civil Liberties Union
J.D.	Juris Doctor (replaced LL.B. in the United States)
J.S.D.	Juridicae Scientiae Doctor or Doctor of Juridical Science
JSTOR	journal storage
J.U.D.	Juris Utriusque Doctor or Doctor of Both Laws (Roman and canon)
KMT	Kuomintang or Nationalist Party (China)
LA	Los Angeles
LC	Library of Congress
LDP	Liberal Democratic Party (Japan)
LL.B.	Legum Baccalaureus or Bachelor of Laws
LL.M.	Legum Magister or Master of Laws
LRS	Legislative Reference Service
LSU	Louisiana State University
MARC	machine-readable cataloging
M.C.L.	Master of Comparative Law
N	number
NGO	nongovernmental organization
NIL	Uniform Negotiable Instruments Law
NPAC	National Program for Acquisitions and Cataloging
NYU	New York University
OECD	Organisation for Economic Co-operation and Development
OEEC	Organisation for European Economic Co-operation
OMGUS	Office of Military Government or AMG
OUP	Oxford University Press
PEU	Pan European Union
Ph.D.	Philosophiae Doctor or Doctor of Philosophy
PRC	People's Republic of China
SCAP	Supreme Commander for the Allied Powers (Japan)
S.J.D.	Scientiae Juridicae Doctor (equivalent to J.S.D.)
SLADE	Studies in Law and Development (Stanford University)

UCLA	University of California, Los Angeles
U.K.	United Kingdom
ULC	Uniform Law Commission
U.N.	United Nations
UNCITRAL	U.N. Commission on International Trade Law
UNESCO	U.N. Educational, Scientific and Cultural Organization
UNIDROIT	International Institute for the Unification of Private Law
U.S.	United States
USA	United States of America
USAID	U.S. Agency for International Development
USSR	Union of Soviet Socialist Republics
WGI	Worldwide Governance Indicators
WJP	World Justice Project
YCC	Younger Comparativists Committee

1
Legal History and Comparative Law

The history of what the law has been is necessary to the knowledge of what the law is.

Oliver Wendell Holmes Jr.[1]

A. Introduction

1. Historical Comparative Law and Comparative Legal History

Legal history and comparative law overlap in important respects.[2] This is more apparent with the use of some methods for comparison, such as legal transplant, natural law, or nation building.[3] M.N.S. Sellers nicely portrayed the relationship:

> The past is a foreign country, its people strangers and its laws obscure.... No one can really understand her or his own legal system without leaving it first, and looking back from the outside. The comparative study of law makes one's own legal system more comprehensible, by revealing its idiosyncrasies. Legal history is comparative law without travel.[4]

Legal historians, perhaps especially in the United States, have been skeptical about the possibility of a fruitful comparative legal history, preferring in general to investigate the distinctiveness of their national experience.[5] Comparatists,

---

[1] OLIVER WENDELL HOLMES, THE COMMON LAW 33 (Mark DeWolfe Howe ed., 1963; 1st ed. 1881).

[2] James Gordley concisely and persuasively made the argument that one should study comparative law and legal history together. James Gordley, *Comparative Law and Legal History*, in THE OXFORD HANDBOOK OF COMPARATIVE LAW 753–73 (Mathias Reimann & Reinhard Zimmermann eds., 2006) [hereinafter OXFORD HANDBOOK]; *see* Charles Donahue Jr., *Comparative Legal History in North America: A Report*, 65 TIJDSCHRIFT VOOR RECHTSGESCHIEDENIS 1 (1997). A recent interesting treatise explored comparative law historically. *See* O.V. KRESIN 1–2 COMPARATIVE LEGAL STUDIES: 1750 TO 1835 (W.E. Butler, ed. & trans., 2019) (Ukrainian orig. 2017).

[3] *See* David S. Clark, *Comparative Law Methods in the United States*, 16 ROGER WILLIAMS U.L. REV.134, 137–38 (2011).

[4] M.N.S. SELLERS, REPUBLICAN LEGAL THEORY: THE HISTORY, CONSTITUTION AND PURPOSES OF LAW IN A FREE STATE 99 (2003); *see* DAVID LOWENTHAL, THE PAST IS A FOREIGN COUNTRY (1985).

[5] Hermann Wellenreuther, *Introduction: German-American Constitutional History—The Past and the Present*, in GERMAN-AMERICAN CONSTITUTIONAL THOUGHT: CONTEXTS, INTERACTION, AND HISTORICAL REALITIES 1, 7–11 (Hermann Wellenreuther ed., 1990); C. Vann Woodward, *Preface*,

however, content with revealing or promoting similarities or differences between legal systems, by their nature strive toward comparison. Some American historians, especially since World War II, see the value in this.[6]

For Europeans, the value in comparative legal history has been evident since World War II with the desire of politicians and jurists in civil law nations to reduce nationalism and to promote a common legal tradition in the interest of peace and economic prosperity. Recalling an earlier period of shared juristic learning associated with the *jus commune* in continental Europe, proponents of emphasizing similarities among nations succeeded in building the institutional framework of the European Union (E.U.). At the doctrinal level, many jurists investigate and compare specific legal issues and even branches of law, often historically, to promote harmonization among E.U. member states. These efforts may originate with the E.U. Commission though the use of directives[7] or with scholars who obtain government or private funding for collaborative projects.[8]

David Ibbetson identified another approach that one might use to combine the comparative method and legal history: "the study of one aspect of a single legal system but from a standpoint outside that system."[9] David Rabban wrote an important book using this method about U.S. legal scholarship from the end of the Civil War until World War I.[10] In general, I study over the course of American history law-trained individuals who utilized their specialized knowledge to consider the desirability of foreign legal ideas, rules, and institutions. After World War II, a new interest in the United States developed to examine the feasibility of promoting legal change in foreign nations toward adoption of American legal institutions, processes, and rules. On some occasions, these persons reflected and reacted to their internal or external social, cultural, political, and economic

---

in THE COMPARATIVE APPROACH TO AMERICAN HISTORY ix-x (Woodward ed., 1968) [hereinafter Woodward, *Preface*]; Woodward, *The Comparability of American History*, in THE COMPARATIVE APPROACH TO AMERICAN HISTORY, *supra*, at 3–11 [hereinafter Woodward, *Comparability*]. In European civil law nations, legal history traces back to a period of relative universality with Roman and canon law prior to the nationalism and statism of the eighteenth century. The European Society for Comparative Legal History has its own journal combining the two disciplines.

[6] Woodward, *Preface*, *supra* note 5, at x-xi; Woodward, *Comparability*, *supra* note 5, at 12–16. Comparisons "compel Americans to see their past in a new light; to revise complacent assumptions of national exclusiveness, uniqueness, or excellence; to reconsider commonplace myths and flattering legends; and to put to the test of comparison many other traditional assumptions that are rarely subjected to such scrutiny." Woodward, *Preface*, *supra*, at xi.

[7] TFEU arts. 288–89.

[8] *See, e.g.*, the nine-volume series, *Comparative Studies in the Development of the Law of Torts in Europe*, with numerous editors, published between 2010 and 2012.

[9] David Ibbetson, *The Challenges of Comparative Legal History*, 1 COMP. LEG. HIST. 1, 3 (2013).

[10] DAVID M. RABBAN, LAW'S HISTORY: AMERICAN LEGAL THOUGHT AND THE TRANSATLANTIC TURN TO HISTORY 1–9 (2013).

environment to initiate the comparison. Thus, the historical investigation in this volume will usually comprise an intellectual factor as well as a social factor.[11]

Moreover, I follow the established pattern in American comparative law and legal history and distinguish between the civil law and common law traditions. Since American legal history until recently began its research with English origins, the task of demonstrating significant continuities between American law and that of Great Britain would be modest.[12] Consequently, I focus on exploring situations in which lawyers[13] and judges investigated or borrowed legal rules and institutions from outside the common law tradition or instances in which Roman law, canon law, natural law, or civil law was already part of the English legal system.[14]

2. Methodological Issues

A typical method in comparative law—legal transplantation—will inform much of the analysis in this book. This method, which may involve importing (borrowing) or exporting (formerly dominant to the process of colonization, but more recently used in nation building), is a tool in intellectual history. On the importing side, some authors emphasize the importance of specific actors, knowledgeable about a foreign system, who were crucial in the introduction or development of a legal ideology, institution, principle, or rule in the recipient country. If they find a similarity, the inference is that the person used this special knowledge to import the legal element.[15] Others first stress ideological, doctrinal,

---

[11] Ibbetson described some examples of institutional or external elements that influenced legal change. Ibbetson, *supra* note 9, at 8–11. For the social factor historically on a global level, *see* David S. Clark, *History of Comparative Law and Society*, in COMPARATIVE LAW AND SOCIETY 1–36 (Clark ed., 2012).

[12] William Nelson found that the primary issue in pre-1960 American legal history concerned the reception of the common law in the United States. William E. Nelson, *Legal History before the 1960s*, *in* THE LITERATURE OF AMERICAN LEGAL HISTORY 1, 7–15 (William E. Nelson & John Phillip Reid eds., 1985) [hereinafter Nelson, *Legal History*]. Some legal historians still value the continuities between English law and American law. JOHN H. LANGBEIN, RENÉE LETTOW LERNER, & BRUCE P. SMITH, HISTORY OF THE COMMON LAW: THE DEVELOPMENT OF ANGLO-AMERICAN LEGAL INSTITUTIONS xxv–xxvi (2009).

[13] I will often use the word lawyers to include all law-trained persons, including judges, law professors, and politicians.

[14] For this purpose, I build on the recent work of several scholars who combine legal history and comparative law—especially Michael Hoeflich and M.N.S. Sellers—but also Daniel Coquillette, Richard Helmholz, David Ibbetson, Mathias Reimann, Peter Stein, and Reinhard Zimmermann.

[15] M.H. HOEFLICH, ROMAN AND CIVIL LAW AND THE DEVELOPMENT OF ANGLO-AMERICAN JURISPRUDENCE IN THE NINETEENTH CENTURY 2–3 (1997); *see id.* at 26–49 (Joseph Story); David S. Clark, *The Civil Law Influence on David Dudley Field's Code of Civil Procedure*, in THE RECEPTION OF CONTINENTAL IDEAS IN THE COMMON LAW WORLD: 1820–1920, at 63 (Mathias Reimann ed., 1993); Michele Graziadei, *Comparative Law as the Study of Transplants and Receptions*, *in* OXFORD HANDBOOK, *supra* note 2, at 441–47.

or institutional similarities between the supposed donor nation or its scholars and the recipient nation, inferring that the transplant must have occurred.[16]

Although legal historians and comparatists have used approaches associated with specific persons or with ideology, doctrine, and institutions, the generally accepted notion of an Anglo-American common law hinders the search for similarities between civil law countries—primarily France, Germany, and Spain—and the United States. In addition, since the American insurgents created the United States as a republic, the prestigious example of Rome (and the lack of convincing contemporary European examples) suggests an important link to republican Rome.[17] Only since the 1960s, however, have classicists surveyed the writings of American framers comprehensively to make the argument.[18]

The issue of influence is a complex one. It appears to concern historians, political scientists, and sociologists more than legal comparatists. The latter may be satisfied to identify, explain, or evaluate similarities and differences between two legal systems, although they too sometimes speak of influence or causation. From the perspective of this book, any of the commonly accepted methods of comparative law that American lawyers have used with foreign law to understand another legal system or to formulate, evaluate, or implement new legal rules or institutions qualifies as comparative law.[19] Two of the most popular contemporary methods that comparatists use are functionalism and formalistic description and analysis. The latter was dominant prior to World War II.[20]

Comparative law functionalists are not much interested in the issue of influence. Their primary concern is with the function that legal rules or institutions serve in the legal systems they investigate. Comparatists using the legal transplant methodology, however, do write about influence. For some scholars, the demonstration that crucial jurists, politicians, or judges cited or promoted foreign legal ideas, rules, or institutions, which then appeared in the home legal system, strongly suggests influence. For others, weaker links, such as a jurist's educational background, reading lists, or personal library is sufficient to show influence. Comparative lawyers have made these connections but some attempt to refute them based on insufficient "proof."

---

[16] HOEFLICH, *supra* note 15, at 2–3; *see* Alan Watson, *The Transformation of American Property Law: A Comparative Law Approach*, 24 GEO. L. REV. 163 (1990). Hoeflich noted that an important difficulty with this approach, beyond examples of direct exportation via conquest or centralized and systematic colonization, is definitively to distinguish between direct influence and parallel development. HOEFLICH, *supra*, at 3.

[17] SELLERS, *supra* note 4, at 6–25.

[18] *See infra* ch. 3, pt. D (republican form of government).

[19] See Graziadei, *supra* note 15, at 461–63, 465–74.

[20] *See* Gerhard Dannemann, *Comparative Law: Study of Similarities or Differences?*, in OXFORD HANDBOOK, *supra* note 2, at 382, 385, 396–408, 412–18; Ralf Michaels, *The Functional Method of Comparative Law*, in OXFORD HANDBOOK, *supra*, at 339, 343–66, 373–76, 378–81.

The debate about foreign law influence has been especially contentious for the crucial American legal documents of the revolutionary period (1776 to 1791). Involving historians, political scientists, lawyers, and classicists, each group has tended to bring its own perspective or perspectives to the question.[21] Many years after Gordon Wood's remarkable book, *The Creation of the American Republic*,[22] he identified two central issues that commentators had raised in reviewing his work. These were, first, the connection between ideology and behavior, and second, the temporal relation between classical republicanism and liberalism. The first point concerns the influence or causation question while the second point illustrates the dynamic character of any foreign influence on the design of a nation's core legal institutions.[23]

The connection between ideology and behavior illustrates the belief in Western social sciences that the mind and body are separate and that ideas or culture may affect action. For some scholars, Wood contended, ideas are discrete things that might "cause" people to act, but usually stronger material "causes," such as social class or economic interest, overwhelm those ideas. Many "realists" believe that legal ideology simply cannot explain much legal or political activity. Wood responded that no one can prove causation one way or the other, but that ideas constantly accompany our actions and give them meaning. "Ideology creates behavior."[24] During the arguments concerning the Constitution, the Federalists ended up being more persuasive, but the Anti-Federalists still believed their evidence that the document was aristocratic and undemocratic. In 1787, as today, there was no one true meaning of the Constitution.[25]

Wood's second issue about the temporal relation between classical republicanism and liberalism involved the relevance of foreign ideas before 1791 and those during the decades following, matters discussed in detail in Chapters 3 and 4. Wood asserted that the contemporary polemic about republicanism and liberalism creates an unnecessary dichotomy that the Constitution's framers did not have. Jefferson, for instance, did not have to choose between Niccolò Machiavelli

---

[21] SELLERS, *supra* note 4, at x–xi, 20–23 (lawyer and historian); PAUL A. RAHE, 3 REPUBLICS ANCIENT AND MODERN (INVENTIONS OF PRUDENCE: CONSTITUTING THE AMERICAN REGIME) 27–30 (1994) (historian); MEYER REINHOLD, CLASSICA AMERICANA: THE GREEK AND ROMAN HERITAGE IN THE UNITED STATES 17–20 (1984) (classicist); MICHAEL P. ZUCKERT, THE NATURAL RIGHTS REPUBLIC: STUDIES IN THE FOUNDATION OF THE AMERICAN POLITICAL TRADITION 92–96 (1996) (political scientist).
[22] GORDON S. WOOD, THE CREATION OF THE AMERICAN REPUBLIC, 1776–1787 (1969).
[23] Gordon S. Wood, *Ideology and Origins of Liberal America*, 44 WM. & MARY Q. 628 (1987).
[24] *Id.* at 631; *see id.* at 628–31. "In 1787–1788 Federalists and Antifederalists argued over the 'aristocratic' and 'democratic' nature of the Constitution. Each side tried to persuade Americans to accept its particular attribution of meaning to the document. The Federalists made a brilliant case for the view that the Constitution was thoroughly republican and democratic, and they could do so because of the way republicanism and democracy had developed by 1787." *Id.* at 631–32.
[25] *Id.* at 632. Lawyers may need the fiction of a "correct" interpretation of the Constitution, but historians should be open to deeper complexities of culture and action. *Id.* at 632–34.

(1469–1527) and John Locke (1632–1704); he could believe that the danger of corruption in American government was as serious as the need to protect individual rights. Nevertheless, the framers did write about "republicanism" in their arguments, but none referred to "liberalism" with the meaning currently ascribed to that term. That does not mean that the framers failed to recognize the self-interested pursuit of happiness; however, the emergence of party competition, the liberal world of business, and an acquisitive society occurred in the early nineteenth century.[26]

Beyond the revolutionary period, the dominant view among American legal historians has been that the significance of Roman and civil law was minor for the origin and development of American law.[27] This applies both to general works in social history as well as to those in intellectual history. Prior to 1960, most American legal history was intellectual history, usually from the professional perspective of lawyers, conservative in nature. It often argued to promote the rule of law and to restrain judicial decision-making but also included the study of constitutional history, a field in which political historians were also active. Since 1960, a more academic tone to intellectual legal history appeared, especially related to constitutional history.[28] In addition, social history—regularly concerned with law and social change—became more important in the 1960s and 1970s.[29] By the twenty-first century, legal history has blossomed in ways unimaginable 50 years earlier.[30]

---

[26] *Id.* at 634–402; *see* John M. Murrin, *Gordon S. Wood and the Search for Liberal America*, 44 WM. & MARY Q. 597–601 (1987).

[27] HOEFLICH, *supra* note 15, at 1, 51, 74, 131 (1997); R.H. Helmholz, *Use of the Civil Law in Post-Revolutionary American Jurisprudence*, 66 TUL. L. REV. 1649, 1650–51 (1992).

[28] HOEFLICH, *supra* note 15, at 3; Nelson, *Legal History*, *supra* note 12, at 1–2, 7, 19–32; *id.*, *Conclusion: Standards of Criticism*, *in* THE LITERATURE OF AMERICAN LEGAL HISTORY 303 (William E. Nelson & John Phillip Reid eds., 1985); *see* G. EDWARD WHITE, TORT LAW IN AMERICA: AN INTELLECTUAL HISTORY (1980) [hereinafter WHITE, TORT LAW]. For constitutional history, *see* CONSTITUTIONALISM AND AMERICAN CULTURE: WRITING THE NEW CONSTITUTIONAL HISTORY (Sandra E. Van Burkleo, Kermit L. Hall, & Robert J. Kaczorowski eds., 2002); WILLIAM M. WIECEK, THE LOST WORLD OF CLASSICAL LEGAL THOUGHT: LAW AND IDEOLOGY IN AMERICA, 1886–1937 (1998).

[29] On the shift in general American history to a social perspective, *see, e.g.*, SOURCES OF THE AMERICAN SOCIAL TRADITION xv–xx (David J. Rothman & Sheila M. Rothman eds., 1975) [hereinafter SOURCES]. It is more accurate to think of an approach to legal history on a continuum between emphasis of intellectual or cultural factors and of social factors, with many scholars utilizing both. Roscoe Pound and Willard Hurst illustrated the variation in the twentieth century. Nelson, *Legal History*, *supra* note 12, at 6.

[30] Michael Grossberg & Christopher Tomlins, *Preface*, *in* 1 THE CAMBRIDGE HISTORY OF LAW IN AMERICA: EARLY AMERICA (1580–1815) vii, xiii–xiv (Michael Grossberg & Christopher Tomlins eds., 2008) [hereinafter 1 CAMBRIDGE HISTORY]; *see* A COMPANION TO AMERICAN LEGAL HISTORY (Sally E. Hadden & Alfred L. Brophy eds., 2013); Michael H. Hoeflich & Steve Sheppard, *Disciplinary Evolution and Scholarly Expansion: Legal History in the United States*, 54 AM. J. COMP. L. 23 (Supp. 2006); Assaf Likhovski, *The Intellectual History of Law*, *in* THE OXFORD HANDBOOK OF LEGAL HISTORY 151–69 (Markus D. Dubber & Christopher Tomlins eds., 2018).

3. Scope of the Book

I divide the history of American comparative law into seven periods.[31] Chapter 2 describes the British colonial period, beginning with a review of the place of Roman, civil, and canon law in English legal history followed by a discussion of what impact those elements plus natural law, particularly through Scotsmen, might have had in America. Self-study and apprenticeship were the avenues to learn law in the colonies. Because the social and physical environment in America was so different from that in England, I examine the importance of social factors on the development of law, especially on lawyers and courts. In addition, I speculate on the relevance for law of the religious and cultural diversity that existed in the 13 North American colonies. Finally, I select John Adams as an exemplary legal comparatist in the pre-revolutionary period and survey his law practice and political writings.

Chapter 3 examines the legal foundation for the new republic established from 1776 to 1791. The Declaration of Independence (1776), the Constitution (1787), and the supplemental Bill of Rights (1791) were all extraordinary legal documents. The men who drafted and defended them, most of whom had studied or practiced law, looked to three major sources beyond those parts of British law that offered promise for a new land. First, the legal structures of classical Greek city-states, their leagues, and the Roman Republic were the most visible and persuasive counterexamples to monarchy. Second, European political philosophy (continental and British) from the sixteenth to eighteen centuries, with its treatment of classical polities and embrace of natural law rules, supplied a modern supplement to Roman law. Third, the ethnic and religious diversity in the 13 colonies presented popular views of law appropriate for a nation founded on the people's will rather than divine delegation. This pluralism further suggested that the framers should layer, balance, and check sovereign power, derived from these different peoples, to avoid the tyranny that drove colonists to rebel in the first place.

Most comparative law activity during this period concentrated on public law, especially the structure for and limits on national government, its relation to the constituent states and to the people, and certain criminal procedure rules. It was

---

[31] My division reflects major changes in comparative law activity. There has been a reassessment since 1980 in the traditional periodization of early American legal history. Stanley Katz, already in the mid-1960s, asserted that the broadening range of source materials suggested significant continuity between the pre-revolutionary period and the early republic. Stanley N. Katz, *Looking Backward: The Early History of American Law*, 33 U. CHI. L. REV. 867, 882–84 (1966) (book review). Legal historians prior to 1980 generally followed Roscoe Pound's thesis of a "formative era" beginning after 1776. James A. Henretta, *Magistrates, Common Law Lawyers, Legislators: The Three Legal Systems of British America*, in 1 CAMBRIDGE HISTORY, *supra* note 30, at 555, 561–62; *see* ROSCOE POUND, THE FORMATIVE ERA OF AMERICAN LAW vii (1938) [hereinafter POUND, FORMATIVE ERA].

a small group of exceptional lawyers, trained as classicists, who succeeded in formulating and enacting the core legal documents. The chapter emphasizes the work of several of these: John Adams, Alexander Hamilton, John Jay, Thomas Jefferson, James Madison, James Wilson, and George Wythe.

Chapter 4 analyzes the period 1791 to the end of the Civil War, what Roscoe Pound described as part of the formative era of American law. Lawyers with knowledge of Enlightenment legal philosophy and Roman and civil law shifted their attention primarily to the task of constructing a system of private law. Nevertheless, comparatists explored penal reform and adopted ideas from European criminology that made Pennsylvania and New York models that French and German jurists then studied. In addition, the expansion of the nation to absorb Louisiana as a territory and later a state provided an important instance of civil law influence, particularly on the matter of legal codification. These decades also saw the beginning of American comparative legal science, which legal education, a growing legal literature—James Kent and Joseph Story stood out—and law libraries amply illustrated. I select a dozen or so legal comparatists for detailed treatment on their contributions to early comparative law. In addition, I explore the diverse important legal sources on the codification and slavery questions.

German historical jurisprudence and learned law took hold in the United States after the Civil War through the remainder of the nineteenth century. Chapter 5 begins with the romanticism and nationalism that infused the historical school and differentiated it from natural law theory. The German version aspired to be both systematic as a science and historical for sources of law. James Carter, a leading American disciple of historical jurisprudence, used it to defeat David Field's ambitious codification program in New York. The learned law aspect of German legal science found fertile ground at Harvard Law School in the 1870s, which transformed American legal education to firmly root its teaching and development at universities with a scientific casebook method of instruction in judicial source materials. Furthermore, significant comparative law libraries emerged during this time.

Roman and civil law survived in this era of industrialization and social transformation. Roman law teaching was a substitute for academic comparative law, a bridge between the classical past and interest in universalism and unification of law in the twentieth century. Legal periodicals provided an outlet for comparative law information and scholarly essays, and a few American jurists were aware of German sociological jurisprudence, which was a forerunner to legal realism. William Hammond, Oliver Wendell Holmes, William Howe, and Christopher Tiedeman afford examples. Finally, comparative law formed as a discipline, first in Europe, then with supporters in the United States, highlighted by the 1900 International Congress of Comparative Law.

At the beginning of the twentieth century, sustained scholarly comparative law activities were largely associated with the successful effort to establish scientific teaching and research at leading law schools, 25 of which created the Association of American Law Schools in 1900. Chapter 6 details the new field of comparative juristic inquiry that emerged from both idealistic as well as practical concerns. The interest of jurists in drawing from history and social science as well as traditional legal sources provided new perspectives for both national and comparative law, especially on the role of law and government in society. Woodrow Wilson, the 28th U.S. president, was a prominent legal comparatist, the first to become president since John Adams, Thomas Jefferson, and James Madison set an impossibly high standard. Hessel Yntema later promoted scientific methods to develop a social science of law.

As an aftermath of the 1898 Spanish-American War, the Treaty of Paris ceded sovereignty over the Philippines to the United States. U.S. foreign policy took a course of indirect and consensual engagement with the legal system in the new territory, especially during Wilson's presidency. A few jurists—some of whom had knowledge of the civil law tradition—worked with American foundations, professional associations, universities, or the U.S. government to support foreign legal reform, including in China after it became a republic in 1912, reflecting the domestic Progressive movement to improve law.

Organized American comparative law began in earnest with the 1904 St. Louis Universal Congress of Lawyers and Jurists. The American Bar Association (ABA) created the Comparative Law Bureau in 1907, with annual meetings and a *Bulletin* from 1908 until 1914, when World War I disrupted cross-Atlantic connections, then continued with special Bureau issues of the *ABA Journal* through 1929. Comparatists developed teaching materials; set up graduate law degree programs that included comparative law, many completed by foreign lawyers; and supported expanded comparative law libraries. In 1925, Bureau members established the American Foreign Law Association in New York City. Americans also took a leading role in forming the International Academy of Comparative Law, with Roscoe Pound and John Wigmore as active members.

Chapter 6 then describes two sides of German-American juristic relations in the 1930s. On the one hand, there was the rise of Nazis in Germany and anti-Semitism in American universities. On the other, several U.S. law schools accepted some émigré legal scholars much to their mutual benefit while a few Catholic-affiliated university law schools and philosophy and government departments took in those who revived an interest in natural law jurisprudence.

Just as the U.S. government undertook legal transplants to the Philippines at the beginning of the twentieth century, it again reengaged in legal reform after 1945 in Germany, Japan, and Korea. Chapter 7 traces those efforts that were similar and distinct among the three countries, dependent on the social, political, economic, and military situation. In addition, during the 1950s, the Cold War ideological threat posed by communism to capitalism and liberal democracy pushed the United States to demonstrate its ability to foster economic and social progress among its allies and nonaligned nations. Comparatists in the ABA and the newly formed American Association for the Comparative Study of Law (AACSL) devoted substantial effort to international unification of commercial and trade law as the government also financed private foreign investment. The 1960s, the decade of development, expanded those efforts to use law to promote modernization among developing countries, which engaged senior and younger comparatists in promoting agrarian reform, judicial independence, active instruction in legal education, and other U.S.-inspired improvements. By the 1970s, the unsatisfactory results for most of these action programs shifted academic concern to scholarly inquiry about the relationship between law and social change. Furthermore, comparative lawyers began to take a greater interest in the amorphous concept of rule of law and in human rights.

The postwar period marked a steady rise of academic quality and interest in comparative law, stimulated by the AACSL, its meetings, journal, and participation in international congresses. American comparatists developed expertise in and promoted subfields, namely, unification of law, private international law, and comparative legal sociology. At the same time, American law schools saw similar trends with more comparative law courses and coursebooks, some specialized in Soviet, Japanese, or Latin American law, or in fields such as comparative constitutional law or European Community law. There also was a proliferation of comparative law journals and degree programs for foreign students and expansion of comparative law libraries and projects to facilitate research into foreign and comparative law. By 1990, the AACSL had 69 sponsor members and had instituted a democratic system of election, which put it on a path toward further growth among U.S. and even foreign law schools.

Chapter 8 presents the 1990s as a decade of opportunities for comparative law as it reacted to accelerated globalization following the collapse of the Soviet Union. Scholars offered a variety of views about the end of the Cold War ranging from characterizing it as the end of history and triumph for Western liberal democracy to maintaining that the West's power was at its peak in relation to other civilizations, which would continue to present challenges to the Western view of law. The tenacity of cultures, with their embedded notions of law, as well as nationalism, meant that world security required acceptance of global multiculturality. In the United States, many more jurists—including government officials and lawyers—engaged in comparative activities often unaware of the difficulties of achieving successful legal transplants. Comparative law scholars had a variety of views about the strength of the American discipline, but any feeling of angst dissipated in the twenty-first century as new pursuits emerged.

Unlike earlier periods, most U.S. comparatists now rejected the idea of legal convergence and universalism and argued instead for an emphasis on exploring differences among legal traditions and national legal systems. Besides traditional research on foreign legal rules and institutions, there was a noticeable growth of interest in legal cultures and contextual interdisciplinary treatment of legal issues and institutions. Geographically, there were more studies about Asian and Latin American law.

The renamed American Society of Comparative Law (ASCL) expanded its institutional membership to around 100, but each law school participating in workshops, special and annual meetings, and other activities now sent more professors to attend those events. The society adopted a long-range planning report to improve the academic value of meetings, expand eligibility to hold office and contribute to editing the *Journal*, and facilitate attendance by foreign comparatists. It augmented the society's role in international congresses through subsidies to participants, financed the continued growth of the ASCL *Journal* until it no longer required a subsidy, created a website, and invited foreign sponsor members. In 2010, the ASCL hosted the Eighteenth International Congress of Comparative Law in Washington, D.C. Shortly thereafter, one of the society's committees, for younger comparatists, transformed itself into a semiautonomous organization with annual meetings and periodic workshops to integrate new scholars into the discipline.

The reality of economic and political globalization affected certain U.S. legal institutions that had a comparative law aspect, primarily law firms and legal education. Thousands of foreign lawyers and law students studied at American universities and worked at U.S. law firms domestically or abroad. Law schools became more cosmopolitan with interchange between U.S. and foreign students, new advanced degrees, and expansion of the comparative law curriculum. American law and development research took on a second life, often with foreign collaborators, and shifted toward a plenary rule of law rhetoric to export an American or European model of legal institutions and processes to newly independent and other developing countries. A noteworthy curriculum development was in the field of comparative constitutional law and constitutionalism, which saw several coursebooks, handbooks, new courses, symposia, and interesting interactions between U.S. legal scholars and legislators, judges, and lawyers.

The debate about global governance, often simplified as rule of law, was one of the surprising new developments in comparative law, consolidating a shift from private to public law. Governmental agencies, multinational and national, nongovernmental organizations (NGOs), especially the ABA, initiated programs to transplant Western ideas about law and government. Much of the activity and research in this area was interdisciplinary and quantitative, sometimes utilizing legal indicators to assess aspects of law in diverse nations, opening a new dimension to comparative law.

By 2005, the optimism of the early 1990s regarding practical comparative law in exporting legal rules and institutions to Eastern Europe, Asia, and Latin America receded. The number of democracies in all regions fell; income inequality increased in developed countries and social change disrupted many developing nations. At the same time, authoritarian countries, particularly China and Russia, became more assertive. The 2016 elections in the United States and the United Kingdom strengthened the spread of nationalism as a reaction to globalization. Identity politics reaffirmed the significance of culture as did resistance from Islamic countries and China to the West's promotion of rule of law. Comparatists worked to explain these developments, while the growing use of methods and perspectives from the social sciences suggested that success in accumulating knowledge about the relationship between law and society could augment the prestige of the discipline.

B. Historiography: 1771 to 1900

1. Establishing an American System of Legal Rules

Drawing distinctions between American books or parts of books intended as *general* legal history or philosophy, including those for students, and those discussing the historical background for particular *practical issues* for lawyers and judges can be difficult.[32] The first American publication of Sir William Blackstone's four-volume *Commentaries on the Laws of England* was a 1771–1772 printing in Philadelphia.[33] The several popular editions of Blackstone served as a surrogate for a general history of law—English law—until American jurists could create their own legal literature in the nineteenth century.[34] Among examples of historical background for a practical legal issue, Alexander Hamilton provided

---

[32] The first law book printed in colonial British America was *The Book of the General Lawes and Libertyes concerning the Inhabitants of the Massachusetts* (1648, facsimile reprint 1975). The General Court ordered 600 copies of the compilation, organized alphabetically, to distribute to magistrates in the colony. LAWRENCE M. FRIEDMAN, A HISTORY OF AMERICAN LAW 51–53 (3d ed. 2005); *see* DAVID M. POWERS, DAMNABLE HERESY: WILLIAM PYNCHON, THE INDIANS, AND THE FIRST BOOK BANNED (AND BURNED) IN BOSTON 79–80, 162–63 (2015). Other colonies copied parts of the Massachusetts's compilation. FRIEDMAN, *supra*, at 52. Friedman described other "practical" law books, mostly on specific subjects, published in the colonies and the new republic. *Id.* at 59–61, 241–46.

[33] Robert Bell was the printer. There was scarcely a mention of the British colonies or American colonial law. WILLIAM BLACKSTONE, 1 COMMENTARIES ON THE LAWS OF ENGLAND 106–09 (1771) (treating the "American plantations").

[34] FRIEDMAN, *supra* note 32, at 59–60, 244–49; *see infra* ch. 4, pts. D, E (law books and other legal literature).

his view of the relevance of the Roman republican division of legislative power between patricians and plebeians as support for the proposed design in the U.S. Constitution of the Senate and House of Representatives.[35]

An early rudimentary attempt at an American general legal history appeared in 1795 when James Kent (1763–1847) published the law lectures he had given at Columbia College in 1794. The second lecture—Of the History of the American Union—seemed most on point.[36] Kent later revised this work in the first part of *Commentaries on American Law*, written while he again was lecturing at Columbia after his retirement from the New York judiciary.[37]

In 1804, the son of James Wilson (1742–1798) edited and published a series of lectures his father had delivered at the College of Philadelphia from 1790 to 1792.[38] Wilson wanted these, like Blackstone's Oxford lectures for English law, to present a comprehensive treatment of American law and jurisprudence. Offered as chapters, the first one reflected on a general American legal history to introduce the student and reader to the study of law in the United States. Nevertheless, its influence was less than that for Kent's effort, which continued via incorporation into the latter's *Commentaries*.[39]

Much more important for the first quarter of the nineteenth century, Henry St. George Tucker (1780–1848) published in 1803 a five-volume edition of Blackstone's *Commentaries* with lengthy annotations and notes referencing the U.S. Constitution, its national law, and the law of Virginia.[40] Tucker based these additions on his law lectures at the College of William and Mary, where he intended to show the value of Blackstone's volumes to American lawyers, making allowance for the Englishman's antidemocratic views. Tucker was the most frequently cited American jurist until 1827, when Kent and then Joseph Story (1779–1845) surpassed him with their publications.[41]

---

[35] THE FEDERALIST NO. 34, at 206 (Alexander Hamilton) (Clinton Rossiter ed. 1961).

[36] JAMES KENT, DISSERTATIONS: BEING THE PRELIMINARY PART OF A COURSE OF LAW 27–49 (1795, reprint 1991); WILLIAM KENT, MEMOIRS AND LETTERS OF JAMES KENT 62–64, 76–77 (1898). John Adams was critical of ideas in Kent's first lecture—"Of the Theory, History and Duties of the Civil Government"—in three letters to his son. See WILLIAM KENT, *supra*, at 64–73.

[37] JAMES KENT, 1 COMMENTARIES ON AMERICAN LAW iii, 189–205 (1826). Kent divided the book by lectures rather than chapters. Lecture 10 had the title "Of the History of the American Union."

[38] Mark David Hall, *Bibliographical Essay: History of James Wilson's Law Lectures, in* 1 COLLECTED WORKS OF JAMES WILSON 401–04, 407–11 (Kermit L. Hall & Mark David Hall eds., 2007) [hereinafter 1 WILSON COLLECTED WORKS]; *see* 1 WILSON COLLECTED WORKS, *supra*, at 427–746; 2 *id.* at 7–315 (lectures); see *infra* ch. 3, pt. G (Wilson).

[39] Kermit L. Hall, *Introduction, in* 1 WILSON COLLECTED WORKS, *supra* note 38, at xiii, xxvii; Mark Hall, *supra* note 38, at 401, 404; 1 WILSON COLLECTED WORKS, *supra* note 38, at 431–63 (introductory chapter). After the 1804 edition of WILSON COLLECTED WORKS, the next one did not appear until 1896. Mark Hall, *supra*, at 404.

[40] ST. GEORGE TUCKER, 1–5 BLACKSTONE'S COMMENTARIES (1803). Blackstone's volumes resulted from his law lectures at Oxford University from 1758 through the 1760s. 1 *id.* at i–ii, 3.

[41] Paul Finkelman & David Cobin, *Introduction, in* TUCKER, *supra* note 40, at i, x, xiii (1996 reprint). There was not another American edition of *Blackstone's Commentaries* until 1852. *Id.* at xiii.

Addressing the shortcomings of the English apprenticeship system of legal education in general and specifically for the United States, David Hoffman (1784–1854) used his appointment in 1814 as the first law professor at the University of Maryland to prepare a systematic course of legal study.[42] Published as *A Course of Legal Study* in 1817, Joseph Story wrote a favorable review and praised its inclusion of material on admiralty, maritime, and the civil law.[43] Lecturers used the published *Course* to guide legal instruction in the 1820s elsewhere, including at Harvard and the University of Virginia.[44] The *Course*, divided into 13 titles, was a list of readings accompanied by extensive notes that formed the basis for developing lectures on various legal and political topics. With a second edition in 1836, revised in 1846, it was the most influential treatise for legal education prior to the Civil War (1861–1865).[45]

Following the literary style first developed in sixteenth-century England, Nathan Dane (1752–1835), a Massachusetts lawyer and politician, published an eight-volume comprehensive abridgment and digest of American law in 1823 and 1824 covering the existing 24 states plus the federal government. Aimed at law students as well as lawyers and judges, it sold well enough for Dane to fund the first law professorship at Harvard intended for Joseph Story.[46] Dane's approach was a historical one that included the colonial charters, state constitutions and statues, as well as reported court cases. He divided his subject into 28 divisions for public and private law with 228 chapters and 1,707 articles.[47]

Story and Kent were the two most significant authors of legal literature in the first half of the nineteenth century.[48] Both were educators as well as judges and cited Roman and civil law in their writing. From 1831 to 1845, Story wrote treatises, which he called commentaries, on nine legal subjects with 11 volumes.

---

[42] Thomas L. Shaffer, *David Hoffman's Law School Lectures, 1822–1833*, 32 J. LEG. EDUC. 127 (1982); see Maryland Carey Law, About, https://www.law.umaryland.edu/about. Based on the reading lists in his *Course*, Hoffman lectured at Maryland from 1822 to 1833. Shaffer, *supra*, at 128, 130. The university appointed its next law professor in 1868. Maryland Carey Law, *supra*.

[43] DAVID HOFFMAN, A COURSE OF LEGAL STUDY; RESPECTFULLY ADDRESSED TO THE STUDENTS OF LAW IN THE UNITED STATES (1817); Joseph Story, 6 N. AM. REV. 45, 63, 75–77 (1817) (book review); *see* Maxwell Bloomfield, *David Hoffman and the Shaping of a Republican Legal Culture*, 38 MD. L. REV. 673, 678–79 (1979).

[44] Shaffer, *supra* note 42, at 130.

[45] Hugh C. MacGill & R. Kent Newmyer, *Legal Education and Legal Thought, 1790–1920*, in 2 THE CAMBRIDGE HISTORY OF LAW IN AMERICA: THE LONG NINETEENTH CENTURY (1789-1920) 36, 45–46 (Michael Grossberg & Christopher Tomlins eds., 2008) [hereinafter 2 CAMBRIDGE HISTORY]. The 1817 edition sold out in a year and a half, although the second edition in 1836 had serious competition from a less scholarly introduction to common law. Bloomfield, *supra* note 43, at 687–88. The *American Jurist* printed a generous review of the second edition. Anon., 15 AM. JURIST & L. MAG. 321 (1836) (book review).

[46] J.H. BAKER, AN INTRODUCTION TO ENGLISH LEGAL HISTORY 184–86 (4th ed. 2002); WIECEK, *supra* note 28, at 40; *see* NATHAN DANE, 1–8 A GENERAL ABRIDGMENT AND DIGEST OF AMERICAN LAW (1823–1824). Dane compiled a supplement volume published in 1829. 9 *id.* (1829).

[47] 1 DANE, *supra* note 46, at iii–vi, ix–xiv.

[48] FRIEDMAN, *supra* note 32, at 246–49.

The seminal work on conflict of laws defined the field in America and illustrated substantial reliance on continental jurists. Story believed that law was a product of history and, as correctly understood, the embodiment of reason. This put American law on a parity with Roman law and natural law. In the equity treatise, Story portrayed the precise development of American law as a specific adaptation of fundamental general principles.[49]

Story's *Commentaries on the Constitution of the United States* (1833)[50] illustrated the difficulty of differentiating between a general historical treatment of American law and one aimed at informing lawyers about a specific field of law. Most of volume 1 described the legal history of the British North American colonies up to 1776, the Revolution, establishment of the confederation, and the adoption of the Constitution. Story then turned to some general issues associated with the Constitution to finish that volume and in volumes 2 and 3 provided detailed analysis and opinion on each clause and institution created in that document. As with the academic efforts of Blackstone, Kent, and Tucker, Story produced his books while lecturing, in his case as Dane Professor of Law at Harvard University.[51]

Timothy Walker (1802–1856) published the first book in 1837 that considered larger issues associated with the common law in the United States in the context of European civil law examples. He wrote it primarily from the perspective of a law teacher. In 1833, Walker with three others had opened the Cincinnati Law School, which in 1835 became the law department of Cincinnati College, where he served as dean until 1844. Walker had studied at Harvard College and Law School, where at the latter he was a student of Joseph Story.[52] Decrying the lack of materials to instruct American students, he wrote *Introduction to American Law* (1837).[53] Little, Brown and Company (Boston) acquired the right to publish the third edition in 1855, which went through 11 editions up to 1905.[54]

Walker explained in the first edition's preface that as a student he had learned too much English law and too little American law. Thus, his book offered "a systematic outline of American instead of English law [since] the two systems differ in nearly as many points as they correspond."[55] The coverage included most public law and private law, including procedure. For organization, Walker

---

[49] *Id.* at 247–48; HOEFLICH, *supra* note 15, at 26–32, 36–43.
[50] JOSEPH STORY, 1–3 COMMENTARIES ON THE CONSTITUTION OF THE UNITED STATES (1833).
[51] 1 *id.* at v.
[52] Bernard J. Hibbitts, *Walker, Timothy*, in 22 AMERICAN NATIONAL BIOGRAPHY 519-20 (John A. Garraty & Mark C. Carnes eds., 1999); University of Cincinnati College of Law, *History*, https://law.uc.edu/about/history.html.
[53] TIMOTHY WALKER, INTRODUCTION TO AMERICAN LAW: DESIGNED AS A FIRST BOOK FOR STUDENTS (Philadelphia: P.H. Nicklin & T. Johnson, 1837); *see id.* at preface. Derby, Bradley & Co. (Cincinnati) published the second edition in 1846.
[54] *Id.* (Clement Bates ed., 11th ed. 1905).
[55] *Id.* at v (4th ed. 1860). Walker dedicated his book to Story. *Id.* at iii.

implied that he followed Blackstone's *Commentaries* as far as useful, but distinguished the American system for its written constitutions and approach toward treaties.

On the "unwritten law"—common law and equity—Walker separated the two sources.[56] He asserted that the first American states retained the common law "that had been much improved under their own legislation," and that among the new states, only Louisiana had preferred a civil code. In resolving a legal question, he suggested that the student look first to a state's written law, then without success in preferential order to its case reports, to other American state reports, to English reports, and finally to "seek light from the civil law, or from any other source which can furnish it."[57] As for equity, Walker mentioned its Roman and canon law antecedents and equity's weaker penetration into some of the American colonies.[58] Nevertheless, all unwritten law shared a characteristic Walker believed debased a legal system—undue complexity, uncertainty, and lack of uniformity. He pointed to the 1,000 volumes of English and 500 volumes of American case reports, digests, and abridgments. The solution was codification, which he supported in much of his writing, citing the successful examples of Justinian's *Corpus juris civilis*, the French and Louisiana civil codes, and to a lesser extent American state criminal law.[59]

2. The Codification Debate and Historical Jurisprudence

To a surprising extent, many of the nineteenth-century general legal history books explicitly referred to Roman or civilian models in developing their subject, perhaps due to the interest in legal codification that characterized much of that century. Little, Brown published James Walker's volume, *The Theory of the Common Law*, in 1852.[60] Walker (1813–1854), a Scottish American, was a lawyer and South Carolina state legislator. He was representative of a circle of jurists in the antebellum South writing about Roman and civil law.[61] In *Theory*, Walker continued the argument he developed in an earlier book[62] that examined the

---

[56] *Id.* at 50–55.
[57] *Id.* at 55.
[58] *Id.* at 56–58.
[59] *Id.* at 58–62, 746–47; see FRIEDMAN, *supra* note 32, at 475 (reporting 800 volumes of American case reports by 1848); KERMIT L. HALL & PETER KARSTEN, THE MAGIC MIRROR: LAW IN AMERICAN HISTORY 140 (2d ed. 2009); Walter Theodore Hitchcock, Timothy Walker: Antebellum Lawyer (1990); *id.*, *Walker, Timothy*, in THE YALE BIOGRAPHICAL DICTIONARY OF AMERICAN LAW 568 (Roger K. Newman ed., 2009).
[60] JAMES M. WALKER, THE THEORY OF THE COMMON LAW (1852) [hereinafter WALKER, THEORY].
[61] HOEFLICH, *supra* note 15, at 50–52, 65, 69–73.
[62] JAMES M. WALKER, INQUIRY INTO THE USE AND AUTHORITY OF ROMAN JURISPRUDENCE IN THE LAW CONCERNING REAL ESTATE (1850). Michael Hoeflich called this "one of the earliest American contributions to the debate among legal historians as to whether substantive Roman law was ever

origin of common law property rules as they related to Roman law. However, he extended it to argue that Roman and civil law (as a form of natural law) could provide the scientific method necessary to organize the common law into a coherent system.[63] In distinguishing English law from that in America, he stated, "The law of the Colonies already conformed to a much greater extent than that of England to the *jus gentium*."[64]

Luther Cushing (1803–1856) in *An Introduction to the Study of the Roman Law* (1854) took a more forceful position for the absorption of Roman law principles into English common law. He traced this influence from the writing of Glanvill and Bracton up to Blackstone's *Commentaries*.[65] *Introduction* was the product of Cushing's lectures at Harvard Law School from 1848 to 1851.[66] Hoeflich placed Cushing midway between the historical school of jurisprudence and the German systematizing Pandectists who desired codification.[67]

Cushing presented three reasons for American law students to study Roman law. First, Roman jurists dealt clearly with the fundamentals of general jurisprudence, as had some eminent American judges, and these principles were part of American law. Second, important doctrines of American substantive and procedural law had their origin in Roman law. Third, the early European inhabitants of Louisiana, Florida, Texas, and California had directly introduced Roman and civil law into those jurisdictions. Finally, Roman law was the basis of the legal systems of civilized countries in Europe and the Americas with which the United States had trade relations as well as the foundation of private and public international law.[68]

In 1848, New York enacted a civil procedure code to simplify and reform one of the most technical and irrational areas of the common law. David Dudley Field (1805–1894) was the driving force behind its drafting and, although Louisiana had adopted a Digest of the Civil Laws in 1808—four years prior to statehood— and other codes in the 1820s, the 1848 New York code marked a bigger success for what became a widespread attempt to codify state private and penal law. The 1848 code, often called the Field Code, was clearly like the French and Louisiana civil procedure codes, which embraced the rationalism and scientific

received into the Anglo-American tradition," mentioning that it predated the efforts of Roscoe Pound by 50 years. HOEFLICH, *supra* note 15, at 63–64, 165 n.70.

[63] WALKER, THEORY, *supra* note 60, at 1, 4–8, 125–30; *see* HOEFLICH, *supra* note 15, at 52, 55, 63–65, 69.
[64] WALKER, THEORY, *supra* note 60, at 123.
[65] LUTHER CUSHING, AN INTRODUCTION TO THE STUDY OF THE ROMAN LAW 168–79 (1854).
[66] HOEFLICH, *supra* note 15, at 85–86. Cushing also served on the editorial board of a German comparative law journal and translated important French and German works on Roman and civil law into English, including those of Domat, Mittermaier, Pothier, and Savigny. *Id.*
[67] *Id.* at 86–87, 89–91.
[68] *Id.* at 3, 180–82.

organization of the European Enlightenment. Although the Field Code did not have initial success in the East, most states west of Ohio adopted it by the end of the century.[69]

Similarly, other jurists promoted ideas of simplifying or codifying parts of or the whole common law as suitable for an age of reason. Civil law jurisdictions provided models for codification. Nevertheless, the notion was not necessarily to import civil law rules, but to use the form of codes to digest and organize American law. In 1865, Field presented his civil code with the first three parts following the organization of the French Civil Code. New York never enacted it, but it had more success in the West, including California.[70]

The primary opponent to Field's civil code in New York was James Carter (1827–1905). He was a founder and longtime president of the Association of the Bar of the City of New York. Carter's influence with the New York legislature, coupled with speeches and pamphlet writing, were instrumental in the code's defeat.[71] He promoted the historical school of jurisprudence, which he first encountered as a Harvard Law School student in the writing of Friedrich Carl von Savigny (1779–1861) against codification in Germany. Carter believed that common law judges were better able than legislatures to conform American law to the fundamentals of justice as legal rules evolved from custom. The careful study of cases over time was an inductive science.[72]

In 1881, Little, Brown published *The Common Law* by Oliver Wendell Holmes Jr. (1841–1935).[73] It covered from a historical perspective criminal law and much of private law, with an occasional reference to Roman law. Within 20 years, jurists considered the book a classic, undoubtedly the most important American work of legal history and philosophy in the nineteenth century.[74] Holmes's education and experience prepared him to be receptive to a comparative perspective on law. His participation in the American Civil War and familiarity with its cruelties supported skepticism toward absolute truth or standards of right and wrong. During his years at Harvard Law School, the admittedly crude organization of private law between common law and equity and its structure within forms of pleading and remedies was breaking down and drowning in an ocean of new cases. Holmes in the early 1870s thought that a new principled order should

---

[69] FRIEDMAN, *supra* note 32, at 293–98. Louisiana adopted the Code of Practice in Civil Cases in 1825.

[70] *Id.* at 302–04.

[71] *See* JAMES COOLIDGE CARTER, LAW: ITS ORIGIN, GROWTH AND FUNCTION iii–v (1907).

[72] RABBAN, *supra* note 10, at 4–6, 31, 35, 356–57, 367–68, 508–09; *see* Mathias Reimann, *The Historical School against Codification: Savigny, Carter, and the Defeat of the New York Civil Code*, 37 AM. J. COMP. L. 95 (1989).

[73] HOLMES, *supra* note 1. This book was the product of a series of lectures Holmes delivered at the Lowell Institute in Boston; it has not been out of print since 1881. The 2009 Belknap Press (Harvard) version has an introduction by G. Edward White.

[74] *Id.* at xi, xx; *see* FRIEDMAN, *supra* note 32, at 479–80.

replace this chaotic situation. He first looked for this order in England under John Austin's analytical method.[75]

Holmes found that Austin's system failed to accommodate Holmes's Darwinian view of law as an evolutionary struggle with the strong prevailing over the weak. Abstraction and logic were inadequate; empirical observation and inductive generalization were necessary to understand living legal systems. Holmes turned to consider what other scholars, including legal scholars, from England and America were then examining—German methods in history, philosophy, and science. He found the German law professors' emphasis on history and science attractive as well as their development of historical jurisprudence. Holmes had studied Roman law and in the early 1870s was reading some German works in translation. By the mid-1870s, he had learned enough German to read the important books of the nineteenth century in law, legal history, and philosophy.[76]

By the time of *The Common Law*'s publication, Holmes rejected the dominant school of German legal conceptualism, the science of Justinian's *Digest* (Pandects) infused with Kantian individualism, as too much like the earlier abstract natural law but without the substantive morality. Although historical jurisprudence was to his liking, he did not acknowledge his resistance to the Romanists' legal formalism that existed within Germany like his own aversion to the formalism that Christopher Langdell's legal science at Harvard represented in America. Rudolf von Jhering, Germany's most famous opponent of *Pandektenwissenschaft*, had published *Der Kampf um's Recht* in 1872, which Holmes read in translation before 1881.[77] Its theme of the struggle for law parallels Holmes's social evolution ideas.[78] Holmes's use of the comparative method to develop his own legal ideas, even when he rejected some of the foreign formulations, was an important example of nineteenth-century American comparative legal history.[79]

---

[75] Mathias W. Reimann, *Holmes's Common Law and German Legal Science*, in THE LEGACY OF OLIVER WENDELL HOLMES, JR. 72, 74–79 (Robert W. Gordon ed., 1992); *see* JOHN AUSTIN, THE PROVINCE OF JURISPRUDENCE DETERMINED (1832); MARK DEWOLFE HOWE, 1 JUSTICE OLIVER WENDELL HOLMES: THE SHAPING YEARS, 1841–1870, at 35–207 (1957).

[76] Reimann, *supra* note 72, at 79–85; *see* MARK DEWOLFE HOWE, 2 JUSTICE OLIVER WENDELL HOLMES: THE PROVING YEARS, 1870–1882, at 135–54 (1963); David S. Clark, *Tracing the Roots of American Legal Education—A Nineteenth Century German Connection*, 51 RABELS ZEITSCHRIFT FÜR AUSLÄNDISCHES UND INTERNATIONALES PRIVATRECHT 313 (1987).

[77] Reimann, *supra* note 72, at 83–85, 91–95, 101–103; *see* RUDOLF VON IHERING, DER KAMPF UM'S RECHT (1872); *id.*, THE STRUGGLE FOR LAW (John J. Lalor ed., translated from the 5th German ed., 1879) [hereinafter IHERING, STRUGGLE].

[78] "The life of the law is a struggle,—a struggle of nations, of the state power, of classes, of individuals." IHERING, STRUGGLE, *supra* note 77, at 1 (2d ed. 1915). Holmes was clearly comfortable with views of the Germanists within the historical school of jurisprudence. Reimann, *supra* note 72, at 96–97.

[79] In Chapter 5, pt. E.6, I more fully develop Holmes's comparative inquiry and conclusions. See the sources cited there.

During the last decade of the nineteenth century, several general legal history books embraced the historical school of jurisprudence, its importance for judge-made law, and rejected the natural law foundation of early nineteenth-century codification. In 1894, Little, Brown published *The Laws and Jurisprudence of England and America*.[80] It comprised the 1891–1892 Storrs Lectures that Yale University established in 1889, delivered by John Dillon (1831–1914) at the law school over the course of that academic year. Dillon, also president of the ABA during his lectureship,[81] exhibited the increasing parochialism characteristic of the historical school, particularly if it adopted some *Volksgeist* ideal for the American people.

> There is one purpose which runs through all the lectures, . . . to exhibit the excellences of our legal system as it now exists, with a view to show that for the people subject to its rule it is, with all its faults, better than the Roman or any other alien system. It is . . . a protest against the *Continentalization* of our law.[82]

Among the faults Dillon identified, the common law's bulk and disorder were its most significant.

> The pressing want of our substantive law is an authoritative, scientific, and comprehensive arrangement of its vast and scattered materials. . . . [F]or this purpose, our law must be treated as substantially unique and distinctive, and arranged according to its real character,—arranged, so to speak, from within and not from without. . . . [I]t seems to be taken for granted that the Roman law will supply all or most of the needed aid and models. This is a radical mistake. Our laws and jurisprudence must be analyzed and resolved into their constituent principles, and these must be arranged according to their own nature and historical development.[83]

---

[80] John F. Dillon, The Laws and Jurisprudence of England and America (1894, reprint 1995).

[81] Friedman, *supra* note 32, at 343; *see id.* at 477–78. Dillon served as a justice on the Iowa Supreme Court (1862–1868), federal judge on the Eighth Circuit Court (1869–1879), and law professor at Columbia Law School (1879–1882) before devoting himself to a lucrative practice in New York representing railroads and financiers. *Id.* at 403; Hall & Karsten, *supra* note 59, at 244; Thomas H. Boyd, *Dillon, John Forest*, in The Yale Biographical Dictionary of American Law 164–65 (Roger K. Newman ed., 2009).

[82] Dillon, *supra* note 80, at viii; *see id.* at 24–26, 143–44, 169–71.

[83] *Id.* at x; *see id.* at 179–86, 242–92, 344–47, 373. Other authors were hostile to codification of the private law in any form. *See, e.g.*, R. Floyd Clarke, The Science of Law and Lawmaking: Being an Introduction to Law, a General View of Its Forms and Substance, and a Discussion of the Question of Codification (1898).

In the last decades of the nineteenth century, some American jurists were not as dismissive of Langdell's formalism as Holmes was, or as nativist as Dillon. For instance, William A. Keener (1856–1913) brought Langdell's case method of teaching to Columbia Law School in 1891 as dean. Keener earned his law degree at Harvard from 1874 to 1877 during the first years of Langdell's innovation and returned to teach there in 1883 (as Story Professor from 1888–1890).[84] He prepared a course book of excerpts on Anglo-American law that was less insular than Dillon's book. West Publishing Co. (St. Paul) printed *Selections on the Elements of Jurisprudence* (1896).[85] Unlike Keener's casebooks on contracts and equity, this volume included materials from books and journals that teachers could use to introduce first-year law students to their new discipline.[86] Although there were many references to Roman law, Keener did not intend by his selections to denigrate or embrace it, but rather to place it in the appropriate historical context. By the end of the nineteenth century, Roman law primarily served for some jurists as an alternative legal system for the emerging academic discipline of comparative law.[87]

Other jurists took a more favorable view toward the usefulness of Roman law (or analogous civil law systems) for the reform of American law or for understanding the nature and evolution of law. For instance, Isaac Russell (1857–1931) compiled 48 lectures in 1894 under the title *Outline Study of Law* that he used in his introduction to American law course at the University of the City of New York.[88] He made many comparative references throughout the book and the 13th lecture carried the heading "A Plea for the Study of Roman Law."[89] Roman law, in particular, would be useful to Americans considering the codification of law.[90]

William Howe (1833–1909) took the Romanist perspective much further in preparing a book, based on his 1894 Storrs Lectures, for a course of study in "comparative jurisprudence." From its title, *Studies in the Civil Law, and Its*

---

[84] FRIEDMAN, *supra* note 32, at 471; Jonathan Lurie, *Keener, William Albert*, in 12 AMERICAN NATIONAL BIOGRAPHY 447 (John A. Garraty & Mark C. Carnes eds., 1999); *see supra* text accompanying note 77 (Holmes's resistance to Langdell's conceptualism). Keener served ten years as dean at Columbia until 1901. Lurie, *supra*, at 447.

[85] WILLIAM A. KEENER, SELECTIONS ON THE ELEMENTS OF JURISPRUDENCE (1896).

[86] *Id.* at iii.

[87] HOEFLICH, *supra* note 15, at 103–07, 112–15, 123–30, 139–40.

[88] ISAAC FRANKLIN RUSSELL, OUTLINE STUDY OF LAW iii (2d ed. 1895), published by Baker, Voorhis & Co. in New York. It published a first edition in 1894 and a third edition in 1900.

[89] *Id.* at 82–90.

[90] *Id.* at 89.

[I]t may be said of Roman law, that it furnishes a key to the whole body of continental legislation, to public and private international law, to much of the admiralty and equity jurisprudence of to-day, to the law of bailments, trusts and succession; it provides us with ... the best known canons of interpretation and construction; and, finally, it exhibits a course of development during a millennium which is full of instruction regarding the forces which make for legal evolution. *Id.*

Relations to the Law of England and America, one could see that Roman and civil law would be central.[91]

> The civil law is also one of the many elements which have concurred in the formation of what we know as the law of England and America. You are not asked to neglect the other elements. I only hope to suggest and to stimulate,—to ask you to study a little, and especially to compare.[92]

The 14 lectures then traced the development of Roman law; its study at universities in Europe; its effect on England; and then, subject by subject, how one might better understand American law by considering its Roman law antecedents and similarities.

C. Historiography: 1900 to 1950

Legal history, and indeed comparative legal history, made a strong appearance at the beginning of the twentieth century. Shortly after the formation of the Association of American Law Schools (AALS) in 1900, designed to represent academic lawyers in their collective endeavor to make legal education more scientific and prestigious,[93] the organization established a committee to collect materials for books that would serve to educate students and the legal profession in legal history, foreign law, and legal philosophy.[94] From 1907 to 1909, Little Brown published three volumes of edited articles and book excerpts with the title *Select Essays in Anglo-American Legal History*.[95] Many of the

---

[91] WILLIAM WIRT HOWE, STUDIES IN THE CIVIL LAW, AND ITS RELATIONS TO THE LAW OF ENGLAND AND AMERICA vii, 1 (1896), published by Little, Brown [hereinafter HOWE, STUDIES]. It published a second edition in 1905 with a slightly modified subtitle. Howe taught the comparative jurisprudence class in 1899–1900 at the Columbian University School of Comparative Jurisprudence and Diplomacy in Washington, D.C. *See id.* COURSE IN COMPARATIVE JURISPRUDENCE: SYNOPSIS (1899). Howe had been a justice on the Louisiana Supreme Court from 1869–1873 and served as ABA president in 1898–1899. HOWE, STUDIES, *supra*, at 1; George Dargo, *Howe, William Wirt*, *in* 11 AMERICAN NATIONAL BIOGRAPHY 345–46 (John A. Garraty & Mark C. Carnes eds., 1999).

[92] HOWE, STUDIES, *supra* note 91, at 2.

[93] ROBERT STEVENS, LAW SCHOOL: LEGAL EDUCATION IN AMERICA FROM THE 1850S TO THE 1980S, at 96–103 (1983).

[94] ASSOCIATION OF AMERICAN LAW SCHOOLS, PROCEEDINGS OF THE ANNUAL MEETING 15–18 (1905). Dean John Henry Wigmore (Northwestern University), an important comparatist, prepared the resolution that the AALS adopted. *Id.* at 15. Wigmore chaired the three-person committee, which included another comparatist, Ernst Freund, a University of Chicago law professor who had received his doctor juris at Heidelberg, and William Mikell, future dean (1914–1929) of the University of Pennsylvania.

[95] 1–3 SELECT ESSAYS IN ANGLO-AMERICAN LEGAL HISTORY (Committee of the Association of American Law Schools ed., 1907–1909, reprint 1992) [hereinafter SELECT ESSAYS].

essays treated the influence of Roman, canon, and civil law on the common law tradition.[96]

1. James Carter

After James Carter's retirement from active law practice, he prepared a series of 13 lectures that he intended to deliver at Harvard Law School.[97] These were published posthumously as *Law: Its Origin, Growth and Function* (1907).[98] Contemporary jurists recognized Carter as the leading proponent of the idea that law, especially private law, developed from evolving custom. He believed that, in general, an enlightened minority in society generates the evolution of custom, which the majority then gradually accepts, typically making it suitable for an effective legal rule. Nevertheless, some custom is more appropriate for moral force alone. Carter indirectly referred to Savigny in explaining his historical jurisprudence. In addition, Carter explicitly rejected natural law (unprovable) and positivism (state force) as viable theories to understand law.[99]

Carter argued that social change subjects custom to transformation so that law should similarly reflect that adjustment. Judges are best able to carry out this task via the doctrine of precedent, which authenticates custom. "A judicial precedent is not law *per se*, but evidence of it only. The real law is custom."[100] Legislation will only be effective when it reinforces custom; in this situation, one may properly call it law. Beyond that, legislation is normally suitable for public law.[101] In developing his position, Carter made numerous references to Roman law and a few to canon law.[102]

---

[96] *E.g.*, Thomas Edward Scrutton, *Roman Law Influence in Chancery, Church Courts, Admiralty, and Law Merchant*, *in* 1 SELECT ESSAYS, *supra* note 95, at 208; William Stubbs, *The History of Canon Law in England*, *in* 1 SELECT ESSAYS, *supra*, at 248; James Bryce, *A Comparison of the History of Legal Development at Rome and in England*, *in* 1 SELECT ESSAYS, *supra*, at 332; Christopher Columbus Langdell, *The Development of Equity Pleading from Canon Law Procedure*, *in* 2 SELECT ESSAYS, *supra*, at 753 (Langdell cited works in Latin and French).
[97] CARTER, *supra* note 71, at iii–iv, vii.
[98] *Id.*
[99] RABBAN, *supra* note 10, at 340–42, 357, 364–65; *see* CARTER, *supra* note 71, at 4–14, 19–20, 129, 118, 120, 173–74, 241–42, 313, 321.
[100] CARTER, *supra* note 71, at 84, cited in RABBAN, *supra* note 10, at 344; *see* CARTER, *supra*, at 65–66, 79–80, 119, 129–30, 320; RABBAN, *supra*, at 343–44, 356–57.
[101] RABBAN, *supra* note 10, at 358–60; *see* CARTER, *supra* note 71, at 115–17, 120, 135–36, 228, 238, 242, 244–45, 253, 257–62, 333–36.
[102] CARTER, *supra* note 71, at 35–37, 88–91, 101–05, 286–301.

2. Roscoe Pound

From the early years of the twentieth century, Roscoe Pound (1870-1964) was a major influence on American legal history, comparative law, and legal philosophy.[103] Writing in 1953, Edwin Patterson, Cardozo Professor of Jurisprudence at Columbia University, concluded:

> Pound's sociological jurisprudence is the most comprehensive, coherent and original philosophy of law yet produced in the United States. Most of its basic beliefs are grounded on pragmatism, much of its constructive apparatus resembles Hegel's dialectical idealism and many of its valuable insights were derived from the Roman and civil law.[104]

Pound's books illustrated significant ways in which history, philosophy, and the comparative method could overlap with each other.[105] In *Readings on the History and System of the Common Law*, Pound in 1904 followed Keener's 1896 model of using book and article excerpts (with the addition of documents and many court cases). Pound wanted to challenge students in liberal arts and law to think about the subject of legal history, the nature of the common law, and its American version modified by local custom and natural law.[106] By the time of the book's second edition in 1913, Pound had already written about the influence of the civil law on American law.[107] He also attempted to introduce that theme in *Readings* by editing excerpts that described the absorption of civil and canon law

---

[103] See HOEFLICH, *supra* note 15, at 2, 116, 125-30; *see generally* N.E.H. HULL, ROSCOE POUND AND KARL LLEWELLYN: SEARCHING FOR AN AMERICAN JURISPRUDENCE (1997); EDWARD B. MCLEAN, LAW AND CIVILIZATION: THE LEGAL THOUGHT OF ROSCOE POUND (1992); PAUL SAYRE, THE LIFE OF ROSCOE POUND (1948).

[104] EDWIN W. PATTERSON, JURISPRUDENCE: MEN AND IDEAS OF THE LAW 509 (1953); *see id.* at 511-13. Patterson noted that Pound's sociological jurisprudence was prescriptive, while sociology of law was descriptive and empirical. *Id.* at 509. This would distinguish Pound's intellectual history from the movement toward social history that gained dominance in the 1970s.

[105] For instance, as dean of the law department at the University of Nebraska (1903-1907), Pound wrote *Outlines of Lectures on Jurisprudence* (67 pp., 1903), *Readings on the History and System of the Common Law* (404 pp., 1904), and *Readings in Roman Law* (234 pp., 1906), all of which Jacob North & Co. in Lincoln published. After Pound accepted a professorship at Harvard Law School in 1910, Harvard University Press continued *Jurisprudence* in a second edition in 1914 through a fifth edition in 1943 (now 244 pp.) and *Roman Law*, broadened to also cover civil law as a course book for comparative law, in a second edition in 1914 (159 pp.). The Boston Book Company published the second edition of *Common Law* in 1913, which Theodore Plucknett joined for a third edition in 1927 (731 pp.) and Lawyers Co-operative Publishing Company (Rochester) printed.

[106] ROSCOE POUND, READINGS ON THE HISTORY AND SYSTEM OF THE COMMON LAW iii-v, 262-304 (Boston Book Co., 2d ed., 1913) (describing the 1904 edition) [hereinafter POUND, READINGS]; see *supra* text accompanying notes 74-77 (Keener).

[107] *Id.* at 289, n.1; *see id.*, *The Influence of French Law in America*, 3 ILL. L. REV. 354 (1908-1909).

into English common law through the ecclesiastical, merchant, and admiralty jurisdictions.[108]

In 1921, Pound delivered a series of lectures at Dartmouth College, which arranged for their publication as *The Spirit of the Common Law*.[109] The book was as much about legal philosophy as legal history. Pound began his first lecture:

> Perhaps no institution of the modern world shows such vitality and tenacity as our Anglo-American legal tradition which we call the common law. Although it is essentially a mode of judicial and juristic thinking, a mode of treating legal problems rather than a fixed body of definite rules, it succeeds everywhere in molding rules, whatever their origin, into accord with its principles and in maintaining those principles in the face of formidable attempts to overthrow or to supersede them.[110]

Pound illustrated this assertion with the success of common law thought over the increasing mass of American legislation and its reception in Texas and California (and inroads in Louisiana) against civil law institutions. Comparative law insights permeated the book from its beginning, as he added additional common law confrontations with the civil law: Québec, Scotland, South Africa, Puerto Rico, and the Philippines.[111]

Pound found the power of the common law "in its treatment of concrete controversies, as the strength of its rival, the modern Roman law, is in its logical development of abstract conceptions."[112] If common law judges control the administration of justice, "their habit of applying to the cause in hand the judicial experience of the past rather than attempting to fit the cause into its exact logical pigeonhole in an abstract system gradually undermines the competing body of rules and makes for a slow but persistent invasion of the common law."[113] Pound wanted to ascertain the *spirit* of the common law in a quest similar to that of Charles-Louis de Montesquieu (1689–1755), Rudolf von Ihering (1818–1892), and Friedrich von Savigny.[114]

---

[108] POUND, READINGS, *supra* note 106, at 26–27, 44–58, 278–83. In Chapter 6, I more fully develop Pound's contributions to comparative law.

[109] ROSCOE POUND, THE SPIRIT OF THE COMMON LAW (1921) [hereinafter POUND, SPIRIT)]. The New Hampshire publisher, Marshall Jones Company, reprinted the book in 1925, 1931, and 1947. Beacon Press reprinted the volume in 1963 (with a preface by Supreme Court Justice Arthur J. Goldberg) as did Transaction Publishers in 1999 (with an introduction by Neil Hamilton and Mathias Alfred Jaren).

[110] *Id.* at 1.

[111] *Id.* at 1–2; *see id.* at 5.

[112] *Id.* at 2.

[113] *Id.* at 3. Pound believed that Japan decided to import German law (over that of England or France) because it was a contest among systems of rules, not modes of judicial administration. "In a contest of abstract systems the common law is at its worst." *Id.*

[114] Edwin W. Patterson, *The Spirit of the Common Law*, 20 MICH. L. REV. 809, 809 (1922) (book review); *see* RUDOLPH JHERING, 1–4 GEIST DES RÖMISCHEN RECHTS AUF DEN VERSCHIEDENEN STUFEN

Pound began his common law history at the same place Holmes did, the Germanic laws and institutions utilized by common law judges.[115] Even though the Norman Conquest of England added some French legal vocabulary, it initially brought little of importance from Roman law.[116] He asserted that scholars had discredited historical jurisprudence, which should be replaced by "sociological legal history; . . . a study not merely of how legal doctrines have evolved and developed as jural materials, but of the social causes and social effects of doctrines and of the relations of legal history to social and economic history."[117] Pound singled out Carter as the leading representative of historical jurisprudence. Pound criticized that theory's evils, especially in promoting excessive individualism and deductive formalism.[118]

Pound identified two central characteristics of the common law tradition. First, there was extreme individualism. Second, pulling in another direction, there was an emphasis on legal relations rather than legal transactions as the basis for legal consequences. This second aspect imposed liability and duty on certain people in a relationship independently of a person's will.[119] Pound discussed these characteristics in the context of seven factors significant in distinct historical periods.[120] Throughout, he made many comparisons with developments in Roman and continental European law with textual references to European jurists.[121]

SEINER ENTWICKLUNG (1852–1865); CHARLES DE SECONDAT MONTESQUIEU, THE SPIRIT OF THE LAWS (Anne M. Cohler et al. eds. & trans., 1989, orig. French ed. 1748, Thomas Nugent orig. English trans., 1900); FREDERICH CHARLES VON SAVIGNY, OF THE VOCATION OF OUR AGE FOR LEGISLATION AND JURISPRUDENCE 24, 27–30 (Abraham Hayward trans., 1831, orig. German ed. 1814) (Savigny's concept of *Volksgeist* or people's spirit). *See generally* Eugen Ehrlich, *Montesquieu and Sociological Jurisprudence*, 29 HARV. L. REV. 582 (1916); PATTERSON, *supra* note 104, at 410–14, 459, 462–63.

[115] POUND, SPIRIT, *supra* note 109, at 16–17; *see* HOLMES, *supra* note 1, at xvi, 5, 17–24. Holmes did call Roman law the other parent of the common law. *Id.* at 17; *see id.* at 6–17.

[116] POUND, SPIRIT, *supra* note 109, at 16. "[O]ur law is today more Germanic than the law of Germany itself." *Id.*

[117] *Id.* at 10. "The most ingrained of the errors which are held about the Common Law is that it consists of the ancient tribal laws of the Anglo-Saxons, brought with them from German forests to England and slowly—but not essentially—modified by the course of events in England and in America." MAX RADIN, HANDBOOK OF ANGLO-AMERICAN LEGAL HISTORY 528 (1936, reprint 1993).

[118] RABBAN, *supra* note 10, at 31, 430–31, 449–50, 465. Rabban detailed the many errors Pound made in his critique of historical jurisprudence in general and Carter in particular. *Id.* at 430–31, 437, 450. Ironically, Harvard Law School appointed Pound to the Carter Professorship of General Jurisprudence in 1913. *Id.* at 437.

[119] POUND, SPIRIT, *supra* note 109, at 13–14.

[120] *Id.* at 14–15. After the Germanic laws and legal institutions came English feudalism, Puritanism in England and America, competition between the Crown and courts, eighteenth-century natural law rights, American pioneer individualism up to the Civil War, and the transformation of these factors by American courts (judicial empiricism). At the time Pound wrote, he believed American law was in a transition between individualist justice to social justice or the socialization of the law. *Id.* at 14–15, 185–216.

[121] *E.g.*, in discussing the jurisprudence of interests: "We owe this way of thinking to Rudolf von Jhering who was the first to insist upon the interests which the legal order secures rather than the legal rights by which it secures them." *Id.* at 203–04. Pound's book had no footnotes.

Soon after Pound completed his time as Harvard Law School's dean, he delivered lectures at Tulane Law School that Little, Brown published in 1938 as *The Formative Era of American Law*.[122] As the title suggests, compared to *The Spirit of the Common Law*, he more narrowly focused this volume to cover America from about 1776 to the end of the Civil War. In addition, in text and footnotes, he more strongly emphasized the importance of Roman and civil law on American legal development.[123]

> In the history of Anglo-American law there are successive borrowings and adaptations from Roman law (*e.g.* the rules as to title by occupation), from the canon law (*e.g.* our law and practice as to marriage and divorce and probate and administration), from the modern Roman law and Continental codes (*e.g.* in our law of riparian rights), and from the commercial law of Continental Europe, as Mansfield's decisions and the decisions and tests of Kent and Story make clear abundantly.[124]

Incorporating that into his legal history, Pound described four major elements that influenced American law: natural law, legislation, case law, and doctrinal writing. Of all the general histories of American law, this volume made the most transparent case for the significant infiltration of continental legal ideas into the U.S. legal system.[125]

3. Max Radin

During the period that Pound's lectures on legal history appeared, another law professor who also had the background to understand civil law developments wrote a general American legal history recognizing both civil law and common law influences. Max Radin (1880–1950), born in East Prussia (now Poland), grew up in the United States and learned Greek and Latin during his classical studies. He taught law at the University of California (Berkeley) from 1919 until his death.[126] After preparing *Handbook of Roman Law* in 1927 for West Publishing

---

[122] POUND, FORMATIVE ERA, *supra* note 31, at vii.
[123] See HOEFLICH, *supra* note 15, at 129–30. At the end of his preface, Pound sardonically stated:

> As I am telling of the reception, adaptation and developing of a taught legal tradition, it has been necessary to say something about recent theories of law as formulated class self-interest, or as a product of individual judicial psychology governing the behavior of the judge, or as a disappearing phenomenon in the society of the future.

POUND, FORMATIVE ERA, *supra* note 31, at vii–viii.
[124] POUND, FORMATIVE ERA, *supra* note 31, at 94.
[125] See examples described and cited in Chapters 2 to 5.
[126] William R. Dennes, Harold F. Cherniss, & Alexander M. Kidd, *Max Radin, Law: Berkeley and Hastings*, in *University of California: In Memoriam, 1950*, at 21–26 (1950), at https://cdlib.org

Company, he continued with West's Hornbook Series to write *Handbook of Anglo-American Legal History* (1936).[127] Radin summarized his view of the development of English common law.

> Besides Anglo-Saxon law, which was . . . "received" into the body of the Common Law, there were other legal systems which to a greater and smaller degree were "received" at different times. These were (1) "feudal law" of Continental, and originally of Lombard, origin; (2) the Canon Law, which was receiving a new formulation just when the Common Law was in its infancy; (3) the Roman or Civil Law; [and] (4) the Law Merchant.[128]

Radin also emphasized the importance of legal literature and how civil and canon law forms influenced common law writers.[129]

4. The Dominance of Intellectual Legal History

In *The Formative Era* Pound had identified the historical school as the major force to turn jurists away from natural law.[130] Of course, by emphasizing philosophies of law, he was engaged in intellectual history. Pound criticized Savigny and by implication those American jurists, especially Carter, supporting historical jurisprudence as unduly individualistic, formalistic, and hostile to legislation. Pound preferred the newer anti-formalist German legal thought illustrated by von Ihering, American philosophical pragmatism, and the promise of emerging social sciences. Pound labeled his approach sociological jurisprudence, but at a philosophical level and not as empirical sociology. It recognized the importance

---

(Google search using authors and title); Richard Hyland, in THE YALE BIOGRAPHICAL DICTIONARY OF AMERICAN LAW 444–45 (Roger K. Newman ed., 2009). Radin earned his law degree at New York University and Ph.D. (in classical philology) at Columbia University, where he published his dissertation, THE LEGISLATION OF THE GREEKS AND ROMANS ON CORPORATIONS (1909). Dennes et al., *supra*, at 23–24. Among other subjects at Berkeley, Radin taught Roman law and comparative law. Hyland, *supra*, at 444.

[127] RADIN, *supra* note 117. It is clear from the footnotes in *Anglo-American Legal History* that Radin could also read French and German. West began the Hornbook Series in 1894 with Benjamin J. Shipman, *Hand-book of Common-Law Pleading*.

[128] RADIN, *supra* note 117, at 41; *see* 107–09, 115–18, 145–51, 486–500. "There is scarcely any one of the specific developments of the Common Law that did not form part of a larger group that extended into the Continent." *Id.* at 529. Nevertheless, Radin was quick to add: "But the core of the Common Law is not to be found in any of these systems. It was created out of the needs of an administrative organization conditioned by the strange and exceptional position of the Norman and Angevin kings." *Id.*

[129] *Id.* at 275–97. Blackstone was the most important example for America. *Id.* at 286–87, 303–304, *see supra* text accompanying notes 33–34 (Blackstone).

[130] *See, e.g.*, POUND, FORMATIVE ERA, *supra* note 31, at 21, 26–27, 63–64, 110–17, 144–45.

of collective interests needed to solve pressing social problems that excessive individualism created.[131]

In 1924, William Walsh, a New York University law professor, adopted that historical school perspective when he wrote the textbook *Outlines of the History of English and American Law*.[132] Walsh took a conservative view of law that made history dominant and legal interpretation backward looking. He stated in the preface to the book's second edition, "Legal education needs more legal history and real understanding and less of modern pragmatic and behavioristic philosophy."[133] By detailing differences between property, tort, contract, and inheritance rules and doctrine in England and the American states, Walsh utilized a type of intra-tradition comparison within the common law.[134]

D. Historiography: 1950 to 2000

1. Perry Miller, Intellectual Legal History, and Its Decline

Perry Miller's (1905–1963) posthumous *The Life of the Mind in America* (1965),[135] which the following year won the Pulitzer Prize for History, contained perhaps the most influential essay on early American legal history in the immediate post–World War II period.[136] Miller wrote in the tradition of Henry Steele Commager, a historian who was also interested in the American mind.[137] Commager described his book as a study in comparative cultural history and stated his major premise to support the notion of American exceptionalism. "[T]here is a distinctively American way of thought, character, and conduct."[138] Commager wrote two chapters on law. The first chapter, as did Miller, emphasized the importance

---

[131] RABBAN, *supra* note 10, at 8, 423, 426–36, 442–62. Rabban convincingly demonstrated that Pound's portrayal of Carter was seriously misleading. *Id.* at 430–31, 523.

[132] WILLIAM F. WALSH, OUTLINES OF THE HISTORY OF ENGLISH AND AMERICAN LAW (New York University Press, 1924). The second edition, which Bobbs-Merrill Company published in 1932, had the title *A History of Anglo-American Law*.

[133] WILLIAM F. WALSH, A HISTORY OF ANGLO-AMERICAN LAW iv (2d ed. 1932, reprint 1993).

[134] "Departure from the English law in special cases in the United States will be referred to hereafter in tracing the history of the law by topics." *Id.* at 97. The comparison of legal rules and institutions between England and one or more American states (or between two other common law jurisdictions) has not engaged most American comparatists, although there is no sound justification for this failure. A notable exception is RICHARD A. POSNER, LAW AND LEGAL THEORY IN ENGLAND AND AMERICA (1996).

[135] PERRY MILLER, THE LIFE OF THE MIND IN AMERICA: FROM THE REVOLUTION TO THE CIVIL WAR (1965).

[136] *Id.* at 97–265 ("The Legal Mentality," in seven chapters).

[137] HENRY STEELE COMMAGER, THE AMERICAN MIND: AN INTERPRETATION OF AMERICAN THOUGHT AND CHARACTER SINCE THE 1880's (1950).

[138] *Id.* at vii; *see id.* at viii, 3–5. The theme of exceptionalism continued into the 1990s and beyond. *See, e.g.*, DOROTHY ROSS, THE ORIGINS OF AMERICAN SOCIAL SCIENCE xiv–xviii, 22–171 (1991).

of natural law, derived from English common law and European civil law, but reformulated by Kent and Story for American conditions in the pre-Civil War period.[139] The second chapter proceeded to Louis Brandeis (1856–1941), Holmes, and Pound. Social, political, and economic circumstances supported a new form of jurisprudence that favored functionalism and devalued formalism.[140]

As described by Stanley Katz, Miller based his analysis on the legal literature developed prior to the Civil War. One can best infer institutional and social development and historical change in general from literary sources relevant to the topic. Consequently, "legal history becomes the study of what lawyers and judges have committed to print."[141] Katz used Miller's chapter on the debate for legal codification to illustrate this point and then proceeded to demonstrate the shortcoming of Miller's persistent use of dualities in his view of American history. In addition, Katz argued that legal history should reorient itself toward a wider range of source materials to demonstrate law's social significance as well as its social origins.[142]

Likewise, but more forcefully, Lawrence Friedman directly took on Miller's approach to legal history. Friedman pointed out that Miller relied primarily on juristic writing rather than statutes or judicial opinions to form generalizations about legal change and the "legal mind."[143] Friedman disagreed that the intellectual elements of law could cause or explain social change; quite the contrary, he saw the causation arrow running from social change to developments in law and legal institutions.[144] The implication was that legal history to be more informative should focus on the social context in which the legal system operated.

Through the end of the 1960s, some legal historians continued to emphasize intellectual history. Bernard Bailyn and Gordon Wood were important examples with their books on early American law.[145] Robert Gordon and Katz later referred to the two principal approaches to writing legal history as internalist (intellectual) and externalist (social).[146] One's preference depends on whether

---

[139] COMMAGER, *supra* note 137, at 359–69; *see* MILLER, *supra* note 135, at 109–50, 156–61, 164–82, 193–95, 207–38.
[140] COMMAGER, *supra* note 137, at 374–90.
[141] Katz, *supra* note 31, at 877–78.
[142] *Id.* at 878–80, 882–83.
[143] Lawrence M. Friedman, *Heart against Head: Perry Miller and the Legal Mind*, YALE L.J. 1244, 1245 (1968) (book review).
[144] *Id.* at 1245–53, 1255–57.
[145] *See* BERNARD BAILYN, THE IDEOLOGICAL ORIGINS OF THE AMERICAN REVOLUTION (1967); GORDON S. WOOD, THE CREATION OF THE AMERICAN REPUBLIC, 1776–1787 (1969).
[146] ROBERT GORDON, TAMING THE PAST: ESSAYS ON LAW IN HISTORY AND HISTORY IN LAW 18–20 (2017) (original article published in 1975); Stanley N. Katz, *Explaining the Law in Early American History: Introduction*, 50 WM. & MARY Q. 3–6 (1993). For a critique of this dichotomy and the misleading application of the internalist label to major legal scholars from the end of the Civil War to World War I, *see* David M. Rabban, *The Historiography of Late Nineteenth-Century American Legal History*, 4 THEORETICAL INQ. L. 541, 544–47, 575–78 (2003).

one believes a nation's law is mostly autonomous from society or thoroughly dependent on it for law's creation and change. The latter view animates the "mirror of society" metaphor.[147]

2. Willard Hurst and the Emergence of Social Legal History

As Gordon, Katz and others foretold, American legal history's dominant perspective was set to change and that occurred with the work of Willard Hurst (1910–1997). The Social Science Research Council provided Hurst one of its "demobilization awards" that assisted in the preparation of *The Growth of American Law: The Law Makers* (1950).[148] This book, which Little, Brown published, adopted a thoroughly social scientific approach to understanding the reality of American law, an approach that fully blossomed in the 1970s. Although Hurst recognized the worth of earlier work by Holmes and Pound,[149] his history of American law would be more fully instrumental and realist in recognizing the significant of legal institutions and their processes, and the dominance of economic interests and values.[150] The social was more important than the legal.[151] Hurst identified three factors that channeled the development of American law: (1) the country's physical setting—geography, distance, and isolation[152]— and natural resources; (2) technology; and (3) the social setting, including people's habits, values, and ideas.[153] He later applied this economic and social approach to law in the lectures he delivered at Northwestern University School of Law that became *Law and the Conditions of Freedom in the Nineteenth-Century United States*.[154] There he argued that Americans used law to release their creative energies.

---

[147] *See* KERMIT L. HALL, THE MAGIC MIRROR: LAW IN AMERICAN HISTORY 3–5 (1989).

[148] JAMES WILLARD HURST, THE GROWTH OF AMERICAN LAW: THE LAW MAKERS (1950) [hereinafter HURST, GROWTH].

[149] *See, e.g., id.* at 171, 184.

[150] *Id.* at 4; *see id.* at 14–16. "We shall get a more realistic grasp of the part law has played in United States history if we keep in mind this readiness of Americans to use it as a means to bring about immediate practical results." *Id.* The institutions Hurst examined were legislatures, courts, constitution-making machinery, the bar, and executive and administrative agencies.

[151] *Id.* at 4. "In the interaction of law and American life the law was passive, acted upon by other social forces, more often than acting upon them." *Id.*

[152] *Id.* at 6–9. "The physical setting worked to free us from legal traditions that might otherwise have bound us. The ocean limited the ideas freighted over from the common law and civil systems, great as was the effect of both." *Id.* at 8.

[153] *Id.* at 9–19.

[154] JAMES WILLARD HURST, LAW AND THE CONDITIONS OF FREEDOM IN THE NINETEENTH-CENTURY UNITED STATES (1956); *see* Carl Landauer, *Social Science on a Lawyer's Bookshelf: Willard Hurst's* Law and the Conditions of Freedom in the Nineteenth-Century United States, 18 LAW & HIST. REV. 59 (2000).

Hurst's emphasis on social factors left little room for the influence of foreign legal ideas on prominent individuals. This was true whether he was discussing David Field and his codification efforts or Christopher Langdell and the reform of legal education, both of which Hurst considered significant.[155] In general, he believed the role of individual lawyers and judges to be minor in the development of American law.[156]

The traditional treatment of American legal history as an extension of English legal history found further support in the mid-1960s with two course books that West published as part of its American Casebook Series.[157] An earlier effort to prepare cases and materials to teach law students chiefly American law did not find a publisher to print the volume. That was Mark Howe's *Readings in American Legal History* (1949).[158] By the early 1960s, only four American law schools taught a course specifically on American legal history.[159]

The first of the West books in the 1960s was Joseph Smith's *Cases and Materials on the Development of Legal Institutions*,[160] which grew out of materials Julius Goebel had used at Columbia University since 1928.[161] Goebel used political, social, economic, and intellectual factors in his historical analysis, which Smith also emphasized.[162] Nevertheless, their treatment of American law still deeply embedded English history. The influence on America of Roman and canon law and the European *lex mercatoria*, Smith argued, came through England.[163]

The second West course book gave more attention to American law and some to non-English sources, but still presented legal history as an Anglo-American process. Spencer Kimball had used cases and extracts at the University of

---

[155] *See* HURST, GROWTH, *supra* note 148, at 18, 71, 76, 86, 88, 91, 184–85, 261–71, 276. Chapters 4 and 5 fully treat civil law influences on the reforms led by Field and Langdell.

[156] *Id.* at 17–18. "We may be especially tempted to put too much weight on individual contributions in the law.... There are very few men in our legal history over whom one hesitates in making this general denial of individual influence." *Id.* at 17. Of the exceptions that Hurst mentioned, Chapters 3 to 5 discuss David Field, Thomas Jefferson, James Kent, Joseph Story, and James Wilson. See Hurst's full list in *id.* at 18.

[157] West began this series in 1908 with WILLIAM E. MIKELL, CASES ON CRIMINAL LAW: SELECTED FROM DECISIONS OF ENGLISH AND AMERICAN COURTS (1908), and EUGENE ALLEN GILMORE, CASES ON THE LAW OF PARTNERSHIP, INCLUDING LIMITED PARTNERSHIPS: SELECTED FROM DECISIONS OF ENGLISH AND AMERICAN COURTS (1908).

[158] Mark DeWolfe Howe, *Readings in American Legal History* (Harvard University Press, mimeographed, 529 pp., 1949). "The study of American legal history is only in its infancy, and any attempt to deal with the subject as a whole seems, for the present, inadvisable." *Id.* at iii.

[159] Edward D. Re, *Legal History Courses in American Law Schools*, 13 AM. U. L. REV. 45–46, 48, 56–59 (1963). One law school, at the University of Miami, taught a comparative legal history course. *Id.* at 51–53.

[160] JOSEPH H. SMITH, CASES AND MATERIALS ON THE DEVELOPMENT OF LEGAL INSTITUTIONS (1965).

[161] MATERIALS FOR THE DEVELOPMENT OF LEGAL INSTITUTIONS (Julius Goebel Jr. ed., 1928, 412 pp.), with seven versions up to 1946.

[162] SMITH, *supra* note 160, at 1–9.

[163] *See id., e.g.*, at 9, 31–33, 494, 635–46.

Michigan since 1961, which led to *Historical Introduction to the Legal System*.[164] He was more sensitive to the direct influence of French and Spanish law in regions that had been subject to the control of those countries[165] and to civilian ideas that clearly played some role in the nineteenth-century American codification debates.[166]

3. Lawrence Friedman and a Comprehensive American Social History of Law

The first comprehensive one-volume treatment of American legal history, Lawrence Friedman's *A History of American Law*, a social history of American law, appeared in 1973.[167] William Nelson's *Americanization of the Common Law* (1975)[168] and Morton Horwitz's *The Transformation of American Law, 1780-1860* (1977)[169] followed shortly thereafter. By the 1980s, American legal history books were taking a social, political, and economic perspective on parts of American law, the most frequent of which dealt with constitutional law.[170]

Friedman found Roman and civil law to be a relatively insignificant part of American legal history. His conclusion was rooted in a thoroughly social perspective on legal history that, at least in the American context, permitted only a small part for tradition. Living law, he asserted, is a continuing present that, decade after decade, replaces in piecemeal fashion the law of the past.

> Some parts of the law are like layers of geological formations. The new presses down on the old, displacing, changing, altering, but not necessarily wiping out *everything* that has gone before. . . . Despite a strong dash of history and idiosyncrasy, the strongest ingredient in American law, at any given time, is the present—current emotions, real economic interests, and concrete political groups.[171]

---

[164] SPENCER L. KIMBALL, HISTORICAL INTRODUCTION TO THE LEGAL SYSTEM (1966).

[165] *Id.* at 309–26.

[166] *Id.* at 357–425. The concerns about the common law that animated the codification debate carried on into the twentieth century and influenced the founding of the American Law Institute. *Id.* at 400–16.

[167] LAWRENCE M. FRIEDMAN, A HISTORY OF AMERICAN LAW 9–10 (1973) [hereinafter FRIEDMAN, HISTORY (1973 ed.)].

[168] WILLIAM E. NELSON, AMERICANIZATION OF THE COMMON LAW: THE IMPACT OF LEGAL CHANGE ON MASSACHUSETTS SOCIETY, 1760–1830 (1975) [hereinafter NELSON, AMERICANIZATION].

[169] MORTON J. HORWITZ, THE TRANSFORMATION OF AMERICAN LAW, 1780–1860 (1977) [hereinafter HORWITZ, TRANSFORMATION].

[170] *E.g.*, MELVIN I. UROFSKY, A MARCH OF LIBERTY: A CONSTITUTIONAL HISTORY OF THE UNITED STATES (1988).

[171] FRIEDMAN, *supra* note 32, at xi–xii (emphasis in original).

Functionalism drove this social history. "Old rules of law and old legal institutions stay alive only when they still have a purpose.... The legal system always 'works': it always functions."[172] This approach minimized the role of inertia, ideology, and intellectual currents, particularly those internal to the legal profession. Individuals have less importance than social forces. Of course, the most significant social forces in the United States are American in the sense they take effect within the country. Even when the origin of the forces is foreign or international, the local legal system processes the forces internally. "[E]nough time has elapsed for American law to be essentially American—the product of American experience."[173]

These views would seem to provide little place for comparative law, or at least that part of comparative law that is interested in ascertaining the influence of foreign law and legal institutions on the development of law in the United States. At most, any influence would be temporary, after which lawyers would deem its continuation Americanized. They could then minimize or deny any foreign influence, or be ignorant of it, and refer to the new legal norm or institution as American. In fact, one can observe this propensity today as an aspect of American legal culture and of American culture in general.[174] This is ironic in a land where most of the inhabitants or their ancestors came from abroad.

Although the process of Americanization in Friedman's *History* was a dominant theme, there were more layers to the story than that. "American law is not an isolate. It has, and has had, close affinities to other legal cultures."[175] This, then, provided an opening for the comparatist. Friedman stated, what legal historians all accept, that the substratum of American law was English (like the language). Of course, before the Europeans arrived, there were native peoples who had their own legal systems. However, the Europeans came in ever-larger numbers as well as from diverse places.

Thus, the Spanish colonized La Florida in the sixteenth century.[176] At the same time, the French began to claim lands that later formed five provinces in the Vice-Royauté de Nouvelle-France, the most significant of which for the future United States was the province of La Louisiane, created in 1682. The French founded Nouvelle Orléans in 1718, which four years later became the capital of Louisiana.[177] In the seventeenth century, the Dutch established forts in

---

[172] *Id.* at xii.
[173] *Id.*
[174] Compare this to attitudes in Spanish American countries toward Spain, in Canada toward England, or in Senegal toward France.
[175] FRIEDMAN, *supra* note 32, at xii.
[176] *See* James Milton Carson, *Historical Background of Florida Law*, 3 MIAMI L.Q. 254 (1949). In 1763, Spain traded Florida to Great Britain in exchange for Havana, Cuba. *See* COLIN G. CALLOWAY, THE SCRATCH OF A PEN: 1763 AND THE TRANSFORMATION OF NORTH AMERICA xviii–xix, 19–46 (2006).
[177] THOMAS L. PURVIS, COLONIAL AMERICA TO 1763, at 45–46 (1999); Jacques Vanderlinden, *Aux origines de la culture juridique française en Amérique du Nord*, 2 J. CIVIL L. STUD. 1, 6–38 (2009);

Delaware, New Jersey, New York, and Connecticut as Nieuw Nederland with its capital at Nieuw Amsterdam. They established liberal policies of religious freedom, free trade, and multilingualism under the administration of the Dutch West-Indische Compagnie, which permitted settlement by diverse peoples. Walloons and Huguenots spoke French, Germans and Scandinavians used their languages, and refugees from Dutch settlements in Brazil spoke Portuguese. The Dutch Company granted residence to Ashkenazi and Sephardi Jews, Quakers, and Anabaptists, among other religious refugees.[178] In 1732, Benjamin Franklin published the first non-English newspaper, the German-language *Philadelphische Zeitung*, in Philadelphia.[179]

Nevertheless, the British along the Atlantic from Maine down to Georgia were dominant.[180] They defeated the Dutch in the seventeenth century. In the eighteenth century, the English, Spanish, and French fought over territory along the Gulf of Mexico, while the English and French contested lands west of the Atlantic settlements. The Treaty of Paris (1763) marked the end of French control in North America: Territory east of the Mississippi River went to Great Britain. New Orleans and lands west went to Spain.[181] In the nineteenth century, English-speaking people settled in the area west of the Mississippi River even when sovereignty belonged to Spain (but Louisiana to France in 1800 to 1803) and later Mexico.[182]

---

see Hans W. Baade, *Marriage Contracts in French and Spanish Louisiana: A Study in "Notarial" Jurisprudence*, 53 TUL. L. REV. 1 (1978); Elizabeth Gaspar Brown, *Law and Government in the "Louisiana Purchase": 1803–1804*, 2 WAYNE L. REV. 169 (1956); Mitchell Franklin, *The Place of Thomas Jefferson in the Expulsion of Spanish Medieval Law from Louisiana*, 16 TUL. L. REV. 319 (1942); id., *Eighteenth Brumaire in Louisiana: Talleyrand and the Spanish Medieval Legal System of 1806*, 16 TUL. L. REV. 514 (1942).

[178] PURVIS, *supra* note 177, at 41–43.

[179] *The First German Newspaper in America*, N.Y. TIMES, 21 Oct. 1900, at 23. From 1700 to 1775, 84,500 Germans immigrated to the American colonies. PURVIS, *supra* note 177, at 164.

[180] The British began settlement in Nova Britannia (Virginia). *See* NOVA BRITANNIA: OFFERING MOST EXCELLENT FRUITS BY PLANTING IN VIRGINIA (London 1609), reprinted in SOURCES, *supra* note 29, at 7–10. The estimated British migration to the American colonies before 1700 was 171,800, 89 percent of which was from England. This percentage plummeted between 1700 and 1775, when 44,100 English, 85,500 Germans, 108,600 Irish, 35,300 Scots, and 29,000 Welsh immigrated. In addition, slave ships brought 278,400 Africans. PURVIS, *supra* note 177, at 164.

[181] PURVIS, *supra* note 177, at 45–49, 163–64. North of Maine, the Scots began settlements in the 1620s in Nova Scotia (New Scotland). Both the French and British controlled the area over the next century. Besides French-speaking Roman Catholic Acadians, Protestant French, Swiss, and Germans immigrated there. In 1755, the British forcibly expelled thousands of Acadians, many of whom fled to Québec or to Louisiana (where the moniker Cajuns took hold). After the British defeat in the American War of Independence, thousands of American Tories settled in Nova Scotia. PURVIS, *supra*, at 167; *see* PETER L. MCCREATH & JOHN G. LEEFE, A HISTORY OF EARLY NOVA SCOTIA (1982); MYTH, MIGRATION AND THE MAKING OF MEMORY: SCOTIA AND NOVA SCOTIA (Michael Vance & Marjory Harper, eds., 1999).

[182] John H. Tucker Jr., *Code and Common Law in Louisiana*, 29 TUL. L. REV. 739, 741–44 (1955); *see* Edward Lee Markham Jr., *Reception of the Common Law of England in Texas and the Judicial Attitude toward That Reception, 1840–1859*, 29 TEX. L. REV. 904 (1951).

Friedman accepted that each "culture group lived by its own legal norms."[183] Today, various Native American "nations" have their own legal systems, with courts, lawmaking bodies, police, and social welfare programs. Some of their traditional elements live on. The district attorney concept may be Dutch in origin.[184] French and Spanish law established dominance in Louisiana, where parts of it remain in English translation. Spanish law controlled much of the West well into the nineteenth century. Its form still affects matrimonial property issues, water rights, and some other land title rights. Friedman mentioned these examples, but concluded that everything else, if not indigenous to the United States, lawyers have built on an English base.[185] It is this conclusion that we will examine in chapters to come.

4. The Rise of American Legal History as a Distinct Discipline

William Nelson subtitled his 1975 book *The Impact of Legal Change on Massachusetts Society, 1760–1830*.[186] Although rich in primary source material and insight on one rapidly changing colony and state, it did not provide fertile ground to show Roman and civil law influence. Much of that occurred at the level of early national constitutional law, or on state criminal law and procedure, or occurred after 1830 in other state law subjects. In Massachusetts, Puritan ideas and a freewheeling jury system dominated criminal law.[187]

Morton Horwitz's 1977 book covered a wider geography for the period 1780 to 1860, but concentrated on the private law fields of tort, contract, property, and commerce, primarily in their judge-made form. He also was not particularly interested in constitutional or criminal law. He demonstrated that lawyers made crucial choices for the law in the post-revolutionary period to promote economic growth that had determinative consequences for wealth and power distribution. While he agreed with consensus historians that American law began with a core regulatory state, and that laissez-faire policies only came to dominate in the second half of the nineteenth century, he rejected their assumption that most regulation was in the public interest. In addition, he did not find the concept of

---

[183] FRIEDMAN, *supra* note 32, at xiii.
[184] LAWRENCE M. FRIEDMAN, CRIME AND PUNISHMENT IN AMERICAN HISTORY 28–29, 479 n.29 (1993); *see* W. Scott van Alstyne Jr., *The District Attorney—A Historical Puzzle*, 1952 WIS. L. REV. 125. The Dutch *schout* was both sheriff and prosecutor. In England during the eighteenth century, there was no paid official to prosecute crime, which was a private function done at private expense. FRIEDMAN, *supra*, at 29.
[185] FRIEDMAN, *supra* note 32, at xiii, 113–20, 273–75, 294–95, 564.
[186] *See* NELSON, AMERICANIZATION, *supra* note 168.
[187] *Id.* at 20–30, 36–40, 109–11, 117–21.

laissez-faire useful when applied to judges who had the task of governmental regulation since it did not distinguish between developmental and distributional goals.[188] Horwitz's sequel volume analyzed the period 1870 to 1960.[189] It had a quite different tone, influenced by critiques of traditional notions of historical explanation, some casting doubt on the very possibility of explanation beyond thick description. Nevertheless, his acceptance of multi-factored complexity did not include a discussion of civil law influence on American law, even though he treated the codification debates and the rise of legal realism.[190]

In 1980, Stephen Presser and Jamil Zainaldin prepared the first commercially published "casebook" on American legal history in the model of law school teaching materials.[191] It was a good example of modern intellectual legal history, which also had provided only a minor place for Roman and civil law. This intellectual legal history dealt with the people who promote ideas and the ideas themselves; it did not ignore material elements but makes them secondary. It concentrated on how culture and environment influenced certain people, especially those deemed of major importance in transforming events, such as particular American Founding Fathers.[192]

Presser and Zainaldin emphasized the primacy of values and ideas to understanding history. In the preface to the book's first edition: "American law mirrors the social values of our culture, and ... American law can also be seen to reflect the economic preferences or the political ideology of particular groups in the polity."[193] They proceeded to identify four transcendent values or ideas expressed in American law. First, there should be restraints on arbitrary power, which the rule of law can facilitate. Second, popular sovereignty should be the ultimate political principle, with the American people responsible for the content of legal rules and the legal system broadly benefiting all the people. Third, law should further economic progress and social mobility, which are the best means to implement democratic theory. Fourth, law should maintain a large sector of private enterprise relatively immune from public regulation.[194]

---

[188] HORWITZ, TRANSFORMATION, *supra* note 169, at xii–xvi.

[189] MORTON J. HORWITZ, THE TRANSFORMATION OF AMERICAN LAW, 1870–1960: THE CRISIS OF LEGAL ORTHODOXY (1992) [hereinafter HORWITZ, CRISIS]. For a review of the 1977 and 1992 Horwitz books, *see* Robert W. Gordon, *Morton Horwitz and His Critics: A Conflict of Narratives*, 37 TULSA L. REV. 915–27 (2002).

[190] HORWITZ, CRISIS, *supra* note 189, at viii–ix, 9–10, 116–21, 169–212.

[191] STEPHEN B. PRESSER & JAMIL S. ZAINALDIN, LAW AND AMERICAN HISTORY: CASES AND MATERIALS (1980). West republished the first edition's preface in *id.*, CASES AND MATERIALS ON LAW AND JURISPRUDENCE IN AMERICAN HISTORY xxi–xxvii (7th ed. 2009) [hereinafter citation is to the 7th ed.].

[192] Much of G. Edward White's work during this period also illustrated intellectual legal history. *See* G. EDWARD WHITE, INTERVENTION AND DETACHMENT: ESSAYS IN LEGAL HISTORY AND JURISPRUDENCE 3–72 (1994).

[193] PRESSER & ZAINALDIN, *supra* note 191, at xxi (7th ed. 2009, reprinting first edition preface).

[194] *Id.* at xxii; *see* Stephen B. Presser, *"Legal History" or the History of Law: A Primer on Bringing the Law's Past into the Present*, 35 VAND. L. REV. 849–66 (1982).

The challenge was to understand how these central ideas developed, functioned, and changed, where they came from, and how that origin affected their form and substance, even as they reflected economic preference or political ideology. Presser and Zainaldin assigned a primary role here to judges and lawyers (including law professors), while not ignoring the influence of executive officials and legislators.[195]

The field of legal history continued to develop in the last decade of the twentieth century as an interdisciplinary endeavor, illustrated by Kermit Hall's *The Magic Mirror: Law in American History*,[196] a general interpretive essay, and his "cases and materials" with William Wiecek and Paul Finkelman.[197] These works, as well as those from the 1970s, drew from the substantial literature that had developed on American legal history as well as from historical documents and other writings. Kermit Hall (1944–2006) and his colleagues considered state law as well as federal law in the development of the American legal system and the interplay between public and private law.[198] These general treatments, like those earlier, were predisposed to ignore any contribution that Roman and civil law might have made to American law and legal institutions. However, they varied in their openness to consider non-English legal sources for rules and institutions. As social history, they tended to regard non-English developments as indigenous, as adaptations to the New World environment, or as influences from religion, such as that of the Puritans or Quakers. Some authors seemed at times to forget that not all European inhabitants of America were English. It is here, among the factors of social history, but leavened with relevant cultural ideas, that the search for Roman and civil law elements appears most promising.

Hall and his colleagues took an intermediate position between social and intellectual history in their teaching materials on American legal history.[199] While Presser and Zainaldin intended their book primarily for law students, Hall, Finkelman, and Ely directed their volume mainly toward history and political science students. The latter authors stated that their "approach stresses the tension inherent in our legal system between law as a technical subject with its own

---

[195] PRESSER & ZAINALDIN, *supra* note 191, at xxi–xxii.

[196] HALL, *supra* note 147, at vii–viii.

[197] KERMIT L. HALL, WILLIAM M. WIECEK, & PAUL FINKELMAN, AMERICAN LEGAL HISTORY: CASES AND MATERIALS (1991).

[198] "[T]he traditional distinction between legal and constitutional history has been often misleading.... Public and private law are best viewed as reciprocal and reinforcing phenomena." KERMIT L. HALL, PAUL FINKELMAN, & JAMES W. ELY, JR., AMERICAN LEGAL HISTORY: CASES AND MATERIALS xxiv (3d ed. 2005) [hereinafter HALL, FINKELMAN, & ELY].

[199] HALL, FINKELMAN, & ELY, *supra* note 198. In the 1991 and 1996 editions, William M. Wiecek coauthored the book with Hall and Finkelman.

internal logic and law as a scheme of social choice responsive to a host of political, social, and economic pressures."[200] Comparative law has developed methods to deal with both perspectives. Hall and his colleagues appeared the most willing to entertain the influence of Roman and civil law on early American law, but they do not substantially develop that theme.[201] For instance, in the second edition of the *The Magic Mirror*, Hall and Peter Karsten stated, "Legal systems composed part of the cultural baggage of colonial expansion; the English settlers not only came in larger numbers, but they came to stay with concentrated settlement on the vital Atlantic beachhead."[202] They went on to comment that although the Dutch in 1624 brought their civil law system with them to Novum Belgium (New Netherland) and its capital and most important settlement, Nieuw Amsterdam, the transfer to the English in 1664 brought that area also under the common law.[203]

Robert Gordon offered a different perspective on socio-legal history, using the intellectual tools of critical legal studies. He criticized the evolutionary functionalism of most social history applied to law, which he saw as the successor to legal realism. Nevertheless, he also found formalist legal history, which would include Pound, as subject to the same criticisms. There are important differences between formalism and realism. The former analyzes legal doctrine, while the latter considers doctrine as only one component of a general social framework. Although Gordon found more value in social history, it was necessary to point out its shortcomings. "[I]ts essential working assumptions misleadingly objectify history, making highly contingent developments appear to have been necessary."[204] Socio-legal scholars understand society as constructed by impersonal social forces and largely ignore the insight that people manufacture these inevitable processes. As social creatures, humans reflect their cultural milieu.[205] This latter notion might support the work of some comparatists who prefer to understand law as symbols and rituals, a kind of cultural anthropology.[206]

---

[200] *Id.* at xxiv.
[201] *See id., e.g.,* at 2–3, 37–38, 333–34.
[202] HALL & KARSTEN, *supra* note 59, at 8; *see id.* at 10–27.
[203] *Id.* at 8. The Dutch West India Company, founded in 1621, administered Nieuw Amsterdam, which expanded from Governors Island (Noten Eylant) to lower Manhattan. In 1658, the Dutch established Nieuw Haarlem. These settlements were pluralistic, with about half of the émigrés from Scandinavia to France. *See generally* JAAP JACOBS, NEW NETHERLAND: A DUTCH COLONY IN SEVENTEENTH-CENTURY AMERICA (2005); RUSSELL SHORTO, THE ISLAND AT THE CENTER OF THE WORLD: THE EPIC STORY OF DUTCH MANHATTAN AND THE FORGOTTEN COLONY THAT SHAPED AMERICA (2004).
[204] Robert W. Gordon, *Critical Legal Histories*, 36 STAN. L. REV. 57, 70 (1984); *see id.* at 57–70, 108.
[205] *Id.* at 70–71.
[206] *Id.* at 95–96, 98–101.

E. Historiography: The Twenty-First Century

1. Eclecticism, Culture, and Thick Description: The Return of Intellectual Legal History

Social legal history, broadened by accepting cultural legal history, has continued its importance in the current century.[207] Richard Ross, writing in 1993, believed that legal culture studies could provide a bridge between social and intellectual history. Scholarship in cultural legal history typically uses race, ethnicity, religion, or gender to distinguish its research.[208] A good example is Barbara Welke's analysis of social and legal treatment of personhood and citizenship from 1789 to 1920 based on race, gender, ability, and other characteristics of identity.[209] Bruce Mann and Christopher Tomlins preferred the term "legalities" to consider both the cultural and social, since multiple legalities may exist at one time in the same place.[210] By 2012, G. Edward White adopted a third perspective that combined the internalist intellectual approach with a historical social context analysis.[211] His broad conception of law included "cultural customs or traditions or practices that were deeply and broadly enough held to amount to legal rules."[212] This allowed him to treat the influence that Amerindian cultures and non-English populations had on colonial legal history and law. For American history, however, White took a narrow non-globalist conception, which, as with Commager, embraced exceptionalism as "one of the foundational themes of American culture."[213] Today, the legal literature on American exceptionalism and its implications is substantial.[214]

---

[207] E.g., Mary Sarah Bilder, *English Settlement and Local Government*, in 1 CAMBRIDGE HISTORY, supra note 30, at 63, 90–91; Grossberg & Tomlins, supra note 30, at xiii. Friedman had early on made legal culture a part of his social history. FRIEDMAN, HISTORY (1973 ed.), supra note 167, at 13–16, 21.

[208] Richard J. Ross, *The Legal Past of Early New England: Notes for the Study of Law, Legal Culture, and Intellectual History*, 50 WM. & MARY Q. 28, 32–41 (1993).

[209] See BARBARA YOUNG WELKE, LAW AND THE BORDERS OF BELONGING IN THE LONG NINETEENTH CENTURY UNITED STATES (2010); id., *Law, Personhood, and Citizenship in the Long Nineteenth Century: The Borders of Belonging*, in 2 CAMBRIDGE HISTORY, supra note 45, at 345–86.

[210] Bruce H. Mann, *Afterword*, in THE MANY LEGALITIES OF EARLY AMERICA 442–47 (Christopher L. Tomlins & Bruce H. Mann eds., 2001); Christopher L. Tomlins, *Introduction*, in id. at 1–20; see Scott D. Gerber, *Bringing Ideas Back In—A Brief Historiography of American Colonial Law*, 51 AM. J. LEG. HIST. 359, 364–65 (2011).

[211] G. EDWARD WHITE, LAW IN AMERICAN HISTORY, VOLUME 1: FROM THE COLONIAL YEARS THROUGH THE CIVIL WAR 7–10 (2012). The third perspective "allows historians to read legal materials from the past simultaneously as intraprofessional documents and historical artifacts." Id. at 9.

[212] Id. at 4; see id. at 3, 7–10.

[213] Id. at 5; see id. at 5–6, 18–41; see supra text accompanying note 137 (Commager). White writes, "by 'American' history I mean, on the whole, the playing out of themes connected to American exceptionalism. . . . By American exceptionalism I mean a singular combination of optimism, self-confidence, parochialism, and insularity." White, supra, at 6.

[214] See, e.g., Steven G. Calabresi, *"A Shining City on a Hill": American Exceptionalism and the Supreme Court's Practice of Relying on Foreign Law*, 86 BOSTON U.L. REV. 1335, 1344–1416 (2006) (surveying the reality and ideology of exceptionalism).

In general, intellectual legal history has experienced a resurgence as some historians recognize that ideas or internal legal processes matter for the development of legal rules and legal institutions. This does not deny that social and cultural elements are also important; it simply asserts that ideas, ideology, and internal legal culture are also important or even primary to legal change.[215]

A variant of this approach emerged during the last quarter of the twentieth century through the work of Alan Watson and his method of legal transplants.[216] This approach de-emphasized social context and asserted that important features of a country's legal institutions and rules can arise by legal transplant from a donor nation. The donor might impose legal elements on a host by military, political, or economic pressure. Alternatively, the recipient country might borrow legal elements from a donor due to the latter's prestige, a common language, an earlier colonial relationship, or the simple efficiency of borrowing.[217] Furthermore, Watson contended that although the creation of legal rules and institutions might occur because of social factors, one could explain the persistence of dysfunctional law by the force of inertia, by internal legal factors such as lawyer self-interest or fascination with technicalities, or by the absence of effective institutions for meaningful change.[218] Legal transplant continues as an important method for legal history and comparative law.[219]

2. Legal History Meets Comparative Law

By the end of the twentieth century, legal history and comparative law in the United States had developed sufficiently that the two academic disciplines could more fruitfully consider the other's perspectives and interests. For instance, in 1997, Anthony Chase wrote an idiosyncratic essay, *Law and History: The Evolution of the American Legal System*.[220] Without an index to check for references to Roman, French, German, civil, or comparative law, one might expect to find

---

[215] Gerber, *supra* note 210, at 359, 367, 371–74; *see, e.g.*, KENNETH W. MACK, REPRESENTING THE RACE: THE CREATION OF THE CIVIL RIGHTS LAWYER (2012); KAREN M. TANI, STATES OF DEPENDENCY: WELFARE, RIGHTS, AND AMERICAN GOVERNANCE, 1935–1972 (2016).

[216] *See* ALAN WATSON, LEGAL TRANSPLANTS: AN APPROACH TO COMPARATIVE LAW (1974, 2d ed. 1993); *id.*, SOCIETY AND LEGAL CHANGE (1977, 2d. ed. 2001). The idea of legal borrowing or imposition (reception) across legal systems was an old one in comparative law. *E.g.*, Edward M. Wise, *The Transplant of Legal Patterns*, 38 AM. J. COMP. L. 1, 7–10, 14, 20–22 (Supp. 1990) (mentioning POUND, FORMATIVE ERA, *supra* note 31, at 93–94).

[217] WATSON, SOCIETY AND LEGAL CHANGE, *supra* note 216, at 102–05, 140–41 (2d. ed. 2001).

[218] *Id.* at 7–8.

[219] *See* Graziadei, *supra* note 15, at 465–74.

[220] ANTHONY CHASE, LAW AND HISTORY: THE EVOLUTION OF THE AMERICAN LEGAL SYSTEM (1997). Chase was concerned that providing an index to his book would prompt readers to review only portions of his book and dissuade them from digesting the whole argument. Thus, there was no index. *Id.* at 8.

nothing that would interest a comparatist. Surprisingly, in the final chapter, "Wake of the Flood," the longest section is entitled "The German Ideology."[221] Chase had read in an earlier book review by Gordon[222] a passage that led him to the work of two English comparatists on nineteenth-century German tort law.[223] Chase asked:

> Why did industrialization, he [Gordon] wants to know, produce a fault approach in the U.S. and yet its seeming opposite, a strict liability approach, at about the same time in Germany? This is an excellent question and one, I suspect, few American law professors would think to ask.... Most American law professors are not comparativists and Gordon understandably provides a footnote.[224]

Chase proceeded to explain how the comparative analysis helped to understand the American legal issue.[225] It is precisely this point, among others, that *American Comparative Law: A History* tries to develop.

Two years later, in 1999, Daniel Coquillette took the comparative inquiry further in *The Anglo-American Legal Heritage*.[226] He stated in the introduction to his collection of teaching materials,

> Early English and American lawyers built their rule of law from whatever materials were at hand. The English settlers of Massachusetts, clinging to a hostile shore in 1641, were often fluent in Latin, and the opening lines of their first legal treatises borrowed not only from the *Magna Carta* of 1215 A.D., but also from the Digest of the Emperor Justinian, completed in 533 A.D.[227]

To make the point even stronger, Coquillette entitled the book's first chapter "The Glory That Was Rome."[228] This included a section on "John Adams as Roman Lawyer."[229] In this chapter, Coquillette made two important points. First: "In

---

[221] *Id.* at 167–94.
[222] Robert W. Gordon, *Book Reviews*, 94 HARV. L. REV. 903, 907 (1981) (reviewing WHITE, TORT LAW, *supra* note 28).
[223] The English sources analyzing German law were F.H. LAWSON, NEGLIGENCE IN THE CIVIL LAW: INTRODUCTION AND SELECT TEXTS (1950) and F.H. LAWSON & B.S. MARKESINIS, TORTIOUS LIABILITY FOR UNINTENTIONAL HARM IN THE COMMON LAW AND THE CIVIL LAW (1982).
[224] CHASE, *supra* note 220, at 168.
[225] *Id.* at 170–86.
[226] DANIEL R. COQUILLETTE, THE ANGLO-AMERICAN LEGAL HERITAGE: INTRODUCTORY MATERIALS (1999). There was a second edition without significant change, published in 2004. Citation is to this second edition.
[227] *Id.* at xix.
[228] *Id.* at 1–35
[229] *Id.* at 33–35. Coquillette based this excerpt on research that earlier led to Daniel R. Coquillette, *Justinian in Braintree: John Adams, Civilian Learning, and Legal Elitism, 1758-1775*, in LAW IN COLONIAL MASSACHUSETTS: 1630–1800, at 359 (Coquillette, Robert J. Brink, & Catherine S. Menand eds., 1984).

every century, whether it be the age of Bracton, Bacon or of Bentham, Roman law influenced English law because it influenced educated English jurists and judges."[230] Second:

> America was influenced, too. Recent research has now begun to uncover the full extent of Roman law influence on the early development of American law. We have always known that Roman law texts were found in the best colonial libraries, such as at Harvard, but it now appears that early colonial attempts at treatise writing and codification were directly influenced by the *Institutes*.[231]

In 2002, the *Oxford Companion to American Law* attempted an encyclopedic approach to the subject, often from a historical and interdisciplinary perspective, with 468 entries written by over 300 contributors.[232] The editors described the organizing principles. "American law has not historically been independent, nor does it today exist in isolation from legal developments in other countries and at the international level.... Many contributors, therefore, have approached their subjects from a cultural, comparative, and international perspective."[233] Nevertheless, the small number of entries that either directly treated comparative law topics or discussed legal subjects or institutions comparatively provided only a beginning toward a true comparative awareness.[234]

---

[230] COQUILLETTE, *supra* note 226, at 3. The treatise known as *Bracton* followed by several decades the important practitioner's book of royal court procedure called *Glanvill*, written in Latin between 1187 and 1189 and named for King Henry II's chief justiciar, Ranulf de Glanvill, who likely was not the true author. Its Latin title was *Tractatus de legibus et consuetudinibus regni Angliae*. Several authors, some using Roman and canon law for concepts or comparison, wrote the more sophisticated *Bracton* from 1220 to 1230, which perhaps Judge Henry de Bracton (c. 1210–1268) revised and updated. Based in part on Bracton's notebook of earlier cases, it used Roman law categories, especially from Justinian's *Institutes*, to organize the judge-made royal law and to treat legal and constitutional theory, which later influenced the crucial constitutional debates between Crown and Parliament in the seventeenth century. Its Latin title was *De Legibus et Consuetudinibus Angliae*. *Id.* at 61–63; BAKER, *supra* note 46, at 174–77; *see* THOMAS EDWARD SCRUTTON, THE INFLUENCE OF THE ROMAN LAW ON THE LAW OF ENGLAND (1885).

Francis Bacon (1561–1626), in addition to his writing as a scientist and philosopher, was a barrister who studied Justinian's *Corpus juris civilis*, became Lord Chancellor, and wrote in both Latin and English. COQUILLETTE, *supra* , at 9; *see id.*, FRANCIS BACON 105–17 (1992). Jeremy Bentham (1748–1832), a legal and moral philosopher, tried to reduce English jurisprudence to the principles of natural science, in particular by applying his felicific calculus for utilitarianism that could yield a civil-law type codification. COQUILLETTE, *supra*, at 500–12, 515–16, 523–29; *see* GERALD J. POSTEMA, BENTHAM AND THE COMMON LAW TRADITION (1986); BENTHAM: MORAL, POLITICAL, AND LEGAL PHILOSOPHY (Gerald J. Postema ed., 2002).

[231] COQUILLETTE, *supra* note 226, at 4.

[232] OXFORD COMPANION TO AMERICAN LAW (Kermit L. Hall et al., eds. 2002). Editors David S. Clark, James W. Ely, Jr., Joel Grossman, and H.E.H. Hull assisted Hall as editor-in-chief.

[233] *Id.* at ix.

[234] There were entries on Canon Law (*id.* at 82–83), Civil Law in America (*id.* at 107–10), Codification (*id.* at 120–21), Comparative Law (at 130–34), and German Legal Philosophy, Influence of (*id.* at 331–33) as well as Common Law (*id.* at 125–30).

In 2009, John Langbein, Renée Lerner, and Bruce Smith authored *History of the Common Law: The Development of Anglo-American Legal Institutions*.[235] Like the Coquillette book, it was a mixture of historical documents, excerpts from scholarly literature, and the authors' own text intended for courses in legal history. Similarly, it was in the "legal institutions" tradition explicitly to explore those institutions that distinguish the common law tradition from the civil law.[236] Consequently, their emphasis was on differences between the two major traditions rather than their similarities and cross-influences. Nevertheless, there were some sections where they mentioned Roman, canon, and civil law traces, such as in English procedure, the careers of civilians in England, and the impact of a European institutionalist tradition on Blackstone's *Commentaries* and its effect in America.[237]

Almost a decade later, in 2018, the *American Journal of Comparative Law* published symposium papers under the title, "Legal History and Comparative Law: A Dialogue in Times of the Transnationalization of Law and Legal Scholarship."[238] In the preface, Thomas Duve argued that comparative law and legal history were undergoing reorientation of their methods and even their disciplinary identities. Both disciplines now recognized the importance of context and traditions.[239] Heikki Pihlajamäki presented a more ambitious desire, the merger of the two disciplines. In defending this proposition, he detailed the shared elements existing in the nineteenth century between the two fields, how they split apart, and what for the future might foster merger in research and teaching.[240]

---

[235] LANGBEIN ET AL., *supra* note 12.
[236] *Id.* at xxv–xxvi. In the United States, they traced this tradition back to JULIUS GOEBEL, CASES AND MATERIALS ON THE DEVELOPMENT OF LEGAL INSTITUTIONS (1929).
[237] LANGBEIN ET AL., *supra* note 12, at 125–39, 190–98, 838–44.
[238] 66 AM. J. COMP. LAW 727–830 (2018).
[239] Thomas Duve, *Preface, id.* at 727; *see id., Legal Traditions: A Dialogue between Comparative Law and Comparative Legal History*, 6 COMP. LEG. HIST. 15–33 (2018).
[240] Heikki Pihlajamäki, *Merging Comparative Law and Legal History: Towards an Integrated Discipline*, 66 AM. J. COMP. L. 733–50 (2018).

2
British Colonization in North America

> There is a latent spark in the breasts of the people, capable of being kindled into a flame, and to do this has always been the employment of the disaffected. What is this latent spark? The love of liberty. *A Deo hominis est indita naturæ.* Human nature itself is evermore an advocate for liberty.
>
> John Adams (1775)[1]

A. Prelude: Comparative Law in England

1. Legal Education and Literature

Comparative law as a subject did not exist in colonial British America or in Great Britain prior to 1783, when the Treaty of Paris recognized the United States of America as a sovereign country. Although a person could study Roman, civil, and canon law in Britain at its two universities (Oxford and Cambridge), which might lead one to comparative inquiry, most lawyers trained by reading or with an apprenticeship. Barristers also socialized at the Inns of Court, while attorneys and solicitors joined in 1729 to form the Society of Gentlemen Practisers (incorporated as the Law Society in 1826).[2] Nevertheless, advocates and judges who practiced in English ecclesiastical and admiralty courts did study at the universities in Oxford and Cambridge. Prior to the reign of Henry VIII (1509–1547), they took degrees in canon law, but after Henry closed the canon law faculties, they became doctors of civil law. Many advocates joined Doctors' Commons in

---

[1] *Novanglus: Or, a History of the Dispute with America, in* JOHN ADAMS, THE REVOLUTIONARY WRITINGS OF JOHN ADAMS ch. 8 (C. Bradley Thompson ed., 2000) [hereinafter ADAMS, REVOLUTIONARY WRITINGS], https://oll.libertyfund.org (extracted from CHARLES FRANCIS ADAMS, 4 THE WORKS OF JOHN ADAMS 3 (1865, orig. 1851); select People, then John Adams); *see infra* pt. F.4 (*Novanglus* letters).

[2] J.H. BAKER, AN INTRODUCTION TO ENGLISH LEGAL HISTORY 155, 160–64 (4th ed. 2002); *see* PAUL M. HAMLIN, LEGAL EDUCATION IN COLONIAL NEW YORK 12–17 (1939); LAWYERS IN EARLY MODERN EUROPE AND AMERICA 16–128 (Wilfrid Prest ed., 1981); FRANCIS DE ZULUETA & PETER STEIN, THE TEACHING OF ROMAN LAW IN ENGLAND AROUND 1200 (1990); Ralph Michael Stein, *The Path of Legal Education from Edward I to Langdell: A History of Insular Reaction*, 57 CHI. KENT L. REV. 429–36 (1981) [hereinafter Ralph Stein]. The division between barristers and solicitors replicated the Roman distinction between *advocatus* and *procurator*. BAKER, *supra*, at 163.

London, near St. Paul's Cathedral, where they collected a significant library of foreign law books.[3] William Blackstone at Oxford presented university lectures on English law in 1753, which were successful enough for him to become the initial recipient of the recently endowed Vinerian Professorship in 1758. According to Sir John Baker, Blackstone's efforts were the first to try to systematize the whole of English law since Henry de Bracton in the thirteenth century.[4]

A few English books did explore and compare the civil law and the common law. The earliest popular book, which used the literary form of dialogues to introduce students to English law, was Christopher St. German, *Dialogus de fundamentis legum Angliæ et de conscientia* (1523–1530). He wrote the first part in Latin, but the second part was in English. The first part was soon translated into English with additional chapters and until 1815 enjoyed over 30 printings.[5] In 1601 and 1602, William Fulbecke also prepared dialogues to compare legal systems, *A Parallele or Conference of the Civill Law, the Canon Law, and the Common Law of this Realme of England*.[6] Both of these authors asserted that a statute against natural law (or the law of reason) was void and not a law, a view that the American colonists would later find useful in their disputes with England and in accepting judicial review of legislation.[7]

An important eighteenth-century example comparing civil law and common law was Thomas Wood's *A New Institute of the Imperial or Civil Law* (1704).[8] Until 1730, there were four editions with significant circulation in America.[9]

---

[3] BAKER, *supra* note 2, at 169; Daniel R. Coquillette, *The Civilian Writers of Doctors' Commons, London: Three Centuries of Juristic Innovation in Comparative*, COMMERCIAL AND INTERNATIONAL LAW 24–32 (1988) [hereinafter Coquillette, *Civilian Writers*]; see R.H. HELMHOLZ, CANON LAW AND THE LAW OF ENGLAND (1987); Brian P. Levack, *The English Civilians, 1500–1750*, *in* LAWYERS IN EARLY MODERN EUROPE AND AMERICA, *supra* note 2, at 108–28. The Oxford degree was D.C.L, while the Cambridge degree was LL.D. BAKER, *supra*, at 169.

[4] BAKER, *supra* note 2, at 170–71. Baker found Edward Coke's *Institutes of the Law of England* (1628–1644) to be too disordered and wandering. *Id.* at 189–90. Within 50 years, benefactors established similar English law chairs at Cambridge and at Trinity College Dublin. *Id.* at 170.

[5] A 1721 edition carried the title DOCTOR AND STUDENT: OR DIALOGUES BETWEEN A DOCTOR OF DIVINITY AND A STUDENT IN THE LAWS OF ENGLAND, CONTAINING THE GROUNDS OF THOSE LAWS, TOGETHER WITH QUESTIONS AND CASES CONCERNING THE EQUITY AND CONSCIENCE THEREOF; ALSO COMPARING THE CIVIL, CANON, COMMON AND STATUTE LAWS, AND SHOWING WHEREIN THEY VARY FROM ONE ANOTHER. William Muchall edited an American edition in 1874, which he had published in Cincinnati. The best modern edition is CHRISTOPHER SAINT GERMAN'S DOCTOR AND STUDENT (T.F.T. Plucknett & J.L. Barton eds., 1974). *See* Coquillette, *Civilian Writers*, *supra* note 3, at 46–57, 94–95.

[6] The second edition was WILLIAM FULBECKE, A PARALLELE OR CONFERENCE OF THE CIVIL LAW, THE CANON LAW, AND THE COMMON LAW OF THIS REALME OF ENGLAND (2d ed. 1618). *See* Coquillette, *Civilian Writers*, *supra* note 3, at 46–48, 71–79, 94–95.

[7] BAKER, *supra* note 2, at 210, 210 n.97.

[8] THOMAS WOOD, A NEW INSTITUTE OF THE IMPERIAL OR CIVIL LAW: WITH NOTES, SHEWING IN SOME PRINCIPAL CASES, AMONGST OTHER OBSERVATIONS, HOW THE CANON LAW, THE LAWS OF ENGLAND, AND THE LAWS AND CUSTOMS OF OTHER NATIONS DIFFER FROM IT (1704).

[9] There is a 2007 reprint of Wood's 1721 edition. For Wood's importance, *see* Coquillette, *Civilian Writers*, *supra* note 3, at 198–203; Robert B. Robinson, *The Two Institutes of Thomas Wood: A Study in Eighteenth Century Legal Scholarship*, 35 AM. J. LEG. HIST. 432 (1991).

John Adams (1735–1826), second president of the United States, referred to it frequently in his admiralty law practice.[10] In Pennsylvania, with the oldest appellate court among the 13 colonies, Supreme Court Chief Justice James Logan (served 1731–1739) had a copy in his library, as did Justice Jasper Yeates (served 1791–1817).[11] In the preface, Wood asserted, "a great part of the Civil Law, is part of the Law of *England*, and interwoven with it throughout. I hope therefore that the study of it may be encouraged amongst us as in other Nations ... for the better understanding of the *Common* Law of *England*."[12]

Another significant book was William Strahan's 1722 English translation of Jean Domat's five-volume *Les Loix civiles dans leur ordre naturel* (1689).[13] Domat's volumes put Roman law as used in France into the rational order that natural law writers suggested. This work was one of the major influences on the 1804 French *Code civil*. In America, John Adams owned a French edition of Domat, while Thomas Jefferson (1743–1826), third president of the United States; John Jay (1745–1829), first chief justice of the U.S. Supreme Court; and Jasper Yeates had the Strahan translation.[14] Luther Cushing published an American edition in 1850.[15]

2. Roman and Canon Law Influence in England

What do we know about Roman, civil, and canon law influence on the English legal system? Charles Donahue asked this question and found civilian influence on Ranulf de Glanvill and Henry de Bracton in the twelfth and thirteenth centuries, on sixteenth-century Renaissance jurists, and on commercial law from

---

[10] Coquillette, *Civilian Writers*, supra note 3, at 200 n.231; *see infra* pt. F (Adams).

[11] *Id.* Logan (1674–1751), a Scottish Quaker, also had diverse scientific and philosophical interests. He translated two of Cicero's works from Latin and bequeathed his 3,000-book library for public use, later residing at The Library Company of Philadelphia. Jeffrey B. Webb, *Logan, James*, in 13 AMERICAN NATIONAL BIOGRAPHY 833–34 (John A. Garraty & Mark C. Carnes eds., 1999); *see infra* note 128 and accompanying text (The Library Company).

[12] WOOD, *supra* note 8, at viii (2d ed. 1712), reprinted in Coquillette, *Civilian Writers*, supra note 3, at 200–01 n.232.

[13] JEAN DOMAT, 1–2 THE CIVIL LAW IN ITS NATURAL ORDER, TOGETHER WITH THE PUBLICK LAW ... WITH ADDITIONAL REMARKS ON SOME MATERIAL DIFFERENCES BETWEEN THE CIVIL LAW AND THE LAW OF ENGLAND (William Strahan trans., 1722). A 2008 reprint is available. Domat's volumes 4 and 5 in the 1695 edition also carried the title *Droit Public*. Strahan was a member of Doctors' Commons. For Strahan's importance, *see* Coquillette, *Civilian Writers*, supra note 3, at 203–09; Peter Stein, *The Attraction of the Civil Law in Post-Revolutionary America*, 52 VA. L. REV. 403, 406–07 (1966). Another comparative book was GILES JACOB, A TREATISE OF LAWS, OR A GENERAL INTRODUCTION TO THE COMMON, CIVIL, AND CANON LAW (1721).

[14] Coquillette, *Civilian Writers*, supra note 3, at 204 n.244, 209. Ralph Assheton, an influential judge on the Pennsylvania chancery court and later common pleas between 1730 and 1746, also had the Strahan translation. *Id.*

[15] JEAN DOMAT, 1–2 THE CIVIL LAW IN ITS NATURAL ORDER (William Strahan trans., Luther S. Cushing ed., from the 2d London ed. of 1737, 1850).

the late seventeenth to the eighteenth century, particularly on Lord Mansfield (1705–1793).[16] In *The Civilian Writers of Doctors' Commons, London*,[17] Daniel Coquillette provided intriguing insights into possible pathways, primarily on English law. American colonists likely also then adopted some of these civilian elements.

For the better part of the three centuries up to the time of American independence, English civilians, about one-tenth the number of common law lawyers, dominated debates about legal issues in family and inheritance law as well as in admiralty and many mercantile matters. In addition to ecclesiastical courts, civilians practiced in the secular courts of chancery (and requests), admiralty, and chivalry. They considered their work more rational and scientific than the fragmented development of rules in common law courts, since civilian doctrine was subject to a universal test of reason based on *ius gentium*, natural law, or *ratio scripta*.[18] Perhaps one can make the best case for doctrinal transplant with English *lex mercatoria*.[19] In addition to civilian influence on substantive rules, Coquillette argued that it affected the ideas of important common law lawyers such as Francis Bacon and Jeremy Bentham and their attitudes toward legal method, procedure, and codification.[20]

David Ibbetson, Regius Professor of Civil Law at Cambridge, examined the early modern English situation in the larger context of European legal history. He reassessed Thomas Wood's view about the seepage of Roman civil law into English common law.[21]

> [T]he *ius commune* constituted ... the background to the operation of local statutes and customs, an interpretative framework within which sense could be made of these and a source of norms which could be called upon or dug into to fill in gaps in individual legal systems. *Iura propria*, particular laws, continued to have force, and the balance between these and the principles of the *ius commune* could and did vary substantially from place to place.[22]

---

[16] Charles Donahue Jr., *The Civil Law in England*, 84 YALE L.J. 167, 168–70, 178–81 (1974) (book review); *see* JOHN L. BARTON, ROMAN LAW IN ENGLAND (1971).

[17] Coquillette, *Civilian Writers*, *supra* note 3.

[18] *Id.* at 7–9, 18–20, 32–34, 37–39, 51–54, 296–301; *see* BRIAN P. LEVACK, THE CIVIL LAWYERS IN ENGLAND 1603–1641: A POLITICAL STUDY (1973).

[19] Coquillette, *Civilian Writers*, *supra* note 3, at 97–303. For the significance of Lord Mansfield, *see id.* at 282–96.

[20] *Id.* at 20–21, 98–99, 257–59, 299–302; *see id.*, FRANCIS BACON (1992); Dean Alfange Jr., *Jeremy Bentham and the Codification of Law*, 55 CORNELL L. REV. 58 (1969).

[21] DAVID IBBETSON, COMMON LAW AND *IUS COMMUNE* (2001); *see supra* text accompanying notes 8, 12 (Wood).

[22] *Id.* at 6.

Ibbetson described what comparatists know about Europe prior to the French Revolution—that virtually everywhere courts cited their previous decisions and those of other courts in searching for justification in reaching a judgment. This was as true of the Paris *parlement* as it was of courts in Germany, Holland, Italy, Portugal, and Spain. It might take two or three prior consistent decisions, rules differed on what was binding or only persuasive, but the English view of precedent was not unique to England.[23]

Ibbetson listed four features that marked commonality among continental European legal systems. He then asked whether each element existed in England. These features were (1) advocates and judges educated in the learned law; (2) Romanization of legal literature; (3) use of learned law in legal argument; and (4) internationalism. He found that, although there was evidence for the first two elements, outside ecclesiastical and admiralty courts, there was little use of Roman and canon law in common law argument, while common law courts were distinctly insular in their attitude toward continental legal authority.[24]

B. Roman and Civil Law in Colonial British America

1. Natural Law, the Law of Nations, and Moral Philosophy

What do we know about Roman, civil, and perhaps canon law influence on the legal systems of colonial British America? Besides the work of Coquillette on John Adams,[25] the terrain is virtually *terra incognita*. A probable avenue for continental European law ideas into America was through writing on natural law,[26] the law of nations (*ius gentium*),[27] and moral philosophy generally. Peter Stein

---

[23] Id. at 7-9; see JOHN P. DAWSON, THE ORACLES OF THE LAW (1968).

[24] IBBETSON, supra note 21, at 9-27; see id., English Law and the European Ius Commune 1450-1650, 8 CAMBRIDGE Y.B. EUR. LEGAL STUD. 115 (2005-2006).

[25] Daniel R. Coquillette, *Justinian in Braintree: John Adams, Civilian Learning, and Legal Elitism, 1758-1775*, in LAW IN COLONIAL MASSACHUSETTS: 1630-1800, at 359 (1984) [hereinafter Coquillette, *John Adams*]; see MAX RADIN, HANDBOOK OF ANGLO-AMERICAN LEGAL HISTORY 109-10 (1936) (minimal transplant of rules of English ecclesiastical courts) [hereinafter RADIN, HANDBOOK]. For the influence of canon law procedure on the concept of appeal in colonial Massachusetts and Rhode Island, see Mary Sarah Bilder, *Salamanders and Sons of God: The Culture of Appeal in Early New England*, in THE MANY LEGALITIES OF EARLY AMERICA 47 (Christopher L. Tomlins & Bruce H. Mann eds., 2001).

[26] Max Radin, *The Rivalry of Common-Law and Civil Law Ideas in the American Colonies*, in 2 LAW: A CENTURY OF PROGRESS 1835-1935, at 404, 405-07, 420-28 (Alison Reppy ed., 1937). "It was clothed in a garb that had so much in it of the Roman law that natural law and Roman law could almost be used interchangeably." *Id.* at 405. "[A] conception of an ideal of comparative law as declaratory of natural law gave direction to judicial development of the law." ROSCOE POUND, THE FORMATIVE ERA OF AMERICAN LAW 107 (1938); see RADIN, HANDBOOK, supra note 25, at 117-18, 259.

[27] James Muldoon provided an interesting example of canon law influence on the English charters authorizing the occupation of North America, which John Adams then parsed in legal

mentioned four standard law treatises by European scholars that, through their English translations, had substantial circulation in America during the eighteenth century.[28] These were Hugo Grotius, *De iure belli ac pacis* (1625);[29] Samuel von Pufendorf, *De jure naturae et gentium* (1672);[30] Johann Heineccius, *Elementa iuris naturae et gentium* (1737);[31] and Jean-Jacques Burlamaqui, *Principes du droit naturel* (1747).[32] Beginning in 1756, the College of Philadelphia (later the University of Pennsylvania) assigned the books by Grotius and Pufendorf for a course that included instruction in the civil law and King's College (later Columbia University) in 1763 required those books in the fourth year curriculum.[33] The English translation of Burlamaqui was so popular that it had American printings in Boston, Cambridge, and Philadelphia between 1792 and 1823 and one in Ohio in 1859. These books adopted the position that Roman law was written reason (*ratio scripta*) and humans should form their rules of conduct through the exercise of reason.[34]

Many of the influential moral philosophers in British America were Scotsmen, that is, men who came from a nation where lawyers learned civil law.[35] A leading example was Francis Hutcheson, who divided *A Short Introduction to Moral Philosophy* (1747)[36] into a part on ethics and a part on the law of nature. The latter

---

argument during the 1760s. This authority served as a counterpoint to the emerging *ius gentium*. James Muldoon, *Discovery, Grant, Conquest, or Purchase: John Adams on the Legal Basis for English Possession of North America*, in THE MANY LEGALITIES OF EARLY AMERICA, *supra* note 25, at 25, 27–32, 43–46; *see infra* text accompanying notes 185–86 (Adams).

[28] Peter Stein, *supra* note 13, at 404–06; *see* DAVID J. BEDERMAN, THE CLASSICAL FOUNDATIONS OF THE AMERICAN CONSTITUTION: PREVAILING WISDOM 11 (2008); HERBERT A. JOHNSON, IMPORTED EIGHTEENTH-CENTURY LAW TREATISES IN AMERICAN LIBRARIES, 1700–1799, at xxiii–xxv, xxxvi, 27, 30, 46 (1978).

[29] Published in Latin in a single volume with three parts (books) under the name Hugonis Grotii (Dutch name Hugo de Groot), book one dealt with Grotius's theory of natural justice. The first English translation appeared in 1654. George Washington (1732–1799), first president of the United States, had a copy of the 1738 London translation titled *The Rights of War and Peace* (reprint 2004).

[30] Published in Latin under the name Samuelis Pufendorfij. The first English translation was *Of the Law of Nature and Nations* (Oxford 1703).

[31] George Turnbull translated this as 1–2 *A Methodical System of Universal Law, or, The Laws of Nature and Nations* (London 1763, reprint 2008). He added his own 80-page "Discourse upon the Nature and Origin of Moral and Civil Laws."

[32] Thomas Nugent translated this as THE PRINCIPLES OF NATURAL LAW: IN WHICH THE TRUE SYSTEMS OF MORALITY AND CIVIL GOVERNMENT ARE ESTABLISHED (London 1748, reprint 2003). Burlamaqui, four years after his first book, published 1–2 *Principes du droit politique* (1751). Nugent translated this volume as *The Principles of Politic Law* (1752) and later combined it with natural law as 1–2 *The Principles of Natural and Politic Law* (2d ed. 1763, reprint 2006).

[33] Coquillette, *John Adams*, *supra* note 25, at 367 n.8.

[34] Peter Stein, *supra* note 13, at 404–05.

[35] *See* Murdoch, *The Advocates, the Law and the Nation in Early Modern Scotland*, in LAWYERS IN EARLY MODERN EUROPE AND AMERICA, *supra* note 2, at 147.

[36] FRANCIS HUTCHESON, A SHORT INTRODUCTION TO MORAL PHILOSOPHY. . . . CONTAINING THE ELEMENTS OF ETHICKS AND THE LAW OF NATURE (1747). This was Hutcheson's translation of his earlier *Philosophiae moralis institutio compendiaria, ethices & jurisprudentiae naturalis elementes continens* (1742).

part (in book 2) discussed natural law, human rights, liberty, and legal rights very much as would a contemporary book on Roman or civil law. Thomas Jefferson recommended Hutcheson's *Introduction* in a course for prospective lawyers.[37]

2. Self-Study and Legal Apprenticeship

In the second half of the eighteenth century, legal education in the 13 colonies was rudimentary and often part of one's general liberal education. Important college teachers included the Scotsmen William Small (College of William and Mary) and John Witherspoon (president, College of New Jersey, now Princeton University), who taught or recommended one or more of the natural law books in English translation to students. Thomas Jefferson studied under Small while James Madison (1751–1836), fourth president of the United States, read under Witherspoon from 1769 to 1771.[38] Witherspoon's moral philosophy course connected natural law, radical republicanism, and Christian virtue. In 1774, he published an essay encouraging Americans never to submit to Parliament's claim to full sovereignty, followed in 1776 with a printed sermon appealing to Scots to join with Americans in their resistance to England.[39]

James Wilson (1742–1798), also born in Scotland, studied the Scottish Enlightenment at the Universities of St. Andrews, Glasgow, and Edinburgh before he immigrated to America in 1765, settling in Philadelphia. There he began teaching at the College of Philadelphia, founded by Benjamin Franklin (1706–1790), while at the same time reading law at the office of John Dickinson (1732–1808).[40] Wilson was among the most influential of the Founding Fathers.

---

[37] Peter Stein, *supra* note 13, at 405.

[38] Bederman, *supra* note 28, at 7–9; Peter Stein, *supra* note 13, at 405; *see* IRVING BRANT, JAMES MADISON: THE VIRGINIA REVOLUTIONIST, 1751–1780, at 76 (1941); DUMAS MALONE, JEFFERSON, THE VIRGINIAN 51–55 (2005, vol. 1 of the series JEFFERSON AND HIS TIME, orig. 1948).

[39] Mark A. Noll, *Witherspoon, John, in* 23 AMERICAN NATIONAL BIOGRAPHY, *supra* note 11, at 704, 706–07. Witherspoon (1723–1794) was a New Jersey delegate to the Continental Congress (1776–1782) and was the only clergyman to sign the Declaration of Independence. *Id.* at 706. Nevertheless, most Scots were loyalists to the Crown during the events leading up to the Revolution. T.M. DEVINE, TO THE ENDS OF THE EARTH: SCOTLAND'S GLOBAL DIASPORA, 1750–2010, at 136–39 (2011).

[40] PAGE SMITH, JAMES WILSON: FOUNDING FATHER, 1742–1798, at 8, 12–16, 24, 37 (1956); Penn University Archives and Records Center, *James Wilson*, https://archives.upenn.edu (search James Wilson). Franklin founded the College in 1755, for which the State of Pennsylvania reissued a charter in 1791 to merge with another institution to become the University of Pennsylvania. James Wilson served as its first law professor from 1790 to 1798. Penn University Archives and Records Center, *Penn in the 18th Century*, https://archives.upenn.edu (search Penn eighteenth century). Dickinson wrote *Letters from a Farmer in Pennsylvania* (1767), one of the most widely circulated tracts in the colonies contesting Parliament's right to tax the colonies and to quarter troops. In the 1780s, he served as president of Delaware and then of Pennsylvania. He was one of Delaware's delegates to the Constitutional Convention and supported the Constitution's adoption in a series of letters (by Fabius) first published in the *Delaware Gazette* (1788). Elaine K. Ginsberg, *Dickinson, John, in* 6 AMERICAN NATIONAL BIOGRAPHY, *supra* note 11, at 566–68; *see* CRAIG YIRUSH, SETTLERS, LIBERTY, AND EMPIRE: THE ROOTS OF EARLY AMERICAN POLITICAL THEORY, 1675–1775, at 36–37 (2011).

He participated in national and state constitutional deliberations, signed the Declaration of Independence, principally drafted the Pennsylvania Constitution of 1790, initiated law teaching at the College of Philadelphia in 1790, and served as associate justice of the U.S. Supreme Court from 1789 until his death.[41]

In addition to study, to become a lawyer, men typically had to clerk or apprentice with a senior lawyer, which involved paying a fee in exchange for the promise to train the aspiring jurist. Besides copying documents and pleadings, the apprentice had an opportunity to read the lawyer's law books.[42] Jeremiah Gridley, a leading Boston lawyer, for instance, suggested to John Adams that he study the civil law and natural law to gain a better understanding of the logic and system of law, which Adam's diary reveals he accomplished.[43]

William Smith Jr. (1728–1793), a prominent New York lawyer, similarly advocated an ambitious study plan for law students in 1756 that reflected the desire to foster an increasingly sophisticated, broadly educated, colonial bar. In his seven-part plan, one element was English law, but three other elements included Latin and French, logic and rhetoric, and the "law of nature and nations."[44] Smith recommended that, after one had his liberal education, he begin with a general knowledge of law by reading Wood's *A New Institute* or Domat's *The Civil Law*.[45] Next, for an overview of natural law, the student should turn to Pufendorf's *De officio hominis et civis* (1673), which was an abridgement of *De jure naturae et gentium* (1672).[46] After completing the core English texts on the common law,

---

[41] Bederman, *supra* note 28, at 11–12; Stephen A. Conrad, *Wilson, James*, in THE OXFORD COMPANION TO THE SUPREME COURT OF THE UNITED STATES 932–33 (Kermit L. Hall et al., eds., 1992); Peter Stein, *supra* note 13, at 407.

[42] LAWRENCE M. FRIEDMAN, A HISTORY OF AMERICAN LAW 55–57 (3d ed. 2005); Ralph Stein, *supra* note 2, at 437–40.

[43] Peter Stein, *supra* note 13, at 405–06; L. Kinvin Wroth, *Gridley, Jeremiah*, in 9 AMERICAN NATIONAL BIOGRAPHY, *supra* note 11, at 579–80: *see infra* notes 142–52 and accompanying text (Gridley and Adams).

[44] HAMLIN, *supra* note 2, at 61–62, 80, 82–83, 197; *see id.* at 160–62. Smith graduated from Yale College, as had his father who also was a lawyer, and served as a justice on the New York Supreme Court. Smith apprenticed with his father, as had William Livingston, another Yale graduate and prominent New York lawyer. Livingston used a study plan for his apprentices like the one Smith used. The New York governor appointed Smith to the Executive Council in 1767, after which his political sentiments sided more often with the Crown. His reward was appointment in 1780 as chief justice, but he fled to England in 1783 when loyalists evacuated the province. He served as chief justice of Lower Canada from 1786 to 1793. Livingston, however, remained a patriot and became the first governor of the State of New Jersey. Milton M. Klein, *The Rise of the New York Bar: The Legal Career of William Livingston*, 15 WILLIAM & MARY Q. 334, 336, 356–58 (1958); L.F.S. Upton, *Smith, William*, in 4 DICTIONARY OF CANADIAN BIOGRAPHY ONLINE (John English & Réal Bélanger eds., 2000), http://www.biographi.ca/en/bio.php?&id_nbr=2171.

[45] HAMLIN, *supra* note 2, at 62, 197–98; *see supra* notes 8–15 and accompanying text (Wood and Domat).

[46] HAMLIN, *supra* note 2, at 198. The first English translation of *De officio hominis et civis* was THE WHOLE DUTY OF MAN ACCORDING TO THE LAW OF NATURE (Andrew Tooke trans., 1691, reprint 2003); *see* SAMUEL PUFENDORF, ON THE DUTY OF MAN AND CITIZEN ACCORDING TO NATURAL LAW (James Tully ed. & Michael Silverthorne trans., 1991); *supra* note 30 and accompanying text (Pufendorf).

including St. German's *Doctor and Student*,[47] the student should return to the laws of nature and civil law, studying the full version of Pufendorf, *De jure naturae*; rereading Wood and Domat; and finishing Grotius's *De iure belli ac pacis*.[48]

The discussion of legal literature and law study, as well as civil law (or common law) influence, depends on the presence of lawyers, a group that members of society consider expert in the law and perhaps government. From this perspective, legal literature, study, and influence are part of intellectual history. Societies, however, exist without lawyers, though not without law, or at least law as anthropologists consider the term. Thus, a social legal history of colonial British America would likely take a quite different approach to the issue of foreign influence.

C. Social Factors Affecting Law

George Haskins set out a framework to develop such a social history for the seventeenth century. He contended that each colony evolved its own individual legal system just as it did for its political and social systems. These depended on the conditions of settlement and subsequent developments: geography, climate, time of settlement, degree of external supervision, people's attitudes, and so on.[49] There were three basic sources of early colonial law: (1) the local English rules (not from the royal London courts) that settlers brought with them; (2) indigenously developed norms to cope with colonial situations, such as relations with Native peoples; and (3) ideologically or religiously derived rules (such as those of the Puritans) that supported settlers' beliefs.[50]

Courts played an important governing role in colonial life and existed in great diversity.[51] They serve to illustrate how Haskin's list of sources could expand to include non-English law. For instance, before the English defeated the Dutch in

---

[47] HAMLIN, *supra* note 2, at 198; *see supra* note 5 and accompanying text (St. German).

[48] HAMLIN, *supra* note 2, at 199. One of Smith's apprentices, Peter van Schaack (1747–1832), grew up in Dutch country near Albany, New York, where from 1786 to 1828 he accepted over 100 apprentices, including James Kent and Theodore Sedgwick, to whom he taught the law. He followed Smith with a broad curriculum that included the seven liberal arts as well as law. MAXWELL BLOOMFIELD, AMERICAN LAWYERS IN A CHANGING SOCIETY, 1776–1876, at 2–8, 25–26 (1976); Daniel J. Helsebosch, *Van Schaack, Peter*, *in* THE YALE BIOGRAPHICAL DICTIONARY OF AMERICAN LAW 560–61 (Roger K. Newman ed., 2009).

[49] GEORGE LEE HASKINS, LAW AND AUTHORITY IN EARLY MASSACHUSETTS: A STUDY IN TRADITION AND DESIGN 4–6, 163, 188 (1960); *see* KERMIT L. HALL & PETER KARSTEN, THE MAGIC MIRROR: LAW IN AMERICAN HISTORY 10–13 (2d ed. 2009); MELVIN I. UROFSKY & PAUL FINKELMAN, 1 A MARCH OF LIBERTY: A CONSTITUTIONAL HISTORY OF THE UNITED STATES (FROM THE FOUNDING TO 1890) 7–15 (2d ed. 2002).

[50] FRIEDMAN, *supra* note 42, at 4–7; *see* WILLIAM F. WALSH, A HISTORY OF ANGLO-AMERICAN LAW 85–92 (2d ed. 1932).

[51] FRIEDMAN, *supra* note 42, at 7–16.

New York, the Court of Burgomasters, Schepens, and Schout from 1653 heard criminal matters and most civil cases in New Amsterdam.[52] The court used Dutch substantive and procedural law, suitably modified to cope with the reality of frontier life.[53] After the English arrived in 1664, the Duke of York appointed Richard Nicolls governor, who authorized the preparation of *Duke's Laws* (1665), which changed the court's name to Mayor's Court.[54] The new court structure was similar to that used in New Netherland, but most commercial law cases remained with the Mayor's Court.[55] Just as the English used the Mayor's Court of London to develop the European *lex mercatoria* into modern English commercial law, so too did the New York City Mayor's Court carry out that function for the New York economy, which by 1730 had one of the three most important ports in colonial North America. The court's procedure (adding the English jury) maintained Dutch emphasis on arrest, attachment, and arbitration into the early eighteenth century, recognizing foreign law and mercantile custom. By this time, England had received most of the *lex mercatoria* so that the increased number of New York lawyers who had read English law did not upset the mercantile Dutch transplant.[56]

William Nelson, in the first of four volumes, began to test the following hypothesis. "The thirteen mainland American colonies were founded by different

---

[52] HERBERT ALAN JOHNSON, THE LAW MERCHANT AND NEGOTIABLE INSTRUMENTS IN COLONIAL NEW YORK: 1664 to 1730, at 22–23, 64 n.1 (1963). The Burgomasters' Court, like many European courts, also had certain administrative and legislative power, such as the regulation of bread prices. JOHNSON, THE LAW MERCHANT, *supra*, at 6–7.

[53] JOHNSON, THE LAW MERCHANT, *supra* note 52, at 23; *see* WILLIAM E. NELSON, 2 THE COMMON LAW IN COLONIAL AMERICA: THE MIDDLE COLONIES AND THE CAROLINAS, 1660-1730, at 9–25, 32–37 (2013) [hereinafter cited as NELSON, 2 THE COMMON LAW]. The court's library had texts on Dutch admiralty law, procedure, States General ordinances, and Amsterdam bylaws. JOHNSON, THE LAW MERCHANT, *supra*, at 62 nn.1–2. It also included HUGO DE GROOT, INLEIDING TOT DE HOLLANDSCHE RECHTS-GELEERTHEYD (1631). This was the first legal treatise written in Dutch rather than Latin. R.W. Lee translated Grotius's work as *The Jurisprudence of Holland* in 1926 (reprint 1977). JOHNSON, THE LAW MERCHANT, *supra*, at 62.

[54] JOHNSON, THE LAW MERCHANT, *supra* note 52, at 23. For *Duke's Laws*, *see infra* note 62.

[55] *Id.* at 23–25, 31. The new vice-admiralty court for the Province of New York primarily handled criminal prosecutions for violation of the English Acts of Trade and Navigation. *Id.* at 24–25. "Dutch civil law experienced no difficulty in absorbing the law merchant into its fabric. Its philosophic bases in natural law and its ready acceptance of changes made in the law by the practices of the people made it much more receptive to change than the common-law system." *Id.* at 62 n.4.

[56] *Id.* at 14–21, 25–27, 37–38, 40; NELSON, 2 THE COMMON LAW, *supra* note 53, at 45–48; RADIN, HANDBOOK, *supra* note 25, at 500–01. Grotius's *Jurisprudence of Holland* included the *lex mercatoria*, which by the end of the seventeenth century was approximately the same as commercial law in England. JOHNSON, THE LAW MERCHANT, *supra* note 52, at 16. For other Dutch legacies, *see* CHARLES W. MCCURDY, THE ANTI-RENT ERA IN NEW YORK LAW AND POLITICS: 1839–1865 (2001) (Dutch land tenure law in the Hudson River Valley); DENNIS SULLIVAN, THE PUNISHMENT OF CRIME IN COLONIAL NEW YORK: THE DUTCH EXPERIENCE IN ALBANY DURING THE SEVENTEENTH CENTURY (1997); OPENING STATEMENTS: LAW, JURISPRUDENCE, AND THE LEGACY OF DUTCH NEW YORK (Albert M. Rosenblatt & Julia C. Rosenblatt eds., 2013). The traditional view was that New York "was the first American success of common-law imperialism; the process would be later repeated with varying results, in Louisiana, Florida, Illinois, Texas, and California." FRIEDMAN, *supra* note 42, at 13.

groups—indeed, by different nations—for many different purposes. Insofar as law reflects the societal conditions under which it operates, tremendous differences had to exist among the legal systems of the early colonies."[57] Nelson documented these differences and described how, as early as the 1660s, two regional patterns among the New England legal systems and the Chesapeake (Maryland and Virginia) legal systems emerged. The North's system was more egalitarian; moderate in the treatment of women, children, and servants; and focused on family farms except for the three port towns supporting mercantile capitalism. In contrast, the South's system was more hierarchical, harsh in permitting brutal master control of servile labor, and aimed toward the export of tobacco. These two legal cultures shared a commitment to govern by rule of law (to prevent tyranny) and to rely on their English legal heritage. Local legislatures were the most authoritative legal institutions in each colony and they all had asserted the right to make law, marking the colonies as distinctively American.[58]

During this early period, leaders drafted simple, systematic compilations of written law. Each had its own peculiarities, but by the second half of the seventeenth century, there was substantial copying by one colony of the work of another. The earliest compilation occurred in 1636 in New Plymouth, which set out limits on magistrate power with rules of procedure. The same motivation—to constrain elite power—led to the Massachusetts General Court's *Body of Liberties* (1641).[59] *The Laws and Liberties of Massachusetts* (1648) was more comprehensive, including a system of government and courts; relations between state and church; along with diverse subjects such as crime, property, trade, and family law, ordered alphabetically.[60] Puritans believed in the importance of the written word,

---

[57] WILLIAM E. NELSON, 1 THE COMMON LAW IN COLONIAL AMERICA: THE CHESAPEAKE AND NEW ENGLAND, 1607–1660, at 6 (2008) [hereinafter NELSON, 1 THE COMMON LAW]; see id. at vii, 7–11.

[58] *Id.* at 125–31.

[59] FRIEDMAN, *supra* note 42, at 50–51; Daniel R. Coquillette, *Radical Lawmakers in Colonial Massachusetts: The "Countenance of Authoritie" and the Lawes and Libertyes*, 67 NEW ENG. Q. 179, 189–94 (1994) [hereinafter Coquillette, *Lawes and Libertyes*]. Nathaniel Ward (1578–1652), a Puritan minister who had studied law was the principal drafter of *Body of Liberties*. He graduated from Cambridge and traveled widely in German lands before emigrating to America. He preferred theocracy, drew freely from Mosaic law for his rules, and believed law and justice were essential to liberty. FRIEDMAN, *supra*, at 51, 55; Mary Rhinelander McCarl, *Ward, Nathaniel*, in 22 AMERICAN NATIONAL BIOGRAPHY, *supra* note 11, at 646.

[60] FRIEDMAN, *supra* note 42, at 51; George L. Haskins, *Codification of the Law in Colonial Massachusetts: A Study in Comparative Law*, 30 IND. L.J. 1, 3, 5, 8–9 (1954); Coquillette, *Lawes and Libertyes*, *supra* note 59, at 194–202. In its alphabetical organization, e.g., Ana-Baptists followed Age. FRIEDMAN, *supra*, at 51. For illustrations of the influence of religion on crimes, *see* LAWRENCE M. FRIEDMAN, CRIME AND PUNISHMENT IN AMERICAN HISTORY 32–44 (1993). Henry E. Huntington in 1911 purchased (in England) the only known surviving copy of *Laws and Liberties* and had Harvard University Press publish a facsimile in 1929 (Max Farrand introduction, reprint 1998). *The Book of the General Lawes and Libertyes concerning the Inhabitants of the Massachusets* was the first compilation of laws and constitutional rights printed in British America, with most of the 600 copies provided free of charge to court magistrates and deputies. Professor Haskins originally presented his paper in French at the Fourth Congress of the International Academy of Comparative Law in Paris

evidenced by the Bible's literal authority, to organize the church and its believers. *Laws and Liberties* in principle repudiated the authority of English law.[61]

Other colonies copied substantial parts of the Massachusetts 1648 compilation. These included Connecticut (1650), New Haven (1656), New York (1665), New Hampshire (1680), and Pennsylvania in the late seventeenth century. The borrowing, however, was always selective with an eye to local circumstances. For instance, Quakers in Pennsylvania disagreed with certain norms that served Puritans in Massachusetts or Anglicans in New York.[62]

By the eighteenth century, the royal English contribution to law had become more important and standardized for the various colonies, supplementing American law making and inter-colonial borrowing.[63] The Privy Council in London, which could review colonial statutes for conformity with the Crown's law, influenced their substance and style. There remained considerable variety among the colonies. For instance, in the province of Carolina, named after King Charles I of Great Britain, Chief Justice Nicholas Trott in Charles Towne compiled what he considered 150 acceptable English statutes (*Trott's Laws*) in 1712. Informally divided into south and north, the former's assembly approved the *Laws*, but since there was no local printer until the 1730s, they remained unpublished until 1736.[64]

In 1760, the 13 North American British colonies that would declare their independence from Great Britain had a total population of 1.6 million.[65] They extended along the Atlantic coast from Maine (then part of Massachusetts) south to Georgia with few settlements more than 75 miles inland.[66] The economy of

(1954). *See generally* David S. Clark, *American Participation in the Development of the International Academy of Comparative Law and Its First Two Hague Congresses*, 54 AM. J. COMP. L. 1 (Supp. 2006).

[61] HASKINS, *supra* note 49, at 6–7; Coquillette, *Lawes and Libertyes*, *supra* note 59, at 197, 202; *see* NELSON, 1 THE COMMON LAW, *supra* note 57, at 49–79.

[62] FRIEDMAN, *supra* note 42, at 52. After King Charles II of Great Britain captured the province of Nieuw Nederland in 1664, he granted governing authority to his brother, James, Duke of York. James appointed Richard Nicolls governor, who renamed the colony and its principal city New York. The law-trained Matthias Nicolls and the governor prepared *Duke's Laws* (1665), some of which they copied from *Laws and Liberties*. Pennsylvania borrowed from *Duke's Laws* as well as *Laws and Liberties*. *Id.* at 52, 57; *see* George L. Haskins, *Influences of New England Law on the Middle Colonies*, 1 LAW & HIST. REV. 238–50 (1983).

[63] FRIEDMAN, *supra* note 42, at 5, 14–22, 40, 52.

[64] *Id.* at 52–53, 56–57; EDWARD MCCRADY, THE HISTORY OF SOUTH CAROLINA UNDER THE ROYAL GOVERNMENT: 1719–1776, at 4–7, 144–48, 414, 462, 483 (1899). Trott trained as a barrister at Inner Temple before his career in the colonies. For his legal writing, Oxford University awarded him the D.C.L (doctor of civil law) in 1720, since there was no academic degree for achievement in the common law. L. Lynn Hogue, *Trott, Nicholas*, *in* 21 AMERICAN NATIONAL BIOGRAPHY, *supra* note 11, at 840–41.

[65] U.S. BUREAU OF THE CENSUS, HISTORICAL STATISTICS OF THE UNITED STATES: COLONIAL TIMES TO 1970, at 1168 (part 2, bicentennial ed., 1975) [hereinafter HISTORICAL STATISTICS]. This included 326,000 Black persons, but excluded Native Americans. *Id.* There were about 150,000 Indians east of the Mississippi River, a dramatic decline from 1600 caused mainly by European viral disease. THOMAS L. PURVIS, COLONIAL AMERICA TO 1763, at 34, 36 (1999).

[66] PURVIS, *supra* note 65, at 18, 46.

these colonies was largely agricultural with few towns. The largest towns in 1760 were Philadelphia (23,000), New York (18,000), and Boston (16,000).[67] Only Virginia and Massachusetts had a population exceeding 200,000.[68]

In the 1760s, transportation between colonies could be difficult with the sea and rivers constituting the main channels of commerce. Some colonies had more commerce with Great Britain than with other colonies. Ships brought most of the books available in the colonies from England. In 1760, nine colonies still had established churches, only six colleges existed, and local printers had published only a few American law books, mostly manuals for justices of the peace or sheriffs.[69]

D. Lawyers and Courts

The story of colonial diversity is much the same if we consider legal practitioners.[70] In the early seventeenth century, social attitudes and some laws, such as clause 26 of the *Body of Liberties* in Massachusetts, proscribed lawyer participation in dispute resolution, at least for a fee and in court. Puritans, abused in England, distrusted servants of the state, including lawyers with their peculiar discourse and privileges (unnecessary in a godly society). In addition, Quakers favored peace and harmony and opposed the adversary procedural system in principle.[71]

Attitudes toward lawyers and the English common law were different in Virginia. More of its men studied law at the Inns of Court in London—60 in

---

[67] WILLIAM E. NELSON, AMERICANIZATION OF THE COMMON LAW: THE IMPACT OF LEGAL CHANGE ON MASSACHUSETTS SOCIETY, 1760–1830, at 1 (1975) [hereinafter NELSON, AMERICANIZATION]. Compare population figures in 1750 with Europe (86.6 million), including England (5.8 million) and London (675,000). E. Anthony Wrigley, *Urban Growth and Agricultural Change: England and the Continent in the Early Modern Period*, 15 J. INTERDISC. HIST. 683, 686, 688, 709 (1985).

[68] HISTORICAL STATISTICS, *supra* note 65, at 1168. The 1760 populations were Virginia, 340,000 (141,000 Black), Massachusetts, 203,000 excluding Maine (5,000 Black), Pennsylvania, 184,000 (4,000 Black), Maryland, 162,000 (49,000 Black), and Connecticut, 142,000 (4,000 Black). *Id.*

[69] NELSON, AMERICANIZATION, *supra* note 67, at 2; PURVIS, *supra* note 65, at 242–46; Mary Sarah Bilder, *English Settlement and Local Governance* [hereinafter Bilder, *Local Governance*], *in* 1 THE CAMBRIDGE HISTORY OF LAW IN AMERICA: EARLY AMERICA (1580–1815) 63, 102 (Michael Grossberg & Christopher Tomlins eds., 2008) [hereinafter CAMBRIDGE HISTORY]; *see* CHARLES WARREN, A HISTORY OF THE AMERICAN BAR 157–63 (1911, reprint 1980).

[70] Attorneys, the preferred term, meant that the person had some knowledge of the law. Licensing rules took hold in most colonies by 1710. Bilder, *Local Governance*, *supra* note 69, at 93–96.

[71] FRIEDMAN, *supra* note 42, at 53–54; UROFSKY & FINKELMAN, *supra* note 49, at 30–32; Stephen Botein, *The Legal Profession in Colonial North America*, *in* LAWYERS IN EARLY MODERN EUROPE AND AMERICA, *supra* note 2, at 129, 130–33; James A. Henretta, *Magistrates, Common Law Lawyers, Legislators: The Three Legal Systems of British America*, *in* CAMBRIDGE HISTORY, *supra* note 69, at 555, 563–64. The Massachusetts General Court promulgated the *Body of Liberties* as a legal code in 1641. However, after 1660, Massachusetts began to receive the common law, at least for procedural rules. WILLIAM E. NELSON, 3 THE COMMON LAW IN COLONIAL AMERICA: THE CHESAPEAKE AND NEW ENGLAND, 1660–1750, at 69–71, 85–87, 92–94, 110–12 (2016) [hereinafter NELSON, 3 THE COMMON LAW].

total—than in any other colony. Rather than practice law upon their return to Virginia, however, most of these wealthy men served on county courts. They tended to justify their decisions based on equity and good conscience rather than on common law technicalities. Maryland and South Carolina were similar in their view of the common law and law training, as they ranked second and third among the colonies associated with London law study.[72]

As we saw earlier, the Dutch settled in what they called New Netherland beginning in 1614.[73] From at least 1625, the government and courts used civil-law style notaries (*secretarissen*) as a European type of legal professional. For the next 50 years, about 100 of them worked in the colony. Trained through apprenticeship, they prepared legal documents for commercial, property, family, inheritance, and administrative law matters.[74] After complaints from the colonists, the Dutch government permitted private notaries (*beroepsnotissen*) in the 1650s. Petrus Stuyvesant, who served (1647–1664) in Manhattan (New Amsterdam) as the last director-general of the colony for the Dutch West India Company, protested since he did not want to lose control over document authentication. Nevertheless, records indicate that the Dutch *Staten Generaal* and provincial authorities appointed 17 of these private notaries who served clients until the 1680s.[75] With the arrival of British control in the renamed colony of New York, the usefulness of Dutch notaries with a knowledge of Dutch law ended. The British had their own legal practitioners.[76]

In general, however, animosity toward lawyers continued in the colonies into the eighteenth century. Artisans, merchants, farmers, and sailors viewed lawyers as upper class. Governors and royalists, however, could not always depend on the loyalty of lawyers and, due to their connection to law and authority, feared their possible influence. Lay judges naturally resented the growing power of lawyers over the judiciary. The periodic popular hatred of lawyers expressed in pamphlets was sometimes graphic. Nevertheless, as Lawrence Friedman concluded, colonists determined that with the growth in land transactions, general commercial activity, and issues associated with greater social complexity, lawyers were a "necessary evil."[77] There was a gradual professionalization of the bar with

---

[72] NELSON, 2 THE COMMON LAW, *supra* note 53, at 78–81; NELSON, 3 THE COMMON LAW, *supra* note 71, at 14, 47–50.

[73] *See supra* text accompanying notes 52–56 (Dutch colony).

[74] Mathias Reimann, *The Notary in American Legal History: The Fall and Rise of the Civil Law Tradition?*, in HANDBUCH ZUR GESCHICHTE DES NOTARIATS DER EUROPÄISCHEN TRADITIONEN 559, 571–72, 575–76 (Mathias Schmoeckel & Werner Schubert eds., 2009). New France (Louisiana) and New Spain (Florida and the Southwest) also utilized notaries as a type of legal professional. *Id.* at 564–71, 574–75, 577–79.

[75] *Id.* at 570–73. Private notaries advised clients, authenticated witness statements for use in court, and sometimes mediated disputes. *Id.* at 572.

[76] *Id.* at 573–76.

[77] FRIEDMAN, *supra* note 42, at 54. *See generally* WARREN, *supra* note 69, at 39–145 (describing lawyers in each of the 13 colonies).

men engaged in local study and apprenticeship with senior lawyers, while some read law and trained in England. By 1750, each major city had a professional bar with a few financially successful lawyers.[78]

Each colony determined its own bar admission standards. In 1709, New York City established the first bar association in the colonies.[79] Some had a select group of senior lawyers conduct an examination, or its high court pass on admission, or local court-by-court decentralized admission. The usual requirement was a fixed period of apprenticeship, which examiners might reduce if the applicant had graduated from college. The number of full-time lawyers was small, and sometimes a group would take guild-like action to try to keep the bar that way. Although many in the bar were loyalists, those lawyers who supported the break with Great Britain were disproportionately influential. Thus, lawyers were 25 of the 56 signers of the Declaration of Independence and 31 of the 55 delegates to the Constitutional Convention. American lawyers led the movement for national independence.[80]

Court organization developed along the same lines as the legal profession. In general, seventeenth-century courts were instruments in the hands of a colony's officials and freemen, typically not law trained. They were not a separate branch of government defined by function. For instance, in Massachusetts, the General Court performed the functions of a legislature and high court of appeals; the Court of Assistants heard some first instance cases and appeals; and county courts tried other civil and criminal matters as well as carried out numerous administrative tasks. There were also at times special courts and magistrates.[81]

By the late seventeenth century, English models and customs had more influence, promoted especially by landowners and merchants. Colonies realized that by charter or patent they were subject to English law, but that they were different from England and often needed their own rules and institutions. In addition, the Crown in Great Britain took more interest in governing America. County courts continued to be influential in resolving disputes, but also in general administrative duties. Usually staffed with lay judges, they reflected and protected local

---

[78] FRIEDMAN, *supra* note 42, at 54–56; HAMLIN, *supra* note 2, at 15–23; Botein, *supra* note 71, at 133–39; Henretta, *supra* note 71, at 566–74, 583; *see* WARREN, *supra* note 69, at 146–208. The Inns of Court in London after 1640 no longer provided structured legal education and served primarily as eating clubs. DAVID LEMMINGS, GENTLEMEN AND BARRISTERS: THE INNS OF COURT AND THE ENGLISH BAR, 1680–1730, at 78, 98–99 (1990).

[79] NELSON, 2 THE COMMON LAW, *supra* note 53, at 58.

[80] FRIEDMAN, *supra* note 42, at 57–59; HAMLIN, *supra* note 2, at 160–64 (Agreement of the Bar of New York City, 1756); Roscoe Pound, *A Hundred Years of American Law*, *in* 1 LAW: A CENTURY OF PROGRESS 1835–1935, *supra* note 26, at 8, 10; Botein, *supra* note 71, at 136–37, 139–42; *see* WARREN, *supra* note 69, at 211–24.

[81] FRIEDMAN, *supra* note 42, at 8–10; HALL & KARSTEN, *supra* note 49, at 16–19; NELSON, AMERICANIZATION, *supra* note 67, at 14–17; Bilder, *Local Governance*, *supra* note 69, at 91, *see supra* notes 51–56 and accompanying text (Dutch Court of Burgomasters).

political and economic power. Governors appointed most judges for a term. In the eighteenth century, vice-admiralty and chancery courts demonstrated the increasing English authority and complexity in the colonial legal system.[82]

E. Religious and Cultural Variation

1. Religious Establishment and Attempts at Tolerance

Of all the overseas colonies European empires established before 1760, only the 13 British mainland colonies had substantial religious pluralism. This element of pluralism in American society suggests that law and dispute resolution similarly might have displayed such diversity.[83] For religion, this was fortuitous since most settlers up to the end of the colonial period did not believe in the separation of church and state or in the freedom of worship. Governments required tax support and regular attendance, but some colonies allowed multiple establishment through local option. In New England, Puritans (Congregationalists) dominated. Otherwise, the Church of England (Anglican) was the principal established religion in America, which competed with the powerful Roman Catholicism in the French and Spanish empires.[84] These dominant Christian organizations taught that to protect one's soul, an individual's spiritual (and at times complete) loyalty was to the church. Church and state had been rivals as much as cooperating entities in Europe since Christianity's emergence during the Roman Empire.[85] The Church of England, catholic and reformed, with the Crown as its supreme governor, also distrusted minority Protestant groups—as potential sources of political subversion—because of the Puritan role in the regicide of Charles I in 1649.[86]

---

[82] FRIEDMAN, *supra* note 42, at 14–21; HALL & KARSTEN, *supra* note 49, at 18–23; NELSON, AMERICANIZATION, *supra* note 67, at 32–35; Bilder, *Local Governance*, *supra* note 69, at 92; *see* Stanley N. Katz, *The Politics of Law in Colonial America: Controversies over Chancery Courts and Equity Law in the Eighteenth Century*, in LAW IN AMERICAN HISTORY 257–84 (Donald Fleming & Bernard Bailyn eds., 1971). In New England, town assemblies also had substantial governing power. HALL & KARSTEN, *supra*, at 23–26.

[83] LAUREN BENTON, LAW AND COLONIAL CULTURES: LEGAL REGIMES IN WORLD HISTORY, 1400–1900, at 7–12 (2002) (legal pluralism); *see id.* at 1–7, 12–30.

[84] PURVIS, *supra* note 65, at 178; Mark McGarvie & Elizabeth Mensch, *Law and Religion in Colonial America*, in CAMBRIDGE HISTORY, *supra* note 69, at 324, 326–27, 329; *see* JON BUTLER, BECOMING AMERICA: THE REVOLUTION BEFORE 1776, at 185–204 (2000). The only two colonies that never imposed religious establishment were Pennsylvania and Rhode Island. McGarvie & Mensch, *supra*, at 326–27. For an example of the legal culture in northern New Spain, *see* James F. Brooks, *"Lest We Go in Search of Relief to Our Lands and Our Nation": Customary Justice and Colonial Law in the New Mexico Borderlands, 1680–1821*, in THE MANY LEGALITIES OF EARLY AMERICA, *supra* note 25, at 150.

[85] *See, e.g.*, David S. Clark, *The Medieval Origins of Modern Legal Education: Between Church and State*, 35 AM. J. COMP. L. 653 (1987).

[86] PURVIS, *supra* note 65, at 178.

In 1690, 90 percent of all colonial congregations were either Puritan or Anglican. Over the next 80 years, that dominance diminished substantially as German, French, Irish, and Scot immigrants settled in the Middle Colonies. By 1770, Puritans represented only 20 percent and Anglicans 15 percent of the total colonial population. Beyond an increase in religious diversity, commercialism strengthened the role of law to regulate property and contract relationships in a more heterogeneous society. Communitarianism weakened and the acceptance of an individualist ideology supported later efforts toward political revolution.[87]

Some point to Maryland with its 1649 Act concerning Religion as an early example of religious tolerance in America.[88] After Charles I (who was married to a French Catholic) gave the province to the Catholic Cecilius Calvert (Lord Baltimore) in 1629, many of that faith settled there. Calvert used his proprietary authority to manage the colony as a profit-making enterprise, but to attract laborers (who were mainly Protestant) he encouraged religious diversity. Many younger sons of the English Catholic gentry found Maryland attractive since they could freely practice their religion and Calvert accommodated them with large land tracts and better political positions. This religious diversity, however, only meant toleration in the weaker sense of forbearance. Events in England associated with the Civil War and Charles I's conviction of treason (and beheading) in 1649 led Calvert to support the Act concerning Religion to protect the minority Catholic population.[89] The Act criminalized speech against or denial of the Trinity (punishable with death and property forfeiture to Lord Baltimore), speech disgraceful of the Virgin Mary (£5 the first time, £10 the second time, and property forfeiture and banishment the third time), and derogatory speech toward the religion of any Christian believing in the Trinity (10 shillings for each offense).[90]

Calvert's regime was short-lived. By 1651, Protestants controlled the Assembly, which in 1654 repudiated Lord Baltimore's authority to govern and later made Catholicism a crime. Puritans plundered the homes of Catholics and forced many into exile. Thereafter, until the American Revolution, the legal position of Catholics in Maryland vacillated with political developments in England and in the colony. When a later Lord Baltimore converted to the Anglican Church in the eighteenth century, Maryland acquired an established religion and flourished

---

[87] McGarvie & Mensch, *supra* note 84, at 329.
[88] Id. at 357; BRADLEY T. JOHNSON, THE FOUNDATION OF MARYLAND AND THE ORIGIN OF THE ACT CONCERNING RELIGION 5–12, 15–17 (1883). For the Act, *see* JOHNSON, *supra*, at 185–89; Yale Law School (Avalon Project), Maryland Toleration Act (September 21, 1649), https://avalon.law.yale.edu/18th_century/maryland_toleration.asp [hereinafter Maryland Toleration Act].
[89] McGarvie & Mensch, *supra* note 84, at 357–59.
[90] Maryland Toleration Act, *supra* note 88. This might be the first American example of "three strikes and you are out" punishment, perhaps derived from the game of cricket or rounders.

along its populated coast. After 1720, in western Maryland the immigrants were Germans, French Huguenots, and Scotch Irish, who brought with them their allegiance to the Lutheran, Moravian, Mennonite, Dutch Reformed, Baptist, or Methodist denominations.[91]

The Dutch charter founding New Amsterdam stipulated that the Dutch Reformed Church would be the official religion, which Governor Stuyvesant interpreted by punishing dissidents. However, the social reality by 1650 included Catholics, Jews, and numerous Protestant denominations. Interested in profits, the West India Company directed Stuyvesant to permit religious diversity and to promote free trade.[92] When the English took over, they continued a limited toleration of non-Anglican Protestant churches, but Dutch resentment was strong through the end of the seventeenth century.[93] For instance, Dutch women owned property, traded in their own names, and enjoyed civil-law protections from inheritance law. English coverture law ended these advantages since women lost their legal identity upon marriage. Nevertheless, by 1750, the colony's emphasis on commerce encouraged more attention to law and less importance to religion.[94]

After the Glorious Revolution in England (1688–1689), Parliament issued the Act of Toleration 1689,[95] which could apply in the colonies by charter or by act of a royal governor. The Act permitted freedom of worship for certain non-Anglican Trinitarian Protestants, such as Puritans and Baptists, who accepted an oath of loyalty to the British monarch, but excluded Catholics. It had a mixed and limited reception in the colonies. Massachusetts implemented it in 1692. In other colonies, such as New York and Pennsylvania, there was substantial de facto toleration of religious diversity.[96]

---

[91] McGarvie & Mensch, *supra* note 84, at 359–62; *see* GREGORY A. WOOD, THE FRENCH PRESENCE IN MARYLAND: 1525–1800, at 16–23, 26, 56–58 (1978). In 1750, 85 percent of the few Catholic churches in the 13 colonies were in Maryland or Pennsylvania. PURVIS, *supra* note 65, at 181. From 1680 to 1700, most Huguenots settled in South Carolina and New York. BUTLER, *supra* note 84, at 20–22.

[92] McGarvie & Mensch, *supra* note 84, at 343; *see* Simon Middleton, *Order and Authority in New Netherland: The 1653 Remonstrance and Early Settlement Politics*, 67 WM. & MARY Q. 31–68 (2010) (describing the social reality of that period and the 1653 protest by English and Dutch settlers filed against Stuyvesant's administration). *See also* Harrop A. Freeman, *A Remonstrance for Conscience*, 106 U. PA. L. REV. 806–30 (1958) (the 1657 Flushing Remonstrance).

[93] McGarvie & Mensch, *supra* note 84, at 344.

[94] *Id.* at 344–46.

[95] 1688, 1 W. & M., c. 18 (An Act for Exempting their Majestyes Protestant Subjects dissenting from the Church of England from the Penalties of certaine Lawes).

[96] McGarvie & Mensch, *supra* note 84, at 337, 343–45, 347, 349, 352, 360–61; Laura Zwicker, *The Politics of Toleration: The Establishment Clause and the Act of Toleration Examined*, 66 IND. L.J. 773, 777–84 (1991). *See generally* RICHARD S. KAY, THE GLORIOUS REVOLUTION AND THE CONTINUITY OF LAW (2014).

2. Regional and Intraregional Religious Differences

Beyond religious diversity within a single colony, Mark McGarvie and Elizabeth Mensch described major regional and intraregional variations. In New England, Puritan doctrine was a force that frequently subordinated civil government to religious orthodoxy, illustrated by the struggle against the amoral effects of commerce on many communities. Even here, however, disagreements led to new religions. The Puritan Roger Williams, for instance, after banishment from Massachusetts, founded the first Baptist congregation in Rhode Island. Church and state were to be separate, although by the eighteenth century, Baptists were using property and trust law to serve their aims. New England towns supported a common Reformation heritage, communitarian in nature, marked by Puritan (Pilgrim, Congregational) and Baptist churches, and a few Quaker meetinghouses. Puritans believed that God endowed humans with reason to comprehend the world and they wanted their civil government to serve scripture and the church. Up to the 1670s, clergymen resolved most disputes using religious norms to preserve the community's unity. Liberty was the freedom to conform to God's scripture. Until the 1740s, judges charged juries to use law to create a civil and Christian state. Religious establishment lasted longest in this region, for example in Massachusetts, which continued until 1833 the public support of churches.[97]

In the Middle Colonies, Pennsylvania's legal history, influenced by Quakers, was different from that in New York, where the Anglican establishment imposed in the eighteenth century ran up against Dutch resistance. Many of the immigrants to these two colonies, as well as New Jersey and Delaware, were German, Dutch, Scottish, and Irish.[98] Anglicans lived among Presbyterians, Baptists, Lutherans, Quakers, and Dutch and German Reformed parishioners. The resulting religious diversity, including the revivalists of the Great Awakening (1730s–1740s), together with the substantial economic activity in Philadelphia and New York, weakened the power of religion over law. These colonies disestablished their churches in the 1770s and removed core functions such as poor relief, education, and record keeping from religious authorities.[99]

---

[97] PURVIS, *supra* note 65, at 181–83, 186; McGarvie & Mensch, *supra* note 84, at 331–43.

[98] PURVIS, *supra* note 65, at 164, 181, 183–84, 186; McGarvie & Mensch, *supra* note 84, at 331–32, 344–53. The 1628 charter founding New Amsterdam established the Dutch Reformed Church as the sole official religion, which the West India Company was to staff under supervision from the Church's Classis in the Dutch Republic. The Company, eager for population growth and trade, liberalized the practice of religion by the mid-seventeenth century, which the English tolerated after their takeover in 1664. McGarvie & Mensch, *supra*, at 343–44; *see infra* text accompanying notes 135–36 (the Middle Colonies).

[99] PURVIS, *supra* note 65, at 179–82, 184–85; McGarvie & Mensch, *supra* note 84, at 329–30, 343–53; *see* BUTLER, *supra* note 84, at 185–86; *supra* text accompanying note 87 (greater importance of law).

In the Chesapeake area and in the South, Anglicans dominated and spiritualized the legal order, including slave laws, promoting a paternalistic and honor-based culture. In Virginia, the gentry refused to convert slaves to Christianity, despite the English clergy's pressure to do so, partly to justify slavery over heathens. Property ownership provided social rank with landed gentry acting like feudal manor lords. By 1700, economic matters, especially related to labor, prevailed over the founders' strict religious prescriptions. This permitted toleration of religious dissenters, who nevertheless had to contribute to the support of Anglican churches. In the eighteenth century, most growth in religious affiliation occurred among rural Baptists and Methodists. The diversity and economic interests in this region led the states to disestablish religion during the early republic.[100]

3. The Anglicization Thesis

Did the American colonies show the same degree of pluralism in law, legal control, lawmaking, and dispute resolution as they did in religion? Demographic data reveal that from 1700 to 1775, 84,500 Germans and 35,300 Scots immigrated to the American colonies compared to 73,100 English and Welsh and 108,600 Irish (some of whom were Catholic, while others had recently left Scotland and were thus Calvinists). By contrast, prior to 1700, most settlers were British, numbering 171,800, 89 percent of whom were from England with another 6 percent from Wales.[101] Should we expect eighteenth-century ethnic, religious, and cultural diversity substantially to have affected the reality of the various legal systems? Alternatively, did the earlier British settlers so firmly establish the governmental and legal structure during the seventeenth century that the newer immigrants had to accept and adapt to it or move to a new territory?

Craig Yirush has presented a promising view of American political thought in the late eighteenth century for comparative law. He argued that it was the result of a settler vision of the British Empire in the larger context of competing colonial empires in the Atlantic region. Immigrants lived in a world of jurisdictional plurality and contested sovereignty. "[T]he American colonies [are] now seen as

---

[100] PURVIS, *supra* note 65, at 181–82; McGarvie & Mensch, *supra* note 84, at 331–32, 353–57.
[101] PURVIS, *supra* note 65, at 164 (derived from Aaron Fogelman, *Migrations to the Thirteen British North American Colonies, 1770–1775*, 22 J. INTERDISC. HIST. 691, 698 (1992)); McGarvie & Mensch, *supra* note 84, at 329; *see* BUTLER, *supra* note 84, at 16–36. In addition, some Dutch and Germans had arrived in the seventeenth century and a group of Quakers and Mennonites established Germantown, Pennsylvania, in 1683. *See* WILLIAM I. HULL, WILLIAM PENN AND THE DUTCH QUAKER MIGRATION TO PENNSYLVANIA (1935, reprint 1970); *infra* text accompanying notes 111-112 (the Dutch and Germans). A.G. Roeber estimated the number of immigrants from the Holy Roman Empire between 1683 and 1783 at 120,000. A.G. ROEBER, PALATINES, LIBERTY, AND PROPERTY: GERMAN LUTHERANS IN COLONIAL BRITISH AMERICA ix (1993).

integral parts of a broader British world of commerce, religion, culture, law, and politics. This Atlantic turn in the study of early America is itself part of a broader trend toward transnational and comparative histories of the United States."[102] Yirush emphasized the revival of Roman law, natural law, and the law of nations by English jurists in the sixteenth and seventeenth centuries. This was part of a larger embrace of reason in transnational legal doctrines.[103]

Most legal historians recognize that there was diversity in American colonial law. The largely unexplored issue is whether the significant number of Germans and Scots affected the development of colonial law.[104] James Henretta posed the question as whether the "Anglicization thesis" of eighteenth-century British America withstands scrutiny.[105] He rejected the idea that imperial officials or sympathizers increasingly dominated the colonies. Rather, he saw Anglicization as limited to a few developments. First, the English legal regime of New York incorporated the pre-1664 Dutch law of New Netherland. Second, the German immigrant's inheritance customs were gradually adapted to fit within English legal categories. Third, the critical Puritan and Quaker attitude toward lawyers and colonial courts gave way to the emergence of a professional bar, especially in Boston and Philadelphia. Finally, the widespread formation of a new type of common law within the American legal system did provide a more pervasive Anglicization. That, however, did not mean royalization. Rather, Whig lawyers in the 1760s and 1770s used English common law against imperial officials and American jurors thwarted criminal and civil actions with their own customary norms.[106]

Nelson agreed with Henretta's conclusion that British colonial policy in America after the Glorious Revolution led to a reversal of Charles II's imperial initiatives. Nevertheless, Nelson emphasized other British developments that affected colonial law. Primary among them was support for non-Anglican Protestants, increased power for Parliament in governance, growth in the empire's commercial economy, and intermittent warfare to thwart French imperial pretensions. These developments, in turn, fostered the maturation of British nationalism. The peoples of the empire believed that they enjoyed a liberty and fortune unique among Europeans. Americans read the British literature expressing

---

[102] YIRUSH, *supra* note 40, at 5; *see id.* at 4–11, 19, 25–26; THOMAS BENDER, A NATION AMONG NATIONS: AMERICA'S PLACE IN WORLD HISTORY (2006).
[103] YIRUSH, *supra* note 40, at 12–15, 264–67.
[104] An exception is Alfred L. Brophy, *"Ingenium est Fateri per quos profeceris:" Francis Daniel Pastorius' Young Country Clerk's Collection and Anglo-American Legal Literature, 1682–1716*, 3 U. CHI. L. SCH. ROUNDTABLE 637 (1996); *see infra* notes 113–21 and accompanying text (Pastorius). Brophy found Pastorius's *Collection* to be the oldest law treatise written in British North America. *Id.* at 639, 642.
[105] Henretta, *supra* note 71, at 577–80. Between 1700 and 1775, there "was no anglicization of colonial *society* and *culture*, but rather just the reverse." *Id.* at 577 (italics in original).
[106] *Id.* at 580–82.

this British nationalist ideology of liberty, prosperity, and Protestantism. Unlike in Britain where national institution building succeeded, however, efforts in America to create colony-wide legal institutions largely failed. The eighteenth-century reality continued to be one of local law and government.[107]

G. Edward White viewed Anglicization of colonial legal culture and institutions as more thoroughly successful by 1750 due to the emergence of Britain as the dominant power in North America. By the end of the eighteenth century, the law and legal institutions of the 13 American states "much more closely resembled their counterparts in late eighteenth-century England than their seventeenth-century colonial predecessors. The Anglicization of the colonial American legal system had become pervasive."[108] White attributed this change to the development of learned groups of lawyers, illustrated by the early eighteenth-century formation of the New York City bar association.[109] However, the important role of colonial courts in the formation and ratification of local legal customs undermined Anglicization, driven by the divergence principle found in all colonial charters. This principle permitted local courts to accept legal norms that diverged from those in England as social conditions of colonial life varied. In opposition, the repugnancy principle, also present in the charters, prohibited colonial laws repugnant or incompatible with English law. During the eighteenth century, the former principle became more prominent than the latter principle. Land law and succession law were important examples.[110]

4. Eighteenth-Century Immigrants: The Germans and Scots

The issue of civil law influence remains. Germans, of course, emigrated from the German-speaking lands of Europe, all of which were civil law based in the seventeenth and eighteenth centuries. They constituted the largest group from continental Europe and were the most different from the English. The prejudice they experienced influenced the community and group identity they formed. Over two-thirds of the eighteenth-century German immigrants went to Pennsylvania.[111]

---

[107] NELSON, 3 THE COMMON LAW, *supra* note 71, at 1–10, 24–25, 86–88, 97. Nelson concluded, "The North American colonies had become common law, nonhierarchical Protestant societies that provided a bulwark ensuring that Roman Catholic monarchism championed by France and Spain could never dominate the continent's Atlantic coast." *Id.* at 10.

[108] G. EDWARD WHITE, LAW IN AMERICAN HISTORY, VOLUME 1: FROM THE COLONIAL YEARS THROUGH THE CIVIL WAR 42 (2012); *see id.* at 42–55, 489–90 n.45.

[109] *Id.* at 42, 46–48.

[110] *See id.* at 48–54, 487–88 n.24. "As it evolved, the common law of American courts would diverge significantly from that being handed down by their English counterparts." *Id.* at 49.

[111] BUTLER, *supra* note 84, at 29–32; JOHN HENRY MERRYMAN, DAVID S. CLARK & JOHN OWEN HALEY, COMPARATIVE LAW: HISTORICAL DEVELOPMENT OF THE CIVIL LAW TRADITION IN EUROPE, LATIN AMERICA, AND EAST ASIA 352–54, 509–29 (2010). *See generally* Oswald Seidensticker, *Die*

A notable example was Francis Pastorius (1651–c.1720), who founded the first permanent German settlement in the colonies at Germantown, Pennsylvania (now part of Philadelphia). He was a lawyer, trained at Altdorf, Jena, and other German universities, practicing law in Frankfurt-am-Main in 1683 when a group of Quakers, Mennonites, and Lutheran Pietists (Pastorius's religion) approached him about serving as their lawyer to purchase land in Pennsylvania. William Penn (1644–1718) and other Quakers had visited Frankfurt in 1671 and 1677. In 1681, when Charles II granted Penn land in America, Penn founded the colony *sylvania* (Latin for woods) and invited his Dutch and German friends. Pastorius desired a more spiritual life. In 1683, he undertook the ten-week voyage to America and met Penn, from whom he had purchased 23 square miles for the settlement. Pastorius negotiated the details, plotted the land, and remained there until his death.[112]

Pastorius served as the first manager of Germantown, to which Penn in London granted a charter in 1689. The charter, which the keeper of Pennsylvania's great seal recorded in 1691, created the General Court for "German Towne," whose chief officer was the bailiff (Pastorius). The Court could make "good and reasonable Laws . . . necessary and convenient for the Government" of the corporation and should meet every six weeks. Penn had also selected Pastorius as justice for the Philadelphia county court in 1686, which the governor reaffirmed in 1693. Electors sent Pastorius to the Pennsylvania Assembly in 1687.[113] Marion Learned, in her biography of Pastorius, called him a "lawgiver" and concluded that he and the other Germans brought with them their local customs.[114] "In reading the Laws or Ordinances of Germantown, one feels the traditions and atmosphere of a German town with its long experience in matters of town legislation, modified and adapted to the English forms of provincial government."[115]

erste deutsche Einwanderung in Amerika, und die Gründung von Germantown im Jahre 1683 (printed in Philadelphia, 1883).

[112] MARION DEXTER LEARNED, THE LIFE OF FRANCIS DANIEL PASTORIUS: THE FOUNDER OF GERMANTOWN 63–70, 74–79, 85–90, 102–10, 116–21, 126–29, 133–34, 218 (1908); Brophy, *supra* note 104, at 643–50; Marianne S. Wokeck, *Pastorius, Francis Daniel*, *in* 17 AMERICAN NATIONAL BIOGRAPHY, *supra* note 11, at 111–12. Altdorf (Nürnberg) was the first German university to have a chair in public law—*ius publicum*. LEARNED, *supra*, at 67, 82. Regarding Penn, who had lived in France and studied law in England, and his plan for the American colony, *see* McGarvie & Mensch, *supra* note 84, at 347–50.

[113] LEARNED, *supra* note 112, at v, 156, 159–63, 170, 219; Brophy, *supra* note 104, at 651. The Court's minutes between 1691 and 1707 were in German and Dutch. LEARNED, *supra* note 112, at 161. Pastorius served in various Germantown offices using his law training until at least 1707. *Id.* at 163–69. He also used his legal talents to benefit the province. *Id.* at 226. By joint action the governor, Assembly, and Provincial Council naturalized Pastorius and 150 other Germans as English subjects in 1706. *Id.* at 170–72.

[114] LEARNED, *supra* note 112, at 225.

[115] *Id.* Learned found many similarities between the sanitary regulations of Frankfurt and Germantown. *Id.* Pastorius, as Germantown scrivener, kept the *Grund- und Lager-Buch* of land records. *Id.* at 226, 265–67. He also prepared two manuscripts entitled (1) *Copia des Germantownischen*

One can also see some civil law influence in Pastorius's *Young Country Clerk's Collection*, especially for contract law and perhaps a preference for arbitration, but more of the volume was an attempt to mold English law to suit Pennsylvania realities.[116]

Pastorius affiliated spiritually with the Quakers, illustrated by his citations to the Bible when writing about judging, endorsement of natural law to order society, as well as when he and three others signed the first town-meeting objection against slavery in the British colonies in 1688. Pastorius wrote out the protest for the Society of Friends meeting in Germantown.[117] In the document,[118] the signatories presented their reasons against slavery. After referring to the golden rule,[119] they continued:

> Here is liberty of Conscience [which] is right and reasonable; here ought to be lickewise liberty of ye body.... This mackes an ill report in all those Countries of Europe, where they hear off, that ye Quackers doe here handel men licke they handel there ye Cattel. And for that reason some have no mind or inclination to come hither.

The authors concluded that Black slaves had a right to fight for their freedom.[120]

Extensive communication among German Americans began in 1738 when Christoph Sauer in Germantown began publishing in German an almanac (*Calender*) and one year later a newspaper.[121] Benjamin Franklin had published the first German language newspaper in 1732, the *Philadelphische Zeitung*, a biweekly that did not last the year although he later revived it.[122] Sauer's press

---

Charters and (2) *Gesetz, Ordnungen und Statuten der Gemieinden zu Germantown, in denen daselbstigen generalen Raths Versamblungen von Zeit zu Zeit gemacht und plublicirt*. *Id.* at 264. Pastorius wrote in Latin and English as well as German. *Id.* at 226–85.

[116] Brophy, *supra* note 104, at 672, 677–78, 682–86, 725, 727.

[117] LEARNED, *supra* note 112, at 223, 231, 266; Brophy, *supra* note 104, at 654–65.

[118] Pastorius et al., *Germantown Friends' Protest against Slavery, 1688*, *in* LEARNED, *supra* note 112, at 261–62. An original is PASTORIUS ET AL., QUAKER PROTEST AGAINST SLAVERY IN THE NEW WORLD, GERMANTOWN (PA.) 1–2 (1688), Triptych (tri-college digital library), http://triptych.brynmawr.edu (use advanced search).

[119] Pastorius et al., *supra* note 118, at 261. The rule is to treat all people as oneself, found in Leviticus 19:34, Matthew 7:12, and Luke 6:31; *see* Brophy, *supra* note 104, at 654, 659, 685.

[120] Pastorius et al., *supra* note 118, at 261–62. From the monthly Quaker meeting, the four signatories forwarded the document to the Germantown quarterly meeting and from there to the annual meeting in Philadelphia. *Id.* at 262. Later in life, Pastorius wrote the tract: *Good Counsel to Bad Lawyers and Attorneys* (1713). LEARNED, *supra* note 112, at 285.

[121] ROEBER, *supra* note 101, at 5–6, 175, 188–89. Sauer also spelled his name as Saur or Sower. The newspaper was the *Der Hoch-Deutsch Pennsylvanischer Geschichts-Schreiber*. *Id.* at 123. It was a quarterly until 1741, when it continued as a monthly until 1745. Albert Bernhardt Trust, *Christopher Saur*, *in* 18 THE CAMBRIDGE HISTORY OF ENGLISH AND AMERICAN LITERATURE ch. 31, § I.5 (W.P. Trent et al. eds., orig. 1921), online by Bartleby.com, https://www.bartleby.com/228/0805.html (2000).

[122] ROEBER, *supra* note 101, at 178–79; *The First German Newspaper in America*, N.Y. TIMES, 21 Oct. 1900, at 23; *see supra* note 40 (Franklin). Franklin published *Die Hoch Teutsch und Englische*

in the beginning relied on Franklin for its paper and there was some cooperation between the two, although Sauer's Quaker separatist politics conflicted with Franklin's secular progressive views. Sauer's son continued the paper's publication as a weekly until 1777.[123] By 1750, Quakers made up a quarter of Pennsylvania's population while German Lutherans represented about a half, which resulted in a mix of cultural influences. The dominant view of the legal concepts of both liberty and property, however, was that they were to protect the pious household from plunder, not to encourage public virtue. Liberty began as freedom of conscience. The German emphasis on property protection provided Pennsylvania with a more individualist orientation than the seventeenth century communitarianism prevailing elsewhere.[124]

Sauer's newspaper contained advice for German readers about natural law, how to avoid English intestate law, which disfavored widows compared to German law, and how to use English law to avoid escheat and otherwise to protect property.[125] In 1762, Henrich Miller established another German printing office in Philadelphia. He had worked for Franklin in the 1740s and 1750s as a printer and now published *Der Wöchentliche Philadelphische Staatsbote*, which continued as a weekly newspaper until 1767, when it changed name to *Der Wöchentliche Pennsylvanische Staatsbote* (until 1779).[126] The paper published speeches and accounts of political events that connected Christian virtue with a secularized republican society. Both Miller's and Sauer's papers opposed the Stamp Act, but as conditions with Great Britain deteriorated, Sauer took the pacifist Quaker position while Miller supported Franklin and the Revolution. Miller served as the unofficial German language publisher for the First Continental Congress (1774) by printing its minutes and votes. He also printed the pro-Whig pamphlet *Der Alarm* (1776) and the first newspaper

---

Zeitung from 1751–1752 and revived the *Philadelphische Zeitung* from 1755 to 1757, while also backing other German publications. Reimer Eck, *German Language Printing in the American Colonies up to the Declaration of Independence*, http://www.dhm.de/archiv/magazine/unabhaengig/eck_2e.htm (also *id.* at eck_3e.htm).

[123] ROEBER, *supra* note 101, at 177, 197; Eck, *supra* note 122. In 1746, Sauer's paper changed names to *Pensylvanischer Berichte*, with the subtitle *Sammlung wichtiger Nachrichten, aus dem Natur- und Kirchen-Reich*. It became a biweekly in 1748 and the print run was 4,000 (in 1753), distributed in German settlements from Pennsylvania to Georgia. In 1762, it took the name *Germantowner Zeitung*. Trust, *supra* note 121; see HEATHER A. HAVEMAN, MAGAZINES AND THE MAKING OF AMERICA: MODERNIZATION, COMMUNITY, AND PRINT CULTURE, 1741–1860, at 23–54 (2015).

[124] ROEBER, *supra* note 101, at 175–78, 180–82, 310; McGarvie & Mensch, *supra* note 84, at 350–51.

[125] ROEBER, *supra* note 101, at 175–76, 187; McGarvie & Mensch, *supra* note 83, at 351, 353. Sauer in 1743 started to add some of this advice in his annual *Calender*, often in the form of dialectical *Gespräche*. ROEBER, *supra*, at 190–96.

[126] ROEBER, *supra* note 101, at 199, 202–05; Eck, *supra* note 122; McGarvie & Mensch, *supra* note 84, at 351. The newspaper suspended publication for a year beginning in September 1777. In 1763, Miller began publishing his own annual *Calender* to compete with that of Sauer. ROEBER, *supra*, at 203.

announcement of the Declaration of Independence's adoption (in German in the July 5, 1776, issue of the *Staatsbote*).[127] By this time, Pennsylvanians engaged in substantial nonsectarian, voluntary civic cooperation with an ideal of liberty as obligation. Franklin built upon this ideal through interdenominational entities like the Philosophical Society and Library Company to promote progress with reason and science.[128]

Scottish settlers from 1700 to 1775 also came from a largely civil law legal system.[129] Prior to the Treaty of Union (1707), Scotland and England had been independent kingdoms. Hostile English acts at the end of the thirteenth century convinced the Scots that they needed a powerful friend in Europe, which under the Auld Alliance was primarily France until 1560. Scottish law then developed along civil law lines with Scottish law students attending universities in Avignon, Louvain, and Orleans. In the sixteenth century, after Scotland embraced Calvinism in its Reformation, law students studied at the Dutch universities in Groningen, Leiden, and Utrecht. Consequently, by the eighteenth century, Scottish law was a mixture of customary feudal land law, Roman law, statutes from its parliament, and natural law. Lord Stair's *Institutions* (1681) amply demonstrated the Roman, canon, and civil law influence.[130] Even with union, that is, as part of the United Kingdom of Great Britain, Scotland retained its traditional court system and private law through the eighteenth century, after which it lost most of its connection with continental European legal developments.[131]

---

[127] ROEBER, *supra* note 101, at 283–90; Eck, *supra* note 122; McGarvie & Mensch, *supra* note 84, at 351–52. In addition, Miller printed in German the Minutes of the Pennsylvania Constitutional Convention (1776). Eck, *supra*. A new German-language print business in Philadelphia, Steinen & Cist, printed the Declaration in German on July 6. Miller followed with his German version on July 9 in the *Staatsbote*. ROEBER, *supra*, at 283; Deutsches Historisches Museum, *Der deutschsprachige Erstdruck der Unabhängigkeitserklärung der Vereinigten Staaten von Amerika*, https://www.dhm.de/archiv/magazine/unabhaengig/index.html. Melchior Steiner and Carl Cist also published a German translation of Thomas Paine's *Common Sense* in 1776, *Gesunde Vernunft*. ROEBER, *supra*, at 309–10; Eck, *supra*.

[128] ROEBER, *supra* note 101, at 288, 325–31; McGarvie & Mensch, *supra* note 84, at 352–53; see "AT THE INSTANCE OF BENJAMIN FRANKLIN": A BRIEF HISTORY OF THE LIBRARY COMPANY OF PHILADELPHIA (rev. ed. 1995); American Philosophical Society, *About the APS*, https://www.amphilsoc.org/about; *supra* note 11 (The Library Company).

[129] Scots shaped a distinctive ethnic, cultural, and religious identity in America. BUTLER, *supra* note 84, at 24–26; *see* DEVINE, *supra* note 39, at 125–48, 274–77.

[130] KONRAD ZWEIGERT & HEIN KÖTZ, INTRODUCTION TO COMPARATIVE LAW 202 (Tony Weir trans., 3d ed. 1998). *See* SIR JAMES DALRYMPLE OF STAIR, THE INSTITUTIONS OF THE LAW OF SCOTLAND: DEDUCED FROM ITS ORIGINALS, AND COLLATED WITH THE CIVIL, CANON AND FEUDAL LAWS; AND WITH THE CUSTOMS OF NEIGHBOURING NATIONS (1681). Stair revised and edited a second edition in 1693 (reprint 1981, David M. Walker ed., with explanatory material). John Gordon and William Johnstone edited a third edition in 1759.

[131] ZWEIGERT & KÖTZ, *supra* note 130, at 202–04; *see* THE CIVILIAN TRADITION AND SCOTS LAW (David L. Carey Miller & Reinhard Zimmermann eds., 1997); WILLIAM M. GORDON, ROMAN LAW, SCOTS LAW AND LEGAL HISTORY (2007).

5. Regionalism and Legal Diversity

Friedman explained the legal diversity in the British colonies with several factors.[132] First, English law was complex and difficult to ascertain. Authorities did not know which statutes or court cases to apply to their situation. Second, joint stock companies and royal proprietary charters founded or confirmed colonies at different times, with distinct legal forms, reflecting varying English legal regimes.[133] Third, the ocean separating the colonies from England impeded administration from the center to the periphery as well as communication between them. Fourth, the colonial relationship was often not harmonious and colonists quarreled over politics, law, and especially taxation. Fifth, the New England legal cultures differed significantly from those of the southern colonies. Friedman concluded: "The colonies borrowed as much English law as they wanted to take or were forced to take."[134]

As a social historian, Friedman made another important observation. English common law was primarily concerned with two matters: land law and the technical process of the royal central courts in London. From Sir Edward Coke to Sir William Blackstone, the main emphasis was on the law for the nobility and gentry. Except for the harsh criminal justice system, most people were only indirectly under the rule of the common law. When these people settled in America, they brought their local law and customs with them. In addition, seventeenth- and eighteenth-century common law had absorbed many Roman and canon law ideas in equity, admiralty, and commercial law.[135]

David Konig similarly concluded that American regionalism—social, cultural, and legal, reflecting varying influence from England—had its roots in the colonial era. He identified three distinct regions: New England, the Middle Colonies, and the Chesapeake and South.[136] New England, centered in Massachusetts, developed communal ideals stemming from the religious force of Puritanism. Virginia, the dominant culture in the South, supported acquisitive individualism with a repressive authority to control labor, deviating from the common law to establish slavery. The most distinctive variation, however, was in the mid-Atlantic area of New York, New Jersey, Pennsylvania, and Delaware, where the

---

[132] FRIEDMAN, *supra* note 42, at xiii–xiv; *see* UROFSKY & FINKELMAN, *supra* note 49, at 7–12.
[133] Bilder, *Local Governance*, *supra* note 69, at 67–88.
[134] FRIEDMAN, *supra* note 42, at xiii. Blackstone had not completed his *Commentaries* until 1769. SIR WILLIAM BLACKSTONE, 1–4 COMMENTARIES ON THE LAWS OF ENGLAND (1765–1769). Robert Bell printed the first American edition in Philadelphia in 1771 and 1772 and sold 1,557 sets. For the first time in America, a standard version of English law was available and widely disseminated. FRIEDMAN, *supra*, at 59–60. The University of Chicago Press printed a facsimile of Blackstone's first edition in 2002.
[135] FRIEDMAN, *supra* note 42, at xvii–xx; *see* BAKER, *supra* note 2, at 97–134, 169–74.
[136] David Thomas Konig, *Regionalism in Early American Law*, *in* CAMBRIDGE HISTORY, *supra* note 69, at 144–46, 149–56, 177.

former Dutch and Swedish settlements mixed with the eighteenth-century influx of other non-English immigrants. Although English officials succeeded in establishing formal common law institutions, they could not eliminate a cultural legacy of defiance toward authority.[137]

The tolerant policies of the Dutch had encouraged independent local settlements of Scandinavians, Jews, and Muslims that the English had a difficult time controlling. The Dutch also preferred policies that stimulated trade over those that maintained religious conformity. They raised the traditional interest percentage on usury, permitted full rights to assign debt, and favored the Roman law right for women to trade without their husband's approval or to enter into partnership with their husbands to share profit and risk in a family business. German immigrants preferred the mid-Atlantic area because of this freedom and religious tolerance. The Quaker William Penn encouraged ethnic diversity in immigration to Pennsylvania, but his ideal of political harmony did not prevail. Dutch, French, and Scottish settlers along the lower Delaware River and Delaware Bay decided not to merge their counties with Pennsylvania and maintained a separate assembly that served as the basis for a colony.[138]

F. John Adams: An American Comparatist

1. Study of the Civil Law

Legal comparatists sometimes divide their discipline's objectives into three categories: practical or professional, scientific, and cultural.[139] Of these three objectives, the easiest to document before the twentieth century is the professional use of Roman, civil, and natural law materials. Comparatists have not looked, however, for such use prior to the American Revolution with the admirable exception of Daniel Coquillette's research on John Adams.[140]

---

[137] *Id.* at 161–62. Konig summarized St. George Tucker's (1752–1827) 1803 argument against complete colonial acceptance of English law in the context of the great diversity existing among the American colonies, especially between Virginia and Massachusetts. *Id.* at 161–62, 166–69; *see* St. George Tucker, *Of the Unwritten, or Common Law of England: And Its Introduction into, and Authority within the United States*, *in id.*, VIEW OF THE CONSTITUTION OF THE UNITED STATES: WITH SELECTED WRITINGS 313–70 (1999). Tucker was a law professor at the College of William and Mary (1800–1804). Federal Judicial Center, *Tucker, St. George*, https://www.fjc.gov/history/judges/tucker-st-george. For an imaginative social history of colonial New York, finding the roots of numerous legal institutions among the Puritans of Holland, and before them the Romans and Germans, *see* DOUGLAS CAMPBELL, 1–2 THE PURITAN IN HOLLAND, ENGLAND, AND AMERICA: AN INTRODUCTION TO AMERICAN HISTORY (1892).

[138] Konig, *supra* note 136, at 162–64, 176; McGarvie & Mensch, *supra* note 84, at 344; *see supra* text accompanying notes 52–56 (Dutch courts). There were only about 250 Jewish families in the colonies by 1770. BUTLER, *supra* note 84, at 26–28.

[139] MERRYMAN ET AL., *supra* note 111, at 52–53.

[140] Coquillette, *John Adams*, *supra* note 25. Another exception was JOHNSON, *supra* note 52.

After Adams attended Harvard College,[141] he decided to pursue a legal career and wrote in his diary that he believed that a thorough study of the "Civil Law, in its native languages,"[142] would distinguish him in that effort. During his apprenticeship between 1756 and 1758, besides books on English law, he read Wood's *A New Institute* about the civil law.[143] When Adams wanted to join the Suffolk County Bar, he met with one of its leading lawyers, Jeremiah Gridley, who agreed to sponsor his membership and stressed the importance of learning "civil Law, and natural Law, and Admiralty Law."[144] Gridley introduced Adams to his extensive library of Roman, civil, and natural law books and loaned him an abridgement of Justinian's *Institutes*.[145]

Adams continued to educate himself in the civil law during the early years of his law practice. In addition to the works of Justinian and Wood, Adams also read John Cowell's *Institutiones iuris Anglicani* (1605), apparently in the original Latin.[146] Cowell, civil law master at Trinity Hall (Cambridge), presented the English common law within the conceptual framework of Justinian's *Institutes*, maintaining a tradition Bracton had started in the thirteenth century.[147] Adams also read St. German's *Dialogus*[148] and Charles Molloy's *De jure maritimo et navali* (1676),[149] both of which had many references to Roman, canon, and natural

---

[141] Harvard College had a faculty of seven. In Adams's class of 1755, there were 27 students. Adams graduated third in his class academically, but was 14th on the commencement list due to "dignity of family." DAVID MCCULLOUGH, JOHN ADAMS 35, 37 (2001).

[142] 1 DIARY AND AUTOBIOGRAPHY OF JOHN ADAMS 45 (L.H. Butterfield ed., 4 vols. 1961) [hereinafter DIARY], quoted in Coquillette, *John Adams*, supra note 25, at 360.

[143] Coquillette, *John Adams*, supra note 25, at 360, 372-73; *see supra* notes 9-13 and accompanying text (Wood's *A New Institute*). For a similar education including Roman and natural law, *see* Daniel R. Coquillette, *The Legal Education of a Patriot: Josiah Quincy Jr.'s Law Commonplace* (1763), 39 ARIZ. ST. L.J. 317, 322, 326-27, 363-67 (2007).

[144] 1 DIARY 55, *supra* note 142, quoted in Coquillette, *John Adams*, supra note 25, at 363; *see id.* at 366. Gridley recommended that Adams read Grotius and Pufendorf. Coquillette, *supra*, at 363; *see supra* note 43 and accompanying text (Gridley). The court of common pleas admitted Adams to practice in 1758. Coquillette, *supra*, at 366.

[145] Coquillette, *John Adams*, supra note 25, at 363, 372-73. The book was JOHANNES VAN MUYDEN, COMPENDIOSA INSTITUTIONUM JUSTINIANI TRACTATIO: IN USUM COLLEGIORUM (1707), which Adams purchased from Gridley's estate after he died in 1767. Coquillette, *supra*, at 365 n.30; *see* Boston Public Library, *Home*, https://www.bpl.org (search website for John Adams Library) (the Adams Library home page provides tools to browse the collection or search for a book) [hereinafter John Adams Library]. Gridley's library had almost 500 law books plus dictionaries and grammar books for Dutch, French, Greek, Italian, and Latin. Robert St. George, *Gridley, Jeremiah*, in THE YALE BIOGRAPHICAL DICTIONARY OF AMERICAN LAW, *supra* note 48, at 237-38.

[146] Cowell wrote under his Latin name, Iohanne Cowello. There were later Latin editions (1664 and 1676) after Cowell's death in 1611. Adams had the 1676 printing in his library. John Adams Library, supra note 145 (catalog search for Cowell). By an act of Parliament, W.G. translated the book into English as THE INSTITUTES OF THE LAWES OF ENGLAND: DIGESTED INTO THE METHOD OF THE CIVILL OR IMPERIALL INSTITUTIONS (1651).

[147] Coquillette, *John Adams*, supra note 25, at 369-70; *see supra* text accompanying note 4 (Bracton and Blackstone).

[148] *See supra* note 5 and accompanying text (St. German).

[149] CHARLES MOLLOY, DE JURE MARITIMO ET NAVALI: OR, A TREATISE OF AFFAIRES MARITIME AND OF COMMERCE (1676, reprint 2009). There were several editions through the eighteenth century;

law.[150] Adams's diary suggests, in addition, that he read Enlightenment political philosophy, including that of Charles-Louis de Montesquieu.[151] Montesquieu's influence appears in this diary entry:

> The Laws of Britain, should be adapted to the Principle of the british Government, to the Climate of Britain, to the Soil, to its situation, as an Island, and Its Extent, to the manner of living of the Natives as Merchants, Manufacturers and Husbandmen, to the Religion of the Inhabitants.[152]

In 1761, the Boston Superior Court of Judicature admitted Adams to practice before it, which continued his progress at the bar. In 1765, his mentor, Gridley, invited Adams and Samuel Fitch (a future loyalist) to join a law club, called Sodalitas, for the study of law and oratory.[153] The periodic evening meetings ranged widely from the study of Denis Godefroy's annotation on Roman law, Cicero, Blackstone, Coke, feudal law, canon law, and European political philosophy.[154]

2. Law and Politics in Writing and Practice

Adams's first major foray into writing about law and politics resulted from the Sodalitas meetings. He intended to present *A Dissertation on the Canon and Feudal Law* to the club, but the British Parliament's approval of the Stamp Act (1765), which he saw as an "enormous Engine . . . for battering down all the Rights and Liberties of America," motivated him to publish *Dissertation* in the *Boston Gazette*.[155] The newspaper published it without title or attribution in four

---

the one in Adams's library was the eighth edition from 1744, which Adams apparently purchased from Gridley's estate. John Adams Library, *supra* note 145.

[150] Coquillette, *John Adams*, *supra* note 25, at 370, 373. Molloy had a detailed index that would make it very useful to a lawyer practicing in admiralty, commercial, or international law.
[151] *Id.* at 371.
[152] 1 DIARY 117, *supra* note 142, quoted in Coquillette, *John Adams*, *supra* note 25, at 374 n.8.
[153] Coquillette, *John Adams*, *supra* note 25, at 376–77.
[154] *Id.* at 379–82; *see supra* note 134 (Blackstone). The Godefroy volumes could have been the 1756 edition, 1–2 *Corpus juris civilis romani: Cum notis integris Dionysii Gothofredi*. Adams's library had three of Cicero's books, from 1661 in Latin, 1670 in French, and 1702 in English. Its pre-*Commentaries* Blackstone was 1–2 LAW TRACTS (1762). It had all four parts of Coke's *Institutes of the Laws of England*, published in seventeenth-century editions. John Adams Library, *supra* note 145.
[155] Coquillette, *John Adams*, *supra* note 25, at 380–81, 401–04, quoted from 1 PAPERS OF JOHN ADAMS 104 (Robert J. Taylor et al. eds., 1977). Regarding the Stamp Act, *see* Claire Priest, *Law and Commerce, 1580–1815*, *in* CAMBRIDGE HISTORY, *supra* note 69, at 400, 427–28.

parts during 1765 and Thomas Hollis, a wealthy English dissenter who supported republican causes, reprinted it in the *London Chronicle* that same year.[156]

In *Dissertation*, Adams contrasted the corrupt customary laws of Europe with the universal natural law and reason that scholars had built from the classical civilizations illustrated by the Roman *ius gentium*. The feudal system was inconsistent with liberty, the rights of man, and the ideals of righteous American settlers (that is, Puritans). European medieval oppression stemmed equally from feudal regimes and the Roman Church. In Adams's view, the proper relationship of the colonists with the British Crown was direct, with no subordinate agencies. Loyalty to the king did not require acquiescence to Parliament's taxation. Furthermore, a ruler is no more than the people's agent; if an agent betrays the people's trust, they have a right to revoke his authority and to transfer it to abler agents. British liberties are not grants from monarchs or Parliament, but original rights and conditions of an original contract. One finds the foundation of British laws and government in human nature.[157]

During the ten years following the initial publication of *Dissertation*, Adams had many opportunities to put his civil law learning to use in his law practice. Adams knew from his reading of *Coke upon Littleton*[158] and other sources about the continued role for civil and canon law in England in admiralty and ecclesiastical courts.[159] In 1763, America had nine vice-admiralty courts but no ecclesiastical courts or Exchequer (to hear revenue matters). The results of the Seven Years War (French and Indian War) marked a crucial shift in British colonial relations. The Treaty of Paris (1763) recognized Britain's dominance in shipping on the Atlantic as well as sovereignty over more of North America east of the Mississippi River including Florida. British debt, however, was huge and the Crown wanted the colonies to increase their financial contribution to maintain

---

[156] Coquillette, *John Adams, supra* note 25, at 404–07; CHARLES FRANCIS ADAMS, 3 THE WORKS OF JOHN ADAMS 447 (1865, orig. 1851) [hereinafter CHARLES ADAMS]. Hollis reprinted it again in *The True Sentiments of America* (1768) as a chapter, attributing it to Jeremiah Gridley and providing it the title describing its subject. Coquillette, *supra*, at 406–07. *Dissertation* is available online: ADAMS, REVOLUTIONARY WRITINGS, *supra* note 1, at ch. 2 (extracted from volumes 3 and 4 of CHARLES ADAMS, *supra*).

[157] Coquillette, *John Adams, supra* note 25, at 403–06; CHARLES ADAMS, *supra* note 156, at 449–52, 454–57, 460, 462–64. Adams's uneven grasp of history and feudal theory did not dampen his polemic style. Coquillette, *supra*, at 403–04. His fondness for liberty was rooted in the Roman Republic and certainly not in its Empire or in the "papal usurpations" of the Catholic Church. *See* CHARLES ADAMS, *supra*, at 449–51, 453–54; Coquillette, *supra*, at 371–72. Adams's belief in the settlers' righteousness illustrated the periodic assertion of an American exceptionalism as moral superiority. This attitude would support the notion of indigenous laws and legal institutions rather than significant legal transplantation.

[158] EDW. COKE, THE FIRST PART OF THE INSTITUTES OF THE LAWES OF ENGLAND: OR, COMMENTARIE UPON LITTLETON (1628); John Adams Library, *supra* note 145.

[159] Coquillette, *John Adams, supra* note 25, at 383, 387 n.5, 391. For the main elements of Roman-canonic procedure, *see* R.C. VAN CAENEGEM, HISTORY OF EUROPEAN CIVIL PROCEDURE, 16 INTERNATIONAL ENCYCLOPEDIA OF COMPARATIVE LAW 16–23 (ch. 2, 1973).

the empire. The lack of an American exchequer court (with juries) meant that the resolution of tax and customs cases would occur in admiralty courts (without juries).[160]

Coquillette reviewed several cases in which Adams made specific references to civilian legal sources. In *Doane v. Gage* (1766–1769), a vice-admiralty court case (using the Roman-canonic written procedure with positions, objections, witness interrogatories, and judicial examination of English admiralty), Adams represented Captain Doane, whose whaling boat had first harpooned a whale, against the second person to have harpooned the same whale. Adams prepared "notes of authorities" with quotations from Grotius's *De iure belli* and Justinian's *Institutes*, comparing the later to passages from the *Digest*, regarding the ownership of wild animals.[161]

In 1768, Adams had the opportunity to litigate a customs case in admiralty with his representation of John Hancock (1737–1793), a wealthy Boston merchant, the first signer of the Declaration of Independence, and a notorious smuggler. The central factual issue was whether Hancock had smuggled Madeira wine off his boat, *Liberty*, at night to avoid duties, but local observers described various British indignities and Adams argued about the injustice of the vice-admiralty court since it deprived Hancock of his English right of trial by jury.[162]

Adams used his knowledge of the civil law to defend his client. Since the court used Roman-canonic procedure, Adams argued it should also honor the two-witness rule for full proof. Because the Crown presented only a single witness against Hancock, its proof failed. For authority, he quoted from Thomas Wood's *A New Institute*, Justinian's *Code* and *Digest*, and Johannes Calvinus's *Lexicon*. Adams was not beyond omitting certain aspects of his cited sources that were

---

[160] FRIEDMAN, *supra* note 42, at 19–21; Priest, *supra* note 155, at 426. The English Navigation Act of 1696 had established the vice-admiralty courts to enforce the navigation acts in America. In England, these cases would go to Exchequer of Pleas, which provided a jury trial for many of the penal matters that in America had the non-jury admiralty procedure. Until the 1760s, American merchants had reached a workable balance between their interests and the enforcement of customs duties that the British revenue acts of 1763 and 1764 upset. Priest, *supra*, at 414–15. The 1765 Stamp Act drew Adams directly into the fray with the publication of *Dissertation*; *see supra* notes 155–57 and accompanying text (*Dissertation*).

[161] Coquillette, *John Adams*, *supra* note 25, at 383–87; *see* Andrew Lewis, *John Adams and the Whale*, in CRITICAL STUDIES IN ANCIENT LAW, COMPARATIVE LAW AND LEGAL HISTORY 261–65 (John W. Cairns & Olivia F. Robinson eds., 2001).

[162] Coquillette, *John Adams*, *supra* note 25, at 386–87; Priest, *supra* note 155, at 429, quoting 2 LEGAL PAPERS OF JOHN ADAMS 173, 194, 202 (L. Kinvin Wroth & Hiller B. Zobel eds., 1965) [hereinafter ADAMS LEGAL PAPERS] (Adams's draft argument and copy of the information). Adams cited Magna Carta in support of the jury trial right as a bulwark of liberty. Henretta, *supra* note 71, at 581. Hancock graduated from Harvard College in 1754 and served from 1766 to 1774 on the Massachusetts General Court, when it defied the governor by reconstituting as a provincial congress with Hancock as president. The congress selected Hancock a delegate to the Continental Congress, which in 1775 elected him its president. In 1780, Massachusetts voters elected Hancock the first governor of the commonwealth and in 1789, as president of the proposed U.S. Constitution's Massachusetts ratifying convention, he provided the crucial support for its adoption. William M. Fowler Jr., *Hancock, John*, in 9 AMERICAN NATIONAL BIOGRAPHY, *supra* note 11, at 968–70.

inconsistent or disfavored his client.[163] In a second point, Adams contended that in cases in which the penalty is severe, the court should strictly construe the law. For this proposition, he quoted from Jean Domat's *The Civil Law* in its English translation (referring to Justinian's *Digest*) and cited Wood. Although the judge rejected Adams's arguments in an interlocutory decree, the court dropped the case against Hancock in 1769.[164]

Adams could also use his civilian knowledge to represent clients in probate proceedings, which in England ecclesiastical courts would process. In 1767 and 1768, he defended the testament of Samuel Clap against his disinherited eldest son, William. The Supreme Court of Probate in Massachusetts consisted of the governor and his council, where William attacked the will claiming his father was insane when he executed the document. Adams's notes in this case referred to basic civil law books used in Doctors' Commons in London.[165] They supported the presumption of sanity where the court finds that either the testator had periods of lucidity or the will appears coherent.[166]

After Adams wrote *Dissertation* in 1765, he continued his opposition to the Stamp Act by drafting that same year the Braintree Town Instructions to its representative in the Massachusetts colony's legislature, the General Court. The *Boston Gazette* published the document as did other papers and soon 40 towns had adopted the Instructions.[167] Based on the British constitution and the spirit of the common law, the Instructions declared that Parliament had no authority to tax colonists since the colonists had no representation in that body and there should be no taxation without direct or represented consent. In addition, the vice-admiralty court (assessing the tax), Adams argued, was improper. The judge profited from a condemnation and the court lacked a jury procedure. Finally, relying on Magna Carta, the Instructions argued that there should be no fine, forfeiture, imprisonment, or restriction on liberty without a trial of one's peers.[168] Parliament repealed the Stamp Act in 1766.[169]

---

[163] Coquillette, *John Adams, supra* note 25, at 387-88; *see* VAN CAENEGEM, *supra* note 159, at 19-20; JOHANNES CALVINUS, LEXICON JURIDICUM JURIS CAESAREI SIMUL ET CANONICI: FEUDALIS ITEM, CIVILIS, CRIMINALIS, THEORETICI AC PRACTICI (Cologne ed. 1622); John Adams Library, *supra* note 145.

[164] Coquillette, *John Adams, supra* note 25, at 388-90; 2 ADAMS LEGAL PAPERS, *supra* note 162, at 183; *see supra* notes 13-14 and accompanying text (Domat).

[165] Coquillette, *John Adams, supra* note 25, at 391-92; *see* JOHN GODOLPHIN, THE ORPHAN'S LEGACY: OR, A TESTAMENTARY ABRIDGMENT (4th ed. 1701); WILLIAM NELSON, LEX TESTAMENTARIA (2d ed. 1724); HENRY SWINBURNE, HENRY, A TREATISE OF TESTAMENTS AND LAST WILLS: COMPILED OUT OF THE LAWS ECCLESIASTICAL, CIVIL, AND CANON (5th ed. 1728); John Adams Library, *supra* note 145 (Godolphin and Swinburne volumes).

[166] Coquillette, *John Adams*, supra note 25, at 391.

[167] McCULLOUGH, *supra* note 141, at 61.

[168] *Instructions of the Town of Braintree to Their Representative, 1765*, *in* ADAMS, REVOLUTIONARY WRITINGS, *supra* note 1, at ch. 3. A slightly different version of Instructions is in RECORDS OF THE TOWN OF BRAINTREE: 1640 TO 1793, at 404-06 (Samuel A. Bates ed., 1886).

[169] McCULLOUGH, *supra* note 141, at 62.

3. The Boston Declaration of 1772

In the early 1770s, John Adams continued his involvement in defending colonial political and economic interests. His cousin, Samuel Adams (1722–1803), an influential Massachusetts Whig politician, petitioned for a Boston town meeting in 1772, which appointed a committee of correspondence to declare "the Rights of the Colonists, and of this Province."[170] The town meeting approved the committee's report, the Boston Declaration, which it sent to every town in Massachusetts and which suggested they maintain communication of their views and sentiments. After 80 towns had voted resolutions in support of the Boston Declaration, the Massachusetts governor, Thomas Hutchinson, believed that this wide dissemination of seditious ideas required rebuttal at a joint session of the General Court. John Reid characterized the Boston Declaration, along with the Declaration of Independence, as the two most important documents relying on natural rights authority that the colonial Whigs issued.[171]

In Hutchinson's address to the General Court in 1773, his central premise was that the English constitution supported the sovereign supremacy of Parliament over the colonies. Both legislature chambers of Massachusetts—the Council and the House of Representatives—individually responded with an answer to the governor, and then upon his replication, each provided a rejoinder. Along with the governor's final surrejoinder, Reid called these documents—which the *Boston Gazette* printed as a pamphlet—"the briefs of the American Revolution."[172]

John Adams was the primary author of the House's answer and rejoinder. Adams wrote them like judicial briefs, but perhaps due to the short period available to prepare them, provided fewer citations of authority in the answer than in the rejoinder.[173] In essence, the answer adopted a position similar to that Adams would argue two years later in a series of letters with many references to English and civil law authority, while the rejoinder made some use of his *Dissertation*.[174] The answer recognized the God-granted natural rights over property of the heathen American indigenous people at the time of early English settlement. Any transfer of title from these non-Christian people went to the English Crown and not to the "Realm of England," as reflected in various colonial charters. These

---

[170] Boston Declaration iii (1772), quoted in THE BRIEFS OF THE AMERICAN REVOLUTION: CONSTITUTIONAL ARGUMENTS BETWEEN THOMAS HUTCHINSON, GOVERNOR OF MASSACHUSETTS BAY, AND JAMES BOWDOIN FOR THE COUNCIL AND JOHN ADAMS FOR THE HOUSE OF REPRESENTATIVE 1 (John Phillip Reid ed., 1981) [hereinafter BRIEFS]; *see* BRIEFS, *supra*, at 1–2.

[171] BRIEFS, *supra* note 170, at 2–4; *see* RICHARD D. BROWN, REVOLUTIONARY POLITICS IN MASSACHUSETTS: THE BOSTON COMMITTEE OF CORRESPONDENCE AND THE TOWNS, 1772–1774 (1970); WILLIAM V. WELLS, 2 THE LIFE AND PUBLIC SERVICES OF SAMUEL ADAMS 91–99 (1865).

[172] BRIEFS, *supra* note 170, at ix, 4–5 (quotation at 5); *see id.* at 7–14, 160–62.

[173] *Id.* at 46–49, 78, 119–20, 123.

[174] *Id.* at 78–79, 119–21, 126–34; *see infra* pt. F.4 (*Novanglus*).

charters also recognized the Crown's, but not Parliament's, authority to assess colonial legislation as "consonant to Reason" or "not repugnant to the Laws of England." Since the Crown had not annexed America to the English realm, Parliament should not make laws affecting the colonies without their consent.[175] In the rejoinder, Adams amplified on the issue of lack of colonial consent as a basis for resisting intrusive parliamentary legislation.[176]

4. The *Novanglus* Letters of 1775

During the first four months of 1775, Adams wrote a series of 12 anonymous letters that the *Boston Gazette* published, which illustrated his revolutionary thought and reference to natural and civil law authority. These *Novanglus* letters were Adams's response to a series of letters that another lawyer, Daniel Leonard (under the name Massachusettensis), published elsewhere. In these letters, Leonard argued the practical benefits of colonial subordination to the Parliament of Great Britain.[177]

Adams's primary purpose was to justify legally a commonwealth status for American colonies under a constitutional monarch.[178] To that end, he admitted the Crown's theoretical dominion in the colonies, but denied that this dominion brought with it the unbridled power of Parliament. Coquillette found that in *Novanglus*, Adams relied upon three legal principles from the *ius gentium*.[179]

---

[175] BRIEFS, *supra* note 170, at 55–73. The answer concluded: We recognize the "Sense of Allegiance which we owe to the King of Great-Britain, our rightful Sovereign: And should the People of this Province be left to the free and full Exercise of all the Liberties and Immunities granted to them by Charter, there would be no Danger of an Independance [sic] on the Crown. Our Charters reserve great Power to the Crown in its Representative, fully sufficient to balance, analagous [sic] to the English Constitution, all the Liberties and Privileges granted to the People." *Id.* at 73.

[176] *Id.* at 136–43. Adams referred to Grotius, Locke, and Pufendorf, and to the writing of Rousseau and Vattel without name. *Id.* at 127 n.4, 141 n.38. His reference to Locke was to quote a passage from RICHARD HOOKER, OF THE LAWES OF ECCLESIASTICAL POLITIE (1666 ed., orig. eight books 1593–1662) to support the consent theory of legislation. BRIEFS, *supra* note 170, at 142.

[177] Coquillette, *John Adams*, *supra* note 25, at 408–09, 416–17; *Novanglus*, *supra* note 1; *see* YIRUSH, *supra* note 40, at 256–59. After the Parliament passed the Massachusetts Government Act (1774), which terminated the colonial charter and permitted the governor to appoint certain officers that previously the colonists had elected, Leonard accepted the office of mandamus councilor and later served as solicitor to the customs commissioners until he was convinced to sail to Halifax in 1776. Coquillette, *supra*, at 409 n.1; Carol Berkin, *Leonard, Daniel*, *in* 13 AMERICAN NATIONAL BIOGRAPHY, *supra* note 11, at 489.

[178] Coquillette, *John Adams*, *supra* note 25, at 408, 416. Thomas Jefferson had a similar idea. *Id.* at 416 n.6; *see* THOMAS JEFFERSON, A SUMMARY VIEW OF THE RIGHTS OF BRITISH AMERICA (1774, reprint 1976).

[179] Coquillette, *John Adams*, *supra* note 25, at 410–11. Adams also made use of English legal precedents that had developed in the relations of England with Scotland, Wales, and Ireland, but whose applicability to the American colonies was indirect at best. *Id.* at 415–16. *Calvin's Case*, 7 Coke Report 1a, 77 Eng. Rep. 377 (1608) was the most notable example. *See Calvin's Case, or the Case of the Postnati, in* SIR EDWARD COKE, 1 THE SELECTED WRITINGS AND SPEECHES OF SIR EDWARD COKE ch. 1,

First, the law of nature and nations permits lawful resistance to arbitrary power. Second, that same law (as well as the English constitution) recognizes that there is no lawful parliamentary authority over the colonies; rather the colonists are subject to the Crown's law via their own legislative assemblies. Third, therefore, the colonists' resistance to attempted colonial subordination by the Parliament's edicts, as a matter of universal legal principle, was the affirmation of legal order.[180]

Throughout his argument, Adams relied significantly on Roman, civil, and natural law authorities as well as English political theorists. These included Grotius's *De iure belli ac pacis*, Pufendorf's *Law of Nature and Nations*,[181] James Harrington's *The Oceana*,[182] John Locke's *The Second Treatise of Civil Government*,[183] and Algernon Sidney's *Discourses concerning Government*.[184] Adams was attempting to use natural law and *ius gentium* principles to prevent war and to find a compromise that might yield authority to Parliament over the oceans and trade on the high seas and authority to colonial assemblies for internal matters.[185] As on other occasions, Adams drew a comparison with the Roman Republic.

> The Romans continued their colonies under the jurisdiction of the mother commonwealth; but, nevertheless, they allowed them the privileges of cities.

---

pt. 7 (Steve Sheppard ed., 2003), https://oll.libertyfund.org (select People, then Sir Edward Coke). Christopher Tomlins, *Law, Population, Labor*, in CAMBRIDGE HISTORY, *supra* note 69, at 211, 223–26. In *Calvin's Case*, the plenum court of 14 royal justices, convened by Lord Chancellor Ellesmere, clarified the issue of loyalty to the Crown in the context of natural law.

For the Laws: 1. That ligeance, or obedience of the subject to the Sovereign, is due by the Law of nature: 2. That this Law of nature is part of the Laws of England: 3. That the Law of nature was before any judicial or municipal Law in the world: 4. That the Law of nature is immutable and cannot be changed.

Calvin's Case, *supra*, 7 Coke Report 4b, 77 Eng. Rep. 382. For the possible influence of civilian and canon law on the conquest rule in *Calvin's Case*, see Gavin Loughton, *Calvin's Case and the Origins of the Rule Governing Conquest in English Law*, 8 AUSTL. J. LEGAL HIST. 143, 170–75 (2004).

[180] Coquillette, *John Adams*, *supra* note 25, at 410–11. To these I would add the principle that under natural law and *ius gentium*, Parliament cannot legislate for the American colonies without the latter's appropriate representation in that body. *See Novanglus*, *supra* note 1, letters 7–10.

[T]he case of America ... can be determined only by eternal reason and the law of nature. ... [T]he analogy of all these cases of Ireland, Wales, [Isle of] Man, ... etc. clearly concur with the dictates of reason and nature, that Americans are entitled to all the liberties of Englishmen, and that they are not bound by any acts of parliament whatever, by any law known in English records or history, excepting those for the regulation of trade, which they have consented to and acquiesced in.

Novanglus, *supra*, letter 9.

[181] *Supra* notes 29–30 and accompanying text (Grotius and Pufendorf).

[182] JAMES HARRINGTON, THE OCEANA AND OTHER WORKS OF JAMES HARRINGTON (1737, reprint 1963); *see* John Adams Library, *supra* note 145 (1737 and 1771 editions). The Harrington volume included his 1656 essay, *The Commonwealth of Oceana*, which proposed a utopian republic based on classical examples.

[183] LOCKE, 1–3 THE WORKS OF JOHN LOCKE (4th ed. 1740); *see* John Adams Library, *supra* note 145. Volume 2 included *The Second Treatise of Civil Government* (1690).

[184] JOHN ALGERNON SIDNEY, 1–2 DISCOURSES CONCERNING GOVERNMENT (1750, orig. 1698, reprint 1990); *see* John Adams Library, *supra* note 145. The Crown used a draft of *Discourses* as the second witness necessary to convict and hang Sidney of treason.

[185] Coquillette, *John Adams*, *supra* note 25, at 411–16. This division between external affairs and internal colonial affairs was a recurrent theme after the Stamp Act. Jack P. Greene, *Law and the Origins of the American Revolution*, in CAMBRIDGE HISTORY, *supra* note 69, at 447, 456–69.

Indeed, that sagacious city seems to have been aware of difficulties similar to those under which Great Britain is now laboring. She seems to have been sensible of the impossibility of keeping colonies planted at great distances, under the absolute control of her *senatus consulta*.... The senate and people of Rome did not interfere commonly by making laws for their colonies, but left them to be ruled by governors and senates.[186]

James Muldoon demonstrated that Adams also understood canon law (although he did not care to cite it) in investigating whether the colonial charters created a single constitutional unit for the British Empire equal to the king's territories that he ruled together with Parliament, or rather many territories that the king ruled, only some of which Parliament had under its jurisdiction.[187] The crucial document that English monarchs relied upon for colonial charters in the seventeenth century was Pope Alexander VI's *Inter caetera* (1493), which served as the legal basis for Spanish possessions in the Americas.[188]

5. The Advantage of a Comparative Perspective

John Adams loved books and expended much time and money in building what he considered the best law library in Massachusetts. While abroad, he purchased books in England, France, and Spain. Besides a general interest in history, he emphasized what today we would call comparative and foreign law, public international law, and political and moral philosophy.[189] At the age of 86, Adams bequeathed his library of about 3,000 volumes to the town of Quincy and at the end of the nineteenth century, its library supervisors transferred the books to the Boston Public Library, where it remains today as the John Adams Library.[190] Based on the Library's online catalog, I estimate that Adams had a collection of about 750 volumes of the type one might find in a modern university law library.[191] Harvard Law School at the time of Adams's gift (1822) had about 600 volumes in its library.[192]

---

[186] *Novanglus*, *supra* note 1, letter 7. Adams referred to Rome over 20 times in *Novanglus*.
[187] Muldoon, *supra* note 27, at 26–27, 31–32.
[188] *Id.* at 31–35. To avoid the Roman Church's authority (or that of the Holy Roman emperor), the English Crown relied on the *imperium in imperio* maxim that jurists argued made England an empire within its own realm. *Id.* at 36–39, 42–46.
[189] Coquillette, *John Adams*, *supra* note 25, at 399.
[190] John Adams Library, *supra* note 145 (select Internet Archive). An 1823 catalog listed 2,800 books in the gift. *Id.* David McCullough reported that Adams's library had 3,200 volumes. McCullough, *supra* note 141, at 618.
[191] John Adams Library, *supra* note 145 (Internet Archive, browse books by category). The Library classified 254 books in the Law category. I added many of the books listed in Classics, Philosophy and Ethics, and Politics and Government. *Id.*
[192] The Harvard Law School, created in 1817, initially located the library in the office of the university professor of law. Harvard Law School, *History of the Harvard Law School Library*, https://hls.harvard.edu/library/about-the-library (select History of the Library). Harvard College in the eighteenth

Coquillette summarized several additional examples of Adams's use of civil law sources in his law practice not detailed here. He suggested that a close reading of the voluminous and detailed materials that Adams left would find more. In addition, other colonial lawyers collected European law books.[193] The field of colonial American law is open for future investigators to search for materials that might demonstrate other colonial lawyers who could meet the modern standard for the professional use of comparative law.

The evidence in this chapter is insufficient to show that Roman, civil, and natural law *directly* influenced the formation of colonial American legal institutions and norms beyond what the English legal system had already incorporated. Nevertheless, those European sources *may* have had that effect. The point is that prior to the American Revolution at least one, and probably several legal comparatists existed who used their knowledge in the professional application of civilian learning. Yet, one must not assume, of course, that because someone knows a foreign legal system, he would then prefer elements from that foreign system to the ones in the system in which he operates. John Adams, for instance, in *Dissertation* railed against popish corruption in European legal systems[194] and would have preferred a British jury trial in his defense of Hancock rather than rely on the admiralty court's civilian procedure.[195]

In summary, comparison offered two important advantages to colonial legal scholars. First, it provided one with a more complete and accurate understanding of a past or present reality. Second, for comparatists with an activist agenda, it afforded the perspective to assess which of two or more existing alternatives

---

century had the largest library in the 13 colonies, with almost 3,000 titles in 1723 (including many pamphlets). Most of these titles dealt with theology, but about 100 treated law and government, with another 220 on philosophy. The total number of titles by 1763 had increased to 4,700. PURVIS, *supra* note 65, at 250. Charles Warren for this early period reported a much smaller number of law "books." WARREN, *supra* note 69, at 164. An estimate was 12 English and American law books (mostly statutes) and a larger number of Roman and civil law books. Coquillette, *Lawes and Libertyes*, *supra* note 59, at 179, 181 n.1, 196.

[193] Coquillette, *John Adams*, *supra* note 25, at 394–95.
[194] Nelson summed up the view of most colonists after the Glorious Revolution in England. "[I]t mattered to be British and Protestant rather than French and Roman Catholic: The British, as they saw it, enjoyed liberty and self-government, whereas the French lived under arbitrary, hierarchical rule." NELSON, 3 THE COMMON LAW, *supra* note 71, at 4.
[195] See *supra* text accompanying notes 162–64 (Adams's use of civil law). In arguing for the two-witness rule, Adams pleaded:

> Shall We say that We are to be governed by some Rules of the common Law and some Rules of the civil Law, that the Judge at his Discretion shall choose out of each system such Rules as please him, and discard the rest. . . . Shall We suffer under the odious Rules of the civil Law, and receive no advantage from the beneficial Rules of it?

Coquillette, *John Adams*, *supra* note 25, at 389, quoting 2 ADAMS LEGAL PAPERS, *supra* note 162, at 207.

would be best for a defined purpose, rather than settling for the default indigenous solution or to have to imagine a better alternative. Adams had that comparative perspective, which he continued to utilize during the remainder of his career.[196] With John Adams, American comparative law predated the American republic.

---

[196] *See, e.g.*, John Adams, *Thoughts on Government: Applicable to the Present State of the American Colonies* (1776), *in* ADAMS, REVOLUTIONARY WRITINGS, *supra* note 1, at ch. 9. Adams initially wrote this as a letter in response for assistance with state constitution drafting. George Wythe of Virginia and others prevailed on Adams to publish it as a pamphlet. MCCULLOUGH, *supra* note 141, at 101.

3
Legal Foundation for the New Republic: 1776 to 1791

To comprehend modern times well, it is necessary to comprehend ancient times well; it is necessary to follow each law in the spirit of all the ages.

Charles-Louis de Secondat, Baron de la Brède et de Montesquieu[1]

What chiefly attracts and chiefly benefits students of history is just this—the study of causes and the consequent power of choosing what is best in each case. Now the chief cause of success or the reverse in all matters is the form of a state's constitution.

Polybius[2]

A. Inventing a New Nation: A Golden Age of Comparative Law

Declaring political independence and creating the successful framework for a new legal order are two distinct matters. Both occurred, nevertheless, in only 16 years from 1776 to 1791. Although the new nation was in large part heir to the English legal tradition, American law diverged from English law from the beginning.[3] Perhaps most important, America would have no monarch. This provided

---

[1] Montesquieu, 2 Oeuvres Completes de Montesquieu 1103 (Roger Caillois ed., 1951), quoted in Paul A. Rahe, 3 Republics Ancient and Modern (Inventions of Prudence: Constituting the American Regime) xxvii (1994).

[2] Polybius, 3 Histories 271 (vi.2.9) (W.R. Paton trans., 1923), quoted in David J. Bederman, The Classical Foundations of the American Constitution: Prevailing Wisdom vi (2008).

[3] Comparative law considers differences and similarities between two or more legal systems. I focus on differences between English law and the new American law. I also attempt to identify similarities in eighteenth-century English law and European civil law that could have influenced Americans as examples of Western or "universal" law. I do not deny that the "British constitution" or English common law rights overall had substantial influence on American legal institutions and norms. See John Phillip Reid, *The Irrelevance of the Declaration*, in Law in the American Revolution and the Revolution in the Law: A Collection of Review Essays on American Legal History 46–69 (Hendrik Hartog ed., 1981).

law a place of special prominence as the reigning sovereign authority.[4] In fact, lawyers were the largest group signing the Declaration of Independence and participating at the Constitutional Convention.[5]

However, where should one look for ideas and examples for legal institutions and rules beyond the parts of British law that offered promise in a new land? My argument in this chapter is that the founders, most of whom had studied or practiced law, looked to three additional sources. First, the legal structures of classical Greek city states, their leagues, and the Roman Republic were the most visible and persuasive counterexamples to monarchy. Second, European political philosophy (continental and British) from Niccolò Machiavelli (1469-1527) through the eighteenth century, with its treatment of classical polities and its embrace of natural law rules, supplied a modern supplement to Roman law.[6] Third, the ethnic and religious diversity in the 13 colonies presented popular views of law appropriate for a nation founded on the people's will rather than divine delegation. This pluralism further suggested that the framers should layer, balance, and check sovereign power, derived from these different peoples, to avoid the tyranny that drove colonists to rebel in the first place.[7]

Thomas Jefferson (1743-1826) and James Madison (1751-1836) worked to prevent religious authoritarianism from achieving legal establishment. Jefferson's draft Declaration of Independence revealed his heterodox theology, emphasizing its deistic, universal, and impartial God.[8] In 1777, Jefferson drafted the Bill for Establishing Religious Freedom, which his legislative committee introduced to the Virginia House of Delegates in 1779. Although tabled, Madison reintroduced a slightly modified version to the General Assembly, which enacted it in 1785.

---

[4] Nan Goodman, *Law in Popular Culture, 1790-1920: The People and the Law*, in 2 THE CAMBRIDGE HISTORY OF LAW IN AMERICA: THE LONG CENTURY (1789-1920) 387, 393 (Michael Grossberg & Christopher Tomlins eds., 2008). Even if one insists on the fiction that the American people are the sovereign, they must exercise that authority through representatives, who express its details with law.

[5] Richard D. Brown, *The Founding Fathers of 1776 and 1787: A Collective View*, 33 WM & MARY Q. 465, 467 (1976). During the presidential administrations of John Adams and Thomas Jefferson (1797-1809), 75 percent of high-level executive appointees were lawyers. *Id.* at 468.

[6] This period extended from the Renaissance, through the Age of Reason, to the Enlightenment. For reliance on British and Continental authors and intermingling customary rights with deductive natural law during the revolutionary period, *see* James Q. Whitman, *Why Did the Revolutionary Lawyers Confuse Custom and Reason?*, 58 U. CHI. L. REV. 1321 (1991). *See generally* THOMAS E. RICKS, FIRST PRINCIPLES: WHAT AMERICA'S FOUNDERS LEARNED FROM THE GREEKS AND ROMANS AND HOW THAT SHAPED OUR COUNTRY (2020).

[7] General anti-lawyer sentiment reinforced the popular consensus that lawmaking and administration should be accessible to the white, male population without the intermediation of a professional bar. <Goodman, *supra* note 4, at 393-94. Political elections and the use of civil and penal juries supported pluralism, as did the importance of the "reasonable man" standard for legal and social conduct. *Id.* at 394.

[8] ALLEN JAYNE, JEFFERSON'S DECLARATION OF INDEPENDENCE: ORIGINS, PHILOSOPHY AND THEOLOGY xi-xii, 6-8, 19-40, 139-67 (1998). Since God created nature, God's law and the law of nature were the same. PAULINE MAIER, AMERICAN SCRIPTURE: MAKING THE DECLARATION OF INDEPENDENCE 132-33, 148 (1997).

The statute explicitly asserted its natural law origin, in effect disestablishing the Church of England in Virginia, and explicitly guaranteed all individuals freedom of religion.[9] The United States Congress gave Madison the task of drafting the Constitution's initial amendments. The first one that the states ratified in 1791 restrained Congress in dealing with religion.[10]

One might argue that this initial period of U.S. legal history was a golden age of comparative law.[11] It is remarkable that five of the first six presidents of the United States were lawyers, schooled in classical studies. Several of them could read Latin or Greek, although some primarily learned about Greek and Roman legal institutions through translations.[12] Those men influential in framing basic legal principles, rules, and institutions for the United States often cited the legal comparatist Baron de Montesquieu (1689–1755).[13] In 1776, the United States had only a small corpus of indigenous written law that would be usable in the republic. There had been only a few judicial case reports and no legal literature such as the English institutionalist commentaries by Sir William Blackstone (1723–1780). Continental European states also had institutionalist legal writing, characterized by its comprehensiveness, national unification, didactic purpose, and rational organization.[14]

---

[9] JACK N. RAKOVE, JAMES MADISON AND THE CREATION OF THE AMERICAN REPUBLIC 13–14, 30, 34–36 (1990) [hereinafter RAKOVE, JAMES MADISON]; Thomas Jefferson, *A Bill for Establishing Religious Freedom (1779)*, in ENCYCLOPEDIA VIRGINIA (2020), https://www.encyclopediavirginia.org (search for the title).

[10] Saul Cornell & Gerald Leonard, *The Consolidation of the Early Federal System, 1791–1812*, in 1 THE CAMBRIDGE HISTORY OF LAW IN AMERICA: EARLY AMERICA (1580–1815) 518, 522 (Michael Grossberg & Christopher Tomlins eds., 2008) [hereinafter 1 CAMBRIDGE HISTORY]; *see* Rodney A. Grunes, *James Madison and Religious Freedom*, in JAMES MADISON: PHILOSOPHER, FOUNDER, AND STATESMAN 105–14 (John R. Vile et al. eds., 2008) [hereinafter JAMES MADISON (Vile ed.)]. "Congress shall make no law respecting an establishment of religion, or prohibiting the free exercise thereof." U.S. Const. amend I.

[11] "[W]e cannot properly understand the political choices and claims made by the American revolutionaries unless we realize that to them, in many ways, the world of the ancient Mediterranean was as vivid and recognizable as the world in which they were living." ERAN SHALEV, ROME REBORN ON WESTERN SHORES: HISTORICAL IMAGINATION AND THE CREATION OF THE AMERICAN REPUBLIC 2 (2009); *see id.* at 2–8.

[12] George Washington, the first president (1789–1797), was a surveyor and soldier, with little if any study of classical studies. JOSEPH J. ELLIS, HIS EXCELLENCY: GEORGE WASHINGTON 8–18 (2004). Madison, the fourth president (served 1809–1817), was not a lawyer since he had no bar membership, but he studied law and was a legal scholar. Mary Sarah Bilder, *James Madison, Law Student and Demi-Lawyer*, 28 LAW & HIST. REV. 389–403 (2010); *see infra* pt. H.1 (Madison).

John Quincy Adams, the sixth president (served 1825–1829), was only 24 when admitted to the Massachusetts bar in 1791, the year of the Bill of Rights' ratification. When he entered Harvard, he could fluently read Greek and Latin, in part, because his father had enrolled him in a Latin grammar school during his stay in France. In 1806, Adams held the chair of rhetoric and oratory at Harvard while he was a U.S. senator. CARL J. RICHARD, THE FOUNDERS AND THE CLASSICS: GREECE, ROME, AND THE AMERICAN ENLIGHTENMENT 32–34 (1994).

[13] *See infra* pt. D.4 (Montesquieu's *Spirit of the Laws*).

[14] JOHN H. LANGBEIN, RENÉE LETTOW LERNER, & BRUCE P. SMITH, HISTORY OF THE COMMON LAW: THE DEVELOPMENT OF ANGLO-AMERICAN LEGAL INSTITUTIONS 838–41 (2009); *see infra* ch. 4, pt. D.2 (Blackstone and the American institutionalist literature). To access case reports, one

Either Americans could invent their own government structure, legal institutions, processes, types of professions, appropriate education, and legal principles and rules, or they could borrow bits and pieces or intact elements from one or more foreign legal systems, past or contemporary. As suggested earlier,[15] and as the remainder of this chapter will illustrate, the small number of Americans involved with formulating a new legal system primarily relied on borrowing or inertia. With the former, we have comparative law as legal transplant; with the latter, we usually find English law and institutional forms. In the 1770s and 1780s, Blackstone's *Commentaries* provided the central channel by which Americans could learn about English law and jurists could find material for legal argument or judicial decision.[16]

B. Learning Foreign Law and Political Theory: George Wythe

In the 1960s, some legal historians and political scientists began a sustained attack on the prevalent economic interpretation of the American Constitution and the nation's founding. They preferred an ideological approach, which for certain scholars, especially since the 1980s, put the explanatory emphasis on the classical republicanism or civic humanism of ancient Rome and Greece.[17] Mortimer Sellers is a good illustration of this group. He did not deny that among those who discussed, wrote, and ratified the Constitution, some were familiar with the writings of the European Renaissance and Enlightenment, and that those sources were influential on American constitutional opinion.[18] His point was that, like many Europeans, a sufficient number of Americans—both Federalists and Anti-Federalists—were educated in Roman classics and history as well as

---

would have to travel to the court or the office of the reporter. *E.g.*, VIRGINIA GENERAL COURT, CASES ADJUDGED IN THE GENERAL COURT OF VIRGINIA, 1733-1741 (Gustavus Myers made a copy of Edward Barradall's reports in the possession of Conway Robinson; Harvard Law School Library acquired the copy in 1903).

[15] See *supra* text accompanying notes 6-7 (sources of law).
[16] SIR WILLIAM BLACKSTONE, 1-4 COMMENTARIES ON THE LAWS OF ENGLAND (1765-1769). Robert Bell printed the first American edition in Philadelphia in 1771 and 1772 and sold 1,557 sets. LAWRENCE M. FRIEDMAN, A HISTORY OF AMERICAN LAW 59-60 (3d ed. 2005).
[17] ALAN GIBSON, UNDERSTANDING THE FOUNDING: THE CRUCIAL QUESTIONS 9, 91-93, 131-36, 144-47, 238 n.1, 258-61 n.54-55 (2007); *e.g.*, 3 RAHE, *supra* note 1, at 39-44, 60-63. See *generally* THOMAS JEFFERSON, THE CLASSICAL WORLD, AND EARLY AMERICA (Peter S. Onuf & Nicholas P. Cole eds., 2011).
[18] M.N.S. SELLERS, AMERICAN REPUBLICANISM: ROMAN IDEOLOGY IN THE UNITED STATES CONSTITUTION x-xi, 20-21, 133-41, 163-71, 226-44 (1994) [hereinafter SELLERS, AMERICAN REPUBLICANISM]. Sellers mentioned Beccaria, Burlamaqui, Grotius, Locke, Montesquieu, Pufendorf, Rousseau, Vattel, and Voltaire. *Id.* at 20. All but Locke were continental Europeans.

Latin (and Greek) and could make use of that learning for their political thinking and decisions.

David Bederman expressed the same opinion. "[C]lassicism provided the common political vocabulary for participants in the constitutional deliberations of 1787. Even if there was a backlash against the over-use of certain kinds of ancient references, the classics still structured and conditioned the debate."[19] Americans could and did independently derive the lessons of Roman republicanism, which they brought to the task of designing the framework for a new nation. Their knowledge of Rome was not only derivative from European political philosophy, but from the direct study of books about Rome and Roman literature.[20] Although this distinction is central to Sellers's thesis, American use of both Roman and continental European ideas about law and legal institutions were each illustrations of comparative law.[21]

The American revolutionary period, as suggested, was a golden age of comparative law.[22] To understand this assertion it is useful to reflect on what type of educational or experiential background a lawyer would need intelligently to write about or to compare foreign law.[23] Clerkship was the typical form of legal education.[24] In 1963, Richard Gummere first presented the general case for Greek and Roman influence on the North American colonial mind. Almost all the nation's founders had some college education, much of which dealt with Greek and Roman authors. Relying on the colonists' writings themselves, Gummere found their references to classical ideas pragmatic rather than philosophical, since they addressed current concerns.[25] College education in the eighteenth century largely consisted of learning Greek and Latin to study the classics with exercises

---

[19] BEDERMAN, *supra* note 2, at 44.
[20] SELLERS, AMERICAN REPUBLICANISM, *supra* note 18, at 5–7, 20–23, 219 (classical republicanism). English political theory and England's institutional framework after 1688 were also influential with some of the Americans involved with the new nation's founding legal documents. *Id.* at 50–51, 55, 61–62, 105, 140–41, 225–31 (Glorious Revolution). Sellers identified as a third source of republican principles the mixed governments of the 13 American states, some of which had governors, presidents, and senates from 1776 on. Federalists saw the principal infirmity of these examples in weak senates. *Id.* at 42, 51–56, 61, 65, 204, 222–23, 232–37, 243–46. Sellers, following John Adams, deemphasized the influence of Hellenic republican models. *Id.* at 37–38; *see id.* at 99–101.
[21] *See* ch. 1, § A.1 (American comparative law's distinction between civil law and common law).
[22] *See supra* text accompanying notes 11–13 (golden age).
[23] For the importance of classical studies as part of eighteenth-century legal education, *see* BEDERMAN, *supra* note 2, at 9–12. Today, most American comparative law focuses on rules and institutions from civil law nations, which include most of Europe, Latin America, and East Asia. The jurists who engage in this activity almost always have foreign language fluency gained by parental heritage, education, or significant foreign residence. The history of American legal comparatists involves a varying mixture of immigrant jurists and indigenous lawyers who developed the appropriate background to engage in comparative law.
[24] Craig Evan Klafter, *The Influence of Vocational Law Schools on the Origins of American Legal Thought, 1779-1829*, 37 AM. J. LEG. HIST. 307, 311–12 (1993).
[25] RICHARD M. GUMMERE, THE AMERICAN COLONIAL MIND AND THE CLASSICAL TRADITION: ESSAYS IN COMPARATIVE CULTURE vii–xii, 1, 3 (1963); *see* MEYER REINHOLD, THE CLASSICK PAGES: CLASSICAL READING OF EIGHTEENTH-CENTURY AMERICANS 1–3 (1975)

in rhetoric and logic.[26] In addition, literacy was prevalent among white male colonists, which supported the growing newspaper, magazine, and pamphlet materials circulating in the colonies. Michael Warner explored what he termed the "*res publica* of letters" in eighteenth-century America, when the relation between print and political culture transformed the "public sphere" to one of a discourse on republicanism.[27] Bederman ably summarized the literature describing classical education prevalent during the eighteenth century.[28]

Meyer Reinhold prepared an anthology excerpting the most significant Greek and Roman authors that the educated person read in grammar (that is, secondary) school and college before and during the revolutionary period. These works consisted of texts, translations, and histories typically found in private and college libraries and in booksellers' catalogues.[29] Relevant to legal and political theory, three of the most extensive private libraries were those of John Adams (1735-1826), Benjamin Franklin (1706-1790), and Jefferson. In 1776, there were nine colleges distributed from New England to Virginia and many grammar schools that prepared young men for college. The grammar school curriculum typically lasted seven years, centered on the classics, and, by the mid-eighteenth century, had somewhat secularized toward morals and history. Nevertheless, while classical works were significant in colonial libraries of the 1770s, and particularly important for political discourse, they were never dominant by volume count. In addition, most Americans—including the nation's founders—often relied on translations of Greek and Roman authors or secondary works of ancient history.[30]

Reinhold demonstrated that reading classics was selective, reflecting American pragmatic humanism, "the immediate goals of freedom and the establishment of a new republic, and the contemporary nationwide quest for 'useful

---

[hereinafter REINHOLD, CLASSICK PAGES]; *id.*, CLASSICA AMERICANA: THE GREEK AND ROMAN HERITAGE IN THE UNITED STATES 286-89 (1984) [hereinafter REINHOLD, CLASSICA AMERICANA]. Some of those who did not attend college, such as Benjamin Franklin, learned Latin by self-study. GUMMERE, *supra*, at 174. Gummere refuted the consensus among political scientists that the colonists derived their ideas primarily through European Renaissance writers. Rather, he found the original classical authors equally consulted. *Id.* at xi, 174.

[26] Joe W. Kraus, *The Development of a Curriculum in the Early American Colleges*, 1 HIST. EDUC. Q. 64-76 (no. 2, June 1961). Philosophy (moral), natural science, geography, and mathematics supplemented the curriculum. *Id.* at 67-68. Some colleges devoted significant time to Hebrew and biblical studies. French was the most common modern language added at some colleges. *Id.* at 69-70, 72.

[27] MICHAEL WARNER, THE LETTERS OF THE REPUBLIC: PUBLICATION AND THE PUBLIC SPHERE IN EIGHTEENTH-CENTURY AMERICA xi-xiii, 34-72 (1990).

[28] BEDERMAN, *supra* note 2, at 3-9.

[29] REINHOLD, CLASSICK PAGES, *supra* note 25, at viii-ix, 4-8; *see* CAROLINE WINTERER, THE CULTURE OF CLASSICISM: ANCIENT GREECE AND ROME IN AMERICAN INTELLECTUAL LIFE, 1780-1910, at 11-13 (2002) [hereinafter WINTERER, CLASSICISM].

[30] BEDERMAN, *supra* note 2, at 12-14; REINHOLD, CLASSICK PAGES, *supra* note 25, at 4-10; *see* REINHOLD, CLASSICA AMERICANA, *supra* note 25, at 26-32, 295-300. Grammar school or private tutoring typically began at age eight. RICHARD, *supra* note 12, at 12-13, 17-18. The first college

knowledge."[31] The classics prepared colonists for intelligent living and were an agent for individual and social progress guided by virtue and taste. They were not merely ornamental, but useful in the affairs of daily life. Practical knowledge thus included the classics as well as natural philosophy or science.[32] Of all subjects, ancient history appeared central to the interests of mid-eighteenth-century Americans. They learned most of their history through independent reading; many thought it a guide to distinguish virtue from vice with the examples of heroic or tragic persons.[33]

For legal and political theory, Reinhold found that classical influence during the American revolutionary era was at its apogee, a golden age. The founders read ancient history and political theory as a "lamp of experience." Of the 55 men who attended the Constitutional Convention, 31 were college graduates. The lessons served as authoritative precedent to validate conclusions already reached through reason and from other reading. Above all, the Roman Republic was an exemplar for republicanism, liberty, and the control of corrupting vice with civic virtue.[34] In general, the framers carried out this effort in comparative law and politics, not directly from Greek and Roman authors, but through translations, modern histories of the ancient world, British Whig writers, and continental jurists.[35] Reinhold asserted, "It is clear that the precedents, analogies, and lessons Madison and others quarried from antiquity were not mere window dressing or 'pedantry in politics,' but solemn exercises in comparative political institutions and history."[36] In addition, the classical idea of natural law

---

was Harvard, founded in 1636. The other eight were Dartmouth, Yale, Rhode Island (later Brown), King's (later Columbia), Queen's (later Rutgers), New Jersey (later Princeton), Philadelphia (later Pennsylvania), and William and Mary. REINHOLD, CLASSICK PAGES, *supra*, at 4.

[31] REINHOLD, CLASSICK PAGES, *supra* note 25, at 10.
[32] *Id.* at 11–16, 19–20; REINHOLD, CLASSICA AMERICANA, *supra* note 25, at 32–37, 301; WINTERER, CLASSICISM, *supra* note 29, at 15–16. In 1769, two scholarly societies merged into the American Philosophical Society, held at Philadelphia for Promoting Useful Knowledge. Several founders were members. The 1776 state constitutions of North Carolina and Pennsylvania had the same provision: "all useful learning shall be duly encouraged and promoted in one or more universities." REINHOLD, CLASSICK PAGES, *supra*, at 12–13; *see* American Philosophical Society, *History*, https://www.amphilsoc.org/about/history.
[33] REINHOLD, CLASSICK PAGES, *supra* note 25, at 16–18; Reinhold, Classica Americana, *supra* note 25, at 37–39, 301.
[34] REINHOLD, CLASSICA AMERICANA, *supra* note 25, at 94–95, 97–98; *see* WINTERER, CLASSICISM, *supra* note 29, at 15–29. "The Founding Fathers ransacked the ancient world as a usable past for guidelines, parallels, analogies to present political problems." REINHOLD, CLASSICA AMERICANA, *supra*, at 95. On the quest for virtue, *see id.* at 142–63.
[35] REINHOLD, CLASSICA AMERICANA, *supra* note 25, at 96, 301. As John Adams wrote in 1765 in his *Dissertation on the Canon and Feudal Law*, "Let us study the law of nature; search into the spirit of the British Constitution; read the histories of the ancient ages; contemplate the great examples of Greece and Rome." *Quoted in id.* at 96, 110.
[36] REINHOLD, CLASSICA AMERICANA, *supra* note 25, at 102. Gummere found that the three most important classical authors for issues of legal structure were Aristotle, Cicero, and Polybius. Richard M. Gummere, *The Classical Ancestry of the United States Constitution*, 14 AM. Q. 3, 4–8 (1962).

served to contest repugnant enactments of the British Crown and Parliament. Although colonists cited Aristotle (384–322 BCE), the Stoics, and Marcus Tullius Cicero (106–43 BCE), they again relied largely on British and continental political theorists and jurists.[37]

George Wythe (1726–1806), a noted classics scholar proficient in Latin and Greek, was a Virginia lawyer, judge, and legislator, who stood out as a teacher of law and the classical political and legal traditions. Among Wythe's famous pupils that he had accepted in legal apprenticeship were Jefferson and St. George Tucker (1752–1827). The latter became an important legal educator and scholar after 1790. The Virginia General Assembly in 1778 selected Wythe as one of three judges for the High Court of Chancery.[38] Jefferson repaid his mentor in 1779, when he became governor of Virginia. The governorship led him to board membership at the College of William and Mary. Under Jefferson's leadership, the board reorganized the college and modernized its curriculum. It created professorships in law, medicine, and modern languages, with Wythe named the first professor of law and police in America.[39] Now, rather than one or two apprentices reading law with Wythe, he taught 40 or so students in law at the college. Besides the English common law, Wythe was the first to lecture on constitutional law. He also directed some students in general studies, which included the ancient classics, and the fundamentals of Greek and Latin. His most notable student was John Marshall (1755–1835), fourth chief justice of the U.S. Supreme Court. In 1790, Wythe resigned his professorship to work as sole chancellor for the Court of Chancery, where he served until his death.[40]

Wythe not only used his knowledge of the ancient classics in education, but also as a judge on the state equity court. Wythe had one of the largest libraries in colonial America, estimated at 478 titles.[41] Virginia lawyers other than Wythe

---

Bederman provided a comprehensive list of the most cited authors of ancient political theory and history. BEDERMAN, *supra* note 2, at 14–18.

[37] REINHOLD, CLASSICA AMERICANA, *supra* note 25, at 96–97, 302; *see* SUSAN FORD WILTSHIRE, GREECE, ROME, AND THE BILL OF RIGHTS 13–34 (1992). Reinhold mentioned the British writers Coke, Locke, Milton, and Sidney and continental jurists such as Burlamaqui, Pufendorf, and Vattel. *Id.* at 97, 302. In 1774, Adams summarized these sources in his *Novanglus*, referring to Aristotle, Plato, Livy, Cicero, Harrington, Locke, and Sidney. REINHOLD, *supra*, at 97, 110.
[38] ALONZO THOMAS DILL, GEORGE WYTHE: TEACHER OF LIBERTY 20, 40, 60 (1979); ROBERT B. KIRTLAND, GEORGE WYTHE: LAWYER, REVOLUTIONARY, JUDGE 29–33, 45–46, 111, 118–22 (1986); *see infra* text accompanying note 48 (Wythe and Jefferson). Wythe also heard cases in the Court of Appeals where he participated ex officio until 1788. DILL, *supra*, at 60.
[39] DILL, *supra* note 38, at 41–42; KIRTLAND, *supra* note 38, at 114–16. Blackstone, as holder of the Vinerian chair at Oxford University, had the first law professorship in the common law world. DILL, *supra*, at 42.
[40] DILL, *supra* note 38, at 43, 54–57; KIRTLAND, *supra* note 38, at 136, 158–59.
[41] College of William and Mary Law Library, *Wythepedia: Home*, http://lawlibrary.wm.edu/wythepedia (select Wythe's Library). Wythe's will left Jefferson his library. *Id.* (select Jefferson's Inventory).

also cited Roman and civil law authorities in courts during the eighteenth century. This was most common for cases dealing with intestate succession, commercial law, admiralty, and equity.[42] Nevertheless, Wythe was the most prolific enthusiast of civilian legal sources. He considered Roman law to be of equal value with English common law as a source of legal ideas for courts so long as there was not a direct binding legal precedent.[43] During Wythe's years on the High Court of Chancery, he made at least 85 classical references in 21 different cases. About half are in the text of judicial opinions and half are in published notes for the cases. About a quarter of the references are to Justinian's *Corpus Juris Civilis*. His ability to marshal argument from the ancient Greek and Roman sources undoubtedly added to the high prestige Wythe enjoyed among his law-trained colleagues.[44]

At the time of the Constitutional Convention and subsequent state ratifying debates, classical and renaissance legal institutions related to federalism were especially relevant. Adams had addressed this and other issues from Europe in his three-volume *Defence* of the American experience.[45] Reinhold also identified Alexander Hamilton (1757–1804), Madison, and James Wilson (1742–1798) as diligent students of the classical legal structures that Rome and various Greek republics and leagues utilized. *The Federalist* (1788) had many extracts from translations of classical authors and even more from contemporary works on ancient history and legal and political theory.[46] In general, the founders were aware of the failures and deficiencies of the classical examples they used in debate; however, it was this information that would allow them to form that more perfect union.[47]

---

[42] W. Hamilton Bryson, *The Use of Roman Law in Virginia Courts*, 28 AM. J. LEG. HIST. 135, 139–41, 143, 145 (1984) [hereinafter Bryson, *Roman Law*]. Several private libraries in the eighteenth century included books on Roman law, natural law, and European civil law. Bryson, *supra*, at 136–37; *see* BRYSON, CENSUS OF LAW BOOKS IN COLONIAL VIRGINIA (1978).

[43] Bryson, *Roman Law, supra* note 42, at 141–44; Richard J. Hoffman, *Classics in the Courts of the United States, 1790–1800*, 22 AM. J. LEG. HIST. 55, 70–75, 80–81 (1978).

[44] Hoffman, *supra* note 43, at 57–59. Jefferson called Wythe the Cato of the eighteenth century. *Id.* at 61–62.

[45] REINHOLD, CLASSICA AMERICANA, *supra* note 25, at 102–03; *see* JOHN ADAMS, 1–3 A DEFENCE OF THE CONSTITUTIONS OF GOVERNMENT OF THE UNITED STATES OF AMERICA (London, 1787–1788) [hereinafter ADAMS, DEFENCE]; *see infra* text accompanying notes 118–19, 140–46 and note 126 (DEFENCE). *See generally* LUKE MAYVILLE, JOHN ADAMS AND THE FEAR OF AMERICAN OLIGARCHY (2016); RICHARD ALAN RYERSON, JOHN ADAMS' REPUBLIC: THE ONE, THE FEW, AND THE MANY (2016).

[46] REINHOLD, CLASSICA AMERICANA, *supra* note 25, at 102–03. For *The Federalist*, Reinhold listed Aristotle, Cicero, Demosthenes, Livy, Plato, Plutarch, Polybius, Sallust, Strabo, and Tacitus among the ancients; and for the Europeans, Adam Ferguson, John Gillies, Abbé Mably, Conyers Middleton, Claude Millot, William Mitford, Edward Montagu, Walter Moyle, Charles Rollin, and René-Aubert Vertot. *Id.* at 102.

[47] *Id.* at 103–05. Madison in *The Federalist* (No. 18) summed up the mix of empiricism and rationalism, the compromise among ancient institutions, reason, and American distinctiveness. REINHOLD, CLASSICA AMERICANA, *supra* note 25, at 105. Other founders, nevertheless, such as Franklin, were hostile toward too much use of or deference toward illustrations from antiquity. *Id.* at 105–06, 120–21.

C. Thomas Jefferson, Natural Law, and Independence

In 1760, Jefferson was already proficient in Greek, Latin, and classical study when, at the age of 17, he enrolled at the College of William and Mary. Later in life, he identified two persons who most influenced him in developing his worldview. First, the Scot William Small (1734–1775), Professor of Natural Philosophy, was Jefferson's primary teacher at the college for two years. Small, influenced by the Scottish Enlightenment, emphasized the study of nature, including natural law. From the Scottish view, natural law favored Roman and civil law, useful as a tool to resist and to encroach upon English common law. Second, Wythe, Small's friend, took over Jefferson's education for five years as both an apprentice in law and a student of the classics. Wythe sponsored him for bar membership before the Virginia General Court in 1767. Both Wythe and Jefferson were active at the Second Continental Congress (1775–1776), which adopted the Declaration of Independence.[48]

Greek and Roman Stoics developed a philosophy centered on nature, whose principles based on reason permeated the whole universe. Humans, peculiarly endowed with reason, should conduct themselves according to the laws derived from their nature. This required disengaging from passion and emotion, recognizing the inherent equality of humans, and striving to attain inner tranquility, harmony, and virtue. Reason was the universal basis of law and justice, valid everywhere and eternally. Cicero, the great Roman jurist, adopted many ideas from Stoicism for his own legal philosophy. The principle of equality in Stoic and Roman *jus naturale* ameliorated Roman ideas about slavery—contained in both the *jus civile* and the *jus gentium*—during the empire.[49]

In British North America, natural law competed with or infused local or customary law, which might be unique to a region or people and reflected the diversity of the 13 British colonies.[50] Natural law, of course, even against general

---

[48] DILL, *supra* note 38, at 19–20; JEFFERSON'S LITERARY COMMONPLACE BOOK 6–8, 227–28 (Douglas L. Wilson ed., 1989); KIRTLAND, *supra* note 38, at 44–46; CHARLES A. MILLER, JEFFERSON AND NATURE: AN INTERPRETATION 14 (1988); RICHARD, *supra* note 12, at 18, 22, 181; Merrill D. Peterson, *Jefferson, Thomas*, in 11 AMERICAN NATIONAL BIOGRAPHY 909 (John A. Garraty & Mark C. Carnes, gen. eds., 1999); see RICKS, *supra* note 6, at 65–86, 121–32, 264–73. Wythe signed the Declaration of Independence, briefly represented Virginia at the Constitutional Convention, and played an important role in gaining Virginia's ratification of the Constitution in 1788. DILL, *supra*, at 63–70; KIRTLAND, *supra*, at 92–99, 123–24, 128–31.

[49] EDGAR BODENHEIMER, JURISPRUDENCE: THE PHILOSOPHY AND METHOD OF THE LAW 13–20, 224 (rev. ed. 1974); RICHARD, *supra* note 12, at 170–72, 184–85. Cicero added virtue as an element, derived from the social nature of humans, which, in any case, they must nurture by reason. RICHARD, *supra*, at 171–72, 184.

[50] RICHARD, *supra* note 12, at 169; JACK P. GREENE, THE CONSTITUTIONAL ORIGINS OF THE AMERICAN REVOLUTION xiii–xiv, 48–54, 75–76, 81–87, 91–92 (2011) [hereinafter GREENE, CONSTITUTIONAL ORIGINS].

English common law, is universal as well as eternal. Natural law rules and rights are inherent in human nature, endowed by nature or nature's God. These rules and rights are self-evident to learned persons who understand them using reason. Consequently, natural law exists independently of political authority or legal custom.[51] John Locke (1632–1704), Montesquieu, Algernon Sidney (1623–1683), and Emer de Vattel (1714–1767)—philosophers the founders were familiar with—all had similar foundations for their theories of natural law, even though the consequences of their analysis might be different.[52]

David Konig argued that some of the new nation's founding fathers constructed a misleading narrative of legal uniformity to represent the actual variation that existed in the American colonies. It was true that merchants were likely to have more contact with their counterparts in London, Glasgow, or the West Indies than with the other Atlantic colonies, so that they would not be familiar with the diversity of governmental institutions in mainland colonies. The issue of colonial diversity or uniformity became relevant in mobilizing resistance in the 1770s to Parliament's assertion of full sovereignty and compliance with English law. The American Whig view, however, was that the relationship was based on a charter or patent with the subsequent colonial statutes and court practice that had adapted law to peculiar American needs.[53]

Jefferson contended that American legal development from the seventeenth century had been a process of amateurs simplifying English law. The colonists devised a purer, generic law better suited to North American realities. They were "farmers, not lawyers," who devised rules and institutions by right of nature as the product of nature. Jefferson invoked a mythic Saxon past prior to feudalism similar to what the American "farmers" created in reducing American law to its common elements.[54] Konig concluded: "Out of that process emerged a shared foundation of truly American law, rid of English corruptions and based on the universal 'laws of nature & of nature's god.'"[55]

---

[51] RICHARD, *supra* note 12, at 174; *see* JAYNE, *supra* note 8, at 22–29, 39–40, 122–26; MORTON WHITE, THE PHILOSOPHY OF THE AMERICAN REVOLUTION 142–84 (1978); CAROLINE WINTERER, AMERICAN ENLIGHTENMENTS: PURSUING HAPPINESS IN THE AGE OF REASON 15–16, 175–78, 225–26 (2016) [hereinafter WINTERER, ENLIGHTENMENTS].

[52] RICHARD, *supra* note 12, at 174–75. Sidney, for instance, thought the British Parliament, the true representative of the people, could accurately reflect natural law in its enactments. *Id.* at 175.

[53] David Thomas Konig, *Regionalism in Early American Law*, *in* 1 CAMBRIDGE HISTORY, *supra* note 10, at 144, 145–46; *see* Jack P. Greene, *Law and the Origins of the American Revolution*, *in* 1 CAMBRIDGE HISTORY, *supra*, at 447, 469–74 [hereinafter Greene, *Law*] (importance of local law).

[54] Konig, *supra* note 53, at 146–47, quoting Jefferson's 1774 draft of instructions to the Virginia delegates in the Continental Congress.

[55] *Id.* at 147, quoting Jefferson's draft for the Declaration of Independence. Jefferson, the Virginian, changed his opinion on the diversity issue in the 1780s when the problem facing representatives of the new states was to accommodate their distinct concerns in a national constitution to replace the Articles of Confederation. *Id.* at 147–49.

Consequently, popular law could return us to a version of natural law.[56]

The Declaration of Independence explicitly relied upon a natural law and natural rights theory.[57] Historians disagree about whether that matters or not for intellectual history. The substantial majority emphasize the two introductory paragraphs and the concluding paragraph, which contain the natural law language and statements about collective and individual natural rights. A few historians view the Declaration as primarily a legal text and focus on the other paragraphs as a bill of indictment against King George III. Even those concerned with law and constitutionalism recognize that the Declaration's political philosophy was purposely unexceptional. Indeed, this would be necessary to gain acceptance by the 56 delegates to the Continental Congress who signed the document in 1776.[58]

The separation of a new republic from Great Britain, the Declaration stated, "deriving [its] just powers from the consent of the governed," was justified by "the Laws of Nature and of Nature's God."[59] During the Second Continental Congress, the Declaration's drafting committee in June 1776 consisted of Adams, Franklin, Jefferson, Robert Livingston (1746–1813), and Roger Sherman (1721–1793). Jefferson probably wrote the first draft after the committee outlined its desired

---

[56] Some during the revolutionary period understood natural law and rights as a historical process rather than transcendent principles. British policies threatened American rights accepted and practiced for so long that they were the constitution of society. Lester H. Cohen, *The American Revolution and Natural Law Theory*, 39 J. HIST. IDEAS 491, 493, 500–02 (1978). For the perspective of Adams and Wilson on this issue, *see id.* at 497–99.

[57] GREENE, CONSTITUTIONAL ORIGINS, *supra* note 50, at 185–86; Greene, *Law, supra* note 53, at 481; GUMMERE, *supra* note 25, at 97–119. Gummere asserted that the two most important classical ideas relevant to 1776 were Roman natural law, superior to human law, and the Greek concept of a colony substantially independent from its colonizing polity. GUMMERE, *supra*, at 97–98, 110–11, 179–84.

[58] MAIER, *supra* note 8, at xvi–xvii, 245 n.11; REID, *supra* note 3, at 79–81, 84. Most of the substantive edits to Jefferson's draft Declaration concerned the content and desirability of injuries that Congress alleged against King George. MAIER, *supra*, at 236–41. The strongest statement for the minority position was REID, *supra*, at 47–69. Maier tended toward this camp. MAIER, *supra*, at xvii–xix, 206. The majority approach focused on the nature law ideology, although different scholars disagreed about which European or British political philosophers were most influential for crucial delegates to the Congress or debates regarding the Declaration.

Jack Greene extended this dichotomy between an ideological orientation versus a legal and constitutional approach to the origins of the American Revolution in general. Greene, following Reid in his substantial body of research, argued that the colonists had an equally strong legal argument regarding the issues of legislation and taxation separating them from Great Britain as did the imperial jurists. GREENE, CONSTITUTIONAL ORIGINS, *supra* note 50, at ix–xxiii, 149–90; *see, e.g.*, JOHN PHILLIP REID, CONSTITUTIONAL HISTORY OF THE AMERICAN REVOLUTION: THE AUTHORITY OF LAW (1993).

[59] The Declaration of Independence paras. 1, 2 (U.S. 1776). For spelling, punctuation, and capitalization, I rely on the transcription of the stone engraving of the parchment Declaration of Independence on display in the Rotunda at the National Archives Museum. *See* U.S. National Archives, *Declaration of Independence: A Transcription*, https://www.archives.gov/founding-docs. (select Declaration, Read a Transcript). Jefferson's draft was identical, but it did not capitalize "laws of nature" or "nature's god." MAIER, *supra* note 8, at 235–36.

contents. Following discussion by the Congress as a committee of the whole, it adopted the final version on July 4.[60] The ideas in the Declaration's preamble (before the bill of particulars listing King George's "injuries and usurpations" that had established an "absolute Tyranny" over the 13 colonies) were generally known and accepted by the Congress's delegates. Jefferson's task was to formulate these principles into language for a legal document. For the preamble, the draft Virginia Declaration of Rights by George Mason (1725-1792) was most useful.[61]

Where did the asserted right of revolution, justified on reasonable grounds, and the right to create a new sovereign, free, and equal nation, originate?[62] The Declaration (and Jefferson's draft) stated that these collective rights were justified by natural law.[63] In addition, the Declaration continued that individual natural rights were "self-evident, that all men are created equal, that they are endowed by their Creator with certain unalienable Rights, that among these are Life, Liberty and the pursuit of Happiness."[64]

The right of revolution certainly could not come from Blackstone's *Commentaries*.[65] In his public law, Blackstone adopted the principle of parliamentary supremacy, stated that Englishmen owed homage to the English Crown rather than a feudal allegiance to the king's person, and concluded that the Bill of Rights resulting from the Glorious Revolution did not apply to colonists.[66]

---

[60] MAIER, *supra* note 8, at xiii–xiv, 43–46, 97–105, 143, 150. In writing the draft Declaration, Jefferson probably consulted his draft preamble to the Virginia Constitution, which relied on the English Declaration of Rights, as well as George Mason's preliminary version of the Virginia Declaration of Rights. *Id.* at 104–05, 125–26. Most of the debate in Congress about the Declaration's wording concerned the list of grievances against the king. *See id.* at 105–23, 143–50. Congress had affirmed that the united colonies were free and independent states on July 2; it took two more days finally to approve the Declaration. *Id.* at 143.

[61] *Id.* at 122–29, 138–39, 268 n.59; *see* George Mason's Gunston Hall, Home: *Virginia Declaration of Rights—First Draft* (2026 May 1776), https://www.gunstonhall.org (search Virginia Declaration) [hereinafter Mason, *Draft Virginia Declaration*]. Contra JAYNE, *supra* note 8, at 132. For the bill of particulars, Jefferson began with his June 1776 preamble draft to the Virginia Constitution. It opened with a list of King George's "detestable" acts, constituting tyranny, which the Virginia Convention adopted as the first part for its Constitution. MAIER, *supra* note 8, at 48, 55–57, 105–16; *see Virginia Constitution: 29 June 1776* [hereinafter *Virginia Constitution*], *in* 1 THE FOUNDERS' CONSTITUTION 6, 7 (Philip B. Kurland & Ralph Lerner eds., 1987) (paras. 2–23) [hereinafter FOUNDERS' CONSTITUTION].

[62] "We, therefore, the Representatives of the united States of America, in General Congress ... declare, That these United Colonies are, and of Right ought to be Free and Independent States." THE DECLARATION OF INDEPENDENCE para. 33 (U.S. 1776).

[63] MAIER, *supra* note 8, at 132–33. White also referred to natural law influence on Adams, Hamilton, and Wilson. WHITE, *supra* note 51, at 4–5.

[64] THE DECLARATION OF INDEPENDENCE para. 2 (U.S. 1776); see MAIER, *supra* note 8, at 133–36, 189–97. "Unalienable" appeared in the printed version, although the approved Declaration used "inalienable." MAIER, *supra*, at 144, 236. For the source and meaning of the pursuit of happiness, *see* Carl N. Conklin, *The Origins of the Pursuit of Happiness*, 7 WASH. U. JURIS. REV. 195 (2014).

[65] See *supra* note 16 and accompanying text (BLACKSTONE).

[66] BEVERLY ZWEIBEN, HOW BLACKSTONE LOST THE COLONIES: ENGLISH LAW, COLONIAL LAWYERS, AND THE AMERICAN REVOLUTION 117–21 (1990). Ireland, Scotland, and Wales were also outside constitutional protection. *Id.* at 140, n.7. Colonists carried certain private common law from England, but otherwise Parliament could act to legislate in the colonies. *Id.* at 119–20.

Instead, Adams used Roman law, natural law, and *jus gentium* authorities as well as English sources. Some colonial lawyers relied primarily on English history back to the Germanic peoples prior to William's invasion in 1066. A mythic ancient constitution balanced power between the ruler and the ruled. People expressed their will through representatives while the king was subject to customary law. The colonists' English nationality stemmed from ties to the king, but those existed from the feudal concept of allegiance to his person. He could not legislate for them; they had their own assemblies for that. When George III failed in his obligation to protect the colonists in 1775, their only alternative to parliamentary authority, a body excluding their presence, was independence.[67]

Other colonial lawyers, such as Wilson and John Dickinson relied on Jean-Jacques Burlamaqui's *Principes du droit naturel* (1747) and *Principes du droit politique* (1751) in English translation,[68] among other sources, to conclude that Parliament could not legislate for America since colonists did not participate in that body. It did not meet Burlamaqui's first test of government—happiness of the governed. Parliament was a tool for tyranny and they hoped that a mythic image of the king could redress the balance of power.[69]

Twentieth-century historians who have supported the Declaration as an Enlightenment document stating ideological principles typically turned for interpretive meaning to the systematic European political and juristic treatises of the seventeenth and eighteenth centuries as source material familiar to Americans. They also reviewed the writing of Jefferson and other principal delegates to Congress.[70] Allen Jayne divided these scholars between two groups. First, those who preferred the liberal interpretation of Locke or other empiricist or natural law philosophers stated that nations should form government to protect the natural rights of individuals. Second, revisionists minimized Locke's importance and emphasized a communitarian, republican view, promoting virtue and subordinating individual rights and interests to the well-being of the community.[71]

Carl Becker established the first camp with his seminal 1922 book on the Declaration, which argued that Jefferson largely copied Locke.[72] Morton

---

[67] ZWEIBEN, *supra* note 66, at 4–19; *see* J.G.A. POCOCK, THE ANCIENT CONSTITUTION AND THE FEUDAL LAW: A STUDY OF ENGLISH HISTORICAL THOUGHT IN THE SEVENTEENTH CENTURY (revised ed. 1987). Zweiben identified the American lawyers John Dickinson, Thomas Jefferson, and James Wilson. ZWEIBEN, *supra*, at 9–19.

[68] JEAN-JACQUES BURLAMAQUI, 1–2 THE PRINCIPLES OF NATURAL AND POLITIC LAW (Thomas Nugent trans., 2d ed. 1763, reprint 2006).

[69] ZWEIBEN, *supra* note 66, at 86–89, 95, 98–111, 121–39.

[70] JAYNE, *supra* note 8, at 1–2; MAIER, *supra* note 8, at 117, 123–25, 135; *see* WHITE, *supra* note 51, at 3–8; GARRY WILLS, INVENTING AMERICA: JEFFERSON'S DECLARATION OF INDEPENDENCE 109–10, 120–24, 186–87, 365–66 (1978).

[71] JAYNE, *supra* note 8, at 1–6, 41–42.

[72] CARL BECKER, THE DECLARATION OF INDEPENDENCE: A STUDY IN THE HISTORY OF IDEAS 24–37, 53–79 (1922); *see* JAYNE, *supra* note 8, at 41–51.

White considered a wider range of European writers beyond Locke, especially Burlamaqui, whom he called the "founding forefathers."[73] Garry Wills believed the dominant influence on Jefferson came from Scottish philosophers, especially David Hume (1711–1776) and Francis Hutcheson (1694–1746).[74]

Bernard Bailyn's *The Ideological Origins of the American Revolution* (1967) represented the second camp in the form of classical republicanism or civic humanism, showing that Jefferson, Adams, and other delegates at the Second Continental Congress were familiar with the Greek and Roman classics. Nevertheless,

The classics of the ancient world are everywhere in the literature of the Revolution, but are everywhere illustrative, not determinative, of thought. They contributed a vivid vocabulary but not the logic or grammar of thought. . . . More directly influential in shaping the thought of the Revolutionary generation were the ideas and attitudes associated with the writings of Enlightenment rationalism.[75]

In the end, Bailyn found seventeenth- and eighteenth-century radical English Whig and Scottish works most influential for concepts related to mixed government, liberty, and the contractual basis of society and government.[76]

In 1975, J.G.A. Pocock went further in reducing the inspiration from Locke on the American Declaration and Revolution, calling it a myth and quasi-rhetoric. The lasting influence was classical republicanism and renaissance civic humanism (rooted in the Roman Republic as described by Polybius), rejecting English corruption, justifying by legal right the establishment of sovereignty, and using virtue to promote liberty.[77] Both Richard Gummere and Meyer Reinhold believed that of all the founders, Adams and Jefferson best demonstrated their

---

[73] WHITE, *supra* note 51, at 5, 15–19, 23–52, 61–78, 107–27, 136–41, 163–70. Other major "forefathers" included Aquinas, Grotius, Hooker, Hutcheson, and Pufendorf. WHITE, *supra*, at 5; BODENHEIMER, *supra* note 49, at 23–26, 35–39. *See generally* WHITE, *supra*, at 11–272.

[74] WILLS, *supra* note 70, at 192–206, 367–68. *But see* Ronald Hamowy, *Jefferson and the Scottish Enlightenment: A Critique of Garry Wills's Inventing America*, 36 WM & MARY Q. 503–23 (3d series, 1979).

[75] BERNARD BAILYN, THE IDEOLOGICAL ORIGINS OF THE AMERICAN REVOLUTION 26 (enlarged ed. 1992; 1st ed. 1967); *see id.* at 23–29, 48–50. *But see* RICHARD, *supra* note 12, at 1–2, 121. For natural law, Bailyn mentioned Burlamaqui, Grotius, Locke, Pufendorf, and Vattel. BAILYN, *supra*, at 27–29.

[76] BAILYN, *supra* note 75, at xii, 34–54; *see id.* at 55–93; MAIER, *supra* note 8, at 135–38. In 1992, Bailyn published an enlarged edition of *Ideological Origins* that argued that classical republicanism carried forward to influence the state constitutions from 1776 to the 1780s as well as the U.S. Constitution itself. BAILYN, *supra*, at 321–79; *see infra*, pts. D and E (republics and liberty).

[77] J.G.A. POCOCK, THE MACHIAVELLIAN MOMENT: FLORENTINE POLITICAL THOUGHT AND THE ATLANTIC REPUBLICAN TRADITION 506–10, 522–25, 545–49, 551 (1975). Pocock made the case against Locke's impact more strongly in J.G.A. POCOCK, VIRTUE, COMMERCE, AND HISTORY: ESSAYS ON POLITICAL THOUGHT AND HISTORY 120–21, 266–67 (1985), described in JAYNE, *supra* note 8, at 2–4.

humanist classical learning in the revolutionary discourse about republicanism and civic virtue.[78]

In an attempt at synthesis, Carl Richard stated that the Stoic view of natural law and their optimistic image of human nature furnished the underpinning for modern natural law and the liberal idea of social progress. Thus, Stoic natural law was an important bridge between classical republicanism and nineteenth-century liberalism.[79] If one can distinguish between Jefferson in 1776 and Jefferson in 1801, we may see both ends of the bridge—republicanism and mixed government versus the more representative and democratic program of the Republican Party.[80] Alternatively, perhaps a better natural law synthesis is to view classical republicanism as a component of the dominant Lockean political philosophy, even in 1776.[81]

Jayne's research into the source material that Jefferson had available to him in considering what to include in the Declaration revealed that he actively studied the public law of the Scandinavian countries, Poland, and Great Britain. In this comparative law investigation, Jefferson used Locke's *Second Treatise of Government* to support the latter's view of England's ancient constitution, which included the people's authority over the legislature and indirectly the monarch. This natural right, requiring the consent of the people, formed the basis of government in America. In addition, the Declaration took the natural right of government dissolution directly from Locke.[82] As Locke stated, "Self-defence is a part of the Law of Nature; nor can it be denied the Community, even against the King himself."[83]

Jefferson followed Locke's idea that all people by nature are equal and that God created them that way. This status of equality, besides providing people with certain permanent rights such as life, liberty, and the pursuit of happiness, was necessary for Locke's consent theory of government. In addition, it gave ordinary people a basis to resist and ultimately to overthrow a government that

---

[78] GUMMERE, *supra* note 25, at 191–97; REINHOLD, CLASSICK PAGES, *supra* note 25, at 2–3, 21 n.15, 228–31.

[79] RICHARD, *supra* note 12, at 169, 180–81.

[80] *Id.* at 123, 131–34, 157–58, 166–68. *See generally* REASON AND REPUBLICANISM: THOMAS JEFFERSON'S LEGACY OF LIBERTY (Gary L. McDowell & Sharon L. Noble eds., 1997); THOMAS JEFFERSON AND THE POLITICS OF NATURE (Thomas S. Engeman ed., 2000).

[81] MICHAEL P. ZUCKERT, THE NATURAL RIGHTS REPUBLIC: STUDIES IN THE FOUNDATION OF THE AMERICAN POLITICAL TRADITION 4–8, 31–40, 92–96, 208–19, 239–43 (1996).

[82] JAYNE, *supra* note 8, at 42–51. Jayne quoted several sections from Locke's *Second Treatise* (*An Essay Concerning the True Original Extent and End of Civil Government*) for support, using JOHN LOCKE, TWO TREATISES OF GOVERNMENT 356, 362, 380, 398–99, 405, 407–08, 414 (Peter Laslett ed., 2d ed. 1988); *see infra* notes 270–272 and accompanying text (Locke's *Second Treatise*).

[83] LOCKE (Laslett ed.), *supra* note 82, at 420, quoted in JAYNE, *supra* note 8, at 51. Jayne listed several of Locke's general ideas that Jefferson borrowed for the Declaration as well as elements for the list of specific English abuses. JAYNE, *supra*, at 42–51.

did not have their consent.[84] The French physiocrats (*économistes*) in the 1750s and 1760s similarly supported the idea that the immutable laws of nature drove people to live in society and to become enlightened enough to foster happiness.[85] The Italian Beccaria wrote in the same vein to advocate reform in penal law and procedure, a position Jefferson, Madison, and Wythe endorsed in Virginia.[86]

D. A Republican Form of Government

1. The Roman Republic and Early Principate

The United States Constitution guarantees each of its constituent states a "Republican Form of Government,"[87] while most historians describe the Constitution's national government as a federal democratic republic. Sellers analyzed the meaning and influence of republican ideology on the Constitution from the perspectives of historians, lawyers, and classicists. Historians usually tied American republican ideology to British and European examples as part of a historical continuum and de-emphasized what the republican authors wrote. Lawyers focused on the content of the historical materials, possibly as a source of law for new legislation or judicial argument. Classicists, for their part, used the Roman sources to link to Greek politics and tended to overlook the English

---

[84] JAYNE, *supra* note 8, at 109, 112–20, 122–25, 168–70; *see* LOCKE (Laslett ed.), *supra* note 82, at 304; *supra* text accompanying note 64 (Declaration's text). Jayne believed that although Locke was the most influential philosopher on Jefferson for the language "pursuit of happiness," Jefferson's reading of Blackstone, Beccaria, Burlamaqui, and the Scots Henry Home (Lord Kames), David Hume, and Francis Hutcheson, among others, was also useful. JAYNE, *supra*, at 128–38.

[85] WINTERER, ENLIGHTENMENTS, *supra* note 51, at 202–04. The physiocrats' laissez-faire attitude toward trade weakened mercantilism and found a sympathetic response by Adam Smith in his *Wealth of Nations* (1776). Franklin in America had strong ties to the physiocrats. *Id.* at 203–09. In the nineteenth century, Jefferson popularized the free trade notions of the French *idéologues* supporting social happiness in *A Treatise on Political Economy* (1817), the English translation that Jefferson edited of Antoine Louis Claude Destutt de Tracy's work, *Traité de la Volonté et de ses Effets*. *Id.* at 219–21. *Traité* was the final part of *Élémens d'Idéologie*, published in four volumes in France between 1801 and 1815.

[86] Jefferson copied 26 extracts from Beccaria between 1774 and 1776 in his commonplace book. As a member of Virginia's law revision committee, Jefferson in 1778 proposed the Bill for Proportioning Crimes and Punishments in Cases heretofore Capital, which would restrict the use of capital and corporal punishment. Madison, with support from Wythe, introduced the bill to the Virginia House in 1785, which rejected it. The bill followed Beccaria, reflecting his dislike for capital punishment, and adopted the proportionality principle between crime and punishment. Jefferson would have limited the death penalty to the crimes of treason and murder. JOHN D. BESSLER, THE BIRTH OF AMERICAN LAW: AN ITALIAN PHILOSOPHER AND THE AMERICAN REVOLUTION 182–84, 187, 189–90, 205–07 (2014); MARCELLO MAESTRO, CESARE BECCARIA AND THE ORIGINS OF PENAL REFORM 141–42 (1973).

[87] U.S. Const. art. IV, § 4.

common law tradition that complemented the founders' classical eighteenth-century education.[88]

Sellers's aim was to develop all three perspectives and to show that Americans selectively used their European sources to develop a less democratic distinctively American republicanism, somewhat like the senatorial class during the early Roman Principate. The American references to Cicero, Titus Livius (Livy, 59 BCE–12 CE), and Cornelius Tacitus (56–120 CE) were part of their form of political debate before 1789.[89] Most American political thinkers in the period from 1776 to 1789 knew the basic story of the Roman Republic. It began as the *res publica* (implying government in the public interest) when the Roman people replaced the king with two annually elected consuls. The consuls, soon subjected to a written compilation of laws, ruled in the name of the people and the existing senate. The senate proposed new laws, which the people could enact in popular assemblies. "This was America's conception of the Roman constitution at what Americans would have considered the height of Rome's glory, power and virtue. 'Monarchical' consuls balanced an 'aristocratic' senate and 'democratic' people to establish justice and secure the blessings of liberty to all the citizens of Rome."[90]

The success of the Roman example and the prominent place for law provided Americans with a precedent that they could suitably modify to reflect their own social conditions.[91] This suggested a balanced republic, but with a senate that should predominate. Nevertheless, the descent of the Roman Republic into authoritarian rule during the Principate, plus the example of England's failed attempt at republican government, placed an emphasis on the lessons of history and understanding Rome's trajectory. Sellers proposed six required elements that America's framers took from the Roman story. These were (1) the pursuit of justice and the common good, through (2) the rule of law under (3) a mixed and balanced government, consisting of (4) a sovereign people, (5) deliberative senate, and (6) elected magistracy. All American political factions understood this conception of republican government and the desirability of a patrician flavor of ordered liberty and public virtue. However, the factions differed on the

---

[88] SELLERS, AMERICAN REPUBLICANISM, *supra* note 18, at x–xi. Gummere, a classicist, argued that the influence of the classics was at its height when the delegates to the Constitutional Convention assembled. GUMMERE, *supra* note 25, at 173–74. For examples, *see id.* at 174–90.

[89] SELLERS, AMERICAN REPUBLICANISM, *supra* note 18, at xi, 3–4, 20, 28. Sellers stated that he situated his approach in time and place. He limited his analysis of the meaning of republics and republican government to the framers and ratifiers of the American Constitution up to 1789. This permitted use of documents associated with the ratifying conventions in Massachusetts, New York, Pennsylvania, and Virginia. *Id.* at 4–5.

[90] *Id.* at 5–6, 46. The American understanding of the Roman constitution was primarily through the writing of Polybius, who wrote a history of the Roman Republic as a model for the Greeks. It emphasized the importance of checks and balances among the political interests of the one, the few, and the many. *Id.* at 46–50; *see* BEDERMAN, *supra* note 2, at 59–75.

[91] *See* SHALEV, *supra* note 11, at 10–39.

causes of Rome's fall and how best to preserve a republic. Federalists, who drafted the Constitution, most feared the intemperance and passions of the people.[92]

Federalists labeled their principal opponents during the Constitutional Convention Anti-Federalists, some of whom believed that revision of the Articles of Confederation would be adequate. However, most of the state delegates supported working with the Virginia Plan, based on republican principles, which James Madison inspired and Edmund Randolph introduced. Randolph saw the chief danger to the America union in the democratic parts of constitutions. The Virginia Plan suggested that the national legislature should have two chambers, one elected by the people, but the other (a senate) nominated by state legislatures, in addition to an independent judiciary and a national executive. Randolph made it clear that the senate would serve as a check on the more democratic chamber and restrain the "fury of democracy."[93]

2. Republican Images

Sellers built his case for the usefulness of knowledge about Roman legal institutions and laws during the Constitution's adoption and ratification debates on several factors. First, most Americans for and against the Constitution who used historical pseudonyms chose the names of Roman republican heroes, such as Lucius Junius Brutus (co-founder of the Republic, consul 509 BCE), Marcus Junius Brutus (85–42 BCE, conspirator against Julius Caesar), Marcus Porcius Cato (234–149 BCE, censor to restore discipline and virtue), Cicero (consul 63 BCE, legendary jurist and advocate), Lucius Quinctius Cincinnatus (519–430 BCE, senate supporter and virtuous military leader), and Publius (Valerius Publicola, co-founder of the Republic, consul 509 BCE). Those selected from the early Principate were in opposition to the Roman emperor.[94]

Second, federal political iconography was decidedly Roman and mottoes were in Latin. Government symbols reaching the public, such as those on currency, expressed a republican theme or revolutionary struggle in Latin. This shift also occurred with state symbols and slogans, which altered the prior use of English on colonial paper money and coins. The Roman goddess *Libertas* became

---

[92] SELLERS, AMERICAN REPUBLICANISM, *supra* note 18, at 6–7. Sellers was careful to note that Roman republicanism was not the primary influence on the U.S. Constitution, but only that the framers used Roman imagery in their arguments and were impressed with the success of the Roman example. *Id.* at 7.

[93] *Id.* at 58; *see id.* at 58–61; Nicholas P. Cole, *American Bicameralism and the Legacy of the Roman Senate*, 7 CLASSICAL RECEPTIONS J. 79–96 (2015).

[94] SELLERS, AMERICAN REPUBLICANISM, *supra* note 18, at 8–10, 27, 70–75, 90–98, 218, 223–25; *see* SHALEV, *supra* note 11, at 151–87. Hamilton, Madison, and Jay wrote as Publius. SELLERS, *supra*, at 213–14; *see infra* pt. H (Publius).

particularly common, as did the motto *e pluribus unun*. Both early state seals and the Great Seal of the United States (adopted in 1782) expressed republican attitudes in Latin, some derived from Virgil's poetry.[95]

3. The Debate about Republics and Democracies

Delegates at the Constitutional Convention clearly distinguished republicanism and democracy. Federalists supported the senate as a republican protection against the leveling spirit of unchecked democracy. Anti-Federalists felt that mixed government had insufficient corrective power for corruption and that public virtue and civic equality were necessary for America to avoid the fate of the Roman Republic. The two sides agreed on more than what separated them.[96]

Benjamin Rush (1746–1813), who signed the Declaration of Independence and represented Pennsylvania at the Continental Congress, illustrated the dominant Federalist concern with the weak national government in the Articles of Confederation. Rush preferred a stronger central government and feared placing too much power directly in the people. He worried about the Roman Republic's fate due to corruption and *licentia* and wanted the new American Constitution to have protections against the people's own ignorance and licentiousness. In a magazine article, Rush argued, "power should not be *in* the people, but *derived* from them."[97] Cicero and Montesquieu also drew that conclusion from the fall of the Roman Republic and it was a central element of Federalist republicanism.[98]

William Barton (1754–1817), a Philadelphia lawyer who helped to design the nation's great seal, wrote of the Roman Cato's worry about the erosion of *virtus* among the people associated with clashing interests, political parties, and corruption. Like Federalists in general, he wanted a stronger central government to promote the common weal and control selfish state interests. Like the Roman aristocracy, an American senate of worthy leaders through their moral authority could preserve virtue. Adams made similar arguments to support ratification in his defense of the Constitution.[99]

Anti-Federalists also used Roman pseudonyms in their tracts against ratification of the Constitution. However, they followed Tacitus, glossed by Montesquieu, in their principal objection that the Constitution's central

---

[95] SELLERS, AMERICAN REPUBLICANISM, *supra* note 18, at 11–19, 27, 29. Virgil's Latin name was Vergilius Maro. *Id.* at 348. The first committee that designed the national seal included Adams, Franklin, and Jefferson. *Id.* at 18.
[96] *Id.* at 242–46.
[97] *Id.* at 24; *see id.* at 28, 58.
[98] *Id.* at 24, 228.
[99] *Id.* at 24–26, 28–29, 74; *see* ADAMS, 1–3 DEFENCE, *supra* note 45.

government would embrace too large a republic to maintain democratic representation.[100] A remote authority would need military force to implement its policies. In the absence of a bill of rights, people would be without protection from venality and corruption. Anti-Federalists disliked the idea of too much power in an aristocratic senate. A strict separation of powers would better balance government power. They preferred a confederation of republics to represent the local interests of the people.[101]

4. Baron de Montesquieu

Charles-Louis de Secondat, Baron de la Brède et de Montesquieu, published his most noteworthy book, *The Spirit of the Laws*, in 1748.[102] Concerned with understanding different human laws, social systems, and forms of government, he explored their causes and relationship to climate, geography, demography, commerce, and religion. *Spirit of the Laws* was perhaps the finest comparative law book of the eighteenth century and the one most referenced in America. Illustrated by historical examples, he explained how three distinct types of governments might protect themselves from corruption, which would otherwise breed despotism, the worst form of government for its subjects. Relevant to Americans tasked with forming their own legal and political system were Montesquieu's democratic republic and aristocratic republic.[103]

Each governmental structure had a dominant principle and passions that establish it, which if that principle weakens will lead to corruption.[104] In a democratic republic, the people are sovereign, so laws controlling suffrage are

---

[100] SELLERS, AMERICAN REPUBLICANISM, *supra* note 18, at 152–54, 161, 163–68; *Republican Government: Introduction, in* 1 FOUNDERS' CONSTITUTION, *supra* note 61, at 96, 97–98. Montesquieu argued that the contiguity of private and public interests would only be visible in a small state of homogeneous free men. REPUBLICAN GOVERNMENT, *supra*, at 97. Hamilton and Madison responded that enlightened friends of liberty and proper elections could promote virtue and sustain a republic. *Id.* at 98.

[101] SELLERS, AMERICAN REPUBLICANISM, *supra* note 18, at 149, 156–62, 211–12, 231, 241.

[102] MONTESQUIEU, THE SPIRIT OF THE LAWS (Anne M. Cohler et al. ed. & trans., 1989, original French ed., 1748). Thomas Nugent first translated *De l'Esprit des Lois* into English in 1750. For Montesquieu's importance during the American revolutionary period, *see* Paul A. Rahe, *Montesquieu and Constitution of Liberty, in* AMERICAN AND ENLIGHTENMENT CONSTITUTIONALISM 123–55 (Gary L. McDowell & Johnathan O'Neill eds., 2006).

[103] MONTESQUIEU, *supra* note 102, at 8–17, 112–16 [hereinafter also cited in bk. & ch.] (1.3, 2.1–2.3, 8.1, 8.2, 8.5). "The more an aristocracy approaches democracy, the more perfect it will be." *Id.* at 17 (2.3). For the importance and influence of *Spirit of the Laws*, *see* ANNE M. COHLER, MONTESQUIEU'S COMPARATIVE POLITICS AND THE SPIRIT OF AMERICAN CONSTITUTIONALISM 1, 4, 148–69 (1988); RAHE, *supra* note 1, at 40–46, 49–50, 57–59, 152–53; SELLERS, AMERICAN REPUBLICANISM, *supra* note 18, at 20–21, 24, 28, 163–71, 211–14, 228, 244; David S. Clark, *Comparative Legal Systems, in* 1 ENCYCLOPEDIA OF LAW AND SOCIETY: AMERICAN AND GLOBAL PERSPECTIVES 224, 226 (2007). *See generally* PAUL MERRILL SPURLIN, MONTESQUIEU IN AMERICA: 1760–1801 (1940).

[104] MONTESQUIEU, *supra* note 102, at 21, 112 (3.1, 8.1).

fundamental. Its principle is political virtue embracing the rule of law and loyalty to the constitution, the nation, equality, and frugality. This virtue is unnatural to humans, since it requires a preference for public rather than private interests. Citizen education is central to help them identify their larger interests with those of the nation. The nation's territory should be small, making it easier for citizens to connect with others. Property laws should strive to promote equal benefits.[105]

By contrast, for an aristocratic republic, a select group—the nobility, usually in a senate—governs the others. Its principle is moderation; this virtue controls the rulers from oppressing the people and acquiring too much power. Here laws must restrain the rulers, such as short terms of office for magistrates (perhaps one year) or denying them exemptions from taxes or allowing special stipends. Furthermore, nobles should act with modesty to disguise the class structure present in society. Laws should promote equality among the nobility so that it does not lose the spirit of moderation.[106]

The creation of either type of republic would be difficult and unusual. Its legal structure and laws must foster the appropriate virtue and balance government powers so that no single agency subverts its ruling principle. Humans abuse authority when they have it, so power must check power. A legal system could accomplish this by separating the functions of government into legislative, executive, and judicial branches. Merging two powers would subvert political liberty.[107] Madison, for instance, relied in *Federalist* No. 47 on the "celebrated Montesquieu," an "oracle ... in the science of politics," to defend the Constitution's blend of separation of powers with checks and balances.[108] In addition, Montesquieu proposed an alternative form, a confederation, a society of societies. If composed of small republics, it would enjoy the benefits of republics, while the association could have the same defensive force as a large monarchy.[109]

Anti-Federalists such as Mason found much to their liking in *Spirit of the Laws*. They preferred a democratic republic with sovereignty in the people. They identified with the safeguard of annual terms of office for magistrates, restraints on a senate, and the need for vigilance against the natural tendency toward

---

[105] *Id.* at xli-xlii, 10-15, 22-24, 35-36, 38-39, 42-48, 124-25 (foreword, 2.2, 3.3, 4.5, 4.7, 5.2-5.6, 8.16). Frugality limits the desire to possess; otherwise, equality would erode. *Id.* at 43 (5.3-5.4). Law should support frugality and equality via redistribution policies. *Id.* at 44-48 (5.5, 5.6).

[106] *Id.* at 15-17, 24-25, 51-55, 115-16 (2.3, 3.4, 5.8, 8.5); see COHLER, *supra* note 103, at 68-71, 75-85, 95-96. Nobles should not levy taxes nor engage in commerce; those powers should reside in the popular class. MONTESQUIEU, *supra* note 102, at 53 (5.8).

[107] MONTESQUIEU, *supra* note 102, at 155-66 (11.4, 11-6); see COHLER, *supra* note 103, at 104-14. "Political liberty is found only in moderate governments. . . . It is present only when power is not abused, but it has eternally been observed that any man who has power is led to abuse it; he continues until he finds limits. . . . So that one cannot abuse power, power must check power by the arrangement of things." MONTESQUIEU, *supra*, at 155 (11.4).

[108] THE FEDERALIST PAPERS: ALEXANDER HAMILTON, JAMES MADISON, JOHN JAY viii-xi (Clinton Rossiter ed., New American Library, 1961) [hereinafter THE FEDERALIST].

[109] MONTESQUIEU, *supra* note 102, at 131-33 (9.1-9.3).

corruption. Siding with Montesquieu's view that democratic republics must remain small to maintain political virtue, the 13 states individually were already at the limit for viable republics. Matters such as collective defense could be satisfied with a confederation of republics.[110]

5. Diverse Influences

Some scholars, such as Bailyn, have suggested that information available in colonial British American before and after 1776 about the Roman Republic as well as notions of liberty came from English authors writing from the Interregnum (1640–1660) until after the Glorious Revolution (1688). They wrote with a renewed interest in Roman history and may have had an independent influence on American republicanism. Adams himself suggested in a 1776 essay that three English authors—James Harrington (1611–1677), Locke, and Sidney—were important in convincing skeptics of the desirability of republicanism.[111] For constitutionalism at the state and federal levels, Horst Dippel added Blackstone to this list, especially his treatment in the *Commentaries* of checks and balances, judicial independence, impeachment, executive pardon, and certain individual rights.[112] Richard adopted an eclectic approach, finding that the classics directly exerted the formative influence, but also through the mediation of Whig and American perspectives. The classics contributed to mixed government theory and to the founders' view of human nature and the character and role for virtue in civil society.[113]

Gordon Wood had another perspective on the importance of Adams and his writing for the content and meaning of the U.S. Constitution.[114] Although Wood agreed, "no American was more deeply involved in the constitutionalism of the American Revolution," he concluded that it was "Adams's unfortunate

---

[110] SELLERS, AMERICAN REPUBLICANISM, *supra* note 18, at 149–50, 163–64, 168–69; *see supra* text accompanying notes 93, 96, 100–1 (Anti-Federalists).

[111] BAILYN, *supra* note 75, at 35–37, 53–54; SELLERS, AMERICAN REPUBLICANISM, *supra* note 18, at 27–28, 105, 133, 226–28; *see id.* at 34, 118–45; John Adams, *Thoughts on Government: Applicable to the Present State of the American Colonies* (1776) [hereinafter Adams, *Thoughts*], *in* ADAMS, THE REVOLUTIONARY WRITINGS OF JOHN ADAMS 242, 243 (C. Bradley Thompson ed., 2000) [hereinafter ADAMS, REVOLUTIONARY WRITINGS], https://oll.libertyfund.org (extracted from CHARLES FRANCIS ADAMS, 4 THE WORKS OF JOHN ADAMS (1850); select People, then John Adams). Adams also included excerpts from these English authors in *Defence*. 1 ADAMS, DEFENCE, *supra* note 45, at 125–27, 134–38, 148–52, 158–69, 365–71.

[112] Horst Dippel, *Blackstone's* Commentaries *and the Origins of Modern Constitutionalism, in* REINTERPRETING BLACKSTONE'S COMMENTARIES: A SEMINAL TEXT IN NATIONAL AND INTERNATIONAL CONTEXTS 199, 201–14 (Wilfred Prest ed., 2014).

[113] RICHARD, *supra* note 12, at 7–11.

[114] GORDON S. WOOD, THE CREATION OF THE AMERICAN REPUBLIC: 1776–1787, at 567–92 (1969) ("The Relevance and Irrelevance of John Adams").

fate to have missed the intellectual significance of the [Constitution]."[115] Wood believed that Adams clung to the traditional oligarchic eighteenth-century view of politics that no society could ever be truly egalitarian and that he was pessimistic about the difficulties Americans would have to face in its new nation. In short, Adams did not believe that America was exceptional or that Americans had a special public virtue that could sustain the republic. People, he thought, could not alter their basic nature.[116]

Unlike Jefferson and Rush, Adams did not think that education could discipline the people's emotions. Wood agreed with Sellers that for Adams only a balanced constitution could maintain the social order.[117] However, Wood disagreed that Adams was in the mainstream of American constitutional thought in the late 1780s. Wood felt that Adams's *Defence* was rooted in the local opinion of Massachusetts and its 1780 Constitution, which Adams largely drafted, as well as the European political attitudes he absorbed during his nearly ten years holding American overseas positions in France, Holland, and Great Britain. Adams's advocacy of a bicameral legislature with an independent executive sharing lawmaking power coincidentally mirrored the Federalist position.[118]

Sellers replied that Wood's analysis of a democratic republic properly belonged to the events of Jefferson's presidency beginning in 1801. By then, American opinion had turned away from the elitist republicanism informing the 1787 Constitution. The Constitution had adopted the checks and balances Adams supported including an independent executive embodied in the president's office furnished with a legislative veto. In addition, both Federalists and Anti-Federalists praised Adams's *Defence* and recognized its influence on the Constitution.[119]

Finally, Bederman contended that for some elements of what he called the structural constitution, Greek examples were more persuasive to the framers than those of Rome were. This included the place of colonies within an imperial system, since America had just emerged from its colonial relationship with Great Britain. Although most of the American writing on this subject, including its comparison with the British Empire, occurred during the 1760s and 1770s, the topic reoccurred in 1787 and 1788 related to the question of potential powers that the Constitution should grant to the national government. Greek examples

---

[115] *Id.* at 567; *see id.* at 567–69.

[116] *Id.* at 569–70, 572, 575, 588, 592; *see id.* at 48–82, 93–107; SELLERS, AMERICAN REPUBLICANISM, *supra* note 18, at 35. Wood entitled the subchapter "No Special Providence for Americans." WOOD, *supra* note 114, at 569–74.

[117] WOOD, *supra* note 114, at 575–80; *see id.* at 197–214. "Nothing 'but three different orders of men, bound by their interests to watch over each other, and stand the guardians of the laws' could maintain social order." *Id.* (quoting Adams).

[118] *Id.* at 580–86.

[119] SELLERS, AMERICAN REPUBLICANISM, *supra* note 18, at 35, 250 n.16; RICHARD, *supra* note 12, at 235–38 (agreeing with Sellers).

were also important in debating the inadequacies of the pre-convention confederacy.[120]

E. The Sacred Fire of Liberty

The principle of liberty[121] has a long history in philosophy, politics, and theology.[122] It was the core concern of America's founders in their design for a new government. British constitutional scholars and philosophers as well as European political philosophers shared the desire to protect liberty. One of the central purposes of the U.S. Constitution was to "secure the Blessings of Liberty to ourselves and our Posterity."[123] This fulfilled the 13 British colonies' 1776 call for independence from Great Britain. That declaration stated the self-evident premise that the Creator had endowed all men with the unalienable right of liberty. It was the task of government to secure this natural right. The appropriate form of government to accomplish this would derive just powers from consent of the governed—that is, the framers believed, a republic.[124] Thus, Americans knew that they desired a republican liberty.[125]

Sellers maintained that the nature of republican liberty was essentially a Roman idea with its basic formulation in the writing of Cicero and Livy. The idea re-emerged in Renaissance Italy and later in England prior to its impact on American and French revolutionary debate.[126] Montesquieu distinguished

---

[120] BEDERMAN, *supra* note 2, at ix, 50–59, 111–18, 224, 227.

[121] In 1789, George Washington warned the citizenry that their new free government was a departure from history such that "the preservation of the sacred fire of liberty, and the destiny of the republican model of government, are . . . staked on the experiment entrusted to the hands of the American people." George Washington, *The First Inaugural Speech*, *in* GEORGE WASHINGTON: A COLLECTION 460, 462 (William Barclay Allen ed., 1988), *quoted in* SELLERS, AMERICAN REPUBLICANISM, *supra* note 18, at 3; *see* M.N.S. SELLERS, THE SACRED FIRE OF LIBERTY: REPUBLICANISM, LIBERALISM AND THE LAW (1998) [hereinafter SELLERS, LIBERTY]. James Madison drafted Washington's address. LANCE BANNING, THE SACRED FIRE OF LIBERTY: JAMES MADISON AND THE FOUNDING OF THE FEDERAL REPUBLIC vi (1995).

[122] The Roman Emperor Marcus Aurelius (ruled 161–180 CE), for instance, wrote of "the idea of a polity in which there is the same law for all, a polity administered with regard to equal rights and equal freedom of speech, and the idea of a kingly [ruled by reason] government which respects most of all the freedom of the governed." THE MEDITATIONS OF MARCUS AURELIUS: SELECTIONS ANNOTATED & EXPLAINED 211 (George Long trans., Russell McNeil annotator, 2007). *See id.* at 210.

[123] U.S. Const. preamble.

[124] The Declaration of Independence para. 2 (U.S. 1776). For a thorough discussion of the idea and sources of liberty as a natural right, *see* Philip A. Hamburger, *Natural Rights, Natural Law, and American Constitutions*, 102 YALE L.J. 907 (1993).

[125] SELLERS, LIBERTY, *supra* note 121, at 1, 38–40, 73–77, 127; *see* U.S. Const. art. 4, § 4 (Republican Form of Government).

[126] SELLERS, LIBERTY, *supra* note 121, at 2, 11, 23, 30, 32–33, 38–40, 73; *see id.* at 43–46. Adams's *Defence* primarily had source materials concerning Rome, Italy, and England. *Id.* at 17. Sellers defined liberty as the "status of citizens in a republic, whom no one restricted, except to serve the common good." *Id.* at 3. Republicanism implements liberty in resolving conflicts among unfettered individuals

political liberty in its relation to the constitution from liberty's relation to the citizen. For the former, existing only in democracies and republics, it was "the right to do everything the laws permit." For the latter, it consisted of one's opinion of her security, primarily protected by beneficial criminal laws and procedures.[127]

The nostalgia of Roman historians during the Principate portrayed *libertas* associated with *res publica*, protected by annual popular elections, limited terms of office, the rule of law, mixed and balanced government, and a deliberative senate. Liberty and the republic were born together in 509 BCE and died simultaneously in 27 BCE when the senate proclaimed Octavian Augustus the *princeps*. The original meaning of *libertas* was the position of a free (*liber*) person in a political community; it included the rights one could exercise by being a Roman citizen. The history of the nearly 500-year republic unfolded as the proper balance between authority (*auctoritas*) of the *senatus* and sovereignty (*imperium*) or power (*potestas*) of the *populus*. The republic needed senatorial authority to preserve liberty—and avoid license (*licentia*)—without compromising the sovereignty and equal rights (*aequare ius*) of the people.[128]

Americans could only begin to develop republican liberty openly in 1776. Adams provided the most influential early illustration in *Thoughts on Government* directed to Virginia in framing its constitution. Adams's view of liberty as embracing free and happy people connected with his proposal for a republic that included a bicameral legislature, an elected governor to check the legislature, an independent judiciary, and liberal funding for general education.[129] Adams asserted that the "happiness of the individual is the end of man. . . . [T]he form of government which communicates ease, comfort, security, or, in one word, happiness to the greatest number of persons, and in the greatest degree, is the best."[130] He concluded his short essay, "A constitution founded on these [republican] principles introduces knowledge among the people, and inspires them with a conscious dignity becoming freemen."[131]

---

by appealing to the common good or by supporting a judicial system to adjudicate difficult cases based on law. *Id.*

[127] MONTESQUIEU, *supra* note 102, at 155 (11.3); SELLERS, AMERICAN REPUBLICANISM, *supra* note 18, at 169–70; *see* MONTESQUIEU, *supra*, at 154–56, 187–207 (11.1–11.4, 12.1–12.21); Cohler, *supra* note 103, at 98–104. Montesquieu also discussed liberty in Rome. MONTESQUIEU, *supra*, at 170–86 (11.12–11.19).

[128] SELLERS, LIBERTY, *supra* note 121, at 7–11. In addition to the senate and popular assemblies, magistrates acted in the name of the senate and the people of Rome, the *senatus populusque Romanus* (SPQR). *Id.* at 8–9.

[129] *Id.* at 23–25, 27, 67–69, 75; *see* Adams, *Thoughts, supra* note 111, at 242–43, 245–48. A people cannot be free or happy if the government is in a single representative assembly. Adams, *Thoughts, supra*, at 244. Thompson (the editor) suggested that *Thoughts* also influenced the constitutions of Massachusetts, New Jersey, New York, and North Carolina. *Id.* at 242.

[130] Adams, *Thoughts, supra* note 111, at 243.

[131] *Id.* at 247.

By 1787, the most persuasive advocate for republican liberty was Madison. Writing as Publius in letters to the public printed by New York newspapers during the Constitution's ratification debates, Madison supported the Constitution's adoption of representation as a republican solution to turbulent democracies of the past. It would prevent the domination of any single locality and encourage the common good. Short terms of office and numerous officeholders could prevent any individual or group from developing a monopoly of power, the very embodiment of tyranny. One should divide and balance government powers and be able to check each one to guarantee liberty. A bicameral legislature would guard against each chamber's ambition and corruption.[132]

F. John Adams

By 1751, Adams had learned enough Latin and Greek from tutors and the Braintree Latin grammar school to pass the Harvard entrance examination at age 15. For four years at Harvard, besides more Latin and Greek, he studied rhetoric, logic, natural philosophy (science), and moral philosophy. Shortly after Adams graduated in 1755, he chose law as a career and apprenticed for two years until 1758.[133] Jeremiah Gridley, a leading Boston lawyer, sponsored Adams for admittance to the court of common pleas in Suffolk County, encouraged him to learn Roman civil law, natural law, and admiralty, and provided a library full of the books he would need. Adams's use of this knowledge in his law practice in Braintree and legal and political writing was extensive during the colonial period, which would make him the most important early American legal comparatist.[134] Adams's reference to foreign law in his briefs, letters, essays, pamphlets, and books continued after 1776, both in his law practice to represent clients and in his activity to promote American constitutionalism.

In 1779, the Town of Braintree selected Adams as a delegate to the Massachusetts state constitutional convention. The 250 delegates assembled in Cambridge, where they chose Adams for a drafting committee of 30. It, in turn, created a subcommittee of three, which gave Adams the task of writing the constitution. Since he could work at home, he had the comfort of his extensive library, including many books on comparative law and political theory. Adams reread some of his earlier writing, such as *Thoughts on Government*, studied the

---

[132] SELLERS, LIBERTY, *supra* note 121, at 2, 70–72, 75–76; *see The Federalist* Nos. 10, 14, 20, 37, 47, 51, 62, 63 (Madison, except No. 20 co-authored with Hamilton).

[133] RICHARD, *supra* note 12, at 19, 21; John Adams Historical Society, *Education*, http://www.john-adams-heritage.com/early-life-education; *see* DAVID MCCULLOUGH, JOHN ADAMS 33–44 (2001). At Harvard, Adams discovered Cicero and Sallust, two of his favorite classical writers. RICHARD, *supra*, at 21, 25.

[134] *See* RICKS, *supra* note 6, at 41–64, 107–20; ch. 2, pt. F (John Adams).

state constitutions already approved, and prepared his draft constitution in a few weeks.[135]

The drafting committee with two minor additions sent Adams's draft to the convention, which after several changes approved it in 1780.[136] After a preamble reciting reliance on the people's natural rights, the Constitution's part 1 set out a declaration consisting of 30 articles of specific rights and protections that the people of Massachusetts retained. Article 1 stated, "All men are born free and equal, and have certain natural, essential, and unalienable rights, among which may be reckoned the right of enjoying and defending their lives and liberties; that of acquiring, possessing, and protecting their property; in fine, that of seeking and obtaining their safety and happiness."[137] Adams derived several provisions in part I's "Declaration of the Rights of the Inhabitants" from other state constitutions. For instance, he borrowed freedom of speaking (removed by the convention delegates) and liberty of the press from Pennsylvania. Many of the rights listed found their way into the first eight amendments to the national Constitution in 1791, which we explore later.[138] Adams also included in the Declaration as rights of the people the principle of separation of powers and components for the rule of law.[139]

---

[135] McCullough, *supra* note 133, at 220–21; Adams, *Thoughts*, *supra* note 111. Adams initially wrote *Thoughts* as a letter in response for assistance with state constitution drafting. Wythe of Virginia and others prevailed on Adams to publish it as a pamphlet. McCullough, *supra*, at 101.

[136] John Adams, *The Report of a Constitution, or Form of Government, for the Commonwealth of Massachusetts* [hereinafter Adams's Mass. Const.], *in* Adams, Revolutionary Writings, *supra* note 111, at 249; McCullough, *supra* note 133, at 224.

[137] *Massachusetts Constitution: 2 Mar. 1780, in* 1 Founders' Constitution, *supra* note 61, at 11. Adams's draft declaration had 31 articles. The convention eliminated his article 14 formulating a general due process clause for "life, liberty, or estate." Adams's Mass. Const., *supra* note 136, at 253. In article 1, Adams had used the phrase "born equally free and independent," a clause he took from Mason's draft Virginia Declaration of Rights. The convention delegates preferred Jefferson's slightly different idea of "created equal" from the Declaration of Independence. Adams's Mass. Const., *supra*, at 251; McCullough, *supra* note 133, at 221, 224.

[138] McCullough, *supra* note 133, at 221–22, 224; *see infra* pt. I (Bill of Rights). The Declaration contained free elections (art. 9); the right of private property, except for public use upon payment of reasonable compensation (art. 10); no denial or delay of justice (art. 11); a privilege against self-incrimination and rights to prosecution notice, a defense assisted with counsel, confrontation of adverse witnesses, and jury trial in capital or infamous cases (art. 12); the right against unreasonable search and seizure of one's person, house, papers, or possessions, plus search warrants that required specificity and an officer's oath (art. 14); the right to a civil jury (art. 15); liberty of the press (art. 16); a right to keep and bear arms for the common defense (art. 17); and rights to peaceful assembly and petition government (art. 19); no excessive bail or cruel or unusual punishment (art. 26); and no obligation to quarter soldiers in one's houses during peace (art. 27). Massachusetts Constitution, *supra* note 137, at 12–13.

Adams omitted the article 10 public use exception. The convention deleted Adams's article 12 for speedy and public trial by an impartial jury requiring unanimity to convict, which Adams had extended broadly to "any crime." It also dropped Adams's freedom to speak and write (in his art. 17). Adams's Mass. Const., *supra* note 136.

[139] Adams's Mass. Const., *supra* note 136, at 254 (arts. 30–31); Massachusetts Constitution, *supra* note 137, at 13–14. The rule of law would be supported by the right to require government officials properly to perform their duties under the constitution (art. 18); prohibition of government suspension, except by the legislature (art. 20); legislator immunity from judicial proceedings for conduct in

Adams wrote a series of letters in 1786 and 1787 (originally published in London, then reprinted in Boston, New York, and Philadelphia) in three volumes as *A Defence of the Constitutions of Government*.[140] It was the most comprehensive American sourcebook and commentary for illustrations of republican institutions and attitudes available to those for and against the U.S. Constitution. Volume one, the most important of the three volumes, arrived from London in time for the Philadelphia Convention. It included descriptions of the classical republics of Greece and Rome, philosophical opinion from that time, and subsequent analysis and comment. In addition, it sketched the Swiss, Dutch, and northern Italian republics (among some others). Since Adams was popular among many of the patriots, some of his views prevailed at the Constitutional Convention.[141]

Defence divided republics into three main categories—democratic, aristocratic, and monarchical. Adams believed in the progressive improvement of human society over the preceding few centuries (documented primarily with European examples) and preferred a balanced or mixed political system. He set out his central views in the first volume's 26-page preface. Adams began with the basic spirit of republics, which comprised the rule of law, checks and balances, property security, religious toleration, and personal liberty. Even monarchies could become "republican" by adopting checks and balances.[142]

---

the legislature (art. 21); prohibition of ex post facto laws (art. 24) and martial law for civilians, except as set by the legislature (art. 28); an impartial and independent judiciary in which judges have "honorable salaries" and hold office while they "behave themselves well" (art. 29); and separation of three branches of government (art. 30). *Id.*

[140] 1-3 ADAMS, DEFENCE, *supra* note 45; *see* SELLERS, AMERICAN REPUBLICANISM, *supra* note 18, at 33.

[141] SELLERS, AMERICAN REPUBLICANISM, *supra* note 18, at 33-34, 38, 57, 63-65, 220. Volumes 2 and 3, which continued with Italian republics and included commentary on the English civil war and interregnum, was available during the state ratification debates. *Id.* at 34, 38-39. In the preface to volume 1, Adams metaphorically made the traditional argument supporting the value of comparative law.

> Called without expectation... to erect suddenly new systems of laws for their future government, [delegates of the American people] adopted the method of a wise architect, in erecting a new palace for the residence of [their] sovereign. They determined to consult... writers of reputation in the art; to examine the most celebrated buildings,... compare these with the principles of writers; and enquire how far both the theories and models were founded in nature.... [W]hen this should be done, as far as their circumstances would allow, [they would] adopt the advantages, and reject the inconveniences, of all.

1 ADAMS, DEFENCE, *supra* note 45, at xvii.

[142] SELLERS, AMERICAN REPUBLICANISM, *supra* note 18, at 34, 36, 233-35; *see* 1 ADAMS, DEFENCE, *supra* note 45, at i-ii, xxi-xxii; *Balanced Government: Introduction*, in 1 FOUNDERS' CONSTITUTION, *supra* note 61, at 336, 337-38, 356. *See generally* LUKE MAYVILLE, JOHN ADAMS AND THE FEAR OF AMERICAN OLIGARCHY (2016); RICHARD ALAN RYERSON, JOHN ADAMS' REPUBLIC: THE ONE, THE FEW, AND THE MANY (2016).

The checks and balances of republican governments have been in some degree adopted by the courts of princes. By the erection of various tribunals, to register the laws, and exercise the judicial power—by indulging the petitions and remonstrances of subjects, until by habit they are regarded as rights—a [control] has been established over ministers of state, and the royal councils, which approaches, in some degree, to the spirit of republics. Property is generally secure, and personal liberty seldom invaded.[143]

Adams cited the Greek historian, Herodotus (484–425 BCE), for a discussion of the nature of monarchy, aristocracy, and democracy with the advantages and disadvantages of each as well as various mixtures of the three types. Adams believed this understanding was as thorough for the Greeks in the fifth century BCE and the Romans during the Republic as during his era. A free government meant one "of laws and not of men," which would promote the "happiness of life, and even the further progress of improvement in education and society."[144]

Adams felt a simple democracy was inappropriate for the United States since compared to Swiss cantons or Greek city states it was heterogeneous, populous, and rapidly growing. He proposed separating the three functional branches of government, making them equal in status, and creating a system of checks and balances. The monarchical element would be in the executive, the aristocratic element in the lawmaking senate (which could also advise ministers), and the democratic element in the larger legislative assembly with representatives directly chosen by the people. This mixture would protect liberty and people's rights.[145]

Defence was a refinement of Roman ideas and institutions, particularly as Cicero and Tacitus described them. Government should be an empire of laws (*imperium legum*). The preferred republic for America required a balanced constitution with a bicameral legislature to represent democratic and aristocratic features in society. People must act for the common good and share a sense of

---

[143] 1 ADAMS, DEFENCE, *supra* note 45, at i.

[144] *Id.* at ii. Adams included the same ideas in his draft Massachusetts Constitution. Article 30 of the final Declaration of Rights, after requiring separation of powers, concluded, "to the end it may be a government of laws and not of men." Massachusetts Constitution, *supra* note 137, at 14. Adams in his draft had put that language in the second sentence of part II's Frame of Government, immediately following the Declaration of Rights. Adams's Mass. Const., *supra* note 136, at 255.

[145] 1 ADAMS, DEFENCE, *supra* note 45, at iii–v, viii, x, xiii; *see* MCCULLOUGH, *supra* note 133, at 375–78, 406; SELLERS, AMERICAN REPUBLICANISM, *supra* note 18, at 36–38. Adams relied substantially on Cicero for the three governmental powers, with emphasis on the legislature through laws to protect property and provide the rules for justice. This was the essence of a republic. 1 ADAMS, DEFENCE, *supra*, at xix–xxii; *see* MCCULLOUGH, *supra*, at 375; SELLERS, *supra*, at 36–37, 90–99.

justice. The Roman Republic failed when the popular assemblies gained too much power, which permitted tyranny to prevail.[146]

G. James Wilson

James Wilson, born in Scotland in 1742, first learned Latin and Greek in grammar school. He then studied for five years those languages and other traditional university subjects for that era, including moral and political philosophy. Scottish Enlightenment writers were a prominent part of that curriculum. In 1765, at the age of 23, Wilson immigrated to Philadelphia, where he tutored students in Latin at the Academy and College of Philadelphia.[147] After a year, Wilson began a legal apprenticeship with John Dickinson (1732–1808), who became a major political figure during the revolutionary period. Admitted to the Philadelphia bar in 1767, Wilson set up a successful law practice in Reading and later in Carlisle. In Carlisle, he became involved in politics and in 1774, published a tract challenging British parliamentary authority in the colony, which established him as Whig leader. In 1775, voters elected Wilson to the Pennsylvania assembly, which in turn sent him to the Continental Congress, where he signed the Declaration of Independence in 1776.[148]

In 1778, Wilson moved to Philadelphia. Four years later, the Pennsylvania legislature selected him as a delegate to the Continental Congress, where he served intermittently through 1786. As a Pennsylvania delegate to the 1787 Constitutional Convention to remedy deficiencies in the national government, Wilson played an active role. The large-state delegates supported the May 1787

---

[146] SELLERS, AMERICAN REPUBLICANISM, *supra* note 18, at 38, 40. Adams summarized the eventual structure of the U.S. Constitution with a president, senate, and democratic assembly of representatives. *Id.* at 38.

[147] William Ewald, *James Wilson and the Drafting of the Constitution*, 10 U. PA. J. CONST. L. 901, 902–04 (2008) [hereinafter Ewald, *James Wilson*]; *id., James Wilson and the Scottish Enlightenment*, 12 U. PA. J. CONST. L. 1053, 1055–58, 1060–64, 1112 (2010); *see* CHARLES PAGE SMITH, JAMES WILSON: FOUNDING FATHER: 1742–1798, at 1–89 (1956). Scots schooled in Scotland also taught Jefferson and Hamilton. Roman law was at the heart of the Scottish Enlightenment, connecting Scotland to the universities in continental Europe. Ewald, *Scottish Enlightenment*, *supra*, at 1058–60, 1092–1101, 1105–06, 1108, 1113–14; *see supra* note 48 and accompanying text (Jefferson).

Franklin wrote a constitution for the academy in 1749 and the first class graduated in 1757. Nine men who signed the Declaration of Independence were either alumni or trustees of the college, including Franklin and Wilson. *The Early Years: The Charity School, Academy and College of Philadelphia* 2–3 (1972), https://archives.upenn.edu (search "early years").

[148] Kermit L. Hall, *Introduction, in* 1 COLLECTED WORKS OF JAMES WILSON xiii, xvi–xvii (Kermit L. Hall & Mark David Hall eds., 2007); Ewald, *James Wilson, supra* note 147, at 904–05; *see* Wilson, *Considerations on the Nature and Extent of the Legislative Authority of the British Parliament, 1774, in* COLLECTED WORKS OF JAMES WILSON, *supra*, at 3–31 (originally written in 1768). Jefferson copied extracts from *Considerations* into his commonplace book, which may have influenced his opening paragraphs in the Declaration. Ewald, *supra*, at 904–05. The 2007 Hall edition of *Collected Works* is also available at https://oll.libertyfund.org (select People, then James Wilson).

Virginia Plan and its 15 resolutions through mid-June, after which, in July, the small states reached a compromise for equal state representation in the senate. At that point, the convention elected five members, four of whom were lawyers, to the Committee of Detail. Its mandate was to prepare the Constitution's draft text based on decisions made in the previous two months. Wilson was the dominant figure among the four lawyers—three of whom were also destined to sit on the U.S. Supreme Court.[149]

William Ewald, in his careful research on Wilson, concentrated on the period of the committee's work from late July to early August 1787. Ewald argued that the committee engaged in substantial rewriting of the convention's decisions for the draft it presented on August 6, followed by a month of debate over final details, stylistic polishing, signing, and ratification. Wilson continued to contest committee provisions he disliked, sometimes successfully, such as a property qualification for members of Congress.[150]

Ewald concluded that Madison and Wilson were the two dominate figures at the convention and, in general, were in close alliance for the major issues debated in Philadelphia. Furthermore, Wilson was not a mere follower of Madison, but diverged on some important matters, such as the selection and nature of the national executive and senate as well as the judiciary's jurisdiction. Finally, the two lawyers' constitutional theories were distinct. Madison favored a strong and virtuous senate, the central institution in the national government, while Wilson preferred popular sovereignty and the functional separation of government tasks. For this era, Wilson had a deep conception of human equality, disfavoring property or other qualifications, such as a long period of citizenship for government office. Unlike Madison, Wilson rejected the notion that the senate protected the interest of states, which Wilson called "imaginary beings," basing his view of democracy as one founded on popular sovereignty.[151]

Wilson was the principal Federalist supporter in Pennsylvania for ratification of the 1787 Constitution, the first state to call a convention for that purpose. On October 6, 1787, his Philadelphia "state house yard" speech, reprinted in 34 newspapers and distributed as a pamphlet throughout the United States, set the terms of debate with Anti-Federalists.[152] Wilson aimed to refute three

---

[149] Ewald, *James Wilson*, supra note 147, at 906, 910–12, 934–35, 937–40, 982–84; Kermit Hall, supra note 148, at xviii–xx.

[150] Ewald, *James Wilson*, supra note 147, at 936–38, 983–1003. *See generally id., The Committee of Detail*, 28 CONST. COMMENT. 197 (2012). The August 6 committee draft was three times the length of the convention resolutions. Ewald, *James Wilson*, supra, at 993.

[151] Ewald, *James Wilson*, supra note 147, at 962–67, 970, 973, 977, 996–1009. For Wilson's theory of popular sovereignty and its origin in the Scottish Enlightenment, *see* Ian Bartrum, *James Wilson and the Moral Foundations of Popular Sovereignty*, 64 BUFF. L. REV. 225, 231–35, 256–300 (2016).

[152] 2 THE DOCUMENTARY HISTORY OF THE RATIFICATION OF THE CONSTITUTION 56, 128 (Merrill Jensen ed., 1976) (Pennsylvania) [hereinafter 2 DOCUMENTARY HISTORY OF RATIFICATION]; *James Wilson's State House Yard Speech October 6, 1787* [hereinafter *Wilson's State House Yard Speech*], in 1 COLLECTED WORKS OF JAMES WILSON, supra note 148, at 171–77. The speech is also available in 2

major Anti-Federalist arguments against ratification. First, the document did not include a bill of rights. Second, there was too much power in an "aristocratic" senate. Third, reflecting Montesquieu's view that republics were only viable for a small territory and homogeneous population, the national government's sovereignty would cover too much area and too many people. Its dominance, the Anti-Federalists believed, would lead to the annihilation of the states, which would become mere "corporations."[153]

Wilson's response was, first, that popular sovereignty and the national government's checks, balances, and limited powers obviated the need for a bill of rights. Later, he added that enumeration was susceptible to the argument that those natural rights not on a list did not receive protection or that they did not even exist. Second, the federal Senate could not act alone; it would have a legislative check by the more democratic House of Representatives and an executive check by the president. Third, the new national government would still be "confederated," since local power remained dominant. The states retained all three branches of government, chose the president and members of the Senate, and determined the qualifications of the federal electorate. Furthermore, the people themselves voted for their representatives to the legislative House.[154]

At the Pennsylvania ratification convention, Wilson's stature in debate was dominant since he was the only one who had participated in the Constitution's drafting. Wilson expanded on the views expressed in his statehouse yard speech, repeatedly referring to the writings of Montesquieu and occasionally Tacitus related to republics.[155] For instance, Wilson contended that Montesquieu

DOCUMENTARY HISTORY OF RATIFICATION, supra, at 167–72. Bailyn contended that Wilson's speech was a more influential Federalist statement than The Federalist. Bailyn, supra note 75, at 328.

[153] SELLERS, AMERICAN REPUBLICANISM, supra note 18, at 172–73; Wilson's State House Yard Speech, supra note 152, at 172–75; see BEDERMAN, supra note 2, at 85–90. Wilson also explained why the Constitution lacked civil jury trial protection, provided for a standing army during peacetime, and authorized direct taxation. Wilson's State House Yard Speech, supra, at 173–75. In arguing against including a bill of rights, Wilson contended that even the European jurists Grotius, Pufendorf, and Vattel could not construct a complete list of human and citizen rights. James Wilson, Convention Debates on 4 December [hereinafter Wilson, 4 December], in 2 DOCUMENTARY HISTORY OF RATIFICATION, supra note 152, at 465, 470.

[154] Kermit Hall, supra note 148, at xxii; SELLERS, AMERICAN REPUBLICANISM, supra note 18, at 173; Wilson's State House Yard Speech, supra note 152, at 172–75. Wilson concluded his speech: "I am satisfied that any thing nearer to perfection could not have been accomplished.... [I]t is the best form of government which has ever been offered to the world." Id. at 176–77.

[155] Ewald, James Wilson, supra note 147, at 913; SELLERS, AMERICAN REPUBLICANISM, supra note 18, at 173–74. The classical references are evident in Wilson's speech on 24 November 1787. Numerous newspapers from northern states published a summary, which also circulated widely in pamphlet form. It evoked a variety of partisan responses that contributed to the ratification debates in several states. James Wilson's Speech on 24 November [hereinafter Wilson, 24 November], in 2 DOCUMENTARY HISTORY OF RATIFICATION, supra note 152, at 339–40, 343, 354, 363.

Wilson prepared an outline of objections and support for the Constitution prior to his convention speech on December 4. On his list of "reasons for adoption," Wilson cited Montesquieu for six

suggested that a "federal republic" might be the solution for a large polity that consolidated distinct societies. Wilson found the political configurations of German states, Swiss cantons, United Netherlands, and some classical examples either too loosely confederated or lacking reliable information to serve as useful illustrations for America.[156] He argued, "representation ... is the true chain between the people and those to whom they entrust the administration of the government."[157] The proposed Constitution's popular sovereignty and division of power between the states and national government would facilitate harmony among diverse peoples and an aggregation of liberty.[158]

Wilson then explored what he considered the four options available to the delegates at Philadelphia drafting the Constitution. Rejecting a consolidated empire, division into 13 independent commonwealths, or separation into two or more confederacies, he argued that the Constitution wisely formed a "comprehensive federal republic."[159] A mixed government, as supported by Tacitus and Montesquieu, protected against tyranny as well as licentiousness. The people, the "fountain of government," created their states as well as the separate branches of national government to promote their own liberty and happiness.[160] The Constitution explicitly derived every kind of authority by representation from the people. Checks and balances were more important to republican liberty than separation of powers alone. Thus, a unicameral legislature could foster licentiousness or tyranny; the Constitution's bicameral legislature provided a middle course between those dangers.[161]

The years 1789 to 1792 were busy for Wilson. President Washington appointed him to the U.S. Supreme Court in 1789. He was the principal architect of the new Pennsylvania Constitution of 1790 as well. In that year, trustees at the College of Philadelphia chose Wilson to present a series of lectures on law. More significant

provisions in the Constitution and Burlamaqui for one provision. Wilson, *4 December, supra* note 153, at 485–86, 493.

[156] SELLERS, AMERICAN REPUBLICANISM, *supra* note 18, at 174–75, 177–78; Wilson, *24 November, supra* note 155, at 341–43, 352–53.
[157] Wilson, *24 November, supra* note 155, at 344.
[158] SELLERS, AMERICAN REPUBLICANISM, *supra* note 18, at 174–75, 177–78; Wilson, *24 November, supra* note 155, at 345.
[159] Wilson, *24 November, supra* note 155, at 345; *see id.* at 345–46, 349, 357–58, 362–63. Wilson pointed to the failure of imperial Rome as a consolidated empire. *Id.* at 345.
[160] SELLERS, AMERICAN REPUBLICANISM, *supra* note 18, at 175; Wilson, *4 December, supra* note 153, at 472; *see* SELLERS, *supra*, at 176–78; Wilson, *24 November*, supra note 155, at 361–62. Wilson referred to Locke for the theory of sovereignty residing with the people. Wilson, *4 December, supra*, at 472. "Liberty has a formidable enemy on each hand; on one there is tyranny, on the other licentiousness. In order to guard against the latter, proper powers ought to be given to government; in order to guard against the former, those powers ought to be properly distributed." James Wilson, *Convention Debates on 28 November*, *in* 2 DOCUMENTARY HISTORY OF RATIFICATION, *supra* note 152, at 382, 400.
[161] SELLERS, AMERICAN REPUBLICANISM, *supra* note 18, at 174–78. The Constitution guaranteed every state a "republican form of government." *Id.* at 176.

than his few opinions on the Court were these *Lectures on Law*, over 1,100 pages of text in the 1804 edition, which he presented from 1790 to 1792. In 1792, the college became the University of Pennsylvania, which appointed Wilson its first professor in the Law Department.[162]

Pennsylvania was the first state to adopt a constitution after the Declaration of Independence. Thoroughly democratic, the 1776 Constitution contained no elements of "aristocracy." There were no effective checks on the powerful unicameral assembly, such as an upper legislative chamber, executive veto, or judicial review, which could be impediments to the people's will. The franchise to elect legislators to one-year terms had no property requirement.[163]

The Pennsylvania Constitution was controversial from the beginning, not only at home but also in other states. By 1777, both Dickinson and Rush attacked it in pamphlets. Adams, in his *Thoughts on Government*, proposed instead a balanced government of checks and balances with a bicameral legislature and property requirements for voting and holding office. Wilson came out publicly against the Pennsylvania Constitution after the mob violence during the 1779 Fort Wilson Incident. These framers and their writings were influential at the Philadelphia Convention in 1787 to create a different framework for government.[164]

In 1789, the Pennsylvania assembly called for a convention to replace the 1776 Constitution with a new model. The delegates succeeded in 1790, substituting a governor with veto power for the weak plural executive, a bicameral legislature for the single assembly, and direct popular election of the governor and both legislative chambers. Wilson was the leader of the victorious Republicans. He allied with the opposing Constitutionalists to support the popular election for members of the senate.[165]

---

[162] Ewald, *James Wilson, supra* note 147, at 913–14, 927; Kermit Hall, *supra* note 148, at xx; Mark David Hall, *Bibliographical Essay: History of James Wilson's Law Lectures*, *in* 1 COLLECTED WORKS OF JAMES WILSON, *supra* note 148, at 402–03; *see* 1 *id.* at 427–746; 2 *id.* 7–315. Wilson intended to publish these lectures as a treatise on American law. He died before that happened, but his son, Bird Wilson, edited and published them in 1804. Mark Hall, *supra*, at 401–04, 407–11; *see* 1–3 THE WORKS OF THE HONOURABLE JAMES WILSON (Bird Wilson ed., 1804).

[163] Robert F. Williams, *The State Constitutions of the Founding Decade: Pennsylvania's Radical 1776 Constitution and Its Influences on American Constitutionalism*, 62 TEMP. L. REV. 541, 547, 550, 554, 556–57, 582 (1989). Pennsylvania's Constitution contained a Declaration of Rights, patterned after that of Virginia. The second part of the Constitution was a frame of government. Duquesne University School of Law, *Constitution of the Commonwealth of Pennsylvania—1776*, https://www.paconstitution.org (select Texts, then 1776) [hereinafter Pennsylvania Constitutions]; Williams, *supra*, at 555. The other 12 state constitutions had a property qualification for those elected to public office. Joseph S. Foster, *The Politics of Ideology: The Pennsylvania Constitutional Convention of 1789-90*, 59 PENN. HIST. 122, 123–24 (1992).

[164] Williams, *supra* note 163, at 558–69, 574–76, 580, 583–84; *see supra* note 111 and text accompanying notes 129–131, 135 (*Thoughts on Government*).

[165] Foster, *supra* note 163, at 122–25, 127, 129, 131–32, 137. Wilson's backing for popular election to the senate failed to gain adoption in the 1787 U.S. Constitution. *Id.* at 129.

The convention elected a Committee of Nine, including Wilson, to draft the constitution. The initial effort failed, but the delegates then favored Wilson's principle of popular sovereignty for wide popular authority over three independent government branches, including the judiciary, as well as the need for a bicameral legislature. Sovereignty resided in the people, who could assign it to dual governments, that is, a state and national government. Because judges were agents of the people, they could nullify unconstitutional statutes, but only in a constrained manner since they should rely upon constitutional text and structure.[166]

Wilson's philosophy of law, which owed much to the Scottish Enlightenment and to Locke, guided the substance of his 1790–1792 *Lectures*. Wilson quoted and cited most commonly the Scots Hutcheson and Thomas Reid; the Englishmen Richard Hooker, Locke, and Blackstone; and the continental Europeans Hugo Grotius and Samuel von Pufendorf.[167] In addition, he referred to the writing of the Romans Cicero, Justinian, Pliny the Younger, and Tacitus and the historians of Greek and Roman law and politics Thomas Bever, Edward Gibbon, John Gillies, John Potter, Charles Rollin, and Ubbo Emmius. Finally, he cited continental jurists and philosophers Jean-Jacques Barthélemy, Cesare Beccaria, Jacques Pierre Brissot, Burlamaqui, Jean Domat, Johann Heineccius, Montesquieu, Jean-Jacques Rousseau, and Vattel.[168] Aaron Knapp maintained that Wilson's *Lectures* gave birth to American jurisprudence and served as an important rejoinder to the influential ideas in Publius's *The Federalist*.[169]

In Wilson's introductory lecture, after referring to Rome and Greece, he stated, "Were I called upon for my reasons why I deem so highly of the American character, I would assign them in a very few words: . . . the love of liberty, and the love of law."[170] This lecture proposed a plan of study for legal education, a science of law, proceeding from the general to the specific. Wilson contended that the principles of American constitutions and laws were materially better than those principles of England, and that American legal material should form the basis for legal education. He disagreed with Blackstone's dismissal of popular sovereignty, embraced in America. "[T]he supreme or sovereign power of the society

---

[166] *Id.* at 129–31, 133–34, 140; Kermit Hall, *supra* note 148, at xx–xxiv. The Constitution's article 9, section 2, stated, "That all power is inherent in the people, and all free governments are founded on their authority, and instituted for their peace, safety and happiness." Pennsylvania Constitutions, *supra* note 163 (select Texts, then 1790).

[167] Mark Hall, *supra* note 162, at 406–11.

[168] Mark David Hall, *Bibliographic Glossary*, *in* 2 COLLECTED WORKS OF JAMES WILSON, *supra* note 148, at 316–23.

[169] Aaron T. Knapp, *Law's Revolutionary: James Wilson and the Birth of American Jurisprudence*, 29 J.L. & POL. 189, 194–96, 300–07 (2014); *see* BEDERMAN, *supra* note 2, at 125–26; *infra* pt. H (*The Federalist*).

[170] 1 COLLECTED WORKS OF JAMES WILSON, *supra* note 148, at 431, 432; *see id.* at 435.

resides in the citizens at large; and that, therefore, they always retain the right of abolishing, altering, or amending their constitution."[171]

Cicero was important for Wilson's views on natural law; he cited Cicero repeatedly in his lectures and other writing. Wilson held the view common among the founders that both reason and intuition (conscience) were necessary to understand natural law.[172] In addition, Wilson in his lecture on natural law broadly explored a variety of European views, including those of Burlamaqui, Grotius, Heineccius, and Pufendorf.

> "[O]bligation is nothing more than a restriction of liberty produced by reason.... [Nevertheless,] obligation and duty depend on the intervention of a superiour, whose will is manifested by law.... On this distinction, the kinds of obligation, external and internal, are founded. These two principles must be united.... As a rational being, [man] is subject to reason: as a creature of God, to his supreme will. Thus, reason and the divine will are perfectly reconciled."[173]

Richard contended that those framers with a background in the Scottish Enlightenment supported natural law in a manner like the customary Scottish resistance to the automatic adoption of English legal principles for Scotland. Scots preferred Roman law to English law as truer natural law. Wilson's first lecture rejected slavish adoption of English legal principles before a truly American legal education could develop. Law students often had some familiarity with Justinian's *Corpus Juris* and it was clear that English common law had no guidance for issues such as federalism in the new republic. Adams, Jefferson, Hamilton, and Wythe also expressed this skepticism toward the common law.[174]

H. Publius: *The Federalist*

Along with Wilson's *State House Yard Speech*, printed in newspapers and as a pamphlet,[175] the most influential Federalist defense for ratification of the U.S. Constitution was a series of newspaper essays published as *The Federalist*.

---

[171] *Id.* at 440–41; *see id.* at 458–60. For private law, Wilson indicated he would follow the Roman division used in Justinian's *Institutes* separating the law of persons, things, and actions. *Id.* at 459–63.

[172] RICHARD, *supra* note 12, at 175–79. Jefferson agreed with Wilson on this point. *Id.* at 188. *See generally* James Wilson Institute on Natural Rights and the American Founding, *Home*, https://www.jameswilsoninstitute.org.

[173] 1 COLLECTED WORKS OF JAMES WILSON, *supra* note 148, at 506; *see id.* at 503–09, 521, 523. Wilson also contended that the law of nations was of divine origin. *Id.* at 527. For other parallels between natural law and the law of nations, *see id.* at 527–33.

[174] RICHARD, *supra* note 12, at 181–83.

[175] *See* BAILYN, *supra* note 75, at 327–29; note 152 and accompanying text (*State House Yard Speech*).

The authors of the essays, signed as Publius, were James Madison, Alexander Hamilton, and John Jay.[176] All three were lawyers who had a classical education.[177] Each deserves discussion in this section.

Taking *The Federalist* as a whole, the 85 essays displayed substantial classical influence of a type common for educated discussion and persuasion at the end of the eighteenth century. The subject was the core public law document intended for a national government in a new era and the style was argument to persuade ratification. Since many essays utilized Greek and Roman references to law and government, either directly from classical texts or indirectly through British and European writers, we have the practical use of comparative law. George Kennedy found that 29 of the essays fall into this category, with six containing major references to classical antiquity and 23 less so.[178] Madison and Hamilton more commonly utilized these historical and comparative models, Greek more than Roman, primarily to defend a mixed constitution with balanced authority, support a strong national government, or justify specific federal powers. Classical comparison was less relevant, in general, to the essays concerning details of the executive or judicial branches.[179]

1. James Madison

James Madison, at the age of 11, began five years of rigorous classical study at the boarding school of Donald Robertson, a Scotsman. He taught the boy Greek, Latin, and French aided with selections from numerous Greek and Roman authors. In 1767, Madison returned home for two more years of study with a tutor, after which he enrolled at the College of New Jersey, easily passing the exams in Greek and Latin. John Witherspoon, also a Scotsman, was the college's

---

[176] *The Federalist, supra* note 108. A printer published the essays in two volumes, the first one in March 1788, and the second volume in May of that year. *Id.* at viii. Hamilton, who wrote two-thirds of the essays, conceived the plan to use short essays or letters to explain and support the proposed Constitution, particularly aimed at ratification in New York. *Id.* at ix. Madison, a demi-lawyer (see *supra* note 12) and the other two authors selected Publius as their pseudonym, referring to Publius Valerius Publicola, one of the first consuls of the Roman republic in 509 BCE. SELLERS, AMERICAN REPUBLICANISM, *supra* note 18, at 70–72, 199, 218.

[177] RICHARD B. MORRIS, WITNESSES AT THE CREATION: HAMILTON, MADISON, JAY, AND THE CONSTITUTION 16, 31–32, 99–100 (1985); George Kennedy, *Classical Influences on The Federalist*, in CLASSICAL TRADITIONS IN EARLY AMERICA 119–20, 135–38 (John W. Eadie ed., 1976).

[178] Kennedy, *supra* note 177, at 120. Those with major classical discussion and citation were *Federalist* Nos. 6, 8, 9, 18, 38, and 63. Reinhold had a similar list, but added No. 70. REINHOLD, CLASSICA AMERICANA, *supra* note 25, at 102. Kennedy's 23 other examples contained passing mention or clear implicit allusion to a classical source. Kennedy, *supra*, at 120.

[179] REINHOLD, CLASSICA AMERICANA, *supra* note 25, at 100–08; SELLERS, AMERICAN REPUBLICANISM, *supra* note 18, at 199–210; Kennedy, *supra* note 178, at 120–22. An exception, related to executive power, was Hamilton's No. 70, which repeatedly referred to the Roman Republic. *The Federalist, supra* note 108, at 423–31.

president and Madison's special tutor for an additional year in law, political philosophy, and theology after Madison's graduation in 1771.[180] Madison then read law in 1773 and 1774 prior to his election to the Virginia legislature.[181]

In 1776, county electors chose Madison to represent them as a delegate to the Virginia Provincial Convention, which began in May to draft a state constitution on the structure of government, a task principally carried out by George Mason. Adopted in June, Virginia's Constitution reflected institutional forms from the Roman Republic. Beyond a Senate with members serving for four years, the Constitution called for annual election of the governor and members of the House of Delegates.[182] Mason, as with other influential framers, had a Scottish tutor; learned Latin; and was familiar with Greek, Roman, and Enlightenment classics so that he could utilize their insights in legal and political debate.[183] In addition to the Constitution, the convention debated a Declaration of Rights to enumerate the values and principles underlying the new republican government. Again, Mason was the primary author, but Madison succeeded in adding language in the final paragraph for the "free exercise of religion, according to the dictates of conscience," which converted Mason's conditional privilege to a right. Nevertheless, Mason had views like Madison as well as Jefferson on appropriate church-state relations.[184]

From 1781 to 1783, Madison served in the Congress of the Confederation. When county voters elected Madison to the Virginia House of Delegates from

---

[180] RICHARD, *supra* note 12, at 18–20, 25–26; Lance Banning, *Madison, James, in* 14 AMERICAN NATIONAL BIOGRAPHY, *supra* note 48, at 306; *see* RICKS, *supra* note 6, at 87-106, 193-218. Madison began keeping a commonplace book at the age of eight, which illustrated his early interest in Greek and Roman authors. RICHARD, *supra*, at 25–26, 51.

[181] Bilder, *supra* note 12, at 403. Madison again studied law books in 1783 and 1784. During the Virginia legislative sessions from 1784 to 1786, he served on committees charged with revising Virginia law and organizing its courts, chairing the Courts of Justice Committee in 1784. The College of William and Mary, on Wythe's recommendation, granted Madison an LL.D. law degree in 1785. *Id.* at 394, 396–99, 402–03.

[182] RAKOVE, JAMES MADISON, *supra* note 9, at 10–13; SELLERS, AMERICAN REPUBLICANISM, *supra* note 18, at 53; *see Virginia Constitution, supra* note 61, at 7–9. The bicameral legislature elected the governor. *See id.* at 8.

The convention added Jefferson's list of grievances against King George as a preamble to the Constitution when his draft arrived from Philadelphia. Thomas Jefferson, *Proposed Constitution for Virginia, in* 2 THE WORKS OF THOMAS JEFFERSON 160 (Paul Leicester Ford ed., 1904); *see id.* at 158–64.

[183] JEFF BROADWATER, GEORGE MASON, FORGOTTEN FOUNDER 3–4, 7, 9, 68–69 (2006); RICHARD, *supra* note 12, at 31, 35, 95–96, 103, 108, 112; SPURLIN, *supra* note 103, at 58 (Montesquieu). Although Mason was never a member of the Virginia bar, he read legal and political theory in preparation for political office, for service as justice of the peace in county court, and for business pursuits. Neighbors sought out his legal advice and often mistook him for a lawyer. BROADWATER, *supra*, at 91; ROBERT ALLEN RUTLAND, GEORGE MASON: RELUCTANT STATESMAN 23–25 (1961).

[184] BROADWATER, *supra* note 183, at 12–13; RAKOVE, JAMES MADISON, *supra* note 9, at 13; *see Virginia Declaration of Rights: 12 June 1776* [hereinafter *Va. Declaration Rts.*] art. 16, *in* 1 FOUNDERS' CONSTITUTION, *supra* note 61, at 7. Madison proposed the change when the delegates refused to disestablish the Anglican Church in Virginia. RAKOVE, *supra*, at 13.

1784 to 1786, he continued his battle to disestablish religion in Virginia. Jefferson had earlier proposed and Madison promoted the Bill for Establishing Religious Freedom, which the legislature enacted in 1785. Had Article V of the Articles of Confederation not precluded Madison from representing Virginia as a delegate to Congress for more than three out of six years, he would have remained there. Madison's main source of information about national politics in the mid-1780s, consequently, came from Jefferson. When Congress sent Jefferson to France in 1785, he joined Franklin and Adams as ministers in Europe to negotiate trade agreements with Britain, France, and Spain.[185] James Monroe (1758–1831), Jefferson's successor in the Virginia congressional delegation, fulfilled the function of providing news. Monroe, the fifth U.S. president, had a lifelong friendship with Madison shaped by shared political views. During Madison's years in the Virginia legislature, he committed to an intense study of law and political theory; the classical and Enlightenment texts Jefferson sent him from France—some 200 books—had an important influence.[186]

Virginia again appointed Madison to represent it in Congress in 1786 as well as to attend the Annapolis Convention and the Philadelphia Convention. Madison was convinced the delegates could not adequately remedy the Articles of Confederation to satisfy the requirements for a national government. His years of study of classical governments as well as knowledge of the failures of the American state constitutions persuaded him of the need for a new federal constitution. The state defects were structural in nature: too much power in popularly elected legislative assemblies and too little authority in an executive and judiciary to assist in lawmaking or to check the assembly. The challenge for a national government was to fuse republicanism with federalism.[187]

In 1786, Madison reduced to paper his research and thinking on these issues of legal structure in "Notes on Ancient and Modern Confederacies."[188] They illustrate an approach commonly used in comparative legal research that has a pragmatic aim. Madison investigated six historical confederacies and, after a

---

[185] Peterson, *supra* note 48, at 912; RAKOVE, JAMES MADISON, *supra* note 9, at 33–37; *see supra* text accompanying note 9 (religious freedom). The trade commission met in Paris. Jefferson replaced Adams as minister to France and Jefferson lived in Paris until 1791. Peterson, *supra*, at 912.

[186] RAKOVE, JAMES MADISON, *supra* note 9, at 35, 37, 44, 46; ROBERT ALLEN RUTLAND, JAMES MADISON: THE FOUNDING FATHER 12 (1987) [hereinafter RUTLAND, JAMES MADISON]; J.W. Schulte Nordholt, *The Example of the Dutch Republic for American Federalism*, *in* FEDERALISM: HISTORY AND CURRENT SIGNIFICANCE OF A FORM OF GOVERNMENT 65, 71 (J.C. Boogman & G.N. van der Plaat eds., 1980); *see* James Madison, *Notes on Ancient and Modern Confederacies*, *in* 9 THE PAPERS OF JAMES MADISON 3–23 (Robert A. Rutland & William M. E. Rachal eds., 1975) [hereinafter Madison, *Confederacies*, Rutland & Rachal ed.], National Archives, *Founders Online*, https://founders.archives.gov/volumes/Madison/01-09.

[187] RAKOVE, JAMES MADISON, *supra* note 9, at 40–46.

[188] James Madison, *Of Ancient & Modern Confederacies* [hereinafter Madison, *Confederacies*, Hunt ed.], *in* 2 THE WRITINGS OF JAMES MADISON 243, 289 (Gaillard Hunt ed., 1901) (Madison's notes were on 39 handwritten pages).

brief description, organized his information under the categories of federal authority and constitutional vices. He relied on 21 different European sources and presented the most detail on the Holy Roman Empire of the early modern era and the Dutch Republic (including the 1579 Union of Utrecht). Madison and Adams, as with Hume and other Enlightenment authors, studied the past to avoid the vices of human nature in formulating law and government. For Madison, the common problem in confederacies was their weakness and tendency toward dissolution. His challenge at Philadelphia was how to maintain central authority against member state demands.[189]

Madison used his research on confederations for speeches at the Philadelphia Convention, the Virginia ratifying convention, and in several essays for *The Federalist* (primarily Nos. 18 to 20, with Hamilton's collaboration).[190] For instance, in *Federalist* No. 20, Madison described the evils and weaknesses of the United Netherlands, "a confederacy of republics."[191] Furthermore, a year after his confederation research, Madison prepared a memorandum to use at the convention, "Vices of the Political System of the United States."[192] In several places, it illustrated Madison's insight formed by comparative analysis to arrive at what he perceived to be the best solution for a new American national government.

Madison listed 12 vices (11 with commentary) in the existing confederation at the levels of the national government, the states, and the people. First, the confederation government was weak: it lacked general coercive power and control over commerce and naturalization; its requests to the states often went unanswered and it could not guarantee state constitutions and laws against internal violence; the states encroached on national authority, violated treaties and the laws of nations, and trespassed on other states' rights. Second, there were too many state laws, frequently unjust in nature, which changed too often, leading to instability. This resulted in citizen noncompliance, weakening the rule of law. State legislative majorities went unchecked as they passed laws violating minority and individual rights, undercutting the republican form of government. Third, in some

---

[189] RAKOVE, JAMES MADISON, *supra* note 9, at 46, 50; Madison, *Confederacies*, Rutland & Rachal ed., *supra* note 186 (editorial note); Madison, *Confederacies*, Hunt ed., *supra* note 188, at 249–59; Nordholt, *supra* note 186, at 65–77; *see* J.C. Boogman, *The Union of Utrecht: Its Genesis and Consequences, in* FEDERALISM, *supra* note 186, at 5–35 (Republic of the United Netherlands). "History is philosophy teaching by examples." Nordholt, *supra*, at 65.

[190] BEDERMAN, *supra* note 2, at 119–22.

[191] *The Federalist* No. 20, *supra* note 108, at 134–38 (Madison with Hamilton) (defects of the confederation); Madison, *Confederacies*, Rutland & Rachal ed., *supra* note 186 (editorial note); Nordholt, *supra* note 186, at 75–76. Madison returned to the example of the Netherlands and the vice of its factions in *Federalist* No. 37. *The Federalist* No. 37, *supra*, at 224, 231.

[192] James Madison, *Vices of the Political System of the United States, in* 2 THE WRITINGS OF JAMES MADISON 236–42 (Gaillard Hunt ed., 1901).

states, the people had not ratified the Articles of Confederation through state constitutional recognition; rather it was a matter of legislative discretion.[193]

Madison formulated his major recommendation to remedy these defects in the American legal structure from the study of previous confederacies, which had a tendency toward anarchy among the divisions rather than tyranny by the central government. The solution, he believed, was a federal veto—exercised by the senate—over state laws. With supremacy in a large indivisible republic, this "negative" would also secure minority and private rights at the local level. A national government would be a disinterested umpire in state disputes involving different passions and interests. This answer for a republic differed from that of Montesquieu, who felt that the passions of human nature could only support a homogeneous citizenry in a small republic.[194]

Madison and other Virginians arrived at the Philadelphia Convention early in May 1787 before a quorum was present. They used that time to discuss and draft a plan of action that ultimately included 15 items to introduce at the convention. The Virginia Plan was a collective document that largely represented Madison's concerns for a new constitution.[195] The convention adopted several of the Plan resolutions for the Constitution,[196] but Madison's core desire for a federal legislative veto over any state law violating the new national Constitution failed to gain acceptance.[197]

Madison was somewhat disheartened with the Constitution's final version since he felt it should have included more authority for the national government and better control over mischief he expected from the states related to individual and minority rights. Nevertheless, he enthusiastically supported the ratification effort with his involvement in *The Federalist*.[198] Madison's first contribution to the collective series of essays, and the one for which he is best known, was No. 10. Here he hid his doubts about the national government and argued that it would cure the problem of faction, that is, self-interested political behavior and

---

[193] RAKOVE, JAMES MADISON, *supra* note 9, at 46–47; James Madison, *Vices of the Political System of the United States*, *in* 9 THE PAPERS OF JAMES MADISON 345–58 (Robert A. Rutland & William M. E. Rachal eds., 1975) (editorial note), National Archives, *Founders Online*, https://founders.archives.gov/volumes/Madison/01-09.

[194] RAKOVE, JAMES MADISON, *supra* note 9, at 48–52; *see supra* text accompanying note 109 (Montesquieu).

[195] *Virginia Plan: 29 May 1787*, *in* 1 FOUNDERS' CONSTITUTION, *supra* note 61, at 251–52; BANNING, *supra* note 121, at 113–16, 369–70; RAKOVE, JAMES MADISON, *supra* note 9, at 53–55. Rutland contended Madison was the primary author. RUTLAND, JAMES MADISON, *supra* note 186, at 15–17.

[196] *See supra* text accompanying note 195 (Virginia Plan).

[197] *Virginia Plan*, *supra* note 195, at 251 (para. 6); RAKOVE, JAMES MADISON, *supra* note 9, at 63; Charles F. Hobson, *The Negative on State Laws: James Madison, the Constitution, and the Crisis of Republican Government*, 36 WM & MARY Q. 215–35 (1979). Instead, the delegates voted to make national laws and treaties the "supreme law." RAKOVE, *supra*, at 63.

[198] RAKOVE, JAMES MADISON, *supra* note 9, at 66–68, 70–71.

its aggregation into groups or parties. In all, Madison contributed 29 essays to *The Federalist* over a period of four months.[199]

In *Federalist* No. 10, Madison restated the points he had originally made in the memorandum, "Vices of the Political System." He rejected Montesquieu's notion that only a small republic could be stable and contended that an extensive republic could control better the effects of factions and the local demagogues who support them. The two structural features for the extensive republic he foresaw would be popular representation in a small body of citizens and an increased diversity of interests in a larger population and territory. He also contended that voters in large districts would be more likely to elect leaders with enlightened views.[200] Even if that did not happen, Madison explained in later essays how national separation of powers, checks and balances among government functions, along with the division of authority between the federal and state governments, would promote virtuous sentiments, prevent the accumulation of power, and protect individual and minority rights.[201]

For four months in Philadelphia beginning in December 1791, Madison compiled "Notes on Government" as a preliminary step toward a comprehensive, comparative study on republican government. He intended to analyze the conditions for stability in a political system necessary to promote liberty and the happiness of its citizens. Madison divided his outline into three parts. The first part projected chapters on the appropriate size for a nation, how that would influence the perception of external danger, and what today we would call the role for legal or political culture. The latter were peoples' views, beliefs, mores, and manners and the influence of public opinion on government. The second part sketched structural elements that a legal system could utilize to filter or modulate public opinion and its effect on popular government. These factors included checks on officials, separation of powers, and federalism. The concluding part anticipated a plan for a free and virtuous republic.[202]

---

[199] *Id.* at 71–72.

[200] *The Federalist* No. 10, *supra* note 108, at 77–84; *see* BANNING, *supra* note 121, at 202–14, 219; MORRIS, *supra* note 177, at 117–18, 195; Alan Gibson, *Inventing the Extended Republic*, in JAMES MADISON (Vile ed.), *supra* note 10, at 63–66, 75–81. Madison argued that removing the *causes* of factions would be futile, since latent causes were rooted in man's human nature. *The Federalist* No. 10, *supra*, at 78–80. In considering the *effects* of factions, he distinguished between democracies and republics. Only in a republic, and better an extensive republic, could the structure of government protect the rights of individuals and minorities. *Id.* at 81–84. For Hume's likely influence on Madison, *see* John Allphin Moore, Jr., *James Madison, David Hume, and Modern Political Parties*, in JAMES MADISON (Vile ed.), *supra*, at 209, 214–19, 220–26 nn.16–53.

[201] RAKOVE, JAMES MADISON, *supra* note 9, at 71–74; *see* BEDERMAN, *supra* note 2, at 123–24; Cohler, *supra* note 103, at 148–65; MORRIS, *supra* note 177, at 14, 195.

[202] <COLLEEN A. SHEEHAN, THE MIND OF JAMES MADISON: THE LEGACY OF CLASSICAL REPUBLICANISM ix–x, 4–8, 10–11, 13, 15–18 (2015); *see id.* at 123–65; BANNING, *supra* note 121, at 348–65; James Madison, *Notes for the National Gazette Essays*, in 14 THE PAPERS OF JAMES MADISON 157–69 (Robert A. Rutland & Thomas A. Mason eds., 1983), National Archives, *Founders Online*, https://founders.archives.gov/volumes/Madison/01-14.

"Government Notes" revealed Madison's extensive knowledge useful in preparation of a treatise on comparative law and politics. He cited the commonly used Greek, Roman, British, and European authors familiar to his contemporaries. In addition, most of his references were to a recently published four-volume French work by Jean-Jacques Barthélemy on ancient Greek civilization and culture.[203] In 1789, Jefferson, while in Paris as a representative of the United States, sent Madison Barthélemy's *Voyage du Jeune Anacharsis en Grèce*, remarking on its popularity in France. Madison saw Barthélemy's intellectual journey through ancient Greece as relevant to his own philosophical interest in the causes that tend to preserve or destroy republics, a subject he also found in Aristotle's *Politics* and Montesquieu's *Spirit of the Laws*.[204]

Barthélemy used the device of Anacharsis's fictive travels in Greece commenting on all features of Greek law and politics as well as geography, culture, and society in the fourth century BCE.[205] This was similar to Montesquieu's portrayal of two Persians visiting Europe and commenting on features of eighteenth-century society, culture, politics, and law.[206] Barthélemy's *Voyage*, with over 2,000 citations to Greek writers, was a comprehensive reference source to Hellenic culture and philosophy. Madison could use this information as a guide to primary Greek sources. Sheehan argued that Madison used Barthélemy's insights from the golden age of classical Greece to refashion his view of republicanism. Madison perceived a modern republic improved by science and technology that could buttress inner stability threatened by domestic factions and support external strength against foreign enemies. Slavery, a destabilizing institution, would not be necessary for social prosperity, while improvement in communication—newspapers and mail post—could enable liberty to survive in an empire. Public opinion would be decisive to preserve constitutional order.[207]

---

[203] SHEEHAN, *supra* note 202, at 15–16, 19; *see* Jean-Jacques Barthélemy, 1–4 *Voyage du Jeune Anacharsis en Grèce, dans le Milieu du Quatrième Siècle avant l'Ére Vulgaire* (Paris 1788). Subsequent French editions appeared with a different number of printed volumes. There was an English translation in 1790, published in London in eight volumes. An American edition of four volumes, published in 1804 in Philadelphia, copied the English translation by William Beaumont.

[204] SHEEHAN, *supra* note 202, at 11–13, 15–17; *see id.* at 25–113; ARISTOTLE, ARISTOTLE'S POLITICS (Carnes Lord trans. & intro., 2d ed. 2014); MONTESQUIEU, *supra* note 102. In 1792, a year after Madison prepared "Government Notes," he and Jefferson founded the Republican Party in opposition to the Federalist agenda of Adams and Hamilton. SHEEHAN, *supra*, at 12.

[205] SHEEHAN, *supra* note 202, at 11, 19.

[206] MONTESQUIEU, PERSIAN LETTERS (Margaret Mauldon trans., 2008, original French ed., 1721).

[207] SHEEHAN, *supra* note 202, at 19, 24.

2. Alexander Hamilton

Alexander Hamilton was born in British West Indies, outside the 13 North American British colonies. During his early years, he primarily taught himself with books he read from the library of a Presbyterian cleric, Hugh Knox. In 1773, he arrived in New York City with letters of introduction from Knox to two clergymen, who sent Hamilton to a preparatory academy across the Hudson River in New Jersey. There he learned Greek, Latin, and French and met influential lawyers, including Elias Boudinot and William Livingston, both active patriots during the American Revolution.[208]

Hamilton entered King's College in New York in 1774 and continued with a classical education. During the same year, when the First Continental Congress was meeting in Philadelphia, Hamilton determined that the colonists had legitimate grievances against Great Britain. In response to a Tory pamphlet (signed A W[estchester] Farmer) published in New York against the Congress, he responded in kind with a 35-page piece that he signed "A Friend of America."[209] An exchange continued and in February 1775, at the age of 18, Hamilton published *The Farmer Refuted*. In this lengthier pamphlet, he expounded on notions common among the American patriots associated with natural law and rights, liberty, British tyranny, and the right of revolution.[210] These were the same ideas that Jefferson would include in the Declaration of Independence. Hamilton grounded his argument on natural rights, referring the reader to Grotius, Pufendorf, Locke, Montesquieu, and Burlemaqui while also quoting Blackstone's *Commentaries*. He denied Parliament's right to legislate for America since the colonists did not have their own representatives. For comparative purposes, he utilized the example of the Roman Republic and its colonies.[211]

Later in 1775, Hamilton began his military career by joining a volunteer company of rebels, became captain in the Continental Army in 1776, and

---

[208] JAMES THOMAS FLEXNER, THE YOUNG HAMILTON: A BIOGRAPHY 18, 46–47, 52–56, 157 (1997); DARREN STALOFF, HAMILTON, ADAMS, JEFFERSON: THE POLITICS OF ENLIGHTENMENT AND THE AMERICAN FOUNDING 46, 50 (2005). The Hamilton Papers at the Library of Congress has Hamilton's 1773 list of 27 books and subjects on ancient and medieval history and philosophy, illustrating what he studied. List of Books (1773), *in* 1 THE PAPERS OF ALEXANDER HAMILTON, 1768–1778, at 42 (Harold C. Syrett ed., 1961), National Archives, Founders Online, https://founders.archives.gov/volumes/Hamilton/01-01.

[209] FLEXNER, *supra* note 208, at 58–62, 65–70; *see* BEDERMAN, *supra* note 2, at 53–54 (references to the Roman Republic's colonial practice).

[210] FLEXNER, *supra* note 208, at 70–75; *see* Alexander Hamilton, *The Farmer Refuted* [hereinafter Hamilton, *Farmer Refuted*], *in* THE REVOLUTIONARY WRITINGS OF ALEXANDER HAMILTON 47–135 (Richard B. Vernier ed., 2008).

[211] Hamilton, *Farmer Refuted*, *supra* note 210, at 51–53, 57–58, 61–71, 90, 120, 125, 134. The "intention of this right [to elect representatives to Parliament] is to preserve the life, property, and liberty of the subject from the encroachments of oppression and tyranny." *Id.* at 62. The right of revolution is inherent in divine natural law. *Id.* at 89–90, 105.

aide-de-camp to George Washington in 1777, whom he served until 1781.[212] During these years, Hamilton found time to keep a commonplace book, in which he wrote extracts from some Greek authors, such as Plutarch (46–120 CE).[213] In 1782, Hamilton petitioned the New York Supreme Court to delay lapse of a rule applied to soldiers who had studied law that exempted them from a mandatory three-year apprenticeship in a law office. The court granted him a stay until October and, after examination, admitted Hamilton to the bar. He practiced law in New York City for much of the period until his death in 1804.[214]

Beyond considering a new career in 1781, Hamilton read widely in political economy and finance. He then wrote a series of six newspaper essays that collectively constitute *The Continentalist*. He began with the premise that the Congress created by the recently ratified Articles of Confederation was entirely too weak and that it required a strong national government and finance system. He filled the first three essays with historical illustrations from the classical Greeks onwards; the core problem was disassociating central power from tyranny. The last three essays listed and explained Hamilton's recommendations for a stronger Congress and federal republic.[215]

In *Continentalist* No. 1, the aim was to formulate a government to promote and protect liberty. "In a government framed for durable liberty, not less regard must be paid to giving the magistrate a proper degree of authority to make and execute the laws with rigor, than to guard against encroachments upon the rights of the community. As too much power leads to despotism, too little leads to anarchy, and both, eventually, to the ruin of the people."[216] Hamilton then surveyed the commonwealths of ancient Greece, the Roman Republic, and more recent illustrations such as the German Diet, Helvetic League, and United Netherlands.[217] Hamilton used several of these same examples to demonstrate

---

[212] FLEXNER, *supra* note 208, at 77–79, 91–93, 135–37, 143, 336–37. Hamilton, according to his account, qualified for a bachelor's degree from King's College in 1776 (although not granted) and had already begun the study of law. He was referring to the natural law sources he mentioned in *Farmer Refuted*, plus Sir Edward Coke's *Reports* and Wyndham Beawes's *Lex Mercatoria Rediviva* (6th ed. 1773). *Id.* at 375. A 1776 edition of Coke was in three volumes, consisting of 13 parts.

[213] BEDERMAN, *supra* note 2, at 21. From Plutarch's *Lives*, he copied information about two Greek and two Roman leaders who founded republics: Theseus and Lycurgus compared to Romulus and Numa Pompilius. *Id.* There was an English translation from the Greek available: 1–6 *Plutarch's Lives* (John Langhorne & William Langhorne trans., 1770).

[214] FLEXNER, *supra* note 208, at 374–79, 433–34, 444–45.

[215] *Id.* at 342–46, 400; *see* Alexander Hamilton, *The Continentalist* [hereinafter Hamilton, *Continentalist*], *in* THE REVOLUTIONARY WRITINGS OF ALEXANDER HAMILTON, *supra* note 210, at 165, 169–200.

[216] Hamilton, *Continentalist*, *supra* note 215, at 171.

[217] *Id.* at 171–72, 175–77, 180 (Nos. 1–3). In the essays on Hamilton's recommendations, he particularly relied on the United Provinces for comparison with the United States. *Id.* at 184–86, 189, 193 (Nos. 4, 5). Nevertheless, by referring to classical examples, he intended to warn rather than suggest emulation. *Id.* at 197.

the consequence of a weak confederation during his effort in support of the Constitution at the New York ratifying convention.[218]

Of course, Hamilton's effort to convince New Yorkers to ratify the U.S. Constitution with *The Federalist* was his greatest contribution of a scholarly nature to the new republic. As with the other two authors, Hamilton relied on his wide reading in legal and political history and philosophy to help persuade his readers. Hamilton presented the question in *Federalist* No. 1. You should decide "whether societies of men are really capable or not of establishing good government from reflection and choice, or whether they are forever destined to depend for their political constitutions on accident and force."[219] In *Federalist* No. 9, he developed an argument in support of a confederate republic, an assemblage of societies, based on his reading of Montesquieu. This form had the advantage of suppressing factions, maintaining internal tranquility in the political units, and increasing external security. The constituent republics would enjoy their own internal happiness. Hamilton referred to Montesquieu's endorsement of the Lycian confederacy as support for the Constitution's plan for the federal government.[220]

3. John Jay

John Jay (1745–1829) received his classical training at King's College where he graduated in 1764. In addition to Latin, he studied French and in the fourth-year curriculum read Grotius and Pufendorf. In June 1764, Jay began clerking for a New York City lawyer as an apprentice, where he participated in an active commercial practice. However, he could not ignore the political developments in 1765 associated with the effective date for implementation of the Stamp Act, which New York City lawyers determined to resist by refusing to file litigation papers that required the stamp.[221] The Stamp Act crisis led to civil rioting in New York and general disfavor toward the British. During the lapse in litigation, Jay had the opportunity to continue with his reading, which included Plato and Montesquieu. He maintained an interest in classical studies through 1767, when

---

[218] *Convention Debates, 20 June 1788*, in 22 THE DOCUMENTARY HISTORY OF THE RATIFICATION OF THE CONSTITUTION 1704, 1722, 1725–26 (John P. Kaminski ed., 2008) (New York).

[219] *The Federalist, supra* note 108, at 33.

[220] *Id.* at 73–76; MORRIS, *supra* note 177, at 18–19, 228. Hamilton used one part of *Spirit of the Laws* (bk. 9, ch. 1) to defeat another part, that is, the notion that republics are only sustainable over a small territory and population. *The Federalist, supra*, at 73–74. Hamilton continued with the discussion of Greek leagues (Lycian and Achaean) and their comparison with the Constitution in *Federalist* No. 16.

[221] HERBERT A. JOHNSON, JOHN JAY: COLONIAL LAWYER 1–2, 7–9, 12–16, 20–22, 27, 31–32, 46, 50 (1989); Jerald A. Combs, *Jay, John*, in 11 AMERICAN NATIONAL BIOGRAPHY 891–92 (John A. Garraty & Mark C. Carnes, gen. eds., 1999). In March 1766, Britain's Parliament repealed the Stamp Act of 1765 (5 George III, c. 12). News of repeal did not reach New York until May, when litigation resumed. JOHNSON, *supra*, at 37–40.

King's College awarded him a Master of Arts degree. By 1768, Jay had qualified for admittance to the New York bar.[222]

The New York advocate bar during Jay's clerkship period was small, 36 attorneys in 1765, and elite with connections to the leading landowning and mercantile families. Of the 36, with an average age of 38, 16 had degrees from King's College, the College of New Jersey, or Yale. By 1770, there were 60 advocates admitted to practice before the Supreme Court. New York's inferior courts, such as the mayor's court of New York City or common pleas courts in each county, could each admit others deemed qualified to practice before it. Jay practiced law before the supreme court, the city mayor's court, and Westchester County common pleas until 1776, when British forces entered New York City.[223] He acquired an extensive law library, including works on civil law, natural law, and international law. Jay had made frequent classical references in court pleadings during his legal career. Some of the library books would prove useful as Jay began to wind down his practice and became active politically as a delegate to the First and Second Continental Congress.[224]

Jay's political duties in New York prevented him from voting for the Declaration of Independence, which he supported. In July 1776, the New York Provincial Congress authorized a committee to prepare the New York Constitution, largely drafted by Jay, which the Congress (constituting itself as a convention) approved in 1777. Under the Constitution, a council of senators elected Jay chief justice of the Supreme Court, an office he held for two years. Jay continued to be active in national politics. The New York legislature sent him to the Continental Congress in 1779, which elected him president of the Congress, and appointed him minister to Spain (from 1779 to 1782). The successor Confederation Congress selected Jay secretary of foreign affairs, an office he held until 1790. Washington nominated Jay to be the first chief justice of the U.S. Supreme Court, where he served until voters elected him governor of New York in 1795.[225]

Jay's contribution of a scholarly nature to comparative law was modest, consisting primarily of five essays in *The Federalist*, a task he had to abandon due

---

[222] JOHNSON, *supra* note 221, at 31–32, 34–36, 58–59.

[223] *Id.* at 60–63, 79, 93–95, 116, 158, 166–69. The New York Supreme Court of Judicature had the same jurisdiction as England's King's Bench, Common Pleas, and Exchequer. Those admitted to the Supreme Court could litigate in any New York court after requesting formal admission to the local court. *Id.* at 79, 91.

[224] BEDERMAN, *supra* note 2, at 23; JOHNSON, *supra* note 221, at 114–16, 124, 151, 154–58. The library included works, many in translation, from Domat, Jacob (*Lex Mercatoria*), Justinian, Pufendorf, Rutherford, and Vattel. JOHNSON, *supra*, at 114, 186, 191–92. Jay had some cases before civil law courts in New York, including Chancery, the Prerogative Court and, when he was an apprentice, the Vice-Admiralty Court. *Id.* at 50–54, 125–37.

[225] JOHNSON, *supra* note 221, at 159; Combs, *supra* note 221, at 891–92; *see* The Avalon Project, *The Constitution of New York: April 20, 1777*, at https://avalon.law.yale.edu/18th_century/ny01.asp; MORRIS, *supra* note 177, at 70 (for the Constitution, Jay drew on Adams's mixed government ideas).

to illness. The New York newspaper letters to the public were Hamilton's idea. As it became clear he would need assistance, he first enlisted Jay and later Madison to write some of the essays.[226] Jay first met Hamilton in 1774 while the latter was in preparatory school in New Jersey; they became lifelong friends and allies in New York.[227]

Jay began his contribution with *Federalist* No. 2, which contained an implicit reference to Montesquieu's reliance on geography and cultural homogeneity as elements to support a republic and effective national government. Providence gave "one connected country to one untied people ... similar in their manners and customs, and who ... have notably established their general liberty."[228] In No. 4, Jay argued for a strong federal government as superior to 13 independent republics or three or four confederacies, especially related to collective defense. He then relied on the history of ancient Greek states and the many instances of inadequate defense due to interstate competition and mutual jealousies.[229] Jay continued along this line in No. 5, adding the positive example of England's union with Scotland and the negative one of Rome's treachery toward colonies it purported to treat as allies.[230]

I. The Bill of Rights

The motivation for and origin, rendition, and approval of the first ten amendments to the U.S. Constitution, ratified in 1791, brought together the themes of natural rights, republican liberty, and English civic rights with Madison's desire adequately to satisfy Anti-Federalists so that the new federal government would be a success.[231] Madison, perhaps the most scholarly and effective comparative lawyer during the revolutionary period, became the primary author of the Bill of Rights.[232]

Massachusetts, with significant Anti-Federalist resistance, was the sixth state to ratify the Constitution in early 1788. The majority Federalists accomplished this result by permitting the Massachusetts convention conclusively to ratify the Constitution while recommending amendments for future consideration. This

---

[226] BANNING, *supra* note 121, at 196–98.
[227] FLEXNER, *supra* note 208, at 54, 75; MORRIS, *supra* note 177, at 31.
[228] *The Federalist*, *supra* note 108, at 37, 38; *see* MORRIS, *supra* note 177, at 48–49.
[229] *The Federalist*, *supra* note 108, at 45, 46–49; MORRIS, *supra* note 177, at 50–51.
[230] *The Federalist*, *supra* note 108, at 50, 52–53; *see* MORRIS, *supra* note 177, at 52.
[231] *See supra* parts C, E, and H.1.
[232] Madison disparaged the need for a bill of rights when he wrote in defense of ratification for the Constitution. RICHARD LABUNSKI, JAMES MADISON AND THE STRUGGLE FOR THE BILL OF RIGHTS 62 (2006). *See generally The Federalist* Nos. 38, 44, 46, and 48, *supra* note 108. The other principal author of *The Federalist*, Hamilton, remained satisfied with his defense of the original Constitution omitting a list of rights. *The Federalist* No. 84, *supra*, at 510–20; *see* LABUNSKI, *supra*, at 9–10, 22.

strategy precluded contingent ratification and proved decisive for Federalist success in New Hampshire, Virginia, and New York. Nevertheless, a recurrent concern was the omission of an enumeration of natural and fundamental rights. Mason, most notably, had already raised the issue at the Constitutional Convention in Philadelphia, arguing to place the rights as a preface. Furthermore, Adams and Jefferson, both on diplomatic assignment in Europe, supported such a list. Although Federalists convincingly won in the national elections of 1788-1789, Madison, in his race for a seat in the House of Representatives, changed his mind about the usefulness of including further fundamental rights to protect individuals. He publicly committed to leading an effort for such inclusion, although he preferred to place the amendments within the existing Constitution itself.[233]

In June 1789, with Congress meeting in New York, Madison presented his amendments to the House, which referred them to a committee including Madison. That committee reported the amendments back to the full House, which approved 17 of them to proceed to the Senate. This version altered two principal elements of Madison's proposal, omitting a preamble concerning natural rights and endorsing the list as supplemental to the Constitution's seven articles. The Senate, for its part, removed Madison's effort to protect rights of conscience, a free press, and criminal jury trials from *state* infringement.[234] In the reduction to 12 amendments, the Senate also eliminated Madison's statement regarding separation of powers.[235]

The bill of rights now went to a conference committee, from which it emerged as 12 amendments, approved by both chambers. President Washington transmitted them to the states for ratification. Anti-Federalists were concerned that the referral contained none of the structural changes—public rights—which

---

[233] LABUNSKI, *supra* note 232, at 9–10, 59, 62–63, 103; LEONARD W. LEVY, ORIGINS OF THE BILL OF RIGHTS 25–26, 31–34 (1999); ROBERT ALLEN RUTLAND, THE BIRTH OF THE BILL OF RIGHTS: 1776–1791, at 107–10, 190–97 (rev. ed. 1983) [hereinafter RUTLAND, BILL OF RIGHTS]; THE ANNOTATED U.S. CONSTITUTION AND DECLARATION OF INDEPENDENCE 56–60 (Jack N. Rakove ed., 2009) [hereinafter ANNOTATED CONSTITUTION]. Jefferson's correspondence with Madison from December 1787 to early 1789 might have aided Madison's thinking, especially the argument that a bill of rights could provide the judiciary with a check on an oppressive majority impinging minority rights. LEVY, *supra*, at 32–33.

[234] ANNOTATED CONSTITUTION, *supra* note 233, at 59–61; *see* LABUNSKI, *supra* note 232, at 178–212, 216–40; LEVY, *supra* note 233, at 34–40. The Senate, as guardian of state legislative authority, rejected Madison's desire for federal oversight of states to protect some rights. The amendments would only apply against action by the national government. ANNOTATED CONSTITUTION, *supra*, at 61; *see infra* notes 237–241 and accompanying text (Madison's proposed amendments from 8 June 1789).

[235] *See* LABUNSKI, *supra* note 232, at 202, 236–37, 274–77. Madison might have included this statement, in his amendment 8, to remind the state ratifying conventions that the national government adopted the doctrine of separation of powers as a safeguard against tyranny. *Id.* at 35–36, 202. One could read Madison's language, however, as weakening the checks and balances of mixed government.

the state ratifying conventions had recommended. Even so, by December 1791, Virginia became the 11th state to ratify, enough for the addition of the rights to the Constitution. As finally ratified, the ten amendments protected only private civil and natural rights.[236]

Madison initiated the amendment process on June 8, 1789, by presenting the first Congress a list of eight amendments to consider.[237] Amendment 1 would add to the Constitution's "we the people" preface natural rights language like Jefferson's first two paragraphs in the Declaration of Independence. "[A]ll power is originally vested in, and consequently derived from, the people." Government is instituted and "exercised for the benefit of the people; which consists in the enjoyment of life and liberty, with the right of acquiring and using property, and generally of pursuing and obtaining happiness and safety." People have an "unalienable . . . right to reform and change their Government whenever it be found adverse or inadequate to the purposes of its institution."[238]

Madison thought that Congress should insert most of his civil and natural rights into the Constitution's Article I, section 9. Amendment 4 (in Madison's wording) included:

(1) The civil rights of none shall be abridged on account of religious belief or worship, nor shall any national religion be established, nor shall the full and equal rights of conscience be in any manner, or on any pretext, infringed.

(2) The people shall not be deprived or abridged of their right to speak, to write, or publish their sentiments; and the freedom of the press, as one of the great bulwarks of liberty, shall be inviolable.

(3) The people shall not be restrained from peaceably assembling and consulting for their common good; nor from applying to the Legislature by petitions, or remonstrances, for redress of their grievances.

(4) The right of the people to keep and bear arms shall not be infringed; a well armed and well regulated militia being the best security of a free country: but no person religiously scrupulous of bearing arms shall be compelled to render military service in person.

(5) No soldier shall in time of peace be quartered in any house without the consent of the owner; nor at any time, but in a manner warranted by law.

---

[236] ANNOTATED CONSTITUTION, *supra* note 233, at 62–63; *see* LEVY, *supra* note 233, at 40–43. The states rejected the original first two amendments: one related to the population ratio for the House; the other for congressional pay raises. ANNOTATED CONSTITUTION, *supra*, at 63.

[237] House of Representatives, *Amendments to the Constitution: 8 June 1789* [hereinafter *Madison's Amendments*], *in* 5 FOUNDERS' CONSTITUTION, *supra* note 61, at 20, 25–26. The amendments also appear in LABUNSKI, *supra* note 232, at 265–68; LEVY, *supra* note 233, at 281–83.

[238] *Madison's Amendments*, *supra* note 237, at 25.

(6) No person shall be subject, except in cases of impeachment, to more than punishment or one trial for the same offence; nor shall be deprived of life, liberty, or property, without due process of law; nor be obliged to relinquish his property, where it may be necessary for public use, without a just compensation.

(7) Excessive bail shall not be required, nor excessive fines imposed, nor cruel and unusual punishments inflicted.

(8) The rights of the people to be secured in their persons, their houses, their papers, and their other property, from all unreasonable searches and seizures, shall not be violated by warrants issued without probable cause, supported by oath or affirmation, or not particularly describing the places to be searched, or the persons or things to be seized.

(9) In all criminal prosecutions, the accused shall enjoy the right to a speedy and public trial, to be informed of the cause and nature of the accusation, to be confronted with his accusers, and the witnesses against him; to have a compulsory process for obtaining witnesses in his favor; and to have the assistance of counsel for his defence.

(10) The exceptions here or elsewhere in the Constitution, made in favor of particular rights, shall not be so construed as to diminish the just importance of other rights retained by the people, or as to enlarge the powers delegated by the Constitution.[239]

In addition, three other matters that Madison proposed found their way into the final version of the Bill of Rights. First, he sought protection in amendments 6 and 7 for the English civil jury right for most cases arising under the common law, but not for those in admiralty or equity. Second, in amendment 7 he stated that persons tried for crimes have a right to a preliminary grand jury determination and an impartial jury at trial. Third, Madison provided in amendment 8 that the "powers not delegated by this Constitution, nor prohibited by it to the States, are reserved to the States respectively."[240] Madison recognized that his proposal constituted a "bill of rights"; he contrasted it to the English Declaration of Rights (1689) that restrained only the Crown and not Parliament. A bill of rights would "raise barriers against power in all forms and departments of Government."[241]

---

[239] *Id.*; *see* LEVY, *supra* note 233, at 241–60 (rights retained by the people).
[240] *Madison's Amendments*, *supra* note 237, at 25–26; *see* U.S. Const. amends. V, VI, VII, X. Madison also stated the separation of powers principle in amendment 8, derived from language in both Virginia's Declaration of Rights (art. 5) and its Constitution.
[241] *Madison's Amendments*, *supra* note 237, at 26; *see* JACK N. RAKOVE, ORIGINAL MEANINGS: POLITICS AND IDEAS IN THE MAKING OF THE CONSTITUTION 296–97 (1996) [hereinafter RAKOVE, ORIGINAL MEANINGS]; *infra* note 244 (1689 Declaration). Madison recognized the difference between natural rights existing in nature, such as freedom of conscience or pursuit of happiness, and fundamental rights modified by the existence of society. "Trial by jury cannot be considered a natural right, but a right resulting from a social compact, . . . [it] is as essential to secure the liberty

Madison did not consider his offering especially controversial, since seven states already had bills of rights and delegates thoroughly debated the issue of their usefulness, "parchment barriers," at the Philadelphia Constitutional Convention and state ratifying conventions.[242] What were the sources that Madison used to formulate the civil and natural rights that eventually found their way into the first ten amendments to the U.S. Constitution? Broadly, given the short time available, Madison considered the seven state bills of rights and 11 state constitutions existing in early 1789, many of which largely copied other states and particularly the two public law documents from Virginia. Mason, a lifetime proponent for the importance of a bill of rights to a republic, was the primary author for both Virginia's Declaration of Rights (1776) and Constitution (1776).[243]

Beyond the Virginia texts and the English 1689 Declaration of Rights,[244] Madison read widely classical and Enlightenment authors. As a comparatist, he could select which rights were, to his thinking, most significant for the defense of liberty in a republic and thus for inclusion in the Constitution. Jack Rakove stated that this was part of the debate from 1787 to 1789: "to identify, enumerate, and define with textual precision the rights that Americans most valued."[245] However, that was only one element. As this chapter indicates, the founders—with a common education in classical and Enlightenment texts—entered the revolutionary crisis in the 1770s confident they knew what their rights were. This attitude changed little up to 1791.[246]

What did evolve, Rakove contended, "were their ideas of *where* the dangers to rights lay and of *how* rights were to be protected."[247] At the beginning of this

---

of the people as any one of the pre-existent rights of nature." *Madison's Amendments, supra*, at 26 (Madison, 8 June 1789).

[242] LABUNSKI, *supra* note 232, at 62–66, 108, 114–15; 159–62; LEVY, *supra* note 233, at 24, 32–39; see *The Federalist* No. 48 (Madison), *supra* note 108, at 308 (referring to the Constitution's separation of powers principle set out in articles I, II, and III as a parchment barrier).

[243] See *supra* notes 182–84 and accompanying text (Virginia Constitution and Declaration); LEVY, *supra* note 233, at 263–68 (various provisions and sources).

[244] After King James II (reigned 1685–1688), who had tried to reinstate Catholic worship in England, fled to France, Prince William of Orange, invited to England, summoned a special parliament, a "convention." It prepared a declaration of the events by which James had subverted the laws and liberties of England along with a list asserting 13 ancient rights and liberties. William, husband of James's elder daughter, Mary, both implicitly agreed to preserve those rights. Parliament offered them the crown. Parliament incorporated the declaration with some amendments into an Act of Parliament, 1 W. & M, 2d sess., c.2, 16 Dec. 1689. Although technically a declaration since Parliament worded its title, "An act for declaring the rights and liberties of the subject," authors commonly refer to it as a bill or rights. See *Bill of Rights: 16 Dec. 1689* [hereinafter *Eng. Declaration Rts.*], in 5 THE FOUNDERS' CONSTITUTION, *supra* note 61, at 1–3; LOIS G. SCHWOERER, THE DECLARATION OF RIGHTS, 1689 (1981).

[245] RAKOVE, ORIGINAL MEANINGS, *supra* note 241, at 289.

[246] See *id.* at 290–93.

[247] *Id.* at 289 (emphasis in original).

period, the British government and its officials were the arbitrary and tyrannous actors; the colonists' best protection would be in rights of political representation and jury trial. By 1787, Madison perceived different dangers, which called for public rights, such as separation of powers, and more elaborate private rights, such as the rights of conscience and worship. These newly perceived threats more commonly came from state and local despotism than from the central government, and comprised factious popular majorities harming minority groups as well as individuals. In addition, Madison now believed that the abuse of legislative power was more menacing than arbitrary executive acts. During the post-1791 period, this perception shifted attention away from the jury as the original Whig legal institution for protection of rights toward an independent judiciary with judicial review over legislature measures as well as executive acts.[248]

Although the ancient Greek and Roman authors wrote about natural law, they never developed a theory of natural rights that the framers believed helpful.[249] For material useful in a declaration of rights, the founders—Mason and Madison, in particular—relied on the foreign legal and political ideas of Enlightenment figures from the seventeenth and eighteenth centuries.[250] Mason, to illustrate, suggested for the Virginia Declaration of Rights, "[A]ll Men are born equally free and independent, and have certain inherent natural Rights, ... among which are the Enjoyment of Life and Liberty, with the Means of acquiring and possessing Property, and pursuing and obtaining Happiness and Safety."[251] Significantly, Mason did have one paragraph in his draft that connected Roman liberty, its republic, and civic virtue with Enlightenment authors. "[N]o free Government, or the Blessings of Liberty can be preserved to any People, but by a firm adherence to Justice, Moderation, Temperance, Frugality, and Virtue and by frequent Recurrence to fundamental Principles."[252] Tacitus, available through Thomas Gordon's English translation, wrote about the loss of the Roman Republic

---

[248] *Id.* at 289–90; *see id.* at 293–338; SCOTT DOUGLAS GERBER, A DISTINCT JUDICIAL POWER: THE ORIGINS OF AN INDEPENDENT JUDICIARY, 1606–1787 (2011).

[249] BODENHEIMER, *supra* note 49, at 31–35; Richard Kraut, *Are There Natural Rights in Aristotle?*, 49 REV. METAPHYSICS 755–74 (1996). *Contra* FRED D. MILLER, JR., NATURE, JUSTICE, AND RIGHTS IN ARISTOTLE'S POLITICS (1995); WILTSHIRE, *supra* note 37, at 99–183 (Bill of Rights reflected issues raised in classical Greece and Rome).

[250] BODENHEIMER, *supra* note 49, at 49–52; *see id.* at 35–39, 45–49; BROADWATER, *supra* note 183, at 37, 41–45, 87–88 (Mason); *supra* pt. H.1 (Madison).

[251] Mason, *Draft Virginia Declaration*, *supra* note 61, at para. 1. Mason, Jefferson, and Madison opposed slavery on principle, although most influential Virginians were in favor. The language that "all men are by nature equally free" provoked great concern at the Virginia convention that it would provoke civil conflict. The delegates' solution was to add after "inherent rights" the clause, "when they enter into a state of society," suggesting that African American slaves did not yet meet that condition. RAKOVE, JAMES MADISON, *supra* note 9, at 176–77; RUTLAND, BILL OF RIGHTS, *supra* note 233, at 35–37; *Va. Declaration Rts.* art. 1, *supra* note 184, at 6.

[252] Mason, *Draft Virginia Declaration*, *supra* note 61, at para. 8; *Va. Declaration Rts.* art. 15, *supra* note 184, at 7; *see supra* pt. D.1 (Roman republic and virtue).

through avarice and corruption, while Montesquieu warned of the need for virtue to maintain a republic (plus frugality in its democratic form and moderation in its aristocratic form).[253]

From the English Declaration of Rights, there were several provisions on common law civic rights that likely influenced language in the U.S. Bill of Rights.

(1) [I]t is the right of the subjects to petition the King. . . . [F]or redress of all grievances . . . parliaments ought to be held frequently.[254]
(2) [F]reedom of speech, and debates or proceedings in parliament, ought not to be impeached.[255]
(3) [T]he subjects which are protestants, may have arms for their defence suitable to their conditions, and as allowed by law.[256]
(4) [Penal] jurors ought to be duly impaneled and returned.[257]
(5) [E]xcessive bail ought not to be required, nor excessive fines imposed; nor cruel and unusual punishments inflicted.[258]

By 1776, this set of relatively limited and conditional rights, asserted as "ancient rights and liberties," agreed to by Prince William and Princess Mary of Orange, transformed in Virginia into more numerous "inherent rights" that all men had, which the state might not deprive or divest them. Representatives of the voting people of Virginia confirmed these rights.[259]

The approved Virginia Declaration of Rights contained a preamble and 16 articles, nine as basic principles for a republic and seven to enumerate citizen rights.[260] Mason's draft contained a similar preamble and 11 paragraphs. The catalogued individual rights in the Declaration's language that found their way as modified into the 1791 Bill of Rights encompassed protection for the following.

---

[253] SELLERS, AMERICAN REPUBLICANISM, *supra* note 18, at 83–86, 87–89, 100, 105, 166–67, 224, 228; *see* MONTESQUIEU, *supra* note 102, at 42–44, 47–48, 51–54, 122 (5.2–5.4, 5.6, 5.8, 8.13); *supra* pt. D.4 (Montesquieu). Among Roman sources, American founders most often cited Tacitus and Cicero. SELLERS, AMERICAN REPUBLICANISM, *supra*, at 83; *see Thomas Gordon, 1–4 The Works of Tacitus: With Political Discourses upon That Author* (Thomas Gordon trans., 3d ed. 1753); *supra* text accompanying notes 89, 100, 146, 160 (Tacitus).
[254] *Eng. Declaration Rts.* §§ 5, 13, *supra* note 244, at 2; U.S. Const. amend. I.
[255] *Eng. Declaration Rts.* § 9, *supra* note 244, at 2; U.S. Const. amend. I.
[256] *Eng. Declaration Rts.* § 7, *supra* note 244, at 2; U.S. Const. amend. II.
[257] *Eng. Declaration Rts.* § 11, *supra* note 244, at 2; U.S. Const. amend. VI.
[258] *Eng. Declaration Rts.* § 10, *supra* note 244, at 2; U.S. Const. amend. VIII.
[259] *Eng. Declaration Rts.* preamble, *supra* note 244, at 2; *Va. Declaration Rts.* art. 1, *supra* note 184, at 6. "[A]ll power is vested in, and consequently derived from, the People." *Id.* art. 2.
[260] RUTLAND, BILL OF RIGHTS, *supra* note 233, at 35–36, 38–39. Rutland did not consider item (3) in Mason's list (*infra* at note 263 and accompanying text) a citizen right. *Id.* at 38. Jefferson's two-paragraph preamble in the Declaration of Independence owed much to Mason's draft Virginia Declaration, paras. 1–3, which the Virginia convention largely adopted as articles 1–3. See *supra* text accompanying note 61 (Mason's draft).

(1) [A]ll men are equally entitled to the free exercise of religion, according to the dictates of conscience.[261]
(2) [The] freedom of the Press is one of the great bulwarks of liberty.[262]
(3) [A] well-regulated Militia, composed of the body of the people, trained to arms, is the proper, natural, and safe defence of a free State; the military should be under strict subordination to, and governed by, the civil power.[263]
(4) [G]eneral warrants, whereby any officer or messenger may be commanded to search suspected places without evidence of a fact committed, or to seize any person or persons not named, or whose offence is not particularly described and supported by evidence, are grievous and oppressive.[264]
(5) [I]n all capital or criminal prosecutions a man hath a right to demand the cause and nature of his accusation, to be confronted with the accusers and witnesses, to call for evidence in his favour, and to a speedy trial by an impartial jury of his vicinage, without whose unanimous consent he cannot be found guilty, nor can he be compelled to give evidence against himself; that no man be deprived of his liberty except by the law of the land, or the judgment of his peers.[265]
(6) [A]ll men ... cannot be taxed or deprived of their property for publick uses without their own consent or that of their Representative so elected.[266]
(7) [In] controversies respecting property, and in suits between man and man, the ancient [civil] trial by Jury is preferable ... and ought to be held sacred.[267]

---

[261] *Va. Declaration Rts.* art. 16, *supra* note 184, at 7; Mason, *Draft Virginia Declaration*, *supra* note 61, at para. 9 ("fullest Toleration in the Exercise of Religion"); U.S. Const. amend. I; *see supra* note 10 and accompanying text (Madison).

[262] *Va. Declaration Rts.* art. 12, *supra* note 184, at 6 (only "despotick Governments" would restrain the press); Mason, *Draft Virginia Declaration*, *supra* note 61, at para. 11; U.S. Const. amend. I.

[263] *Va. Declaration Rts.* art. 13, *supra* note 184, at 6–7; U.S. Const. amend. II; *see* Levy, *supra* note 233, at 133–49. As expressed in Virginia, this was not a citizen right "to keep and bear Arms." However, the Pennsylvania Declaration of Rights (1776) did include that individual right. "[T]he people have a right to bear arms for the defence of themselves and the state." *Pennsylvania Constitution of 1776, Declaration of Rights* art. 13, in 5 FOUNDERS' CONSTITUTION, *supra* note 61, at 6, 7. Beccaria also supported a personal right to carry arms. "The laws that forbid the carrying of arms ... disarm those only who are neither inclined nor determined to commit crimes.... Such laws make things worse for the assaulted and better for the assailants; they serve rather to encourage than to prevent homicides." CESARE BECCARIA, ON CRIMES AND PUNISHMENTS 87–88 (Henry Paolucci trans., 1963) (ch. 38); *see* BESSLER, *supra* note 86, at 391–93; *infra* note 279 and accompanying text (Beccaria's influence).

[264] *Va. Declaration Rts.* art. 10, *supra* note 184, at 6; U.S. Const. amend. IV; *see* Levy, *supra* note 233, at 150–79. *See generally* WILLIAM J. CUDDIHY, THE FOURTH AMENDMENT: ORIGINS AND ORIGINAL MEANING, 602–1791 (2009).

[265] *Va. Declaration Rts.* art. 8, *supra* note 184, at 6; Mason, *Draft Virginia Declaration*, *supra* note 61, at para. 7; U.S. Const. amends. V, VI; *see* Levy, *supra* note 233, at 180–202.

[266] *Va. Declaration Rts.* art. 6, *supra* note 184, at 6; Mason, *Draft Virginia Declaration*, *supra* note 61, at para. 6; U.S. Const. amend. V.

[267] *Va. Declaration Rts.* art. 11, *supra* note 184, at 6; Mason, *Draft Virginia Declaration*, para. 10, *supra* note 61; U.S. Const. amend. VII.

(8) "[E]xcessive bail ought not to be required, nor excessive fines imposed, nor cruel and unusual punishments inflicted."[268]

The influence of Mason's draft on the Virginia convention delegates in 1776 and the resultant Virginia Declaration's similarity with much of Madison's proposed amendments in 1789 is striking. An important difference is that Madison did not endorse the "ought to be" language used in England or Virginia, but strengthened it with "shall" or "shall not." Of the first eight U.S. Amendments, all have portions that are recognizable from the Virginia Declaration except for the Third Amendment. Behind this impact was Enlightenment natural rights theory and principles that Mason and Madison both knew. Locke's natural rights theory coupled with Montesquieu's concept of separation of powers formed a coherent philosophical basis for American government after 1791. The link between the two was judicial authority to defend natural rights, a view supported by Jefferson, Madison, Hamilton, and Wilson.[269]

Although Locke's natural rights theory supported legal argument from 1776 to 1791, he supplied few details that would be useful in drafting a list of rights. His primary contribution elaborated the natural right that persons in society had in property. In the *Second Treatise of Government*, Locke's chapter on the limit of legislative power described principles related to government appropriation and taxation of property.[270] The legislative power "cannot take from any Man any part of his Property without his own consent. For the preservation of Property being the end of Government, and that for which Men enter into Society, it necessarily supposes and requires, that the People should have Property."[271] Since government requires revenue to act, part of which is to protect peoples' property, it follows that a property owner "should pay out of his Estate his proportion for the maintenance of it. But still it must be with his own Consent, i.e. the Consent of the Majority ... or their Representatives."[272]

The style, detail, and organization of Montesquieu's *Spirit of the Laws*,[273] unlike Locke's lack of detail, provided several important examples related to

---

[268] Va. Declaration Rts. art. 9, *supra* note 184, at 6; U.S. Const. amend. VIII; *see* Levy, *supra* note 233, at 231–40.

[269] BODENHEIMER, *supra* note 49, at 46, 49–52; *see id.* at 52 n.15 (Jefferson in a 1789 letter to Madison); *The Federalist* No. 78 (Hamilton), *supra* note 108, at 467; *supra* text accompanying note 166 (Wilson) and 248 (Madison). Locke wrote that authorized judges would dispense justice and determine natural rights in a less biased and emotional manner than a legislature would. JOHN LOCKE, THE SECOND TREATISE OF GOVERNMENT AND A LETTER CONCERNING TOLERATION 69 (ch. 11, § 136) (3d ed., J.W. Gough ed., 1966) (first published as *Two Treatises of Government* (1690)).

[270] LOCKE, *supra* note 269, at 67–73 (ch. 11). Locke often used "property" as it existed in nature to mean "life, liberty, and estate." *Id.* at 43 (ch. 7, § 87), 63 (ch. 9, § 123), 68 (ch. 11, § 135); *see* BODENHEIMER, *supra* note 49, at 45–46.

[271] LOCKE, *supra* note 269, at 71 (ch. 11, § 138).

[272] *Id.* at 72 (ch. 11, § 140).

[273] MONTESQUIEU, *supra* note 102.

government and individual rights. He wrote about the role of the state in toleration for religion. Outside of theocracies and monotheistic states, the general principle should be state toleration toward religion. "When the laws of a state have believed they should allow many religions, they must also oblige them to tolerate each other." Here "is the fundamental principle for political laws in religious matters. When one is master of the state's accepting a new religion, or not accepting it, it must not be established; when it is established, it must be tolerated."[274] Locke also defended government toleration of religion and asserted that "liberty of conscience is every man's natural right."[275]

Montesquieu reflected on judicial process concerning life and property. "[I]n moderate states where the head of even the lowest citizen is esteemed, his honor and goods are removed from him only after long examination; he is deprived of his life only when the homeland itself attacks it [and] gives him every possible means of defending it."[276] He proposed a maxim, "it is never in the public good for an individual to be deprived of his goods ... by a political law.... [I]t is necessary to observe strictly the civil law which is the *palladium* of property.... If the political magistrate wants to build some public edifice, some new road, he must pay compensation."[277]

Finally, Montesquieu contemplated the role of punishment in law. "Men must not be led to extremes; one should manage the means that nature gives us to guide them. If one examines the cause of every instance of laxity, one will see that it is unpunished crimes and not moderated penalties.... It is essential for penalties to be harmonious among themselves, because it is essential that the greater crime be avoided rather than the lesser one."[278] The founders were also familiar with Beccaria's *On Crimes and Punishments*.[279] His proportionality principle between the seriousness of crime in its harm to society and the appropriate punishment, based on utilitarian theory, provided theory and illustration to the Eighth Amendment's general prohibition of "cruel and unusual punishments."[280]

---

[274] *Id.* at 487–88 (25.9, 25.10). Compare: "Congress shall make no law respecting an establishment of religion, or prohibiting the free exercise thereof." U.S. Const. amend. I.

[275] LOCKE, *supra* note 269, at 125, 135, 148, 159 (*A Letter Concerning Toleration*).

[276] MONTESQUIEU, *supra* note 102, at 75 (6.2). Compare: "No person shall ... be deprived of life, liberty, or property, without due process of law." U.S. Const. amend. V.

[277] MONTESQUIEU, *supra* note 102, at 510 (26.15) (emphasis in original). Compare: "[P]rivate property [shall not] be taken for public use without just compensation." U.S. Const. amend. V.

[278] MONTESQUIEU, *supra* note 102, at 85, 91 (6.12, 6.16). Compare: "[E]xcessive fines [shall not] be imposed, nor cruel and unusual punishments." U.S. Const. amend. VIII.

[279] CESARE, MARCHESE DI BECCARIA, DEI DELITTI E DELLE PENE (published anonymously 1764, first translated into English as *An Essay on Crimes and Punishments*, 1767). Several founders cited Beccaria in their legal argument, among them Adams, Jefferson, Madison, and Wilson. *See* BESSLER, *supra* note 86, at 163–69, 173–95, 205–09; *supra* notes 86, 263 and accompanying text (Beccaria).

[280] BESSLER, *supra* note 86, at 36–38, 179–80, 368–75. Beccaria wrote "It is to the common interest not only that crimes not be committed, but also that they be less frequent in proportion to the harm they cause society. Therefore, the obstacles that deter men from committing crimes should be stronger in proportion as they are contrary to the public good, and as the inducements to commit

J. Classical Legal Models

Classical history and philosophy provided the constitutional framers four sets of values that together influenced the debate and ultimately the U.S. Constitution. First, historical perspective offered insight into ancient rationalism and useful knowledge. Second, the sources illustrated a political ethic and morality necessary for the personal integrity and trust associated with the framers' relationships as well as examples of virtue, fame, and honor. Third, the classics gave a political vocabulary for advocates and detractors—and their readers—to communicate and receive ideas useful to achieve agreement on the Constitution. There was a significant anticlassicist faction—exemplified by Franklin—while even the most learned in ancient writers sometimes had doubt about a classical comparison to American reality. However, overall, classical public law comparison was pervasive.[281] Thus, Hamilton could write in *Federalist* No. 70 in support of a strong executive that even the "least conversant in Roman history knows how often that republic was obliged to take refuge in the absolute power of a single man ... as against the invasions of external enemies who menaced the conquest and destruction of Rome."[282] Fourth, the classics offered a style and mode of thinking helpful to understand Enlightenment political philosophy and especially principles of natural law and rights.[283]

Bederman argued that classical legal and political literature was instrumental for two central elements of the structural Constitution: (1) the Senate's role in checking the popularly elected assembly and (2) selection of the president. The founders intended the Senate to be an elite institution, informed by the experience of Sparta, Carthage, and Rome. The Roman Senate allowed the election of plebians based on age and public experience, which avoided the hereditary aristocracy in the British House of Lords. The Electoral College system for president, although against Wilson's desire for direct, popular election, had some resemblance to Roman voting assemblies, reducing sectional rivalries and electoral corruption. Both Federalists and Anti-Federalists believed that limited government best protected liberty—separated and checked—and layered as federal, state, and local. Classical polities provided the examples.[284]

---

them are stronger. There must, therefore, be a proper proportion between crimes and punishments."
BECCARIA, *supra* note 263, at 62 (ch. 23).

[281] BEDERMAN, *supra* note 2, at 26; *see id.* at 26–44, 223.
[282] *The Federalist, supra* note 108, at 423.
[283] BEDERMAN, *supra* note 2, at 26, see id. at 45–49.
[284] *Id.* at 223–25. Classical ideas also informed the Constitution's Guarantee Clause in both the provision (1) to guarantee every state a republican form of government and (2) to protect each state against invasion. U.S. Const. art. IV, § 4; BEDERMAN, *supra*, at 209–21, 227. Bederman did not claim that classical antiquity provided the chief inspiration for constitutional text. "The Framing generation's use of classical authority in designing not only the broad contours of the constitutional

Richard largely supported this view of the place for the classics during the revolutionary period. Its ideas formed the basis for theories of government structure, social responsibility, human nature, and virtue. They facilitated communication by providing a common set of illustrations that both Federalists and Anti-Federalists could reference. Furthermore, they served as precedent for a Whig politics that the American revolutionaries were preserving liberty, defending natural rights, and not upsetting the natural order. They had ready symbols for friend and foe: Jefferson as Cato or Cicero, while George III could be Nero or Caligula. Patriots invoked classical history at the Constitutional Convention and subsequent ratifying conventions regarding political theory on mixed government and republics, the dangers of democracy, as well as the Constitution's specific clauses.[285]

How should we assess the foremost lawyers who created the legal documents that declared the United States an independent nation and then wrote the principal public law instruments for the states, the confederation, and the federal republic? The argument in this chapter is that most of these individuals were engaged in professional comparative law. Bederman contended that with the primary sources available to them, the founders did a reputable job in attempting to understand the legal structure of antiquity and apply it to the task. He identified, among those discussed here, Adams, Hamilton, Jefferson, Madison, Wilson, and Wythe as the best classicists. Largely influenced by Whig politics, they read critically, checked historical institutions in separate accounts, and strategically assessed the social and political differences between ancient Greece and Rome compared to America.[286] As expressed on the Great Seal, approved by the first U.S. Congress in 1789, America would be *novus ordo seclorum*, a new order for the ages.[287]

---

scheme and drafting particular clauses ... should be considered as a coequal body of originalist literature." *Id.* at 227.

[285] RICHARD, *supra* note 12, at 232–37.
[286] BEDERMAN, *supra* note 2, at 228–29, 231.
[287] U.S. Dept. State, *The Great Seal of the United States* (2003), https://2009-2017.state.gov/documents/organization/27807.pdf; *see* FORREST MCDONALD, NOVUS ORDO SECLORUM: THE INTELLECTUAL ORIGINS OF THE CONSTITUTION (1985).

4
The Formative Era: 1791–1865

Why might we not have *comparative law*, to place the legal systems of different countries and ages side by side, that the lawyer may profit by the history of the world? He is, perhaps the only man of science who does not look beyond his own commonwealth, and to whom the history of other countries is as a sealed book.

David Dudley Field[1]

A. The Shift from Public to Private Law

After the impressive creativity demonstrated from 1776 to 1791 in formulating the central public law documents required to organize and to constrain federal and state governments, American lawyers with knowledge of Enlightenment legal philosophy and Roman and civil law turned primarily to the task of constructing a system of private law. This chapter will concentrate on investigating that activity prior to the end of the Civil War. Nevertheless, there were exceptions to interest in private law, which we will also consider. For instance, European Enlightenment writing about reform of penal justice rules and practices—the traditional core of public law—affected legislation at the state level in that field. Furthermore, the United States Supreme Court— Joseph Story (1779–1845) in particular—undertook the responsibility of providing detailed meaning to clauses in the U.S. Constitution and its amendments.

George Dargo investigated the antebellum period after 1790 with emphasis on courts, litigation, and common law doctrine. First, he recognized that government stimulus for economic activity—banking and finance, patent and monopoly protection, surveying, and shipping as well as construction of roads, canals, harbors, and railroads—was crucial in early economic development of competitive agriculture and later manufacturing.[2] Second, however, there was

---

[1] David Dudley Field, *Study and Practice of the Law* (1844), *in* 1 Speeches, Arguments, and Miscellaneous Papers of David Dudley Field 484, 491 (A.P. Sprague ed., 1884) (emphasis in original).

[2] George Dargo, Law in the New Republic: Private Law and the Public Estate 2, 4–5 (1983) [hereinafter Dargo, Private Law]; Mark R. Wilson, *Law and the American State, from the Revolution to the Civil War: Institutional Growth and Structural Change*, *in* 2 The Cambridge History of Law in America: The Long Century (1789–1920) 1, 13–15, 17–20 (Michael Grossberg & Christopher Tomlins eds., 2008) [hereinafter 2 Cambridge History of Law].

a decided cultural shift from public values and virtue toward private decision-making, the private sector, and individualism. The early nineteenth century saw the emergence in America of the distinction between public and private in law.[3] Meyer Reinhold found the same change in interest associated with the decline in classical learning to support public morality. After 1790, classical literature and languages seemed less useful for individuals, elitist, and an impediment to science and practical studies.[4]

Natural law did not suddenly dissipate as a legal philosophy in 1791 after its impressive influence on public law during the Revolutionary Era. Rather its effect among lawyers swung toward private law as embodied in legislative reform efforts and in legal treatise and periodical writing.[5] Furthermore, R.H. Helmholz contended that natural law affected important American case law. These cases included contracts, the family, inheritance, and personal and real property. There was no accepted catalog of natural rights; instead, the rules operated as principles to apply to specific situations. They also often confirmed a rule of the common law or statutory interpretation. In fact, lawyers conversant with natural law, which in theory was superior to positive law, typically sought that solution.[6]

Despite a decline of interest in classical studies and a cultural move toward private interests, Michael Hoeflich identified four developments that expanded interest in Roman and civil law in the United States during the first half of the nineteenth century. First, a general hostility toward English culture and law increased after the War of 1812, during which Americans lost several battles and suffered numerous hardships including the British burning of the capital at Washington. After the Treaty of Ghent in 1815, ending hostilities, American jurists were more willing to consider Roman and civil law solutions to private law

---

An illustration involved Robert Livingston, whom the New York legislature provided a monopoly for steamboat use on the Hudson River. While Livingston served as minister to France in 1803, Robert Fulton tested a steamboat on the River Seine. Livingston contracted with Fulton to use his steam engine design for a commercial steamboat on the Hudson between Albany and New York City. Passenger service began on the *North River Steamboat* in 1807 and was an economic success. *See* KIRKPATRICK SALE, THE FIRE OF HIS GENIUS: ROBERT FULTON AND THE AMERICAN DREAM (2001); *infra* notes 17, 20 and accompanying text (Livingston in Paris).

[3] DARGO, PRIVATE LAW, *supra* note 2, at 4–5, 8–9.
[4] MEYER REINHOLD, CLASSICA AMERICANA: THE GREEK AND ROMAN HERITAGE IN THE UNITED STATES 174–83, 194 (1984). The classical decline was not immediate after 1790, but took hold in the early nineteenth century. *See* Richard J. Hoffman, *Classics in the Courts of the United States, 1790–1800*, 22 AM. J. LEG. HIST. 55 (1978) [hereinafter Richard Hoffman]. Hoffman compared the U.S. Supreme Court to the Virginia High Court of Chancery, the latter due to the importance of its first chancellor, George Wythe. *Id.* at 56–58, 65.
[5] ROSCOE POUND, THE FORMATIVE ERA OF AMERICAN LAW 3–6, 12–13, 20, 23–24, 27 (1936) [hereinafter POUND, FORMATIVE ERA]; R.H. Helmholz, *The Law of Nature and the Early History of Unenumerated Rights in the United States*, 9 U. PA. J. CONST. L. 401–03, 407 (2007) [hereinafter Helmholz, *Law of Nature*].
[6] Helmholz, *Law of Nature*, *supra* note 5, at 408–11, 413–18, 420–21. From 1789 to 1825, the U.S. Supreme Court cited Grotius, Pufendorf, or Vattel at least 90 times. *Id.* at 407.

issues that arose. Second, Congress incorporated new territory as states into the Union, especially Louisiana (1812) and Florida (1845), which had been subject to a civil law system. Jurists in those regions faced legal problems that required attention to both civil law and common law traditions. Third, as tensions grew between the interests of northern and southern states, a distinct southern literary and legal culture emerged that drew inspiration from Roman and European sources, including from Scotland. Finally, legal education became more rigorous and sophisticated, leading jurists to turn toward Roman and civil law to formulate a more scientific approach to private law than the common law provided for legal doctrine.[7]

B. Territorial Expansion: Jefferson and the Louisiana Purchase

The Treaty of Paris (1783), ending the Revolutionary War, established the initial territorial boundaries of the United States on terms beneficial to the new nation.[8] Because the Treaty's article 1 released British claims to the several American states, it took two decades for them and the federal government to resolve issues of boundaries and sovereignty over territorial claims, especially related to western lands extending to the Mississippi River.[9] The Congress of the Confederation enacted several statutes to facilitate this, including the Land Ordinance (1784) and the Northwest Ordinance (1787). The former provided some geographical guidelines for state lands ceded to the national government that Congress contemplated would eventually form new states. The more detailed Northwest Ordinance asserted national sovereignty over western territory north of the Ohio River (article 4) and foresaw the admittance of three to five new states, constituted as republics (article 5). It also protected religious freedom, private contracts, and various individual rights like those in the 1791 Bill of Rights (articles 1 and 2), emphasized Native American rights (article 3), and prohibited the establishment of slavery (article 6).[10] In 1798, Congress

---

[7] M.H. HOEFLICH, ROMAN AND CIVIL LAW AND THE DEVELOPMENT OF ANGLO-AMERICAN JURISPRUDENCE IN THE NINETEENTH CENTURY 1–2, 7–8 (1997) [hereinafter HOEFLICH, ROMAN AND CIVIL LAW]. The Treaty of Ghent between Great Britain and the United States, once ratified in February 1815, ended the War of 1812, and provided terms facilitating amity between the two nations. Both agreed to use their "best endeavors" to end slave trade, as "irreconcileable with the principles of humanity" (art. 10). See 8 Stat. 218 (1814). Law schools that developed in the early nineteenth century were not much more than law training offices. This was true even at Harvard until Story provided a more scholarly focus. See infra pt. D.1 (legal education).
[8] The Definitive Treaty of Peace 1783 art. 2, Gr. Brit.-U.S., 3 Sept. 1783, T.S. No. 104, 8 Stat. 80, 12 Bevans 8; see National Archives, https://www.ourdocuments.gov (search Treaty of Paris 1783).
[9] Congress was the only federal institution under the Articles of Confederation (arts. 2, 13).
[10] See National Archives, supra note 8 (search Land Ordinance 1784 or Northwest Ordinance 1787); Wilson, supra note 2, at 28–29.

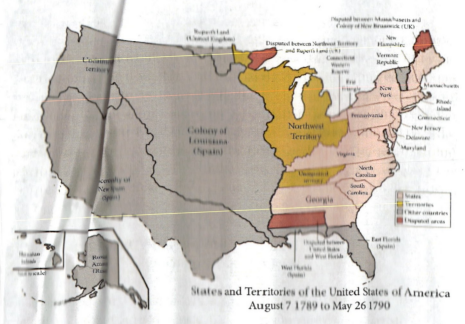

States and Territories of the United States of America
August 7 1789 to May 26 1790

Figure 4.1 U.S. States and Territories in 1790

extended the Northwest model (but permitting slavery) to the southern territory of Mississippi, which would later form that state and Alabama.[11]

The Louisiana Purchase in 1803[12] was the first substantial addition to national territory, more than doubling the U.S. land and inland waterways from 1790.[13] France had asserted sovereignty since 1682 over New Orleans and the surrounding area of *La Louisiane*, named after King Louis XIV (ruled 1643–1715). However, France (and Spain) lost the Seven Years' War (1756–1763) and in the Treaty of Paris (1763), France relinquished Louisiana territory east of the Mississippi River (excluding New Orleans) to Great Britain. Spain, which claimed *La Florida* from the sixteenth century, ceded that land to Britain, which divided these territories into East and West Florida.[14] In 1762, the Spanish had joined

---

[11] LAWRENCE M. FRIEDMAN, A HISTORY OF AMERICAN LAW 105 (3d ed. 2005) [hereinafter FRIEDMAN, HISTORY]. For the comparative law dimension related to slave law, see infra pt. I (slavery).

[12] Golbez created Figure 4.1 and placed it in the public domain. See https://en.wikipedia.org/wiki/Northwest_Ordinance.

[13] BUREAU OF THE CENSUS, HISTORICAL STATISTICS OF THE UNITED STATES: COLONIAL TIMES TO 1970 (part 1) 428 (1975) [hereinafter HISTORICAL STATISTICS]. In 1803, the population of Lower Louisiana was approximately 27,500: 15,000 of European ancestry, 11,000 slaves, and 1,500 free persons of African or Native American ancestry. PETER J. KASTOR, THE NATION'S CRUCIBLE: THE LOUISIANA PURCHASE AND THE CREATION OF AMERICA 30–31, 33, 242 n.40 (2004).

[14] Junius P. Rodriguez, *Introduction*, in THE LOUISIANA PURCHASE: A HISTORICAL AND GEOGRAPHIC ENCYCLOPEDIA xvii, xviii–xx (Junius P. Rodriguez ed., 2002) [hereinafter LOUISIANA PURCHASE]; Rory T. Cornish, *Paris, Treaty of (1763)*, in LOUISIANA PURCHASE, supra, at 272–73. France also gave Britain Québec under the Treaty. The French loss of Québec and eastern Louisiana

---

Due to a production error, this figure was omitted from the first printing of this book; subsequent printings include the figure as intended.

France in the war, but Britain defeated France that year in the war's last major battle in North America. Since both France and Spain had monarchs from the House of Bourbon and in exchange for Spain's assistance in Europe, France had already given western Louisiana to Spain in the secret Treaty of Fontainebleau (1762).[15] Spain effectively incorporated New Orleans and western Louisiana (*Luisiana*) into its colonial viceroyalty system in 1768, which continued until 1803. Nevertheless, Spain in two treaties from 1800 and 1801 promised to return its Louisiana territory to France. Spain also agreed to continue administering the area until delivery occurred.[16]

In 1801, Thomas Jefferson, the third U.S. president (1801–1809), appointed Robert Livingston as minister to France.[17] He and envoy James Monroe offered Napoléon Bonaparte, First Consul of the French Republic, up to $10 million for the purchase of New Orleans and adjacent Gulf coastal areas from France. Napoléon needed funds to finance his military campaigns and, with other difficulties in French American colonies, offered to sell all of Louisiana for $15 million in cash and debt forgiveness. The American delegates accepted this surprising proposal. Jefferson ignored political dissent at home that the Constitution did not list land purchase among the president's or Congress's powers, contending that the provision authorizing the president to negotiate treaties implied such authority.[18] In November 1803, Spain fulfilled its treaty promise to France of retrocession of Louisiana, three weeks prior to France's ceremony in New Orleans ceding Lower Louisiana to the United States. The conveyance of Upper Louisiana,

---

in 1763 initiated the Acadian (Cajun) migration from the north and French settlers from the east side of the Mississippi River to New Orleans and western Louisiana. Cornish, *supra*, at 273.

[15] Rodriguez, *supra* note 14, at xx; F.F. Stone, *The Reception of Law in Louisiana*, in LEGAL THOUGHT IN THE UNITED STATES OF AMERICA UNDER CONTEMPORARY PRESSURES 127, 130–31 (John H. Hazard & Wenceslas J. Wagner eds., 1970). The North American component of the Seven Years' War was the French and Indian War. Spain did not contest British sovereignty in eastern Louisiana after 1763 and only revealed its claim to New Orleans and western Louisiana in 1764. *Id.*; Elizabeth Pugliese, *Fontainebleau, Treaty of (1762)*, in LOUISIANA PURCHASE, *supra* note 14, at 112–13.

[16] Rodriguez, *supra* note 14, at xx; Stone, *supra* note 15, at 131–34. Spain's treaties with France were the secret Treaty of San Ildefonso (1800), confirmed by the Treaty of Aranjuez (1801). Rodriguez, *supra*, at xxii–xxiii; Thomas C. Sosnowski, *San Ildefonso, Treaty of (1800)*, in LOUISIANA PURCHASE, *supra* note 14, at 305–06.

[17] Regarding Livingston's life and family history in New York, *see* James Brown Scott, *Robert R. Livingston, 1746–1813*, *in* 1 GREAT AMERICAN LAWYERS 435–72 (William Draper Lewis ed., 1907).

[18] KASTOR, *supra* note 13, at 39–41; Rodriguez, *supra* note 14, at xxiii–xxiv; *see* Act of 31 Oct. 1803, ch. 1, 2 Stat. 245, Library of Congress, *The Louisiana Purchase: A Legislative Timeline*, https://memory.loc.gov/ammem/amlaw/louisiana2.html [hereinafter *LC Louisiana Timeline*]. James Madison was secretary of state during Jefferson's presidency. GEORGE DARGO, JEFFERSON'S LOUISIANA: POLITICS AND THE CLASH OF LEGAL TRADITIONS 38–39 (rev. ed. 2009) [hereinafter DARGO, JEFFERSON'S LOUISIANA]. The Senate ratified the Louisiana Purchase Treaty and both legislative chambers appropriated the necessary money: $11.3 million in cash and $3.7 million to pay U.S. citizens who had claims against the French government. Acts of 10 Nov. 1803, chs. 2–3, 2 Stat. 245, 247.

furthermore, occurred on two days in March 1804 in St. Louis as a transfer from Spain to France to the United States.[19]

Even before Livingston and Monroe signed the Louisiana Purchase Treaty on behalf of the United States in April 1803,[20] Jefferson had sent a secret letter to Congress in January requesting $2,500 for an expedition of 10 to 12 men to explore Western lands "even to the Western Ocean," to negotiate with Native Americans, and to extend commerce.[21] Congress approved the request in February.[22] Jefferson selected Meriwether Lewis, his secretary, to lead the exploration party, the Corps of Discovery. Lewis contacted an army friend, William Clark, to help lead the group. After witnessing the St. Louis ceremony transferring Upper Louisiana, the Corps departed in May 1804 for its two-year trip West over the Rocky Mountains until it reached the Columbia River's end at the Pacific Ocean in 1805 and wintered at Fort Clatsop.[23] After the Treaty of Ghent (1815), American relations with Great Britain were sufficiently amiable that the two countries signed a treaty in 1818 that agreed to a boundary line in the Pacific Northwest at the 49th parallel north latitude. The treaty called for joint occupancy (for ten years) in the southern region (Oregon Country for Americans and Columbia District for the British). The Oregon Treaty (1846) confirmed the reality of American immigration to the area, giving the United States sovereignty to Oregon Country.[24]

As mentioned earlier, France and Spain ceded territory east of the Mississippi River to Great Britain that then proceeded, in 1763, to divide into East and West Florida. These colonies remained loyal to Britain during the Revolutionary War. However, under the 1783 Treaty of Paris, Britain returned these lands to Spain, which loosely administered parts of them until the Adams-Onís Treaty (1819), which in 1821, transferred what remained of Spain's territory in that area to the United States.[25] The residual of Spanish

---

[19] Junius P. Rodriguez, *Saint Louis*, in LOUISIANA PURCHASE, *supra* note 14, at 304; *see supra* text accompanying notes 15–16 (Spain's administration of Louisiana until 1803). Congress divided the new land into two U.S. territories: Orleans and the district of Louisiana. Act of 26 Mar. 1804, ch. 38, §§ 1, 12, 2 Stat. 283, *LC Louisiana Timeline*, *supra* note 18. Orleans became the State of Louisiana in 1812, at which time Congress renamed the latter Missouri Territory. Rodriguez, *supra* note 14, at xxvi.

[20] Treaty of 30 Apr. 1803, 8 Stat. 200, 206, *LC Louisiana Timeline*, *supra* note 18.

[21] *Letter of 18 Jan. 1803*, in LOUISIANA PURCHASE, *supra* note 14, at 404–05; *LC Louisiana Timeline*, *supra* note 18.

[22] Act of 28 Feb. 1803, ch. 12, 2 Stat. 206, *LC Louisiana Timeline*, *supra* note 18.

[23] Rodriguez, *supra* note 14, at xxiv–xxv.

[24] Douglas W. Dodd, *Oregon Country*, in LOUISIANA PURCHASE, *supra* note 14, at 263, 265; Melinda Marie Jetté, *Convention of 1818*, in LOUISIANA PURCHASE, *supra*, at 85; *see supra* note 7 and accompanying text (Treaty of Ghent). In 1845, there were 5,000 Americans in Oregon compared to only 750 British subjects. In 1848, Congress created the Oregon Territory. Dodd, *supra*, at 265.

[25] Scott D. Wignall, *Transcontinental Treaty (1819)*, in LOUISIANA PURCHASE, *supra* note 14, at 336–37. The Senate ratified the treaty a second time in 1821, the same year Mexico gained its independence from the Spanish Empire. Spain gave up its claim to Oregon Country while the United States relinquished its claim to most of Texas and agreed to pay up to $5 million in American claims against Spain. In 1822, Congress organized the Florida land as a new U.S. territory. *Id.* at 336–38.

law in East Florida, including that of the Cádiz Constitution (1812), was slight.[26]

Because of these developments, by 1821, the United States had expanded to 24 states from the original 13 states in 1791. The census population during this time grew from 4 million to 9.9 million inhabitants.[27] Substantial parts of the southern tier from Florida to Louisiana had been under Spanish and French rule immediately prior to accession to the United States. This presented lawyers in those regions, especially the new state of Louisiana, with potential comparative law issues associated with the civil law tradition. The Spanish provinces of Texas, New Mexico, and California had very few lawyers or administrators, notaries, or judges with even a partial training in Roman and civil law. Nevertheless, some Spanish legal texts and commentaries circulated in northern New Spain and influenced the magistrates tasked with judicial duties. Thus, the Spanish legal system did have a noticeable effect on the law of real property, water rights, marriage, and inheritance that found its way into American jurisprudence.[28]

The most important early civil law influence in this newly acquired region occurred in Louisiana when it was still Orleans Territory, shortly after acquisition by the United States.[29] In 1803, Jefferson appointed William Claiborne, a successful lawyer from Tennessee, territorial governor. Claiborne held that office until 1812, when voters elected him Louisiana's first governor.[30] In 1804, Congress enacted legislation to define the boundaries of Orleans and establish the details of local government. In addition to executive power, the act provided the governor primary authority to approve, alter, or repeal laws, with the advice and consent of a 13-person legislative council that the president annually appointed.[31] The majority French-speaking population in Lower Louisiana was disappointed in the act, since it did not provide a timetable for statehood,

---

[26] M.C. Mirow, *The Constitution of Cádiz in Florida*, 24 FLA. J. INT'L L. 271, 328–29 (2012).

[27] HISTORICAL STATISTICS (part 1), *supra* note 13, at 8, 38.

[28] CHARLES R. CUTTER, THE LEGAL CULTURE OF NORTHERN NEW SPAIN, 1700–1810, at 3–4, 6, 36–37, 69, 82, 96, 99–102 (1995); DARGO, JEFFERSON'S LOUISIANA, *supra* note 18, at 21–31; *see* Hans W. Baade, *The Formalities of Private Real Estate Transactions in Spanish North America*, 38 LA. L. REV. 655 (1978); *id.*, *Marriage Contracts in French and Spanish Louisiana: A Study in "Notarial" Jurisprudence*, 53 TUL. L. REV. 1 (1978); *id.*, *The Form of Marriage in Spanish North America*, 61 CORNELL L. REV. 1 (1975); Stuart Banner, *Written Law and Unwritten Norms in Colonial St. Louis*, 14 LAW & HIST. REV. 33 (1996); FRIEDMAN, HISTORY, *supra* note 11, at 113–17; Mathias Reimann, *The Notary in American Legal History: The Fall and Rise of the Civil Law Tradition?*, *in* HANDBUCH ZUR GESCHICHTE DES NOTARIATS DER EUROPÄISCHEN TRADITIONEN 559, 565–70 (Mathias Schumoeckel & Werner Schubert eds., 2009).

[29] FRIEDMAN, HISTORY, *supra* note 11, at 116–17.

[30] DARGO, JEFFERSON'S LOUISIANA, *supra* note 18, at 43–50; Kastor, *supra* note 13, at 149–51. Claiborne, the national government's chief legal representative while he was territorial governor, made regular reports to Madison, then Secretary of State. DARGO, JEFFERSON'S LOUISIANA, *supra*, at 44, 47, 49–50, 77.

[31] DARGO, JEFFERSON'S LOUISIANA, *supra* note 18, at 50–52, 186–87; Act of 26 Mar. 1804, *supra* note 17, § 4. Congress could also veto the territory's legislation. *Id.* § 4.

self-government, or for continued importation of slaves. Edward Livingston (1764–1836), younger brother of Robert Livingston, had recently arrived from New York and took the local side in drafting the *Louisiana Remonstrance* (1804), a memorial of grievances forwarded to Congress.[32]

Congress responded to the *Remonstrance* with a revised territorial statute in 1805, permitting an elected 25-member general assembly.[33] The new assembly selected ten local persons, whose names it forwarded to President Jefferson. He then submitted five to the Senate for approval to serve on the Orleans legislative council. When the first council met in 1806, all members were French. It soon passed a bill declaring the civil law in force within the territory. The bill named civilian legal authorities applicable, pending the completion of a private law codification. Claiborne vetoed this and other council bills, provoking local outrage and threatening a collapse of government. He was in a difficult position, since his power depended on pleasing the federal government, but stability in the region required local support. After the 1806 crisis, Claiborne shifted his policy more toward local interests, highlighted by his approval in 1808 of the territorial legislature's adoption of America's first private law codification, a civil law digest.[34]

Livingston's background, growing up in a wealthy and influential New York family, included private tutoring, education at the College of New Jersey, and law training with John Lansing. Lansing, of Dutch ancestry, taught Livingston Roman law, which likely predisposed him toward the systematic coherence of the civil law.[35] Lansing, New York chancellor from 1801 to 1814, followed New York's first chancellor, Robert Livingston, who James Kent (1763–1847) in turn succeeded.[36] Edward Livingston's first effort at codification occurred after nine years as a lawyer in New York when voters elected him to the U.S. House

---

[32] DARGO, JEFFERSON'S LOUISIANA, *supra* note 18, at 32–33, 51–56, 61–62, 164, 196, 204–05, 209–10; *see supra* text accompanying notes 17–20 (Robert Livingston). French speakers in Lower Louisiana consisted of creoles (born in Louisiana), Acadians (who left Canada from the 1760s to the 1790s), and people born in France, who were mostly refugees from the French Revolution and civil strife in the Caribbean. DARGO, JEFFERSON'S LOUISIANA, *supra*, at 12–13. Edward Livingston also undertook to harmonize various elements of Orleans law. He authored the Practice Act (1805), a simplified system of procedure, and about the same time translated parts of the *Corpus Juris Civilis* into English. *Id.* at 180–81, 196–97; *see infra* at notes 38–39 and accompanying text (1805 Practice Act).

[33] Act of 2 Mar. 1805, ch. 23, §§ 2, 4, 2 Stat. 322, *LC Louisiana Timeline, supra* note 18. Congress also provided for Lower Louisiana to petition for statehood upon reaching a population of 60,000 free inhabitants. Act of 2 Mar. 1805, *supra* § 7.

[34] DARGO, JEFFERSON'S LOUISIANA, *supra* note 18, at 83–87, 131, 188–90, 223–66, 269. In 1803, Jefferson supported importation of the common law to Orleans since he felt the nation would develop more easily with a similar legal system throughout. He maintained that position until 1808. DARGO, JEFFERSON'S LOUISIANA, *supra*, at 181, 188–93, 267, 270, 294, 304.

[35] MARK F. FERNANDEZ, FROM CHAOS TO CONTINUITY: THE EVOLUTION OF LOUISIANA'S JUDICIAL SYSTEM, 1712–1862, at 58, 74 (2001).

[36] Historical Society of the New York Courts, *New York State Court of Chancery*, https://www.nycourts.gov/history/legal-history-new-york/history-legal-bench-court-chancery.html.

of Representatives (serving 1795–1801). For two years following his election, he proposed federal penal reform in the style of a code enlightened toward criminal rehabilitation and reduced use of capital punishment. The House committees he chaired were unsuccessful in that effort.[37]

Livingston's second attempt at codification followed in the civil-law friendly Orleans Territory. There he drafted a simplified procedure for the Practice Act of 1805, which the Legislative Council adopted for use in the territorial superior court as well as in county and justice of the peace courts. Consisting of 22 sections, it required a petition stating a cause of action followed by an answer admitting, avoiding, or denying facts. Both parties could conduct discovery with written interrogatories, but had to submit all facts to the judge prior to a jury trial. Important portions of the act carried over to the 1825 Louisiana Code of Practice.[38] Livingston's sources likely included a mixture of Spanish and French procedure modified to reflect U.S. common law sovereignty with its support for jury trial, open court oral testimony, and extraordinary writs. Most Louisiana jurists have contended that Spanish norms were dominant even though the legislature promulgated the 1805 Act in French and English. Congress also provided for general continuity of legal norms until altered, which supported principally Spanish law. The Orleans legal profession accepted Spanish procedure as the primary basis for the act, which remained in effect (until 1825) into early statehood.[39]

The most significant civil law influence in pre-statehood Louisiana involved the *Digest of the Civil Laws* (1808).[40] After Governor Claiborne's 1806 veto of the territorial assembly's bill to declare the applicable law in Orleans—Roman and

---

[37] FERNANDEZ, *supra* note 35, at 75; CHARLES HAVENS HUNT, LIFE OF EDWARD LIVINGSTON 83–84, 96–97 n.* (1864).

[38] Henry G. McMahon, *The Proposed Louisiana Code of Practice: A Synthesis of Anglo-American and Continental Civil Procedures*, 14 LA. L. REV. 36, 42–43 (1953) [hereinafter McMahon, *Procedure I*]; An Act Regarding the Practice of the Superior Court in Civil Causes, ch. 26, 10 Apr. 1805, *in* ACTS PASSED AT THE FIRST SESSION OF THE LEGISLATIVE COUNCIL OF THE TERRITORY OF ORLEANS 210–60 (1805) [hereinafter 1805 Practice Act]; see *infra* text accompanying notes 318–326 (Louisiana Code of Practice).

[39] Act of 26 Mar. 1804, *supra* note 17, § 11; McMahon, *Procedure I*, *supra* note 38, at 43–46, 49; Henry G. McMahon, *The Louisiana Code of Civil Procedure*, 21 LA. L. REV. 1, 7–9 (1960) [hereinafter McMahon, *Procedure II*]; Stone, *supra* note 15, at 135–38. In 1769, General Alejandro O'Reilly firmly established Spanish rule through a *cabildo*, *regidores*, *alcaldes*, and inferior courts with appeal to the *cabildo*, then to the *audiencia* in Havana. O'Reilly authorized two procedural ordinances in French, utilizing Spanish sources. Stone, *supra*, at 132–34. The relevant Spanish laws in force in Louisiana appeared in John H. Tucker, Jr., *Source Books of Louisiana Law: Part III—Spanish Laws*, 8 TUL. L. REV. 396–400 (1934) [hereinafter Tucker, *Spanish Laws*].

Another view was that the 1805 Act was a simplification of American chancery practice, which derived from English equity jurisdiction administered by ecclesiastics schooled in Roman-canonic procedure pervasive in continental Europe. In any case, the existence of jury trial and open court testimony required the development of evidence rules. McMahon, *Procedure I*, *supra*, at 43–44, 49; McMahon, *Procedure II*, *supra*, at 8.

[40] John W. Cairns, *Blackstone in the Bayous: Inscribing Slavery in the Louisiana Digest of 1808*, *in* RE-INTERPRETING BLACKSTONE'S COMMENTARIES: A SEMINAL TEXT IN NATIONAL AND

Spanish law—aided by the interpretation of reputable civilian commentators, it passed a resolution that Claiborne approved, appointing James Brown and Louis Moreau-Lislet to prepare a civil code utilizing civil law. Brown had moved to New Orleans from Kentucky in 1804, where he had been a lawyer. President Jefferson initially appointed him territorial secretary and later U.S. district attorney. Despite his common law background, Brown's knowledge of French and Spanish aided his successful practice in Louisiana courts. Moreau-Lislet studied law in Paris prior to his practice in Saint Domingue (later Haiti). He arrived in New Orleans in 1805.[41] Brown was the territory's attorney general from 1807 to 1809, while Moreau-Lislet held that office from 1810 to 1812 and for the state from 1817 to 1818.[42]

The assembly enacted Brown and Moreau-Lislet's Digest in 1808. Consisting of 2,160 articles, it took the form and structure of the 1804 French *Code civil* and its 1800 *Projet du Gouvernement*. As with the *Code*, which had 2,281 articles, the Digest's drafters also divided it into a preliminary title and three books, with titles, chapters, and sections as further divisions (each with a heading). The governor, jurists, and citizenry all considered the Digest to be a compilation of preexisting law whose aim was to make that law known and readily available.[43]

Jurists have had differing opinions about what was the preexisting law of Orleans. Dargo believed it to be Spanish law, modified as it applied to the Indies. He referred to the 1812 publication of the commander of Upper Louisiana, who stated that the Spanish had changed most French colonial law. Particularly important sources were the *Siete Partidas* and *Recopilacíon de las Leyes de Indias*.[44] Lawyers and judges in Lower Louisiana agreed. In 1819, the state legislature authorized an English translation for the *Siete Partidas*, which Moreau-Lislet and Henry Carleton edited to include those rules still in force in Louisiana, published in two volumes in 1820.[45] Dargo concluded that the prevailing juristic opinion today remains that Spanish law was predominant in early Louisiana, reflected

---

INTERNATIONAL CONTEXTS 73, 79–80 (Wilfrid Prest ed., 2014) [hereinafter Cairns, *Blackstone*]; *see* Digest of the Civil Laws Now in Force in the Territory of Orleans (1808), at LSU Law, Digest Online, https://www.law.lsu.edu/clo/digest-online.

[41] Dargo, Jefferson's Louisiana, *supra* note 18, at 60, 201, 244–45, 268–69; Cairns, *Blackstone*, *supra* note 40, at 79–81; Mitchell Franklin, *Libraries of Edward Livingston and Moreau Lislet*, 15 Tul. L. Rev. 401, 404–09 (1941).

[42] National Association of Attorneys General, *Louisiana Former Attorneys General*, https://www.naag.org (select Attorneys General, then Research & Data, then Former Attorneys General). Brown served twice as a U.S. senator after Louisiana became a state: 1813 to 1817 and 1819 to 1823. He was then U.S. minister to France until 1829. Cairns, *Blackstone*, *supra* note 40, at 81; Biographical Directory, *Brown, James (1766–1835)*, https://bioguide.congress.gov/search/bio/B000921.

[43] Dargo, Jefferson's Louisiana, *supra* note 18, at 271–74; Cairns, *Blackstone*, *supra* note 40, at 88–89.

[44] Dargo, Jefferson's Louisiana, *supra* note 18, at 275 (Major Amos Stoddard).

[45] *Id.* at 275–78; 1–2 Laws of Las Siete Partidas, Which Are Still in Force in the State of Louisiana (L. Moreau-Lislet & Henry Carleton trans., 1820); Tucker, *Spanish Laws*, *supra* note 39, at 401–03.

in the Digest. He accepted that the drafters used Roman, French, and English sources for some articles.[46]

An earlier view, now in resurgence, recognized that the Digest's structure was French and asserted that its rules likewise mainly came from French sources.[47] Recent proponents of the French thesis included legal comparatists Vernon Palmer and John Cairns, who emphasized the cultural background of francophone residents and the availability of French treatises as well as the French *Code* and *Projet*.[48]

In addition, Cairns contended that Brown and Moreau-Lislet used William Blackstone's *Commentaries*—probably some combination of the London, Philadelphia, and Paris editions (the latter in French)—as a source for many of the universal rules in the Digest. These rules were common to English and French law, some rooted in natural law, and appeared in the preliminary title and in three titles of book one dealing with persons. A supporting source for these articles was Jean Domat's seventeenth-century treatise, *Les Loix Civiles dans Leur Ordre Naturel* (1689), which Blackstone, Brown, and Moreau-Lislet all probably read in one of its editions.[49] Mark Fernandez took this argument further and suggested that the Anglo-American common law was influential enough so that Louisiana, although a mixed-tradition jurisdiction for some legal matters, was similar to other American states. The adoption of a unified judicial system, capped by a supreme court with the power of stare decisis, along with English-speaking judges

---

[46] DARGO, JEFFERSON'S LOUISIANA, *supra* note 18, at 202, 230, 278–80, 293, 296; *see* RICHARD HOLCOMBE KILBOURNE, JR., A HISTORY OF THE LOUISIANA CIVIL CODE: THE FORMATIVE YEARS, 1803–1839, at 61–95 (1987); Robert A. Pascal, *Sources of the Digest of 1808: A Reply to Professor Batiza*, 46 TUL. L. REV. 603 (1972); Robert A. Pascal, *A Recent Discovery: A Copy of the "Digest of the Civil Laws" of 1808 with Marginal Source References in Moreau Lislet's Hand*, 26 LA. L. REV. 25 (1965) (De la Vergne manuscript).

[47] Henry Plauché Dart, *The Influence of the Ancient Laws of Spain on the Jurisprudence of Louisiana*, 6 TUL. L. REV. 83, 87–88, 90 (1931); John H. Tucker, *Source Books of Louisiana Law: Civil Code*, 6 TUL. L. REV. 280, 283–84 (1932) [hereinafter Tucker, *Civil Code*]. The principal scholarly proponent of the French thesis was Rodolfo Batiza, who published his results in 1971. DARGO, JEFFERSON'S LOUISIANA, *supra* note 18, at 278–86; *see* Rodolfo Batiza, *The Louisiana Civil Code of 1808: Its Actual Sources and Present Relevance*, 46 TUL. L. REV. 4 (1971).

[48] John W. Cairns, *Spanish Law, the Teatro de la Legislación universal de España e Indias, and the Background to the Drafting of the Digest of Orleans of 1808*, 31 TUL. EUR. & CIV. L.F. 79, 81–82, 108–09, 118–20 (2017); VERNON VALENTINE PALMER, THE LOUISIANA CIVILIAN EXPERIENCE: CRITIQUE OF CODIFICATION IN A MIXED JURISDICTION 19–36, 52–55, 60–61 (2005); *see* JOHN W. CAIRNS, CODIFICATION, TRANSPLANTS AND HISTORY: LAW REFORM IN LOUISIANA (1808) AND QUEBEC (1866), at 137–234, 357–96, 427–33 (2015). *See generally* Mitchell Franklin, *Some Considerations on the Existential Force of Roman Law in the Early History of the United States*, 22 BUFF. L. REV. 69 (1972) (tension between the French-Romanist bourgeois influence and the Spanish-Romanist feudal influence).

[49] Cairns, *Blackstone*, *supra* note 40, at 80, 82–91, 94; *see* Stephen M. Sheppard, *Legal Jambalaya*, *in* RE-INTERPRETING BLACKSTONE'S COMMENTARIES, *supra* note 40, at 95; Thomas W. Tucker, *Sources of Louisiana's Law of Persons: Blackstone, Domat, and the French Codes*, 44 TUL. L. REV. 264 (1970); *see infra* notes 153, 217, 221, 323, 388 and accompanying text (Domat). For the general importance of Blackstone in America, *see infra* pt. D.2 (Blackstone and institutionalist literature).

and lawyers and a public law rooted in American institutions and legal principles, made this Americanization inevitable.[50]

C. Resistance to English Law and the Beginning of American Legal Science

Roscoe Pound (1870–1964), perhaps the leading legal comparatist in the first half of the twentieth century, pointed to several factors that impeded an easy American reception of English law after the War of Independence. First, English law seemed to embrace medieval scholasticism. Its presentation was often alphabetical, abridged, and disorganized. This contrasted with the order and system of continental treatises, which influenced Joseph Story and others. Second, American social and economic conditions, emphasizing individualism in a pioneer society, were very different from those in England, which was in the process of industrialization and urbanization. American lawyers felt they had to work out their own rules supporting the exploitation of abundant natural resources. Third, Puritans, reacting against their hostile treatment in England, tended to distrust lawyers and disfavor lawyers' law. Fourth, many Americans were bitter at the English after the war. Since some states had lay judges even in their high courts, they expressed this sentiment by preferring French or natural law. Fifth, an economic depression followed the War of 1812. Lawyers, active in collecting debts, enforcing the British subjects' treaty rights, and invoking English criminal law against persons involved in disturbances, provoked some politicians to resist using English law.[51]

A few states either passed a statute or adopted a court rule forbidding English judicial citations, at least to those from cases after 1776.[52] Some states rejected the English court structure and procedural system of writs for private law as unduly complicated for American jurisdictions, particularly where most judges were laypersons or there were few adequately trained lawyers. Georgia, the last of the original 13 British North American colonies, enacted a statute to revise

---

[50] Fernandez, *supra* note 35, at 16–18, 21, 31–45, 105–11, 113–16; *id.*, Edward Livingston, *America, and France, in* EMPIRES OF THE IMAGINATION: TRANSATLANTIC HISTORIES OF THE LOUISIANA PURCHASE 268, 279–81 (Peter J. Kastor & François Weil eds., 2009).

[51] POUND, FORMATIVE ERA, *supra* note 5, at 6–8, 11–12, 21–22, 40–43, 91–92, 107, 147–50, 154–56, 159 (1936); ROSCOE POUND, THE SPIRIT OF THE COMMON LAW 14–15, 35–39, 44–45, 55–58, 112–20, 128–29 (1921) [hereinafter POUND, COMMON LAW]; *see* FRIEDMAN, HISTORY, *supra* note 11, at 65–71; GRANT GILMORE, THE AGES OF AMERICAN LAW 19–20 (2d ed. 2014); PERRY MILLER, THE LIFE OF THE MIND IN AMERICA: FROM THE REVOLUTION TO THE CIVIL WAR 105–09 (1965); *see* MAXWELL BLOOMFIELD, AMERICAN LAWYERS IN A CHANGING SOCIETY, 1776–1786, at 32–58 (1976) [hereinafter BLOOMFIELD, AMERICAN LAWYERS] (anti-lawyer sentiment).

[52] David J. Seipp, *Our Law, Their Law, History, and the Citation of Foreign Law*, 86 B.U.L. Rev. 1417, 1426–28 (2006).

its judicial system in 1799. The 1798 Constitution had already merged law and equity in general jurisdiction superior courts, authorized to hear both civil and criminal cases, supplemented by various inferior courts. Voters elected superior court judges for a term of three years.[53] The 1799 Act called for simple pleading in civil cases, for both the plaintiff and defendant, with dilatory pleas discouraged.[54] The Constitution foresaw a digest of the civil and criminal law by 1803.[55]

Despite the pervasive reference to natural law and rights during the Revolutionary Era, David Konig asserted that natural law did not offer practical guidance for the formation of a new American private law legal system in the first half of the nineteenth century. He held this view despite continued rhetorical invocation of natural justice by influential jurists and judges.[56] Other jurists, such as Kent, accepted natural law but found the common law, suitably modified for America's republican principles, better able to protect a uniform liberty of personal and property rights. Kent was willing to incorporate French and Roman law to improve American common law, particularly for commercial matters.[57] Hoeflich maintained that Roman law and its terminology provided the basis for natural law argument as well as for the substance of natural law rules.[58]

Pound believed that natural law, "at work in legislation . . . , in judicial decision, and in doctrinal writing, guided the creative process of applying reason to experience which has been the life of the law. . . . Reason demonstrating and expressed in natural law replaced authority."[59] The differing views of Konig, Hoeflich, and Pound about the importance of natural law might be reconciled if one changed perspective to use natural law to de-emphasize English common law and explore Roman and European civil law for solutions to American legal issues. Pound saw natural law as

---

[53] Ga. Constitution of 1798 art. III, §1; An Act to Revise and Amend the Judiciary System of this State, no. 633, 16 Feb. 1799 [hereinafter Ga. Judiciary Act (1799)], arts. 1, 3, 53, *in* A DIGEST OF THE LAWS OF THE STATE OF GEORGIA 31, 39, 689, 691, 706–07 (1800).

[54] Ga. Judiciary Act (1799), *supra* note 53, at 692–93, 706–07, arts. 8–9, 53. "[T]he plaintiff's charge, allegation or demand [shall be] plainly, fully and distinctly set forth" (art. 8). "The defendant . . . shall appear at the court [and] shall make his . . . defence in writing, which shall plainly, fully and distinctly set forth the cause of his defense." Errors of form or other defects unrelated to the merits should be corrected by motion to the court for amendment (art. 9). Persons desiring an equitable remedy should use a bill, with the response in an answer (art. 53).

[55] Ga. Constitution of 1798, *supra* note 53, at 40, art. III, §8 ([T]he body of our laws, civil and criminal, shall be revised, digested and arranged, under proper heads").

[56] David Thomas Konig, *Jurisprudence and Social Policy in the New Republic*, in DEVISING LIBERTY: PRESERVING AND CREATING FREEDOM IN THE NEW AMERICAN REPUBLIC 178, 184–85 (Konig ed., 1995).

[57] KUNAL M. PARKER, COMMON LAW, HISTORY, AND DEMOCRACY IN AMERICA, 1790–1900: LEGAL THOUGHT BEFORE MODERNISM 1–2, 87–88, 105, 113–16, 141 (2011). The notion of using the common law method to protect local custom was deemphasized. *Id.* at 103–04, 112–13.

[58] HOEFLICH, ROMAN AND CIVIL LAW, *supra* note 7, at 12. Helmholz would agree with this point. R.H. HELMHOLZ, NATURAL LAW IN COURT: A HISTORY OF LEGAL THEORY IN PRACTICE 17–20 (2015) [hereinafter HELMHOLZ, NATURAL LAW].

[59] POUND, FORMATIVE ERA, *supra* note 5, at 12–13, 15. Pound recognized that there were many versions of natural law, typically "a body of ideal legal precepts by which the precepts of positive law are to be criticized and . . . made to conform." *Id.* at 15; *see id.* at 56–57.

a comparative law method to change existing legal rules—the creative role—and to systematize and organize rules—the stability role. He referred to Kent, Livingston, and Story as jurists who understood comparative law in these ways.[60]

Helmholz supported Pound's view for the usefulness of civil law in improving American law beyond that of promoting systematic thinking in legal education.[61] Helmholz read judicial decisions between 1790 and 1825 from 14 local jurisdictions and from federal courts, excluding Louisiana, to determine if American judges used civil law sources.[62] His survey revealed that in all the jurisdictions, American lawyers used Roman law texts and civil law treatises in their forensic practice and judges cited them in their opinions. Consequently, the practical use of comparative law occurred in northern as well as southern states and as far west as Kentucky and Tennessee. Nevertheless, English case citation predominated and near the end of the period, reference to civil law materials fell as citation to American cases filled the gap. The range of civil law authorities that lawyers and judges used was extensive, from Roman law texts and their commentaries' natural law authors such as Burlamaqui, Grotius, and Pufendorf; European writers on the law of nations; to specialized books by Ulrich Huber (for conflict of laws); Beccaria (for criminal law); and Robert Pothier (for commercial law). Some Americans preferred English authors writing on the European *jus commune*, natural law, and civil law. Jurists also frequently relied upon the American Thomas Cooper's volume on Justinian's *Institutes*, which among other useful features, specifically related American case law to the civil law.[63]

Helmholz identified three functions for the use of civil law in judicial processes. First, it provided solutions to legal questions where the English common law was nonexistent, inconclusive, or considered inappropriate. Second, civil law offered additional support related to fundamental principles of justice. Finally,

---

[60] *Id.* at 16–17, 20–21, 94, 102–10, 146–48, 166–67. Pound found that these jurists made a "skilful use of comparative law, seeming to show the identity of an ideal form of the English common law rule with an ideal form of the Roman law or civil law rule, and thus demonstrating the identity of each with a universally acknowledged law of nature." *Id.* at 12.

[61] In addition, Helmholz made the argument for the significance of natural law in American legal education before the Civil War. HELMHOLZ, NATURAL LAW, *supra* note 58, at 131–41.

[62] R.H. Helmholz, *Use of the Civil Law in Post-Revolutionary American Jurisprudence*, 66 TUL. L. REV. 1649–52, 1682, 1684 (1992) [hereinafter Helmholz, *Use of the Civil Law*]. Helmholz undertook a similar survey regarding the use of natural law in American courts prior to the Civil War. HELMHOLZ, NATURAL LAW, *supra* note 58, at 142–72. For Louisiana, *see* Shael Herman, *The Contribution of Roman Law to the Jurisprudence of Antebellum Louisiana*, 56 LA. L. REV. 257, 264–315 (1995).

[63] Helmholz, *Use of the Civil Law*, *supra* note 62, at 1653–55, 1683; *see* THOMAS COOPER, THE INSTITUTES OF JUSTINIAN WITH NOTES (1812) [hereinafter COOPER, INSTITUTES]. Cooper added over 250 pages of notes and references about the civil law to the translation of the *Institutes*. The thorough 18-page index to those notes included mention of nearly 200 American cases. COOPER, *supra*, at 698–700. In the preface, Cooper wrote:

> I have said nothing about the utility of a knowledge of the Civil Law. Professional men who carefully peruse the reported cases, whether of the British or the American courts, will find from the frequency of reference to the Justinian Collections, that a competent knowledge of

and like the second purpose, civil law reinforced the common law rule in situations in which jurists believed that was necessary.[64]

Grant Gilmore contended that after the early period of hostility to English law, lawyers and judges returned to an Americanized version of the common law in the 1820s. This encompassed a partial borrowing of English law, particularly significant for commercial law and those legal subjects influenced by industrialization. Some jurists, such as Kent and Story, believed that the nation would benefit from a uniform private law. Story, a U.S. Supreme Court justice from 1812 until 1845, favored the study of foreign law and limited codification at the state level to improve law and promote uniformity. In 1837, he collaborated with Simon Greenleaf and Luther Cushing in proposing the codification of parts of Massachusetts's common law.[65] Massachusetts, from 1790 to 1830, had transformed its agrarian subsistence society, with a few coastal commercial towns, into a statewide industrializing, market economy. The reception of English common law was only partial, as state judges created their own precedents to meet local economic and social needs and conditions. As in Georgia, Massachusetts jurists found English procedure particularly incompatible with the American entrepreneurial spirit of the early nineteenth century.[66]

It is important to distinguish English common law as substance from common law as a logical method. As a method, many jurists considered it the

> the general principles of the Civil Law, is expected as a matter of course among the Bar, as well as upon the Bench.
>
> COOPER, *supra*, at viii.

[64] Helmholz, *Use of the Civil Law*, *supra* note 62, at 1664-82. The legal subject with the most common law gaps was conflict of laws, which Story, Supreme Court justice from 1812, was content to fill with civil law doctrine. *Id.* at 1666-68. For fundamental principles, European natural law and Roman *jus gentium* supplied additional backing. *Id.* at 1671-76. The most frequent American use of civil law occurred where the common law rule was the same or similar to the civil law solution, buttressing its validity. The jurists' justification could have been ornamentation, demonstrating classical learning, or belief that the common law had incorporated the Roman law, justifying reliance on the original. Maritime, conflicts, and testamentary succession rules illustrated the latter reason. *Id.* at 1677-81.

[65] GILMORE, *supra* note 51, at 20-24; SEE POUND, FORMATIVE ERA, *supra* note 5, at 107, 144-45, 153; *id.*, *A Hundred Years of American Law*, *in* 1 LAW: A CENTURY OF PROGRESS, 1835-1935, at 8, 14-19 (Alison Reppy ed., 1937); Joseph Story, *Progress of Jurisprudence*, *in* THE MISCELLANEOUS WRITINGS OF JOSEPH STORY 198, 213-24, 234-35, 237-39 (William W. Story ed., 1852) [hereinafter STORY'S WRITINGS] (1821 speech to the Suffolk Bar Association); *id.*, *Codification of the Common Law*, *in id.* at 698, 715-16, 726-33 (1837 commission report proposing a series of codes to the Massachusetts governor). Rather than a civilian style code, Story preferred a digest consistent with his idea of legal science, entailing ordered categories and principles derived from judicial decisions. STEVEN J. MACIAS, LEGAL SCIENCE IN THE EARLY REPUBLIC: THE ORIGINS OF AMERICAN LEGAL THOUGHT AND EDUCATION 162-65 (2016); Alfred S. Konefsky, *The Legal Profession: From the Revolution to the Civil War*, *in* 2 CAMBRIDGE HISTORY OF LAW, *supra* note 2, at 68, 98-99.

[66] WILLIAM E. NELSON, AMERICANIZATION OF THE COMMON LAW: THE IMPACT OF LEGAL CHANGE ON MASSACHUSETTS SOCIETY, 1760-1830, at 5-10, 69-88, 165-70 (1975).

least arbitrary and most scientific and systematic process of lawmaking. The common law judge was better able than an elected legislature or bureaucratic department to ascertain community values and the direction of social change presented to him in the courtroom.[67] What America had to add to the process in the 1820s until the Civil War was codification of the rules. Many were aware of Jeremy Bentham's (1748–1832) support for codification and of the new codes in France. Expansion of the electorate in the 1820s and 1830s to include all white male adults, who at the state level increasingly could vote for judges, provided a democratic spirit to the new common law. Legal science, as supported by Kent and Story, could supply a bridge between the work of judges and the reasonableness and simplification of digests, treatises, and codes.[68]

Most juristic writing in the early decades of the nineteenth century asserted that law was a science.[69] Steven Macias contended that legal elites insisted on building American law from eclectic sources. Frequently, this included European civil law, natural law philosophy (especially important for rules in equity), and Roman law. Some also wanted to borrow methods from the natural sciences, placing law on a sounder foundation, or improve the connection between law and society with the emerging discipline of political economy.[70] Certain jurists contrasted methods from the natural sciences with those from the moral sciences used by Kent, Story, St. George Tucker, Wythe, and continental civil law writers. Among law teachers who drew inspiration from the natural sciences, and who were conversant in Roman and civil law, were David Hoffman (University of Maryland) and Nathan Beverly Tucker (William and Mary College).[71] Hoeflich

---

[67] PARKER, supra note 57, at 16, 22, 124, 281–83.
[68] R. KENT NEWMYER, SUPREME COURT JUSTICE JOSEPH STORY: STATESMAN OF THE OLD REPUBLIC 271–81 (1985); PARKER, supra note 57, at 114–16, 124–26, 139–58. Kent spent most of his legal career resisting populist tendencies in legal administration and promoting learned law. The latter included both English law principles and civil law rules as examples of a universal natural law. John H. Langbein, *Chancellor Kent and the History of Legal Literature*, 93 COLUM. L. REV. 547, 566–71, 584, 594 (1993).
[69] MACIAS, supra note 65, at 1–3, 7, 13–16, 32–34; ELLEN HOLMES PEARSON, REMAKING CUSTOM: LAW AND IDENTITY IN THE EARLY AMERICAN REPUBLIC 4–8 (2011) (using the civil law term legist); WILLIAM M. WIECEK, THE LOST WORLD OF CLASSICAL LEGAL THOUGHT: LAW AND IDEOLOGY IN AMERICA, 1886–1937, at 38–40 (1998); Langbein, supra note 68, at 566–70, 594 (learned law).
[70] MACIAS, supra note 65, at 2–3, 10, 40, 123. For political economy, Macias cited the lawyers DANIEL RAYMOND, THOUGHTS ON POLITICAL ECONOMY (1820, 4th ed. 1840, adding the title: ELEMENTS OF CONSTITUTIONAL LAW); THOMAS COOPER, LECTURES ON THE ELEMENTS OF POLITICAL ECONOMY (1826); and WILLARD PHILLIPS, A MANUAL OF POLITICAL ECONOMY (1828). MACIAS, supra, at 2, 16. *See generally id.* at 117–33 (Cooper).
[71] Howard Schweber, *The "Science" of Legal Science: The Model of the Natural Sciences in Nineteenth-Century American Legal Education*, 17 LAW & HIST. REV. 421–25, 429–31, 437–39, 451, 453–54 (1999). An early effort to reach aspiring American law students, simplify Blackstone and Kent into one volume, and to present law as a traditional moral science, was Francis Hilliard's *Elements of Law* (1835). FRANCIS HILLIARD, THE ELEMENTS OF LAW; BEING A COMPREHENSIVE SUMMARY OF AMERICAN CIVIL JURISPRUDENCE: FOR THE USE OF STUDENTS . . . iii–v (1835). "[I]n law, as in other sciences, there are certain broad and fixed principles, which embody the essence of the system." *Id.* at v.

argued that the dominant form of legal science in the first half of the nineteenth century was based on mathematics, first principles, syllogistic logic, and deduction. European Romanists studying Justinian's *Digest* influenced Americans in this view of law. In addition to Hoffman, Hoeflich identified Hugh Legaré as an American supporter of law as a deductive science.[72]

Ellen Pearson emphasized the foundations of English common law, portrayed through Blackstone's *Commentaries*, affecting American juristic literature. The legists she considered were reacting against the push for codification of rules to achieve a more rational and scientific order. They considered the common law sufficiently rational and preferred judges over legislators making law. Jurists such as Kent were skeptical about codification, even though they might point out similarities between the civil and common law. Kent preferred a digest to simplify the increase in judicial precedents and to maintain the common law's flexibility.[73]

D. Legal Education and Law Books

1. Training American Lawyers

Apprenticeship training was the predominant avenue to become a lawyer from the 1790s until the Civil War. At the beginning of this period, the profession established the rules, with the norm being three years of reading about the law and carrying out tasks assigned by a lawyer. Typically, local courts appointed a committee of lawyers to administer a perfunctory oral examination, which few failed to pass. The principal weakness of this law-office education was its failure to teach law as a coherent system or, as scholarly jurists claimed, a science. Lawyers expected apprentices, after reading, to organize their learning by compiling commonplace books, which formed the foundation of their knowledge.[74]

A secondary limitation to the pure apprenticeship method was the shortage of lawyers willing and capable of supervising students in learning law. The American solution to these difficulties initially was proprietary law office-type schools. The paradigm was Tapping Reeve's Litchfield Law School, which he founded in Connecticut in 1784. James Gould, his student, joined him and took over teaching in 1823 until the school closed in 1833. During the school's

---

[72] M.H. Hoeflich, *Law & Geometry: Legal Science from Leibniz to Langdell*, 30 Am. J. Leg. Hist. 95, 96–99, 112–15 (1986). The jurists Francis Bacon and Blackstone adopted a deductive approach for the common law in England. Wiecek, *supra* note 69, at 39; Hoeflich, *supra*, at 108; *see infra* text accompanying notes 265–71 (Legaré).

[73] Pearson, *supra* note 69, at 7, 12–30, 173–78, 181–86, 192–93; *see* David W. Raack, *"To Preserve the Best Fruits": The Legal Thought of Chancellor James Kent*, 33 Am. J. Leg. Hist. 320, 351–65 (1989).

[74] Konefsky, *supra* note 65, at 79; Hugh C. MacGill & R. Kent Newmyer, *Legal Education and Legal Thought, 1790–1920*, *in* 2 Cambridge History of Law, *supra* note 2, at 36, 37–41.

existence, the pair trained about 1,000 lawyers. Students took notes for 14 months based on a comprehensive set of lectures organized around the legal principles in Blackstone's *Commentaries*. There were weekly tests and forensic exercises. Other lawyers and judges in seven states attempted to earn a living by teaching law with the Litchfield model, but none equaled its success. By 1850, there were still 20 proprietary law schools of various types. After that, they declined faced with the competition of university law schools.[75]

Early attempts at the end of the eighteenth century to interest students in law lectures delivered at a college or university were largely unsuccessful.[76] St. George Tucker (1752–1827), a student of Wythe at William and Mary College, initiated what a university-based lecture system in law could entail. Tucker was professor of law and police and his notes from the 1790s formed the basis for his 1803 five-volume Americanized version of Blackstone's *Commentaries*, explaining how American law differed from Blackstone's portrayal of English law.[77]

In 1793, the trustees at Columbia College had appointed Kent to its first law professorship. For the 1794–1795 academic term, he prepared elementary lectures on government, the law of nations, state and federal constitutional law, and real property. Only seven college students and 36 New York lawyers and aspiring apprentices attended. The lectures were sufficiently uninspiring that the next term Kent taught in his office and afterward resigned in 1797.[78]

From 1790 to 1820, the number of lawyers increased dramatically to about 6,000, faster than the rapidly growing population. In the original states, the per capita expansion was double to four times over the 30-year period.[79] By the 1820s, some

---

[75] Konefsky, *supra* note 65, at 81–82; MacGill & Newmyer, *supra* note 74, at 46; *see* ALFRED ZANTZINGER REED, TRAINING FOR THE PUBLIC PROFESSION OF THE LAW: HISTORICAL DEVELOPMENT AND PRINCIPAL CONTEMPORARY PROBLEMS OF LEGAL EDUCATION IN THE UNITED STATES WITH SOME ACCOUNT OF CONDITIONS IN ENGLAND AND CANADA 128–33, 431–38 (1921).

[76] There were only 20 colleges in 1800, which, however, grew in number to 217 by 1860, mostly after 1830 and in Midwestern states. Likewise, the number of students increased from 1,000 to 16,000, doubling the percentage of white males aged 15 to 20 attending, but still less than 2 percent of that population. CAROLINE WINTERER, THE CULTURE OF CLASSICISM: ANCIENT GREECE AND ROME IN AMERICAN INTELLECTUAL LIFE, 1780–1910, at 44 (2002).

[77] CHARLES T. CULLEN, ST GEORGE TUCKER AND LAW IN VIRGINIA: 1772–1804, at 116–41 (1987, reprint of 1971 PhD dissertation); MACIAS, *supra* note 65, at 24–25, 29; ST. GEORGE TUCKER, 1–5 BLACKSTONE'S COMMENTARIES: WITH NOTES OF REFERENCE (1803); *see* Craig Evan Klafter, *St. George Tucker: The First Modern American Law Professor*, 6 J. HIST. SOC'Y 133 (2006). Wythe, the first law professor in the United States, was Tucker's law tutor (apprenticeship) from 1773–1775. ALONZO THOMAS DILL, GEORGE WYTHE: TEACHER OF LIBERTY 42 (1979); Konefsky, *supra* note 65, at 80–81. For Tucker's notes, *see* VIEW OF THE CONSTITUTION OF THE UNITED STATES: WITH SELECTED WRITINGS (1999), https://oll.libertyfund.org (select People, then St. George Tucker).

[78] Langbein, *supra* note 68, at 548, 558–60; *see* MACIAS, *supra* note 65, at 29. Another example of poorly attended lectures in the 1790s were those of James Wilson (University of Pennsylvania). MacGill & Newmyer, *supra* note 74, at 45.

[79] DARGO, PRIVATE LAW, *supra* note 2, at 48–49; *Intelligence*, 2 AM. JURIST & L. MAG. 400 (1829). In 1821, New York had the largest number of lawyers (1,391), followed by Virginia (483), and Pennsylvania (417). Even Louisiana had 106 lawyers. *Intelligence*, *supra*.

colleges decided to offer a way for proprietary law schools to compete for those interested in learning law and entering the profession. Private law schools wanted affiliation with a college or university since it provided prestige and permitted the school to issue a law degree, something most states only permitted colleges and universities to do. For their part, educational institutions increased their scope of influence without cost since the schools were self-financing. Yale undertook this route in 1824 by making the local school's owner, a judge, the law professor. More importantly for the development of legal education, Harvard, which had created a law department in 1817, reorganized its law-related offerings in 1829. The Harvard Law Department brought in Supreme Court Justice Joseph Story to teach (a condition of Nathan Dane's endowed professorship) for prestige and John Ashmum, a practitioner who owned Northampton Law School, for bringing his students. Story intended to develop an elite education that included a comparative law element with a practical purpose.[80]

Story saw law as a set of ideals, embodying eternal and universal principles of natural justice. From this perspective, law was a moral science designed to guide human behavior. In a republic such as the United States, specially trained lawyers could protect against perceived excesses of democracy, meaning Jacksonian democracy after the mid-1820s. University law schools should instill republican virtue. Story's influence was national, promoted via his treatises on various legal subjects, such as the volume endorsing constitutional nationalism.[81] The fees Harvard collected from additional law students allowed Story to acquire books for an outstanding law library, including civil law treatises, necessary for the scientific study of law. Harvard, as its enrollment grew from 24 in 1830 to 166 in 1860, became the country's first national law school.[82] By the late 1830s, Harvard had switched from the lecture method of teaching to a text and recitation pedagogy using commentaries and treatises, particularly those by Story.[83]

---

[80] ROBERT STEVENS, LAW SCHOOL: LEGAL EDUCATION IN AMERICA FROM THE 1850S TO THE 1980S, at 5, 15 n.46, 26–27 (1983); Daniel R. Coquillette, *"Mourning Venice and Genoa": Joseph Story, Legal Education, and the Lex Mercatoria*, in FROM LEX MERCATORIA TO COMMERCIAL LAW 11, 17–26, 40 (Vito Piergiovanni ed., 2005); *see* NEWMYER, *supra* note 68, at 241–48; REED, *supra* note 75, at 137–42. Samuel Livermore's bequest of his civil and mercantile law library to Harvard provided Story with many of the books he used to write his commentaries. HOEFLICH, ROMAN AND CIVIL LAW, *supra* note 7, at 29, 56; Coquillette, *supra*, at 23–24, 39.

[81] Konefsky, *supra* note 65, at 82–83; MacGill & Newmyer, *supra* note 74, at 47–48.

[82] REED, *supra* note 75, at 451; MacGill & Newmyer, *supra* note 74, at 47; *see* ARTHUR E. SUTHERLAND, THE LAW AT HARVARD: A HISTORY OF IDEAS AND MEN, 1817–1967, at 92–139 (1967). The quality of students at Harvard Law School steadily deteriorated from its early years as a department. Even in 1829, students whom the college would not admit were welcome at the law school. In the 1830s, a law degree took only 18 months and the school eliminated examinations. REED, *supra*, at 143, 149; STEVENS, *supra* note 80, at 15 n.46; *see* SUTHERLAND, *supra*, at 62–63, 77–78, 123–24, 141.

[83] Coquillette, *supra* note 80, at 29, 43–46; *see infra* pt. D.3 (Story's commentaries).

One of Story's students, Timothy Walker (1802–1856), co-founded the Cincinnati Law School in 1833 to emulate Story's vision. Shortly thereafter, the school merged with Cincinnati College and Walker served as law department dean until 1843. Based on his lectures and desiring to distinguish American from English law, Walker prepared *Introduction to American Law*. Enormously successful, the text saw 11 editions through 1905 and informed generations of Americans about law.[84] Walker distrusted judges and favored some state law codification and national penal law codification. He initiated the *Western Law Journal* in 1843, which he edited until 1853, occasionally writing articles in support of law reform, including codification.[85]

As the nineteenth century unfolded, lawyers and judges gradually lost control over the admission and practice standards for law under political pressures associated with Jacksonian democracy. From the common three-year requirement for apprenticeship in the first decade, reduced in some states for college education, only 11 of 30 states in 1840 prescribed a minimum period of law study or apprenticeship. That number fell to nine of 39 states in 1860. Furthermore, university law study did not serve as much of a social filter to bar entry, since it was slow to meet demand. There were only 15 university law schools in 1850. Meanwhile, the number of lawyers had reached 24,000 nationwide.[86]

Since a law degree was not necessary to become a lawyer, universities needed to convince students that their law schools' value justified the time and expense of attending. The reason they used—that law was a science—required theoretical training as well as the practical information obtained through apprenticeship. University law schools could prepare citizen lawyers in a republic to become leaders, reformers, and, with knowledge of legal history and philosophy, public

---

[84] REED, *supra* note 75, at 184 n.2, 432, 455; Gordon A. Christenson, *A Tale of Two Lawyers in Antebellum Cincinnati: Timothy Walker's Last Conversation with Salmon P. Chase*, 71 U. CIN. L. REV. 457, 471, 479–80, 489 (2002); *see* TIMOTHY WALKER, INTRODUCTION TO AMERICAN LAW, DESIGNED AS A FIRST BOOK FOR STUDENTS (1837); *id.* (11th ed., Clement Bates ed., 1905) [hereinafter WALKER, INTRODUCTION]. Walker dedicated his book to Story. National journals favorably reviewed the volume. G[eorge] S. H[illard], *Walker's Introduction to American Law*, 18 AM. JURIST 375–90 (1838); *Introduction to American Law, Designed as a First Book for Students*, 45 NORTH AM. REV. 485–88 (1837).

[85] POUND, FORMATIVE ERA, *supra* note 5, at 145, 159–60; Christenson, *supra* note 84, at 479–80, 485, 492; *e.g.*, Timothy Walker, *Codification*, 1 WESTERN L.J. 433–40 (1844) (author's support for common law codification); 5 *id.* at 335, 337, 385 (1848) (report on the New York Code of Civil Procedure); 7 *id.* at 199–217 (1850) (Kentucky legislative debates on codification). For the argument in favor of codification in Walker's treatise, *see* WALKER, INTRODUCTION, *supra* note 84, at 59–62, 490–92, 746–47 (4th ed., Edward L. Pierce ed., 1860).

[86] STEVENS, *supra* note 80, at 7–8; Konefsky, *supra* note 65, at 83–85; *see* REED, *supra* note 75, at 68–71, 82–93, 152–59, 442, 444. There were 21 university law schools in 1860 and 35,000 lawyers. REED, *supra*, at 153, 442, 451.

intellectuals.[87] Story, in his 1817 review of David Hoffman's *Course of Legal Study*, praised his ambitious plan for university legal education.

> [I]t contains by far the most perfect system for the study of the law, which has ever been offered to the publick. . . . [Hoffman's] notes are composed in a tone of the most enlarged philosophy . . . calculated to elevate the moral as well as intellectual character of the profession. . . . No work can sooner dissipate the common delusion, that the law may be thoroughly acquired in the immethodical, interrupted and desultory studies of the office of a practising counsellor. Such a situation is indispensable after the student shall have laid a foundation in elementary principles under the guidance of a leaned and discreet lecturer.[88]

Hoffman's (and Story's) views on the importance of university legal education for legal science, in addition to Harvard, influenced two other successful law schools in the antebellum period. One was Transylvania University's Law Department, created in 1821, in Lexington, Kentucky. The other was Columbia School of Jurisprudence in New York City, which Theodore Dwight established in 1858. Both schools accepted the notion that an appropriate education included both theory and practice.[89]

An unusual example was the University of Louisiana, established by the state and partially funded with a poll tax. The university created a law department in 1847 with four professors, consisting of two judges and two lawyers. Indigent students paid no tuition. By 1890, the law department had graduated 673 students with bachelor degrees. During the period 1847 to 1890, apart from the Civil War interruption (1862–1865), the school continuously taught Roman law and maintained at least one professor of civil law. Paul Tulane's donation of land

---

[87] M.H. Hoeflich, *Plus ça Change, Plus C'est la Même Chose: The Integration of Theory & Practice in Legal Education*, 66 TEMP. L. REV. 123, 125–28, 135, 137 (1993) [hereinafter Hoeflich, *Theory & Practice*].

[88] [Joseph Story], *A Course of Legal Study Respectfully Addressed to the Students of Law in the United States*, 6 N. AM. REV. & MISC. J. 45, 76–77 (no. 1, 1817) (*reprinted in* STORY'S WRITINGS, *supra* note 65, at 66–92; *see id.* at 63–64, 75–77. "What particularly pleases us is the enlarged and liberal view with which Mr. Hoffman recommends the student of the common law to a full and careful study of the admiralty, maritime and civil law. If the note on the excellence of the civil law were not too long, we should gladly insert it in this place." *Id.* at 75–76. *See* DAVID HOFFMAN, A COURSE OF LEGAL STUDY; RESPECTFULLY ADDRESSED TO THE STUDENTS OF LAW IN THE UNITED STATES (1817) [hereinafter HOFFMAN, COURSE].

[89] Hoeflich, *Theory & Practice*, *supra* note 87, at 133–35, 139. Transylvania hired its first law professor in 1799. It graduated its first class from a law department in 1823, at which time there were 44 students enrolled. *Id.* at 133 n.50; REED, *supra* note 75, at 450. Harvard offered a course on civil law in the 1830s. CHARLES WARREN, 1 HISTORY OF THE HARVARD LAW SCHOOL AND OF EARLY LEGAL CONDITIONS IN AMERICA 437 (1908); Peter Stein, *The Attraction of the Civil Law in Post-Revolutionary America*, 52 VA. L. REV. 403, 425 (1966). Dwight was the foremost legal educator of the 1850s. Columbia hired him from Hamilton College, where he had taught law and political economy since 1847. Dwight was one of the founders of the Bar of the City of New York; he continued teaching law at Columbia until 1891. STEVENS, *supra* note 80, at 21–24.

and money in the 1880s led to re-establishment in 1884 as Tulane University of Louisiana, absorbing the law department.[90]

A final avenue for insight into Roman and civil law occurred with Americans studying at German university law faculties. During the nineteenth century after 1815, perhaps hundreds of Americans matriculated at German law faculties.[91] One of those was Philip Kaufmann, a New York lawyer who had earned a law doctorate at the University of Freiburg. In 1845, he translated from German a popular student treatise on the history of Roman law and its fundamental modern principles and rules.[92] For American lawyers interested in the rising German historical school of jurisprudence, this was a valuable resource.

2. William Blackstone and the American Institutionalist Literature: St. George Tucker and James Kent

Alfred Konefsky identified three categories of juristic literature that could establish an American legal science: court reports, commentaries and treatises, and periodicals. Republican lawyers, in particular, wanted to ground public and private decision-making in scientifically derived principles.[93] The type of literature most relevant for comparative law that drew upon Roman and European civil law included commentaries and treatises.[94] However, it was not until the 1820s and 1830s that academic law study, together with increased law book publishing, was sufficiently common that one could point to the beginning of American legal science.[95]

The earliest remedy for the disjointed attribute of English common law was Blackstone's *Commentaries*. Lawyers who provided this resource to apprentices

---

[90] Lamar C. Quintero, *The Law School of the Tulane University of Louisiana*, 2 GREEN BAG 116–19, 123 (1890); *see* Robert Feikema Karachuk, *A Workman's Tools: The Law Library of Henry Adams Bullard*, 42 AM. J. LEG. HIST. 160, 186 (1998).

[91] David S. Clark, *Tracing the Roots of American Legal Education—A Nineteenth Century German Connection*, 51 RABELS ZEITSCHRIFT FÜR AUSLÄNDISCHES UND INTERNATIONALES PRIVATRECHT 313, 320–21 (1987); *see* JÜRGEN HERBST, THE GERMAN HISTORICAL SCHOOL IN AMERICAN SCHOLARSHIP: A STUDY IN THE TRANSFER OF CULTURE 1–2 (1965); POUND, COMMON LAW, *supra* note 51, at 154.

[92] FERDINAND MACKELDEY, 1–2 COMPENDIUM OF MODERN CIVIL LAW (trans. & ed., Philip Ignatius Kaufmann, 1845) (from *Lehrbuch des heutigen Römischen Rechts*, 12th ed., 1842; 1st ed., 1814).

[93] Konefsky, *supra* note 65, at 91–95. In addition to the dominant republican view emphasizing civil virtue, Jacksonians wanted a legal science rooted in the people's will and political science, borrowing inductive methods from the natural sciences. *Id.* at 92.

[94] Between 1790 and 1840, American publishers printed 410 legal monographs in 675 editions. By contrast, from 1790 to 1830, only 12 American legal periodicals appeared. Konefsky, *supra* note 65, at 93–94.

[95] M.H. HOEFLICH, LEGAL PUBLISHING IN ANTEBELLUM AMERICA 11–12, 14–27 (2010); MACIAS, *supra* note 65, at 29, 32–35.

were free to carry on their practice without taking much time and effort to teach the law. The *Commentaries* introduced the study of law and its nature followed by systematic and comprehensive coverage of English public and private law. It did more than any other single work to shape legal education during the formative era. By the early nineteenth century, jurists wrote Americanized versions of Blackstone's work that students and lawyers could use. Of these, the commentaries by St. George Tucker and Kent—America's institutionalist literature—were the most influential.[96]

Blackstone's *Commentaries* emulated the civilian institutionalist writing in Europe during the seventeenth and eighteenth centuries. Its defining characteristics were comprehensiveness in describing private and some public law, with a rational systematic organization, to serve a didactic purpose, and to unify national law. As European nation-states consolidated and Roman-canonic *jus commune* weakened, the challenge for European institutionalists was to integrate *jus commune*, local customary law, and emerging national positive law. This literature typically appeared in a national vernacular instead of the universal Latin *jus commune* jurists utilized. However, the organizational framework came from Justinian's *Institutes*, which in turn borrowed from the classical Gaius's *Institutes* (c. 160 CE). The legal subject categories of persons, things, and actions pervaded this juristic literature.[97]

American classical and juristic interest in Roman law and its perceived natural legal order led Cooper to publish a translation of Justinian's *Institutes* (533 CE) in 1812. He based it on the Englishman George Harris's translation, first published in 1756.[98] The *Institutes* divided into four books, but European jurists tended to emphasize three divisions: persons; things and property transfer (gifts and succession); and obligations and actions. Book 1 of Justinian's *Institutes* had two titles on the nature of law and 22 titles on the law of persons (status, family law, and slavery). Book 2 treated things, gifts, and wills (25 titles). Book 3 continued with intestate succession (12 titles) and contractual obligations (17 titles). Finally, book 4 concerned delictual obligations (five titles) and civil actions (13 titles).[99]

The Roman tripartite pattern influenced Blackstone's first three volumes.[100] Blackstone used his fourth volume for criminal law and procedure, which

---

[96] Konefsky, *supra* note 65, at 78–80; MacGill & Newmyer, *supra* note 74, at 40–41; *see* Dennis R. Nolan, *Sir William Blackstone and the New American Republic: A Study of Intellectual Impact*, 51 N.Y.U. L. REV. 731, 737, 747–59 (1976).

[97] Langbein, *supra* note 68, at 585–90; *see* John W. Cairns, *Blackstone, An English Institutist: Legal Literature and the Rise of the Nation State*, 4 OXFORD J. LEG. STUD. 318 (1984).

[98] COOPER, INSTITUTES, *supra* note 63 (Philadelphia, 1812) (2d ed. 1841).

[99] *Id.* The final title in book 4 dealt with public prosecutions.

[100] *See* SIR WILLIAM BLACKSTONE, 1–4 COMMENTARIES ON THE LAWS OF ENGLAND (1765–1769). In 1771 and 1772, Robert Bell printed the first American edition in Philadelphia and sold 1,557 sets. SIR WILLIAM BLACKSTONE, 1–5 COMMENTARIES ON THE LAWS OF ENGLAND (Robert Bell ed.,

was only a minor part of the Roman legal system during its classical period.[101] Alan Watson persuasively demonstrated that the organization of Blackstone's *Commentaries*—its structure—was derived from Justinian's sixth-century *Institutes*[102] through the modifications later developed by Dionysius Gothofredus[103] and Sir Matthew Hale.[104] Hale's earlier eighteenth-century treatment of English law was itself modeled on Justinian's *Institutes*. Given the more casuistic character of English law compared to civil law, Blackstone's accomplishment in presenting English law was impressive.[105] Even so, this was an important transplant from the civil law to both British common law and for common law in the new American republic.

Blackstone did not have another easy option. English common law had no structure itself. The centuries of case law yielded no obvious system and England did not have a tradition of scholars working together to develop such a system as did Roman law, canon law, and civil law. Parliament had not enacted important private law statutes that Blackstone could follow to organize his volumes. Consequently, he needed an external structure, and the most popular one that jurists used on the European continent and in Scotland was Justinian's

---

1771-1772) [hereinafter BLACKSTONE, COMMENTARIES (Bell ed.)]. Bell reported that the first four volumes were an accurate copy of the latest English edition, while the 288-page fifth volume was an appendix for a few English arguments, remarks, and letters concerning the *Commentaries*. I cite the American edition in this chapter. Blackstone abandoned the English writ system, with its emphasis on procedure, as obsolete to organize his classification. Instead, he relied on Roman law and European natural law to emphasize concepts of substantive law. Langbein, *supra* note 68, at 586-88, 590-91. The French Civil Code of 1804 also followed the Roman pattern with three books: persons, property and property rights, and modes of acquiring property rights. Book 3 included successions, gifts, and contractual and delictual obligations.

[101] Thus, the four books of Justinian's *Institutes* dedicated only one title at the end of book 4 to public prosecutions.

[102] Alan Watson, *The Structure of Blackstone's Commentaries*, 97 YALE L.J. 795-98, 813-15 (1988) [hereinafter Watson, *Blackstone*]; *see* Calvin Woodard, *Sir William Blackstone and Anglo-American Jurisprudence, in* THE POLITICAL THEORY OF THE CONSTITUTION 67, 76-78 (Kenneth W. Thompson ed., 1990) (Gaius).

[103] Watson, *Blackstone*, *supra* note 102, at 806-11, 817-21; *see* 1-2 CORPUS JURIS CIVILIS ROMANI: CUM NOTIS INTEGRIS DIONYSII GOTHOFREDI (1756, orig. Geneva ed. 1583). Gothofredus wrote the most widely circulated editions of Justinian's *Corpus juris* (including the *Institutes*). Watson, *supra*, at 806. Scholars also referred to Gothofredus as Dionysii Gothofredi or Denis Godefroy. John Adams had studied Gothofredus. *See supra* ch. 2, § F.1 (civil law).

[104] Watson, *Blackstone*, *supra* note 102, at 799, 810-11 (Blackstone's preface recognized his debt to Hale); *see* [MATTHEW HALE], THE ANALYSIS OF THE LAW: BEING A SCHEME, OR ABSTRACT, OF THE SEVERAL TITLES AND PARTITIONS OF THE LAW OF ENGLAND, DIGESTED INTO METHOD (1713).

[105] Watson, *Blackstone*, *supra* note 102, at 799-806. Watson set out Blackstone's challenge. English law prominently featured land based on an old feudal system. Substantive law, inextricably intertwined with a complicated procedure and its writs, would make the presentation of substantive law as its own subject difficult. Contract law and tort law were primitive compared to Roman law. *Id.* at 798, 810.

Institutes.[106] Blackstone's civil law degree from Oxford acquainted him with this literature and he did own a copy of Justinian's *Institutes*.[107]

The first Americanized version of Blackstone's work that students and lawyers could use was Tucker's 1803 edition of the *Commentaries*.[108] Hoeflich argued that Tucker's notes and narrative appendices on U.S. and Virginia law utilized a style developed by medieval European glossators to respect the original text while modifying its meaning or utility with commentary for an American audience.[109] Tucker, relying on many European jurists, developed this material from his law lectures at William and Mary during the 1790s.[110] Prior to the Civil War, other Americanized versions of Blackstone appeared, some as abridgments or reflecting later English editions, primarily aimed toward law students but also cited by lawyers desiring to appear learned.[111]

As with many others, Tucker believed that some English common law was inappropriate for the different social and political circumstances in republican America. Blackstone's views and superficial treatment of certain issues, Tucker believed, threatened to return America to monarchy. Tucker's edition of the *Commentaries* contained appendices supporting Virginia's rejection of Blackstone's anti-republican suggestions.[112] After Wythe resigned from law teaching, he became chief judge of the Virginia High Court of Chancery. In 1790, he began citing Justinian's *Corpus Juris* as precedent for his rulings. By 1795, he was criticizing the slavish adherence to English authorities, since he believed Roman law provided a more rational model. During the 1790s, Wythe wrote 21 judicial opinions with 85 examples of classical sources or references.[113]

James Kent's *Commentaries*,[114] like those of Tucker, evolved from law teaching and purported to be a comprehensive treatment of American law. In 1823, at age 60, Kent was subject to New York's mandatory retirement age, which ended

---

[106] Watson, *Blackstone*, *supra* note 102, at 796–98, 802.

[107] ANTHONY TAUSSIG, BLACKSTONE AND HIS CONTEMPORARIES 2, 5 (2009); Watson, *Blackstone*, *supra* note 102, at 809.

[108] *See supra* note 77 and accompanying text (Tucker's Blackstone).

[109] Michael Hoeflich, *American Blackstones*, *in* BLACKSTONE AND HIS COMMENTARIES: BIOGRAPHY, LAW, HISTORY 171–73 (Wilfrid Prest ed., 2009) [hereinafter Hoeflich, *American Blackstones*].

[110] CULLEN, *supra* note 77, at 142–49, 157–63, 205–06; Davison M. Douglas, *Foreword: The Legacy of St. George Tucker*, 47 WM. & MARY L. REV. 1111–15 (2006).

[111] Hoeflich, *American Blackstones*, *supra* note 109, at 174–78, 180. During the first decades of the nineteenth century, booksellers continued to offer both literal American reprints of Blackstone and imported English editions. *Id.* at 176–80, 183.

[112] Konig, *supra* note 56, at 180–82, 192–93, 212.

[113] CARL J. RICHARD, THE FOUNDERS AND THE CLASSICS: GREECE, ROME, AND THE AMERICAN ENLIGHTENMENT 182 (1994); *see* Richard Hoffman, *supra* note 4, at 57, 62, 68–73.

[114] JAMES KENT, 1–4 COMMENTARIES ON AMERICAN LAW (1826–1830) [hereinafter KENT, COMMENTARIES]; *see supra* text accompanying notes 57–58, 65, 68, 71, 73, 78 (Kent).

his tenure as chancellor. Columbia College reappointed Kent law professor and he began work on his second attempt at law lectures, which he delivered during two terms from 1824 to 1826.[115] After the fourth volume of the *Commentaries* appeared in 1830, the work became the most influential American law book in the antebellum period.[116] Oliver Wendell Holmes Jr. edited the twelfth edition in 1873.[117]

Kent began his law practice in 1785 together with a member of the New York Livingston family. At the same time, Kent—in contact with Edward Livingston—maintained a disciplined reading regimen utilizing his knowledge of French, Greek, and Latin to study English and European law as well as classical literature. He brought this learning to the *Commentaries*, which benefited from his library of 3,000 volumes.[118] Kent valued Roman law, not for its structure of government, criminal law, or civil and political liberty, but for many subjects of private law. These included guardianship in family law, real and personal property, trusts and life estates, gifts, inheritance, contracts, and commercial law.[119]

Although Kent believed law students and lawyers could gain insight from the study of civil law, he stood with those jurists who desired to establish a learned American common law, suitably modified from the English version to meet American conditions. He railed against folk law and populist impulses in legal administration. Kent maintained, as had Blackstone, that English legal principles were universal, rooted in natural law. Kent's many references in his law reports and the *Commentaries* to foreign law, especially the Code Napoléon and Dutch and French jurists, served to legitimate English law as another example of natural justice.[120] Perhaps, Kent believed that his citation of Roman and civil law, although sometimes careless, nevertheless helped to persuade fellow jurists of the value of his conclusion on a point of law.[121]

---

[115] Langbein, *supra* note 68, at 548, 564–65, 591–92; *see* KENT, 1 COMMENTARIES, *supra* note 114, at iii–iv. John Jay, governor of New York, appointed Kent to the New York Supreme Court in 1798. In 1814, Kent accepted the post of New York Chancellor. Langbein, *supra*, at 561, 564, 567.

[116] Langbein, *supra* note 68, at 548, 565–66; *see id.* at 585–86, 590–93. For the success of Kent's *Commentaries* abroad, *see id.* at 585.

[117] KENT, 1–4 COMMENTARIES, *supra* note 114 (O.W. Holmes, Jr., ed., 1873).

[118] Langbein, *supra* note 68, at 554–55, 591; *see supra* text accompanying notes 32, 35–39 (Livingston).

[119] KENT, 1 COMMENTARIES, *supra* note 114, at 507–08.

[120] Langbein, *supra* note 68, at 567–72, 594 (Kent); *see* Woodard, *supra* note 102, at 86–91 (Blackstone): KENT, 1 COMMENTARIES, *supra* note 114, at 439–41. "A great proportion of the rules and maxims which constitute the immense code of the common law . . . was the application of the dictates of natural justice, and of cultivated reason, to particular cases." *Id.* at 439. *See also* Carl F. Stychin, *The Commentaries of Chancellor James Kent and the Development of an American Common Law*, 37 AM. J. LEG. HIST. 440, 448–51, 453–55 (1993).

[121] Alan Watson, *Chancellor Kent's Use of Foreign Law, in* THE RECEPTION OF CONTINENTAL IDEAS IN THE COMMON LAW WORLD: 1820–1920, at 45, 52, 61–62 (Mathias Reimann ed., 1993) [hereinafter RECEPTION (Reimann ed.)]; *see* HOEFLICH, ROMAN AND CIVIL LAW, *supra* note 7, at 28–29, 39.

Kent's *Commentaries* were more thoroughly American than Tucker's endeavor. Both were institutionalist since they were comprehensive in describing private and some public law and served a didactic purpose. However, Tucker used only the fifth volume of his set to begin to unify a national law, while Kent's effort encompassed his four volumes. Kent also deviated for his topic organization from the tripartite division adopted by Justinian's *Institutes* and Blackstone's *Commentaries*. Kent had six parts in his work: (1) law of nations; (2) national constitutional law; (3) sources of state law;[122] (4) persons, including the family, master-servant, slavery, and corporations; (5) personal property, together with contracts, gifts, partnership, and maritime and commercial law; and (6) real property, including estates, trusts, inheritance, and deeds.[123]

3. American Legal Treatises: Joseph Story

Recall that the type of literature in early America most significant for comparative law, which utilized Roman and European civil law sources, included treatises as well as institutionalist commentaries.[124] Simpson, relying on Plucknett, described treatises as monographs, dealing with a single branch of law, possessing sufficient coherence that the author could begin with basic principles and deduce logical categories, concepts, and rules.[125] European jurists, in an effort to further legal science, had been writing treatises since the seventeenth century.[126] The first notable treatise in the United States was Story's *Bailments* (1832).[127] Story recognized his debt to French civilian treatises and their vision

---

[122] This part included a lecture on the history and importance of Roman law. KENT, 1 COMMENTARIES, *supra* note 114, at 481–508.

[123] *See* HOEFLICH, ROMAN AND CIVIL LAW, *supra* note 7, at 35; Langbein, *supra* note 68, at 591–93.

[124] *See supra* pt. D.2 (commentaries); Stein, *supra* note 89, at 417–27.

[125] A.W.B. Simpson, *The Rise and Fall of the Legal Treatise: Legal Principles and the Forms of Legal Literature*, 48 U. CHI. L. REV. 632–33 (1981); *see* T.F.T. PLUCKNETT, EARLY ENGLISH LEGAL LITERATURE 19 (1958); HOEFLICH, ROMAN AND CIVIL LAW, *supra* note 7, at 32–33.

[126] HOEFLICH, ROMAN AND CIVIL LAW, *supra* note 7, at 33–34.

[127] JOSEPH STORY, COMMENTARIES ON THE LAW OF BAILMENTS, WITH ILLUSTRATIONS FROM THE CIVIL AND THE FOREIGN LAW (1832) [hereinafter STORY, BAILMENTS]. Story noted with criticism that he had consulted the 1781 English essay on bailment by William Jones, who also treated Roman and civil law in comparison to English law. *Id.* at v–vi; *see* Simpson, *supra* note 125, at 651–52, 659–60, 668.

Simpson identified Zephaniah Swift, *System of the Law of Connecticut* (1795–1796), as America's first treatise author. Simpson, *supra*, at 669. Pound chose Tapping Reeve, *The Law of Baron and Femme* . . . (1816) (dealing with family law) as the first textbook in the United States. POUND, FORMATIVE ERA, *supra* note 5, at 140; *see* Angela Fernandez, *Tapping Reeve, Coverture and America's First Legal Treatise*, *in* LAW BOOKS IN ACTION: ESSAYS ON THE ANGLO-AMERICAN LEGAL TREATISE 63–67, 80–81 (Angela Fernandez & Markus D. Dubber eds., 2012).

of systematization.[128] For the remainder of the nineteenth century and into the twentieth, the best of the treatise tradition was associated with the efforts of professors at university law schools. Teaching and research were symbiotic.[129]

Story began teaching at Harvard in 1829 as the first Dane Professor (while also serving as Supreme Court justice) until his death in 1845. During this time at Harvard, he completed eight additional treatises,[130] covering American constitutions (1833),[131] conflicts (1834),[132] equity jurisprudence (1836),[133] equity pleading (1838),[134] agency (1839),[135] partnership (1841),[136] bills of exchange (1843),[137] and promissory notes (1845).[138] These treatises collectively saw 75 editions up to 1900, speaking to their importance throughout the nineteenth century.[139] From the full titles to Story's commentaries, one can see that, except for constitutional law and equity pleading, seven works covering commercial law, conflict of laws, and equity were explicitly comparative law endeavors. Story's comparative approach to law teaching and scholarly presentation was important for promoting juristic exchange between American and European

---

[128] STORY, BAILMENTS, *supra* note 127, at vi–ix. Story stated that he benefited greatly from the French jurists Domat and Pothier. *Id.* at vi–vii; *see* HOEFLICH, ROMAN AND CIVIL LAW, *supra* note 7, at 34–36. *See generally* MICHAEL H. HOEFLICH & KAREN S. BECK, CATALOGUES OF EARLY AMERICAN LAW LIBRARIES: THE 1846 AUCTION CATALOGUE OF JOSEPH STORY'S LIBRARY (2004).

[129] Simpson, *supra* note 125, at 670–71; Stein, *supra* note 89, at 423 (civil law study). For Story's interest in legal science and his involvement at Harvard Law School, *see supra* text accompanying notes 80–83, 88–89; Simpson, *supra*, at 672–74.

[130] NEWMYER, *supra* note 68, at 240–42, 263, 281–300.

[131] JOSEPH STORY, 1–3 COMMENTARIES ON THE CONSTITUTION OF THE UNITED STATES; WITH A PRELIMINARY REVIEW OF THE CONSTITUTIONAL HISTORY OF THE COLONIES AND STATES ... (1833) (250 pages in volume 1 dealt with the colonies before 1776 and the national government from 1776 until 1787).

[132] *Id.*, COMMENTARIES ON THE CONFLICT OF LAWS, FOREIGN AND DOMESTIC... (1834).

[133] *Id.*, 1–2 COMMENTARIES ON EQUITY JURISPRUDENCE, AS ADMINISTERED IN ENGLAND AND AMERICA (1836). "I have endeavoured to show the reasons, upon which these doctrines are founded; and to illustrate them by principles drawn from foreign jurisprudence, as well as from the Roman Civil Law." 1 *id.* at vi; *see* MACIAS, *supra* note 65, at 161–62 (*jus gentium*).

[134] JOSEPH STORY, COMMENTARIES ON EQUITY PLEADINGS ... (1838).

[135] *Id.*, COMMENTARIES ON THE LAW OF AGENCY, AS A BRANCH OF COMMERCIAL AND MARITIME JURISPRUDENCE, WITH OCCASIONAL ILLUSTRATIONS FROM THE CIVIL AND FOREIGN LAW (1839).

[136] *Id.*, COMMENTARIES ON THE LAW OF PARTNERSHIP, AS A BRANCH OF COMMERCIAL AND MARITIME JURISPRUDENCE, WITH OCCASIONAL ILLUSTRATIONS FROM THE CIVIL AND FOREIGN LAW (1841). "The Roman Law is an inexhaustible treasure of various and valuable learning; and the principles applicable to the Law of Partnership are stated with uncommon clearness and force in the leading title of the Institutes (De Societate), and those of the Digest and the Code of Justinian (Pro Socio), and in the very able Commentaries of Vinnius, Heineccius, and John Voet thereon. *Id.* at vii.

[137] *Id.*, COMMENTARIES ON THE LAW OF BILLS OF EXCHANGE, FOREIGN AND INLAND, ... WITH OCCASIONAL ILLUSTRATIONS FROM THE COMMERCIAL LAW OF THE NATIONS OF CONTINENTAL EUROPE (1843).

[138] *Id.*, COMMENTARIES ON THE LAW OF PROMISSORY NOTES, ... WITH OCCASIONAL ILLUSTRATIONS FROM THE COMMERCIAL LAW OF THE NATIONS OF CONTINENTAL EUROPE (1845).

[139] G. Blaine Baker, *Story'd Paradigms for the Nineteenth-Century Display of Anglo-American Legal Doctrine*, *in* LAW BOOKS IN ACTION, *supra* note 127, at 82.

legal scholars.[140] For instance, Francis Lieber asked Story in 1834 to write an article on American law for Carl Mittermaier's German comparative law journal, which Story did.[141] Story had earlier written 18 entries for Lieber's ambitious *Encyclopædia Americana* utilizing a comparative law approach.[142]

Story believed that federal judges should take the lead in working toward a national and even global conflict of laws and commercial law. To achieve this goal, American lawyers would need to read continental European legal treatises and study Roman law.[143] In *Swift v. Tyson* (1842), Story wrote, "The law respecting negotiable instruments may be truly declared in the language of Cicero ... to be in a great measure, not the law of a single country only, but of the commercial world."[144] However, most of the law teachers that followed Story after 1845 lacked his knowledge and language abilities to pursue his vision founded on the natural law premise of universal law.[145] Nevertheless, many other lawyers wrote about natural law in their scholarly works during the first half of the nineteenth

---

[140] Hoeflich detailed some of Story's European legal sources and circle of friends who supported his cosmopolitan writing. HOEFLICH, ROMAN AND CIVIL LAW, *supra* note 7, at 30–32, 53–54. However, Hoeflich adopted a twentieth-century view of legal comparison to criticize Story's effort as "mere juxtaposition of legal rules with little attempt at synthesis," concluding that Story "was not truly a comparativist." *Id.* at 152. I would resist holding Story to a standard not commonly achieved even since World War II. *See* Kurt H. Nadelmann, *Joseph Story's Sketch of American Law*, 3 AM. J. COMP. L. 3 (1954) (Story's "masterly use—of the comparative method," referring to the conflicts commentary). In 1947, Edouard Lambert called Story the American ancestor of comparative law. *Id.* at 8.

[141] Nadelmann, *supra* note 140, at 4–5; Morris L. Cohen, *Introduction*, *in* THE UNSIGNED ESSAYS OF SUPREME COURT JUSTICE JOSEPH STORY: EARLY AMERICAN VIEWS OF LAW xi, xxix–xxx (Valerie L. Horowitz ed., 2015) [hereinafter UNSIGNED ESSAYS]; *see* NEWMYER, *supra* note 68, at 287, 290. It appeared in German as the lead article in 9 *Kritische Zeitschrift für Rechtswissenschaft und Gesetzgebung des Auslandes* 1 (1836), reproduced in 3 AM. J. COMP. LAW 9–26 (1954) and UNSIGNED ESSAYS, *supra*, at 343–60. In 1835, Story also wrote an article on national courts for a French comparative law journal, *Revue Étrangère et Française de Législation et d'Économie Politique*. Nadelmann, *supra*, at 4 n.17.

[142] John C. Hogan, *Joseph Story's* Encyclopedia Americana *"Law Articles,"* 48 LAW LIBR. J. 117–21 (1955) *see* UNSIGNED ESSAYS, *supra* note 141, at 3–326; *infra* text accompanying notes 247–250 (Lieber's encyclopedia). "The treatises, like his contributions to the *Encyclopedia Americana* were marked by Story's comparative law approach whereby American law was viewed in a larger context and related to English law, the law of various civil law countries, Roman law and other ancient legal systems." Cohen, *supra* note 141, at xii–xiii; *see id.* at xxv–xxvii.

[143] MACIAS, *supra* note 65, at 165–70; NEWMYER, *supra* note 68, at 287; Coquillette, *supra* note 80, at 26–27. *See id.* at 46 (course on civil and foreign law). Coquillette found that Story's judicial opinions on *lex mercatoria* used civilian legal sources primarily for an ornamental flourish rather than for governing authority (which was largely English common law). *Id.* at 33–38. Hoeflich, likewise, saw Story's use of Roman and civil law in the commentaries as generally illustrative or comparative in confirming the universality of a common law rule. Nevertheless, at times, especially for conflict of laws, Story would use the civilian rule to fill a gap in the common law. HOEFLICH, ROMAN AND CIVIL LAW, *supra* note 7, at 37–44, 46–48. *See generally* ALAN WATSON, JOSEPH STORY AND THE COMITY OF ERRORS: A STUDY IN CONFLICT OF LAWS (1992).

[144] 41 U.S. (16 Pet.) 1, 19 (*quoted in* Coquillette, *supra* note 80, at 26); *see* NEWMYER, *supra* note 68, at 334–43.

[145] Coquillette, *supra* note 80, at 30–33; *see* John C. Hogan, *Joseph Story's Essay on "Natural Law,"* 34 OR. L. REV. 88 (1955).

century.[146] Moreover, Story's ideas persisted through the many editions of his commentaries.[147]

4. David Hoffman's Plan for Legal Education

David Hoffman (1784–1854), a Maryland lawyer, believed that a thorough knowledge of Roman and civil law should be a significant part of any American lawyer's training. He helped to establish the University of Maryland, which in turn appointed him professor of law in 1814. Hoffman then spent three years devising an ambitious curriculum that he felt appropriate for American law study.[148] In 1817, he published the *Course of Legal Study*, the same year Harvard created its law department. Story anonymously praised the work. In 1822, Hoffman began using his *Course* at an institute he created, loosely associated with the University of Maryland, and continued teaching until 1832.[149] Other teachers also used his *Course* at Harvard, Virginia, and Columbia. Later, Hoffman pursued his interest in Roman and civil law at the University of Göttingen, which awarded him a doctorate degree in law, a fact he listed on the title page of the expanded second edition of *Course*.[150]

The *Course* was part detailed bibliography and part discursive notes based on the readings. For instance, title 10 dealt with the "civil or Roman law." It consisted of three pages of readings, referenced to notes 1 to 7, which occupied 19 pages following the bibliography.[151] Hoffman justified this civilian chapter for American students on the ground that Roman (or civil law) was *ratio scripta*,

---

[146] HELMHOLZ, NATURAL LAW, *supra* note 58, at 139. Helmholz provided a list of 62 such lawyers. *Id.* at 139–40.

[147] NEWMYER, *supra* note 68, at 301–04.

[148] Maxwell Bloomfield, *Hoffman, David* [hereinafter Bloomfield, *Hoffman*], *in* 10 AMERICAN NATIONAL BIOGRAPHY 938 (John A. Garraty & Mark C. Carnes eds., 1999) [hereinafter AMERICAN NATIONAL BIOGRAPHY]; *see* Maxwell Bloomfield, *David Hoffman and the Shaping of a Republican Legal Culture*, 38 MD. L. REV. 673, 678, 683 (1979) [hereinafter Bloomfield, *Shaping*]. Hoffman was an early advocate of historical jurisprudence; he viewed legal issues in evolutionary terms that required close study of social context. *Id.* at 681–82, 686.

[149] Bloomfield, *Hoffman*, *supra* note 148, at 938; Hoeflich, *Theory & Practice*, *supra* note 87, at 124, 128–29; *id.*, *Roman and Civil Law in American Legal Education and Research prior to 1930: A Preliminary Survey*, 1984 U. ILL. L. REV. 719, 723 [hereinafter Hoeflich, *American Legal Education*]; Thomas L. Shaffer, *David Hoffman's Law School Lectures, 1822–1833*, 32 J. LEG. EDUC. 127, 128–29 (1982); *see supra* text accompanying notes 88–89 (Hoffman's *Course* and Story's review).

[150] Hoeflich, *American Legal Education*, *supra* note 149, at 723, 725; REED, *supra* note 75, at 454–55; Shaffer, *supra* note 149, at 130, 138; *see* DAVID HOFFMAN, 1–2 A COURSE OF LEGAL STUDY, ADDRESSED TO STUDENTS AND THE PROFESSION GENERALLY (2d ed., 1836). For a review of this edition, *see* F.J.T., *Hoffman's Course of Legal Study*, 15 AM. JURIST & L. MAG. 321–42 (1836).

[151] HOFFMAN, COURSE, *supra* note 88, at 251–72; *see* Hoeflich, *American Legal Education*, *supra* note 149, at 724.

THE FORMATIVE ERA: 1791–1865   175

which virtually all enlightened nations had adopted as the foundation of their legal systems.[152] In addition, he felt that Roman and civil law were sources for particular common law subjects. Consequently, for the chapter on contracts, Hoffman cited 35 continental authors, such as Domat and Pothier, compared to 38 common law authors.[153]

The civilian orientation of Hoffman's *Course* made it attractive in Louisiana. In 1840, the Louisiana Supreme Court issued a course of studies necessary for those who aspired to become Louisiana lawyers. The court's rule required— beyond familiarity with Louisiana's codes, statutes, and case law—knowledge of Justinian's *Institutes*, Domat on civil law, and Pothier on obligations. The compromise rule also mandated reading the commentaries of Blackstone and Kent. François Martin (1762–1846), an émigré from France, was instrumental in bringing Hoffman's vision to Louisiana. Martin was one of three judges on the court from 1815 until 1845. He was sympathetic to Hoffman's notion that the civil law and common law were not hostile rivals but complementary to each other.[154]

Hoffman's publication of *Legal Outlines* in 1829 amply demonstrated his theoretical approach to legal education. He drew upon history, philosophy, and political science, and provided a list of books, from which he drew the contents of ten lectures.[155] The ninth lecture began with the division between public or political law and private or civil law. For over 100 pages, Hoffman described a variety of historical forms of government that had existed or philosophers had imagined from Greek city states to contemporary France. A commentator used that lecture to emphasize Hoffman's position that American private law owed a substantial debt to rules and concepts the Romans had developed centuries ago.[156]

---

[152] HOFFMAN, COURSE, *supra* note 88, at 254–56. Hoffman elaborated: "No nation has been more copiously supplied from the purest streams of the Civil Law, and has at the same time given it so little credit for what it had received, as Great Britain." *Id.* at 257; *see* Hoeflich, *American Legal Education*, *supra* note 149, at 723–25.

[153] Hoeflich, *American Legal Education*, *supra* note 149, at 724.

[154] Warren M. Billings, *A Course of Legal Studies: Books That Shaped Louisiana Law*, in A LAW UNTO ITSELF? ESSAYS IN THE NEW LOUISIANA LEGAL HISTORY 25–26, 28–29, 31–33, 37 (Warren M. Billings & Mark F. Fernandez eds., 2001); *see infra* note 206 and accompanying text (Martin).

[155] Bloomfield, *Shaping*, *supra* note 148, at 681; see DAVID HOFFMAN, 1 LEGAL OUTLINES, BEING THE SUBSTANCE OF A COURSE OF LECTURES NOW DELIVERING IN THE UNIVERSITY OF MARYLAND (1829; reprinted 1836) [hereinafter HOFFMAN, OUTLINES]. There were two reviews, which were generally favorable to Hoffman's efforts. *Hoffman's Legal Outlines*, 3 AM. JURIST & L. MAG. 86–100 (1830); [Joseph K. Angell], *Hoffman's* Legal Outlines, 1 U.S. LAW INTELLIGENCER & REV. 264–67 (1829).

[156] *The Civil Law*, 8 AM. JURIST 203–13 (1832); *see* HOFFMAN, OUTLINES, *supra* note 155, at 363–484. Some of that Roman law influence filtered through absorption in English law and equity. *The Civil Law*, *supra*, at 203–04.

E. Other Legal Literature Depicting Roman and Civil Law

1. Periodicals with Legal Content

A common thread for periodicals with legal content during the first half of the nineteenth century was that each editor was a lawyer knowledgeable in one or more foreign languages—usually a Romance language. Consistent with American legal culture these editors found it useful to include translations or articles about Roman and civil law. The first law periodical in the United States was the *American Law Journal and Miscellaneous Repertory*, which included several translations of foreign law and jurists.[157] The editor, John Hall (1783–1829), a Baltimore lawyer, published six volumes between 1808 and 1817. In the first three volumes, he translated portions of Justinian's *Digest* related to maritime law.[158] Although most of the journal printed American court decisions, especially on admiralty matters, Hall wrote several articles about civilian publications useful to American lawyers. To illustrate, he reviewed a book about the French Council of State's discussions of the 1804 Civil Code.[159]

With Hall's interest in maritime law, he undertook to translate into English portions of a French edition of the fourteenth-century *Consulate of the Sea*, originally written in Catalan. Derived from usages and customs shared by several nations, it served to govern sea trade in the Mediterranean and was the basis for modern maritime law.[160] He followed that with a translation of excerpts from the French ordinance of the sea related to maritime loans.[161] In 1811, Hall published his translation of Balthazard Emérigon's French essay on maritime loans to

---

[157] M.H. Hoeflich, *Translation & the Reception of Foreign Law in the Antebellum United States*, 50 AM. J. COMP. L. 753, 762–63 (2002) [hereinafter Hoeflich, *Translation*]. The *Journal* was based on the English endeavor, the *Law Journal*, which issued three volumes from 1804 to 1806. See [John Hall], *Preface*, 1 AM. L.J. & MISC. REPERTORY v–vi (1808).

[158] [John Hall], *Civil Law*, 2 AM. L.J. & MISC. REPERTORY 491–96 (1809) (book 4, title 9); *id.* at 250–51 (book 47, title 5); *id.* at 462–72 (book 14, title 1); 3 *id.* at 14–21 (1810) (book 14, title 2); *id.* at 151–55 (book 22, title 2); *see* Stein, *supra* note 89, at 413–14. Hall reprinted his translation in Emérigon, *infra* note 162.

[159] [John Hall], *Review*, 2 AM. L.J. & MISC. REPERTORY 472–83 (1809) (Regnaud, 1–2 *Discussions du Code Civil dans le Conseil d'État* (1805)); 3 *id.* at 72–80 (1810). Livingston submitted an article to the *Journal* about the litigation concerning the Batture in New Orleans. Edward Livingston, *Examination of the Title of the United States to the Land Called The Batture*, 2 *id.* at 307–42. Hall dedicated two issues of volume 5 (1814) to this litigation.

[160] [John Hall], *Il Consolato del Mare: The Judicial Order of Proceedings before the Consular Court*, 2 AM. L.J. & MISC. REPERTORY 385–91 (1809); 3 *id.* at 1–13 (1810); 4 AM. L.J. at 299–304 (no. 2, 1813); *see* [John Hall], *Legal Bibliography*, 4 *id.* at 160–68 (issue 2, 1813) (book review of Antonio de Capmany, 1–2 *Libro del Consulado* (1791)).

[161] [John Hall], *Translation*, 3 AM. L.J. & MISC. REPERTORY at 156–58 (1810); 4 AM. L.J. at 464–66 (1813) (Louis XIV Ordonnance de la Marine, book 3, title 5).

which he added notes and his earlier *Journal* translations of Roman and French maritime law.[162]

The War of 1812 with the United Kingdom interrupted publication of the *Journal* and the flow of translations. Nevertheless, Hall resumed publication in 1813 with volume 4 issued as a new series. In the preface, he remarked on the value of foreign law. "The legal lore of former ages and foreign nations is an abundant treasury, to which the scientific lawyer can always resort for those abstract principles of right which are applicable at all times and in all places."[163] Hall presented an article on French criminal procedure based on the recent French Code, in particular comparing the use of criminal jury trial in France and America.[164] In the *Journal's* final volume in 1817, Hall provided a forum for James Workman (d. 1832), a Louisiana judge who had emigrated from Ireland. Workman had a scholarly interest in Spanish America and offered to write a digest of the laws of Castile and the Spanish Indies, providing Hall a summary of the subject. He also translated a Spanish royal edict on the treatment of slaves in the Indies.[165]

Several lawyers served as editors to commence a new periodical in 1822, the *United States Law Journal and Civilian's Magazine*, which, although it had a short run of two volumes, attempted to carry on the pattern of its predecessor. The first issue presented a translation of André Dupin's historical sketch of Roman law, stating that every young lawyer should gain an acquaintance with the civil law.[166] Issue 2 included a summary of Edward Livingston's 1822 report to the Louisiana legislature proposing a penal code.[167] Issue 3 offered a translation of Cuba's 1794 statute creating a commercial tribunal with accompanying rules.[168] There followed a translation of the 1814 French Constitution and the 1810 French Penal Code.[169] After a lapse of four years, a different mix of editors published a second volume that dropped the "civilian's magazine" portion of the title.

---

[162] BALTHAZARD-MARIE EMÉRIGON, AN ESSAY ON MARITIME LOANS (Hall trans., 1811) (*Traité des Assurance et des Contrats a la Grosse* (1783)); *see* Stein, *supra* note 89, at 414.

[163] [John Hall], *Advertisement*, 4 AM. L.J. v, vii (no. 1, 1813).

[164] *Id., Review*, 305–19, 588–617 (1813).

[165] [James Workman], *Laws of the Spanish Indies*, 6 AM. L.J. 285–307 (1817); *id., For the Good Government and Protection of Slaves in the Spanish Colonies*, at 465–73 (cédula of 31 May 1789); *see id., The Civil Law* (excerpt from Justinian's *Digest*), *id.* at 307–12.

[166] M. *Dupin's Sketch of the History of the Roman Law*, 1 U.S. L.J. & CIVILIAN'S MAG. 110, 111–34 (1822); *see* Simeon E. Baldwin, *The United States Law Journal of 1822*, 4 A.B.A. J. 37, 39, 51 (1918). For a review of Dupin's pamphlet, *see infra* note 178.

[167] *Penal Jurisprudence*, 1 U.S. L.J. & CIVILIAN'S MAG. 259–80 (1822); *see* Baldwin, *supra* note 166, at 43. The editors printed Livingston's full 106-page report in 1826. Edward Livingston, *Report Made to the General Assembly of the State of Louisiana, on the Plan of a Penal Code for the Said State*, 2 U.S. L.J. 1–106 (Supp. 1826). They also included certain draft articles for the code. *Id.* at 107–59 (Supp. 1826).

[168] Andrew S. Garr, *Commercial Code of Havana*, 1 U.S. L.J. & CIVILIAN'S MAG. 357–66 (1823).

[169] *Constitution and Penal Code of France*, 1 *id.* at 405, 406–45.

The most successful of the early law periodicals was the *American Jurist and Law Magazine*, which appeared regularly in 28 volumes from 1829 to 1843. Unlike Hall's journal, *American Jurist* had a series of editors. It also had a strong connection to the Boston legal community, Harvard Law School, and especially Joseph Story.[170] Three of the editors from 1834—Luther Cushing, George Hillard, and Charles Sumner—were good friends with Story and the latter two had been his students. Cushing (1803-1856) was to become the most important for the field of comparative law and was the principal editor after 1838.[171] Not surprisingly, Story offered the first article, his 1821 speech to the Suffolk Bar, for volume 1.[172] Story saw that the increasing mass of court reports from 23 American jurisdictions threatened to bury lawyers and judges in the "labyrinths of the law." Contemporary jurists, as with Romans in the ancient world, should find "general principles to guide us in new and difficult cases.... The whole continental jurisprudence rests upon this broad foundation of Roman wisdom."[173]

In 1829, *American Jurist* demonstrated its interest in Roman law with a review of two recent books on the subject, one published in England and other in France.[174] This attention continued until the 1840s.[175] It began to list a few books and legal developments from France, Germany, and the Netherlands along with the usual publications and other legal matters in America and the United Kingdom.[176] The magazine entertained the codification question that Bentham

---

[170] The initial editors until 1834 were successful Boston lawyers: Willard Phillips (1784–1873) and Samuel Sewall (1799–1888, Harvard Law School degree, 1820), who carried the principal workload, with John Davis (1787–1854, U.S. House of Representatives 1825–1834, then governor of Massachusetts) and Richard Fletcher (1788–1869, U.S. House of Representatives 1837–1839). *Notices of New Books*, 6 LAW REPORTER 234 (1843); *see Willard [Phillips], in* 4 APPLETONS' CYCLOPEDIA OF AMERICAN BIOGRAPHY 763 (James Grant Wilson et al. eds., 1888), http://famousamericans.net/willardpiiillips; NINA MOORE TIFFANY, SAMUEL E. SEWALL: A MEMOIR 12–13, 17–18 (1898); Kinley Brauer, *Davis, John, in* 6 AMERICAN NATIONAL BIOGRAPHY, at 206–07; Biographical Directory, *Fletcher, Richard*, https://bioguide.congress.gov/search/bio/F000203.

[171] HOEFLICH, ROMAN AND CIVIL LAW, *supra* note 7, at 85; Nadelmann, *supra* note 140, at 6; *see* NEWMYER, *supra* note 68, at 265, 268, 279. Hillard graduated from Harvard Law School in 1832 and began practicing law in Boston in 1833, the year Sumner graduated from the Law School. He joined Hillard in private practice until 1837, when Sumner departed for Europe for three years, learning French, German, Italian, and Spanish. Frederick J. Blue, *Sumner, Charles, in* 21 AMERICAN NATIONAL BIOGRAPHY, *supra* note 148, at 137; Charles H. Brichford, *Hillard, George Stillman*, 10 *id.* at 806.

[172] Joseph Story, *An Address Delivered before the Members of the Suffolk Bar*, 1 AM. JURIST & L. MAG. 1–34 (1829) [hereinafter Story, *Suffolk Bar*]; *see supra* note 65 (Suffolk address entitled "Progress of Jurisprudence" reprinted in STORY'S WRITINGS).

[173] Story, *Suffolk Bar*, *supra* note 172, at 13–14, 31.

[174] [John Pickering], *The Civil Law*, 2 AM. JURIST & L. MAG. 39–65 (1829) (book review of EDMUND PLUNKETT BURKE, AN HISTORICAL ESSAY ON THE LAWS AND THE GOVERNMENT OF ROME: DESIGNED AS AN INTRODUCTION TO THE STUDY OF THE CIVIL LAW (1827); and ANDRÉ-MARIE DUPIN, PRÉCIS HISTORIQUE DU DROIT ROMAIN, DEPUIS ROMULUS JUSQU'À NOS JOURS (4th ed., 1822)).

[175] *E.g.*, *On the Influence of the Stoic Philosophy on the Roman Law*, 25 *id.* at 47–65 (1841); *On the Influence of Christianity on the Roman Law*, *id.* at 280–96.

[176] *E.g.*, *Intelligence*, 2 *id.* at 189, 198–99 (1829); *Quarterly List of Law Publications*, 3 *id.* at 416–18 (1830); *Intelligence and Miscellany*, *id.* at 158–63, 177–80; 4 *id.* at 208–14, 225–29 (1830); 5 *id.* at

presented and Story recognized in his 1821 address as a force relevant to counteract the accelerating mass of legal authority. In 1831, it published an essay about the codification debate in Germany between law professors Thibaut and Savigny and its relevance to England and the United States.[177] It also reported on the situation in France related to increased citation of judicial authority.[178] By 1835, even some conservative jurists, such as Cushing, believed that legal science supported selected use of codification among American states as a means of law reform.[179] The debate continued into the 1840s.[180]

Beyond reviews of European books about Roman and civil law, *American Jurist* published translations of certain primary and secondary legal authority originating in Europe. These excerpts ranged from Spanish prescription law to French copyright law.[181] As a new editor, Cushing began writing articles about civil law topics that he believed would interest American lawyers. The first was about the civilian approach to contracts of sale.[182] Another concerned the movement of European and American penal law theories of punishment away from vengeance.[183]

402–04 (1831); 6 *id.* 459–61 (1831). Other countries included Chile and India. 4 *id.* at 215–17 (1830). After a gap, the listing of continental books resumed in 1835. *E.g.*, 13 *id.* at 241–42 (1835); 14 *id.* at 251, 489–94 (1835).

[177] *Written and Unwritten Systems of Laws*, 5 *id.* at 23–51 (1831); 9 *id.* at 5–36 (book review of J.D. Meyer, *De la Codification en Général, et de Celle de l'Angleterre* . . . (1830)); *see Letter of Jeremy Bentham*, 27 *id.* at 62–79 (1842) (publication of Bentham's 1818 letter to a representative of the New Hampshire legislature regarding its rejection of his offer regarding codification).

[178] *The Citing of Authorities*, 8 *id.* at 111–17 (1832) (book review of ANDRÉ DUPIN, DE LA JURISPRUDENCE DES ARRÊTS (1825) and JOHN JAMES PARK, CONTRE-PROJET TO THE HUMPHREYSIAN CODE... (1828)).

[179] CHARLES M. COOK, THE AMERICAN CODIFICATION MOVEMENT: A STUDY OF ANTEBELLUM LEGAL REFORM 164–81 (1981); *see, e.g.*, S.F. [Dixon], *Codification, and Reform of the Law*, 14 AM. JURIST & L. MAG. 280–302 (1835); 15 *id.* at 16–42 (1836); 16 *id.* at 59–87, 289–315 (1836–1837; 17 *id.* at 71–93 (1837); 20 *id.* at 305–24 (1839); 21 *id.* at 352–72 (1839); 22 *id.* at 282–303 (1840); 24 *id.* at 32–62 (1840). Dixon, a New York lawyer, began writing articles for the journal in 1835 and became associate editor in 1841. *Intelligence and Miscellany*, 26 *id.* at 262 (1841).

[180] J. Louis Tellkampf [incorrectly spelled Telkampf], *On Codification, or the Systematizing of the Law*, 26 AM. JURIST & L. MAG. 113–45 (1841); 26 *id.* at 283–329 (1842).

[181] *On the Plan and Objects of the American Jurist and Law Magazine*, 19 AM. JURIST & L. MAG. 1, 7–8 (1838) [hereinafter *Plan and Objects*] (foreign law policy); *see, e.g.*, *Spanish Law of Prescription*, 10 *id.* at 268–73 (1833); L.S. [Cushing], *Theory of the Rights of Authors*, 22 *id.* at 39–92 (1839) [hereinafter Cushing, *Rights of Authors*], *republished as* AUGUSTIN-CHARLES RENOUARD, THEORY OF THE RIGHTS OF AUTHORS IN LITERATURE, SCIENCES, AND IN FINE ARTS (L.S. Cushing trans., 1839) (56-page pamphlet of extracts from 1 *Traité des Droits d'Auteurs, dans la Littérature, les Sciences et les Beaus-Arts* (1838)). Cushing added an analysis of Kant's doctrine of author rights. Cushing, *Rights of Authors*, *supra*, at 40, 88–92.

[182] [Luther Cushing], *The Nature of the Contract of Sale—Civil Law*, 11 *id.* at 271–89 (1834); 13 *id.* at 247–71 (1835); 15 *id.* at 43–60 (1836). Although the journal's editors usually did not list their authorship of articles, the series on contracts was likely by Cushing, since he published a translation of Pothier's treatise on that subject in 1839. *See Critical Notices*, 21 *id.* at 455–59 (1839) (book review); R.J. POTHIER, TREATISE ON THE CONTRACT OF SALE (L.S. Cushing trans., 1839). *See also Plan and Objects*, *supra* note 181, at 7 (attribution policy).

[183] L.S. [Cushing], *A Sketch of the Various Theories concerning the Rightful Foundation and the Object of Punishment*, 22 AM. JURIST & L. MAG. 359–73 (1840).

In 1833, Carl Mittermaier, co-founder of the world's first comparative law periodical and a law professor at the University of Heidelberg, wrote a review of German legislation for *American Jurist*.[184] With the German journal, the *Kritische Zeitschrift für Rechtswissenschaft und Gesetzgebung des Auslandes*, and its editors, began a period of interchange between Germany and the United States that jurists and Story, in particular, found useful for his treatise writing.[185] For instance, *American Jurist* published Cushing's translation of Mittermaier's three-part comparative and empirical German article on the death penalty[186] as well as Mittermaier's article on drunkenness and criminal responsibility.[187] Mittermaier wrote an original article for the *American Jurist* on current German penal legislation.[188] He also agreed to provide translations to the first French comparative law journal, the *Revue Étrangère de Législation et d'Économie Politique*.[189] Perhaps Mittermaier's most impressive contribution was to illustrate the careful and comprehensive effort of one of the nineteenth century's greatest comparatists encompassed within a critical analysis of penitentiary reform in Europe and America.[190]

In addition to Cushing's knowledge of French law, he had an interest in the German historical school of jurisprudence, its cultural specificity, and the shift away from natural law.[191] For instance, he translated an article by Gustav

---

[184] Carl Mittermaier, Miscellany and Intelligence, 9 id. at 234–38 (1833); see, e.g., Intelligence and Miscellany, 17 id. at 484, 488–99 (summary of articles from the periodical); 17 id. at 499–500 (German advertisement of a translation of Story's conflicts treatise); Critical Notices, 19 id. at 482 (1838); 21 id. at 475–77 (1839) (list of journal articles). Mittermaier, with Karl Zachariä, founded the Kritische Zeitschrift in 1829. It issued until 1856. KONRAD ZWEIGERT & HEIN KÖTZ, INTRODUCTION TO COMPARATIVE LAW 54–55 (Tony Weir trans., 3d ed., 1998); see Notices of New Books, 12 AM. JURIST & L. MAG. 229–30 (1834) (review of Kritische Zeitschrift).

[185] In 1834, Francis Lieber translated a letter that Mittermaier wrote to Story, praising the latter's conflict of laws treatise and wondering whether Harvard might grant the German a doctorate degree. Harvard Law Library, https://hollis.harvard.edu (search 990119834440203941); see Intelligence and Miscellany, 14 AM. JURIST & L. MAG. 247 (1835) (Mittermaier's German review of Story's treatise); German Criticism of Mr. Justice Story's Commentaries on the Constitution of the United States, id. at 330–44 (1835); 15 id. at 1–13 (1836).

[186] Mittermaier, On the Latest Progress of Legislation and Science in Europe and America, concerning the Abolition of the Punishment of Death, 18 AM. JURIST & L. MAG. 334–75 (L.S. [Cushing] trans., 1838), original in Archiv des Criminalrechts 1–30, 292–322 (new series 1836).

[187] C.J.A. Mittermaier, On the Effect of Drunkenness upon Criminal Responsibility and the Application of Punishment, 23 AM. JURIST & L. MAG. 290–332 (1840), original in Archiv des Criminalrechts 1–52 (new series, 1839).

[188] C.J.A. Mittermaier, On the Present State of Criminal Legislation in Germany, 24 AM. JURIST & L. MAG. 62–79 (1840).

[189] Miscellany and Intelligence, 11 id. at 495–96 (1834); Intelligence, 13 id. at 236–38 (1835) (review of Story's conflicts treatise); Intelligence and Miscellany, 13 id. at 483–84 (1835). Jean-Jacques Foelix, the founder of French scientific comparative law, was the first editor for the Revue, which issued from 1834 to 1843. ZWEIGERT & KÖTZ, supra note 184, at 55–56; see, e.g., Critical Notices, 19 AM. JURIST & L. MAG. 483–84 (1838); 21 id. at 238–39 (1839); 22 id. at 490 (1840) (list of Revue articles).

[190] Mittermaier, On the Progress of Penitentiary Improvement in Europe and North America, 28 AM. JURIST & L. MAG. 110–49 (1842); 28 id. at 340–87 (1843) (analyzing 60 publications on prisons).

[191] [Luther Cushing], The German Historical School of Jurisprudence, 14 id. at 43–62 (1835) (book review of E.[ugène] Lerminier, Introduction Générale à l'Histoire du Droit (2d ed., 1835)); see L.S.

von Hugo, founder of the historical school, from a German journal, about the German approach to the citation of Roman law.[192] Furthermore, Cushing translated a French analysis of Savigny's *Das Recht des Besitzes* (1803), a classic of the historical school dealing with the law of possession.[193] The *American Jurist*, however, did not abandon reporting on natural law.[194] An illustration of Cushing's eclectic comparative law interests were two book reviews he translated that had appeared in the *Revue Étrangère*. Both concerned Mittermaier's publications: the first a two-volume work comparing German, French, and English criminal procedure and the second a book comparing the theory of proof in criminal proceedings in the same systems.[195]

The earliest occasion in the United States to use the phrase "science of comparative law" appeared in Cushing's 1839 preface to a translation he made of a French report that André Dupin had presented to the Académie des Sciences Morales et Politiques in Paris.[196] Dupin, a Romanist and president of the Chamber of Deputies, wrote about a collection of national civil and penal laws that Victor Foucher had translated and compared to the French codes. Dupin

---

[Cushing], *Reddie's Historical Notices of the Roman Law*, 15 *id.* at 342–62 (1836) (book review); *Critical Notices*, 25 *id.* at 244–46 (1841) (review of a French translation of Friedrich Carl von Savigny, 1 *System des heutigen römischen Rechts* (1840)).

[192] L.S. [Cushing], *Citation of the Roman Law*, 15 *id.* at 63–72 (1836). In the second part of this article, Cushing translated a chapter in French regarding the French style of citing Roman law. *Id.* at 72–81.

[193] L.S. [Cushing], *On the Law of Possession: Analysis of Savigny's Treatise on the Law of Possession*, 19 *id.* at 13–49, 257–91 (1838). L.A. Warnkönig wrote the French analysis published in both a periodical and as a pamphlet, which in its third edition used Friedrich Carl von Savigny, *Das Recht des Besitzes: Eine civilistische Abhandlung* (5th ed. 1827) (624 pages). Cushing, *supra*, at 13–14.

[194] *Jouffroy on Natural Law*, 18 Am. Jurist & L. Mag. 11–36 (1837) (book review of 1–2 *Cours de Droit Naturel* (1835), lectures at the University of Paris by the French philosopher, Théodore Simon Jouffroy); *see Notes*, 18 *id.* at 521, 532 (book review of J.-F.-M. Bussard, *Elémens de droit naturel privé* (1836)); *Critical Notices*, 24 *id.* at 504–05 (1841) (review of Heinrich Ahrens, *Cours de Droit Naturel ou de Philosophie du Droit* (1836–1839)).

[195] L.S. [Cushing], *Criminal Procedure of Germany, France, and England*, 19 *id.* at 332–49 (1838) (review of 1–2 *Das deutsche Strafverfahren* ... (2d ed. 1832-1833)); 20 *id.* at 94–101 (1838) (review of *Die Lehre vom Beweise* ... (1834)); *see Influence of Insanity on Criminal Responsibility*, 21 *id.* at 468–70 (1839) and 22 *id.* at 311–29 (1840) (review of Mittermaier's dissertation); *Critical Notices*, 21 *id.* at 224 (1839) (review of *Die gemeine deutsche bürgerliche Prozess* ... (1838)); *Critical Notices*, 21 *id.* at 475–77 (1839) (review of Mittermaier's German article on the progress of codification in the United States, mentioning Kent and Story).

[196] L.S. [Cushing], *Civil and Criminal Laws of Modern States* [hereinafter Cushing, *Civil and Criminal Laws*], 21 *id.* at 56 (1839) (book review of 1–4 *Collection des Lois Civiles et Criminelles des États Modernes* (Victor Foucher ed., 1833–1838)). Napoléon suppressed the Académie in 1803, but it was re-established in 1832. *Cf.* Hannis Taylor, *A Comparative Study of Roman and English Law, in the Old World and the New*, 7 Am. Law. 473, 477 (1899) ("The science of comparative law is yet in its infancy."). Taylor supported merging comparative politics with comparative jurisprudence, borrowing the phrase from an 1886 address presented at the Tulane University Law Department. *Id.*

asserted that in the 1830s nations were mutually profiting from the study of their different experiences.[197]

> [T]he science of law cannot remain isolated within the borders of each particular state.... [H]enceforward, the study of comparative law is called to form an essential and important element of the science. This study enlarges and elevates the idea of law; it raises it from the narrow sphere of private and local right, and teaches it to generalize; whilst, in the details, it points out deficiencies and defects, and prepares reforms. Finally, regarded in a practical point of view, and in reference to the multiplied relations, which commerce, travel, and mutual exchanges establish among the inhabitants of different countries, this study is every day becoming more necessary.[198]

The first attempt at a comparative law periodical in the United States was the *Louisiana Law Journal*, edited by Gustavus Schmidt from 1841 to 1842. The world's first comparative law journal had appeared in Germany in 1829, followed five years later by one in France.[199] Schmidt had emigrated from Sweden in 1815 at the age of 20. After a few years, he studied law and joined the Virginia bar, where he practiced until 1829. At that time, he moved to New Orleans, where his knowledge of French, German, and Spanish facilitated his law practice there.[200] The *Journal* appeared in four issues totaling more than 600 pages. Schmidt wrote most of the articles and book reviews, reflecting his interest in Roman, European civil, and Louisiana law. These included reviews of books by Savigny and Story. He reported on noteworthy cases from France, Spain, and Scotland, legal reform in Russia, and the Code Napoléon. In the final issue, he outlined the history of Roman law and took up the issue of French versus Spanish law in Louisiana.[201]

In addition to law journals, there were literary periodicals that on occasion presented articles related to Roman and civil law, especially on the civilian method emphasizing the principles and classifications of law. The *North American Review*, founded in 1815, tended to reflect interests at Harvard and, for legal issues, Story's influence. To illustrate, in 1817 and 1818, Story wrote reviews

---

[197] Cushing, *Civil and Criminal Laws*, supra note 196, at 57. Dupin reviewed the first six installments of Foucher's project (four of which he translated and edited), which included codes and statutes from Austria, Brazil, Geneva, Naples and Sicily, and Spain. *Id.* at 58–75.

[198] *Id.* Dupin clarified that he believed a truly scientific comparison required a jurist to study legal systems, not simply isolated rules, and in relation to government and public manners. *Id.* at 58, 69.

[199] *See supra* notes 185–189 and accompanying text (*Kritische Zeitschrift* and *Revue Étrangère*).

[200] M.H. Hoeflich & Louis de la Vergne, *Gustavus Schmidt: His Life & His Library*, 1 ROMAN LEG. TRAD. 112–13, 116 (2002); Agustín Parise, *Gustavus Schmidt, The Civil Law of Spain and Mexico* (1851), 2 J. CIVIL L. STUD. 183–85 (2009) (book review) [hereinafter Parise, *Schmidt*].

[201] Hoeflich & De la Vergne, supra note 200, at 113–14; *Critical Notices*, 26 AM. JURIST & L. MAG. 492–93 (1842).

of Hoffman's *Course* and of a German maritime law treatise (in American translation).[202] In 1820, Caleb Cushing published an article on the usefulness of the civil law. "[I]t is by comparison of our rules and practice with those of foreigners, that we become fully sensible of what is defective or excellent. . . . Nothing more inevitably checks improvement than a jealous or contemptuous rejection of foreign, and an over weening admiration of domestic habits, customs, and principles."[203] In 1828, Hugh Legaré, principal co-founder of the *Southern Review*, modeled it on the Boston version. Early on, he iterated the common view that the civil law was most useful for its method of constructing a legal science.[204]

2. Other American Translations

Translation of legal materials has always been an adjunct to comparative law. It extends the scope of comparison to legal systems otherwise beyond an analyst's reach. In addition to publication of translations in law journals during the nineteenth century, the American interest in Roman and European civil law stimulated translation of important longer works on foreign law, which facilitated comparative law writing. After the French Revolution, some liberal sentiment preferred French law over English law.[205] Robert Pothier (1699–1772) was the most distinguished and prolific of the French civilians. In 1802, François Martin was the first American to translate Pothier's *Traité des Obligations* (1761).[206] We noted earlier the 1820 translation of the *Siete Partidas* in Louisiana and Cooper's 1812 translation of Justinian's *Institutes*.[207] Harvard Law School required students to read both

---

[202] Stein, *supra* note 89, at 415–18; *see* [Joseph Story], Frederick J. Jacobsen, *Laws of the Sea with Reference to Maritime Commerce* (William Frick trans., 1815), 7 N. Am. Rev. & Misc. J. 323–47 (1818) (book review). Willard Phillips, later co-editor of the *American Jurist*, was an editor in 1816 and contributed legal articles until 1834. *Phillips, Willard, supra* note 170.

[203] [Caleb Cushing], *On the Study of the Civil Law*, 11 N. Am. Rev. & Misc. J. 407, 408 (1820). Cushing listed the several areas of law in which the civil law would be advantageous and called for its study early in an American lawyer's education. *Id.* at 408–12. Stein identified the anonymous author as Cushing. Stein, *supra* note 89, at 420.

[204] Stein, *supra* note 89, at 427–31; John R. Welsh, *An Early Pioneer: Legaré's Southern Review*, 3 Southern Literary J. 79–84, 88 (no. 2, Spring 1971). Legaré wrote most of the essays during the *Review*'s four-year existence (of eight volumes). *Id.* at 80, 86.

[205] Hoeflich, *Translation, supra* note 157, at 753–54, 757–59.

[206] Stein, *supra* note 89, at 412; *see* Robert J. Pothier, 1–2 A Treatise on Obligations, Considered in a Moral and Legal View (F.X. Martin trans., 1802); *see supra* text accompanying note 154 (Martin). In 1789, Martin became a lawyer in North Carolina, where he published the Pothier volume, and then moved to Louisiana in 1809. There he served as a judge from 1815 on the Louisiana Supreme Court. Michael Chiorazzi, *Francois-Xavier Martin: Printer, Lawyer, Jurist*, 80 Law Libr. J. 63, 65, 70, 73–74, 76, 78, 80, 92 (1988).

[207] *See supra* note 45 (Moreau-Lislet & Carleton's Siete Partidas) and note 63 (Cooper's Institutes) with accompanying text. Hoeflich, *Translation, supra* note 157, at 765–67. Cooper was Thomas Jefferson's choice to be the first law professor at the University of Virginia, but clerical opposition precluded him. Stein, *supra* note 89, at 419–20.

Cooper's translation of Roman law and Cushing's later translation of Pothier's treatise on sales contracts in the foreign law block of courses.[208]

Hoeflich divided antebellum translations into five groups: (1) by Americans, including recent arrivals from Europe; (2) by Englishmen, reprinted in the United States, some edited with notes to appeal to American readers; (3) British imports; (4) commissioned works, such as those from German that Story requested; and (5) shorter pieces in legal and other periodicals.[209] One subject important for comparative law and useful to Story was conflict of laws. Peter Du Ponceau, a French émigré, had a background like that of Martin. Classically educated in France, Du Ponceau joined the Philadelphia bar in 1785 and in his active practice before the U.S. Supreme Court had an opportunity in 1797 to translate Ulric Huber's *De Conflictu Legum*.[210] In addition, in 1811, Du Ponceau translated the French penal code and commercial code.[211]

Most interest in foreign law centered on maritime law and commercial law, but translations also appeared on other legal subjects such as conflict of laws, copyright, and mining.[212] To illustrate, besides Hall's work in the *American Law Journal*, he published *The Practice and Jurisdiction of the Court of Admiralty*.[213] William Johnson and Joseph Ingersoll also published civilian maritime law translations.[214]

---

[208] Hoeflich, *Translation, supra* note 157, at 773 n.96; *see* REED, *supra* note 75, at 456; *infra* note 218 and accompanying text (Pothier's *Traité du Contrat de Vente*).

[209] Hoeflich, *Translation, supra* note 157, at 760, 766–67, 769.

[210] Stein, *supra* note 89, at 413. Generally known as *De Conflictu Legum Diversarum in Diversis Imperiis* or simply *De Conflictu Legum*, Huber's short seventeenth-century presentation on conflict of laws, of all continental civilians, had the greatest impact on American and British jurists. It was printed in *Emory v. Grenough*, 3 U.S. (3 Dall.) 369, 370–77 (1797) (Supp.). D.J. Llewelyn Davies, *The Influence of Huber's De Conflictu Legum on English Private International Law*, 18 BRIT. Y.B. INT'L L. 49–50, 53–56, 60 (1937); Ernest G. Lorenzen, *Huber's* De Conflictu Legum, 13 ILL. L. REV. 375, 393–94, 397–98 (1919). It is possible Du Ponceau relied for his translation on Ulrici Huberi, 2 *Praelectionum Juris Romani et Hodierni* 30–36 (Frankfurt, 1689) (book 1, title 2), but several other seventeenth-century versions also existed. *E.g.*, Lorenzen for his translation relied on *Praelectionum Juris Civilis* (Leipzig, 1707). Lorenzen, *supra*, at 401–18. Davies's translation borrowed substantially from Lorenzen. Davies, *supra*, at 64–78.

[211] *The Penal Code of the French Empire*, 2 AM. REV. HIST. & POL. app. at 1–69 (no. 1, July 1811); *The Commercial Code of the French Empire*, 2 *id.* at 91–203 (no. 2, Oct. 1811) (with the translator's explanatory notes), *cited* in Peter Stephen Du Ponceau & James L. Whitehead, *The Autobiography of Peter Stephen Du Ponceau*, 63 PA. MAG. HIST. & BIOGRAPHY 189, 191 (1939).

[212] Hoeflich, *Translation, supra* note 157, at 760–62, 768–69, 771; Stein, *supra* note 89, at 413.

[213] JOHN E. HALL, THE PRACTICE AND JURISDICTION OF THE COURT OF ADMIRALTY (1809). Part 2 of this three-part volume was Hall's translation of Francis Clerke, *Praxis Supremae Curiae Admiralitatis* (1679), using the improved 1791 edition. HALL, *id.* at iii–iv. Hall wrote an essay on the history of admiralty jurisdiction in part 1 and presented the form of a libel, followed by examples and precedents, in part 3.

[214] DOMENICO ALBERTO AZUNI, THE MARITIME LAW OF EUROPE (William Johnson trans., 1806), orig. Sistema Universale dei Principi del Diritto Maritimo dell' Europa, 1795); Johnson used a 1797

THE FORMATIVE ERA: 1791–1865   185

There were more British than U.S. translations, but the British exports to the libraries of American lawyers demonstrated interest and practical need. Often, an American reprint followed.[215] For example, perhaps unaware of Martin's 1802 translation, William Evans translated Pothier's *Traité des Obligations* in England in 1806, which was reprinted in Philadelphia in 1826.[216] Luther Cushing edited William Strahan's British translation of Jean Domat's four-volume *Les Lois Civiles dans Leur Ordre Naturel* and *Le Droit Public* (1689, 1697) to improve the translation and eliminate some of the translator's notes related to English law.[217] Cushing also translated Pothier's *Traité du Contrat de Vente* (1762).[218]

Hoeflich analyzed the citation of foreign legal translations in American judicial decisions prior to 1860. The leading subject matter for these references was commercial and maritime law. Pothier was the author with the most mentions at 265. Besides his volumes on obligations and sales contracts, they also included Pothier's treatise on maritime contracts.[219] Second in citation at 144 was Balthazard-Marie Emérigon, including Hall's translation on maritime loans and an English translation on insurance law.[220] Third was the writing of Domat at 105, and fourth, Roccus at 43.[221]

French version for the translation; FRANCESCO ROCCI, A MANUAL OF MARITIME LAW (Joseph Ingersoll trans., 1809, from the original Latin of Roccus, 1655); *see* Hoeflich, *Translation, supra* note 157, at 761; Stein, *supra* note 89, at 412–13.

[215] Hoeflich, *Translation, supra* note 157, at 760–62, 764–65, 770; *e.g.*, 1–2 THE CODE NAPOLEON (Bryant Barrett trans., London 1811); THE CODE NAPOLEON (anonymous trans., London, 1824); CODE NAPOLEON (George Spence trans., London, 1827), reprinted in New York in 1841; THE COMMERCIAL CODE OF FRANCE (John Rodman trans., New York, 1814).
[216] Stein, *supra* note 89, at 412–13.
[217] Hoeflich, *Translation, supra* note 157, at 767; *see* JEAN DOMAT, 1–2 THE CIVIL LAW IN ITS NATURAL ORDER (William Strahan trans., 2d. ed. 1737, Luther S. Cushing ed., 1850); *see supra* note 49 and accompanying text (Domat).
[218] R.J. POTHIER, TREATISE ON THE CONTRACT OF SALE (L.S. Cushing trans., 1839), derived from OEUVRES DE POTHIER, CONTENANT LES TRAITES DU DROIT FRANÇAIS (Andre Dupin ed., 9th ed. 1827) (vol. 2 included Pothier's 1762 *Du Contrat de Vente*); *see* CHARLES PURTON COOPER, CATALOGUE OF BOOKS ON FOREIGN LAW 160–62 (F.W.H. ed., 1849); *supra* note 208 and accompanying text (Pothier).
[219] Hoeflich, *Translation, supra* note 157, at 761, 772–73; Stein, *supra* note 89, at 422; *see* ROBERT JOSEPH POTHIER, A TREATISE ON MARITIME CONTRACTS OF LETTING TO HIRE (Caleb Cushing trans., 1821) (from *Traité du Contrat de Louage*, 1771).
[220] Hoeflich, *Translation, supra* note 157, at 761, 772–73; *see* Stein, *supra* note 89, at 414; BALTHAZARD MARIE EMÉRIGON, A TREATISE ON INSURANCES (Samuel Meredith trans., London, 1850) (from 1–2 *Traité des Assurances et des Contrats à la Grosse*, 1783); *supra* note 146 and accompanying text (Hall).
[221] Hoeflich, *Translation, supra* note 157, at 761, 773; *see* text accompanying note 214 (Roccus).

3. Law Libraries

In the first half of the nineteenth century, a few individual lawyers—such as Adams, Kent, Livermore, and Story—collected personal libraries of law materials with 1,000 or more books and pamphlets. These included volumes on foreign law, history, and political theory.[222] Other lawyers who needed access to books for their law practice formed bar association libraries, as in Europe, or pooled their resources for membership libraries. The most notable was the Boston Social Law Library, founded in 1803. Many state and county governments also created law libraries servicing lawyers and public officials. A few of these had foreign law materials.[223]

Prior to the Civil War, Harvard University had the largest library in the United States. Furthermore, the Law School had the leading law library not counting some law books in the university's collection.[224] Since Harvard had received many books on Roman and civil law from Livermore's 1833 bequest and Story's gifts, Harvard also had the principal comparative law library in the country.[225] Both Adams and Jefferson took an interest in the establishment of the Library of Congress. In 1800, Congress appropriated funds to purchase books for the use of members. The British pillaged that library in 1814 when they invaded the Capitol. Jefferson offered his personal library of 6,500 volumes, which Congress purchased. The universality of Jefferson's collection set the standard for building a comprehensive national library including foreign publications. Among social libraries of this era, the Library of Congress had the largest proportion of law books.[226]

In 1832, Congress created the Law Library of Congress as a separate administrative unit to service both members of Congress and justices of the Supreme

---

[222] David S. Clark, *Nation Building and Law Collections: The Remarkable Development of Comparative Law Libraries in the United States*, 109 LAW LIBR. J. 499, 527 (2017) [hereinafter Clark, *Nation Building*]; *see supra* note 80 (Livermore).

[223] Clark, *Nation Building*, *supra* note 222, at 528–29. Benjamin Franklin organized the first quasi-public social library in 1731, chartered as the Library Company of Philadelphia. It served as the de facto library for members of the Continental Congress prior to 1791. New York City had a social library from 1754 with 3,500 volumes in 1776. *Id.* at 512. Philadelphia also created a subscription law library in 1803, the Law Library Company of the City of Philadelphia, which had 391 volumes by 1805. Regina L. Smith, *America's First Law Library*, Philadelphia Law 112, 114 (Winter 2002).

[224] Clark, *Nation Building*, *supra* note 222, at 513–15, 527 (2017). The Law Library had 600 books in 1817. *Id.* at 527.

[225] Michael H. Hoeflich, *Annals of Legal Bibliography: J.G. Marvin*, 96 LAW LIBR. J. 333, 335, 337–38, 340–41 (2004); *see Critical Notices*, 26 AM. JURIST & L. MAG. 237, 254–61 (1841) (criticism of the law librarian's exaggeration of the relative size and breadth of Harvard Law School's library collection).

[226] Clark, *Nation Building*, *supra* note 222, at 516–17, 544; *see* THOMAS JEFFERSON'S LIBRARY: A CATALOG WITH THE ENTRIES IN HIS OWN ORDER (James Gilreath & Douglas L. Wilson eds., 1989). In 1858, the Library of Congress had 63,000 volumes, the seventh largest in the United States. Clark, *Nation Building*, *supra*, at 515.

Court. At that time, the new library had 2,011 volumes, one-third of which had belonged to Jefferson. In 1834, Congress passed a resolution authorizing its library committee to use 25 copies of each government printed or financed volume to exchange for other publications. Congress regularized this exchange with the French government in 1837, expanded to 50 copies plus library duplicates in 1840, and broadened to include other governments and foreign libraries. In 1860, the Law Library had 16,000 books, many published in Europe and Mexico, plus additional international law and law-related political science books in the general Library of Congress collection.[227]

F. Other Legal Comparatists

The primary American locus for comparative law activity during the first half of the nineteenth century, except for Louisiana, was in the North, from Boston to Baltimore. The two dominant figures—Kent and Story—illustrated this with Harvard Law School serving as the institutional center. Table 4.1[228] sets out comparative statistics for the U.S. population, the number of lawyers, law schools,[229] and select city sizes in the North and South in 1820 and 1850.

1. Boston: Luther Cushing

Luther Cushing had an active interest in Roman and civil law from a young age. He graduated from Harvard Law School in 1826 and soon contributed to comparative law with his articles and translations about both French and German law, typically published in the *American Jurist*. Like Story, Cushing served on the editorial board of Mittermaier's *Kritische Zeitschrift*.[230] After Story died in 1845, several persons undertook teaching responsibilities during a period of transition

---

[227] Clark, *Nation Building, supra* note 222, at 544–46. About half of Jefferson's law books came from continental Europe. *Id.* at 545. In 1857, Congress transferred administration of the document distribution and exchange system to the State and Interior Departments. *Id.* at 546.

[228] HISTORICAL STATISTICS (part 1), *supra* note 13, at 8; U.S. Census Bureau, *Population of the 100 Largest Cities and Other Urban Places in the United States: 1790 to 1990*, https://www.census.gov/library/working-papers/1998/demo/POP-twps0027.html (Campbell Gibson, working paper no. POP-WP027, June 1998); REED, *supra* note 75, at 442, 444, 446; *see* note 79 and accompanying text (lawyers in 1820).

[229] The three law schools in 1820 were in Massachusetts, Virginia, and Kentucky. By 1850 there were 15 law schools with a total of 400 students, but of the cities in Table 4.1, only Boston and New Orleans had a law school. REED, *supra* note 75, at 442, 446.

[230] HOEFLICH, ROMAN AND CIVIL LAW, *supra* note 7, at 85; *see supra* notes 170–98 and accompanying text (Cushing and the *American Jurist*).

Table 4.1 U.S. Population, Lawyers, Law Schools, and Select City Size, 1820 and 1850

	1820	1850
Total U.S. Population	9,618,000	23,261,000
Lawyers	6,000	23,939
Law Schools	3	15
City Size		
Baltimore	62,738	169,054
Boston	43,298	136,881
New Orleans	27,176	116,375
Charleston	24,780	42,985

at Harvard Law School. Since there was substantial student interest in Roman, civil, and international law, the school hired Cushing as a lecturer in civil and parliamentary law for the term beginning in 1848. He continued to teach until 1851.[231]

One of the courses Cushing taught was on Roman law. From those lectures, he developed enough material to publish in 1854 *An Introduction to the Study of the Roman Law*. Intended for students or lawyers unfamiliar with Roman law literature, Cushing did make some use of Mackeldey's treatise, citing the German version.[232] Nevertheless, the volume is peculiarly American, differing from the German Pandectist literature or English summaries of Roman substantive law. Rather, *Introduction* dealt with the philosophy and sources of Roman law, emphasizing the practical utility of its study. Cushing argued that many American legal rules and institutions derived from Roman law, although he rejected the notion that it was *ratio scripta*. He also pointed out that several American jurisdictions such as Louisiana, Florida, Texas, and California had civilian systems.[233]

---

[231] 2 WARREN, *supra* note 89, at 95–98, 111, 126, 128–129, 132, 204, 344, 346–47, 353.

[232] LUTHER S. CUSHING, AN INTRODUCTION TO THE STUDY OF THE ROMAN LAW v–vii, 113, 143–45 (1854) [hereinafter CUSHING, ROMAN LAW]; *see supra* note 92 and accompanying text (Mackeldey). Cushing stated that the American translation of Mackeldey was the best available for students. CUSHING, ROMAN LAW, *supra*, at 144 n.1.

[233] HOEFLICH, ROMAN AND CIVIL LAW, *supra* note 7, at 86–87, 90–91. The one extended treatment Cushing provided for substantive law was for bailment. HOEFLICH, *supra*, at 88–89; *see* CUSHING, ROMAN LAW, *supra* note 232, at 183–200.

2. New Orleans: Samuel Livermore and Gustavus Schmidt

Samuel Livermore (1786–1833) was a transitional figure, since he spent half his career as a lawyer in Boston and Baltimore and the other half in New Orleans, where he moved in 1819. While in Boston he wrote a book on agency law that in addition to English case law utilized British and civilian treatises on mercantile law, such as those by Gerard de Malynes, Wyndham Beawes, and Pothier.[234] After moving to Baltimore in 1815, Livermore expanded his agency treatise to two volumes, including a more thorough comparative treatment of Roman, Dutch, French, and Italian jurists on mercantile law.[235]

While practicing law in New Orleans, the Louisiana Supreme Court provoked Livermore into writing a volume on conflicts law. The court had refusal to accept his argument relying on Italian and French statutists to resolve a choice of law issue. In *Dissertations on the Questions which Arise from the Contrariety of the Positive Laws of Different States and Nations* (1828), Livermore utilized a comparative methodology to thoroughly investigate his two dissertations.[236] He reviewed the doctrine of many European jurists, beginning with Charles Dumoulin in the sixteenth century through Louis Boullenois in the eighteenth century, before presenting his own approach.[237]

Livermore's conflicts treatise, based on the commentator statutist theory, did not have a significant impact in the United States. Rather, it was Story's commentary on conflict of laws, utilizing Huber's Dutch comity approach, which elevated territorialism and prevailed to influence common law conflicts doctrine

---

[234] Rodolfo de Nova, *The First American Book on Conflict of Laws*, 8 AM. J. LEG. HIST. 136 n.1 (1964); *see* SAMUEL LIVERMORE, A TREATISE ON THE LAW RELATIVE TO PRINCIPALS, AGENTS, FACTORS, AUCTIONEERS, AND BROKERS (1811).

[235] Gino Gorla, *Samuel Livermore (1786–1833): An American Forerunner to the Modern "Civil Law-Common Law Dialogue," in* COMPARATIVE AND PRIVATE INTERNATIONAL LAW: ESSAYS IN HONOR OF JOHN HENRY MERRYMAN ON HIS SEVENTIETH BIRTHDAY 121, 123-26, 128-32, 134-35 (David S. Clark ed., 1990); *see* SAMUEL LIVERMORE, 1-2 A TREATISE ON THE LAW OF PRINCIPAL AND AGENT; AND OF SALES BY AUCTION (1818). "I have drawn freely from the works of the ancient Roman lawyers collected in the *Corpus Juris Civilis*, and from the modern French, Italian, and Dutch commentators." *Id.* at vi; *see id.* at viii-xi.

[236] De Nova, *supra* note 234, at 137, 143-45; Gorla, *supra*, note 235, at 123, 132-34; *see* SAMUEL LIVERMORE, DISSERTATIONS ON THE QUESTIONS WHICH ARISE FROM THE CONTRARIETY OF THE POSITIVE LAWS OF DIFFERENT STATES AND NATIONS (1828) [hereinafter LIVERMORE, DISSERTATIONS]. Bartolus was the most important of the early Italian statutists. One could divide local laws (statutes) between real and personal rules, with French jurists later adding a third category, mixed. Real and mixed laws applied territorially, while personal laws could operate extraterritorially to control those who owed allegiance to a polity. PETER HAY, PATRICK J. BORCHERS, & SYMEON C. SYMEONIDES, CONFLICT OF LAWS 10-14 (5th ed. 2010).

[237] LIVERMORE, DISSERTATIONS, *supra* note 236, at 5-12, 16; *see Livermore's Dissertations*, 1 AM. JURIST & L. MAG. 132-40 (1829) (book review). Livermore dismissed Ulricus Huberus and early American court opinions as superficial. LIVERMORE, DISSERTATIONS, *supra*, at 12-13.

in the nineteenth and early twentieth century.[238] However, Livermore and Story respected each other's comparative law efforts as illustrated in their writing. Significantly, Livermore devised his huge 400-volume collection of European law books, printed from the invention of the press until 1800, to Harvard University. Story relied on this collection in writing his *Commentaries*.[239]

Gustavus Schmidt (1795–1877) arrived in New Orleans in 1829. With a scholarly interest in the law and multilingual in French, German, and Spanish, he established the *Louisiana Law Journal* in 1841 and three years later the Louisiana Law School. In 1847, the University of Louisiana absorbed Schmidt's private school into its new law department.[240] In 1851, relying on his extensive comparative law library, Schmidt wrote *The Civil Law of Spain and Mexico*. In that volume, he cited 55 different legal sources and established himself as an American authority on Spanish and colonial Mexican law. The book had two parts. First, there was a 100-page summary of Spanish legal history from the Roman occupation of the Iberian Peninsula, the Visigothic and Muslim periods, through the colonial era ending with Mexican independence in the nineteenth century. Second, Schmidt set out in 300 pages a proposed civil code (1,439 articles) based on Spanish texts using the organization of the French civil code and an 1832 Spanish draft code. The book ended with 50 pages of appendices of Mexican statutes and Spanish court decisions. The periodic citation of *The Civil Law* in federal and state judicial opinions reflected its usefulness to lawyers.[241]

3. Charleston and Columbia: Francis Lieber, Hugh Legaré, and James Walker

In general, southern jurists tended to take a broader view of law and its role in society than the perspective prevalent in northern states. Perhaps not a coincidence, the South led the nation in fostering legal education as a comprehensive and cosmopolitan discipline. When the College of William and Mary reorganized its curriculum in 1779, it selected Wythe as the first full-time professor of law

---

[238] Davies, *supra* note 210, at 49–50; De Nova, *supra* note 234, at 137–38, 153–56; HAY ET AL., *supra* note 236, at 14–15, 18–24; *see supra* notes 63, 210, and accompanying text (Huber). Story did cite *Dissertations* about 60 times. De Nova, *supra*, at 138.

[239] HOEFLICH, ROMAN AND CIVIL LAW, *supra* note 7, at 29–30, 42, 56; Gorla, *supra* note 235, at 126–28. Livermore had graduated from Harvard College in 1804 and later read law. HOEFLICH, *supra*, 163 n.37.

[240] STEVENS, *supra* note 80, at 5; A.N. Yiannopoulos, *Louisiana Civil Law: A Lost Cause*, 54 TUL. L. REV. 830, 838–39 (1980); *see supra* text accompanying note 90 (University of Louisiana) and notes 199–201 (Schmidt).

[241] Parise, *Schmidt, supra* note 200, at 185–90. Parise counted 65 federal and state court references to the book. *Id.* at 191; *see* GUSTAVUS SCHMIDT, THE CIVIL LAW OF SPAIN AND MEXICO, ARRANGED ON THE PRINCIPLES OF THE MODERN CODES, WITH NOTES AND REFERENCES (1851).

THE FORMATIVE ERA: 1791–1865   191

(and police) in the United States. During his ten years as professor and earlier affiliation teaching Greek and Latin classics at the college, his students and apprentices included Thomas Jefferson, John Marshall, James Monroe, and St. George Tucker. Tucker followed Wythe as the college's law professor in 1790. The University of Virginia and the University of Georgia followed the Wythe model, while other southern law schools were successful in New Orleans (Tulane) and Lexington, Kentucky (Transylvania).[242]

European literature, including on law, was an important part of the southern legal tradition. Many lawyers from the South traveled to Europe for the university experience and, especially in Louisiana, South Carolina, and Virginia, were familiar with Roman and civil law. Two South Carolina library collections of Roman, natural, and civil law contained most of the same works available to Virginia jurists during the revolutionary period. This broad exposure complemented the practical interest of some Louisiana and Texas lawyers with European civil law solutions toward local private law issues. Hoeflich identified three South Carolina jurists, two born there, who had the background and interest to qualify as legal comparatists. They were Story's friend Francis Lieber (1798–1872), Hugh Legaré (1797–1843), and James Walker (1813–1854).[243]

Story was the leading American comparatist in the juristic exchange with European scholars. Besides Lieber, Story was friends with two Boston Romanists, John Pickering (1777–1846) and Charles Follen (1796–1840).[244] Follen and Lieber were German émigrés. Follen was a Roman law lecturer (*Privatdocent*) at the University of Jena, but political events forced him to leave and he eventually arrived to the United States. In 1825, he began teaching German at Harvard and later also lectured on Roman and civil law.[245] Lieber, born in Berlin and educated in Germany, immigrated to Boston in 1827 where he met Story. Lieber kept Story current on German scholarship and introduced him by mail to Mittermaier, who made Story an editor and contributor to *Kritische Zeitschrift*.[246]

In Boston, Lieber determined that his new country needed an encyclopedia to summarize existing knowledge, so he began work on a project based on the

---

[242] HOEFLICH, ROMAN AND CIVIL LAW, *supra* note 7, at 50–51, REED, *supra* note 75, at 116–19, 155–59; *see* Wythepedia, *Wythe the Teacher*, http://lawlibrary.wm.edu/wythepedia (search Teacher); *supra* text accompanying notes 71, 77 (Wythe and Tucker).

[243] HOEFLICH, ROMAN AND CIVIL LAW, *supra* note 7, at 51–52, 56–57; *see id.*, *Roman and Civil Law in the Anglo-American World before 1850: Lieber, Legaré and Walker, Roman Lawyers in the Old South*, in RECEPTION (Reimann ed.), *supra* note 121, at 19–43.

[244] HOEFLICH, ROMAN AND CIVIL LAW, *supra* note 7, at 30–31; see *supra* note 166 (Pickering).

[245] HOEFLICH, ROMAN AND CIVIL LAW, *supra* note 7, at 30–31, 106–07; *see* CHARLES FOLLEN, SUMMARY OF A COURSE OF LECTURES ON THE CIVIL LAW (1830). In 1830, Harvard appointed Follen professor of German literature, a position he resigned in 1835. Harvard Square Library, *Follen, Charles Theodore Christian (1796–1840)*, https://www.harvardsquarelibrary.org (search Follen).

[246] HOEFLICH, ROMAN AND CIVIL LAW, *supra* note 7, at 31, 52–54; PARKER, *supra* note 57, at 159–61.

German *Conversations-Lexikon*, which Friedrich Brockhaus had completed in 1811.[247] Lieber finished editing the first volume of *Encyclopædia Americana* in 1829, concluding with volume 13 in 1833. The work was enormously successful, selling 100,000 copies.[248] Partly translations from the German *Conversations-Lexikon*, for which Lieber hired a dozen translators in Boston, much of the work also included original articles.[249] For instance, Story contributed 18 entries ranging from subjects such as the common law, natural law, criminal law, contracts, evidence, and the jury. Particularly relevant for codification was Story's article on law, legislation, and codes.[250]

Lieber broadly viewed law and government and favored public law over the usual law school concern with private law. In 1833, he translated an empirical and comparative study of the American penitentiary system by Gustave de Beaumont and Alexis de Tocqueville. In Lieber's 30-page preface and introduction, he praised early American prison reform as illustrative of the "progress of mankind from physical force to the substitution of moral power in the art and science of government; . . . it must be regarded as a new victory of mind over matter."[251] He dedicated his translation to Edward Livingston and the German comparatist Mittermaier, both widely known for proposing reform of criminal procedure, punishment, and prisons. Beyond making this important French volume more widely accessible to American jurists and criminologists, Lieber reprinted in the appendix his encyclopedia entry on the Eastern State Penitentiary of Pennsylvania, which had opened in 1829. Using a hub-and spokes design to facilitate surveillance of prisoners confined in separate cells, it resembled Bentham's Panopticon, never implemented in England.[252]

---

[247] M. Russell Thayer, *The Life, Character, and Writings of Francis Lieber, in* 1 THE MISCELLANEOUS WRITINGS OF FRANCIS LIEBER: REMINISCENCES, ADDRESSES, AND ESSAYS 13, 22–23 (Daniel C. Gilman ed., 1880) [hereinafter MISCELLANEOUS WRITINGS] (Gilman was the founding president of Johns Hopkins University). Brockhaus purchased an incomplete Leipzig encyclopedia begun in 1796 and finished it with two supplemental volumes in 1811. *Encyclopaedia, in* 9 THE ENCYCLOPAEDIA BRITANNICA 369, 381 (11th ed. 1910). The 21st edition of *Brockhaus Enzyklopädie* began publication in 2005 and is now entirely online. Brockhaus, *Über uns*, https://brockhaus.de/info/information/ueber-uns.

[248] NEWMYER, *supra* note 68, at 275; Cohen, *supra* note 141, at xviii–xix. 1–13 ENCYCLOPÆDIA AMERICANA: A POPULAR DICTIONARY OF ARTS, SCIENCES, LITERATURE, HISTORY, POLITICS AND BIOGRAPHY . . . ON THE BASIS OF THE SEVENTH EDITION OF THE GERMAN CONVERSATIONS-LEXIKON (Francis Lieber ed., 1829–1833); *see* [John Neal], *Encyclopaedia Americana*, 34 N. AM. REV. 262–68 (1832) (book review). The set cost $30 to $32 from 1832 to 1833. *Id.* at 266; *see* Cohen, *supra*, at xviii–xix.

[249] Cohen, *supra* note 141, at xvii–xix.

[250] *Id.* at xx–xxiii; *see* UNSIGNED ESSAYS, *supra* note 141, at 3–326.

[251] G. DE BEAUMONT & A. DE TOCQUEVILLE, ON THE PENITENTIARY SYSTEM IN THE UNITED STATES, AND ITS APPLICATION IN FRANCE viii (Francis Lieber trans., 1833) (translation of *Du Système Pénitentaire aux États-Unis, et de Son Application en France*, 1833).

[252] *Penitentiary System of Pennsylvania, in id.* at 287–302 (article plus comments); *see infra* pt. G (penal reform). In addition to statistical information on prisons in Connecticut, Maryland,

The *Encyclopædia Americana* brought Lieber prominence that led to a scholarly career. In 1833, he moved to Philadelphia where the encyclopedia publisher was located. After some unsuccessful efforts to find a teaching position, in 1835, Lieber accepted an appointment as professor of history and political economy at South Carolina College (in Columbia), successor to Cooper.[253] Lieber's first major scholarly publication was on political and legal philosophy, historical and comparative in scope, directed toward college and law students. Both Kent and Story praised the two-volume *Manual of Political Ethics*.[254] Lieber defined natural law as rational law, derived from the elements of human nature, and politics as the science of discovering the institutions and rules required to protect those rights inherent in natural law. The state could not impose satisfactory rules, which must organically emerge from society over time. With this orientation, one can see influence from the German historical school of jurisprudence.[255]

Lieber's principal Romanist book was *Legal and Political Hermeneutics* (1839), which synthesized numerous sources and perspectives, including ethics, on the proper interpretive principles to use in reading legal materials, including constitutions, treaties, statutes, precedents, and documents. Lieber often relied on Roman and civilian sources, which had a longer history and more reliance on textual legal enactments and commentaries than did the common law tradition. He also compared these sources to American judicial review of legislation for constitutionality. Lieber contended that rules of legal interpretation were universal—suitable in any legal system relying on text—akin to natural law principles.[256]

Massachusetts, New York, and Pennsylvania, Beaumont and Tocqueville had a section comparing data from France and the U.S. *Id.* at 244–74.

[253] Paul D. Carrington, *The Theme of Early American Law Teaching: The Political Ethics of Francis Lieber*, 42 J. LEG. EDUC. 339, 361, 366 (1992); Cohen, *supra* note 141, at xix–xx; John Martin Vincent, *Lieber, Francis, in* 11 DICTIONARY OF AMERICAN BIOGRAPHY 236–37 (Dumas Malone ed., 1933); *see supra* notes 63, 98, 208, and accompanying text (Cooper). The title of Lieber's professorship added political philosophy in 1849. REED, *supra* note 75, at 155 n.2.
[254] PARKER, *supra* note 57, at 159–61; *see* FRANCIS LIEBER, 1–2 MANUAL OF POLITICAL ETHICS, DESIGNED CHIEFLY FOR THE USE OF COLLEGES AND STUDENTS AT LAW (1838-1839) [hereinafter LIEBER, MANUAL].
[255] LIEBER, MANUAL, *supra* note 254, at 58–63; *see* C.B. Robson, *Francis Lieber's Theories of Society, Government, and Liberty*, 4 J. POL. 227–31, 236, 239–42 (1942).
[256] HOEFLICH, ROMAN AND CIVIL LAW, *supra* note 7, at 57–59; *see* FRANCIS LIEBER, LEGAL AND POLITICAL HERMENEUTICS, OR PRINCIPLES OF INTERPRETATION AND CONSTRUCTION IN LAW AND POLITICS (enlarged ed., 1839). Lieber published a preliminary version of this work in *American Jurist*, which Cushing praised and summarized. Lieber, *On Legal Hermeneutics, or on Political Interpretation and Construction, and Also on Precedents*, 18 AM. JURIST & L. MAG. 37–101, 281–94 (1837–1838); *see* L.S. C[ushing], *Lieber's Hermeneutics*, 21 *id.* at 388 (1839). William Hammond published a third edition with his comments in 1880, which 16 *Cardozo L. Rev.* 1883–2105 (1995) republished together with ten articles commenting on *Hermeneutics* plus a Lieber bibliography. *Id.* at 2107–2351. An admirable summary of *Hermeneutics*'s coverage and significance is Michael Herz, *Rediscovering Francis Lieber: An Afterword and Introduction*, *id.* at 2107, 2120–34.

In 1844, the king of Prussia invited Lieber to visit and offered him an appointment at the University of Berlin. Lieber spent a year in Berlin, advised the king on penology, but elected to return to South Carolina.[257] He resumed teaching and, in 1853, published his lectures in a volume entitled *On Civil Liberty and Self Government*. A historical and comparative treatment of constitutional law and government, professors assigned the text in colleges nationwide for much of the nineteenth century.[258] Influenced by German historiography, Lieber took a broad look at European and American history up to the republican experiments in France and the United States, which represented the spirit of the age. As society progressed, law should necessarily follow. In the common law, to illustrate, precedent was not absolute.[259]

> Everything that is a progressive continuum requires the precedent. A precedent in law is an ascertained principle applied to a new class of cases, which in the variety of practical life has offered itself. It rests on law and reason, which is law itself. It is not absolute.... A precedent can be overruled. But again, it must be done by the law itself, [which becomes] precedent in turn.[260]

Perhaps the failure of European revolutions in 1848 stimulated Lieber to expand his treatment of liberty from the *Manual of Political Ethics*. In *Civil Liberty*, he had chapters on Anglican, "Gallican," and American liberty.[261] In aiming for a systematic and objective study of social phenomena, he utilized political and social empirical data that he had collected from questionnaires and a variety of printed sources.[262] Good government should be measured by the degree to which it permits the gradual clarification of ideas and objects that persons in society desire. The state, that is, jural society, should defer to self-government, permitting rules and institutions to grow and develop themselves.[263]

---

[257] Carrington, *supra* note 253, at 363.

[258] FRANCIS LIEBER, ON CIVIL LIBERTY AND SELF GOVERNMENT (1853) [HEREINAFTER LIEBER, CIVIL LIBERTY]. Lieber enlarged the second edition in 1859. Theodore Woolsey edited the third edition, reprinted repeatedly from 1874 to 1891. Woolsey also edited the second edition of Lieber's *Manual of Political Ethics* in 1875, reprinted in 1890. Woolsey studied for three years at universities in France, Germany, and Italy before he became professor of Greek at Yale College in 1831 and then college president from 1846 to 1871 (while also teaching constitutional law). He taught constitutional and international law at the law school until his death in 1889. Carrington, *supra* note 253, at 364; Louise L. Stevenson, Woolsey, Theodore Dwight, 23 AMERICAN NATIONAL BIOGRAPHY, *supra* note 148, at 863–64.

[259] PARKER, *supra* note 57, at 159–61.

[260] LIEBER, CIVIL LIBERTY, *supra* note 258, at 171–72.

[261] *Id.* at 68–72, 277–86, 298–319; *see* PARKER, *supra* note 57, at 161–63.

[262] Robson, *supra* note 255, at 232–33, 242–44, 246. In 1836, Lieber proposed to the U.S. Senate that Congress prepare and publish a comprehensive statistical survey dealing with geography, economics, politics, and social conditions of the sort France, Great Britain, and Prussia had begun. *Id.* at 233–36.

[263] Lieber had earlier developed many of these views in MANUAL OF POLITICAL ETHICS, *supra* note 254. Robson, *supra* note 255, at 235–240, 242.

In 1856, Lieber left South Carolina and in 1857, accepted the chair of history and political science at Columbia College. A year later, Lieber and Theodore Dwight reinstituted the law school with the latter teaching doctrinal private law. Lieber continued his broader comparative approach to public law, including when he taught exclusively at the law school from 1865 until his death in 1872.[264]

Legaré was born in Charleston and graduated from South Carolina College in 1814. Early in his training, he immersed himself in classical studies and at college continued to improve his Greek, Latin, and knowledge of Romance languages. Rather than engage in a standard law office apprenticeship, Legaré convinced his former teacher, a Charleston attorney, to serve as patron so that he could read law at home. After three years, he was ready to travel to Europe to learn civil law, which he did at Edinburgh University during 1818 and 1819. By the time he returned to South Carolina, he considered Roman and civil law an attractive alternative to the common law system.[265]

Legaré took up politics in the early 1820s and voters elected him to the South Carolina House of Representatives. In 1826, the House named him chair of a committee to explore codification of state law. His report took a position somewhat like that of Story's view for Massachusetts in 1837, which favored partial or moderate compilation of statutes. Legaré concluded that consolidating the state's public law statutes in a logical arrangement with simpler and more concise phrasing was worthwhile, while comprehensive codification including private law was not. Furthermore, he wanted judicial interpretation presented with a statute's language due to the statute's inevitable ambiguity.[266]

In 1827, Legaré co-founded the *Southern Review*, a popular literary magazine that contained significant material about law. A frequent contributor, he elaborated there on his views of codification in 1831.[267] Unlike Lieber, Legaré was not a prolific writer, but his erudition in Roman and civil law impressed Story. Legaré wrote a review of the first two volumes of Kent's *Commentaries* in the journal. With some criticism of Kent's knowledge of Roman private law, Legaré favored Kent's endorsement of the value of Roman law to aid development of American common law as a legal

---

[264] REED, *supra* note 75, at 158–59, 303 n.1; *see* Francis Lieber, *History and Political Science, Necessary Studies in Free Countries: An Inaugural Address (1858), in* 1 LEIBER'S WRITINGS, *supra* note 247, at 329–68. Columbia revived Lieber's chair in history and political science in 1876, expanding the scope to include international law, and hired the German-trained John Burgess to teach at the law school and, after 1880, at the new school of political science. This was part of an attempt to emulate German university ideals of science. REED, *supra*, at 334–36.

[265] HOEFLICH, ROMAN AND CIVIL LAW, *supra* note 7, at 54–55; MACIAS, *supra* note 65, at 141–42; Stein, *supra* note 89, at 427.

[266] MACIAS, *supra* note 65, at 146–49; *see supra* note 65 and accompanying text (Story).

[267] *Id.* at 146; *see* Hugh S. Legaré, *Codification*, 7 SOUTHERN REV. 395 (no. 14, 1831) [hereinafter Legaré, *Codification*], *reprinted in* 2 THE WRITINGS OF HUGH SWINTON LEGARÉ 482–501 (Mary Legaré ed., 1846) [hereinafter LEGARÉ'S WRITINGS]; *supra* text accompanying note 204 (*Southern Review*).

science.[268] Legaré's expertise as a Romanist especially revealed itself in his article on the origin, history, and influence of Roman legislation. He surveyed contemporary civilian scholarship on Roman law derived from five recent publications, including Story's commentary on conflicts. He saw Roman law, particularly its notion of *jus gentium*, as a model for advanced legal systems. The article on codification rejected wholesale incorporation of civilian codes, recognizing the virtues of common law flexibility and reliance on judges.[269]

In 1832, Legaré took the position of U.S. chargé d'affaires to Brussels, which allowed him to travel widely for four years, buying law books, including in Germany where he met Savigny. Legaré later claimed allegiance to Savigny's historical school of jurisprudence. By this time, he was conversant with both German and French as well as the classical languages.[270] In addition, while Legaré was U.S. attorney general from 1841 to 1843, he argued several cases before the Supreme Court involving disputed land grants in territories formerly under French or Spanish rule. Justice Story found his adaption of Roman law principles into American property law impressive. As with other American jurists during this period who had a knowledge or Roman and civil law, Legaré wanted to improve American private law through selective incorporation of civilian ideas.[271]

James Walker, as with Legaré, was born in Charleston, graduated from South Carolina College in 1830, and was capable of reading Latin. The college and the Charleston bar association both had adequate libraries in civil and natural law. In 1850, Walker published a book on Roman substantive law and its relationship to the origins of English common law property rules. As a work in comparative legal history, it attempted to refute an English author's conclusion that Roman law had no influence on the common law.[272] Walker's second book, *The Theory of the Common Law* (1852), argued that Roman and civil law could serve as the basis for a scientific analysis of the common law. To do this, he organized

---

[268] MACIAS, *supra* note 65, at 149–50; Stein, *supra* note 89, at 427–31; *see* Legaré, *Kent's Commentaries*, 2 SOUTHERN REV. 77 (no. 3, 1828), *reprinted in* 2 LEGARÉ'S WRITINGS, *supra* note 267, at 102–41; Joseph Story, *Sketch of the Character of Hugh S. Legaré*, in STORY'S WRITINGS, *supra* note 65, at 820–24.

[269] HOEFLICH, ROMAN AND CIVIL LAW, *supra* note 7, at 52–53, 60–63, 67–68; MACIAS, *supra* note 65, at 148–49; Stein, *supra* note 89, at 428; *see* Legaré, *The Origin, History and Influence of Roman Legislation*, 5 N.Y. REV. 284 (no. 10, 1839), reprinted in 1 Legaré's Writings, *supra* note 267, at 502–58; *id.*, Legaré, *Codification*, *supra* note 267.

[270] HOEFLICH, ROMAN AND CIVIL LAW, *supra* note 7, at 54–56, 76; *see* LINDA RHEA, HUGH SWINTON LEGARÉ: A CHARLESTON INTELLECTUAL 51–59, 131–55 (1934). In the 1830s, Legaré had the second largest Roman and civil law book collection in the United States, behind only Harvard. M.H. Hoeflich, *Roman Law in American Legal Culture*, 66 TUL. L. REV. 1723, 1741–42 (1992).

[271] HOEFLICH, ROMAN AND CIVIL LAW, *supra* note 7, at 67–68; RHEA, *supra* note 270, at 91–101, 111–30, 200–15.

[272] HOEFLICH, ROMAN AND CIVIL LAW, *supra* note 7, at 55–57, 63–64, 69; *see* JAMES M. WALKER, AN INQUIRY INTO THE USE AND AUTHORITY OF ROMAN JURISPRUDENCE IN THE LAW CONCERNING REAL ESTATE (1850).

common law real and marital property rules, together with U.S. political rights, according to Roman law concepts. The method aimed to Romanize English property law into a coherent system. Walker contended this would be easier in America than in England.[273] "The law of the Colonies already conformed to a much greater extent than that of England to the *jus gentium*."[274]

G. Penal Reform: Law and Punishment

Initial efforts toward law reform in eighteenth-century America concentrated largely on constitutional law and penal procedure. Driven by resentment against English oppression and a preference toward Enlightenment political philosophy and natural law theory, these efforts resulted in republican forms of government, characterized by separation of powers with checks and balances, as well as explicit legal limits on all branches of government in the definition, investigation, prosecution, and punishment of crime. The U.S. Constitution of 1789, supplemented by the Fourth to Eighth Amendments of 1791, illustrated these reform initiatives. Where this public law reform did not already exist at the state level, the federal pattern provided an example. However, most activity in this field occurred with states.[275] We earlier saw that the specific protections for penal procedure contained in the U.S. Bill of Rights, and a few years before in the Virginia Declaration of Rights, derived from the English Declaration of Rights and from Enlightenment political philosophers such as Montesquieu and Beccaria.[276]

Some European jurists and social philosophers in the eighteenth century criticized the brutality of prevailing penal punishments based on humanitarian concerns, the desirability of social reform, and the usefulness of a rational approach to crime reduction. Montesquieu, for instance, believed that human liberty was a legal system's foremost goal, best achieved under conditions of peace, popular sovereignty, and with due regard for human nature. Among

---

[273] Hoeflich, Roman and Civil Law, supra note 7, at 64–65, 68–69; MILLER, supra note 51, at 161, 168; see JAMES M. WALKER, THE THEORY OF THE COMMON LAW (1852) [hereinafter WALKER, COMMON LAW].

[274] WALKER, COMMON LAW, supra note 273, at 123 (italics in original); see id. at 1–5 (method of legal science).

[275] LAWRENCE M. FRIEDMAN, CRIME AND PUNISHMENT IN AMERICAN HISTORY 63–64, 72–73 (1993) [hereinafter FRIEDMAN, CRIME]; see James Q. Whitman, The Comparative Study of Criminal Punishment, 1 ANN. REV. L. & SOC. SCI. 17–18 (2005). To illustrate, the 1776 Pennsylvania Constitution, § 38, placed a duty on the legislature to reform penal law. FRIEDMAN, HISTORY, supra note 11, at 207.

[276] JOHN D. BESSLER, CRUEL AND UNUSUAL: THE AMERICAN DEATH PENALTY AND THE FOUNDERS' EIGHTH AMENDMENT 8–9, 31–43, 47–58 (2012); see supra ch. 3, note 86 and accompanying text (Beccaria); ch. 3, text accompanying notes 236–240, 244–63, 267–74 (Madison and Mason).

governmental powers, the legislature should determine penal sanctions, not judges.[277]

In 1764, Beccaria published *Dei Delitti e delle Pene*, the first book (anonymous and a mere 104 pages) dedicated to penal reform that endorsed rational Enlightenment values. He agreed with Montesquieu that it was a legislative role to specify sanctions, generally milder than the prevailing situation, without regard to station to avoid arbitrary judicial variation. Beccaria criticized contemporary criminal law and procedure, arguing against secret accusation, torture, and indiscriminate capital punishment. He emphasized the concepts of equal punishment for all perpetrators, regardless of social rank, and proportionality between the gravity of crime and the severity of punishment.[278]

Jeremy Bentham borrowed from Beccaria[279] and added his system of utilitarian analysis to reduce the social problem of crime. Security of one's person, property, and honor preceded liberty. Punishment should be an empirical issue between the actor's desire versus the infliction of adequate pain to provide a deterrent. Penal severity, thus, was not an abstract label, but rather the use of excessive pain unnecessary to deter action. Sanctions, for instance, might include monetary compensation. In general, a legal system should foster a society's happiness.[280] Bentham's emphasis on the security of person and property, in fact, described the American (or at least Massachusetts) shift of criminal law by 1810

---

[277] JAMES Q. WHITMAN, HARSH JUSTICE: CRIMINAL PUNISHMENT AND THE WIDENING DIVIDE BETWEEN AMERICA AND EUROPE 50, 144, 184 (2003) [hereinafter WHITMAN, HARSH JUSTICE]; *see* MONTESQUIEU, THE SPIRIT OF THE LAWS 82–86, 91–93 (Anne M. Cohler et al. ed. & trans., 1989, original French ed., 1748) (bk. 6, ch. 9–12, 16–18).

[278] WHITMAN, HARSH JUSTICE, *supra* note 277, at 50–51, 114, 163, 169, 183–84; JEROME HALL, GENERAL PRINCIPLES OF CRIMINAL LAW 602–03 (2d ed., 1960) (1st ed., 1947) [hereinafter HALL, CRIMINAL LAW]; Harry Elmer Barnes, *The Historical Origin of the Prison System in America*, 12 J. CRIM. L. & CRIMINOLOGY 35, 40–42, 47 (1921). The first English language edition of Beccaria's essay appeared in London in 1767, *An Essay of Crimes and Punishments* (179 pages, translated from Italian, plus a 79-page commentary attributed to Voltaire, translated from French). American printers in Philadelphia (1776) and Charleston (1777) made this available in the United States. BESSLER, *supra* note 276, at 31.

[279] Bentham and Beccaria both set out the intellectual foundation for the later economic analysis of criminal law in the twentieth century. Beccaria based his proportionality principle on an early cost-benefit analysis to achieve deterrence. Bentham tied proportionality, deterrence, and certainty systematically to utility. MARK TUNICK, PUNISHMENT: THEORY AND PRACTICE 69–78 (1992); Talia Fisher, *Economic Analysis of Criminal Law*, in THE OXFORD HANDBOOK OF CRIMINAL LAW 38, 43–45 (Markus D. Dubber & Tatjana Hörnle, eds., 2014). For differences between Beccaria and Montesquieu, *see* James Q. Whitman, *The Transition to Modernity*, in THE OXFORD HANDBOOK OF CRIMINAL LAW, *supra*, 84, 104–07.

[280] HALL, CRIMINAL LAW, *supra* note 278, at 312–13; WHITMAN, HARSH JUSTICE, *supra* note 277, at 23, 197; Margery Fry, *Bentham and English Penal Reform*, in JEREMY BENTHAM AND THE LAW: A SYMPOSIUM 20, 25–33, 42–45 (George W. Keeton & Georg Schwarzenberger eds., 1948); *see* BENTHAM, AN INTRODUCTION TO THE PRINCIPLES OF MORALS AND LEGISLATION (1789) (first printed in 1780); *id.*, TRAITÉS DE LÉGISLATION CIVILE ET PÉNALE (Étienne Dumont trans, 1802) (published in English as *Theory of Legislation* (1840)); *id.*, THÉORIE DES PEINES ET DES RÉCOMPENSES (Étienne Dumont trans, 1811) (published in English as *The Rational of Punishment* (1830)).

away from enforcement of morals and religion toward protection of physical safety and property enjoyment.[281]

In addition, Blackstone was a source of ideas for penal reform.[282] Volume 4 of his *Commentaries* covered public wrongs and penal procedure. As he described in the first chapter, "[I] proceed to the consideration of public wrongs, or crimes and misdemeanors; with the means of their prevention and punishment."[283] Jerome Hall demonstrated that as one under the influence of natural law writers, Blackstone's contribution toward definitions and classification was essentially derivative of European jurists. The criminal law "should be founded upon principles that are permanent, uniform, and universal; and always conformable to the . . . feelings of humanity, and the [indelible] rights of mankind." Blackstone then referred to Montesquieu and Beccaria.[284]

By the 1790s, some state legislatures undertook to reform substantive penal law to make it less harsh with fewer capital crimes and less physical and bloody in the punishment levied. There were even advocates to abolish the death penalty.[285] In general, the reform movement accepted the proper aim of criminal law to deter crime and rehabilitate criminals. Central to these efforts was the principle of proportionality, which the Eighth Amendment expressed by prohibiting cruel and unusual punishment.[286]

Another Enlightenment-inspired reform was to "codify" criminal law, which usually meant the conversion of common law crimes into a statutory form. Influenced by the general distrust of government and the view that checks and balances could control executive and judicial abuse, a legislative check would resolve the retroactivity issue of judges creating new crimes. When a judge determined that a novel common law crime existed during a criminal proceeding,

---

[281] William E. Nelson, *Emerging Notions of Modern Criminal Law in the Revolutionary Era: An Historical Perspective*, 42 N.Y.U. L. REV. 450–66, 481–82 (1967).

[282] WHITMAN, HARSH JUSTICE, *supra* note 277, at 41–42, 152–53; *see supra* pt. D.2 (Blackstone's Commentaries).

[283] Blackstone, 4 *Commentaries* (Bell ed.), *supra* note 100, at 1. Chapters 19 to 32 described penal procedure.

[284] *Id.* at 3, 7, 16–18; HALL, CRIMINAL LAW, *supra* note 278, at 9–10; WHITMAN, HARSH JUSTICE, *supra* note 277, at 49, 53, 158, 163. To the influence of Montesquieu and Beccaria on Blackstone, Hall added Domat, Grotius, and Pufendorf. Hall found that Blackstone's systematization left criminal law in England better organized. HALL, *supra*. Gerhard Mueller agreed with Hall's assessment on both the civil law inspiration and its consequent systematization. GERHARD O.W. MUELLER, CRIME, LAW AND THE SCHOLARS: A HISTORY OF SCHOLARSHIP IN AMERICAN CRIMINAL LAW 19–21 (1969). On Hall's significance, *see id.* at 210–14.

[285] FRIEDMAN, HISTORY, *supra* note 11, at 208–10; FRIEDMAN, CRIME, *supra* note 275, at 73–75; *see* David Brion Davis, *The Movement to Abolish Capital Punishment in America, 1787–1861*, 63 AM. HIST. REV. 23–46 (1957). The first state to abolish capital punishment was Michigan, in 1847. FRIEDMAN, HISTORY, *supra*, at 209. In 1852 and 1853, Rhode Island and Wisconsin followed Michigan's example. Davis, *supra*, at 43–44.

[286] FRIEDMAN, HISTORY, *supra* note 11, at 207–08, 210; Kathryn Preyer, *Crime, the Criminal Law and Reform in Post-Revolutionary Virginia*, 1 LAW & HIST. REV. 53–85 (1983) (proportionality in Virginia).

it was ex post facto in the sense that the accused had no notice that his action was culpable. There was widespread agreement that legislatures should reduce to statute the criminal substantive law and some procedure to support the principle of *nulla poena sine lege*. The Supreme Court declared as much for federal law in 1812 and most states followed that lead either explicitly or de facto. Philosophical argument for this reform came from Enlightenment jurists such as Montesquieu, Beccaria, and Bentham.[287]

A third change, related to making substantive criminal law less harsh, was the replacement of shaming, whipping, branding, and infliction of other physical pain with penitentiaries—modern prisons. Shaming became less effective as urbanization progressed, while reduction in the use of death as a punishment raised the question of what to do with convicted felons. At the same time, progressive opinion began to blame economic and social conditions as agents causing corruption, theft, and other criminal acts. Reformed prisons—houses for penitence—could rehabilitate bad actors for re-entry into society. The central concept behind this transformation required individual isolation of prisoners.[288]

In 1795, the first reformed prison opened in Philadelphia with 16 individual cells as an addition to the Walnut Street jail. Good hygiene, hard work to instill discipline, silence, and solitary confinement with reflection and remorse were the goals. Western Penitentiary in Pittsburgh opened in 1826 modeled after Bentham's round Panopticon. Guards could constantly watch prisoners since the design placed cells in spokes around a hub. In 1829, Eastern State Penitentiary, also in Philadelphia, instituted the Walnut Street concept. Advocates referred to it as the separate system, since inmates worked, ate, and slept in their individual cells.[289]

In 1821, an alternative prison model based on instilling useful values through collective work done in silence opened in Auburn, New York. The state replicated this idea in 1826 at the larger Sing Sing prison it built along the Hudson

---

[287] FRIEDMAN, HISTORY, *supra* note 11, at 215–17, 435–36; FRIEDMAN, CRIME, *supra* note 275, at 62; *see* HALL, CRIMINAL LAW, *supra* note 278, at 27–69 (*nulla poena*). In *United States v. Hudson and Goodwin*, 11 (7 Cranch) 32, 34 (1812), the U.S. Supreme Court rejected the notion of federal common law crimes and determined that Congress must first make an act criminal, establish a penalty, and provide a federal court with jurisdiction. FRIEDMAN, HISTORY, *supra*, at 215–16; FRIEDMAN, CRIME, *supra*, at 64, 71. The number of crimes in state penal codes expanded from the 1820s to the Civil War. FRIEDMAN, HISTORY, *supra*, at 442–43.

[288] FRIEDMAN, HISTORY, *supra* note 11, at 219–20, 453; FRIEDMAN, CRIME, *supra* note 275, at 77–78; *see* BEAUMONT & TOCQUEVILLE, *supra* note 251, at 1–130; ADAM J. HIRSCH, THE RISE OF THE PENITENTIARY: PRISONS AND PUNISHMENT IN EARLY AMERICA (1992) (origin of penitentiaries was in sixteenth-century English ideology of hard labor).

[289] FRIEDMAN, HISTORY, *supra* note 11, at 219–20; FRIEDMAN, CRIME, *supra* note 275, at 78–79; Barnes, *supra* note 278, at 44–45; *see* Francis Lieber, *Penitentiary System of Pennsylvania*, *in* BEAUMONT & TOCQUEVILLE, *supra* note 251, at 287–301 (modified version of the author's *Encyclopædia Americana* article). *See also* ASHLEY T. RUBIN, THE DEVIANT PRISON: PHILADELPHIA'S EASTERN STATE PENITENTIARY AND THE ORIGINS OF AMERICA'S PENAL SYSTEM, 1829-1913 (2021).

River. In subsequent decades, the Auburn or congregate model came to prevail as reformers determined that it was better than the Pennsylvania system in rehabilitating prisoners, not to mention providing inexpensive or free labor. Friedman found that by the 1840s inadequate resources and administrative failure led to relapse toward physical punishment in maintaining discipline. Local jails at the city and county level were generally worse. The average citizen was not particularly concerned, however, since deviants and criminals were off the streets.[290]

Edward Livingston's writing supported all three of these penal reform efforts.[291] For instance, he was a central figure in the anti-gallows movement in the 1820s and 1830s.[292] Livingston's penal code, which was actually a system of penal law, prepared for the Louisiana legislature, demonstrated a sophisticated comparative law knowledge of penal law developments in Europe and illustrated the attempt to bring crime and punishment into a systematic statutory form. He began the project in 1820 and completed it in 1824. It reflected a utilitarian approach that adopted moderate punishments (thus excluding the death penalty) and emphasized crime prevention and the legality principle. Although the Louisiana legislature rejected the code in 1825, Livingston's influence in Maine, New York, and Pennsylvania was significant. Kent took a direct interest in the work. Overseas, Livingston's effort directly inspired the penal codes of Brazil, Guatemala, Russia, and India and he was one of America's best-known jurists in Europe.[293]

---

[290] FRIEDMAN, HISTORY, *supra* note 11, at 220–22, 454; FRIEDMAN, CRIME, *supra* note 275, at 79–82, 155–58, 166–68. Europeans and Latin Americans tended to favor the Pennsylvania system since reformers believed that solitary confinement promoted reformation. John H. Cary, *France Looks to Pennsylvania: The Eastern Penitentiary as a Symbol of Reform*, 82 PA. MAG. HIST. & BIO. 186–203 (1958); *see* Barnes, *supra* note 278, at 40–50.

[291] See *supra* text accompanying notes 32–39 (Livingston and codification).

[292] Philip English Mackey, *Edward Livingston and the Origins of the Movement to Abolish Capital Punishment in America*, 16 LA. HIST. 145, 148–49, 152–56, 158–60, 162–64 (1975). For the socio-political context in the United States, England, France, and Germany during the period in which Livingston worked on his codes, *see* Mitchell Franklin, *Concerning the Historic Importance of Edward Livingston*, 11 TUL. L. REV. 163–79 (1937) [hereinafter Franklin, *Livingston's Importance*].

[293] Davis, *supra* note 285, at 31–34, 36; Franklin, *Livingston's Importance*, *supra* note 292, at 212; James Kent, *Letter from Chancellor Kent to Edward Livingston—Penal Code*, 16 AM. JURIST & L MAG. 361–71 (1837); MUELLER, *supra* note 284, at 22, 25–26, 29; Agustín Parise, *Codification of the Law in Louisiana: Early Nineteenth-Century Oscillation between Continental European and Common Law Systems*, 27 TUL. EUR. & CIV. L. F. 133, 144–45 (2012) [hereinafter Parise, *Codification*]. The *United States Law Journal* published Livingston's 1822 penal code plan to the Louisiana legislature and certain portions of the draft legislation. 2 U.S. L.J. 1–159 (Supp. 1826); *see Penal Jurisprudence*, 1 *id.* 259–80 (1822); 17 N. AM. REV. 242–68 (1823). The French Academy of Moral and Political Science published a two-volume translation of Livingston's penal law writing into French in 1872. *See* EDWARD LIVINGSTON, 1–2 EXPOSÉ D'UN SYSTÈME DE LÉGISLATION CRIMINELLE POUR L'ÉTAT DE LA LOUISIANE ET POUR LES ÉTATS-UNIS D'AMÉRIQUE (1872).

Livingston's code proposed to replace capital punishment with a penitentiary system. Overall, the code was a blueprint to reduce crime, promote certainty of punishment, and provide opportunities for reformation. Measures included religious training for all children; reformatories for problem juveniles; state industrial houses for the unemployed and idle; separation of those *accused* of crime, from those *convicted* of misdemeanors and those *convicted* of felonies; as well as post-release assistance to prisoners.[294]

Livingston presented his system as four codes and a book of definitions. The codes, which Jerome Hall characterized as original and enlightened, covered crimes and punishments, crime prevention and penal procedure, evidence rules, and prison discipline and prisoner reform. The dominant methodological approach followed Bentham and was comparative, eclectic, and empirical, referring to European jurists and French, Roman, Russian, Tuscan, and English law.[295] Livingston was consequently suspicious of judicial supremacy and judge-made law and supportive of the legislature's role in penal law.[296] The reports and complete text of the codes were only widely available after 1833 once published in Philadelphia.[297] However, in 1828, Livingston, as one of Louisiana's members in the U.S. House of Representatives, presented the chamber with a similar package of penal law reforms intended for federal authority.[298] National interest in foreign penal law again appeared in 1854 with the U.S. Senate's publication of a historical and comparative survey of European penal codes.[299] Livingston's influence on the reform of penal law and prisons continued after the Civil War, illustrated by the U.S. national prison association's publication of his complete works on penal law.[300]

---

[294] Ginger Roberts, *Edward Livingston and American Penology*, 37 LA. L. REV. 1037, 1043–52 (1977); Mackey, *supra* note 292, at 154–56.

[295] Jerome Hall, *Edward Livingston and His Louisiana Penal Code*, 22 A.B.A. J. 191–96 (1936); Sanford H. Kadish, *Codifiers of the Criminal Law: Wechsler's Predecessors*, 78 COLUM. L. REV. 1098–1104 (1978); Elon H. Moore, *The Livingston Code*, 19 J. AM. INST. CRIM. L. & CRIMINOLOGY 344, 347–48 (1928) (Bentham and other European sources of inspiration); Parise, *Codification*, *supra* note 293, at 143–44 (2012); *see* EDWARD LIVINGSTON, A SYSTEM OF PENAL LAW, FOR THE STATE OF LOUISIANA 5–46 (1833) [hereinafter LIVINGSTON, LOUISIANA]. Moore referred to Livingston as the father of sociological jurisprudence and American penal reform. Moore, *supra*, at 344, 357.

[296] Franklin, *Livingston's Importance*, *supra* note 292, at 180–94.

[297] LIVINGSTON, LOUISIANA, *supra* note 295; *see Book Review*, 43 N. AM. REV. 297–336 (1836); L.S. C[ushing], *Livingston's Penal Codes*, 22 AM. JURIST & L. MAG. 395–401 (1840).

[298] EDWARD LIVINGSTON, A SYSTEM OF PENAL LAW FOR THE UNITED STATES OF AMERICA (1828). Livingston formulated a concise list of the modern principles he followed in the codes in *id.* at 1–4.

[299] H.S. SANFORD, THE DIFFERENT SYSTEMS OF PENAL CODES IN EUROPE (1854). In 1854, Sanford was U.S. chargé d'affaires to Paris; in 1855, Heidelberg University granted him the J.U.D. degree in civil and canon law. *See* JOSEPH A. FRY, HENRY S. SANFORD: DIPLOMACY AND BUSINESS IN 19TH CENTURY AMERICA 35–65 (1982).

[300] EDWARD LIVINGSTON, 1–2 COMPLETE WORKS OF EDWARD LIVINGSTON ON CRIMINAL JURISPRUDENCE; CONSISTING OF SYSTEMS OF PENAL LAW FOR THE STATE OF LOUISIANA AND FOR THE UNITED STATES OF AMERICA (1873).

From the 1830s to the 1850s, American jurists maintained their interest in comparative penology. Luther Cushing in his role as editor of the *American Jurist* opened the journal to important writing by the comparatist Carl Mittermaier.[301] Mittermaier served as a channel to transmit information about the work of Paul Johann Anselm von Feuerbach (1775–1833) to Americans. A German law professor, he was notable for his formulation and defense of the legality principle and for his draft of the Bavarian Penal Code, promulgated in 1813. Feuerbach's *Lehrbuch des gemeinen in Deutschland geltenden peinlichen Rechts* appeared in 1801 at the height of European revolutionary liberalism. His theory restricted statutory penal enactment to acts that violate liberty, protected by strict judicial interpretation rejecting analogy. As with Beccaria and Bentham, he believed that legislatures should delineate crime, which would decrease as humans reacted psychologically to the threat of punishment.[302] Markus Dubber identified Feuerbach as the father of comparative criminal law.[303]

Francis Lieber was a leading American comparatist proposing prison reform and reducing the harshness of punishment. He wrote a 30-page essay on comparative penal systems in Europe and America, which prefaced his translation of Beaumont and Tocqueville's comparative law book on prisons in the United States and France.[304] In addition, Lieber added notes where he believed clarification required, where he disagreed with the authors, plus relevant appendices.[305]

The materials presented by Lieber, Beaumont, and Tocqueville were extraordinary for their time in the use of statistical and other empirical data to analyze prisons. The American prison examples were in Connecticut, Maryland, Massachusetts, New York, and Pennsylvania. For instance, one learns that in 1830, among the U.S. states studied, about ten times as many persons sentenced to prison for one year or more had convictions for crimes against property compared to crimes against persons. The same ratio in France was seven to one.

---

[301] See *supra* notes 184–190 and accompanying text (Cushing and Mittermaier).

[302] HALL, CRIMINAL LAW, *supra* note 278, at 34–35; Guyora Binder, *Homicide*, in THE OXFORD HANDBOOK OF CRIMINAL LAW, *supra* note 279, at 702, 708–09; Lindsay Farmer, *Codification*, in *id.*, at 379, 385–86, 390–91, 395; Daniel Ohana, *Regulatory Offenses and Administrative Sanctions: Between Criminal and Administrative Law*, in *id.* at 1064, 1066–68; Werner S. Landecker, *Criminology in Germany*, 31 J. CRIM. L. & CRIMINOLOGY 551, 554 (1941).

[303] Markus D. Dubber, *Comparative Criminal Law*, in THE OXFORD HANDBOOK OF COMPARATIVE LAW 1276, 1280–84 (Mathias Reimann & Reinhard Zimmermann eds., 2d ed. 2019). The roots of the legality principle were Roman, which had prohibited retroactive laws. Heikki Pihlajamäki, *Medieval Canon Law: The Origins of Modern Criminal Law*, in THE OXFORD HANDBOOK OF CRIMINAL LAW, *supra* note 279, at 201, 207–08.

[304] BEAUMONT & TOCQUEVILLE, *supra* note 251, at v–xxxv; *see supra* notes 251–252 and accompanying text (Lieber's translation). Lieber's preface was a comparative treatment of European punishment and prisons in contrast to the American experiments with penitentiaries. Along the way, he offered his ideas about male and female criminality. BEAUMONT & TOCQUEVILLE, *supra*, at viii–xxix, xxxii–xxxv.

[305] BEAUMONT & TOCQUEVILLE, *supra* note 251, at vi, 151–66. Lieber also updated certain statistical information. *Id.* at vii.

Turning to the proportion of women sentenced to prison in the two nations, the ratio was 22 percent in France, but only 9 percent among the American states.[306]

Lieber refined his views on what he termed the science of penology in a 90-page essay published in 1838. Beginning with a historical and comparative discussion of theories of punishment, drawing variously from Feuerbach, Beccaria, and others, he then compared the separate and congregate prison systems operating in Pennsylvania and New York.[307]

H. Codification: Edward Livingston to David Dudley Field

Codification, in the form and substance of early nineteenth-century French codes, was a defining characteristic of civil law legal systems from that era. More generally in Europe and among proponents in the United States, codification of law was associated with progress toward modernity. Typical features for codification of an area of the law were completeness, simplicity, certainty, system, and authority. Beccaria, Bentham, and Feuerbach supported such a science of legislation.[308]

The most important advocate of Bentham's ideas in American was Edward Livingston, evident as early as his congressional service from 1795 to 1801. His reading of Dumont's 1802 French translation of Bentham's *Theory of Legislation* convinced him that only comprehensive codification could remedy the anomalies of law. That influenced Livingston in drafting the Louisiana Practice Act (1805), a copy of which he sent to Bentham, as well as his proposed penal code for Louisiana.[309] But Livingston was more generally interested in comprehensive codification and Louisiana provided the jurisdiction to demonstrate its value. In

---

[306] BEAUMONT & TOCQUEVILLE, *supra* note 251, at 266–67, 269; *see* FRIEDMAN, CRIME, *supra* note 275, at 108–11, 233–34. The authors (and translator) explained why a comparison of the incidence of incarceration in the two countries was difficult due to the source materials available. Nevertheless, it appeared that in 1830 the number of persons per 100,000 population sentenced to prison in the United States was no greater, and probably somewhat less, than in France. BEAUMONT & TOCQUEVILLE, *supra*, at 272–74.

[307] FRANCIS LIEBER, POPULAR ESSAY ON SUBJECTS OF PENAL LAW, AND ON UNINTERRUPTED SOLITARY CONFINEMENT AT LABOR, AS CONTRADISTINGUISHED TO SOLITARY CONFINEMENT AT NIGHT AND JOINT LABOR BY DAY (1838). Lieber's collected writings included portions of the penal law pamphlet, with the author's additions. *Id.*, *Contributions to Political Science*, *in* 2 LIEBER'S WRITINGS, *supra* note 247, at 470–94.

[308] Farmer, *supra* note 302, at 384–93; Gunther A. Weiss, *The Enchantment of Codification in the Common-Law World*, 25 YALE J. INT'L L. 435, 454–70 (2000); *see* Andrew P. Morriss, *Codification and Right Answers*, 74 CHI.-KENT L. REV. 355–56, 369–76 (1999).

[309] Dean Alfange, Jr., *Jeremy Bentham and the Codification of Law*, 55 CORNELL L. REV. 58, 63, 65–68, 70–74 (1969); C.W. Everett, *Bentham in the United States of America*, *in* JEREMY BENTHAM AND THE LAW, *supra* note 280, at 185, 193–94; Roberts, *supra* note 294, at 1055; *see supra* notes 38–39, 293–300 and accompanying text (Practice Act and penal code) and note 280 (Dumont translation).

1822, the Louisiana legislature authorized revision into code form of the 1808 civil law Digest,[310] the 1805 Practice Act, and commercial law. It gave the task to Livingston, Moreau-Lislet (1808),[311] who had worked on the earlier Digest, and Pierre Derbigny.[312] In 1825, the trio presented the legislature with a commercial code, based largely on the French commercial code, but it took no action.[313]

The Civil Code of 1825, alternatively, with 3,522 articles was a major success that served to define Louisiana as a civil law jurisdiction for generations. Professors Batiza and Palmer from Tulane Law School have traced the contents of both the Louisiana 1808 Digest and its successor 1825 Civil Code. About 85 percent of the Digest's content came from French sources.[314] The Civil Code, in turn, took 75 percent of the Digest's 2,160 articles, maintaining its French ancestry. In addition, for approximately 1,000 of the new code articles, the dominant origin was French treatise writers.[315] Palmer also illustrated how the Louisiana code in general following the structure, form, and style of the *Code Napoléon*. Deviation occurred largely to educate Louisiana lawyers and judges in civil law methodology, since some of them came from common law jurisdictions. These code articles included definitions, illustrations, and instructions to judges regarding sources of law and code interpretation. The code (in article 3521) intended to improve certainty of law by explicitly repealing prior Roman, Spanish, and French laws. The code's French legacy remained essentially intact for the next 150 years.[316] Livingston's principal concern, as one of the code's three redactors, was to diminish judicial lawmaking discretion, which would reduce corruption and improve legal certainty.[317]

---

[310] See *supra* notes 40–50 and accompanying text (1808 Digest of the Civil Laws).

[311] See *supra* notes 41–42 and accompanying text (Moreau-Lislet).

[312] McMahon, *supra* note 38, at 46–47; Tucker, *Civil Code*, *supra* note 47, at 286–87. In 1823, the legislature approved the jurists' plan for three codes: civil law, commerce, and civil procedure. It approved the French language civil law *projet* in 1824 for translation into English and promulgation in 1825. Tucker, *supra*, at 287–88, 290–91.

[313] Parise, *Codification*, *supra* note 293, at 160–62. Scholars disagreed about whether Livingston was the primary drafter of the commercial code. Compare McMahon, *supra* note 38, at 46 n.29 (yes) with RICHARD HOLCOMBE KILBOURNE, LOUISIANA COMMERCIAL LAW: THE ANTEBELLUM PERIOD 34 (1980) (probably yes); Parise, *supra*, at 159–60 (probably no).

[314] PALMER, *supra* note 48, at 52, 54; see Tucker, *Civil Code*, *supra* note 47, at 289–90; *supra* notes 46–48 and accompanying text (French thesis). The *Code Napoléon* and the code's 1800 *Projet* provided respectively 709 and 807 provisions in the Digest for a total of 70 percent. Another 15 percent came from Domat and Pothier's treatises, the Custom of Paris, and the Ordonnance of 1667. PALMER, *supra*, at 54–55.

[315] PALMER, *supra* note 48, at 55; *see* Rodolfo Batiza, *The Actual Sources of the Louisiana Projet of 1823: A General Analytical Survey*, 47 TUL. L REV. 1–115 (1972).

[316] PALMER, *supra* note 48, at 56–69, 83–84, 99. In 1828, the legislature repealed "all civil laws" in force before 1825. *Id.* at 58. Kilbourne argued that the pre-codal sources of Spanish laws and jurisprudence persisted in Louisiana after the 1825 Civil Code. KILBOURNE, *supra* note 46, at xiv, 96–164; see FERNANDEZ, *supra* note 35, at 79.

[317] FERNANDEZ, *supra* note 35, at 78–80. Livingston did not appreciate the Louisiana Supreme Court's tenacity in maintaining Anglo-American patterns of judicial decision-making. *Id.* at 80–88.

The Louisiana legislature in 1825 also enacted a Code of Practice in French with an English translation, which blended French, Spanish, Roman, and common law forms. The redactors noted in the 1823 *projet* the sources they used. The consensus is that Livingston led the drafting.[318] The Code of Practice in style, structure, and some content followed the 1806 French Code of Civil Procedure. The French code consolidated state control over court jurisdiction and simplified Louis XIV's *Ordonnance Civile* of 1667. Government officials had observed the Ordinance in Louisiana during the French period from 1699 to 1769.[319] The French commission drafting the civil procedure code primarily relied for its structure and much of its content on the Ordinance, so that this codal framework easily carried over to the Louisiana Code of Practice.[320]

Nevertheless, the Code of Practice was truly a mixture of common law and civil law elements related to Louisiana's peculiar legal history. On the surface the form appeared French, since both codes had two parts. The heading for the French part I and the Louisiana part II were both "procédure devant les tribunaux." The French part then divided into books, titles, and articles. The Louisiana part divided into titles, sections, subsections, and articles. The other part of each code was "actions civiles" in Louisiana and "procédures diverses" in France. Beyond that, the similarity weakens.[321] In addition to important common law and civilian provisions from the 1805 Practice Act,[322] the primary Spanish authorities were the *Siete Partidas* (1265), the *Recopilación de las Indias* (1680), Juan de Hevia Bolaños's *Curia Philípica* (1767), and José Febrero's *Adicionado: Librería de*

---

[318] McMahon, Procedure I, supra note 38, at 36, 48–49, 61; McMahon, Procedure II, supra note 39, at 1; Parise, Codification, supra note 293, at 151–52; John H. Tucker, Jr., Source Books of Louisiana Law: The Code of Practice, 7 TUL. L. REV. 82, 85–86 (1932) [hereinafter Tucker, Code of Practice]. The Louisiana legislature authorized republication of the commission's projet for the Code of Practice. 1–2 LOUISIANA LEGAL ARCHIVES (1937) [hereinafter ARCHIVES]. The Code's official name was Traité sur les Règles des Actions Civiles et de la Procédure à suivre dans les Tribunaux, commonly referred to as the Code of Practice.

[319] Rodolfo Batiza, Origins of Modern Codification of the Civil Law: The French Experience and Its Implications for Louisiana Law, 56 TUL. L. REV. 477, 579–80 (1982). The French Procedure Code went into effect on 1 January 1807. The full name of the Code Louis was Ordonnance civile touchant la réformation de la justice (1667).

[320] McMahon, Procedure II, supra note 39, at 4; Tucker, Code of Practice, supra note 318, at 85–86; see, e.g., DANIEL JOUSSE, 1–2 NOUVEAU COMMENTAIRE SUR L'ORDONNANCE CIVIL (1767). The Ordinance and commentary organized rules into 35 titles with articles as subdivisions.

[321] See McMahon, Procedure I, supra note 38, at 47; McMahon, Procedure II, supra note 39, at 10–11; Tucker, Code of Practice, supra note 318, at 90.

[322] The three major common law institutions from the 1805 Practice Act were extraordinary writs (habeas corpus, mandamus, prohibition, certiorari, and quo warranto), the right of jury trial, and the requirement that available witnesses provide testimony in open court. McMahon, Procedure I, supra note 38, at 45–46, 49; McMahon, Procedure II, supra note 39, at 7; see supra notes 38–39 and accompanying text (1805 Practice Act).

Escribanos (1806–1808). The principal French sources were Domat and Pothier, the latter commenting on Louis XIV's 1667 Ordinance.[323]

The code's drafting commission inserted comments to many of the code's articles, giving reasons for inclusion as well as a source. Divided by legal system, the *projet* referred to Justinian's *Digest* eight times and the *Institutes* three times. For Spanish law, there were 63 references to procedure writers and statutory compilations, but one should add the majority of the 45 references to the 1805 Practice Act, which was largely based on Spanish law. For French law, there were 26 citations to the 1808 Louisiana Digest, largely derived from the French Civil Code, and 30 to French legal commentators. In addition, French civil procedure influenced the Louisiana articles regulating injunctions, succession practice, interrogatories, and executory procedure (creditor seizure of property).[324]

Another approach to assessing the civil law impact on the Code of Practice is to list the issues derived from civil law and those whose origin came from the common law. Civil law doctrine influenced articles on jurisdiction, civil actions in general and their types (including personal and real), pleadings (demand and answer), claim and party joinder, claim consolidation, *litis contestatio* (establishing issues in contention), provisional remedies (injunction, arrest, sequestration), interrogatories, judgments, and special procedures for summary, executory (for debt collection), and succession matters. Anglo-American law affected court organization and administration, judicial officers, civil jury trial, evidence, new trial, judgment execution, attachment, and extraordinary remedies. Both legal traditions shaped process and its service, depositions, and appellate procedure.[325] In the decades up to the Civil War, the Louisiana Supreme Court read common law solutions into some articles and used it to fill gaps in the code. The proliferation of common law publications in the state along with the decline in use of French and Spanish supported that trend.[326]

---

[323] David S. Clark, *The Civil Law Influence on David Dudley Field's Code of Civil Procedure*, in RECEPTION (Reimann ed.), *supra* note 121, at 63, 74 [hereinafter Clark, *Field Code*]; McMahon, *Procedure I*, *supra* note 38, at 48, 50, 61; McMahon, *Procedure II*, *supra* note 39, at 5; Tucker, *Code of Practice*, *supra* note 318, at 85–87; *see* ROBERT POTHIER, 1–2 TRAITÉ DE LA PROCÉDURE CIVILE (9th ed. 1776).

[324] Henry Plauché Dart, *The Place of the Civil Law in Louisiana*, 4 TUL. L. REV. 163, 171–72 (1930); McMahon, *Procedure I*, *supra* note 38, at 47–48; McMahon, *Procedure II*, *supra* note 39, at 11; *see* WILLIAM KERNAN DART, THE LOUISIANA JUDICIAL SYSTEM 36–37 (1917). Henry Dart found the source of interrogatories in the 1667 Ordinance, but the redactors cited the Practice Act, the Civil Code, Bolaños, Febrero, and Pothier. Henry Dart, *supra*, at 172; ARCHIVES, *supra* note 318, at 60–62 (arts. 347–356).

[325] McMahon, *Procedure I*, *supra* note 38, at 48–49, 52–53; McMahon, *Procedure II*, *supra* note 39, at 12. For instance, the Louisiana Supreme Court and successive constitutions affirmed the civilian appellate review of facts. McMahon, *Procedure I*, *supra*, at 49–50.

[326] McMahon, *Procedure I*, *supra* note 38, at 50, 61; McMahon, *Procedure II*, *supra* note 39, at 2, 13–14; *see* McMahon, *Procedure I*, *supra*, at 45–46; Parise, *Codification*, *supra* note 293, at 151; *supra* note 322 (common law influence).

In 1821, Story had identified the proliferation of American case reports as a problem requiring a solution. Already, American law needed clarification and systemization. Federalism, with each state formulating its own version of the common law, only made the situation worse.[327] Thomas Cooper shared Story's concern and saw codification as the answer to provide law with certainty and simplicity. In addition, democratic legitimacy required legislative law, reducing the role for unelected judges. In 1819, Cooper took a position as professor at South Carolina College, where he was president from 1820 to 1833.[328]

The governor of South Carolina in 1821 asked the legislature to carry out a general revision of state law, referring to the French Civil Code as an example. Lawyers, including Cooper, in the 1820s heatedly debated the question of codification, whether against, or in favor of only statutory law or the whole common law.[329] Thomas Grimké, a successful Charleston lawyer and state senator, supported complete codification of the common law. Application of the scientific method would reduce common law rules to general principles that one could order into a system. After his speech on the subject to the South Carolina bar association in 1827, the state senate appointed him chair of a committee for law reform and then published the committee's report. However, the legislature let the matter die in subsequent sessions.[330]

Prior to 1830, the principal sources of inspiration for jurists concerned with improving the clarity and certainty of American law were the French codes of the first decade of the nineteenth century, the Louisiana codes from the 1820s, and Bentham's philosophical support for codification.[331] In 1816, Bentham prevailed on John Quincy Adams, then ambassador to Great Britain, to send sets of Bentham's published works to state governors and a few prominent jurists, including Cooper. In addition to Livingston and Cooper, Macias argued that Bentham's influence affected the writing of Hoffman and Timothy Walker.[332] William Sampson, delivered in 1823 the influential *Anniversary Discourse* criticizing English common law and proposing American codification. He and other

---

[327] COOK, *supra* note 179, at 104–06; NEWMYER, *supra* note 68, at 272–74; *see supra* notes 66, 172 (Suffolk Bar address). Other concerns about the common law were that its technicalities served the interest of lawyers and not the public, it promoted inequality, and judge-made law was undemocratic. Konefsky, *supra* note 65, at 95–98.

[328] COOK, *supra* note 179, at 56–58, 86–88, 90, 92, 123; MACIAS, *supra* note 65, at 55–56; *see supra* notes 63, 70, 98, 253 and accompanying text (Cooper).

[329] COOK, *supra* note 179, at 123–30, 136.

[330] *Id.* at 78, 81, 90, 121–30; MACIAS, *supra* note 65, at 26, 30; MILLER, *supra* note 51, at 246–49; George M. Hezel, *The Influence of Bentham's Philosophy of Law on the Early Nineteenth Century Codification Movement in the United States*, 22 BUFF. L. REV. 253, 260–62 (1972); *see* THOMAS S. GRIMKÉ, AN ORATION ON THE PRACTICALITY ... OF A CODE 28–30 (1827).

[331] COOK, *supra* note 179, at 70–92, 97–104.

[332] MACIAS, *supra* note 65, at 45, 56–57; COOK, *supra* note 179, at 100–02; *see supra* pt. D.4 (Hoffman); notes 84–85 and accompanying text (Walker).

jurists were ardent Francophiles who considered Napoléon's codes as models for American reform.[333]

The 1820s and 1830s witnessed Jacksonian democracy and attacks on the judiciary as elitist. If judges were supposed to generate the principles necessary for scientific codification, but political power was shifting to state legislatures and their politicians, legislative codification could become too radical. Story presented his answer in "Law, Legislation, Codes," published in Lieber's *Encyclopædia Americana*.[334] He primarily addressed the argument to conservative lawyers who resisted any reform, making use of historical jurisprudence. If legal development was incremental, "no legislature can make a system half so just . . . or harmonious, both from want of time . . . and opportunity of knowledge, as judges, who are successively called to administer justice, and gather light from the wisdom of their predecessors."[335]

In 1836, the Massachusetts governor requested that the legislature codify the common law to make it more accessible to the citizenry. It authorized a commission and the governor appointed Story to lead it. Story supported moderate codification to save the common law from more radical experimentation.[336] "We ought not to permit ourselves to indulge in the theoretical extravagance of some well-meaning philosophical jurists [thinking of Bentham], who believe that all human concerns for the future can be provided for in a code." The legislature should limit codification to those parts of the common law, "which under the forming hand of the judiciary, shall from time to time acquire scientific accuracy."[337] Story understood that the common law served American republicanism since judges could restrain excessive democratic impulses. Conservatism and reform could coexist; codification if it was moderate was acceptable. Story drew the line between radical Benthamism and conservative codification. Nevertheless, the Massachusetts legislature decided not even to pursue Story's restrained role for codification.[338]

---

[333] BLOOMFIELD, AMERICAN LAWYERS, *supra* note 51, at 59, 69, 75–82; COOK, *supra* note 179, at 58–60, 106–10, 164.

[334] Joseph Story, *Law, Legislation, Codes, in* 7 ENCYCLOPÆDIA AMERICANA, *supra* note 246, at 576–92 [hereinafter Story, *Law, Legislation, Codes*]; *see* COOK, *supra* note 179, at 158–63; NEWMYER, *supra* note 68, at 277.

[335] Story, *Law, Legislation, Codes*, *supra* note 334, at 588; *see* NEWMYER, *supra* note 68, at 275–76; UNSIGNED ESSAYS, *supra* note 141, at 195–234.

[336] Konefsky, *supra* note 65, at 98–99; NEWMYER, *supra* note 68, at 273, 277–79; Morriss, *supra* note 308, at 360–61; Weiss, *supra* note 308, at 502–03; *see* Joseph Story et al., *Codification of the Common Law, in* STORY'S WRITINGS, *supra* note 65, at 698 (Luther Cushing was a co-author of the commission report); *supra* note 65 and accompanying text (Massachusetts commission).

[337] NEWMYER, *supra* note 68, at 274, quoting from Story's 1821 Suffolk Bar address. STORY'S WRITINGS, *supra* note 65, at 237–38. A century later, the American Law Institute wrote something similar in its founding document.

[338] COOK, *supra* note 179, at 171–81; NEWMYER, *supra* note 68, at 271–74, 279–81.

Story presented a division of labor between judges and legislators. The former would create (or discover) principles of law in their case-by-case method. Legislators or their commissions would subsequently clarify and refine them. After that, judges could apply the resulting codes or digests uniformly with objectivity according to rules of interpretation that Story set forth.[339] Macias found that the political divide in the 1820s and 1830s over codification and the modest legislative reforms achieved outside Louisiana did not end interest in the subject. Codification was part of a larger jurisprudential reform based on reasoned law within the framework of legal science.[340]

The most successful American code of the nineteenth century in terms of its widespread adoption was the 1849 New York Code of Civil Procedure. Already by the 1820s, some jurists in New York advocated codification as a legal reform to solve the problems of judicial inefficiency and case law proliferation. Most considered legislation as the only viable avenue toward simplicity of the law. Sampson in his 1823 *Anniversary Discourse* before the New York Historical Society further stoked the flames. By 1828, the legislature enacted a partial compilation of rules, with some simplification, as New York Revised Statutes. Nevertheless, this reform did not sufficiently reduce the delay and cost associated with litigation. Complaints continued into the 1830s and 1840s about the unduly complex appellate and first instance court system, incompetent judges, and antiquated procedural rules.[341]

By this time, Americans had learned more about the desirability of codification from the writing of German legal scientists. Louis (Johann Ludwig in Germany) Tellkampf provides a good example with his arrival in New York in 1838. He had earned a position as *Privatdozent* at the University of Göttingen law faculty after completing his habilitation book in 1835 about improving law in the German states by creating law reform commissions.[342] In 1837, the new English king of Hanover dismissed seven Göttingen professors for refusing to sign a loyalty oath; Tellkampf also refused, left the university, and moved to Prussia. There, the Prussian government approved a teaching and research position at one of its universities and a Prussian ministry provided him letters of introduction to facilitate research on prison discipline in America.[343]

---

[339] NEWMYER, *supra* note 68, at 276–77.
[340] MACIAS, *supra* note 65, at 54–55.
[341] COOK, *supra* note 179, at 58, 134–36, 140–53, 168–69, 185–87; Clark, *Field Code*, *supra* note 323, at 67, 69–72; *see supra* text accompanying note 333 (Sampson).
[342] James R. Maxeiner, *J.L. Tellkampf: German Legal Scientist in the U.S. (1839–47) in an Age of Reform*, 50 Y.B. GERMAN-AM. STUD. 1, 5 (2015) [hereinafter Maxeiner, *Tellkampf*]; id., *The First Humboldtian Research Trip into the Polis: J.L. Tellkampf in the United States, 1838–1847*, in RECHTSSTAATLICHES STRAFEN 771–73, 775, 777 (Jan C. Joerden und Kurt Schmoller eds., 2017) [hereinafter Maxeiner, *Research Trip*].
[343] Maxeiner, *Tellkampf*, *supra* note 342, at 6–7; Maxeiner, *Research Trip*, *supra* note 342, at 772, 775–76. As a comparatist, Tellkampf argued for importing elements of U.S. constitutional law during

Tellkampf was in contact with Mittermaier, Germany's leading penologist and comparatist, before his trip to New York. In 1838, after meeting Story in Cambridge, Tellkampf lectured in upstate New York on Roman law and political economy. The next year, Union College offered him a professorship where he taught law, history, and political economy for five years. During this period, Tellkampf met Lieber, researched prison discipline, and published a two-part article based on his habilitation in the *American Jurist*. He reported on his prison research in German journals and was a co-founder in 1844 of the Prison Association of New York. By 1847, Tellkampf returned to Prussia for a law professorship at the University of Breslau.[344]

Our primary interest here is Tellkampf's article in the *American Jurist* on the need for system to correctly codify legal rules. He based his approach on natural law as the embodiment of reason applied to the external affairs of humans. Referring to Hoffman's perception that since the mid-eighteenth-century Roman law had influenced the development of American common law, Tellkampf suggested Roman law in fact provided an excellent example of system in organizing legal rules.[345] Anticipating resistance to his recommended codification of American common law, Tellkampf provided a list of objections and their rebuttal. He then offered a specific plan to codify civil, penal, and procedural law in a scientific manner both in form and substance. Citing Montesquieu, Savigny, and Thibaut, this method allowed for climatic, historical, and cultural peculiarities. Philosophy and history could go hand in hand. A government-appointed commission of jurists should undertake the task of codification.[346]

In 1839, David Dudley Field (1805–1894) joined the fight for legal reform. He was familiar with Louisiana's simplified pleadings that required only a petition and answer and had read Livingston's work. This would prove useful for legal reform and especially codification in New York. Field had studied French and Spanish, spent 14 months traveling in Europe, and was familiar with European law.[347] His chance came in 1846, when public dissatisfaction led to

---

the German debates about a new constitution in 1848 and 1849. The resulting *Paulskirchenverfassung* became the model for German constitutional development for a century. Bernd J. Hartmann, *How American Ideas Traveled: Comparative Constitutional Law at Germany's National Assembly in 1848-1849*, 17 TUL. EUR. & CIV. L.F. 23, 40–42, 63–70 (2002).

[344] Maxeiner, *Tellkampf, supra* note 342, at 6–7, 9–14, 21–23, 29–30; Maxeiner, *Research Trip, supra* note 342, at 776–78, 788–93; *see* Maxeiner, *Tellkampf, supra*, at 12, 18–20 (Lieber); *supra* text accompanying notes 184–190, 301 (Mittermaier).

[345] Tellkampf, *supra* note 180, at 113–14, 120–25, 137–38. As examples of progress in the United States, Tellkampf referred to Louisiana's codes and the attempts to organize statutes since the 1820s in New York and Massachusetts. *Id.* at 143–44, 289; *see supra* note 65 and accompanying text (Story and Massachusetts).

[346] Tellkampf, *supra* note 180, at 283–304, 318–19; *see* Maxeiner, *Research Trip, supra* note 342, at 781–84.

[347] Clark, *Field Code, supra* note 323, at 73–74.

a constitutional convention. Field and others promoted judicial change as the means to streamline litigation. The new 1846 Constitution combined law and equity jurisdiction into one court structure; however, it did not reform procedure. Rather, the constitution required the legislature to appoint three commissioners "to revise, reform, simplify and abridge the rules of practice, pleadings, forms and procedures" for the consolidated court system.[348]

After a resignation from the commission, the New York legislature in 1847 appointed Field, who joined two other commissioners supportive of codification. The three prepared a draft code of civil procedure in less than half a year. They considered it a partial codification of remedial law, since it excluded testimony and evidence rules. The legislature enacted this partial code of 391 sections in 1848.[349] With Field as the pivotal member of the commission, it continued with revisions and amendments that the legislature adopted in 1849 totaling 473 sections. Finally, the commission's final report, published in 1850, included a Code of Civil Procedure (with evidence rules) and a Code of Criminal Procedure, both of which the legislature rejected.[350]

The success of the New York Code of Civil Procedure, in one of its three forms, was widespread and embodied the single most significant transplant of civil law ideas to the United States in this period. For procedure, it was revolutionary since it abolished the English feudal writ and bill system of pleading, replacing it with a single civil action guided by "code" pleading. It implemented the merger of law and equity, a distinction peculiar to English history that was the source of great confusion and delay. In 1849, Missouri began the American emulation when it enacted the code's 1848 version. Field's brother, Stephen (later a U.S. Supreme Court justice), persuaded the California legislature in 1851 to enact a procedure code based on the 1850 model. By 1873, more than half the American states and territories had embraced civil procedure codes grounded on one of the New York models or the California code.[351]

David Clark investigated the way the civil law influenced Field's Code. Based on an analysis of the 1806 French and 1825 Louisiana Codes of Civil Procedure, he found that their effect related to codification's ideology, its structure with

---

[348] N.Y. Const. art. 6, § 24 (1846); COOK, *supra* note 179, at 187–90; Clark, *Field Code*, *supra* note 323, at 65, 70, 75; *see* CHARLES Z. LINCOLN, 2 THE CONSTITUTIONAL HISTORY OF NEW YORK 164 (1905). In 1846 and 1847, Field lobbied the bar and public to explicitly require simplification of the law to take the form of a systematic code. Clark, *supra*, at 75; *see* N.Y. Const. art. 1, § 17 (1846) ("reduce [the law] into a written and systematic code").

[349] COOK, *supra* note 179, at 190–91. The code was a scientifically arranged set of reasoned principles, unlike a typical common law statute and more like a code in the French style. FRIEDMAN, HISTORY, *supra* note 11, at 293.

[350] Clark, *Field Code*, *supra* note 323, at 65, 76 n.62. For discussion and analysis in this part, I rely on the 1849 Code, the final one of the three that the New York legislature adopted. *Id.* at 76 n.62.

[351] *Id.* at 65; *see* FRIEDMAN, HISTORY, *supra* note 11, at 295–98.

scientific categories and definitions, and borrowed provisions.[352] After decades of fighting for codification of New York law and in America more generally, Field presented four reasons for his endorsement of codification. First, it supported the separation of powers principle, which reduced the role for judges in ex post facto lawmaking, preferring the legislative process. Second, it provided citizens with better information about the laws they should obey. Third, it improved legal certainty, permitting lawyers to operate more efficiently. And fourth, history taught that no society adopting codification ever returned to case-by-case "guess-law."[353]

Field, the intellectual leader on New York's commission, took the constitution's mandate to merge law and equity jurisdictions as support for adopting a uniform procedure for both types of lawsuits. Like the French and Louisiana codes, Field divided New York's 1849 Code into two parts: (1) courts of justice and their jurisdiction; and (2) civil actions. Part I had seven titles beginning with courts in general followed by six titles treating specific courts in detail. Of more interest, Part II had 15 titles, eight with chapters, which tracked the typical way a lawyer would organize his litigation. To illustrate, title 6 on pleadings had six functional chapters: complaint; demurrer; answer; reply; general rules; and mistakes in pleading and amendments. By analyzing the French, Louisiana, and New York codes as to structural division, scientific categories, and definitions, Clark concluded that it was more likely that the Livingston code rather than the French code influenced Field in drafting the New York Code of Procedure.[354] After considering the substance of Field's major reforms on simplified pleading, liberal joinder of parties, and appeals, the same conclusion remained. Much of the French influence probably made its way to New York via Louisiana, making Louisiana the cultural intermediary between civil law Europe and common law America.[355]

Amalia Kessler explored a separate issue related to the Field Code: its adoption of an oral adversarial procedure for both equity and common law matters. In 1817, Chancellor Kent had opened the door to oral testimony before New York equity masters with parties and lawyers present, purportedly to make equity

---

[352] Clark, *Field Code, supra* note 323, at 65–66, 68–69.

[353] *Id.* at 74; *see* David Dudley Field, *Codification*, 20 AM. L. REV. 1–7 (1886).

[354] Clark, *Field Code, supra* note 323, at 76–81. The commission called the 1849 draft as adopted the Code of Procedure even though it only dealt with civil litigation. It was the 1850 unratified draft that divided into two codes: one on civil procedure and the other on criminal procedure. Nevertheless, jurists henceforth referred to the 1849 version as the Code of Civil Procedure. *Id.* at 65, nn.8–9.

[355] *Id.* at 81–86. For earlier recognition of the influence of Livingston's code on Field's code, *see* CHARLES E. CLARK ET AL., HANDBOOK OF THE LAW OF CODE PLEADING 28 n.70 (2d ed. 1947); J. Newton Fiero, *Report of Committee on Uniformity of Procedure and Comparative Law*, 19 A.B.A. ANN. REP. 411, 427 (1896), *reprinted in* 54 ALB. L.J. 198, 204 (1896); McMahon, *Procedure I, supra* note 38, at 51; McMahon, *Procedure II, supra* note 39, at 14.

more efficient and thus less costly.[356] From the 1820s, lawyers pushed to move away from the secret, written inquisitorial aspects of equity procedure to embrace adversarial orality. This facilitated law and equity's merger in 1848. Given the code's influence in other states, the feature of American adversarial legal culture prevailed as a salient discriminant between the United States and countries with the civil law tradition.[357] Nevertheless, the success of Field's structure of a code to adopt this merger, already prevalent in Europe with a common procedure for Roman-canonic law, reflected a comparative law transplant of French legal ideas indirectly to New York.[358]

Ironically, the enduring effect of this civil law import was stronger in newer states from Iowa west than in New York. There, a resurgence of the common law legislative style gradually eroded the Field Code's civilian characteristics supported by the power of a narrowly educated bench and bar that clung to traditional modes of thought, suspicious of the civilian values of simplicity, order, and predictability in legal rules. In the years following the New York legislature's rejection of the 1850 draft codes, the bar attempted to return to their familiar practice by amending the 1849 Code. By the time the legislature repealed it in 1877, it had over 3,000 articles. Nevertheless, by 1865, 16 states or territories, more recently populated by settlers, had less interest in established property rights or common law intricacies. Lawyers who traveled west tended to be young and from various jurisdictions. Codified procedure, simple to understand and promising order and certainty, was attractive.[359]

I. Slavery

Slavery has been part of human existence for thousands of years, predating recorded history, found in all climates and among all races. Every major religion has sanctioned it and civilizations have depended upon it.[360] The Hammurabi Code mentioned slavery and Greek and Roman law extensively regulated it. For European

---

[356] AMALIA D. KESSLER, INVENTING AMERICAN EXCEPTIONALISM: THE ORIGINS OF AMERICAN ADVERSARIAL LEGAL CULTURE, 1800–1877, at 2–5, 13–14, 83, 86–89, 329 (2017); see Remsen v. Remsen, 2 Johns. Ch. 495 (N.Y. Ch. 1817) (deviating from the tradition of secrecy and written interrogatories to prevent perjury). Kessler suggested there was some deviation before 1817. KESSLER, supra, at 82–86.

[357] KESSLER, supra note 356, at 9–13, 17, 89–111, 136–50.

[358] See id. at 325–28; id., Our Inquisitorial Tradition: Equity Procedure, Due Process, and the Search for an Alternative to the Adversarial, 90 CORNELL L. REV. 1181, 1260–75 (2005).

[359] COOK, supra note 177, at 193–98; Clark, Field Code, supra note 323, at 86–87. California and Arizona's prior experience with the civil law might have eased early enactment. Clark, supra, at 87 n.85.

[360] For Montesquieu's view of slavery, which influenced Jefferson, see CAROLINE WINTERER, AMERICAN ENLIGHTENMENTS: PURSUING HAPPINESS IN THE AGE OF REASON 153–57 (2016) [hereinafter WINTERER, ENLIGHTENMENTS]. See generally HeinOnLine Databases, Slavery in America and the World: History, Culture & Law, https://home.heinonline.org/content (select Special Collections).

law, the Roman example would seem most relevant due to Roman law's general influence after the twelfth century. By that time, nevertheless, European society had largely developed based on feudalism, so lesser forms of subservience such as serfdom largely replaced slavery. European law by the sixteenth century reflected the distinction between serfdom and slavery and slave law dealt with European colonization and the bondage of indigenous people in Africa, the Americas, and Asia. Portuguese explorers at that time began buying slaves from African slave traders, transporting them initially to Portugal and later to Brazil. The Spanish, Dutch, and French saw the advantage of added coerced labor for their own colonies, with the British and Americans eventually entering the market for slaves. From 1500 to 1870, when the trade from west Africa closed, slavers shipped between ten and 15 million people to the colonies.[361] An unusual example of slavery in what became the American southwest was the Spanish enslavement of Indians, known as *genízaros*. In 1776, about one-third of the population there was *genízaro*.[362]

The economic importance of slavery varied by century among the British North American colonies. There were about 30,000 slaves by 1700, which number grew to 450,000 in 1776, with approximately 90 percent in the South throughout the eighteenth century. It was of little significance in New England, but considered essential in Virginia and Maryland, especially for tobacco planters. In those places where slavery was prevalent, racism against African Blacks was strongest, already stringent by the end of the seventeenth century.[363] There was considerable diversity among the other colonies. New York, New Jersey, and Delaware began as the Dutch colony of New Netherlands, incorporating Roman law to regulate a mild form of slavery until the English ousted the Dutch in 1664. After that, New York colonial law implemented a harsher version of slavery for its Black population.[364] By 1810, the slave population in the United States had grown to 1.2 million, reaching 3.9 million in 1860.[365]

---

[361] Sally E. Hadden, *The Fragmented Laws of Slavery in the Colonial and Revolutionary Eras*, in 1 THE CAMBRIDGE HISTORY OF LAW IN AMERICA: EARLY AMERICA (1580–1815) 253–58 (Michael Grossberg & Christopher Tomlins eds., 2008); William M. Wiecek, *The Origins of the Law of Slavery in British North America*, 17 CARDOZO L. REV. 1711, 1713–15 (1995) [hereinafter Wiecek, *Origins*]; see id. at 1715–25 (England), 1735–42 (Portuguese, French, Spanish, and English colonization). There was no slavery in England, which had not received Roman law. ALAN WATSON, SLAVE LAW IN THE AMERICAS 63 (1989) [hereinafter WATSON, SLAVE LAW].

[362] BILL PIATT & MOISES GONZALES, SLAVERY IN THE SOUTHWEST: GENÍZARO IDENTITY, DIGNITY AND THE LAW 4–6, 20–26 (2019). In addition, Indians used other Indians and later Black Americans as slaves. *Id.* at 6–7, 20–22.

[363] Hadden, *supra* note 361, at 263–64; Wiecek, *Origins*, *supra* note 361, at 1742–1763; THOMAS D. MORRIS, SOUTHERN SLAVERY AND THE LAW, 1619–1860, at 9–11 (1996); see id. at 17–36. Pennsylvania was like New England, while Carolina and Georgia followed Virginia and Maryland with a strict slavery law. Wiecek, *supra*, at 1768–73.

[364] Wiecek, *Origins*, *supra* note 361, at 1763–68, 1770–71; *see* WATSON, SLAVE LAW, *supra* note 361, at 102–14. For slavery in states that joined the Union after 1790, *see* MORRIS, *supra* note 363, at 4–6, 8–9.

[365] Hadden, *supra* note 361, at 254.

Some modern researchers have contended that the English common law of property regulated slave law in the United States, supplemented by certain equity principles and by American statutory law to control slave behavior.[366] William Wiecek rejected this view, noting that Blackstone and many English judges denied that the common law recognized slavery. English law acknowledged the special status of servants, apprentices, and certain agricultural workers, but all these individuals had rights as persons; the law treated none as chattel. The colonists, thus, had three options: invent slave law de novo, borrow from some legal system that had already developed slave law, or allow social and economic custom to dictate the appropriate legal rules. Some scholars have embraced the borrowing thesis, with sources varying from Roman law, Spanish law, to the law of Barbados. From that initial importation, other American colonies could copy their sister legal systems.[367]

The essence of American slave law was that Black Africans were chattel, personalty. As property, one could purchase, own, sell, mortgage, warranty, and devise another human. Since slaves were Black, their property status allowed white racism to further degrade their humanity. Carolina had perhaps the strictest deprivation of freedom in the colonies and for a time prior to 1740 treated slaves as realty for some purposes. By the mid-eighteenth century, legislators settled on the classification of slaves as chattel. However, in general they left it to courts to elaborate rights and relationships, using the common law mode of incremental lawmaking. Among the many incongruities of American slave law was emancipation or manumission, which permitted property to become a free person, creating a category of free Blacks.[368] Even some southern states permitted a slaveowner's manumission or the government's emancipation of a slave. In 1796, St. George Tucker wrote a tract proposing the gradual abolition of slavery in Virginia.[369]

---

[366] Wiecek, *Origins, supra* note 361 at 1775, *see* MORRIS, *supra* note 363, at 6–8, 39, 42–45, 47, 54. Thomas Morris suggested that Louisiana and Texas did derive their slavery law, perhaps indirectly, from Roman law. *Id.* at 8, 47–48.

[367] Wiecek, *Origins, supra* note 361, at 1775–77; MORRIS, *supra* note 363, at 37, 46–47, 49, 56; *see* J.H. BAKER, AN INTRODUCTION TO ENGLISH LEGAL HISTORY 475–77 (4th ed. 2002); WATSON, SLAVE LAW, *supra* note 361, at 63–65. Many of the early settlers to South Carolina were from Barbados and they brought their slaves and slave customs with them. WATSON, *supra*, at 67–68; *see* Hadden, *supra* note 361, at 260–64. Sally Hadden argued that colonial slave law was largely rooted in cultural and social custom. Hadden, *supra*, at 254–55, 264–66.

[368] Wiecek, *Origins, supra* note 361, at 1777–79, 1782–85; MORRIS, *supra* note 363, at 42, 61–80, 371–84, 392–98, 425–26, 435. Virginia classed slaves as realty and personalty, sometimes simultaneously. Wiecek, *Origins*, at 1779. A legislature would intervene to modify common law if necessary when the master's self-interest interfered with public order. An example of this was the creation of slave tribunals to levy punishment or ascertain value of a condemned slave. *Id.* at 1780, 1788.

[369] MORRIS, *supra* note 363, at 371–404, 440; WINTERER, ENLIGHTENMENTS, *supra* note 360, at 166–70; *see, e.g.*, An Act to Authorize the Manumission of Slaves (Va. 1782), *in* 11 The STATUTES AT LARGE 39–40 (William Waller Hening ed., 1821); ST. GEORGE TUCKER, DISSERTATION ON SLAVERY: WITH A PROPOSAL FOR THE GRADUAL ABOLITION OF IT, IN THE STATE OF VIRGINIA

In the early nineteenth century, the consensus regarding the origin of American slave law was that it evolved from social custom. The U.S. Supreme court accepted this view for slave trade in 1825.[370] Certain antebellum abolitionists, however, argued that American slave law was rooted in Roman law and the civil law monarchies of Europe, inconsistent with the individual liberty the American founders supported. Slave state jurists did not draw that conclusion but in South Carolina agreed that its slave law followed the civil law.[371] Some American state appellate courts began to refer to Roman law to solve legal issues involving slave relations.[372]

Alan Watson argued, however, that colonial and then state legislatures created the bulk of American slave law, which had a strong public law dimension that was lacking in Roman law. Roman slave law was largely private law, non-racist (since it applied to various ethnicities), putting slaves under the control of a *pater familias* who exercised authority over the *familia*. By contrast, the public law aspect of British American slave law stemmed from the government's obligation to maintain order among Black slaves, which also required white citizens to assist in enforcement of the restrictive rules. South Carolina's first statute on slavery in 1690 and subsequent enactments, derived from slave statutes in Barbados, illustrated those features.[373]

The new American legal system absorbed Enlightenment political philosophy and natural law theory, including republican forms of government and the core principle of liberty. These were in direct conflict with slavery as it had evolved. The tension between slavery abolitionists and apologists persisted with

---

(106 pp., 1796) [hereinafter TUCKER, SLAVERY]. Pennsylvania, where Tucker published his volume, enacted such a statute in 1780. An Act for the Gradual Abolition of Slavery (Pa. 1780), https://www.ushistory.org/presidentshouse/history/gradual.php. For more on Tucker and the circulation of his views in other states, *see* PEARSON, *supra* note 69, at 117–35; Michael Kent Curtis, *St. George Tucker and the Legacy of Slavery*, 47 WM & MARY L. REV. 1157–1212 (2006), Paul Finkelman, *The Dragon St. George Could Not Slay: Tucker's Plan To End Slavery*, id. at 1213–43.

[370] Wiecek, Origins, *supra* note 361, at 1773. John Marshall noted that all the European nations with colonies had engaged in the African slave trade and thus it did not violate the positive law of nations by usage and custom. Nevertheless, the United States and Great Britain had enacted laws to suppress slave trade, while natural law condemned it. The Antelope, 23 U.S. (10 Wheat) 66, 115–24 (1825) (Marshall, C.J.).

[371] Wiecek, Origins, *supra* note 361, at 1774.

[372] MORRIS, *supra* note 363, at 37, 49–52; WATSON, SLAVE LAW, *supra* note 361, at 64–65. Judges referred to available reference volumes on Roman law, especially JOHN TAYLOR, ELEMENTS OF THE CIVIL LAW (1755) and COOPER, *supra* note 63. MORRIS, *supra*, at 37, 51; WATSON, *supra*, at 65.

[373] WATSON, SLAVE LAW, *supra* note 361, at 67–76; Act for the Better Ordering of Slaves (S. Car. 1690); *see* Matthew H. Jennings, *Slave Codes* (2018), at South Carolina Encyclopedia, http://www.scencyclopedia.org/sce/entries/slave-codes; Hadden, *supra* note 361, at 270–74. Other scholars agreed that Roman law had little influence on the slave law of the original 13 states. VERNON VALENTINE PALMER, THROUGH THE CODES DARKLY: SLAVE LAW AND CIVIL LAW IN LOUISIANA 160–61 (2012) [hereinafter PALMER, SLAVE LAW]; MARK V. TUSHNET, SLAVE LAW IN THE AMERICAN SOUTH 7 (2003).

the Euro-American racism prevalent throughout the nation. From an apologist perspective, the United States established liberty for Euro-Americans based on the enslavement of Afro-Americans.[374] Two fundamental national public law documents adopted in 1787 illustrated this tension—the Northwest Ordinance and the Constitution. The former prohibited the extension of slavery into the Northwest Territory but did not call for emancipation of slaves already owned by settlers.[375] The latter adopted the Three-Fifths Compromise, which James Wilson proposed to gain southern support for the new framework of national government. Southerners believed by counting slaves they would have more members in the House of Representatives, which also would provide disproportionate power to elect presidents.[376] The Constitution also had the Importation Clause, which prohibited Congress from controlling migration of "persons" (slaves) into states until 1808[377] and the Fugitive Slave Clause, which forbade states from emancipating a fugitive "Person held to Service or Labour" (slave) whom a master demanded returned.[378]

Most historians contend that the role for comparative law in the construction and eventual abolition of slavery was small. As Wiecek has shown, in the 40 years following the ratification of the U.S. Constitution, there was a "federal consensus" supporting the legitimacy of slavery. Its tenets were that only states could regulate or abolish slavery within their respective jurisdictions. The national government's authority only extended to regulation of the international slave trade, fugitive slaves, and slave insurrections.[379] Before 1833, organized antislavery was moderate and focused on ameliorating slavery at the state and local levels. The founding of the American Anti-Slavery Society (AASS) at that time began to direct its concern toward federal action through constitutional amendment and demanded the abolition of slavery as illegitimate. The AASS Constitution (1833) promised pacifism and declared that slavery violated God's

---

[374] Hadden, *supra* note 361, at 276–83, 286–87; Jan Lewis, *The Problem of Slavery in Southern Political Discourse*, in DEVISING LIBERTY, *supra* note 56, at 265, 267–76; Wiecek, *Origins*, *supra* note 361, at 1790–92. "Whilst America hath been the land of promise to Europeans, and their descendants, it hath been the vale of death to millions of the wretched sons of Africa. The genial light of liberty, which hath here shone with unrivalled lustre on the former, hath yielded no comfort to the latter." TUCKER, SLAVERY, *supra* note 369. at 9.

[375] Northwest Ordinance (1787), § 14, art. 6. The Confederation Congress adopted this statute. *See supra* text accompanying notes 10–11 (Northwest Ordinance).

[376] U.S. Const. art. I, § 2 (Enumeration Clause, in which the census counts three fifths of "other persons" [slaves] to apportion representation in the House, amended by the Fourteenth Amendment).

[377] *Id.* at art. I, § 9; *see* WILLIAM M. WIECEK, THE SOURCES OF ANTISLAVERY CONSTITUTIONALISM IN AMERICA, 1760–1848, at 70–78, 117–18 (1977) [hereinafter WIECEK, SOURCES]. In fact, Congress prohibited slave trade from that date. Act to Prohibit the Importation of Slaves of 1807, 2 Stat. 426.

[378] U.S. Const. art. IV, § 2; Fugitive Slave Act of 1793, 1 Stat. 302; *see* WIECEK, SOURCES, *supra* note 377, at 97–100, 156–57, 197–200. Congress in effect repealed this clause with the Thirteenth Amendment.

[379] WIECEK, SOURCES, *supra* note 377, at 15–16. The U.S. Constitution set out the federal government's authority. U.S. Const. art. I, §§ 2, 8, 9; art. IV, §§ 2, 4; WIECEK, SOURCES, *supra*, at 62–83.

law, natural law, and the American Declaration of Independence. In the beginning the organization directed its effort toward preventing the extension of slavery into new states and abolishing it in the territories. Within a few years, the AASS had over a thousand local chapters with perhaps 250,000 members.[380]

In contesting slavery, natural law's principles that all humans are created equal and entitled to inalienable rights provided a viable comparative basis to attack slave law in a manner like natural law's support for republican government against the tyranny of King George in the Declaration of Independence.[381] In the decades after 1791, nevertheless, slavery spread into free states and territories. Although the U.S. Congress conceded to antislavery sentiment in its slave trade statutes, it protected slavery in federal territories (other than the Northwest Territory) through the Fugitive Slave Act (1793), which required return of escaping slaves. Because territories created their own law, those with slavery could borrow a southern state's slave code, which typically carried over into the territory's statehood.[382]

Louisiana provided an interesting example of borrowing, including the importation of slave law from civil law jurisdictions. Over the course of its history as a colony, territory, and state, it imported slave law concepts and provisions from the French Lesser Antilles islands of Martinique, Guadeloupe, and St. Christophe; Spain (with its transplanted Roman law); and sister states. Vernon Palmer investigated not only the positive law of these places as brought to Louisiana, but also the economic and cultural practices of masters and slaves. These customs often subverted and reworked positive law, sometimes to benefit slaves.[383]

Comparatists interested in Louisiana slave law have thoroughly investigated its sources. Nevertheless, there remains significant disagreement about whether the primary civil law origins of early Louisiana rules were from Roman law (either through French or Spanish borrowing) or from the compiled customs of the French Antilles colonies.[384] Leaving that debate aside, we consider here the

---

[380] WIECEK, SOURCES, *supra* note 377, at 16–17, 167–71; AASS Constitution, arts. I, II, IV, V, quoted in *id.* at 168–69.

[381] The Declaration of Independence para. 2 (U.S. 1776); *see* HELMHOLZ, NATURAL LAW, *supra* note 58, at 161–65; WIECEK, SOURCES, *supra* note 377, at 20–22, 26–27, 30–32, 38, 42–43, 45, 47–48, 143, 192, 241, 259–61, 265, 274–75, 286.

[382] WIECEK, SOURCES, *supra* note 377, at 97–105, 108–09. From 1819 to 1821, the process of slavery's westward expansion led to Missouri's statehood crisis, yielding the Missouri Compromise. To maintain parity in the U.S. Senate between northern and southern states, Congress only admitted Missouri as a slave state with an agreement to admit Maine as a free state. In addition, Congress would permit slavery thereafter only south of the 36th parallel latitude. *Id.* at 106–25.

[383] PALMER, SLAVE LAW, *supra* note 373, at xiii–xv, 3, 7–8, 54–64, 74, 79–85, 118.

[384] *Id.* at 4–9, 20, 22, 35, 40–41, 54–60, 74, 112–15; WATSON, SLAVE LAW, *supra* note 361, at 83–90, 128; Hans W. Baade, *Law of Slavery in Spanish Luisiana, 1769-1803*, in LOUISIANA'S LEGAL HERITAGE 43–86 (Edward I. Haas ed., 1983); *id.*, *The Gens De Couleur of Louisiana: Comparative Slave Law in Microcosm*, 18 Cardozo L. Rev. 535–86 (1996).

comparative law aspects of introducing slave law into the 1808 Louisiana Digest, enacted shortly before statehood.[385]

Louisiana had less volatility in its slave law than some other southern colonies and states. Prior to its codification in the 1808 Digest, Louisiana had two slave law compilations—the *Code Noir* in 1724 with 59 provisions and the Black Code in 1806 with 39 articles.[386] Palmer pointed out, however, that a clearer picture of the treatment of slaves by law required consideration of customs and judicial decisions. Custom was dynamic and supplied competing norms for behavior that influenced lawmakers in formulating or revising statutes.[387] The Digest was the first modern code to incorporate slavery with 45 such articles into its structure, consistent with the Spanish *Siete Partidas* but distinct from the French decision to maintain slavery outside the civil law. Palmer concluded that the evidence to support incorporation of Spanish norms for slavery into the Digest was substantial. Moreau-Lislet, the primary drafter, included mainly private law rules, leaving the public law norms for special statutes.[388]

The Digest's principal treatment of slaves was in book I (persons), title 6 (master and servant), chapter 3 (slaves), but there were also important articles in books II (property) and III (modes of acquiring property). Overall, the treatment of slaves was much harsher in the Digest that under Roman or Spanish law.[389] In the years after statehood in 1812, the Louisiana Supreme Court repeatedly referred to Roman and Spanish authorities in expanding slavery law, sometimes in a fashion benefiting slaves as with emancipation, personal property ownership (*peculium*), and limited forms of contracting and succession. The three compilers of the 1825 Louisiana Civil Code, including Moreau-Lislet, incorporated these liberalizing elements into the code.[390] For instance, the code allowed slaves to enter into a contract for their freedom or to initiate a lawsuit toward the same end.[391]

---

[385] *See supra* text accompanying notes 40–50 (Louisiana Digest).

[386] PALMER, SLAVE LAW, *supra* note 373, at 43. By contrast, Virginia from 1689 to 1865 enacted 130 slave statutes. *Id.* Louis XIV introduced the *Code Noir* for the French Antilles in 1685, which Louisiana adopted with a few changes in 1724. *Id.* at 49–54.

[387] *Id.* at 44–49, 65, 85–93, 100–101.

[388] *Id.* at 61–62, 103–06, 110, 123–29, 141. The Digest declared slaves to be immovables by operation of law. Art. 19 (book II, title 1, chap. 2); *see* art. 13 (book I, title 1, chap. 2) (a slave is in the power of a master). Moreau-Lislet also took some provisions from the French jurist, Jean Domat. PALMER, SLAVE LAW, *supra* note 373, at 127–28.

[389] PALMER, SLAVE LAW, *supra* note 373, at 129–34.

[390] *Id.* at 64, 99, 134–38; *see supra* text accompanying notes 310–16 (Louisiana Civil Code).

[391] Judith Kelleher Schafer, *"Forever Free from the Bonds of Slavery": Emancipation in New Orleans, 1855–1857*, in A LAW UNTO ITSELF?, *supra* note 154, at 142–43.

THE FORMATIVE ERA: 1791–1865   221

For the remainder of the antebellum period, civil litigation concerning slaves was the largest category of the Louisiana Supreme Court's caseload. To maintain consistency in its rulings, the court interpreted slave articles in the Digest and code together with adjacent articles while referring to Spanish, Roman, and French *jus commune* jurists. Using contextual or historical interpretation, to illustrate, the justices liberalized the slave law of manumission.[392]

---

[392] PALMER, SLAVE LAW, *supra* note 373, at 142–49, 153–56, 160. The code permitted owners to emancipate their slaves. Schafer, *supra* note 391, at 143–47. From 1804 (when Louisiana was a territory) until 1865, about 1,200 slavery-related appeals went to the state supreme court, in some years representing a quarter of its caseload. PALMER, SLAVE LAW, *supra*, at 142–43; *see* JUDITH KELLEHER SCHAFER, SLAVERY, THE CIVIL LAW, AND THE SUPREME COURT OF LOUISIANA 10–27, 61–63 (1994).

5
Historical Jurisprudence and Learned Law: 1865–1900

[T]he entire Germanic family, in its earliest known stage of development, placed the administration of law, as it placed the political administration, in the hands of popular assemblies composed of the free, able-bodied members of the commonwealth.... [T]he slender thread of political and legal thought ... leads [the researcher] out upon the wide plains of northern Germany, and attaches itself at last to the primitive popular assembly, parliament, law-court, and army in one; which embraced every free man, rich or poor, and in theory at least allowed equal rights to all.

Henry Adams[1]

A. Science and Romanticism: German Historical Jurisprudence

From early in the nineteenth century, many jurists embraced the aim of simplifying law and organizing legal rules into coherent structures. They typically saw this objective as part of legal science but might disagree on whether it should take the form of codes, digests, or treatises. What was different about the post-Civil War period was the shift from natural law to historical jurisprudence—predominantly the German version—as the philosophical basis for legal science. Germany had an even stronger reaction than the English to the principles of rationalism and universalism characteristic of the French Revolution. The historical turn was romantic, irrational, and strongly nationalistic in character. For law, this directed scientific research into law-shaping forces rather than the earlier inquiry into its ideal nature and purposes.[2]

---

[1] Henry Adams, *The Anglo-Saxon Courts of Law*, in ESSAYS IN ANGLO-SAXON LAW 1–54 (1876); see *infra* note 12 and accompanying text (*Essays*) and text accompanying notes 171–72 (Adams).

[2] EDGAR BODENHEIMER, JURISPRUDENCE: THE PHILOSOPHY AND METHOD OF THE LAW 70–71, 73–74 (rev. ed. 1974); DAVID M. RABBAN, LAW'S HISTORY: AMERICAN LEGAL THOUGHT AND THE TRANSATLANTIC TURN TO HISTORY 4–5, 63–80, 92–93 (2013); Mathias Reimann, *Nineteenth Century German Legal Science*, 31 B.C. L. REV. 837–38 (1990) [hereinafter Reimann, *German Legal Science*].

Friedrich Carl von Savigny (1779-1861) was the leading proponent of the historical school.[3] His position as Roman law professor at the University of Berlin from 1810 to 1842 gave him enormous influence, which continued in his scholarship through the end of the nineteenth century. In 1814, Savigny wrote a pamphlet rejecting a proposal to codify law among the German states according to the arrangement implemented by the French. He saw law as the result of internal, cultural forces, deeply rooted in a nation's past. Legal rules derived from popular custom and the common consciousness of a people. Law was like language, determined by people's usage and character and, above all, by a community's spirit (*Volksgeist*).[4]

In 1815, Savigny with two colleagues published a journal of historical jurisprudence, the *Zeitschrift für geschichtliche Rechtswissenschaft*, which saw 15 volumes through 1848. He contributed articles in all but one of the volumes up to his university retirement in 1842. Savigny illustrated his critical approach to primary sources with the six-volume *Geschichte des römischen Rechts im Mittelalter* (1815-1831), which became the foundation for the further study of Roman law and Roman *jus commune*. He believed that legal science should be both historical and systematic; it should reveal the inner coherence of legal materials developed in historical sources. As applied to the civil law, Savigny demonstrated the Roman basis of modern European law in the eight-volume treatise *System des heutigen römischen Rechts* (1840-1849).[5]

---

[3] David S. Clark, *Tracing the Roots of American Legal Education—A Nineteenth Century German Connection*, 51 RABELS ZEITSCHRIFT FÜR AUSLÄNDISCHES UND INTERNATIONALES PRIVATRECHT 313, 322-24 (1987) [hereinafter cited as Clark, *Roots*], reprinted in 1 THE HISTORY OF LEGAL EDUCATION IN THE UNITED STATES: COMMENTARIES AND PRIMARY SOURCES 495-508 (Steve Sheppard ed., 1999). Reimann concisely explained Savigny's historical theory of law. Reimann, *German Legal Science, supra* note 2, at 851-58.

[4] BODENHEIMER, *supra* note 2, at 71-73; M.H. HOEFLICH, ROMAN AND CIVIL LAW AND THE DEVELOPMENT OF ANGLO-AMERICAN JURISPRUDENCE IN THE NINETEENTH CENTURY 75-77 (1997) [hereinafter HOEFLICH, ROMAN AND CIVIL LAW]; Reimann, *German Legal Science, supra* note 2, at 852-54; *id., The Historical School against Codification: Savigny, Carter, and the Defeat of the New York Civil Code*, 37 AM. J. COMP. L. 95, 97-98 (1989) [hereinafter Reimann, *Historical School*]; *see* SAVIGNY, VOM BERUF UNSERER ZEIT FÜR GESETZGEBUNG UND RECHTSWISSENSCHAFT (1814), which Abraham Hayward translated from the second edition (1828) as OF THE VOCATION OF OUR AGE FOR LEGISLATION AND JURISPRUDENCE (1831) [hereinafter SAVIGNY, VOCATION].

Savigny summarized, "[A]ll law is originally formed in the manner ... by custom and popular faith, next by jurisprudence, ... therefore, by internal silently-operating powers, not by the arbitrary will of a law-giver." SAVIGNY, VOCATION, *supra*, at 30; *see id.* at 24.

[5] Reimann, *German Legal Science, supra* note 2, at 852, 854-58; *see* RABBAN, *supra* note 2, at 93-101. Reimann pointed out that there were many inconsistencies in American understanding of German legal science related to the historical school. Reimann, *supra*, at 838-41. *See generally* MATHIAS REIMANN, HISTORISCHE SCHULE UND COMMON LAW: DIE DEUTSCHE RECHTSWISSENSCHAFT DES 19. JAHRHUNDERTS IM AMERIKANISCHEN RECHTSDENKEN (1993).

In 1842, Savigny accepted a ministerial post to lead a new department to reform Prussian law. The 1848 revolution ended his career there, so he returned to writing scholarly works. The principal consequence was a treatise on contract law, 1-2 Das Obligationenrecht (1851-1853), which supplemented his work on modern European law.

Natural law jurists considered the rules they had discovered by reason to be universal and eternal. In eighteenth-century Germany, Christian Wolff was its leading scholar.[6] As a revolutionary force exemplified by the French and dispersed militarily by Napoleon, these jurists looked toward the future. In contrast, historical jurists believed in the national character of law, special to a people's culture, romantic in spirit, derived from the past. It could change, but only slowly by silent forces related to incremental social adjustment. The historical school after 1815 was the legal counterpart to the politics of Napoleon's defeat and the restoration of aristocratic regimes in Europe.[7]

As Savigny illustrated, German jurists in the early nineteenth century searched for a new systematic foundation for legal science (*Rechtswissenshaft*), which became a science of positive law. From a Kantian perspective, this legal science had to use empirical methods to discover positive law and had to organize its findings to provide the inherent structure of the subject. As objective knowledge, not as a means but as an end, *Wissenschaft* took on a normative meaning that indicated the intellectual dignity of a discipline. Once the historical work of discovery had identified a community's customary rules and induced the major legal principles, in advanced civilizations, academic jurists could turn their attention to construction of a system to categorize the levels of principles. Legal rules still emerged organically and might over time demand juristic reconsideration of the systematic structure of principles. This required that scientists remain connected to a culture's *Volksgeist*.[8]

In the United States, before 1860, natural law in general continued to be a creative theory that could work hand in hand with comparative law by borrowing from civil law jurisdictions. Nevertheless, some American jurists, such as Luther Cushing, Francis Lieber, and Hugh Legaré utilized the German historical school as an important philosophical approach to legal development. This was apparent as early as the 1830s with Cushing's articles and book reviews in the *American Jurist*.[9] In addition,

---

[6] Reimann, *German Legal Science*, supra note 2, at 843–44. The search for a new basis of legal science came from the practical need to clarify the diverse laws in German lands and the philosophical criticism by the Prussian Immanuel Kant. *Id.* at 843–46; *see* IMMANUEL KANT, CRITIK DER REINEN VERNUNFT (1781).

[7] BODENHEIMER, *supra* note 2, at 73. The historical school divided early between the Romanists and the Germanists. The latter focused on German legal customs historically in a traditional way, adopted romantic notions of lay justice, and reduced, without rejecting, Savigny's preference for a special role for academic scientific jurists promoting the task of systematizing concepts. Reimann, *German Legal Science*, supra note 2, at 868–71; RABBAN, *supra* note 2, at 101–06.

[8] Reimann, *German Legal Science*, supra note 2, at 846–48, 852–56. From the data of positive laws, a jurist could induce principles, which would serve as the organizing criteria for a rational system. *Id.* at 849.

[9] *See supra* ch. 4, pts. G and H (natural law with penal reform and codification); ch. 4, pt. F (Cushing, Lieber, and Legaré).

Cushing's 1849 lectures at Harvard sympathetically expounded Savigny's ideas.[10]

After 1865, in both Europe and the United States, jurists more often looked inward and reveled in the specific over the universal. Italy in 1861 and Germany in 1871 coalesced to become modern nation-states. Lawyers, along with others, emphasized the uniqueness and virtue of their national culture, language, and law. The most famous in the United States was James Carter, who had been one of Cushing's students at Harvard. Carter became a distinguished New York lawyer and leader of the American bar. He embraced Savigny's historical orientation and was David Field's primary critic in the latter's attempt to codify New York's civil law.[11]

An impressive American scholarly contribution to historical jurisprudence was the volume that Henry Adams at Harvard organized with three of his history graduate students, *Essays in Anglo-Saxon Law* (1876). Adams had studied law at Berlin and other universities in Germany for two years after graduating from Harvard College. In 1870, Charles Eliot, the new president of Harvard University, hired Adams as an assistant professor of history. Adams introduced German teaching and scholarship standards, worked from original Anglo-Saxon, German, and Latin sources, and financed *Essays* as the first original legal history published in America. The volume emphasized the Teutonic origins of English and American law and legal institutions.[12]

Consequently, in the latter third of the nineteenth century, the primary jurisprudential theories that replaced natural law were either historical and scientific, searching for law in a people's spirit, or analytical, organizing legal rules, developing concepts, and discovering principles in a formalistic manner.[13] Neither

---

[10] HOEFLICH, ROMAN AND CIVIL LAW, *supra* note 4, at 89–91; *see supra* ch. 4, pt. F.1 (Cushing). Hoeflich identified Savigny's translated works as important sources of information about historical jurisprudence. Michael H. Hoeflich, *Savigny and His Anglo-American Disciples*, 37 AM. J. COMP. L. 17–23, 26–30, 32–36 (1989).

[11] BODENHEIMER, *supra* note 2, at 76–77; JAMES E. HERGET, AMERICAN JURISPRUDENCE, 1870–1970, at 120–30 (1990) [hereinafter cited HERGET, JURISPRUDENCE]; *see infra* pt. D (Carter and Field).

[12] RABBAN, *supra* note 2, at 44–48; *see id.* at 153–86; *infra* text accompanying notes 33–37, 41–43 (Eliot). In the Works Cited section of *Essays* most of the listed books were in German. ESSAYS IN ANGLO-SAXON LAW vii–xii (1876). The authors dedicated the volume to Eliot.

[13] RABBAN, *supra* note 2, at 6–7; HERGET, JURISPRUDENCE, *supra* note 11, at 12–30 (evolutionary or expository); *id., The Influence of German Thought on American Jurisprudence, 1800–1918* [hereinafter Herget, *German Thought*], *in* THE RECEPTION OF CONTINENTAL IDEAS IN THE COMMON LAW WORLD: 1820–1920, at 203 (Mathias Reimann ed., 1993); Roman J. Hoyos, BEYOND CLASSICAL LEGAL THOUGHT: LAW AND GOVERNANCE IN POSTBELLUM AMERICA, 1865–1920, *in* A COMPANION TO AMERICAN LEGAL HISTORY 86–90, 94–96, 100 (Sally E. Hadden & Alfred L. Brophy eds., 2013); James D. Schmidt, *American Jurisprudence in the Nineteenth and Early Twentieth Centuries*, *in* A COMPANION TO AMERICAN LEGAL HISTORY, *supra*, at 506, 512–14; *see* Mathias Reimann, *Historical Jurisprudence*, *in* THE OXFORD HANDBOOK OF LEGAL HISTORY 397–410 (Markus D. Dubber & Christopher Tomlins eds., 2018) [hereinafter Reimann, *Historical Jurisprudence*]; Michael Lobban, *Legal Formalism*, *in* OXFORD HANDBOOK, *supra*, at 419–31.

of these approaches seemingly left much room for valuing how other societies solved legal problems. Roscoe Pound saw this period as a nadir in American comparative law activities.[14] This chapter assesses whether that judgment was accurate.

B. German Legal Science

By 1865, the Romanist branch of historical jurisprudence dominated the Germanist branch in German law faculties. Each side contributed to legal doctrine that eventually found its way into Germany's civil and commercial codes, both effective in 1900. However, where the Roman sources were plentiful, that is, most of private law, Romanists prevailed. In fields where those sources were scarce, such as business enterprises, insurance, and admiralty, Germanists succeeded in devising the doctrine for those codes.[15] In addition, both groups spent less effort working with their primary source materials once they had established doctrine, leaving the source material to legal historians. Instead, the scientists concentrated on the conceptual and systematic aspects of materials already recognized. Legal science then became a system of timeless logic.[16]

The shared German concept of legal science had its roots in Savigny's historical theory of law. Its fundamental ideas were that law was a product of history, it was a system, and combined, it was a science of positive law. Accordingly, legal science, as a cultural phenomenon, contrasted clearly with natural law. Law was not universal and eternal; it was specific to a society and changed over time. Earlier, we saw these elements in Montesquieu's writing. For nineteenth-century legal scientists, law had its roots in the past, which could serve as a reference point in analytical jurisprudence. Furthermore, law evolved organically, which scientists could perceive and explain as doctrine, which legislators should not subject to erratic alteration. The statutory form tended to impede further growth consonant with society in whatever field of private law the legislature invaded. Finally, law was positivist, tied to discovered legal facts and principles and not to speculative reason.[17]

---

[14] ROSCOE POUND, THE FORMATIVE ERA OF AMERICAN LAW 148-49, 157, 163-64 (1938) [hereinafter POUND, FORMATIVE ERA]. "The high estimate of the civil law which was formed in [the postrevolutionary] period lingered in this country till the end of the third quarter of the [nineteenth] century." *Id.* at 148.

[15] Reimann, *German Legal Science, supra* note 2, at 870-71; Reimann, *Historical Jurisprudence, supra* note 13, at 411-12; *see supra* note 7 (Romanists and Germanists). Germanists initially prevailed with these fields in the 1861 commercial code of the German Confederation. Reimann, *German Legal Science, supra,* at 871 n.135.

[16] Reimann, *German Legal Science, supra* note 2, at 871-74.

[17] Clark, *Roots, supra* note 3, at 324-25; Reimann, *German Legal Science, supra* note 2, at 875-80, 889-91; Reimann, *Historical School, supra* note 4, at 108-10.

The goal of historical research into a culture's legal rules and principles was to establish the scientific order of law, a system. A scientist could discover the internal order based on positive, historical material. This work was objective, inductive, and scientific. Savigny compared it to geometry to show that the system would be complete and gapless. Once scholars established such a system, a jurist could deduce the logical detailed rules needed to resolve a dispute. Moreover, the system was not static, but slowly evolved organically in a manner that a scientist could explain.[18] Accepting such a vision of law privileged the scholar over the legislator or judge. For Carter, adapting the German argument to American society meant placing leadership in learned judges and diligent practitioners.[19]

Although the dominance of legal science as a philosophy waned in Germany after the codifications of 1900, its influence in the United States was notable in the new model for legal education begun at Harvard Law School. To a lesser extent, analytical jurisprudence, with its emphasis on classification, concepts, and formalistic logic, was also important. Nevertheless, it too had a historical orientation with attention to judicial case law.[20]

C. Making Legal Education Scientific: Harvard Law School

The period after the Civil War saw the complete transformation of American legal education from a modified English apprenticeship approach, even at Harvard Law School, where instruction relied primarily on lectures, memorization, and recitation. The new system embraced university law schools that adopted major elements related to the goals, method, structure, and ceremony of German legal education, the leading European model.[21]

---

[18] Reimann, *German Legal Science, supra* note 2, at 880–89, 893–94; SAVIGNY, VOCATION, *supra* note 4, at 38–39; *see id.* at 45.

[19] Reimann, *Historical School, supra* note 4, at 110–14.

[20] Lobban, *supra* note 13, at 427–31, 435; Reimann, *German Legal Science, supra* note 2, at 838–40, 896–97 n.208; *id.*, *Historical Jurisprudence, supra* note 13, at 397–98, 402–03, 413–14; *see* MELVILLE M. BIGELOW, CENTRALIZATION AND THE LAW: SCIENTIFIC LEGAL EDUCATION 165–67 (1906); Robert W. Gordon, *Legal Thought and Legal Practice in the Age of American Enterprise: 1870–1920*, *in* PROFESSIONS AND PROFESSIONAL IDEOLOGIES IN AMERICA 70, 72–73, 82–89, 98–99 (Gerald L. Geison ed., 1983) (legal science and legal education); *supra* text accompanying note 13 (legal philosophies).

[21] Laura I. Appleman, *The Rise of the Modern American Law School: How Professionalization, German Scholarship, and Legal Reform Shaped Our System of Legal Education*, 39 NEW ENG. L. REV. 251–53, 274–300 (2005); Clark, *Roots, supra* note 3, at 315–17, 321–22; Gail J. Hupper, *The Rise of an Academic Doctorate in Law: Origins through World War II*, 49 AM. J. LEG. HIST. 1, 3–4, 7–13 (2007); Edward Shils & John Roberts, *The Diffusion of European Models outside Europe*, *in* 3 A HISTORY OF THE UNIVERSITY IN EUROPE: UNIVERSITIES IN THE NINETEENTH AND EARLY TWENTIETH CENTURIES (1800–1945), 163, 166–67 (2004).

1. Americans Pursue Post-Secondary Education in Germany

The transformation of legal education was part of a general American reform and growth of graduate university teaching and research, including for the professions. Because German universities had the best reputation in Europe, these were the places most Americans serious about their studies would attend.[22] For the century following 1815, nine to ten thousand Americans matriculated in German universities, many returning with a doctoral degree. Berlin accounted for about half the matriculation, with Heidelberg and Leipzig each enrolling about 10 percent of the total. Prior to 1861, the rudimentary American institutions did not offer a doctoral degree, and during the period up to 1900, the number of earned doctoral degrees was small. German doctorates, alternatively, offered at established research universities provided prestige.[23] The transfer of culture also occurred when Germans took up residence in the United States as teachers in higher education.[24] Hermann von Holst's acceptance of a history professorship at the creation of the University of Chicago in 1892 was a famous example. He established rigorous graduate training in history along German lines.[25]

---

[22] JOHN S. BRUBACHER & WILLIS RUDY, HIGHER EDUCATION IN TRANSITION: A HISTORY OF AMERICAN COLLEGES AND UNIVERSITIES, 1636-1976, at 174-78 (3d ed. 1976); RABBAN, *supra* note 2, at 86-87; Walter Rüegg, *Themes*, *in* 3 A HISTORY OF THE UNIVERSITY IN EUROPE, *supra* note 21, at 3, 5-6, 10-13, 17-18. A small number of Americans enrolled at French and English universities. In 1895, to illustrate, 30 Americans matriculated at the Sorbonne compared to 200 at Berlin. English universities suffered a poor reputation since most science and learning occurred outside their walls. JÜRGEN HERBST, THE GERMAN HISTORICAL SCHOOL IN AMERICAN SCHOLARSHIP: A STUDY IN THE TRANSFER OF CULTURE 8-13 (1965).

[23] HERBST, *supra* note 22, at 1-2, 24; CHARLES F. THWING, THE AMERICAN AND THE GERMAN UNIVERSITY: ONE HUNDRED YEARS OF HISTORY 40-41 (1928); Konrad H. Jarausch, *American Students in Germany, 1815-1914: The Structure of German and U.S. Matriculants at Göttingen University*, *in* GERMAN INFLUENCES ON EDUCATION IN THE UNITED STATES TO 1917, at 195-96 (Henry Geitz et al. eds., 1995). Although there had been a few honorary doctoral degrees awarded in the United States, in 1861, Yale granted the first earned doctorates. Their growth was slow until they exceeded 100 by 1890. Thus, by decade, the number was one (1870), 54 (1880), 149 (1890), and 382 (1900). U.S. BUREAU OF THE CENSUS, HISTORICAL STATISTICS OF THE UNITED STATES, COLONIAL TIMES TO 1970, at 386 (1975) (series H 761); Ralph P. Rosenberg, *The First American Doctor of Philosophy Degree: A Centennial Salute to Yale, 1861-1961*, 32 J. HIGHER EDUC. 387-88, 391, 394 (1961).

[24] About 300 Germans taught at American colleges and universities from 1815 until World War I. THWING, *supra* note 23, at 103. Soon after Michigan joined the Union as a state, its legislature chartered the University of Michigan, which was to emulate the German university research model. Shils & Roberts, *supra* note 21, at 167-68.

[25] Jörg Nagler, *A Mediator between Two Historical Worlds: Hermann Eduard von Holst and the University of Chicago*, *in* GERMAN INFLUENCES ON EDUCATION IN THE UNITED STATES TO 1917, *supra* note 23, at 257, 269-74. Holst illustrated the mixture of law and politics. H. VON HOLST, THE CONSTITUTIONAL LAW OF THE UNITED STATES OF AMERICA (Alfred Bishop Mason trans., 1887); *id.*, 1-8 THE CONSTITUTIONAL AND POLITICAL HISTORY OF THE UNITED STATES (John J. Lalor & Alfred B. Mason trans., 1889-1892).

Up to 1880, law was the second most popular subject, after medicine and the supporting natural sciences, for Americans to study in Germany. After that time, with a successful reform in American legal education at Harvard, the relative importance of law for American students in Germany declined significantly. It varied between 6 and 9 percent at the leading universities in Berlin, Heidelberg, and Leipzig compared with a quarter of the German students at university who enrolled in law.[26] The magnitude of law department size at German universities illustrated the impression it would make on American scholars. In 1892, for instance, there were 6,900 students at 20 law faculties, three of which—Berlin, Leipzig, and Munich—each had over 1,000 law students. Berlin, the largest, had 27 teachers, 11 of whom were full professors. But even the smallest law faculties, with fewer than 100 students, had at least five full professors in residence.[27]

Beyond a knowledge of German law, what could American scholars hope to bring back to the United States? Unlike U.S. legal education in the twentieth century, which emerged as a graduate discipline, German legal education was and is an undergraduate subject. Successful innovations in the early nineteenth century at Berlin University aimed toward humanistic and scientific training of public civil servants in the Kantian concepts of duty. These innovations spread to other German universities by the 1840s. Because the law curriculum included Roman and canon law, it was attractive both as a general education and as preparation for a gentleman lawyer.[28] Americans engaged in the German tradition of switching universities, which widened their exposure to the German concept of science (*Wissenschaft*). For instance, they could hear Heinrich Zachariae (1806–1875) at Göttingen lecture on criminal procedure, Rudolf von Gneist (1816–1895) at Berlin on English constitutional and administrative law, and Johann Bluntschli (1808–1881) at Heidelberg on international law.[29]

---

[26] HERBST, *supra* note 22, at 6–7; Jarausch, *supra* note 23, at 200, 205, 207; *see* Mathias Reimann, *A Career in Itself: The German Professoriate as a Model for American Legal Academica*, in THE RECEPTION OF CONTINENTAL IDEAS, *supra* note 13, at 165, 173–77 [hereinafter Reimann, *German Professoriate*].

[27] RECHTSFORSCHUNG UND RECHTSUNTERRICHT AUF DEN DEUTSCHEN UNIVERSITÄTEN, AT ANHANG 133, 140 (Otto Fischer ed., 1893) [hereinafter RECHTSFORSCHUNG].

[28] HERBST, *supra* note 22, at 6; CHARLES E. MCCLELLAND, STATE, SOCIETY, AND UNIVERSITY IN GERMANY, 1700–1914, at 2, 152–53 (1980); *see* FRANZ WIEACKER, PRIVATRECHTSGESCHICHTE DER NEUZEIT: UNTER BESONDERER BERÜCKSICHTIGUNG DER DEUTSCHEN ENTWICKLUNG 438–49 (2d ed. 1967). For example, Breslau University during the academic year 1892–1893 offered the following courses in the law faculty: introduction to legal science, history of Roman law, Roman law Institutes, Roman law Pandects (Digest), canon law, legal philosophy, political economy, macroeconomics, commercial law, German legal history, German private law, German civil procedure, German constitutional law, German criminal law, German criminal procedure, German administrative law, international law, and Prussian state law. RECHTSFORSCHUNG, *supra* note 27, at 1, 16–17.

[29] HERBST, *supra* note 22, at 15–18.

James Hart (1839-1916), to illustrate, earned a law degree at the University of Göttingen and later wrote a popular book about his experience.[30] He stressed the importance at German universities of the goal of *Wissenschaft*, "knowledge in the most exalted sense of the term, namely, the ardent, methodical, independent search after truth in any and all of its forms, but wholly irrespective of utilitarian application." This goal required the conditions of *Lehrfreiheit*, a professor's freedom "to teach what he chooses, as he chooses," and *Lernfreiheit*, a student's freedom to learn, thus "emancipation . . . from *Schulzwang*, compulsory drill by recitation."[31] Hart emphasized that German universities stressed the theoretical over the practical, since educating thinkers was the aim. Even though only a few would become scientists (jurists), the remainder who graduated would enter the practical disciplines, such as lawyers and judges, with the experience of scientists.[32]

2. Harvard Law School and the Development of Graduate Education: Charles Eliot and Christopher Langdell

Although Yale College, with Theodore Woolsey (1801-1889) as president, awarded the first earned doctorates in the United States in 1861, Harvard University was at the center of the American transformation to a university research mission.[33] This occurred under the presidency of Charles Eliot (1834-1926) and for law, with the school's first dean, Christopher Langdell (1826-1906), who served from 1870 until 1895. Eliot, who had traveled for two years in Europe in the 1860s studying educational systems, was the more important.[34] He actively

---

[30] JAMES MORGAN HART, GERMAN UNIVERSITIES: A NARRATIVE OF PERSONAL EXPERIENCE, TOGETHER WITH RECENT STATISTICAL INFORMATION, PRACTICAL SUGGESTIONS, AND A COMPARISON OF THE GERMAN, ENGLISH, AND AMERICAN SYSTEMS OF HIGHER EDUCATION v, 1-18, 217-46 (1874, printed in 1878).

[31] *Id.* at 249-50. The twin principles of *Lehrfreiheit* and *Lernfreiheit* formed the basis for the general acceptance of academic freedom in American universities, marked by the creation in 1916 of the American Association of University Professors. Elite U.S. universities also accepted the German idea of *Einheit von Forschung und Lehre*, the unity of research and teaching. Shils & Roberts, *supra* note 21, at 169-71.

[32] HART, *supra* note 30, at 251-55, 257-59. "The higher education of the German universities is the best in the world. Yet Americans should beware of entering upon it before they are fully ripe." *Id.* at 393.

[33] ROBERT STEVENS, LAW SCHOOL: LEGAL EDUCATION IN AMERICA FROM THE 1850S TO THE 1980S, at 35 (1983). Woolsey had studied Greek for three years at universities in Berlin, Bonn, and Leipzig. BROOKS MATHER KELLEY, YALE: A HISTORY 171-208 (1974).

[34] STEVENS, *supra* note 33, at 35-36; Appleman, *supra* note 21, at 283-89; Clark, *Roots*, *supra* note 3, at 319; Hugh C. Macgill & R. Kent Newmyer, *Legal Education and Legal Thought, 1790-1920*, in 2 THE CAMBRIDGE HISTORY OF LAW IN AMERICA: THE LONG NINETEENTH CENTURY (1789-1920) 36, 45, 49-54 (Michael Grossberg & Christopher Tomlins eds., 2008); Reimann, *German Professoriate*, *supra* note 26, at 166-67, 184-86; *see* HENRY JAMES, 1 CHARLES W. ELIOT: PRESIDENT OF HARVARD UNIVERSITY, 1869-1909, at 115-17, 121-23, 128, 132-38, 147, 152 (1930).

initiated and supported reform throughout the university and presided over most Law School faculty meetings. He hired law professors who lacked a background of professional practice but could be full-time teachers and scholars.[35]

Langdell, with the help of Eliot's leadership, from 1870 to 1885 institutionalized five important changes: (1) an entrance examination; (2) a progressive three-year curriculum, leading to an undergraduate bachelor of laws degree (LL.B.); (3) requisite annual examinations before students could proceed to the next year's subjects; (4) support for a research function similar to that existing at German universities; and (5) an instructional method utilizing Socratic dialogue to discuss appellate court cases, justified as a scientific process to elaborate general, organic principles of the common law.[36] Langdell was most famous for this last innovation, the introduction of the case method of instruction. He contended that he was trying to put American law faculties on a level with universities in continental Europe. Professors and students should together work through questions and answers to discover common law principles, aided by classroom research manuals called casebooks.[37]

Langdell's theory of legal science and organic development was like that of German historical jurisprudence. As he explained in his 1871 casebook on contracts,

> Law, considered as a science, consists of certain principles or doctrines.... Each of these doctrines has arrived at its present state by slow degrees; in other words, it is a growth, extending in many cases through centuries. This growth is to be traced in the main through a series of cases.... [For contracts, I] select, classify, and arrange all the cases which had contributed in any important degree to the growth, development, or establishment of any of its essential doctrines.[38]

---

[35] BRUBACHER & RUDY, *supra* note 22, at 178, 182–83, 187, 204, 206; STEVENS, *supra* note 33, at 36–37, 51–52; ARTHUR E. SUTHERLAND, THE LAW AT HARVARD: A HISTORY OF IDEAS AND MEN, 1817–1967, at 164, 167 180–84, 186–87, 191, 195 (1967); Clark, *Roots*, *supra* note 3, at 318–19, 326–27; Rosenberg, *supra* note 23, at 387–88, 393–94; *see* 2 JAMES, *supra* note 34, at 62–63 (1930); Shils & Roberts, *supra* note 21, at 169. *See generally* CHARLES A. WARREN, 2 HISTORY OF THE HARVARD LAW SCHOOL AND OF EARLY LEGAL CONDITIONS IN AMERICA 354–418 (1908) (early relationship between Eliot and Langdell).

Eliot had a concept of organicism like that of Savigny and Langdell. The "universe, as science teaches, [is] an organism which has by slow degrees grown to its form to-day on its way to its form to-morrow, with slowly formed habits which we call laws." 1 JAMES, *supra*, at 318 (quoting Eliot).

[36] Clark, *Roots*, *supra* note 3, at 327–28; *see* STEVENS, *supra* note 33, at 51–53, 55, 59–60, 93, 134.

[37] Clark, *Roots*, *supra* note 3, at 327–28; *see* STEVENS, *supra* note 33, at 52–57.

[38] C.C. LANGDELL, A SELECTION OF CASES ON THE LAW OF CONTRACTS: WITH REFERENCES AND CITATIONS vi–vii (1871); *see* Clark, *Roots*, *supra* note 3, at 328–29. *See also* WILLIAM M. WIECEK, THE LOST WORLD OF CLASSICAL LEGAL THOUGHT: LAW AND IDEOLOGY IN AMERICA, 1886–1937, at 89–94 (1998).

For both Savigny and Langdell, the process of initiating legal craftmanship and transforming it into legal science belonged at the university. Thus, both desired to keep legal theory and practical apprenticeship separate.[39]

At the midterm of his career as dean, Langdell made a speech explaining his vision for the Law School.

> [I]n all the rest of Christendom law has always been taught and studied in universities; ... the true interests of legal education in this country required that, in this respect, we should not follow in the footsteps of England, but should bring ourselves into harmony with the rest of the civilized world. ... I have tried to do my part towards making the teaching and study of law [at Harvard] worthy of a university, ... toward placing the law school, as far as differences of circumstance would permit, in the position occupied by the law faculties in the universities of continental Europe.[40]

As dean, Langdell recruited James Barr Ames (1846–1910) as an assistant professor in 1873. Ames was the new breed of academic lawyer, with limited practical experience, who met Eliot's goal for teaching and scholarship. Ames had studied for over a year at German universities. He became a popular instructor with Langdell's Socratic method and produced many casebooks widely used in American law schools. Eliot selected Ames to become dean in 1895. Legal science promised a complete and orderly system of norms; it brought prestige to law as a science.[41]

Eliot had maintained an exchange of educational resources between Germany and Harvard up to his retirement as president in 1909. In that year, the German government conferred the Royal Order of the Prussian Crown on Eliot. In 1911, Eliot received an honorary Ph.D. from Breslau University.[42] Earlier, Eugen Kühnemann, who twice held a German exchange professorship at Harvard, wrote an essay praising Eliot for his leadership, mentioning Harvard's resemblance to a European university, and particularly admiring the accomplishments of the Law School.[43]

---

[39] Clark, *Roots*, *supra* note 3, at 327–29; Reimann, *Professoriate*, *supra* note 26, at 169–71. Langdell wanted legal study to be a graduate curriculum, since American secondary school students were so ill-prepared for academic work. In 1875, the Harvard Board of Overseers overruled his effort to require college graduation for law school admission. Clark, *supra*, at 327 n.70.

[40] Christopher C. Langdell, *The Harvard Law School*, 3 LAW Q. REV. 118, 123–24 (1887) (speech celebrating the 250th anniversary of Harvard College's founding).

[41] STEVENS, *supra* note 33, at 38–39, 51, 54–56, 60; RABBAN, *supra* note 2, at 53–54; Clark, *Roots*, *supra* note 3, at 330.

[42] 2 JAMES, *supra* note 34, at 137–142, 359; see Clark, *Roots*, *supra* note 3, at 332–33. In Harvard's first ceremony to honor a foreign prince with an honorary doctorate of laws in 1902, Eliot had acknowledged Germany's contribution to America's universities. Clark, *supra*, at 333.

[43] Clark, *Roots*, *supra* note 3, at 333. Kühnemann taught at Harvard during the 1906 and 1908 academic years. He also published his essay in German in Berlin. *Id.*

3. The American Bar Association

In 1870, only about one-quarter of the states required apprenticeship or sometimes law school study (which was like apprenticeship) before one could become a lawyer. There were 1,650 law students among 31 law schools at that time aspiring to join the 40,700 lawyers who served a population of almost 40 million. By the end of the decade, 15 of 38 states required some formal preparation to enter law practice, but only six of those allowed law school to substitute for clerkship. Of course, that meant that over half the states had no entry barrier to practice law while the number of lawyers in 1880 expanded to 60,600.[44]

This lax situation concerned urban elite lawyers who believed the profession required entry control to improve prestige. The re-emergence of bar associations in the major commercial centers in the 1870s was one step toward a solution. In 1877, there were municipal bar associations in Boston, Chicago, Cleveland, New York, and St. Louis. Similarly, state and territorial bar associations formed in the 1870s and there were eight by 1878. In 1900, that number of mostly voluntary organizations was 40.[45]

In 1878, Simeon Baldwin (1840–1927) coordinated 14 concerned lawyers from different bar associations who signed a letter calling for a meeting at Saratoga Springs, New York, to establish the American Bar Association (ABA).[46] Its constitution, adopted at the first meeting in 1878, stated as its purpose, "to advance the science of jurisprudence, promote the administration of justice and uniformity of legislation throughout the Union, [and] uphold the honor of the profession of the law."[47]

Baldwin was from an illustrious Connecticut family with Yale College ties going back to the eighteenth century. As a member of the New Haven bar, he accepted teaching responsibility at Yale Law School in 1869 and, with President

---

[44] RICHARD L. ABEL, AMERICAN LAWYERS 40–41, 51–52, 277, 280–81 (1989). In 1870, five of the lawyers were women. *Id.* at 284.

[45] ABEL, *supra* note 44, at 44–46; ALFRED ZANTZINGER REED, TRAINING FOR THE PUBLIC PROFESSION OF THE LAW: HISTORICAL DEVELOPMENT AND PRINCIPAL CONTEMPORARY PROBLEMS OF LEGAL EDUCATION IN THE UNITED STATES WITH SOME ACCOUNT OF CONDITIONS IN ENGLAND AND CANADA 206 (1921); STEVENS, *supra* note 33, at 27, 92–93.

[46] *Call for a Meeting*, 1 A.B.A. [ANN. REP.] 4 (1878); SUSAN K. BOYD, THE ABA'S FIRST SECTION: ASSURING A QUALIFIED BAR 5 (1993); STEVENS, *supra* note 33, at 34 n.60, 103 n.1. According to Baldwin, the idea for the ABA came about after a discussion at the 1877 annual meeting in New York of the American Social Science Association (ASSA, founded in 1865), which had a section on jurisprudence. The initial discussion involved Baldwin, David Field, William Hammond, and Carleton Hunt, but Baldwin took the lead with the Connecticut State Bar Association to organize a solicitation committee. Baldwin was later president of the ASSA. Simeon E. Baldwin, *The Founding of the American Bar Association*, 3 A.B.A. J. 658–60 (1917) [hereinafter Baldwin, *Founding*]; Paul D. Carrington, *William Gardiner Hammond and the Lieber Revival*, 16 CARDOZO L. REV. 2135, 2146 (1995).

[47] *proceedings*, 1 A.B.A. [ANN. REP.] 5, 16, 19 (1878); *see Constitution, id.* at 30. About 100 lawyers attended the ABA organizational meeting in 1878. Baldwin, *Founding, supra* note 46, at 691.

Woolsey's approval, brought in three additional young New Haven lawyers to help with instruction at the school. Although Yale College provided some financial support for administration and the library, the school remained proprietary until the early twentieth century. Baldwin continued as professor until 1919, while building a private and public career as the nation's leading railroad lawyer, ABA president (1890–1891), and Connecticut supreme court justice (1893–1907, chief justice 1907–1910) and governor (1911–1915).[48]

The ABA Committee on Legal Education and Admissions to the Bar, at its first annual meeting in 1879, submitted several resolutions for adoption. Those involving admission to the bar would require either three years of practice in a sister state or a three-year law school education that had at least "four well paid and efficient teachers." The chair of the committee, Carleton Hunt of Louisiana, convinced its members to propose in the law school curriculum resolution inclusion of Roman and civil law, comparative jurisprudence, and political economy. ABA members tabled all these resolutions.[49] Nevertheless, Baldwin considered the ABA Committee's continued efforts to support a rigorous three-year law school education as crucial to its more general acceptance by the end of the century.[50]

Behind the ABA effort to improve legal education was its purpose to "uphold the honor of the profession of the law." This was apparent from the committee's first report in 1879. At that time, 17 states—including Massachusetts, New York, Illinois, and California—admitted law school graduates to the bar without examination. However, the curricula in most law schools was not sufficiently comprehensive and some schools had granted diplomas after only six months study. The problem with raising standards for admission to state bars was that ABA members could not agree on whether law schools should be the dominant

---

[48] John H. Langbein, *Blackstone, Litchfield, and Yale: The Founding of the Yale Law School*, in HISTORY OF THE YALE LAW SCHOOL: THE TERCENTENNIAL LECTURES 17, 58–59, 61–63 (2004); Simeon Eben Baldwin, *Museum of Connecticut History*, https://museumofcthistory.org/2015/08/simeon-eben-baldwin; *see* FREDERICK H. JACKSON, SIMEON EBEN BALDWIN: LAWYER, SOCIAL SCIENTIST, STATESMAN (1955).

[49] *Proceedings*, 2 A.B.A. ANN. REP. 5, 14–15, 18 (1879). The committee's report surveyed the long history of Roman and continental European legal education, including Germany's historical jurisprudence, and its commitment to legal science. It then bemoaned the deficiencies of American law school education and called for a course of comparative jurisprudence, improved methods of instruction, and written examinations. Carleton Hunt, *Report of the Committee on Legal Education and Admissions to the Bar, id.* at 209, 212–23, 227–32. ABA members debated the committee's resolutions again during the 1880 annual meeting, where they tabled them again. 3 A.B.A. ANN. REP. 13–24, 29–46 (1880). Hunt, a law professor at the University of Louisiana, resigned from the committee in 1886. *See* BOYD, *supra* note 46, at 5.

[50] Simeon E. Baldwin, *The Study of Elementary Law: The Proper Beginning of a Legal Education*, 13 YALE L.J. 1, 4 (1903) [hereinafter Baldwin, *Study*]. Baldwin cited the examples of Harvard, Yale, and Boston University that by 1876 had met the ABA's three-year aspiration. *Id.* at 4. In 1904, 19 states required three years of law study to become a lawyer, although not all that time had to be in a law school. ABEL, *supra* note 44, at 52–53.

avenue to bar membership, and if so, what the length of study and curriculum would be, and whether there should be state reciprocity to practice law.[51]

William Hammond, one of the initial supporters of the ABA along with Baldwin, Hunt, and Field, took over as chair of the committee in 1889.[52] In 1891, the committee issued a lengthy report based on answers to questionnaires along with several resolutions for adoption. These recommended that each state supreme court create a board of bar examiners to admit attorneys who satisfied a comprehensive examination of basic legal subjects. States should encourage nonprofit law schools and the endowment of "chairs of elementary law and of scientific jurisprudence in such schools [to permit] teaching of law as a science." Finally, the committee had requested the U.S. Commissioner of Education to facilitate gathering information from foreign common law and civil law countries concerning their systems of legal education, an explicit comparative law effort, to report more fully at a later meeting.[53]

The committee report described a situation in which most applicants to state bars—perhaps 80 percent—had read law with a lawyer rather than attended a law school, of which there were 49 with 293 instructors and 3,667 students at the time of the survey. The report also summarized the literature on European civil law legal education, which demonstrated the "superiority of that system to any now in use in common law countries."[54] It explained that the first semester of a three to five-year civil law curriculum (compared to the usual two-year American law school) emphasized principles and concepts necessary for legal reasoning before studying rules that govern particular facts. Besides an elementary course to introduce legal science, the report favored the case method of instruction over practitioner textbook recitation. It endorsed historical jurisprudence over legal positivism as the correct legal philosophy.[55]

In 1893, the ABA added a bylaw to permit the creation of the Section of Legal Education to meet annually to discuss teaching methods and to make

---

[51] Max Radin, *The Achievements of the American Bar Association: A Sixty Year Record*, 25 A.B.A. J. 903, 1011–13 (1939); *id.* at 26 A.B.A. J. 19 (1940); *see supra* text accompanying note 47 (ABA Constitution). The ABA's efforts to improve legal education and the status of lawyers was the enterprise of elite lawyers, evidenced by the organization's small membership size. From 75 lawyers in 1878, the ABA grew to 750 in 1888 and 1,500 in 1898. James Grafton Rogers, *The American Bar Association in Retrospect*, *in* 1 LAW: A CENTURY OF PROGRESS, 1835–1935, at 166, 178–79 (Alison Reppy ed., 1937).

[52] *Standing Committees*, 12 A.B.A. ANN. REP. 93 (1889); *see* STEVENS, *supra* note 33, at 94–95; *supra* note 46 (Hammond).

[53] *Report of the Committee on Legal Education*, 14 A.B.A. ANN. REP. 301, 325–27, 349–51 (1891) [hereinafter 1891 *Report*]; BOYD, *supra* note 46, at 6; Radin, *supra* note 51, at 19. Sixteen states conferred a diploma privilege on certain law schools automatically admitting their graduates to the state bar. 1891 *Report*, *supra*, at 314. The Bureau of Education was in the U.S. Department of the Interior. The ABA tabled the committee's resolutions until the 1892 meeting. 1891 *Report*, *supra*, at 48–50, 356.

[54] 1891 *Report*, *supra* note 53, at 315–19, 327; Radin, *supra* note 51, at 19–20.

[55] 1891 *Report*, *supra* note 53, at 327–28, 332–33, 338–48.

recommendations that the ABA could refer to the Committee on Legal Education. Baldwin was the section's temporary chair and Hammond wrote its bylaws.[56] Hammond and Field both died in 1894, but a new type of full-time scholarly law professor, often knowledgeable about foreign legal systems, continued their efforts to improve legal education though the ABA's first section. To illustrate, the section elected Henry Rogers (1853–1926) its initial chair. Rogers began teaching as the first full-time professor at the University of Michigan Law Department in 1883, named professor of Roman law in 1885, and then served as dean until 1890. While section chair, Rogers was now Northwestern University president and in 1900, took the professorship of jurisprudence at Yale Law School (dean 1903–1916).[57] Two other examples of important scholars supporting comparative law in the early twentieth century were John Wigmore and Samuel Williston.[58]

In the address that Rogers delivered at the first section meeting, he provided a statistical overview of American legal education, emphasizing that law schools had become the predominant avenue to bar membership. Of the 72 law schools, 65 were affiliated with a university. A concerning fact, however, was that fewer than half the law students enrolled at the country's leading law schools entered with an academic degree. The only exception was Harvard Law School where 76 percent of the entrants had one. Michigan, Iowa, Boston, Yale, and Columbia ranged from 17 to 41 percent. Wade compared this general lack of a liberal education with the situation in continental Europe, where all law students were knowledgeable in foreign languages and the arts and sciences. He noted that Harvard in 1895 would begin to require a specific college degree for regular law students; those without that might enter as special students but must earn high marks to obtain the LL.B. degree.[59]

As the number of full-time law professors gradually increased, their collective interests diverged from those of the practicing bar represented in the ABA and its committees. The Section of Legal Education, with its own meeting of legal educators, was a step toward separation. The next step occurred in 1900 when,

---

[56] *By-Laws*, 16 A.B.A. ANN. REP. 84, 89 (1893) (Bylaw XIV); *Transactions, id.* at 7–10; *Proceedings of the Section of Legal Education, id.* at 366–67 [hereinafter 1893 *Proceedings*]; *see* BOYD, *supra* note 46, at 11–12; Radin, *supra* note 51, at 24. Baldwin and Hammond were among the five organizers of the section and Baldwin served as its first chair. 1893 *Proceedings, supra*, at 366–67.

[57] BOYD, *supra* note 46, at 12; 1893 *Proceedings, supra* note 56, at 368; Federal Judicial Center, *Rogers, Henry Wade*, https://www.fjc.gov/node/1387081; *see* Henry W. Roders, T*he Influence of Roman Law on English Law*, 26 CHAUTAUQUAN 496–500 (1898).

[58] Both graduated from Harvard Law School in the 1880s. STEVENS, *supra* note 33, at 45 n.20. Both presented papers at the ABA annual meeting. Samuel Williston, *Legal Education*, 16 A.B.A. ANN. REP. 391–400 (1893); John H. Wigmore, *A Principle of Orthodox Legal Education*, 17 A.B.A. ANN. REP. 453–59 (1894).

[59] Henry Wade Rogers, *Address*, 17 A.B.A. ANN. REP. 389, 393, 396–98 (1894); *see* Radin, *supra* note 51, at 23–24; *Report of the Committee on Legal Education and Admission to the Bar*, 20 A.B.A. ANN. REP. 349–50, 352–60 (1897).

at the invitation from the section, representatives from certain law schools met shortly before the ABA annual meeting and formed the Association of American Law Schools (AALS). To join this new organization, a law school needed to meet minimum quality standards: (1) require a high school diploma for entrance; (2) own or have access to a law library with basic sets of court reports; and (3) maintain a two-year curriculum, increased within five years to a three-year curriculum.[60] The prestige of the AALS from the beginning would permit market forces to eventually drive out the many low-quality schools then in existence.

4. Other Law Schools Adopt the Harvard Model

Harvard Law School's influence on American legal education up through the twentieth century was unequivocal. By 1900, the professionally oriented curriculum that Langdell and Ames fostered was dominant at other university-affiliated law schools. However, it also included the new type of legal educator, one dedicated to scholarship as well as teaching, course books utilizing the case method of instruction, and the structure of a three-year curriculum as a post-collegiate program.[61]

Initially, it was Harvard's law professors and students who spread the Harvard approach to other schools. These included William Keener in 1891 to Columbia, where he became dean; Eugene Wambaugh to the University of Iowa; and John Wigmore in 1893 to Northwestern University. Nevertheless, the scientific prestige of Harvard was enough for other universities to adopt the Harvard model. These involved Western Reserve and its new Law School in 1892, the University of Cincinnati Law School's 1895 reorganization by Dean William Taft, and Stanford with Law Dean Nathan Abbott hiring five new full-time law professors in 1900.[62]

---

[60] STEVENS, supra note 33, at 96–97; BOYD, supra note 46, at 15–16; E.W. Huffcut, *Association of American Law Schools*, 23 A.B.A. ANN. REP. 569–75 (1900); Radin, supra note 51, at 24–25. The ABA section and the AALS cooperated during the twentieth century to improve American legal education. *Id.* at 25–26. Baldwin and Rogers were AALS presidents in 1902 and 1905 respectively. *Presidents of the Association*, THE AALS DIRECTORY OF LAW TEACHERS 2019–2020, at i (2019).

[61] STEVENS, *supra* note 33, at 38–42, 59–64, 134; James Barr Ames, *Vocation of the Law Professor*, 48 AM. L. REG. 129, 137–39 (vol. 39 n.s., 1900). Ames cited the German use of full-time legal scholar professors as worthy of emulation. He also mentioned the example of Stanford, which hired five recent law graduates to be professors at the law school. *Id.* at 137, 141, 145. In 1895, Harvard had ten professors and more than 400 students; by 1907 those numbers were 14 professors and 700 students. STEVENS, *supra*, at 60.

[62] LAWRENCE M. FRIEDMAN, A HISTORY OF AMERICAN LAW 470–71 (3d ed. 2005) [hereinafter FRIEDMAN, HISTORY]; STEVENS, supra note 33, at 60–64, 73, 84 n.6; *see* A HISTORY OF THE SCHOOL OF LAW: COLUMBIA UNIVERSITY 135–86 (Julius Goebel, Jr., ed., 1955) [hereinafter COLUMBIA LAW SCHOOL]. In 1891, Northwestern University purchased Union College of Law. STEVENS, *supra*, at 77–78.

Another example was the University of Wisconsin's Law School. After its founding in 1868, the curriculum modeled law office subjects to compete with apprenticeship training. However, in 1892, Charles Kendall Adams became university president. Prior to teaching history at Michigan, Adams, like Eliot, had toured European universities in the 1860s. Convinced of their scientific approach, Adams set up research seminars that he characterized as history laboratories, where future historians could work with original documents. At Wisconsin, Adams wanted to improve the Law School. He favored the ideas of a law library serving as a laboratory and using the case method pedagogy. He hired a local attorney as associate dean, Charles Gregory, to carry out the conversion. During the summer, Gregory visited Ames at Harvard and Keener at Columbia. Gregory returned convinced and until his departure in 1901 hired as many new professors trained in the case method as he could. Gregory helped organize the AALS and made Wisconsin a founding member.[63]

William Harper (1856–1906), the first president of the University of Chicago from 1892, similarly wanted a German-style research mission for graduate education at his new institution.[64] When he was ready to open a law school in 1900, he turned to Eliot and Dean Ames at Harvard for advice and support, even inviting the Harvard faculty to teach at Chicago. Harvard's Joseph Beale took the post of dean. Ernst Freund (1864–1932), a political scientist on the Law School's steering committee, promoted the school's obligation to "cultivate and encourage the scientific study of systematic and comparative jurisprudence, legal history, and the principles of legislation."[65]

Freund, raised and educated in Germany, received a J.U.D. doctorate in law at the University of Heidelberg in 1884 and then emigrated to the United States. After practicing law in New York, he taught Roman law in the political economy department at Chicago from 1894 to 1902, and then as the Law School opened in 1902, served there as professor until his death. Freund's interest in comparative legal and political systems, especially the emerging fields of legislation and administrative law, infused his publications from 1897.[66]

---

[63] Macgill & Newmyer, *supra* note 34, at 59–60.

[64] FRANK L. ELLSWORTH, LAW ON THE MIDWAY: THE FOUNDING OF THE UNIVERSITY OF CHICAGO LAW SCHOOL 30–36, 92–98 (1977); Shils & Roberts, *supra* note 21, at 169; *see* JOHN W. BOYER, THE UNIVERSITY OF CHICAGO: A HISTORY 67–148 (2015). "In a few cases, a whole department at the new University was shaped by German paradigms." *Id.* at 139; *see id.* at 139–42 (chemistry, history, and mathematics), To illustrate, Albion Small, the founding professor of the Chicago sociology department, studied in Berlin and Leipzig, interpreted the work of German social scientists, and encouraged his students to study in Germany. *Id.* at 137–38.

[65] ELLSWORTH, *supra* note 64, at 36–40, 52–77, 98–100; STEVENS, *supra* note 33, at 39–40, 60 (quotation at 40); *see id.* at 42 n.2; Ernst Freund, *The Proposed German Civil Code*, 24 AM. L. REV. 237–54 (1890); Reimann, *German Professoriate, supra* note 26, at 175. Freund also recommended the teaching of Roman law. STEVENS, *supra*, at 40.

[66] John C. Reitz, *The Influence of Ernst Freund on American Law*, *in* DER EINFLUSS DEUTSCHEN EMIGRANTEN AUF DIE RECHTSENTWICKLUNG IN DEN USA UND IN DEUTSCHLAND 423–35 (Marcus Lutter et al. eds., 1993); *see* ERNST FREUND, THE LEGAL NATURE OF CORPORATIONS (1897)

In 1913, the Carnegie Foundation brought Josef Redlich, a University of Vienna law professor, to the United States to study the case method of legal instruction. Reviewing its history, he made the comparison to legal science.

> For Anglo-American law, just as much as for the common German law of the nineteenth century, the birth and powerful influence of the new historical method marks the turning-point at which the inheritance of the Middle Ages—legal craftsmanship and practical expertness in law—becomes converted into legal science. What Savigny and his pupils and the entire legal-historical school of Germany accomplished for the common law of Germany has been performed in no less admirable fashion in the last half-century for the English common law by such men as [James] Thayer [at Harvard], Langdell, Ames, and [Melville] Bigelow [as Boston University law dean] in America.[67]

5. Refining Legal Science: Emulating Germany's Law Curriculum

Baldwin was an early advocate for a broader law curriculum than that generally available in American law schools after the Civil War. He was familiar with the wider range of courses offered at German and French law faculties. Thus, he saw merit at Yale and Boston University law schools, which even in 1877 offered as part of their scientific curriculum Roman law, jurisprudence, and international law.[68] By 1891, ten law schools taught Roman law and five had a course in jurisprudence or legal history.[69]

The ABA Committee on Legal Education and Admissions to the Bar led by Hammond took the lead in analyzing law school curricula and proposing

---

(Anglo-American, French, and German corporation law); *id.*, ADMINISTRATIVE POWERS OVER PERSONS AND PROPERTY: A COMPARATIVE SURVEY (1928) (Prussian, German, English, New York, and U.S. federal law). Freund served as president of the American Political Science Association in 1915. Reitz, *supra*, at 432 n.47.

[67] JOSEF REDLICH, THE COMMON LAW AND THE CASE METHOD IN AMERICAN UNIVERSITY LAW SCHOOLS: A REPORT TO THE CARNEGIE FOUNDATION FOR THE ADVANCEMENT OF TEACHING 43 (1914); *see id.* at 54–59; STEVENS, *supra* note 33, at 112–13, 117–20; David M. Rabban, *Melville M. Bigelow: Boston University's Neglected Pioneer of Historical Legal Scholarship in America*, 91 B.U. L. REV. 1–42 (2011); Reimann, *German Professoriate*, *supra* note 26, at 176, 180. *See also* JAMES B. THAYER, LEX AQUILIA [Digest 9.2]: TEXT, TRANSLATION AND COMMENTARY, ON GIFTS BETWEEN HUSBAND AND WIFE [Digest 24.1] (1929, reprint 2008).

[68] Simeon E. Baldwin, *Graduate Courses: At Law Schools*, 11 J. SOC. SCI.123, 131–32, 134–36 (1880). "[N]o one can look over the topics of instruction proposed by the faculty of law at a European University, without observing how many are absent, which are of the first importance to an American lawyer." *Id.* at 135.

[69] REED, *supra* note 45, at 300–01. Columbia, Michigan, and Northwestern offered a course in comparative constitutional law. *Id.* at 302.

reform. In 1892, it found that almost all law schools taught practical private law subjects, using a technical rather than scientific or philosophical view of law. The schools varied in their teaching methods, ranging from textbook recitation, lecture, or case analysis. Since more than two years of study was impracticable at most law schools, the committee recommended that schools (1) tighten entrance requirements; (2) offer electives in public law, the history and philosophy of law and government, and comparative law; and (3) provide post-graduate courses in general jurisprudence and public law.[70]

The committee suggested that law schools could improve the effectiveness of their teaching by adapting the continental European scientific approach. Referring to Savigny's history of Roman law, the committee traced the development of teaching at European law faculties from the time of the glossators until later jurists began systematizing legal principles that could support a theory of law. It then quoted Savigny's notion of historical jurisprudence.[71]

> All of a science that is the product of continuous development forms an organic whole: and no portion of it can be thoroughly understood unless it is studied in connection with the rest. Thus the entire system of legal science which governs our actions can only be thoroughly mastered by historical study, going back to its first beginning and following it into all later ramifications.[72]

Finally, the committee, contrasting American student textbooks intended for practitioners, described nineteenth-century student textbooks, which in Germany were the result of Pandectist legal science that could instruct law students in the basic principles of private law. "[T]he student acquires the law as a whole and not as a congeries of separate and independent doctrines."[73]

The committee insisted that America's best jurists worked with common law principles in their practice, some wrote noteworthy treatises, and that the common law was capable of systematization. Its concern was with the use of textbook practitioner manuals to educate law students. "It is absurd to expect that a

---

[70] *Report of the Committee on Legal Education*, 15 A.B.A. ANN. REP. 317, 319–25, 328–29 (1892) [hereinafter 1892 *Report*]; Radin, *supra* note 51, at 21, 23.

[71] 1892 *Report, supra* note 70, at 330–36. On the advantages of historical jurisprudence in teaching elementary law, *see id.* at 344–48.

[72] 1892 *Report, supra* note 70, at 336 (quoting and citing SAVIGNY, 5 HISTORY OF THE ROMAN LAW IN THE MIDDLE AGES 474) (Cathcart had translated volume 1 of this work into English in 1829); see *supra* text accompanying note 5 (Savigny's German edition). Of the committee members, only Hammond would have had the knowledge required to translate from the German in volume 5.

[73] 1892 *Report, supra* note 70, at 337–38. The committee distinguished its criticism of American textbooks from those materials professors had developed using cases. "We do not mean to underrate ... selected cases as objects of study, either in the deduction of principles ... or (what we regard as of still greater use) as teaching the historical growth and development of such principles." *Id.* at 339. Nevertheless, the case method was inefficient since it could only treat a few topics of a legal subject. *Id.* at 340–41, 361.

class of beginners will strike out a scientific method for themselves in a mass of such 'practical' rubbish, merely because we deafen them with praises of the logical consistency and scientific character of the law."[74] There were two methods to derive legal concepts and principles: the historical and the logical. The first studies the origin and growth of legal terms historically. The second compares the relationship of legal terms to each other, assuming they belong to a harmonious system, and deduce the precise meaning of each term from the relationship.[75] "[T]he most important recommendation we can make is the abandonment of the present method of teaching the law mainly by distinct topics, at least during the first year of the course, and the substitution for it of a careful and systematic study of the system as a whole after the European method."[76]

Baldwin supported Hammond and the committee in its effort to improve American legal education. He argued for one or more introductory courses in the first year of law school, like that offered at German law faculties, to properly orient students toward the study of cases in the diverse subjects covered in the curriculum. "[L]aw schools must set before each incoming class the outlines of law in general, substantive and adjective, in orderly and scientific arrangement."[77] He denied that Langdell's inductive method was the only scientific approach to learning law and described Francis Bacon's empirical approach to distilling legal rules and principles appropriate for an elementary student text of private law. In addition, Baldwin favored historical jurisprudence and referred to the ease of learning legal principles and rules from Justinian's *Institutes* or a civil law codification.[78]

There were a few other jurists promoting legal science who believed that American law schools should broaden their curriculum to approximate the German model. In addition to private law subjects, this would include an introductory course; public law offerings besides criminal and constitutional law; and perhaps a few courses in legal history, legal philosophy, or the social sciences affecting law. Once Harvard introduced electives to the curriculum, that idea spread to other prestigious law schools that were following the Harvard model in other respects.[79] In 1895 and 1897, the ABA Legal Education Committee recommended three years of legal education and raising law school entrance requirements to promote a liberal education among entrants. It supported this

---

[74] *Id.* at 348–51 (quotation at 350).
[75] *Id.* at 352–56. "[T]he historical method commends itself for elementary teaching because it shows the law neither in the form of mere abstraction nor in that of individual cases, but illustrates at every step the process by which it rises from the mere evidential fact to the highest generalization." *Id.* at 344.
[76] *Id.* at 360.
[77] Baldwin, *Study, supra* note 50, at 6. A typical book used at Berlin University was JOSEF KOHLER, EINFÜHRUNG IN DIE RECHTSWISSENSCHAFT (2d ed. 1905, 1st ed. 1901).
[78] Baldwin, *Study, supra* note 50, at 6–12, 14–15.
[79] REED, *supra* note 45, at 306–11, 352–53, 458; STEVENS, *supra* note 33, at 39–41.

position by referring to the superior legal education in Europe, including in Great Britain. It also backed the elective system featuring public law, legal philosophy, and legal history.[80]

Furthermore, in 1895, the ABA created a Special Committee on Uniformity of Procedure and Comparative Law. Woodrow Wilson was an initial member. The impetus behind the committee's formation was to exchange delegates between the newly established Society of Comparative Legislation in London and the ABA.[81] In 1896, the committee reported on the society's research into procedural systems in British colonies, which suggested to the committee that it should make a similar inquiry into the American state procedural regimes. Promoting legal uniformity was the committee's goal.[82]

The ABA committee for the first time recommended that law schools teach civil law or comparative law in 1895. "[T]he Civil law is but one of the many elements which have concurred in the genesis of what we call the law of England and America. Its study should be preliminary or introductory." The committee then detailed what such a course might encompass, including a comparative look at the case law of continental Europe and the United States.[83] In 1894, William Howe, a member of the committee and Louisiana lawyer, had delivered the Storrs lectures at Yale Law School comparing the civil law and common law. His address at the 1895 ABA annual meeting illustrated the prevalence of historical jurisprudence, detailing the impact of Roman law on English law. Howe served as president of the ABA from 1897 to 1898.[84] Charles Needham provided another example.

> Law is a growth, the result of long continued observance of any custom and of legislation, prompted by new conditions and experiences; therefore to understand a rule of law we must know the conditions and causes that brought it into being. For this reason law should be studied historically and comparatively.[85]

---

[80] *Report of the Committee on Legal Education*, 18 A.B.A. ANN. REP. 309, 317–20 (1895) [hereinafter 1895 *Report*]; *id.*, 20 A.B.A. ANN. REP. 349, 352–60, 365–67, 371–74 (1897). In 1895, the committee found that eight law schools taught Roman law, seven jurisprudence, and three historical jurisprudence, and four political science. 1895 *Report*, *supra*, at 318.

[81] *Transactions*, 18 A.B.A. ANN. REP. 3, 33–34, 36–37 (1895); *Special Committees*, *id.* at 115, 117.

[82] *Transactions*, 19 A.B.A. ANN. REP. 3, 22–27, 47, 700 (1896); *see Report of Committee on Uniformity of Procedure and Comparative Law*, *id.* at 411–32. The ABA disbanded the committee in 1898 after resistance from some ABA members that the committee might use its comparative study of foreign procedural systems to attempt to foster codification of federal procedure. *Transactions*, 21 A.B.A. ANN. REP. 33–36, 42–43 (1898); *see Report of the Committee on Uniformity of Procedure*, *id.* at 454–65.

[83] 1895 *Report*, *supra* note 80, at 326–31 (quotation at 328).

[84] Henry Plauché Dart, *William Wirt Howe: Twentieth President of Association*, 14 A.B.A. J. 541, 544 (1928); *see* William Wirt Howe, *The Historical Relation of the Roman Law to the Law of England*, 18 A.B.A. ANN. REP. 275–93 (1895). Howe began his address with a reference to Savigny. *Id.* at 275.

[85] Charles W. Needham, *Schools of Law: The Subjects, Order and Method of Study*, 21 A.B.A. ANN. REP. 615, 621 (1898).

In 1899, Howe, as chair of the Section of Legal Education, delivered his address on comparative jurisprudence. The three other papers presented at that meeting were about legal education in Canada, England, and France.[86] In 1900, the cection chair's address concerned legal education in the world, surveying Brazil, Canada, China, England, France, Germany, India, Japan, Mexico, Russia, and the USA.[87]

6. Law Libraries

By 1875, Harvard Law School had the largest university law collection in the United States with 15,000 volumes, consistent with Harvard's push to develop a scientific approach to scholarship and teaching. Because of the Roman and civil law books from Livermore and Story and other purchases, Harvard was also the principal comparative law library prior to the Civil War. The only other university law school libraries in the top 11 American law libraries were at Yale (8,000 volumes) and Michigan (3,000 volumes).[88]

America's leading law library in 1875 was at the Library of Congress with 35,000 volumes. Its comparative law collection benefited from the 6,500 books that Jefferson sold to the government after the Capitol burned during the British invasion in the War of 1814. In 1832, Congress created the Law Library of Congress as a separate administrative unit to service members of Congress along with Supreme Court justices. In 1837, Congress regularized an exchange of books, serials, and documents with the French government, which broadened to include other governments and foreign libraries after 1840. By 1900, the law library had grown to 103,000 volumes, of which 12 percent were in languages other than English.[89]

Much of the success of the Law Library of Congress after the Civil War was due to Ainsworth Spofford, who served as librarian for the Library of Congress from 1864 to 1897. He had a vision to make it a national library on a par with the leading examples in Europe. In 1897, when the library moved from the Capitol into its own separate building, the largest library building in the world at that

---

[86] William Wirt Howe, *The Study of Comparative Jurisprudence*, 22 A.B.A. ANN. REP. 567–77 (1899); *see id.* at 579–624.

[87] Charles Noble Gregory, *The State of Legal Education in the World*, 23 A.B.A. ANN. REP. 459–74 (1900), *reprinted in* 34 AM. L. REV. 841–55 (1900).

[88] David S. Clark, *Nation Building and Law Collections: The Remarkable Development of Comparative Law Libraries in the United States*, 109 LAW LIBR. J. 499, 527–28, 538, 542–43 (2017) [hereinafter Clark, *Nation Building*]; *see supra* ch. 4, pt. E.3 (Harvard's law collection). In 1845, the foreign and comparative law books in Harvard's library numbered 12,000 volumes, equaling or exceeding the libraries of Europe. Clark, *supra*, at 542.

[89] Clark, *Nation Building*, *supra* note 88, at 516–17, 528, 544–47; *see supra* ch. 4, pt. E.3 (Law Library of Congress).

time, Congress further improved the status of the institution by allowing the librarian to make rules for its own governance. The choice of librarian would also be subject to Senate confirmation.[90]

D. Historical Jurisprudence against Codification: James Carter and David Dudley Field

In addition to its effect on the structure of American universities and law school teaching methods, historical jurisprudence provided a theoretical bulwark against further codification of private law.[91] At the time of the ABA's creation, most lawyers were against new efforts to codify, including in commercial law where the benefits of national uniformity were most obvious.[92] Nevertheless, one of the stated purposes of the ABA was to "advance ... uniformity of legislation."[93]

In the early 1880s, debates in New York concerning codification of private law drew from two major strands of European civil law ideology. On one side was David Field's (1805–1894) systematic projects to codify major areas of New York state law, which derived from the success of French codification, and on the other side was James Carter's (1827–1903) historical jurisprudence influenced by German jurists such as Savigny. The debate between these two New York jurists crystalized the preference for either legislative or judge-made rules.[94]

The idea of codification, illustrated by the French and Louisiana codes, was to simplify the law by gathering legal rules and principles from their various sources, whether treatises in the civil law or judicial reports in the common law, and restating them in a systematic and complete fashion for a general subject of law. The French division into five codes was the predominant model for the nineteenth century. The accomplishment of that task would provide certainty and authority to law.[95]

In 1865, Field published a civil code, divided into four parts analogous to the French Napoleonic Code, which he proposed for New York.[96] The legislature approved the code twice, but governors turned it down, on the last occasion

---

[90] Clark, *Nation Building*, supra note 88, at 517, 545.
[91] *See generally* RABBAN, *supra* note 2, at 325–80.
[92] Radin, *supra* note 51, at 907. For an analysis of the codification debate from the perspective of political interest and emotional commitment, *see* Aniceto Masferrer, *Defense of the Common Law against Postbellum American Codification: Reasonable and Fallacious Argumentation*, 50 AM. J. LEG. HIST. 355–430 (2008–2010).
[93] Radin, *supra* note 51, at 1007; *see supra* text accompanying note 47 (ABA Constitution).
[94] Reimann, *Historical School*, supra note 4, at 99–101; *see* KUNAL M. PARKER, COMMON LAW, HISTORY, AND DEMOCRACY IN AMERICA, 1790–1900: LEGAL THOUGHT BEFORE MODERNISM 238–43 (2011); Andrew P. Morriss, *Codification and Right Answers*, 74 CHI.-KENT L. REV. 355–91 (1999).
[95] *See supra* ch. 4, pt. H (Livingston and Field).
[96] *See* HERGET, JURISPRUDENCE, *supra* note 11, at 356 (outline of code).

in 1885. Nonetheless, Field continued to argue for the code's adoption until his death in 1894. Field had more success in New York with the draft penal code of 1865, which went into effect in 1881 along with the earlier code of criminal procedure. California, where Field's brother Stephen was a prominent lawyer and assemblyman, found codification persuasive. Beginning in 1850, the California legislature adopted Field's two procedure codes, civil code (suitably modified), and penal code.[97]

The victory of Carter and his historical jurisprudence, marked by the defeat of Field's civil code in New York, largely settled the debate among the legal elite in the eastern United States. However, many western states, besides California, adopted some version of one or more of Field's codes.[98] Carter was against private law codification because he believed it would shift the locus of rule-making from the courts to legislatures. The latter, staffed by politicians of various backgrounds, desirous of re-election, relied on passion to please their constituents in the short term. Alternatively, judges—at least appellate judges who authoritatively determined rules—were more likely chosen for their qualifications in working with the law. Codes would impair the gradual growth, development, and improvement of the law. By freezing legal rules, codes prevented natural evolution. Historical jurisprudence, deeply indebted to Savigny, taught that rules should derive from a people's common wisdom. Even codes drafted by legal experts were inferior to rules slowly developed by self-correcting growth. Judges, members of a community, would apply a social standard of justice, a part of culture. Not incidentally, lawyers and judges could also mobilize Carter's philosophy against social and economic legislation, which they did during this period.[99]

Carter presented his criticism against codification as limited to private law. The New York City Bar authorized a pamphlet during the decisive battle against

---

[97] FRIEDMAN, HISTORY, *supra* note 62, at 295–98, 302–03; Reimann, *Historical School*, supra note 4, at 99–101, 103; *see* David Dudley Field, *Law Reform in the United States and Its Influence Abroad*, 25 AM. L. REV. 515–35 (1891); Gunther A. Weiss, *The Enchantment of Codification in the Common-Law World*, 25 YALE J. INT'L L. 435, 508–14 (2000); Code Napoleon, 3 *Am. L. Reg.* 641–50 (1855). Stephen Field was a justice on the California supreme court from 1857 to 1863, when Abraham Lincoln nominated him to the U.S. Supreme Court, where he served until 1897. Paul Kens, *Field, Stephen Johnson (1816-1899)*, *in* THE OXFORD COMPANION TO AMERICAN LAW 309 (Kermit L. Hall et al. eds, 2002).

[98] FRIEDMAN, HISTORY, *supra* note 62, at 295–96, 302–04, 479; William B. Fisch, *The Dakota Civil Code: More Notes for an Uncelebrated Centennial*, 45 N.D. L. REV. 9, 25–53 (1968); Andrew P. Morriss, "THIS STATE WILL SOON HAVE PLENTY OF LAWS,"—LESSONS FROM ONE HUNDRED YEARS OF CODIFICATION IN MONTANA, 56 Mont. L. Rev. 359, 364–65, 372–424 (1995); Radin, *supra* note 51, at 1007. Field's code of civil procedure was the most successful of his codes; thus, besides many western states, North and South Carolina also adopted one of its versions. Before 1900, almost all states had reformed civil procedure, especially related to pleading. FRIEDMAN, *supra*, at 295, 297.

[99] FRIEDMAN, HISTORY, *supra* note 62, at 302–03; RABBAN, *supra* note 2, at 31–32; Reimann, *Historical School*, *supra* note 4, at 103–07; *see* JAMES C. CARTER, THE PROPOSED CODIFICATION OF OUR COMMON LAW (1884) [hereinafter CARTER, PROPOSED CODIFICATION] (Carter prepared this pamphlet for a committee of the Bar Association of the City of New York). Carter argued that common judge-found law was characteristic of societies with popular rule and Anglo-Saxon liberty, while codes had existed in despotic Latin regimes since the period of Roman emperors. *Id.* at 6–9.

Field's civil code, in which Carter framed the debate as one about the desirability of written law versus unwritten law. The former was appropriate for subjects in which certainty was paramount, while the latter fit situations in which the preferred goal was justice. Carter acknowledged that public law and procedure required certainty, but private law, including most of commercial law, required justice to serve a free people.[100]

The ABA membership split on the question of codification. In 1884, it approved a Special Committee on Delay and Uncertainty in the Administration of Justice, with Field as chair. Two years later, the two members of the committee submitted a report and resolution that "The law itself should be reduced, so far as possible, to the form of a statute."[101] In the report, Field and John Dillon, who became ABA president in 1891–1892, reviewed the usual arguments.

> [T]he uncodified portion of the common law, so far as it is settled by judicial decisions, should be enacted by the legislature in as brief a compass as possible and published for the use of judges and lawyers, and for the information of the people. We repel the idea, that the reduction of the law, so far as practicable, to the form of a statute would check the natural growth of law.[102]

The committee contented that centering lawmaking in the legislature was democratic, providing certainty of rules, available for people to know before litigation, and would rightly limit the judicial function to interpretation.[103] Buttressing Field's push for codification, the ABA president-elect, Thomas Semmes, delivered the 1886 annual address on the same topic.[104] He concluded:

---

[100] CARTER, PROPOSED CODIFICATION, supra note 99, at 12–22; id., *The Provinces of the Written and the Unwritten Law*, 24 AM. L. REV. 1–24 (1890); David Dudley Field, *Codification: Mr. Field's Answer to Mr. Carter*, id. at 255–66; Reimann, *Historical School*, supra note 4, at 114–18. Carter thought it preferable that judges formulate written procedural law rather than legislatures. CARTER, PROPOSED CODIFICATION, supra, at 19–20, 83–85.

[101] *Report of the Special Committee on Delay and Uncertainty in the Administration of Justice* [hereinafter *ABA Special Committee*], 9 A.B.A. ANN. REP. 325–27, 356, 387–88 (1886). Field and Dillon explained that the committee selected the word statute instead of code, seemingly to reduce emotional reaction. Id. at 332–33; see *Transactions*, id. at 3, 14–16. For the diverse opinions of ABA members concerning codification, see *Answers*, 9 A.B.A. ANN. REP. 395–402 (1886).

[102] *ABA Special Committee*, supra note 101, at 327; see id. at 327–33.

[103] Id. at 327–29, 333; see *Transactions*, supra note 101, at 11–74; John F. Dillon, *Codification*, 20 AM. L. REV. 1–47 (1886).

[104] Thomas J. Semmes, *Annual Address [Codification: The Natural Result of the Evolution of the Law]*, 9 A.B.A. ANN. REP. 189–214 (1886), see id. at 104, 555. Semmes was a law professor at the University of Louisiana from 1873 to 1899, teaching civil law for many years. Semmes, *Thomas Jenkins*, in A DICTIONARY OF LOUISIANA BIOGRAPHY (Glenn R. Conrad ed., 1988), https://www.lahistory.org (select Resources, then Dictionary, then Semmes). In 1888, George Hoadly, former governor of Ohio and a law professor at the University of Cincinnati for almost two decades, also delivered the ABA annual address promoting legal codification. *Annual Address [Codification]*, 11 A.B.A. ANN. REP. 219–46 (1888); reprinted in George Hoadly, *Codification of the Common Law*, 23 AM. L. REV. 495–520 (1889); see George Hoadly, 1 *Bench and Bar of Ohio: A Compendium of History and Biography* 87–89 (George Irving Reed ed., 1897).

> The history of codification teaches that the task of preparing a code of laws is difficult, that its proper execution is a work of years, to be entrusted not to a deciduous committee of fugitive legislators, but to a permanent commission of the most enlightened and cultivated jurists, whose *projet*, prior to adoption, should be subjected to rigid and universal criticism.[105]

Herget identified further support for systematizing American law from another ABA source, the Committee on the Arrangement of the Law. Henry Terry, teaching American law at the University of Tokyo, sent the committee a letter in 1888 recommending classification using principles and concepts from a treatise he had published. The committee published the letter and later supported a theoretical and a practical classification of American law. Terry, who denied much knowledge of the civil law, must have absorbed certain fundamentals from his experience in Japan during the height of its debate on whether to transplant French, German, or Anglo-American law to buttress its efforts to industrialize and to deal with Western powers.[106] By the early twentieth century, jurists and the ABA had lost interest in pursuing classification of the law as a worthwhile endeavor.[107]

Field, who became ABA president for 1888–1889, also submitted a resolution at the 1886 ABA annual meeting in support of a U.S. Senate bill to create a commission to formulate a federal code of procedure.[108] The next year, Baldwin's Jurisprudence and Law Reform Committee issued a report fully supporting the federal initiative to include both civil and criminal procedure.[109] Baldwin had been a member of that ABA Committee since its creation in 1878. In Field's presidential address at the 1889 ABA annual meeting, he made another argument for the general codification of American law.

> What is required ... is a treble process—the process of elimination, the process of condensation, and the process of classification. This performance would make a code, call it by whatever other name you please. ... Many lawyers are

---

[105] Semmes, *supra* note 104, at 213–14.

[106] HERGET, JURISPRUDENCE, *supra* note 11, at 53–62, 65–73; *see* HENRY T. TERRY, SOME LEADING PRINCIPLES OF ANGLO-AMERICAN LAW: EXPANDED WITH A VIEW TO ITS ARRANGEMENT AND CODIFICATION (1884); *Report of the Committee on Arrangement of the Law*, 12 A.B.A. ANN. REP. 327–38 (1889). Terry taught at the Imperial University (Tokyo) from 1877 to 1884 and 1894 to 1912. HERGET, *supra*, at 54.

[107] HERGET, JURISPRUDENCE, *supra* note 11, at 75–81. Pound explicitly came out against efforts at classification. *Id.* at 78–79.

[108] *Memorandum of Subjects Referred to Committees*, 9 A.B.A. ANN. REP. 551 (1886); *Officers*, 11 A.B.A. ANN. REP. 117 (1888). The ABA tabled Field's procedure resolution and referred it to the Committee on Jurisprudence and Law Reform. *Transactions*, *supra* note 101, at 73, 75, 81.

[109] *Report of the Committee on Jurisprudence and Law Reform Concerning a Federal Code of Procedure*, 10 A.B.A. ANN. REP. 317–20 (1887).

frightened by the idea of a code.... I insist that it is the first duty of a government to bring the laws to the knowledge of the people....

The adversaries of codification stand in this dilemma. They must insist either that there are no old laws as yet unwritten, or that all are written somewhere. Now, if they are written anywhere, they exist for the whole body of citizens, not alone for the lawyers, and therefore should be put into a form where the citizens can find and understand them. This can be accomplished by no other means than by collecting, condensing and arranging them.[110]

In 1890, Carter responded to Field in the ABA's annual address. In addition to codification, Carter also rejected analytical positivism and explained his approach to historical jurisprudence for American law.[111]

That the judge can not *make* the law is accepted from the start.... It is agreed that the true rule must be somehow *found*. Judges and advocates—all together—engage in the *search*.... [It is plain] (1) that the whole process consists in a *search* to find a rule; (2) that the rule thus sought for is the *just* rule...; (3) that it is tacitly assumed... that they have a *common standard of justice*...; (4) that the field of search is the habits, customs, business and manners of the people, and those previously declared rules which have sprung out of previous similar inquiries.... The conclusion is already suggested that our unwritten law—which is the main body of our law—is not a command, or a body of commands, but consists of rules springing from the social standard of justice, or from the habits and customs from which that standard has itself been derived.[112]

Carter then surveyed Roman and English history to show that societies always had judges before they had formal law. But law itself existed, which judges administered derived from the social standard of justice, that is, the habits and customs of the people. Justice was thus an oracle, not a force. Law's true character was that of an inductive science engaged in the observation and classification of facts. In advanced societies, legislation might supplement, but should not counter, the unconscious rules found in society.[113]

After Carter retired from his law practice, Dean Ames at Harvard approved a series of lectures that Carter was to deliver in 1904–1905. Published after his death as *The Origin, Growth and Function of Law* (1907), Carter tracked Savigny's

---

[110] *Address of David Dudley Field*, 12 A.B.A. Ann. Rep. 149, 230–32 (1889); *reprinted in* 23 Am. L. Rev. 946–57 (1889).
[111] James C. Carter, *Annual Address: The Ideal and the Actual in the Law*, 13 A.B.A. Ann. Rep. 217, 222–25 (1890) [hereinafter Carter, *Ideal*]; *reprinted in* 24 Am. L. Rev. 752–78 (1890).
[112] Carter, *Ideal*, *supra* note 111, at 224–25 (italics in original).
[113] *Id.* at 225–45.

historical jurisprudence and legal science and argued that custom furnished the rules governing human conduct. A judicial decision put the stamp of public approval on custom and thus authenticated it. This should settle a dispute, using an appropriate and genuine rule, and determine right and wrong. Courts do not make law; they discover it.[114]

From 1879, those lawyers supportive of the Jurisprudence and Law Reform Committee needed a term to replace "codification," which had become taboo with many of their colleagues. The synonym adopted was "uniformity" and its derivatives. Max Radin found that the "same persons who argued that it was against the genius of the common law to rephrase its rules in statutory form, were equally emphatic against the confusion and disturbances caused by the variety of laws [within and among states] in certain fields."[115] Consequently, in 1889, the ABA approved a Special Committee on Uniform State Laws. The next year, those ABA lawyers supportive of the uniformity goal convinced the New York legislature to adopt an act authorizing appointment of "commissioners for the promotion of uniformity of legislation in the United States." In 1892, nine states sent commissioners to a national conference on uniform legislation that met just prior to the annual ABA meeting.[116]

The National Conference of Commissioners on Uniform State Laws (also known as the Uniform Laws Commission, ULC) became a separate organization, but still connected functionally with the ABA. By 1912, all American states had representatives to the conference. The ULC operated by drafting model laws on subjects of interest, approving them, and then attempting to secure adoption as legislation (preferably as written, but often altered) in as many states as possible. Its most successful project in the nineteenth century was the Uniform Negotiable Instruments Law (NIL, 1896).[117] Williston drafted the Uniform Sales Act, promulgated in 1906, which however, depended on using

---

[114] JAMES COOLIDGE CARTER, THE ORIGIN, GROWTH AND FUNCTION OF LAW: BEING A COURSE OF LECTURES PREPARED FOR DELIVERY BEFORE THE LAW SCHOOL OF HARVARD UNIVERSITY 59, 65, 84–86, 118–20 (1907); see Lewis A. Grossman, *James Coolidge Carter and Mugwump Jurisprudence*, 20 L. & HIST. REV. 577–79, 587–88, 595–619 (2002).

[115] Radin, *supra* note 51, at 1007–08; *Committees*, 1 A.B.A. [ANN. REP.] 38 (1878).

[116] FRIEDMAN, HISTORY, *supra* note 62, at 498; Radin, *supra* note 51, at 1008; *Report of the Committee on Uniform State Laws*, 13 A.B.A. ANN. REP. 336–37 (1890). The ABA Special Committee on Uniform State Laws continued through the end of the century. *Special Committees*, 23 A.B.A. ANN. REP. 99 (1900).

[117] FRIEDMAN, HISTORY, *supra* note 62, at 305–06, 408–09, 498, 563; Radin, *supra* note 51, at 1008. In 1900, 35 states and territories were members of the ULC. The original name of the ULC was the Conference of the State Boards of Commissioners on Promoting Uniformity of Law in the U.S. In 1905, it changed its name to Commissioners on Uniform State Laws, and then in 1915, to National Conference of Commissioners on Uniform State Laws. In 2006, the Conference adopted the informal name, Uniform Law Commission. ROBERT A. STEIN, FORMING A MORE PERFECT UNION: A HISTORY OF THE UNIFORM LAW COMMISSION 19, 28–29, 31 (2013), at Uniform Law Commission, https://www.uniformlaws.org/newsandpublications/publications.

Williston's treatise on sales to provide lawyers meaningful guidance in analyzing cases.[118]

The NIL was an interesting illustration of the circuitous influence of comparative law in the late nineteenth century that drew upon the idea of French codification. Field, as we earlier saw, was familiar with the French and Louisiana codes. Although New York rejected his proposed civil code, California adopted most of it in 1872, including 117 provisions related to negotiable instruments. These articles covered bills of exchange, promissory notes, bank notes, checks, bonds, and certificates of deposit. The NIL split its sections into four titles, taken verbatim and in the same order as the six chapters of the California code. In addition, the NIL copied many articles from California, including the scope of coverage. A practical reason for following the California civil code rather than the English Bills of Exchange Act (1882) was that six states had already enacted the California rules. The hope for success with state adoptions of the NIL to promote the ULC's uniformity depended on the momentum that seven American states would provide.[119]

E. Other Uses of Roman and Civil Law

1. Teaching Roman Law: A Substitute for Academic Comparative Law

As we have seen, scholars continued to teach Roman law after the Civil War in both law schools and liberal arts colleges. In 1891, many colleges and 10 law schools taught the subject.[120] To illustrate, James Hadley (1821–1872) taught Roman law at Yale College, designed to provide budding historians and classicists with an introductory knowledge of the subject. His lectures posthumously published became *Introduction to Roman Law* (1873). The book went through several editions until 1931.[121] About one-third of the volume treated the

---

[118] STEVENS, *supra* note 33, at 133, 144 n.21, 23; *see* SAMUEL WILLISTON, THE LAW GOVERNING SALES OF GOODS AT COMMON LAW AND UNDER THE UNIFORM SALES ACT (1909).

[119] Frederick K. Beutel, *The Development of State Statutes on Negotiable Paper Prior to the Negotiable Instruments Law*, 40 COLUM. L. REV. 836, 850–53 (1940); *see* FRIEDMAN, HISTORY, *supra* note 62, at 408–09. Field explicitly compared the New York civil code to the French civil and commercial codes. New York's code had 2,028 sections while the French civil code had 2,281 articles and the commercial code 648 articles. Breaking out negotiable instruments, New York's code had 117 sections and the French commercial code 80 articles. David Dudley Field, *Codification*, 20 AM. L. REV. 1, 7 (1886).

[120] HOEFLICH, ROMAN AND CIVIL LAW, *supra* note 4, at 108, 112–13; *see supra* text accompanying note 68–69 (law schools).

[121] HOEFLICH, ROMAN AND CIVIL LAW, *supra* note 4, at 105–06, 123; *see* JAMES HADLEY, INTRODUCTION TO ROMAN LAW: IN TWELVE ACADEMICAL LECTURES (1873).

history of Roman law up through European codification and two-thirds dealt with its principal private law subjects.

Hadley on occasion and other professors taught Roman, canon, and civil law at Yale Law School from the 1870s. The Law School required Albert Wheeler's Roman law class from 1876 until his death in 1905 for all doctor of civil law (D.C.L.) candidates. Wheeler taught three courses on Roman law and one on canon law. He used a comparative and historical approach that emphasized the relevance of Roman law not only for civil law countries, but also for Anglo-American law. Other professors lectured on the French codes and Savigny's views on obligations.[122]

As the number of lawyers expanded in the 1870s, most without law school enrollment, an occasional jurist would write in defense of Roman law study.[123] Adolphe Pincoffs wrote about its value as expressed in modern German research, the *usus modernus Pandectarum*. "The merit of the modern German school is that it has done what the Romans have failed to do. It has expressed what was but dimly felt. It has arranged in systematical form the materials which in the *Digest* appear as a confused mass." Beyond the usefulness of principles and system, Pincoffs argued that specific Roman rules were better than common law rules since the social and economic system of Romans in their classical period of the third century was closer to the current American condition than that of feudalistic England.[124]

Hoeflich asserted that Roman law had new importance during this period as part of the developing university disciplines of history and comparative law. While Roman law gained this academic niche, it lost its relevance as a replacement or supplement to the common law. Consequently, one found the new model of scholarly law professor who used Roman or civil law for a useful comparative perspective on contemporary legal issues. Examples included Hammond, Oliver Wendell Holmes, John Pomeroy, and Samuel Williston, some of whom I discuss later.[125]

---

[122] HOEFLICH, ROMAN AND CIVIL LAW, *supra* note 4, at 105–07, 123–25; M.H. Hoeflich, *Roman and Civil Law in American Legal Education and Research Prior to 1930: A Preliminary Survey*, 1984 U. ILL. L. REV. 719, 731–33 (1984) [hereinafter Hoeflich, *Legal Education*]; *see* CHARLES PHINEAS SHERMAN, 1–3 ROMAN LAW IN THE MODERN WORLD (1917).

[123] *E.g.*, W.A. Hunter, *The Place of Roman Law in Legal Education*, 9 W. JURIST 461–72 (1875); *see* HOEFLICH, ROMAN AND CIVIL LAW, *supra* note 4, at 108–10, 112.

[124] Adolphe L. Pincoffs, *The Object and Value of the Study of Roman Law*, 15 AM. L. REV. 555, 565–72 (1881) (quotation at 566–67).

[125] HOEFLICH, ROMAN AND CIVIL LAW, *supra* note 4, at 102–08, 112, 115; *see infra* pt. E.3 and E.6 (Hammond and Holmes). The dominance of historical jurisprudence led some legal scholars to investigate the origin and development of common law rules and institutions in Roman or Germanic law. *Id.* at 106.

In 1897, Munroe Smith (1854–1926),[126] a professor at Columbia who taught at both the Law School and School of Political Science, investigated the question of whether American law schools should continue to offer a Roman law course. He argued that the answer depended on the school's mission. Most law schools, Smith admitted, saw their task as twofold, one part as information and the other part as method. The information for students concerned the principal American private law subjects. Here, although Roman and canon law infiltrated into much English common law, it was not essential that students understand this underpinning of American private law. When one turned to method, however, Smith believed that Roman law offered advantages. These involved Roman juristic sophistication in statutory interpretation and utilizing precedents from both a majority or minority of jurisconsults, analogous to judicial decision-making.[127]

In addition, Smith suggested that the contemporary effort to improve legal education aimed to transform law for a profession serving social welfare. The bar should "shape the new law which the constantly changing needs of social life require." One could only comprehend private law in its relation to public law since they were organically interdependent. Consequently, leading law schools had added constitutional, administrative, and international law to their curriculum. Furthermore, lawyers "really comprehend things only when we know how they have come into existence and how they have grown to their present form." Thus, history along with ethics, politics, and economics were useful. At European law departments, the state always required public law and some were adding economics. A few students at U.S. university law schools were taking those courses in other departments. Roman law would be a valuable elective in these law schools.[128]

Lastly, elite law schools now viewed law as a science, so legal education should be scientific. These schools should teach legal history, public law, economics, and ethics.

---

[126] COLUMBIA LAW SCHOOL, *supra* note 62, at 89–92. Smith earned his law degree at Columbia in 1877, after which he spent three years studying in Berlin, Leipzig, and Göttingen, the latter university awarding him the J.U.D. law degree. In 1880, Columbia College appointed Smith instructor and in 1886, professor of Roman law and comparative jurisprudence in the college's department of political science. At that later time, he became managing editor (until 1893) of the *Political Science Quarterly*. *Id.* at 91; Munroe Smith, 6 COLUM. LAW TIMES 183–84 (1893). Smith also taught courses on European legal history and jurisprudence. COLUMBIA LAW SCHOOL, *supra* note 62, at 149, 167–68; *Smith, supra*, at 183.

[127] Munroe Smith, *Roman Law in American Law Schools*, 45 AM. L. REG. & REV. 175–78 (n.s. vol. 36, 1897); *see* HOEFLICH, ROMAN AND CIVIL LAW, *supra* note 4, at 113–14. Smith identified exceptions for which American students could profitably use a knowledge of Roman law, namely conflicts of laws. Smith, *supra*, at 176–77.

[128] Smith, *supra* note 127, at 178–81 (quotations at 179); *see* COLUMBIA LAW SCHOOL, *supra* note 62, at 96, 148. In 1891, Columbia University made Smith professor of Roman law and comparative jurisprudence. *Id.* at 148.

[E]very true science studies and presents its material in the light of its development and in its relations to allied sciences. But every true science employs a method, . . . [which] is comparison. It is pre-eminently *the* scientific method. . . . Many of the problems with which . . . American lawyers have to deal are problems with which the Roman jurists dealt; all of them are problems with which the jurists of modern Europe are dealing.[129]

Smith concluded that to learn law scientifically, Roman law and the comparative method were essential.[130]

2. Law Journal Literature on Comparative Law

The earliest law journal to explicitly afford support for comparative law, albeit short lived, was the *Southern Law Review* in its 1875 reincarnation as a new series. Seymour Thompson (1842–1904), a scholarly lawyer and St. Louis court of appeals judge, took over the editorship of the quarterly with the intention of discontinuing case digests and providing "the *best legal thought* in America and Europe on all prominent matters of interest to the profession." The *Review* would accept original essays and selections from Europe's leading law periodicals.[131] The first volume had eight articles on Roman or French law, plus Hammond's review of German legal developments that he proposed continuing in future volumes.[132] In fact, Hammond in volume 2 treated French, German, and Swiss law and another lawyer wrote about current jurisprudential controversies in Europe.[133] After two years as editor, Thompson accepted the co-editorship of the *American Law Review*, an office he held from 1883 until 1901 while published in St. Louis. Thompson traveled widely in Europe and carried over his interest in foreign law to the new assignment.[134] He wrote an article on U.S. extradition law for the first volume he edited and later one on Swedish law reform.[135]

---

[129] Smith, *supra* note 127, at 181–82 (quotation at 182).

[130] *Id.* 183–85; *see* HOEFLICH, ROMAN AND CIVIL LAW, *supra* note 4, at 113–14; B.J. Ramage, *The Value of Roman Law*, 48 AM. L. REG. 280–93 (vol. 39 n.s., 1900). Smith preferred a Roman private law course that besides the *Institutes* devoted half its time to the *Digest*. Smith, *supra* note 127, at 185–86.

[131] Preface, 1 SO. L. REV. iii (n.s. 1875) (quotation at iv, italics in original). The *American Civil Law Journal*, an earlier effort, printed only one issue in 1873.

[132] William G. Hammond, *Notes on Current German Law*, 1 SO. L. REV. 653–61 (n.s. 1875).

[133] William G. Hammond, *Notes of Current European Law*, 2 SO. L. REV. 156–67, 533–50, 773–90 (n.s. 1876); U.M. Rose, *Controversies of Modern Continental Jurists*, *id.* at 1–21, 215–46, 551–75, 615–43. Hammond finished his series with *Notes of Current European Law*, 3 SO. L. REV. 753–66 (n.s. 1877) and *Notes of Current Foreign Law*, 4 SO. L. REV. 593–99 (n.s. 1878).

[134] John F. Dillon, *Bar Meeting of the St. Louis Bar in Memory of Hon. Seymour D. Thompson*, 38 AM. L. REV. 699, 705–06, 712 (1904); *Notes: Honorable Seymour D. Thompson*, *id.* at 714–18. Thompson was a delegate to the 1904 Universal Congress of Jurists, held in St. Louis. *Id.* at 718.

[135] Seymour D. Thompson, *Practice in Cases of Foreign Extradition*, 17 AM. L. REV. 315–49 (1883); *id.*, *Swedish Law Reform*, 38 AM. L. REV. 388–401, 674–82 (1904).

The *American Law Review* had a significant role in developing and maintaining comparative law interest. The journal's index from 1866 to 1879 listed nine articles on French law and two on German law.[136] After that, for instance, Émile Stocquart, a Belgian comparatist and specialist in conflicts and family law, published several articles.[137] A Swede wrote about the jury in his country.[138] Two American lawyers working in Paris presented articles on French law with one of them arguing for an American civil code based on the French model.[139] For Germany, C.W. Ernst compared similarities among German, English, and American law with a summary of German codification reforms in the second half of the nineteenth century.[140] Of course, comparative law was of direct interest in Louisiana, where lawyers were familiar with both civil law and common law sources.[141]

Two university law journals also contributed to comparative law literature. *Harvard Law Review* was the first, from 1887, edited by its law school students. The *Yale Law Journal* followed in 1891, with Baldwin writing the first article.[142] Taking the leading publication first, Hoeflich surveyed the *Harvard Law Review*.[143] Most of the civil law articles up to 1904 were historical in treating their subjects, and their authors were academics interested in gaining a comparative perspective on modern common law issues. Prominent young comparatists who wrote articles during this period included Freund, on the new German civil code; John Chipman Gray (1839–1915), on judicial precedent in Roman, German, and the common law; John Wigmore (1863–1943), with a comprehensive comparative survey on the pledge in three articles; and Samuel Williston (1861–1963), with three articles on contracts.[144] The contribution of the *Yale Law Journal* to

---

[136] *Index*, AM. L. REV. at 62, 64, 134 (1879).

[137] Émile Stocquart, *Marriage in Private International Law*, 23 AM. L. REV. 976–92 (1889); id., *Spanish Laws on Marriage and Their Extraterritorial Effect*, 25 id. at 82–95 (1891); id., *The New French Law on Divorce*, 27 id. at 1–13, 876–81 (1893).

[138] Gustaf Edward Fahlcrantz, *The Næmd; or the Remnant of the Jury in Sweden*, 22 AM. L. REV. 837–52 (1888).

[139] George Merrill, *The Bench and the Bar in France*, 11 AM. L. REV. 672–83 (1876); id., *An American Civil Code*, 14 id. at 652–63 (1880); Edmond Kelly, *The French Law of Marriage*, 18 AM. L. REV. 933–60 (1884); id., *The French Law of Evidence*, 19 id. at 380–99 (1885).

[140] C.W. Ernst, *Law Reforms in Germany*, 18 AM. L. REV. 801–13 (1884).

[141] *See, e.g.*, Henry Denis, *The Analogies and Differences of the Civil and the Common Law*, 33 AM. L. REV. 28–41 (1899).

[142] Two earlier efforts by students, at Albany in 1875 and Columbia in 1885, failed. Michael I. Swygert & Jon W. Bryce, *The Historical Origins, Founding, and Early Development of Student-Edited Law Reviews*, 36 HASTINGS L.J. 739, 763–69 (1985).

[143] HOEFLICH, ROMAN AND CIVIL LAW, *supra* note 4, at 115–16, 175–76 n.46; id., *Legal Education*, *supra* note 122, at 733–35.

[144] Ernst Freund, *The New German Civil Code*, 13 HARV. L. REV. 627–37 (1900); John Chipman Gray, *Judicial Precedents: A Short Study in Comparative Jurisprudence*, 9 id. at 27–41 (1895); John H. Wigmore, *The Pledge-Idea: A Study in Comparative Legal Ideas*, 10 id. at 321–50, 389–417 (1896–1897), 11 id. at 18–39 (1897–1898); Samuel Williston, *Risk of Loss after an Executory Contract of Sale in the Civil Law*, 9 id. at 72–79 (1895); id., *Dependency of Mutual Promises in the Civil Law*, 13 id. at 80–109 (1899); id., *Contracts for the Benefit of a Third Person in the Civil Law*, 16 id. at 43–51

comparative law was significantly less, but there were articles on Japan, South America, and Roman law.[145]

In summing up the role served by Roman and civil law in American legal thought during the nineteenth century, Hoeflich found that they gave common lawyers a comparative benchmark by which to analyze their own solutions to problems affecting law and legal institutions. Teachers like Hammond saw the comparative method as a tool for teaching jurisprudence and training law students to be problem-solvers. More particularly, they provided models of systematic legal structure, such as those for codification or those in treatises, by which jurists could organize common law rules. Scientific university legal education was another example. Furthermore, Roman and civil law, in contrast to the medieval flavor of the common law, appeared to have conceptual and linguistic precision. Before the Civil War, scholars such as Lieber had redefined civilian terms and introduced them into the common law. In Latin, they seemed appropriate for university law study and superior to the casuistic nature of law-office training. Finally, Roman and civil law, requiring some knowledge of a foreign language, bestowed intellectual prestige on common lawyers.[146]

3. William Hammond

An important American jurist to embrace comparative law full time as a scholar and teacher was William Hammond (1829–1894). In 1865, Hammond and two Iowa Supreme Court justices began the Iowa Law School. The Iowa State University took it over in 1868 with Hammond as law department chancellor, where he taught civil law and comparative law. In the 1870s, he pushed for a broad, philosophical, and scientific education, including knowledge of Roman law, of the type he had witnessed as a student at Heidelberg, appropriate for a university law school. Savigny's historical approach heavily influenced Hammond in his Roman and civil law work.[147] This was evident in Hammond's 1870

(1902); see supra notes 65–66 and accompanying text (Freund); supra note 58 and accompanying text (Wigmore and Williston).

[145] William Trumbull, *Legal Practice in South America*, 1 YALE L.J. 139–42 (1892); Robert Morris, *Adoption in Japan*, 4 id. at 143–49 (1895); Robert C. Fergus, *The Influence of the Eighteenth Novel of Justinian*, 7 id. at 26–39, 67–74 (1897); W.F. Foster, *The Study of Roman Law*, id. at 207–18.

[146] HOEFLICH, ROMAN AND CIVIL LAW, supra note 4, at 132–44; see Peter Stein, *The Attraction of the Civil Law in Post-Revolutionary America*, 52 VA. L. REV. 403–34 (1966).

[147] David S. Clark, *The Modern Development of American Comparative Law: 1904–1945*, 55 AM. J. COMP. L. 587–89 (2007) [hereinafter Clark, *Modern Development*]; see HOEFLICH, ROMAN AND CIVIL LAW, supra note 4, at 91–93; REED, supra note 45, at 191, 461. See also RABBAN, supra note 2, at 35–39; Emlin McClain, *Law Department of the State University of Iowa*, 1 GREEN BAG 374–94 (1889).

comparative law course at Iowa, which he named "the civil law and its utility in America." In an article describing its introductory lecture, he stated that it was

> *possible* to revive the study of the *civil law*, and [given] opinions expressed by leading jurists, and by bodies like the [American Social Science Association], it seems *probable* that in a very short time we shall learn to regard a legal education as incomplete, if it does not enable the student to make some use of the treasures of jurisprudence garnered up in the [*Corpus juris civilis*].[148]

Between 1876 and 1880, Hammond published an edition of Justinian's *Institutes*,[149] which included a comparative survey of civil and common law classification systems, and his own edition of Lieber's *Legal and Political Hermeneutics*.[150] These and articles appearing in the *Western Jurist* while Hammond was editor (1867–1870) and later through the 1870s demonstrated a historical-comparativist approach to Roman and civil law.[151]

In 1881, Hammond became dean of Washington University Law Department, also known as St. Louis Law School, which the university had acquired. He continued until his death to advocate a more scientific legal education and to write on civil law, comparative law, and legal history.[152] In 1890, he published his own edition of Blackstone's *Commentaries*.[153] Unlike other American editions, Hammond presented the text as an expression of Blackstone's legal ideas between the first edition in 1765 and the eighth edition in 1778, shortly before the author's death. In addition, Hammond used his law students to review 2,500 volumes of American law reports from 1787 to 1890 so that he could include their citation to passages in the *Commentaries*. Finally, he appended his lecture notes after each chapter that treated American developments in that branch of law.[154]

---

[148] W.G. Hammond, *The Civil Law*, 4 W. JURIST 173–80 (1870) (quotation at 175, italics in original); *see* Emlin M'Clain, *William Gardiner Hammond*, *in* 8 GREAT AMERICAN LAWYERS 191, 217, 227–30 (William Draper Lewis ed., 1909); *see infra* pt. F.2 (the ASSA).

[149] THOMAS COLLETT SANDARS, THE INSTITUTES OF JUSTINIAN (William G. Hammond ed., 1876).

[150] FRANCIS LIEBER, LEGAL AND POLITICAL HERMENEUTICS (William G. Hammond ed., 1880); *see* Carrington, *supra* note 46, at 2143–52. For the usefulness of Hammond's appendices in the Lieber volume to study Roman and civil law, see Carrington, *supra*, at 2150–51; Hoeflich, *Legal Education*, *supra* note 122, at 730; M'Clain, *supra* note 148, at 229–30.

[151] HOEFLICH, ROMAN AND CIVIL LAW, *supra* note 4, at 92, 94–95, 97; M'Clain, *supra* note 148, at 213–15. While at Iowa, Hammond accumulated a library of 300 volumes on Roman and civil law. HOEFLICH, *supra*, at 97.

[152] Clark, *Modern Development*, *supra* note 147, at 589. Established in 1867, St. Louis Law School was the first one west of the Mississippi River. *See* STEVENS, *supra* note 33, at 77–78 (1983). For Hammond's comparative approach to legal education, *see* W.G. Hammond, *American Law Schools Past and Future*, 7 So. L. REV. 400–29 (n.s. 1881).

[153] WILLIAM BLACKSTONE, 1–4 COMMENTARIES ON THE LAWS OF ENGLAND (from Blackstone's 8th ed., William G. Hammond ed., 1890) [hereinafter BLACKSTONE (Hammond ed.)].

[154] William G. Hammond, *Preface to This Edition*, *in* 1 BLACKSTONE (Hammond ed.) at xii–xix; Wilfrid Prest, *Editorial Conventions and Practices*, *in* WILLIAM BLACKSTONE, 1 COMMENTARIES ON THE LAWS OF ENGLAND xliii–xlv (Wilfred Prest ed., 2016).

To conclude, Hammond saw the historical approach to American law as linked to comparative analysis of civil and Roman law since they helped the lawyer and law student understand the operations of the common law and how it evolved. This historical and comparative perspective could also serve the jurist interested in legal reform.[155] John Pomeroy (1828–1885), a prolific treatise writer and law professor first at New York University and then from 1878 until his death at Hastings Law College (in San Francisco), took a similar view. In 1878, as Hastings opened, Pomeroy designed a three-year curriculum with the first year dedicated to basic categories and concepts of law as they had developed historically.[156]

4. William Wirt Howe

After the Civil War, William Howe (1833–1909) practiced law in New Orleans and served as a justice of the Louisiana Supreme Court from 1868 to 1872. Interested in history and the civil law, he revived the Louisiana Historical Society as president in 1888. Roman and civil law formed the basis of his Storrs lectures at Yale in 1894.[157] From 1897 to 1898, Howe served as president of the ABA. In addition to his historical interest in the civil law, he was conversant in the modern legal systems of France, Spain, and the nations of Latin America. These were the subject of his comparative law lectures at Boston University, the University of Pennsylvania, and Columbian Law School (George Washington University) in Washington, D.C.[158]

Howe's greatest contribution to comparative law was his book *Studies in the Civil Law* (1896), which served for decades as an introduction for lawyers and students to the civil law.[159] Howe was fluent in French and Latin and could consult original sources in those languages to present his overview of private and procedural

---

[155] HERGET, JURISPRUDENCE, *supra* note 11, at 50–53, 69 n.16 (Hammond's blend of evolutionary theory and sociological jurisprudence); HOEFLICH, ROMAN AND CIVIL LAW, *supra* note 4, at 91–97, 104–05; RABBAN, *supra* note 2, at 39.

[156] HOEFLICH, ROMAN AND CIVIL LAW, *supra* note 4, at 97–101; RABBAN, *supra* note 2, at 32–35.

[157] JAMES GRAFTON ROGERS, AMERICAN BAR LEADERS: BIOGRAPHIES OF THE PRESIDENTS OF THE AMERICAN BAR ASSOCIATION, 1878-1928, at 95–97 (1932) [hereinafter ROGERS, BAR LEADERS]; *see* WILLIAM WIRT HOWE, STUDIES IN THE CIVIL LAW AND ITS RELATIONS TO THE JURISPRUDENCE OF ENGLAND AND AMERICA (1896, 2d ed. 1905) [hereinafter HOWE, STUDIES], based on the Yale lectures. *Id.* at vii. A law journal article summarized his views. William Wirt Howe, *Roman and Civil Law in America*, 16 HARV. L. REV. 342-58 (1903); *see* Hoeflich, *Legal Education*, *supra* note 122, at 734–35.

[158] ROGERS, BAR LEADERS, *supra* note 157, at 95, 98. Between 1899 and 1900, Howe presented 16 lectures on comparative jurisprudence at Pennsylvania, 27 on the same theme at Columbian along with ten on Roman law, and ten on civil law at Boston. During the same period, he delivered addresses on comparative law before the bar associations in Georgia, Indiana, Maryland, Ohio, and Texas. Dart, *supra* note 84, at 544–45.

[159] ROGERS, BAR LEADERS, *supra* note 157, at 97; *see supra* note 157 (*Studies in the Civil Law*).

law as developed by the Romans and later absorbed into the French and Louisiana legal systems. When Howe referred to the German variation of the civil law, it was through French or English translations of German authors. Although the perspective of the volume was historical—the Romans, to Europe (mainly France), then Louisiana—there was no treatment of Savigny's historical jurisprudence. Rather, compilation and codification appeared to be the civil law's end state.[160]

5. Sociological Jurisprudence in Germany

Germans trace the beginning of legal sociology to Rudolf von Ihering (1818–1892) and his two publications, *Der Kampf um's Recht* (1872) and *Der Zweck im Recht* (1877, 1883).[161] His legal philosophy, unlike that of Savigny, asserted that a state's authoritative rules were the result of struggles between conflicting individuals and groups. The subjective goals and desires of groups or individuals comprising them—their social interests—are advanced or not through struggle and conflict. One could view these interests objectively for their social usefulness. Struggle (*Kampf*) was necessary for public policy to reflect a society's most useful rules.[162]

The other principal element to Ihering's legal philosophy was purpose (*Zweck*). As individuals and groups competed to achieve their own egoistic or collective interests, their selfish purpose at the same time attained society's overall purposes. Ihering rejected Savigny's scientific conceptualism for law as a self-contained system. Rather, a true explanation must account for the social needs of people and identify how legal rules and institutions reconcile those social needs.[163] One could perceive Ihering's debt to the English utilitarians, especially Jeremy Bentham, as it related to the mechanism for utility or usefulness. However, Ihering rejected limiting a society's goals to the four that Bentham identified and the latter's narrow concept of justice as simply utility.[164]

---

[160] *See* HOWE, STUDIES, *supra* note 157, at 1–11, 103–08, 131–49, 346–72.

[161] KLAUS R. RÖHL, RECHTSSOZIOLOGIE: EIN LEHRBUCH 15, 44 (1987); ROSCOE POUND, THE SPIRIT OF THE COMMON LAW 203–05 (1921); *see* RUDOLF VON IHERING, DER KAMPF UM'S RECHT (1872) (20th ed. 1921); *id.*, 1–2 DER ZWECK IM RECHT (1877, 1883) (8th ed. 1923).

[162] BODENHEIMER, *supra* note 2, at 89; RABBAN, *supra* note 2, at 106, 109–11, 113; Herget, *German Thought*, *supra* note 13, at 206; *see* RUDOLPH VON IHERING, THE STRUGGLE FOR LAW 29–63 (John J. Lalor trans. of *Der Kampf um's Recht*, 5th German ed. (1878), 1879).

[163] RABBAN, *supra* note 2, at 112–14; Herget, *German Thought*, *supra* note 13, at 206; *see* RUDOLF VON IHERING, LAW AS A MEANS TO AN END 25–70 (Isaac Husik trans. of 1 *Der Zweck im Recht*, 4th German ed. (1903), 1913) (5 The Modern Legal Philosophy Series, edited by a committee of the AALS) [hereinafter IHERING, LAW AS A MEANS].

[164] BODENHEIMER, *supra* note 2, at 84–90. Ihering also denied that the sole purpose of law was to protect liberty, as John Stuart Mill (another utilitarian) had argued. One could not solve the issue of limiting liberty with an abstract formula, such as self-protection or preventing harm to other individuals. For Ihering, the goal of law was to establish an equilibrium between the individual principle and the social principle. An individual existed both for himself and for society. Pound characterized Ihering as a social utilitarian. *Id.* at 88–89.

Finally, Ihering's theory tackled both an explanation of a society's law and its view of justice. Law in the collective sense encompassed the institutions that provide security for the conditions of social life. These include the possibility of attaining many of the valued things in life beyond mere survival. These objects of life vary over time and across societies; thus, the purpose of law was always relative to a specific culture. A just legal system, objectively, would fully accomplish the purposes predominant in that society.[165] Ihering favored legislation over judge-made law, since he believed the former would more likely produce a legal system in conformance with current societal needs than the latter.[166]

6. Oliver Wendell Holmes, Jr.

Pound identified four judges from the latter nineteenth century that he considered most important in developing American law.[167] Only one of them—Oliver Wendell Holmes, Jr. (1841–1935)—had the background to understand Roman and civil law, but given the philosophical tenor of the period, he more subtly incorporated civilian insights into his influential court decisions and writings. Holmes's famous book, *The Common Law* (1881),[168] provided a systematic historical and philosophical critique of its subject, which served as the basis for much of American private law development in the twentieth century. For 20 years as justice and then chief justice of the Massachusetts Supreme Judicial Court, Holmes applied his pragmatic jurisprudence to private law. He then served for 30 more years on the U.S. Supreme Court, where his influence on public law was equally important.[169]

In 1881, Eliot approached Holmes about accepting a newly endowed professorship at Harvard Law School. A year earlier, Holmes had delivered a series of lectures, later published as *The Common Law*, that would make him famous. Without the law faculty's approval, Eliot offered Holmes the position to begin for the fall term in 1882. Holmes received the usual professor's salary, but only had to teach a two-thirds schedule including jurisprudence. As fate had it, in December

---

[165] Herget, *German Thought, supra* note 13, at 206–07.

[166] BODENHEIMER, *supra* note 2, at 90.

[167] POUND, FORMATIVE ERA, *supra* note 14, at 4, 30–31 n.2; *see* Bernard Schwartz, *The Judicial Ten: America's Greatest Judges*, 1979 So. ILL. U.L. REV. 405–06, 420–24 (1979).

[168] OLIVER WENDELL HOLMES, THE COMMON LAW (Mark DeWolfe Howe ed., 1963).

[169] David S. Clark, *Development of Comparative Law in the United States*, *in* THE OXFORD HANDBOOK OF COMPARATIVE LAW 148, 160 (Mathias Reimann & Reinhard Zimmermann eds., 2d ed. 2019); Morton J. Horwitz, *The Place of Justice Holmes in American Legal Thought*, *in* THE LEGACY OF OLIVER WENDELL HOLMES, JR. 31 (Robert W. Gordon ed., 1992). Friedman characterized Holmes's volume as the most distinguished law book of the second half of the nineteenth century. FRIEDMAN, HISTORY, *supra* note 62, at 479–80; *see* RABBAN, *supra* note 2, at 48, 215.

1882, the Massachusetts governor offered Holmes an open judgeship on the Supreme Judicial Court, which Holmes accepted, much to the law faculty's and Eliot's displeasure. Eliot responded by hiring William Keener as an assistant professor for the open post, again without a faculty vote.[170]

Holmes was solidly within the post-bellum American school of historical jurisprudence and owed an intellectual debt to his fellow American, Henry Adams, as well as to Savigny and Henry Maine in England. Maine was the first occupant of the Oxford University historical and comparative jurisprudence chair in 1869, where historical jurisprudence and comparative law were two sides of the same coin.[171] David Rabban contended that, although Holmes anticipated American sociological jurisprudence that took hold in the twentieth century, he never abandoned evolutionary historical jurisprudence. He read the works of both Savigny and Maine, took notes on them, but generally did not acknowledge their influence. For the Teutonic origins of English common law, Adams assisted Holmes with the German scholarship with which Adams was familiar. Holmes also gained insight from communication with Pomeroy and his historical research.[172]

Mathias Reimann found that Holmes in *The Common Law* predominantly relied on the scholarship of German jurists, not to venerate them, but to confront legal science as illustrated by *Pandektenwissenschaft* or as developed by Langdell. The book was an assault on legal formalism.[173] Nevertheless, Holmes drew insight from the historical jurisprudence of Savigny. While Holmes rejected the teleology of a *Volksgeist*, he shared Savigny's view that rethinking a legal system required one to begin with a society's past and that law and morality should be separate.[174]

Holmes kept a journal of his reading. The entries between 1873 and 1876 revealed his interest in historical studies of English, French, German, and Roman law as well

---

[170] G. EDWARD WHITE, 2 LAW IN AMERICAN HISTORY: FROM RECONSTRUCTION THROUGH THE 1920's, at 323–27 (2016); RABBAN, *supra* note 2, at 51, 234. Keener, as assistant professor, received half the pay offered Holmes. WHITE, *supra*, at 324, 326. Dissatisfied with the pay structure at Harvard, Keener brought the case method of instruction to Columbia Law School in 1890. *Id.* at 330.

[171] HERGET, JURISPRUDENCE, *supra* note 11, at 42–46; RABBAN, *supra* note 2, at 216, 220–21; KONRAD ZWEIGERT & HEIN KÖTZ, INTRODUCTION TO COMPARATIVE LAW 58–59 (Tony Weir trans, 3d ed. 1998); *see* HENRY SUMNER MAINE, ANCIENT LAW: ITS CONNECTION WITH THE EARLY HISTORY OF SOCIETY, AND ITS RELATION TO MODERN IDEAS (1st American ed. 1864; London ed. 1861); *supra* text accompanying note 12 (Adams). Theodore Dwight, a law professor at Columbia, wrote the introduction to Maine's American edition. MAINE, *supra*, at ix–lxix. On Maine, *see* HOEFLICH, ROMAN AND CIVIL LAW, *supra* note 4, at 77–85.

[172] RABBAN, *supra* note 2, at 217–24, 229, 261–62; *see supra* text accompanying note 156 (Pomeroy).

[173] Mathias W. Reimann, Holmes's *Common Law* and German Legal Science, in THE LEGACY OF OLIVER WENDELL HOLMES, JR., *supra* note 169, at 72–74, 80–81, 83–85, 91–97, 106–11 [hereinafter Reimann, *Holmes*]. Much of Holmes's criticism of Langdell was undeserved. PARKER, *supra* note 94, at 247–69.

[174] Reimann, *Holmes*, *supra* note 173, at 98–99.

as the type of cultural anthropology that Maine illustrated. Holmes had a reading knowledge of German and he included references to Savigny and Ihering as well as to German Pandectists such as Rudolf Sohm and Bernhard Windscheid. Holmes believed historical analysis rather than logic was important in understanding, organizing, and classifying law. His opening paragraph in *The Common Law* demonstrated this orientation.

> The life of the law has not been logic; it has been experience. The felt necessities of the time, the prevalent moral and political theories, ... even the prejudices which judges share with their fellow-men, have had a good deal more to do than the syllogism in determining the rules by which men should be governed. The law embodies the story of a nation's development through many centuries.[175]

Morton Horwitz took the logic-experience dichotomy as a frontal attack by Holmes against legal formalism, conceptualism, and natural-rights theory. In 1881, historical jurisprudence provided the predominant legal philosophy for that purpose. However, a decade and a half later, when Holmes published his famed "The Path of the Law," he embraced more of Ihering's philosophy of social interests. Horwitz attributed this to the social and economic conflicts occurring in the 1890s. Custom, unconsciously evolving social conventions, could no longer provide the bridge between society and the state. Judicial decision-making could not always depend on common law tradition and would have to consider policy alternatives in framing legal rules. Holmes wrote, "the man of the future is the man of statistics and the master of economics."[176]

Rabban rejected this analysis and contended that Holmes continued in "Path of the Law" and later essays to describe legal history in organic and evolutionary terms consistent with historical jurisprudence.[177] Reimann essentially agreed. He mentioned that Holmes had read Ihering's *Kampf* in translation while he was writing the lectures that became *The Common Law*. Ihering by this time was the principal antagonist to German formalism while Charles Darwin's *Origin of Species* and its theme of the struggle for life inspired both him and Holmes.[178]

---

[175] RABBAN, *supra* note 2, at 231–36, 253–58, 260 (quotation at 234); HOLMES, *supra* note 168, at 5; Reimann, *Holmes*, *supra* note 173, at 80, 98. For a list of the German authors Holmes read, *see* RABBAN, *supra*, at 249–50 n.41.

[176] Horwitz, *supra* note 169, at 31–32, 49–55, 65–69; O.W. Holmes, *The Path of the Law*, 10 HARV. L. REV. 457–78 (1897) (quotation at 469). Holmes also stated that a legal rule "is a concealed, half conscious battle on the question of legislative policy, and if any one thinks that it can be settled deductively, or once for all, I only can say that I think he is theoretically wrong." Holmes, *supra*, at 467. Earlier, Pound had seen a similar transition in Holmes between 1881 and 1897. RABBAN, *supra* note 2, at 261–63, 266.

[177] RABBAN, *supra* note 2, at 263–68.

[178] Reimann, *Holmes*, *supra* note 173, at 102–05; *see* CHARLES DARWIN, ON THE ORIGIN OF SPECIES BY MEANS OF NATURAL SELECTION (1859). *See generally* FREDERIC R. KELLOGG, OLIVER WENDELL HOLMES JR. AND LEGAL LOGIC (2018).

7. Christopher G. Tiedeman

After graduating from college, Christopher Tiedeman (1857–1903) studied law for two years at Göttingen and Leipzig before completing his law degree at Columbia. After practicing law for two years, he began an academic law career, first at the University of Missouri, then New York University, and finally as law dean at the University of Buffalo.[179] At Göttingen Tiedeman had attended Ihering's classes and favored the approach of German legal education. "If I were called upon to establish a course of legal instruction, I would follow the German methods as nearly as the situation and public opinion in America would allow." Tiedeman preferred a three-year curriculum, with the first year dedicated to fundamental legal principles that students would learn by reading treatises and attending class.[180]

Tiedeman was a prolific writer, authoring seven legal treatises on both private and public law. The most successful was *A Treatise on the Limitation of Police Power in the United States* (1886), explicating the power of constitutional limitations (both state and federal) to protect private rights against what he considered radical social reformers. By the end of his career, Tiedeman had come to fear giant institutions—whether corporations or big government—overwhelming smaller enterprises or individuals in a laissez-faire economy.[181]

Tiedeman was less well known for his use of historical analysis of law based on German sources. This use is evident in his principal treatment, published in 1899, of the nature of constitutions, constitutional interpretation, and the parameters of the U.S. Constitution.[182] Ihering perceived law as evolving in response to a society's fluctuating social needs. As applied to a written constitution, Tiedeman contended that jurists should interpret its meaning using unwritten principles derived from changes in the society's prevalent sense of right. Consequently, the U.S. Constitution could change its meaning without formal amendment. He embraced Ihering's view that these adjustments emerged from competition among opposing social, political, economic, and cultural forces in

---

[179] RABBAN, *supra* note 2, at 57.

[180] Christopher G. Tiedeman, *Methods of Legal Education*, 1 YALE L.J. 150, 151, 153, 157–158 (1891) (quotation at 158). "The adjudicated cases constitute nothing more than materials out of which the scientific jurist is to construct a science of jurisprudence. They are not law in themselves." *Id.* at 153–54.

[181] RABBAN, *supra* note 2, at 57–59; Louise A. Halper, *Christopher G. Tiedeman, Laissez-Faire Constitutionalism and the Dilemmas of Small-Scale Property in the Gilded Age*, 51 OHIO ST. L.J. 1349–50, 1353, 1355–59, 1382–84 (1990). The subtitle of the 662-page treatise was "Considered from Both a Civil and Criminal Standpoint."

[182] CHRISTOPHER G. TIEDEMAN, THE UNWRITTEN CONSTITUTION OF THE UNITED STATES: A PHILOSOPHICAL INQUIRY INTO THE FUNDAMENTALS OF AMERICAN CONSTITUTIONAL LAW (1890) [hereinafter TIEDEMAN, UNWRITTEN CONSTITUTION]; PARKER, *supra* note 94, at 244–47, 270; RABBAN, *supra* note 2, at 59. Tiedeman's book was originally prepared as lectures for the Missouri Bar Association in celebration of the U.S. Constitution's centenary. Halper, *supra* note 181, at 1349 n.8, 1363.

society. This deviated from Savigny's position that transformation occurred as a smooth development over decades or longer.[183]

For Tiedeman, neither legislators nor judges made law; rather, they mirrored what the community desired. The Constitution was an organic legal document that changed meaning over time. Thus, it was erroneous for judges to ascribe meaning to a constitutional passage based solely on its language or the framers' intent; instead, they should consider the "present will of the people."[184] As Tiedeman described more generally about law, "the life of a rule of law is derived from its habitual and spontaneous observance by the mass of the people.... The legal rule is, therefore, fashioned after the prevalent sense of right. The Germans call it *Rechtsgefuehl*."[185]

F. Comparative Law Emerges as a Discipline

There were practical comparative law activities—mostly borrowing—in several countries in the latter half of the nineteenth century, associated with newly independent nations in the Americas or with political interest in industrialization in places such as eastern Europe, Russia, Turkey, and Japan. Nevertheless, the home of scholarly comparative law first appeared in Germany and France.[186] Jurists in the United States with a comparative law interest during this period absorbed ideas from civil law Europe that would form their views of law and science.

1. Germany and France

In Germany, especially at the University of Heidelberg, professors took an early interest in foreign law. Some were reacting against the inward-looking nature of historical jurisprudence, which as we have seen searched for rules relevant to each people's specific genius. These comparatists had either the practical aim of using their foreign law knowledge to improve German legislation or

---

[183] RABBAN, *supra* note 2, at 59–60, 329; Halper, *supra* note 181, at 1363; David N. Mayer, *The Jurisprudence of Christopher G. Tiedeman: A Study in the Failure of Laissez-Faire Constitutionalism*, 55 Mo. L. REV. 93, 103–25 (1990). Consider Ihering's definition: "Law is the sum of the conditions of social life in the widest sense of the term, as secured by the power of the State through the means of external compulsion." IHERING, LAW AS A MEANS, *supra* note 163, at 380.
[184] Halper, *supra* note 181, at 1364–65; TIEDEMAN, UNWRITTEN CONSTITUTION, *supra* note 182, at 151; *see id.* at 145–54.
[185] TIEDEMAN, UNWRITTEN CONSTITUTION, *supra* note 182, at 6–7.
[186] 1 LÉONTIN-JEAN CONSTANTINESCO, TRATADO DE DERECHO COMPARADO: INTRODUCCIÓN AL DERECHO COMPARADO 104–203 (Eduardo Freitas da Costa trans., 1981) (translated from the 1972 French version). There was also a 1971 German version. For the Asian examples of Japan and Turkey, *see id.* at 199–203.

the academic aim of simply increasing their understanding of law. The great names involved in this activity during the century's first half included Paul von Feuerbach, Eduard Gans, Karl Mittermaier, Anton Thibaut, and Karl Zachariae. By contrast, the French satisfaction with their civil code and the jurists' interest in its exegesis left little room for comparative law at that time.[187]

After 1850 in Europe, interest in comparative law spread, reflected by the creation of societies and journals of comparative legislation. In 1869, French jurists established the Society of Comparative Legislation to stimulate the knowledge of foreign laws, publish a journal, and create a center in Paris to scientifically study legislation. By 1896, it had 1,400 members and a Paris library of 10,000 volumes.[188] In 1894, 40 German jurists met in Berlin to create the International Association for Comparative Legal Science and Economics, which also published a journal. Within a few years, the association had 800 members.[189]

In Germany, beyond legislation, there was also substantial curiosity about the influence of foreign scholarly doctrine and judicial jurisprudence on legal science. Already, some saw comparative law as an instrument for legal unification. For others the comparative law method could improve legal history and the newly formed legal ethnology. Josef Kohler was a major figure in many of these developments. However, by the end of the nineteenth century, comparative law leadership passed from Germany to France. Partly, this was a consequence of the successful enactment of the *Bürgerliches Gesetzbuch* (1896), the German civil code, and the subsequent juristic concern with exploring its ramifications. Partly, it was due to the failure to have institutionalized comparative law within German universities.[190]

2. Social Science Associations and Comparative Law

The French-speaking region of nineteenth-century Europe took important initiatives to develop comparative law, particularly the institutional aspect of holding international congresses as a mechanism to exchange ideas and opinions. Comparative law themes mixed with history and the social sciences, but had not yet quite emerged as a distinct discipline. The *Association Internationale pour le*

---

[187] David S. Clark, *Nothing New in 2000? Comparative Law in 1900 and Today*, 75 TUL. L. REV. 871, 873 (2001) [hereinafter Clark, *Nothing New*]; *see* CONSTANTINESCO, *supra* note 186, at 105–34.

[188] Henri Lévy-Ullmann, *Account of the French Society of Comparative Legislation*, 10 HARV. L. REV. 161–62, 164 (1896). The journal, which still exists, today is the *Revue international de droit comparé*.

[189] ELMAR WADLE, EINHUNDERT JAHRE RECHTSVERGLEICHENDE GESELLSCHAFTEN IN DEUTSCHLAND 7, 32–35 (1994). The Internationale Vereinigung für vergleichende Rechtswissenschaft und Volkswirtschaftslehre existed until 1926 and continues today as the Gesellschaft für Rechtsvergleichung. *Id.* at 7–9.

[190] Clark, *Nothing New*, *supra* note 187, at 873–74; *see* CONSTANTINESCO, *supra* note 186, at 139–80, 204–09.

Progrès des Sciences Sociales did dedicate one of its five membership and annual meeting sections to comparative legislation.[191] The association held its initial congress in 1862 at its seat in Brussels.[192] The First Section defined its aims as the "study of civil, political, and penal laws in various countries, their effect on people's social condition, their imperfections and resulting evils, and their susceptibility to improvement and reform."[193]

The association's officers lived in several countries other than Belgium: France, Germany, Great Britain, Italy, the Netherlands, Poland, Portugal, Russia, Spain, Switzerland, and the United States. Delegates at the first congress discussed and delivered reports on various topics: (1) the bases and means for a good codification of laws; (2) legislation controlling the press in European countries; (3) improvements in legislation concerning aliens; and (4) international recognition of foreign corporations.[194]

In the United States, this mixing of law, history, and social science occurred in the American Social Science Association (ASSA), created in 1865. The ASSA had four departments, one of which was jurisprudence. Harvard and Yale law professors supplied most of jurisprudence department's leadership up to 1900. The ASSA met periodically, had scholarly sessions with papers presented, and published a journal.[195] Among those playing an important part in the organization were eminent law professors such as Lieber (Columbia), Theodore Dwight (Columbia), Hammond (Iowa), and James Thayer (Harvard). University presidents joined, including Eliot at Harvard and Woolsey at Yale, the latter teaching constitutional law at that time. Woolsey and Eliot served as vice presidents (1865–1866 and 1873–1876, respectively) and Baldwin as president (1897–1899) of the ASSA.[196]

---

[191] 1 ANNALES DE L'ASSOCIATION INTERNATIONALE POUR LE PROGRÈS DES SCIENCE SOCIALES 10–11 (1863) (arts. 15, 19) [hereinafter 1 ANNALES]. One of the association's purposes was "to guide public opinion toward the most practical means for improvement in civil and penal legislation." *Id.* at 9 (art. 2).

[192] Clark, *Nothing New*, supra note 187, at 874. Association annual meetings followed in Ghent (1863), Amsterdam (1864), and Berne (1865). *Id.* at 874 n.5.

[193] 1 ANNALES, *supra* note 191, at 131.

[194] *Id.* at 4–5, 53–66, 133–226.

[195] THOMAS L. HASKELL, THE EMERGENCE OF PROFESSIONAL SOCIAL SCIENCE: THE AMERICAN SOCIAL SCIENCE ASSOCIATION AND THE NINETEENTH-CENTURY CRISIS OF AUTHORITY vi, 87–88, 97–100, 106–09, 111–14, 116, 131 (1977); DOROTHY ROSS, THE ORIGINS OF AMERICAN SOCIAL SCIENCE 63 (1991); Carrington, *supra* note 46, at 2144–45. In 1867, the ASSA department of jurisprudence program had three papers covering prison discipline, crime against property, and the role of law in social reform. HASKELL, *supra*, at 114. The *American Law Review* noted two addresses on law delivered at the ASSA, one on legal education in 1876 and one on constitutional property rights in 1889. Francis L. Wellman, *Admission to the Bar*, 15 AM. L. REV. 295, 319 (1881); *Notes*, 24 *id.* at 107, 112–13 (1890).

[196] HASKELL, *supra* note 195, at 99, 104, 192 n.2, 216, 219–21; Ross, *supra* note 195, at 64; Carrington, *supra* note 46, at 2145–46; *see* George Chase, *The "Dwight Method" of Legal Instruction*, 1 CORNELL L.J. 74–81 (1894); *supra* pt. E.3 (Hammond). Lieber was the first head of the jurisprudence department. Hammond presented a paper on legal education in 1876. Baldwin as president took a conservative position on penal reform. HASKELL, *supra*, at 104, 220–21.

Until 1885, the ASSA prospered as a diverse group concerned with the use of social science to support social reform. As general interest in the social sciences evolved into academic professionalization in separate scholarly organizations and disciplines at universities, the ASSA declined. For instance, John Burgess, who followed Lieber at Columbia Law School, established in 1880 the separate School of Political Science and the independent Academy of Political Science, which published the *Political Science Quarterly* (1886). Burgess had studied in Berlin, Göttingen, and Leipzig prior to accepting the law school appointment in 1876. Frank Goodnow, with a law degree from Columbia and study abroad in Paris and Berlin, joined Burgess on the political science faculty in 1883. He wrote a two-volume comparative treatise on administrative law in 1893.[197] We earlier saw the role of Eliot and Harvard in making legal education scientific. Once the ABA became viable, efforts to enact legislative reform and improve legal education shifted toward that organization.[198] In the early twentieth century, the ABA took a direct interest in comparative law.[199]

The earliest successful publications arising from the mixture of law, history, and social science, using a comparative method, occurred with constitutional law. In 1884, William Crane and Bernard Moses published *Politics: An Introduction to the Study of Comparative Constitutional Law*.[200] Moses was a professor of history and political economy at the University of California. The authors adopted the prevalent historical and scientific approach, emphasizing the organic nature of constitutions as expressions of a national will. In the introductory chapter, they set out a clear distinction between claims that were normative contrasted with those that were descriptive. The realm for political science was descriptive or explanatory.[201] Chapter 2 began, "The nation is an organic social being, a growth, and not an artificial creation."[202] Unlike most of the juristic interest of this era that had a comparative dimension, this volume embraced public law— namely constitutional and administrative law—and its place within a nation. It described the area between power and law. "Every independent political society

---

[197] COLUMBIA LAW SCHOOL, *supra* note 62, at 69–75, 81, 83, 85–89, 148, 167–68; FRANK J. GOODNOW, 1–2 COMPARATIVE ADMINISTRATIVE LAW: AN ANALYSIS OF THE ADMINISTRATIVE SYSTEMS NATIONAL AND LOCAL, OF THE UNITED STATES, ENGLAND, FRANCE AND GERMANY (1893); *see* ESSAYS ON THE LAW AND PRACTICE OF GOVERNMENTAL ADMINISTRATION: A VOLUME IN HONOR OF FRANK JOHNSON GOODNOW v, vii (Charles G. Haines & Marshall E. Dimock eds., 1935). In 1904, Goodnow was the first president of the American Political Science Association. *Id.* at v, viii.

[198] Ross, *supra* note 195, at 63, 72, 78; Carrington, *supra* note 46, at 2145, 2149–50; Political Science Quarterly, *PSQ History*, https://www.psqonline.org/History.cfm; *see infra* note 204–05, 222 and accompanying text (Burgess).

[199] Clark, *Modern Development*, *supra* note 147, at 591–92, 596–600.

[200] WILLIAM W. CRANE & BERNARD MOSES, POLITICS: AN INTRODUCTION TO THE STUDY OF COMPARATIVE CONSTITUTIONAL LAW (1884).

[201] *Id.* at 1–5. The chapter's two citations of authority referred to German authors. *Id.* at 1, 5.

[202] *Id.* at 6.

is an organic body and has a will. This will finds its expression in the organs and institutions of the government, and also in commands or laws."[203]

In 1890, Burgess authored the two-volume *Political Science and Comparative Constitutional Law*. He contended that he would borrow the comparative law method, chiefly followed by German jurists but relatively new to English and French legal literature, from natural science to apply in political science and jurisprudence.[204] Burgess first explained, as had Montesquieu, that he would consider geography, culture, ethnicity, and political psychology, which he did broadly for Europe and North America. He then dealt with theories of the state: its origin, forms, and ends. Nevertheless, most of the text took four principal countries for comparison: France, Germany, Great Britain, and the United States. He separately analyzed them for each of the three branches of government and added comparative law chapters for the legislature, executive, and judiciary.[205]

In 1893, Frederic Coudert wrote a private law book utilizing a comparative political science perspective. He earned two Columbia degrees, one in law (1890) and the other a doctorate in political science (1894). The thesis for the latter was *Marriage and Divorce Laws in Europe, A Study in Comparative Legislation*. Coudert began with a treatment of his topic in Roman and canon law, then surveyed the legislative changes introduced in 11 European countries. Overall this illustrated cultural and legal secularization in Europe during the nineteenth century. Admitted to the New York bar in 1892, Coudert joined the first binational law firm in the United States that could take advantage of comparative law expertise. In the 1850s, three Coudert brothers, sons of an immigrant from France, had begun a New York City law office that primarily served French, Spanish, and Latin American clients. The Coudert Brothers firm in 1879 opened their second office in Paris (Coudert Frères).[206]

By the beginning of the twentieth century, Coudert Brothers was the preeminent transnational law firm in the United States, whose attorneys understood foreign and international law. Their advice and transactions represented the epitome of practical comparative law. In the first half of the new century, Frederic Coudert took the leadership role in developing the firm. To illustrate, the firm early on advised the governments of Belgium, France, Italy, Russia, Turkey, and Venezuela. After the United States annexed Hawaii in 1898 and acquired Puerto Rico, the Philippines, and Guam from Spain after the Spanish-American

---

[203] *Id.* at 38.
[204] JOHN W. BURGESS, 1 POLITICAL SCIENCE AND COMPARATIVE CONSTITUTIONAL LAW vi (1890). The first volume was subtitled, SOVEREIGNTY AND LIBERTY; THE SECOND GOVERNMENT.
[205] *See* 1–2 *id.*
[206] FREDERIC R. COUDERT, JR., MARRIAGE AND DIVORCE LAWS IN EUROPE, A STUDY IN COMPARATIVE LEGISLATION (1893). *See generally* VIRGINIA KAYS VEENSWIJK, COUDERT BROTHERS, A LEGACY IN LAW: THE HISTORY OF AMERICA'S FIRST INTERNATIONAL LAW FIRM, 1853–1993 (1994).

War, Coudert Brothers participated in most of the *Insular Cases* before the U.S. Supreme Court determining the status and rights of the territories.[207]

3. The 1900 International Congress of Comparative Law

During the second half of the nineteenth century, the excitement and pride associated with industrialization in Europe and elsewhere led to a series of national and then international expositions to showcase a nation's technological and social progress.[208] Social science congresses had relied on enlightened cultural nationalism to foster the bonds of human civilization improved by economic and social progress. Expositions proved more successful. In 1851, England sponsored the first of the international expositions, the Great Exhibition of the Works of Industry of All Nations, at the Crystal Palace (Hyde Park, London). Six million people attended over the course of half a year, with 25 nations represented. England and France shared these periodic expositions through 1867. The United States subsidized the first one held outside Europe in 1876, the Centennial International Exhibition commemorating the Declaration of Independence. Ten million people visited Philadelphia with 35 countries hosting pavilions.[209]

The World's Fair, Columbian Exposition, was the second international exposition located in the United States, celebrating in 1893 the discovery of America by Europeans. Held in Chicago, there were 27 million visitors to 19 national displays.[210] The exposition had an auxiliary branch divided into departments. In the government department, Henry Rogers was the chair of the division on jurisprudence and law reform. At that time, Rogers was the president of Northwestern University and chair of the ABA's Section of Legal Education. In an address to jurists of all countries, Rogers described the role of his division. It was "necessary to supplement the primary work of the Columbian Exposition by providing for a proper presentation of the intellectual and moral progress of mankind."[211] The U.S. government was committed to encouraging foreign nations to appoint delegates to the "Congress on Jurisprudence and Law Reform." Rogers anticipated that two themes would define the congress: international law

---

[207] See VEENSWIJK, *supra* note 206.

[208] Entertainment was also a feature. Besides general amusements, colonial pavilions from some nations displayed exotic features from their colonies, including ethnographic characteristics of "primitive" people that demonstrated the social and cultural superiority of industrialized societies. Bureau International des Expositions [hereinafter BIE], *Home*, https://www.bie-paris.org/site/en (select About Us, then A Short History of Expos).

[209] BIE, *Home*, *supra* note 208 (select Expos, then Since 1851).

[210] *Id.* (select Expos, then Since 1851).

[211] Henry Wade Rogers, *Notes: The World's Congress Auxiliary*, 26 AM. L. REV. 866, 874 (1892) hereinafter Rogers, *Notes*]; see *supra* note 57 and accompanying text (Rogers). There were six divisions in the government department. *Id.* at 875.

and the administration of justice. Under those themes, Rogers suggested that jurists could discuss comparatively topics such as legal codification, legal aid to the indigent, barriers to judicial access, and reducing court delay. "To advance the science of jurisprudence, and to promote the administration of justice in all parts of the world, is the leading purpose of this Congress."[212]

In 1900, the *Exposition Universelle* in Paris was the culmination of this nineteenth-century innovation in expositions, with the largest attendance, 51 million, and national participation, 40 nations.[213] In connection with the 1900 Paris World Exposition, and with French ministerial authority, the *Société de législation comparé* held a one-week International Congress of Comparative Law during the summer. There were six sections in this congress, with the greatest emphasis on general theory and method. Reports had to be in French or translated into French.[214]

Professor Raymond Saleilles, University of Paris, prepared a report explaining the congress's usefulness and its four objectives.[215] First, comparative legal science would determine which methods were most appropriate to use in analyzing diverse legislation. This task consisted of three stages: observation, comparison, and adaptation. Observation began with the idea that the text was nothing without interpretation, and that interpretation itself was nothing without consequences. Comparative law aimed to observe beyond text to reach those consequences. At the second stage, comparison considered the rational rapprochement among diverse national legislation, examining their juridical forms as well as practical consequences. A predominant type could then serve as a model. At the third stage, comparative law took that model and adapted it to national, racial, and environmental conditions and important cultural traditions. In this adaptation it was difficult to formulate, a priori, general laws. Here, history could supplement comparative law. History was extremely useful in identifying examples of immature legislation and artificial adaptations, as well as in clarifying which conditions and methods allowed legislation to penetrate national law and the life of a people. These same techniques could also develop scholarly doctrine and determine the legitimacy of judicial interpretation. Comparative

---

[212] Rogers, *Notes, supra* note 211, at 875–76 (quotation at 876). "The lawyers of all countries will be interested in an interchange of views on important questions of comparative jurisprudence; and this Congress... will afford such an opportunity for this purpose as never before existed." *Id.* at 877.

[213] BIE, *Home, supra* note 208 (select Expos, then Since 1851); *see* DANIEL T. ROGERS, ATLANTIC CROSSINGS: SOCIAL POLITICS IN A PROGRESSIVE AGE 8–20 (1998).

[214] Clark, *Nothing New, supra* note 187, at 875. Lévy-Ullmann, *supra* note 188, at 161–62, 164.

[215] R. Saleilles, *Rapport présenté a la Commission d'Organisation sur l'utilité, le but et le programme du Congrès*, 29 BULLETIN DE LA SOCIÉTÉ DE LÉGISLATION COMPARÉ 228–36 (1900); *see* CONSTANTINESCO, *supra* note 186, at 209–17.

law's three stages, applied to legislation, doctrine, and judicial interpretation, might lead, at least partially, to a *droit commun de l'humanité civilisée*.[216]

The congress's second objective, considering doctrine, would be to define comparative law's role as a teaching method. Third, from the viewpoint of practical legal solutions, the congress would discover which comparative law results jurists should utilize via national legislation, judicial interpretation adopting custom or doctrine, or international agreement. Finally, for practitioners, the congress would discover and organize mechanisms for obtaining information about foreign law sources and scholarship.[217] Since the 1870s, the French Society of Comparative Legislation had promoted an exchange of information about national legislation among nations. These reports on legislative reforms permitted French comparatists to track progress on matters such as judicial independence and the autonomy of a private bar association, which strengthened legal defense for individuals.[218]

The congress program included a theoretical part and a practical part, broadly conceived to cover public law and criminology as well as private law and private international law.[219] The congress billed itself as international. However, the program revealed that for the theoretical portion all seven general reporters were French, although 4 of the 12 special reporters were foreigners. Josef Kohler of Berlin and Sir Frederick Pollock of Oxford were the most renown. Almost all reporters were law professors, which gave sessions the scholarly tone typical of the civil law tradition.[220]

The congress itself was more international (basically European) than the reporter system. Foreign delegates represented Belgium, Canada, Germany, Great Britain, Italy, Japan, Luxembourg, Mexico, Monaco, Russia, San Marino, Switzerland, the United States, and Turkey. In addition, jurists from Spain and Sweden served on one of the panels. Delegates were legislators, government officials, and lawyers as well as law professors. They prepared 76 reports and written comments that the society eventually published in two volumes.

---

[216] Saleilles, *supra* note 215, at 230–32; see Clark, *Nothing New, supra* note 187, at 875–76.
[217] Clark, *Nothing New, supra* note 187, at 876.
[218] Jules Le Berquier, *The French Bar*, 19 Am. L. Rev. 90–91 (1885) (Stella A. Kroff trans. from *Revue des Deux Mondes*).
[219] Clark, *Nothing New, supra* note 187, at 877, 887–88. Today, one might consider criminology more appropriate for legal sociology, but recent international comparative law congresses have had criminal law and criminal procedure topics that overlap criminology. *See, e.g.,* Nora V. Demleitner, *Witness Protection in Criminal Cases: Anonymity, Disguise or Other Options?* 46 Am. J. Comp. L. 641 (Supp. 1998).
[220] Clark, *Nothing New, supra* note 187, at 877.

Practically all the reports were prepared by French, Italian, German, and Belgian jurists, with the French writing 46 percent of the total.[221] The two best-known American delegates were the law professors Burgess at Columbia (1876–1912), who taught constitutional law; and Charles Needham, who also served as president of George Washington University (1902–1910).[222]

---

[221] *Id.* at 878–79; *see* 1-2 CONGRÉS INTERNATIONAL DE DROIT COMPARÉ: PROCÈS-VERBAUX DES SÉANCES ET DOCUMENTS (1905, 1907).

[222] Clark, *Nothing New*, *supra* note 187, at 878 n.25; *see* Columbia250, *Home*, http://c250.columbia.edu (search for Burgess); THE GEORGE WASHINGTON UNIVERSITY: STATEMENT OF PRESIDENT NEEDHAM REGARDING THE PLANS AND WORK 3–4 (1909); *supra* text accompanying notes 197, 204 (Burgess). The remaining American delegates included the president of the U.S. Chamber of Commerce and two other attorneys. Clark, *supra*.

6
The Modern Development: 1900–1945

> In the [nineteenth] century we studied law from within. The jurists of today are studying it from without. The past century sought to develop completely and harmoniously the fundamental principles which jurists discovered by metaphysics or by history. The jurists of today . . . insist upon study of the actual social effects of legal institutions and legal doctrines. . . . Where the last century held comparative law the best foundation for wise lawmaking, they hold it not enough to compare the laws themselves, but that even more their social operation must be studied and the effects they produce.
>
> Roscoe Pound[1]

A. Transition into a New Century

At the end of the nineteenth century, sustained scholarly comparative law activities were largely associated with the successful effort to establish scientific teaching and research at leading law schools, 25 of which created the Association of American Law Schools (AALS) in 1900.[2] The new field of comparative juristic inquiry emerged from both idealistic as well as practical concerns. Moreover, it was as successful in the United States as with the much better-known contemporary national developments in Belgium, France, Germany, and Great Britain.[3] The interest of jurists in drawing from history and social science as well as traditional legal sources provided new perspectives for both national and comparative law, especially on the role of law and government in society.[4]

---

[1] Roscoe Pound, The Spirit of the Common Law 212 (1921).
[2] Robert Stevens, Law School: Legal Education in America from the 1850s to the 1980s, at 92–111 (1983). Between 1900 and 1924, eight of the AALS presidents had some connection to comparative law (Thayer, Baldwin, Kirchwey, Pound, Beale, Stone, Gilmore, Lewis).
[3] See The Oxford Handbook of Comparative Law 29–147 (Mathias Reimann & Reinhard Zimmermann eds., 2d ed. 2019); Elmar Wadle, Einhundert Jahre Rechtsvergleichende Gesellschaften in Deutschland 7–43 (1994); 1 Léontin-Jean Constantinesco, Traité de Droit Comparé: Introduction au Droit Comparé 68–126 (1972).
[4] See supra ch. 5, pt. F (comparative law as a discipline).

1. Woodrow Wilson

Woodrow Wilson (1856–1924) provides an interesting illustration since most of his academic career and the book he wrote on comparative law and government occurred during the nineteenth century while he had the opportunity to apply his academic learning in the twentieth century.[5] Wilson grew up and began college in the South during the Civil War and Reconstruction, then transferred to the College of New Jersey, where he received a bachelor's degree in political philosophy and history. In 1879, he attended the University of Virginia Law School, withdrew due to poor health to then read law, and eventually moved to Atlanta to practice law for over a year. In 1883, however, he enrolled in Johns Hopkins University, where he earned a Ph.D. three years later. After teaching at two eastern colleges, in 1890, Wilson accepted the professorship of jurisprudence and political economy at the College of New Jersey. That college became Princeton University in 1896 and its trustees named Wilson president in 1902.[6]

Early in his career, Wilson wrote about the role of law and government in society. The first book after his dissertation, *The State: Elements of Historical and Practical Politics* (1889), was a successful comparative and historical study of law and the structures and procedures of government. Intended as a textbook, it saw many revised editions up to 1918.[7] Wilson used a German model for his text, since nothing like its comprehensiveness had yet been prepared in America. He followed Heinrich Marquardsen's multi-volume *Handbuch des öffentlichen Rechts der Gegenwart in Monographien*.[8] Influenced by the German historical school in jurisprudence and political economy,[9] Wilson began his volume with the origins of the state and then traced community, law, and government in Europe and the United States from the classical period of Greece and Rome,

---

[5] *See* HENRY STEELE COMMAGER, THE AMERICAN MIND: AN INTERPRETATION OF AMERICAN THOUGHT AND CHARACTER SINCE THE 1880'S, at 322–25 (1950).

[6] *Chronology*, in THE WILSON READER 275 (Frances Farmer ed., 1956).

[7] WOODROW WILSON, THE STATE: ELEMENTS OF HISTORICAL AND PRACTICAL POLITICS (1889) [hereinafter WILSON, THE STATE]. "[T]he only thorough method of study in politics is the comparative and historical." *Id.* at xxxv–xxxvi.

[8] *Id.* at xxxiv–xxxvi. Wilson stated that for the "invaluable" volumes available, he had "used it constantly in my preparation of this work." *Id.* at xxxvi. Marquardsen was a public law professor at Heidelberg and then Erlangen who had studied and wrote about English law. He edited the handbook series between 1883 and 1894. Hermann Rehm, *Marquardsen, Heinrich*, in 52 ALLGEMEINE DEUTSCHE BIOGRAPHIE 216–18 (1906). Wilson thanked Munroe Smith for reading portions of his book and mentioned that James Bryce's 1–2 *The American Commonwealth* (1888) appeared too late for Wilson to rely upon it for the U.S. chapter. WILSON, THE STATE, *supra* note 7, at xxxvi.

[9] *See* Joseph Dorfman, *The Role of the German Historical School in American Economic Thought*, 45 AM. ECON. REV. 17–28 (1955); Heino Heinrich Nau, *Gustav Schmoller's Historico-Ethical Political Economy: Ethics, Politics and Economics in the Younger German Historical School, 1860–1917*, 7 EUR. J. HIST. ECON. THOUGHT 507–31 (2000). Columbia University led the movement after 1877 in America. Dorfman, *supra*, at 18.

through Germanic forms during the Middle Ages, until the modern era. Finally, he concluded with some comparative chapters on law and government.

Wilson's treatment of law evidenced his reliance on the historical school and its organic and evolutionary elements.

> Law thus follows in its development, with slow, sometimes with uneven, but generally with quite distinct steps, the evolution of the character, the purposes, and the will of the organized community whose creation it is.... The nature of each State, therefore, will be reflected in its law; in its law, too, will appear the functions with which it [the State] charges itself.[10]

Law, in reflecting the peculiar characteristics of its community, was local or national in scope; universal law was unlikely. "Law thus normally speaks the character, the historical habit and development of each nation. There is no universal law, but for each nation a law of its own which bears evident marks of having been developed along with the national character."[11] For Wilson, sovereignty resided in the community. "[Sovereignty] is the will of an organized independent community, whether that will speak in acquiescence merely, or in active creation of the forces and conditions of politics. The kings or parliaments who serve as its vehicles utter it, but they do not possess it."[12] Nevertheless, anticipating Wilson's presidency during the Great War and his support for a League of Nations, he contended that as with the Roman *jus gentium*, jurists might discover in all national legal systems certain common moral judgments, a "common legal conscience in mankind."[13]

Wilson maintained a connection with the American Bar Association (ABA). For instance, he attended the 1894 annual meeting and delivered a paper to the Section of Legal Education on undergraduate legal studies.[14] While president of Princeton, Wilson presented the ABA's plenary annual address in 1910.[15] He began, "[t]he whole history of society has been the history of a struggle for law." Wilson contended that the old order of contemporary society was changing swiftly with great antagonism; social forces were not willing to accommodate their differences and arrive at a common understanding for mutual benefit. Radical reconstruction was on the horizon.[16] He saw the Civil War as

---

[10] WILSON, THE STATE, *supra* note 7, at 610; *see id.* at 618, 633–35 (historical school); COMMAGER, *supra* note 5, at 323–25, 337 (evolution).

[11] WILSON, THE STATE, *supra* note 7, at 622.

[12] *Id.* at 625.

[13] *Id.* at 625; *see id.* at 628–30 (international law).

[14] 22 WASH. L. REP. 481 (1894); *Proceedings of the Section of Legal Education*, 17 A.B.A. ANN. REP. 351, 364 (1894). The second day of the section's meeting consisted of three papers and discussion by Baldwin, Wilson, and Wigmore. *Id.* at 363–64.

[15] Woodrow Wilson, *The Lawyer and the Community: Annual Address*, 33 A.B.A. ANN. REP. 419–39 (1910).

[16] *Id.* at 419–21, 430, 439 (quotation at 419).

a watershed. "The life of the nation . . . does not center now upon questions of governmental structure or of the distribution of governmental powers. It centers upon economic questions, questions of the very structure and operation of society itself, of which government is only the instrument."[17] He decried the decline of the generalist lawyer-statesman for the lawyer specialized in some aspect of business. People no longer saw lawyers as mediators of progress. Corporate power had decreased liberty for workers, cogs in a machine, or pawns in a game. Wilson believed the present task for law was to rehabilitate the individual and moderate the power of corporations, which the law should not treat as legal persons. "We [lawyers] are the servants of society."[18]

These ideas placed Wilson squarely within the Progressive movement and in the twentieth century along with those jurists such as Roscoe Pound who attacked the administration of justice in state courts.[19] Progressives to varying degrees sought to expand democracy, aid victims of industrialization, and bring order and efficiency to government. They typically were against laissez-faire corporate capitalism and the legal formalism of common law judges. Wilson's solution to economic domination, poverty, and exploitation was to build new government organizations to regulate business and provide social aid. On the international plane, he promoted the principle of people's right of self-determination. This analysis reflected the social nature of human experience.[20]

In 1914, the ABA invited Wilson, who was now the United States president (served 1913–1921), to deliver its opening address at the October annual meeting in Washington, D.C. War had erupted in Europe during August and by October thousands had already died. The ABA president, William Taft, introduced Wilson as a person whom the ABA was "proud to claim as one of us." Wilson began his brief address by comparing evidentiary procedure in the Permanent Court of Arbitration to that used in American judicial systems. For Wilson, law should arise out of human life and reflect changed social circumstances. American judges should be able to modify precedents and adjust the common law to this foundational principle rather than make citizens rely on

---

[17] *Id.* at 424.

[18] *Id.* at 425–29, 431, 433, 437–39 (quotation at 439).

[19] WILLIAM M. WIECEK, THE LOST WORLD OF CLASSICAL LEGAL THOUGHT: LAW AND IDEOLOGY IN AMERICA, 1886–1937, at 188–92 (1998); William E. Forbath, *Politics, State-Building, and the Courts, 1870–1920*, *in* 2 THE CAMBRIDGE HISTORY OF LAW IN AMERICA: THE LONG NINETEENTH CENTURY (1789–1920) 643, 652–53, 658 (Michael Grossberg & Christopher Tomlins eds., 2008) [hereinafter 2 CAMBRIDGE HISTORY]; Russell R. Wheeler, *Roscoe Pound and the Evolution of Judicial Administration*, 48 S. TEX. L. REV. 943–44, 950–57 (2007).

[20] GEORGE ATHAN BILLIAS, AMERICAN CONSTITUTIONALISM HEARD ROUND THE WORLD, 1776–1989: A GLOBAL PERSPECTIVE 251–52, 259–60, 456 n.3 (2009); COMMAGER, *supra* note 5, at 349–50; Forbath, *supra* note 19, at 650–54. Wilson declared that the American state should be Prussianized. *Id.* at 652. However, Wilson the southerner considered African Americans second-class citizens and used executive authority to segregate the federal workforce. LAWRENCE M. FRIEDMAN, A HISTORY OF AMERICAN LAW 525 (3d ed. 2005).

uneven statutes to change law. "[W]e are custodians not of commands, but of a spirit." Judges need not look forward to anticipate change, but they should not retard it and lag the average person's moral judgments.[21]

To further his political agenda, Wilson, against the opposition of the ABA, successfully appointed Louis Brandeis to the U.S. Supreme Court in 1916. A progressive Zionist, Brandeis saw that movement as a solution to European anti-Semitism. Before enrolling at Harvard Law School, he had studied for three years at a *Gymnasium* in Dresden. As a lawyer, Brandeis supported sociological jurisprudence and illustrated that in a 1908 Supreme Court case with a 100-page brief of factual data demonstrating the adverse effects of long hours on women's health.[22]

2. Early Attempts to Transplant American Law Abroad

As an aftermath of the 1898 Spanish-American War, the Treaty of Paris ceded sovereignty over Guam, the Philippines, and Porto Rico to the United States.[23] The Senate ratification debate made it clear that this was a break with the past. America now held territories it did not intend to admit as states. These possessions were colonial and the development might have begun an era of empire.[24] Some lawyers argued that the new possessions were incompatible with America's republican tradition, but the Supreme Court in the *Insular Cases*

---

[21] *Transactions*, 37 A.B.A. ANN. REP. 5–9 (1914) (quotations at 6, 8). Wilson had defeated Taft in the 1912 presidential election. Forbath, *supra* note 19, at 664. In 1916, Wilson nominated Louis Brandeis—a foe of the excesses of capitalism—to the U.S. Supreme Court. LAWRENCE M. FRIEDMAN, AMERICAN LAW IN THE 20TH CENTURY 275 (2002) [hereinafter FRIEDMAN, AMERICAN LAW]; *see* WIECEK, *supra* note 19, at 195–96.

[22] PAUL CARRINGTON, SPREADING AMERICA'S WORD: STORIES OF ITS LAWYER-MISSIONARIES 188–89, 198–99 (2005); Philippa Strum, *Louis Dembitz Brandeis*, *in* BIOGRAPHICAL ENCYCLOPEDIA OF THE SUPREME COURT: THE LIVES AND LEGAL PHILOSOPHIES OF THE JUSTICES 46–48, 52, 54 (Melvin I. Urofsky ed., 2006); William O. Douglas, *Louis Brandeis: Dangerous Because Incorruptible*, N.Y. TIMES, 5 Jul. 1964, § 7, at 3 (book review); *see* BRANDEIS ON ZIONISM: A COLLECTION OF ADDRESSES AND STATEMENTS BY LOUIS D. BRANDEIS (1942). Elihu Root and William Taft, presidents of the ABA, and President Lawrence Lowell at Harvard, opposed Brandeis's nomination. Douglas, *supra*.

[23] Treaty of Peace (Paris), Spain-U.S., arts. 2–3, 10 Dec. 1898, *in* 11 Bevans 615–21. The United States agreed to pay Spain $20 million. *Id.* art. 3, at 616.

[24] BILLIAS, *supra* note 20, at 223–27; FRIEDMAN, AMERICAN LAW, *supra* note 21, at 9, 134–37, 575–76. When the recently declared First Philippine Republic objected to the terms of the Treaty of Paris, fighting began in 1899 against the United States. That war ended in 1902, permitting the U.S. Congress to enact the Philippine Organic Act, which served as the archipelago's basic law including provision for a male Filipino-elected Philippine Assembly. That assembly (implemented in 1907) was the lower chamber in a bicameral legislature with the Philippine Commission (established in 1900), appointed by the U.S. president, as the upper house. The U.S. War Department's Bureau of Insular Affairs had some administrative responsibilities in the islands. BILLIAS, *supra*, at 231; Library of Congress, *United States Rule*, *in* PHILIPPINES: A COUNTRY STUDY (Ronald E. Dolan ed., 1991), http://countrystudies.us/philippines [hereinafter LC, PHILIPPINES].

legitimized the acquisition of colonial territories. Nevertheless, particularly with Wilson, U.S. foreign policy took a course of indirect and consensual engagement with the legal systems in the new territories. A few jurists—some of whom had knowledge of the civil law tradition—working with American foundations, professional associations, universities, or the U.S. government-supported foreign legal reform. These efforts abroad mirrored the Progressive movement to improve law domestically.[25]

When Americans arrived in the twentieth century, the Philippines had a mixed legal system, combining customary usages, Islamic law, civil law, and soon the newly overlaid American common law. On a shrinking indigenous base of customary law, the migration of Malays around 1500 added Islamic law and subsequent colonization by Spain in the sixteenth century and later the United States appended the two European legal traditions.[26] The principal American comparatist involved with the Philippines was Charles Lobingier (1866–1956).

Lobingier was active in both the Comparative Law Bureau and the American Foreign Law Association. He had studied Latin at college, passed the bar examination in Nebraska, earned an LL.M. degree at its university law department, and in 1903, a Ph.D. at the department of American history and jurisprudence. In 1904, the governor general of the Philippine Islands appointed Lobingier judge at its first instance court, which applied Spanish civil and penal law. He held the post until 1914 and, in addition, taught Roman law at the University of the Philippines (1911–1921).[27] In 1908, the Philippine legislature, with support from the United States, had authorized the university at Manila, which included a "college of law and of social and political science."[28] The first dean, George Malcolm

---

[25] BILLIAS, *supra* note 20, at 226–29; Jedidiah Kroncke, *Law and Development as Anti-Comparative Law*, 45 VAND. J. TRANSNAT'L L. 477, 501–03 (2012) [hereinafter Kroncke, *Law and Development*]; *see* A. Caesar Espiritu, *Constitutional Development in the Philippines*, *in* CONSTITUTIONALISM AND RIGHTS, THE INFLUENCE OF THE UNITED STATES CONSTITUTION ABROAD 260–64 (Louis Henkin & Albert J. Rosenthal eds., 1990) [hereinafter INFLUENCE ABROAD]. President William McKinley (1897–1901) was against a policy of colonialism, but felt a duty to govern and protect the Philippines and prepare them for self-governance. CARRINGTON, *supra* note 22, at 87–88, 92; Espiritu, *supra*, at 261–62.

[26] George A. Malcolm, *Constitutional History of Philippines*, 6 A.B.A. J. 109 (1920); *Language Diversity and Uniformity*, *in* LC, PHILIPPINES, *supra* note 24; *Early History*, *in id.* Malcolm was an associate justice on the Supreme Court of the Philippine Islands. Malcolm, *supra*.

[27] TIMOTHY G. KEARLEY, LOST IN TRANSLATIONS: ROMAN LAW SCHOLARSHIP AND TRANSLATION IN EARLY TWENTIETH-CENTURY AMERICA 41–43, 92 (2018); *Lawyers in the News*, 36 A.B.A. J. 63 (1950); *see* CHARLES SUMNER LOBINGIER, THE EVOLUTION OF THE ROMAN LAW: FROM BEFORE THE TWELVE TABLES TO THE CORPUS JURIS (2d ed. 1923) (greatly expanded from his 1915 *Evolution of the Civil Law*). In the 1923 book, Lobingier divided each of 32 chapters between a one-page syllabus followed by text. Kocourek favorably reviewed it. A.K., 19 ILL. L. REV. 396–98 (1925) (book review).

[28] An Act for the purpose of founding a University . . ., Rep. Act No. 1870, §§ 1, 6(b), O.G. 76 (18 June 1908) (Phil.). The university had an academic and administrative structure based on the American model. *Id.* at §§ 4, 6(b), 9–11. In addition, the college of law initiated a student-run journal, the *Philippine Law Journal* in 1914, which continues to this day. *Greetings*, 1 PHILIPPINE L.J. 1, 3 (1914). In 1611, the Spanish king authorized the Colegio de Santo Tomas in Manila, which by

(served 1910-1917), a Michigan law graduate, replicated the American law school model, which allowed the AALS to admit it as a member school.[29] In 1909, the legislature created a code commission, which Lobingier chaired.[30] In 1912 to 1913, Lobingier published nine short articles in the *Philippine Law Review* about cases from the first instance court and on Spanish and Roman law.[31]

The principal American legal transplant to the Philippines, mandated by the U.S. Congress and president, and carried out primarily by U.S. government lawyers, was in public law, especially constitutional and administrative law, but excepting penal law. This held true from the beginning of U.S. administration in the islands through the Filipino drafting of the 1935 Constitution. The Philippine Supreme Court, with justices appointed by the U.S. president, interpreted public law issues considering American jurisprudence. Students at the Philippine law school studied U.S. Supreme Court cases in English. Private law in general continued under Spanish influence, but procedural law became a mixture of American and Spanish rules. Moreover, with the doctrine of judicial precedent and Philippine legislation, many common law rules took hold for commercial law and special contracts. Otherwise, American supervision usually tolerated native customs in rural areas and Islamic law in the Moro regions.[32]

In 1913, Wilson had appointed five Filipinos to the Philippine Commission, the legislature's upper chamber, which gave it a Filipino majority for the first time. He also appointed the governor general, the same term the Spanish had used during its colonial administration. The governor general undertook rapid Filipinization of the civil service, distressing many American officials. This signaled that Filipinos might achieve eventual independence for the islands.[33] In

---

1733 had faculties in law, theology, and liberal arts, based on the European practice. *History of the University of Santo Tomas*, https://thereaderwiki.com/en/History_of_University_of_Santo_Toma.

[29] CARRINGTON, *supra* note 22, at 104-05.
[30] *See* Charles Sumner Lobingier, *Codification in the Philippines*, 3 ANN. BULL. COMP. L. BUREAU ABA 42-47 (1910).
[31] Most of the articles in this bar association journal were in Spanish. Spanish remained an official language for use in courts, along with English, until 1920. George R. Harvey, *The Administration of Justice in the Philippine Islands*, PHILIPPINE L.J. 330, 349-51 (1915). Earlier, Lobingier had published *A Treatise on Philippine Practice* (1907) (156 pp.).
[32] CARRINGTON, *supra* note 22, at 105-06; Espiritu, *supra* note 25, at 264-68, 280-81; Enrique M. Fernando, *An Asian Perspective on the American Constitutional Influence in Asia: Its Impact on the Philippine Legal System*, 18 MALAYA L. REV. 281, 310-13 (1976); Charles Sumner Lobingier, *A Decade of Juridical Fusion in the Philippines*, 3 ANN. BULL. COMP. L. BUREAU ABA 38-42 (1910); id., *Blending Legal Systems in the Philippines*, 21 L.Q. REV. 401-07 (1905); Malcolm, *supra* note 26, at 110-12; H. Lawrence Noble, *Development of Law and Jurisprudence in the Philippines*, 8 A.B.A. J. 226-29 (1922); Andrzej Rapaczynski, *Bibliographical Essay: The Influence of U.S. Constitutionalism Abroad*, *in* INFLUENCE ABROAD, *supra* note 25, at 405, 439-42. Although Filipino jurists, trained in the American educational system, controlled the drafting of the 1935 Constitution, they were aware that the U.S. president had to certify that it provided for a republican form of government and a bill of rights. Fernando, *supra*, at 311.
[33] CARRINGTON, *supra* note 22, at 100-03; *The Jones Act*, *in* PHILIPPINES, *supra* note 24; *see* SERGIO OSMEÑA, THE CONSTITUTIONAL DEVELOPMENT OF PHILIPPINE AUTONOMY (1924). William

1934, the U.S. Tydings-McDuffie Act provided for a 10-year transition period to independence. During this time, the new Commonwealth of the Philippines would be self-governing and have its own constitution.[34]

In China, the Xinhai Revolution in 1911 defeated the Qing rulers, the last imperial dynasty, leading to a republic in 1912. From 1905, authorities allowed a few private and public schools to teach law and government.[35] The most interesting from the legal transplant approach to comparative law was the Soochow Law Department, also known as the Comparative Law School of China, which opened in Shanghai in 1915. As with the law college in the Philippines, Soochow used the American model and lawyers soon organized local and national bar associations. There was no private, independent legal profession in China until the republic: only foreign lawyers in treaty ports and foreign concessions. The ABA expressed some interest in China while the Carnegie Endowment for International Peace funded Frank Goodnow, a Columbia political science professor, to advise on law reform.[36]

In 1913, the Chinese government—at the suggestion of one of the Carnegie Endowment's trustees, Charles Eliot—asked the Endowment to recommend an expert familiar with the French constitution to aid China in drafting its own constitution. The Endowment selected Goodnow and its secretary, James Brown Scott, notified Goodnow that his role was advisory, since the Chinese intended to prepare their own constitution. Goodnow, an expert in administrative and

---

Howard Taft was the first governor general (served 1901–1904), who chaired the commission. The commission established the Philippines Supreme Court to replace the Spanish Audiencia of Manila. CARRINGTON, *supra*, at 98–99. In 1913, 30 percent of government officials were American, which fell to 4 percent by 1921. *Jones Act, supra*.

[34] *The Commonwealth*, in LC, PHILIPPINES, *supra* note 24. The U.S. statute, also know as the Philippine Commonwealth and Independence Act, 48 Stat. 456 (1934), retained U.S. control over foreign policy and U.S. presidential veto over Philippine trade and immigration law. The Philippine constitutional convention drafted the 1935 Constitution, which a plebiscite approved. Delayed by the Japanese occupation during World War II, the Philippine government gained full sovereignty over its republic in 1946. *Id.*

[35] An example was the law department at Peiyang University in Tianjin. Warren Seavey, who later became a Harvard law professor, taught law there using the case method from 1906 until 1911. A few of his students studied for a year at Harvard and later took important positions in the Chinese government. Seavey collected a 5,000-volume library, which he left to the school. It did not long survive the collapse of the imperial regime. CARRINGTON, *supra* note 22, at 121–22; JEDIDIAH J. KRONCKE, THE FUTILITY OF LAW AND DEVELOPMENT: CHINA AND THE DANGERS OF EXPORTING AMERICAN LAW 119–20 (2016) [hereinafter KRONCKE, FUTILITY].

[36] KRONCKE, *Law and Development, supra* note 25, at 505–07; Alison E.W. Conner, *Soochow Law School and the Shanghai Bar*, 23 HONG KONG L.J. 395–97, 410–11 (1993) [hereinafter Conner, *Soochow*]; *see* Edgar Pierce Allen, *Legal Education in China*, 39 A.B.A. ANN. REP. 671–77 (1916); Charles W. Rankin, *China*, 2 A.B.A. J. 284–87 (1916); ch. 5, note 197 and accompanying text (Goodnow). Goodnow also taught some courses at the law school. *A History of the School of Law: Columbia University* 167–68 (Julius Goebel, Jr. ed., 1955) [hereinafter COLUMBIA LAW].

municipal law, was a pragmatic progressive and historicist, who viewed government as an evolving institution that should satisfy the needs of society.[37]

When Goodnow arrived in China, there was turmoil between the president, Yuan Shikai, and the National Assembly's dominant party, the Kuomintang (KMT or Nationalist Party). The Chinese administration assigned Goodnow to the Bureau of Legislation, attached to the cabinet. He had already prepared a draft constitution, based on the American model, which he presented to the bureau. They discussed it and translated it into Chinese. Goodnow lectured on constitutional law at Peking University late in 1913 and a daily newspaper printed the lectures, which gave publicity to Goodnow's ideas. While Goodnow favored a strong executive, the parliament, which had the authority to approve any constitution, preferred a weak executive subject to legislative control.[38]

In 1914, Yuan, with the army's support, expelled the KMT from parliament and later dissolved it. Under Yuan's direction, a conference produced a provisional constitution largely based on Goodnow's 1913 version. However, it added an advisory legislature and council of state, which could not check the executive. This 1914 document became known in the West as Goodnow's Constitution. In his report to the Endowment, an editorial in a Chinese newspaper, and paper delivered at the American Political Science Association, he supported the constitution as consistent with the social, political, and cultural traditions in China. Goodnow left China late in 1914.[39]

Methodists established Soochow University near Shanghai in 1900. Charles Rankin, an American lawyer teaching political science at the university, initiated the law department in 1915 as its dean. Its goal was to instruct Chinese students in the Chinese legal system and those of the principal civil and common law nations. During the early years, nevertheless, most instruction was in Anglo-American law taught by American professors. Lobingier taught Roman law as the civil law element, but that and the jurisprudence course contained comparative analysis.[40] Under the second dean, William Blume (served 1921–1927), the school gained a regional reputation, added more Chinese law courses, used the

---

[37] KRONCKE, FUTILITY, *supra* note 35, at 126–28; Noel Pugach, *Embarrassed Monarchist: Frank J. Goodnow and Constitutional Development in China, 1913–1915*, 42 PAC. HIST. REV. 499, 501–02, 516 (1973). The Endowment funded Goodnow for three years at $12,000 per annum. The Chinese desired its adviser to assist with revisions in the document so that its parts were internally consistent. *Id.* at 502.

[38] KRONCKE, FUTILITY, *supra* note 35, at 132–57; Pugach, *supra* note 37, at 502–03.

[39] Pugach, *supra* note 37, at 503–10. Goodnow returned to China in the summer of 1915 at Yuan's request and prepared a memorandum on comparative government as applied to China. He concluded that a constitutional monarchy with a parliament was better suited to China than a republic. *Id.* at 511–16.

[40] Alison W. Conner, *The Comparative Law School of China*, *in* UNDERSTANDING CHINA'S LEGAL SYSTEM: ESSAYS IN HONOR OF JEROME A. COHEN 210–15, 230–31, 239–40, 244 (C. Stephen Hsu ed., 2003) [hereinafter Conner, *Comparative Law School*]; Rankin, *supra* note 36, at 285–86.

case method of instruction, developed a library, and set up an LL.M. program.[41] Blume also introduced moot court and a student-run periodical, the *China Law Review*, which encouraged comparative research.[42]

In 1927, the leadership at Soochow Law School shifted to two former Chinese graduates of the school, Robert Sheng as dean and John Wu (Wu Jingxiong) as principal. Sheng after graduation had studied at Northwestern with Wigmore. Wu subsequently earned an J.D. at Michigan in 1921, and held research fellowships in Paris and Berlin as well as at Harvard (1923 and 1930). In 1924, he returned to Shanghai to teach at Soochow and to write. Wu became chief justice of the Shanghai Provisional Court in 1927 and, at the behest of the KMT, wrote a draft republican constitution in 1933 that became the basis for the 1947 Chinese Constitution.[43] Wu framed the draft on his knowledge of foreign constitutions and political philosophy as well as China's interests and political culture. In 1947, it gained the praise of Pound who had been advising the Chinese ministry of justice.[44] The Constitution incorporated Sun Yat-sen's three principles— nationalism, democracy, and livelihood (social welfare)—with five branches (Yuan) of government that would operate under checks and balances.[45] The

---

[41] CARRINGTON, *supra* note 22, at 122–23; W.W. Blume, *Legal Education in China*, 1 CHINA L. REV. 305–06 (1923); Conner, *Comparative Law School*, *supra* note 40, at 213–15, 223, 230–32, 235; Conner, *Soochow*, *supra* note 36, at 397–98. In 1930, the Soochow Law School (changing its name from department in 1927) had 594 students enrolled. Conner, *Soochow*, *supra*, at 397 n.11, 399 n.22. In 1928, Blume became a professor at Michigan Law School. ELIZABETH GASPAR BROWN & WILLIAM WIRT BLUME, LEGAL EDUCATION AT MICHIGAN: 1859–1959, at 340 (1959).

[42] Conner, *Comparative Law School*, *supra* note 40, at 224–26; Conner, *Soochow*, *supra* note 36, at 407–08; Alison W. Conner, *Training China's Early Modern Lawyers: Soochow University Law School*, 8 J. CHINESE L. 1, 20–22 (1994) [hereinafter Conner, *Training Lawyers*]; Editorial, 1 CHINA L. REV. 33–34 (1922). Most instruction in the 1920s was by American lawyers and Soochow graduates who had studied in the United States. Blume, *supra* note 41, at 306.

[43] Conner, *Comparative Law School*, *supra* note 40, at 215–16; Conner, *Soochow*, *supra* note 36, at 398–99; Li Xiuqing, *John C.H. Wu at the University of Michigan School of Law*, 58 J. LEGAL EDUC. 545–47, 551–55 (2008) (Nicholas C. Howson ed. & trans.); Xiaomeng Zhang, *John C.H. Wu and His Comparative Law Pursuit*, 41 INT'L J. LEGAL INFO. 196–97, 207, 213, 215 (2013); Robert N. Wilkin, Book Review, 42 A.B.A. J. 260–61 (1956) (reviewing John C.H. Wu, *Fountain of Justice: A Study in Natural Law* (1955)). The Carnegie Endowment financed Wu's Paris and Berlin fellowship. Li Xiuqing, *supra*, at 556; Zhang, *supra*, at 205, Wilkin, *supra*, at 260. At the University of Paris, Wu completed a dissertation, *La Méthode du droit des gens: Essai de la critique juridique*, and at Berlin studied under the legal philosopher Rudolf Stammler. Zhang, *supra*, at 205–06. In 1926, the Provisional Court had taken over the jurisdiction of the Mixed Court of International Settlements, adjudicating cases except where the defendant had the right to a consular court. *Id.* at 212–13.

[44] Zhang, *supra* note 42, at 215–16; Note, *Dr. Wu's Constitution*, 132 HARV. L. REV. 2300–04 (2019); *see* Roscoe Pound, *The Chinese Constitution*, 22 N.Y.U. L.Q. REV. 194, 199 (1947) [hereinafter Pound, *Constitution*]. Pound stated that the framers "have made an intelligent selection of constitutional ideas from the best modern constitutions without slavish following of any . . . to make the whole instrument a Chinese constitution for China." *Id.* at 199; *see* Roscoe Pound, *Comparative Law and History as Bases for Chinese Law*, 61 HARV. L. REV. 749, 751 (1948) [hereinafter Pound, *Comparative Law*].

[45] Pound, *Constitution*, *supra* note 44, at 194–96, 223–30; Zhang, *supra* note 42, at 216 (a balance of individualism and collectivism). When the KMT abandoned mainland China for Formosa (Taiwan) in 1949, it took the 1947 Constitution with them. It remains largely in effect in Taiwan today. Note, *supra* note 44, at 2307.

extensive list of civil liberties, however, was only weakly protected. Nevertheless, as a transplant from Western constitutions of that era and a reflection of Chinese tradition, it met the KMT's requirements.[46]

During Sheng's tenure as dean, he and Wu expanded the comparative law offerings at Soochow, hired European teachers, and by 1930, had expanded the comparative law library to 10,000 volumes in Chinese, English, and European languages. The high point in comparative law instruction occurred from 1927 to 1939. Besides Anglo-American, Chinese, and Roman law, the school now also covered French, German, Japanese, and Soviet law.[47] Wu, while performing administrative duties as principal through 1938, offered courses in Roman law, legal philosophy and history, and comparative law. Where appropriate, he used the case method of instruction since he subscribed to the idea that immersion in details in a historical and comparative manner would lead to a better understanding of a subject matter. Wu was also an adviser for the *China Law Review* and wrote 20 articles until the journal ceased publication in 1940. In 1951, he accepted a law professorship at Seton Hall University.[48] Soochow suffered difficulties after the 1937 commencement of the Second Sino-Japanese War but continued to teach some students. After renewal in 1945, the People's Republic closed the school in 1952. Soochow maintained its comparative law approach to instruction throughout its existence.[49] In 1954, the Republic of China reinstated Soochow Law School in Taipei.[50]

In 1914, President Wilson had nominated Lobingier to a 10-year judicial post at the United States Court for China in Shanghai. While serving there, and teaching at Soochow, he wrote *The Evolution of the Roman Law* (1923), intended as a text for students. Lobingier suggested to Rankin the comparative law name for Soochow Law School and participated in its design when he arrived in Shanghai.[51] Lobingier also established an American law library in Shanghai and

---

[46] Note, *supra* note 44, at 2315–20; *see* Pound, *Constitution*, *supra* note 44, at 219–23.

[47] Conner, *Comparative Law School*, *supra* note 40, at 216–21, 227–28.

[48] Zhang, *supra* note 42, at 207–11, 217, 220–21; Conner, *Training Lawyers*, *supra* note 42, at 23 n.101. As a Soochow administrator, Wu increased the number of Chinese law offerings. Zhang, *supra*, at 209. At Seton Hall, Wu prepared a West Publishing Co. coursebook on jurisprudence. *Id.* at 218; *see* JOHN C.H. WU, CASES AND MATERIALS ON JURISPRUDENCE (1958) (many excerpts from comparatists).

[49] Conner, *Comparative Law School*, *supra* note 40, at 227–29; Conner, *Soochow*, *supra* note 36, at 400–03. For instance, in 1934 the curriculum included Chinese law, civil law (France, Germany, Japan, Soviet Union), Anglo-American law, Roman law, and public and private international law. Conner, *Training Lawyers*, *supra* note 42, at 11. In 1941, the law library had 30,000 volumes, classified using the Dewey system, consisting of two-thirds foreign law books covering 30 countries. Zhang, *supra* note 42, at 211.

[50] Conner, *Training Lawyers*, *supra* note 42, at 43–44.

[51] KEARLEY, *supra* note 27, at 81–85, 88; KRONCKE, FUTILITY, *supra* note 35, at 120; Conner, *Training Lawyers*, *supra* note 42, at 6 n. 16, 22–23; Conner, *Comparative Law School*, *supra* note 40, at 212, 214; Zhang, *supra* note 42, at 200; *see supra* note 27 (Lobingier's book). The United States created the consular court in 1906 and asserted jurisdiction over U.S. citizens (including corporations) in China. The court continued until 1943. Zhang, *supra*, at 199; *see* CHARLES SUMNER LOBINGIER,

led the formation of the Far Eastern American Bar Association with members also from China, Japan, and the Philippines.[52]

In retrospect, the presence of American jurists in the Philippines had a more substantial influence on legal institutions and norms, even if not much on legal culture, than reform activities in China on its legal system. Despite the importance of Soochow Law School, Chinese lawyers found the German civil law tradition, coupled with its Japanese variant, compatible with Chinese political culture, and there was little the U.S. government or American jurists could do about that. The tradition of a Mandarin class governing with a Confucian concept of *li* (proper norms of social behavior) together with *guanxi* (social networks and reciprocity), permitted authoritarian rule and what a Western jurist would call corruption.[53]

When Lobingier returned to the United States in 1924, he continued his interest in Roman and civil law expanded by his experience on the Philippine first instance court and U.S. Court for China. From 1925 to 1927, he served as assistant U.S. attorney general for Cuba while also drafting law reforms of Cuban law for the American Chamber of Commerce in Cuba. In 1926, the dean of National University Law School hired Lobingier to teach civil law. Since National only had a part-time night program, he also held government posts in Washington, D.C., primarily at the Securities and Exchange Commission. He continued to write articles on Roman, civil, and comparative law through the 1930s.[54] In 1946, he lectured on codification projects for the U.S. military government in Korea.[55]

3. A Timeline through Two World Wars

Organized American comparative law began in earnest with the 1904 St. Louis Universal Congress of Lawyers and Jurists, building on the experience in Chicago

---

AMERICAN COURTS IN CHINA (1919) (pamphlet of Lobingier's address as president of the Far Eastern American Bar Association).

[52] CARRINGTON, *supra* note 22, at 120–22; KRONCKE, FUTILITY, *supra* note 35, at 123–25.
[53] CARRINGTON, *supra* note 22, at 96, 106–07, 123–24; KRONCKE, FUTILITY, *supra* note 35, at 122–23; Kroncke, *Law and Development*, *supra* note 25, at 507, 517; Roscoe Pound, *Progress of the Law in China*, 23 WASH. L. REV. & ST. B. J. 345, 354 (1948) [hereinafter Pound, *Progress*]; *see* Teemu Ruskola, *Colonialism without Colonies: On the Extra Territorial Jurisprudence of the U.S. Court for China*, 71 LAW & CONTEMP. PROBS. 217, 234–39, 241–42 (2008). After comparative law in China served the purpose of selecting the framework of codes and provisions for substantive and procedural law, Pound proposed to use comparative law to develop techniques of interpretation and application given the conditions of Chinese life. Pound, *Comparative Law*, *supra* note 44, at 757–60.
[54] KEARLEY, *supra* note 27, at 86–91, 197–98; *see, e.g.*, Charles Sumner Lobingier, *The Value and Place of Roman Law in the Technical Curriculum*, 49 AM. L. REV. 349–74 (1915). National University merged with George Washington in 1954. STEVENS, *supra* note 2, at 85 n.15.
[55] KRONCKE, FUTILITY, *supra* note 35, at 119.

with the 1893 Congress on Jurisprudence and Law Reform. It also drew support and ideas from the justly celebrated 1900 Paris *Congrès international de droit comparé*.[56] The timeline I describe here shows how the discipline of comparative law slowly developed in the United States. The outbreak of the Great War in 1914 was a major choke point to this development. Nevertheless, after the 1918 armistice, optimism for peace and collaboration returned among some comparatists. The Great Depression and political events during the 1930s were another blow to institutional comparative law. Thus, it was not until the early 1950s that academic comparative law achieved a firmer footing.

First, organizational efforts to establish the Comparative Law Bureau started in 1905, which led the ABA to create the bureau as a special section in 1907. Bureau members met annually at the ABA's summer meeting and published a 200-page *Annual Bulletin* from 1908 until 1914, when World War I disrupted cross-Atlantic connections. The *Annual Bulletin* was the first successful comparative law journal in the United States.

Second, academic interest in Roman, civil, and comparative law continued at a few American law schools and professors developed teaching materials in those subjects. Elite schools initiated or expanded graduate law degree programs beyond the LL.B. that emphasized jurisprudence, comparative law, and legal history. American and increasingly foreign jurists enrolled in these programs typically with the goal of teaching or writing about law. Some American professors and graduates translated civil law scholarship into English. Between 1920 and 1939, about 100 foreign lawyers earned the doctorate at the top seven U.S. schools; many of these came from China and the Philippines.[57]

Wang Chung-hui, a graduate student at Yale Law School from 1902 until 1905, provides an illustration of the transplant dimension of comparative law. After Wang received the civil law D.C.L. degree, he returned to China to establish Fudan University's law program, modeled in part on that at Yale with a comparative perspective, and to assist the new republic in constructing a civil law legal system. Wang's LL.M. thesis was on the diplomatic history between China and the United States and his D.C.L. thesis was a comparison of domicile in various legal systems.[58] Professor Edward Raynolds was Wang's favorite mentor.

---

[56] David S. Clark, *Nothing New in 2000? Comparative Law in 1900 and Today*, 75 TUL. L. REV. 871, 875-88 (2001) [hereinafter Clark, *Nothing New*]; *see supra* ch. 5, pt. F.3 (1893 Chicago and 1900 Paris congresses). Germans held their first comparable international congress in Heidelberg in 1911. Forty-four delegates from the United States attended the German congress, a number of foreigners exceeded only by Austria, Hungary, Italy, Russia, and Switzerland. *See* VERHANDLUNGEN DER ERSTEN HAUPTVERSAMMLUNG DER INTERNATIONALEN VEREINIGUNG FÜR VERGLEICHENDE RECHTSWISSENSCHAFT UND VOLKSWIRTSCHAFTSLEHRE IN BERLIN (1912).

[57] Gail J. Hupper, *Education Ambivalence: The Rise of a Foreign-Student Doctorate in Law*, 49 NEW ENG. L. REV. 319, 325 (2015).

[58] Li Chen, *Early Graduate Studies in America and Legal Transplantation: The Case of China's First International and Comparative Legal Scholar*, 68 J. LEG. EDUC. 716-19, 729, 733-39, 742-47 (2019). In 1902, half of Yale's faculty members had an advanced Yale degree. *Id.* at 718. Prior to 1905, the

Raynolds had a D.C.L. in comparative jurisprudence from Yale and offered a course on the German Civil Code. Wang took interest in Germany's new code and began an English translation, which he completed in 1907. Raynolds was a member of the French Society of Comparative Legislation and successfully recommended Wang as its first Chinese member in 1905.[59]

Third, the ABA, although organized in 1878 and publishing reports of its proceedings, only started publishing the *ABA Journal* in 1915. Established as a quarterly, the Comparative Law Bureau's editorial staff controlled the second issue each year, which it devoted primarily to the subjects previously handled in the bureau's *Annual Bulletin*. Bureau members continued to meet annually while the publishing arrangement with the ABA continued through 1929. After that date, there were no more special bureau issues of the *ABA Journal*, but comparative and foreign law articles still appeared there with regularity, about five to ten per volume. In 1931, the bureau made the *Tulane Law Review* its official journal, where it published meeting reports and some of its papers in a special section.[60]

Fourth, since interest in foreign and comparative law was especially strong in New York City during the 1920s, bureau members decided to organize a new entity in lieu of simply creating a New York branch of the bureau in the manner that the International Law Association (headquartered in London) created branches. Therefore, in 1925, they established the American Foreign Law Association (AFLA), which until 2000 was a sponsor member of the American Society of Comparative Law with a special subscription relationship to the *American Journal of Comparative Law*.

Finally, due to the Great Depression, the bureau fell into financial difficulty in the 1930s. It published one more *Annual Bulletin* in 1933, 215 pages long, but neither the annual comparative review nor the bureau itself could survive. To salvage the comparative law enterprise, John Wigmore, a member of the bureau's council, urged the ABA executive committee to sponsor an amendment to the ABA's constitution, which successfully merged the Comparative Law Bureau with the ABA's International Law Section. From 1933, the ABA referred to the

---

only foreign students earning an advanced law degree were Japanese. *Id.* at 728, 740. Among Wang's courses were conflict of laws from Simeon Baldwin and Roman law from Charles Sherman. *Id.* at 740.

[59] Li Chen, *supra* note 58, at 741, 744–45; *see* CHUNG HUI WANG, THE GERMAN CIVIL CODE: WITH AN HISTORICAL INTRODUCTION AND APPENDICES (London 1907). Raynolds also taught a course on the Spanish legal system and nineteenth-century codes. Li Chen, *supra*, at 741.

[60] *See* Jerome Hall, *Report of the Committee on Publications*, PROC. SEC. INT'L & COMP. L. 158, 164 (1946). For instance, the bureau's 1931 annual meeting celebrated the publication of its translation of *Las Siete Partidas*. Henry Plauché Dart, *American Bar Association Bureau of Comparative Law*, 6 TUL. L. REV. 83–93 (1931). Samuel Scott, the translator, had given the bureau the manuscript for his translation in 1913, but the bureau only published it in 1931 after his death. *Antonio S. de Bustamante y Sirvén, Las Siete Partidas*, 6 *id.* at 328 (1932) (book review). Bureau members Charles Lobingier wrote the introduction and John Vance provided a bibliography.

new entity as the Section of International and Comparative Law. Wigmore served as its first chair.[61]

B. The 1904 Universal Congress of Lawyers and Jurists

The St. Louis Universal Congress of Lawyers and Jurists resulted from a proposal that the Louisiana Purchase Exposition Company made to the ABA. After reciting the fact that President Thomas Jefferson purchased the Louisiana Territory for $15 million from France in 1803, the company offered to hold a centennial in St. Louis in 1903. The proposal noted that the "wilderness of 1803 has developed into 14 States and Territories." It stated that the city of St. Louis, with the help of $5 million from the U.S. Congress and $1 million from the state of Missouri, was willing to devote more than the purchase price (that is, $16 million) to a celebration of Louisiana's centennial. The Centennial Exposition contemplated a "World's Fair greater and more wonderful than any ever held," and "to gather together the learned men of the world in the several departments of arts and sciences, including the science of jurisprudence."[62]

The ABA accepted the proposal, which it postponed until 1904 to further coordinate preparations, and which would now celebrate the centennial of the official transfer of sovereignty from Spain to France and then France to the United States. The World's Fair was a great success, attracting 20 million visitors. St. Louis also hosted the third modern Olympics that same year. In 1903, the ABA president had appointed Simeon Baldwin, a law professor at Yale and justice of the Connecticut Supreme Court, to the ABA's executive committee to implement the congress. It took place from September 28 to 30, 1904, immediately after the ABA's annual meeting.[63]

In addition to the many government positions and public service offices Baldwin had held, he was also a member of the *Institut de droit comparé* in Brussels. Baldwin was a natural leader and a crucial figure in the early development of comparative law. For instance, from 1908 to 1919, he was the director of the Comparative Law Bureau. John Langbein described this Yale law professor, appointed in 1869, sometime treasurer, and major benefactor, as the person who carried the law school into the twentieth century.[64] Baldwin taught private

---

[61] WILLIAM R. ROALFE, JOHN HENRY WIGMORE: SCHOLAR AND REFORMER 109, 258–59 (1977).

[62] Universal Congress of Lawyers and Jurists, *History of the Organization of the Congress*, in OFFICIAL REPORT OF THE UNIVERSAL CONGRESS OF LAWYERS AND JURISTS 315, 315–16 (V. Mott Porter ed., 1905) [hereinafter OFFICIAL REPORT].

[63] *Id.* at 317–23, 326–27; *see supra* ch. 5, text accompanying notes 46, 48, 56, 68, 77–78, 140 (Baldwin).

[64] John H. Langbein, *Law School in a University: Yale's Distinctive Path in the Later Nineteenth Century*, in HISTORY OF THE YALE LAW SCHOOL: THE TERCENTENNIAL LECTURES 53, 59–63 (Anthony T. Kronman ed., 2004).

international law using civilian sources, but after the ABA liaison position to the Universal Congress, his principal contribution as bureau director was to lend his prestige as one of America's leading jurists to the development of comparative law and its institutionalization.[65]

The St. Louis Congress's aims, which tracked the major conference sessions, included,

> consideration of the history and efficacy of the various systems of jurisprudence and the discussion of those questions of international, municipal and maritime law which concern the welfare of all civilized nations; the hope of contributing to greater harmony in the principles and the forms of procedure upon which the law of civilized nations should be based; the bringing of lawyers and jurists from all parts of the world into contact for the purpose of exchanging views on the principles and methods of the correct administration of justice.[66]

Unlike the 1900 International Comparative Law Congress in Paris, lawyers and judges organized and ran the St. Louis Congress, with a smaller representation from academia. The Congress president was David Brewer, an associate justice of the U.S. Supreme Court, who was also an international law professor at George Washington University. Brewer was born in Smyrna, Asia Minor (now Turkey), where his father worked as a missionary. His mother was Emilia Field, sister of Supreme Court justice Stephen Field and the New York codifier, David Dudley Field. Brewer's experience in Asia came through in strong dissents in cases limiting the rights of Chinese and Japanese immigrants. His dissent in *Fong Yue Ting v. United States* (1893)[67] illustrated the view that later made him a natural favorite to preside at a congress of comparative lawyers. In *Fong*, the Court determined that Congress's power to deport aliens was plenary and inherent in federal sovereignty. Brewer responded: "In view of this enactment of the highest legislative body of the foremost Christian nation, may not the thoughtful Chinese disciple of Confucius ask, Why do they send missionaries here?" Brewer was an anti-imperialist who believed that the United States should give the Philippines its independence and then guarantee its neutrality.[68]

---

[65] David S. Clark, *The Modern Development of American Comparative Law: 1904-1945*, 55 AM. J. COMP. L. 587, 594 (2007) [hereinafter Clark, *Modern Development*].

[66] Universal Congress of Lawyers and Jurists, *Organization of the Congress*, in OFFICIAL REPORT, supra note 62, at xiii; see *Universal Congress of Lawyers and Jurists*, 38 AM. L. REV. 746-50 (1904) [hereinafter *Universal Congress*].

[67] 149 U.S. 698 (1893).

[68] *Id.* at 744 (quotation); Forbath, supra note 19, at 691-92; Sarah Barringer Gordon, *Law and Religion, 1790-1920*, in 2 CAMBRIDGE HISTORY, supra note 19, at 417, 438-39; see Kunal M. Parker, *Citizenship and Immigration Law, 1800-1924: Resolutions of Membership and Territory*, in 2 CAMBRIDGE HISTORY, supra, at 168, 185-91.

Of the 14 congress vice presidents, one from each of the congress nations, most were judges or lawyers, but four were professors. These 14 persons formed a Committee of Nations and voted on congress propositions. Most of the voting members were European: from Austria, Belgium, the British Empire, France, Germany, Italy, the Netherlands, Sweden, and Switzerland. The remaining congress countries were Argentina, Brazil, China, Mexico, and the United States.[69]

Delegates could present reports and discuss in any language, but Congress staff would make translations into English. Comparative law panels included (1) the preferable method of regulating the trial of civil actions with respect to pleading and evidence, (2) a review of the four Hague Conferences on private international law, and (3) the extent to which local courts should recognize the judicial action of foreign country courts.[70]

There were 481 registered delegates at the congress, which was a huge number for such an event, even though the large majority was from the United States. Forty American law professors attended from almost 30 law schools, including deans from leading law schools such as Chicago (Joseph Beale), Harvard (James Barr Ames), Northwestern (Wigmore), Pennsylvania (William Draper Lewis), and Stanford (Nathan Abbott). Some, in addition to deans Beale, Lewis, and Wigmore, would publish comparative law research or contribute to comparative law activities, such as Eugene Gilmore (Wisconsin),[71] Charles Huberich (Texas), William Mikell (Pennsylvania), James Brown Scott (Columbia), Munroe Smith (Columbia), and William Walz (Maine). The most famous foreign law professors in attendance were Georges Blondel (Paris), Josephus Jitta (Amsterdam), and Friedrich Meili (Zurich).[72]

---

[69] Universal Congress of Lawyers and Jurists, *Officers of the Congress*, in OFFICIAL REPORT, *supra* note 62, at xv–xvi.

[70] Universal Congress of Lawyers and Jurists, *Rules of Organization and Procedure*, in OFFICIAL REPORT, *supra*, at xvii, xviii–xix; *Universal Congress*, *supra* note 66, at 747.

[71] In 1917, Gilmore taught law at the University of the Philippines, where he succeeded in enlarging the curriculum and reorganizing the library. As vice governor general of the Philippines in 1922, his position as chair of the university's board of regents allowed him to introduce a progressive social reform mission for the public university. CARRINGTON, *supra* note 22, at 105. For Beale's conflicts theory in the *Restatement of Conflict of Laws* (1934) and his three-volume treatise on the subject, he translated Savigny's Latin rendition of Bartolus's treatment of choice of law. Albert A. Ehrenzweig, *Beale's Translation of Bartolus*, 12 AM. J. COMP. L. 384–85 (1963); *see* JOSEPH HENRY BEALE, BARTOLUS ON THE CONFLICT OF LAWS (1914).

[72] Universal Congress of Lawyers and Jurists, *List of Delegates Accredited to the Universal Congress of Lawyers and Jurists*, in OFFICIAL REPORT, *supra* note 62, at 270–312. Other registered delegates were professors James Brewster (Michigan) and James Webb (Yale). William Curtis and William Keysor represented Washington University at St. Louis. *Id*. Professors Blondel and Jitta were also honorary chairpersons at the 1911 German international congress. VERHANDLUNGEN, *supra* note 56, at 1.

C. The Comparative Law Bureau

Soon after the 1904 Congress, the question of creating a comparative law society received its first organized recognition by the Pennsylvania State Bar Association in 1905. At the association's annual meeting, the president appointed a committee to study such a project. The committee's report considered the initiative too large for any one state and recommended bringing the matter before the ABA. The ABA in 1906 created the Special Committee on Comparative Law to investigate and recommend the best method to accomplish the goals of comparative law. At its 1907 annual meeting, the ABA authorized the organization of the Comparative Law Bureau, which published its first *Annual Bulletin* surveying foreign legislation and legal literature in July 1908.[73]

It is likely that the French *Société de législation comparée*, founded in 1869, which organized the 1900 Paris Congress, served as the model for the American bureau. In 1896, Henri Lévy-Ullmann (1870–1947), law professor at the University of Montpellier and *avocat* at the Paris *Cour d'appel*, wrote a report describing the French Society in the *Harvard Law Review*.[74]

Lévy-Ullmann served as general reporter to the section on civil law at the Paris Congress, which had five American delegates. He described several elements of the French society that later came to parallel aspects of the American bureau. First, the society's members were lawyers and judges as well as scholars. Second, its principal tasks were to translate and publish interesting foreign laws and to stimulate comparative law studies that could aid legislatures in law reform or simply provide useful information (such as a series of essays on bar organizations in diverse countries). Third, it published a periodic *Bulletin*, which included translated legislation and comparative law studies. Fourth, it provided translations of foreign codes, constitutions, or statutes (by 1896 from England, Germany, Hungary, Italy, Montenegro, Netherlands, Portugal, Russia, Scandinavia, United States, and Zurich) and a few comparative studies, for instance, on the treatment of aliens or on notarial law. He concluded: "Its main object is, by putting the knowledge of the laws of all countries within the reach of everybody, gradually to bring about uniformity in legislation through the

---

[73] William W. Smithers, *Book Reviews: The Civil Code of the German Empire*, 3 ANN. BULL. COMP. L. BUREAU ABA 221 (1910); Hall, *supra* note 60, at 163. Jerome Hall reported that the committee believed there was a "growing feeling that the American bench and bar had something to learn from abroad and that under the program that was envisaged the best fruits of foreign legal thought and experience would be made available to American lawyers." The committee report further stated, "In this utilitarian and constructive age we are bound to recognize that juristic principles are confined to no one people nor to any single era; it is our mission to select from every source that which is best fitted to assure the prosperity and happiness of the American people." Hall, *supra*, at 163.

[74] Henri Lévy-Ullmann, *Account of the French Society of Comparative Legislation*, 10 HARV. L. REV. 161–67 (1896); *see* William W. Smithers, *Editorial Miscellany*, 1 ANN. BULL. COMP. L. BUREAU ABA 5–6 (1908); *supra* ch. 5, pt. F.3 and text accompanying note 186 (French Society and Congress).

development of the science of law; this is pre-eminently a work of civilization and of progress."[75]

The bureau's officers included Simeon Baldwin as director and William Smithers as secretary. Smithers was from Philadelphia, where the International Printing Company published the *Annual Bulletin*, and he also served as the chairman of the *Bulletin*'s editorial staff. The bureau's managers included law school deans James Barr Ames, George Kirchwey (Columbia), William Draper Lewis, who also became the first director of the American Law Institute, and Wigmore.[76] In 1911, Roscoe Pound, then Story professor at Harvard Law School and one of America's great comparatists in the first half of the twentieth century, became a manager.[77]

In the *Bulletin*'s first issue, the bureau presented its aims.[78] These were to (1) publish an annual *Bulletin* with foreign legislation and reviews of foreign legal literature; (2) translate and publish foreign legislation and relevant expert opinions; (3) hold an annual conference to discuss comparative law generally; (4) provide a more thorough means by which foreign laws can become available to American lawyers; (5) promote research in foreign law; (6) establish a list of foreign correspondents; and (7) gather information on foreign law, including bibliographies, for the benefit of practicing lawyers, law teachers, and students.[79]

The bureau circulated the *Bulletin* to all ABA members, numbering over 2,000, and to other subscribers, totaling about 4,500 copies, which rose to 7,000 copies in 1910.[80] The editorial staff in 1908 included Baldwin for general jurisprudence; Robert Shick for Austria-Hungary; Arthur Kuhn for Belgium; Smithers for Egypt, France, and Turkey; Ernest Lorenzen (George Washington University) and Pound (then at Northwestern University) for Germany;[81] Charles Wetherill for China and Great Britain; Masuji Miyakawa (the first Japanese American lawyer admitted to a U.S. state bar, Indiana) for Japan;[82] Leo Rowe (University of

---

[75] Lévy-Ullmann, *supra* note 74, at 166–67.

[76] *Officers and Managers*, 1 ANN. BULL. COMP. L. BUREAU ABA 1 (1908); *see supra* text accompanying notes 63–65 (Baldwin) and text accompanying note 71 (law deans). Other managers were a diverse group that included Andrew Bruce: in 1916, he published an interesting study of property and society in the national social science series. Edgar Farrar became ABA president in 1911. Charles Littlefield was an expert on immigration and citizenship law and a member of Congress. Clifford Walton in 1907 published a five-volume comparative analysis of the commercial and maritime laws of Latin America, Spain, and the United States. *Officers and Managers*, *supra*.

[77] *Officers and Managers*, 4 ANN. BULL. COMP. L. BUREAU ABA 1 (1911).

[78] *Comparative Law Bureau: Objects*, 1 ANN. BULL. COMP. L. BUREAU ABA 2 (1908).

[79] Clark, *Modern Development*, *supra* note 65, at 598.

[80] Hall, *supra* note 60, at 164.

[81] *Editorial Staff*, 1 ANN. BULL. COMP. L. BUREAU ABA 3 (1908); *see* Ernest G. Lorenzen, *Seminary Methods of Legal Instruction in the German Universities*, *in* 1 LAW AND JURISPRUDENCE SERIES 15–33 (1905).

[82] Miyakawa (1870–1916) immigrated to California in 1896. After working various jobs, he earned an LL.M. degree (1903) from Columbian College (later George Washington) and then an LL.B. from Indiana University and a D.C.L. from Illinois College (later DePaul), both in 1904. He lectured on law at the latter two institutions and was the author of several books, including POWERS OF

Pennsylvania) for Latin America; William Hastings (law dean at Nebraska from 1909) for Russia; Samuel Scott for Spain; and Gordon Sherman for Switzerland.[83] There were foreign correspondents from 14 countries, including Gaston de Leval (*avocat* to the Brussels court of appeal) from Belgium and Eugen Huber (law professor at University of Bern) from Switzerland.[84]

In 1910, Smithers added Charles Huberich (then at Stanford University) to the *Bulletin*'s editorial staff for the British colonies and Edwin Borchard and Samuel Williston (Harvard) for Germany.[85] In 1911, he placed Lobingier as editor for the Philippine Islands.[86] Borchard became law librarian at the Library of Congress in 1911 and then librarian and professor at Yale Law School in 1917.[87] In 1910, the bureau had five law libraries and 17 law schools as institutional members. By 1914, that number had grown to 14 law libraries and 20 law school institutional members.[88]

The bureau entered into a publishing arrangement with the Boston Book Company in 1910 for a foreign law series. This included Samuel Scott's translation of *The Visigothic Code* (1910) and Robert Shick's translation of *The Swiss Civil Code* (1915). The latter was a team effort by bureau members, since Wetherill annotated and Huber and Sherman made corrections. Boston Book also published *The Civil Code of the German Empire* (1909), N.M. Korkunov's *General Theory of Law* (1909, Dean Hastings's translation), and 24 volumes (out of 35 projected) of the *Commercial Laws of the World* (1911–1914, with Huberich's general introduction). The German Civil Code was a collaborative effort between the University of Pennsylvania and the Pennsylvania Bar Association. Walter Loewy translated, Smithers wrote a historical introduction, and Wetherill wrote reference notes referring to analogous provisions in other foreign codes.[89]

THE AMERICAN PEOPLE: CONGRESS, PRESIDENT, AND COURTS (ACCORDING TO THE EVOLUTION OF CONSTITUTIONAL CONSTRUCTION) (1906, 2d ed. 1908) and LIFE OF JAPAN (1907, 2d ed. 1910). GREG ROBINSON, THE GREAT UNKNOWN: JAPANESE AMERICAN SKETCHES 153–57 (2016). Illustrative of the prejudice against Asians at that time, *see, e.g., Jap Lawyer is Dead*, L.A. TIMES, Mar. 5, 1916, § 4, at 13. The first Japanese student to earn a law degree at Harvard attended between 1872 and 1874. Bruce A. Kimball & Brian S. Shull, *The Ironical Exclusion of Women from Harvard Law School, 1870–1900*, 58 J. LEG. EDUC. 3, 8 (2008).

[83] *Comparative Law Bureau: Objects*, supra note 78, at 2.
[84] *Foreign Correspondents*, 1 ANN. BULL. COMP. L. BUREAU ABA 4 (1908).
[85] *Editorial Staff*, 3 ANN. BULL. COMP. L. BUREAU ABA 3 (1910).
[86] *Editorial Staff*, 4 ANN. BULL. COMP. L. BUREAU ABA 3 (1911).
[87] William W. Smithers, *Editorial Miscellany*, 4 ANN. BULL. COMP. L. BUREAU ABA 11 (1911) [hereinafter Smithers, 1911 *Miscellany*]. Smithers detailed Borchard's contributions to foreign legal literature guides, portions of which the Bureau printed in the *Bulletin*. *Id.*
[88] *Institutions, Etc., Now Members of This Bureau*, 3 ANN. BULL. COMP. L. BUREAU ABA 8 (1910); 7 *id.* at 5 (1914).
[89] Smithers, 1911 *Miscellany*, supra note 87 at 11; *see* Hall, supra note 60, at 165–66. For the extensive interest in the German Civil Code in the United States, *see* Mathias W. Reimann, *"A Monument of Legal Learning": Anglo-American Perspectives on the German Civil Code*, *in* LAW AND JUSTICE IN A MULTISTATE WORLD 793–809 (James A.R. Nafziger & Symeon C. Symeonides eds., 2002).

In addition, Boston Book (and its successor, Macmillan Company) published 12 volumes in the Modern Legal Philosophy Series between 1911 and 1925, which an AALS committee, chaired by Wigmore and dominated by comparatists, edited. The AALS president selected the committee members in 1910: Albert Kocourek (Northwestern), Ernest Lorenzen (then at the University of Wisconsin), Floyd Mechem (University of Chicago), Pound (Harvard), and Wigmore (Northwestern).[90] Ernst Freund (Chicago) and Huberich (Stanford) joined the committee in 1912, Joseph Drake (University of Michigan) in 1913, and Morris Cohen (College of the City of New York Philosophy Department) in 1922. The volumes primarily consisted of civilian legal science books, articles, and excerpts translated into English. Besides making continental legal theory accessible in English, the editors (who sometimes also translated) and others wrote useful introductions and editorial prefaces.[91] For public law, Little, Brown & Company published the Modern Criminal Science Series, sponsored by the American Institute of Criminal Law and Criminology, organized by Wigmore in 1909. Wigmore chaired the committee on translation of the continental European authors, with Freund, Pound, and Smithers as other committee members.[92]

In 1911, the United States government began to financially support the comparative law movement by devoting resources to the Library of Congress "to collect the essential materials necessary for an accurate knowledge of the legal institutions of every civilized country."[93] Borchard, bureau editor for Germany and law librarian, was supervising the work. The Library also started to publish critical surveys of foreign country legal literature, which the bureau supported, beginning at Germany, with parts also printed in the *Bulletin*. This series, known as *Guide to the Law and Legal Literature*, was very useful for academic comparatists. Borchard published two in this series, one on Germany (1912) and the other on Argentina, Brazil, and Chile (1917) as well as the *Bibliography of International Law and Continental Law* (1913). The Library of Congress finished this run by publishing volumes on Spain (1915) and France (1931). In 1943, the Library picked up the series again with 12 new volumes, this time concentrating

---

[90] *See* FRITZ BEROLZHEIMER, THE WORLD'S LEGAL PHILOSOPHIES v–ix (1912) (vol. 2, The Modern Legal Philosophy Series). Two planned volumes in this series did not appear.
[91] Clark, *Modern Development, supra* note 65, at 599–600; *see supra* ch. 5, pt. C.4 (Freund). Drake taught Roman law, comparative law, and jurisprudence at Michigan (1906–1930). He had both a Ph.D. and an LL.B. BROWN & BLUME, *supra* note 41, at 209–10, 333, 371, 469, 507, 513, 515.
[92] *See, e.g.*, BARON RAFFAELE GAROFALO, CRIMINOLOGY ii, v, ix (Robert Wyness Millar trans., 1914). Nine volumes appeared between 1911 and 1917. Some universities and colleges also taught criminology in sociology departments. *E.g.*, MAURICE PARMELEE, THE PRINCIPLES OF ANTHROPOLOGY AND SOCIOLOGY IN THEIR RELATIONS TO CRIMINAL PROCEDURE (1908) (sociology professor at City College of New York).
[93] Smithers, 1911 *Miscellany, supra* note 87, at 11; *see infra* pt. E.6 (Law Library of Congress).

on Latin America. Helen Clagett, chief of the Hispanic Law Section, authored ten of these books from 1945 to 1948.[94]

D. The Persistence of Roman Law Interest

The teaching of Roman law as a form of academic comparative law continued from the nineteenth century into the mid-twentieth century.[95] For instance, Rudolf Leonhard, a visiting professor from Breslau University, added to the Roman law curriculum at Columbia Law School. Like his colleague Munroe Smith, they both encouraged American study of Roman law for its comparative use to achieve a deeper understanding of the common law. This added to the obvious purpose of learning more about the foundation of the civil law tradition, including its methods of legal interpretation, pervasive in Europe, Latin America, and East Asia. Finally, Leonhard supported a unification of law goal endorsed by some jurists in continental Europe associated with commonalities one could discover in the civil law and common law traditions that would lead to juridical *rapprochement*.[96]

Many of the most influential jurists in the first half of the twentieth century had classically oriented educations that provided them with a background in Roman law. Some also wrote about Roman law, used it to broaden the scope of their teaching and scholarship, or even produced translations of traditional Roman legal literature.[97] Max Radin, to illustrate, a legal comparatist at the University of California, convinced West Publishing to issue a coursebook on Roman law in 1927.[98] Timothy Kearley presented many other examples.

Samuel Scott (1846–1929) had a classical education, read law, and became a lawyer shortly after the Civil War. He left law practice a few years later

---

[94] The first two Latin American volumes covered Colombia (1943, Richard C. Backus & Phanor J. Eder) and Cuba, the Dominican Republic, and Haiti (1944, Crawford M. Bishop & Anyda Marchant). Clagett's single country volumes included: Mexico (1945, with John T. Vance); Bolivia, Chile, Ecuador, the Mexican states, Paraguay, Peru, Uruguay, and Venezuela (all published in 1947); and Argentina (1948). *See* Edwin O. Ford, REPORT OF THE COMMITTEE ON LATIN AMERICAN LAW, PROC. SEC. INT'L & COMP. L. 125, 138 (1947).

[95] *See supra* ch. 5, pt. E.1 (Roman law). Professors also taught Roman law in history departments. *See, e.g.,* ANDREW STEPHENSON, A HISTORY OF ROMAN LAW: WITH A COMMENTARY ON THE INSTITUTES OF GAIUS AND JUSTINIAN (1912).

[96] M.H. HOEFLICH, ROMAN AND CIVIL LAW AND THE DEVELOPMENT OF ANGLO-AMERICAN JURISPRUDENCE IN THE NINETEENTH CENTURY 114–15 (1997); Rudolf Leonhard, *The Vocation of America for the Science of Roman Law*, 26 HARV. L. REV. 389–402 (1913). Leonhard was the Kaiser Wilhelm Professor of Roman Law during the 1907–1908 academic year. *Id.* at 389 n.1, 415. *See also id., Methods Followed in Germany by the Historical School of Law*, 7 COLUM. L. REV. 573–81 (1907). Hessel Yntema was the successor to teach Roman law and comparative jurisprudence at Columbia. COLUMBIA LAW, *supra* note 36, at 278.

[97] KEARLEY, *supra* note 27, at xix.

[98] MAX RADIN, HANDBOOK OF ROMAN LAW (West hornbook series, 1927).

for the banking business, but retained and nurtured an interest in the Iberian Peninsula and Roman Law. In the twentieth century, he served as an editor for the Comparative Law Bureau.[99] Scott's first legal translation was *The Visigothic Code* (1910),[100] which he probably made from the Spanish version published in 1815. The quality of the translation was questionable and the 40-page preface, according to three reviewers, had little historical or legal value. A German jurist had produced a superior Latin edition of the Code, but apparently Scott did not know German. Kearley counted four positive reviews of Scott's volume against the three negative ones, but concluded that overall his errors marred the attempt.[101]

Scott had more success critically with another translation he finished in 1913, the *Siete Partidas*, although there was a delay in its publication since the Comparative Law Bureau lacked necessary funds. Finally, in 1931, the bureau was able to publish it with Lobingier preparing the introduction and index and Vance the bibliography.[102] Scott finished his *magnum opus* in 1922, the 17-volume *Civil Law*. The core of this translation primarily from the Latin comprised all four parts of Justinian's *Corpus juris civilis*, including the Code and Novels, which, until recently, were the only available English version. The principal review of Scott's volumes came from the Romanist, William Buckland, a Cambridge professor, who chided Scott for his use of antiquated Latin texts and failure to utilize recent German scholarship. It fell to Scott's estate to publish this work.[103]

Charles Sherman (1874–1962) took a classical curriculum at Yale College, then an LL.B. at Yale Law School followed by its D.C.L. degree in 1899. In 1905, the Yale law dean hired Sherman to teach Roman law courses, a position he expanded over the next 12 years to include canon law and serve as law librarian. In 1917, Sherman published *Roman Law in the Modern World*.[104] *Roman Law* was an ambitious three-volume work that first surveyed the history of Roman law

---

[99] KEARLEY, *supra* note 27, at 19, 22–23, 25–26, 117.

[100] THE VISIGOTHIC CODE (FORUM JUDICUM) (S.P. Scott ed. & trans., 1910).

[101] *The Visigothic Code*, 45 AM. L. REV. 478–79 (1911) (book review); *see* KEARLEY, *supra* note 27, at 117, 119–21. On the title page, Scott stated that he made the translation from the original Latin. Paul Vinogradoff also wrote a critical review. *The Visigothic Code (Forum judicum)*, 27 L.Q. REV. 373 (1911) (book review). Munroe Smith wrote the third negative review. M.S., *The Visigothic Code (Forum Judicum)*, 11 COLUM. L. REV. 695–96 (1911) (book review).

[102] KEARLEY, *supra* note 27, at 121–24; *see* LAS SIETE PARTIDAS (S.P. Scott ed. & trans., 1931). *E.g.*, Antonio de Bustamante, one of the founders of the International Academy of Comparative Law, wrote a favorable book review.

[103] KEARLEY, *supra* note 27, at 125–31; *see* 1–17 THE CIVIL LAW: INCLUDING THE TWELVE TABLES, THE INSTITUTES OF GAIUS, . . . (S.P. Scott ed. & trans., 1932) (bound in seven volumes); W.W. Buckland, *The Civil Law*, 7 TUL. L. REV. 627–32 (1933) (book review).

[104] HOEFLICH, *supra* note 96, at 123; KEARLEY, *supra* note 27, at 43–45, 93–96; *see* CHARLES PHINEAS SHERMAN, 1–3 ROMAN LAW IN THE MODERN WORLD (1917). Sherman's dissertation for the civil law degree was *The Maritime Law of Rome and Some Comparisons with Modern Jurisprudence* (1899). KEARLEY, *supra*, at 45 n.54.

through its rebirth in Europe and acceptance into modern codes. Furthermore, the second volume presented Roman private law principles, arranged systematically, and illustrated by both civil law and common law systems. The third volume was a bibliography of Roman and civil law by topic. Reviewers had a mixed response to Sherman's effort, but *Roman Law* saw two more editions, in 1924 and 1937.[105] After Sherman left Yale, he held several visiting positions until 1926, when he began teaching Roman law and history regularly at William and Mary School of Jurisprudence and canon law at National University Law School. This continued until 1935, two years after he coauthored a volume of Roman law excerpts intended for teaching.[106]

Fred Blume (1875-1971), born in Germany, emigrated 12 years later to the United States where he learned Latin in high school and at the State University of Iowa, which awarded him a bachelor of philosophy degree in 1898. He apprenticed in a law office for a year and passed the Iowa bar exam in 1899. After a few years of law practice there, Blume moved to Wyoming and began a law practice and political career. After leaving politics in 1912, Blume decided to dedicate himself to self-education in classical civilizations and the European Middle Ages. Since he knew German, he subscribed to the principal German journal on legal history and read the German research literature on the *Corpus juris civilis*. He soon dedicated himself to undertake a translation of Justinian's Code and Novels.[107]

In 1919, Blume became more serious about his desire to translate Justinian's Code into English. He wrote to a New York book dealer to obtain a copy of Paul Krüger's 1877 critical Latin edition of the Code. Blume already had the 1872 volume that Krüger and Theodor Mommsen had prepared for Justinian's Digest and Institutes.[108] In 1921, the Wyoming governor appointed Blume to the state supreme court. Thus, Blume at this point had two tasks, the day job with the court and his spare time for the Code, a draft of which he finished in 1924. Unsatisfied, he continued reading German juristic literature while he revised the manuscript, deviating in the summer of 1929, at Wigmore's invitation, to teach Roman law at Northwestern. Scott's translation of Justinian's *Corpus Juris Civilis* appeared in 1932, but given its mixed reviews, Blume continued his revision sporadically until he sent a final manuscript in 1943 to Clyde Pharr, a Vanderbilt

---

[105] HOEFLICH, *supra* note 96, at 124-25, 143; KEARLEY, *supra* note 27, at 96-100. Illustrative of reviews was the one by Kocourek. A.K., *Roman Law in the Modern World*, 12 ILL. L. REV. 662-66 (1918) (book review).

[106] KEARLEY, *supra* note 27, at 100-104; *see* CHARLES PHINEAS SHERMAN & THOMAS RAYMOND ROBINSON, ROMAN READINGS IN ROMAN LAW (1933). *See also* EPITOME OF ROMAN LAW IN A SINGLE BOOK (Charles Phineas Sherman ed. & trans., 1937) (700 excerpts).

[107] KEARLEY, *supra* note 27, at 37-40, 132, 134-37.

[108] KEARLEY, *supra* note 27, at 136, 140-41; *see* 1 CORPUS IURIS CIVILIS: INSTITUTIONES, DIGESTA (Paul Krüger & Theodor Mommsen eds., 1872); 2 *id*.: CODEX IUSTINIANUS (Paul Krüger ed., 1877). Blume appeared to have the 1914 edition of Krüger's *Codex*. KEARLEY, *supra*, at 142.

classics professor.[109] Nevertheless, Blume's translation and edition of the Code did not appear until long after his death in 2016.[110]

In 1935, the Nazi regime forced Ernst Levy (1881–1968) to retire from his law professorship at Heidelberg. Levy had earned his J.U.D. at Berlin in 1906 and began his teaching career there in 1914, followed by professorships at Frankfurt and Freiburg. An expert in Roman law, he emigrated to the United States in 1936 and accepted a Roman law position at the University of Washington. The next year, the law school hired him to teach comparative law, Roman law, and modern civil law, which he did until his retirement in 1952.[111]

Finally, the bronze doors at the U.S. Supreme Court building illustrate the symbolic status of Roman law in American legal history. From 1800, the Court conducted its business in space that Congress had provided it at the capitol building. Only in 1935 could the Court occupy its own new Corinthian-style marble structure with giant bronze entrance doors weighing 13 tons that depict Roman law on three of their eight panels. These portray the praetor's edict, the jurist Julian with a pupil scholar, and Justinian presenting the *Corpus juris civilis*.[112]

E. American Comparatists Look Abroad and Institutionalize at Home

The 1920s and 1930s were decades during which American comparatists became actively involved in European legal research and European legal conferences, together with substantial interest in Asia and Latin America. An aspect of this appeared in the doctoral programs at leading American law schools. For instance, in 1925, the U.S. government initiated a comparative law series in the Department of Commerce, which continued until 1940 with periodic reports

---

[109] KEARLEY, *supra* note 27, at 142, 144–47, 149–52, 154–55, 169, 171, 179. In 1937, Blume had a library of almost 900 books about Roman law and, by 1943, had finished a translation of Justinian's Novels. *Id.* at 147, 171.

[110] 1–3 THE CODEX OF JUSTINIAN: A NEW ANNOTATED TRANSLATION, WITH PARALLEL LATIN AND GREEK TEXT BASED ON A TRANSLATION BY JUSTICE FRED H. BLUME (Bruce W. Frier gen. ed., 2016). For the origin of the Frier edition, *see* KEARLEY, *supra* note 27, at 179–80.

[111] Dietrich V. Simon, *Levy, Ernst, in* 14 NEUE DEUTSCHE BIOGRAPHIE 403–04 (Fritz Wagner gen. ed., 1985); Robert L. Taylor, *Dr. Ernst Levy*, 27 WASH. L. REV. & ST. B.J. 173–75 (1952); *see* ERNST LEVY, WEST ROMAN VULGAR LAW: THE LAW OF PROPERTY (1951); *id.*, WESTRÖMISCHES VULGARRECHT: DAS OBLIGATIONENRECHT (1956); Stefan A. Riesenfeld, *Book Review*, 57 AM. HIST. REV. 659–61 (1952).

[112] Supreme Court of the United States, *Building History*, at https://www.supremecourt.gov/about/buildinghistory.aspx; *id.*, *Building Features*, at https://www.supremecourt.gov/about/buildingfeatures.aspx. Of the remaining five panels, one represents a trial scene from primitive law, three portray events in English legal history, and one presents John Marshall and Joseph Story. *Building Features, supra*.

on American and foreign commercial law.[113] *ABA Journal* special sections devoted to comparative law also reflected this as did American submissions to foreign legal publications. The 1925 *Journal* reported that foreign law had become increasingly important in the United States, both for the goals of comparative law as well as private international law.[114] The *Journal* went to all ABA members, numbering around 4,000 in 1920, but increasing to 30,000 by 1936. In 1930, 14 law schools reported offering a comparative law course, usually to graduate students.[115]

1. The International Academy of Comparative Law

Although two impressive multinational congresses of comparative law occurred at the beginning of the twentieth century, namely the 1900 Paris Congress and the 1904 St. Louis Congress, neither created the momentum able to replicate periodic congresses in the following years. Then in 1924, Munroe Smith, a professor at Columbia University, together with Élemér Balogh, Antonio de Bustamante, Henri Lévy-Ullmann, Vittorio Scialoja, and André Weiss formed the International Academy of Comparative Law as its first officers in Geneva, which moved its seat in 1925 to The Hague.[116]

Smith was one of three vice presidents of the academy. The number of full titular members was set at a maximum of 30, although they could elect additional correspondent members. Members had to be professors or published scholars, a practice that continues today. The other American members were: John Bassett Moore, teaching at Columbia Law School since 1891 and a judge on the Permanent Court of International Justice from 1921; Pound, dean at Harvard Law School since 1916; James Brown Scott, a law professor at Georgetown University and editor in chief of the *American Journal of International Law* from

---

[113] *See* U.S. Dept. Commerce, Comparative Law Series 1 (C.L. no. 584, May 1936). There was a gap between 1929 and 1932. Id.
[114] G. Evans Hubbard, *American Foreign Law Association*, 11 A.B.A. J. 270–71 (1925).
[115] Walther Hug & Gordon Ireland, *The Progress of Comparative Law*, 6 Tul. L. Rev. 68, n.3 (1931).
[116] David S. Clark, *American Participation in the Development of the International Academy of Comparative Law and Its First Two Hague Congresses*, 54 Am. J. Comp. L. 1, 2–3, 8 (Supp. 2006) [hereinafter Clark, *International Academy*]; *see Annales et Documents*, *in* 1 Actorum Academiae Universalis Iurisprudentiae Comparativae 1, 8–13 (Élemér Balogh ed., 1928) [hereinafter Actorum Academiae]; John Wigmore, *The Movement for International Assimilation of Private Law: Recent Phases*, 20 Ill. L. Rev. 42, 45–48 (1925) [hereinafter Wigmore, *Movement*]; Ernst Heymann, *Vorwort*, *in* Deutsche Landesreferate zum Internationalen Kongress für Rechtsvergleichung im Haag 1932 v (Ernst Heymann ed., 1932). Wigmore was a strong supporter of the Academy. *See* Clark, *International Academy*, *supra*, at 3 n.8; Élemér Balogh, *Speech on the Activities of the Academy and of the Congress*, in 3 Actorum Academiae, *supra*, at 49, 50 (pts. 1 & 2, 1953). I detailed much of the academy's early history, which informed most of this section, in Clark, *International Academy*, *supra*, at 2–12.

1907; and Harlan Stone, dean of Columbia Law School (served 1910–1923) and U.S. Supreme Court justice from 1925.[117]

Three of the original five American members were to play an important role in the academy and its international congresses during the 1920s and 1930s.[118] Of these, Pound was the most famous scholar. He established sociological jurisprudence in the United States and spoke from a position of influence as a professor (1910–1947) and dean (1916–1936) at Harvard Law School.[119] Pound served as an editor for the *Annual Bulletin* of the Comparative Law Bureau from its first issue in 1908 and was a manager on the bureau's council from 1911 until the time of its merger with the American Bar Association's International Law Section in 1933. He became president of the academy's Anglo-American group in 1927 and functioned as president of the academy itself from 1950 to 1955.[120]

Scott, as with Smith, earned a German J.U.D. (at Heidelberg) in 1894. He was a delegate to the 1904 St. Louis Congress, representing Columbia School of Law, where he had been a professor since 1903.[121] Scott's interests, like those of his compatriot, Moore, centered on public international law rather than comparative law. From 1906 to 1910, Scott worked as solicitor at the United States Department of State. He served as founding editor in chief of the *American Journal of International Law* from 1907 to 1924 and was the "guiding force" in the American Society of International Law's creation in 1906.[122] It is likely that Scott and Moore were instrumental in convincing academy members to move the annual meetings and, in fact, the organization itself to The Hague. Scott was a delegate, like Bustamante, to the Second Hague Peace Conference (1907) and to the 1919 Paris Peace Conference. From 1910, when Scott left the government, until 1940, he was a trustee and secretary to the Carnegie Endowment for International Peace in Washington. The academy elected Scott one of its vice presidents in 1932.[123]

---

[117] Clark, *International Academy, supra* note 116, at 4–6; *see supra* ch. 5, text accompanying notes 126–30 (Smith).

[118] Smith died in 1926. Columbia University Press published his lectures on European legal history two years later. MUNROE SMITH, THE DEVELOPMENT OF EUROPEAN LAW (1928).

[119] DAVID M. RABBAN, LAW'S HISTORY: AMERICAN LEGAL THOUGHT AND THE TRANSATLANTIC TURN TO HISTORY 426–30, 432–36, 451–62, 469–71 (2013); *see* Noga Morag-Levine, *Sociological Jurisprudence and the Spirit of the Common Law, in* THE OXFORD HANDBOOK OF LEGAL HISTORY 438–56 (Markus D. Dubber & Christopher Tomlins eds., 2018) (Ihering's influence); *see infra* pt. F.1 (Pound).

[120] Clark, *International Academy, supra* note 116, at 6–7.

[121] Scott was the founding dean of the Los Angeles Law School (1896–1899), which became the University of Southern California School of Law. He left to become law dean at the University of Illinois (1899–1903), followed by a law professorship at Columbia University (1903–1905) and George Washington University (1905–1906). *James Brown Scott, in* 1 ACTORUM ACADEMIAE, *supra* note 116, at 1162.

[122] *History of the Organization of the American Society of International Law*, 1 PROC. AM. SOC'Y INT'L L. 23–26, 34, 37 (1907); Frederic L. Kirgis, *The Formative Years of the American Society of International Law*, 90 AM. J. INT'L L. 559, 562–68 (1996).

[123] Clark, *International Academy, supra* note 116, at 7–8.

Moore, the first professor of international law at Columbia University, maintained that relationship from 1891 to 1924. The academy elected Moore one of its vice presidents in 1927. Like Bustamante, Moore became both a member of the Permanent Court of Arbitration (from 1912 until 1938) and in 1921, the first American judge on the Permanent Court of International Justice (until 1928). The location of both institutions was at the Peace Palace in The Hague.[124]

The story of the academy's move in 1925 from Geneva, a French-speaking city, to The Hague in the Netherlands is an interesting one. The academy from its origin had a distinct French flavor, rooted in the history of international legal institutions supporting both international and comparative law but also in the consequences of World War I. Its official name was French as were two of the original five officers.[125] Of the 30 original titular members, there were five French, five American, four Italian, three English, two German, one Dutch, one Swiss, and the remainder from other places.[126] At the academy's 1925 annual meeting, it amended the statutes to reflect the move and to established itself as an association under Dutch law. The meeting's report gave two principal reasons for the transfer: to placate the English and American members and to strengthen the bonds between the academy and the Permanent Court. In fact, the academy's meeting occurred at the Peace Palace.[127]

I believe that there was an unstated American element to explain the move to The Hague and the use of the Peace Palace for meetings, which was the legacy left by Andrew Carnegie, who died in 1919. At the beginning of the twentieth century, Carnegie was the richest man on the planet, having sold his interest in the eponymous steel company for $225 million, equivalent today to almost $8 billion. Tired of creating wealth, he decided to spend his remaining years trying to donate it to worthy causes. World peace became one of those causes.[128]

In 1904, Carnegie donated $1.5 million to a Dutch entity, the Carnegie Foundation, to build a "temple of peace" for the Permanent Court of Arbitration. The stone-laying ceremony occurred during the Second Hague Peace Conference in 1907 and the building opened in 1913 with Carnegie present. In 1922, the Peace Palace also became home to the Permanent Court of International Justice and in 1923 the Hague Academy of International Law, created in 1914. Funding

---

[124] *Id.* at 8.
[125] *Id.* at 2–3, 8–9. The French officers were Weiss (president) and Lévy-Ullmann (secretary). Bustamante, law professor at the University of Havana, was a vice president who became president in 1927 (until 1950) and Scialoja, professor of Roman law at the University of Rome, was another vice president. Balogh (secretary), a polyglot Hungarian, taught law at many universities and became the permanent general secretary until 1955. *Id.* at 2–5, 8–9.
[126] Wigmore, *Movement, supra* note 116, at 47–48. Of those representing northern Africa, two were French.
[127] Clark, *International Academy, supra* note 116, at 6, 8.
[128] *Id.* at 9.

to support this academy came from the Carnegie Endowment in Washington, of which Scott happened to be secretary. Although the International Academy of Comparative Law, an impecunious institution from its creation until today, did not require substantial funding to continue, the ability to hold annual meetings in the Peace Palace along with whatever assistance Scott might provide must have seemed attractive. In fact, the Carnegie Foundation did provide funding for the First International Congress of Comparative Law in 1932, when Scott became an academy vice president.[129]

Wigmore, who was on the Bureau of Comparative Law's board of managers from 1907 until 1933, was skeptical of the academy's purposes and personnel from its beginning. First, he identified the academy's purposes as two: (1) comparative law study; and (2) improvement of private law legislation, including codification. In a dialectical commentary, Wigmore concluded that the academy was not suited for study. Thirty members were too few. As for private international law, the Hague Academy, housed from 1923 in the Peace Palace, was financially sound and covered the field. He offered as an alternative the creation of an international organization that coordinated the scholarly efforts of already existing national comparative law entities, such as the U.S. Bureau. Many of these published journals. Turning to codification and unification of law as instruments of improvement, Wigmore found the academy inadequate for the task. It had no money or library, and Geneva did not provide the latter for comparative law. Again, only 30 members could not accomplish much. More importantly, as something of a legal realist, he argued that a few lawyers sitting in a room separated from the economic and political interests at stake could not achieve legal unification.[130]

Second, Wigmore considered the academy's membership. Since it could not accomplish its purposes, it served nothing more than an honorary function. The number of members was too small, since there were 60 nations qualified to join the League of Nations. The standard for selection, excellence as a professor or published scholar in the field of comparative or private international law, was too narrow. He then listed suitable candidates with other qualifications. Moreover, he scrutinized the "strict process of selection" that the statutes called for. He pointed out that two of the five American members were not comparatists, but rather distinguished public international lawyers. He then proceeded to review

---

[129] *Id.* at 9–10. The academy held all its annual meetings through the 1930s in the Peace Palace. *Id.* at 12. Carnegie created the Carnegie Foundation for the Advancement of Teaching in 1905; the Carnegie Endowment for International Peace in 1910; and in 1911, an umbrella foundation, the Carnegie Corporation (New York). Carnegie Corporation of New York, *Our History*, at https://www.carnegie.org/about/our-history.

[130] Clark, *International Academy*, *supra* note 116, at 13–14.

the omissions, naming names, associated with various European countries, Latin America, and Asia.[131]

2. The American Foreign Law Association

The Comparative Law Bureau in 1924 adopted a resolution to create a New York section of the bureau. That same year, during a visit of hundreds of American lawyers to the ABA annual meeting held in London, the French *Société de législation comparée* entertained a group of the American lawyers who had traveled to Paris. At that meeting, some suggested that the Americans form a *Société* branch in the United States. There followed a meeting between the president of the New York City Bar Association, the chair of its special committee on private international law and conflicts of law, and the bureau's chairman and vice chairman. They decided to form an organization committee that led to the 1925 founding of the AFLA.[132]

The AFLA's Constitution detailed the aims and objectives of the new organization, which paralleled those of the bureau and later influenced the creation of the American Association for the Comparative Study of Law in 1951. The AFLA Constitution stated:

> The objects of the Association shall be the advancement of the study, understanding, and practice of foreign, comparative and private international law, the promotion of solidarity among members of the legal profession who devote themselves, wholly or in part, to those branches, the maintenance of adequate professional standards relative to members and active cooperation with learned societies, devoted to such subjects, like the Comparative Law Bureau of the ABA [and] the Société de Legislation Comparée.[133]

AFLA dues were set at $10 annually. The first elected president was Smithers. The General Council included Manley Hudson (Harvard), Judge Otto Schoenrich (New York City), Lobingier (U.S. Court for China in Shanghai and professor, Comparative Law School of China), Phanor Eder (New York City), and Arthur Kuhn (New York City). In 1925, the AFLA had 42 American members and nine foreign members.[134]

---

[131] Wigmore, *Movement, supra* note 116, at 42, 52–56.
[132] Phanor J. Eder, *Thirtieth Anniversary of the American Foreign Law Association*, 4 AM. J. COMP. L. 320–22 (1955) (*Bulletin*); Hubbard, *supra* note 114, at 271; *American Foreign Law Association*, 20 ILL. L. REV. 110, 111 (1925).
[133] *American Foreign Law Association, supra* note 132, at 111 (art. II).
[134] Eder, *supra* note 132, at 322; *American Foreign Law Association, supra* note 132, at 110–11.

3. Social Science and the Johns Hopkins Institute of Law

By the beginning of the twentieth century, American judges faced an increasing number of public law disputes, some of which involved overt political issues. In addition, population growth and an increasing number of lawyers precipitated more litigation of all types.[135] John West from 1876 saw the business opportunity of printing state appellate court decisions quickly for lawyers to use in future cases. Forming the West Publishing Company, West added more states with a regional reporter system, which covered the whole country by 1887. The company also developed a digest system prefacing decisions with headnotes categorized by key numbers. In 1908, West introduced indexing for all American law that made its products even more valuable to lawyers.[136] The consequence for the American legal system, however, was an accelerating expansion of authoritative sources for legal rules that obviously undercut any assertion of certainty and predictability of law. Rather than the premise on which law schools were teaching, that the law consisted of stable principles one could learn, jurists increasingly saw judicial precedents as ad hoc rationalizations. Winning a case depended on finding the closest precedent that matched from a reservoir of thousands.[137]

One approach that elite lawyers supported to deal with this crisis of legal uncertainty was the formation of the American Law Institute in 1923.[138] Some professors at a few leading law schools adopted another strategy in the 1920s and 1930s. Robert Stevens identified three strands to this effort: (1) determine how social science might help jurists understand or improve the law, (2) remake the law curriculum, and (3) adopt legal realism as a guiding philosophy. As early as 1910, Pound had argued for law school training in economics, philosophy, and sociology. During that decade, certain Yale law professors, such as Wesley Hohfeld, also proposed broader scholarship and a revised curriculum.[139]

---

[135] STEVENS, *supra* note 2, at 132. In 1910, the population was 92 million served by 122,000 lawyers. *Id.* at 132.

[136] Mnopedia, *West Publishing Company*, https://www.mnopedia.org/group/west-publishing-company. The uniform indexing system for all American law consisted of 412 main topics and 66,000 subtopics. This system enabled a lawyer anywhere in the country with access to West's reporters and indexes to find up-to-date court decisions on every point of law for every state and the federal courts. *Id.*

[137] STEVENS, *supra* note 2, at 132–33.

[138] See *infra* pt. E.4 (ALI).

[139] STEVENS, *supra* note 2, at 134; *see* Roscoe Pound, *Law in Books and Law in Action*, 44 AM. L. REV. 12, 35–36 (1910). "Let us not become legal monks. Let us not allow our legal texts to acquire sanctity and go the way of all sacred writings." *Id.* at 36. In 1914, the AALS had discussed creating a national school of jurisprudence that would have had comparative, historical, and functional dimensions in the effort to improve American law. Wesley Newcomb Hohfeld, *A Vital School of Jurisprudence and Law: Have American Universities Awakened to the Enlarged Opportunities and Responsibilities of the Present Day?*, *in* 14 PROCEEDINGS OF THE FOURTEENTH ANNUAL MEETING OF THE ASSOCIATION OF AMERICAN LAW SCHOOLS 76, 83–96, 107–14 (1914).

With a new law dean in 1916, the Yale faculty submitted a plan to rename it the Yale School of Law and Jurisprudence. The purpose of the newly conceptualized school would incorporate the historical and comparative study of law. Scholarship should include Roman law and teaching such courses as historical, comparative, analytical, and functional jurisprudence. The dean wanted the school to be both professional and academic with comparative study of foreign jurisprudence. Further innovation at Yale, however, had to wait until after 1927, when the school began to add social scientists to the faculty.[140]

Another series of ambitious proposals associated with curriculum reform occurred at Columbia in the 1920s. The central idea was to develop functional courses and teaching materials. Professors wrote some new course books on functional themes that included more than appellate cases. By the end of the decade, the project to transform the law school's primary goal from teaching to research split the faculty and failed.[141]

In 1928, two Columbia law professors left to form with others the Institute of Law at Johns Hopkins University. One was Hessel Yntema (1891–1966), Columbia professor of Roman law and comparative jurisprudence. The institute's mission focused solely on research since it had no students. The institute secured funding for only five years and in 1933, with the economic depression, it closed. Members, including the director who came from Yale Law School, brought a variety of perspectives from philology to economics and physics. The goal was to apply scientific methods to develop a social science of law.[142] Specifically, the institute's aims included simplification and codification of law. "The study of the economic and social effects of law; the clarification and simplification of law; the training of jurists and codifiers; and the guidance of writers of text-books and thinkers upon the human effects of law."[143] With the end of the institute and the

---

[140] STEVENS, *supra* note 2, at 134–35, 145–46 n.35; Manfred Rehbinder, *The Development and Present State of Fact Research in Law in the United States*, 24 J. LEG. EDUC. 567, 575–77 (1972). In 1915, the prior dean had requested money to expand the school for a comparative study of the world's legal systems. STEVENS, *supra*, at 145 n.33.

[141] STEVENS, *supra* note 2, at 137–40; Rehbinder, *supra* note 140, at 569–72; COLUMBIA LAW, *supra* note 36, at 299–302, 305. One study classified law to reflect the connections between law and modern life, such as familial relations, political relations, and business relations. STEVENS, *supra*, at 148–49 n.64.

[142] JAMES E. HERGET, AMERICAN JURISPRUDENCE, 1870-1970: A HISTORY 206, 212 (1990) [hereinafter HERGET, JURISPRUDENCE]; Rehbinder, *supra* note 140, at 572–75; *The Johns Hopkins Institute for the Study of Law*, 6 AM. L. SCH. REV. 336 (1928) [hereinafter *Institute*]; *see* Hessel E. Yntema, *The Rational Basis of Legal Science*, 31 COLUM. L. REV. 925–55 (1931); *id.*, *The Implications of Legal Science*, 10 N.Y.U. L.Q. REV. 279–310 (1933) (both articles defending empirical legal science). At Columbia, Yntema had been a professor at both the law and political science faculties. He had a Ph.D. from Michigan in political science and a S.J.D. from Harvard. COLUMBIA LAW, *supra* note 36, at 278, 305; *Institute*, *supra*, at 338.

[143] *Institute*, *supra* note 142, at 337.

tenacity of the Langdellian tradition at law schools, the promise of a social science of law would have to wait until a more propitious time.[144]

Some of the institute's members incorporated part of Pound's sociological jurisprudence in their writing.[145] James Herget identified four components to Pound's theory, two of which owed a debt to German legal philosophy. First, a nation's legal rules and principles derived their authority from the fact that courts relied upon and elaborated them. They did not meaningfully exist as a body of rules independent from decision makers. Second, the work was pragmatic, a characteristic of American intellectual thought. Third, one could explain social phenomena as a product of conflict among group interests. Fourth, using the free law perspective, one should be skeptical about predicting legal outcomes. The latter two elements were rooted in German legal scholarship.[146]

Herget called the aggregate of these components the Poundian paradigm since Pound presented it first, but recognized that others developed all or part of it further in the 1920s and 1930s under the label sociological jurisprudence, legal realism, free law, functionalism, pragmatism, or jurisprudence of interests.[147] Yntema suggested that legal realism in the United States began with an article

---

[144] In 1960, reassessing legal realism and empirical legal science, Yntema recognized that those foremost in that movement failed to incorporate comparative law perspectives. Hessel E. Yntema, *American Legal Realism in Retrospect*, 14 VAND. L. REV. 317, 330 (1960).

[145] HERGET, JURISPRUDENCE, *supra* note 142, at 206 (Herman Oliphant); Hessel E. Yntema, *Legal Science and Reform*, 34 COLUM. L. REV. 207-08, 222-24 (1934) (Pound's administration of justice reform and Cardozo's recommendation to consider foreign examples for a ministry of justice).

[146] HERGET, JURISPRUDENCE, *supra* note 142, at 148; N.E.H. HULL, ROSCOE POUND AND KARL LLEWELLYN: SEARCHING FOR AN AMERICAN JURISPRUDENCE 242-43 (1997) [hereinafter HULL, POUND AND LLEWELLYN]; James E. Herget, *The Influence of German Thought on American Jurisprudence, 1880-1918*, in THE RECEPTION OF CONTINENTAL IDEAS IN THE COMMON LAW WORLD: 1820-1920, at 203, 215-27 (Mathias Reimann ed., 1993) [hereinafter Herget, *Influence*]; *see* EDGAR BODENHEIMER, JURISPRUDENCE: THE PHILOSOPHY AND METHOD OF THE LAW 115-20, 288-89, 312-13 (3d rev. ed. 1974); RABBAN, *supra* note 119, at 464-66; Edwin G. Baetjer, *Policy and Program of the Johns Hopkins Institute of Law*, 16 A.B.A. J. 312-13, 315-16 (1930); James E. Herget & Stephen Wallace, *The German Free Law Movement as the Source of American Legal Realism*, 73 VA. L. REV. 399, 401-28 (1987); Katharina Isabel Schmidt, *Law, Modernity, Crisis: German Free Lawyers, American Legal Realists, and the Transatlantic Turn to "Life," 1903-1933*, 39 GERMAN STUD. REV. 121-40 (2016).

Herget pointed to Hermann Kantorowicz (1877-1940, law professor at Freiburg, then Kiel until 1933) as a leading frèe law proponent. He taught the 1927 summer term at Columbia, again in 1934 in New York at the New School for Social Research, then in England until his death. Herget, *Influence*, *supra*, at 213; *see* Vivian Grossfeld Curran, *Rethinking Hermann Kantorowicz*, in RETHINKING THE MASTERS OF COMPARATIVE LAW 37 (Annelise Riles ed., 2001) [hereinafter RETHINKING THE MASTERS]; Thomas Raiser, *Hermann Ulrich Kantorowicz*, in DER EINFLUSS DEUTSCHER EMIGRANTEN AUF DIE RECHTSENTWICKLUNG IN DER USA UND IN DEUTSCHLAND: VORTÄGE UND REFERATE DES BONNER SYMPOSIONS IM SEPTEMBER 1991, at 365-81 (Marcus Lutter et al. eds., 1993) [hereinafter DER EINFLUSS]; Herman U. Kantorowicz & Edwin W. Patterson, *Legal Science— A Summary of Its Methodology*, 28 COLUM. L. REV. 679, 707 (1928); Hermann Kantorowicz, *Some Rationalism about Realism*, 43 YALE L.J. 1240-53 (1934).

[147] HERGET, JURISPRUDENCE, *supra* note 142, at 147, 165-66, 170-74, 192-95; WIECEK, *supra* note 19, at 198-99; Herget & Wallace, *supra* note 146, at 432-34, 437-39; *see* COMMAGER, *supra* note 5, at 375, 377-80; HERGET, JURISPRUDENCE, *supra*, at 155-64; RABBAN, *supra* note 119, at 474-75, 485-86; Roscoe Pound, *The Theory of Judicial Decision*, 36 HARV. L. REV. 640-62, 802-25, 940-59 (1923).

that Karl Llewellyn (1893–1962), then on the law faculty at Columbia, published based on an address he gave at the American Association of Political Science.[148] Llewellyn, like Pound, was fluent in German and was influenced both by Pound and German juristic literature.[149]

However, by the 1930s, Pound's belief in the strength of the common law's evolutionary growth, distrust of the administrative state as a fourth branch of government, and rising political conservatism, led him to reject what he considered radical legal realism.[150] Pound saw the expansion of public administrative bureaucracies in Europe and the United States to cope with the industrial era. Unlike the civil law's absorption of social welfare policies into a centralizing state, Pound preferred maintaining social policy functions in courts and private groupings such as employers, the professions, commercial insurers, and philanthropic entities. By the late 1930s, Pound was a reliable critic of the New Deal and its intrusion into the legal system. He stood for pluralism and decentralized state institutions, which the courts and its common law fostered.[151] In 1934, Pound went as far as praising Adolf Hitler for his opposition to international socialism.[152]

4. The American Law Institute and Unification of Law

Comparative law has traditionally included the study, comparison, and use of foreign law, private international law, and unification of law.[153] We saw interest

---

[148] Hessel E. Yntema, *American Legal Realism in Retrospect*, 14 VAND. L. REV. 317–21, 323–24, 328 (1960); *see* BODENHEIMER, *supra* note 146, at 124–25; Karl N. Llewellyn, *A Realistic Jurisprudence—The Next Step*, 30 COLUM. L. REV. 431–65 (1930); HERGET, JURISPRUDENCE, *supra* note 142, at 176–79, 191, 200.

[149] Herget, *Influence*, *supra* note 146, at 227–28; Llewellyn, *supra* note 148, at 433–35, 437; Rehbinder, *supra* note 140, at 568–69. Llewellyn lectured during the 1928–1929 and 1931–1932 academic years at the University of Leipzig on the American doctrine of precedent and sociology of law. WILLIAM TWINING, THE KARL LLEWELLYN PAPERS 31 (1968).

[150] JOHN FABIAN WITT, PATRIOTS AND COSMOPOLITANS: HIDDEN HISTORIES OF AMERICAN LAW 213–17 (2007); Roscoe Pound, *The Call for a Realist Jurisprudence*, 44 HARV. L. REV. 697–711 (1931).

[151] WITT, *supra* note 150, at 228–33, 252, 257–58, 261; *see* HULL, POUND AND LLEWELLYN, *supra* note 146, at 278, 280–81, 302–03, 308–09, 315. Witt found that Edward Ross, a sociologist who had studied for two years in Berlin prior to his doctorate at Johns Hopkins, had a significant impact on Pound's sociological jurisprudence while both were at the University of Nebraska. Ross wrote about the evolution of law as a mechanism for social control. WITT, *supra*, at 220; *see* EDWARD ALSWORTH ROSS, SOCIAL CONTROL: A SURVEY OF THE FOUNDATIONS OF ORDER (1901). The earlier Pound had used sociology to fault the common law system and prefer more efficient techniques of administration. WITT, *supra*, at 221–27, 265.

[152] WITT, *supra* note 146, at 231; see infra pt. G.1 (Nazis and anti-Semitism). In 1951, Pound was vice-chairman of the Council Against Communist Aggression. WITT, *supra*, at 233. After 1934, as Germany's harsh policies toward Jews and dissidents appeared less a temporary phenomenon, Pound became more circumspect in his statements about Germany. By 1942, he blamed philosophical relativism for the rise of force in contrast to the restraints provided by an essentialist theory of law. HULL, POUND AND LLEWELLYN, *supra* note 146, at 301–03, 309, 315–16; *see* ROSCOE POUND, SOCIAL CONTROL THROUGH LAW (1942, reprint 2017).

[153] David S. Clark, *The Stool's Third Leg: Unification of Law in Berlin, Rome, and Washington from the 1920s to the 1940s*, *in* AUFBRUCH NACH EUROPA: 75 JAHRE MAX-PLANCK-INSTITUT FÜR PRIVATRECHT 39 (Jürgen Basedow et al. eds., 2001) [hereinafter Clark, *Unification of Law*].

in the latter element arise out of the codification debates during the second half of the nineteenth century in the United States, culminating in creation of the Uniform Laws Commission.[154] In Europe and elsewhere, this interest was manifest, sometimes called harmonization of law, at the 1900 Paris Congress. Professors Raymond Saleilles (Paris) wrote about a *droit commun de l'humanité civilisée* and Édouard Lambert (Lyon) a *droit commun législatif*.[155]

After the Great War, comparatists expressed renewed concern for legal unification, which led to the establishment of three institutes from 1923 to 1926.[156] These were set up in Philadelphia, Berlin, and Rome and each had its own peculiar reasons for formation. Starting with Germany, the *Kaiser Wilhelm Gesellschaft* created the Institute for Foreign and International Private Law (Berlin) in 1926.[157] Germany was in the unenviable position under part X of the Versailles Treaty (1919), which regulated economic relationships between Germany and its citizens vis-à-vis victor and associate states and their citizens. Since the German translation of the treaty was not authentic, jurists contended that solution of legal questions concerning contracts, debts, property rights, unfair competition, shipping, intellectual property, judgments, prescription, and social insurance lay in French and English legal concepts (such as *dette*, debt), interpretation methods, and legal institutions (*tribunal*, court) and traditions.[158]

The Berlin Institute chose Ernst Rabel (1874–1955), professor of Roman and modern private law at Berlin University, its first director. He had experience with the practical problem of interpreting the Versailles Treaty as a judge on the Italian-German mixed arbitral tribunal. In addition, he had ambitious scientific goals for the new institute. One of these concerned the harmonization and unification of law. Rabel, in the institute's journal (*Zeitschrift*), referred to comparative law's scientific virtues and to the increasing interest in the unification of law via international conventions.[159] Some of the prewar juristic optimism toward legal harmonization shone through Rabel's observation that the journal would summon up a legal science out of all the differences in laws and establish a broader and deeper community of nations (*Gemeinschaft der Völker*), the same as that which developed earlier under Roman law.[160]

---

[154] *See* ROBERT A. STEIN, FORMING A MORE PERFECT UNION: A HISTORY OF THE UNIFORM LAW COMMISSION (2013), at *Uniform Law Commission*, https://www.uniformlaws.org/newsandpublicati ons/publications; *supra* ch. 5, pt. D (codification and unification). Pound, Wigmore, and Williston were ULC members as was Woodrow Wilson. STEIN, *supra*, at 31, 40–41.

[155] Clark, *Unification of Law*, *supra* note 153, at 41–42; *see supra* ch. 5, pt. F.3 (1900 Paris Congress). Some jurists felt that legal harmonization was utopian, since diversity and competition was the law of life. Other jurists believed that unification might be possible for part of or all commercial law and certain civil law contracts. *Id.* at 42.

[156] *E.g.*, Hessel E. Yntema, *Comparative Research and Unification of Law*, 41 MICH. L. REV. 261–68 (1942).

[157] The Kaiser Wilhelm Institut für ausländisches und internationals Privatrecht.

[158] Clark, *Unification of Law*, *supra* note 153, at 42.

[159] *Id.* at 42–43; Ernst Rabel, *Zur Einführung* [hereinafter Rabel, *Einführung*], 1 ZEITSCHRIFT FÜR AUSLÄNDISCHES UND INTERNATIONALES PRIVATRECHT [hereinafter ZEITSCHRIFT] 1–4 (1927).

[160] Clark, *Unification of Law*, *supra* note 153, at 43; Rabel, *Einführung*, *supra* note 159, at 4.

Second, the *Zeitschrift* noted the 1926 creation of the *Institut international pour l'unification du droit privé* (Rome) and included the French text of its *Statut organique*. This statute explicitly stated that the institute's purpose was to study and promote private law harmonization and unification. Vittorio Scialoja, professor of Roman law at Rome University, convinced the Italian government to support the institute's foundation before the League of Nations, which gave its blessing and asserted the power of direction, although the Italian government paid the bills.[161] Rabel was Germany's first representative to the institute (until 1934) and it appointed him to the council of directors. The Rome Institute arranged for Rabel and his Berlin staff to prepare comparative studies aimed toward a uniform international sale of goods law for worldwide application. Rabel published the first volume of his comparative treatise on sale of goods in 1936.[162] Friedrich Kessler (1901-1998), a Berlin Institute *Referent* who later became a Yale Law School professor, wrote in the *Zeitschrift* about the American federal system of judicial and legislative lawmaking and the efforts to bring some coherence to the variability in state rules. He listed the many uniform acts that the Uniform Laws Commission had prepared and those states that had acquiesced to them.[163]

Kessler also reported on the creation of the American Law Institute (ALI) in 1923, the third institute discussed here, whose core purpose was to eliminate the common law's uncertainty (*Unsicherheit des Common Law zu beseitigen*) through the ALI's elaboration of a restatement of the common law. Kessler's article preceded a national report on U.S. legislative developments, which included a section on uniform laws (*einheitliche Gesetze*). Furthermore, U.S. national reports continued periodically in the *Zeitschrift*, such as the one by Yntema on private international law in 1928.[164]

There was a major difference between the Rome Institute and the ALI. The former was Eurocentric in its membership and looked toward supranational unification of law, while the ALI was wholly American in its membership and aimed to simplify the law and increase its certainty within the national legal system.

---

[161] Clark, *Unification of Law*, *supra* note 153, at 43; *Organisationen der Privatrechtsvergleichung in Europa*, 1 ZEITSCHRIFT, *supra* note 159, at 489, 498–500 (1927); Massimo Pilotti, *L'Activité de l'Institut international pour l'unification du droit privé*, *in* 1 L'UNIFICATION DU DROIT/UNIFICATION OF LAW 14, 15–17 (1948). Scialoja was one of the founders of the International Academy of Comparative Law. See *supra* text accompanying note 116 (Scialoja).

[162] Clark, *Unification of Law*, *supra* note 153, at 44; ERNST RABEL, 1 DAS RECHT DES WARENKAUFS: EINE RECHTSVERGLEICHENDE DARSTELLUNG (1936).

[163] Fritz Keßler, *Uniform State Laws in den Vereinigten Staaten*, 1 ZEITSCHRIFT, *supra* note 159, at 185–207, 816–66 (1927).

[164] *Id.*; see J.P. Chamberlain, *Die Entwicklung des Gesetzesrechts in den Vereinigten Staaten 1926*, 1 ZEITSCHRIFT, *supra* note 159, at 794–810 (Hans Mestern trans., 1927); Hessel E. Yntema, *Internationalprivatrechtliche Entscheidungen in den Vereinigten Staaten im Jahre 1926*, 2 ZEITSCHRIFT, *supra* note 159, at 856–62 (1928). Both Chamberlain and Yntema taught law at Columbia. Clark, *Unification of Law*, *supra* note 153, at 44 n.33–34.

In the 1920s, the United States was still primarily an importing nation in terms of ideas about law and legal institutions. In fact, the initial impetus for an institute primarily of legal scholars directed toward improving American law came during the immediate prewar period when German influence on American legal institutions was strong.[165] The Great War ended many of the explicit legal connections, or the willingness to recognize those connections, between Germany and the United States until the *Emigranten* arrived in the 1930s.[166]

It is in this light that one should view the early ALI efforts toward unification of law. An AALS committee established it as a nonprofit organization in 1923 and shortly thereafter, the Carnegie Foundation made a $1.1 million gift to fund operations for ten years.[167] Lewis, one of the managers of the Comparative Law Bureau since 1907, became the first executive director of the ALI. Among the 40-person committee organizing the ALI were four individuals with experience in foreign law: Freund, Pound, Wigmore, and Williston. Williston was the reporter for the ALI's first restatement, on contracts, which appeared in 1932.[168]

The institute completed nine restatements before the end of the Second World War: agency, conflict of laws, contracts, judgments, property, restitution, security, torts, and trusts. Comparatists did not play much of a role in this work.[169] In fact, early on, comparatists criticized the project. Mitchell Franklin (1902–1986), a Romanist at Tulane University, chided the ALI for its unwillingness to admit (what Williston had recognized) that its restatement represented the first step toward codification. He went on,

> Restatements cannot be very creative. Restatement, therefore, is summation; it is an inventory, taken in the twentieth century, of nineteenth century resources. Moreover, due to the unwillingness of the Institute to describe its work as codification, the Restatements are not expected to have political sanctions put behind them. As they are to lack legislative approval, apparently the Restatements

---

[165] *See* John P. Frank, *The American Law Institute 1923–1998*, in THE AMERICAN LAW INSTITUTE SEVENTY-FIFTH ANNIVERSARY 1923–1998, at 3, 9 (1998) [hereinafter AMERICAN LAW INSTITUTE]; N.E.H. Hull, *Restatement and Reform: A New Perspective on the Origins of the American Law Institute*, 8 LAW & HIST. REV. 55, 58–67 (1990).

[166] HOEFLICH, *supra* note 96, at 142–43; *see* DER EINFLUSS, *supra* note 146.

[167] Frank, *supra* note 165, at 9; HERGET, JURISPRUDENCE, *supra* note 142, at 77–78; N.E.H. Hull, *Back to the "Future of the Institute": William Draper Lewis's Vision of the ALI's Mission during Its First Twenty-five Years and the Implications for the Institute's Seventy-fifth Anniversary*, in AMERICAN LAW INSTITUTE, *supra* note 165, at 105, 119 (1998).

[168] 1–2 RESTATEMENT OF THE LAW OF CONTRACTS (1932); *see supra* text accompanying notes 71, 76 (Lewis); ch. 5, text accompanying notes 65–66, 118, 144 (Freund and Williston); *infra* ch. 6, pt. F (Pound and Wigmore).

[169] Clark, *Unification of Law*, *supra* note 153, at 46. An exception was Max Rheinstein, an adviser on the Restatements of Torts (1939) and Property (1944). An original *Referent* at the Berlin Institute, Rheinstein became a Chicago Law School professor. *Id.*

must become efficacious through an eighteenth century view as to the compulsiveness of reason.[170]

At the 1935 AALS annual meeting, Yntema, a comparatist then at Johns Hopkins University, added that restatements were unduly static, since they failed their goal to be "analytical, critical, and constructive, embodying whatever improvements in the law might be recommended by exhaustive study." In addition, the "initial plan made no specific provision for the comparative study of foreign experience or even for the consideration of data accumulated in other sciences."[171]

5. Tulane University College of Law

After 1929, when the ABA discontinued publishing the Comparative Law Bureau's reports,[172] three young Harvard law professors, Walther Hug (1898–1980), Gordon Ireland (1880–1950), and James Thayer (1899–1976), together with the recent Harvard J.S.D. graduate, Mitchell Franklin, convinced the *Tulane Law Review* to provide the bureau a section in the *Review* devoted to comparative law. Franklin had begun teaching at Tulane in 1930, and the bureau selected the *Review* to be its official periodical in 1931.[173] The Law College had developed a special relationship with the bureau dating from 1916, when Tulane began publishing the *Southern Law Quarterly*. Wigmore wrote its lead article, "Louisiana: The Story of Its Legal System," and Lobingier wrote two articles.[174] After 1918, Tulane no longer published the *Quarterly*, but it arose again in 1929 as volume 4 of the *Tulane Law Review*.[175]

In 1931, Ernst Feilchenfeld (1898–1956), assistant professor at Harvard (1926–1932), joined the original Harvard group and the *Review* masthead listed them all as "Comparative Law Editors." Hug and Feilchenfeld earned their doctor of law degrees in Zurich and Berlin, respectively.[176] Bureau reports and papers appeared in the *Review*.[177] After the bureau merged with the ABA International

---

[170] Mitchell Franklin, *Restatement of the Law of Contracts*, 8 Tul. L. Rev. 149, 149–50 (1933) (book review) (quotation at 150). One could also see the interest in Roman law as support for the restatements. Kearley, *supra* note 27, at 70–71.

[171] Hessel E. Yntema, *What Should the American Law Institute Do?*, 34 Mich. L. Rev. 461, 465–66, 471 (1936).

[172] See *supra* note 60 and accompanying text (Bureau's special issues).

[173] Mitchell Franklin, *Editorials*, 6 Tul. L. Rev. 99–100 (1931–32).

[174] John Wigmore, 1 So. L.Q. 1 (1916); Charles Lobingier, *Value and Place of Roman Law in the Technical Curriculum*, 1 So. L.Q. 117 (1916); *id., Evolution of the German Civil Code*, 1 So. L.Q. 330 (1916); see *id., Napoleon and His Code*, 32 Harv. L. Rev. 114–34 (1918). Charles Sherman contributed *The Hexabiblos: A Code of the Roman Empire Still in Use*, 3 So. L.Q. 127 (1918).

[175] Clark, *Modern Development*, *supra* note 65, at 603.

[176] 6 Tul. L. Rev. 279, 301 (1932).

[177] *Id.* at 83–93, 280–300; 7 Tul. L. Rev. 82–97, 235–51, 416–24, 580–84 (1932–1933).

Law Section in 1933, the new Section of International and Comparative Law, with Wigmore serving as its first chair, chose the *Tulane Law Review* to be its "official organ." Section reports included articles by American and foreign comparatists and continued until the section, in 1942, decided to begin its own journal, *Proceedings of the Section of International and Comparative Law*. Besides section reports, the *Review* organized a group of comparatists to contribute to a new part of the journal that digested interesting articles appearing in foreign legal periodicals.[178]

In 1932, the *Tulane Law Review* further expanded its comparative law mission. The faculty editor, James Morrison, announced that if the *Review* was to "fulfill its place as a comparative law journal its organization must be on a broader and more comprehensive basis; it must not only reflect the developments and achievements of comparative law in the United States, but in the rest of the civilized world as well."[179] Morrison went on to describe the new group of contributing editors, which borrowed an approach earlier used by the *Bulletin*:

> The group from the United States is composed of Dean Roscoe Pound, Harvard Law School, Dean Emeritus John H. Wigmore, Northwestern University School of Law, Professors Edwin M. Borchard and Ernest G. Lorenzen of Yale University School of Law, Gordon Ireland, formerly of Harvard Law School, and Mitchell Franklin, Tulane University College of Law.[180]
>
> The group from abroad is composed of Professor Antonio S. de Bustamante, of the University of Havana, Judge of the World Court, and President of the International [Academy] of Comparative Law; Professor Élemér Balogh of the University of Kaunas; Professor Giorgio del Vecchio, Director of the Faculty of Jurisprudence of the University of Rome, and Director of the International Institute for Unification of Private Law at Rome; Professor Ernst Rabel, Director of the Institute of Comparative Law at Berlin; and Professor Edouard

---

[178] *Editorials*, 8 TUL. L. REV. 103, 104; 417, 420; 572 (1933–1934); *see* Ford, *supra* note 97, at 143; *Editor's Note*, A.B.A. SEC. INT'L & COMP. L. PROC. 3 (1943). Section reports, often including more Louisiana than foreign or comparative law, appeared at 8 TUL. L. REV. 396–416, 550–71 (1933–1934); 9 *id.* at 89–103, 244–67, 416–20, 566–83 (1934–1935); 10 *id.* at 69–101, 263–69, 416–33, 604–11 (1935–1936); 11 *id.* at 425–27, 575–605 (1936–1937); 12 *id.* at 108–19, 226–38, 412–17, 552–606 (1937–1938); 13 *id.* at 99–118, 253–68, 416–22, 585–98 (1938–1939); 14 *id.* at 72–92, 225–44, 407–27, 573–99 (1939–1940); 15 *id.* at 75–111, 241–70, 415–34, 567–73 (1940–1941). *See supra* text accompanying note 61 (merger of the Bureau and ABA Section).

[179] James J. Morrison, *Editorials*, 7 TUL. L. REV. 96 (1932).

[180] *Id.* Ireland later taught law at Louisiana State University, Cambridge University, and Catholic University. Ernst Freund, University of Chicago Law School, had accepted the Tulane appointment shortly before his death in 1932. Pound contributed an article in 1934. Roscoe Pound, *The Place of Comparative Law in the American Law School Curriculum*, 8 TUL. L. REV. 161–70 (1934).

Lambert of the University of Lyon, Director of the Institute of Comparative Law at Lyon.[181]

William W. Buckland of Cambridge University joined later. The *Review* continued to list this group, reduced by deaths, until 1955, when it added a new generation of comparatists.[182]

To reflect this new role, the *Review* announced that it was the official "American medium of expression of the International Congress of Comparative Law," held at The Hague in 1932, and that it would publish the official American report of the proceedings and several general reports from that Congress.[183] The *Review* continued this role for reports from the Second International Congress of Comparative Law, held in 1937 at The Hague.[184]

In 1949, the Tulane law dean announced the establishment of the Tulane Institute of Comparative Law, led by Ferdinand Stone (1908–1989), based on the school's early support for comparative law and Louisiana's French and Spanish legal heritage and relationship with Latin America jurists.[185] Stone, who earned a civil law degree at Oxford as a Rhodes Scholar and a J.S.D. at Yale, reported on the 1950 London International Congress of Comparative Law in the *Tulane Law Review*, where he also published the national report he presented in London.[186] In 1956, the Ford Foundation provided the Institute $275,000 to strengthen the Tulane civil and comparative law program and in 1957, the Rockefeller Foundation added $114,000 to establish a program in Latin American legal studies.[187]

6. The Law Library of Congress and Other Law Libraries

By the end of the nineteenth century, the Library of Congress (LC) librarian pressed the idea that it should serve as America's national library, referring to Jefferson's

---

[181] Morrison, *supra* note 179, at 97. Balogh later taught at Witwatersrand University (Johannesburg) and became secretary general of the academy. Rabel subsequently became a researcher at the University of Michigan.

[182] *See* 30 TUL. L. REV. 322 (1955–1956).

[183] 6 TUL. L. REV. 97 (1931); *see* H. Milton Colvin, *The International Congress of Comparative Law*, 7 TUL. L. REV. 53–81 (1932); Carl L.W. Meyer, *International Legal Documentation*, 7 *id.* at 40 (1932); Edwin M. Borchard, *Declaratory Judgments*, 7 *id.* at 183, 388 (1933); Roscoe Pound, *Hierarchy of Sources and Forms in Different Systems of Law*, 7 *id.* at 475 (1933); Ernst Freund, *Responsibility of the State in Internal (Municipal) Law*, 9 *id.* at 1 (1934).

[184] *See, e.g.*, Mitchell Franklin, *The Passing of the School of Montesquieu and Its System of Separation of Powers*, 12 TUL. L. REV. 1 (1937) (general report); H.C. Gutteridge, *The Comparative Aspects of Legal Terminology*, 12 *id.* at 401 (1938); Charles Sumner Lobingier, *The Natural History of the Private Artificial Person: A Comparative Study in Corporate Origins*, 13 *id.* at 41 (1938).

[185] Paul Brosman, *Two Recent Program Additions*, 24 TUL. L. REV. 108–09 (1949).

[186] Ferdinand F. Stone, *The International Congress of Comparative Law*, 25 TUL. L. REV. 98 (1950); *id.*, *The End to Be Served by Comparative Law*, 25 *id.* at 325 (1951).

[187] Ray Forrester, *Editorials: The Tulane Law School: A Report by the Dean*, 31 TUL. L. REV. 313 (1957). John Rockefeller endowed the Rockefeller Foundation as a New York corporation in 1913.

vision of building a collection universal in scope that would serve the whole country.[188] Herbert Putnam, librarian from 1899 to 1939, continued that aim by calling for such a universal collection available to scholars and the public via interlibrary loan. Trained as a lawyer at Columbia University, he put a priority on legal materials, and particularly legislation.[189] He aggressively acquired government documents from Europe, Asia, and Latin America. In Putnam's annual report to Congress in 1928, he mentioned three libraries he was attempting to emulate: the British Museum, the *Bibliothèque Nationale de France*, and the *Staatsbibliothek zu Berlin*.[190]

In 1902, Putnam called for the creation of an Index to Comparative Legislation as appropriate for a national library.[191] He directed the acquisition of research collections representing foreign cultures, including the purchase of complete foreign libraries. In 1901, he had reported that the LC was the first in America to contain one million volumes. The development of a classification scheme and distribution of cataloging information to other libraries moved the LC into a leadership role among the world's libraries. After the end of World War II, the library organized automatic purchase agreements with foreign dealers and expanded international exchange of official publications.[192]

Between 1900 and 1930, the LC Law Library expanded from 103,000 volumes to 240,000 volumes. This was a period of substantial growth in the foreign and comparative law collection. In part the international book and document exchange program administered through the Smithsonian Institution since the 1890s greatly benefited the Library of Congress, but especially the Law Library since its emphasis was on government documents. In addition, copyright deposit continued to be

Rockefeller Foundation, *Our History*, https://www.rockefellerfoundation.org/about-us/our-history. In 1936 Edsel Ford established the Ford Foundation, to which other Ford family members later made large bequests. Ford Foundation, *Our Origins*, https://www.fordfoundation.org/about/about-ford/our-origins.

[188] *See supra* ch. 5, pt. C.6 (Library of Congress).

[189] JAMES CONAWAY, AMERICA'S LIBRARY: THE STORY OF THE LIBRARY OF CONGRESS, 1800–2000, at 98–99 (2000). For the idea of a universal library, *see* MATTHEW BATTLES, LIBRARY: AN UNQUIET HISTORY 9–10, 12, 16, 206, 210–12 (2003).

[190] John Y. Cole, *The Library of Congress Becomes a World Library*, 40 LIBR. & CULTURE, 385, 388–90.

[191] REPORT OF THE LIBRARIAN OF CONGRESS FOR THE FISCAL YEAR ENDING JUNE 30, 1902, at 15 (1902). Congress did not act on this proposal until it created the Center of Latin American Legal Studies.

[192] JOHN Y. COLE, JEFFERSON'S LEGACY: A BRIEF HISTORY OF THE LIBRARY OF CONGRESS 27–28, 31, 59 (1993); *id., Library of Congress of the United States, in* INTERNATIONAL DICTIONARY OF LIBRARY HISTORIES 407–09 (David S. Stam ed., 2001) [hereinafter COLE, LIBRARY OF CONGRESS]; *see also* CONAWAY, *supra* note 189, at 99–111; JANE AIKEN ROSENBERG, THE NATION'S GREAT LIBRARY: HERBERT PUTNAM AND THE LIBRARY OF CONGRESS, 1899–1939 (1993). Putnam had been superintendent of the Boston Public Library. COLE, LIBRARY OF CONGRESS, *supra*, at 408. The LC also benefited from participation in the Farmington Plan (54 American libraries in 1950) for the cooperative acquisition of foreign publications. Its goal was to have at least one copy of every current foreign publication of research value available somewhere in the United States. ANNUAL REPORT FOR THE LIBRARIAN OF CONGRESS FOR THE FISCAL YEAR ENDING JUNE 30, 1950, at 115 (1951).

important.[193] Congressional appropriations to the Law Library for books and serials in the twentieth century began at $3,000 annually in 1902, but in 1930 ballooned to $50,000 to support aggressive acquisition of foreign legal materials.[194]

During this time, the Law Library made the transition from a legislative, court, and government reference library to become also a legal research center. This entailed preparing written legal reports and comparative studies for Congress to use in its efforts to legislate more effectively. The staff of five, which increased to 13 by 1932, also wrote bibliographic studies and scholarly analyses useful for lawyers, judges, and academics.[195]

Edwin Borchard (1884–1951), law librarian from 1911 to 1916, proposed using the growing wealth of foreign legal materials to prepare a series of guides to the legal literature of individual countries that would serve as introductions to foreign law for American lawyers and judges. In 1910, as an assistant in law for the Law Library, he had toured the major European capitals seeking advice about what foreign law literature the Law Library should acquire. The first guide covered Germany, published in 1912.[196] In 1915, Borchard made an acquisitions trip to 11 nations in Latin America, which greatly improved the Hispanic holdings.[197] Although he took a position as law professor at Yale Law School in 1917 (until 1950), Borchard continued to supervise and assist in the foreign law guide series, which the government printed.[198]

---

[193] David S. Clark, *Nation Building and Law Collections: The Remarkable Development of Comparative Law Libraries in the United States*, 109 LAW LIBR. J. 499, 522–23, 545–47 (2017) [hereinafter Clark, *Nation Building*]. By comparison, in 1911, the State Library of Massachusetts had a foreign law collection of 10,000 volumes from 260 political units. *See* ELLEN M. SAWYER, CATALOGUE OF THE LAWS OF FOREIGN COUNTRIES IN THE STATE LIBRARY OF MASSACHUSETTS (1911).

[194] Library of Congress, LAW LIBRARY, 1832–1982: A BRIEF HISTORY OF THE FIRST HUNDRED AND FIFTY YEARS 11 (1982) [hereinafter LC, LAW LIBRARY]; William D. Murphy, *The Library of Congress and Its Influence on Law Librarianship*, 69 LAW LIBR. J. 554, 559 (1976); John T. Vance, *The Law Library of Congress*, 28 LAW LIBR. J. 148, 154 (1935). The law librarian, George Scott, acquired major foreign and comparative law collections beginning in 1904. LC, LAW LIBRARY, *supra*, at 12–13.

[195] LC, LAW LIBRARY, *supra* note 194, at 13, 21, 28. In 1906, the title law librarian replaced assistant at law or custodian in law, which the Law Library had used in the nineteenth century. *Id.* at 13, 29.

[196] *Id.* at 14; EDWIN M. BORCHARD, GUIDE TO THE LAW AND LEGAL LITERATURE OF GERMANY (1912); *see supra* notes 85, 87, 94 and accompanying text (Borchard and the Comparative Law Bureau). Borchard's father had emigrated from Prussia to New York. Borchard's subsequent books in this genre included THE BIBLIOGRAPHY OF INTERNATIONAL LAW AND CONTINENTAL LAW (1913), COMMERCIAL LAWS OF ENGLAND, SCOTLAND, GERMANY AND FRANCE (with Archibald J. Wolfe, 1915), and GUIDE TO THE LAW AND LEGAL LITERATURE OF ARGENTINA, BRAZIL AND CHILE (1917). Borchard supervised THOMAS W. PALMER, GUIDE TO THE LAW AND LEGAL LITERATURE OF SPAIN (1915).

[197] LC, LAW LIBRARY, *supra* note 194, at 14.

[198] Michael S. Mayer, *Borchard, Edwin Montefiore*, in AMERICAN NATIONAL BIOGRAPHY (1999), at http://www.anb.org/articles/11/11-00081.html; *see also* LC, LAW LIBRARY, *supra* note 194, at 18; GEORGE WILFRED STUMBERG, GUIDE TO THE LAW AND LEGAL LITERATURE OF FRANCE (1931). Borchard was the first U.S. professor to lecture (in 1925) at the University of Berlin after World War I. Mayer, *supra*.

In 1914, Congress established the Legislative Reference Service (LRS), which the law librarian supervised until 1921, when the directorship became a separate position. Both entities handled congressional American law reference questions, but the Law Library was responsible for foreign law reference and research inquiries while LRS processed research on American law.[199]

John Vance became law librarian in 1924 (serving until 1943), one year after he made a book acquisition trip to Latin America on behalf of the Law Library. He continued the emphasis on improving the foreign law collection. Vance emphasized the goal of building good working collections of every legal system in the world. This meant legislation, court decisions, and a reasonable number of legal treatises, dictionaries, digests, journals, and law society publications. In the 1920s, the Law Library had a smaller book budget than the law schools at Columbia, Harvard, Michigan, or Yale. Vance argued that mere law library parity was something the U.S. government should not tolerate.[200] With significantly increased funding in 1930, thanks in part to lobbying by U.S. Justices Louis Brandeis and Harlan Stone, Vance made the Law Library an impressive foreign and comparative law research center, doubled the collection size, and renewed interest in the foreign law guide series in 1943. The series, substantially financed by the U.S. State Department, resulted in 12 new volumes, most covering Latin America and authored by Helen Clagett, chief of the Latin American Law Section.[201] In 1942, the U.S. Congress authorized the Center of Latin American Legal Studies in the Law Library of Congress with its first task begun in 1949 to index and digest laws from Latin American countries. Active in the ABA's Section of International and Comparative Law, Vance had supported the establishment of the center at the Law Library.[202]

In 1942, the law librarian was able to organize the Law Library into specialties, with the goal of hiring staff who had the language and cultural competence

---

[199] LC, LAW LIBRARY, *supra* note 194, at 15–16. In 1970, Congress gave the LRS more autonomy and renamed it the Congressional Research Service (CRS). *Id.* at 16. The CRS today has a staff of 600 reference librarians, lawyers, economists, and social and natural scientists. Library of Congress, *CRS: Organizational Structure*, http://www.loc.gov/crsinfo/about/structure.html. The Law Library continued to process foreign law reference, research, and English language translations of foreign legal materials for Congress. LC, LAW LIBRARY, *supra*, at 16.

[200] 1930 LAW LIBR. CONG. ANN. REP. 19, 22–24.

[201] Clark, *Modern Development*, *supra* note 65, at 600; LC, LAW LIBRARY, *supra* note 194, at 17–18, 21–22; Murphy, *supra* note 194, at 559–60; 1930 LAW LIBR. CONG. ANN. REP. 20. In 1930 and 1931, the Law Library purchased Paul Krüger's Roman law books, pamphlets, and manuscripts—totaling 4,700 volumes—and Nicholas II's Winter Palace Library of Russian materials. LC, LAW LIBRARY, *supra*, at 17. In 1935, Vance described issues facing the Law Library and acquisitions to the comparative and foreign law collection. Vance, *supra* note 194, at 154–56.

[202] Victor C. Folsom, *Report of the Committee on Latin American Law*, PROC. SEC. INT'L & COMP. L. 93, 103–04 (1950); John Thomas Vance, *Need for a Center of Latin-American Legal Study*, 26 A.B.A. J. 705 (1940); *see* ANNUAL REPORT OF THE LIBRARIAN OF CONGRESS FOR THE FISCAL YEAR ENDING JUNE 30, 1942, at 85–86 (1943) (Congressional authorization in 1942).

to pursue the LC's ambition to have a universal collection. The five law sections were British, Foreign (meaning traditions other than the common law), American, International, and Jurisprudence. The next year, the librarian merged the International Law and Jurisprudence sections and added a Latin American Law Section. In 1946, further consolidation yielded a staff of 30 working in the Anglo-American, Latin American, and Foreign (now including international law) sections and two processing and technical services sections. With further adjustments, the five divisions in 1960 became (1) American-British, (2) European, (3) Far Eastern, (4) Hispanic (Latin American), and (5) Near Eastern and North African. Each division had a chief and staff of experts in the division's specialization. By 1960, the Law Library was the largest comparative law library in the world and included literature for most of the world's countries.[203]

Many foreign-born law librarians have staffed the Law Library since the 1850s. As the importance of foreign and comparative law grew, these librarians educated a national audience of librarians about acquiring and using a comparative law collection. In addition, through exchange programs, international meetings, and book-purchase trips, they assisted legal researchers worldwide. In 1942, the Law Library opened a Foreign Law Reading Room and, as mentioned, created a Foreign Law Section within the administrative organization.[204]

During the first half of the twentieth century, four distinct types of law libraries proliferated in the United States, a process that accelerated after World War II with the dramatic growth in the number of lawyers and the size of government. All these types had the potential to be comparative law libraries depending on their size and purpose. These four categories were, first, academic libraries associated with separately administered law schools, typically part of a university. Universities might be private or public, but their law school mission focused on legal education and scholarly research. Second, government law libraries—financed mainly by taxpayers—served a national, state, county, or citywide combination of legislators, administrators, judges, lawyers, and the public. Third, state, county, or city bar association libraries—paid for by attorney bar membership dues—provided books, serials, and today online services, for

---

[203] ANNUAL REPORT OF THE LIBRARIAN OF CONGRESS FOR THE FISCAL YEAR ENDING JUNE 30, 1946, at 402–03, 405 (1947); LC, LAW LIBRARY, *supra* note 194, at 22; Murphy, *supra* note 194, at 559–60; Kurt Schwerin, *Law Libraries and Foreign Law Collections in the U.S.A.*, 11 INT'L & COMP. L.Q. 537, 547 (1962). In 1954, the Law Library created the Far Eastern Law Section after the U.S. State Department had funded research by Asian lawyers in the library for several years. In 1959, it added the Near Eastern and North African Law Division. In a 1957 reorganization, the Law Library had put the foreign and geographical area sections into divisional status. The Foreign Law Section, for instance, became the European Law Division. LC, LAW LIBRARY, *supra*, at 23.

[204] Lorraine Kulpa, *The Contributions and Unique Role of Foreign-Born, Foreign-Educated Law Librarians*, *in* LAW LIBRARIANSHIP: HISTORICAL PERSPECTIVES 203, 206 (Laura N. Gasaway & Michael G. Chiorazz eds., 1996) [hereinafter LAW LIBRARIANSHIP].

that constituency. Fourth, private law libraries existed in law firms and large corporations with legal departments to offer legal materials for their lawyers.[205]

By 1938, the leading U.S. law libraries had collections of at least 100,000 volumes, as reported in Table 6.1.[206] Of the 15 libraries listed,[207] eight were university law libraries located and administered at the institution's law school. In fact, the AALS required approved law schools to "own a law library" as early as 1926.[208] The development of university law schools in the nineteenth century had set the tradition of law libraries distinct from the university or liberal arts college library.[209]

After World II, American law libraries established a commanding worldwide lead in the size and diversity of their collections.[210] In 1950, 31 U.S. law libraries had more than 100,000 volumes, and by 1960, 57 libraries had reached that threshold.[211] Table 6.2[212] reflects that growth, which for the largest libraries

---

[205] See Julius J. Marke, *Law Libraries: Purposes and Objectives*, in WORLD ENCYCLOPEDIA OF LIBRARY AND INFORMATION SERVICES 436, 436–37 (Robert Wedgeworth ed., 3d ed. 1993); Velvet E. Glass & Michael L. Richmond, *Administration of Private Law Libraries*, in 1 LAW LIBRARIANSHIP: A HANDBOOK 69, 69–70 (Heinz Peter Mueller et al. eds., 1983). The proliferation of law firm libraries was impressive. In 1950, there were 60; by the end of the twentieth century, there were more than 1,000. Their size was also significant. In the 1930s, the largest New York firms had libraries of 10,000 volumes. In 1995, the big U.S. firms had upward of 70,000 volumes. Gitelle Seer & Jill Sidford, *The Evolution of Law Firm Libraries: A Preliminary History*, in LAW LIBRARIANSHIP, supra note 204, at 77, 79, 88. Baker & McKenzie, the world's largest global law firm in 1972, had a foreign and comparative law collection of 7,000 books (with another 100 books on international law) at its headquarters in Chicago. Igor I. Kavass, *Foreign and International Law Collections in Selected Law Libraries of the United States: Survey 1972–1973*, 1 INT'L J.L. LIBR. 117, 128 (1973).

[206] ANNUAL REPORT OF THE LIBRARIAN OF CONGRESS FOR THE FISCAL YEAR ENDED JUNE 30, 1938, at 72 (1939) [hereinafter 1938 ANN. REP. LIBR. CONG.]; Thomas S. Dabagh, *Law Library News Notes*, 15 L.A. BAR BULL. 51 (1939), as reprinted in Gail H. Fruchtman, *The History of the Los Angeles County Law Library*, 84 LAW LIBR. J. 687, 692 n.38 (1992). The American Association of Law Libraries (AALL) prepared the list of holdings. Fruchtman, supra, at 692 n.38.

[207] The New York Law Institute listed in Table 6.1 is the oldest circulating law library in New York City, founded by two lawyers in 1828 as a membership library to facilitate the practice of law. New York Law Institute, *Our History*, http://www.nyli.org/history.

[208] ALFRED Z. REED, REVIEW OF LEGAL EDUCATION IN THE UNITED STATES AND CANADA FOR THE YEARS 1926 and 1927, at 7 (1928). The ABA amended its standards for approved law schools in 1940 to support the same idea as the AALS. New standard IV read: "[T]he library is the heart of a law school and is a most important factor in training law students and in providing faculty members with materials for research and study. Therefore, it is a cardinal requirement of the American Bar Association that an adequate library be maintained, consisting of not less than 7,500 well-selected, usable volumes, . . . kept up to date and owned or controlled by the law school." Cindy Hirsch, *The Rise and Fall of Academic Law Library Collection Standards*, 31 LEGAL REFERENCE SERVS. Q. 65, 68 (2012).

[209] Columbia, Harvard, Michigan, and Yale all had separate law libraries established prior to 1860. Stephen B. Griswold, *Law Libraries*, in PUBLIC LIBRARIES IN THE UNITED STATES OF AMERICA: THEIR HISTORY, CONDITION, AND MANAGEMENT pt. 1, at 161, 169 (S.R. Warren & S.N Clark eds., 1876).

[210] Even by 1970, in Germany, Italy, and the United Kingdom, the largest law libraries contained between 100,000 and 200,000 volumes. INTERNATIONAL ASSOCIATION OF LAW LIBRARIES, EUROPEAN LAW LIBRARIES GUIDE 249, 258–59, 275–76, 281, 412, 606, 621, 629 (1971).

[211] Schwerin, supra note 203, at 541–42.

[212] ANNUAL REPORT OF THE LIBRARIAN OF CONGRESS FOR THE FISCAL YEAR ENDED JUNE 30, 1950, at 65 [hereinafter 1950 Ann. Rep. Libr. Cong.]; Schwerin, supra note 203, at 543–44, 547–48.

Table 6.1. U.S. Law Library Size in 1938, by Institution and Volumes

Harvard University	532,000
Library of Congress	404,000
Yale University	245,000
Columbia University	225,000
New York City Bar Association	220,000
University of Michigan	200,000
New York State	127,000
Los Angeles County	120,000
New York Law Institute	120,000
Northwestern University	112,000
Connecticut State	110,000
University of Minnesota	106,000
San Francisco County	106,000
University of Chicago	101,000
University of Pennsylvania	100,000

occurred primarily at university law schools. The principal exception was the Law Library of Congress,[213] which by 1950 had overtaken Harvard Law School Library as the largest one in the United States. Congress had increased its law library funding since the 1930s as it recognized the importance of broadening the foreign law collection from a half dozen European nations to all the countries of the world.[214]

Besides Harvard that had a comparative law collection in the nineteenth century, a few U.S. law libraries, mostly associated with a university, determined at the beginning of the twentieth century to make foreign and comparative law an important component. For academic law libraries, this decision typically

---

[213] The LC Law Library figures for 1950 and 1960 exclude 300,000 law-related volumes in the general collection. 1950 ANN. REP. LIBR. CONG., supra note 212, at 65; ANNUAL REPORT OF THE LIBRARIAN OF CONGRESS FOR THE FISCAL YEAR ENDING JUNE 30, 1960, at 45 (1961); Schwerin, supra note 203, at 543, 547.

[214] 1938 ANN. REP. LIBR. CONG., supra note 206, at 72; 1950 ANN. REP. LIBR. CONG., supra note 212, at 69, 75–76 (1951); see also id. at 67–71 (foreign law collection).

Table 6.2. U.S. Law Library Size in 1950 and 1960, by Institution and Volumes

Law Library	1950	1960
Library of Congress	805,000	1,020,000
Harvard University	656,000	933,000
Yale University	327,000	393,000
Columbia University	300,000	387,000
New York City Bar Association		308,000
Los Angeles County		308,000
University of Michigan	210,000	276,000
University of Minnesota	172,000	244,000
San Francisco County		195,000
Northwestern University	144,000	181,000
New York Law Institute		165,000
New York University	100,000	165,000
Ohio State University	85,000	154,000
University of Pennsylvania	121,000	145,000
Cornell University	114,000	144,000
University of Washington	111,000	135,000
University of California	91,000	135,000
University of Chicago	125,000	134,000
University of Illinois	95,000	130,000

required cooperation between the law dean and a law librarian, at least one of whom needed the special background required to build such a collection.[215]

Wigmore, who served as law dean from 1901 to 1929 at Northwestern University, illustrated the situation in which a dean had the necessary background and took the lead to build a comparative law collection.[216] In 1901, the law school library had only 3,000 volumes. Wigmore began a worldwide book acquisition initiative, obtained the money and book donations for a comprehensive library, and appointed the school's first librarian in 1907. Some of the books

---

[215] Clark, *Nation Building*, supra note 193, at 538.
[216] *See infra* pt. F.2 (Wigmore).

came from the Chicago Law Institute, a membership library for Chicago attorneys. By 1910, the law school library had 40,000 volumes and at the end of his deanship about 100,000 volumes. By the 1970s, about one-third of the books and serials dealt with foreign, comparative, and international law. Wigmore's interest in anthropology and legal history added important materials in primitive, ancient, customary European, and Tokugawa Japanese law.[217]

At the University of Michigan Law School, the dean and librarian formed a cooperative team in the 1920s. Henry Bates became law dean in 1910 (until 1939) with a vision to build a world-renowned law school. The library was one part of this plan.[218] Once Bates had the opportunity to attract private money to support a major library, he hired as law librarian Hobart Coffey (served 1926–1966), who emulated the approach used by Harvard Law Library. Coffey had studied at the law faculties in Paris, Berlin, and Munich. He developed the foreign law collection using a variety of methods: faculty assistance, travel abroad, developing foreign relationships, collaborating with university librarians, exchanging and selling duplicates, and encouraging gifts. During his tenure, the law school library expanded from 55,000 to 330,000 volumes and in 1960 had a comparative law collection of 150,000 books.[219] In 2002, the foreign, comparative, and international law portion of the law library represented 33 percent of all books and serials at 300,000 volumes.[220]

F. Roscoe Pound and John Wigmore

Among the many academic comparatists placed among a variety of American law schools and the occasional one at a university's political science department, two played a central role in the institutional development of comparative law in the United States. Roscoe Pound (1870–1964) and John Wigmore (1863–1943) were both deans at leading law schools, but in addition, they were both important national scholars who influenced how jurists thought about comparative law.

---

[217] Rolf H. Erikson, *Northwestern University Libraries, in* 20 ENCYCLOPEDIA OF LIBRARY AND INFORMATION SCIENCE 200, 237–39 (Allen Kent et al. eds., 1977); Emily Kadens, *A Hidden Treasure: The Law School's Rare Book Collection*, 2 Nw. L. RPTR. 11, 14 (Fall 2013).

[218] Margaret A. Leary, *Building a Foreign Law Collection at the University of Michigan Law Library, 1910–1960*, 94 LAW LIBR. J. 395, 397 (2002).

[219] BROWN & BLUME, *supra* note 41, at 370–71, 379–80; Leary, *supra* note 218, at 404–20; *Hobart Coffey: Memorial Address*, 14 LAW QUADRANGLE NOTES 16 (Winter 1970). In the 1920s and 1930s, the foreign, comparative, and international law collection grew significantly through the purchase of several private law libraries. Leary, *supra*, at 408.

[220] Leary, *supra* note 218, at 397 n.3.

1. Roscoe Pound

Pound was America's most distinguished comparatist during the first half of the twentieth century. After attending Harvard Law School, he began his academic career at the University of Nebraska in 1895, where he taught Roman law in the Latin department. In 1899, he continued teaching that course even after his appointment as professor in the law department, where he became dean in 1903. In 1907, he joined the law faculty at Northwestern University and later the University of Chicago, after which he accepted the Story professorship at Harvard Law School in 1910. There he served as dean from 1916 until 1936. His term as head of the nation's leading law school gave him significant national as well as international visibility and influence. Pound continued to lecture and publish at Harvard until 1947 and elsewhere nearly until his death in 1964.[221]

Pound learned German in his youth, earned a Ph.D. in botany that involved reading the work of German scientists, and minored in Roman law. Michael Hoeflich divided Pound's scholarship into three areas: (1) legal philosophy, where he was especially interested in Rudolf von Ihering's (1818–1892) jurisprudence of interests (*Interessenjurisprudenz*) and other civilian jurists' writing about sociological jurisprudence; (2) the development of Roman law into modern civil law and its use for comparison; and (3) the influence of Roman and civil law on United States law. All these areas were significant examples of American comparative law scholarship broadly conceived. Pound influenced comparative law not only through his writing but also from his administrative position at Harvard by inviting foreign legal scholars to lecture and research there.[222] In 1936, Pound delivered four lectures at Tulane Law School on the centennial of Edward Livingston's death, published as *The Formative Era of American Law*, which became a standard work on American legal history while emphasizing the importance of comparative law in the early United States.[223]

---

[221] HOEFLICH, *supra* note 96, at 125–26; HERGET, JURISPRUDENCE, *supra* note 142, at 2–3, 164; RABBAN, *supra* note 119, at 424–26; ARTHUR E. SUTHERLAND, THE LAW AT HARVARD: A HISTORY OF IDEAS AND MEN, 1817–1967, at 199–204, 236–40, 244, 282–83, 288–89, 293, 296–98 (1967). John Witt stated that by 1950, many considered Pound the "world's greatest living legal scholar." WITT, *supra* note 150, at 211; *see* FRIEDMAN, AMERICAN LAW, *supra* note 21, at 489 (most prolific and celebrated figure in American jurisprudence).

[222] HOEFLICH, *supra* note 96, at 126–30; *see* HERGET, JURISPRUDENCE, *supra* note 142, at 164–70; HULL, POUND AND LLEWELLYN, *supra* note 146, at 79, 82–83, 254; WIECEK, *supra* note 19, at 192; Herget, *Influence*, *supra* note 146, at 203–05, 208–09, 211, 215; *supra* ch. 5, pt. E.5 (Ihering). Good illustrations of the historical and comparative aspects of Pound's sociological jurisprudence appeared in *Liberty of Contract*, 18 YALE L.J. 454–87 (1908) and *Theories of Law*, 22 YALE L.J. 114–50 (1912). For a postmodern critique of Pound's late work, namely 1–5 JURISPRUDENCE (1959), which some scholars found inferior to his earlier writings, *see* HULL, POUND AND LLEWELLYN, *supra* note 146, at 283, 326–30; Mitchel Lasser, *Comparative Readings of Roscoe Pound's Jurisprudence*, 50 AM. J. COMP. L. 719 (2002).

[223] ROSCOE POUND, THE FORMATIVE ERA OF AMERICAN LAW vii (1938); *see* STEPHEN B. PRESSER, LAW PROFESSORS: THREE CENTURIES OF SHAPING AMERICAN LAW 115–19 (2017). Presser divided Pound's scholarship into three categories: evolutionary and organic legal change; legal history; and sociological jurisprudence. *Id.* at 113–22.

Pound's 1914 teaching materials deserve recognition as the first published comparative law student textbook used in the United States. The Harvard University Press edition entitled it *Readings in Roman Law and the Civil Law and Modern Codes as Developments Thereof: An Introduction to Comparative Law*.[224] In the preface, Pound explained his frustration when he first taught Roman law in 1899 by using Justinian's Institutes (following his own teacher's example). Likewise, reliance on English language treatment of Roman law included too much history and too little law for Pound's purpose. Consequently, in 1902, he collected excerpts from Roman texts (especially Justinian's Digest), modern (meaning mainly European) juristic scholarship, and civil codes (including the new German and Japanese codes). "The purpose of this collection was to afford the basis for class discussion of concrete cases so that through tracing the development of modern doctrines and comparing the Roman and modern solutions with those of our own law the course might serve as an introduction to comparative law."[225] After enrollment in the class increased, Pound had the book of 234 pages first published in 1906. In the second edition of 1914, Pound updated the English translations of mostly German jurists (with some excerpts from French, English, and Scottish legal scholars).[226]

Pound divided the 1914 *Readings* into three parts. Part one covered the sources, forms, and interpretation of the law. Part two dealt with juristic acts, reflecting Pound's interest in German law. This included their nature, requirements for their creation, the declaration of will, and problems of duress, mistake, and fraud. Finally, part three treated the exercise and protection of rights, which encompassed about half of the book. The orientation was procedural, including self-help, Roman law, canon law, and modern civil law examples.[227]

Pound served as an editor for the *Annual Bulletin* of the Comparative Law Bureau from its first issue in 1908 and was a manager on the bureau's council from 1911 until the time of its merger with the American Bar Association's International Law Section in 1933. In 1924, the founders of the *Académie internationale de droit comparé* invited Pound to join that organization as one of its first 30 titular members. Pound became president of the academy's Anglo-American

---

[224] ROSCOE POUND, READINGS IN ROMAN LAW AND THE CIVIL LAW AND MODERN CODES AS DEVELOPMENTS THEREOF: AN INTRODUCTION TO COMPARATIVE LAW (2d ed. 1914). The title page labeled this the second edition of part one.

[225] *Id.* at iii.

[226] *Id.* at iii-iv. Pound wrote the reference notes to French and German legal literature primarily for the instructor. *Id.* J. North & Company published the 1906 book, *Readings in Roman Law*, in Lincoln, Nebraska.

[227] Clark, *Modern Development*, supra note 65, at 607.

group in 1927 and served as president of the academy itself from 1950 to 1955.[228] He also actively contributed articles to its publications.[229]

Reflecting Pound's prestige, the editorial board of the *American Journal of Comparative Law* asked him to write the introduction to its first issue in 1952.[230] The ten-page essay was a *tour d'esprit* of Pound's lifelong commitment to comparative law and its importance to American legal history.[231] In a symbolic way, the article marked the closing of modern American comparative law's first half century and its resurgence through the *Journal* and its supporting institution, the American Association for the Comparative Study of Law.[232]

2. John Wigmore

Another major American comparatist with a worldwide reputation during this period was John Wigmore. He began his comparative law career when Harvard's president, Charles Eliot, selected him in 1889 to be the first professor of Anglo-American law at Keio University in Tokyo. Japan at the time was intensely interested in transplanting the best features of Western law. Wigmore became an expert in Tokugawa law and corresponded with scholars such as Josef Kohler (University of Berlin), who was a German delegate at the Paris Congress.[233] Wigmore, intrigued by the legal transplantation theory of Gabriel de Tarde, a French delegate at the Paris Congress, felt that Tarde, by emphasizing imitation, had completely failed to account for the example of Japanese legal evolution.[234]

In 1893, Wigmore joined the Northwestern University Law School faculty, holding the deanship from 1901 to 1929.[235] He attended the 1904 St. Louis Congress and was on the founding Board of Managers of the Comparative Law Bureau in 1907, remaining until its merger in 1933. Wigmore chaired the AALS editorial committee (all typically bureau members), created in 1909, that

---

[228] Clark, *International Academy, supra* note 116, at 6–7.
[229] *See* Roscoe Pound, *Introduction*, 1 AM. J. COMP. L. 1–10 (1952) (articles listed in the editorial note, at 1); Roscoe Pound, *Lo sviluppo e la deviazione del diritto americano dal diritto inglese, in* 3 ACTORUM ACADEMIAE, *supra* note 116, at 27–48 (pts. 1 & 2, 1953); Roscoe Pound, *Comparative Law,* 4 AM. J. COMP. L. 70–84 (1955).
[230] Pound, *Introduction, supra* note 229.
[231] *Id.* The editorial note listed some of Pound's books and articles developing this theme. *Id.* at 1.
[232] Clark, *Modern Development, supra* note 65, at 607.
[233] JOHN HENRY WIGMORE, 1–4 MATERIALS FOR THE STUDY OF PRIVATE LAW IN OLD JAPAN (1892); *see* Clark, *Nothing New, supra* note 56, at 878 n.25.
[234] John H. Wigmore, *Comparative Law: Jottings on Comparative Legal Ideas and Institutions,* 6 TUL. L. REV. 48–49 (1931) [hereinafter Wigmore, *Jottings*]; *see* G[abriel] de Tarde, LES TRANSFORMATIONS DU DROIT: ÉTUDE SOCIOLOGIQUE (1893, 8th ed. 1922).
[235] PRESSER, *supra* note 223, at 101–03. Wigmore was one of the founding members of the *Harvard Law Review* in 1886 and was enthusiastic to bring the case method supported by Eliot and Langdell to Northwestern. ROALFE, *supra* note 61, at 11, 33.

oversaw the publication of the extremely useful ten-volume Continental Legal History Series. The other committee members were usually the same persons who organized and edited the Modern Legal Philosophy Series. The history volumes provided translated excerpts from books and articles and some original material on important aspects of European legal history and jurists. There were separate volumes on French, German, and Italian law as well as on civil procedure and criminal law and procedure. Wigmore was actively involved—editing, translating, and writing prefatory and introductory material.[236]

Wigmore continued until his death an interest in translation of civil law philosophers to benefit Anglo-American lawyers as well as to promote comparative law. In 1939, the AALS authorized the creation of a committee, with Wigmore as honorary chair, to secure translations of major twentieth-century civil law jurists. This would update the Modern Legal Philosophy Series, which consisted primarily of nineteenth-century jurists.[237] The majority of the editorial committee were comparatists with a philosophical interest in the field, such as Lon Fuller, Jerome Hall, Edwin Patterson, and Max Rheinstein. Harvard University Press published the series, which numbered eight volumes appearing between 1945 and 1970. They took either a geographical focus, such as philosophers in France (institutionalists), Latin America, or the Soviet Union; thematic emphasis (jurisprudence of interests, neo-Kantianism); or individual legal philosophers (Hans Kelsen, Leon Petrażycki, Max Weber).[238]

Between 1915 and 1918, Wigmore and Albert Kocourek (also at Northwestern) compiled and edited the three-volume *Evolution of Law*, bringing into one place English language excerpts and translated foreign writing about ancient and primitive legal systems; the rules themselves; and the physical, biological, and social factors influencing legal development.[239] The authors intended the first volume, carrying the specific subtitle *Sources of Ancient and Primitive Law*, to be used as a book of materials to accompany the case method of teaching originally

---

[236] Little, Brown & Company (Boston) published the series between 1912 and 1928. However, it never published the planned volume 10 on commercial law. See ROALFE, *supra* note 61, at 87–90, 92. In 1909, Wigmore organized the effort to establish comparative criminal law and criminology in the United States, centered at Northwestern University. Wigmore was the first president of the American Institute of Criminal Law and Criminology, which began a journal still in existence today. Huberich, Pound, and Wigmore, active in the Comparative Law Bureau, were among the journal's associate editors. GERHARD O.W. MUELLER, CRIME, LAW AND THE SCHOLARS: A HISTORY OF SCHOLARSHIP IN AMERICAN CRIMINAL LAW 78–80 (1969); *Editorials*, 1 J. AM. INST. CRIM. L. & CRIMINOLOGY 1–7 (1910); *see supra* text accompanying note 92 (Wigmore and criminology).

[237] E.g., LUIS RECASÉNS SICHES ET AL., LATIN-AMERICAN LEGAL PHILOSOPHY vii, ix–xi (Gordon Ireland et al. trans., vol. 3, 20th Century Legal Philosophy Series, 1948), *see supra* text accompanying notes 90–91 (Modern Legal Philosophy Series).

[238] RECASÉNS SICHES, *supra* note 237, at i–iii, x–xii.

[239] ALBERT KOCOUREK & JOHN H. WIGMORE, 1–3 EVOLUTION OF LAW: SELECT READINGS ON THE ORIGIN AND DEVELOPMENT OF LEGAL INSTITUTIONS (1915, 1918); *see* ROALFE, *supra* note 61, at 92; HERGET, JURISPRUDENCE, *supra* note 142, at 98–101, 108–12, 136–41, 146.

developed at Harvard. Consequently, *Sources*, published in 1915, was the world's first published comparative law "casebook."[240] Although it is commonplace to think of comparative law as the study of similarities and differences in the laws of distinct systems, Kocourek and Wigmore were concerned primarily with similarities. Like other comparatists of their era, they saw unification of law as an important task (or at least insight) for the discipline.[241] As with other comparatists in America and Europe, they also viewed the discipline broadly to include history, jurisprudence, and ethnology.[242]

In 1928, Wigmore published the three-volume *A Panorama of the World's Legal Systems*,[243] an attempt to open comparative law to a broader understanding beyond that provided by merely textual exegesis. Wigmore decried the narrowness of most foreign law studies.[244] He defined comparative law to mean: "tracing of an identical or similar idea or institution through all or many systems, with a view to discovering its differences and likenesses in various systems, . . . in short, the evolution of the idea or institution, universally considered." He then added: "Modern scientific thought has made it generally understood that a legal institution can be fully [comprehended] only in the light of the social, economic, religious, political, racial, and climatic circumstances which surround it."[245]

Wigmore wanted comparatists to have as much contact with the living law of a foreign system as possible, preferably learning the foreign language and residing in

---

[240] *See* 1 KOCOUREK & WIGMORE, *supra* note 239, at ix-x. "Primarily these readings have been projected, as an introduction to the study of specific legal systems, for use in law schools which are now limited to the classic text of Maine's *Ancient Law*. . . . With the successful issue of the case method before our eyes . . . we begin by placing in the hands of the reader the best evidence of ancient law, either the law itself, when there is written law, or an ancient record from general literature of customary law, when there is no written law." *Id.*; *see* 2 *id.*, at v; Annelise Riles, ENCOUNTERING AMATEURISM: JOHN HENRY WIGMORE AND THE USES OF AMERICAN FORMALISM, IN RETHINKING THE MASTERS, *supra* note 146, at 94, 108, n.62, 117-24.

[241] 1 KOCOUREK & WIGMORE, *supra* note 239, at viii, xi (universal legal ideas); *see* Clark, *Unification of Law*, supra note 153, at 39-50. "[A]n intermediate working thesis is necessary to vindicate the very existence of this compilation. It is found in the essential unity of human nature. This is explanatory of the existence of a similarity of institutions among a diversity of peoples where the principle of imitation is inadmissible." 1 KOCOUREK & WIGMORE, *supra*, at viii.

[242] 1 KOCOUREK & WIGMORE, *supra* note 239, at vii; Riles, *supra* note 240, at 106-11.

[243] West Publishing Co. issued these volumes. The Washington Law Book Co. published a single volume library edition (with additional citations) in 1936.

[244] Wigmore, *Jottings, supra* note 234, at 49-51; *see* PRESSER, *supra* note 223, at 106-07.

[245] Wigmore, *Jottings, supra* note 234, at 51. Hug and Ireland presented a similar definition of comparative law, although it seemed more rule-bound. "To understand the history of the rule, to trace its principal sources, its developing vicissitudes, and its final formation and acceptance, to appreciate its relation to other parts of the instant system and, most important of all, to learn its actual operation, to see what it does as distinct from what it says, by consultation of the commentators and more importantly by examination of the actual decisions of the courts, to carry through this analysis for each of the great systems of law, classifying and discussing as many of the subdivisions as circumstances permit, to discover and set forth the similarities and differences of the existing solutions, and then to make a summation of the whole resultant with a view to an at least partial and temporarily valid prediction as to the tendency of current doctrine and lines of decision, more correctly constitutes the real purpose of comparative law." Hug & Ireland, *supra* note 115, at 73.

the country. Since he knew that this was often not possible, and if so, only for one or two countries, he advised scholars, in preparing their comparative studies, to adopt three perspectives. First, learn about the ethical, economic, and social background of their subject legal system. Second, review legal materials used in everyday social life such as deeds and contracts as well as travelers' accounts of legal places and events such as courthouses and trials. Finally, use pictures so that a reader can visualize the legal reality.[246]

Wigmore argued for a methodology that he applied in his *Panorama*. There he surveyed 16 principal legal systems, past and present: Egyptian, Mesopotamian, Hebrew, Chinese, Hindu, Greek, Roman, Japanese, Mohammedan, "Keltic," Slavic, Germanic, maritime, papal, Romanesque, and Anglican. To bring his subject to life he incorporated 500 illustrations. He followed this in 1941 with *A Kaleidoscope of Justice: Containing Authentic Accounts of Trial Scenes from All Times and Climes*. The book's subtitle suggests the author's intent, which was to "tell us of Justice as it is done, not of Justice as by the books."[247] Predating television broadcasting, Wigmore relied on the "records of travel and adventure by eye-witnesses of the scenes described" to provide "informational entertainment" and a "collection of pen-pictures." Nevertheless, Wigmore the scholar, could not restrain the temptation to "draw inferences from these scattered instances to some general truths, truths of evolution and principles of policy," which he did in his 24-page epilogue.[248]

G. Two Sides of German-American Relations: The Nazis, Anti-Semitism, and Natural Law

1. The Nazis and Anti-Semitism at American Universities

In early 1933, Adolf Hitler and the National Socialist Workers' Party consolidated their power over the legislative and executive branches of the German government. The Reichstag enacted an enabling act that provided Chancellor Hitler and his cabinet the ability to issue laws without parliament that could subvert the constitution.[249] Hitler used that authority to promulgate the Law for the Restoration of the Professional Civil Service. The Civil Service Law expelled most Jews and many dissidents from government employment, including 1,200

---

[246] Wigmore, *Jottings, supra* note 234, at 262–66; *see* ROALFE, *supra* note 61.

[247] JOHN H. WIGMORE, A KALEIDOSCOPE OF JUSTICE: CONTAINING AUTHENTIC ACCOUNTS OF TRIAL SCENES FROM ALL TIMES AND CLIMES vii (1941).

[248] *Id.* at v, vii–viii, *see* 713–36; *see* ROALFE, *supra* note 61, at 260–62. For a critique of these methods, *see* Riles, *supra* note 240, at 94–126.

[249] *See* GORDON A. CRAIG, GERMANY: 1866–1945, at 569–90 (1978). The Nationalsozialistische Deutsche Arbeiterpartei (NSDAP) orchestrated the March 1933 enabling act, whose official title was Gesetz zur Behebung der Not von Volk und Reich, which reflected its aim to relieve Germany's distress.

professors in all fields.[250] By 1935, the regime had expelled 132 persons from law faculties, 69 of whom went into exile. Sixty of those who left were Jewish or of Jewish descent. The remainder were social democrats, communists, or other dissidents.[251]

Shortly thereafter, in the United States, the Institute of International Education along with the aid of several Jewish donors established the Emergency Committee in Aid of Displaced German Scholars. It and the Rockefeller Foundation, believing the German crisis would soon pass, created complementary programs to encouraged U.S. universities to host displaced German scholars by subsidizing their salaries for one or two years.[252] Since Harvard's president, Lawrence Lowell, was hostile toward the Emergency Committee as a propaganda tool, law professor Felix Frankfurter, the only Jew on the law faculty, became the relief organization's chief Cambridge contact to place professors. Borchard and Llewellyn carried out a similar role at Yale Law School, although Dean Charles Clark was not initially enthusiastic. The lack of law school commitment was the same with Dean Marion Kirkwood at Stanford and Dean Leon Green at Northwestern.[253]

Anti-Semitic attitudes, deeply entrenched in American academia, substantially affected the response of university presidents and law school deans during the 1930s toward the plight of refugee scholars, who were typically Jewish.[254] At the same time, some of these academic leaders wanted to maintain relations with Europe including German-American student exchange. To illustrate, Harvard's president, James Conant (served 1933-1953), repeatedly ignored opportunities to stand against the Hitler regime while his administration invited Nazi leaders to the campus and to social events, continuing friendly relations with German universities under Nazi control. Furthermore, Conant personally invited Benito Mussolini's U.S. ambassador to his university office.[255]

---

[250] Kyle Graham, *The Refugee Jurist and American Law Schools, 1933–1941*, 50 AM. J. COMP. L. 777, 782 (2002); *see* Gesetz zur Wiederherstellung des Berufsbeamtentums, 7 Apr. 1933, RGBl. I at 175. In 1936, the Emergency Committee published a list of 100 displaced European jurists who were searching for permanent employment. Graham, *supra*, at 817 n.276.

[251] Reinhard Zimmermann, *"Was Heimat hieß, nun heißt es Hölle," The Emigration of Lawyers from Hitler's Germany: Political Background, Legal Framework, and Cultural Context*, in JURISTS UPROOTED: GERMAN-SPEAKING ÉMIGRÉ LAWYERS IN TWENTIETH-CENTURY BRITAIN 1, 8, 25–26, 34–35, 43, 50–51, 53–54, 61 (Jack Beatson & Reinhard Zimmermann eds., 2004).

[252] STEPHEN H. NORWOOD, THE THIRD REICH IN THE IVORY TOWER: COMPLICITY AND CONFLICT ON AMERICAN CAMPUSES 31–33 (2009); Graham, *supra* note 250, at 785–86, 795–98. In 1938, as Nazi aggression spread in Europe, the Emergency Committee changed its name to substitute Foreign for German. Graham, *supra*, at 785 n.45; *see* New York Public Library: Manuscripts & Archives, *Emergency Committee in Aid of Displaced Foreign Scholars Records*, https://archives.nypl.org/mss/922.

[253] NORWOOD, *supra* note 252, at 32–33, 38; Graham, *supra* note 250, at 786–89.

[254] *See* NORWOOD, *supra* note 252, at 29–35; Bruce A. Kimball & Daniel R. Coquillette, *History and Harvard Law School*, 87 FORDHAM L. REV. 883, 897, 905, 907–09 (2018) [hereinafter Kimball & Coquillette, *Harvard*].

[255] NORWOOD, *supra* note 252, at 33, 36–40, 59–60, 73. In 1934, Conant's administration welcomed Ernst Hanfstaengl, Hitler's foreign press chief (1933–1937) and a German-American Harvard graduate, to commencement. Between 1935 to 1937, Conant allowed the German consul general in

While Pound was still dean at Harvard, he toured the Austro-German border in 1934, visiting with various university leaders and ministry of justice officials and reporting on the peaceful scene. Back in the United States, he faced a largely hostile reaction.[256] Later that year, the German ambassador presented Pound an honorary degree from Berlin University at Harvard Law School, which President Conant permitted although the presentation infuriated Frankfurter.[257] Pound was a Germanophile dating from his childhood, due in part to his mother's fluency in German.[258] Through 1934, he may well have supported an authoritarian policy as appropriate in Germany, but there is no evidence he was anti-Semitic.[259]

Llewellyn's relationship with Germany made him potentially subject to more criticism than Pound received. Before enrolling at Yale Law School, Llewellyn attended a German academy, was fluent in German, and enlisted in the Kaiser's army when the Great War broke out. Injured, he received the Iron Cross and returned to the United States in 1915. When America entered the War, Llewellyn volunteered but the army rejected him, so he completed his law studies. As a Columbia law professor, Llewellyn lectured at Leipzig University in 1928 and 1931; the lectures formed the basis for a German language book on the American case law system.[260] A colleague at Columbia, Sam Klaus, chided Llewellyn that

---

Boston to lay a swastika wreath at the university's chapel and sent a delegate and greetings to the universities at Heidelberg and Göttingen on their respective anniversaries. *Id.* at 37, 47–56, 58–60, 63, 65–67, 70–74. Hanfstaengl was the only person, ironically, who worked directly for Hitler and later for Franklin Roosevelt. *See* Steven Casey, Franklin D. Roosevelt, *Ernst "Putzi" Hanfstaengl and the "S-Project," June 1942-June 1944*, 35 J. CONTEMP. HIST. 339–59 (2000).

[256] NORWOOD, *supra* note 252, at 56; Graham, *supra* note 250, at 789–90; Peter Rees, *Nathan Roscoe Pound and the Nazis*, 60 B.C. L. REV. 1313–14, 1317–18, 1325, 1327 (2019). Pound also visited various cities in Germany for a few days in 1936 and 1937. Rees, *supra*, at 1332.

[257] NORWOOD, *supra* note 252, at 57; Graham, *supra* note 250, at 790; Rees, *supra* note 256, at 1315–16, 1325–29. *See generally* BRUCE A. KIMBALL & DANIEL R. COQUILLETTE, THE INTELLECTUAL SWORD: HARVARD LAW SCHOOL, THE SECOND CENTURY 259–67 (2020) [hereinafter KIMBALL & COQUILLETTE, INTELLECTUAL SWORD].

[258] Rees, *supra* note 256, at 1325.

[259] HULL, POUND AND LLEWELLYN, *supra* note 146, at 238 n.39; Kimball & Coquillette, *Harvard*, *supra* note 254, at 905, 907–08; Rees, *supra* note 256, at 1330–32, 1347. Kimball and Coquillette were aware of the pitfall of presentism, faulting individuals for decisions made without information or values only apparent after the time they acted. Kimball & Coquillette, *Harvard*, *supra*, at 884, 902 (politically correct criticism of historical events); *see* JAMES Q. WHITMAN, HITLER'S AMERICAN MODEL: THE UNITED STATES AND THE MAKING OF NAZI RACE LAW 136 (2017) (the USA was not responsible for what happened in Germany); DAVID S. WYMAN, THE ABANDONMENT OF THE JEWS: AMERICA AND THE HOLOCAUST, 1941–1945, at 326 (1984) (not until 1942 was the Holocaust generally known in the USA). Pound condemned totalitarian philosophies, whether fascism or communism. HULL, POUND AND LLEWELLYN, *supra* note 146, at 245, 301–02.

[260] HULL, POUND AND LLEWELLYN, *supra* note 146, at 136–38, 168–69, 224–25; Ulrich Drobnig, *Llewellyn and Germany*, *in* RECHTSREALISMUS, MULTIKUTURELLE GESELLSCHAFT UND HANDELSRECHT: KARL N. LLEWELLYN UND SEINE BEDEUTUNG HEUTE 17–43 (Ulrich Drobnig & Manfred Rehbinder eds., 1994); *see* KARL N. LLEWELLYN, PRÄJUDIZIENRECHT UND RECHTSPRECHUNG IN AMERIKA: EINE SPRUCHAUSWAHL MIT BESPRECHUNG (1933); *id.*, THE CASE LAW SYSTEM IN AMERICA (Paul Gewirtz ed., Michael Ansaldi trans., 1989).

the Nazis praised his book and that "you have been accepted as a true Nazi, fit to be amalgamated into the lifeblood of the new Reich." The connection between legal realism and amorality led another professor to label Llewellyn a "fascist and a pillar of the fascist New Deal." The irony was that Llewellyn spoke against Hitler from the beginning of his rise to power in 1933.[261]

From 1906 until the early 1930s, Pound maintained a network of progressive pragmatic scholars, helping to make Harvard the country's foremost research university. He also provided material assistance to younger legal scholars, some of whom were his former students, hoping they would further his jurisprudential aims.[262] One of those law students was Anton Chroust,[263] who was a German exchange student at Harvard Law School from 1932 to 1934. Chroust received his S.J.D. degree in 1933 and had returned to Germany when Pound met with him briefly during his summer tour in 1934.[264] Later that year, Chroust emigrated to the United States, where Pound assisted him during the 1930s and 1940s to obtain academic employment and sometimes hired him for research projects. Pound also defended Chroust before U.S. immigration authorities, even after agents arrested him in 1941 as an enemy alien and detained him until 1943. In 1946, at a repatriation hearing, the U.S. government allowed Chroust to remain in the United States and Notre Dame hired him as a professor.[265]

After Pound's retirement as dean in 1936, he had more time to travel, responding to invitations and honors. His Asian students invited him to China and Japan, which he visited in 1936 and 1937. He toured Europe and the Near East shortly before Hitler invaded Poland, but was aware that jurisprudence could not prevent war.[266] Pound first met John Wu, a Chinese legal scholar at Harvard as a research fellow, in 1923. The pair maintained a lifelong correspondence. In 1932, Pound accepted an invitation to join the trustees of Soochow's Comparative Law School. That set the stage for his first trips to China.[267]

---

[261] HULL, POUND AND LLEWELLYN, *supra* note 146, at 237–38 (quotations at 237).

[262] *Id.* at 6–8, 122–23, 224, 281.

[263] *See infra* notes 290–292 and accompanying text (Chroust).

[264] Rees, *supra* note 256, at 1315, 1333–36. In July 1934, Pound met Chroust in Munich. *Id.* at 1318, 1326. *See generally* KIMBALL & COQUILLETTE, INTELLECTUAL SWORD, *supra* note 257, at 267–71.

[265] Rees, *supra* note 256, at 1335–41. The U.S. Department of Justice accused Chroust of membership in the NSDAP and serving before 1936 as a propagandist for Hitler. *Id.* at 1341–44. Rees suggested that Chroust was a more fervent Nazi than Pound portrayed in his defense of Chroust. *Id.* at 1346–47. Rees supported his argument with the file that the Federal Bureau of Investigation (FBI) had with hearsay statements against Chroust. Rees did not mention that during this era Pound (and later Llewellyn) also had FBI files. HULL, POUND AND LLEWELLYN, *supra* note 146, at 317–21.

[266] HULL, POUND AND LLEWELLYN, *supra* note 146, at 281–82, 302. In the early 1950s, Pound spent a year in India. *Id.* at 314.

[267] Jedidiah J. Kroncke, *Roscoe Pound in China: A Lost Precedent for the Liabilities of American Legal Exceptionalism*, 38 BROOK. J. INT'L L. 77, 87–89, 98 (2012) [hereinafter Kroncke, *Pound in China*]; *see* KRONCKE, FUTILITY, *supra* note 35, at 201–22; Zhang, *supra* note 43, at 206, 217; *see supra* text accompanying notes 43–48 (John Wu and Soochow Law School).

In 1945, the Republic of China's ministry of justice invited Pound, who had learned some Mandarin, to formulate plans to reform the judiciary, which he agreed to do with trips to eastern China in 1946 and 1947. Unlike Pound's trip to Germany in 1934, the Chinese visits elicited praise in the United States. Its policy in support of Chiang Kai-shek's Kuomintang (KMT), the party controlling the Republic, was to thwart Russian influence.[268] Pound organized a survey of criminal justice, requested statistics, and relied on the Nationalist government to gather information. Since he could read the Chinese civil code in Mandarin, he used the code's Roman law structure to collect statutes and commentaries available at Harvard's library. He also gave lectures at Chinese universities and was a spokesman for the Nationalist cause in the United States. When the Nationalist regime collapsed in 1949, Pound blamed the U.S. State Department and the Soviets for arming the Chinese Communists.[269]

In 1934, Yale's president, James Angell (in office 1921–1937), took a position like that of Conant, disinterested in accepting German refugee scholars but otherwise maintaining European academic relations. In 1934, for instance, he welcomed a delegation of Italian Fascist students representing Mussolini to campus and in 1936, sent a representative to the University of Heidelberg's anniversary commemoration.[270]

The situation at Columbia University was more complicated, in part due to the resistance of Columbia's Jewish Students Society to the implicit anti-Semitism associated with the university's action after Hitler's rise to power in 1933. In November 1933, President Nicholas Butler (served 1902–1945) welcomed Hans Luther, Germany's ambassador to the United States, to lecture to Columbia students. Butler also established important ties between Columbia and Italian Fascist leaders and a German and Italian student exchange. Through 1937, Butler refused to criticize Hitler's policies in Germany, which he considered temporary, even though there was student, faculty, and public pressure to do so. His anti-Semitism and belief that Columbia should be a Christian institution led him to institute a Jewish quota, which nevertheless failed to reduce Jewish enrollment due to the preference of elite Protestant families for Harvard and Yale.[271]

---

[268] HULL, POUND AND LLEWELLYN, *supra* note 146, at 311; Kroncke, *Pound in China*, *supra* note 267, at 94–97.

[269] HULL, POUND AND LLEWELLYN, *supra* note 146, at 311–15; Kroncke, *Pound in China*, supra note 267, at 97–99, 117–24, 128; Pound, *Progress*, *supra* note 53, at 345–52, 356–62; *see* ROSCOE POUND, THE LAW IN CHINA AS SEEN BY ROSCOE POUND (Tsao Wen-yen ed., 1953).

[270] NORWOOD, *supra* note 252, at 15, 32–33, 57–58, 60, 70. Earlier, President Conant had individually greeted each of the 160 Italian Fascist students visiting Harvard. *Id.* at 58.

[271] NORWOOD, *supra* note 252, at 76–85, 89–92, 102; Kimball & Coquillette, *Harvard*, *supra* note 254, at 908–09. Butler also sent a delegation to the Heidelberg anniversary. NORWOOD, *supra*, at 93–97.

One should not believe that elite U.S. universities were more callous than the general American public during the period between 1933 and 1938, when in November Nazi storm troopers and German civilians destroyed 7,000 Jewish businesses, killing 100 and imprisoning 30,000 Jews (*Kristallnacht*).[272] Anti-Semitism and anti-immigration attitudes were widespread and dominated the U.S. Congress even after the U.S. declaration of war in 1941. President Franklin Roosevelt (in office 1933–1945), other political leaders, most mass media, and Christian church leaders were, in general, silent about the tragedy in Germany and later in Europe. There was plenty of blame about indifference and even hostility to the Jewish plight to go around.[273]

2. Émigré Legal Scholars and U.S. Law Schools

Within the American social and university environment, law school response to displaced German and Austrian legal scholars prior to 1945 was pragmatic. The number that could reach the United States was small and most schools were indifferent to the refugee plight. Measures varied among those schools that took any action at all, reflecting the economic realities of the Great Depression (1929–1939), a foreigner's ability in English and experience as a scholar or professor, a school's finances, its curricular or scholarly orientation toward foreign and comparative law, and its level of anti-Semitism.[274]

It was only around 1938, particularly after *Kristallnacht*, that American law professors collectively began to denounce the Nazis and as a counterpoint to identify and promote democracy-enhancing legal philosophies. This included idealizing the lawyer-citizen as the appropriate law school aim and criticizing certain versions of legal realism and legal positivism as amoral.[275] Ironically, the reform literature embracing civic mindedness and pragmatism in law schools,

---

[272] NORWOOD, *supra* note 252, at 230–42; WYMAN, *supra* note 259, at 9, 12, 14–15. From 1933, the American Jewish press reported on the plight of Jews in Germany. The *New York Times* described Jewish beatings with economic and political discrimination and threats of worse. By 1934, prominent journalists, politicians, and Jewish leaders published books on Nazi atrocities. NORWOOD, *supra*, at 1–11.

[273] WYMAN, *supra* note 259, at x–xi, 5–15, 55–58, 101–03. Wyman placed the primary responsibility for U.S. inaction on Roosevelt and his administration. *Id.* at xi, 311–17, 327, 331–37. Nevertheless, the United States eventually accepted 130,000 persons, about a quarter of all German-speaking refugees. Zimmermann, *supra* note 251, at 39.

[274] Graham, *supra* note 250, at 790, 793–94, 814. Of the 69 refugees from German-language law faculties, 24 settled in the United States. That number is slightly larger if one includes postdoctoral assistants. Zimmermann, *supra* note 251, at 54.

[275] Graham, *supra* note 250, at 803–07; *see* NORWOOD, *supra* note 252, at 220–42 (*Kristallnacht*); Harold D. Lasswell & Myers S. McDougal, *Legal Education and Public Policy: Professional Training in the Public Interest*, 52 YALE L.J. 203–92 (1943); *infra* pt. G.3 (natural law). "[I]f legal education in the contemporary world is adequately to serve the needs of a free and productive commonwealth, it must be conscious, efficient, and systematic training for policy-making." Lasswell & McDougal, *supra*, at 206.

which sometimes explicitly compared European legal education as inferior, worked against the few foreign law professors who typically had to teach jurisprudence, Roman law, or comparative law.[276]

Most law schools aiding émigré scholars and professors offered short-term lecture, research, or library positions. The one or two-year grants by the Rockefeller Foundation and Emergency Committee to rescue science and learning made law school decisions easier. Occasionally, a law school would have its own funds. For instance, the University of California due to the effort of Max Radin, a Berkeley comparatist who had emigrated from Germany in the nineteenth century, hired Stefan Riesenfeld (1908-1999) as a research associate in 1935. Riesenfeld had obtained his doctorate in law from Breslau University in 1932. In 1933, his German professors helped him find a research position at the University of Milan, where he received the J.U.D. degree in 1934. After earning an LL.B. from Berkeley, Riesenfeld accepted a professorship at the University of Minnesota in 1938.[277]

There was minimal success for established German law professors fired in 1933 for their Jewish heritage or activities as social democrats, who then desired to emigrate. For the 1934-1935 academic year, Columbia hired Arthur Nussbaum (1877-1964), a Jew from the Berlin law faculty; and Michigan accepted Rudolf von Laun, a social democrat and public law scholar at Hamburg University. While Laun had to return to Germany, Nussbaum was able to maintain marginal employment at Columbia until 1939, when the university hired him as a research professor.[278]

Nussbaum was 57 years old when he arrived in New York, which realistically precluded him from pursuing Riesenfeld's path of relearning law as a student in the United States. Llewellyn shared Nussbaum's interest in legal realism and was one of the Columbia professors who helped find gift and grant money to support Nussbaum at the law school. In 1914, Nussbaum had published *Die Rechtstatsachenforschung*, a short pamphlet setting out his philosophy of economic and social fact research regarding legal issues and institutions.[279] He

---

[276] Graham, *supra* note 250, at 806-09, 816.

[277] Richard W. Jennings, *Stefan A. Riesenfeld-In Tribute*, 63 CAL. L. REV. 1387-89 (1975); *see supra* ch. 5, note 51 and text accompanying note 115; ch. 6, note 98 and accompanying text (Radin). Harvard awarded Riesenfeld a J.S.D in 1940 for work he finished there. Jennings, *supra*, at 1389; *see id.* at 1391 n.8 (Riesenfeld's comparative law articles from 1937 to 1973). Additional illustrations of younger émigré comparatists follow, *infra*, at pt. G.3.

[278] Graham, *supra* note 250, at 791-93, 809-10. Laun returned to Germany; in 1945, Hamburg University named him vice-rector and then rector from 1947 to 1949, a post he had held from 1924 to 1925. Georg Stadtmüller, *Laun, Rudolf Edler von, in* 13 NEUE DEUTSCHE BIOGRAPHIE 715-17 (1982), https://www.deutsche-biographie.de/pnd118570188.html.

[279] Graham, *supra* note 250, at 791-92; Elliott E. Cheatham et al., *Arthur Nussbaum: A Tribute*, 57 COLUM. L. REV. 1, 3-4 (1957); *see* Arthur Nussbaum, DIE RECHTSTATSACHENFORSCHUNG: IHRE BEDEUTUNG FÜR WISSENSCHAFT UND UNTERRICHT (1914) (48 pp.); *id., Fact Research in Law*, 40 COLUM. L. REV. 189-219 (1940).

carried this method through his best-known comparative law book, *Money in the Law* (1950). Nussbaum began his interest in this subject in 1920, a response to the postwar inflation in Germany.[280] Finally, Nussbaum maintained his pursuit of a comparative approach to private international law that he first exhibited in 1932 in Germany, since he followed it with an English-language book on that subject in 1942. That comparative focus was also evident in the Parker School of Foreign and Comparative Law's Bilateral Studies in Private International Law, which Nussbaum edited.[281]

Ernst Rabel was one of the last German Jewish law professors to escape Germany, when in the summer of 1939 he left Berlin for the Netherlands, then Brazil, arriving in the United States in September at the age of 65. Yntema arranged Rabel's research associate position at Michigan Law School, where Rabel published three volumes of *The Conflict of Laws* between 1945 and 1950. In the last two years of his life, he returned to Tübingen, where the university made him an honorary professor and his Berlin institute had relocated. Rabel spent a few months at the Berlin Free University, which appointed him professor emeritus.[282]

3. Natural Law

The oldest jurisprudential theories were some form of natural law, which merged morality and law. In the West, beginning with the Greeks and Romans, development later passed to the Roman church. St. Thomas Aquinas combined Christian theology with Aristotelian ethics to provide natural law in the thirteenth century with its most sophisticated elaboration. However, Thomistic philosophy failed to cope adequately with the European scientific revolution, Protestant Reformation, and Enlightenment. Theorists such as Descartes and Bacon developed an alternative epistemology based on rationalism, while jurists like Grotius, Locke, Pufendorf, and Burlamaqui placed ethics and law into a secular natural law. By

---

[280] ARTHUR NUSSBAUM, MONEY IN THE LAW, NATIONAL AND INTERNATIONAL: A COMPARATIVE STUDY IN THE BORDERLINE OF LAW AND ECONOMICS iii–vii (2d ed. 1950, 1st ed. 1939); Cheatham, *supra* note 279, at 1–2, 5.

[281] Cheatham, *supra* note 279, at 4–6; see ARTHUR NUSSBAUM, DEUTSCHES INTERNATIONALES PRIVATRECHT: UNTER BESONDERER BERÜCKSICHTIGUNG DES ÖSTERREICHISCHEN UND SCHWEIZERISCHEN RECHTS (1932); *id.*, PRINCIPLES OF PRIVATE INTERNATIONAL LAW (1943). In 1951, Nussbaum authored the first volume in the Parker School series on American-Swiss conflicts law.

[282] David S. Clark, *The Influence of Ernst Rabel on American Law*, in DER EINFLUSS, *supra* note 146, at 107, 109–110, 118 [hereinafter Clark, *Rabel*]; Zimmermann, *supra* note 251, at 47, 52, 63. Yntema wrote the foreword to volume 1. For volume 4, published in 1958, Rabel had worked at Harvard Law School. Clark, *Rabel*, *supra*, at 110, 121. Rabel was one of 14 émigré law professors or postdoctoral researchers expelled from German universities who returned to Germany as rémigrés after the war. Zimmermann, *supra*, at 53, 28–29, 63.

the eighteenth century, Kant, Hume, Adam Smith, and Bentham presented ideas about morality and law independent of religion. Thus, it was Jeffersonian natural rights, Protestant theology, and utilitarianism that dominated the thinking of American jurists during the early years of the new republic.[283]

From the American Revolution forward, secular natural law and rights, positivism, historical jurisprudence, or sociological jurisprudence were dominant theories of law. Thomistic natural law ideas only began to regularly appear in America around 1940.[284] In the late 1930s and 1940s, some jurists and philosophers, including Pound at times, argued for a moral theory of law, one that could justify American democracy against the tyranny of totalitarian regimes in Europe and the Soviet Union. In addition, there was general dissatisfaction expressed against extreme empiricism and ethical relativism associated with some proponents of legal realism. These concerns continued into the 1950s.[285]

Jacques Maritain (1882–1973), for instance, a French Thomistic philosophy professor, gave lectures regularly in Toronto between 1933 and 1940, when he moved to New York to teach at Columbia University until 1944. Following the liberation of France from German occupation in 1944, the French government named Maritain ambassador to the Holy See (through 1948) and a member of the French delegation to UNESCO, where he was involved in drafting the Universal Declaration of Human Rights (1948). In 1948, Maritain accepted a philosophy professorship at Princeton, where he taught until 1952, continuing as an emeritus professor until 1959 when he returned to France.[286]

Maritain's philosophy of law, derived from St. Thomas Aquinas, posited an idea of law in human nature, immanent and derivative, but separate from, eternal law. Nature has a teleological character and a person can know what a thing should do or how one should use it by examining its end and the normality of its

---

[283] HERGET, JURISPRUDENCE, *supra* note 142, at 8–9, 228–29; *see supra* ch. 3 (1776–1791).

[284] BODENHEIMER, *supra* note 146, at 134–35; HERGET, JURISPRUDENCE, *supra* note 142, at 9–12, 229. Scholars at Catholic universities were an exception, since they more often had expounded Thomistic ideas. *Id.* at 9, 229, 231; *see, e.g.*, RENE I. HOLANIND, NATURAL LAW AND LEGAL PRACTICE (1899) (Holainind was a professor at Georgetown University).

[285] CARRINGTON, *supra* note 22, at 218–19; HERGET, JURISPRUDENCE, *supra* note 142, at 229–30; HULL, POUND AND LLEWELLYN, *supra* note 146, at 248–54; *see* BODENHEIMER, *supra* note 146, at 142–47. This included a critique of the ethical component of Pound's pragmatism and social interest theory. Karl Kreilkamp, *Dean Pound and the Immutable Natural Law*, 18 FORDHAM L. REV. 173–203 (1949). "Pound confines [jurisprudence] to the quite as amoral technique [of positivism] of applying an arbitrarily given set of moral and social ideals, issuing from society." *Id.* at 203.

[286] William Sweet, *Jacques Maritain*, in THE STANFORD ENCYCLOPEDIA OF PHILOSOPHY (2019), https://plato.stanford.edu/entries/maritain; *see* JACQUES MARITAIN, LES DROITS DE L'HOMME ET LA LOI NATURELLE (1942), which Doris C. Anson translated as *The Rights of Man and Natural Law* in 1943. Maritain delivered nine lectures at the University of Chicago in 1938, published as *Scholasticism and Politics* (Mortimer J. Adler ed. & trans., 1940). The United Nations created the Educational, Scientific, and Cultural Organization (UNESCO) in 1945.

functioning. Human reason can discover rules, according to which the human will must act, to accord with the necessary ends of a human being. Natural law includes rights, specifically in relation to the common good. This good, and not individual rights, is the basis of the state; thus, there can be a hierarchical ordering of these rights. Maritain preferred a liberal democratic state, with positive freedoms, and rejected fascism and communism as dehumanizing secular religions.[287]

With the revival of natural law, Herget identified four elements that most of its variations adopted. First, human nature is immanent. Humans have a basic biological and psychological nature that is constant over time and environments. Second, society should prohibit or require certain human conduct to foster human life. Third, ordinary humans can understand these mandates, which society can organize into a system of principles and rules. Finally, these principles and rules—natural law—provide a basis to test the validity of the state's positive law.[288]

Among those encouraging a revival of Thomistic natural law was Karl Kreilkamp. In 1939, he published his dissertation prepared for the philosophy department at Catholic University. Relying on the work of St. Thomas and subsequent European scholars, Kreilkamp explained the relationship between natural and human laws in terms of thirteenth-century concepts and terminology. Based on an epistemology of essentialism, he emphasized the similarities among humans, their nature, rather than accidental differences. Their shared rationality can appreciate human good, which is the proper end of moral obligation. The mind, using reason and avoiding animal inclinations, can organize principles in a hierarchy from general to specific. The ultimate principle, which is universal, is to do good and avoid evil. Precepts at lower levels combine contingent knowledge of human nature with the ultimate principle, which as one descends the hierarchy, may include economic, social, and cultural elements that are not universal. Lower-level precepts are subject to correction through rational argument and experience. Human laws, beneath natural law, may serve many goals but should not contravene natural law.[289]

---

[287] Sweet, *supra* note 286; *see* JACQUES MARITAIN, MAN AND THE STATE (1951). Since 1957, there has been a Jacques Maritain Center at the University of Notre Dame, where he had lectured during his years living in the United States. Jacques Maritain Center, *Introduction*, https://maritain.nd.edu/jmc/brochure.htm.
[288] HERGET, JURISPRUDENCE, *supra*, note 142, at 230.
[289] HERGET, JURISPRUDENCE, *supra* note 142, at 232–35; *see* KARL KREILKAMP, THE METAPHYSICAL FOUNDATIONS OF THOMISTIC JURISPRUDENCE (1939). Kreilkamp's bibliography listed works in Latin, German, French, and English. *Id.* at 178–80. See also Karl Kreilkamp, *Dean Pound and the Immutable Natural Law*, 18 FORDHAM L. REV. 173 (1949).

Like Kreilkamp, who became a Notre Dame philosophy professor (1946 to 1958), Anton Chroust (1907–1982) taught there as a professor of law, philosophy, and history from 1946 to 1972. Chroust, born in Germany, emigrated to the United States in 1934 and had Pound as a mentor. During the war years, he wrote five articles supporting Thomism and thereafter continued with his writing on jurisprudence and natural law until 1954, when he turned his attention primarily to the legal profession.[290] From 1971 until 1981, Chroust returned to writing about legal philosophy, mostly in the *American Journal of Jurisprudence*.[291]

Chroust earned his law doctorate at the University of Erlangen and philosophy doctorate at the University of Munich. After arriving in the United States, he studied under Pound at Harvard and received the S.J.D. degree. His debt to Pound is evident in a 1945 article Chroust wrote entitled "Law and Morals." In the initial footnote, he referred to Pound's earlier article of the same title as a "masterly presentation." Chroust's presentation reflected more the philosopher than the jurist, but its basis of Thomistic and Kantian essentialism, combined with the dominant reliance on Germanic and Latin sources, was evident.

> For the last moral, social, and, therefore, jural unit in this world of ours is, and always shall be, the individual human being in his infinite moral worth and dignity expressed in the Idea of man's moral freedom. The maintenance, protection, and promotion of the individual human being in his moral aspect constitute the end of the Law. In this the Law must always remain subservient to the moral interests of rational man.[292]

Another German émigré who supported natural law was Heinrich Rommen (1897–1967). He received a doctorate in political economy at Münster, followed by a doctorate in civil and canon law at Bonn in 1929. For the next four years, he led the social department of the *Volksverein für das katholische Deutschland*, an association that addressed social problems from a Catholic perspective to counter the anti-clerical policies of the Social Democratic Party. In 1933, the German government banned the *Volksverein's* activities, arrested and jailed Rommen for a month, but he was able to move to Berlin to work as legal counsel in a corporation. Concerned with political harassment, he emigrated in 1938 to the United States. Rommen taught at a Connecticut college until 1946, when he

---

[290] HERGET, JURISPRUDENCE, *supra* note 142, at 235–36; *see* Anton-Hermann Chroust & Frederick A. Collins, *The Basic Ideas in the Philosophy of Law of St. Thomas Aquinas as Found in the* Summa Theologica, 22 MARQ. L. REV. 11–30 (1941); Anton-Hermann Chroust, *Some German Definitions of Law and Legal Philosophy from Kant to Kelsen*, 22 NOTRE DAME LAW 365–99 (1947).

[291] *See, e.g.*, Anton-Hermann Chroust, *The Philosophy of Law of St. Thomas Aquinas: His Fundamental Ideas and Some of His Historical Precursors*, 19 AM. J. JURIS. 1–38 (1974).

[292] Anton-Hermann Chroust, *Law and Morals*, 25 B.U. L. REV. 348, 364 (1945); *see id.* at 351–68.

became a political science professor at St. Thomas College in Minnesota. In 1953, he joined the government department at Georgetown University, where he was a professor until his death.[293]

While in Germany, Rommen published two books on law and government that served as the basis for his academic career in the United States. The first, published in 1935, came from his commitment to Catholic social action and the distress caused during the dissolution of the Weimar Republic and rise of the Nazi Party. Rommen expanded this as *The State in Catholic Thought: A Treatise in Political Philosophy* (1945).[294] In *Political Philosophy*, Rommen set forth a comprehensive treatment of the relationship between humans and the various communities that comprise a good life. Man, born into society, is by nature social and learns to act in and through communities, each of which has its own common good. To illustrate, the family by its nature seeks to prosper by developing relationships over generations and assisting members to prosper. The same dynamic applies to clubs, associations, churches, and business entities: communities flourish when members flourish. Persons and communities are interdependent and the pursuit of the common good relates to personal virtue. Communities, each with its common good, exist in a hierarchy; the state facilitates the ordered pursuit among communities of common goods. Rommen preferred constitutional democracy, since the state could foster pluralism and subsidiarity to allow these communities to promote human dignity. Conversely, totalitarianism—fascism or communism—required the state to subsume all communities in service to the aims of the state.[295]

Rommen's second German book, in 1936, dealt with the revival of natural law; after his arrival in America, he revised and expanded it as *The Natural Law* (1947).[296] The National Socialist Party's deft use of German legislative, administrative, and judicial institutions to impose totalitarian rule alarmed Rommen. Hitler was a master of legality, what Rommen called *Adolf Légalité*. German lawyers, trained in positivism—the command of the sovereign—seemed at a loss to stem the tide. The problem was the separation of ethics from law.[297]

---

[293] Vernon J. Bourke, *In Memoriam: Heinrich Albert Rommen (1897–1967)*, 12 Nat. L.F. v–vi (1967); Thomas R. Hanley, *Translator's Preface, in* HEINRICH A. ROMMEN, THE NATURAL LAW: A STUDY IN LEGAL AND SOCIAL HISTORY AND PHILOSOPHY iii–iv (Thomas R. Hanley trans., 1947) [hereinafter ROMMEN, NATURAL LAW].

[294] HEINRICH A. ROMMEN, DER STAAT IN DER KATHOLISCHEN GEDANKENWELT (1935); *id.*, THE STATE IN CATHOLIC THOUGHT: A TREATISE IN POLITICAL PHILOSOPHY (1945) [hereinafter ROMMEN, POLITICAL PHILOSOPHY]; *see* Leo Strauss, Book Review, 13 SOC. RES. 250–52 (1946) (*The State in Catholic Thought*).

[295] Bruce P. Frohnen, *Introduction to the 2016 Edition, in* ROMMEN, POLITICAL PHILOSOPHY, *supra* note 294, at iii–v, vii–viii (2016 ed.); Waldemar Gurian, Book Review, 9 REV. POL. 381–83 (1947) (*The State in Catholic Thought*).

[296] HEINRICH ALBERT ROMMEN, DIE EWIGE WIEDERKEHR DES NATURRECHTS (1936); ROMMEN, NATURAL LAW, *supra* note 293, at iii.

[297] Russell Hittinger, *Introduction, in* ROMMEN, NATURAL LAW, *supra* note 293, at xi–xiii (Liberty Fund reprint, 1998), https://oll.libertyfund.org (select People, then Rommen).

Rommen, Maritain, and other German émigrés such as political philosophers Leo Strauss and Eric Vögelin who were not Catholics, strove to explain the European problem with totalitarianism as a warning to Americans. In the later 1930s, American jurists considered natural law antiquated but never acquiesced completely to positivistic analytical jurisprudence. Sociological jurisprudence and legal realism, for many, filled the gap. Rommen and Maritain adopted a neo-scholastic Thomistic version of natural law as the basis of a living tradition.[298]

For Rommen, the central question in *Natural Law* was how law binds the conscience of individuals as free agents. He contended that answers group around one of two poles: *lex ratio* or *lex voluntas*. The book explored the answers historically and systematically or philosophically. The *lex-ratio* tradition accepted the primacy of reason to make sense of law as obligation. Alternatively, the *lex-voluntas* tradition held that law binds human liberty because of a legal authority's superior power; reason or intellect is secondary. For Rommen, the Enlightenment weakened the natural law tradition by favoring *lex voluntas* so that natural law was unable to resist the positivism and nominalism of the twentieth century.[299] Rommen concluded, "Modern totalitarianism with its depersonalization of man ... is molded and remolded in accordance with the shifting policy of the 'Leader,' is of its very nature extremely voluntaristic. *Voluntas facit legem*: law is will. How seldom the theorists and practitioners of totalitarianism mention reason, and how frequently they glory in the triumph of the will."[300]

Nevertheless, Rommen foresaw a future for natural law as reason.

[T]he rule of law, the paramount law binding both the ruler and the ruled, necessarily implies the idea of natural law as the critical norm for the existing positive legal order and for the demand to change it, if it has become unjust. The hope of a peaceful change of the legal *status quo* within each nation as well as in the community of nations depends on the acceptance of such a higher law that measures both the legal rights of the *status quo* and the claims of those who would alter it; and it measures them because it is based on natural reason, in which all men participate. For the natural law, ultimately of divine origin but revealed in the very order of being, is but the rule of reason founded upon the rational and social nature of man. *Veritas facit legem*: law is truth.[301]

---

[298] Hittinger, *supra* note 297, at xiii–xvi, xx, xxiii–xxiv. Rommen's *The Natural Law*, Strauss's *National Right and History* (1950), and Voegelin's *New Science of Politics* (1952) treated the problem of the moral foundations of law and politics speculatively, broadly, and classically. Hittinger, *supra*, at xx.
[299] Hittinger, *supra*, at xxv–xxix.
[300] ROMMEN, NATURAL LAW, *supra* note 293, at 264.
[301] *Id.* at 266.

H. The 1930s and 1940s: Achievement during a Difficult Period

1. The ABA Section of International and Comparative Law

In 1933, the ABA merged the Comparative Law Bureau with the International Law Section, whose first chair was Wigmore.[302] The new Section of International and Comparative Law provided useful articles and information in its official journal, the *Tulane Law Review*, until the section began its own publication in 1940, *Proceedings*.[303] From 1943 until 1950, *Proceedings* typically contained about 100 to 200 pages of section business, annual meeting speeches, committee reports, and foreign legislative updates and surveys as well as international law articles. The section's annual meetings and an increasing number of regional meetings had sessions for academic comparatists, especially at the Comparative Philosophy and History of Law (later the Comparative Jurisprudence) Committee, with Pound initially as chair, and the Teaching of International and Comparative Law Committee, with Jerome Hall as chair.[304]

The ABA Section, reorganized in 1937, elected Phanor Eder (one of the AFLA Council's founding members) vice chair and John Vance secretary. Vance became section chair in 1940; he had served as law librarian at the Library of Congress since 1924 with the vision of making it America's leading foreign law resource center.[305] Wigmore was on the Section Council; its Advisory Committee included Frederic Coudert Jr. (1898–1972), a partner in the Coudert Brothers law firm in New York (then America's leading firm for foreign law issues); Edwin

---

[302] See supra text accompanying notes 61, 178 (Wigmore and the ABA Section).

[303] The first issue of 63 pages covered the section's work for 1938–1939 (published in 1940), titled *Selected Papers and Reports*. There was no volume for 1939–1940. The 1940–1941 volume of 120 pages carried the title *Selected Papers and Reports of the Section of International and Comparative Law on Current Latin-American, European and Asiatic Legislation, and a Discussion of Vital Topics on International Law*. See Harry C. Shriver, *Editor's Note*, SEC. INT'L & COMP. L. ANN. PROC. 3 (1943). David E. Grant and William E. Masterson wrote a summary of the section's proceedings for 1941–1942 as *The Work of the Section of International and Comparative Law of the American Bar Association, 1941–1942*, 36 AM. J. INT'L L. 664–85 (1942). The next year, the journal became regularized as PROCEEDINGS OF THE SECTION OF INTERNATIONAL AND COMPARATIVE LAW until 1951 (although the title page was slightly different for 1942–1943). From 1952 until its last volume in 1965, the journal had the title SECTION OF INTERNATIONAL AND COMPARATIVE LAW: PROCEEDINGS [hereinafter ABA SEC. INT'L & COMP. L. PROC.].

[304] See, e.g., Roscoe Pound, *Report of the Committee on Comparative Philosophy and History of Law*, ABA SEC. INT'L & COMP. PROC., supra note 303, at 299 (1942–1943). On Hall, see HERGET, JURISPRUDENCE, supra note 142, at 239–42. Besides books on jurisprudence, Hall wrote *Comparative Law and Social Theory* (1963).

[305] Guerra Everett, *Report of the Committee on Comparative Civil and Commercial Law*, ABA SEC. INT'L & COMP. L. PROC., supra note 303, at 82, 82–83 (1943); Library of Congres, *The Law Library of Congress at 175: A Timeline*, http://www.loc.gov/loc/lcib/07012/law3.html (see 1924). By coincidence, Vance and Wigmore died the same month in 1943. See Everett, supra, at 82–83.

Dickinson, a professor at the University of California, Berkeley who had attended the 1932 Hague Congress while at the University of Michigan; and Pound.[306]

In 1941, the section authorized Vance, for the duration of the war, to offer that the section would publish the English *Journal of the Society of Comparative Legislation*, but that society decided to continue publishing from London.[307] By 1942, the section's Comparative Law Division had eight committees.[308] The ABA recognized in 1942 the expanded activity of the section, which had about 550 members,[309] and permitted it to levy dues of $2.[310] By 1945, the section had about 970 members, a number that declined to 835 by 1950.[311] In 1950, the section had ten committees in the Comparative Law Division and another three general committees that were indirectly concerned with foreign and comparative law.[312]

2. The 1932 and 1937 International Congress of Comparative Law

The International Academy of Comparative Law continued to hold annual meetings at the Peace Palace in The Hague through the 1920s. In 1927, it elected Pound the president of the Anglo-American group and replaced Smith (who had died) as an American titular member with Borchard, who was then librarian and professor at Yale Law School.[313] At the 1929 meeting, members discussed plans for an international congress of comparative law and the academy secretary sent out requests for topics to national committees, including the Comparative Law Bureau. During the next two meetings, the academy adopted procedures for the congress and granted national committees some voting rights. The academy's executive committee selected one or two general reporters who were to synthesize

---

[306] *The House of Delegates Perfects Its Organization and Proceeds to Business*, 22 A.B.A. J. 688, 691, 694 (1936); *Officers of Sections*, 22 A.B.A. J. 827 (1936); *see supra* ch. 5, text accompanying notes 206–07 (Coudert Sr.).

[307] *Announcement*, 15 TUL. L. REV. 494 (1941).

[308] ABA SEC. INT'L & COMP. L. PROC., *supra* note 303, at 11–13 (1943). Eder became division director in 1945. *Id.* at ix (1945).

[309] Charles W. Watson, *Address of Welcome...*, ABA SEC. INT'L & COMP. L. PROC., *supra* note 303, at 16 (1943).

[310] Grant & Masterson, *supra* note 303, at 684.

[311] William B. Cowles, *Report of the Committee on Membership*, ABA SEC. INT'L & COMP. L. PROC., *supra* note 303, at 135, 136 (1945); *Members*, ABA SEC. INT'L & COMP. L. PROC., *supra*, at 127–38 (1950).

[312] *List of Chairmen of Committees*, ABA SEC. INT'L & COMP. L. PROC., *supra* note 303, at 6–7 (1950).

[313] Clark, *International Academy*, *supra* note 116, at 12.

national reports for 20 topics. It expected national committees to publish their national reports in a law journal.[314]

In 1932, Wigmore wrote an article in the *ABA Journal* titled "An American Lawyer's Pilgrimage on the Continent."[315] His purpose was to interest lawyers in attending the upcoming congress at The Hague. In the notice following this article, he explained:

> This is the first Congress of this kind to be held since the International Congress of Lawyers at the Louisiana Purchase Exposition in 1904 in St. Louis. It is organized by the International Academy of Comparative Law, of which the American members are Edwin Borchard, John Bassett Moore, Roscoe Pound, James Brown Scott, and Justice Harlan F. Stone.[316]

Wigmore had translated Edouard Lambert's report in 1930 calling for such a congress.[317] Wigmore mentioned that 40 countries had formed national committees. Those would designate national reporters for the topics in which they cared to participate. Although the U.S. Attorney General William Mitchell headed the American committee, and 40 state, county, and city bar associations appointed delegates, Wigmore was the driving force in soliciting attendance. At the congress, Americans contributed nine general reports and 20 national reports, thereby covering all available topics.[318]

At the end of 1932, Wigmore dutifully reported about the Hague Congress and the major American presence. Delegates represented 31 countries. Of the 305 delegates registered in attendance, 72 came from the United States. Of these, at least 28 were professors who represented 16 law schools or university faculties. The second largest contingent of 52 participants came from France.[319] The *Tulane Law Review* expanded its comparative law mission by announcing that it would be the official "American medium of expression of the International Congress of Comparative Law" and that it would publish the official American report

---

[314] *Id.* at 12–14. The U.S. national committee primarily consisted of law professors and the heads of organizations such as the Bureau, ALI, ABA, and AALS. *Id.* at 14.

[315] John H. Wigmore, *An American Lawyer's Pilgrimage on the Continent*, 18 A.B.A. J. 88–92 (1932).

[316] *Id.*, *International Congress of Comparative Law*, 18 A.B.A. J. 92 (1932); *see* ROALFE, *supra* note 61, at 263–64.

[317] Edouard Lambert & John H. Wigmore, *An International Congress of Comparative Law in 1931*, 24 ILL. L. REV. 656 (1930).

[318] Clark, *International Academy*, *supra* note 116, at 13–14. Both Mitchell and Stone were trustees of the Parker School of Foreign and Comparative Law at Columbia University, created in 1931. COLUMBIA LAW, *supra* note 36, at 330. Wigmore wrote to 800 law faculty members and 1,200 bar association presidents and secretaries. ROALFE, *supra* note 61, at 263.

[319] John H. Wigmore, *Representatives at International Congress of Comparative Law*, 18 A.B.A. J. 359 (1932); *id.*, *Report of Committee of State Bar Delegates on 1932 International Congress of*

about the proceedings and several general reports from that congress.[320] The academy also held its annual meeting at the time of the congress. The Carnegie Foundation (or the Carnegie Endowment) provided a $5,000 grant to cover congress expenses and to publish its proceedings. The academy elected Wigmore as a titular member and instated Scott as a vice president on the executive committee. In gratitude for Balogh's excellent service to the academy, members elected him "*secrétaire perpetual*," the beginning of a tradition of lifetime power that moved the academy away from its original democratic principles.[321]

In Wigmore's report on the 1932 Congress, he praised the preparations, concept, Dutch social arrangements, and delegate quality as a sign of comparative law progress, but found much to criticize in its execution. He suggested that for any future congress, an Anglo-American member of the organizing committee could bring "modern methods of efficiency." The next year, an English member tried to dissociate the Anglo from Wigmore's less-than-diplomatic remarks.[322]

In 1935, the academy called for a second international congress at The Hague for 1937 with 57 topics, almost triple the number available in 1932. Wigmore was the chair of the United States committee and actively encouraged attendance.[323] The United States again had the largest national contingent of delegates among the 35 nations represented, 47 out of 240 jurists in attendance.[324] It also had the largest number of universities represented, 11 compared to the next highest national group, which was Germany with professors from seven universities. Americans wrote general reports for 12 of the topics. Among these who attended were Eder, Franklin (Tulane), Hall (Louisiana State), Kocourek (Northwestern), Lobingier (National University), Paul Sayre (Iowa), and Yntema (Michigan).

Comparative Law, 18 A.B.A. J. 673–75 (1932) [hereinafter Wigmore, *Report on 1932 Congress*]; see ROALFE, *supra* note 61, at 264–65. Germany published 20 national reports from this congress. DEUTSCHE LANDESREFERATE ZUM INTERNATIONALEN KONGRESS FÜR RECHTSVERGLEICHUNG IM HAAG 1932, at 1–293 (Ernst Heymann ed., 1932).

[320] Morrison, *supra* note 179, at 96–97; *see supra* pt. E.5 (Tulane). For a list of the general and national reports published at the 1932 and 1937 congresses, *see* Charles Szladits, *A Bibliography of Reports of the International Congresses of Comparative Law 1932–1974*, 25 AM. J. COMP. L. 684–93 (1977).

[321] Clark, *International Academy*, *supra* note 116, at 16; *see supra* note 129 (Carnegie Corporation).

[322] Clark, *International Academy*, *supra* note 116, at 16–18; Wigmore, *Report on 1932 Congress*, *supra* note 319, at 674–75 (quotation at 674).

[323] ROALFE, *supra* note 61, at 271–72; Clark, International Academy, *supra* note 116, at 18; John H. Wigmore, *Second International Congress of Comparative Law To Be Held at the Hague, July 26-August 1, 1937*, 22 A.B.A. J. 428 (1936). The German national reports were available in DEUTSCHE LANDESREFERATE ZUM II. INTERNATIONALEN KONGRESS FÜR RECHTSVERGLEICHUNG IM HAAG 1937 (Ernst Heymann ed., 1937).

[324] Clark, *International Academy*, *supra* note 116, at 18. The next largest group of 31 participants came from France. After that, the numbers were Germany (29), Great Britain (29), Netherlands (23), and Italy (14). Most delegates preparing reports were professors, but there still were many appellate judges and practitioners attending as delegates. *Id.*

Pound also wrote a general report but did not attend. American professors present who wrote national reports were Borchard, Harriet Daggett (Louisiana State), the first female U.S. academic comparatist, and Karl Loewenstein (Amherst College), a refugee from the University of Munich. Other American professors who attended, besides Wigmore, came from law schools at George Washington, Valparaiso, William and Mary, Cincinnati, and Wisconsin.[325]

Wigmore felt that the 1937 Congress was far superior to the 1932 Congress. This time he named Balogh as the person responsible, through his diligence, for achieving such a task.[326] If the delegates carried home optimism regarding the use of comparative law in achieving a world of cooperating nations, buttressed by mutual understanding, it disappeared in 1939. It was not until 1950 that the Third International Congress assembled, when Pound served as the academy's president. Although originally planned for The Hague, financial and logistical circumstances required its transfer to London.[327] This set the tradition of holding congresses in varied venues, which have since occurred every four years.[328]

3. Domestic American Comparative Law Activities

Near the end of his deanship, Pound gave the address at the 1935 annual meeting of the newly constituted ABA Section of International and Comparative Law. In magisterial form, he surveyed the history of comparative law since the twelfth century, described its importance for development of law in nineteenth-century America, and argued that current comparative law was one of five universalizing elements helping to break the cult of local law. As we saw, he supported comparison beyond mere legal rules to embrace legal systems, and described the utility of the functional method of comparison.[329]

Although the Great Depression and later World War II made serious comparative law research difficult, there was a surprising amount of important activity in the United States, partly supported by the wave of émigré legal scholars from Germany and Austria. Scholars examined this fascinating process of legal transplantation, which fully blossomed in the postwar period, through the stories

---

[325] John H. Wigmore, *The Congress of Comparative Law*, 23 A.B.A. J. 783, 786 (1937) [hereinafter Wigmore, *1937 Congress*]. Robert Millar (Northwestern) and James Thayer (Harvard) also wrote national reports. John Vance, Library of Congress law librarian, attended but did not write a report. *Id.* at 786. As a law instructor at Northwestern, Millar had translated Garofalo's *Criminology* (1914). *See supra* note 92 and accompanying text (Modern Criminal Science Series); text accompanying notes 134, 305 (Eder).
[326] Wigmore, *1937 Congress*, *supra* note 325, at 783.
[327] Clark, *International Academy*, *supra* note 116, at 19–20.
[328] *Id.*
[329] Roscoe Pound, *What May We Expect from Comparative Law?* 22 A.B.A. J. 56–60 (1936).

of individual scholars at a conference held in Bonn in 1991.[330] Refugee jurists had a very difficult time finding positions in American law schools and often succeeded, if at all, only after a period of "re-education" in American law. Even then, since only about 15 law schools offered a course in comparative or Roman law, most refugees had to settle for a research or other legal position, at least during the 1930s and early 1940s.[331]

A few examples illustrate the situation. Edgar Bodenheimer (1908–1991) earned a doctorate in law at Heidelberg in 1932 and shortly thereafter emigrated to the United States. After receiving an LL.B. at the University of Washington in 1937, he worked for the U.S. government during World War II and assisted in the Nuremberg war crimes trials. During that time, he wrote a treatise on jurisprudence, one of only a few in the United States devoted to the subject and the first one from a continental European perspective. In 1946, he began his academic career at the University of Utah.[332] The experience of Heinrich Kronstein (1897–1972) was similar. As a lawyer in Germany, he wrote several articles stressing the importance of values in law. He left for the United States in 1935, enrolled at Columbia Law School, and after graduation worked for the U.S. Justice Department during the war. In 1946, he began law teaching at Georgetown and in 1949 also at the University of Frankfurt. An expert in antitrust law, he brought a comparative perspective to both countries.[333]

Friedrich Kessler was a Berlin Institute *Referent* when Hilter rose to power in Germany in 1933.[334] He had written his doctorate thesis on American family law and *Habilitationsschrift* on U.S. tort law. With the aid of a Rockefeller Foundation fellowship, he emigrated to America in 1934 and was fortunate to obtain an instructor position at Yale Law School, were he taught from 1934 to 1938, after which he moved to the University of Chicago Law School as associate, then full professor. In 1947, he returned to Yale until his retirement in 1970. Kessler specialized in contract law and beginning in the 1940s, set out elements of a grand theory. His work and teaching demonstrated the influence of Max Weber, his

---

[330] *See Der Einfluß, supra* note 146.

[331] Edward D. Re, *Comparative Law Courses in the Law School Curriculum*, 1 AM. J. COMP. L. 233, 241 (1952); *see supra* pt. G.2 (refugee jurists).

[332] HERGET, JURISPRUDENCE, *supra* note 142, at 262–65; EDGAR BODENHEIMER, JURISPRUDENCE (1940, 2d ed. 1962, 3d rev. ed. 1974); W. Cole Durham, Jr., *Edgar Bodenheimer: Conservator of Civilized Legal Culture, in Der Einfluß, supra* note 146, at 127–43. Jerome Hall had earlier published *Readings in Jurisprudence* (1938).

[333] David J. Gerber, *Heinrich Kronstein and the Development of United States Antitrust Law, in* DER EINFLUSS, *supra* note 146, at 155–69; *see e.g.*, Heinrich Kronstein, *The Dynamics of German Cartels and Patents*, 9–10 U. CHI. L. REV. 643–71, 49–69 (1942); HEINRICH KRONSTEIN & JOHN MILLER, REGULATION OF TRADE: A CASE AND TEXTBOOK (1953).

[334] Graham, *supra* note 250, at 796; *see supra* text accompanying notes 163–164 (Kessler).

teacher in Munich, the civil law as a counterpoint to the common law, and inclusion of economic and social context to contract doctrine.[335]

Like Kessler, Max Rheinstein (1899-1977) worked at the Berlin Institute until 1933, when the Rockefeller Foundation offered him a fellowship in the United States. He also was an admirer and student of Weber in Munich. His doctorate was about English tort law and the *Habilitationsschrift* about the structure of contractual obligations in Anglo-American law. The fellowship permitted Rheinstein to teach at Chicago and research law at Columbia and Harvard until 1935, when the University of Chicago offered him a visiting professorship. The next year, the law school promoted him to assistant professor and in 1940 to an endowed professorship. Rheinstein specialized in family and comparative law and applied a sociological approach to both subjects. He also wrote on textual interpretation and the administration of estates.[336]

Most of the work for organized comparative law in the late 1930s and 1940s fell to the AFLA and to the ABA Section on International and Comparative Law. Some other organizations, however, also helped. In 1939, Lewis at the ALI created a research position in Philadelphia for perhaps Europe's most famous comparatist, Ernst Rabel, the director until 1937 of the Kaiser Wilhelm Institute in Berlin. Yntema helped to arrange a two-year stipend to pay Rabel while he prepared a companion volume to the *Restatement of Conflict of Laws* (1934). Although this project to present the conflicts rules of major countries according to the Restatement's arrangement was a promising opportunity for the ALI explicitly to embrace the comparative method, Rabel simply could not complete the book in such a short time. His efforts returned to his four-volume magnum opus, *The Conflict of Laws: A Comparative Study* (1945-1958), which the University of Michigan financed.[337]

---

[335] Herbert Bernstein, *Friedrich Kessler's American Contract Scholarship and Its Political Subtext*, in DER EINFLUSS, *supra* note 146, at 85-93; Graham, *supra* note 250, at 797-98; Anthony T. Kronman, *My Senior Partner*, 104 YALE L.J. 2129-31 (1995); John K. McNulty, *A Student's Tribute to Fritz Kessler, id.* at 2133-36; *see* FRIEDRICH KESSLER, CONTRACTS: CASES AND MATERIALS (1953) (2d ed. 1970 and 3d ed. 1986 with co-authors); *id.*, *Contracts of Adhesion—Some Thoughts about Freedom of Contract*, 43 COLUM. L. REV. 629-42 (1943). During Kessler's first stay at Yale, he taught comparative law among other courses. Graham, *supra*, at 801-02.

[336] Mary Ann Glendon, *The Influence of Max Rheinstein on American Law*, in DER EINFLUSS, *supra* note 146, at 171-79; Graham, *supra* note 250, at 795-96, 88-01; Farnsworth Fowle, *Max Rheinstein, Law Professor*, 78, N.Y. TIMES, 12 Jul. 1977, at 32; *see* MAX WEBER, MAX WEBER ON LAW IN ECONOMY AND SOCIETY (Max Rheinstein trans. & ed. with Edward A. Shils trans., 1954); Max Rheinstein, *Comparative Law—Its Functions, Methods, and Usages*, 22 ARK. L. REV. 415 (1968). In 1934, Lewis at the ALI had Rheinstein participate in multiple Restatement working groups. Graham, *supra*, at 795. After the war, Rheinstein spent a year in Germany at the U.S. Office of Military Government. Fowle, *supra*.

[337] Clark, Rabel, *supra* note 282, at 107, 109-11, 118-23; *id.*, *Unification of Law*, *supra* note 153, at 49; *see supra* pt. E.4 (ALI); text accompanying notes 159-160, 282 (Rabel and the Institute). Yntema assisted Rabel on *Conflict of Laws*, which won the Harvard faculty Ames Prize as the most meritorious English language legal publication during the preceding five years. BROWN & BLUME, *supra* note 41, at 354.

Columbia Law School supported the teaching of comparative law by three of its professors who developed American-style comparative law course materials in the 1930s. Other than the volumes on the evolution of law by Kocourek and Wigmore,[338] it is probable that the first comparative law "cases and materials" of the modern type appeared at Columbia. Francis Deák (1898–1972), an authority on French and Hungarian law; Arthur Schiller (1902–1977), an expert on Roman, African, Coptic, and *adat* law; and Milton Handler (1903–1998), knowledgeable on trademark law, assembled translated cases and excerpts primarily from France and Germany. They used the first mimeographed version in 1930 in their introductory comparative law course.[339] By 1932, the authors had split these materials into three mimeographed volumes, now more readily available in American and European libraries than the 1930 version. One volume was entitled *Introductory Readings and Materials to the Study of Comparative Law*,[340] and the other two had the title *Cases and Material on Selected Topics in the Law of Trademarks and Unfair Competition in the United States, France and Germany*.[341]

In 1934, Deák prepared and used at Columbia another American-style casebook for a comparative law class. He used many author's notes as well as sections of notes and questions. Although focusing only on torts, it examined selected statute or code articles; legislative debates, *projets*, and *motifs*; American restatements; and judicial decisions of England, France, Germany, and the United States. Its innovative synthesis of the civilian emphasis on legislation (but without the scholarly overlay) and common law reliance on cases was only part of its distinctiveness. It also included briefs, references to other materials, hypothetical cases, and questions for the students.[342]

---

[338] See *supra* text accompanying notes 239–242 (*Evolution of Law*).

[339] FRANCIS DEÁK, MILTON HANDLER & A. ARTHUR SCHILLER, CASES AND MATERIALS SERVING AS AN INTRODUCTION TO THE STUDY OF COMPARATIVE LAW AT COLUMBIA LAW SCHOOL (mimeo., 389 pp., 1930). Deák immigrated to America from Hungary in 1925 and earned an S.J.D. at Harvard Law School in 1927. After researching and teaching at Columbia, he became an assistant professor in 1931. COLUMBIA LAW, *supra* note 36, at 329–30. Pound's earlier book did not include cases unless one characterized the excerpts from Justinian's Digest as cases. See *supra* text accompanying notes 224–227 (*Readings*).

[340] Handler was not an author for this volume, which had 187 pages. Deák and Schiller divided it into three sections: (1) judicial organization, (2) use of continental legal material, and (3) judicial precedent. The first two sections comprised primarily French and German materials while the third section also had English, United States, Swiss, and Philippine examples.

[341] These two volumes (160 pages and 343 pages) were primarily cases and statutes along with author notes and questions. There were also a few excerpts from scholars.

[342] FRANCIS DEÁK, CASES AND MATERIALS ON SELECTED TOPICS IN THE LAW OF TORTS IN THE UNITED STATES, ENGLAND, FRANCE AND GERMANY (mimeo. 1930); *see* James J. Morrison, *Comparative Law: Cases and Materials on Selected Topics in the Law of Torts in the United States, England, France and Germany* (2 vols., 315 pp., unpublished, 1935), 11 TUL. L. REV. 154–58 (1936) (book review).

The sun was setting on the first sustained period of organized comparative law in the United States. Teachers, scholars, and practitioners had accomplished much that would not have been possible during the nineteenth century. There were now comparative law organizations, journals, book series, extensive library collections, and innovative teaching materials. A new dawn waited at the creation of the American Association for the Comparative Study of Law in 1951. At that time, Edward Re (1920-2006), ABA section chair of its Comparative Civil Procedure and Practice Committee, estimated that about 26 law schools offered a comparative law course.[343]

---

[343] *Re, supra* note 331, at 241; see John N. Hazard, *Comparative Law in Legal Education*, 18 U. CHI. L. REV. 264 (1951); Edward D. Re, *Report of the Committee on Comparative Civil Procedure and Practice*, ABA SEC. INT'L & COMP. L. PROC., *supra* note 303, at 90-93 (1951).

7
Postwar Legal Transplants and Growth of the Academic Discipline: 1945–1990

> [A]ll good legal systems, with their varying histories and environments, serve justice as their people see it; and the best of them serve the great tradition of government under law. But as languages can enrich and extend communication by translations and borrowings, so too can legal systems. The promotion of law in the world will therefore benefit from a revival of comparative jurisprudence, a revival in which American lawyers are already taking an active part.
>
> Earl Warren[1]

A. Government Supervision of American Legal Exports

The first 125 years of U.S. history saw some exportation of American laws and legal institutions, primarily to the newly independent Latin American nations in the 1820s. These included concepts from the Constitution of 1789; the 1791 Bill of Rights; and public law structures such as federalism, a presidential executive, and judicial review of legislative and executive action. American comparatists did not pay much attention to this process of outbound law, but concerned themselves with comparison as a filter for the importation of rules and structures meant to serve an emerging nation in the new world.

1. The Early Postwar Period

At the beginning of the twentieth century, the United States was already a powerful nation with a small overseas empire reluctantly ruled, but with a far greater

---

[1] Earl Warren, *The Law and the Future*, 52 FORTUNE 106 (Nov. 1955), reprinted as *Revival of Comparative Jurisprudence*, 5 AM. J. COMP. L. 1 (1956).

reach for economic hegemony. After finishing on the winning side of two world wars, America emerged as the world's leading economic and military power, which after the collapse of Soviet communism in 1989 confirmed that the United States was the unitary superpower.[2] During the second half of the twentieth century, consistent with this new superpower status, American comparatists—both scholars and practicing lawyers—engaged more actively in the exportation of American law and legal institutions in contrast to the net importation of law and legal philosophy that had occurred prior to 1945.[3]

Early American influence stemmed from its military occupation in the late 1940s and 1950s in part of Germany, Japan, and South Korea. One can see the impact in public law, especially constitutional law, and in institutions such as judicial review. The transplantation of legal norms and institutions was stronger in Japan and Korea, the two non-Western nations.[4] However, after a short discussion of the political context, I begin with Germany, which was the only one of the three occupied lands where several American academic legal and political comparatists were actively involved.[5]

American popular sentiment toward Germany and Japan in 1945 ranged from hostility to a desire for revenge, which made the Allied demand for unconditional surrender politically necessary. For instance, the Suggested Post-Surrender Program for Germany, devised by Treasury Secretary Henry Morgenthau (served 1934–1945) and his assistant secretary (a probable Soviet agent), called for German deindustrialization, partition, and push toward a pastoral society. Fortunately for the postwar situation, the plan became a campaign issue in the 1944 presidential election and Henry Stimson, secretary of war (1940–1945), and John McCloy, assistant war secretary (1941–1945), opposed it. Both were Harvard-educated lawyers with extensive government experience.[6]

President Franklin Roosevelt died in April 1945 and Harry Truman, the vice president, became president. Since both were Democrats, Truman initially

---

[2] LAWRENCE M. FRIEDMAN, A HISTORY OF AMERICAN LAW 503–04 (3d ed. 2005) [hereinafter FRIEDMAN, HISTORY]; see GEORGE ATHAN BILLIAS, AMERICAN CONSTITUTIONALISM HEARD ROUND THE WORLD, 1776–1989: A GLOBAL PERSPECTIVE 276–79 (2009).

[3] There were some minor examples of exported American legal institutions or concepts in the first half of the twentieth century, such as in China, Latin America, and the Philippines. LAWRENCE M. FRIEDMAN, AMERICAN LAW IN THE 20TH CENTURY 574–76 (2002) [hereinafter FRIEDMAN, AMERICAN LAW]; see supra ch. 6, pt. A.2 (American transplants).

[4] BILLIAS, supra note 2, at 279; FRIEDMAN, AMERICAN LAW, supra note 3, at 576–77.

[5] See, e.g., CARL J. FRIEDRICH, THE IMPACT OF AMERICAN CONSTITUTIONALISM ABROAD (1967) [hereinafter FRIEDRICH, IMPACT]. Friedrich identified three key aspects of American constitutionalism: presidentialism, federalism, and judicial review of legislation (and human rights protection). Id. at 8–10.

[6] PAUL CARRINGTON, SPREADING AMERICA'S WORD: STORIES OF ITS LAWYER-MISSIONARIES 223–27, 257–58 (2005); see Anthony Kubek, The Morgenthau Plan and the Problem of Policy Perversion, 9 J. HIST. REV. 287–303 (1989). President Franklin Roosevelt endorsed the Treasury Plan in 1944, but his Republican adversary in the presidential election, Thomas Dewey, was against it. CARRINGTON, supra, at 258.

retained Roosevelt's cabinet and in late April, Stimson informed him about the Manhattan Project that was about to test the first atomic bomb. Victory in Europe occurred in May and Allied leaders of the Soviet Union, United Kingdom, and United States met in Potsdam, Germany, during July to determine how to administer Germany and resolve a variety of peacetime issues. During 1945, the Soviet army occupied eastern and central Europe and established a subservient communist government in Poland, justified as defensive action to thwart a future attack from the west. Truman was more suspicious of Joseph Stalin's motives than Roosevelt had been and after the Potsdam Conference, the stage was set for commencement of the Cold War between the United States and the Soviet Union.[7]

As Stimson and McCloy had insisted at Potsdam and Truman's secretary of state James Byrnes (served 1945–1947) came to believe by 1946, the Allied occupying governments should not seek to destroy the German economy, but rather allow Germans the opportunity to rebuild their country on a peaceful basis. The Allies, including France, divided Germany into four zones. The American zone in central and south Germany (plus the city state of Bremen) authorized municipal and regional elections that led to constitutional conventions in those areas by the end of 1946. At that time, General Lucius Clay became deputy military governor in the American zone and supported the reformed view of Byrnes to encourage German economic and political development, which undercut the earlier policy from the Morgenthau Plan. The United States proposed in 1948 that the three Western sectors permit their 11 *Länder* to call a national convention to draft an instrument to protect state rights, provide an adequate central authority, and guarantee individual liberties.[8]

Truman and his foreign policy advisers—particularly George Marshall, secretary of state (1947–1949) and Dean Acheson, undersecretary (1945–1947), later secretary of state (1949–1953)—took a hard line against the Soviets, consistent with American public opinion that feared they were intent upon world domination.[9] Since Republicans controlled Congress in 1947 and 1948, Truman worked with Arthur Vandenburg, chair of the Senate Foreign Relations Committee. This provided bipartisan support for both the Truman Doctrine, which formalized a policy of Soviet containment; and the Marshall Plan (1948–1952), which

---

[7] Library of Congress, *Postwar Occupation and Division*, in GERMANY: A COUNTRY STUDY (Eric Solsten ed., 1995), http://countrystudies.us/germany; *see* CARRINGTON, *supra* note 6, at 228–33 (Red Scare).

[8] CARRINGTON, *supra* note 6, at 260–61, 265. General Dwight Eisenhower was the American zone's military governor from May to November of 1945. The U.S. Army promoted Clay to general in 1947, when he became military governor until 1949.

[9] General Marshall was U.S. army chief of staff from 1939 to 1945 and secretary of defense from 1950 to 1951.

specifically rejected the Morgenthau Plan and instead sought to help rebuild postwar Europe including Germany.[10] The 1952 *Deutschlandvertrag* (in force 1955) allowed the Federal Republic of Germany to regain its sovereignty from the three occupying powers.[11]

The Potsdam Declaration outlined Japan's terms of unconditional surrender, which the Japanese prime minister ignored. To carry out the ultimatum of prompt destruction, Truman approved dropping atomic bombs on Hiroshima and Nagasaki in early August 1945 as the alternative to an Allied ground invasion of mainland Japan. Stimson and McCloy opposed use of the bomb, but Stimson changed his mind and acquiesced. Shortly thereafter, Emperor Hirohito ordered the Japanese military to accept the terms of surrender.[12]

Stimson was acquainted with Japanese culture and prevented the destruction of the historic city of Kyoto. He had been governor-general of the Philippines from 1927 to 1929. With McCloy, the two advocated rebuilding Japan and McCloy was in favor of retaining the emperor as a constitutional monarch. In addition, Byrnes, Truman's secretary of state, saw Japan's unconditional surrender and physical and political destruction as an invitation to assist the Japanese. Like Germany, Japan had experience with the idea of a constitution and parliamentary democracy. Since in both countries defeat completely discredited the ruling elite, new leaders supportive of democracy, with American assistance, might succeed with reform.[13]

After Japan's surrender, Truman appointed General Douglas MacArthur Supreme Commander for the Allied Powers (SCAP) and he became a kind of proconsul or de facto emperor in Japan. At MacArthur's order, Emperor Hirohito remained in office, but the new constitution would strictly limit his power. SCAP replaced the wartime cabinet with one committed to implementing the Potsdam Declaration that called for democracy and fundamental rights. SCAP directives in 1945 eliminated restraints on political expression and abolished Shinto as a state religion. Moreover, with SCAP's guidance, the Japanese government introduced sweeping economic and social reforms based primarily on American

---

[10] U.S. Department of State, *Containment, in* UNITED STATES HISTORY (n.d.), http://countrystudies.us/united-states.

[11] *See* Vertrag . . . Drei Mächten, 26 May 1952, BUNDESGESETZBLATT 1955 II, S. 306–20, http://www.documentarchiv.de/brd/dtlvertrag.html.

[12] CARRINGTON, *supra* note 6, at 258–59; Library of Congress, *World War II and the Occupation* [hereinafter *Occupation in Japan*], *in* JAPAN: A COUNTRY STUDY (Ronald E. Dolan & Robert L. Worden eds., 1994), http://countrystudies.us/japan; *see* THEODORE MCNELLY, THE ORIGINS OF JAPAN'S DEMOCRATIC CONSTITUTION 175–76 (2000) (text of Potsdam Declaration, 26 July 1945).

[13] CARRINGTON, *supra* note 6, at 259–61; *see* R.W. KOSTAL, LAYING DOWN THE LAW: THE AMERICAN LEGAL REVOLUTIONS IN OCCUPIED GERMANY AND JAPAN 1–19, 30–32, 53–54, 61, 332–53 (2019) (generally critical of the American occupations based on the unfulfilled premise that an efficient and complete legal transplantation of liberal democracy was possible under the circumstances); *see supra* text accompanying note 8 (Byrnes).

models. Unlike in Germany, where there was direct military rule to reconstitute government structures, the U.S. military in Japan supervised an existing Japanese government.[14] The 1951 Treaty of San Francisco (in force 1952) on behalf of the United Nations ended Allied occupation of the principal islands, allocated compensation, and returned sovereignty to Japan.[15]

The U.S. Joint Chiefs of Staff prepared its first order in August 1945 that prescribed separate surrender procedures for Japanese forces in Korea north and south of the 38th parallel latitude. The Allied foreign ministers had envisioned a trusteeship by the United States, United Kingdom, Soviet Union, and Republic of China that would prepare for Korean independence. U.S. armed forces landed near Seoul, Korea, in September 1945 and established a military government shortly thereafter. Lieutenant General John Hodge was the military governor of South Korea from 1945 to 1948. He had to deal with hostile political groups—most of which wanted immediate independence and thus were against the trusteeship plan—the Soviet consolidation of power in North Korea, an influx of Koreans from Japan and the Soviet zone, and an economy and society in disarray. Rather than fund economic development, in September 1947, the United States submitted the Korean problem to the United Nations. The General Assembly recognized Korea's claim to independence and sent a temporary commission to oversee national elections in May 1948. The Soviet Union objected and refused to permit the commission into the north.[16]

After the 1948 elections, the newly constituted National Assembly adopted a constitution that contemplated a presidential executive with a four-year term. Syngman Rhee became leader of the assembly, which proclaimed in August the Republic of Korea with Rhee as president. A month later, Kim Il-sung declared himself premier of the Democratic People's Republic of Korea. U.S. occupation forces withdrew by June 1949 and the next year Kim invaded South Korea. In the early weeks of the war, North Koreans easily pushed back their southern counterparts. Truman called for a naval blockade of Korea, only to learn that due to budget cutbacks, the U.S. Navy could not enforce such a measure. Truman

---

[14] BILLIAS, supra note 2, at 284; JOHN W. DOWER, EMBRACING DEFEAT: JAPAN IN THE WAKE OF WORLD WAR II, at 80–84 (1999); MCNELLY, supra note 12, at 2; Occupation in Japan, supra note 12; see KOSTAL, supra note 13, at 61–63, 97–105.

[15] DOWER, supra note 14, at 552–55. The United States returned the Ryukyu Islands, including Okinawa, to Japan in 1972. Id. at 224, 434, 552–54; see Agreement... Ryukyu Islands, Japan-U.S., 17 June 1971, 23 U.S.T. 449.

[16] Library of Congress, South Korea under United States Occupation, 1945–48 [hereinafter Korean Occupation], in SOUTH KOREA: A COUNTRY STUDY (Andrea Matles Savada & William Shaw eds., 1990), http://countrystudies.us/south-korea [hereinafter SOUTH KOREA]. See generally ROBERT T. OLIVER, SYNGMAN RHEE AND AMERICAN INVOLVEMENT IN KOREA, 1942–1960: A PERSONAL NARRATIVE 15–139 (1978). The Republic of Korea (South Korea) and the Democratic People's Republic of Korea (North Korea) were proclaimed in 1948. Both claimed authority over all of Korea. Korean Occupation, supra.

promptly urged the United Nations to intervene; the Security Council—with the Soviet Union boycotting and the Republic of China representing that nation—authorized troops under the U.N. flag led by General MacArthur. Truman decided he did not need formal authorization from Congress for a U.N. police action, which ended with an armistice in July 1953.[17]

2. New Constitutions in Germany, Japan, and Korea

From 1946 to 1949, Carl Friedrich (1901–1984), a Harvard professor expert in German law, served as constitutional and governmental affairs adviser to the American military governor (AMG) in Germany, General Clay.[18] Friedrich, born in Leipzig to a wealthy family, graduated from Heidelberg University in 1925 in social and political studies, followed by a doctorate in 1928. During 1922 and 1923, Friedrich had studied in the United States, where he organized, with support from the Institute of International Education in New York, scholarships for 13 German students to study in America. Upon his return to Heidelberg, the university founded the *Akademischer Austauschdienst* to facilitate student and academic exchange.[19] In 1926, Harvard University appointed Friedrich a lecturer in the government department. His expertise at Harvard, where he taught most of his career, developed in comparative political institutions, political ideology, philosophy of law, and public administration.[20]

The Potsdam Agreement addressed a future German constitution and certain political principals, including political decentralization and increased local governmental responsibility. The 1945 Joint Chiefs of Staff directive, amended in 1947, continued those themes and emphasized democratization including

---

[17] *Korean Occupation, supra* note 16; *The Korean War, 1950–53, in* SOUTH KOREA, *supra* note 16. *See generally* OLIVER, *supra* note 16, at 167–431.

[18] Joseph Berger, *Carl J. Friedrich Dies at 83: Influential Harvard Professor,* N.Y. TIMES, 22 Sept. 1984, § 1, at 32; *see supra* note 8 and accompanying text (Clay). AMG also referred to American Military Government. In the 1950s, Friedrich was a constitutional adviser to Puerto Rico, Israel, and to the European Constituent Assembly. In 1956, he accepted a professorship at the Heidelberg law faculty, where he founded a political science institute and taught several semesters through 1966. Berger, *supra.*

[19] DAAD, *History,* https://www.daad.de/en. (select The DAAD, then History). By 1930, the German organization, now in Berlin and with support from the Association of German Universities, had exchanges in France, Great Britain, and the United States. In 1931, it merged with the Alexander von Humboldt Foundation to form the *Deutscher Akademischer Austauschdienst* (DAAD). In 1950, the British and American military governments facilitated the reestablishment of DAAD in Bonn. John McCloy then received an honorary DAAD scholarship. In 1952, the Fulbright exchange program accepted West Germany as a member country. *Id.; see supra* text accompanying notes 6, 8, 12–13 (McCloy).

[20] Berger, *supra* note 18, at 32; *see* CARL J. FRIEDRICH, THE PHILOSOPHY OF LAW IN HISTORICAL PERSPECTIVE (1957); *id.*, DIE PHILOSOPHIE DES RECHTS IN HISTORISCHER PERSPEKTIVE (1955). Friedrich became a U.S. citizen in 1938. Berger, *supra*, at 32.

separation of powers and periodic elections. Law must guarantee individual rights and freedoms. The British and American position was that, within these parameters, Germans should draft their constitutions, which the French at the 1948 London Conference accepted. One of the conference's recommendations was that the national constitution should contemplate eventual German reunification with the Soviet zone.[21]

From late in 1945, the collective American-British aim had been to permit Germans to solve their own constitutional issues, which delegation of authority largely occurred. General Clay determined that for the American zone, the *Länder* would by the end of 1946 hold local elections, constitute constitutional conventions, and ratify state constitutions. Clay's chief adviser on German politics, James Pollock (1898–1968), a comparative government professor on leave from the University of Michigan, devised the plan for a political and governmental framework. An expert on German political history, Pollack served as liaison between Clay and the state ministers-president.[22] It was likely that Pollack's view on postwar German occupation, consistent with that of Clay, prompted his appointment. Pollock believed that a democratic state in Germany was possible, but the Germans must formulate it themselves. He lectured and wrote offering various concrete proposals, all of them involving the direct participation of non-Nazi Germans in the government at an early stage, geared toward rapid reconstruction.[23] For instance, in 1944, Pollock presented a military occupation plan for American, British, and Soviet zones remarkably like that implemented in 1945. It "would be well calculated to serve as the territorial foundation for a new German government, once the Nazis are eradicated and the German people are again enabled and empowered to create their own system of self-government."[24]

In July 1946, Friedrich arrived in Germany to take up his AMG post as constitutional adviser to Clay. He also agreed with Clay's approach to provide Germans primary responsibility in drafting democratic state constitutions quickly. When the *Länder* constitutional assemblies presented their drafts, Friedrich and Pollock found them acceptable, although others complained about the speed, process,

---

[21] Carl J. Friedrich, Rebuilding the German Constitution, I, 27 AM. POL. SCI. REV. 461, 465–67, 469 (1949) [hereinafter Friedrich, REBUILDING I]; see JOHN FORD GOLAY, THE FOUNDING OF THE FEDERAL REPUBLIC OF GERMANY 1–13, 92–94 (1958); FRIEDRICH, IMPACT, supra note 5 at 38–39 (rejection of presidentialism); U.S. Department of State, Office of the Historian, Potsdam Agreement (Protocol), at https://history.state.gov/historicaldocuments/frus1945Berlinv02/d1383.

[22] KOSTAL, supra note 13, at 119, 137–42; University of Michigan Digital Library, James K. Pollock Papers, at https://quod.lib.umich.edu/b/bhlead/umich-bhl-8635?view=text [hereinafter Pollock Papers]. Pollack earned a Ph.D. in political science from Harvard in 1925, when he began teaching at the University of Michigan. He was president of the American Political Science Association in 1950 and of the International Political Science Association from 1955 to 1958. Pollock Papers, supra.

[23] Pollock Papers, supra note 22.

[24] James K. Pollock, A Territorial Pattern for the Military Occupation of Germany, 38 AM. POL. SCI. REV. 970–75 (1944) (quotation at 972).

or content. Despite objection, AMG approved, the assemblies in October 1946 adopted, and in December plebiscites ratified, the constitutions.[25]

The counterpoint to Friedrich and Pollock was the irascible Karl Loewenstein (1891–1973), a comparative law and government professor from Amherst College. He was firmly against delegating constitutional drafting to German jurists.[26] In 1943, the U.S. Justice Department Special War Section had hired him to prepare a memorandum on German legal denazification. Loewenstein's report blamed the evils of the Nazi justice system on the German legal profession, largely antidemocratic conservatives, for the perversion of law and justice. Nazi ideology irredeemably contaminated most judges and lawyers in the early 1940s. He concluded that an eventual Allied military occupation must directly impose reform from outside without listening to pleas from German jurists. This memorandum competed with other reports, some indexing or analyzing German laws or planning legal system changes, commissioned from the War Department Civilian Affairs Division, the Federal Economic Administration (FEA), the Office of Strategic Services, and ad hoc governmental entities.[27]

Loewenstein received his doctorate (1919) and *Habilitation* (1931) in law at the University in Munich, writing both theses on constitutional law. The latter degree qualified him as a *Privatdozent* on the Munich law faculty. In 1933, with Hitler's rise to power, Loewenstein decided to emigrate. The Emergency Committee in Aid of Displaced German Scholars aided him with the offer of a two-year teaching position in government at Yale University.[28] In 1936, Amherst College hired Loewenstein as a visiting professor and from 1940, as professor of jurisprudence and political science, a position he retained until 1961. He taught and wrote about political theory, the history of government, and international and comparative law. In 1939, Lowenstein had become a naturalized U.S. citizen and member of the Massachusetts bar association. Guggenheim awarded him a fellowship to travel to Latin America and write about its government and law and the risks of fascism. This led to positions with the Justice Department (1942–1944), the FEA (1943–1944), and as consultant to AMG's Legal Division (1945–1946).[29]

---

[25] KOSTAL, *supra* note 13, at 147–58, 161–63.

[26] *Id.* at 143–47.

[27] *Id.* at 35–51, 77–78; *see* Karl Loewenstein, *Law in the Third Reich*, 45 YALE L.J. 779–815 (1936). In 1944, for instance, the comparatist Mitchell Franklin (Tulane) consulted for the joint British-American Allied Expeditionary Force Legal Branch. KOSTAL, *supra* note 13, at 41; *see supra* ch. 6, pt. E.5 (Franklin at Tulane). Both Franklin and Loewenstein prepared reports for and attended the 1937 International Congress of Comparative Law at The Hague. *See supra* ch. 6, text accompanying note 325 (American delegates).

[28] Amherst College Archives & Special Collections, *Karl Loewenstein Papers*, at https://archivessp ace.amherst.edu (select Collections, then search Loewenstein) [hereinafter *Loewenstein Papers*]; *see supra* ch. 6, text accompanying notes 252–53, 277 (Emergency Committee).

[29] *Loewenstein Papers*, *supra* note 28. From 1948 to 1949, Loewenstein was a visiting expert with AMG's Civil Administration Division, continuing in 1949 and 1950 with the U.S. High

In 1948, the 11 *Länder* established a parliamentary council that produced a draft *Grundgesetz* (Basic Law).[30] General Clay insisted that the draft was insufficiently federal with too much central authority at the expense of *Länder*.[31] The U.S. position aimed to prevent a recurrence of concentrated power in a central executive. Friedrich mediated between Clay and the German drafters, who prepared an acceptable text that took effect in 1949. The German authors relied on comparative constitutional study and incorporation of features from German law and culture. The inclusion of an extensive bill of rights and a strong constitutional court to check legislation were notable elements.[32]

The direction that Clay's office provided the German parliamentary council was only general: prepare a democratic framework with a federal structure, bicameral legislature to support federalism, and judicial review of legislation. This permitted German jurists discretion to select details based on their own history and comparative study of constitutional ideas. The German tradition of federalism went back to the Holy Roman Empire. Germans, for instance, insisted on use of the term Basic Law rather than Constitution (*Verfassung*), since the latter was only appropriate for a sovereign nation, not a land under military occupation. When it came to judicial review, the Germans were familiar with U.S. Supreme Court constitutional jurisprudence, which likely shaped some features, but Hans Kelsen's centralized constitutional court provided the institutional structure.[33]

Commissioner for Germany. In 1956, he returned to Munich to lecture at the university law faculty, which later granted him a full professorship. From 1956 to 1958, he was visiting professor of political and legal science at Yale Law School. *Id.*; *see* KARL LOEWENSTEIN, POLITICAL POWER AND THE GOVERNMENTAL PROCESS (1957) (six lectures presented at the University of Chicago); *id.*, *Law and the Legislative Process in Occupied Germany: I & II*, 57 YALE L.J. 724–60, 994–1022 (1948).

[30] GOLAY, *supra* note 21, at 17–26. The 65 members of the parliamentary council represented Germany's political parties as selected by the 11 *Landtage* (legislatures). Many were law professors and almost all were lawyers, often with doctorate law degrees. Konrad Adenauer, a lawyer, was the council's president. *Id.* at 18–20, 265–75.

[31] *Id.* at 96–108; *see id.* at 58–66, 74–92. Edmund Spekack suggested that Clay gave American economic, political, and military interests priority over German concerns and that U.S. influence on the Basic Law was substantial. Edmund Spekack, *American Pressures on the German Constitutional Tradition: Basic Rights in the West German Constitution of 1949*, 10 INT'L J. POL., CULTURE, & SOC'Y 411, 423–30 (1997).

[32] BILLIAS, *supra* note 2, at 279; CARRINGTON, *supra* note 6, at 265–67; KOSTAL, *supra* note 13, at 288–92; Friedrich, *Rebuilding I*, *supra* note 21, at 478–82; Helmut Steinberger, *American Constitutionalism and German Constitutional Development*, in CONSTITUTIONALISM AND RIGHTS: THE INFLUENCE OF THE UNITED STATES CONSTITUTION ABROAD 199, 212–16 (Louis Henkin & Albert J. Rosenthal eds., 1990) [hereinafter INFLUENCE ABROAD]; *see* Carl J. Friedrich, *The Development of the Executive Power in Germany*, 27 AM. POL. SCI. REV. 185–203 (1933); *id.*, *Rebuilding the German Constitution, II*, 43 *id.* 704–20 (1949) (Basic Law's provisions); *id.*, *The Political Thought of Neo-Liberalism*, 49 *id.* 509–25 (1955).

[33] BILLIAS, *supra* note 2, at 280–83; Andrzej Rapaczynski, *Bibliographical Essay: The Influence of U.S. Constitutionalism Abroad*, in INFLUENCE ABROAD, *supra* note 32, at 405, 436–39; *see* FRIEDRICH, IMPACT, *supra* note 5, at 62–64, 66–68 (German federalism), 85–89 (judicial review); *id.*, *Rebuilding I*, *supra* note 21, at 475, 477 (Kelsen).

The path toward a new constitution in Japan involved more American input than what occurred in occupied Germany.[34] The 1889 Meiji Constitution for the Japanese empire, under the influence of German jurists, formulated a constitutional monarchy. In theory, the emperor was supreme leader with a subservient cabinet, but as practiced, the emperor was head of state while a prime minister was head of government. There was an independent judiciary, an imperial Diet initially representing a tiny male electorate, and an executive headed by ministers of state and an advisory privy council. The bicameral legislative Diet, with a House of Representatives and a House of Peers, could limit constitutional liberties by statute. The armed forces wielded substantial independent power.[35]

SCAP, also known as General Headquarters (GHQ), invited a series of Japanese governmental officials to rewrite the Meiji Constitution, while political parties and private groups also published proposals. MacArthur rejected these efforts and, in February 1946, assigned the task to General Courtney Whitney, a lawyer, and chief of GHQ's government section. Whitney convened a steering committee with lawyers and others more knowledgeable in Japanese culture. Colonel Charles Kades, a Harvard law graduate, led the drafting team adhering where possible with the Meiji Constitution. This version narrowly prescribed the emperor's powers, expanded the Diet's legislative authority along lines of the British Parliament, created local authorities, and prohibited aggressive war. The Supreme Court had jurisdiction to enforce separation of powers, but its judges, after appointment, had to stand for election. Whitney presented the draft to the Japanese committee with the threat that, if they rejected it, SCAP would take the matter to the Japanese people and not support the emperor's limited role in the document. With minor revisions, the committee acquiesced. The Diet, whose election occurred in April, made minimal changes and approved the

---

[34] BILLIAS, *supra* note 2, at 294–95; KYOKO INOUE, MACARTHUR'S JAPANESE CONSTITUTION: A LINGUISTIC AND CULTURAL STUDY OF ITS MAKING 1–2, 13 (1991); Rapaczynski, *supra* note 33, at 436. *See generally* DOWER, *supra* note 14, at 346–404. Several factors affected the different treatment in Japan and Germany. First, Americans had a freer hand in Japan than in Germany, since the British and French focused primarily on Europe. Second, American juristic experience with and admiration for German legal tradition and culture was extensive, but thin when it came to Japan. Third, the different treatment during the war of German Americans from Japanese Americans suggested racial bias. Fourth, the personalities of Generals Clay and MacArthur reflected a lack of patience by the latter. Fifth, the Cold War intensified between the time of drafting the Japanese Constitution until the German Basic Law, providing the latter more bargaining power in the postwar world. BILLIAS, *supra*, at 284, 294–95; Rapaczynski, *supra*, at 436 n.136.

[35] BILLIAS, *supra* note 2, at 283; CARRINGTON, *supra* note 6, at 262, 267; INOUE, *supra* note 34, at 51–55, 69–70; Lawrence W. Beer, *Constitutionalism and Rights in Japan and Korea*, *in* INFLUENCE ABROAD, *supra* note 32, at 223, 229–30; *see* Yasuhiro Okudaira, *Forty Years of the Constitution and Its Various Influences: Japanese, American, and European*, 53 LAW & CONTEMP. PROB. 17, 19 (Winter 1990) (Japanese use of the 1850 Prussian Constitution and other German constitutions).

Constitution, the House of Peers dissolved itself, and the emperor promulgated the Constitution in November 1946, effective the following year.[36]

The Kades committee considered earlier Japanese drafts of constitutions as well as about a dozen foreign constitutions. It wanted a constitution consistent with Japanese liberal traditions toward democracy and equal rights for all. After completion of the steering committee draft, "the revised constitution became the creation of a joint enterprise of Japanese and Americans working together under the inauspicious circumstances of a foreign occupation to establish a political and social system which could be the prelude to a treaty of peace."[37] The American military occupation achieved its two major objectives: democratization and demilitarization. The Constitution implemented popular sovereignty by making all three government branches directly or indirectly subject to electoral control. The Constitution's Article 9 renounced Japan's sovereign right to threaten or wage war in settling international disputes or to rearm for that purpose.[38] A Japanese analysis suggested American influence on the 1947 Constitution extended to the concept of democracy, with sovereignty in the people, natural-law type fundamental individual rights, and judicial review.[39]

---

[36] BILLIAS, *supra* note 2, at 284–87; CARRINGTON, *supra* note 6, at 262–65; INOUE, *supra* note 34, at 9–18, 20–26, 73–80, 171–73, 206–10; KOSTAL, *supra* note 13, at 120–37; MCNELLY, *supra* note 12, at 2–25; Beer, *supra* note 35, at 232–34; Rapaczynski, *supra* note 33, at 431–33; *see* INOUE, *supra*, at 303–14 (American draft); Charles L. Kades, *The American Role in Revising Japan's Imperial Constitution*, 104 POL. SCI. Q. 215, 235–41 (1989) (Diet's proposed amendments). *See also* RAY A. MOORE & DONALD L. ROBINSON, PARTNERS FOR DEMOCRACY: CRAFTING THE NEW JAPANESE STATE UNDER MACARTHUR (2002); Theodore H. McNelly, *"Induced Revolution": The Policy and Process of Constitutional Reform in Occupied Japan*, *in* DEMOCRATIZING JAPAN: THE ALLIED OCCUPATION 79–110 (Robert E. Ward & Sakamoto Yoshikazu eds., 1987). On 1 January 1946, the emperor publicly renounced his divinity. McNelly, *supra*, at 4. The retention of the emperor as the symbol of the state and unity of the people, permitting him to present the Constitution as a revision of the Meiji Constitution and his gift to the people, allowed the Japanese to save face under their difficult circumstances. BILLIAS, *supra*, at 286–87; *see* INOUE, *supra*, at 160–205, 219–20.

[37] Kades, *supra* note 36, at 227–28 (quotation at 228); *see id.* at 228–35; BILLIAS, *supra* note 2, at 293–94; MCNELLY, *supra* note 12, at 55–88 (steering committee's deliberations); Alfred C. Oppler, *The Reform of Japan's Legal and Judicial System under Allied Occupation*, 24 WASH. L. REV. & ST. B.J. 290, 299–300 (1949) [hereinafter Oppler, *The Reform*]. Two other American lawyers involved with drafting on the Kades committee were Alfred Hussey and Milo Rowell. INOUE, *supra* note 34, at 16, 26, 127. *See generally* INOUE, *supra* (diverse U.S. and Japanese cultural understanding of the Constitution's two language versions).

[38] BILLIAS, *supra* note 2, 287–91; DOWER, *supra* note 14, at 73–80; JOHN OWEN HALEY, AUTHORITY WITHOUT POWER: LAW AND THE JAPANESE PARADOX 147 (1991); *see* BILLIAS, *supra*, at 291–94; KOSTAL, *supra* note 13, at 158–62; INOUE, *supra* note 34, at 205–19 (popular sovereignty); MCNELLY, *supra* note 12, at 105–28 (article 9); ALFRED C. OPPLER, LEGAL REFORM IN OCCUPIED JAPAN: A PARTICIPANT LOOKS BACK 43–49 (1976) [hereinafter OPPLER, LEGAL REFORM] (debate on whether SCAP imposed the Japanese Constitution or collaborated with Japanese officials and jurists).

[39] Okudaira, *supra* note 35, at 22–24; *see* MCNELLY, *supra* note 12, at 28–29; Beer, *supra* note 35, at 235–39; Hidenori Tomatu, *Constitutional Law*, 26 LAW IN JAPAN 14–16, 20–21 (2000). The 1947 Constitution's list of human rights, under inspiration from the U.S. New Deal and Weimar Constitution, included social and economic rights. In 1972, the Supreme Court adopted a two-tier scrutiny level of government action like that of the U.S. Supreme Court, with more discretion in political powers to affect socioeconomic rights. Okudaira, *supra*, at 24–25. The enumeration of criminal procedure rights was more detailed in Japan (but excluded jury trial) to implement the American

Perhaps the steering committee's most ambitious legal transplant from American law was the U.S. court structure of pervasive decentralized judicial review, unusual for a civil law country.[40] Naturally, it has not functioned as the drafters might have expected. Initially, Japanese Supreme Court precedent and scholarly juristic opinion supported a narrow jurisdiction in cases involving administrative authorities. This, together with the lack of certain common law remedies against administrative action, paralleled the civil law tradition of separate courts for civil and criminal matters and for administrative actions. Similarly, the Court has given the legislature significant discretion to act, thus avoiding constitutional decisions even in cases involving freedom of expression. Last, cultural or political reasons might explain what Yasuhiro Okudaira, a law professor at Tokyo University, labeled "judicial negativism."[41]

Historically, Japanese legal culture has favored mediation and cooperation over confrontation and litigation. In addition, for most of the period since 1955, the conservative Liberal Democratic Party (LDP) controlled the legislature and executive. The cabinet, preferring conservative, pro-LDP candidates, selects Supreme Court justices. However, even though Japanese courts do not often use the Constitution to nullify legislative and executive action, it does not mean that fundamental rights are unprotected. Okudaira argued that economic, political, and cultural factors protect those rights, primarily by extrajudicial means. Dramatic economic growth fostered modernized labor-management relations. There is almost no direct restraint by the government on political freedom and people may criticize politicians and bureaucrats. SCAP eliminated many repressive laws during its occupation, making it difficult to reintroduce those measures after 1952. Unlike Korea, Japan has been involved in little international conflict. Finally, Japanese consciousness toward the importance of human rights, promoted by a favorable media, restrains the government from attempted intrusion.[42]

---

adversarial system of criminal justice. The civil law tradition was too entrenched to permit this transplant to take root. *Id.* at 28.

[40] BILLIAS, *supra* note 2, 288–91; Beer, *supra* note 35, at 234–35, 239; *see* Okudaira, *supra* note 35, at 32. See generally *Decision Making on the Japanese Supreme Court*, 88 WASH. U.L. REV. 1365–1780 (2011) (symposium). Besides decentralized review of legislation for constitutionality, the Japanese court system exhibits bureaucratic control by the Supreme Court over the judges in lower courts, a civil-law type career judiciary, and a reluctance by the Supreme Court to exercise its constitutional review of legislation. David S. Law, *Decision Making on the Japanese Supreme Court: Introduction*, id. at 1365–68.

[41] Okudaira, *supra* note 35, at 34–41. By 1990, Japanese courts had expanded their review of administrative action. *Id.* at 35. From 1947 until 2010, the Japanese Supreme Court declared only eight statutory provisions unconstitutional. David S. Law, *Why Has Judicial Review Failed in Japan?*, 88 WASH. U.L. REV. 1425–26 (2011).

[42] Okudaira, *supra* note 35, at 41–49.

The U.S. military occupation in Korea from 1945 to 1948 met a completely different set of circumstances from that in Japan. The Potsdam Declaration affirmed that the terms of the 1943 Cairo Declaration, which stated that "in due course Korea shall become free and independent," would continue.[43] However, in August 1945, partly to induce the Soviet Union to enter the war against Japan, the United States proposed that the two allies would divide Korea at the 38th parallel to administer Japan's surrender. The Soviets soon occupied North Korea and, almost a month later, Hodge arrived in Seoul under orders from MacArthur to serve as military governor of South Korea for the United States Army Military Government in Korea (AMGK).[44]

As with American military control in the U.S. German sector, AMGK ruled South Korea directly through 211 legislative ordinances through 1948. However, most administrative and enforcement personnel, including police, were Koreans who had worked for the Japanese during colonial rule from 1910 to 1945. In 1945, the Korean population associated these officials with the hated Japanese and not with nationalist democratic interests. In addition, lack of Korean prosecutors, judges, and lawyers hampered AMGK's efforts in developing the Korean legal system. Hodge and his staff were generally unprepared by training or experience for the complexity of the Korean situation and had no Western expert on Korean or Japanese law to aid them.[45]

AMGK, after initially repealing the most repressive Japanese laws, operated on the assumption that formulation and implementation of democratic legal reforms and human rights protections rested on Koreans, whom the Americans had liberated from Japanese rule. Consequently, in November 1945, AMGK issued an ordinance that continued Japanese law in effect until repealed by competent Korean authority.[46] Its effort to form a consensus government among rival political parties and factions failed, so AMGK in July 1946 established an interim legislative assembly, half elected and half appointed by Hodge, to formulate draft reform laws, subject to Hodge's veto.[47] In March 1948, the assembly voted in favor of holding an election for a Korean constitutional assembly. The next month, AMGK issued an ordinance on rights for the Korean people to guide Korean drafters of the pending constitution; another ordinance granted the franchise to women before the national election in May.[48]

---

[43] Beer, *supra* note 35, at 245.
[44] *Id.* at 245; see *supra* text accompanying notes 16–17 (division and occupation of Korea).
[45] Beer, *supra* note 35, at 228, 245–46. In 1945, among Koreans who worked during Japanese control of the peninsula, there were eight prosecutors, 46 judges, and 195 lawyers. *Id.* at 246.
[46] *Id.* at 246.
[47] OLIVER, *supra* note 16, at 48–55, 63, 81; *Korean Occupation, supra* note 16.
[48] BILLIAS, *supra* note 2, at 301–02; OLIVER, *supra* note 16, at 148–50; Beer, *supra* note 35, at 246–47.

From 1946 to 1950, Ernst Fraenkel (1898–1975), an American comparative lawyer expert in German law and politics, served as a legal adviser to AMGK. He described his job as explaining U.S. occupation law to Korean lawyers and Korean private law (that he characterized as essentially German except for family and succession law) to American occupation officers.[49] Fraenkel, born in Cologne, studied law and history at the University of Frankfurt, where he earned a law doctorate in 1923 with a dissertation on labor law. During the Weimar Republic, he became a leading labor union lawyer and member of the Social Democratic Party, positions he lost in 1933 when Hitler's regime dissolved the Party and unions. The regime allowed Fraenkel, who participated in the resistance movement, to continue working as a lawyer in Berlin since he was a veteran of the Great War. He fled Germany in 1938 and the next year emigrated to the United States.[50]

Fraenkel enrolled at the University of Chicago Law School and received his degree in 1941. While working in New York City to assist Jewish refugees from Eastern Europe, he also taught at the New School for Social Research. During this time, he embraced New Deal progressivism and dropped his support for Marxism. In 1944, Fraenkel became a U.S. citizen and the FEA in Washington, D.C., hired him to develop plans for an occupied Germany. He was friends with Alfred Oppler at the FEA. After the war ended, Fraenkel declined an offer to work for the U.S. government in Germany and, after failing to find an academic post, took a position as a legal adviser with AMGK's general affairs section. Fraenkel as well taught constitutional and international law at Seoul University.[51] He also advised Syngman Rhee on legal and constitutional matters. Rhee had attended universities in the United States and had a master's in European history from Harvard and a doctorate in political science from Princeton.[52]

---

[49] Chongko Choi, *Western Jurists on Korean Law: A Historical Survey*, 2 J. KOREAN L. 167, 178–79, 182 (2002) (letter from Fraenkel to Gustav Radbruch, a renowned legal philosopher).

[50] Hubertus Buchstein, *Political Science and Democratic Culture: Ernst Fraenkel's Studies of American Democracy*, 21 GERMAN POL. & SOC'Y 48, 52 (no. 3, Fall 2003). *See generally* VOM SOZIALISMUS ZUM PLURALISMUS: BEITRÄGE ZU WERK UND LEBEN ERNST FRAENKELS (Gerhard Göhler & Hubertus Buchstein, eds., 2000).

[51] Buchstein, *supra* note 50, at 53–54; OPPLER, LEGAL REFORM, *supra* note 38, at 9–10, 70; *see supra* text accompanying note 27 (FEA); *infra* text accompanying notes 76–79 (Oppler). In 1946, Fraenkel took a leave from his Korean activities to work with Oppler in Japan at the courts and law division. OPPLER, *supra*, at 70. When Fraenkel left Korea in 1950, the U.S. State Department hired him as a consultant for reports on the political situation in Berlin while embedded with the American High Commission for Germany. From 1951 to 1953, he also taught political science at the Deutsche Hochschule für Politik. He left U.S. employ and took a professorship at the Hochschule, which later became an institute and merged with the Free University of Berlin. Fraenkel emerged in the 1960s as a leading comparative political scientist in West Germany, adopting a neo-pluralist democratic theory that critiqued the conservative emphasis on the central state. Buchstein, *supra*, at 54.

[52] OLIVER, *supra* note 16, at 4; Choi, *supra* note 49, at 182 n.35 (quoting Oppler); *see supra* text accompanying note 17 (Rhee).

An army colonel led the general affairs section of fewer than a dozen officers, Fraenkel, and some Korean jurists and translators. The section's responsibility was to draft ordinances related to proposed Korean constitutional, criminal, civil, and commercial law. Frankel reported to the section chief using his educational background on constitutions to comment on the draft Korean Constitution and his German law expertise to inform Korean code reform. The colonel had a Yale D.C.L. degree in international and comparative law. After 30 years in legal practice, he was convinced of the superiority of codification and believed the section should thoroughly revise the Korean codes, which had led the War Department to hire Fraenkel.[53]

AMGK's April 1948 ordinance on rights of the Korean people, derived from the American Bill of Rights, had a major impact on Korea's Constitution according to its principal drafter, Yu Chin-o. These rights in the ordinance fell into two groups. First, substantive freedoms of expression, assembly, association, and religion. Second, procedural rights to a speedy and fair trial, legal counsel, due process of law before deprivation of liberty or property, equal protection under law, and prohibition of torture. In addition, Yu incorporated socioeconomic rights into the Constitution based on provisions from the Weimar Constitution.[54]

There were also similarities between the Japanese and Korean constitutions, which suggests that Yu relied on it for organization and some details and thus some indirect U.S. influence.[55] To illustrate, besides each constitution's length (103 articles) and chapter structure, there is striking coincidence in certain detail. Both constitutions root sovereignty in the people, renounce the sovereign prerogative of aggressive war, and contain a supremacy clause for the constitution.[56] In each chapter on rights and duties, the equal protection clause is similar, covering "political, economic, and social" relations.[57] In addition, the two constitutions cover socioeconomic, worker, and property rights.[58]

---

[53] Buchstein, *supra* note 50, at 54; Choi, *supra* note 49, at 182–83. Fraenkel made the first translation of the 1948 Korean Constitution into English. Choi, *supra*, at 183. *See generally* ERNST FRANKEL, 3 GESAMMELTE SCHRIFTEN: NEUAUFBAU DER DEMOKRATIE IN DEUTSCHLAND UND KOREA (Gerhard Göhler ed., 1999) (writing about a proposed 1950 amendment to the Korean Constitution, the structure of AMGK, and other matters of Korean law and politics). Choi, *supra* note 49, at 184 n.43 (list of 16 writings).

[54] BILLIAS, *supra* note 2, at 302; Beer, *supra* note 35, at 247, 250.

[55] *Compare* Amos J. Peaslee, *The Constitution of Japan: Promulgated November 3, 1946*, in 2 CONSTITUTIONS OF NATIONS 307–17 (1950) [hereinafter *Japanese Const.*], *with id.*, *The Constitution of the Republic of Korea: July 12, 1948*, in 2 *id.* 338–48 [hereinafter *Korean Const.*].

[56] *Japanese Const.*, *supra* note 55, preamble, arts. 9, 98; *Korean Const.*, *supra* note 55, preamble, arts. 2, 6, 100. Literally, the Japanese article on war prohibited the maintenance of land, sea, or air forces, but Japanese authorities with the acquiescence of the United States have interpreted it to allow defensive armed forces. DOWER, *supra* note 14, at 394–99.

[57] *Japanese Const.*, *supra* note 55, art. 14; *Korean Const.*, *supra* note 55, art. 8. The *Korean Constitution* in article 8 excludes discrimination by race. Both constitutions declare the equality of husband and wife in marriage. *Japanese Const.*, *supra*, art. 24; *Korean Const.*, *supra*, art. 20.

[58] *Japanese Const.*, *supra* note 55, arts. 22, 25–29; *Korean Const.*, *supra* note 55, arts. 10, 15–19.

Beyond fundamental rights, the structure of government set out in the Constitution was a compromise between AMGK suggestions for a parliamentary system coupled with a supreme court that had judicial review versus Rhee's preference for a dominant presidential executive power. Rhee's status as Korea's leading politician stemmed from his long anti-Japanese and pro-republican activities, including service as president of the Provisional Government of the Republic of Korea from 1919 to 1925 in Shanghai. As approved, the Constitution endorsed a hybrid arrangement with the president elected by two-thirds of legislators in the National Assembly together with a prime minister that the president selected and the assembly confirmed. Furthermore, the president appointed supreme court justices for a court without jurisdiction to review legislation for constitutionality. The Constitution also authorized state ownership and control on major natural resources and businesses. Unfortunately, with the many economic, political, and security problems facing Korea, Rhee's administration soon slipped into authoritarianism.[59]

3. Other U.S. Government-Sponsored Legal Reforms in Germany, Japan, and Korea

As envisioned in early 1945, the U.S. military's primary task for legal reform in Germany—besides new state and federal constitutions—would be denazification of its legal rules, justice system, and legal personnel. During the 12 years of Nazi rule, the government had enacted almost 9,600 laws, about a third of which were discriminatory or infused with Nazi ideology. AMG's Legal Division had this complex and difficult assignment for both American zone reforms and co-ordination within the Allied Control Council (ACC).[60] Legal Division's director selected two experts in German law: Max Rheinstein, a legal comparatist from the University of Chicago; and Loewenstein.[61]

---

[59] BILLIAS, supra note 2, at 302–03; OLIVER, supra note 16, at 5, 140; Beer, supra note 35, at 244, 247, 250, 253.

[60] KOSTAL, supra note 13, at 70–76, 189–90, 251–53. Initially, the army's legal division of U.S. Group Control Council had the denazification mission, which in October 1945, General Clay transferred to the Legal Division of Office of Military Government (OMGUS or AMG). The U.S. High Commissioner for Germany assumed control of AMG's functions in December 1949. The Soviets withdrew from the ACC in March 1948 and then in June blocked land transport to Berlin, precipitating a crisis. Id. at 251, 271, 285, 296.

[61] Id. at 76–78, 85; see Max Rheinstein, *The Legal Status of Occupied Germany*, 47 Mich. L. Rev. 23–40 (1948); supra text accompanying notes 26–29 (Loewenstein); ch. 6, note 169 and text accompanying note 336 (Rheinstein). Rheinstein represented the American zone in the ACC's project to abrogate Nazi racial or political rules from German criminal law and procedure. KOSTAL, supra, at 252–60, 265–66; Max Rheinstein, 25 AM. J. COMP. L. 681–82 (1977). In 1947, the Berlin office of AMG's Legal Division appointed Arthur von Mehren, who had just completed a year of legal study at Zürich University, acting chief of the legislative branch. ARTHUR E. SUTHERLAND, THE LAW AT

When Clay arrived as AMG deputy military governor in 1945, given Germany's physical destruction, social collapse, and the Legal Division's scant resources, he realized its mission of American-led legal reform was not sustainable. The only viable alternative was to allow Germans to lead the denazification program. This would parallel AMG's decision that Germans would draft new constitutions, with some AMG oversight, to implement democratization and fundamental rights. Loewenstein was against this approach since he believed German jurists would thwart the effort. Rheinstein sided with Clay.[62]

In addition to the 1945 Potsdam Agreement's political principles, which the 1949 German Basic Law substantially incorporated, important economic principles included German demilitarization, decartelization, and economic decentralization.[63] Decartelization or antitrust was a legal field in which the United States took a direct interest. In this area, a German American comparatist, Heinrich Kronstein (1897-1972) and a German-British comparatist who taught most of his career at Columbia Law School, Wolfgang Friedmann (1907-1972), performed important roles. The place of competition in a market economy was not even a recognized legal subject in Germany until 1923, when the Reich chancellor issued a regulation to combat the part cartels served in hyperinflation.[64]

Kronstein earned his doctorate in law at Berlin University in 1924 and practiced law until 1935, when he emigrated to the United States. He partly blamed the rise of National Socialism on the failure of positivism to protect the legal system's core values. He enrolled in Columbia Law School where he graduated in 1939, earning a J.S.D. in 1940. In 1941, he began at the U.S. Justice Department, working primarily in the antitrust division. At that time, given his experience in Germany, he converted from Judaism to Roman Catholicism with its emphasis on the place of natural law and human values in a just legal system.[65]

HARVARD: A HISTORY OF IDEAS AND MEN, 1817-1967, at 382 (1967); James R. Gordley, *Arthur Taylor von Mehren*, 53 AM. J. COMP. L. 527 (2005) [hereinafter Gordley, *Von Mehren*].

[62] KOSTAL, *supra* note 13, at 80-97, 139-40, 192-203, 273-74; *see supra* text accompanying notes 8, 22-25, 31-33 (Clay). Another German émigré lawyer, Fritz Oppenheimer, who arrived from England to America in 1942, supported Clay's denazification approach. KOSTAL, *supra*, at 41-42, 68, 82, 91-92; *see* ERNST C. STIEFEL & FRANK MECKLENBURG, DEUTSCHE JURISTEN IM AMERIKANISCHEN EXIL (1933-1950) 129-31 (1991).

[63] MARK GILBERT, EUROPEAN INTEGRATION: A CONCISE HISTORY 24 (2012); *Potsdam Agreement*, *supra* note 21, §§ II.11 to 19; *see* Ivo E. Schwartz, *Antitrust Legislation and Policy in Germany—A Comparative Study*, 105 U. PA. L. REV. 617, 642 (1957).

[64] David J. Gerber, *Heinrich Kronstein and the Development of United States Antitrust Law*, in DER EINFLUSS DEUTSCHER EMIGRANTEN AUF DIE RECHTSENTWICKLUNG IN DER USA UND IN DEUTSCHLAND: VORTÄGE UND REFERATE DES BONNER SYMPOSIONS IM SEPTEMBER 1991, at 155-56, 158, 161 (Marcus Lutter et al. eds., 1993) [hereinafter DER EINFLUSS]; *see* Verordnung gegen Mißbrauch wirtschaftlicher Machtstellungen von 1923, RGBL. I, S. 1067 (2 Nov. 1923).

[65] Gerber, *supra* note 64, at 156-60, 162-63, 167; Eckard Rehbinder, *Heinrich Kronstein: Sein Einfluß auf das deutsche Rechtsdenken und die Fortentwicklung des deutschen Rechts*, in DER EINFLUSS, *supra* note 64, at 383-84; *see supra* ch. 6, pt. G.3 (natural law).

In 1946, Kronstein joined the Georgetown University Law School faculty and from 1949 to 1967 also taught on the Frankfurt law faculty. At Georgetown, he was the director of the Institute for International and Foreign Trade Law and at Frankfurt the director of the *Institut für ausländisches und internationals Wirtschaftsrecht*. Those positions allowed him to influence European antitrust law and to participate in the lengthy effort to reform corporation law and enact antitrust law in West Germany as a comparative jurist familiar with both the American and German experience. It was only in 1957 that the German Bundestag enacted a competition statute.[66] The federal government first introduced the legislation in 1952, which largely adopted the policies underlying American antitrust law as interpreted by U.S. federal courts. The 1957 statute ended application of three 1947 AMG laws dealing with cartels and special laws to deconcentrate coal, steel, and chemicals that the German ministry of economics administered beginning in 1955.[67]

Friedmann studied under the leading German comparatist, Ernst Rabel, at Berlin University, completing his law doctorate in 1930 at Rabel's Institute.[68] Friedmann left Germany for England in 1934, earned an LL.M. at the University of London, and became a barrister. He took British nationality in 1939 and joined the army during the war, serving with the British Foreign Office in intelligence and then German reconstruction. From 1938, he taught law at universities in London, Melbourne, and Toronto before settling at Columbia Law School from 1955 until 1972, where he found the academic rigor more extensive.[69]

From 1944 to 1947, the British army sent Friedmann to assist the Allied military command on German reconstruction, first with the Allied Expeditionary Force under General Dwight Eisenhower and then the British Control Commission. Friedmann's orientation, like that of most German experts working for the Americans and British, was toward rehabilitation rather than punishment. He eventually led the British sector's Office for Economic

---

[66] Gerber, *supra* note 64, at 160–61; Rehbinder, *supra* note 65, at 384–85, 393–95; *see* Gesetz gegen Wettbewerbsbeschränkungen von 1957, BGBl. I, S. 1081 (9 Aug. 1957); Heinrich Kronstein, *Cartels under the New German Cartel Statute*, 11 VAND. L. REV. 271–302 (1958) [hereinafter cited as Kronstein, *Cartels*].

[67] Kronstein, *Cartels*, *supra* note 66, at 271, 273, 301; Schwartz, *supra* note 63, at 643–48, 652–83, 688–90.

[68] Michael I. Sovern, *Wolfgang Gaston Friedmann*, 10 COLUM. J. TRANSNAT'L L. 4 (1971). The thesis, published as a book, *Die Bereicherungshaftung im angloamerikanischen Rechtskreis in Vergleichung mit dem deutschen bürgerlichen Recht* (1930), was a comparative study of British, German, and American unjust enrichment law. *Id.*

[69] John Bell, *Wolfgang Friedmann (1907-1972), with an Excursus on Gustav Radbruch (1978-1949)*, *in* JURISTS UPROOTED: GERMAN-SPEAKING ÉMIGRÉ LAWYERS IN TWENTIETH-CENTURY BRITAIN 517–20 (Jack Beatson & Reinhard Zimmermann eds., 2004); KOSTAL, *supra* note 13, at 42. At Columbia, Friedmann was director of international legal research and founder of what became the *Columbia Journal of Transnational Law*. Preface, 1 COLUM. J. TRANSNAT'L L. vii (1961).

Reconstruction.[70] Friedmann's catholic interests extended from comparative law, jurisprudence, legal sociology, to international law. While teaching comparative law at the University of Toronto, he referred to the service of lawyers in Allied military governments and international organizations in Europe. "Many blunders could . . . have been avoided in the Allied administration of Germany had there been a little more knowledge of Germany's legal system and structure."[71]

Friedmann's involvement in German reconstruction and partiality toward social democracy contributed to his interest in a legal system's structures and the part an interventionist state might serve. For legal theory, he believed that one could best understand legal change in the context of social and political developments. This view informed his publications on public corporations and antitrust law.[72]

The U.S. military occupation of Japan lasted from 1945 until 1952, when Japan regained its sovereignty.[73] During the first three years, SCAP supported numerous legal reforms, primarily to buttress the Constitution's goal of democracy and to support fundamental civil and social rights. Beyond thorough defeudalization and demilitarization, it required opening the political system to free assembly and expression. SCAP's revolution from above was idealistic and evangelistic, bringing a Western legal system to an Oriental nation. In October 1945, a SCAP directive ordered the Japanese government to extend the franchise to women, liberalize education with more schools and new curricula, promote labor organization, and democratize the economy by breaking industrial monopolies and family-controlled holding companies (*zaibatsu*). In 1946, there were initiatives to decentralize government, including the police, and expand local autonomy.[74] By 1948, the Japanese government carried out

---

[70] Bell, *supra* note 69, at 518; Sovern, *supra* note 68, at 6; *Wolfgang Gaston Friedmann*, 10 COLUM. J. TRANSNAT'L L. 1 (1971); *see* Wolfgang Friedmann, *Legal and Political Aspects of the Berlin Crisis*, 1 COLUM. J. TRANSNAT'L L. 3–8 (1961).

[71] W. Friedmann, *Teaching and Research in Comparative Law: Recent Developments at the University of Toronto School of Law*, 10 U. TORONTO L.J. 245–47 (1954) (Friedmann's 1954 national report to the Fourth International Congress of Comparative Law at Paris; quotation at 245); *see* Bell, *supra* note 69, at 520–24, 528–29. For Friedmann's comparative law publications, *see Wolfgang Gaston Friedmann: A Selective Bibliography*, 10 COLUM. J. TRANSNAT'L L. 32–44 (1971) [hereinafter cited as *Friedmann Bibliography*].

[72] Bell, *supra* note 69, at 521–27; *Friedmann Bibliography, supra* note 71, at 32–33; *see, e.g.*, ANTITRUST LAWS: A COMPARATIVE SYMPOSIUM (Wolfgang Friedmann ed., 1956).

[73] *See supra* text accompanying note 15 (Treaty of San Francisco).

[74] DOWER, *supra* note 14, at 73–84, 244, 525; Oppler, *The Reform, supra* note 37, at 290–91, 296. Agrarian land reform dispossessed the rural landlord class and replaced it with owner-farmers. DOWER, *supra*, at 82; Oppler, *supra*, at 295. Some U.S. State Department officials and Japan experts were disdainful of SCAP's efforts to change the Japanese legal system toward democracy. However, New Deal liberals, China experts, and an influential group of behavioral scientists minimized cultural impediments and prevailed with Dean Acheson, whom Truman appointed as Under Secretary of State in August 1945. DOWER, *supra*, at 217–24; *see* THEODORE COHEN, REMAKING JAPAN: THE

the economic reforms, including for antitrust, and many have had surprising durability.[75]

SCAP coordinated the contribution of American comparative lawyers to reform the Japanese legal system. Three jurists stand out: Alfred Oppler, Kurt Steiner, and Thomas Blakemore.[76] All had studied law outside the United States and worked collaboratively with Japanese lawyers to revise the traditional codes and statutes such as the court organization law consistent with the 1947 Constitution and sensitive to the civil law, common law, and Japanese customary law traditions. To promote new fundamental rights, in 1947, they co-founded with Japanese lawyers the Japan Civil Liberties Union (JCLU). That same year, Oppler assisted the justice minister, Yoshio Suzuki, in establishing the Civil Liberties Bureau (CLB), which was like the Civil Rights Section within the U.S. Department of Justice.[77] Suzuki saw that the bureau's resources were inadequate, leading him to propose the 1949 Civil Liberties Commissioner Law, which Steiner helped implement. By the end of the twentieth century, the CLB had 200 bureaucrats served by 13,000 lay commissioners and the Japanese considered it a success in promoting awareness of human rights. Commissioners handled about 16,000 citizen complaints emphasizing conciliation, half a million inquiries providing advice, along with educational projects in schools and communities.[78]

Oppler (1893–1982) was born in Alsace-Lorraine and studied law in Germany, including at Berlin University. After passing the German second state exam for law in 1922, Oppler worked as a government lawyer and, in 1927, began at the Prussian supreme administrative court (*Oberverwaltungsgericht*) as a research

AMERICAN OCCUPATION AS NEW DEAL 3–48, 214–39 (Herbert Passin ed., 1987). Oppler compared the American reform effort to Napoléon's dissemination of French legal codes in conquered lands. Oppler, *supra*, at 290.

[75] HALEY, *supra* note 38, at 147–50; Thomas L. Blakemore, *Japanese Commercial Code Revisions Concerning Corporations*, 2 AM. J. COMP. L. 12–14 (1953) [hereinafter Blakemore, *Corporations*]; Akira Negishi, *Economic Law*, 26 LAW IN JAPAN 34–41 (2000).

[76] HALEY, *supra* note 38, at 105; Beer, *supra* note 35, at 240.

[77] DOWER, *supra* note 14, at 224; Beer, *supra* note 35, at 240–41; OPPLER, LEGAL REFORM, *supra* note 38, at 107, 173, 177; Oppler, *The Reform*, *supra* note 37, at 292, 295, 301–02, 306–11, 323; Kenneth O'Reilly, *The Roosevelt Administration and Black America: Federal Surveillance Policy and Civil Rights during the New Deal and World War II Years*, 48 PHYLON 12, 15 (1987). In 1939, U.S. Attorney General Frank Murphy established the Civil Liberties Unit (renamed Civil Rights Section in 1941) within the criminal division of the Department of Justice. Organized civil rights groups and labor organizations wanted the federal government to act against lynching and violence toward labor organizers. *Id.* at 15–18. Roger Baldwin, executive director (1917–1950) of the American Civil Liberties Union (ACLU), led the effort to establish the JCLU. OPPLER, LEGAL REFORM, *supra*, at 23, 179–80.

[78] Beer, *supra* note 35, at 241; Ian Neary, *The Civil Liberties Commissioners System and the Protection of Human Rights in Japan*, 9 JAPAN FORUM 217–19, 223–25, 228, 230–31 (1997). Even if the American Section inspired the CLB, it soon took on Japanese characteristics with its large lay support system. Consistent with SCAP's emphasis on local government for Japan, village and city mayors nominated commissioners to the minister of justice, who served three-year renewable terms. *Id.* at 219, 221.

assistant and then judge. In 1932, he served as vice president of the Berlin supreme disciplinary court until Hitler's 1933 civil service law demoted him for his Jewish heritage. In 1938, Oppler decided to emigrate. Since he was born in Alsace, which now belonged to France, he came within that country's quota for immigrants to the United States, where he arrived in 1939. During the 1940s, he served as a research assistant and instructor at Harvard University, sponsored by Carl Friedrich. In 1945, Oppler became a U.S. citizen and a year later joined SCAP's effort to reform certain Japanese laws as chief of the new government section's courts and law division. In 1948, GHQ named him chief of the legal section's legislation and justice division.[79]

Kurt Steiner (1912–2003) was born in Vienna, where he graduated from the university law faculty in 1935, emigrating to the United States after Hitler's 1938 annexation (*Anschluß*) of Austria. In 1944, Steiner joined the U.S. Army, studied Japanese at its Military Intelligence School, then transferred to SCAP in 1945. He worked on the American team revising the Japanese Constitution and became chief of the civil affairs and civil liberties branch of the legislation and justice division. From 1948 to 1949, he prosecuted war criminals in Tokyo and departed SCAP in 1951. In 1955, Stanford University awarded him a political science doctorate and hired him for the political science department, where he taught comparative politics and Japanese politics until 1977.[80]

Steiner wrote the foreword to Oppler's memoir, where Steiner's analysis illustrated their sophistication as comparatists. They both were jurists from German-speaking civil law countries, emigrated to the common law United States, and then worked for that government's effort to reform the legal and political system of a defeated East Asian nation that had absorbed important Germanic elements. This would require structural and cultural change, which would have a more durable impact if the United States carried out its guidance with sensitivity to Japanese tradition.[81]

Thomas Blakemore (1916–1994) earned his law degree at the University of Oklahoma in 1938 and then pursued post-graduate law studies at Cambridge

---

[79] OPPLER, LEGAL REFORM, *supra* note 38, at 4–13, 17, 67–68, 220–22; M.E. Grenander Department of Special Collections and Archives, *Alfred C. Oppler Papers, 1908-1982*, https://archives.albany.edu/description/catalog/ger016; *see supra* text accompanying notes 18–20 (Friedrich). In 1946, Whitney was chief and Kades deputy chief of the government section. OPPLER, LEGAL REFORM, *supra*, at 18, 20. After Japan regained its sovereignty in 1952, Oppler remained in government service in East Asia writing reports on Japan and Korea until he returned to the United States in 1959. Oppler Papers, *supra*.

[80] Lisa Trei, *Kurt Steiner* (14 Jan. 2004), https://news.stanford.edu/pr/2004/steinerobit114.html. Steiner authored *Local Government in Japan* (1965), *Politics in Austria* (1972), and *Political Opposition and Local Politics in Japan* (1979). See R.P. Dore, *Local Government in Japan*, 25 J. ASIAN STUD. 771–73 (1966) (book review); Byung Chul Koh, *Local Government in Japan*, 28 J. POL. 441–43 (1966) (book review).

[81] OPPLER, LEGAL REFORM, *supra* note 38, at vii–xiii, 83–84.

University and Tokyo Imperial University until 1941. During the war he was a captain in the U.S. Army with the Office of Strategic Services in China. From 1946 to 1949, Blakemore began as Oppler's deputy in the courts and law division and later worked at GHQ's economic and scientific section. Blakemore's experience with Japanese culture led him to a conservative position in contrast to Oppler's view promoting progressive Western values. Blakemore felt that Japanese jurists and politicians should resolve legal issues on their own where constitutional mandates were not directly involved. Blakemore went on to complete his legal studies at Tokyo University and, in 1950, became a *bengoshi* allowing him to represent clients in Japanese courts. He founded a Tokyo law firm where he practiced for almost four decades.[82]

Japanese bureaucrats, activists, and scholars together with American officials and jurists worked productively under the GHQ's umbrella to reform law. Oppler considered revision of the criminal procedure code central to GHQ's task of bringing codes and statutes into conformity with the Constitution. The task took weeks of meetings with Japanese politicians, judges, lawyers, and the JCLU before the committee in 1948 submitted the draft to the Diet.[83] A similar process occurred with the reform of other codes and many statutes. For instance, after more than a year of meetings and parliamentary proceedings, the Diet enacted the revised civil code in 1947, effective in 1948.[84] GHQ also sided with Japanese sentiment to reform the practicing bar in 1949 by raising qualification standards, removing it from ministry of justice supervision, and giving it self-governing autonomy under the judiciary.[85]

In 1946, GHQ civil code reform focused on books 4 and 5, which reflected Japanese customary law on families and inheritance, and largely ignored the first three books derived primarily from German law.[86] The primary concern of

---

[82] HALEY, *supra* note 38, at 105–06; Kurt Steiner, *The Occupation and the Reform of the Japanese Civil Code*, in DEMOCRATIZING JAPAN, *supra* note 36, at 188, 215–17, 504–05 nn.70–71 [hereinafter Steiner, *Occupation*]; Thomas L. Blakemore, *Post-War Developments in Japanese Law*, 1947 WISC. L. REV. 632–53 (1947); Blakemore, *Corporations*, *supra* note 75, at 12; T.L. Blakemore, 78, *Expert on Japan's Law*, N.Y. TIMES, 4 Mar. 1994, § B, at 8.

[83] OPPLER, LEGAL REFORM, *supra* note 38, at 105–06, 136–48; *id.*, *The Reform*, *supra* note 37, at 302–04.

[84] Steiner, *Occupation*, *supra* note 82, at 206–07; Kurt Steiner, *Postwar Changes in the Japanese Civil Code*, 25 WASH. L. REV. & ST. B.J. 286, 296–97 (1950) [hereinafter Steiner, *Postwar*]. Japanese initiatives for labor and education reforms were especially comprehensive. DOWER, *supra* note 14, at 245–51.

[85] HALEY, *supra* note 38, at 106–07 (*bengoshi* law); OPPLER, LEGAL REFORM, *supra* note 38, at 107–10. Rande Kostal considered Oppler an over-optimistic apologist for GHQ's legal reform initiatives. KOSTAL, *supra* note 13, at 171–85.

[86] OPPLER, LEGAL REFORM, *supra* note 38, at 111; Steiner, *Postwar*, *supra* note 84, at 288, 296; *see* Mikihiko Wada, *Abolition of the House (ie) under the Occupation—Or the Two Faces of Koseki: A Janus*, 26 LAW IN JAPAN 99–127 (2000). For the debate involving the family, marriage equality, and individual dignity in the 1947 Constitution, *see* INOUE, *supra* note 34, at 221–65. For the 1955 civil code revision, *see* Toshio Fueto, *Japan: Revision of the New Civil Code*, 6 AM. J. COMP. L. 559–65 (1957).

Oppler, then with the government section, was the code's Confucian feudalistic household system (*ie*), which gave the family unit—a house or *koshu*—legal autonomy. *Ie* subordinated individuals hierarchically to the house, with an inferior role for women. The head of the house was usually the eldest male, a grandfather or granduncle, who controlled decisions about changing residence, marriage, adoption, or divorce. He also owned most family property. Inheritance rules reinforced the *ie*, including selection of a new *koshu* head (*pater*). Filial obedience and piety to the *pater* were virtues, and he had a duty to support needy family members. The sanction for disobedience was expulsion from the *koshu*. The Constitution's principles of individual dignity and equality, and requirement of marriage based on consent, necessitated a thorough reform. Oppler contended the replacement of *ie* with Western nuclear family rules, spousal equality, and equal inheritance, was a Japanese initiative, but John Dower contended that since the American-Japanese relationship was inherently unequal, the latter knew they could not ignore GHQ suggestions.[87]

Like Japan's other codes, German influence during the Meiji era on the commercial code was dominant. In 1948, GHQ, through its economic and scientific section, took an interest in restructuring the rules for corporations as part of antitrust reform.[88] The section notified Japanese officials and scholars to join a committee with GHQ representatives to strengthen the status of shareholders in the commercial code to foster corporate democracy. Between 1949 and 1950, the committee met in over 50 sessions to debate and formulate revisions, which took effect in 1951. U.S. pressure for these reforms, which included introduction of a board of directors as a collective entity with managerial authority, reduced auditor power, and rules to increase stock ownership among the population, was stronger than in some other legal areas, since the Japanese resisted several of these changes.[89]

Japan had adopted its first criminal procedure code as part of the five-code European package in 1890. In 1922, informed by German legal doctrine, a reformed code maintained the standard inquisitorial civil law model for the

---

[87] Dower, *supra* note 14, at 245; Oppler, Legal Reform, *supra* note 38, at 111–20; *id.*, *The Reform*, *supra* note 37, at 292, 317–18; Steiner, *Occupation*, *supra* note 82, at 188–90, 192–205, 212–17; Steiner, *Postwar*, *supra* note 84, at 288–94, 299–300, 308–09. Blakemore joined Oppler in some of the family law negotiations. Steiner, *Occupation*, *supra*, at 198–99, 206. The revised code made control over children parental, exercised jointly, rather than paternal. *Id.* at 205–06; Steiner, *Postwar*, *supra*, at 304–06. GHQ also reformed the family registration system (*koseki*). Oppler, *The Reform*, *supra*, at 319; Steiner, *Postwar*, *supra*, at 292, 297, 309–10.

[88] Blakemore, *Corporations*, *supra* note 75, at 13–14; Kenjiro Egashira, *Commercial Law*, 26 Law in Japan 50–58 (2000). In addition to GHQ's legal section, reform proposals emanated from other staff sections, such as the economic and scientific section, and GHQ favored coordination among sections. Blakemore, *supra*, at 12; Section of General Staff, Reports of General MacArthur: MacArthur in Japan 71–80 (vol. 1 supp., 1994 ed).

[89] Blakemore, *Corporations*, *supra* note 75, at 14–24. The American models for reform were the Uniform Stock Transfer Act (1909) and the Illinois Business Corporation Act (1933). *Id.* at 15.

ministry of justice, judges, prosecutors, and defense lawyers. Political events in the 1920s and 1930s, however, subverted protections for those accused of crime. The situation changed with the American occupation. To further civil liberties the Japanese government abrogated oppressive laws and released thousands of political prisoners. The Constitution's chapter 3, rights and duties of the people, followed the U.S. Constitution's fourth to eighth amendments as a criminal procedure bill of rights.[90] In 1948, the Diet enacted a new code of criminal procedure, effective in 1949, consistent with the Constitution. Along with other new statutes, Japan now had common law institutions such as habeas corpus, grand jury, and a more adversarial trial mixed with civil law elements like intermittent trial, government appeal, and the role for judges, judicial police, and prosecutors in the procedural system.[91]

The revolution from above largely ended by 1949, when Japanese political realities and Cold War events convinced MacArthur and GHQ that a new approach was necessary. In 1947, food shortages and high inflation led the newly created labor unions to call for a general strike. MacArthur stopped it, but resentment from communists and radical elements in labor became more militant. In 1948, he modified occupation labor policy to prohibit public employees from striking and by 1949, GHQ implemented a "red purge" with cooperation from conservative politicians and government bureaucrats. Initially resulting in dismissal of 11,000 leftist public employees, after the Korean War started in June 1950, it extended to an equal number in the private sector including mass media. The Korean conflict convinced SCAP that Japanese remilitarization was necessary, which had the collateral benefit of stimulating the anemic economy. A reversal of course on economic deconcentration allowed large firms to continue in business.[92]

In Korea, as we saw for its Constitution, political circumstances were fundamentally different. For private law, Meiji jurists during Japanese occupation had compiled Korean popular practices and usages with the aim of turning them into

---

[90] Richard B. Appleton, *Reforms in Japanese Criminal Procedure under Allied Occupation*, 24 WASH. L. REV. & ST. B.J. 401–05 (1949); *see* Kenpō arts. 31–39. Appleton worked for SCAP's legislation and justice division. Appleton, *supra*, at 401.

[91] OPPLER, LEGAL REFORM, *supra* note 38, at 86–106, 132–33, 136–49; Appleton, *supra* note 90, at 406–12, 414, 416–18, 420–26; *see* Steiner, *Postwar*, *supra* note 84, at 288. The code also provided for summary proceedings like the Austrian or German penal order (*Mandatsverfahren* or *Strafbefehlsverfahren*). Appleton, *supra*, at 419–20.

[92] DOWER, *supra* note 14, at 267–73, 526, 528, 532–36, 542; OPPLER, LEGAL REFORM, *supra* note 38, at 196–210; Fujio Hamada, *Labor Law*, 26 LAW IN JAPAN 42–49 (2000). Before the Korean War, Soviet repression in Eastern Europe, communist victory in mainland China, and the nuclear arms race defined the Cold War. Dower credited Marxist influence in Japan to a style of capitalism distinct from that in the United States, characterized by regular state intervention in the economy, job security, and reduced economic disparities. Corporate executives collaborated with union leaders to foster enterprise unionism. Communists and socialists continued in the Diet and to participate in policy debates. DOWER, *supra*, at 272–73, 526.

binding customary law. However, resistance in Japan to a separate legal regime for Korea led the Japanese to impose their civil code in Korea in 1912, except for legal relations involving family matters, succession, certain property rights, and other areas not implicating public order. For these relations, Korean customary rules applied, but as interpreted by Japanese-trained judges sympathetic to the French and German civil law tradition.[93] By August 1948, at the inception of the Republic of Korea, 95 percent of its statutes and regulations were those left by the Japanese.[94]

Besides Fraenkel, the only other academic comparatist who might have influenced law in Korea during the American occupation government beyond the Constitution was Charles Lobingier.[95] In 1946 and 1947, Lobingier visited Korea where he lectured on Korean customary law and guidelines for drafting a new civil code. He believed in incorporating portions of commercial law into the code and maintaining Korean customs for family and succession law.[96] He relied on the civil codes of France, California, and China in his drafting enterprise. Korean jurists, however, preferred the German civil code's structure and its use of a general part. When Korea finally adopted a new civil code in 1958, the drafters based it principally in structure and content on the Japanese civil code.[97] Finally, there was some American influence stemming from the occupation period on the new Korean codes of criminal law and criminal procedure in the early 1950s.[98]

4. Federalism and Antitrust Reform for Western Europe

Ideas about European unity have a long history reaching back to the Romans. Despite the efforts of Napoléon in the nineteenth century and Hitler with his Third Reich, the successful movement for consensual supranational cooperation

---

[93] Marie Seong-Hak Kim, *Law and Custom under the Chosŏn Dynasty and Colonial Korea: A Comparative Perspective*, 66 J. ASIAN STUD. 1067, 1069–70, 1072–73, 1077–84, 1088–89 (2007); see id., *Customary Law and Colonial Jurisprudence in Korea*, 57 AM. J. COMP. L. 205–48 (2009); supra pt. A.2 (Korean constitutional law).

[94] Beer, *supra* note 35, at 246.

[95] *See supra* text accompanying notes 49–53 (Fraenkel); ch. 6, *supra* pt. A.2 (Lobingier).

[96] Choi, *supra* note 49, at 185–86; Helen Clagett, *Korean Code*, 5 LAW. & L. NOTES 2 (1951). Between 1946 and 1949, Lobingier, who took the title honorary consultant in civil law, prepared 1,305 articles divided into four books for the proposed code. Clagett, *supra*, at 2; *see* Charles S. Lobingier, Proposed Civil Code for Korea (1949) (unpublished manuscript in the Far Eastern Law Division, Library of Congress); Choi, *supra*, at 185 n.48.

[97] Keechang Kim, *Codification in the 21st Century—A View from Korea*, in CODIFICATION IN EAST ASIA 19–21 (Wen-Yue Wang ed., 2014).

[98] Beer, *supra* note 35, at 247; *see* Paul Kichyun Ryu, *New Korean Criminal Code of October 3, 1953: An Analysis of Ideologies Embedded in It*, 48 J. CRIM. L., CRIMINOLOGY & POLICE SCI. 275, 278–95 (1957).

among European states required the catastrophes of the 1920s to 1940s. This included fascism, the Great Depression, and war throughout Europe. Christian Democrat leaders elected after 1945 believed that, despite the moral and economic disaster, they could collaborate effectively. By 1950, representatives from six nations—France, West Germany, and Italy at the core, with Belgium, Luxembourg, and the Netherlands—were negotiating to put their coal and steel industries under a high authority with supranational powers. Some referred to and advocated for a United States of Europe.[99]

Did American jurists and government lawyers participate meaningfully in this European process? One's answer to this question depends on the perspective she takes in analyzing the circumstances.[100] Furthermore, an unusual association existed between the two continents at New York University (NYU) from 1942 to 1946. Richard Coudenhove-Kalergi, a classically educated Austrian aristocrat who had taught history at Vienna University, accepted a history lectureship at NYU to initiate a research seminar about a federative postwar Europe. After the Great War, his interest in that subject developed, which he presented in *Pan-Europa* (1923), a German-language volume with seven editions through 1938 and translated into many languages, including English in 1926 as well as Chinese, Japanese, and Arabic.[101]

The success of Coudenhove's manifesto led to the creation of the Pan European Union (PEU) with support from German industrialists such as Robert Bosch.

---

[99] GILBERT, *supra* note 63, at 4, 9–11. Konrad Adenauer became chancellor of West Germany in 1949. He believed that cooperation was essential, a view supported by the Italian Alcide de Gasperi and Frenchman Robert Schuman. *Id.* at 9–10.

[100] *See, e.g.*, Daniel J. Elazar & Ilan Greilsammer, *Federal Democracy: The U.S.A. and Europe Compared, A Political Science Perspective*, in 1 INTEGRATION THROUGH LAW, EUROPE AND THE AMERICAN FEDERAL EXPERIENCE: METHODS, TOOLS AND INSTITUTIONS 71–168 (bk 1, *A Political, Legal and Economic Overview*) (Mauro Cappelletti, Monica Seccombe & Joseph Weiler eds., 1985) [hereinafter INTEGRATION THROUGH LAW]; Francis G. Jacobs & Kenneth L. Karst, *The "Federal" Legal Order: The U.S.A. and Europe Compared, A Juridical Science Perspective*, in *id.* at 169–243; Thomas Heller & Jacques Pelkmans, *The Federal Economy: Law and Economic Integration and the Positive State—The U.S.A. and Europe Compared in an Economic Perspective*, in *id.* at 245–412.

[101] Daniel C. Villanueva, *Richard von Coudenhove-Kalergi's "Pan-Europa" as the Elusive "Object of Longing,"* 59 ROCKY MOUNTAIN REV. LANGUAGE & LITERATURE, 67–69, 76 n.1 (2005); MICHAEL J. HOGAN, THE MARSHALL PLAN: AMERICA, BRITAIN, AND THE RECONSTRUCTION OF WESTERN EUROPE, 1947–1952, at 28 (1987); Robert H. Ferrell, *The Truman Era and European Integration*, in THE UNITED STATES AND THE INTEGRATION OF EUROPE: LEGACIES OF THE POSTWAR ERA 25, 36 (Francis H. Heller & John R. Gillingham eds., 1996) [hereinafter INTEGRATION OF EUROPE]; *see* RICHARD N. COUDENHOVE-KALERGI, PAN-EUROPA (1923).

In *Pan-Europa*, Coudenhove presented a future world with five major geographical and cultural units. In addition to Pan Europa, which would include the continent's colonial empires, there was Pan America, East Asia, the Russian federation, and the British empire. *Id.* at 14–17, 20–23, 29–31, 36–38, 173–74. Europe needed to bind itself together economically and politically to defend against a Russian military threat and American cultural influence. For Europe to survive culturally, there had to be Franco-German reconciliation. Success for economic and political Europe would require an American-style United States of Europe. New Europe would be organic, democratic, Christian, and federal. *Id.* at x–xi, 14–17, 34–35, 53–57, 67–70, 119–30, 166–68.

In 1926, the PEU held its first congress in Vienna with 2,000 participants from 24 nations. The PEU elected Coudenhove president (served until his death in 1972), French foreign minister Aristide Briand honorary president, and set up national affiliates in many countries including the United States. Other notable PEU members sympathetic to the idea of an integrated Europe were Konrad Adenauer, Winston Churchill, and Georges Pompidou. While in America, Coudenhove continued to crusade for a federated Europe with government officials and the public. He also formulated the idea of a European constituent assembly, which influenced the establishment of the parliamentary assembly in the postwar Council of Europe.[102]

For its part, the U.S. State Department was supportive of economic and political integration in Europe as the Cold War emerged to divide Americans and Soviets. Since West European countries were dependent on U.S. foreign aid for recovery, they had little choice but to follow America's projection of its own cooperative model of federalism to serve for Europeans. Nevertheless, the French were resistant at first since its leaders wanted France to lead the economic recovery. American continued insistence on economic and political reform to rebuild West Germany, however, finally made Franco-German rapprochement essential.[103] In particular, the U.S. High Commissioner for Germany, John McCloy (served 1949-1952), broke resistance from German industry by skillfully wielding political and economic pressure that assisted agreement in 1951 on the European Coal and Steel Community (ECSC).[104]

In 1947, Secretary of State George Marshall in a speech at Harvard University had proposed that European nations create a plan for their economic reconstruction, for which the United States would provide financial assistance. The strategy

---

[102] DEREK W. URWIN, THE COMMUNITY OF EUROPE: A HISTORY OF EUROPEAN INTEGRATION SINCE 1945, at 5, 9 (2d ed. 1995); Villanueva, *supra* note 101, at 68; Konrad Adenauer Stiftung, *Coudenhove-Kalergi, Richard Nikolaus Graf*, https://www.kas.de/en/web/geschichte-der-cdu/home (select Significant Figures, then Coudenhove); International Paneuropean Union, *Pan-Europa: The Parent Idea of a United Europe*, http://www.international-paneuropean-union.eu (select English); *see* R.N. COUDENHOVE-KALERGI, AN IDEA CONQUERS THE WORLD (1953) (Churchill wrote the preface).

[103] GILBERT, *supra* note 63, at 10-12, 27; HOGAN, *supra* note 101, at 35-39, 293-95, 424-30; *see* GILBERT, *supra*, at 16-20 (European proposals and political parties for supranational federalism during the 1930s and 1940s); Frederico Romero, *U.S. Attitudes towards Integration and Interdependence: The 1950s*, *in* INTEGRATION OF EUROPE, *supra* note 101, at 103-21. *See generally* PETER HAY, FEDERALISM AND SUPRANATIONAL ORGANIZATIONS: PATTERNS FOR NEW LEGAL STRUCTURES (1966); Carl H. Fulda, *Book Review*, 15 AM. J. COMP. L. 583-85 (1967). After Winston Churchill's Conservative Party lost the 1945 U.K. election, he made a speech at the University of Zürich that called for a United States of Europe. In 1947, he founded the United Europe Movement to resist Soviet encroachment in Western Europe. GILBERT, *supra*, at 18.

[104] HOGAN, *supra* note 101, at 287-88, 311, 356, 366-67, 377-78; ALAN S. MILWARD, THE RECONSTRUCTION OF WESTERN EUROPE: 1945-51, at 383-84 n.32, 387, 391, 397-98, 427 (1984); Karl Lowenstein, *Union of Western Europe: Illusion and Reality I—An Appraisal of the Methods*, 52 COLUM. L. REV. 55, 94-95 (1952); *see id.* at 81-86, 89-99; *supra* text accompanying notes 6, 8, 12-13 (McCloy).

was that political stability would follow, thwarting the incursion of Soviet communism.[105] President Truman sent Marshall's ideas to Congress to provide European economic aid, which Congress enacted as the Economic Cooperation Act of 1948 (Marshall Plan). It specifically declared that European unification was a U.S. foreign policy objective.[106] The act authorized the Economic Cooperation Administration (ECA), which reported to both the State Department and Commerce Department. The ECA had an office in each of 16 European nations participating in the Marshall Plan, which aimed to rebuild infrastructure, expand production, and encourage more open European markets.[107] Parallel to the ECA, European countries set up the Organisation for European Economic Cooperation (OEEC) to help coordinate distribution under the Marshall Plan.[108]

In June 1948, the Soviet blockade of Berlin convinced France to acquiesce to the Anglo-American plan to rebuild West Germany's economy. In exchange, the German Ruhr region's steel and coal cartel opened to France and offered other European access. The U.S. State Department used Marshall Plan funds to coax France into cooperation with the newly established West German government. In March 1950, Konrad Adenauer, German chancellor, suggested a Franco-German economic union with its own executive responsible to the two nations' legislatures. Robert Schuman, French foreign minister, was receptive. In May 1950, he read a statement prepared by Jean Monnet, Planning Commissariat

---

[105] GILBERT, *supra* note 63, at 13–14; HOGAN, *supra* note 101, at 40–45, 52–54. Marshall made it clear in 1947 that a recovery plan should be European. "The initiative . . . must come from Europe. The role of this country should consist of friendly aid in the drafting of a European program and of later support of such a program so far as it may be practical for us to do so. The program should be a joint one, agreed to by a number, if not all, of European nations." THE COLD WAR: A HISTORY IN DOCUMENTS AND EYEWITNESS ACCOUNTS 105, 122 (Jussi M. Hanhimäki & Odd Arne Westad eds., 2003).

[106] HOGAN, *supra* note 101, at 88–109; Karl Lowenstein, *Union of Western Europe: Illusion and Reality II—An Appraisal of the Motives*, 52 COLUM. L. REV. 209, 238 (1952). The act's preamble stated:

> Mindful of the advantages which the United States has enjoyed through the existence of a large domestic market with no internal barriers to trade or the free movement of persons, and believing that similar advantages can accrue to the countries of Europe, it is declared to be the policy of the people of the United States to encourage these countries through their joint organization to exert sustained efforts to achieve speedily that economic cooperation in Europe which is essential for lasting peace and prosperity. It is further declared to be the policy of the people of the United States to encourage the further unification of Europe.

Subsequent security and assistance acts, and statements by General Eisenhower, repeated the objective as European economic cooperation and political federation. *Id.* at 238–40 (quotation at 238).

[107] GILBERT, *supra* note 63, at 15; Economic Cooperation Act, 62 Stat. 137 (1948). The ECA was a predecessor to the U.S. Agency for International Development, formed in 1961 by President John Kennedy's executive order. U.S. AID, *USAID History*, at https://www.usaid.gov/who-we-are/usaid-history.

[108] GILBERT, *supra* note 63, at 10, 15, 36, 45–46; OECD, *A Brief History*, https://www.oecd.org/60-years/#d.en.194377. In 1960, a new convention, signed also by Canada and the United States, added the word development (OECD), which led the organization toward a global mission. *Id.*; *see* DIANE B. KUNZ, BUTTER AND GUNS: AMERICA'S COLD WAR ECONOMIC DIPLOMACY (1997); *supra* text accompanying notes 10–11 (Marshall Plan).

chief, which proposed to place French and German coal and steel production under a common high authority open to other West European countries. Besides Adenauer, another four nations responded favorably. The Paris Treaty of 1951 then created the ECSC.[109]

The ECSC's most distinctive institution was the High Authority. Consisting of nine members, it reflected the size differential between the Benelux countries and France, Germany, and Italy. The latter three each had two representatives and the others one, who collectively selected the ninth member. They served six-year terms, elected officers—with Monnet the first president (1952-1955)—and enjoyed some independence from their home government and other entities reflective of a supranational body. The authority had significant antitrust power to protect the common market in coal and steel from anticompetitive mergers or price and wage fixing.[110]

Quasi-legislative authority existed in two ECSC entities. The first was the assembly, which consisted of 78 representatives drawn from the members' parliaments. Its power over the authority included participation in the ECSC budget, supervision of authority members by requesting information, and censure that could dissolve the authority. The second was the Council of Ministers, an instrument of federalism, at which the national governments' economics or industry minister represented it. The council harmonized authority initiatives with national economic policies regarding labor, pricing, and transport. The council controlled the budget and could block authority action.[111]

A final check on the authority was from the Court of Justice, originally with seven judges serving six-year terms, independent from the countries that selected them. A member state or the council could lodge an action with the court to question an authority decision or recommendation based on violation of the ECSC Treaty, law, or procedure.[112] The transitory period for implementing a common market from 1953 to 1958 was a limited success. Production expanded considerably, but governments often defended their national champions as coal

---

[109] GILBERT, *supra* note 63, at 10, 24-29, 33, 35; HOGAN, *supra* note 101, at 128-34, 304, 364-68, 372-78; *see* 46 AM. J. INT'L L. 107-48 (Supp. 1952) (English translation of ECSC Treaty) [hereinafter ECSC Treaty]. *See generally* ERNST B. HAAS, THE UNITING OF EUROPE: POLITICAL, SOCIAL, AND ECONOMIC FORCES, 1950-1957 (1958). Schuman was prime minister (1947-1948) and then minister of foreign affairs (1948-1953). Monnet was head of the Plan Commission (*Commissariat Général du Plan*, 1946-1952) and then president of the European Coal and Steel Community High Authority (1952-1955). MILWARD, *supra* note 104, at 129 n.7, 153 n.43.

[110] GILBERT, *supra* note 63, at 35-36; *see* ECSC Treaty, *supra* note 109, arts. 8-19; HAAS, *supra* note 109, at 75-83.

[111] GILBERT, *supra* note 63, at 36-37; see ECSC Treaty, *supra* note 109, arts. 20-30.

[112] GILBERT, *supra* note 63, at 37; *see* ECSC Treaty, *supra* note 109, arts. 31-45; Eric Stein, *The European Coal and Steel Community: The Beginning of Its Judicial Process*, 55 COLUM. L. REV. 985-99 (1955).

lost market share to oil. Near the end of the period, the authority was reluctant to act without prior approval from the council.[113]

Unlike American military occupation in Germany, Japan, and Korea, the U.S. State Department's endorsement of European federalism and antitrust reform relied more subtly on economic and political pressure. Mark Gilbert contended that U.S. President Dwight Eisenhower's administration (1953-1961) was strongly committed to European unity with financial and political support through defense, trade, and monetary entities that promoted trade liberalization despite a detrimental impact on U.S. steel exports. European integration in the 1950s was a collaborative effort between the United States and European nations.[114]

Turning to antitrust law, we saw how the Potsdam Agreement's economic principles included German decartelization and decentralization. German jurists supportive of an effective competition law, including Kronstein, helped shape Allied economic policy for European antitrust law, first set out in the ECSC Treaty.[115] Kronstein's relationship to Walter Hallstein, a colleague on the Frankfurt law faculty and state secretary at the German foreign ministry from 1951 to 1958, facilitated Kronstein's influence on European cartel law, especially for the 1958 Rome Treaty creating the European Economic Community (EEC). Hallstein became the first president of the EEC Commission (1958-1967).[116]

Kronstein's writing in the United States analyzed the control model of cartels, dependent on administrators. Germany and a few smaller nations had used it during the 1920s and 1930s. He concluded that it was ineffective in preventing massive concentration of economic power and subsequent economic and social chaos. The task of regulating cartels proved too complex for administrators, whom the cartels also unduly influenced, and courts were usually unwilling to intervene. The American prohibition system was better suited for modern industrial economies. It assumed that preserving economic freedom and equal bargaining power for contractual relationships best served the public interest.[117]

---

[113] GILBERT, *supra* note 63, at 38-39.

[114] *Id.* at 58-59. "European integration, like most exotic blooms, needed a favorable climate to be able to grow: the United States built and maintained the glass house necessary for its survival." *Id.* at 59.

[115] Gerber, *supra* note 64, at 162; Rehbinder, *supra* note 65, at 395; ECSC Treaty, *supra* note 109, arts. 2-5, 65-67; *see supra* text accompanying notes 63-67 (Kronstein and German antitrust law).

[116] GILBERT, *supra* note 62, at 55, 78-83; MILWARD, *supra* note 104, at 412 n.114 (Hallstein); Rehbinder, *supra* note 65, at 384-85, 395; see EEC Treaty, *supra* note 109, arts. 85-90.

[117] Gerber, *supra* note 64, at 162-67; *see* Heinrich Kronstein & Gertrude Leighton, *Cartel Control: A Record of Failure*, 55 YALE L.J. 297-335 (1946); Kronstein, *The Dynamics of German Cartels and Patents I & II*, 9 U. CHI. L. REV. 643-71 (1942); 10 *id.* at 49-69 (1942).

Friedmann's service in the Allied military government in Germany probably affected his scholarship on public corporations in a national economy, cartels and antitrust law, and supranational organizations such as the ECSC. However, his commitment to common law nations reduced the influence his writing might have had in Germany or continental Europe.[118] In 1954, he published an article on the ECSC, which he found rejected previous European economic philosophy and derived its key provisions from U.S. law on free trade, cartels, and antitrust dating back to the 1890 Sherman Act. He believed the ECSC's dual aims of creating limited supranational government and fostering decartelization and deconcentration in the coal and steel industries was overly ambitious. The latter goal stemmed from policy that the Allied military government implemented as a central part of German reorganization. When Germany joined the European initiative, either the antitrust goal would recede or would apply to the entire community to avoid discrimination. German Chancellor Adenauer and his influential minister of economics, Ludwig Erhard, favored the open, integrated common market option.[119]

B. Re-establishing Comparative Law as an Academic Discipline

By the twentieth century, American comparative law began to form as an organized activity, with its own structure, journal, and annual meetings. This process was uneven, but steady. When the Comparative Law Bureau folded into a more comprehensive ABA Section, the American Foreign Law Association (AFLA) kept the flame alive. Comparatists dealt with more complex methods and issues, some debated at international meetings. They developed the first American comparative law casebooks to educate students in the discipline. Nevertheless, the full flowering of American comparative law bloomed only after the Second World War, with a healthy push by émigré scholars from Europe. This process accelerated with the economic and cultural impetus of globalization after 1990, which involved most aspects of law ranging from business, the family, and individual human rights as well as larger issues of legal institution building.

---

[118] *See* W. FRIEDMANN, THE ALLIED MILITARY GOVERNMENT OF GERMANY (1947); *supra* text accompanying notes 68–72 (Friedmann).
[119] W. Friedmann, *The European Coal and Steel Community*, 10 INT'L J. 12–15, 17–19, 23 (1954); *see* Gerhard Bebr, *The European Coal and Steel Community: A Political and Legal Innovation*, 63 YALE L.J. 1–10, 36–44 (1953). The United States had a permanent representative at the ECSC's High Authority. *Id.* at 41.

1. The ABA Section of International and Comparative Law

Shortly after the end of World War II, American and European comparatists made concerted efforts to place comparative law studies on a firmer institutional basis. The principal U.S. national organization for comparative law was the ABA Section of International and Comparative Law (ABA Section). In 1945, among the section's committees in the Comparative Law Division were those suggesting its ambition associated with the world's regions: European Law, Far Eastern Law, Latin American Law, and Near Eastern Law. Phanor Eder (1880–1971), a New York lawyer specializing in Latin America, was director of the division. There were 967 members in the entire section at that time.[120] In 1946, a new committee, Teaching of International and Comparative Law, had 11 professors from different law schools as members plus William Bishop, assistant legal adviser at the U.S. State Department, who joined the Michigan law faculty in 1948.[121]

In 1947, John Hazard (1909–1995), professor at Columbia Law School and chair of the ABA Section's Committee on European Law,[122] arranged with the *Wisconsin Law Review* to print eight papers on trends in foreign law in European countries, explaining that he included Japan due to the impact of German law plus the recent overlay of U.S. law on the Japanese legal system. Reflecting the influence of legal realism on American comparative law, Hazard, an expert on

---

[120] ABA SEC. INT'L & COMP. L. PROC. ix–xi (1945); William B. Cowles, *Report of the Committee on Membership*, id. at 135, 136. In 1945, the section's periodical had the title *Proceedings of the Section of International and Comparative Law*, which it maintained until 1951. From 1952 until its last volume in 1965, the title was *Section of International and Comparative Law: Proceedings* [hereinafter ABA SEC. INT'L & COMP. L. PROC.]; *see supra* ch. 6, pt. H.1 (ABA Section).

Eder, a U.S. citizen, was born in Columbia and later educated in New York, England, and Belgium before he earned his law degree in 1903 at Harvard. A lifelong supporter of comparative law, he participated in the Comparative Law Bureau and then the ABA Section, helped organize the 1932 and 1937 Hague international congresses, and served as AFLA president in 1934. He also taught at New York University's Inter-American Law Institute. His books included *A Comparative Survey of Anglo-American and Latin-American Law* (1950) and *American-Colombian Private International Law* (1956). *Phanor James Eder*, 18 AM. J. COMP. L. 479–81 (1970) [hereinafter *Eder*]; *see supra* ch. 6, text accompanying notes 134, 305, 325 (Eder).

[121] ABA SEC. INT'L & COMP. L. PROC. vii (1946). Bishop and John Dawson at Michigan prepared *Materials on Comparative Law* (1935) (411 pp.). ELIZABETH GASPAR BROWN & WILLIAM WIRT BLUME, LEGAL EDUCATION AT MICHIGAN: 1859–1959, at 823 (1959).

[122] John N. Hazard, *UNESCO and the Law*, 4 REC. ASS'N B. CITY N.Y. 291 (1949). After Hazard's graduation from Harvard Law School in 1934, he studied Soviet law at the Moscow Juridical Institute until 1937. During the war, he served as deputy director of the USSR Branch of the FEA. When he joined the Columbia faculty in 1946, he founded the Russian Institute, which carried out legal and political studies. Hazard published many books on Soviet law and politics, notably *Law and Social Change in the U.S.S.R.* (1953), *The Soviet System of Government* (1957, 5th ed. 1980), and *The Soviet Legal System: Post-Stalin Documentation and Historical Commentary* (with Isaac Shapiro, 1962). Edward Re, *John N. Hazard*, 43 AM. J. COMP. L. xiii–xiv (1995); Hazard, *supra*, at 291; *see supra* text accompanying note 27 (FEA).

Soviet law, stated, "the analysis of law cannot be separated from the economic and political conditions existing in a country."[123] Since several postwar regimes in Europe had increased the role of the state in the general economy or in certain industries or economic sectors, including nationalization of the central bank, committee members speculated on whether these changes would continue based on the pattern set in the Soviet Union.[124]

John Tucker of Louisiana, chair of the Committee on Comparative Civil Procedure and Practice, presented a resolution in 1947 to appoint a special committee to study separation of the Comparative Law Division from the ABA Section and creation of a periodical devoted to comparative law. He noted that some comparatists believed that the section ignored valid interests that their field required. The European Law and Far Eastern Law committee chairs endorsed the resolution.[125]

The ABA Section's Committee on Latin American Law reported that the Law Library of Congress, in 1949, had established the Center of Latin American Legal Studies. Its first project was to index and digest legal norms from Latin American countries buried in almost 11,000 official gazettes as well as legal commentary in an equal number of daily newspapers that the Law Library received in fiscal year 1950.[126] Through the 1950s, the Comparative Law Division within the ABA Section remained active with an increasing number of committees, a few of which continued a scholarly perspective or interest in comparative jurisprudence or foreign law in the principal regions of the world.[127]

---

[123] John N. Hazard, *Trends in Foreign Law: Foreword*, 1947 WISC. L. REV. 6 (1947) [hereinafter Hazard, *Trends*]; *see id.*, *Report of the Committee on European Law*, ABA SEC. INT'L & COMP. L. PROC. 90–91 (1947) (among countries studied, the "trends toward socialism have been so extensive as to become dominant.").

[124] Hazard, *Trends*, *supra* note 123, at 6. In his essay on the Soviet Union, Hazard pointed out that recent changes in the law did not affect the basic Marxist theses on which it existed. Jurisprudence reflected the will of the ruling class it served, determined by the economic conditions of the class. Law was politics and the Soviet state was an apparatus for the proletariat to achieve a socialist and ultimately a communist economy. John N. Hazard, *The Trend of Law in the U.S.S.R.*, 1947 WISC. L. REV. 223–24, 243 (1947); *see* Benjamin H. Conner, *The Trend of the Law in France*, *id.* at 19, 29–30; Henry Van Dam, *The Trend towards Nationalization in the Law of the Netherlands*, *id.* at 244–60; Angelo Piero Sereni, *Legislative Trends of Democratic Italy*, *id.* at 357, 361–63; Paul J. Edwards, *The Trend of Law in Czechoslovakia*, *id.* at 654, 674–79.

[125] Lyman M. Tondel, Jr., *Summary of Cleveland, Ohio Meeting*, ABA SEC. INT'L & COMP. L. PROC. 6, 8 (1947); John H. Tucker, Jr., *Report of the Committee on Comparative Civil Procedure and Practice*, *id.* at 89.

[126] Victor C. Folsom, *Report of the Committee on Latin American Law*, ABA SEC. INT'L & COMP. L. PROC. 93, 103–04 (1950).

[127] *Committees of the Section*, ABA SEC. INT'L & COMP. L. PROC. 6, 7 (1960). In 1960, there were 12 comparative law committees plus the international and comparative law teaching committee in the General Committees Division. *Id.* at 7–8.

2. UNESCO, the AFLA, and the AALS

In 1949, Hazard and other U.S. comparatists decided to take advantage of working with the United Nations Educational, Scientific, and Cultural Organization (UNESCO) to institutionalize comparative law. The UNESCO deputy director had written Hazard, as chair of the ABA Section's Committee on Comparative Jurisprudence, to ask for guidance as to what the organization could do in the field of comparative law to aid international understanding and peace. This was part of a broader UNESCO program to develop international institutes of social science. Professors Hazard, Arthur von Mehren (Harvard), Ernst Rabel (Michigan), and leading comparatists from other nations met in Paris in 1949 to discuss the possibilities. As a result, UNESCO created and funded the International Committee for Comparative Law (ICCL) to coordinate activities among national organizations, which would be ICCL members. The latter's aims were to disseminate information about national law via research guides, exchange students and professors, and encourage law school teaching of foreign and comparative law. At the ABA's Section meeting in 1949, it adopted a resolution pledging support to the ICCL for its purposes within the United States.[128]

In 1950, the ICCL held its first meeting in London and then in Paris, where it admitted 13 national committees including one for the United States represented by the AFLA. The AFLA (with Eder as president at the time), began in the New York City area as an entity for practitioners interested in foreign law.[129] It needed to broaden its membership (about 170 in 1950) to include both more law professors (represented by Hessel Yntema, Michigan) and more residents

---

[128] John N. Hazard, *Report of the Committee on Comparative Jurisprudence*, ABA SEC. INT'L & COMP. L. PROC. 145–46 (1949) [hereinafter Hazard, *1949 Jurisprudence Report*]; *id.*, ABA SEC. INT'L & COMP. L. PROC. 86–87 (1950) [hereinafter Hazard, *1950 Jurisprudence Report*] (Hazard referred to the ICCL as an association in 1949); *id.*, UNESCO, *supra* note 122, at 295–304; Hessel E. Yntema, *The American Journal of Comparative Law*, 1 AM. J. COMP. L. 11–12 (1952) [hereinafter Yntema, *Journal*]; Imre Zajtay, *The International Association of Legal Science: Its Contribution to Comparative Law*, 26 AM. J. COMP. L. 441–42 (1978); *see supra* ch. 6, text accompanying notes 159–60, 282 (Rabel). Hazard also forwarded the UNESCO request to the Committees on European Law and Teaching International and Comparative Law for their responses. Hazard, *1949 Jurisprudence Report, supra*, at 145. He again expressed the realist position that the committee believed that "law as it is currently understood in the United States is more than a body of rules. It is a reflection of political, economic, sociological and philosophical conditions . . . properly the subject for research and study as an integral part of law itself." *Id.* The ICCL could admit international organizations, such as the Rome International Institute for the Unification of Private Law, as associate members. IALS, *Members*, http://www.aisj-ials.net/home/IALS_members.html (Rome Institute).

[129] Hazard, *1950 Jurisprudence Report, supra* note 128, at 86–87; *see* Leon H. Doman, *50th Anniversary of the American Foreign Law Association, Inc.*, 23 AM. J. COMP. L. 132–38 (1975) (AFLA history); *supra* ch. 6, pt. E.2 (AFLA). Hazard also reported on the Third International Congress of Comparative Law held in London in 1950. Most European delegates favored a return to some form of natural law to preserve Western values; some American representatives supported another legal philosophy to achieve that goal. Hazard, *supra*, at 86.

from beyond the Eastern Seaboard. In 1951, it organized chapters in Chicago and Miami, and by 1952, it listed 38 law professors out of a total membership of 253.[130] Both Germany and the United Kingdom in 1950 also created national committees for comparative law.[131] The AFLA appointed Alexis Coudert (1914–1980), a partner in the Coudert Brothers law firm in New York City, as delegate who became a member of the ICCL's executive bureau.[132]

By 1952, the committee had accepted 20 national members and one associate member, the Rome Institute.[133] A council and bureau conducted the ICCL's business. Each national committee had one delegate to the council, which elected the rotating members of the seven-person bureau. The bureau took on an organizational element from the U.N. Security Council: it had three permanent members—France, the United States, and the United Kingdom. The bureau's first secretary-general was René David, an eminent French comparatist. The ICCL determined to concentrate its activity on comparative law publications and bibliographies since most of its budget depended on UNESCO and contributions by national representatives.[134]

Comparative law also moved forward on other fronts. In a 1951 survey of AALS member schools, 26 reported that they offered at least one course in comparative law broadly defined, which could include Roman law, Latin American law, or introduction to the civil law.[135] Although that was only half of the number of schools teaching international law, due to Hazard's initiative, the AALS in 1950 created the Committee on Comparative Law, which was now independent

---

[130] Bernhard C.H. Aubin, *Mitteilungen: American Foreign Law Association*, 16 ZEITSCHRIFT FÜR AUSLANDISCHES UND INTERNATIONALS PRIVATRECHT [hereinafter RABELSZ] 179 (1951) (Rabel's name first used for volume 26 in 1961); Phanor J. Eder, *Reports: American Foreign Law Association*, 1 AM. J. COMP. L. 190 (1952); *American Foreign Law Association Membership List*, 1 *id*. at 468–73 [hereinafter *AFLA Membership*].

[131] C.J. Hamson, *International Committee for Comparative Law*, 2 INT'L & COMP. L.Q. 112, 117–18 (1953); ELMAR WADLE, EINHUNDERT JAHRE RECHTSVERGLEICHENDE GESELLSCHAFTEN IN DEUTSCHLAND 73–87 (1994).

[132] John N. Hazard, *Report of the Committee on Comparative Jurisprudence*, ABA SEC. INT'L & COMP. L. PROC. 93 (1951); *see American Foreign Law Association*, 2 AM. J. COMP. L. 294–96 (1953) (revised AFLA constitution and bylaws); VIRGINIA KAYS VEENSWIJK, COUDERT BROTHERS, A LEGACY IN LAW: THE HISTORY OF AMERICA'S FIRST INTERNATIONAL LAW FIRM, 1853–1993 (1994).

[133] Bernhard Aubin, *Mitteilungen: Internationales Komitee für Rechtsvergleichung*, 18 RABELSZ 331–32 (1953); Alexis Coudert, *International Committee of Comparative Law*, 2 AM. J. COMP. L. 128 (1953). From mid-1956 through 1963, Yntema served as the AFLA's delegate to the ICCL. In 1956, Coudert, Hazard, and Yntema were vice presidents of the AFLA. *See Reports: American Foreign Law Association*, 5 AM. J. COMP. L. 333 (1956); H.E. Y[ntema], *Reports: International Committee of Comparative Law*, 5 *id*. at 704; Hessel E. Yntema, MICH. L. REV. 977, 980–81 (1966) [hereinafter *Yntema 1966*].

[134] Hans Dölle, *Mitteilungen: Vorbereitung einer internationalen Vereinigung für Rechtsvergleichung durch die UNESCO*, 15 RABELSZ 186 (1949–1950); Hamson, *supra* note 131, at 113–16; *Mitteilungen: Internationales Komitee für Rechtsvergleichung*, 16 RABELSZ 331–32 (1951); *see* IALS, *Statutes*, http://www.aisj-ials.net (select Statutes) [hereinafter *IALS Statutes*] (arts. 4, 9, 15).

[135] Edward D. Re, *Report of the Committee on Comparative Civil Procedure and Practice*, ABA SEC. INT'L & COMP. L. PROC. 90–93 (1951).

of the AALS International Law Committee. The Comparative Law Committee's primary responsibility was to organize one or two panels of experts to present reports or commentary at the AALS annual meeting of law professors on salient foreign and comparative law matters. Hazard was the first committee chair in 1951 and Von Mehren chaired the committee's annual program from 1952 to 1953.[136]

C. The American Association for the Comparative Study of Law

1. Structure and Membership of the Organization

Many of the law school affiliated members of the AFLA believed that comparative law needed an organization principally of law school sponsors, which could support a quality journal dedicated to the subject, like those existing in France, Germany, Great Britain, and Italy. Since the United States did not have a funded institute or center of comparative law like those in Berlin or Paris, Americans would need to invent the functional equivalent. The result was a journal and sponsoring organization much like Rabel's Institute in Berlin.[137] In 1950, Kurt Nadelmann (1900–1984), a visiting law professor at the University of Pennsylvania, initiated the AFLA *Bulletin* to report on comparative law activities, publications, and relevant judicial decisions. Nadelmann had received his law doctorate from Freiburg University in 1921, followed by a career in the German judiciary. In 1933, he left for Paris, where after earning the *licence en droit* the bar admitted him to practice law, but he fled to the United States in 1941. The *Bulletin* served as the forerunner for an American comparative law journal. Hazard and Yntema, then an AFLA vice president, took the lead in soliciting comparatists at a few leading law schools in the effort to create the journal and a supporting organization.[138]

---

[136] ASSOCIATION OF AMERICAN LAW SCHOOLS: 1951 PROCEEDINGS 1, 95, 137–39, 346, 51 (1952); John N. Hazard, *Reports: Committee on Comparative Law, Association of American Law Schools*, 1 AM. J. COMP. L. 191 (1952); *Reports: Association of American Law Schools*, 2 *id.* at 293 (1953).

[137] David S. Clark, *The Influence of Ernst Rabel on American Law*, in DER EINFLUSS, *supra* note 64, at 107, 116–17; Yntema, *Journal, supra* note 128, at 13–15, 17–19.

[138] Aubin, *supra* note 130, at 179–80; Eder, *supra* note 120, at 480; Phanor J. Eder, *Greetings*, 1 AM. J. COMP. L. 188 (1952); *Kurt Hans Nadelmann*, 32 AM. J. COMP. L. 402 (1984) [hereinafter *Nadelmann*]; Yntema, *Journal, supra* note 128, at 21; *see supra* ch. 5, pt. F.1 (France and Germany). Eder and Yntema agreed that the AACSL and its journal should reflect both the academic and practical dimensions of comparative law. Eder, *supra*, at 188; Yntema, *supra*, at 14–15. Nadelmann began teaching as a visiting law professor at Pennsylvania (1947–1950), then as a lecturer at NYU (1949–1963) and research scholar at Harvard (1961–1965), achieving a professorship in 1965. He continued editing the *Bulletin* for publication in the *American Journal of Comparative Law*. Nadelmann, *supra*, at 402.

The new entity was the American Association for the Comparative Study of Law (AACSL), whose directors filed its certificate of incorporation with the New York Department of State in 1951.[139] The founders believed that comparative law was too vast a field for a single institution to preempt it, and, even if possible, it would be undesirable in a nation as diverse as the United States. Some also thought the president should not be a full-time professor, again to avoid capture by that person's law school. These attitudes precluded tying the association or its journal financially to the Parker School of Foreign and Comparative Law at Columbia University or the new Tulane Institute of Comparative Law and the *Tulane Law Review*. Although the Parker School was a founding AACSL member, Tulane only joined in 1956.[140]

The AACSL held its first meeting in July 1951 during the ABA annual meeting. Representatives of 20 law schools met at NYU Law School to discuss joining the association. Ten schools (Columbia through the Parker School) plus the AFLA joined as sponsor members, each with one director who enjoyed governance responsibility for the AACSL and one editor, who could be the same person. To provide adequate funding for a journal, this membership level had annual dues of $500 and was also open to institutes, bar associations, and other entities with a comparative law interest. Law firms, corporations, schools, or individuals could join as sustaining members with dues set at $100. Lawyers and law school faculty members not otherwise participating could join for $25 as associate members. Without a fee, the directors could admit relevant foreign entities as corresponding members.[141]

---

[139] Yntema, *Journal*, *supra* note 128, at 16. The association's incorporation certificate stated its purpose: "to promote the comparative study of law and the understanding of foreign legal systems; to establish, maintain, and publish without profit a comparative law journal; and to provide for research and the publication without profit of writings, books, papers, and pamphlets relating to comparative, foreign, or private international law." Quoted in Yntema, *Journal*, *supra*, at 16.

[140] *Board of Editors*, 1 AM. J. COMP. L. ii (1952); 5 *id.* at ii (1956); Arthur T. von Mehren, *The American Society of Comparative Law: The Early Days*, 10 WILLAMETTE J. INT'L L. & DISP. RESOL. 7, 8–9 (2002); *see supra* ch. 6, notes 281, 318 and accompanying text (Parker School); text accompanying notes 185–87 (Tulane Institute). Judge Edwin Parker left most of his estate in trust to support a school that would train students in foreign affairs. The trustees, including Supreme Court Justice Harlan Stone, Henry Stimson (secretary of state), and William Mitchell (attorney general and head of the American delegation to the 1932 Hague Congress), exercised their power in 1931 to select Columbia University as the site for what would be the Parker School of Foreign and Comparative Law. In the 1950s, the Parker School had an ambitious publication program that resulted in twelve books on foreign and comparative law. Columbia Law School, *About the Parker School*, https://parker-school.law.columbia.edu/content/about-parker-school.

[141] *Reports: American Association for the Comparative Study of Law*, 1 AM. J. COMP. L. 189–90 (1952) [hereinafter 1952 *Reports*]. The initial sponsor members and their directors and editors were the AFLA (Eder, Nadelmann), Chicago (Rheinstein), Columbia's Parker School (Coudert, Hazard), Georgetown (Kronstein), Harvard (Cavers, Von Mehren), Indiana (Jerome Hall), Louisiana State University (LSU, Joseph Dainow), Miami (Russell Rasco, David Stern), Michigan (Yntema), NYU (Miguel de Capriles, Walter Derenberg), and Yale (Myres McDougal). *Id.* By the time the association's *Journal* published its first issue in 1952, two more schools had joined as sponsor members, making a total of 13: California (Albert Ehrenzwieg) and Cornell (Rudolf Schlesinger). 1 *id.* at ii, 189–90.

Until 1970, the AACSL held its half-day or evening annual meeting in New York City.[142] During the first two decades, most directors and editors lived near the East Coast, which also provided convenient access to AFLA meetings. In fact, a series of AFLA presidents were influential AACSL representatives and officers. Those included AFLA presidents, all who worked in New York City, Eder (1948–1952), Coudert (1959–1963), Willis Reese (1966–1969), Edward Re (1971–1973), and Hazard (1973–1975).[143]

As the AACSL's incorporation certificate stated, its purpose was "to promote the comparative study of law and the understanding of foreign legal systems." This would include research about "comparative, foreign, or private international law."[144] The parameters for this conception of comparative law likely came from the leading research entity of comparative law, the Institute for Foreign and International Private Law, created in Berlin in 1926.[145] Moved to Tübingen during the war, thereafter it prospered as a comparative law institute and library under the umbrella of the Max Planck Gesellschaft when it moved to Hamburg.[146] Several of the association's founders, familiar with the institute and its first director, Rabel, followed the pattern of its research coverage. Thus, most of the AACSL's members, activities, and journal articles in the first two decades focused on private rather than public law. In addition, they saw comparative law broadly conceived as including unification of law and private international law (usually called conflict of laws in the United States) as well as foreign and comparative law strictly defined.[147]

The AACSL directors elected Eder president, Yntema (1891–1966) vice president, Coudert secretary, and David Cavers (1902–1988) treasurer.[148] This election continued the pattern of mixing scholarly and practice-oriented interests that had characterized American comparative law since its beginning. Both Eder and Coudert were prestigious New York City attorneys involved in foreign practice, although all the remaining directors were full-time law professors. Coudert

---

[142] AACSL minutes of the sponsor members and board of directors [hereinafter AACSL minutes], author's copy.

[143] [AFLA] *President's Report 1983/84*, 32 Am. J. Comp. L. 610, 613 (1984).

[144] *See supra* note 139 (incorporation certificate).

[145] *See supra* ch. 6, text accompanying notes 156–59 (Berlin Institute).

[146] *See* Robert A. Riegert, *The Max Planck Institute for Foreign and International Private Law*, 21 Ala. L. Rev. 475–500 (1969).

[147] *See, e.g.*, T.H. Reynolds, *Book Notice*, 25 Am. J. Comp. L. 596–97 (1977); *infra* pts. F.2 and 3 (unification of law and private international law). In 1977, the Hamburg Institute published a bibliography, derived from its library resources, of 9,600 articles, book chapters, and congress reports that had appeared over the preceding five years. The volume's title mirrored the AACSL's research concerns, absent public law. Reynolds, *supra*, at 596.

[148] 1952 *Reports*, *supra* note 141, at 190; *see supra* ch. 6, pt. E.3 (Yntema). Cavers was a Harvard Law School professor from 1945 to 1969. His principal field was conflict of laws and he was best known for his volume, *The Choice of Law Process* (1965), which developed his principles of preference. Erwin N. Griswold, *David F. Cavers*, 51 Law & Contemp. Prob. i, iv (no. 3, 1988).

was also a law professor at Columbia and acting director of its Parker School from 1949 to 1955, when he succeeded Eder as AACSL president.[149] Eder then held the status of honorary president until his death in 1971.[150]

The central figures in forming the AACSL, implementing its journal, and assisting U.S. comparative law, private international law, and the gradual expansion of the association up to 1970 were a mixture of native-born and émigré comparatists.[151] Two in the latter category—Kronstein (Georgetown) and Rheinstein (Chicago)—had earlier served the United States with its law reform efforts in occupied Germany and those related to German and European cartel law.[152] Four other initial émigré representatives also had significant influence: Miguel de Capriles (NYU), Albert Ehrenzweig (California Berkeley), Nadelmann (AFLA, NYU, Harvard), and Rudolf Schlesinger (Cornell). Among the principal initial indigenous comparatists were Coudert (Parker School, AFLA), Eder (AFLA), Hazard (Columbia), Cavers (Harvard), Von Mehren (Harvard), and Yntema (Michigan).[153]

The association grew slowly through the 1950s and 1960s. In 1955, directors voted to establish a comparative law book prize for outstanding publications. It awarded the first prize to the French legal scholars André and Suzanne Tunc.[154] In 1958, the Ford Foundation provided a two-year $20,000 grant to study improvement in the scholarly dimension of the organization, including an annual program for comparatists, translation or bibliography projects, and aid toward comparative law teaching materials. By 1960, the AACSL had 20 sponsor members, all law schools except the AFLA, and the representatives discussed the possibility of it joining the American Council of Learned Societies.[155]

---

[149] A HISTORY OF THE SCHOOL OF LAW: COLUMBIA UNIVERSITY 366 (Julius Goebel, Jr. ed., 1955) [hereinafter COLUMBIA LAW]; *Reports: American Association for the Comparative Study of Law*, 4 AM. J. COMP. L. 482 (1955); *Board of Editors*, 5 AM. J. COMP. L. ii (1956). In 1955, Willis Reese became director of the Parker School and its director to the AACSL, while Coudert became the AFLA's director. *Reports, supra*, at 482.

[150] Eder, *supra* note 120, at 479.

[151] *See supra* note 141 (1952 list of directors and journal editors with their affiliation). For a valuable study of the influence of émigré jurists on American legal education, see Mathias W. Reimann, *We Are All Globalists Now—The Heritage of the Émigré Jurists for American Legal Education in the Second Half of the Twentieth Century*, in GLOBALIZATION AND THE U.S. LAW SCHOOL: COMPARATIVE AND CULTURAL PERSPECTIVES, 1906–2006, at 101–19 (Stephen C. Hicks & Kjell Å. Modéer eds., 2009) [hereinafter Reimann, *Globalists*].

[152] *See supra* text accompanying notes 64–67, 115–17 (Kronstein) and text accompanying notes 61–62 (Rheinstein).

[153] *See* AACSL minutes, *supra* note 142.

[154] *Comparative Law Prize*, 5 AM. J. COMP. L. 168 (1956); *see* ANDRÉ TUNC & SUZANNE TUNC, 1–2 LE SYSTÈME CONSTITUTIONNEL DES ÉTATS-UNIS D'AMÉRIQUE (1954), *id.*, LE DROIT DES ÉTATS-UNIS D'AMÉRIQUE: SOURCES ET TECHNIQUES (1955); Hessel E. Yntema, *Book Review*, 5 AM. J. COMP. L. 673–78 (1956) (reviewing all three volumes).

[155] Alexis C. Coudert, *American Association for the Comparative Study of Law, Inc.*, 3 SEC. INT'L & COMP. L. BULL. 27–28 (no. 2, May 1959); 9 AM. J. COMP. L. ii (1960); *see* AACSL minutes, *supra* note 142. There were two sustaining university law schools, Puerto Rico and Utah. *Id.*

During the 1950s, the association was small enough that the actual number of representatives who attended an annual meeting—typically a dozen—approximated a collegial social gathering. Regular attendees who had joined included Edward Re (St. John's, AFLA) and Willis Reese (1913–1990). Reese became director of the Parker School in 1955, which he represented as its AACSL director until 1981. Directors typically re-elected officers for one-year terms so long as they participated. In 1960, the directors amended the bylaws to authorized an executive committee (consisting of the officers and the editor in chief) to exercise authority between meetings.[156]

In 1960, AACSL directors elected Miguel de Capriles (1906–1981) president after Coudert became AFLA president. De Capriles had previously served as secretary and was the founder in 1947 of NYU's Inter-American Law Institute. Reese (Parker School) took the office of secretary and Yntema remained as vice president and William Barnes (Harvard) as treasurer.[157] De Capriles had emigrated from Mexico to New York at the end of World War I, earned a law degree from NYU, served with the Department of Justice, and then accepted a law professorship at NYU after World War II. He was NYU law dean from 1964 to 1967, when he became university general counsel.[158]

For the association's first decade, given member backgrounds, their interests focused on the German and French legal systems, with secondary concern for the legal systems of the Soviet Union (Hazard) and Latin American (Eder and De Capriles). Latin America in this context primarily meant Mexico, Argentina, Colombia, and Cuba. In addition, several representatives contributed significantly to private international law or unification of law. Notably, Nadelmann was indefatigable in involving the AACSL in those two subjects.[159] In 1963, the ICCL (now the International Association of Legal Science), named the AACSL its American delegate and national committee despite its small number of members.[160]

During the 1960s, new law schools that joined as sponsor members included representatives who actively participated in the AACSL and broadened its

---

[156] AACSL minutes, *supra* note 142; *Willis L.M. Reese*, 38 AM. J. COMP. L. following 422 (1990). Reese had joined the Columbia law faculty in 1946. COLUMBIA LAW, *supra* note 149, at 362–63.

[157] *Reports: American Association for the Comparative Study of Law*, 9 AM. J. COMP. L. 328 (1960); *Varia: Inter-American Law Institute of New York University School of Law*, 2 AM. J. COMP. L. 293 (1953). It is likely Cavers recommended Barnes, who was an administrator at Harvard, for treasurer. Barnes had earned a law doctorate at the University of Geneva. SUTHERLAND, *supra* note 61, at 334–35.

[158] Josh Barbanel, *Miguel de Capriles, Ex-Dean of N.Y.U. Law School*, N.Y. TIMES, 28 May 1981, § D, at 21. De Capriles was on the U.S. Olympic fencing team in 1932 and 1948, winning the bronze medal both times. *Id.*

[159] *See infra* pts. F.2 and 3 (unification of law and private international law).

[160] Hessel E. Yntema, *Reports: International Committee of Comparative Law*, 12 AM. J. COMP. L. 456–57 (1963).

coverage of the world. John Merryman (Stanford), Keith Rosenn (Ohio State), and Wenceslas Wagner (Indiana and Detroit) added Italy, Brazil, and Poland respectively. Friedrich Juenger (Wayne State) and Courtland Peterson (Colorado) later served as association officers and wrote about private international law.[161] In 1964, the AACSL registered its first female representative from a sponsor member, Ruth Bader Ginsburg (1933–2020) at Rutgers University, who served as editor from 1964 to 1972.[162]

By 1970, the association had 34 sponsor members.[163] In 1971, Boston College selected the second woman as director or editor, Mary Ann Glendon. In 1980, the AACSL elected Glendon the organization's secretary. She was the successor to Reese who had carried out that office from 1960.[164] During the 1970s, several of the new active directors and editors had studied comparative law with those who had earlier built the organization. Some learned foreign law when they participated in U.S. governmental or nongovernmental programs of legal development abroad. This second generation of postwar comparatists who attended law school during the 1960s often had a distinct orientation toward the role of law in society and what they could learn from foreign legal systems.

In 1970, the AACSL held its first annual meeting outside New York City, at the University of Michigan. This had the largest attendance up to that time with 30 professors representing 24 sponsors. Meetings typically now took the entire day as the activities of the association had expanded. Elections of officers continued to be pro forma, with annual re-election the general rule without opposition. However, in 1971, Edward Re (1920–2006) replaced Coudert as president and the executive committee expanded to seven members.[165] In 1970, AACSL finances were barely adequate with assets around $55,000. The *Journal* publication cost more to produce than subscription revenue so the association subsidized it with dues from sponsor members. There was also reimbursement for expense of running the *Journal* office and the editors' meeting, which ranged between $8,000 and $12,000. The situation would require adding more sponsor members, raising dues to more than $500, or increasing the *Journal*'s subscription cost.[166]

---

[161] AACSL minutes, *supra* note 142.

[162] Ruth Bader Ginsburg, "A Decent Respect to the Opinions of [Human]Kind": The Value of Comparative Perspective in Constitutional Adjudication, 26 Am. U. Int'l L. Rev. 927 (2011) [hereinafter Ginsburg, *Comparative Perspective*]; AACSL minutes, *supra* note 142.

[163] AACSL minutes, *supra* note 142. There were three sustaining law members, the Fletcher School (Tufts) and the state university law schools of Mississippi and Puerto Rico. *Id.*

[164] 19 Am. J. Comp. L. at ii (1971); *American Association for the Comparative Study of Law*, 29 *id.* at 172–73 (1981).

[165] AACSL minutes, *supra* note 142. Re was born in Italy, moved to the United States and earned a law degree in 1943 at St. John's University and a J.S.D. from NYU in 1950. He taught at St. John's School of Law until he began a judicial career in 1968 with the U.S. Customs Court and then the U.S. Court of International Trade (chief judge 1980–1991). Federal Judicial Center, *Re, Edward Domenic*, https://www.fjc.gov/node/1392896.

[166] AACSL minutes, *supra* note 142. Treasurer Barnes's oral and sometimes written reports lacked clarity, so the true situation was difficult to ascertain. In 1971, Barnes left his administrative post at

In 1976, the directors created a special committee to examine AACSL finances. That committee recommended, to take effect in 1979: (1) selling stock funds and investing in bonds; (2) raising sponsor member dues to $700; and (3) prohibiting law schools from the sustaining member category (whose dues would rise to $500). In 1977, another special committee recommended that the school hosting an annual meeting provide a half-day scholarly program. Directors endorsed these proposals. The pattern of rotating the location of the joint annual meeting of directors and editors at a member school, usually held in the fall, had already begun after 1970, sometimes involving a comparative law presentation.[167]

In 1971, to encourage attendance at annual meetings, the directors set a total reimbursement budget for representatives at $4,000. With John Fleming (California Berkeley) the new editor in chief and the shift of editorial offices, the AACSL also established a subsidy to the editor of $7,500 (increased to $12,500 in 1972 and $15,000 in 1977) plus reimbursement for office and secretarial costs. By 1974, the total annual meeting expenses reimbursed to members increased to $9,300. In 1979, the scholarly program (at Harvard) was the *Journées Juridiques Franco-Américaines*, the first bilateral meeting of the AACSL with the *Société de Législation Comparée*. That year, the association admitted its first foreign sponsor member, the *Universidad Nacional Autónoma de México Instituto de Investigaciones Jurídicas*.[168]

The association continued to grow steadily with 42 sponsor members in 1980. During this decade there was an increased number of American law schools and interest in comparative law. By 1990, the AACSL had 69 sponsor members.[169] Courtland Peterson (1930–2010), treasurer since 1979, began to put the association's finances in order with interim and annual transparent reports on assets, revenues, and expenses. In 1980, the organization had a cash balance of $23,000 and $37,000 in reserves. The directors approved a standard meeting reimbursement policy to attract attendance, which was a ceiling of $500 to a sponsor member director or editor. Dues were now $700. In addition, the association would reimburse officers and invited speakers up to $500. The subsidy

---

Harvard for a professorship at Tufts University Fletcher School of Law and Diplomacy, which joined the AACSL as a sustaining member. This allowed Barnes to maintain his AACSL position, but with some malfeasance in collecting dues, questionable reports, and failure to file required IRS nonprofit tax forms, the Fletcher School resigned and the directors elected Courtland Peterson treasurer effective January 1979. *Id.*; *see* Detlev F. Vagts, *Foreword*, *in* THE LAW & POLICY OF INTERNATIONAL BUSINESS, SELECTED ISSUES: A FESTSCHRIFT FOR WILLIAM SPRAGUE BARNES (John R. Lacey ed., 1991).

[167] AACSL minutes, *supra* note 142. Schools willing to host an annual meeting needed to submit a proposal to the AACSL executive committee. *Id.*

[168] AACSL minutes, *supra* note 142; *Journées Juridiques Franco-Américaines*, 28 AM. J. COMP. L. 150 (1980); *see* George Ginsburgs, *Journées Juridiques*, 18 AM. J. COMP. L. 621–22 (1970) (book review). Due to Mexico's 1982 debt crisis, the institute was a member only until 1983. AACSL minutes, *supra*.

[169] 28 AM. J. COMP. L. at ii (1980); 38 *id.* at ii (1990); AACSL minutes, *supra* note 142.

to Berkeley for the release time of the *Journal*'s editor and assistant increased to $17,500.[170]

With the expanded number of representatives attending AACSL meetings and the rotation among member schools with a variety of comparative law emphases, the quality and diversity of scholarly programs improved during the 1980s. Beyond Europe and Latin America, participating comparatists added specialties in East Asian legal systems. From 1980 to 1990, the association held meetings at Berkeley, Tulane (twice), Colorado (and Denver), Columbia (twice), Louisiana State, Washington (with a program on Japanese law), Brigham Young (BYU), Puerto Rico, and Montréal. Organization reserves grew to $112,000 despite the increased *Journal* subsidy to $25,000 and meeting expenses varying between $11,000 and $29,000.[171]

AACSL initiatives and foundation grants assisted an improved financial stability. David Clark (Tulsa) and Stephen Wood (BYU) in 1981 solicited large corporations with foreign trade to become sustaining members, gaining ten new ones paying $500 annual dues. The Dana Foundation awarded $10,800 to support members attending the International Academy of Comparative Law quadrennial congress in Caracas (1982) and $10,000 for the bilateral *Journées Juridiques* in Paris (1983). New members supported making the association attractive to more institutions. In 1982, directors amended the bylaws to permit membership for ABA-approved schools that did not have AALS certification and in 1987, expansion of the executive committee to include four non-officer members serving a two-year term. In 1989, the directors elected two younger representatives, Cole Durham (BYU) as secretary and Clark as treasurer.[172]

Finally, in 1990, the AACSL established a democratic system of election after study by Peterson and the executive committee (officers, editor in chief, and four representatives) still in place in 2020. First, all offices except *Journal* editor would be for two-year terms filled by director vote between two candidates selected by the nominating committee. Second, new bylaws created the office of honorary president and staggered terms of office so that only half the posts were up for election in each year. Third, the president, vice president, secretary, and treasurer were eligible for a second term, capping service in those positions at four years.

---

[170] AACSL minutes, *supra* note 142. Peterson earned his law degree at the University of Colorado in 1953 and joined the law faculty in 1959. He continued his studies at the University of Chicago, receiving a master's in comparative law and a Dr. Jur. at the University of Freiburg. His primary field of scholarship was private international law. See *University of Colorado School of Law: Faculty*, 51 U. COLO. L. REV. at x (1979).

[171] AACSL minutes, *supra* note 142. In 1987, the University of Saskatchewan College of Law was the first Canadian school to join the AACSL, followed by McGill University Institute of Comparative Law in 1989. *Id.*

[172] AACSL minutes, *supra* note 142. In 1970, the American Council of Learned Societies provided $5,000 for AACSL members to attend the 1970 IACL congress in Pescara, Italy. AACSL minutes, *supra*.

This replaced the prior system of generally maintaining officers indefinitely for annual terms. In 1998, sponsor members approved a bylaws amendment that made the secretary and treasurer eligible for up to four terms for a maximum of eight years. Incumbent officers did not require an opponent. Fourth, the bylaws clarified the responsibilities of each office and permitted any director or editor to serve in a position. Under this system the directors elected Re honorary president, Friedrich Juenger (1930–2001, California Davis) president, Von Mehren (1922–2006) vice president, Durham secretary, and Clark treasurer.[173]

2. The *American Journal of Comparative Law*

Plans for the *American Journal of Comparative Law* began even before the AACSL's creation. The first meeting occurred at the Parker School in April 1950, followed a year later by a similar meeting at Harvard. The initial convening of the *Journal*'s board of editors took place at the University of Michigan in November 1951. By the first issue in 1952, two more sponsor members had joined—that is, paid their $500 annual dues—to the original 11 in the AACSL, each of which had the right to select one editor for the board (who could also be its association director).[174] Although all were full-time law professors, Yntema, the editor in chief, emphasized both the practical and scientific objectives of the *Journal*.[175]

Pound wrote the lead article in the *Journal*'s first issue.[176] Reminiscent of the earlier Comparative Law Bureau's *Bulletin* and its continuation in the *Tulane*

---

[173] AACSL minutes, *supra* note 142; *see* Gordley, *Von Mehren*, *supra* note 61, at 527; *supra* note 165 and accompanying text (Re).

[174] Yntema, *Journal*, *supra* note 128, at 16–17; *see* Vera Bolgár, *The American Journal of Comparative Law 1952–1966*, 15 Am. J. Comp. L. 21, 24–25 (1966). Michigan's Yntema was editor in chief. Most of the other editors were also directors. However, five members selected a different editor: the AFLA (Nadelmann), the Parker School (Hazard), Harvard (Von Mehren), Miami (David Stern), and NYU (Walter Derenberg). Derenberg (1903–1975) was NYU's editor from 1952 until 1970. Born in Hamburg and educated in law at its university, he emigrated to the United States in 1934. At NYU he earned an LL.B. in 1938 and after the war became a law professor there. In 1946, he served as special counsel at the Nuremburg war crime trials. Peter B. Flint, *Prof. Walter J. Derenberg Dies; Lawyer Was Copyright Expert*, N.Y. Times, 10 Sept. 1975, at 48; Robert B. McKay, *Walter J. Derenberg*, 24 Am. J. Comp. L. 366–67 (1976).

[175] Yntema, *Journal*, *supra* note 128, at 11, 23. The "practical and scientific objectives of comparative law, are twofold: on the one hand, to encourage *general* investigation of legal problems, whether theoretical or empirical, as essential to the advancement of legal science and, on the other, to provide information respecting foreign legal developments, as increasingly requisite in legal practice and for legal reform." *Id.* at 11. Vera Bolgár (1913–2003) was the *Journal*'s first executive secretary, serving from 1951 to 1971 while its office remained at Michigan. Bolgár, *supra* note 174, at 24–25. Bolgár, educated in what remained of the Austro-Hungarian empire, gained fluency in several languages, and lived through military occupations by Hitler and Stalin, escaping to Vienna. She contacted Rheinstein who, realizing her value to a potential journal, put her in contact with Yntema, who bought her to Michigan as a research assistant in 1949. Brown & Blume, *supra* note 121, at 776, 783; Alfred F. Conard, *Vera Bolgar*, 52 Am. J. Comp. L. 5–7 (2004).

[176] Roscoe Pound, *Introduction*, 1 Am. J. Comp. L. 1–10 (1952).

Law Review during the 1930s, the *Journal* had sections on documents, foreign law case digests, and book reviews and notices. The AFLA printed its *Bulletin*, which Nadelmann had begun in 1950, in the *Journal*.[177] The *Bulletin* primarily carried announcements of comparative and international law entities or conferences or summaries of the latter. Most of the *Journal*, however, had a distinctly scholarly tone dedicated to articles, comments, and reviews. It was a quarterly, priced at $5 per volume to encourage wide readership.[178]

Beginning in 1956, the *Journal* offered space for interim bibliographies of foreign and comparative law in English that Charles Szladits at the Parker School provided as a special editor. These gave comparatists early information to aid their research before the bibliographies appeared in book form.[179] By 1959, the *Journal*, supported by AACSL sponsor member dues and subscription fees, had a circulation of 1,200. For most of the publication's existence, the association has provided a subsidy to finance its circulation worldwide at a reasonable price.[180]

In 1961, the *Journal*'s board of editors presented a *Festschrift* of 38 essays to honor Yntema's service to comparative and conflicts law. Most editors wrote an article for the volume as did many foreign comparatists representing 15 countries, writing in French, German, and Spanish as well as English. Rheinstein wrote what probably was the longest book review to that date appearing in the *Journal*. Insightful, his survey of the varied contributions served to elucidate the value and orientation of comparative law at mid-century.[181] He illustrated how his own knowledge of comparative law had served him well when he advised the Allied Control Council in Germany shortly after the end of the war.[182] In 1965, Yntema, just before his death, edited a collection of articles that had appeared in the *Journal* intended for foreign jurists or law school comparative law courses

---

[177] Yntema, *Journal*, *supra* note 128, at 21. Volume 1 also had a brief description of foreign law periodicals, listed by country. *Foreign Legal Periodicals*, 1 Am. J. Comp. L. 329–40 (1952).

[178] *See* 1 Am. J. Comp. L. ii–vi (1952).

[179] *E.g.*, Charles Szladits, *Current Literature on Foreign and Comparative Law*, 5 Am. J. Comp. L. 341–90 (1956); *see infra* pt. F.1 (projects to facilitate research); *infra* text accompanying notes 344–47 (Szladits). The supplements continued annually in the *Journal* through 1986, missing only a few years. *See Charles Szladits—Bibliography*, 34 Am. J. Comp. L. 825, 826 (1986) [hereinafter *Szladits Bibliography*].

[180] Coudert, *supra* note 155, at 27. In 1960, the AACSL increased the annual subscription price to $7.50 and in 1964 to $10. 9 Am. J. Comp. L. ii (1960); AACSL minutes, *supra* note 142. The association provided a $4,000 subsidy to Michigan in 1960 to cover clerical expenses, increased to $5,000 in 1964 with an honorarium of $2,000 to the editor. Of the *Journal*'s subscriptions, 400 went to AFLA members as part of their dues. AACSL minutes, *supra*, 140.

[181] XXth Century Comparative and Conflicts Law: Legal Essays in Honor of Hessel E. Yntema (Kurt H. Nadelmann, Arthur T. von Mehren, & John N. Hazard eds., 1961); Max Rheinstein, *How to Review a Festschrift*, 11 Am. J. Comp. L. 632–68 (1962).

[182] Rheinstein, *supra* note 181, at 644–45; *see supra* notes 60–62 and accompanying text (denazification of German law).

dealing with two themes: rule of law and the new supranational European communities.[183]

When the ABA Section of International and Comparative Law, with Edward Re as chair, established the *International Lawyer* as a quarterly in 1966, it relieved any remaining pressure on the *Journal* to achieve a balance between practical and scholarly concerns. From 1966 until 1970, there were two short-term chief editors of the *Journal*. John Fleming (1919–1997) then took the post from 1971 to 1987.[184] Fleming was born in Berlin but at the age of 15 his parents sent him to England to finish his education. After enrolling at Oxford, he briefly suffered internment as an enemy alien, but then continued and in 1941 obtained a B.A. in jurisprudence. Afterward, he served in the British Royal Tank Corps in North Africa and Italy during the war. In 1946, he became a barrister and law lecturer in King's College at the University of London. In 1949, he emigrated to Australia, took a law professorship at the new Australian National University, where he later became dean. In 1957, Fleming published *The Law of Torts*, a comparative treatment of the field in the Anglo-American world. He joined the law faculty at Berkeley in 1961.[185]

During the transition period after Yntema and continuing with Fleming, the *Journal* devoted the bulk of several quarterly issues to symposia.[186] A notable example was the 1972 symposium on the status of women. Ginsburg wrote the introduction. After a brief statement about the economic, technological, and medical changes that had altered the situation of women in developed nations, she described the symposium's articles that portrayed how various countries had implemented legal policies to reduce the distance between the principle of equality for men and women and traditional practices.[187] A year earlier, Ginsburg

---

[183] 1–2 THE AMERICAN JOURNAL OF COMPARATIVE LAW READER (Hessel E. Yntema ed., 1966); *see* Mauro Cappelletti, *Book Review*, 14 AM. J. COMP. L. 701–02 (1966). The rule of law volume had three parts, treating human rights, constitutional review, and control of legality. The volume on European communities had institutions, remedies, and legal harmonization. *Id.* at 701.

[184] ASCL, *American Journal of Comparative Law*, at https://ascl.org (select Publications, then The Journal). B. James George was editor in chief from 1966 to 1968 and Alfred Conard from 1968 to 1970, both at Michigan. *Id.* In 1967, *Journal* subscriptions numbered 1,930, 60 percent domestic and 40 percent foreign to 83 countries. Beginning in 1969, the annual price was $12.50 ($10 to AFLA members). AACSL minutes, *supra* note 142.

[185] Richard M. Buxbaum, *John G. Fleming*, 45 AM. J. COMP. L. 645 (1997); *see* JOHN G. FLEMING, THE LAW OF TORTS (1957, 9th ed. 1998, rev. 10th ed. 2011). In the United States, the government had also detained a German-born future comparatist as an enemy alien, Anton Chroust. *See supra* ch. 6, text accompanying notes 262–65 (Pound and Chroust).

[186] *See, e.g.*, 16 AM. J. COMP. L. 1–218 (1968) (international unification of law); 17 *id.* at 1–60 (1969) (creditors in bankruptcy proceedings); *id.* at 331–417 (student power in universities); 18 *id.* at 1–168 (1970) (trends in tort law); *id.* at 233–366 (European Convention of Human Rights); *id.* at 483–548 (prosecutor discretion); *id.* at 689–774 (judicial conflicts of interest); 19 *id.* at 1–120 (1971) (choice of law for torts); *id.* at 431–574 (law and development in Latin America); *id.* at 615–785 (next 30 years in comparative law).

[187] Ruth Bader Ginsburg, *Introduction*, 20 AM. J. COMP. L. 585–91 (1972); *see supra* text accompanying note 162 (Ginsburg as *Journal* editor). Ginsburg quoted an 1837 letter to the Boston Female Anti-Slavery Society, "I ask no favor for my sex.... All I ask of our brethren is that they take their feet

had written the introduction to another symposium on women and the law. She began her remarks with Sweden's treatment of women as independent and equal in the law, contrasting American paternalistic legal discrimination in many fields.[188]

Ginsburg began her law studies at Harvard in 1956 at a time when about 2 percent of the students were female. In 1958, she transferred to Columbia, graduating at the top of her class but was unable to find employment with a law firm. Consequently, Ginsburg worked as a clerk for a New York City federal district judge until 1961.[189] That helped her secure an associate position with Strasser & Spiegelberg, a New York law firm. At the same time, Hans Smit, a law professor at Columbia and director of the Project on International Procedure, funded by the Carnegie Corporation, offered her the opportunity of researching law in Sweden, which had in 1948 adopted a new procedure code with elements of both the civil law and common law systems. The research associate position had funding to learn Swedish and to live in Sweden long enough to complete the investigation with a Swedish appellate judge in Lund, Anders Bruzelius. Smit already had studies underway on French and Italian law and the Swedish publication would be a nice complement.[190]

Ginsburg obtained a two-year leave from the law firm and began studying Swedish law at the project. Smit promoted her to associate director, introduced her to comparative law scholars, and allowed her to occasionally lecture his civil procedure class. By 1962, Ginsburg was ready to travel to Sweden, where she met Bruzelius and settled into comfortable accommodations.[191] By 1968, this team had two books published, which established Ginsburg's credentials as a comparatist.[192]

---

off our necks." *Id.* at 589-90. The symposium had articles on France, Great Britain, Israel, Norway, Senegal, the Soviet Union, and Sweden. *Id.* at 592-715.

[188] Ruth Bader Ginsburg, *Introduction*, 25 RUTGERS L. REV. 1-11 (1970). Ginsburg proposed a future where "the prospect of life for women beyond Kinder, Kirche, and Küche takes on a new, attractive dimension." *Id.* at 10.

[189] Gerald Gunther, *Ruth Bader Ginsburg: A Personal, Very Fond Tribute*, 20 HAW. L. REV. 583-84 (1990). Harvard Law School did not admit women until 1953. Gunther, a Columbia law professor, had to threaten Judge Edmund Palmieri to never recommend another Columbia law graduate for his clerkship unless he permitted Ginsburg a trial run as clerk. *Id.* at 583-84.

[190] JANE SHERRON DE HART, RUTH BADER GINSBURG: A LIFE 82-86 (2018); RUTH BADER GINSBURG & ANDERS BRUZELIUS, CIVIL PROCEDURE IN SWEDEN vii-ix (1965). Smit knew Bruzelius, who could coauthor a volume resulting from the research. DE HART, *supra*, at 85-86.

[191] DE HART, *supra* note 190, at 86-87.

[192] GINSBURG & BRUZELIUS, *supra* note 190 (history of Sweden's legal and procedural system, legal assistance, the judiciary, judicial jurisdiction and parties, and the adjudicatory process from first instance, appeal, to enforcement); THE SWEDISH CODE OF JUDICIAL PROCEDURE (Anders Bruzelius & Ruth Bader Ginsburg, trans. & introduction, 1968) (15 American Series of Foreign Penal Codes). The code contained provisions on the organization of courts and on civil and penal procedure in first instance and appeal. *Id.* at 5-6. On behalf of the AALS Comparative Law Committee, Ginsburg published A SELECTIVE SURVEY OF ENGLISH LANGUAGE STUDIES ON SCANDINAVIAN LAW (1970).

In 1963, Rutgers University Law School in Newark offered Ginsburg a tenure-track assistant professorship, with annual renewal, to teach civil procedure and conflict of laws.[193] She accepted and in 1965 became pregnant with her second child, a status that some New Jersey schools considered inappropriate for the classroom. Giving birth in early September, she was in the classroom at the beginning of the fall semester, now also teaching comparative law. In 1966, Rutgers promoted Ginsburg to associate professor and in 1969, full professor with tenure.[194] The New Jersey affiliate of the American Civil Liberties Union (ACLU) asked Ginsburg to litigate cases involving employed pregnant women who had lost their jobs, a task that led to work with the national ACLU filing constitutional cases in the U.S. Supreme Court involving gender discrimination and to a professorship at Columbia Law School.[195]

During the Fleming years as the *Journal*'s chief editor, it prospered and took a position among the world's leading comparative law journals. It provided the center for discussion in the United States of important issues related to comparative law and private international law and many foreign comparatists published their work there. Subscriptions rose to 1,900 in 1973, even at a price increase to $15 ($12 to AFLA members). By 1981, paid circulation was 2,100 with 50 copies provided gratis to deserving institutions in poorer nations. In 1988, Richard Buxbaum (California Berkeley) took over as editor in chief at a time when subscriptions numbered 2,200.[196]

3. Participation in International Congresses

Beyond contributing articles to the *Journal* and participating in annual AACSL scholarly programs, representatives took an active role in international comparative law congresses. In 1956, the International Association of Legal Science

---

[193] DE HART, *supra* note 190, at 90–91. At the time, there were only 18 tenured female law professors in the United States. *Id.* at 91.

[194] *Id.* at 91–93, 98, 136.

[195] *Id.* at 101–03, 107, 137–39, 148–59; Gunther, *supra* note 189, at 585–86; Philippa Strum, *Ginsburg, Ruth Bader, in* THE YALE BIOGRAPHICAL DICTIONARY OF AMERICAN LAW 221–23 (Roger K. Newman ed., 2009). After Ginsburg's brief in *Reed v. Reed*, 404 U.S. 71 (1971) led the Court to overturn a state statute preferring men over women as estate executors, the ACLU created a Women's Rights Project. She left Rutgers to work in New York City half time at the Project and half at Columbia Law School. Between 1973 and 1976, Ginsburg won five of six gender equality cases filed before the Supreme Court. President Jimmy Carter appointed her to a judgeship at the federal court of appeals in Washington, DC, in 1980, which President Bill Clinton followed with nomination to the Supreme Court in 1993. Ginsburg's judicial philosophy was that high courts should follow and reinforce social change, but also give lower courts and other government branches an opportunity to consider responses to new values or circumstances. Gunther, *supra*, at 584–86; Strum, *supra*, at 222.

[196] AACSL minutes, *supra* note 142; 30 AM. J. COMP. L. 216 (1982). The *Journal* later added $1.50 for foreign delivery and the annual price increased to $20 in 1982. AACSL minutes, *supra*.

(IALS), formerly the ICCL, held its first international congress in Barcelona with 200 jurists participating from 37 countries. Comparative law topics at plenary sessions and colloquia ranged from general system matters such as legal education and legal transplant to private and public law topics.[197] Article 3 of the IALS statutes expressed the organization's purpose. "The Association fosters the Development of legal science throughout the world through the study of foreign laws and the use of the comparative method." Although initially comparatists from several countries hoped that the entity might serve as a vehicle to develop more interest in comparative law worldwide and perhaps bridge the Cold War divide through understanding and respecting differences between socialism and capitalism, that did not occur.[198]

The IALS suffered from three main defects that kept it from reflecting the growing interdependence of nations economically, politically, and culturally during the postwar period up to 1990. First, it had no reliable source of funding to develop and present international programs. Money from UNESCO was intermittent and the national committees themselves could not afford financing the endeavor. Second, the IALS was functionally non-democratic. In 1963, the Soviet national committee had proposed changes to the election procedure for the bureau and secretary-general. The delegate complained that there was no opportunity to discuss the secretary-general's proposed candidates to the bureau.[199] Third, both international and national bureaucracies and jealousies at UNESCO and the national comparative law member organizations inhibited participation by comparatists other than the leaders of local entities who spoke French, the IALS's official language. These factors effectively barred younger comparatists who then sought other outlets for their scholarly activities. After the 1956 Barcelona congress, the IALS could not itself sponsor any other general congresses. It largely lent its name to comparative law activities others financed, the most notable of which was the *International Encyclopedia of Comparative Law*. Even by 2020, the association remained essentially a small social clique irrelevant for international comparative law.[200]

---

[197] Carolyn Royall Just, *Report of the Committee on Relations with International Bar Organizations*, ABA SEC. INT'L & COMP. L. PROC. 161–62 (1957); H.E. Y[ntema], *Reports: Barcelona Comparative Law Congress*, 5 AM. J. COMP. L. 704–05 (1956). The IALS adopted its new name in 1955, making the ICCL its executive bureau. IALS, *Home*, http://www.aisj-ials.net.

[198] IALS, *Statutes*, supra note 134; *see* Zajtay, *supra* note 128, at 142–43. Article 3 continued that the association's "ultimate object [was] to aid the mutual knowledge and understanding of nations." IALS, *Statutes*, *supra*.

[199] Hessel E. Yntema, *International Committee of Comparative Law*, 12 AM. J. COMP. L. 456–57 (1963); AACSL minutes, *supra* note 142. The Soviet delegate insisted that the members revise the IALS statutes "assurer une plus grande démocratisation." AACSL minutes, *supra*.

[200] IALS, *Main Activities*, http://www.aisj-ials.net (select Main Activities); *see* Zajtay, *supra* note 128, at 143–45; J.N. Hazard, *Reports: International Committee of Comparative Law*, 13 AM. J. COMP. LAW 337 (1964); *International Association of Legal Science*, AM. J. COMP. LAW 151–54 (1979); Ulrich Drobnig, *The International Encyclopedia of Comparative Law: Efforts toward a Worldwide Comparison of Law*, 5 CORNELL INT'L L.J. 113–29 (1972); *Varia: International Encyclopedia of Comparative Law*,

More significant for the wider development of comparative law was the International Academy of Comparative Law (IACL), which had held two international congresses at The Hague in the 1930s and sponsored its third congress in London in 1950.[201] The academy had selected Élemér Balogh permanent secretary-general in 1932, establishing a tradition of elite non-democratic control and lack of transparency like that of the IALS. The IACL secretary-general (with an office in Paris) dominated decision-making and the first three secretaries through 1973 died in office.[202] The AACSL did its best to work with the IACL to develop a meaningful scholarly program at the congresses, but by the 1960s there was significant American discontent that continued through 1990.

Hazard from the beginning of the AACSL took responsibility for coordinating U.S. relations with the IACL. He solicited U.S. national reports on almost 80 topics for the 1954 Fourth International Congress of Comparative Law in Paris. Most participating countries had a national committee to select reporters. The congress pattern was to have a general reporter for each topic who would condense information provided by national reporters for a panel session led by a session chair (president). For 1954, in addition to sections for civil, commercial, and public law issues, the general section included reports on legal history, ethnology, and philosophy, Oriental and canon law, unification of law, and legal education.[203] Out of some 250 jurists attending, 30 delegates came from the United States with 47 American reports contributed.[204]

The 1958 Congress took place in Brussels. These congresses, typically during a week in August to accommodate the European academic calendar, followed a standard format of periodic social gatherings, three or four days of sessions, and a day for excursions. There were 44 topics on the agenda, almost all with a general report, and 400 national reports. The United States committee (AACSL) sent 40 participants, while there was a total of 350 registrants from 38 nations.

---

15 AM. J. COMP. L. 412–15 (1966). In 1980, the IALS co-sponsored the program on co-habitation held at California Berkeley during the AACSL annual meeting and in 2000, the Centennial World Congress on Comparative Law, financed by Tulane Law School. IALS, *Main Activities, supra*.

[201] Ferdinand F. Stone, *The International Congress of Comparative Law*, 25 TUL. L. REV. 98 (1950); see supra ch. 6, pts. E.1 and H.2 (IACL and congresses). There were 176 registrants for the 1950 congress, eight from the United States including Hazard, Pound, and Yntema. 3 MÉMOIRES DE L'ACADÉMIE INTERNATIONAL DE DROIT COMPARÉ lxi–lxx (Elemér Balogh ed., pts. 1–2, 1953) [hereinafter MÉMOIRES].

[202] H.E. Y[ntema], *In Memoriam: Élemér Balogh*, 5 AM. J. COMP. L. 174 (1956); John N. Hazard, *Felipe de Solá Cañizares*, 14 id. at 212–13 (1965); see IACL, Secretary General, https://aidc-iacl.org/secretary-general (Gabriel Marty). Balogh, a Hungarian teaching law in Berlin, left for Paris in 1933 until he took a law professorship at the University of Witwatersrand (Johannesburg) from 1938 to 1947, when he returned to Paris to administer the IACL. Yntema, *supra; see supra* ch. 6, text accompanying notes 116, 321, 326 (Balogh).

[203] *Fourth International Congress of Comparative Law*, 2 AM. J. COMP. L. 137–39 (1953).

[204] John N. Hazard, *Fourth International Congress of Comparative Law*, 3 AM. J. COMP. L. 614–15 (1954).

Nadelmann complained that there were too many simultaneous sessions, IACL appointment of general reporters was too late for some to compile a thorough report, some general reporters did not appear, and many national reports were not available.[205]

The Sixth Congress was in Hamburg in 1962. The IACL reduced the total topics to 34 while the number of registrants increased to 400. There were 17 national committees publishing their reports in a national volume, more than at Brussels, although the publication of general reports was piecemeal in journals or otherwise. The academy meeting of titular members, coordinated by the secretary-general, instituted certain reforms for future international congresses. First, the secretary-general should ask national committees and academy members to propose topics, which experts would review. Second, academy members would meet to select topics and suggest general reporters, which the executive committee (*bureau*) would choose. The IACL would expect general reporters to prepare an outline for their subjects communicated in enough time to national reporters.[206]

In 1966, the Seventh International Congress of Comparative Law occurred in Uppsala. National reporters submitted 420 reports.[207] The AACSL at its 1964 annual meeting had discussed the possibility of preparing a volume of the U.S. reports, but that idea only came to fruition for the 1970 international congress.[208] At its 1966 annual meeting, AACSL representatives expressed their dissatisfaction with the Uppsala Congress, not for its hospitality, but with growth in the number and variability of topics, too often treated superficially. The directors authorized the president to write the IACL secretary-general about these concerns.[209]

To influence the IACL more effectively regarding issues of organization, topics, and costs for future congresses, the AACSL created an international meetings committee in 1967. The chair was Wenceslas Wagner (1917–2013), who represented Indiana University, assisted by the committee's secretary Hazard as well as Rheinstein and Von Mehren. The committee had the responsibility to

---

[205] *International Academy of Comparative Law*, 6 Am. J. Comp. L. 435–37 (1957); Kurt H. Nadelmann, *Fifth International Congress of Comparative Law*, 7 *id.* at 645–46 (1958). "These defects have been noted at the earlier conferences sponsored by the Academy and have long been criticized." Nadelmann, *supra*, at 646.

[206] *International Academy of Comparative Law*, 9 Am. J. Comp. L. 862–63 (1960); John N. Hazard, *Sixth Congress of Comparative Law*, 11 *id.* at 506–08 (1962); AACSL minutes, *supra* note 142.

[207] [VIIth] *Congress of the International Academy of Comparative Law*, 13 Am. J. Comp. L. 142–44 (1964); Vera Bolgár, *Seventh International Congress of Comparative Law*, 14 *id.* at 743–44 (1966).

[208] Legal Thought in the United States of America under Contemporary Pressures (John N. Hazard & Wenceslas J. Wagner eds., 1970) [hereinafter Legal Thought]; *see* AACSL minutes, *supra* note 142. Etablissements Émile Bruylant (Brussels) published the volume, which sold for $20. It cost the association $7,000, for which it received 200 copies to distribute to reporters and members. AACSL minutes, *supra*.

[209] AACSL minutes, *supra* note 142.

coordinate selection of U.S. national reporters for 1970 and planned for their reports to appear in a U.S. volume. It recommended to the IACL that it encourage national reporters to make available copies of their report and to use a functional rather than legalistic approach to their topic, considering social, economic, and historical factors. Furthermore, the IACL should publish more than solely the title of topics to guide reporters and consider offering some panel presentations by topic experts.[210]

The IACL originally scheduled the 1970 Eighth Congress for Athens, but due to political uncertainty it had to move it, ending up in Pescara, Italy. There were 41 topics at the Congress and 35 U.S. national reporters submitted their contribution in time for the editors of a U.S. volume of reports to include them. Fifteen countries, including the United States, published a national reports volume. The American Council of Learned Societies provided a $5,000 grant to the AACSL to finance U.S. attendance. After the IACL titular members voted regarding candidates for membership, there were 44 titular members (Americans Hazard, Von Mehren, Rheinstein, and Schlesinger) and 35 associate members (Harold Berman, Conard, Dainow, Ehrenzweig, and Wagner from the USA).[211] Ginsburg attended three IACL general congresses between 1962 and 1970, at Hamburg, Uppsala, and Pescara, which added to her growing appreciation for the value of a comparative perspective on law. She also delivered the keynote speech for the American delegation at the 2010 international congress in Washington, D.C.[212]

In 1974, the IACL again had to change the venue for its international congress: from Viña del Mar, Chile, to Teheran. Very few Americans could attend, since the IACL scheduled the Ninth Congress in early October. The publisher Bruylant for the second time prepared the U.S. volume of 34 national reports, which cost the AACSL $6,000 and sold for around $50, a high price impeding

---

[210] *VIII Congress of the International Academy of Comparative Law—1970*, 16 AM. J. COMP. L. 304–05 (1968); W.J. Wagner, *International Academy of Comparative Law*, 20 AM. J. COMP. L. 221–22 (1972); AACSL minutes, *supra* note 142; *see* LEGAL THOUGHT, *supra* note 208. Wagner, born in Poland, participated during World War II in the resistance movement against German occupation, for which he spent time in concentration camps. Afterwards, he emigrated to the United States and began his academic career at the University of Notre Dame (1953–1962). He then was a law professor at Indiana University, leaving for the University of Detroit (1971–1989), were he authored W.J. WAGNER, 2 POLISH CIVIL LAW: OBLIGATIONS IN POLISH LAW (Dominik Lasok ed., 1973). SNAC, *Wagner, Wenceslas J.*, https://snaccooperative.org/ark:/99166/w6ps1hqz (Wagner's papers are in the United States Holocaust Memorial Museum).

[211] *International Academy of Comparative Law*, 18 AM. J. COMP. L. 884 (1970); AACSL minutes, *supra* note 142; *see* LEGAL THOUGHT, *supra* note 208; Stephen Gorove, *Book Review*, 20 AM. J. COMP. L. 349–51 (1972). There were 28 IACL titular members in 1950, four of whom were Americans. MÉMOIRES, *supra* note 201, at xi–xii.

[212] Ginsburg, *Comparative Perspective*, *supra* note 162, at 927. Ginsburg submitted a report for the U.S. volume of national reports: *Recognition and Execution of Foreign Civil Judgments and Arbitration Awards*, *in* LEGAL THOUGHT, *supra* note 208, at 237–60.

sale.[213] The IACL, at the suggestion of the AACSL and others, arranged for Bruylant to publish a volume of the Teheran Congress general reports in 1977.[214]

The Tenth International Congress of Comparative Law took place in Budapest in 1978. The AACSL had determined to use its *Journal* publisher to print the volume of U.S. national reports since it could maintain a lower sale price, which was $20. Even including 200 complimentary copies, the association made a small profit. The volume included 33 reports.[215] America's chief comparative law bibliographer, Szladits, compiled the authoritative list of the general and national reports issued pursuant to IACL congresses from the first one at The Hague in 1932 until the tenth one at Budapest in 1978.[216]

Caracas was the location of the 1982 quadrennial Eleventh Congress, the first one held in Latin America. This resulted in fewer European comparatists attending and only two from socialist nations. The AACSL sent the largest foreign delegation of 33 reporters, subsidized by the Dana Foundation, and printed its 36 national reports as a supplement to the *Journal* sent to subscribers.[217]

In 1983, the AACSL appointed a special committee chaired by Merryman to propose changes to the IACL congresses. The directors unanimously adopted a resolution that it sent to the IACL *secrétaire général perpétuel*, Roland Drago, who took that position in 1973 and held it until 2006.[218] The resolution proposed that the IACL (1) set 20 as the maximum number of congress topics; (2) select topics that have a problem focus suitable for comparative analysis; (3) choose panel presidents at the same time as general reporters so that they may consult with each other; and (4) pick general reporters who have expertise in the topic and who can administer a timely schedule with national reporters. Furthermore, for

---

[213] *International Academy of Comparative Law*, 20 Am. J. Comp. L. 579-80 (1972); Michael Reisman, *Ninth Congress of Comparative Law in Teheran*, 23 *id.* at 161-62 (1975); AACSL minutes, *supra* note 142; *see* Law in the United States of America in Social and Technological Change (John N. Hazard & Wenceslas J. Wagner eds., 1974); Spiros Simitis, *Book Review*, 23 Am. J. Comp. L. 559-67 (1975). Simitis called on the IACL to undertake the responsibility of publishing a congress's general reports. Fleming added his support to Simitis's suggestion. *Id.* at 559-60, 567-68.

[214] J.G. F[leming], *Rapports Generaux au IXe Congrès International de Droit Comparé* (1977), 28 Am. J. Comp. L. 147 (1980) (book review). The volume included 36 of the 39 reports submitted, ten in English and 26 in French.

[215] *X Congress of Comparative Law—1978*, 24 Am. J. Comp. L. 583-85 (1976); AACSL minutes, *supra* note 142. The association investment in the national volume was $11,400, which it recouped in sales. AACSL minutes, *supra*; *see* Law in the U.S.A. in the Bicentennial Era (John N. Hazard & Wenceslas J. Wagner eds., 1978) (26 Am. J. Comp. L. Supp.).

[216] Charles Szladits, *A Bibliography of Reports of the International Congresses of Comparative Law 1932-1974*, 25 Am. J. Comp. L. 684-819 (1977); *id.*, *A Bibliography of Reports of the International Congress of Comparative Law 1978*, 30 Am. J. Comp. L. 709-56 (1982) (included addendum for earlier congresses).

[217] *International Academy of Comparative Law*, 28 Am. J. Comp. L. 534-35 (1980); W.J. Wagner, *The XI International Congress of Comparative Law*, 31 *id.* at 205-06 (1983); AACSL minutes, *supra* note 142; *see* Law in the U.S.A. for the 1980s (John N. Hazard & Wenceslas J. Wagner eds., 1982) (30 Am. J. Comp. L. Supp.); *supra* text accompanying note 172 (Dana Foundation).

[218] AACSL minutes, *supra* note 142; *see supra* note 202 and accompanying text (IACL and secretaries-general).

the congress itself, the resolution urged that that the IACL provide all registrants with the general reports, require general reporters and presidents (or adequate substitutes) to show up for their session, and that national committees also provide their reports at the congress.[219]

In 1986, the Twelfth International Congress was, for the first time, located at two venues in Australia: Sydney and Melbourne. There were 400 registrants, the most ever from Asia, Oceana, and Africa, from 42 countries attending 32 sessions. Most national committees now made a volume of national reports available for purchase. The U.S. reports had 29 contributions.[220] In 1984, the IACL had replaced Rheinstein with Conard as one of the four U.S. titular members. The IACL bylaws capped the number of titular members at 50, with a de facto preference for francophone comparatists. It aimed for 75 non-voting associate members.[221]

The IACL held the Thirteenth International Congress in 1990 for the first time in North America, at Montréal. There were 456 registrants from 37 nations attending 37 panels and two plenary sessions. The U.S. volume of national reports had 32 entries. Although the congresses had gradually improved in scholarly usefulness, it was apparent that IACL secretary-general Drago did not accept most of the American proposal for improvement in the congresses.[222]

D. Developments in American Law Schools

1. Comparative Law Courses and Institutes

Edward Re estimated that in 1951 about 26 law schools offered some version of a comparative law course, which included Roman law offerings.[223] Earlier surveys

---

[219] AACSL minutes, *supra* note 142.

[220] *International Congress of Comparative Law*, 34 AM. J. COMP. L. 827-28 (1986); *XII Congress of Comparative Law—Publications*, 35 *id.* at 863-64 (1987) (national reports); LAW IN THE U.S.A. FACES SOCIAL AND SCIENTIFIC CHANGE (John N. Hazard & Wenceslas J. Wagner eds., 1986) (34 AM. J. COMP. L. SUPP.).

[221] *International Academy of Comparative Law*, 27 AM. J. COMP. L. 150 (1979); *International Academy of Comparative Law*, 32 *id.* 613-15 (1984); *see supra* note 211 and accompanying text (titular members). In 1987, the IACL added Fleming as a titular member. *International Academy of Comparative Law*, 36 AM. J. COMP. L. 391 (1988).

[222] *XIII Congress of Comparative Law*, 35 AM. J. COMP. L. 864 (1987); *XIII Comparative Law Congress Agenda*, 36 *id.* at 609-11 (1988); *id.* at 813-15 (U.S. national and general reporters); *XIII Congress of Comparative Law*, 38 AM. J. COMP. L. final pp. (1990); *see* U.S. LAW IN AN ERA OF DEMOCRATIZATION (John N. Hazard & Wenceslas J. Wagner eds., 1986) (38 AM. J. COMP. L. SUPP.); *supra* text accompanying notes 218-19 (Drago and U.S. proposal).

[223] Edward D. Re, *Comparative Law Courses in the Law School Curriculum*, 1 AM. J. COMP. L. 233, 241 (1952). By comparison, 55 law schools offered a course on international law broadly defined. William Tucker Dean, Jr., *Report of the Committee on Teaching of International and Comparative Law*, ABA SEC. INT'L & COMP. L. PROC. 127 (1951). *See also* Arthur Lenhoff, *Committee on Teaching of International and Comparative Law*, 1 SEC. INT'L & COMP. L. BULL. 8-9 (no. 1, May 1957).

showed somewhat fewer schools teaching comparative or foreign law, but interestingly, one already taught comparative constitutional law. In 1950, nine schools had multiple courses or seminars in the field.[224] Up to 1990, European émigré jurists arriving in the 1950s and later continued to gravitate toward teaching and research in comparative law in addition to mainstream legal subjects.[225]

The Ford Foundation was the principal nongovernmental organization (NGO) supporting comparative law in the 1950s. This support went to individuals and to law schools. In 1951, Ford implemented a program of fellowships and grants to increase knowledge about countries in Africa, Asia, the Near East, and Eastern Europe as well as the Soviet Union. The focus was on area studies that could include economic, political, social, and cultural matters.[226] In 1955, Ford's education for democracy category recognized the importance of international legal studies, including comparative law, to train future jurists and lawyers in the issues of international trade, investment, and organizations. This training should include the social context in which law operates. The first grants for a ten-year period totaled $7.8 million to seven law schools, with Harvard receiving $2.1 million.[227] In 1956 and 1957, Ford made smaller awards to seven additional law schools. The program ended in 1958.[228]

To illustrate, in 1950, Harvard had seven courses in international legal studies, which included comparative law and private international law (later called conflicts of law). By 1955, that number reached 21 involving 11 professors. Von Mehren had joined the faculty in 1946 and Harold Berman, a specialist in Soviet law, in 1948.[229] Michigan began in 1946 to teach introduction to civil law, one of four enrichment courses among which each student should elect one. It had

---

[224] John R. Stevenson, *Comparative and Foreign Law in American Law Schools*, 50 COLUM. L. REV. 613 (1950). The university law schools at Catholic, George Washington, Harvard, LSU, New York, Pennsylvania, Tulane, and Washington (Seattle) taught two or more comparative law courses. Columbia offered seven courses and seminars. Alabama offered comparative constitutional law. *Id.* at 623–28.

[225] Reimann, *Globalists*, *supra* note 151, at 106–08. Examples included Hans Baade, Herbert Bernstein, Mauro Cappelletti, Mirjan Damaška, Friedrich Juenger, Walter Weyrauch, and A.N. Yiannopoulos. *Id.* at 107.

[226] THE FORD FOUNDATION REPORT FOR 1954, at 25–39 (1954) [hereinafter FORD REPORT]; *id.* 71–78 (1955). For instance, Ford contributed to the University of Chicago's Project in Intercultural Studies, which attempted to "discover and define the essential similarities and differences among the more important cultures of the world." FORD REPORT, *supra*, at 57 (1955).

[227] FORD REPORT, *supra* note 226, at 57–59 (1955). Ford provided Chicago, Columbia, and Yale each over $1 million, with lesser amounts to California, Michigan, and Stanford. *Id.* at 58.

[228] FORD REPORT, *supra* note 226, at 98–99, 180 (1956) (Cornell, NYU, Southern Methodist, Texas, and Tulane); *id.* at 41, 86–87 (1957) (Northwestern and Pennsylvania); *id.* at 78 (1958).

[229] SUTHERLAND, *supra* note 61, at 333–34, 336–37, 380–81. Von Mehren earned two degrees at Harvard, the LL.B. (1945) and a Ph.D. in government (1946). From 1946 to 1949, he studied law at Zürich University, followed by work with the U.S. military in Berlin and study at the University of Paris. *Id.* at 336, 382; *see supra* note 61 (Von Mehren in Berlin). In 1958, Harvard completed a building wing for international legal studies, which housed the comparative and international library in addition to reading and seminar rooms and offices. *Id.* at 352–53.

offered a course on private international law since 1894 and taught comparative law since early in the twentieth century. In 1955, the Ford Foundation granted the law school $500,000 to enlarge its program of international and comparative legal studies, which encompassed 11 courses by 1958.[230]

As for law school comparative law institutes to coordinate research and teaching, the two most prominent ones were at Columbia and Tulane. In 1931, the Parker School of Foreign and Comparative Law affiliated with Columbia University and by the 1950s coordinated its activities with the law school.[231] Reese was its director from 1955 until 1981.[232] Hans Smit then served as director until 1996. From 1950 until 2000, the Parker School published 100 volumes, including the 22-volume Szladits's *Bibliography*.[233] Recall also that Ruth Ginsburg, specializing in Swedish law, had worked with Smit at the Parker School.[234]

At Tulane, the Ford and Rockefeller Foundations funded the Institute of Comparative Law, which Ferdinand Stone directed from 1949 to 1979. Thereafter, an influential New Orleans attorney endowed the Eason Weinmann Center for International and Comparative Law together with a research chair.[235] One might also include here the University of Washington's East Asian Law Program, founded in 1962, and Harvard's East Asia Legal Studies Program, created in 1964. By the 1980s, schools funded additional centers and institutes, for instance at Columbia, one for Chinese and another for Japanese legal studies.[236]

2. General Comparative Law Coursebooks

In 1950, Rudolf Schlesinger (1909–1996) prepared a printed comparative law coursebook that was the first one widely used among American law schools, which facilitated offering an introductory comparative law course. Using cases,

---

[230] BROWN & BLUME, *supra* note 121, at 130–31, 143, 164. In 1956, 25 students enrolled in principles of comparative law, 42 in British and French legal methods, and 11 in a seminar on comparative constitutional law. In 1958, the faculty added seminars on comparative criminal procedure and comparative business associations. *Id.* at 144, 146. In 1956, Ford provided Cornell a $390,000 grant to develop international and comparative law. ROBERT STEVENS, LAW SCHOOL: LEGAL EDUCATION IN AMERICA FROM THE 1850S TO THE 1980S, at 222 n.42 (1983).

[231] *See supra* note 140 and accompanying text (Columbia and Tulane).

[232] *See supra* text accompanying notes 143, 156–57 (Reese).

[233] HeinOnline, *Parker School Publications*, https://home.heinonline.org (select Databases, then International Resources) [hereinafter Hein, *Parker School*]; *see supra* note 179 and accompanying text (Szladits).

[234] *Supra* text accompanying notes 189–92 (Ginsburg and Smit); *see* Ruth Ginsburg, *Proof of Foreign Law—Sweden*, A.B.A. SEC. INT'L & COMP. L. PROC. 129–32 (1963); Ruth B. Ginsburg, *Civil Procedure—Basic Features of the Swedish System*, 14 AM. J. COMP. L. 336–45 (1965).

[235] Tulane University Law School, *History*, https://law.tulane.edu/centers/eason/history.

[236] John O. Haley, *The First Decades: 1961–2000*, *in* LEGAL INNOVATIONS IN ASIA: JUDICIAL LAWMAKING AND THE INFLUENCE OF COMPARATIVE LAW 7–21 (John O. Haley & Toshiko Takenaka eds., 2014).

statutes, juristic excerpts, text, and questions, he skillfully presented materials primarily from civil law nations—principally France and Germany, but some from Italy, Spain, and Switzerland—often taking a procedural and practical perspective. In his teaching, Schlesinger used a Socratic case method to develop class discussions.[237] Rheinstein believed that the book served the purpose of training American law students to spot a foreign law problem as it might arise in law practice and to engage an expert to avoid misunderstanding across legal systems. However, it could not educate an American about any foreign law system since the volume only included 18 foreign cases. Most of the excerpted cases were from U.S. jurisdictions and several involved proof of foreign law in U.S. courts.[238]

The popularity of Schlesinger's coursebook continued throughout the postwar period as he edited five versions, the final one with coauthors in 1988. According to reviewers, he incrementally improved each edition and adjusted it to legal change, the burgeoning literature on comparative law, and his own and other's experience with teaching the course in American law schools.[239] To illustrate, for the second edition in 1959, Schlesinger replaced most of the excerpts from books and journals with his own text, some in note form; this allowed him more clearly to make a pedagogical point he desired. Furthermore, he added new foreign judicial opinions, so that the text and decisions constituted the bulk of the volume. In the section on civil procedure, he presented a fictional dialogue occurring between two American attorneys and Professor Comparovich surveying issues in an imaginary civil law Ruritania associated with the selection of counsel to finality of judgments.[240] In the 1990s, three professors undertook a sixth edition, which appeared in 1998. That edition retained the basic structure of previous versions, but thoroughly revised the material so that in some portions of the now

---

[237] RUDOLF B. SCHLESINGER, COMPARATIVE LAW: CASES AND MATERIALS (1950); Ulrich Drobnig, *Memorial Address for Rudolf Schlesinger*, 21 HASTINGS INT'L & COMP. L. REV. 765-67 (1998); *see* Nora V. Demleitner, *Comparative Law in Legal Education*, *in* THE OXFORD HANDBOOK OF COMPARATIVE LAW 320, 334-35 (Mathias Reimann & Reinhard Zimmermann eds., 2d ed. 2019) [hereinafter OXFORD HANDBOOK]. Schlesinger, born in Munich, had dual German and American citizenship. He earned his law doctorate at the University of Munich in 1932 and took an in-house counsel position at a Munich bank, where he worked until his emigration to New York in 1938. After receiving his Columbia LL.B. and some years as a judicial clerk and Wall Street lawyer, Cornell hired him in 1948 to teach comparative law. Drobnig, *Memorial, supra*, at 765-66.

[238] Max Rheinstein, *Teaching Tools in Comparative Law: A Book Survey*, 1 AM. J. COMP. L. 95, 106-07 (1952); *see* John N. Hazard, *Comparative Law in Legal Education*, 18 U. CHI. L. REV. 264-66 (1951) [hereinafter Hazard, *Legal Education*]; Edgar Bodenheimer, *Book Review*, 3 STAN. L. REV. 755-58 (1951).

[239] The subsequent editions of *Comparative Law* appeared in 1959, 1970, 1980, and 1988. In 1988, the three coauthors were Hans W. Baade, Mirjan R. Damaška, and Peter E. Herzog. *See* Edgar Bodenheimer, *Book Review*, 37 AM. J. COMP. L. 819-21 (1989).

[240] Edgar Bodenheimer, *Book Review*, 8 AM. J. COMP. L. 525-28 (1959). Anthony Hope invented Ruritania as a fictional country for his novel *The Prisoner of Zenda* (1894), which David Selznick made into a 1937 film starring Douglas Fairbanks, Raymond Massey, and David Nivin.

1,013-page book (almost twice the length of the 1950 original), the notes overtook the text in the glossator manner.[241]

There were other comparative law coursebooks available in 1950, but generally mimeographed and typically used at one law school. For instance, Rheinstein had a volume on comparative torts for use at Chicago and Hazard and Morris Weisberg prepared one on Soviet law for Columbia.[242] Yntema commissioned the foreign law section chief at the Library of Congress to prepare materials on Soviet law to use at Michigan.[243] Some of these found a commercial publisher so that it could print volumes and make them widely available, even if the subject was one for area specialists. Hazard's Soviet law book was one of those, as he expanded the coverage to the Soviet legal system, found coauthors who could use the materials at their law schools, and promoted Soviet law study as important through the 1980s.[244]

In 1957, Von Mehren prepared the second major comparative law coursebook, *The Civil Law System*. It almost exclusively dealt with French and German law utilizing the American teaching method of relying substantially on judicial decisions to stimulate class discussion. But as the subtitle suggested it also included juristic extracts, statutes, text, and questions. Overall, the bulk of cases were French. The book's tone was more academic that the Schlesinger volume, divided into (1) the historical and institutional context of separation between common law legislation and civil law codes and their courts administering the codes; (2) French public law; and (3) the private law of torts and contracts.[245] Von Mehren cooperated with James Gordley for a second edition in 1977. It was a thorough updating of the original framework, adding the legal profession, first

---

[241] *See* RUDOLF B. SCHLESINGER, HANS W. BAADE, PETER E. HERZOG & EDWARD M. WISE, COMPARATIVE LAW: CASES, TEXT, MATERIALS (6th ed. 1998).

[242] Hazard, *Legal Education, supra* note 238, at 264, 266–67; *see* John N. Hazard & Morris L. Weisberg, Cases and Readings on Soviet Law (mimeo. 1950); Max Rheinstein, The Law of Torts: Cases and Materials from Common Law and Civil Law Countries (mimeo. 1947); René David, Book Review, 51 COLUMB. L. REV. 914–16 (1951) (Hazard & Weisberg). *See also* Douglas W. LIND, BIBLIOGRAPHY OF AMERICAN LAW SCHOOL CASEBOOKS, 1870–2004, at 412–13 (2006).

[243] VLADIMIR GSOVSKI, 1–2 SOVIET CIVIL LAW: PRIVATE RIGHTS AND THEIR BACKGROUND UNDER THE SOVIET REGIME (1948) (used at Michigan); *see* L. Hart Wright, *Gsovski's Soviet Civil Law: A Synopsis*, 28 MICH. ST. B.J. 15–20 (no. 4, Apr. 1949).

[244] *See, e.g.*, JOHN N. HAZARD, WILLIAM E. BUTLER & PETER B. MAGGS, THE SOVIET LEGAL SYSTEM: FUNDAMENTAL PRINCIPLES AND HISTORICAL COMMENTARY (3d ed. 1977) (1st ed. 1962 with Isaac Shapiro, 2d ed. 1969 with Shapiro & Maggs) (cases and materials); WILLIAM E. BUTLER, THE SOVIET LEGAL SYSTEM: SELECTED CONTEMPORARY LEGISLATION AND DOCUMENTS (1978); Dietrich A. Loeber, *Book Review*, 27 AM. J. COMP. L. 142–45 (1979). The coauthored volume was a textbook intended for American law students. Thus, over half the book contained 260 court procuracy cases while the other half was statutes, juristic excerpts, and explanatory text. Loeber, *supra*, at 143.

[245] ARTHUR TAYLOR VON MEHREN, THE CIVIL LAW SYSTEM: CASES AND MATERIALS FOR THE COMPARATIVE STUDY OF LAW (1957); *see* W. Friedman, *Book Review*, 11 J. LEGAL EDUC. 117–26 (1958); Gino Gorla, *Book Review*, 7 AM. J. COMP. L. 602–08 (1958). A chapter on the judicial process concluded the volume.

instance procedure, and substituting more text for juristic excerpts with Gordley providing extra historical context and German materials.[246]

In 1978, Merryman and Clark prepared the third principal coursebook, *Comparative Law: Western European and Latin American Legal Systems*, intended as a general introduction to the subject. It reoriented the scope of comparative law in two ways. Geographic coverage included Italy and Spain as well as the traditions of France and Germany. Moreover, the authors added cases and materials from various Latin American countries illustrating their connection to the European civil law tradition plus their distinctive characteristics. For methodology, the authors de-emphasized legal rules and doctrine and focused on intellectual history, professional actors, structure, and processes characteristic of civil law systems. Thus, although the formal rules of the civil codes of France and Chile might be similar, understanding what lawyers and judges did with those rules required social, cultural, and legal context.[247] In 1994, the second edition of this coursebook added John Haley, an expert on East Asian law, to acknowledge the contribution of the civil law tradition to contemporary East Asian legal systems.[248]

The fourth of the major coursebooks, *Comparative Legal Traditions*, appeared in 1985, extending coverage for an introductory book beyond the civil law of France and Germany to English common law and Soviet socialist law. The authors—Glendon, Michael Gordon, and Christopher Osakwe—desired to show that these three legal traditions were all Western with their intellectual origins in Europe.[249] They borrowed the concept of legal tradition that Merryman popularized and the legal systems approach of the Merryman and Clark coursebook to cover the cultural background of legal traditions, legal actors, structures, and

---

[246] ARTHUR TAYLOR VON MEHREN & JAMES RUSSELL GORDLEY, THE CIVIL LAW SYSTEM: AN INTRODUCTION TO THE COMPARATIVE STUDY OF LAW ix (2d ed. 1977). The ASCL presented von Mehren its Lifetime Achievement Award in 2004. In 2006, Gordley and Von Mehren prepared a successor edition, adding materials on the common law but limiting coverage to private law. *See id.*, AN INTRODUCTION TO THE COMPARATIVE STUDY OF PRIVATE LAW: READINGS, CASES, MATERIALS xxiii (2006).

[247] JOHN HENRY MERRYMAN & DAVID S. CLARK, COMPARATIVE LAW: WESTERN EUROPEAN AND LATIN AMERICAN LEGAL SYSTEMS: CASES AND MATERIALS ix-x (1978); *see* Dale B. Furnish, *Book Review*, 28 AM. J. COMP. L. 344–47 (1980). The book also included a chapter on pleading and proof of foreign law, recognizing Schlesinger's insight about American student need for practicality, and introduced quantitative comparative law. MERRYMAN & CLARK, *supra*, at x-xiii. Merryman's *The Civil Law Tradition: An Introduction to the Legal Systems of Western Europe and Latin America* (1969) provided the framework for the coursebook.

[248] JOHN HENRY MERRYMAN, DAVID S. CLARK & JOHN O. HALEY, THE CIVIL LAW TRADITION: EUROPE, LATIN AMERICA, AND EAST ASIA (1994). The East Asian coverage included Japan, South Korea, Taiwan, Thailand, and Indonesia.

[249] MARY ANN GLENDON, MICHAEL WALLACE GORDON & CHRISTOPHER OSAKWE, COMPARATIVE LEGAL TRADITIONS: TEXT, MATERIALS AND CASES . . ., at xviii (1985). The authors had earlier prepared a student text using the same framework as the coursebook. *Id.*, COMPARATIVE LEGAL TRADITIONS IN A NUTSHELL (1982); *see* MARY ANN GLENDON, PAOLO G. CAROZZA & COLIN PICKER, *id.* (4th ed. 2016).

processes with a de-emphasis of legal rules. The book's second edition dropped coverage of socialist law, but added a chapter on European law.[250]

3. Specialized Comparative Law Coursebooks

In addition to comparative law pedagogy aimed at developing diverse approaches for an introductory course, some comparatists preferred to engage with the legal aspects of foreign area studies or comparative treatment of a doctrinal field or specific legal topic. Beginning in the 1960s, publishing books with these aims supported the growth and significance of comparative law in the United States.

First, regarding the law of a country or region, the most common books dealt with the socialist legal systems of the Soviet Union or China or with the civil law systems in Japan or Latin America. Hazard was the principal proponent of materials on Soviet law that one could use in law schools beyond casebooks; he authored or coauthored several books or editions for that subject from 1960 until 1984.[251] Some professors wanted to broaden coverage to include area studies in Eastern Europe to investigate a common core of Marxist law.[252] However, by 1990, there was little prospect in American law schools for Soviet, Russian, or East European legal studies, just as the potential for teaching and research on the legal system of the People's Republic of China (PRC) was emerging.[253]

The dominant American comparatist for the PRC in the postwar period was Jerome Cohen. In 1959, he accepted a law professorship at California Berkeley, where an opportunity afforded by the Rockefeller Foundation allowed him to study Chinese. Since the U.S. State Department prohibited travel to China using an American passport (until 1971), Cohen visited Hong Kong to interview refugees from the mainland about its criminal justice system. This resulted in *The Criminal Process in the People's Republic of China* (1968), a text that law professors could use in Chinese law and government courses. In 1964, Cohen moved to Harvard, where he established the East Asia Legal Studies Program, the first of its type in the United States.[254]

---

[250] GLENDON ET AL., *supra* note 249 (2d ed. 1994) (coursebook).

[251] *E.g.*, JOHN N. HAZARD, SETTLING DISPUTES IN SOVIET SOCIETY: THE FORMATIVE YEARS OF LEGAL INSTITUTIONS (1960); *id.*, THE SOVIET SYSTEM OF GOVERNMENT (4th ed. 1968, 5th ed. 1980); *id.*, WILLIAM E. BUTLER & PETER B. MAGGS, THE SOVIET LEGAL SYSTEM: THE LAW IN THE 1980's (1984). *See also* HAROLD J. BERMAN, JUSTICE IN THE U.S.S.R. (2d ed. 1963) (text).

[252] John N. Hazard, *Area Studies and Comparison of Law: The Experience with Eastern Europe*, 19 AM. J. COMP. L. 645, 649–54 (1971); *see id.*, COMMUNISTS AND THEIR LAW: A SEARCH FOR THE COMMON CORE OF THE LEGAL SYSTEMS OF THE MARXIAN SOCIALIST STATES (1969).

[253] *See, e.g.*, RALPH H. FOLSOM & JOHN H. MINAN, LAW IN THE PEOPLE'S REPUBLIC OF CHINA: COMMENTARY, READINGS AND MATERIALS (1989); WILLIAM C. JONES, BASIC PRINCIPLES OF CIVIL LAW IN CHINA (1989).

[254] Jerome A. Cohen, *Law and China's "Open Policy": A Foreigner Present at the Creation*, 65 AM. J. COMP. L. 729–31 (2017) [hereinafter Cohen, *Creation*]; James V. Feinerman, *Pioneering the Study*

Cohen advocated normalizing U.S. relations with China. In 1972, the year U.S. President Richard Nixon met Mao Zedong, chairman of the Chinese Communist Party, Cohen was able to travel with other scientists to mainland China where he met Premier Zhou Enlai. Continuing negotiations between the two countries in the 1970s led to Vice Premier Deng Xiaoping's 1979 meeting in the United States with President Jimmy Carter to normalize relations. Deng, de facto leader, opened China to foreign investment and global trade. In 1979, Cohen accepted an offer to teach American contract and commercial law in Beijing. He decided to remain and work with the recently established Beijing office of a New York law firm, which closed after the military suppression of student protests in Tiananmen Square in 1989. In 1990, Cohen returned to the United States to teach law at NYU, having earlier coauthored a text on Chinese contract law.[255]

For the civil law tradition, Japan and Latin America were the two most popular choices for comparatists with expertise in those areas. In the early 1970s, only three law schools regularly offered a course on Japanese law: Columbia, Harvard, and the University of Washington. An argument for using Japanese law as a productive subject for comparative law, beyond Japan's success with modernization in East Asia, was that it blended German, American, and traditional customary law, introducing the U.S. student to both the civil law and indigenous law.[256] At this time, teaching materials were scarce. Von Mehren had an edited volume, *Law in Japan*, and Dan Henderson (1921–2001) at Washington's Asian Law Program had published books, parts of which one could use for an introductory Japanese law course.[257] By 1979, Henderson and his colleague, John Haley,

---

of Chinese Law in the West, id. at 739–40, 742–43; *see* JEROME ALAN COHEN, THE CRIMINAL PROCESS IN THE PEOPLE'S REPUBLIC OF CHINA, 1949–1963: AN INTRODUCTION (1968). As far back as 1961, Cohen and Hazard had collaborated in teaching a course comparing the Chinese and Soviet legal systems. Over that decade, Cohen's introductory course on Chinese law evolved as his appreciation for Chinese legal history grew so that in 1971, with about 30 students, he titled it Modernization of Law in East Asia. Jerome Alan Cohen, *On Teaching Chinese Law*, 19 AM. J. COMP. L. 655, 659–63 (1971).

[255] Cohen, *Creation, supra* note 254, at 729–37; Feinerman, *supra* note 254, at 739–43; *see* JEROME A. COHEN, CONTRACT LAWS OF THE PEOPLE'S REPUBLIC OF CHINA (with assistance of Yvonne Y.F. Chan & Ho Yuk Ming, 1988); ESSAYS ON CHINA'S LEGAL TRADITION (Jerome Alan Cohen, R. Randle Edwards & Fu-mei Chang Chen eds.,1981). At NYU, Cohen established the U.S.-Asia Law Institute. Feinerman, *supra*, at 743.

[256] Charles R. Stevens, *Modern Japanese Law as an Instrument of Comparison*, 19 AM. J. COMP. L. 665–82 (1971). The Parker School first funded the course at Columbia and the Ford Foundation at Washington. *Id.* at 665. Harvard had the East Asia Legal Studies Program from 1964. *See supra* text accompanying note 236 (Harvard). Columbia founded the Center for Japanese Legal Studies in 1980 and its Toshiba Library for Legal Research has the largest collection of Japanese legal materials in an American university. The Center for Chinese Legal Studies followed in 1983. Columbia Law School, *Our History*, https://www.law.columbia.edu/about/our-history.

[257] LAW IN JAPAN: THE LEGAL ORDER IN A CHANGING SOCIETY (Arthur Taylor von Mehren ed., 1963); DAN FENNO HENDERSON, 1–2 CONCILIATION AND JAPANESE LAW: TOKUGAWA AND MODERN (1965); THE CONSTITUTION OF JAPAN: ITS FIRST TWENTY YEARS, 1947–67 (Henderson ed., 1969). When the U.S. army drafted Henderson during World War II, it offered him the alternative of studying Japanese at its University of Michigan language school, which he accepted. From 1946 to

had prepared more comprehensive teaching materials.[258] There was an unusual situation for Japanese law, since two law reviews regularly provided updated materials that comparatists could incorporate into their Japanese law courses.[259] By the mid-1990s, over a dozen law schools had a professor knowledgeable in Japanese teaching a course on the Japanese legal system.[260]

Two AACSL founders, Eder and De Capriles, had their primary interest in Latin American law, both at NYU's Inter-American Law Institute in the 1950s.[261] Nevertheless, that attention did not circulate to the curricula of other law schools to generate published teaching materials until 1966.[262] Kenneth Karst (1929–2019, UCLA) and Keith Rosenn (Ohio State) viewed the study of Latin American legal systems as an opportunity to investigate the role of law in rapidly changing societies. Presenting their perspective in 1971 as one of law and development, it encompassed a reorientation away from preoccupation with the substance of legal rules and attention to legal institutions and processes as well as legal culture.[263] This approach to law and social change was characteristic of teaching Latin American law from the 1970s on, often using selected problems, such as land reform, and empirical methodologies.[264]

1947, he served as censorship officer for Hokkaido and Kyushu, afterward earning his law degree at Harvard. He continued his academic studies in political science at California, finishing in 1955 with a Ph.D. His dissertation developed into the Japanese conciliation and law volumes. Henderson affiliated with a San Francisco law firm that had an office in Tokyo where he qualified as *bengoshi*, permitting him to practice law in Japan. In 1962, the University of Washington Law School hired him to teach Japanese law and with the aid of a Ford Foundation grant, he established the Asian Law Program. Daniel H. Foote, *Dan Fenno Henderson: A Tribute, in* LAW IN JAPAN: A TURNING POINT 623–24 (Daniel H. Foote ed., 2011).

[258] John O. Haley, *Educating Lawyers for the Global Economy*, 17 MICH. J. INT'L L. 733, 737–38 (1996) (book review) [hereinafter Haley, *Educating*]; *see* Dan Fenno Henderson & John Owen Haley, Law and the Legal Process in Japan: Materials for an Introductory Course on Japanese Law (rev. ed. 1979) (2 vol. 1988 ed.) (photocopied ed.). A Japanese professor published materials in Tokyo that he used at Harvard in 1974. Haley, *Educating, supra*, at 738; *see* THE JAPANESE LEGAL SYSTEM: INTRODUCTORY CASES AND MATERIALS (Hideo Tanaka ed. with assistance of Malcolm D.H. Smith, 1976).

[259] The Japanese American Society for Legal Studies (founded 1964), with its U.S. office initially at Harvard, was responsible for *Law in Japan: An Annual* beginning in 1967. Henderson took over as editor in chief in 1968–1970 and had also set up an annual symposium on Japanese (later Asian) law that the *Washington Law Review* published. Foote, *supra* note 257, at 625–26; David F. Cavers, *Messages from the Representative Directors*, 1 LAW IN JAPAN ii–iv (1967). Haley was editor of *Law in Japan* from 1974 to 1977 and 1983 to 1987.

[260] Haley, *Educating, supra* note 258, at 736–37 n.5, 738–41.

[261] *See supra* note 120 (Eder); supra text accompanying notes 157–59 (De Capriles).

[262] Dale B. Furnish, *Book Review*, 16 AM. J. COMP. L. 629, 631–32 (1968); *see* KENNETH L. KARST, LATIN AMERICAN LEGAL INSTITUTIONS: PROBLEMS FOR COMPARATIVE STUDY (1966).

[263] Kenneth L. Karst & Keith S. Rosenn, *Law and Development in Latin America: Introduction*, 19 AM. J. COMP. L. 431 (1971).

[264] Kenneth L. Karst, *Teaching Latin American Law*, 19 AM. J. COMP. L. 685–90 (1971); *see* Keith S. Rosenn, *Teaching Latin American Law, id.* at 692–93, 697–99. Karst and Rosenn implemented their approach in *Law and Development in Latin America: A Case Book* (1975); *see* John E. Huerta, *Book Review*, 25 AM. J. COMP. L. 582–89 (1977). In 1975, at least ten law schools offered a course on Latin American law. *Id.* at 582 n.3.

The initial doctrinal field that U.S. jurists developed for comparative treatment was constitutional law, the area most distinctive in the American legal system. One could date that from the creation of the new republic between 1776 and 1791.[265] However, after the original enthusiasm, jurists shifted their comparative law interest to private law and, to a lesser extent, penal law.[266] When Harvard reformed legal education in the 1870s, Langdell's model of studying judicial decisions remained primarily with private law. Some schools also offered courses in constitutional law or criminal law. Nevertheless, it was not until the 1920s that public law generally entered the curriculum in an expanding number of law schools.[267]

Law professors mimeographed the earliest teaching materials for comparative constitutional law, generally for use by the students at a single school. Paul Kauper, for instance, in 1956, developed readings in the subject for a seminar at Michigan.[268] The leading comparative constitutionalist in the postwar period, however, taught in the government department at Harvard. Carl Friedrich in his popular book for comparative law and government students promoted a historical, philosophical, and empirical approach to the subject. He discussed the origin of constitutional government, its structures, processes, tensions, and breakdowns. This was not a common method in comparative law until the 1970s and 1980s with law and development studies of developing nations or with some jurists for comparative constitutional law in the twenty-first century.[269]

In 1963, Harry Groves (1921–2013), an African American, published the first comparative constitutional law coursebook of cases and materials. For selected constitutional issues he chose to compare the United States and British Commonwealth countries, namely Burma, Ceylon, India, Malaysia, and Pakistan.[270] Groves earned his law degree at Chicago in 1949, after which the

---

[265] Mark Tushnet, *Comparative Constitutional Law*, in OXFORD HANDBOOK, *supra* note 237, at 1193–94; *see supra* ch. 3 (the early republic).

[266] *See* JEROME HALL, GENERAL PRINCIPLES OF CRIMINAL LAW (1947, 2d ed. 1960) (comparing European, English, and U.S. criminal law); *supra* ch. 4, pts A, G (private and penal law).

[267] STEVENS, *supra* note 230, at 39, 41–42, 48 nn.38–39, 50 nn.58–59, 159, 167–68 n.37.

[268] Paul G. Kauper, 1–2 Readings in Comparative Constitutional Law (mimeo. 1956, 2d ed. 1961); *see supra* note 230 (Michigan's seminars).

[269] CARL J. FRIEDRICH, CONSTITUTIONAL GOVERNMENT AND DEMOCRACY: THEORY AND PRACTICE IN EUROPE AND AMERICA (4th ed. 1968) (the 1st ed. in 1937 had the title *Constitutional Government and Politics: Nature and Development*); *see* RAN HIRSCHL, COMPARATIVE MATTERS: THE RENAISSANCE OF COMPARATIVE CONSTITUTIONAL LAW 13–15, 157–89, 226–29, 242–44, 279–81 (2014); *supra* notes 18–20 and accompanying text (Friedrich). *See generally* DEFINING THE FIELD OF COMPARATIVE CONSTITUTIONAL LAW (Vicki C. Jackson & Mark Tushnet eds., 2002); David Fontana, *The Rise and Fall of Comparative Constitutional Law in the Postwar Era*, 36 YALE J. INT'L L. 1–14, 17–23 (2011).

[270] HARRY E. GROVES, COMPARATIVE CONSTITUTIONAL LAW: CASES AND MATERIALS (1963); Cornelius J. Peck, *Book Review*, 17 J. LEGAL EDUC. 481–84 (1965). *See also* THOMAS M. FRANCK, COMPARATIVE CONSTITUTIONAL PROCESS, CASES AND MATERIALS: FUNDAMENTAL RIGHTS IN THE COMMON LAW NATIONS (1968).

Ford Foundation provided him a fellowship to study at Harvard where he developed an interest in Asian constitutional law. He was law dean at Texas Southern University from 1956 to 1960, when he accepted a professorship at the University of Malaya (renamed University of Singapore in 1962), later serving as dean of its law faculty until 1965. For 20 years, he worked with Malaysian government officials regarding interpretation of and amendments to its 1957 Constitution. Upon returning to the United States, Groves held a variety of law teaching and administrative positions ultimately at the University of North Carolina, but continuing as emeritus to visit at law schools until 1993.[271]

In 1967, Friedrich prepared the first general volume on the American Constitution's influence abroad, discussing constitutions in numerous legal systems.[272] A more ambitious study on the same theme organized geographically for emerging nations was a 1970 book by Richard Morris.[273] American books more narrowly aimed, particularly on comparative judicial review, appeared about the same time.[274] A high point for celebrating the export of U.S. constitutionalism with volumes exploring the topic occurred during the bicentennial activities in the United States. A prominent illustration was the series of colloquia that the Miller Center of Public Affairs at the University of Virginia held that resulted in seven volumes of essays and transcribed interviews with jurists, political scientists, and public officials.[275] Donald Kommers (1932–2018), a political scientist with a joint appointment in law at Notre Dame, from 1976 wrote a series of authoritative and insightful books on the German Constitutional Court that provided material for monolingual American constitutionalists to engage in comparative constitutional law.[276]

From the late 1970s, professors in political science and in law also prepared casebooks comparing constitutions and the courts adjudicating their provisions in civil law and common law countries. Nevertheless, the two disciplines

---

[271] John Charles Boger, *Harry Edward Groves, Late Emeritus Henry Brandis Professor of Law: In Memoriam*, 92 N.C. L. Rev. 1041, 1043–47 (2014); *see* L.A. Sheridan & Harry E. Groves, The Constitution of Malaysia (rev. ed. 1967).

[272] Rapaczynski, *supra* note 33, at 413; *see* Friedrich, Impact, *supra* note 5 (Bacon Lectures delivered at Boston University).

[273] Rapaczynski, *supra* note 33, at 413; *see* Richard B. Morris, The Emerging Nations and the American Revolution (1970).

[274] *E.g.*, Mauro Cappelletti, Judicial Review in the Contemporary World (1971). Foreign authors had books on this subject earlier. *E.g.*, Edward McWhinney, Judicial Review in the English-Speaking World (1956).

[275] *E.g.*, The U.S. Constitution and the Constitutions of Asia (Kenneth W. Thompson ed., 1988); The U.S. Constitution and Constitutionalism in Africa (Kenneth W. Thompson ed., 1990); The U.S. Constitution and the Constitutions of Latin America (Kenneth W. Thompson ed., 1991).

[276] Donald P. Kommers, Judicial Politics in West Germany: A Study of the Federal Constitutional Court (1976); *id.*, The Constitutional Jurisprudence of the Federal Republic of Germany (1989, 3d ed. 2012); R. Taylor Cole, *Book Review*, 25 Am. J. Comp. L. 427–29 (1977).

generally remained separate with political scientists comfortable with their categories of analysis, examining judicial policymaking, sometimes with empirical research, while jurists emphasized institutional structures and doctrine. Walter Murphy and Joseph Tanenhaus wrote text and edited cases from Germany and Japan on the civil law side and Australia, Canada, Ireland, and the United States for common law examples. In addressing 11 topics, the authors' aim was to show that judicial decisions are an integral part of governmental policymaking in nations other than the United States.[277] The casebook by Mauro Cappelletti (1927–2004) and William Cohen was narrower in scope, focusing on the comparative control of constitutionality. They approached this theme historically, describing how control evolved in civil law Europe from political to judicial, and then illustrated modern judicial control primarily in Austria, France, Germany, Italy, the European Communities, and the United States for seven legal issues.[278]

The other distinctive doctrinal field that U.S. comparatists developed was supranational European law for its economic and political communities. At Michigan, Eric Stein (1913–2011) and Peter Hay (Illinois) took the lead with course materials in the early 1960s.[279] In 1963, their coursebook *Law and Institutions of the Atlantic Area* utilized scholarly excerpts from law and political science, legal rules, and court cases illustrating European legal integration in a comprehensive manner. This was a thoroughly comparative enterprise, examining each of the six EEC members, the role of their national law in this process, and discussing analogous materials for Austria, the British Isles, Scandinavia, Switzerland, and the United States. There were chapters on European community legal institutions, rulemaking, adjudication, and thematic international and comparative treatment for free movement of goods, competition, access to capital and economic activities, social policy and civil rights, and military coordination. A second volume of documents included, among other institutions, the ECSC, EEC, European Free Trade Association, and European Convention for the Protection of Human Rights and Fundamental Freedoms.[280]

---

[277] COMPARATIVE CONSTITUTIONAL LAW: CASES AND COMMENTARIES (Walter F. Murphy & Joseph Tanenhaus eds., 1977); see Kristine L. Olsen, *Book Review*, 31 WEST. POL. Q. 132–33 (1978); Edward McWhinney, *Book Review*, 26 AM. J. COMP. L. 645–47 (1978).

[278] MAURO CAPPELLETTI & WILLIAM COHEN, COMPARATIVE CONSTITUTIONAL LAW: CASES AND MATERIALS (1979); see Edward McWhinney, *Book Review*, 29 AM. J. COMP. L. 169–71 (1981). Cappelletti had a joint appointment at Stanford Law School (from 1970) and the University of Florence (from 1962).

[279] Anne Boerger, *At the Cradle of Legal Scholarship on the European Union: The Life and Early Work of Eric Stein*, 62 AM. J. COMP. L. 859, 861, 870, 880, 889 (2014). At Michigan, Stein began teaching a course on European international organizations in 1958. BROWN & BLUME, *supra* note 121, at 525, 783, 789. For Stein's ideas on comparative law, *see Uses, Misuses, and Nonuses of Comparative Law*, 72 NW. U.L. REV. 198–216 (1977). The ASCL presented Stein its Lifetime Achievement Award in 2004.

[280] CASES AND MATERIALS ON THE LAW AND INSTITUTIONS OF THE ATLANTIC AREA (Eric Stein & Peter Hay eds., prelim. ed. 1963) (457 pp.); *see* Boerger, *supra* note 279, at 877; Hugo J. Hahn, *Book Review*, 13 AM. J. COMP. L. 489–91 (1964); *supra* pt. A.4 (ECSC and EEC). *See also* Francis G. Jacobs,

By 1965, 25 law schools used the Stein and Hay coursebook.[281] In 1967, the authors doubled the size of the principal volume with more text, adding materials comparing the six national civil law EEC members and expanding discussion of the Council of Europe. In 1976, they took on Michel Waelbroeck, a Belgian law professor, to update their coursebook to cover the then nine EEC members, further updating it with a supplement in 1985.[282] It was not until 1993 that a second American coursebook on European Community law appeared, the popular one prepared by four professors that carried over with subsequent editions as the subject became European Union law into the twenty-first century.[283]

Stein received his J.U.D. degree from Charles University (Prague) in 1937. After the Nazis annexed Sudetenland in 1938, Stein fled the next year to Italy where the U.S. consulate granted him a visa to the United States. In 1942, he earned his J.D. degree at Michigan and enlisted in the U.S. Army, which facilitated his U.S. citizenship. He served in the law department of the Allied Commission for Italy until 1946 when he joined the U.S. State Department, employed in various positions related to the United Nations. In 1956, Michigan Law School, facilitated by a Ford Foundation grant, hired him to teach and work in the international and comparative legal studies program, where he remained active into his nineties.[284] Stein's coedited volume of essays in 1960 on the EEC helped to establish his reputation in Europe and the United States in that field.[285] Peter Hay, a German-born law student at Michigan, began his collaboration with Stein in 1957 as a research assistant. They coauthored a chapter in the volume of essays and Hay wrote another chapter.[286] In 1966, Hay authored *Federalism and*

Comparative Law and European Union Law, in OXFORD HANDBOOK, *supra* note 237, at 524–27, 548–49.

[281] Boerger, *supra* note 279, at 877 n.108.

[282] ERIC STEIN & PETER HAY, LAW AND INSTITUTIONS IN THE ATLANTIC AREA: READINGS, CASES AND PROBLEMS (1967) (1,152 pp.); ERIC STEIN, PETER HAY & MICHEL WAELBROECK, EUROPEAN COMMUNITY LAW AND INSTITUTIONS IN PERSPECTIVE: TEXT, CASES AND READINGS (1976); *see* Jacques H.J. Bourgeois, *Book Review*, 26 AM. J. COMP. L. 333–35 (1978). Stein et al. with Joseph H.H. Weiler assisting prepared a 508-page supplement to the 1976 volume in 1985. HANS-ERIC RASMUSSEN-BONNE ET AL., BALANCING OF INTERESTS: LIBER AMICORUM, PETER HAY ZUM 70. GEBURTSTAG 519 (2005).

[283] GEORGE A. BERMANN, ROGER J. GOEBEL, WILLIAM J. DAVEY, & ELEANOR M. FOX, CASES AND MATERIALS ON EUROPEAN COMMUNITY LAW (1993) (4th ed. 2015, with six authors).

[284] Boerger, *supra* note 279, at 863–65, 868–69, 876, 878–79, 890; *Eric Stein: Vita*, 82 MICH. L. REV. 1149 (1984). Michigan Law School began to grant the J.D. degree in 1910; it was an alternative to the LL.B. and required the student to already hold a B.A. degree and earn in law school a B average. BROWN & BLUME, *supra* note 121, at 738, 740, 744.

[285] 1–2 AMERICAN ENTERPRISE IN THE EUROPEAN COMMON MARKET: A LEGAL PROFILE (Eric Stein & Thomas L. Nicholson, eds., 1960); *see* Boerger, *supra* note 279, at 870–71.

[286] Boerger, *supra* note 279, at 872; *see* 1 AMERICAN ENTERPRISE, *supra* note 285, at 459–510 (coauthored chapter); 2 *id.* at 647–86 (Hay chapter). Stein and Hay published the coauthored chapter as *Legal Remedies of Enterprises in the European Economic Community*, 9 AM. J. COMP. L. 375 (1960). Hay received his Michigan J.D. in 1958 and studied at the law faculties of Göttingen and Heidelberg in 1959–1960. He taught a semester each year on the law faculty at Dresden from 1994 to 2000.

Supranational Organizations, comparing the federal systems of Germany and the United States with the rapidly emerging structure of the European communities as a continuing process.[287]

4. Comparative Law Journals and Projects

After World War II, every ABA accredited law school continued or began a general student-run law journal for pedagogical purposes and to serve the information and research needs of the legal profession. The first specialized journals, almost always administered by students, covered international law broadly defined so that some foreign and comparative law articles appeared there as well as in general law reviews. The initial reviews for foreign law or explicitly including comparative law (usually together with international law) emerged in the late 1960s. The student-edited international and comparative law type appeared at Georgia (1970), Boston College and Hastings (1977), Loyola of Los Angeles (1978), New York Law School (1979), Arizona (1982), and Temple (1985).

Journals for a single country's legal system or for those of countries in a region arrived a little earlier. Some were associated with a law school and made use of students; others had editorial boards of professors and sometimes lawyers and generally rotated editorial offices. The first reviews for East Asia, *Law in Japan* (1967–2001)[288] and *Chinese Law and Government* (1968),[289] largely consisted of articles or legal materials translated into English. The ABA Section of International Law sponsored the *China Law Reporter* (1980–1999).[290] The remaining reviews were an addition to a law school's program in comparative law. These included *Lawyer of the Americas* (1969, Miami),[291] *Canada-United States Law Journal* (1978, Case Western Reserve), *UCLA Pacific Basin Law Journal* (1982), and *Chinese Law* (1987, Columbia).[292]

As for comparative law projects centered at American law schools, Michigan took the lead during World War II in anticipation of the war's end and likely

---

[287] Peter Hay, Federalism and Supranational Organizations: Patterns for New Legal Structures (1966); see Carl J. Friedrich, *Book Review*, 61 Am. J. Int'l L. 636–37 (1967); Dennis Thompson, *Book Review*, 80 Harv. L. Rev. 1372–75 (1967).

[288] *Law in Japan* was a yearbook of the Japanese American Society for Legal Studies that professors edited. From 1968 to 1995, the University of Washington hosted its editorial office. After 1991, it appeared irregularly, in 1995 and finally 2000–2001. *See* David F. Cavers, *The Japanese American Society for Legal Studies*, 13 Am. J. Comp. L. 661–62 (1964); *supra* note 257 and accompanying text (Asian Law Program).

[289] *Chinese Law and Government*, a peer-reviewed journal, began at NYU and rotated editorial offices among law schools and political science departments.

[290] *China Law Reporter* had a board of editors consisting of law professors and lawyers practicing in the United States.

[291] From 1984, *Miami Inter-American Law Review*.

[292] From 1996, *Columbia Journal of Asian Law*.

emergence of the United States in a leadership position. Yntema, as director of research in inter-American law from 1942, with the cooperation of the U.S. State Department, brought young Latin American jurists to Michigan to prepare articles and books on different topics of their countries' negotiable instruments, since this was a technical and nonpolitical area of commercial law. He felt it was a "promising field to test comparative methods and to explore the possibility of legislative unification."[293]

There were a variety of other such projects, typically directed at both practicing lawyers as well as academic comparatists. Some of these involved translations of foreign primary legal sources. A large endeavor was the Comparative Criminal Law Project, directed by Gerhard Mueller (1926–2006) at NYU from 1960 to 1977, with the first two volumes as translations of the French and Korean penal codes. Each translation included an introduction describing the history, ideology, and structure of the foreign criminal substantive or procedural law system.[294] In 1978, Edward Wise (1938–2000) translated *The Italian Penal Code*.[295] He then took on the enterprise at Wayne State and by 1987, the project had translated 28 foreign penal law and procedure codes and statutes. In addition, it published 15 studies on comparative and foreign criminology, criminal law, and procedure.[296]

The Parker School under Coudert as acting director organized another substantial program, bilateral studies in private international law. Arthur Nussbaum wrote the first study in 1951 on Swiss law.[297] There were eventually 19 volumes by

---

[293] Hessel E. Yntema, *Research in Inter-American Law at the University of Michigan*, 43 MICH. L. REV. 549, 552, 554–56, 558 (1944) (quotation at 555); *see Yntema 1966, supra* note 133, at 978–79.

> Under the tremendous impact of the present world conflict, the people of the United States have come to a stern realization of their international commitments.... In this light, comparative study of the laws of the Americas, especially those affecting international commerce, is of special and immediate interest.... Only by ... careful scientific comparison of the existing institutions, as contrasted with unilateral efforts to propagate a particular system, can a sound basis be laid for such reconciliation of the laws in this hemisphere.

Yntema, *Research, supra*, at 552–53.

[294] Gerhard O.W. Mueller, *Foreword*, THE FRENCH PENAL CODE xi, xiii–xiv (Jean F. Moreau & Gerhard O.W. Mueller trans., 1960). Marc Ancel wrote the introduction and was the co-director of a European penal code series at the Paris Institute of Comparative Law; the NYU project also cited the Freiburg Max Planck Foreign and International Penal Law Institute series and the Ibero-American series from Argentina. *Id.* at xiii. *See also* ESSAYS IN CRIMINAL SCIENCE (Gerhard O.W. Mueller ed., 1961) (scholars from ten countries contributed chapters). Mueller enrolled in law at Kiel University, finishing his study in 1949, when he emigrated to the United States. He received his J.D. at Chicago in 1953, after which he taught law, accepting a post at NYU in 1958. He also served as chief, United Nations Crime Prevention and Criminal Justice Branch (1974–1982) and president, American Society of Criminology (1968). Mahmoud Cherif Bassiouni, *In Memoriam: Gerhard O.W. Mueller*, 77 REVUE INTERNATIONALE DE DROIT PÉNAL 9–10 (2006); DIRECTORY OF LAW TEACHERS IN AMERICAN BAR ASSOCIATION APPROVED LAW SCHOOLS: 1960, at 245 (1959).

[295] THE ITALIAN PENAL CODE (Edward M. Wise trans., 1978). Wise also wrote the introduction. *Id.* at xxi–xlvi.

[296] PENAL CODE OF THE FEDERAL REPUBLIC OF GERMANY iii–v (Joseph J. Darby trans., 1987); *see, e.g.*, STUDIES IN COMPARATIVE CRIMINAL LAW (Edward M. Wise & Gerhard O.W. Mueller eds., 1975).

[297] ARTHUR NUSSBAUM, AMERICAN-SWISS PRIVATE INTERNATIONAL LAW 3 (1951); *see supra* ch. 6, text accompanying notes 278–81 (Nussbaum).

1972. Although each publication's title juxtaposed the United States with a foreign country, the studies largely presented the private substantive or procedural law of that nation and how its treaties, statutes, or courts directed a decision between competing laws and about proof of foreign law, jurisdiction, and enforcement of judgments. Later in the series, the volumes included certain public law subjects such as antitrust, crime, social security, or taxation.[298] The Parker School sponsored many other foreign and comparative law books as well as the Szladits bibliographies.[299]

5. Degree Programs for Foreign Students

At the end of World War II, an AALS committee considered that the American postwar geopolitical situation would require leading law schools to encourage graduate law study for foreign lawyers. Due to the immediate influx of returning American veterans financed by the G.I. Bill,[300] it was only in the 1950s that schools could reinstitute their graduate programs and host foreign students, both non-degree and LL.M. and J.S.D. degree candidates and equivalents. The motivation for individual law schools was a combination of the dean's own experience earning a graduate law degree, institutional prestige, and the usefulness of foreign graduate students; it was not financial reward. Columbia, Harvard, Michigan, and Yale spent about 40 percent of their fellowship aid on graduate students even though they represented a mere 6 percent of enrolled students. By the 1960s, as American students lost interest in a graduate degree, there was more availability for foreign students to enroll.[301]

In 1964, a Harvard faculty report recommended three fields for enhancement, one of which was foreign and comparative law. This involved hiring faculty whose primary duty would be graduate training and research and creating special graduate fellowships. Von Mehren directed this initiative and, to illustrate, Harvard awarded a comparative law fellow, Robert Means, who in 1970 joined the Texas law faculty, a S.J.D. in 1967. In 1969, USAID funded the Law and Modernization Program at Yale centered on Africa and Latin America, which a few students

---

[298] *See, e.g.*, ULRICH DROBNIG, AMERICAN-GERMAN PRIVATE INTERNATIONAL LAW (2d ed. 1972). On the bilateral and private law aspect of coverage, *see id.* at 3.

[299] *See* Hein, *Parker School, supra* note 233; supra note 233 and accompanying text (Szladits).

[300] Servicemen's Readjustment Act of 1944, Pub. L. No. 78–346, 58 Stat. 284.

[301] Gail J. Hupper, *Education Ambivalence: The Rise of a Foreign-Student Doctorate in Law*, 49 NEW ENG. L. REV. 319, 326–31, 396, 402–04 (2015). Seven law schools conferred the bulk of J.S.D. or equivalent graduate law degrees: Columbia, George Washington, Harvard, Michigan, NYU, Wisconsin, and Yale. *Id.* at 321. In the 1950s, the Ford Foundation made large grants to these schools to expand their international legal studies, for instance, Harvard ($2.1 million), Columbia ($1.5 million), Yale ($700,000), Michigan ($500,000), and NYU ($450,000). *Id.* at 399.

used to earn the J.S.D. However, by the 1980s, U.S. students accounted for only a quarter of law doctorates earned.[302]

As the transition from domestic to foreign student enrollment in graduate law programs occurred, some professors interested in law and development saw foreign matriculation as an opportunity, and perhaps an obligation, to disseminated American ideas about law and legal systems to lawyers in developing nations. In the 1970s, foreign students earned two-thirds of the law doctorates, driven largely in the next decade by increasing globalization, prominence of the U.S. economy and its concomitant legal rules, and improved academic quality of American legal education. Furthermore, NGO funding allowed schools to expand their comparative and international offerings, sometimes aimed at foreign student LL.M. programs. In some cases, professors used these students for their own research projects, such as Yntema for Latin American commercial law. From the late 1960s through the 1980s, over half of the doctoral graduates at the leading law schools came from developing countries.[303] Growth in foreign student enrollment doubled in the 1980s, from 1,080 (1980) to 1,720 (1985) to 2,200 (1990), and then accelerated so that by 1995 there were 3,453 enrollees.[304]

E. The Role of American Governmental and Nongovernmental Organizations in Legal Transplants

1. Origins and Progression up to 1960

Interest in political, economic, and social development was a component of the European Enlightenment. It manifested itself in law with French legal codes in the early nineteenth century and later in German legal science. For the United States, the result of the Spanish-American War presented the national government with questions of what to do with lands of the defeated Spanish empire. The Philippine Islands was central to the political debate. The primary legal transplant fostered by U.S. government lawyers was in Philippine constitutional and administrative law. In addition, the new Republic of China after 1912 offered opportunities for exploitation or reform by the United States and European countries vying for influence. Jurists affiliated with nonprofit entities, such as the

---

[302] Hupper, *supra* note 301, at 392–94, 445–46; *see* ROBERT CHARLES MEANS, UNDERDEVELOPMENT AND THE DEVELOPMENT OF LAW: CORPORATIONS AND CORPORATION LAW IN NINETEENTH-CENTURY COLOMBIA (1980); *infra* pt. E.2 (USAID).

[303] Hupper, *supra* note 301, at 395–419, 423–24, 430–34.

[304] David S. Clark, *Transnational Legal Practice: The Need for Global Law Schools*, 46 AM. J. COMP. L. 261, 270 (Supp. 1998). In 1994, the countries that sent more than 100 students were Canada, China, Germany, Japan, Korea, and Taiwan. *Id.*

Carnegie Endowment for International Peace, the ABA, and a few universities, participated, especially in legal education.[305]

After the Second World War, American influence stemmed from its military occupation in part of Germany, Japan, and South Korea. One can see the impact in public law, especially constitutional law, and in institutions such as judicial review. The transformation of legal norms and institutions was strongest in Japan and Korea. Many more American comparative lawyers were involved with these legal transplants than with the earlier legal developments in the Philippines and China.[306]

By the 1950s, American concern with foreign development—often then referred to as modernization, including for law and legal institutions—was associated with the ideological threat posed by communism to capitalism and liberal democracy. The Cold War required each side to demonstrate its ability to foster economic and social progress. One could trace the roots of this competition in the United States to the New Deal and worldwide to economic and political crises of the 1930s.[307] With Eisenhower taking the presidency in 1953, his administration was less enthusiastic with non-military foreign aid and multilateral coordination to promote development. The shift was toward trade and private foreign investment. For instance, comparative law jurists in the AACSL and ABA devoted substantial effort to international unification of commercial and trade law. In addition, NGOs and UNESCO continued supporting conferences and studies concerning modernization. The IALS illustrated that for legal science.[308]

A few legal comparatists in the 1950s had argued for use of the field's methodology, in conjunction with public international law, to formulate and improve human rights norms and to enhance basic democratic values. Myres McDougal set out this initiative in the *American Journal of Comparative Law*'s first issue. He declared that the use of the comparative method for value clarification in different communities was necessary to enhance democratic values in a peaceful world.[309] Yntema, the *Journal*'s head editor, in delivering the presidential address at the 1958 International Congress of Comparative Law in Brussels, surveyed the

---

[305] See supra ch. 6, pt. A.2 (early U.S. legal transplants). See generally DAVID EKBLADH, THE GREAT AMERICAN MISSION: MODERNIZATION AND THE CONSTRUCTION OF AN AMERICAN WORLD ORDER 14–37 (2010).

[306] See supra pt. A (U.S. military occupation). See generally EKBLADH, supra note 305, at 121–52 (Korea).

[307] CARRINGTON, supra note 6, at 271–73; EKBLADH, supra note 305, at 4–9.

[308] EKBLADH, supra note 305, at 155–58, 167–72, 185–89; see supra text accompanying note 114 (Eisenhower); infra pt. F.2 (unification of law).

[309] Myres S. McDougal, *The Comparative Study of Law for Policy Purposes: Value Clarification as an Instrument of Democratic World Order*, 1 AM. J. COMP. L. 24–27, 34–38, 56–57 (1952); see id. at 33 n.31 (survey of 18 books and articles treating the purposes of comparative law). The 1948 United Nations Universal Declaration of Human Rights demonstrated this strategy. Id. at 34 n.34.

use of comparison to now develop a worldwide version of the earlier European *jus commune*.

> [T]he immediate motive for comparative law frequently has been utilitarian. It is much easier to imitate a successful foreign model of legislation than to originate a new one. And in international practice as in private international law some knowledge of foreign legal systems is indispensable. But even such practical considerations reflect the perception that a particular system of law gives a partial view; that the essential principles of law transcend political frontiers; that legal science does not admit chauvinistic isolation. It imports the humanistic conception of universal justice, of a law of nature and of nations.... In perpetuating [the *jus commune*] tradition, the comparative study of law, through objective observation of historical phenomena, seeks to ascertain and to formulate in rational terms the common elements of human experience that relate to law and justice.[310]

John McCloy exemplified the foreign policy establishment with his service in the U.S. government and supportive NGOs toward human rights in the 1950s and 1960s. During the war, McCloy was part of a task force that created the Office of Strategic Services, which later became the Central Intelligence Agency (CIA). He also backed the United Nations and use of war crimes tribunals. From 1947 to 1949, McCloy was president of the World Bank, followed by tenure as U.S. High Commissioner for Germany until 1952. He was head of the Ford Foundation from 1956 to 1965 while also chairing the Council on Foreign Relations (CFR) in New York from 1954 to 1970. As commissioner in Germany, McCloy along with Allen Dulles, who was deputy director of the CIA and chair of the CFR, established the International Commission of Jurists (ICJ) to reclaim from a Soviet-supported organization the high moral ground for peace, freedom, and justice.[311] The ICJ's principal focus was to promote the rule of law and its constituent elements.[312]

---

[310] Hessel E. Yntema, *Comparative Law and Humanism*, 7 AM. J. COMP. L. 493, 498 (1958).

[311] Yves Dezalay & Bryant G. Garth, *Law, Lawyers, and Empire*, in 3 THE CAMBRIDGE HISTORY OF LAW IN AMERICA: THE TWENTIETH CENTURY AND AFTER (1920–) 718, 735 (Michael Grossberg & Christopher Tomlins eds., 2008); *see* KAI BIRD, THE CHAIRMAN: JOHN J. MCCLOY, THE MAKING OF THE AMERICAN ESTABLISHMENT (1992); THOMAS ALAN SCHWARTZ, AMERICA'S GERMANY: JOHN J. MCCLOY AND THE FEDERAL REPUBLIC OF GERMANY (1991); see *supra* text accompanying notes 6, 104 (McCloy). The CIA funded and provided administrative support to the ICJ, which became public knowledge in 1967, almost terminating the organization and forcing Seán MacBride, the ICJ's secretary general (1963–1970) and one of the founders of the Council of Europe, to eventually resign. Dezalay & Garth, *supra*, at 735; see HOWARD B. TOLLEY, JR., THE INTERNATIONAL COMMISSION OF JURISTS: GLOBAL ADVOCATES FOR HUMAN RIGHTS 17, 97–139 (1994). John Foster Dulles, the brother of Allen Dulles, was Eisenhower's secretary of state from 1953 to 1959. CARRINGTON, *supra* note 6, at 272–73.

[312] *See, e.g.*, Dudley B. Bonsal, *International Congress of Jurists in New Delhi*, 8 AM. J. COMP. L. 258–59 (1959). The format for the congress was like that utilized by the International Academy of

2. The 1960s: Decade of Development

In 1961, the United Nations declared the 1960s the decade of development, announced by President John Kennedy (served 1961-1963) at the U.N. He had campaigned on restoring American leadership on development to meet the global revolution of rising expectations and to exceed Soviet aid expenditures in developing nations, many newly emergent from colonialism. To coordinate assistance, Congress authorized the creation of the Agency for International Development (USAID).[313] As part of this initiative, Kennedy established the Peace Corps and, to confront Fidel Castro's influence in Latin America, the Alliance for Progress.[314]

The Ford Foundation was instrumental in efforts to improve the quality and independence of lawyers and judges in poorer countries, sometimes supported by USAID and other NGOs. These organizations considered this essential to foster rule of law and human rights protections. The strategy involved sending established American law professors with experience abroad to assist local lawyers in reforming legal education. Ford, the Peace Corps, and the Fulbright fellowship program also financed young law graduates with an interest in foreign nations to participate in a range of legal reform activities.[315] In 1966, Ford awarded $3 million to set up a separate NGO for this activity, the International Legal Center (ILC). Its purpose was to "support systematic study of the role of law in . . . the development of modern nations, . . . expand the ranks of lawyers, social scientists, and others qualified to work on problems of law and development," and "help developing countries establish legal institutions essential to the functioning of modern, free societies."[316]

Comparative Law, but concerned with a questionnaire to solicit answers about the principles that constituted rule of law in various legal systems of the free world. *Id.* at 259.

[313] JAMES A. GARDNER, LEGAL IMPERIALISM: AMERICAN LAWYERS AND FOREIGN AID IN LATIN AMERICA 6-8, 27-40 (1980); EKBLADH, *supra* note 305, at 190-92; James M. Hagen & Vernon W. Ruttan, Development Policy under Eisenhower and Kennedy, 23 J. DEVELOPING AREAS 1 (1988); *see* Foreign Assistance Act of 1961, Pub. L. No. 87-195, 75 Stat. 424.

[314] EKBLADH, *supra* note 305, at 192-93, 195; *see* Michael Dunne, *Kennedy's Alliance for Progress: Countering Revolution in Latin America, Part I—From the White House to the Charter of Punta del Este*, 89 INT'L AFF. 1389-1409 (2013). Kennedy created the Peace Corps in 1961 by executive order, confirmed by Congress. *See* Peace Corps Act, Pub. L. No. 87-293, 75 Stat. 612 (1961).

[315] CARRINGTON, *supra* note 6, at 276-77. The Mutual Educational and Cultural Exchange Act of 1961 expanded the original 1946 Fulbright Program to include research visits of foreigners at American law schools and U.S. legal scholars abroad. *See* Pub. L. No. 87-256, 75 Stat. 527. The Ford Foundation and later USAID financed this author's residence in Costa Rica for two and a half years (1969-1971) to work with Costa Rican lawyers and economists in an agrarian reform institute and to teach that subject from an interdisciplinary perspective at the university law school. In 1999, the Fulbright program provided the author a distinguished chair award to teach transnational litigation at the University of Trento.

[316] FORD REPORT, *supra* note 226, at 23 (1966); *see* GARDNER, *supra* note 313, at 48-49, 126-45, 212-17, 225-26, 233-35; *International Legal Center*, 15 AM. J. COMP. L. 608-09 (1967).

Many of these legal missionaries went to Anglophonic Africa, typically due to insufficient French or other foreign language capability. James Paul (1926-2011) illustrated this group. While a law professor at Pennsylvania, Paul made several trips to Ethiopia and other African nations sponsored by Eisenhower Fellowships, an NGO, and the Peace Corps to promote legal education. In 1963, Haile Selassie University invited him to oversee the creation of a law school, where he served as law dean for four years and then as the university academic vice president until 1969. Paul became law dean and professor at Rutgers-Newark in 1970 and served on the Ethiopian Constitutional Commission (1974-1987), where he assisted in drafting the 1987 Constitution's bill of rights.[317]

In 1965, Arthur Schiller established the African Law Center at Columbia and, with professors from other law schools, the African Law Association in America (ALAA). The latter's aim was to promote the study and development of legal systems—especially legal education and the profession—in Africa.[318] Schiller had a long history teaching comparative and Roman law and this new field expanded his impressive domain of foreign law.[319] He staked a position against efforts at modernizing Ethiopian and Eritrean law along Western lines and preferred a pluralism based on a local *Volksgeist* supporting traditionalism, evidenced by restatements of customary law.[320]

In 1969, the African Law Center began publishing *African Law Studies*, which changed its name in 1981 to *Journal of Legal Pluralism* to capture a larger audience and reflect its new corporate independence.[321] Similarly, recognizing

---

[317] CARRINGTON, *supra* note 6, at 276-77; Sally A. Downey, James C.N. Paul . . ., *Philadelphia Inquirer*, 22 Sept. 2011 (posted); THE AALS DIRECTORY OF LAW TEACHERS [hereinafter AALS DIRECTORY]: 1990-91, at 671 (1990); *see* GARDNER, *supra* note 313, at 40-45; Jayanth K. Krishnan, *Academic SAILERS: The Ford Foundation and the Efforts to Shape Legal Education in Africa, 1957-1977*, 52 AM. J. LEGAL HIST. 261, 263-64, 268-300 (2012). Paul was a founding member of the International Third World Legal Studies Association. 1990 AALS DIRECTORY, *supra*, at 671. Other U.S. law professors who provided legal assistance to African nations were William Harvey (Michigan) to Ghana, Ian Macneil (Cornell) to Tanzania, Jack Koons (Northwestern) to Uganda. CARRINGTON, *supra*, at 277. The ILC sent American lawyers to Africa and brought African students and lawyers to the United States. Krishnan, *supra*, at 312-24.

[318] A. Arthur Schiller, *The African Law Association in America*, 14 AM. J. COMP. L. 378-79 (1965); *see A.A. Schiller, at 74, Retired Law Expert*, N.Y. TIMES, 12 July 1977, at 28.

[319] COLUMBIA LAW, *supra* note 149, at 321-22, 497 n.52; 1930 AALS DIRECTORY, *supra* note 317, at 95; *see* Hessel E. Yntema & A. Arthur Schiller, Source Book of Roman Law (mimeo. 1929); A. Arthur Schiller, Texts and Commentary for the Study of Roman Law: Mechanisms of Development (mimeo. 1936); *supra* ch. 6, notes 339-341 and accompanying text (Schiller). Schiller had studied at Munich University in 1929 and Erlangen University awarded him an honorary Dr. Jur. in 1950. He wrote about Coptic law as well as Indonesian *adat* law. 1960 AALS DIRECTORY, *supra* note 317, at 291-92.

[320] Kaius Tuori, *Legal Pluralism and Modernization: American Law Processors in Ethiopia and the Downfall of the Restatements of African Customary Law*, 62 J. LEGAL PLURALISM & UNOFFICIAL L. 43-70 (2010).

[321] A. Arthur Schiller, *African Law Studies: A New Publication of the African Law Center*, 1 AFR. L. STUD. iii-iv (1969); J[ohn] Griffiths, *From the Editor*, 19 J. LEGAL PLURALISM v-vi (1981). Marc Galanter wrote the lead article in volume 19. *Id.* at 1-48. In 1985, the *Journal* added "and Unofficial Law."

the broader interests of its members, the ALAA in 1980 altered its name to International Third World Legal Studies Association. It provided a forum for annual meetings, collaboration among scholars interested in law and social change, and published *Third World Legal Studies* from 1982 to 2003. The 1982 editorial board consisted of four U.S. law professors assisted by advisory editors who resided abroad. This pattern continued until the journal's demise.[322]

American law professors and recent graduates also went to India, generally to improve legal education. Marc Galanter and Julius Getman illustrated this contingent. After Galanter taught as a Bigelow Fellow at Chicago, he took a Fulbright award in 1957 to the law faculty at the University of Delhi. Employing a social science perspective on law, his career took him to Wisconsin in 1976. As America's leading scholar utilizing law and society methods to analyze law and legal institutions in India, Galanter demonstrated that the overseas experience might change the missionary more than the host legal system.[323] Beginning in 1955, Ford took an interest in supporting the creation by Indians of a legal research institute modeled on the American Law Institute (ALI) adapted to local Indian conditions. The Indian Law Institute in New Delhi opened in 1956, determined to first concentrate on constitutional and administrative law, and shortly thereafter commenced building an important law library and journal. In 1962, Ford sent Von Mehren to the institute, where he organized a seminar to instruct resident scholars in empirical research. Nevertheless, by 1969, reports of dysfunction and political interference at the institute led Ford to commission Von Mehren to critically evaluate its usefulness. When he confirmed that the institute had failed to connect with India's law schools or produce meaningful scholarship, Ford began to phase out funding.[324]

While a law professor at Indiana, the Ford Foundation financed Julius Getman from 1967 to 1968 to consult on legal education at the College of Banaras Hindu University and the Indian Law Institute in New Delhi. During his stay he visited many law schools and at Banaras assisted young instructors in preparing a legal method course. Getman was highly critical of the law school lecture system and the quality of law teachers, students, and administrators. Some government authorities were aware of these deficiencies and wanted the U.S. government

---

[322] A. Peter Mutharika, Foreword: Introducing INTWORLSA, THIRD WORLD LEGAL STUD. i–ii (1982); *see id.* at vii (board of editors); *id.* at iv (2000–2003) (editorial office at Valparaiso).

[323] CARRINGTON, *supra* note 6, at 277–78, 281; 1990 AALS DIRECTORY, *supra* note 317, at 365–66; *see* MARC GALANTER, COMPETING EQUALITIES: LAW AND THE BACKWARD CLASSES IN INDIA (1984); *id.*, LAW AND SOCIETY IN INDIA (Rajeev Dhavan ed., 1989) (compilation of certain Galanter articles and chapters on India). Galanter's first journal publication was *Caste Disabilities and Indian Federalism*, 3 J. INDIAN L. INST. 39 (1961). *See also* Jayanth K. Krishnan, *Professor Kingfield Goes to India*, 46 AM. J. LEGAL HIST. 449 (2005).

[324] Jayanth K. Krishnan, *From the ALI to the ILI: The Efforts to Export an American Legal Institution*, 38 VAND. J. TRANSNAT'L L. 1255, 1262–91 (2005). Ford sent U.S. law professors from 1958 to 1970 to evaluate the institute's performance. *Id.* at 1274–75, 1281–88.

and NGOs, especially Ford, to provide funding for improvement. Ford tied its aid to new instructional materials, use of the case method, and student class participation. While English was the principal legal language, most major law schools were in northern India where Hindi or Hindustani was lingua franca. When instructors attempted an active teaching method, most students and some teachers with poor English skills rebelled. Getman believed the only viable path forward was to support a single law college, the one at Delhi University, where English was generally prevalent.[325]

Various Latin American countries were also host to U.S. law professors with aid directed toward legal education, the court system, or land reform. Ford financed Karst (Ohio State) who studied land reform in Argentina (1962–1963) and Rosenn (Ohio State) who helped to establish graduate legal education in Rio de Janeiro (1966–1968), a period in Brazil subject to military rule. Several legal scholars went to Colombia to assist with reform of legal institutions. Stanford Law School with Ford aid established ties to law faculties in Chile.[326]

Most of the American missionary lawyers of the 1950s and 1960s accepted the prevalent social engineering paradigm taught in U.S. law schools. However, the tradition in host countries, whether their colonial past was common law or civil law, was one of lawyers as technicians serving a bureaucratic state or the private sector in enforcing contracts and property rights. Legal rules and institutions retained colonial roots and seldom reflected the legal cultures or interests of most people. Proposals for reform inevitably lacked local political support and often, when attempted, made social conditions worse. By 1970, donors and missionaries alike sensed that their approach to build a bulwark against the attraction of communism was not working.[327] Comparatists and others concluded

---

[325] CARRINGTON, *supra* note 6, at 278; 1990 AALS DIRECTORY, *supra* note 317, at 377; Julius G. Getman, *The Development of Indian Legal Education: The Impact of the Language Problem*, 21 J. LEGAL EDUC. 513–22, 513 n.* (1969). Others in the India group included John Jackson (Michigan), Harry Jones (Columbia), Kenneth Pye (Duke), and Von Mehren. CARRINGTON, *supra*, at 278; *see* Arthur von Mehren, *Law and Legal Education in India: Some Observations*, 78 HARV. L. REV. 1180 (1965).

[326] CARRINGTON, *supra* note 6, at 279; M.C. MIROW, LATIN AMERICAN LAW: A HISTORY OF PRIVATE LAW AND INSTITUTIONS IN SPANISH AMERICA 187–91 (2004); John Henry Merryman, *Law and Development Memoirs I: The Chile Law Program*, 48 AM. J. COMP. L. 481–99 (2000); 1990 AALS DIRECTORY, *supra* note 317, at 489, 734 (1990); *see* GARDNER, *supra* note 313, at 53–109, 126–45; *supra* text accompanying note 263 (Karst, Rosenn). David Trubek, a recent law graduate, advised USAID in Brazil from 1962 to 1966, after which he began his law teaching career. GARDNER, *supra*, at 66–79; 1990 AALS Directory, *supra*, at 853. Dennis Lynch, another young law graduate, worked as an adviser to the Ford Foundation in Bogotá (1969–1972) before beginning law teaching. GARDNER, *supra*, at 199–210; 1990 AALS DIRECTORY, *supra*, at 566.

[327] CARRINGTON, *supra* note 6, at 280–82; GARDNER, *supra* note 313, at 9–15, 24–26; John Henry Merryman, *Comparative Law and Social Change: On the Origins, Style, Decline & Revival of the Law and Development Movement*, 25 AM. J. COMP. L. 457, 459–60, 480–83 (1977) [hereinafter Merryman, *Social Change*]; *see* GARDNER, *supra*, at 247–81.

that the enterprise was ethnocentric and naïve in its premise about the efficacy of American legal institutions. It was time to forego action and try investigation.[328]

3. Assessment and the Emergence of Human Rights Law

In 1970, John Merryman (1920-2015) convinced Ford and USAID to fund an assessment of law and development activities and to conduct an empirical study comparing legal institutions and processes to learn what best promotes economic development. The Stanford team selected six civil law nations in various stages of economic development that shared a Mediterranean legal culture. By the end of the decade, the conclusion was that associations between law and development—economic, political, or social—were exceedingly complicated and mediated by culture, geography, and other factors.[329]

The Stanford project, called SLADE, defined development as social change, which it measured quantitatively over time (1945-1970) and across socioeconomic regions within a nation. It defined law as legal systems consisting of institutions, processes, and actors that in the aggregate consumed resources, measured by budgets and fees. Each of these categories had a quantitative dimension that varied by region and over time. The institutions were legislative, administrative, judicial, private ordering, law enforcement, and legal education and professions. SLADE collected data on these institutions, their processes, the actors involved, and resources consumed. With the six nations and total of 24 regions for annual data points, SLADE could engage in quantitative comparative law that was both synchronic and diachronic. With numeric social and legal variables or indicators, one could formulate and test hypotheses about the relationship between society and its legal system, thus clearly bringing the enterprise within the field of law and society. Often the analysis of different results would require knowledge of the attitudes and values of legal actors—an internal legal culture—and the population's values and attitudes—an external legal culture—toward individual legal institutions and processes. By 1976, SLADE completed the field research and the USAID grant expired. There was no further funding for systematic study and interpretation of the data. It published the data and there were several national and comparative studies utilizing them.[330]

---

[328] CARRINGTON, *supra* note 6, at 281-82; *see* GARDNER, *supra* note 313, at 211-30; David M. Trubek & Marc Galanter, *Scholars in Self-Estrangement: Some Reflections on the Crisis in Law and Development Studies in the United States*, 1974 WIS. L. REV. 1062, 1080-85 (1974).

[329] CARRINGTON, *supra* note 6, at 281-82; John Henry Merryman, *Law and Development Memoirs II: SLADE*, 48 AM. J. COMP. L. 713-15 (2000) [hereinafter Merryman, SLADE]. The USAID grant was for $750,000. GARDNER, *supra* note 313, at 225. SLADE was the acronym for empirical investigations, Studies in Law and Development. This author was associate director of SLADE from 1973 to 1976.

[330] Merryman, SLADE, *supra* note 329, at 715-27; *see id.* at 724-27 nn.11-12 (published studies); JOHN HENRY MERRYMAN, DAVID S. CLARK, & LAWRENCE M. FRIEDMAN, LAW AND SOCIAL

The tide had shifted from action programs for developing countries that aimed to transplant elements of the American legal system to inquiry about the relationship between law and social change. In 1971, the *American Journal of Comparative Law* published a symposium on law and development in Latin America that illustrated that shift, with articles that emphasized the historical, cultural, and social reality for foreign legal systems.[331] In 1974, Galanter and David Trubek, two comparatists with programmatic experience concluded that the field was in crisis. As scholars subjected U.S. development assistance to critical scrutiny, they concluded that the purported goals of protecting individual freedom, enhancing social equality, and expanding citizen participation in the political system had failed.[332]

By the 1970s, the dominant U.S. foreign policy ideology had shifted from realism, discredited by the failed Bay of Pigs coup against Cuba in 1961 and hostility toward the Vietnam War, to idealism, undercutting the power of the foreign policy establishment. Many disfavored even the concept of modernization due to its connection with the Cold War, ethnocentrism, and cultural imperialism. Already in the 1960s, the International Commission of Jurists, limiting its membership to 60 elite lawyers, judges, and academics, proceeded to authorize national branches and train a staff with legal expertise in human rights and the rule of law. Those individuals with an idealistic orientation went to work for governments and NGOs that facilitated the growing institutionalization of human rights. For example, Amnesty International grew out of the United Kingdom section of the ICJ in 1961 and fostered an image of neutrality that helped its legitimacy as the Cold War intensified. After the mid-1960s, the Ford Foundation under George Bundy began to fund universities and NGOs to support human rights and rule of law projects abroad.[333]

In 1973, two émigrés from Europe, Louis (Ludwig) Sohn (1914–2006) and Thomas Buergenthal, prepared the first U.S. coursebook on international human

---

Change in Mediterranean Europe and Latin America: A Handbook of Legal and Social Indicators for Comparative Study (1979); *see* Stewart Macaulay, *Book Review*, 29 Am. J. Comp. L. 542–47 (1981). *E.g.*, David S. Clark, *Civil Litigation Trends in Europe and Latin America since 1945: The Advantage of Intracountry Comparisons*, 24 Law & Soc'y Rev. 549–69 (1990).

[331] Karst & Rosenn, *supra* note 263, at 431–33.
[332] Trubek & Galanter, *supra* note 328, at 1062–64, 1070–80, 1089–93; *see supra* note 323 and accompanying text (Galanter); *supra* note 326 (Trubek).
[333] Ekbladh, *supra* note 305, at 9–11, 238–44, 258–59; Dezalay & Garth, *supra* note 311, at 719, 731–32, 735–38; *see* Ekbladh, *supra*, at 226–27, 230–38, 244–56; *supra* text accompanying notes 311–12 (ICJ). *See also* International Commission of Jurists, Rule of Law and Human Rights: Principles and Definitions as Elaborated at the Congresses and Conferences Held under the Auspices of the International Commission of Jurists, 1955–1966 (1966). A high point of idealistic human rights in the United States came during the presidency of Jimmy Carter (1977–1981). Dezalay & Garth, *supra*, at 739–40.

rights, drawing substantial material from European developments.[334] Sohn, born in Lviv, Ukraine (then Poland), earned his law degree there and worked at a university institute on comparative conflict of law issues. In 1939, he left on the last ship departing Poland ahead of the invading German army. Joseph Beale had invited Sohn to take a research position at Harvard, but as it turned out, he became a student assistant to Manley Hudson while he worked on his S.J.D. studies. This relationship transformed Sohn's interest in private international law to public international law. He began his teaching career at Harvard Law School, where he remained until 1981, with the country's first course on United Nations law. In 1991, he co-founded the International Rule of Law Center at George Washington University Law School.[335]

Buergenthal, born in 1934 to Polish-Jewish parents in Czechoslovakia, survived Auschwitz, and after the war, attended a *Realgymnasium* in Göttingen. In 1951, he arrived in the United States, finished high school and college, then graduated from NYU Law School. In 1960, Buergenthal entered the LL.M. program at Harvard Law School, where he met Sohn. Based on his writing at Harvard, he published two articles in the *American Journal of Comparative Law* on the European Court of Justice.[336] After beginning a teaching career, Buergenthal returned to Harvard for the S.J.D. and more work with Sohn. Buergenthal had broadened his interest to the European Convention on Human Rights and wrote an article about its application in national legal systems that caught the attention of the ICJ and provided him an introduction to ICJ jurists.[337] He served as a judge from 1979 to 1991 on the Inter-American Court of Human Rights and from 2000 to 2010 on the International Court of Justice, while holding professorships in several American law schools.[338] In 2020, he was Lobingier Professor Emeritus of Comparative Law and Jurisprudence at George Washington University.

---

[334] Dezalay & Garth, *supra* note 311, at 736–37; *see* LOUIS B. SOHN & THOMAS BUERGENTHAL, INTERNATIONAL PROTECTION OF HUMAN RIGHTS (1973). The book was based on prior course materials by Sohn and Buergenthal's efforts at the American Society of International Law's committee on human rights, supported by a grant from the MacArthur Foundation. *Quellen zur Geschichte der Menschenrechte, Thomas Buergenthal* https://www.geschichte-menschenrechte.de/personen/thomas-buergenthal (2015) [hereinafter *Buergenthal Interview*].

[335] Thomas Buergenthal, *Louis B. Sohn (1914–2006)*, 100 AM. J. INT'L L. 623–25 (2006); *see* Louis B. Sohn, *New Bases for Solution of Conflict of Laws Problems*, 55 HARV. L. REV. 978 (1942). Sohn maintained a European approach to teaching that assisted many foreign students who earned their advanced degrees at Harvard. Detlev F. Vagts, *Louis B. Sohn*, 48 HARV. INT'L L.J. 19–21 (2007).

[336] *Buergenthal Interview*, *supra* note 334; *see* Thomas Buergenthal, *Appeals for Annulment by Enterprises in the European Coal and Steel Community*, 10 AM. J. COMP. L. 227–52 (1961); *id.*, *The Private Appeal against Illegal State Activities in the European Coal and Steel Community*, 11 *id.* at 325–47 (1962).

[337] *Buergenthal Interview*, *supra* note 334; *see* Thomas Buergenthal, *The Domestic Status of the European Convention on Human Rights*, 13 BUFF. L. REV. 354–92 (1964), *reprinted in* 7 J. INT'L COMM. JURISTS 55–96 (1966).

[338] *Buergenthal Interview*, *supra* note 334.

By the 1980s, human rights law had both international and comparative dimensions and its inclusion in law school curricula solidified the idealists' hold on the subject. Human Rights Watch, with funding from the Ford Foundation and George Soros's Open Society Foundations, illustrated the symbiotic relationship between activist professionals and philanthropic managers. Both were dependent on law professors and lawyers for selection of overseas projects and their evaluation. In turn, foundations provided funds for university seminars, courses, and NGO internships for the human rights field.[339]

F. Themes in Comparative Law Research

Many diverse themes in comparative law developed after 1945. Some were new and others traditional as illustrated by those that follow. The *International Encyclopedia of Comparative Law*, an ambitious attempt in 17 volumes imagined in the 1960s and early 1970s to compare private law worldwide, included a volume on unification of law and another on private international law, both traditional subjects discussed here.[340] Projects to facilitate comparative research, exemplified by Szladits's bibliographic guides to comparative law books and journal articles or the Index to Foreign Legal Periodicals, were impressive initiatives. Comparative legal sociology, although typified earlier by Montesquieu and Weber, found new support among American comparatists as a better method to understand legal systems. American law and development began as a counterpoint to the role of the U.S. government and NGOs in attempting to transplant elements of Western law—mostly American—in developing countries.

1. Comparative Law Libraries and Projects to Facilitate Research

After World War II, American law libraries established a commanding worldwide lead in the size and diversity of their collections. In 1950, 31 U.S. law libraries had more than 100,000 volumes, and by 1960, 57 libraries had reached that threshold. Most of this growth occurred at university law schools with the notable exceptions of the Law Library of Congress, which by 1950 had overtaken Harvard Law School Library as the largest, and Los Angeles County Law

---

[339] Dezalay & Garth, *supra* note 311, at 737–38, 741–43, 756; *see* Open Society Foundations, *Our History*, https://www.opensocietyfoundations.org/who-we-are/our-history.

[340] *See supra* note 200 and accompanying text (*Encyclopedia*). Of the 17 chief editors for the volumes—as of 2004—five were Americans and four Germans.

Library.[341] It was at these large law libraries that comparative law collections grew remarkably. Prominent comparatists who facilitated this activity included Helen Clagett at the Law Library of Congress, Szladits at Columbia's Parker School, and William Stern at LA County Law Library.

From 1945 to 1948, Clagett (1905–1989), chief of the Hispanic Law Section, authored or coauthored ten bibliographic volumes covering Latin America in the Library of Congress *Guide to the Law and Legal Literature* series.[342] In 1952, in addition, she published a comparative treatment of judicial systems in Latin America. Clagett, born in Puerto Rico, graduated from George Washington University Law School (1941) and was a member of the AFLA and active in the ABA Section, serving as secretary and on the council in the 1950s.[343]

Charles Szladits (1911–1986) was an associate professor of law at the University of Budapest when, with the Soviet takeover of Hungary in 1946, he left for London. There he earned an LL.M. at the London School of Economics before settling in New York in 1949. Szladits affiliated with the Parker School and began work on a bibliography of English language works concerning foreign and comparative law. He took a broad view of the comparative law terrain, including jurisprudence and political philosophy, legal history and sociology, and private international law. He started with publications from 1790 and worked forward. He had nearly completed coverage for 1983 when he died, so the sixth cumulative bound volume covered 1978 to 1983.[344] Szladits found time to publish *Guide to Foreign Legal Materials: French, German, Swiss* (1959). The value of this volume led to a second coauthored edition in two books separately treating publications about the legal systems of France and Germany.[345] He also assisted

---

[341] See supra ch. 6, pt. E.6 (law library growth).

[342] Clagett's single country volumes included Mexico (1945, with John T. Vance); Bolivia, Chile, Ecuador, the Mexican states, Paraguay, Peru, Uruguay, and Venezuela (all published in 1947); and Argentina (1948). See supra ch. 6, note 94 (Clagett's volumes).

[343] HELEN L. CLAGETT, THE ADMINISTRATION OF JUSTICE IN LATIN AMERICA (1952); see Phanor J. Eder, Book Review, 2 AM. J. COMP. L. 274–76 (1953); AFLA Membership, supra note 130, at 468–69; ABA SEC. INT'L & COMP. L. PROC. 20 (1953); John N. Hazard, Reports: ABA Section, 4 AM. J. COMP. L. 644 (1955); Edward D. Re, Reports: ABA Section, 7 id. at 645 (1958).

[344] George A. Berman, Charles Szladits (1911–1986), 34 AM. J. COMP. L. 822–23 (1986); see CHARLES SZLADITS, 1–6 A BIBLIOGRAPHY ON FOREIGN AND COMPARATIVE LAW (1955–1989); supra note 179 and accompanying text (Journal supplements). A mimeographed predecessor to the bibliography began in 1952. The law library staffs at Columbia and NYU issued periodic lists of articles concerning foreign, comparative, and private international law published outside the United States and Great Britain. Formulated as an index, it included English and foreign language articles from about 120 journals. K.H. N[adelmann], Varia: First Cumulation, 3 AM. J. COMP. L. 310 (1954); see, e.g., Columbia University Law Library, Selected List of Articles: International Law and Relations, Comparative and Foreign Law, First Cumulation (1952–1953) (61 pages).

[345] CHARLES SZLADITS & CLAIRE M. GERMAIN, GUIDE TO FOREIGN LEGAL MATERIALS: FRENCH (2d ed. 1985); TIMOTHY KEARLEY & WOLFRAM FISCHER, CHARLES SZLADITS' GUIDE TO FOREIGN LEGAL MATERIALS: GERMAN (2d ed. 1990); see Edgar Bodenheimer, Book Review, 9 AM. J. COMP. L. 134–35 (1960). Szladits also edited two other Parker School guides to foreign legal materials, one for Italy and one for the Benelux countries. Szladits Bibliography, supra note 179, at 825.

the American Association of Law Libraries (AALL) in consulting on its project to guide law schools in developing their comparative law library collections.[346]

Due to the rapidly expanding publication in English of comparative law articles and books from the 1960s, Szladits's *Bibliography* volumes for periods after 1965 issued in book-length parts. The next two intervals, 1966 to 1977, each had two and then three parts respectively and the final coverage for 1978 to 1983 had five parts. After Szladits's death, the Parker School continued with the *Bibliography* including coverage through 1998 with 19 volumes. It published these with single or multi-year cumulations of two or three book-length parts illustrating the proliferation of comparative law literature.[347]

In 1959, the AALL was instrumental in establishing the International Association of Law Libraries (IALL). From 1990 to 2016, the IALL had between 400 and 600 members from 50 countries, with 150 to 180 of those from America. This reflected both the increased importance of foreign, comparative, and international law and its central locus in the United States. Among the largest U.S. comparative law libraries, which typically have less than a quarter of their volumes covering international law, designated librarians, expert in foreign and international law—often foreign born—assist users and coordinate interests through the IALL.[348]

Stern (1910–1972) built the LA County Law Library into a major foreign, comparative, and international law library with his efforts as head cataloger from 1939 to 1945, when he became the foreign law librarian until 1971. In 1933, he completed his J.U.D. law degree at Würzburg University. With Hitler's rise to power, he emigrated to the United States in 1935, taking a position with the Library of Congress. In 1937, he joined the staff at the University of Chicago Law Library, where he developed its foreign law classification system, and then moved to Los Angeles.[349]

In 1958, Stern proposed an *Index to Foreign Legal Periodicals*. The Ford Foundation provided $12,000 for the initiative, whose first annual volume of quarterly issues appeared in 1960 with support from the AALL. With continued Ford Foundation support, the series indexed by subject and geography mostly non-English periodical articles and book reviews of a minimum length in 250 journals from 50 countries plus collections of essays (such as *Festschriften*)

---

[346] Vera Bolgár, *Book Review*, 16 AM. J. COMP. L. 644 (1968) (Law Books Recommended for Libraries, 1968).

[347] SZLADITS' BIBLIOGRAPHY ON FOREIGN AND COMPARATIVE LAW (1990–2001) (Vratislav Pechota compiled and annotated the volumes up to 1990).

[348] David S. Clark, *Nation Building and Law Collections: The Remarkable Development of Comparative Law Libraries in the United States*, 109 LAW LIBR. J. 499, 537, 539–41, 550 (2017) [hereinafter Clark, *Nation Building*].

[349] Clark, *Nation Building*, supra note 348, at 544; Forest S. Drummond, *In Memory of William B. Stern*, 65 LAW LIBR. J. 471 (1972).

dealing with legal history, foreign, comparative, and private and public international law.[350] The *Index* also came out as cumulated three-year volumes through 1983, when due to the rapid increase of foreign publications, a new editor, Thomas Reynolds, comparative and foreign law librarian at the University of California Berkeley, then published quarterly issues cumulated in annual volumes.[351] These were of immense value to comparative law jurists worldwide.

By 1950, the Library of Congress (LC) Law Library was the nation's largest at 805,000 volumes. In 1960, the Law Library had over a million volumes, 475,000 of which dealt with foreign, comparative, and international law. Half of those concerned the law of European countries and Roman and canon law. Another quarter covered the legal systems of the Iberian Peninsula and Latin America. Many foreign lawyers worked at the Law Library, and several held important posts. For instance, Werner Ellinger, with a Heidelberg law doctorate, oversaw the LC classification for American law, class KF, completed in 1967. Jolande Goldberg, also had a Heidelberg law doctorate, and was primarily responsible for creating the K schedules for foreign law holdings. Finally, the Librarian of Congress appointed Rubens Medina, who had a law degree from the Universidad Nacional de Asunción (Paraguay) and had worked at the LC since 1971, Law Librarian of Congress in 1994, serving to 2008.[352]

After the war, Congress more enthusiastically supported the LC's goal of achieving a universal collection. Quincy Mumford, librarian from 1954 to 1974, oversaw this expansion. Appropriations during his tenure grew from $9 million to $96 million with a staff increase from 1,500 to 4,200. In 1958, Congress authorized the library to acquire books and serials from other countries by using excess foreign currency that the United States earned from its overseas sales of surplus agricultural commodities. By 1961, the LC had created acquisition centers in India and Egypt. In 1965, Congress enacted the Higher Education Act, which approved appropriations to the library for what became the National Program for Acquisitions and Cataloging (NPAC).[353]

---

[350] Charles Szladits, *Book Review*, 9 AM. J. COMP. L. 311-12 (1960); *Miscellany*, 2 SEC. INT'L & COMP. L. BULL. 31, 32 (no. 3, July 1958); 1-3 INDEX TO FOREIGN LEGAL PERIODICALS: 1960-62, at i-vi (1964); *see* Drummond, *supra* note 349, at 471. In 1964, the Institute of Advanced Legal Studies (London) published the first cumulation covering 1960-1962 in cooperation with the AALL, which held the copyright. Stern was the chair of the committee of librarians. The *Index* provided titles in the original language if it used the Roman alphabet, but transliterated if another alphabet or translated if an Oriental language. The *Index* complemented the *Index to Legal Periodicals*, which included only English language items, including those from the British empire. 1-3 INDEX, *supra*, at i-ii, vi, 25.

[351] INDEX TO FOREIGN LEGAL PERIODICALS: CUMULATION 1984, at ii, iv (1986). The *Index*'s editorial office remained at Boalt Hall through 2020.

[352] Clark, *Nation Building*, *supra* note 348, at 532, 550-51. In 1950, Harvard Law School's library had 656,000 volumes while Columbia had 300,000. *Id.* at 532.

[353] *Id.* at 518; *see* Pub. L. No. 89-329, 79 Stat. 1219, 1228 (1965) (codified at 20 U.S.C. § 1041 (1970)).

From 1965 to 1975, the library established ten overseas offices and, after 1976, ran the program under its own authority until the money ran out in 1987. Under these programs, the LC also distributed foreign books and serials to other research libraries and centers. Furthermore, the LC took the leadership role in developing international bibliographic standards from the 1960s with MARC, which communicated bibliographic data in machine-readable form. This became the official national standard in 1971 and an international standard in 1973.[354]

In 1972, the Law Library spent half its acquisitions budget on foreign books and journals and could also depend on copyright deposit, foreign exchanges, and transfers from federal agencies. The comparative law collection was 750,000 volumes, 60 percent of the total Law Library volume count. Its reputation as unique, both in the United States and abroad, rested largely on its non-American holdings and staff. Furthermore, in the 1970s, a staff of around 80 produced about 500 congressional studies annually analyzing how foreign governments used law to address social problems. This importance of foreign and comparative law continued through the 1980s.[355]

The evolution of the LC and its Law Library was the product of Thomas Jefferson's vision of universality, American cultural nationalism, and the initiative of librarians of Congress since Ainsworth Spofford.[356] In any case, since World War II, the LC has become the world's largest and most comprehensive library, which occupies a unique space in American civilization. In 2017, it had 36 million cataloged books and other print materials in 460 languages, including 2.9 million print volumes at the Law Library. Two-thirds of the books and serials were in languages other than English.[357] The LC well represented the position of the United States in the world.

2. Unification of Law

Unification of law was a significant activity of comparative law in the first half of the twentieth century. The primary supportive entity was the International Institute for the Unification of Private Law in Rome. Part of the League of

---

[354] Clark, *Nation Building*, supra note 348, at 518. NPAC evolved into the Cooperative Acquisitions Program, under which the library in 2017 maintained six overseas offices in Africa, Asia, and Latin America. Collectively, they acquired materials from 60 nations. At its height, the LC had 24 overseas field offices. *Id.*

[355] *Id.* at 551–52.

[356] *Id.* at 518–19; John Y. Cole, *Library of Congress of the United States*, in 1 INTERNATIONAL DICTIONARY OF LIBRARY HISTORIES 407, 409–12 (David S. Stam ed., 2001); *see supra* ch. 5, text accompanying note 90 (Spofford).

[357] Clark, *Nation Building*, supra note 348, at 518–19, 553. The Law Library collected the legal literature from 240 jurisdictions, including some that were historical. *Id.* at 553.

Nations with national members, the Italian government re-established it in 1940 with a multilateral treaty. Some Americans, such as Edwin Borchard (Yale) and Francis Deák (Columbia) served as experts during the 1930s and 1940s. Now generally known as UNIDROIT, the United States joined in 1964 with the State Department's legal adviser as its representative.[358]

Interest in international legal unification continued after 1945.[359] U.S. government policy was to simplify international trade by supporting international organizations for that aim as well as fostering unification of national commercial law. At the international level, some believed this would reduce tensions that could otherwise lead to armed conflict; others aspired to world peace. Comparative law could educate future diplomats and trade lawyers in the unification movement.[360] Specifically, comparative law would allow jurists to extrapolate general principles to solve individual legal issues. The aggregate of principles would serve to reform national law or as the foundation for transnational rules.[361]

The most important American unification project has been the Uniform Commercial Code, which Llewellyn led as chief reporter from its commencement in 1940.[362] Comparatists traced his inspiration and specific details for the code to German Romanticism, particularly the writing of Levin Goldschmidt on German customary *lex mercatoria*, and provisions from the German Commercial and Civil Codes.[363] Llewellyn had completed his book on sales law[364] when Rabel in 1931 asked him to participate with the Rome Institute on its project for a unified sales law. Since the United States was not a member of

---

[358] David S. Clark, *The Stool's Third Leg: Unification of Law in Berlin, Rome, and Washington from the 1920s to the 1940s*, in AUFBRUCH NACH EUROPA: 75 JAHRE MAX-PLANCK-INSTITUT FÜR PRIVATRECHT 39, 48 (Jürgen Basedow et al. eds., 2001) [hereinafter Clark, *Unification of Law*]; UNIDROIT, *Overview*, https://www.unidroit.org/about-unidroit/overview; *see* Stevenson, *supra* note 224, at 614–16; *supra* chap. 6, pt. E.4 (unification of law).

[359] In 1952, Yntema mentioned it as one of six important uses of comparative law that the new *Journal* could satisfy. Yntema, *Journal*, *supra* note 128, at 21–22.

[360] Hazard, *Legal Education*, *supra* note 238, at 270.

[361] Demleitner, *supra* note 237, at 323.

[362] Robert Braucher, *The Legislative History of the Uniform Commercial Code*, 58 COLUM. L. REV. 798–800 (1958); Zipporah Batshaw Wiseman, *The Limits of Vision: Karl Llewellyn and the Merchant Rules*, 100 HARV. L. REV. 465–70 (1987). Llewellyn's initial work was for the Uniform Law Commission (UCL) on the Revised Uniform Sales Act, which the ALI joined in 1942. The ULC approved the Revised Act in 1943 and the ALI in 1944. Braucher, *supra*, at 800; *see supra* ch. 6, text accompanying note 154 (ULC). In 1958, the ULC and ALI published a final version of the more comprehensive commercial law text and commentary. Braucher, *supra*, at 804; *see id.* at 812–14 (good faith).

[363] James Whitman, *Commercial Law and the American Volk: A Note on Llewellyn's German Sources for the Uniform Commercial Code*, 97 YALE L.J. 156–60, 162–75 (1987); *see* Ulrich Drobnig, *Llewellyn als Transformator deutschen Rechts zum amerikanischen Kaufrecht?*, in RECHTSREALISMUS, MULTIKUTURELLE GESELLSCHAFT UND HANDELSRECHT: KARL N. LLEWELLYN UND SEINE BEDEUTUNG HEUTE 187–95 (Ulrich Drobnig & Manfred Rehbinder eds., 1994) [hereinafter RECHTSREALISMUS]; Wiseman, *supra* note 362, at 514–15.

[364] KARL LLEWELLYN, CASES AND MATERIALS ON THE LAW OF SALES (1930).

the League of Nations, it had no representation at the Institute and Llewellyn consulted as a private expert. In 1932, Llewellyn visited Rome for an institute session and later Rabel's Berlin Institute where he assisted with the Anglo-American portions of Rabel's comparative law treatise on sales law.[365]

Llewellyn taught commercial law most of his career and used his sales casebook to criticize Williston's 1906 Sales Act for being out of date related to current marketplace transactions and for providing rules and principles instead of permitting judges to use customary trade practices for remedies. As a Uniform Law Commission (ULC) member in the 1930s, Llewellyn pushed to modernize the Uniform Sales Act; when that stalled, he argued for a federal sales act. Equally unsuccessful, he turned toward the idea of a commercial code that would include sales, secured transactions, and other commercial transactions. He found allies in the ULC, which provided him staff, and in the merchant community. As reporter for the project, he drafted three versions of a sales act between 1940 and 1943, treating merchant sales separately from non-merchant sales. The project's reform elements ran headlong into banking interests. In 1951, Llewellyn resigned from the ULC but remained as reporter for the ALI drafting team.[366]

Yntema and Nadelmann were two other comparatists who advocated for unification of law with the idea that comparative methodology would facilitate the process. Yntema spent the better part of the 1940s and 1950s working with Latin American jurists to harmonize the financial and commercial laws of the Americas.[367] In 1962 and 1963, the ABA House of Delegates passed resolutions to support U.S. membership in the Hague Conference of Private International Law and in the Rome Institute. The international unification committee chair in the ABA Comparative Law Division subsequently lobbied the U.S. Congress successfully so that the United States became a member of both organizations in 1964.[368] The State Department's legal adviser, Abram Chayes, permitted several

---

[365] Clark, *Unification of Law*, supra note 358, at 48; Ulrich Drobnig, *Llewellyn and Germany*, in RECHTSREALISMUS, supra note 363, at 17, 33–34; *see supra* text accompanying notes 68, 137, 147 (Rabel).

[366] N.E.H. HULL, ROSCOE POUND AND KARL LLEWELLYN: SEARCHING FOR AN AMERICAN JURISPRUDENCE 295–300 (1997); *see supra* ch. 5, notes 117–18 and accompanying text (ULC).

[367] BROWN & BLUME, supra note 121, at 782–83; Hessel E. Yntema, *Comparative Research and Unification of Law*, 41 MICH. L. REV. 261–68 (1942) [hereinafter Yntema, *Comparative Research*]; *see supra* note 293 and accompanying text (Michigan's inter-American law program). In the 1940s, Yntema was the U.S. representative to the Permanent Committee of Habana on Comparative Legislation and the Unification of Legislation. Yntema, *Comparative Research*, supra, at 267.

[368] Clifford J. Hynning, *Report of Committee on International Unification of Private Law*, ABA SEC. INT'L & COMP. L. PROC. 259–60 (1964); Kurt H. Nadelmann, Book Review, 11 AM. J. COMP. L. 112–15 (1962) (ABA, *Unification of International Private Law*, 1961); *id., The United States to Join . . .*, 12 AM. J. COMP. L. 629 (1963); *see* Pub. L. 88–244, 77 Stat. 775 (1963). The State Department, AACSL (Nadelmann and Reese), and ULC had sent observers to the Hague Conference and Rome Institute since 1956 and in 1958, the ULC recommended to the ABA that it create the international unification committee. Nadelmann, Book Review, supra, at 112; *see* Kurt H. Nadelmann & Willis L.M. Reese, *The American Proposal at the Hague Conference on Private International Law to Use the Method of Uniform Laws*, 7 AM. J. COMP. L. 239–47 (1958).

organizations, including the AACSL, to name representatives to the department's advisory committee on private international law. The AACSL initially named Yntema and in 1969, Nadelmann.[369] Von Mehren served with the U.S. delegation to the Hague Conference from 1966 to 2006 and was *rapporteur* for the Hague Convention on the Law Applicable to Contracts for the International Sale of Goods (1986), now in force.[370]

The United States sent a delegation to the Hague Conference in 1964, including John Honnold (Pennsylvania), an AACSL director and *Journal* editor. The conference approved two conventions on international sale of goods, one on the obligations of performance and the other on contract formation. Work on the former had begun in the 1930s at the Rome Institute, including the efforts of Rabel. Honnold was the U.S. member of the 1964 Hague drafting committee.[371]

In 1967, the AACSL and AFLA co-sponsored a forum on international unification of law, which Nadelmann introduced. The AFLA had held a series of forums on this subject since 1960.[372] One paper described the creation in 1966 of the U.N. Commission on International Trade Law (UNCITRAL), which signaled the U.N.'s entry into private law and aimed to support international conventions as well as model and uniform laws, especially for international trade.[373] The *American Journal of Comparative Law* in 1968 also published a symposium, with Peter Hay as editor, on the international unification of law. Three years earlier, Hans Baade had edited a similar symposium for *Law and Contemporary Problems*.[374] All this activity illustrated the substantial shift in attitudes that the American bar and government took toward the unification issue in the 1960s, thanks largely to the efforts of comparatists.[375]

---

[369] Hynning, *supra* note 368, at 260–61; *Yntema 1966*, *supra* note 133, at 980; AACSL minutes, *supra* note 142. The act provided up to $25,000 annually for expenses in the two international entities. Pub. L. 88-244, *supra* note 368.

[370] Gordley, *supra* note 61, at 528; Symeon C. Symeonides, *Arthur Taylor von Mehren: A Gentle Giant*, 53 AM. J. COMP. L. 531, 540–41 (2005). Nadelmann was also a delegate to the Hague Conference. Nadelmann, *supra* note 138, at 402.

[371] John Honnold, *The 1964 Hague Conventions and Uniform Laws on the International Sale of Goods*, 13 AM. J. COMP. LAW 451–53 (1965); *see id.* at 453–77 (text of the conventions); Kurt H. Nadelmann, *The United States and Plans for a Uniform (World) Law on International Sales of Goods*, 112 U. PA. L. REV. 697–709 (1964); John Honnold, *A Uniform Law for International Sales*, 107 U. PA. L. REV. 299–330 (1959). Rabel worked on the institute's 1935 draft and represented it when the Hague Conference discussed his draft uniform sales law in 1951. Clark, *Unification of Law*, *supra* note 358, at 48; Honnold, *A Uniform Law*, *supra*, at 302 n.5.

[372] Kurt H. Nadelmann, *Introducing the Forum: The United States and International Unification of Law*, 15 AM. J. COMP. L. 622–26 (1967).

[373] John Carey, *UNCITRAL: Its Origins and Prospects*, 15 AM. J. COMP. L. 626–39 (1967). In 1968, the AFLA held a forum dedicated to UNCITRAL. Paolo Contini, *Proceedings...*, 16 AM. J. COMP. L. 666–80 (1968).

[374] Peter Hay, T*he International Unification of Law: A Symposium*, 16 AM. J. COMP. L. 1–3 (1968) *see id.* at 4–218 (1968) (nine articles); Hans W. Baade, *Unification of Law: Foreword*, 30 LAW & CONTEMP. PROBS. 231–32 (1965); *see id.* at 233–460 (1965) (eight articles).

[375] Kurt H. Nadelmann, *The United States Joins the Hague Conference on Private International Law: A "History" with Comments*, 30 LAW & CONTEMP. PROBS. 291–325 (1965).

In 1979, Honnold introduced a *Journal* symposium on UNCITRAL, detailing its progress in adopting uniform rules for a variety of matters associated with international trade, including the 1978 uniform law for the international sale of goods (the latter approved as a draft convention). "The preparation of uniform law for international trade is comparative law in action—in its most fascinating and productive dimensions."[376] The United Nations approved the Convention on Contracts for the International Sale of Goods (CISG) in 1980, the United States ratified it in 1986, and it entered into force in 1988.[377] By the end of the 1980s, there were countless international conventions, uniform laws, and rules of conduct, but the real challenge lay in the implementation of these documents in a uniform manner across multiple jurisdictions.[378]

A different variety of unification of law began in the 1950s, when Schlesinger undertook at Cornell the ambitious comparative study to enunciate the common core of contract formation rules. He aimed to identify rules that many legal systems shared, using multilateral and topically broad comparisons, reminiscent of the universalistic spirit of the Paris comparative law congress in 1900. Rabel had illustrated the method in his four-volume treatise, *The Conflict of Laws: A Comparative Study*. Notably, Schlesinger wanted to use a case-oriented factual approach that rejected abstract formulations.[379]

Schlesinger began the ten-year study with a hypothesis that among the world's major legal systems, common ground existed. Otto Kahn-Freund found this notion unexceptional among comparatists, who need some basis of commonality to begin a meaningful comparison. Schlesinger's achievement was to demonstrate quantitatively that there was substantial similarity among contract formation rules for nations classified as civil law, common law, and socialist law.[380] Some critics found the accomplishment limited in scope. Thus, the law of offer

---

[376] John Honnold, *The United Nations Commission on International Trade Law: Mission and Methods*, 27 AM. J. COMP. L. 201–11 (1979) (quotation at 201–02). The symposium extended over two *Journal* issues (at 201–564).

[377] John Honnold, *Introduction to the Symposium*, 21 CORNELL INT'L L.J. 419–22 (1988); see JOHN O. HONNOLD, UNIFORM LAW FOR INTERNATIONAL SALES UNDER THE 1980 UNITED NATIONS CONVENTION (1982); UNCITRAL, *CISG*, https://uncitral.un.org/en/texts/salegoods (select CISG 1980).

[378] Michael Joachim Bonell, *International Uniform Law in Practice—Or Where the Real Trouble Begins*, 38 AM. J. COMP. L. 865–88 (1990).

[379] Drobnig, *Memorial*, supra note 237, at 768–69; *see* supra ch. 6, text accompanying notes 282, 337 (Rabel's *Conflict of Laws*); *see* 1–2 FORMATION OF CONTRACTS: A STUDY OF THE COMMON CORE OF LEGAL SYSTEMS (Rudolf B. Schlesinger gen. ed., 1968) [hereinafter FORMATION OF CONTRACTS]. The Ford Foundation provided $1,000,000 for the project. Drobnig, *Memorial*, supra, at 769. The common core approach influenced the 1994 Common Core of European Private Law project centered at the University of Trento involving 200 comparatists. Ugo Mattei, *The Comparative Jurisprudence of Schlesinger and Sacco: A Study in Legal Influence*, in RETHINKING THE MASTERS OF COMPARATIVE LAW 238, 249–51 (Annelise Riles ed., 2001).

[380] Otto Kahn-Freund, *Comparative Law in Action*, 18 AM. J. COMP. L. 429–30 (1970) (book review); *see* Rudolf B. Schlesinger, *Introduction*, in FORMATION OF CONTRACTS, supra note 379, at 1–65. *See also id.* at 22–29 (insightful discussion of the inclusion of socialist law systems).

and acceptance is formalistic and disconnected from a legal system's social environment. Nevertheless, the method of beginning an inquiry with fact situations rather than rules avoided doctrinal mischaracterization prior to data collection. After research, the team could recast issues in doctrinal form, first as national reports and then synthesizing issues in general reports.[381]

Hazard utilized the common core concept to analyze the family of socialist legal systems. He argued that such a tradition existed distinct from the civil law tradition and insisted on incorporating economic, political, and social context to provide meaningful results. However, in the end, Hazard concluded that although socialist law was a separate legal family, the type of common core Schlesinger was searching for did not exist among the Soviet Union, its European satellite states, China, and African experiments in adopting socialist law.[382] Rheinstein, in his review of Schlesinger's project, found that "no consistent effort has been made to explore the relationship between law and social reality." He noted that the sociological approach would require a team that included some representatives of disciplines other than law.[383]

3. Private International Law

Besides comparative law, European émigré jurists often migrated toward private international law as a subject of primary scholarly and teaching interest. Their contribution to the field was to broaden it from a focus on American interstate conflicts of law to include international conflicts like the European approach obvious from its name. Rabel led the way in this endeavor accompanied by Ehrenzweig, Nadelmann, and Hay. Some indigenous Americans, such as Von Mehren, joined these comparatists through their activities in international organizations, coursebooks, or publications.[384] Mathias Reimann contended that comparative law and private international law were intimately related since they both dealt with foreign legal systems.[385]

---

[381] Kahn-Freund, *supra* note 380, at 430–34, 441; *see* BASIL MARKESINIS, COMPARATIVE LAW IN THE COURTROOM AND CLASSROOM: THE STORY OF THE LAST THIRTY-FIVE YEARS 7–8 (2003). *But see* Mattei, *supra* note 379, at 240–44.

[382] JOHN N. HAZARD, COMMUNISTS AND THEIR LAW: A SEARCH FOR THE COMMON CORE OF THE LEGAL SYSTEMS OF THE MARXIAN SOCIALIST STATES vii–xii, 3–33, 481–528 (1969); Kazimierz Grzybowski, *Socialist Law and Institutions*, 18 AM. J. COMP. L. 662–67 (1970) (book review).

[383] Max Rheinstein, *Book Review*, 36 U. CHI. L. REV. 448, 453 (1969).

[384] Reimann, *Globalists*, *supra* note 151, at 110–11; *see supra* text accompanying notes 151–153 (émigré jurists and comparative law).

[385] Mathias Reimann, *Comparative Law and Private International Law*, *in* OXFORD HANDBOOK, *supra* note 237, at 1339–42, 1346, 1355–62 [hereinafter Reimann, *Private International Law*]. Reimann pointed to the importance of Rabel's volumes on comparative conflict of laws as a definitive example. *Id.* at 1344. Freiburg awarded Reimann a J.U.D. in 1982, where he was a research assistant until 1984. He emigrated to the United States in 1985 and accepted a law professorship at Michigan. 1990 AALS DIRECTORY, *supra* note 317, at 711.

The Parker School's program of bilateral studies in private international law, which yielded 19 volumes between 1951 and 1972, illustrated the relationship. Many American comparatists, most of whom were émigré jurists, prepared volumes in the Parker series, including Henry de Vries (Columbia), Eder, Ehrenzweig, Hazard, Martin Domke (NYU), Nussbaum (Columbia), Reese, and Szladits.[386]

In 1966, Von Mehren made a significant contribution to private international law in the United States with a seminal coauthored article on judicial territorial jurisdiction that rejected the traditional categories and divided it between general and specific jurisdiction, a distinction the U.S. Supreme Court later adopted.[387] That same year, he delivered an expanded version for the Hague Academy of International Law's general lectures on private international law, which some decades later it published as a comparative analysis.[388] The Hague Academy also published his lectures on foreign judgments in 1980.[389] In addition, from 1966 to 2006, Von Mehren was a member of the U.S. delegation to the Hague Conference of Private International Law.[390]

From the 1960s to 1980s, most U.S. literature on private international law turned inward with attention toward theoretical debates on the domestic choice of law revolution against the original *Restatement of Conflicts*. Ultimately, with Reese the reporter for the *Restatement Second of Conflicts* (1971), it became the dominant source for rules among American states. It reflected a less dogmatic and more open analysis in choice of law rules for contracts and torts, using enumerated principles and the "most significant relationship" formula between a state and a transaction or occurrence. By 1990, conflicts scholars, reflecting

---

[386] Hein, *Parker School, supra* note 233; John H. Langbein, *The Influence of the German Emigrés on American Law: The Curious Case of Civil and Criminal Procedure, in* Der EINFLUSS, *supra* 64, at 321, 325 n.9; *see supra* text accompanying notes 297-98 (Parker series). In 1957, Athanassios Yiannopoulos (LSU) was a coauthor with Ehrenzweig on the Greek volume. Hein, *Parker School, supra*.

[387] Arthur T. von Mehren & Donald T. Trautman, *Jurisdiction to Adjudicate: A Suggested Analysis*, 79 HARV. L. REV. 1121, 1164-1179 (1966); *see* Symeonides, *supra* note 370, at 534-35. The coauthors von Mehren and Trautman also had a coursebook for conflict of laws that advocated a functional approach for choice of law permitting judicial policy weighing. ARTHUR T. VON MEHREN & DONALD T. TRAUTMAN, THE LAW OF MULTISTATE PROBLEMS: CASES AND MATERIALS ON CONFLICT OF LAW (1965); *see* Symeonides, *supra*, at 537.

[388] Arthur Taylor von Mehren, *Theory and Practice of Adjudicatory Authority in Private International Law: A Comparative Study of the Doctrine, Policies and Practices of Common- and Civil-Law Systems. General Course on Private International Law (1966), in* 295 COLLECTED COURSES OF THE HAGUE ACADEMY OF INTERNATIONAL LAW 9-432 (2002) (also published as a book in 2003); *see* Peter Šarčević, *Book Review*, 5 Y.B. PRIV. INT'L L. 393-96 (2003).

[389] Arthur T. von Mehren, *Recognition and Enforcement of Foreign Judgments: General Theory and the Role of Jurisdictional Requirements, in* 167 COLLECTED COURSES OF THE HAGUE ACADEMY OF INTERNATIONAL LAW 9-112 (1980).

[390] Symeonides, *supra* note 370, at 540. Von Mehren was *rapporteur* for the 1986 Hague Convention on the Law Applicable to Contracts for the International Sale of Goods, now in force for the signatory nations. *Id.* at 540; *see Convention*, 24 INT'L LEGAL MATERIALS 1573 (1986).

the challenges of economic globalization, had returned to discuss European developments, especially those related to European integration.[391]

Two exceptions to this parochialism in private international law were Ehrenzweig and Nadelmann. Ehrenzweig (1906–1974) earned his Dr. Jur. degree at Vienna in 1928 and joined its law faculty in 1937. After Hitler's *Anschluß* of Austria, Ehrenzweig emigrated to the United States and initiated law study at Chicago in 1939, receiving the J.D. in 1941 and then a J.S.D. at Columbia. He joined the California Berkeley law school faculty in 1948 and was a founding member of the AACSL.[392] In 1962, Ehrenzweig published a treatise on conflict of laws, which Brainerd Currie called the most learned and original in English since the 1930s. Ehrenzweig repudiated both the first and draft second *Restatements* on conflicts and presented a *lex fori* theory for choice of law together with a small number of true (and formulated) rules. He also preferred the separation of interstate and international conflicts issues. For territorial jurisdiction, Ehrenzweig argued for the civil law competence concept that promoted defendant convenience, either domicile or significant in-state contacts.[393] He completed his comparative treatment of private international law in a three-volume treatise shortly before his death.[394]

Reimann classified Ehrenzweig as a realist, grounded in the history of ideas, with a propensity toward systematization characteristic of a civil law jurist, and with attention to the international dimension of private international law in the European tradition. As a realist influenced by Llewellyn, he battled against conceptualism and proposed instead true rules related to the solution of specific problems. These rules, such as the rule of validation, were emerging from court

---

[391] Reimann, *Private International Law*, supra note 385, at 1346–48; *see* 1–3 RESTATEMENT OF THE LAW SECOND, CONFLICT OF LAWS (1971); J.H.C. Morris, *Conflict of Laws*, 21 AM. J. COMP. L. 322, 326–27 (1973) (book review). Reese served as reporter from 1952 until the restatement's publication and jurists found the reporter's notes a useful addition. Morris, *supra*, at 323–25. In 1964 and 1976, the Hague Academy of International Law published Reese's lectures. Willis L.M. Reese, *Discussion of Major Areas of Choice of Law*, in 111 COLLECTED COURSES OF THE HAGUE ACADEMY OF INTERNATIONAL LAW 311–418 (1964); *id.*, *General Course on Private International Law*, in 150 *id.* at 1–194 (1976).

[392] Edward C. Halbach, Jr., *Foreword*, 54 CALIF. L. REV. 1419–21 (1966); *see supra* text accompanying note 141 (AACSL). From 1961 until his death, Ehrenzweig was also honorary professor of private international law at Vienna. Halbach, *supra*, at 1420.

[393] Brainerd Currie, *Book Review*, 13 DUKE L.J. 424–37 (1964) (*A Treatise on the Conflict of Laws*, 1962, West Publishing); see Albert A. Ehrenzweig, *Second Conflicts Restatement: A Last Appeal for Its Withdrawal*, 113 U. PA. L. REV. 1230–44 (1965). West had issued an earlier partial version in 1959, covering jurisdiction, judgment recognition, and a treatment of divorce and annulment. Brainerd Currie, *Book Review*, 73 HARV. L. REV. 801–09 (1960) (*Conflict of Laws*, 1959). The comparatist "often pays American readers the undeserved compliment of assuming an acquaintance with foreign legal institutions and a facility in the use of foreign languages." *Id.* at 807.

[394] ALBERT A. EHRENZWEIG, 1–3 PRIVATE INTERNATIONAL LAW: A COMPARATIVE TREATISE ON AMERICAN INTERNATIONAL CONFLICTS LAW, INCLUDING THE LAW OF ADMIRALTY (1967–1973) (Erik Jayme coauthored volume 2). In 1968, the Hague Academy of International Law published Ehrenzweig's lectures. Albert A. Ehrenzweig, *Specific Principles of Private Transnational Law*, in 124 COLLECTED COURSES OF THE HAGUE ACADEMY OF INTERNATIONAL LAW 167–370 (1968).

decisions. *Lex fori* was the basic rule when a court properly exercised judicial jurisdiction and there was no applicable formulated or true rule.[395]

Nadelmann's contribution to U.S. private international law was more diffuse than that of Ehrenzweig and related to his many articles and continual support for the subject, especially within the AFLA and AACSL, and successful effort toward U.S. membership in the Hague Conference of Private International Law. He often served on the U.S. delegation to that Conference and reported on its activity.[396] In 1972, three of Nadelmann's colleagues at Harvard edited a *Festschrift* for him, *Conflict of Laws: International and Interstate*, which consisted of 15 of his articles originally published in foreign periodicals. Nadelmann typically took a historical perspective on U.S. and European conflicts law and had a special interest in Joseph Story's contribution.[397]

Two postwar German émigrés who took a comparative interest in conflict of laws in the two decades after 1960 were Peter Hay and Friedrich Juenger. Hay, whose primary interest prior to 1980 was European Community law and institutions, also wrote some articles on conflicts from a comparative perspective.[398] In 1991, the Hague Academy of International Law published Hay's conflicts lectures.[399] Juenger completed law studies at Frankfurt and Berlin and passed the exam to become a German lawyer in 1955. With a Fulbright grant, he left for Michigan, receiving an M.C.L. degree in 1957, but then decided to remain in the United States and completed the J.D. program at Columbia in 1960. He worked at Baker & McKenzie for a few years and accepted a professorship at Wayne State in 1966, then joined the California Davis law faculty in 1975. Active in the AACSL, he published numerous articles on conflict of laws.[400] In 1983,

---

[395] Mathias Reimann, *Albert A. Ehrenzweig and the American Conflict of Laws: A Major Player with a Minor Influence*, in DER EINFLUSS, *supra* note 64, at 397–408. With Ehrenzweig's many references to European legal literature and his contacts with scholars and students, he built important bridges between U.S. and European jurists interested in private international law as well as comparative law. *Id.* at 420–21.

[396] See *supra* notes 138, 159, 367–372 and accompanying text (Nadelmann); Kurt H. Nadelmann & Arthur T. von Mehren, *The Extraordinary Session of the Hague Conference on Private International Law*, 60 AM. J. INT'L L. 803, 804 n.2 (1966).

[397] KURT H. NADELMANN, CONFLICT OF LAWS: INTERNATIONAL AND INTERSTATE (David F. Cavers, Arthur T. von Mehren & Donald T. Trautman eds., 1972); Max Rheinstein, *Book Review*, 22 AM. J. COMP. L. 387–91 (1974); *see* Kurt H. Nadelmann, *Bicentennial Observations on the Second Edition of Joseph Story's Commentaries on the Conflict of Laws*, 28 AM. J. COMP. L. 67–78 (1980).

[398] See Peter Hay, *International and Interstate Conflicts Law in the United States: A Summary of the Case Law*, 35 RABELSZ 429–495 (1971); *id.*, *Unjust Enrichment in the Conflict of Laws: A Comparison of German Law and the Restatement 2d*, 26 AM. J. COMP. L. 1–49 (1978); *id.* & Wolfram Müller-Freienfels, *Agency in the Conflict of Laws and the 1978 Hague Convention*, 27 AM. J. COMP. L. 1–49 (1979); *supra* text accompanying notes 279–82, 286–89 (Hay).

[399] Peter Hay, *Flexibility versus Predictability and Uniformity in Choice of Law: Reflections on Current European and United States Conflicts Law*, in 226 COLLECTED COURSES OF THE HAGUE ACADEMY OF INTERNATIONAL LAW 281–412 (1991).

[400] Courtland H. Peterson, *Friedrich Klaus Juenger, 1930–2001*, 49 AM. J. COMP. L. xv–xvi (2001); *see, e.g.*, Friedrich Juenger, *Choice of Law in Interstate Torts*, 118 U. PA. L. REV. 202–35 (1969); *id.*, *Trends in European Conflicts Law*, 60 CORNELL L. REV. 969–84 (1975); *id.*, *The Conflicts Statute of the*

Juenger delivered the Hague Academy's general lectures on private international law.[401]

During the 1980s, a hybrid field began to coalesce from conflict of laws and civil procedure. Comparative lawyers took an active interest in this practical discipline that often required some knowledge of foreign law. Labeled transnational litigation or international civil procedure, it took comparatists into the courtroom as experts or the law office as arbitration experts or decision makers.[402]

Finally, in an initiative extremely important for both private international law and transnational litigation in the United States, Symeon Symeonides (LSU) dedicated substantial effort to tracking and reporting annually on American case law to later develop an empirical approach for choice of law. This began in 1989 in conjunction with the AALS section on conflict of laws and utilized a comprehensive research methodology to capture both state and federal developments. Symeonides organized the report by subject matter, but also provided a methodological map or list of the states by conflicts approach.[403] Early on, he preferred a legislative solution for certain choice of law issues, illustrated by his drafting expertise in Puerto Rico and Louisiana.[404]

4. Comparative Legal Sociology and Law and Development

In 1947, Llewellyn created a new course at Columbia, law in society, consisting of readings and lectures derived from sociological jurisprudence, sociology, and ethnology. Its emphasis was on legal professionals, law jobs, and conflict solving.[405] Several law schools offered such a course, some of which used

---

German Democratic Republic: An Introduction and Translation, 25 AM. J. COMP. L. 332–53 (1977); *id.*, *American and European Conflicts Law*, 30 AM. J. COMP. L. 117–34 (1982); *supra* text accompanying notes 279–82, 286–89 (Juenger).

[401] Friedrich K. Juenger, *General Course on Private International Law (1983)*, *in* 193 COLLECTED COURSES OF THE HAGUE ACADEMY OF INTERNATIONAL LAW 119–387 (1985).

[402] Hans W. Baade, *Comparative Law and the Practitioner*, 31 AM. J. COMP. L. 499–510 (1983); *see* GARY B. BORN & DAVID WESTIN, INTERNATIONAL CIVIL LITIGATION IN UNITED STATES COURTS: COMMENTARY AND MATERIALS (1989); Gordon D. Schaber, *Preface*, 1 TRANSNAT'L LAW. xi–xii (1988).

[403] Symeon Symeonides, *Choice of Law in the American Courts in 1988*, 37 AM. J. COMP. L. 457–94 (1989); *see* Herma Hill Kay, *Theory into Practice: Choice of Law in the Courts*, 34 MERCER L. REV. 521, 591–92 (1983). John Kozyris presented a somewhat different type of survey in 1988. P. John Kozyris, *Choice of Law in the American Courts in 1987: An Overview*, 36 AM. J. COMP. L. 547–63 (1988).

[404] Symeon Symeonides, *Problems and Dilemmas in Codifying Choice of Law for Torts: The Louisiana Experience in Comparative Perspective*, 38 AM. J. COMP. L. 431–73 (1990); *see* Russell J. Weintraub, *The Contributions of Symeonides and Kozyris to Making Choice of Law Predictable and Just: An Appreciation and Critique*, *id.* at 511–20.

[405] COLUMBIA LAW, *supra* note 149, at 369; *see* KARL N. LLEWELLYN & E. ADAMSON HOEBEL, THE CHEYENNE WAY: CONFLICT AND CASE LAW IN PRIMITIVE JURISPRUDENCE (1941); Maria Borucka-Arctowa, *Llewellyn's Concept of Law Jobs and Recent Approaches to the Function of Law*, *in*

materials from two or more legal systems.[406] Hazard had pointed out that comparative law could be a tool to teach legal philosophy and he cited the three-volume West Publishing coursebook on law and society as the materials to accomplish that.[407] Two law professors, Sidney Simpson (NYU) and Julius Stone (University of Sidney), both earlier law professors at Harvard, prepared the coursebook.[408] A tour de force, the authors explained that the materials drew from 4,000 years of legal history and that the method was comparative. The course would "give an understanding of the part law has played in the social, economic and cultural history of mankind." About one-third of the readings were from the social sciences and modern legal materials illustrated the common law, civil law, and socialist law traditions.[409]

Rheinstein also illustrated a comparative law and society interest. He had been a student of Max Weber during his student days at the University of Munich and later was an assistant to Ernst Rabel in Berlin. After he emigrated to the United States, he taught for 42 years at the University of Chicago Law School, where he built his career as a comparatist and legal sociologist. As with Rabel, Rheinstein contended that legal theory should serve practical ends. He brought foreign lawyers from many lands to learn about Anglo-American law and took a broad view of comparative law to include Asian and African legal systems and customary law.[410]

Rheinstein's seminal contribution to legal sociology was his editing, translation, and annotation (together with a Chicago colleague) of Weber's chapter on sociology of law from the formidable *Wirtschaft und Gesellschaft* (1925), making

---

RECHTSREALISMUS, *supra* note 363, at 113–24; Wolfgang Fikentscher, *Die Erforschung des lebenden Rechts in einer multikulturellen Gesellschaft: Karl N. Llewellyns Cheyenne- und Pueblo-Studien*, in *id.* at 45–70.

[406] Max Rheinstein, *Book Review*, 17 U. Chi. L. Rev. 422–23 (1950).

[407] Hazard, *Legal Education, supra* note 238, at 268. In 1953, Hazard published *Law and Social Change in the U.S.S.R.* He took the view that Soviet law had a social reality expressed in judicial decisions and was not a simple façade to obscure political power. The regime used law to implement its nationalization program, increase labor productivity, reward elites, and end political opposition. *See* Harold J. Berman, *Book Review*, 63 YALE L.J. 1044–49 (1954); Julian Towster, *Book Review*, 42 Calif. L. Rev. 204–05 (1954).

[408] SIDNEY POST SIMPSON & JULIUS STONE, 1–3 CASES AND READINGS ON LAW AND SOCIETY (1948–1949); *see* 3 *id.* at v, ix.

[409] 3 *id.* at vii–x (quotation at vii). Pound wrote the general introduction and Hazard collaborated on the Soviet materials. *Id.* at xi, xiii–xviii. As Pound cryptically mentioned, "Law is a word of more than one meaning." *Id.* at xiv.

[410] Mary Ann Glendon, *Max Rheinstein*, 45 U. CHI. L. REV. 516 (1978); *see supra* note 61 and text accompanying notes 61–62, 152, 181–82, 211, 378 (Rheinstein). Rheinstein illustrated his practical and sociological attitude toward law in a coursebook on decedents' estates. The first three chapters dealt with the social function of inheritance law, machinery of inheritance, and problems of policy. MAX RHEINSTEIN, THE LAW OF DECEDENTS' ESTATES: INTESTACY, WILLS, PROBATE, AND ADMINISTRATION 1–47 (2d ed. 1955; 1st ed. 1947). Glendon coauthored the 1971 edition of the coursebook.

it accessible to English language readers as well as to Germans due to its scholarly clarifications.[411] Rheinstein took an empiricist approach toward legal research, illustrated by his comparative inquiry into marriage stability and whether divorce law was strict or liberal. He analyzed the incidence of divorce in several developed nations by considering legislation, statistics, and cultural variables.[412]

In the 1960s, a few law schools created programs based on the relationship between law and social science disciplines. The impetus for this initiative stemmed from increasing political dissensus associated with the civil rights movement and the Vietnam War, rapid social and technological change, and some doubt about the relevance of traditional legal education. Interdisciplinary efforts involved creating joint degree programs, hiring social scientists for law faculties, and establishing research and graduate law specializations.[413] In 1964, a small group of sociologists joined by a few legal scholars decided to form the Law and Society Association, which held annual meetings and created the *Law & Society Review*. Foreigners interested in the field joined the association and contributed to the journal, providing it a comparative flavor.[414]

This activity generated a popular coursebook used in law schools: *Law and the Behavioral Sciences* (1969). Unlike typical instruction materials, the volume used excepts, some comparative, from books and journals.[415] The methodologies presented or implied came from social sciences that transcended legal rules or even states, contrasting with the usual rule-orientation of law studies. "The living law of a society, its *legal system* . . ., is the law as actual process. It is the way in which structural, cultural, and substantive elements interact with each other, under the influence too, of external *situational* factors, pressing in from the larger society."[416] In 1975, Lawrence Friedman followed up with a comprehensive theory of the legal system that could be applied to any society, modern or traditional.[417]

---

[411] Gerhard Casper, *Max Rheinstein*, 45 U. CHI. L. REV. 511 (1978); *see* MAX WEBER, MAX WEBER ON LAW IN ECONOMY AND SOCIETY (Max Rheinstein, ed. & annotator, Edward Shils & Rheinstein trans., 1954). Rheinstein wrote the 47-page introduction. The translation included a few other excerpts related to the sociology of law chapter.
[412] Casper, *supra* note 411, at 512; *see* MAX RHEINSTEIN, MARRIAGE STABILITY, DIVORCE, AND THE LAW (1972).
[413] Hupper, *supra* note 301, at 386–88.
[414] Lawrence M. Friedman, *Law and Society Association, The*, *in* 2 ENCYCLOPEDIA OF LAW & SOCIETY: AMERICAN AND GLOBAL PERSPECTIVES 922–24 (David S. Clark ed., 2007).
[415] LAWRENCE M. FRIEDMAN & STEWART MACAULAY, LAW AND THE BEHAVIORAL SCIENCES (1969) (2d ed. 1977).
[416] FRIEDMAN & MACAULAY, *supra* note 415, at 1000, 1004 (italics in original) (paper later published as Lawernce M. Friedman, *Legal Culture and Social Development*, 4 LAW & SOC'Y REV. 29–44, 1969).
[417] LAWRENCE M. FRIEDMAN, THE LEGAL SYSTEM: A SOCIAL SCIENCE PERSPECTIVE (1975). "[L]aw is only one of many social systems and that other social systems in society give it meaning and effect. . . . No experiment or study can be rigorous, if it is not comparative across space, or time, or both." *Id.* at vii–viii.

For some law professors, the leadership position of the United States in the Cold War competition with the Soviet Union and its allies suggested that a law and society approach to fostering economic, political, and social development in former colonies and other poorer non-allied nations could prove useful. Those who were not already comparatists, if their activities were to have value, would have to learn something about the culture and law of their target countries. The label to identify this group's action and research was usually law and development.[418] This specialization in comparative law coalesced around the idea of progress, the desire for law reform, the adoption of law and society methods, and the belief in social engineering through law.[419]

Harvard, Wisconsin, and Yale took special interest in law and development for their foreign student doctoral programs. As described before, the U.S. government had augmented its development assistance awards to many countries after Fidel Castro came to power in Cuba in 1959. The Ford Foundation targeted its grants for foreign legal development at several law schools. These U.S. and NGO funds could finance foreign student study in the United States. USAID's law and modernization grant to Yale, to illustrate, specifically supported generous fellowship funding.[420]

For the development side of the endeavor, jurists recognized the principal issues as political instability associated with ethnic or social conflict, endemic government and business corruption, hierarchical and authoritarian political and social structures, and cultures of tradition and corporatism. In general, these elements were hostile toward democracy, market capitalism, and free trade, which these jurists believed could improve the economic living conditions and general social welfare of the citizenry. For the law side, jurists believed that rational legal structures, processes, and rules—conflated into the label rule of law—should be an important part of society. The rule of law could foster social change toward higher economic output distributed to all social classes, integration of ethnic and religious minorities into mainstream society, and improved social mobility and equal opportunity.[421]

---

[418] See supra pts. E.2 and E.3 (development decade and assessment). The U.N. Charter anticipated decolonization of the remaining overseas empires of France, Great Britain, the Netherlands, and Portugal, which yielded many new sovereign nations that the United States or the Soviet Union sought to align. FRIEDMAN, HISTORY, supra note 2, at 504; U.N. Charter art. 1(2) (principle of equal rights and self-determination of peoples) and chs. XI–XIII; see Declaration on the Granting of Independence to Colonial Countries and Peoples, G.A. Res. 1514 (XV) (14 Dec. 1960).

[419] Merryman, Social Change, supra note 327, at 461–66. See also Lawrence M. Friedman, On Legal Development, 24 RUTGERS L. REV. 11–64 (1969); David M. Trubek, Toward a Social Theory of Law: An Essay on the Study of Law and Development, 82 YALE L.J. 1–50 (1972).

[420] Hupper, supra note 301, at 434–39, 442. Prior to 1990, about 20 law schools had J.S.D. programs, primarily for foreign students, awarding a small but growing number of degrees in the 1980s: thus, 19 (1980), 29 (1985), and 34 (1990). Gail J. Hupper, The Academic Doctorate in Law: A Vehicle for Legal Transplants, 58 J. LEGAL EDUC. 413, 415–16 (2008).

[421] CARRINGTON, supra note 6, at 275; Merryman, Social Change, supra note 327, at 471–72; see GARDNER, supra note 313, at 261–81. See also JAMES P. ROWLES, LAW AND AGRARIAN REFORM IN

Galanter listed 11 salient features of modern law as an ideal type, dividing them between rules, structures, processes, and professionals. Furthermore, law must be changeable, the state supreme, and reflect separation of authority by function. Modernization is movement toward characteristics of unity, uniformity, and universalism and reflects a tendency to replace local and popular law with official lawyers' law. Nevertheless, each "society must find for itself an appropriate balance between unity and diversity."[422]

A few American jurists identified lawyers and judges who had a reliable moral tradition to withstand corruption as central to implementing rule of law—with a constitution, human rights norms, and private property and contract rules at its core—to assist in appropriate social change. The task required that American jurists train enough local lawyers and law students who would then as law professors educate future morally adequate lawyers and judges needed for rule of law. In addition, this would require institutional reform so that law faculties would have a corps of full-time professors and courts would have judges independent of hostile political and economic forces. Other comparatists viewed the legal profession in most developing countries as an impediment to social progress.[423]

During the postwar period, American comparative law expanded beyond its usual attention to European civil law in Germany and France, civil law variants in Latin America and Japan, and socialist law in the Soviet Union. To illustrate, Merryman made his initial argument for the study of Italian law in 1965, in part for its relevance to law and development activities. "What is going on in western Europe today *is* economic and social development; the differences between Europe and Africa or South Asia or Latin America, in this sense are of degree."[424] He and colleagues extended this idea to Botswana, the People's Republic of China, and Egypt with interdisciplinary case studies to illustrate legal similarities and differences among these radically different cultures. The authors selected

---

COSTA RICA (1985); David S. Clark, *Book Review*, 35 AM. J. COMP. L. 405–08 (1987) (successful agrarian reform and legal stability).

[422] Marc Galanter, *The Modernization of Law*, in MODERNIZATION: THE DYNAMICS OF GROWTH 153–65 (Myron Weiner ed., 1966) (quotation at 165); *see supra* note 323 and accompanying text (Galanter). Galanter was president of the Law and Society Association from 1983 to 1985.

[423] CARRINGTON, *supra* note 6, at 275–76; *see* C.J. DIAS ET AL., LAWYERS IN THE THIRD WORLD: COMPARATIVE AND DEVELOPMENTAL PERSPECTIVES (1981); Steven Lowenstein, *Book Review*, 30 AM. J. COMP. L. 692–97 (1982). These programs sought to implant certain American legal features such as active teaching in law schools, social engineering for lawyers and judges, and augmented judicial power to review political decisions as a spur to economic and political development. *See* GARDNER, *supra* note 313, at 247–61.

[424] John Henry Merryman, *Book Review*, 14 AM. J. COMP. L. 507–11 (1965) (Cappelletti & Perillo, *Civil Procedure in Italy*, 1965) (quotation at 507).

a common problem associated with inheritance, embezzlement, breach of contract, and population control.[425]

Some individual comparatists cooperated with colleagues abroad who were interested in legal developments in the United States. One of those areas of interest was constitutional criminal procedure, particularly vibrant during the tenure of Chief Justice Earl Warren (served 1953-1969) on the U.S. Supreme Court. Warren and other justices were concerned with police and prosecutorial misconduct at the state level, where most criminal proceedings occurred. The U.S. Constitution's due process clause in the 14th Amendment provided an avenue to incorporate the criminal procedure clauses of the Bill of Rights against state governments, guaranteeing fair police investigation, search, and arrest, providing defendants access to a lawyer, and assuring evenhanded prosecutor conduct from arraignment to trial.[426]

Stephen Thaman identified two U.S. principles that gained acceptance abroad, especially in Europe. One was the standard requiring exclusion of evidence that the police obtained during an arrest or search in a manner violating rules the U.S. Supreme Court enunciated. The other was exclusion of confessions or admissions that a suspect made while in police custody prior to advising her of the right to remain silent and to have counsel present. Whatever transplant occurred from the United States to European countries filtered through the latter's parallel development of constitutional courts as a reaction against the human rights abuses prior to 1945 and the influence of international treaties and supranational tribunals for human rights. However, over time, these exclusionary rules have weakened both in the United States and overseas.[427]

Another field of cooperation between American and European comparatists formed in the late 1970s to study issues of European supranational integration through law. The approach adopted involved discussion of the required structure and process of legal institutions and legal rules within the European social, political, and economic context. The Integration Through Law Project published seven books from 1985 to 1988, which coincided with the European Community's Single European Act that aimed to accomplish a single internal market by 1992. The project included separate volumes considering the

---

[425] JOHN H. BARTON ET AL., LAW IN RADICALLY DIFFERENT CULTURES (1983); Luis M. Negron, Book Review, 36 AM. J. COMP. L. 385-87 (1988). The ASCL presented Merryman its Lifetime Achievement Award in 2004.

[426] FRIEDMAN, HISTORY, supra note 2, at 571-73, 575; Stephen C. Thaman, "Fruits of the Poisonous Tree" in Comparative Law, 16 Sw. J. INT'L L. 333-37 (2010).

[427] Thaman, supra note 426, at 335-38, 383-84. Similar procedural reforms occurred in Latin America after 1990 and to a lesser extent in East Asia. Id. at 338. See also Jacqueline E. Ross & Stephen C. Thaman, Introduction: Mapping Dialogue and Change in Comparative Criminal Procedure, in COMPARATIVE CRIMINAL PROCEDURE 1-31 (Jacqueline E. Ross & Stephen C. Thaman eds., 2016); Máximo Langer, From Legal Transplants to Legal Translations: The Globalization of Plea Bargaining and the Americanization Thesis in Criminal Procedure, 45 HARV. INT'L L.J. 1-64 (2004).

environment, consumer law, corporate law and capital market harmonization, and energy markets.[428]

Mauro Cappelletti, the project's organizer at the European University Institute, believed that national legal systems needed to converge toward a *jus commune* and, under the right social conditions, would do so. Harmonization, coordination, and interdependence were objective requirements. In addition, he supported a higher law of human rights rather than national solutions subject to local politics. Because political events could overwhelm or distract state legislatures, judicial activism through a European court would be an instrument for change. American comparatists and project collaborators interested in European law, such as Hay, Kommers, and Stein, supported the constitutional nature of the emerging European legal structure.[429]

5. Other Landmark Comparative Law Books

Many comparatists mentioned in this chapter and the books they wrote had an important impact on comparative law as a discipline as well as on other subjects of law. Two notably, Mirjan Damaška and Mary Ann Glendon, significantly altered the approach to procedure and family law respectively. Damaška, born in 1931 in the Kingdom of Yugoslavia, grew up in Zagreb, Croatia, where he graduated in law from its university in 1955. He was able to study in Luxembourg and the Netherlands prior to earning his Ph.D. in Ljubljana (now in Slovenia) as the prelude to teaching at the law faculty in Zagreb from 1960 to 1971. Dissatisfied with the socialist state, Damaška emigrated to the United States, where he first taught law at Pennsylvania and then, from 1976, at Yale.[430]

In *Faces of Justice and State Authority* (1986), Damaška rejected the traditional comparative law distinction in procedure between the common law's adversarial process versus the civil law's inquisitorial process. Instead, he adopted a Weberian

---

[428] Rebekka Byberg, *The History of the Integration Through Law Project: Creating the Academic Expression of a Constitutional Legal Vision for Europe*, 18 GERMAN L.J. 1531–32, 1537–38, 1549–50 (2017); *see* Single European Act, 1986 O.J. (L 169) 1 (effective 26 June 1987); 1–5 INTEGRATION THROUGH LAW, *supra* note 100 (1985–1988) (volume 1 had three books).

[429] Mauro Cappelletti, *Foreword to the Florence Integration Project Series*, 1 INTEGRATION THROUGH LAW, *supra* note 100, at bk. 1, v–xix (1985); Byberg, *supra* note 428, at 1534–45, 1550–52, 1556; see *supra* note 278 and accompanying text (Cappelletti); *supra* text accompanying notes 276, 279–82, 284–87 (Hay, Kommers, and Stein). The Ford Foundation financed elements of the Institute's project. Byberg, *supra*, at 1541–42.

[430] Harold Hongju Koh, *Mirjan Damaška: A Bridge between Legal Cultures*, in CRIME, PROCEDURE AND EVIDENCE IN A COMPARATIVE AND INTERNATIONAL CONTEXT: ESSAYS IN HONOUR OF PROFESSOR MIRJAN DAMAŠKA 29–31 (John Jackson, Máximo Langer, & Peter Tillers eds., 2008); *see* Máximo Langer, *Interview with Mirjan Damaška*, in *id.* at 415–38. At the end of World War II, Yugoslavia became a federal people's republic. MARIE-JANINE CALIC, A HISTORY OF YUGOSLAVIA 176–91 (Dona Geyer trans., 2019).

methodology that used ideal types to externally view actual procedural systems using two axes, each with a continuum that one could simplify to four cells. The first axis was hierarchical-coordinate, which reflected how a state might organize its judiciary. Hierarchical states structured their judicial officials with stratified authority and rigid roles, while coordinate states authorized the judiciary loosely with overlapping authority and concentrated, informal decision-making. The second axis involved state ideology that ranged from activist to reactive generally reflective of policy-implementing versus conflict-solving processes. The former sought to achieve substantive values in various manners including the judicial process. The latter endorsed no specific vision of the good life and its judiciary acted as neutral arbiter of private disputes, deferring to party autonomy, and enforcing their bargains.[431]

With the model abstracted from any actual legal system, Damaška used it to analyze civil, common, socialist, and religious law countries with originality and insight. He showed that a state's authority structure and ideology substantially determine the procedural rules it developed. These rules were deeply rooted in a society's history and culture and thus were resistant to transplant from one legal tradition to another.[432] Inga Markovits defended the use of dichotomies as a method to bring enlightenment and order from chaos against some who criticized their utility. Nevertheless, she found the dichotomy of policy implementing and conflict solving less able to distinguish clearly among the major legal traditions. The path forward for proceduralists could be to pursue, in addition to a decontextualized model, an immersive cultural or empirical inquiry into the subject.[433]

Glendon wrote a quartet of books from 1977 to 1989 that transformed the comparative study of family law. A student of Rheinstein,[434] she utilized a historical legal sociology that drew from him and Weber and emphasized Clifford Geertz's cultural view of law. All these sources understood that comparison was essential to accumulating meaningful knowledge. In *Abortion and Divorce in Western Law* (1987), Glendon surveyed 20 Western nations relative to their

---

[431] MIRJAN R. DAMAŠKA, THE FACES OF JUSTICE AND STATE AUTHORITY: A COMPARATIVE APPROACH TO THE LEGAL PROCESS 1–46, 71–96 (1986); Koh, *supra* note 430, at 31; *see, e.g.*, Arthur Taylor von Mehren, *The Importance of Structures and Ideologies for the Administration of Justice*, 97 YALE L.J. 341–51 (1987) (book review).

[432] Koh, *supra* note 430, at 31–32, 34.

[433] Inga Markovits, *Playing the Opposites Game: On Mirjan Damaška's The Faces of Justice and State Authority*, 41 STAN. L. REV. 1313–41 (1989). The Free University of Berlin granted Markovits a Dr. Jur. in 1966. She emigrated to the United States and accepted a law professorship at Texas in 1976. 1990 AALS DIRECTORY, *supra* note 317, at 578.

[434] *See* Mary Ann Glendon, *The Influence of Max Rheinstein on American Law*, *in* DER EINFLUSS, *supra* note 64, at 171–81; Max Rheinstein, Foreword, *in* MARY ANN GLENDON, STATE, LAW AND FAMILY: FAMILY LAW IN TRANSITION IN THE UNITED STATES AND WESTERN EUROPE vii–x (1977) [hereinafter GLENDON, STATE, LAW AND FAMILY]; *see supra* note 410 and text accompanying notes 164, 249–50 (Glendon).

legal treatment of abortion, divorce, and dependency associated with pregnancy, marriage, and child rearing. In comparative perspective, she discovered that the American approach to these issues was anomalous and hoped comparison would aid in explaining its unusual situation. She identified for abortion rules the rhetoric supporting individual rights and no-fault divorce together with submersion of relevant social values.[435] The method was a type of cultural hermeneutics first illustrated by Plato's *Laws*.[436]

As a prelude to *Abortion and Divorce*, Glendon published *State, Law and Family* in 1977. Primarily limited to four legal systems—England, France, the United States, and West Germany—with occasional mention of Sweden, it analyzed the law of marriage, its dissolution, and interspousal relations and the emerging role for the state. The coverage was comparative, historical, and sociological.[437] Four years later, Glendon added more material from Sweden and introduced the concept of new property to explore the legal aspects between family and economic structural relationships. She described the decline of marriage and family cohesion as support institutions and status determinants, replaced by the concomitant growth in work and government in providing economic security and social standing. Thus, one should add employment and welfare law to comprehend what constituted the new property.[438]

---

[435] Mary Ann Glendon, Abortion and Divorce in Western Law: American Failures, European Challenges 1-4, 8-9, 58, 60, 62, 66, 106-14, 131-38 (1987) [hereinafter Glendon, Abortion]; *see* Clifford Gertz, *Local Knowledge: Fact and Law in Comparative Perspective, in* Local Knowledge: Further Essays in Interpretive Anthropology 167-234 (1983); *id., Thick Description: Toward an Interpretive Theory of Culture, in* The Interpretation of Cultures 3-30 (1973). One of the book's aims was to "make a case for wider attention to and greater use of comparative legal analysis, by showing how awareness of foreign experiences can illuminate our own situation and contribute in a modest way to our own law reform efforts." *Id.* at 3.

[436] Glendon, Abortion, *supra* note 435, at 5-9, 45, 111, 114, 142; *see* Merryman, Clark, & Haley, *supra* note 248, at 48-50, 54 (hortatory comparative law); Thomas L. Pangle, The Laws of Plato: Translated with Notes and an Interpretive Essay (1980).

[437] Glendon, State, Law and Family, *supra* note 434, at 1-4, 13-20, 289-96, 304-30. What is essentially an updated second edition to this volume appeared in 1989. Mary Ann Glendon, The Transformation of Family Law: State, Law, and Family in the United States and Western Europe ix-x, 1, 3 (1989).

[438] Mary Ann Glendon, The New Family and the New Property 6-8, 91-97, 143-76, 185-245 (1981); *see* Martha Minow, *The Properties of Family and the Families of Property*, 92 Yale L.J. 376-95 (1982) (book review).

8
Between Globalization and Nationalism: A History of the Future after 1990

> [A] remarkable consensus concerning the legitimacy of liberal democracy as a system of government [has] emerged throughout the world over the past few years, as it conquered rival ideologies like hereditary monarchy, fascism, and most recently communism. . . . [W]hile earlier forms of government were characterized by grave defects and irrationalities that led to their eventual collapse, liberal democracy was arguable free from such fundamental internal contradictions. . . . [While some countries] might lapse back into other, more primitive forms of rule like theocracy or military dictatorships, the *ideal* of liberal democracy could not be improved on.
>
> Francis Fukuyama[1]

> In the post-Cold War world, the most important distinctions among peoples are not ideological, political, or economic. They are cultural. Peoples and nations are attempting to answer the most basic question humans can face: Who are we? . . . People define themselves in terms of ancestry, religion, language, history, values, customs, and institutions. They identify with cultural groups: tribes, ethnic groups, religious communities, nations, and, at the broadest level, civilizations. We know who we are only when we know who we are not and often only when we know whom we are against.
>
> Samuel Huntington[2]

---

[1] FRANCIS FUKUYAMA, THE END OF HISTORY AND THE LAST MAN xi (1992) (italics in original) [hereinafter FUKUYAMA, LAST MAN].

[2] SAMUEL P. HUNTINGTON, THE CLASH OF CIVILIZATIONS AND THE REMAKING OF WORLD ORDER 21 (1996) [hereinafter HUNTINGTON, CLASH AND REMAKING].

A. The 1990s as a Decade of Opportunities

1. The Triumph of Globalization?

The decade of the 1980s began with general economic malaise in most of Europe and the Americas associated with slow economic growth and a debt crisis in Latin America.[3] This led to conservative politicians winning office in the United States, Germany, and the United Kingdom.[4] Their policies of deregulating the marketplace and reducing the government's role in the economy succeeded in improving growth and maintaining moderate inflation. Alternatively, the strain of producing growth in the Soviet Union's inflexible economic and political system took its toll. Reformers such as Mikhail Gorbachev tried to alter the situation with economic restructuring (*perestroika*) and political openness (*glasnost*). Despite the revenue gained from exporting oil, the reforms hastened the collapse of the USSR. Many in the Soviet Union and its satellite countries no longer believed communism could deliver the benefits of modernization. In 1989, when given the chance to leave, millions voted with their feet for the liberal West.[5]

The way the Cold War ended surprised most scholars. It set off a wave of writing, some of which attributed it to a vindication of modernization theory. The challenge of state communism appeared defeated. Liberal concepts infused views of political economy and the future of globalization. It required free markets, trade and investment, and open societies. The Washington Consensus emerged supporting these elements, which the U.S. Treasury, World Bank, and International Monetary Fund could buttress. Japan's economic stagnation in the 1990s further tainted statist policies. There were many opportunities for comparative jurists to advise states abandoning communism and developing countries in general about institutional reforms toward judicial independence and legislative changes to contract and property law needed for successful trade and investment. Experts recommended market deregulation and privatization of state enterprises. Some in the 1990s criticized this approach as neoliberal, a theme that broadened in the next century.[6]

Francis Fukuyama illustrated the optimistic forecasts for market capitalism and political democracy in support of globalization. With the Russian Federation

---

[3] DAVID EKBLADH, THE GREAT AMERICAN MISSION: MODERNIZATION AND THE CONSTRUCTION OF AN AMERICAN WORLD ORDER 259–60 (2010); World Bank, *Home*, https://www.worldbank.org/en/home (select Data/By Indicator, then Economy & Growth/GDP Growth, then Country).

[4] Margaret Thatcher in the U.K. (1979–1990), Ronald Reagan in the USA (1981–1989), and Helmut Kohl in Germany (1982–1998), with years in office.

[5] EKBLADH, *supra* note 3, at 259–60.

[6] EKBLADH, *supra* note 3, at 260–61; *see* IVAN KRASTEV & STEPHEN HOLMES, THE LIGHT THAT FAILED: HOW THE WEST IS LOSING THE FIGHT FOR DEMOCRACY 4–11 (2019); WORLD BANK, ECONOMIC GROWTH IN THE 1990S: LEARNING FROM A DECADE OF REFORM (2005).

and the People's Republic of China (PRC) opening their economies to trade from the capitalist West, he found that no alternative to liberal ideology had global legitimacy. This was "the end of history as such: that is, the end point of mankind's ideological evolution and the universalization of Western liberal democracy as the final form of human government."[7] Fukuyama's use of evolutionary stages of history with an eventual endpoint differed from the cyclical stages, the ebb and flow of history, proposed by Arthur Schlesinger to explain American political culture as a pendulum between conservatism and liberalism.[8] Both the evolutionary and cyclical theories had their counterpart in legal scholarship and influenced comparative law. As the title to this chapter suggests, the author favors a cyclical theory whose dialectic alternates between periods when globalization or universalism dominates and those when nationalism or nativism controls. The former provides more fertile ground for comparative law activities.

The nature of classical dialectic involved a proposition and a counterproposition to contradict it. Fukuyama argued for globalization based on liberalism, but discussed forces that could undercut it.[9] Foremost among those were national cultures whose values did not place tolerance for others as the chief virtue. Cultural obstacles to stable democratic capitalism could include a legal system's discrimination by race, ethnicity, or nationality; a dominant religion's unwillingness to permit freedom of conscience; a highly unequal social structure; or a lack of private associations and a strong civil society.[10] Similarly, traditional forms of nationalism acted to contradict universalism. This was obvious with monarchy, feudalism, colonialism, or fascism. However, it was also the case with democratic nationalism that failed to recognize universal human dignity, instead promoting dignity for their own group. That would lead other nations to seek recognition for their group's dignity, fostering conflict or imperialism.[11]

In 1993, Samuel Huntington rejected the inevitability of globalization based on liberalism and instead identified the tenacity of human cultures in all their

---

[7] Francis Fukuyama, *The End of History?* NAT'L INTEREST 3–4, 11–14 (no. 16, Summer 1989) (quotation at 4). Fukuyama borrowed the concept of the end of history from the dialectical materialism of Karl Marx and Georg Wilhelm Friedrich Hegel. *Id.* at 4–6.

[8] *See* ARTHUR M. SCHLESINGER, JR., THE CYCLES OF AMERICAN HISTORY (1999) (private interest versus public action), which modified his father's conservative-liberal pattern of cycles presented in ARTHUR M. SCHLESINGER, SR., PATHS TO THE PRESENT (1949). Samuel Merrill III et al., *Cycles in American National Electoral Politics, 1854–2006: Statistical Evidence and an Explanatory Model*, 102 AM. POL. SCI. REV. 1–2 (2008).

[9] FUKUYAMA, LAST MAN, *supra* note 1, at 126–30. "[T]here has emerged in the last few centuries something like a true global culture, centering around technologically driven economic growth and the capitalist social relations necessary to produce and sustain it." *Id.* at 126.

[10] *Id.* at 215–19, 222. Religion and nationalism were not per se obstacles to liberalism. *Id.* at 215–17.

[11] *Id.* at 266–75. "If nationalism is to fade away as a political force, it must be made tolerant like religion before it. National groups can retain their separate languages and senses of identity, but that identity would be expressed primarily in the realm of culture." *Id.* at 271.

variety of values, norms, and institutions as the central force for the future.[12] This future would be a "politics of identity."[13] More generally, groups of similar cultures had cohered into larger civilizations that people could identify with more broadly, usually with a shared religion. Consequently, religion had been and would be more significant to a civilization than a common language or ethnicity. A civilization, such as the Western, Hindu, or Chinese, was the highest cultural grouping of people and broadest level of cultural identity. The world's major civilizations had evolved and endured for long periods; they had merged and divided and risen and fallen. Since civilizations were cultural and not political entities, the systems of law each contained might be diverse.[14]

Huntington asserted that there were perhaps nine major civilizations: Western, Chinese-Confucian, Japanese, Buddhist, Islamic, Hindu, Slavic-Orthodox Christian, Latin American, and African. Most serious conflict in the future would occur along the cultural fault lines separating these civilizations from one another. Modern communication and transportation among peoples of different civilizations enhanced a person's civilization-consciousness, which augmented differences and animosities stretching into the past. At the same time, modernization separated people from prior local or regional identities, weakening the nation-state and often strengthening religion.[15]

In contrast with Fukuyama, which saw a rosy future for the United States if it maintained liberalism, Huntington predicted that the West in the 1990s was at the peak of its power in relation to other civilizations. The United States was the superpower and, together with a few European nations plus Japan, effectively controlled economic and security questions. They had presented their political and legal solutions as reflecting the "world community." Huntington pointed out that Western culture and its basic principles, other than at a superficial level, had not in general permeated other civilizations. He listed individualism, liberalism (democracy and free markets), constitutionalism, human rights, equality, liberty, rule of law, and separation of church and state. "The very notion that there could be a 'universal civilization' is a Western idea." For comparative law, he stated that U.S. and European efforts to induce other peoples to adopt Western ideas

---

[12] Samuel P. Huntington, *The Clash of Civilizations?* 72 FOREIGN AFFAIRS 22–23, 42, 48 (no. 3, Summer 1993).

[13] *See* HUNTINGTON, CLASH AND REMAKING, *supra* note 2, at 125–54, 266–72.

[14] HUNTINGTON, CLASH AND REMAKING, *supra* note 2, at 20, 40–44; *id.*, FOREIGN AFFAIRS, *supra* note 12, at 24–25. "Non-Western civilizations have attempted to become modern without becoming Western." Japan had been the most successful example. *Id.* at 49.

[15] HUNTINGTON, CLASH AND REMAKING, *supra* note 2, at 20–21, 26–29, 36, 45–48; *id.*, FOREIGN AFFAIRS, *supra* note 12, at 25–26, 29. With Japan as an example, it was possible for a nation to coincide with a civilization. *Id.* at 27–28. "Even more than ethnicity, religion discriminates sharply and exclusively among people. A person can be half-French and half-Arab and simultaneously even a citizen of two countries. It is more difficult to be half-Catholic and half-Muslim." *Id.* at 27.

concerning democracy and human rights usually failed; historically, where they succeeded, it was typically by colonialism or imposition.[16]

Huntington had additional advice about where comparatists should turn their attention. Countries that had large numbers of peoples of different civilizations, such as the Soviet Union and Yugoslavia, had dismembered or would do so. The new political units could have very different legal systems. There were numerous future candidates. Another type of country to study would be one with significant cultural homogeneity but divisions concerning which civilization was the best fit. Turkey provided the division between the West and Islam. With Mexico's entry into NAFTA, it was between Latin American and Western civilization.[17] Already in 1993, Huntington foresaw that the greatest competition for Western civilization in the twenty-first century would come from the Confucianist-Chinese sphere and from Islam. This would entail a direct challenge to Western interests, values, and military power.[18]

At the end of Huntington's 1996 book on the clash of civilizations, he directly provoked his critics with a final broadside against international universalism and those in the United States who supported domestic multiculturalism.

> Multiculturalism at home threatens the United States and the West; universalism abroad threatens the West and the world. Both deny the uniqueness of Western culture. The global monoculturalists want to make the world like America. The domestic multiculturalists want to make America like the world. A multicultural America is impossible because a non-Western America is not American. A multicultural world is unavoidable because global empire is impossible.[19]

Huntington believed that world security required acceptance of global multiculturality. In a sentiment shared by those who criticized U.S. law and development activities of the 1960s, he questioned whether the quest for universalism legitimated imperialism.[20] "Instead of promoting the supposedly universal features of one civilization, the requisites for cultural coexistence demand

---

[16] HUNTINGTON, CLASH AND REMAKING, supra note 2, at 31–32; id., FOREIGN AFFAIRS, supra note 12, at 39–41 (quotation at 41). "The forces of integration in the world are real and are precisely what are generating counterforces of cultural assertion and civilizational consciousness." HUNTINGTON, CLASH AND REMAKING, supra, at 36; see id. at 56–101.

[17] HUNTINGTON, CLASH AND REMAKING, supra note 2, at 28, 37; id., FOREIGN AFFAIRS, supra note 12, at 27, 42–44.

[18] HUNTINGTON, CLASH AND REMAKING, supra note 2, at 20–21; id., FOREIGN AFFAIRS, supra note 12, at 45–46; see HUNTINGTON, CLASH AND REMAKING, supra, at 183–98, 209–45.

[19] HUNTINGTON, CLASH AND REMAKING, supra note 2, at 318–21 (quotation at 318).

[20] Id. at 310–11, 318. "Normatively the Western universalist belief posits that people throughout the world should embrace Western values, institutions, and culture because they embody the highest, most enlightened, most liberal, most rational, most modern, and most civilized thinking of humankind." Id. at 310.

a search for what is common to most civilizations. In a multicivilizational world, the constructive course is to renounce universalism, accept diversity, and seek commonalities."[21] At the national level in a heterogeneous society, the prescription was to promote shared values among diverse cultural, racial, and religious groups: commonality over difference.[22]

In general, the period after 1990 witnessed a burst of activity by U.S. comparative lawyers who mostly saw opportunity to benefit from, influence, and for academics, study the altered legal systems resulting from the collapse of Soviet hegemony. In addition, the American Society of Comparative Law expanded its membership and became an international organization for the first time. Its journal served as the world's leading source of discussion about comparative law issues. Undeniably, globalization affected important U.S. legal institutions. In the 1990s, United States NGOs and the national government seemed to have learned very little from earlier law and development initiatives or from Huntington's warning about universalism. New challenges appeared in the twenty-first century, which interested legal comparatists and broadened their writing about legal cultures previously discounted or ignored.

Huntington did not believe nationalism was dead or would die anytime soon. "Nation states remain the principal actors in world affairs." They pursue power and wealth that partially determine their status; each of the world's civilizations has one or more core nations. Cultural preferences, commonalties within a civilization, and differences with competing civilizations shape their nature and the future of their civilization.[23]

2. Initial Comparative Law Reaction to Accelerated Globalization

After the Soviet Union's disintegration, globalization accelerated in economic, political, social, and cultural life during the 1990s. These global forces affected comparative law primarily through improvements in information

---

[21] *Id.* at 318.

[22] Huntington described the effort to formulate cultural identity in Singapore. In a society of Chinese, Malay, Muslim, and Hindu components, the government selected nation before ethnicity, society above self, family as the basic social unit but with regard for the individual, consensus instead of contention, and racial and religious harmony. HUNTINGTON, CLASH AND REMAKING, *supra* note 2, at 318–19. By contrast, Huntington felt that multiculturalists were sowing discord and disunity within the United States. "[T]hey have attacked the identification of the United States with Western civilization, denied the existence of a common American culture, and promoted racial, ethnic, and other subnational cultural identities and groupings." They have substituted "for the rights of individuals the rights of groups, defined largely in terms of race, ethnicity, sex, and sexual preference." *Id.* at 305–06.

[23] HUNTINGTON, CLASH AND REMAKING, *supra* note 2, at 21, 28–29, 33–35, 125–26, 231–35; *see id.* at 272–91.

dissemination, international travel, and academic collaboration, supplemented by the spread of American-style law firms worldwide. American lawyers were at the front of the expansion in transnational legal services, earning billions of dollars. Comparatists often replaced the term modernization with globalization after 1990.[24]

At the same time as there seemed to be many indicators of success for American comparative law, there were skeptics of its position in legal education or more generally its influence on American legal life. Measured from the 1930s, there appeared little doubt that there had been important progress in the acceptance of foreign and comparative law teachers and journals in United States law schools. Academic comparatists were involved with the U.S. government and NGOs in exporting U.S. law and legal institutions to developing countries. In addition, American lawyers and judges dealt with foreign law issues every day. By 2000, the globalized law firm was a fact of modern legal practice.[25]

What was the case for skepticism? By 2000, no U.S. law school made comparative law a core discipline or put comparatists at the center of scholarly debate. This was true even at NYU School of Law, which claimed to be the country's pre-eminent global law school.[26] In the United States, the center of greatest attention at most schools was either constitutional law—the various subdisciplines that it permeated, with U.S. Supreme Court case law—or perhaps business law broadly construed. Faculty hiring decisions and budget allocations reflected this situation, which was simply a reality of American legal history and culture. Another complaint was that domestic American law students were generally ill prepared to take on serious comparative law study, since they lacked a rigorous background in geography, history, philosophy, or languages. This critique had some merit, but might be changing as law faculties hired more professors with doctoral degrees outside law and created more post-J.D. degree programs, and as students came to appreciate the demands of global legal practice. American law schools were also willing to hire a few foreign-trained professors, which added to the school's global perspective.[27]

In 1996, Mathias Reimann presented an informed, comprehensive attack on American comparative law teaching as it had developed since the 1950s in

---

[24] One German-Swiss comparatist used the term Americanization to refer to this dynamic. *See* Wolfgang Wiegand, *Americanization of Law: Reception or Convergence?*, in LEGAL CULTURE AND THE LEGAL PROFESSION 137–52 (Lawrence M. Friedman & Harry N. Scheiber eds., 1996). *See also* R. Daniel Kelemen & Eric C. Sibbitt, *The Americanization of Japanese Law*, 23 U. PA. J. INT'L ECON. L. 269–323 (2002).

[25] *See infra* pt. C (globalization of American legal institutions).

[26] *See* John Edward Sexton, *The Global Law School Program at New York University*, 46 J. LEGAL EDUC. 329–35 (1996).

[27] David S. Clark, *Development of Comparative Law in the United States* [hereinafter Clark, *Development*], in THE OXFORD HANDBOOK OF COMPARATIVE LAW 148, 178 (Mathias Reimann & Reinhard Zimmermann eds., 2d ed. 2019) [hereinafter OXFORD HANDBOOK].

U.S. law schools. His proposal to end its marginality was to replace an autonomous comparative law course with incorporation of a comparative perspective in mainstream courses from the beginning of instruction in the first-year program. Leading comparatists had made this recommendation before, but it never gained success with law school colleagues. Reimann contended that globalization of law offered a new opportunity and demanded the shift. He believed current comparative law courses were poor in quality and design; foreign law courses, such as those treating German law, Japanese law, or Latin American legal systems, should replace them. Furthermore, newly prepared core courses with a foreign law component would permit true comparison with American law and expose more students to the discipline.[28]

Broader criticism of comparative law occurred at two law school conferences held in 1996 and 1997. The first, at Utah College of Law, drew a mixed group of foreign and U.S. participants, most of whom had little experience with comparative law, and reflected nominalist approaches toward understanding law then growing in acceptance at American law schools.[29] Some older comparatists pointed out that many of the papers used approaches that were hardly new, but rather solid examples that drew from the toolbox already available for comparative research.[30] Others borrowed heavily from the jargon of critical legal studies, identity politics, literary theory, or feminism to criticize what most comparatists do.[31] From much of that, it would be hard to map a path forward. Basil Markesinis saw postmodernism as a direct threat to American comparative law. He had three principal objections: it involved sloppy theorizing; unclear concepts; and neologisms and verbose language, which were useless for practical comparative law.[32]

The second conference took place at Michigan Law School and Hastings College of Law and included mid-career comparatists who had taught in the United States. The organizers asserted that the discipline lacked theoretical and methodological foundations and had no accepted standards of quality.

---

[28] Mathias Reimann, *The End of Comparative Law as an Autonomous Subject*, 11 TUL. EUR. & CIV. L.F. 49–56, 58–59, 61–65, 69–70 (1996). For a rare coursebook that integrated a comparative dimension, see SYMEON C. SYMEONIDES, WENDY COLLINS PERDUE, & ARTHUR T. VON MEHREN, CONFLICT OF LAWS: AMERICAN, COMPARATIVE, INTERNATIONAL, CASES AND MATERIALS (1998) (4th ed. 2019).

[29] *Foreword*, 1997 UTAH L. REV. 255–57 (symposium on new approaches to comparative law).

[30] Paolo G. Carozza, *Continuity and Rupture in New Approaches to Comparative Law*, 1997 UTAH L. REV. 657–63.

[31] *See, e.g.*, Günter Frankenberg, *Stranger than Paradise: Identity & Politics in Comparative Law*, 1997 UTAH L. REV. 259–74. The popularity of critical legal studies declined after the collapse of the Soviet Union and the viability of state socialism. STEPHEN B. PRESSER, LAW PROFESSORS: THREE CENTURIES OF SHAPING AMERICAN LAW 277–83, 290–92 (2017).

[32] Sir Basil Markesinis, *Understanding American Law by Looking at It through Foreign Eyes: Towards a Wider Theory for the Study and Use of Foreign Law*, 81 TUL. L. REV. 123, 140–48 (2006); *see id.*, COMPARATIVE LAW IN COURTROOM AND CLASSROOM: THE STORY OF THE LAST THIRTY-FIVE YEARS 51–54 (2003) [hereinafter Markesinis, COMPARATIVE LAW]. Markesinis was a law professor at University College London and the University of Texas School of Law.

Some papers called for more attention to the diversity of human cultures, promoting tolerance for differences in how law operates; or for more jurisprudence or interdisciplinarity; or for a broader conception of law as a system of norms, institutions, and processes, perhaps generating testable hypotheses.[33]

Not all the participants agreed with the organizers about the dire state of American comparative law. John Reitz, for instance, believed there was a large degree of consensus about the essentials of the comparative method, perhaps a canon. He offered nine principles to follow to achieve quality comparative law scholarship.[34] David Gerber argued that although the usual comparative law methods served traditional objectives adequately, new objectives had emerged that required additional methods to go beyond study of legal rules.[35] These new aims included both scientific comparative law, seeking knowledge about how legal systems operate; and practical comparative law for the use of lawyers, judges, and legislators. He proposed to examine over time the decisions of legal actors, schooled in common cognitive patterns, in the context of a legal system composed of rules, institutions, and processes that would capture causal factors affecting results. The benefit, as with other sciences, would be the accumulation of knowledge.[36]

Reimann, one of two organizers of the second conference, took a decidedly more pessimistic view of American comparative law. He found it marginal and in crisis, having somehow missed opportunities offered by globalization. It was derivative of European comparative law, out of date, and unable to serve global or American needs. This Eurocentric discipline had three major features impeding its development in the United States.[37] First, it had a predominantly private law orientation, although Reimann recognized that was no longer the U.S. situation.

---

[33] Ugo Mattei & Mathias Reimann, *Introduction*, 46 Am. J. Comp. L. 597–606 (1998) (symposium on new directions in comparative law). Most American comparatists see comparative law as a collection of methods from which the investigator selects one to meet the requirements for a specific study. Each method or approach, such as legal transplant, functionalism, unification of law, historical jurisprudence, natural law, economic analysis, cultural hermeneutics, or legal sociology has its assumptions and techniques. In the 1990s, for instance, some believed legal transplant was the predominate and preferred method. Ugo Mattei, *Why the Wind Changed: Intellectual Leadership in Western Law*, 42 Am. J. Comp. L. 195–218 (1994).

[34] John C. Reitz, *How to Do Comparative Law*, 46 Am. J. Comp. L. 617–35 (1998).

[35] David J. Gerber, *System Dynamics: Toward a Language of Comparative Law?*, 46 Am. J. Comp. L. 719–24 (1998). Gerber associated traditional objectives with the concerns of private international law, unification of law, and legal transplants. Common to them was the focus on legal rules. *Id.* at 720–21; *see supra* ch. 7, pts. E.1, F.2, F.3 (activity associated with those objectives).

[36] Gerber, *supra* note 35, at 724–37. Gerber did not refer to the work of comparative legal sociology or pre-1990 law and development. *See supra* ch. 7, pt. F.4 (describing that work).

[37] Mathias Reimann, *Stepping Out of the European Shadow: Why Comparative Law in the United States Must Develop Its Own Agenda*, 46 Am. J. Comp. L. 637–39, 645 (1998). Reimann and other comparatists mistakenly believed that the history of American comparative law began with the émigré group in the late 1930s and 1940s. Thus, it was easy to conclude that the discipline was mostly a German import that never really fit American circumstances and in 1996 was badly out of date. *See id.* at 638–39.

Second, its approach was to compare Anglo-American law with European civil law. Again, he mentioned that two of the four U.S. law school coursebooks he cited also compared other legal systems or regions. Third, the discipline continued to emphasize traditional sources of law: codes, legislation, and case law. Although these were important, the U.S. study of Latin American and Asian legal systems demonstrated that cultural sources of rules were also relevant.[38] In short, the premise that U.S. comparative law had been or was hostage to European comparative law was false.

Perhaps surprisingly, with historical perspective, there was a sense in which American comparative law today is less significant in legal academia than it was in the first quarter of the twentieth century. This assessment would consider the national leadership of American law schools, persons with whom all law teachers would be familiar, and ask whether those leaders were active in organized comparative law. In recent decades, the answer in general would be no. Looking at the first quarter of the twentieth century, however, seven of the first 25 presidents of the AALS were active in comparative law activities.[39]

As American comparative law progressed in the early twenty-first century, major scholarly conferences of external or self-reflective criticism of the discipline faded in relevance as the field faced the practical realities of globalization and reactions manifested against legal uniformity, absorbed new members with interests outside Europe, and experimented with interdisciplinary methodologies. One could assert that U.S. comparative law, rather than being marginal, was ascending.[40] Instead of lining it up against other American legal or allied disciplines, or contrasting it with some mythical scholarly universe, one could measure its activity relative to the strength of comparative law in foreign countries. For instance, in the first edition of the influential *Oxford Handbook of Comparative Law* (2006), one of the two co-editors held his academic position in the United States and 16 authors of its 43 chapters affiliated with American universities. Germany, the next most represented country, had eight authors.[41]

---

[38] *Id.* at 639–43; *see supra* ch. 7, text accompanying notes 247–250 (U.S. comparative law coursebooks).

[39] Those AALS presidents, with presidency year and affiliation, were Simeon Baldwin (1902, Yale, the Comparative Law Bureau's director), George Kirchwey (1907, Columbia, Bureau manager), Roscoe Pound (1911, Harvard, Bureau manager and original member of the International Academy of Comparative Law), Joseph Beale (1913, Harvard), Harlan Stone (1916–1919, Columbia, original member of the International Academy), Eugene Gilmore (1920, Wisconsin), and William Draper Lewis (1924, Pennsylvania, Bureau manager). *See supra* ch. 6, pt. C (Comparative Law Bureau).

[40] MARKESINIS, COMPARATIVE LAW, *supra* note 32, at 61–64.

[41] OXFORD HANDBOOK OF COMPARATIVE LAW ix–xv (Mathias Reimann & Reinhard Zimmermann eds., 2006) [hereinafter OXFORD HANDBOOK 2006]. "[C]omparative law has become a vibrant and intellectually stimulating field of study and research and it has advanced our knowledge in a variety of areas and contexts." Preface, in *id.* at v.

In 2000, Tulane hosted the Centennial World Congress on Comparative Law to commemorate a century of organized comparative law activities since the famed 1900 Paris International Congress of Comparative Law.[42] The fact that the celebration occurred in the United States rather than France reinforced the notion that American comparative law had a leadership role in the discipline. The U.S. papers tended to support Fukuyama's view of the reality of globalization, but without typically embracing universalism.[43] A few presenters reminded the audience of the diversity of existing legal systems and decried the hegemony of Western law, offering the idea of the moral equivalency of legal cultures.[44]

3. The Tenacity of Traditions, Cultures, and Legal Pluralism

Huntington rejected the possibility of one world, one law: the dream of some comparatists at the end of the nineteenth century. In his view, once humans invented language and writing, there evolved a multicivilizational world. Civilizations rose and fell, replaced by new or altered civilizations. This cycle of history fascinated Europeans who studied the 1,000-year history of the Roman Republic and Empire. Law played an important part in that history, which carried over as a major characteristic of Western civilization through the eras of colonialism, nationalism, and globalization.[45] For the United States, the legal elements unifying its national identity were liberty, democracy, individualism, equality in law, constitutionalism, and private property.[46]

---

[42] David S. Clark, *Nothing New in 2000—Comparative Law in 1900 and Today*, 75 TUL. L. REV. 871, 875–88 (2001).

[43] *E.g.*, David J. Gerber, *Globalization and Legal Knowledge: Implications for Comparative Law*, 75 TUL. L. REV. 949–76 (2001); Mathias Reimann, *Beyond National Systems: A Comparative Law for the International Age*, 75 *id.* at 1103–20. Gerber identified three dimensions of globalization: economic activity, information technology, and regulatory or normative development. Gerber, *supra*, at 951–53. Reimann recommended adding comparison of transnational law—international trade, European Union, and human rights—to the national legal systems. Reimann, *supra*, at 1115–20.

[44] Franz Werro, *Notes on the Purpose and Aims of Comparative Law*, 75 TUL. L. REV. 1225, 1230–34 (2001). Markesinis rejected the usefulness of equating the history and culture of Asian or Islamic law with the reality of Western law influence on the world's legal systems. MARKESINIS, COMPARATIVE LAW, *supra* note 32, at 50–51.

[45] HUNTINGTON, CLASH AND REMAKING, *supra* note 2, at 301–02, 311. No one doubts that the West has had an enormous impact on other civilizations from 1500, since it initiated the processes of modernization and industrialization. Adopting what was useful from these processes, but maintaining core cultural values, non-Western nations have attempted, with some success, to catch up with the West in social organization and wealth. *Id.* at 302; *see* ROBBIE ROBERTSON, THE THREE WAVES OF GLOBALIZATION: A HISTORY OF A DEVELOPING GLOBAL CONSCIOUSNESS (2003). Robertson dated the first globalization wave from 1500, based on colonialism and regional trade. The second began around 1800, aided by industrialization. Finally, the third wave originated after 1945, centered in the United States and derived from the West's economic, political, and legal architecture for the postwar order. ROBERTSON, *supra*, at 4–13.

[46] HUNTINGTON, CLASH AND REMAKING, *supra* note 2, at 305.

After 1990, although doubted by some, leaders within a few civilizations—especially those of the Chinese and Muslims—made renewed efforts to resist Westernization, including individualism, rule of law, separation of church and state, freedom of expression, and democracy. Huntington believed that the West could be at that stage in its history, self-confident and congratulatory, where its officials operated with the assumption that its system and values were universal and would remain dominant. This universal stage could continue for a long time but it would eventually end, either by external force or internal disintegration.[47]

What does this analysis signal to legal comparatists? The existence of numerous civilizations, each with its own conception of the role for law and legal institutions, provides challenging opportunities to understand a foreign civilization and report on the place and function of law in the nations that comprise a single civilization. Obviously, the researcher would require a social and cultural perspective to comprehend those legal systems. This is true for comparison even within the Western civilization at the national level. Italy is not Germany, which is not the United Kingdom. Comparison among civilizations, where the reality of legal pluralism is evident, would be more ambitious, particularly in determining a common frame of reference.

In 2001, Patrick Glenn (1940–2014) tackled the question of incommensurability across legal traditions. He suggested that the issue's emergence in comparative law during the 1990s might be a reaction against challenges to Western law. For some, the concept was equivalent to incomparability.[48] Glenn took the position that the world's major legal traditions do not exist in isolation from one another since they consist of large amounts of detailed and communicable information that a tradition's jurists cannot rigidly control. Furthermore, each tradition must be tolerant of internal diversity if it aspires to transnational status. It cannot acknowledge incommensurability; each tradition has "developed doctrines of accommodation of conflicting inner doctrines or schools or

---

[47] *Id.* at 301–03. "The central issue for the West is whether, quite apart from any external challenges, it is capable of stopping and reversing the internal processes of decay." *Id.* at 303. Robertson stated the idea differently. "No wave has ever been the product of one 'civilization' or one culture alone. Waves encompass many cultures; they enable them to interact, although not necessarily as equals. They enable cross-fertilization. Exclusivity, on the other hand, denies mutual benefit and is difficult to sustain." ROBERTSON, *supra* note 45, at 4.

[48] H. Patrick Glenn, *Are Legal Traditions Incommensurable?*, 49 AM. J. COMP. L. 133–40 (2001) [hereinafter Glenn, *Incommensurable*]; *see* Vivian Grosswald Curran, *Cultural Immersion, Difference and Categories in U.S. Comparative Law*, 46 AM. J. COMP. L. 43, 90–92 (1998). One might point out that Glenn was a Canadian citizen who taught at McGill University in Montréal. However, he studied at Harvard Law School (LL.M in 1966) and was president of the American Society of Comparative Law from 2012 to 2014. McGill University, *Institute of Comparative Law*, https://www.mcgill.ca/icl (select Glenn).

declarations of autonomy.... Legal traditions are thus externally open and internally accommodating. They both represent and preserve diversity."[49]

Glenn also recognized legal culture as a major tool for comparative law analysis, reflective of a legal tradition. A tradition might include multiple cultures consisting of discrete legal ideas, values, and practices. Within the Western legal tradition, culture evolved in the nineteenth century as a concept to differentiate human groups, particularly the French and Germans, to contest claims of convergence or universalism. However useful it might be as a description, it has not carried much explanatory power due to its ambiguity. Today, most comparatists consider legal culture as holistic and society specific, although for heterogenous societies one could investigate subcultures associated with the idea of legal pluralism. Nevertheless, a consequence of accepting the intransigence of culture within a legal system is that the difference with foreign legal systems likely leads to competition, conflict, and possibly dominance. Convergence and universalism are not realistically achievable. Glenn rejected the essentialist dimension of legal culture and argued that legal tradition—as multinational, a result of history, alterable, and porous—offered potential conciliation among legal traditions.[50]

Glenn had earlier, in 2000, presented a thorough interdisciplinary treatment of the issues associated with comparison of the legal systems of civilizations in *Legal Traditions of the World*. The volume was a success, appearing in five editions through 2014.[51] According to a reviewer, Glenn offered a "humanistic framework for addressing cultural and ethnic diversity in the law and the phenomenon of globalization among legal systems."[52] Rather than Huntington's nine civilizations, Glenn selected seven legal traditions, dividing the Western legal tradition into the civil law and common law and grouping indigenous legal cultures subjected to European colonization into a chthonic or customary law

---

[49] Glenn, *Incommensurable, supra* note 48, at 140–42 (quotation at 142). Glenn's list of principal transnational legal traditions included chthonic (customary) law, Talmudic law, civil law, common law, Islamic law, Hindu law, and Asian law. *Id.* at 140. To avoid an external, objective structure of reality—monism—the comparatist should explore the data provided by the concepts and normative structures of the competing traditions. *Id.* at 144–45.

[50] H. Patrick Glenn, *Legal Cultures and Legal Traditions, in* EPISTEMOLOGY AND METHODOLOGY OF COMPARATIVE LAW 7–20 (Mark van Hoecke, ed., 2004); *see* Elizabeth Kiss, *Is Nationalism Compatible with Human Rights? Reflections on East-Central Europe, in* IDENTITIES, POLITICS, AND RIGHTS 367–402 (Austin Sarat & Thomas R. Kearns eds., 1995) (universalistic human rights and ethnic nationalism).

[51] H. PATRICK GLENN, LEGAL TRADITIONS OF THE WORLD: SUSTAINABLE DIVERSITY IN LAW (4th ed. 2010) [hereinafter GLENN, LEGAL TRADITIONS] (1st ed. 2000, 5th ed. 2014); *see* Thomas E. Carbonneau, *Book Review*, 48 AM. J. COMP. L. 729–31 (2000); H. Patrick Glenn, *Comparative Legal Families and Comparative Legal Traditions, in* OXFORD HANDBOOK 2006, *supra* note 41, at 421–40. In 1998, the International Academy of Comparative Law awarded Glenn's manuscript its grand prize at the quadrennial congress. Carbonneau, *supra*, at 729.

[52] Carbonneau, *supra* note 51, at 731.

tradition. Three other traditions paralleled Huntington's civilizations: Islamic, Hindu, and Confucian.[53]

Both Glenn and Huntington held out hope for the world's civilizations to promote peace via their legal and political systems rather than engage in conflict to gain advantage. Huntington believed religion had a significant place in the peace process. "[W]hatever the degree to which they divided humankind, the world's major religions—Western Christianity, Orthodoxy, Hinduism, Buddhism, Islam, Confucianism, Taoism, Judaism—also share key values in common. If humans are ever to develop a universal civilization, it will emerge gradually through the exploration and expansion of these commonalities." Nevertheless, he foresaw the rise of China in the twenty-first century as a dangerous source of international instability that could lead to intercivilizational war.[54] Glenn also promoted the search for commonalities and rejected the universalism of any legal tradition as unacceptable domination. Toleration of other legal traditions would be necessary. "Whether a given tradition is universalizing ... will be a question of how it reconciles its own normativity with its own tolerance of other traditions." Normativity, complexity, and multivalence characterized all of Glenn's traditions and he predicted they one day would be interdependent with sustainable diversity in law.[55]

Beyond the several major legal traditions that American comparatists studied,[56] some also adopted the concept of legal culture in their research.[57] Of course, there are, in the aggregate, hundreds of regional, national, local, ethnic, religious, gender, and social class cultures and group subcultures that have a set of attitudes and values about law and the legal system that identify these cultures. A few examples should suffice.

Alan Watson was concerned with legal culture at the national level and its role in legal change. He argued that a satisfactory approach to the question required a combination of the methods of comparative law, legal history, and legal sociology

---

[53] GLENN, LEGAL TRADITIONS, *supra* note 51, at 61–360; *see id.* at 99–132 (Talmudic tradition); *supra* note 15 and accompanying text (Huntington's classification). Huntington distinguished between African and Latin American civilizations instead of Glenn's chthonic tradition, while the latter added a Talmudic legal tradition that Huntington implicitly included in Western civilization.

[54] HUNTINGTON, CLASH AND REMAKING, *supra* note 2, at 312–17, 320 (quotation at 320).

[55] GLENN, LEGAL TRADITIONS, *supra* note 51, at 49–54, 365–85 (quotation at 365). "[T]here will be sustainable diversity in law in the world, and . . . all the efforts of all of the universalizers (of all traditions) will now not succeed in disrupting it." *Id.* at 377.

[56] *See supra* ch. 7, text accompanying notes 247–250, 409 (comparative law coursebooks oriented around the concept of legal tradition).

[57] *E.g.*, DAVID M. ENGEL, TORT, CUSTOM, AND KARMA: GLOBALIZATION AND LEGAL CONSCIOUSNESS IN THAILAND (2010); James Q. Whitman, *The Two Western Cultures of Privacy: Dignity versus Liberty*, 113 YALE L.J. 1151–1222 (2004); LEGAL CULTURE IN THE AGE OF GLOBALIZATION: LATIN AMERICA AND LATIN EUROPE (Lawrence Friedman & Rogelio Perez-Perdomo eds., 2003) [hereinafter AGE OF GLOBALIZATION]; *see supra* ch. 7, notes 263–64, 329–31, 432–36 and accompanying text (comparative law research utilizing the concept of legal culture).

studying several legal systems. He believed sociologists overly devalued the role of positive law and its sources, with their common longevity and dysfunction, even for social elites, attempting to explain legal change solely with political, economic, and social factors.[58] "[L]aw exists and flourishes at the level of idea, and is part of culture." Lawmakers—legislators, judges, or jurists—are the principal agents for legal change, so their culture is central to how that process occurs. However, attitudes toward and values about law and the legal system among lawyers and the general population are also relevant. Lawyers are often resistant to legal change, since making legal rules or processes simpler or less ambiguous could adversely affect their income. When economic or social reasons suggest that law should change, that pressure affects the overall culture. Nevertheless, the impetus for legal change and its timing, nature, and success or failure must mediate through lawmakers and sometimes lawyers.[59]

Most comparatists who used legal culture in their research were writing about national legal cultures or sometimes regional legal cultures, in which case the analysis approached the idea of a legal tradition.[60] Nevertheless, there were a few studies of subnational legal cultures that would implicate the concept of legal pluralism.[61] Often this was the work of anthropologists.[62] In addition, some American jurists investigated the legal norms—customary and written—of U.S. native peoples whose tribes had a limited form of sovereignty that permitted them to apply their law to members of their own group. Although this was a type of comparative law, these scholars created their own associations.[63] Comparatists interested in legal pluralism concentrated their attention on foreign countries

---

[58] Alan Watson, *Legal Change: Sources of Law and Legal Culture*, 131 U. PA. L. REV. 1121, 1125–26, 1134–36, 1151–52 (1983). Watson did not deny the relevance of social variables, simply that they were not exclusive. "All legal rules are created by a cause; and this cause of creation is commonly, but not always, rooted in social, economic, or political factors ... [but today] may be rooted in transnational aspects of the legal tradition.... Once created, legal rules tend to live on." *Id.* at 1135.

[59] *Id.* at 1152–57 (quotation at 1152).

[60] *See, e.g.*, MARY SARAH BILDER, THE TRANSATLANTIC CONSTITUTION: COLONIAL LEGAL CULTURE AND THE EMPIRE (2008); AMALIA D. KESSLER, INVENTING AMERICAN EXCEPTIONALISM: THE ORIGINS OF AMERICAN ADVERSARIAL LEGAL CULTURE (2017); Hannah L. Buxbaum, *German Legal Culture and the Globalization of Competition Law: A Historical Perspective on the Expansion of Private Antitrust Enforcement*, 23 BERKELEY J. INT'L L. 474–95 (2005); Boris Kozolchyk, *A Roadmap to Economic Development through Law: Third Parties and Comparative Legal Culture*, 23 ARIZ. J. INT'L & COMP. L. 1–36 (2005); Lawrence Rosen, *Law and Custom in the Popular Legal Culture of North Africa*, 2 ISLAMIC L. & SOC'Y 194–208 (1995); Keith S. Rosenn, *Brazil's Legal Culture: The Jeito Revisited*, 1 FLA. INT'L L. J. 1–44 (1984).

[61] *E.g.*, David S. Clark, *Italian Styles: Criminal Justice and the Rise of an Active Magistracy*, in AGE OF GLOBALIZATION, *supra* note 57, at 239–84 (using several legal and social indicators comparing Italy south of Rome (Mezzogiorno) with the region of Rome and north Italy); *see supra* ch. 7, notes 320–21 and accompanying text (legal pluralism).

[62] *E.g.*, Sally Engle Merry, *Legal Pluralism*, 22 LAW & SOC'Y REV. 869–96 (1988).

[63] *See* RENNARD STRICKLAND, FIRE AND THE SPIRITS: CHEROKEE LAW FROM CLAN TO COURT (1975). Organizations that support legal research include the American Indian Law Center and the National Native American Bar Association.

with heterogenous populations, often the result of colonialism.[64] This work typically involved sensitively toward the foreign subnational legal system. "There is much to learn from indigenous cultures about the nature and function of law in society. The dangers of moral relativism in this context are fewer than those of manifest destiny. Accommodation is preferable to assimilation and extinction."[65]

Vivian Curran advocated a cultural immersion approach to comparative law, which considered historical, political, economic, and linguistic contexts of law. She criticized the postwar comparatists for emphasizing similarities among countries in their research and felt that the emphasis during a period of globalization should be on differences. This orientation would be difficult because cultural contexts result from substructural patterns of classification in each culture, some of which are imperceptible to natives so that comparatists must discover them on their own. Curran rejected strict relativism and believed proper inquiry would lead to knowledge based on symbiotic concepts derived from the systems studied. She also suggested her approach could apply to subnational marginalized groups, defined by race or gender, which cohered sufficiently in a cultural sense. Acceptance of multiculturalism, studying differences rather than similarities, could achieve greater understanding, tolerance without uniformity.[66]

Nora Demleitner agreed with Curran on that last point: American comparative law should recognize multiculturalism in society and a more integrated world to overcome prejudice and stereotyped notions of other cultures and legal systems. A sociolegal approach to groups in societies would also require attention to the group's attitudes toward and values relevant to law and the legal system. Comparatists should avoid projecting their own legal rules, institutions, and values on other legal systems; in short, they should reject ethnocentrism. Western lawyers during the 1990s too often were legal missionaries in Eastern Europe, the former USSR, and elsewhere. "After recognizing commonalities and similarities, it is then necessary to manage the difference, not to abolish it." Legal integration would require mutual appreciation of the cultural embeddedness of law.[67]

---

[64] *See, e.g.*, PLURALISM, TRANSNATIONALISM AND CULTURE IN ASIAN LAW: A BOOK IN HONOUR OF M.B. HOOKER (Gary F. Bell ed., 2017); David S. Clark, *Witchcraft and Legal Pluralism: The Case of Célimo Miquirucama*, 15 TULSA L.J. 679-80, 682-83, 692-98 (1980) [hereinafter Clark, *Witchcraft*]. *See also* M.B. HOOKER, LEGAL PLURALISM: AN INTRODUCTION TO COLONIAL AND NEO-COLONIAL LAWS (1975).

[65] Clark, *Witchcraft, supra* note 64, at 698.

[66] Curran, *supra note* 48, at 51-57, 59, 61-66, 83-88. "The immersion approach in comparative legal analysis suggests the importance of trying to understand foreign legal cultures in an *untranslated* form; i.e., through the prisms that shape perceptions in the target legal culture." *Id.* at 57 (italics in original). For the application of this approach to modern China, *see* Donald Clarke, *Anti Anti-Orientalism, or Is Chinese Law Different?*, 68 AM. J. COMP. L. 55-94 (2020).

[67] Nora V. Demleitner, *Combating Legal Ethnocentrism: Comparative Law Sets Boundaries*, 31 ARIZ. ST. L.J. 737 739-55, 762 (1999) (quotation at 746). Demleitner believed that the application

James Whitman saw the approach of Curran and Demleitner, a kind of cultural anthropology suggesting more sensitivity to deep differences in human normative orders, as neo-Romanticism. Other American comparatists were in this camp, reminiscent of the cultural specificity of historical jurisprudence and its idea of *Volksgeist*. These scholars were concerned with understanding the inner perspective of a legal system, what the actors within that system believe, as well as the implicit assumptions that motivate activity in a legal system. Whitman did not want to take the hermeneutical approach to its logical extreme that one could never understand the "other." For him, law was an activity that aimed at normative justification of certain human acts and the exercise of authority. Different societies offered varying normative justifications that were in flux. Comparatists could comprehend these and make the information available to jurists.[68]

B. The American Society of Comparative Law

By 1990, the influx of younger comparatists as directors and editors within the American Association for the Comparative Study of Law (AACSL), with sympathetic older allies, successfully instituted a democratic system of officer election. Based on the concept of competitive offices set at two-year terms with limited renewal, the idea was to rotate diverse talent through the organization to improve its relevance to developments in the discipline.[69] At that time, the association had 69 sponsor members. Sponsor dues were set at $700 with standard reimbursement of up to $600 for editor or director attendance at the annual meeting. These dues provided 83 percent of AACSL income with the remainder from diversified investments. The principal expenses included a $25,000 subsidy to produce the association's *Journal* (at California Berkeley) and $23,000 to support the annual meeting (at Montréal). Revenues exceeded expenses by $5,000, which brought the reserves in 1990 to $112,000.[70]

The officers in 1990 were Friedrich Juenger (California Davis), president; Arthur von Mehren (Harvard), vice president; Cole Durham (Brigham Young, BYU), secretary; and David Clark (Tulsa), treasurer. Together with four elected

---

of feminism, critical race theory, and economics to legal issues in the United States offered valuable methodological perspectives for comparative law. *Id.* at 746–47.

[68] James Q. Whitman, *The Neo-Romantic Turn, in* COMPARATIVE LEGAL STUDIES: TRADITIONS AND TRANSITIONS 312–29, 336–44 (Pierre Legrand & Roderick Munday eds., 2003).

[69] *See supra* ch. 7, text accompanying note 173 (amendments to AACSL bylaws).

[70] AACSL minutes of the sponsor members and board of directors [hereinafter ASCL minutes], author's copy; *see supra* ch. 7, text accompanying notes 169–171 (Association in 1990).

members of the executive committee plus the editor in chief and honorary president, they administered the association's business between annual meetings.[71] Richard Buxbaum (California Berkeley) was the *Journal*'s editor in chief (until 2003).[72] They with others continued efforts to improve governance, expand membership, and develop programs.

The society encouraged comparatists to participate in its programs through meeting expense reimbursement and to submit manuscripts to the *American Journal of Comparative Law* with monetary prize awards. The 1990 Montréal meeting was the first held outside the United States and the first in conjunction with the International Association of Comparative Law's (IACL) quadrennial congress. With the impetus of Gerber (Illinois Institute of Technology, Chicago Kent) the association established its first periodic award—the Hessel Yntema Prize—in 1991, which it offered annually at $1,500 for the best *Journal* article by a scholar under the age of 40.[73] It also increased its subsidy for the *Journal* to $30,000 for two years rather than raise the annual subscription price of $30 ($32 foreign) and to pay for the *Journal*'s publication of the Montréal national reports as a supplement to volume 38.[74]

In 1992, the AACSL changed its name to the American Society of Comparative Law (ASCL) to parallel the *Journal* and its older sister organization, the American Society of International Law (ASIL).[75] The IACL held its Fourteenth International Congress in Athens in 1994. Again, the ASCL decided to hold its annual meeting during the congress outside the United States. To encourage American attendance, the society increased its meeting reimbursement rate to $800. To boost American participation as national reporters for congress topics, the *Journal* determined to publish those reports in a supplemental volume, priced at $30. The congress was very successful with a U.S. delegation of over 70 attending 34 panels presenting general and national reports.[76]

---

[71] Juenger served as honorary president from 1994–1996. Courtland H. Peterson, *Friedrich Klaus Juenger, 1930–2001*, 49 AM. J. COMP. L. xv (2001); *see supra* ch. 7, text accompanying note 173 (executive committee officers and members).

[72] George A. Bermann, James R. Gordley, & Mathias W. Reimann, *Our Thanks to Richard Buxbaum*, 52 AM. J. COMP. L. 3–4 (2004); *see supra* ch. 7, text accompanying note 196 (*Journal*). The AACSL bylaws provided for election of the editor in chief to a five-year term, renewable. ASCL minutes, *supra* note 70.

[73] ASCL minutes, *supra* note 70; *Prize Announcement*, 39 AM. J. COMP. L. n.p. (1991); *see Winner of Hessel Yntema Prize*, 40 AM. J. COMP. L. 539 (1992); *Prize Announcement*, 41 AM. J. COMP. L. 151 (1993).

[74] ASCL minutes, *supra* note 70; 41 AM. J. COMP. L. n.p. (1993); *see supra* ch. 7, text accompanying note 222 (Montréal meeting). In 1990, the *Journal* subscription price was $20. 38 AM. J. COMP. L. n.p. (1990).

[75] 40 AM. J. COMP. L. n.p. (1992).

[76] ASCL minutes, *supra* note 70; 42 AM. J. COMP. L. 686 (1994); Photini Pazartzis, *XIVth Congress of the International Academy of Comparative Law*, 42 *id.* at 827–30; *see* 42 *id.* (Supp.). At the Athens Congress, the United States provided six general reports, the largest number of any nation. *Id.* at n.p. The Society provided $15,000 for the *Journal*'s supplemental volume. ASCL minutes, *supra*.

In 1995, the society's officers were Von Mehren, president; George Bermann (Parker School), vice president; Symeon Symeonides (Louisiana State University), secretary; and Clark, treasurer. The society's directors amended the bylaws to add another office, parliamentarian, and elected Courtland Peterson (Colorado). They selected half the officers and two additional executive committee members for two-year terms at each annual meeting.[77] Clark recommended that the society apply for membership in the American Council of Learned Societies (ACLS), which supported the advancement of humanistic studies. The application was successful and the president appointed Clark the society's delegate. The council's annual meeting concerned electronic communications, which prompted Clark to recommend ASCL support for a society website. The directors approved $3,000 in 1997 and Clark teamed with Durham in setting up the initial websites. In 1998, Clark accepted primary responsibility as webmaster and Durham co-edited a society newsletter.[78] As copyright holder of its *Journal* articles, the society in 1993, first with West Publishing Co.'s computer database, had begun to license permission to reproduce electronically the *Journal*'s contents in exchange for royalties.[79]

At the 1997 ASCL annual meeting, the directors, on the executive committee's recommendation, voted to establish a long-range planning committee to examine broad membership and program issues. The president appointed Bermann chair of the nine-person committee. That committee issued its final report in 1998 after soliciting opinions of ASCL representatives and presented it for discussion at the annual meeting later held in Bristol, United Kingdom. At a delayed 1999 annual meeting, directors approved the committee's recommendations and sponsor members amended the bylaws as required to implement the membership changes.[80]

Under membership, the principal goal was to diversify and increase it. Among the recommendations were the following. Maintain the ASCL's structure of

---

[77] ASCL minutes, *supra* note 70. The parliamentarian, as an elected officer, also served on the executive committee. ASCL Bylaws. Peterson served as honorary president from 1996–1998. ASCL minutes, *supra*; *see supra* ch. 7, note 170 and accompanying text (Peterson).

[78] ASCL minutes, *supra* note 70. In 1995 and in 2000, the council had only five law-related members. See ACLS, *Member Societies*, https://www.acls.org/Member-Societies. Durham and Stephen Wood (BYU) co-edited the newsletter. Clark prepared a brochure providing the ASCL's history, makeup, and program for circulation at scholarly meetings and to interested institutions. ASCL minutes, *supra*.

[79] ASCL minutes, *supra* note 70. Before the advent of online databases, the *Journal* received small annual royalties from University Microfilms International and from Fred B. Rothman & Co. for selling back issues. *Id*. In 2000, William S. Hein & Co. began to handle the *Journal*'s back issues. 48 Am. J. Comp. L. iv (2000).

[80] ASCL minutes, *supra* note 70. Committee members also included Clark, Frances Foster (Washington St. Louis), Gerber, Michael Gordon (Florida), Hilary Josephs (Syracuse), Reimann, Reitz, and Joachim Zekoll (Tulane). Reitz took over as chair of the long-range planning committee in late 1998. Airport closures associated with a hurricane caused delay of the 1999 annual meeting until 8 January 2000. ASCL minutes, *supra*.

sponsor law schools rather than the individual members characteristic of the ASIL. Since some law schools had more than two comparatists (who could serve as director and editor), add the category of delegate, permitting a school to name those interested for an additional payment of $50 each. This new category of representative could attend and participate at meetings and would be eligible to hold ASCL office. Reimbursement for meeting attendance would continue at a maximum per sponsor member. Furthermore, the committee favored creation of an associate membership largely for comparatists at law schools not ASCL sponsor members. It expected the number in this category to be small; these associates would pay about $90 annually to cover the cost of the *Journal* plus added administrative and meeting expenses. Associates could participate in society meetings and committees but could not hold office or vote at annual meetings.[81]

For program development, the committee included the annual meeting, the *Journal*, and other scholarly activities. Regarding the first item, ASCL had begun a scholarly component to its annual meeting in the late 1970s. To improve that aspect, directors created a program committee in 1997 to advise the host school on what a rotating group of diverse representatives believed would constitute stimulating sessions. The long-range committee wanted to extend the program committee's mandate, once it and the directors had selected a host school, to take an affirmative role in choosing the program's subject or orientation. This might involve a workshop or subsidized guests. For the *Journal*, the long-range committee suggested that the executive committee form an executive editorial board of rotating ASCL representatives to assist the editor in chief. Members of this board would have specific responsibilities from soliciting book reviews to organizing special issues. Finally, the committee proposed that the ASCL sponsor certain research and publication projects, none of which came to fruition as envisioned.[82]

The 1998 annual meeting, in Bristol, took place during the Fifteenth International Congress of Comparative Law. Of the 37 topics that the IACL selected, Americans submitted national reports on 29 that the *Journal* published in a supplemental volume. The ASCL directors elected Bermann president, Clark vice president, and Symeonides secretary while Nafziger remained as treasurer.[83]

---

[81] ASCL, *Report on Membership and Program* (6 Apr. 1998), author's copy [hereinafter *Membership Report*]. Although delegates would have broad participation rights, only a school's director or editor (or proxy) could vote in the respective director or editor meeting. Since the internal politics of a sponsor member might convince a law school dean to preclude a comparatist from the list of director, editor, or delegate, the excluded person could join the ASCL as an associate. *Id.*

[82] *Membership Report, supra* note 81.

[83] ASCL minutes, *supra* note 70; George A. Bermann & Symeon C. Symeonides, *Preface*, 46 Am. J. Comp. L. v (Supp. 1998). The ASCL reimbursement for attendance in Bristol was $1,000 per sponsor member. Bermann served as honorary president from 2002–2004 and received the society lifetime achievement award in 2016. ASCL minutes, *supra*.

Symeonides recommended that the society co-sponsor the centennial celebration of the 1900 Paris International Congress of Comparative Law. Since neither the IACL, the IALS, nor the French *Société de législation comparé* was able to host this celebration in Paris, the proposal was that the society and Tulane Law School would undertake in 2000 major responsibility for a suitable scholarly program in New Orleans. Directors approved this initiative and decided to hold its annual meeting in conjunction with the three-day centennial world congress.[84]

In 2000, the society had 97 sponsor members, all law schools or their institutes plus the Law Library of Congress that joined in 1997. This was a 41 percent expansion in just a decade. The dues and standard meeting reimbursement to directors and editors remained constant. Dues generally covered ASCL's two major expense items, the annual meeting plus a *Journal* subsidy that was usually $25,000 but on occasion $30,000. The increased revenue came mainly from the growth in sponsor members. Reserves between 1990 and 2000 increased 111 percent to $236,000, a result of the society's favorable investment policy.[85] The society had 13 corresponding institutional members from nine countries plus from an international organization. These non-paying comparative law organizations received ASCL information and invitations to participate in the society.[86]

As the twenty-first century began, the society's role in developing American comparative law was dominant. The addition of delegates to sponsor member representatives expanded attendance at annual meetings and together with committee activities provided a crucial network for both senior and younger comparatists. The annual meeting typically took the pattern of participant arrival on Thursday evening, informal reception, full day of scholarly panels on Friday, formal dinner, some scholarly presentations on Saturday (morning or afternoon) along with the business meeting.[87] As before 1990, ASCL-affiliated

---

[84] ASCL minutes, *supra* note 70; *see supra* ch. 5, pt. F.3 (1900 Congress). Tulane's director to the ASCL, A.N. Yiannopoulos, organized most details for the November congress through the Eason-Weinman Center of Comparative Law that he led. K.D. Kerameus, *Comparative Law and Comparative Lawyers: Opening Remarks*, 75 TUL. L. REV. 865–70 (2001).

[85] ASCL minutes, *supra* note 70; *see supra* text accompanying notes 69–70 (ASCL in 1990). The *Journal*'s subsidy also covered the unmet costs of quadrennial supplements. ASCL minutes, *supra*.

[86] The corresponding members in 2000 were Law Asia (Australia), Canadian Society of Comparative Law and Québec Society of Comparative Law (Canada), Société de Législation Comparé (France), Gesellschaft für Rechtsvergleichung and Max-Planck-Institut für ausländisches und internationals Privatrecht (Germany), Hellenic Institute of International and Foreign Law (Greece), Associazione Italiana di Diritto Comparato (Italy), Academia Mexicana de Derecho Internacional Privado y Comparado (Mexico), Nederlandse Vereniging voor Rechtsvergelijking (Netherlands), Institut suisse de droit comparé (Switzerland), British Institute of International and Comparative Law and Institute of Advanced Legal Studies (United Kingdom), International Institute for the Unification of Private Law (UNIDROIT). ASCL minutes, *supra* note 70.

[87] ASCL minutes, *supra* note 70. The Saturday program might include, for instance, works in progress. *Id.* As the scholarly meetings became more extensive, Nafziger, as treasurer, successfully recommended that the Society increase its payment to the host school to $4,000. *Id.*

comparatists continued to publish their lectures delivered at the Hague Academy of International Law. These included Bermann (twice), Hannah Buxbaum (Indiana Bloomington), Glenn, Peter Herzog (Syracuse), and Symeonides (twice).[88]

The *Journal* was the leader in comparative law scholarship within the United States at a time when there were 17 peer and 71 student-edited publications specializing in comparative and international law.[89] Its circulation continued at around 2,200, with almost 900 of those subscriptions from foreign countries.[90] Furthermore, the society's role as organizer of the U.S. national committee to the quadrennial international congresses of comparative law had in the 1990s led to substantial growth of American attendance, which usually represented the largest foreign contingent at these meetings.[91] The high participation level for national and general reports continued up to 2020.

In 2001, sponsor members elected its first member from outside North America, Bucerius Law School (Hamburg). Bucerius was Germany's first private law school and emphasized comparative studies in its curriculum. This precedent established the principle that, although the society had American in its name, permitting a foreign law school, institute, or organization to join as a core sponsor member signaled the global scope of the ASCL.[92] In addition, during this decade, the society expanded its co-sponsorship of comparative law

---

[88] *See* George A. Bermann, *Regulatory Federalism: European Union and United States*, in 263 COLLECTED COURSES OF THE HAGUE ACADEMY OF INTERNATIONAL LAW 9–148 (1997); *id.*, *Arbitration and Private International Law*, in 381 COLLECTED COURSES OF THE HAGUE ACADEMY OF INTERNATIONAL LAW 41–484 (2015); Hannah L. Buxbaum, *Public Regulation and Private Enforcement in a Global Economy: Strategies for Managing Conflict*, in 399 COLLECTED COURSES OF THE HAGUE ACADEMY OF INTERNATIONAL LAW 267–442 (2018); H. Patrick Glenn, *La conciliation des lois*, in 364 COLLECTED COURSES OF THE HAGUE ACADEMY OF INTERNATIONAL LAW 187–470 (2012); Peter E. Herzog, *Constitutional Limits on Choice of Law*, in 234 COLLECTED COURSES OF THE HAGUE ACADEMY OF INTERNATIONAL LAW 239–330 (1992); Symeon C. Symeonides, *The American Choice-of-Law Revolution in the Courts: Today and Tomorrow*, in 298 COLLECTED COURSES OF THE HAGUE ACADEMY OF INTERNATIONAL LAW 9–448 (2002); *id.*, *Idealism, Pragmatism, Eclecticism*, in 384 Collected Courses of THE HAGUE ACADEMY OF INTERNATIONAL LAW 9–385 (2016); *supra* ch. 7, pt. F.3 (private international law).

[89] Gregory Scott Crespi, *Ranking International and Comparative Law Journals: A Survey of Expert Opinion*, 31 INT'L LAW. 869, 871–74, 879 (1997). In 2000, the *Journal* was starting to receive significant revenue from electronic databases and from the Copyright Clearance Center. To illustrate, royalties were $6,500 in 2003. ASCL minutes, *supra* note 70.

[90] ASCL minutes, *supra* note 70.

[91] John C. Reitz & David S. Clark, *Preface*, 54 AM. J. COMP. L. v (Supp. 2006).

[92] ASCL minutes, supra note 70. In 2001, the ASCL committee on prizes proposed a resolution to add a $1,500 prize for the best article by a senior scholar published in the *Journal* during the previous year. The directors adopted it. The committee would name the prize in honor of a recently deceased ASCL member. In 2002, its first award was to Symeonides named for Juenger's scholarship in private international law. *Id.*

conferences, including those formulated by foreign organizations, with a reimbursement policy to encourage ASCL representative participation.[93]

Since the society adopted a democratic governance structure in 1990, the idea of backing that form for the IACL took on renewed emphasis. ASCL members had discussed it in 2000 (with Juenger taking a leadership role) and again in 2001. They considered this reform essential to achieving better IACL leadership, programs, and diverse membership. The IACL had selected Brisbane for the Sixteenth International Congress in 2002; only titular IACL members (of which there were 50) could achieve the reform by academy bylaw amendment at its Brisbane meeting.[94] For the 34 topics at the congress, Americans submitted a national report for almost all the panels, while 26 were prepared in sufficient time for inclusion in the *Journal*'s printed volume to be circulated at the congress.[95] The U.S. IACL titular members, hampered by a controlling secretary for life who ran the business meeting in Brisbane, failed to gain much support for their proposed reform.

At the Brisbane meeting, ASCL directors elected Clark president, Symeonides vice president, and Curran secretary.[96] In 2003, since Buxbaum was completing his term as *Journal* editor in chief, the editors at the annual meeting voted upon the recommendation of a screening committee and the executive committee to select three representatives to share the responsibilities of editor in chief: Bermann, James Gordley (California Berkeley), and Reimann.[97] They implemented in 2004 the newly approved executive editorial board with eight members. This expanded responsibility was due to the widening scope of comparative law—both in subject matter as well as methodology—and the increased number of article submissions.[98]

At the 2003 annual meeting, Clark took the initiative to recommend that the society periodically offer a lifetime achievement award to one or more of its senior U.S. comparatists. The directors approved and the first three recipients were

---

[93] In 2003, ASCL directors approved a reimbursement policy of $600 for U.S. conferences and $1,000 for foreign events. The joint meetings committee initially determined which events to co-sponsor. ASCL minutes, supra note 70.

[94] ASCL minutes, *supra* note 70; *see supra* text accompanying notes 69, 71–72 (1990 reform and officers).

[95] Symeon C. Symeonides & John C. Reitz, *Preface*, 50 AM. J. COMP. L. 1 (supp. 2002).

[96] ASCL minutes, *supra* note 70. Directors elected Symeonides for one year to fill Clark's remaining term as vice president. They had renewed Nafziger as treasurer in 2001. *Id.*; *see supra* text accompanying note 83 (1998 election).

[97] ASCL minutes, *supra* note 70. The *Journal*'s administration initially remained at Berkeley. The directors elected Buxbaum honorary president for 2004–2006. *Id.*

[98] George A. Bermann, James R. Gordley, & Mathias W. Reimann, *Introduction*, 52 AM. J. COMP. L. 1–2 (2004); ASCL minutes, *supra* note 70. Francesco Parisi (ASCL director for George Mason) ran an electronic comparative law journal, the Social Science Research Network (SSRN) eLibrary: Comparative Law. It accepted any comparative law academic paper for posting. ASCL minutes, *supra*.

John Merryman (Stanford), Eric Stein (Michigan), and Von Mehren (Harvard), who all enhanced the 2004 society dinner with remarks about their careers.[99] Furthermore, the executive committee in 2004 approved Clark's idea to increase the *Journal*'s visibility by signing agreements with Hein Online and JSTOR to provide electronic access to their subscribers for the *Journal*'s past volumes.[100] Clark appointed members to two new committees—the finance committee to review the treasurer's reports and investments, and the younger comparatists committee that Colin Picker (Missouri Kansas City) had advocated. These complemented the already effective committees for annual meeting programs, nominations, joint meetings, prizes, and research and service.[101] Finally, as the task of maintaining the society's business had grown, Clark successfully proposed the creation of the office of executive assistant, who would carry out administrative duties for the society's officers and be located at one of the officer's law schools.[102] The directors elected Leila Sadat (Washington University) secretary and approved its third foreign sponsor member, the *Institut Suisse de droit comparé*.[103] The next year, HEC School of Management (Paris), National University of Singapore Law Faculty, and Trento University Law Faculty joined as sponsor members.[104]

In 2005, the directors ratified the executive committee's decision to transfer the *Journal*'s administrative office to Michigan, making Reimann the responsible editor in chief (of the three), and to resolve continuing financial shortfalls by increasing the annual subscription rate to $52.[105] In addition, the Seventeenth International Congress of Comparative Law (in Utrecht) was coming up in 2006. The directors passed a resolution of support for the ASCL president's efforts with national committees of comparative law (and their titular members) to amend the academy's statutes at its Utrecht general meeting. Bermann, who was president of the academy's common law group, agreed to aid Clark in that long-standing endeavor to democratize and diversify the academy as the best

---

[99] ASCL minutes, *supra* note 70.

[100] ASCL minutes, *supra* note 70. Clark was also ASCL delegate to the ACLS, which was an early sponsor of JSTOR. As webmaster, Clark oversaw the creation on the ASCL website of an index, by author or title, to all the *Journal*'s volumes since 1952. *Id.*

[101] ASCL minutes, *supra* note 70. The finance committee, Richard Kay (Connecticut) chair, drafted a set of audit and investment guidelines that covered the treasurer and the *Journal*'s editor in chief. *Id.*

[102] ASCL minutes, *supra* note 70. The executive assistant position would be part time with a society subsidy to the host school of $10,000. ASCL discontinued the previous $500 subsidy to each of the schools of the president, secretary, and treasurer.

[103] ASCL minutes, *supra* note 70. The other two foreign members were McGill's Institute of Comparative Law and Bucerius Law School.

[104] ASCL minutes, *supra* note 70. In 2005, the directors elected Kay treasurer and Reitz parliamentarian. *Id.*

[105] ASCL minutes, *supra* note 70. For foreign subscribers, the annual subscription price was $55. The *Journal* set the price for the 2006 Utrecht national reports supplement at $35 (and $40 for foreign recipients). *Id.*

approach to improve quadrennial meetings.[106] For the *Journal*'s supplement of U.S. national reports at the Utrecht meeting, 37 Americans wrote on 33 topics.[107]

The American initiative for academy reform yielded some success. At the 2006 Utrecht meeting, the French secretary general, Roland Drago, resigned, while the executive committee recommended adoption of the U.S. (with its co-sponsors') amendments. The titular members voted to affirm and approved the executive committee's nominees, Bermann for president and a co-director of the Hamburg Max Planck Institute, Jürgen Basedow, as secretary general, both to serve a four-year renewable term. Each held his office for two terms until 2014. Basedow and his successor, Diego Fernández Arroyo, at the IACL's principal leadership position, have in addition to the other officers done an admirable job by 2020 in making the academy—with its transparent website, quadrennial meetings, and extensive membership—a much better comparative law organization.[108]

At the ASCL business meeting in Utrecht, the directors elected Symeonides president, Reitz (Iowa) vice president, and Sadat secretary. The U.S. delegation to the international congress was the largest, at 50 registrants from 44 ASCL member schools, after the host delegation from the Netherlands. Oxford University Press (OUP) approached the society about assuming responsibility for the *Journal*'s publication and made a presentation that began a discussion within the executive committee about its merits compared to ASCL publication. In 2007, the ASCL announced its intention to host the Eighteenth International Congress of Comparative Law in 2010 at one or more of its sponsor members in the United States. After considering applicants, the directors selected a consortium of three Washington, D.C., schools, American, George Washington, and Georgetown.[109]

For the remainder of the century's first decade, the ASCL continued to improve as it fully implemented the changes that had begun in 1990. The number

---

[106] ASCL minutes, *supra* note 70; ASCL Resolution of Support... to Improve Future Congresses. Several of the national committees that Clark contacted were ASCL corresponding foreign institutional members. The proposal was to amend two articles of the academy's statutes. As they stood, all academy offices were for a four-year term except secretary general, which was for life. Since 1924, all secretaries general had died in office, after which the other officers named his successor. The secretary screened proposed candidates for other offices one month prior to the quadrennial general meeting when only one name went forward. The amendments would make the secretary general subject to a four-year term and permit any three titular members to propose a candidate for office at the general meeting, where a simple majority would determine the winner. *Id.*

[107] Reitz & Clark, *supra* note 89, at v–vi. There were four American general reporters out of a total of 35. *Id.* at v. The ASCL provided, as customary, a $5,000 subsidy to the *Journal* for printing and distributing the national reports volume. ASCL minutes, *supra* note 70.

[108] IACL, *Home*, https://aidc-iacl.org (select Menu/Secretary General). The IACL statutes now authorize the executive committee to create a five-person nominating committee to present a slate of candidates for office prior to the quadrennial meeting. In addition, any three titular members may propose additional candidates. *Id.* (select Menu/Statutes).

[109] ASCL minutes, *supra* note 70. The directors elected Clark honorary president (2006–2008); he served as chair of the ad hoc committee to find a host school for the congress. *Id.*

of sponsor members remained around 100, but now with a foreign contingent representing the globalization affecting academic disciplines. The annual meetings from the 1950s had a few foreign comparatists participate; after 1990, their number significantly increased providing depth to the discussions of current methodological and substantive topics. Furthermore, the society awarded more prizes to comparatists.[110] It also co-sponsored comparative law conferences and workshops every year, which gave more opportunities, especially for younger comparatists, to engage with the discipline.[111] Finally, the *Journal* was in transition to financial independence from the ASCL subsidy, which had declined to $13,000 in fiscal 2008, when the board of editors elected Reimann sole editor in chief for five years. In part due to the price increases, subscribers to the paper version at that time declined to 1,500 (about one-third foreign), but electronic access was growing every year. Royalties to the ASCL were $25,000, primarily from JSTOR, Hein, and West Group.[112]

By 2010, the society had reached a mature level of activity in service to U.S. comparative law that would characterize the 2010s. It had 105 sponsor members, including seven foreign organizations. The Eighteenth International Congress in Washington, D.C., was a great success.[113] It was the first time since the IACL's founding that it held the congress in the United States. The ASCL introduced some innovations to the week-long program beyond the standard panels of general and national reports. There were sessions about underrepresented regions such as Africa and Latin America and special panels on law and development, Islamic finance and banking, and international government procurement reform (reflecting the presence of the World Bank in Washington). There were 27 published U.S. national reports (out of a total of 31 topics), with 33 authors.[114]

---

[110] ASCL minutes, *supra* note 70. Prior to 2006, the ASCL had awarded senior prizes named in honor of Herbert Bernstein (Duke), Juenger, and Edward Wise (Wayne State); after 2006, there were prizes honoring Dan Henderson (Washington), Stefan Riesenfeld (Berkeley), and Rudolf Schlesinger (Hastings). *Id.*; *see supra* ch. 7 text accompanying note 154 (one-time 1954 prize).

[111] ASCL minutes, *supra* note 70. The society began to co-sponsor an annual workshop (for works in progress) in 2006, initially in cooperation with its sponsor members Illinois (Jacqueline Ross) and Michigan (Reimann). Later, Princeton (Kim Scheppele) and Yale (Whitman) replaced Michigan as co-sponsors. The ASCL financed up to $600 for attendance of authors and commentators at the host school. Announcement and Call for Papers. *Id.*

[112] ASCL minutes, *supra* note 70; *see supra* note 105 (2005 *Journal* price). In 2006, Bermann resigned as co-editor in chief as did Gordley in 2008, leaving Reimann as the *Journal's* editor in chief. In 2008, the *Journal* subscription price was $62 ($65 foreign); the $10 increase would include the 2010 supplement. Copyright Clearance Center paid almost $8,000 for reprint permissions. The *Journal* reported its finances for the calendar year beginning in 2009. ASCL minutes, *supra*.

[113] ASCL minutes, *supra* note 70; see George A. Bermann et al., *Comparative Law: Problems and Prospects*, 26 AM. U. INT'L L. REV. 935–68 (2011). Ruth Bader Ginsburg, U.S. Supreme Court associate justice, delivered the Friday general luncheon address. *See* Supreme Court of the United States, Home, https://www.supremecourt.gov (select News Media, then Speeches, 30 July 2010).

[114] John C. Reitz & Symeon C. Symeonides, *Preface*, 58 AM. J. COMP. L. v–vi (supp. 2010).

At the ASCL business meeting in Washington, the directors elected Reitz president, Glenn vice president, Alison Conner (Hawaii) secretary, and Symeonides honorary president. They had elected Kay treasurer in 2009. The *Journal* was now self-sufficient financially based on its subscriptions and royalty revenue. The ASCL, free of the need to subsidize its publication, had augmented resources to finance periodic programs and workshops beyond the annual meeting. ASCL reserves in 2010 were $302,000, about four times its annual expenses.[115] Bermann, president of the IACL, alerted ASCL titular members that he, together with Basedow, the IACL general secretary, had pushed its executive committee to support a thorough reform of its statutes to restructure the association. The U.S. members agreed and the IACL adopted the changes. They eliminated the fixed *numerus clausus* on titular members, permitted associate members to vote on all matters short of electing new titular members, abolished regional groups, and established a nominating committee to select a slate of officers prior to elections.[116]

A welcome development during the 2010s was the rise and success of the Younger Comparativists Committee (YCC), which served to provide the society with future generations of scholars for its discipline. Formed in 2004 as an ASCL committee, with its first allocated panel session at an annual meeting in 2009, it transformed itself as an organization under the leadership of Richard Albert (Boston College) from 2011 to 2015. Albert initiated the YCC global annual conference, periodic workshops, an inventory of course syllabi, and a mentorship program pairing senior and junior comparatists from many countries. Some of the annual conferences had over 100 participants with multiple concurrent panels.[117]

In 2011, ASCL directors created the office of information officer (webmaster), made the occupant an elected executive committee member, and provided up to $1,500 for expenses. It also confirmed Gerber as parliamentarian. The next year, directors elected Glenn president, Gerber vice president, Franklin Gevurtz (McGeorge) secretary, Wulf Kaal (St. Thomas) information officer, and Reitz

---

[115] ASCL minutes, *supra* note 70. The *Journal* subscription for 2010 cost $77 ($80 foreign). The ASCL presented Symeonides its lifetime achievement award in 2019. *Id.*

[116] ASCL minutes, *supra* note 70. The ASCL titular members were Richard Buxbaum, Clark (Willamette), Joseph Darby (San Diego), Gerber, Mary Ann Glendon (Harvard), Gordley (Tulane), Peter Hay (Emory), Vernon Palmer (Tulane), Reimann, Reitz, and Symeonides. Bermann email letter to U.S. members, 16 June, 2010, author's copy. The IACL had 80 titular members in 1998, which progressively increased to 110 by 2001. Art. 6(2), IACL Statutes.

[117] Richard Albert, *Third Annual YCC Global Conference and the Future of Comparative Law*, INT'L J. CONST. L. BLOG (3 Apr. 2014), at http://www.iconnectblog.com/2014/4; *see* ASCL, *YCC@ASCL*, https://ascl.org/yccascl. In 2011, ASCL directors approved a $1,000 subsidy to the YCC for its first conference, held at George Washington University in April 2012. ASCL minutes, *supra* note 70; *see supra* text accompanying note 101 (committee's origin).

honorary president. With the success of ASCL-sponsored meetings and the website, the society approved $3,000 for annual meeting speakers, $2,600 to the YCC, $3,000 for the work in progress workshop, and $1,000 for web maintenance. In 2013, it elected Mortimer Sellers (Baltimore) treasurer and William Fisch (Missouri) parliamentarian, while it increased expense reimbursement for YCC events to $6,000. The *Journal* editors supported a proposal, subject to final executive committee approval, from James Feinerman and Franz Werro (Georgetown) and Helge Dedek (McGill) to serve as co-editors in chief with shared administration.[118]

In 2014, the ASCL annual meeting took place in Vienna in conjunction with the Nineteenth International Congress of Comparative Law. To encourage attendance, the society reimbursed sponsor member representatives $1,200 per school, with 54 sending one or more participants, a number comparable to those attending a U.S. annual meeting. The directors approved a proposal by Sellers that would allow the executive committee to create a book series—ASCL Studies in Comparative Law—with Cambridge University Press under appropriate conditions. The three new editors in chief worked through coordination issues for the *Journal*'s 2014 volume, with Feinerman resigning in 2015. The two editors who persevered and agreed to a second five-year term from the society in 2019 accepted a noticeably higher percentage of articles from comparatists located outside the United States. Just as the ASCL had more foreign sponsor members during this period than before, the foreign participation in the *Journal* reflected the globalized character of both.[119]

With Glenn's death in late 2014, ASCL directors the next year elected Gerber president and Curran vice president as well as John Haskell (Mississippi College) information officer. They also voted to empower the executive committee to partner with OUP in production of the *Journal*. This would relieve the editors in chief of administrative tasks, reduce cost to the host law school, and improve electronic access and market distribution (especially to China and India) of the *Journal*. The two parties signed an agreement in 2016 and Oxford published its first volume in 2017.[120] For the 2014 and 2018 IACL congress (in Vienna and Fukuoka), the U.S. national reports were only available electronically, initially

---

[118] ASCL minutes, *supra* note 70. In 2012, the ASCL approved up to $3,000 for recipients of its prizes, an amount generally authorized during the 2010s. *Id.*

[119] ASCL minutes, *supra* note 70; see Helge Dedek, James V. Feinerman, & Franz G. Werro, *Editors' Note*, 62 AM. J. COMP. L. ix (2014). From 2014 to 2020, the ASCL increased the annual YCC subsidy to $7,000. ASCL minutes, *supra*. By 2020, Cambridge had published six volumes in the comparative law series. *Id.* The publisher also initiated a Comparative Constitutional Law and Policy series.

[120] ASCL minutes, *supra* note 70; Helge Dedek & Franz Werro, *Editors' Note*, 65 AM. J. COMP. L. vii (2017). For 2018, OUP set the print subscription price at $130 ($3 less for online access only). 66 AM. J. COMP. L. ii (2018).

on the ASCL website. Since OUP produced the 2018 volume, it continued free access to the reports on its website through 2020.[121]

In 2016, ASCL directors elected Curran president; Kay vice president; and in 2017, Sally Richardson (Tulane) parliamentarian. Curran decided to serve only one term and in 2018, directors chose Kay president, Máximo Langer (UCLA) vice president, and Curran honorary president. In 2019, directors elected Ronald Scalise treasurer and Boris Mamlyuk (Memphis) information officer; and in 2020, Langer president, Hannah Buxbaum vice president, Virginia Harper Ho (Kansas), secretary, and Kay honorary president. With the large number of mostly foreign associate members, they amended the bylaws to make it clear that the renamed individual members could participate on ASCL committees and at meetings.[122]

By 2020, the society was on solid financial and administrative ground as the leading organization to support academic comparative law. It had 100 law school and institute sponsor members (most with multiple representatives). These included members from Canada, China, Croatia, Ireland, Italy, Mexico, Portugal, Serbia, Singapore, and the United Kingdom. Furthermore, there were 24 foreign and international corresponding institutional members representing 14 nations.[123] Its *Journal* had the highest ranking of any periodical specializing in comparative law, including foreign journals.[124] Besides its annual scholarly meeting, the society co-sponsored more academic conferences than ever before, both in the United States and abroad. Moreover, society members were active in establishing student-run comparative and international law journals at their home institutions. Most ABA accredited law schools now have one of these journals, which provide a written outlet for Americans and others to express their every thought related to foreign and comparative law.

C. Globalization of American Legal Institutions

1. Global Law Schools and Law Firms

The concept of a global law school arose in the 1990s associated with the economic and political changes happening during that decade. American

---

[121] See Franklin A. Gevurtz & Vivian Grosswald Curran, *Preface*, 66 AM. J. COMP. L. vii (supp. 2018); Helge Dedek & Franz Werro, *Editors' Note*, 67 *id.* at vii (2019). The ASCL reimbursement at Fukuoka was $1,400. ASCL minutes, *supra* note 70.

[122] ASCL minutes, *supra* note 70. The bylaws divided individual members into two categories, one to pay $160 and receive the *Journal* and the other to pay $75 without the *Journal*. *Id.*

[123] ASCL, *Home*, https://ascl.org (select Membership/Current).

[124] Washington and Lee Law Library, *Home*, https://law.wlu.edu/library (select Law Journal Rankings, enter comparative law). OUP had set the *Journal* price at $168.

comparatists discussed where such an institution might emerge and what form its structure and program should take. One view was that initially the United States would be the ideal locale, but that demand for such places would allow them to prosper elsewhere, particularly in Europe.[125] The United States had certain structural advantages since it had more law schools than in other countries, the majority of which were private, thus freeing them from as much bureaucratic and political influence characteristic of public law schools or university law faculties. In addition, the United States by the 1990s allowed more foreign lawyers to offer transnational legal services—usually in rapidly expanding global law firms—than in other nations. A successful global law school would attract the diverse students needed to populate these multinational law firms locally as well as abroad. To illustrate, New York in 1995 had 60 foreign law firms from 20 countries.[126]

In 1994, NYU School of Law announced the creation of the world's first global law school program. Supported by a large endowment, the initiative intended to invite foreign law professors (most to teach for a full or half semester), foreign scholars (professors, judges, and government officials for one to six months), and foreign graduate students to NYU to interact and collaborate with resident professors and students. Some of the endowment would generate innovations in the curriculum and finance conferences that reflected the impact of an emerging global economy. In 1997, NYU had almost 225 enrolled foreign citizens—representing over 50 countries—out of 1,500 students. At this level of commitment, as foreign and American faculty and students spent time together, they both learned about the international legal order in a more denationalized manner as well as gained new comparative perspectives on American and foreign law.[127]

In 1995, there were almost 3,500 foreign lawyers and students enrolled in U.S. law schools. Those countries that sent more than 100 (other than Canada) were China, Germany, Japan, Korea, and Taiwan. The total represented 59 percent

---

[125] David S. Clark, *Transnational Legal Practice: The Need for Global Law Schools*, 46 AM. J. COMP. L. 261-66 (Supp. 1998) [hereinafter Clark, *Transnational*]; *see* Mathias W. Reimann, *We Are All Globalists Now—The Heritage of the Émigré Jurists for American Legal Education in the Second Half of the Twentieth Century*, *in* GLOBALIZATION AND THE U.S. LAW SCHOOL: COMPARATIVE AND CULTURAL PERSPECTIVES, 1906-2006, at 101, 115-16 (2009) [Reimann, *Globalists*]. Clark based the argument for the United States on its contribution to world trade and private direct foreign investment, the multicultural nature of its society, its dominance in higher education including law, and that instruction and research would be in English, the world's lingua franca. Clark, *Transnational*, *supra*, at 261-64.

[126] Clark, *Transnational*, *supra* note 125, at 263, 267-68, 273-74. Between 1990 and 1994, U.S. export of legal services tripled to $1.6 billion, which represented about 10 percent of the largest 100 law firms' total revenue. Both the ABA and the AALS recognized this transformation and sponsored programs on the global law school. *Id.* at 268-69, 273; Reimann, *Globalists*, *supra* note 125, at 115.

[127] David S. Clark, *American Law Schools in the Age of Globalization: A Comparative Perspective*, 61 RUTGERS L. REV. 1037, 1046 (2009) [hereinafter Clark, *Globalization*].

of all law students in post-J.D. or other special programs. By the end of the decade, a substantial number of schools made a significant commitment to comparative and international law by establishing institutes, law journals, summer or semester abroad programs, and faculty exchanges. Schools saw that augmenting the multinational mix of its student body improved the quality of teaching since students learned from each other and teachers learned from students. Foreign students challenged usual assumptions about law; they reminded others that each culture might have a distinctive way of dealing with conflict and human behavior in general.[128] In 2000, almost 550 American law professors listed one or more comparative law courses or seminars that they had taught. Over half of those came to the subject in the prior five years.[129]

American lawyers have been very successful worldwide, both in establishing branch law firms or alliances abroad as well as in obtaining foreign clients for domestic offices. In 1998, of the world's top 50 law firms, 43 in terms of revenue and 30 by size were U.S. firms.[130] They (and English firms) benefited from business internationalization, the dominance of U.S. and U.K. investment banks, and the crucial role New York and London capital markets played in the world economy. These global firms handled merger and acquisition deals, privatizations in countries increasing market competition, and project financing in developing nations. Many U.S. firms abroad employed substantial numbers of foreign-trained lawyers. Baker & McKenzie, long ago, established the model of using primarily locally licensed lawyers in its many offices around the world.[131] Smaller companies also needed transnational legal services; they often bypassed the largest firms and turned to less expensive firms that had created professional networks linking their members across jurisdictions. In 2000, Lex Mundi, for instance, had 152 firms in its network.[132]

In 2018, America exported $10.3 billion in legal services and imported $3.4 billion. This illustrated the global interchange among large law firms, but with continued dominance in the United States. The trade surplus in legal services existed for every year between 2006 and 2018. At the end of the 2010s, America accounted for half of the world's nearly $600 billion global legal services

---

[128] Clark, *Transnational*, supra note 125, at 269–72; *see* James Gordley, *Comparative Law and Legal Education*, 75 TUL. L. REV. 1003–14 (2001); supra ch. 7, text accompanying note 304 (foreign students, 1980 to 1995). Reimann estimated that in 2006 there were more than 150 law journals specializing in comparative and international law. Reimann, *Globalists*, supra note 125, at 115 n.53.

[129] THE AALS DIRECTORY OF LAW TEACHERS [hereinafter AALS DIRECTORY]: 2000–2001, at 1182–86 (2000).

[130] Carole Silver, *Internationalizing U.S. Legal Education: A Report on the Education of Transnational Lawyers*, 14 CARDOZO J. INT'L & COMP. L. 143, 146 (2006).

[131] Clark, *Transnational*, supra note 125, at 273–74; Susan van Syckel, *Strategies for Identifying Sources of Foreign Law: An Integrated Approach*, 13 TRANSNAT'L LAW. 289, 300 (2000).

[132] Van Syckel, supra note 131, at 300; Laurel S. Terry, *Global Networks and the Legal Profession*, 53 AKRON L. REV. 137, 159–69 (2019). In 2020, Lex Mundi listed 700 firm offices in its network with 22,000 lawyers from 130 countries. Lex Mundi, *Home*, https://www.lexmundi.com.

revenue.[133] Much of this activity occurred within the top 200 U.S. law firms, which in the aggregate had 25,000 lawyers who practiced in 70 foreign countries. In addition, the activity was diffuse across America with 47 states that had law firms with a foreign office.[134] Many U.S. law firms claimed to be global organizations, often by referring to the American LL.M. credential for its non-U.S. lawyers working in overseas offices.[135]

At the turn of the century, U.S. law schools had many diverse one-year LL.M. programs as well as study abroad and foreign cooperative programs that encouraged American law students to travel overseas and foreigners to study in America. In 2000, to illustrate, there were 33 LL.M. programs designed specifically for foreign lawyers and another 178 specialty LL.M. programs open to foreigners ranging from admiralty to taxation as well as general advanced legal studies. The ABA had approved 34 cooperative programs with foreign universities, nine semester abroad programs organized on the U.S. model, and 146 summer programs that 76 law schools sponsored outside the United States in 43 countries.[136] There were 5,800 international students enrolled in American law study, some in J.D. programs.[137]

The first postwar peak in J.D. student enrollment at 183 ABA-approved law schools had occurred in 1995 with 129,000 persons, falling to 125,000 in 2000 primarily due to a saturated lawyer market. However, a 2,100-student increase in post-J.D. programs during the 1990s to 7,300 in 2000 partially compensated law schools for the J.D. decline. Over half of that latter figure consisted of foreigners.[138] Of programs with a topical focus, the most common in 2004 was for international and comparative law.[139] Part of the motivation for some foreign lawyers to enroll in an American LL.M. course was to use the degree to qualify for a U.S. state bar examination, which cannot under the U.S. Constitution require

---

[133] Terry, *supra* note 132, at 143–44.
[134] *Id.* at 164.
[135] Carole Silver, *The Variable Value of U.S. Legal Education in the Global Legal Services Market*, 24 GEO. J. LEGAL ETHICS 1–58 (2011) (China and Germany). The ABA Section of International Law served as a forum for many of these transnational lawyers. In 2020, it had 18,000 members from 90 countries and provided committees for foreign and comparative law. See ABA, *International Law Section*, https://www.americanbar.org/groups/international_law.
[136] David S. Clark, *American Legal Education: Yesterday and Today*, 10 INT'L J. LEG. PROFESSION 93, 101 (2003) [hereinafter Clark, *Legal Education*]; *see* Silver, *supra* note 130, at 146–54. By 2004, there were 66 LL.M. programs designed exclusively for foreign lawyers who often took courses with J.D. students. Silver, *supra*, at 153, 155.
[137] Institute of International Education, *Number of International Students by Field of Study, 1998/99 to 2019/20* (2020), https://opendoorsdata.org (use search categories) [hereinafter IIE, *International Students*].
[138] Clark, *Legal Education*, *supra* note 136, at 97–98, 101; ABA, *Statistics Archives*, https://www.americanbar.org/groups/legal_education/resources/statistics [hereinafter ABA, *Statistics*] (select Archives, then Total Enrollment 1963–2013). In 2004, 4,500 foreigners were in post-J.D. programs. Silver, *supra* note 130, at 149.
[139] Silver, *supra* note 130, at 161–62 (28 programs).

U.S. citizenship. In 2000, 23 states permitted foreign lawyers to take its bar examination (usually with an American LL.M. degree) and thus to become an attorney in that state. New York has dominated this development, passing 1,093 foreign lawyers, who succeeded at a 41 percent rate in 2000.[140] In 2019, New York allowed 6,400 U.S. and 3,000 foreign applicants to take its bar examination with a pass rate for all first-timers at 74 percent. For the foreigners, the pass rate was 51 percent.[141]

By 2019, J.D. enrollment at 197 schools was only 113,000, while U.S. and foreign post-J.D. students numbered 20,000. The J.D. figure had declined from the second peak of 148,000 reached in 2010.[142] Among J.D. and LL.M. students in 2019, 14,200 were foreign lawyers or students, representing a majority among the post-J.D. student body. Moreover, many more foreigners enrolled in J.D. programs than in 2000.[143] In 2008, for instance, only 2,017 foreign nationals had enrolled in American J.D. programs, with 582 earning the degree.[144]

About 20 U.S. law schools, beyond program development in foreign and comparative law, have aspired to become multinational—with substantial foreign student enrollment and teaching staff—providing graduates for global American law firms and foreign firms with offices in the United States.[145] This primarily occurred with LL.M. programs. Nevertheless, the schools most integrated with foreigners also enrolled around 5 percent or more of their student body in the competitive J.D. course.[146] In 2019, for example, a few elite schools took the lead with 10 percent or more of their J.D. matriculation foreign: Columbia, Cornell, Northwestern, and Washington St. Louis (Illinois and NYU had 9 percent). A unique case was Detroit Mercy Law School, which had a 43 percent foreign J.D. population, almost all of it Canadian. Located across the Detroit River from Windsor, Ontario, the school offered a three-year dual degree with the University of Windsor Law Faculty that offered courses comparatively examining both

---

[140] Clark, *Legal Education*, supra note 136, at 107; *see* Silver, supra note 130, at 165–67.

[141] New York State Board of Law Examiners, *NYS Bar Exam Statistics*, https://www.nybarexam.org/ExamStats/Estats.htm.

[142] ABA, *Statistics*, supra note 138. Of the 20,000 non-J.D. students, 7,400 participated in classes online. A few schools had more non-J.D. students than J.D. students. Arizona was an extreme example, with a ratio of 1,203 non-J.D. (of whom only 182 students were online) to 375 J.D. students. *Id.*

[143] IIE, *International Students*, supra note 137; *see* Clark, *Globalization*, supra note 127, at 1050–53 (for 2008).

[144] Clark, *Globalization*, supra note 127, at 1051. In 2015, about a quarter of ABA law schools offered a J.S.D. or equivalent degree program, almost solely for foreign students. Gail J. Hupper, *Education Ambivalence: The Rise of a Foreign-Student Doctorate in Law*, 49 New Eng. L. Rev. 319, 323 (2015); *see id.*, *The Academic Doctorate in Law: A Vehicle for Legal Transplants*, 58 J. Legal Educ. 413–54 (2008).

[145] In 1998, for example, 13 percent of J.D. graduates started work at law firms of more than 250 lawyers. David S. Clark, *Legal Education and the Legal Profession*, *in* Introduction to the Law of the United States 13, 29 (David S. Clark & Tuğrul Ansay eds., 2d ed. 2002).

[146] Clark, *Globalization*, supra note 127, at 1051–53 (for 2008).

U.S. and Canadian law and satisfied both American state and Canadian provincial licensure authorities.[147]

By 2020, many law schools had institutes or centers for research and teaching on globalization, foreign law, and comparative law. The oldest was the Parker School at Columbia. Tulane had the Eason-Weinmann Center for International and Comparative Law, founded in 1981, and before that the Institute of Comparative Law. Both schools had long histories of foreign and comparative law research and teaching. Some new law schools made comparative law a specialty, such as California-Irvine, which had the umbrella Center on Globalization, Law, and Society to administer the study of international, transnational, and comparative law.[148] In 2018, the number of American law professors who offered one or more comparative law courses or seminars was only slightly higher than in 2000—at 580—but more had taught the subject for longer than ten years.[149]

Finally, the Law Library of Congress continued its commitment to foreign and comparative law and initiated services in support of globalization. The *Global Legal Monitor*, commenced in 2006, was an online publication covering legal news and developments worldwide. The Legal Research Institute offered law schools and the public research classes on foreign and comparative law as well as webinars.[150]

2. Academic Law and Development Programs

Law and development activity at a few American law schools began in the 1960s as an aspect of Cold War competition with the Soviet Union. The social revolution in Cuba in 1959 gave the initiative immediate importance as part of an effort to slow or halt the spread of communism in the Americas, although comparatists later gave their attention also to Africa and Asia. The U.S. government and NGOs financed law school programs including foreign student and lawyer study in the United States and scholarly theorizing about the rule of law and its place in political and economic development to improve general social welfare in developing nations.[151] In

---

[147] ABA Section of Legal Education and Admissions to the Bar, *503 Required Disclosures*, http://www.abarequireddisclosures.org/Disclosure509.aspx (select School). Law schools with 4 percent or more foreign J.D. enrollment were California (Berkeley, Davis, Irvine, and Los Angeles), Cardozo, Fordham, Georgetown, George Washington, Miami, and Yale. *Id.*

[148] UCI Law, *Center on Globalization, Law, and Society*, https://www.law.uci.edu/centers/glas; *see supra* ch. 7, note 140 and accompanying text (Columbia and Tulane).

[149] AALS DIRECTORY: 2018–2019, *supra* note 129, at 1428–33; *see supra* text accompanying note 129 (for 2000).

[150] Library of Congress, *Global Legal Monitor*, https://www.loc.gov/collections/global-legal-monitor; *id.*, *Home*, https://www.loc.gov (search for Legal Research Institute). *See also* Andrew Winston et al., *The Law Library of Congress: A Global Resource for Legal Education*, 67 J. LEGAL EDUC. 962–69, 971–75, 977, 982 (2018); *supra* ch. 7, text accompanying notes 352–57 (Law Library of Congress).

[151] *See supra* ch. 7, text accompanying notes 418–425 (law and development).

addition, the U.S. Agency for International Development (USAID), the Peace Corps, Fulbright fellowship program, and Ford Foundation directly financed legal reform efforts in developing countries. In general, American missionary lawyers accepted the prevalent social engineering model taught in U.S. law schools. Unsophisticated about target cultures and history, reform proposals inevitably lacked local political support and sometimes made social conditions worse. Comparatists determined the enterprise was ethnocentric and naïve in its premise about the efficacy of American legal institutions. By 1970, academic interest declined. It either shifted away from action or for some toward empirical study and assessment influenced by the recently created law and society discipline.[152]

The 1990s, with the end of the Cold War and Soviet support to affiliated nations, gave law and development a second life, seemingly without regard to the failures of its first life. The initial iteration primarily concentrated on reforming legal education toward a U.S. model of full-time professors engaged in active teaching methods to promote policy change within a local legal system. The idea was that these new law graduates, some also educated in the United States, would become the lawyers, judges, and professors to implement social change. The second wave, by contrast, encompassed a plenary rule of law rhetoric to export an American or European model of legal institutions and processes to newly independent and other developing countries. Moreover, strengthening political democracy and market capitalism went along with rule of law, since together they would result in improved social conditions.[153] An economic historian, Douglass North, provided a theory for the new version of law and development. His study revealed that those countries that protected property rights and established predictable rules for resolving contract disputes were more likely to experience economic growth than those that did not. Nevertheless, some comparatists questioned whether this neoliberal model could explain economic success in East Asia and introduced concepts such as Asian values and thin rule of law.[154]

---

[152] See supra ch. 7, pts. E.2 and E.3 (development decade and assessment).

[153] Bryant G. Garth & Yves Dezalay, Introduction, in GLOBAL PRESCRIPTIONS: THE PRODUCTION, EXPORTATION, AND IMPORTATION OF A NEW LEGAL ORTHODOXY 1–3, 5 (Yves Dezalay & Bryant G. Garth eds., 2002); Michael J. Trebilcock, The Rule of Law and Development: In Search of the Holy Grail, 3 WORLD BANK LEGAL REV. 207–39 (2012); Jeremy Waldron, The Rule of Law and the Importance of Procedure, in GETTING TO THE RULE OF LAW 3–5 (James E. Fleming ed., 2011); see infra pt. D (government and NGO rule of law programs). See also Thomas Carothers, The Rule of Law Revival, 77 FOREIGN AFFAIRS 95–106 (no. 2, 1998); Amy L. Chua, Paradox of Free Market Democracy: Rethinking Development Policy, 41 HARV. INT'L. L.J. 287–380 (2000) (tension between market capitalism and democracy, making them difficult to successfully transplant in developing nations).

[154] Tom Ginsburg, Does Law Matter for Economic Development? Evidence from East Asia, 34 LAW & SOC'Y REV. 829–34 (2000); Randall Peerenboom, Varieties of Rule of Law: An Introduction and Provisional Conclusion, in ASIAN DISCOURSES OF RULE OF LAW: THEORIES AND IMPLEMENTATION OF RULE OF LAW IN TWELVE ASIAN COUNTRIES, FRANCE, AND THE U.S. 1–55 (Randall Peerenboom

Comparatists split on whether it was realistically possible to transfer Western ideas about rule of law, constitutionalism, democracy, independent judiciaries, and human rights to most developing countries.[155] Since so much of the comparative law literature of the twenty-first century had been a combined effort of North Americans and Europeans, furthered by multinational membership in the ASCL, it would be difficult to categorize a line of argument, for instance, as American comparative law versus German or Italian comparative law. For law and development (or rule of law), at least, the term Western comparative law reflected this legal globalization better.[156]

To illustrate, Mauro Bussani, an Italian comparatist, contended that legal scholars could be powerful agents for legal transplants, referring to the writing of a U.S. comparatist, Bryant Garth, and to other Americans. The argument was that local communities did not perceive scholars, unlike government officials, as attempting to impose their legal policies. When the scholars' ideas appeared persuasive, local elites could adopt some version of them as their own. Thus, there would be less resistance.[157] Bussani emphasized that the effective transplant of rule of law and democracy would require a deep cultural understanding of a recipient nation's legal and social situation as well as better awareness of the circumstances—historical, economic, and cultural—affecting successful democracy and rule of law in the West. This compelled less ethnocentrism and deglobalizing many Western jurists' views that some of their legal principles and institutions should be universal.[158]

On the other side, Jedidiah Kroncke took the position that attempts by U.S. politicians and comparatists to export elements of American law to Asia, especially China, were futile as confirmed by the history of the relationship between China and the United States in the twentieth century.[159] The failure was due to a combination of American ignorance of its own legal system, but

---

ed., 2004); see DOUGLASS NORTH, INSTITUTIONS, INSTITUTIONAL CHANGE, AND ECONOMIC PERFORMANCE (1990).

[155] See Kevin E. Davis & Michael J. Trebilcock, *The Relationship between Law and Development: Optimists versus Skeptics*, 56 AM. J. COMP. L. 895–946 (2008) (reviewing three books and other writing on the subject).

[156] See, e.g., THE RULE OF LAW IN COMPARATIVE PERSPECTIVE (Mortimer Sellers & Tadeusz Tomaszewski eds., 2010).

[157] Mauro Bussani, *Deglobalizing Rule of Law and Democracy: Hunting Down Rhetoric through Comparative Law*, 67 AM. J. COMP. L. 701, 710–12 (2019); see Garth & Dezalay, *supra* note 153 (cited in Bussani, *supra*, at 711 n. 34).

[158] Bussani, *supra* note 157, at 704–08, 739–44.

[159] JEDIDIAH J. KRONCKE, THE FUTILITY OF LAW AND DEVELOPMENT: CHINA AND THE DANGERS OF EXPORTING AMERICAN LAW (2016); see *supra* ch. 6, pt. A.2 (legal transplants) and text accompanying notes 267–69 (Pound in China). See also Jedidiah Kroncke, *Law and Development as Anti-Comparative Law*, 45 VAND. J. TRANSNAT'L L. 477–555 (2012) (century of failure).

a faith nevertheless in the system's virtues, and a missionary mentality to save the Chinese people from their corrupt leaders and inadequate law and legal institutions. In reviewing Kroncke's book on law and development, Timothy Webster stated that the author overused the missionary metaphor and that simple paternalism and amnesia explained much U.S. law and development activities in Africa, Asia, and Latin America. Moreover, China in recent decades had solicited collaboration on many legal concepts and institutions from the United States. Granted, this included NGOs, specific lawyers, and academic comparatists as well as the U.S. State Department.[160]

In 2011, Garth and Yves Dezalay edited a volume to explore the role of lawyers in promoting rule of law abroad.[161] Their thesis was that the contemporary interest in exporting rule of law served the globalization of market economies by adopting a global language. Large corporations, law firms, and investment banks desired to expand the domain in which they operated with their own instruments, while those actors outside that language—such as Japanese and Korean conglomerates—sought access to compete effectively in global capitalism. An assumption of rule of law advocates was that reform of corporate and commercial law would spill over to state governance and legal process. Lawyers held a central role in this transfer as brokers who negotiated between their clients and target governments. Law, thus, embedded itself in social relations.[162]

Garth and Dezalay found most law and development activity and literature defective since it ignored the relation between law and social relations. To illustrate, the ABA World Justice Project ranked countries using indicators to measure rule of law, such as perceived judicial independence and impartiality. Scholarship on the judicialization of politics argued that as courts took on more public law disputes, they would resolve some political issues with legal rules, improving the place of law in that society. These examples missed the social context in which legal processes operated and the role of lawyers in building social capital through their brokered negotiations. While exporting support for rule of law had some measure of success in many developing nations, this was less true in parts of Asia, particularly in China and Japan.[163]

---

[160] Timothy Webster, *Book Review*, 65 Am. J. Comp. L. 968–72 (2017). Organizations that consulted with China on legal reform included the ABA, Ford Foundation, Open Society Foundation, Public Interest Law Initiative, and centers at NYU and Yale. *Id.* at 973 n.13.

[161] Lawyers and the Rule of Law in an Era of Globalization (Yves Dezalay & Bryant Garth eds. 2011) [hereinafter Lawyers and Globalization].

[162] Yves Dezalay & Bryant Garth, *Introduction: Lawyers, Law, and Society*, in Lawyers and Globalization, *supra* note 161, at 1–2.

[163] Dezalay & Garth, *supra* note 162, at 2–5, 17–18; *id.*, *Conclusion: How to Convert Social Capital into Legal Capital and Transfer Legitimacy across the Major Practice Divide*, in Lawyers and Globalization, *supra* note 161, at 260–65.

Ronald Gilson and Curtis Milhaupt took a less sanguine view. They believed that after 1945, few poorer countries successfully developed. Among those that succeeded, many were authoritarian regimes that entered global commerce by transitioning from small-scale, relational exchange, to government-directed exchange based either on the threat of informal sanctions or on formal third-party enforcement. They tested their hypothesis with three case studies: Chile, South Korea, and China (PRC). Although many international organizations, such as the World Bank and International Monetary Fund (IMF), contended that an impartial judiciary was the key to transition from relational to market exchange, Gilson and Milhaupt thought authoritarian and other alternatives were possible.[164]

By choosing three diverse countries, the authors were able to show that benevolent authoritarian economic development could follow different strategies, none particularly relying on law. Chile used Chicago School ideas for shifting to open markets. Korea had an export-oriented economy with government-supported champions (*chaebol*) selected from among the elite together with domestic market protection. China utilized a state-led export policy with relatively open domestic markets. For all, governments had to make a credible commitment to economic actors that governments would respect the actors' investments in physical and human capital and that they could keep substantial gains from their efforts.[165] Finally, Gilson and Milhaupt considered what options might be available to developing democracies that desired economic growth. Scholars should shift focus from the character of institutions for growth to their functions. One alternative would be to create a regional entity, such as a commercial court, which could enforce agreements against an entrenched national elite. Another would be for a government to delegate enforcement of contracts to an independent NGO, as in Korea and Taiwan.[166]

The rule of law approach that Randall Peerenboom and colleagues advocated illustrated the current multinational nature of comparative law collaboration.[167]

---

[164] Ronald J. Gilson & Curtis J. Milhaupt, *Economically Benevolent Dictators: Lessons for Developing Democracies*, 59 AM. J. COMP. L. 227–29, 238–40 (2011). The autocracies that succeeded had leaders who placed national development with widely shared wealth ahead of their own family's or friends' enrichment. Gilson and Milhaupt added Singapore and Taiwan to the list. *Id.* at 229–30.

[165] *Id.* at 233–35, 241–77. Investors needed protection from direct government expropriation, indirect regulatory expropriation, and opportunism from contracting parties. For the latter, government assistance in contract enforcement was useful. *Id.* at 235–40.

[166] *Id.* at 278–81. The authors also considered whether a nation that first develops economically would usually liberalize toward rule of law and democracy. They considered the evidence mixed. *Id.* at 281–88.

[167] André Nollkaemper (University of Amsterdam) & Michael Zürn (Free University of Berlin) co-edited with Peerenboom the volume, RULE OF LAW DYNAMICS: IN AN ERA OF INTERNATIONAL AND TRANSNATIONAL GOVERNANCE xii–xiv (Michael Zürn, André Nollkaemper, & Randall Peerenboom eds., 2012) [hereinafter RULE OF LAW DYNAMICS]. Peerenboom was a law professor at UCLA Law School from 1998 to 2007, when he left for La Trobe University. He received his Ph.D. in philosophy

Modifying legal transplant methodology, it considered how international and national lawmaking interacted dynamically. It disaggregated the transplant into rule of law promotion, mechanisms for its diffusion (by sanctions, persuasion, or emulation), and then its conversion (by reception, resistance, or adaptation). Qualitative inquiry complemented quantitative indicators through the three dimensions and utilized multiple disciplinary methods.[168]

Finally, there were a few American academic centers, programs, or courses that supported research on law and development. The Center on Democracy, Development and the Rule of Law at Stanford University was an example. It illustrated the interdisciplinary nature of legal issues by including their social, political, and economic dimensions. In addition, besides research and education, it supported the training of civic leaders and social entrepreneurs from many countries.[169] Among the center's research programs was the Governance Project that Fukuyama began in 2012. Its scholars sought to conceptualize and measure governance in China and the United States. They analyzed legal institutions, accountability, and administrative capacity to understand the relationship between governance and democracy.[170]

3. Constitutional and Judicial Globalization

American comparative constitutional law was the first subject matter systematically studied as an aspect of the new republic's creation. Thereafter, isolated comparatists and the gradually emerging law schools tended to shift their interest to private law and, to a lesser extent, penal law. Late in the nineteenth century, research in comparative constitutional law developed primarily in political science departments.[171]

With the concern of East European and other nations to draft new constitutions after 1990, U.S. comparatists engaged in consulting with foreign

---

from the University of Hawaii in 1990 and three years later his law degree from Columbia. He was an adviser to Stanford's China Guiding Cases Project, which works to develop a more transparent and accountable judiciary in China. Stanford University, *CGCP Directory*, https://cgc.law.stanford.edu/directory/randall-peerenboom.

[168] Michael Zürn, André Nollkaemper, & Randall Peerenboom, *Introduction: Rule of Law Dynamics in an Era of International and Transnational Governance*, in RULE OF LAW DYNAMICS, *supra* note 167, at 3–8; *see id.*, *Conclusion: From Rule of Law Promotion to Rule of Law Dynamics*, in *id.* at 305–23.
[169] Stanford University, *Center on Democracy, Development & the Rule of Law*, https://cddrl.fsi.stanford.edu.
[170] Stanford University, *The Governance Project*, https://cddrl.fsi.stanford.edu/governance.
[171] *E.g.*, JOHN W. BURGESS, POLITICAL SCIENCE AND COMPARATIVE CONSTITUTIONAL LAW (1890); *see supra* ch. 7, text accompanying notes 265–67 (1776 to 1920s).

jurists in that activity and in studying the new development.[172] Along with comparative constitutional law, which already had some law school supporters from the 1950s,[173] a few U.S. Supreme Court justices as well as academic comparatists participated in domestic and international conferences and wrote about comparative judicial review and other topics such as the judicial treatment of foreign law.[174]

After 2005, there was something of a tempest in a teapot fostered by comparatist scholars and judges writing about reliance on or citation of foreign law in American courts, especially in the U.S. Supreme Court, outside the field of conflict of laws. A few legislatures also took up the issue, contemplating or passing legislation to ban the use of foreign law in that jurisdiction's courts.[175] When the matter concerned *shari'a*, hostility toward Islamic law continued. Between 2010 and 2018, 43 legislatures introduced anti-*shari'a* measures and 14 enacted such statutes. Some of these included choice of law issues, but in general were meaningless since they duplicated enunciating a public policy position that state courts almost certainly would adopt.[176]

Nevertheless, by 2015, most U.S. jurists accepted that high courts had globalized in the sense that they were aware of the activities of foreign courts and many judges took that activity into account in reaching their decisions. Stephen Breyer, Supreme Court associate justice, for instance, wrote *The Court and the World: American Law and the New Global Realities*. It recognized the interdependence of the world's nations economically, politically, and ecologically as well as increasingly, culturally. There was no reason for law not to follow.[177]

---

[172] See HERMAN SCHWARTZ, THE STRUGGLE FOR CONSTITUTIONAL JUSTICE IN POST-COMMUNIST EUROPE (2000).

[173] See supra ch. 7, text accompanying notes 268–278 (postwar developments).

[174] ELAINE MAK, JUDICIAL DECISION-MAKING IN A GLOBALIZED WORLD: A COMPARATIVE ANALYSIS OF THE CHANGING PRACTICES OF WESTERN HIGHEST COURTS 88–90, 99–101, 154–58, 187–90 (2013); see, e.g., Yale Law School, Global Constitutionalism Seminar, https://law.yale.edu (search Global Constitutionalism Seminar) (annual event from 1996 with published materials since 2012).

[175] David S. Clark, Development of Comparative Law in the United States, in OXFORD HANDBOOK 2006, supra note 41, at 175, 178–80; see CHRISTOPHER ROBERTS, FOREIGN LAW? CONGRESS V. THE SUPREME COURT (2014); Steven G. Calabresi, A Shining City on a Hill: American Exceptionalism and the Supreme Court's Practice of Relying on Foreign Law, 86 B.U. L. REV. 1335–1446 (2006); Mark C. Rahdert, Exceptionalism Unbound: Appraising American Resistance to Foreign Law, 65 CATH. U.L. REV. 537–604 (2016).

[176] Swathi Shanmugasundaram, Anti-Sharia Law Bills in the United States (5 Feb. 2018), at Southern Poverty Law Center, Home, https://www.splcenter.org (search Anti-Sharia Law).

[177] STEPHEN BREYER, THE COURT AND THE WORLD: AMERICAN LAW AND THE NEW GLOBAL REALITIES (2015). "[T]he Supreme Court must increasingly consider the world beyond our national frontiers. In its growing interdependence, this world of laws offers new opportunities for the exchange of ideas, together with a host of new challenges that bear upon our job of interpreting statutes and treaties and even our Constitution." Id. at 281.

Mark Tushnet dated the current vibrant field of comparative constitutional law from the 1990s, with interest in the addition of new democratic constitutions in Canada, South Africa, Latin America, and East Asia to those from Eastern Europe. Furthermore, there was debate about whether the European Community needed a proper constitution to further federalism and protect human rights. In 2003, Norman Dorsen and Michel Rosenfeld created the *International Journal of Constitutional Law*, which intended to publish transnational and comparative research utilizing legal and social science perspectives.[178]

As Tushnet pointed out, and as the history of U.S. academic constitutional law suggested, constitutions lay at the intersection of law and politics. Comparatists held positions in law schools as well as in political science departments. To appropriately analyze and compare constitutions on topics such as separation of powers, federalism, and judicial review, scholars required concepts suitable for interdisciplinary research.[179] There was also the distinction between constitutional law and constitutionalism. The former was a descriptive field that primarily examined written documents, including for totalitarian and failed states, along with the doctrinal and institutional structure surrounding them. However, especially for fundamental human rights encased within a constitution, the subject inclined toward universalism and thus would be normative. Constitutionalism, alternatively, was a full-blown normative model that assumed universalism with a Western bias. It required certain minimum requirements, which could vary in the manner that rules, structures, and processes satisfied them. Although jurists might disagree, in general, those requirements were rule of law, an independent judiciary, and regular, open elections with a widespread franchise.[180]

Another theme in comparative constitutional law centered around discussion of which rights legislators should include in a constitution. Here, there was substantial difference between the U.S. Constitution and the constitutions of European nations. The former was associated with classical liberalism that had government structures designed to minimize abusive legislation or executive action along with a bill of rights enumerating specific protected matters that government should not impinge. In Europe, the rise of socialism in the early twentieth century led to constitutions that added rights for political participation, equality, and—requiring government action—social and economic protection. After World War II, group rights to cultural preservation and environmental quality joined the list.[181]

---

[178] Mark Tushnet, *Comparative Constitutional Law, in* OXFORD HANDBOOK, *supra* note 27, at 1193, 1195; Norman Dorsen & Michel Rosenfeld, *Note to Readers*, 1 INT'L J. CONST. L. 1 (2003).

[179] Tushnet, *supra* note 178, at 1196–97; *see* TOM GINSBURG, JUDICIAL REVIEW IN NEW DEMOCRACIES: CONSTITUTIONAL COURTS IN EAST ASIA (2003).

[180] Tushnet, *supra* note 178, at 1197–1200.

[181] *Id.* at 1198–99.

Of the two leading early twenty-first century coursebooks on comparative constitutional law, one emphasized constitutional law and the other constitutionalism. Tushnet and Vicki Jackson prepared the first volume, *Comparative Constitutional Law*, in 1999, with a third edition by 2014.[182] In the third edition, they described the evolution of the field over 15 years as reflected in their editions. This included the dramatic increase in new and amended national constitutions, their interpretation by national and international courts, growth of supranational organizations, and supporting secondary literature. New issues emerged, such as unconstitutional constitutional amendments, public participation in constitution making, and illiberal, authoritarian constitutions. There were also important changes in the treatment of religious liberty, freedom of expression, and social welfare rights. The coverage in 2014 was worldwide in its illustrations, including Africa.[183]

In 2003, Dorsen, Rosenfeld, and colleagues offered a competitor, *Comparative Constitutionalism*. It also saw three editions through 2016.[184] The authors shared the view that the field had expanded remarkably and in a global fashion, so that the term transnational constitutionalism was appropriate. In the first chapter, they used materials to demonstrate what they meant by constitutionalism. Rosenfeld stated that constitutionalism's three essential features were rule of law, limitations on government power, and protection of fundamental rights. Of these, rule of law was the most expansive and malleable and could include the other two features. It was apparent, consequently, that the normative theory of constitutionalism overlapped contemporaneous efforts in law and development. The prescriptive nature of constitutionalism distinguished those constitutions that satisfied its requirements in substantial measure versus façade or illiberal constitutions. The coursebook emphasized fundamental rights that supported constitutionalism's universalistic aspirations.

The authors included materials from more than 50 jurisdictions worldwide. Illustrating the shared interest in constitutionalism between the United States and Europe, two authors were American and three others were jurists in Germany, Hungary, and Italy.[185]

Among general U.S. comparative law coursebooks, *The Contemporary Civil Law Tradition* (2015) provided extensive coverage of comparative constitutional law, demonstrating the shift away from the usual private law

---

[182] VICKI C. JACKSON & MARK TUSHNET, COMPARATIVE CONSTITUTIONAL LAW (3d ed. 2014) (1st ed. 1999, 2d ed. 2006).

[183] *Id.* at v–vii.

[184] NORMAN DORSEN, MICHEL ROSENFELD, ANDRÁS SAJÓ, SUSANNE BAER, & SUSANNA MANCINI, COMPARATIVE CONSTITUTIONALISM: CASES AND MATERIALS (3d ed. 2016) (1st ed. 2003, 2d ed. 2010). Mancini joined the third edition.

[185] *Id.* at iii, 41–42, 73, 78–79; *see* Davis & Trebilcock, *supra* note 155, at 905–11 (law and development).

orientation characteristic of the twentieth century.[186] After 2000, there were so many monographs on foreign or comparative constitutional law and edited comparative volumes with U.S. authors that one might conclude that it was the dominant American comparative law subject of the twenty-first century. In 2011, Tom Ginsburg and Rosalind Dixon described the collaborative and interdisciplinary nature of the newly energized field. Lawyers, political scientists, sociologists, and economists participated in research with interest from courts, legislators, and jurists involved with constitution making or interpretation. Regional and international associations offered fora for the exchange of ideas and collaborative projects. At the same time, judges took on more active participation, especially in new constitutional courts. Judicialization, consequently, sided with constitutionalism.[187] Dixon and Ginsburg followed with edited volumes on East Asia (2014) and Latin America (2017).[188]

Since 2012, three publishers—Oxford, Cambridge, and Routledge—commissioned handbooks on comparative constitutional law.[189] Many more books on the subject also appeared during this period. Ran Hirschl's volume was a good example. He called for an interdisciplinary approach incorporating methodologies from law, history, and the social sciences.[190] Jurists organized symposia.[191] As noted, much of this literature discussed judges and courts and their role in globalized constitutional law. *Comparative Judicial Review*, which Dixon and Erin Delaney edited in 2018, illustrated that contribution.[192]

---

[186] *See* JOHN HENRY MERRYMAN, DAVID S. CLARK, & JOHN OWEN HALEY, THE CONTEMPORARY CIVIL LAW TRADITION: EUROPE, LATIN AMERICA, AND EAST ASIA 11–20, 59–208, 247–308, 403–592 (2015). The other major public law treatment was for criminal law and procedure. *Id.* at 891–998.

[187] Rosalind Dixon & Tom Ginsburg, *Introduction, in* COMPARATIVE CONSTITUTIONAL LAW 1, 3–4, 12 (Tom Ginsburg & Rosalind Dixon eds., 2011). The authors proposed more methodological variety in comparative constitutional law, including empirical studies, experiments, surveys, and ethnography. *Id.* at 13. The volume had 33 chapters with authors from many countries.

[188] COMPARATIVE CONSTITUTIONAL LAW IN ASIA (Rosalind Dixon & Tom Ginsburg eds., 2014); COMPARATIVE CONSTITUTIONAL LAW IN LATIN AMERICA (Rosalind Dixon & Tom Ginsburg eds., 2017).

[189] THE OXFORD HANDBOOK OF COMPARATIVE CONSTITUTIONAL LAW (Michel Rosenfeld & András Sájo eds., 2012) (64 chapters); THE CAMBRIDGE COMPANION TO COMPARATIVE CONSTITUTIONAL LAW (Roger Masterman & Robert Schütze eds., 2019) (22 chapters) [hereinafter CAMBRIDGE COMPANION]; ROUTLEDGE HANDBOOK OF COMPARATIVE CONSTITUTIONAL CHANGE (Xenophon Contiades & Alkmene Fotiadou eds., 2021) (26 chapters). Authors were professors of law or political science, high court judges, or researchers at law and policy institutes and worked in many countries, illustrating the ecumenical nature of the subject matter.

[190] RAN HIRSCHL, COMPARATIVE MATTERS: THE RENAISSANCE OF COMPARATIVE CONSTITUTIONAL LAW 6, 13–15, 157–89, 226–29, 242–44, 279–81 (2014) [hereinafter HIRSCHL, COMPARATIVE MATTERS]; *see The Future of Constitutional Comparison: A Colloquy on Ran Hirschl's Comparative Matters*, 64 AM. J. COMP. L. 191–218 (2016). *See also* COMPARATIVE CONSTITUTIONAL DESIGN (Tom Ginsburg ed., 2012); CONSTITUTIONS IN AUTHORITARIAN REGIMES (Tom Ginsburg & Alberto Simpser eds., 2014).

[191] *E.g.*, Symposium on Comparative Constitutional Law, 62 AM. J. COMP. L. 493–686 (2014).

[192] COMPARATIVE JUDICIAL REVIEW (Erin F. Delaney & Rosalind Dixon eds., 2018); *see* CULTURES OF LEGALITY: JUDICIALIZATION AND POLITICAL ACTIVISM IN LATIN AMERICA (Javier A. Couso, Alexandra Huneeus, & Rachel Sieder eds., 2010); COURTS AND COMPARATIVE LAW (Mads Andenas

Finally, there were associations and university and law school institutes that promoted comparative constitutional law. The most prominent international organization was the International Association of Constitutional Law, founded in 1981. Eurocentric and modeled on the International Academy of Comparative Law, it held quadrennial world congresses and periodic workshops and roundtables. One American, Rosenfeld, served as president from 1999 to 2004, but many U.S. academics have participated in its programs.[193]

In 2005, Ginsburg, Zachary Elkins, and James Melton initiated the Comparative Constitutions Project (CCP) at the University of Illinois as a joint effort in the law school and political science department. The goal was to investigate the sources and consequences of constitutional choices by empirically analyzing the contents of all constitutions written in independent states since 1789. In 2009, they published *The Endurance of National Constitutions* to investigate empirically the risks to constitutions and what made them survive. Examining environmental and design factors related to almost 1,000 constitutions from 200 countries, they found that the average life span was 19 years. In 2013, CCP partnered with Google Ideas to make the data about and texts of constitutions publicly accessible. They formulated Constitute, a website that thoroughly indexed the texts for nearly every national constitution in the world.[194]

D. Rule of Law Programs: Governments, the ABA, and NGOs

1. Conceptualization and Timeline from 1990 to 2020

The debate about global governance was one of the surprising new developments in comparative law after 1990.[195] Often simplified as rule of law, it was a nebulous phrase that according to many of its advocates has represented the achievements

---

& Duncan Fairgrieve eds., 2015); Ruth Bader Ginsburg, "*A Decent Respect to the Opinions of [Human] Kind*": *The Value of Comparative Perspective in Constitutional Adjudication*, 26 AM. U. INT'L L. REV. 927–34 (2011).

[193] International Association of Constitutional Law, *Home*, http://iacl-aidc.org; Cardozo School of Law, *Michel Rosenfeld*, https://cardozo.yu.edu/directory/michel-rosenfeld.

[194] Comparative Constitutions Project, *Home*, http://comparativeconstitutionsproject.org (select About); ZACHARY ELKINS, TOM GINSBURG, & JAMES MELTON, THE ENDURANCE OF NATIONAL CONSTITUTIONS 2–6, 9, 65–121 (2009); Constitute, *Home*, https://constituteproject.org. An interesting feature of CCP was its presentation of constitution rankings, which presented an empirical value to executive and legislative power and judicial independence. CCP, *Home, supra* (select Data & Analysis, Constitution Rankings).

[195] Mathias Siems, *New Directions in Comparative Law*, in OXFORD HANDBOOK, *supra* note 27, at 852–53, 863–64, 870–73 [hereinafter Siems, *New Directions*].

of Western civilization in the realm of governance, the supremacy of law, and human rights. The term no longer belonged primarily with attempted legal transplants from the United States associated with periodic law and development efforts in the twentieth century. The United Nations, World Bank, Council of Europe, other international organizations, and national governments, including the U.S. government, adopted rule of law as part of their programs.[196] The activity of American comparatists promoting or researching the concept overlapped that of government and NGO programs supporting rule of law and that of jurists involved with the revival of law and development or with comparative constitutional law.[197] Beyond the international entities promoting rule of law, European and American comparatists often collaborated on books and articles about the subject so that it appeared to some to be part of world culture.[198]

Rule of law was imprecise as an idea in a variety of ways.[199] Many agreed it included human rights, but which ones? National constitutions, and often legislation, recognized some combination of civil, political, economic, social, cultural, or collective rights. Nevertheless, they did not agree on the correct list. Should the consensus view of Western nations control? That would make the enterprise ethnocentric (and messianic) as the West pushed other countries to adopt its list. Should the West accept a thin rule of law that limited itself to a common set of rights also found in Islamic and authoritarian states? Would governments in fact need to enforce the rights? To what degree? Another approach would be to make rule of law an ideal that no country could attain, but worth striving for to attain peace and justice in society. Assuming one could define and measure it, the world's nations would lie on a spectrum ranging from no rule of law to a close

---

[196] Bussani, *supra* note 157, at 712–14; *see* Tom Ginsburg, *In Defense of Imperialism? The Rule of Law and the State-Building Project*, in GETTING TO THE RULE OF LAW, *supra* note 153, at 224–26, 230–31; Martin Krygier, *Four Puzzles about the Rule of Law: Why, What, Where? And Who Cares?*, in *id.*, at 64–91; Richard W. Miller, *Might Still Distorts Right: Perils of the Rule of Law Project*, in *id.*, at 265–86; Christopher May & Adam Winchester, *Introduction to the* Handbook on the Rule of Law, *in* HANDBOOK ON THE RULE OF LAW 1, 2–3, 6–7 (Christopher May & Adam Winchester eds., 2018) [hereinafter RULE OF LAW HANDBOOK]; United Nations, *UN System and the Rule of Law*, https://www.un.org/ruleoflaw/un-and-the-rule-of-law. *See generally* THE CAMBRIDGE COMPANION TO THE RULE OF LAW (Jens Meierhenrich & Martin Loughlin eds., 2021); RULE OF LAW: CASES, STRATEGIES, AND INTERPRETATIONS (Barbara Faedda ed., 2021); BRIAN Z. TAMANAHA, ON THE RULE OF LAW: HISTORY, POLITICS, THEORY (2004).

[197] René Urueña, *Indicators and the Law: A Case Study of the Rule of Law Index* [hereinafter Urueña, *Indicators*], *in* The QUIET POWER OF INDICATORS: MEASURING GOVERNANCE, CORRUPTION, AND RULE OF LAW 75, 78–80, 94–95 (Sally Engle Merry, Kevin E. Davis, & Benedict Kingsbury eds., 2015) [hereinafter QUIET POWER]; *see* CONSTITUTIONALISM AND THE RULE OF LAW: BRIDGING IDEALISM AND REALISM (Maurice Adams, Anne Meuwese & Ernst Hirsch Ballin eds., 2017); *supra* pts. C.2 and C.3 (law and development and comparative constitutionalism).

[198] Frank Schimmelfennig, *A Comparison of the Rule of Law Promotion Policies of Major Western Powers*, in RULE OF LAW DYNAMICS, *supra* note 167, at 111–13.

[199] *See* Rachel Kleinfeld, *Competing Definitions of the Rule of Law*, *in* PROMOTING THE RULE OF LAW ABROAD: IN SEARCH OF KNOWLEDGE 31–65 (Thomas Carothers ed., 2006) [hereinafter PROMOTING THE RULE OF LAW].

actualization of the ideal.[200] We will see that governments and NGOs tended to utilize either an ethnocentric universalistic approach or a spectrum model for rule of law.[201]

Another notion associated with rule of law was that judicialization of politics would benefit society since it would transform political issues into legal issues that courts could resolve with legal principles. This ignored the social context in which officials utilized courts to unfairly punish opponents or in which judges were otherwise corrupt. If activists depended on national and international NGOs—civil society—to protect rule of law and judicial independence, they typically failed to empirically examine the action of lawyers who translated aspirational norms into legal processes and rules. Lawyers involved in legal transplants acted as brokers between various economic and political interests tied to the transfer, including their own.[202] In China, for instance, support by international aid donors and NGOs to modernize the legal profession and judiciary did more for economic development than for political liberalism or human rights. China impeded political lawyering and lawyers themselves did not generally welcome liberal democracy. It illustrated thin rule of law that excluded liberal democracy or some human rights popular in Western societies.[203]

Consequently, assertions of a global consensus about rule of law—perhaps a natural convergence toward unification of law—usually appeared with international governmental organizations or NGOs. The gulf on understandings of the concept were typically with domestic governmental agencies and national NGOs or with scholars, who might be jurists, economists, political scientists, or more recently anthropologists. Scholars accused national governments of externalizing their domestic rule of law system. A standard dichotomy of views was between thin and thick rule of law. A thin rule of law stressed its formal aspects, which any system of law required to function effectively. It did not depend on

---

[200] Bussani, *supra* note 157, at 716–17, 720–21, 724–26, 739–43. Other issues were whether governance must be democratic or utilize an independent judiciary. Scholars concerned with law and development generally preferred market capitalism while rule of law scholars had a wider range of views on the economy. *Id.* at 718–20, 723–24, 726–30; see Thomas Carothers, *Rule of Law Temptations*, 33 FLETCHER F. WORLD AFF. 49–61 (no. 1, 2009).

[201] May & Winchester, *supra* note 196, at 7–10; *see* Mona Rishmawi, *The Rule of Law and Human Rights*, in RULE OF LAW HANDBOOK, *supra* note 196, at 357–79; Peer Zumbansen, *The Rule of Law, Legal Pluralism, and Challenges to a Western-Centric View*, in *id.* at 57–74. Another rule of law scale could be between thin and thick versions of rule of law. May & Winchester, *supra*, at 10.

[202] Dezalay & Garth, *supra* note 162, at 2–7, 9–11; *see* Thomas Carothers, *The Problem of Knowledge*, in PROMOTING THE RULE OF LAW, *supra* note 199, at 15, 20–21; César Rodríguez-Garavito, *Toward a Sociology of the Global Rule of Law Field: Neoliberalism, Neoconstitutionalism, and the Contest over Judicial Reform in Latin America*, in LAWYERS AND GLOBALIZATION, *supra* note 161, at 156–78.

[203] Randall Peerenboom, *Searching for Political Liberalism in All the Wrong Places: The Legal Profession in China as the Leading Edge of Political Reform?*, in LAWYERS AND GLOBALIZATION, *supra* note 161, at 239–43, 246–55; see *supra* text accompanying note 154 (thin rule of law). There was a strong correlation between GDP per capita and lawyers per capita, litigation rates, and the quality of the judiciary. Peerenboom, *supra*, at 241–42; see Dan Banik, *The Legal Empowerment of the Poor*, in RULE OF LAW HANDBOOK, *supra* note 196, at 419–20.

whether the society was democratic or capitalist. Some contended that its rules must be general, public, prospective, clear, consistent, stable, and enforced. For institutions, there should be courts and enforcement agencies. Thick or substantive rule of law theories added political morality to the thin version, requiring a certain economic system, form of government, or conception of human rights.[204]

By the end of the 1990s, criticism of foreign development efforts, whether by the U.S. government, NGOs, or the World Bank, had grown.[205] George W. Bush, who became U.S. president in 2001 (until 2009), had campaigned in 2000 against policies of nation building. However, after the terrorist attacks on the United States in September 2001, an altered development policy returned to U.S. foreign relations that affected the agendas of comparative jurists in the new century. The 2004 National Commission report on the attacks found that Middle Eastern state-centered regimes had been unable to produce dynamic economies adequate for their populations, leaving young men susceptible to Islamic radicalism promoted by Al Qaeda. The Bush administration committed to development aid, especially through the World Bank, to raise living standards and reform political and economic structures.[206]

Furthermore, for recalcitrant governments, Bush promised to transform societies with a war on terror. After demolishing a malevolent regime, the United States would reconstruct it as a liberal society, even though it had never existed in that form. Afghanistan and Iraq were the laboratories, with NGO and some multilateral support. The rhetoric of nation building returned. There continued an emphasis on privatization in reconstruction and avoidance of state-centered policies. The security situation deteriorated and partners abandoned their projects so that a comparison with Vietnam was inevitable. U.S. president Barack Obama (served 2009–2017) and his administration attempted to reconceptualize development, regain NGO support, and encourage greater state involvement in the target societies. Nevertheless, international distaste for what most of the

---

[204] Adriaan Bedner, *The Promise of a Thick View*, in RULE OF LAW HANDBOOK, *supra* note 196, at 34–47; Ronald J. Daniels & Michael Trebilcock, *The Political Economy of Rule of Law Reform in Developing Countries*, 26 MICH. J. INT'L L. 99–134 (2004); Jørgen Møller, *The Advantage of a Thin View*, in *id.*, at 21–33; Daniel B. Rodriguez, Matthew D. McCubbins, & Barry R. Weingast, *The Rule of Law Unplugged*, 59 EMORY L.J. 1455–94 (2010); Schimmelfennig, *supra* note 198, at 113–17; Zürn et al., *supra* note 168, at 1 n.1.

[205] *See, e.g.*, Amy L. Chua, *Markets, Democracy, and Ethnicity: Toward a New Paradigm for Law and Development*, 108 YALE L.J. 1–107 (1998) (failure to consider host country's diverse ethnicities); Jacques deLisle, *Lex Americana? United States Legal Assistance, American Legal Models, and Legal Change in the Post-Communist World and Beyond*, 20 U. PA. J. INT'L ECON. L. 179–204, 226–308 (1999).

[206] EKBLADH, *supra* note 3, at 264–66; Joseph S. Nye, Jr., *The Rise and Fall of American Hegemony from Wilson to Trump*, 95 INT'L AFF. 63, 69–70 (2019) [hereinafter Nye, *American Hegemony*]; *see* NATIONAL COMMISSION ON TERRORIST ATTACKS UPON THE UNITED STATES, THE 9/11 COMMISSION REPORT: FINAL REPORT OF THE NATIONAL COMMISSION ON TERRORIST ATTACKS UPON THE UNITED STATES (2004).

public saw as America's unilateral wars discredited broad foreign development endeavors in a manner reminiscent of the period following the Vietnam War.[207]

2. Specific Programs and Activities

The World Bank was a leader in the rule of law movement. An international financial institution that made loans and grants to member nations, it began operations in 1946 as the International Bank for Reconstruction and Development (IBRD). Located in Washington, D.C. (as was the IMF), its president traditionally had been an American and U.S. influence over its policies continued to be dominant as the bank's largest shareholder.[208] Based on U.S. proposals, the bank's board of governors in 1960 created the International Development Association (IDA) to provide interest-free loans and grants to poorer countries. In 1980, the PRC took over representation of China's membership and became one of the IDA's largest borrowers. Then, in 1992, Russia and 12 former Soviet republics joined the World Bank, making it a near-universal institution.[209]

During the 1980s, the bank played a leading role in identifying disabilities in local legal systems as impediments to the functioning of markets in global economic development. Bank economists and lawyers coupled advice with loans to stimulate wealth creation, with less attention to its distribution or to human rights, and recommended an independent judiciary and an emphasis on private law reforms.[210] In 1992, the World Bank published its first report on governance and its relationship to development. For sustainable economic and social development to occur, which was necessary for a country to repay its loans, good governance would require predictable and transparent legal rules and institutions for private and public business. Summarized as rule of law, its components were a professional bureaucracy, accountable executive branch, and strong civil society participating in public affairs. Since the bank's Articles of Agreement prohibited it from interfering in a nation's internal political affairs, the call for rule of law only concerned its contribution to social and economic development and poverty reduction.[211]

---

[207] EKBLADH, *supra* note 3, at 269–73.

[208] WORLD BANK, A GUIDE TO THE WORLD BANK 10–12, 17–18, 209, 219 (3d ed. 2011) [hereinafter WORLD BANK GUIDE]; World Bank, *History*, https://www.worldbank.org/en/about/history.

[209] WORLD BANK GUIDE, *supra* note 208, at 209, 212. The IDA is part of the World Bank. It utilizes the same headquarters and staff as the IBRD to evaluate projects in less credit-worthy countries. World Bank Group, *What is IDA?*, http://ida.worldbank.org/about/what-is-ida.

[210] PAUL CARRINGTON, SPREADING AMERICA'S WORD: STORIES OF ITS LAWYER-MISSIONARIES 283–84 (2005); *see supra* text accompanying notes 6, 164 (World Bank); Frank Upham, *Mythmaking in the Rule-of-Law Orthodoxy, in* PROMOTING THE RULE OF LAW, *supra* note 199, at 75, 77–79.

[211] WORLD BANK, GOVERNANCE: THE WORLD BANK'S EXPERIENCE vii (1994); *see id.* at 1–36, 53–54.

By 1994, the bank was providing advice to borrowers requiring a certain legal framework for development. This included new laws on property rights, business, bankruptcy, banking, antitrust, foreign investment, and regulatory bodies. For some countries, there was assistance for legal training and judicial infrastructure. It limited human rights to those necessary for poverty reduction. From the mid-1980s, the bank had emphasized privatization of state enterprises, public sector reform, and support for functioning market economies.[212] In its 1994 report on governance, the bank concluded:

> The legal framework in a country is as vital for economic development as it is for political and social development. Creating wealth through the cumulative commitment of human, technological, and capital resources depends greatly on a set of rules securing property rights, governing civil and commercial behavior, and limiting the power of the state.[213]

After 2000, the bank expanded its concern for what it called justice institutions—courts, their processes, and informal dispute resolution—and their place in development.[214] Nevertheless, much of the aid for the justice sector had little success measured by institutional change in the host nations. Courts welcomed the buildings and equipment, but judges were not necessarily more productive or honest.[215]

From 1990 to 2020, the World Bank approved 125 projects related to rule of law, access to justice, and law reform. Eighteen were grants and the remainder loans about equally divided between the IBRD and IDA. The bank distributed the aid evenly among countries in East and South Asia, Europe and Central Asia, Latin America, and Sub-Saharan Africa, with somewhat fewer in the Middle East and North Africa.[216] Estimates on the amount of development aid varied widely, but one put it at $18 billion on projects with a law and justice subsector component and around $48 billion on projects coded as having some rule of law

---

[212] *Id.* at xvii–xviii, 4–9, 23.

[213] *Id.* at 23; *see id.* at 24–29.

[214] WORLD BANK, WORLD DEVELOPMENT REPORT 2017: GOVERNANCE AND THE LAW 83–108 (2017); *id.*, *Justice and Development*, https://www.worldbank.org (search Justice and Development); *see id.*, LEGAL AND JUDICIAL REFORM: STRATEGIC DIRECTIONS (2003) [hereinafter BANK REFORM].

[215] Linn Hammergren, *Rule of Law Challenges in Middle-Income Countries and Donor Approaches to Addressing Them*, *in* RULE OF LAW DYNAMICS, *supra* note 167, at 181, 184–89; Mariana Prado & Michael Trebilcock, *Path Dependence, Development, and the Dynamics of Institutional Reform*, 59 U. TORONTO L.J. 341–79 (2009) (usefulness of path dependence theory for rule of law reform to transform dysfunctional legal institutions).

[216] World Bank, *Home*, *supra* note 3 (select What We Do/Projects/By Country/World/ProjectList, enter Filters). Bolivia and Indonesia had the largest number of projects, at seven and eight respectively. *Id.* Especially during the 1990s, the bank was satisfied with changes to constitutions or laws, but donee countries did not always carry out the reform after the bank disbursed aid. Hammergren, *supra* note 215, at 183–84.

thematic impact.[217] The 2009 loan to Colombia for judicial reform was illustrative. It involved a five-year disbursement plan of $20 million through 2014 with the Colombian government providing $10 million. The goal was to reduce case processing time in civil, family, and labor courts and the judiciary exceeded its target objective. In addition, Columbia decentralized court locations, retrained staff, and set up mediation centers while the legislature reformed the judicial code.[218]

The bank also took on the task of evaluating legal and judicial reforms to improve market economies in a systematic manner and globally. It utilized statistically relevant evidence that such reforms influenced individuals and firms, leading to increased investment, wealth creation, and equitable distribution of resources.[219] Perhaps the most ambitious of those efforts was the *Doing Business* series that it commenced in 2004. In 2020, it documented regulations and changes for 12 areas of business activity in 190 economies. By using indicators and numeric scores, it yielded an aggregate ease of doing business assessment and ranking.[220]

However, in 2021, with the discovery of data irregularities and staff ethical misconduct, the World Bank discontinued the series.[221] After an internal and external investigation of the 2018 *Doing Business* indicators, it appeared that the bank's president, Jim Yong Kim, had directed staff to change its methodology to improve China's ranking at the request of Li Keqiang, China's State Council premier. Kristalina Georgieva, the bank's vice president, led the team that found it could raise China's pending ranking by altering calculations for three indicators: ease of starting a business, obtaining credit, and paying taxes. The episode revealed that there was inherent tension between the bank's diplomatic duties and its scientific aspirations, that national leaders (and investors) paid attention to the rankings, and that some leaders had initiated genuine reforms in

---

[217] Deval Desai, *Power Rules: The World Bank, Rule of Law Reform, and the World Development Report 2017*, in HANDBOOK ON THE RULE OF LAW, *supra* note 195, at 217, 219–21.

[218] World Bank, *Home*, supra note 3 (search P083904). In the end, the IBRD disbursed $18.4 million and Columbia repaid $13.8 million through 2021. *Id.*

[219] BANK REFORM, *supra* note 214, at 16–24; Monika Heupel, *Rule of Law Promotion through International Organizations and NGOs*, in RULE OF LAW DYNAMICS, *supra* note 167, at 133, 143–44. From the 1990s, the bank often made the disbursal of loans and aid subject to commitment to rule of law reform or to good governance reforms more broadly, an approach known as conditionality. Heupel, *supra* at 135–36, 145–46.

[220] WORLD BANK GROUP, DOING BUSINESS 2020: COMPARING BUSINESS REGULATION IN 190 ECONOMIES 1–15 (2020).

[221] World Bank Group, *World Bank Group to Discontinue Doing Business Report*, https://www.worldbank.org (select Who We Are, then News, search 16 September 2021). An external review found that a major defect was to rely on de jure rules rather than the de facto reality in a jurisdiction. LAURA ALFARO ET AL., DOING BUSINESS: EXTERNAL PANEL REVIEW (2021), at https://apo.org.au/node/314345.

legal regulations and processes. A solution to the dilemma might be to let an NGO or university oversee the indicator results.[222]

USAID began its rule of law programs in Latin America in the mid-1980s. Its aim at that time was to expand democracy and free markets, combat crime, fight corruption, and reduce human rights violations in countries that would improve the legal infrastructure for trade with an independent judiciary and civilian police force. In the 1990s, USAID added programs in Eastern Europe and Central Asia aimed at refashioning legal norms, institutions, and processes to support democracy and market capitalism. These projects encompassed new legislation and initiatives with law schools, bar associations, and entities for judicial training and court management. Overall themes were transparency, access to justice, and building civil society constituencies for legal reform.[223] As with the World Bank, USAID rule of law projects were an instrumental goal, a means to achieve their primary objectives. For USAID, that objective was democracy, so that its rule of law measure had a larger political component than that of the World Bank. USAID also suffered the problem of inadequate donee institutional follow-through, although it had some success in reforming criminal procedure with support from local jurists, shifting it toward an accusatorial system.[224]

From 1993 to 1998, there were 35 entities within the U.S. government that had rule of law programs, mostly law enforcement agencies providing training and technical assistance to overseas counterparts. Nevertheless, measured by direct funding, USAID conducted half the activities, the Justice Department 20 percent, and the Departments of State and Defense 10 percent each. In fact, USAID provided a larger

---

[222] *Why Georgieva Should Go*, 440 ECONOMIST, 25 Sept. 2021, at 14; *How World Bank Leaders Put Pressure on Staff to Alter a Global Index*, ECONOMIST, 17 Sept. 2021, at https://www.economist.com (search Georgieva). Bank staff also altered the scores for Azerbaijan, Saudi Arabia, and the United Arab Emirates. *Id.* Another episode involving China that illustrated the power of legal indicators occurred with Transparency International (TI). In 2014, TI's release of its annual Corruption Perceptions Index angered Chinese officials since the Index moved China down 20 places from 80 to 100 in its ranking of countries, even though China had publicly initiated an anti-corruption campaign aimed at high officials and their activities and assets abroad. Alexander Cooley, *How International Rankings Constitute and Limit Our Understanding of Global Governance Challenges: The Case of Corruption*, in THE PALGRAVE HANDBOOK OF INDICATORS IN GLOBAL GOVERNANCE 49–50, 59–60, 62 (Debora Valentina Malito, Gaby Umbach, & Nehal Bhuta eds., 2018) [hereinafter PALGRAVE HANDBOOK].

[223] Carothers, *Knowledge*, *supra* note 201, at 15–17; Steven E. Hendrix, *USAID Promoting Democracy and the Rule of Law in Latin America and the Caribbean*, 9 Sw. J.L. & TRADE AM. 277–83, 307–20 (2002); USAID, USAID and the Rule of Law 1–4 (2001) (typescript), at https://gsdrc.org/document-library/usaid-and-the-rule-of-law. More challenging aid projects existed in Africa, the Near East, and other parts of Asia. *Id. See also* Lisa Bhansali & Christina Biebesheimer, *Measuring the Impact of Criminal Justice Reform in Latin America*, in PROMOTING THE RULE OF LAW, *supra* note 199, at 301–21.

[224] Hammergren, *supra* note 215, at 181, 184, 202–04; Máximo Langer, *Revolution in Latin American Criminal Procedure: Diffusion of Legal Ideas from the Periphery*, 55 AM. J. COMP. L. 617–76 (2007); Daniel Palacios Muñoz, *Criminal Procedure in Chile: New Agents and the Restructuring of a Field*, in LAWYERS AND GLOBALIZATION, *supra* note 161, at 112–28; Schimmelfennig, *supra* note 198, at 129–30.

share via interagency transfers primarily through its Rule of Law Division within the Office of Democracy and Governance (later adding Human Rights to its name).[225]

Reitz presented a thoughtful analysis of U.S. rule of law projects during the 1990s within a comparative context. Utilizing the transplant metaphor of legal export, he evaluated the activities and strategies in terms of coercion, chauvinism, backlash, and waste. Some of the early projects were amateurish and ephemeral. Reitz preferred a universalistic definition for rule of law that would minimize the critique of imperialism for its export. He found that to consist of belief in, and the actual limitation of governmental power by, legal rules that restrict official discretion. Nevertheless, most export strategy aimed at institutionalization, such as judicial independence, jurisdiction over public law disputes, legal education, and mechanisms to reduce corruption.[226]

In the 1990s, there were three principal goals for the importation of foreign legal models in Eastern Europe and Eurasia. First, the leaders of post-communist countries thought that rapid legislative changes were necessary to smooth the transition toward a market economy, democracy, and rule of law. Second, importers might simply be looking for new ideas; the foreign example would then be subject to considerable modification to fit the local legal culture. Third, a faction within a country might believe that the prestige of foreign legal institutions or rules could provide it an advantage in its struggle with another faction. Exporters, for their part, had some mix of altruism or self-interest related to commercial benefit or national prestige.[227]

After 2003, rule of law appeared as a factor in American military strategy in response to the insurgencies in Afghanistan and Iraq that erupted after the U.S. invasion of Iraq. For the military command, rule of law was necessary to build legitimacy for the U.S.-supported governments.[228] Considering the history of imposed rule of law attempts, the projects were unrealistic and ultimately doomed to fail, but Stanford Law School tried to foster indigenous support for the goal through its Afghanistan Legal Education Project partially funded by the State Department.[229] This project was part of Stanford's Rule of Law Program,

---

[225] Schimmelfennig, *supra* note 198, at 117–18; *see* USAID, RULE OF LAW PRACTITIONER'S GUIDE (2020) [HEREINAFTER USAID ROL GUIDE]. In 2020, the State Department's rule of law program was primarily under the Bureau of Democracy, Human Rights, and Labor. U.S. Department of State, *Home*, https://www.state.gov (select Bureaus & Offices).

[226] John C. Reitz, *Export of the Rule of Law*, 13 TRANSNAT'L L. & CONTEMP. PROBS. 429–32, 435–41, 451–58, 460–62, 464–67, 472, 474–77, 481–84 (2003).

[227] *Id.* at 448–51.

[228] Tilmann J. Röder, *Civil-Military Cooperation in Building the Rule of Law*, *in* RULE OF LAW DYNAMICS, *supra* note 167, at 206, 210–12, 214, 223–26; *see id.* at 215–23, 226–32. During the 2000 presidential election campaign, the chair of the Joint Chiefs of Staff had rejected nation building as an appropriate military activity. *Id.* at 210.

[229] Stanford University, *Afghanistan Legal Education Project (ALEP)*, https://law.stanford.edu/alep. The $3,000,000 State Department grant came from its Bureau of International Narcotics and Law Enforcement Affairs. *Id.*; *see* Röder, *supra* note 228, at 221.

which began in 1999, offering students the opportunity to learn the theory and practice of state-building through coursework, experiential learning, and research.[230]

In 2010, USAID adopted a rule of law framework that had five essential elements: order and security; (2) legitimate constitutions, laws, and legal institutions; (3) strengthened checks and balances; (4) fairness and human rights; and (5) effective application of the law.[231] Rule of law was also one of five components needed to achieve effective democracy, human rights, and governance. Human rights had taken on increased importance in the agency's aid programs and pushed it toward a thicker version of rule of law.[232] Under pressure from the U.S. Congress to meaningfully evaluate the success or failure of USAID's programs, the latter adopted outcome indicators and measurements for various rule of law components.[233]

The ABA became involved with the export of rule of law in the 1990s in Eastern Europe with funding largely from USAID and the Departments of Justice and State. Unlike the rule of law activities of West European nations plus the European Community, which were direct government programs, the American efforts resulted from the initiative of commercial lawyers within the ABA. The ABA's Central and East European Law Initiative (CEELI), begun in 1990 and purporting to promote the rule of law, in the first decade provided the aid of 5,000 judges, attorneys, and professors to help write constitutions and laws in Russia, its former republics, and a few other developing nations.[234]

CEELI's first office was in Bulgaria in 1991 and by 2006, it had established 30 offices staffed with liaison officers in the target nations. The Washington, D.C., home office had 40 employees.[235] The ABA's initiative in the 1990s illustrated a

---

[230] Stanford University, *Rule of Law Program*, https://law.stanford.edu/rule-of-law-program. Erik Jensen was the program director and professor of the practice of law since 2012, but he had worked part time at the program after 1999 while also employed as an advisor to the World Bank and other international development banks. Program funding came from Microsoft, the Law School, and the University's Center on Democracy, Development and Rule of Law. *Id.*; *see supra* text accompanying notes 169–170 (Center).

[231] USAID ROL GUIDE, *supra* note 225, at 3.

[232] USAID, DEMOCRACY, HUMAN RIGHTS, AND GOVERNANCE STRATEGIC ASSESSMENT FRAMEWORK iv, 18–23, 34–35 (2014); *see id.*, *Democracy, Human Rights, and Governance*, https://www.usaid.gov/democracy; text accompanying note 223 (human rights).

[233] USAID ROL GUIDE, *supra* note 225, at 31–34.

[234] ABA CEELI, PROMOTING THE RULE OF LAW 1 (n.d., c. 2002); Ole Hammerslev, *The European Union and the United States in Eastern Europe: Two Ways of Exporting Law, Expertise and State Power*, *in* LAWYERS AND GLOBALIZATION, *supra* note 161, at 134–35, 137–39, 141, 148. "All candidates must be interested in making a difference." ABA CEELI, *supra*, at 2; *see* Hammerslev, *supra*, at 142. The program was ambitious, including reform of the judiciary, legal profession and education, commercial, criminal, and environmental law, plus influencing gender issues. ABA CEELI, *supra*, at 3–9; Hammerslev, *supra*, at 143.

[235] ABA, RULE OF LAW INITIATIVE, ANNUAL REPORT 2019, at 2, 72 (2019) [hereinafter RULE OF LAW ANNUAL REPORT], at https://www.americanbar.org/advocacy/rule_of_law/publications (search annual report 2019); Hammerslev, *supra* note 234, at 136, 140–42.

shallow understanding of how legal systems function, or the importance of culture within a society, along with a high degree of hypocrisy about the American legal system itself. Recognition of these factors would have led those involved with rule of law export to exhibit more humility, diffidence, and willingness to understand the recipient's reality.[236]

In 2004, USAID commissioned a study to evaluate its rule of law programs during the 1990s in Eastern Europe, both direct and indirect via NGOs such as the ABA. One of its findings was that the agency failed to grasp the core differences between the United States and the target nations, which had a civil law foundation, affecting the relation between courts, the legislature, and the civilian style of drafting legislation. Among the eight countries evaluated, Bulgaria was the most successful.[237]

In 2007, the ABA established the Rule of Law Initiative to consolidate its five existing overseas rule of law programs. Today, it participates with a professional staff of 500 together with partners in over 100 countries to strengthen foreign legal professionals and institutions toward an idealized natural-law type vision of rule of law and respect for human rights.[238] It might well be that with the experience of the 1990s, the ABA's professional staff directing the rule of law programs have learned the importance of culture and local commitment in designing and implementing their legal transplants. In 2019, the Rule of Law Initiative had a $33 million budget with programs in 40 countries.[239]

3. The Emergence of Legal Indicators

With so many government agencies and public and private institutions utilizing rule of law rhetoric in their programs as a desirable feature of government, one might believe there had been progress toward a consensus on what the term entailed. However, too many conceptualizations, especially those with normative content in a thick version, vied for acceptance. Comparative law scholars,

---

[236] CARRINGTON, supra note 210, at 291–300; Upham, *supra* note 210, at 83–88, 98–101. For the United States, Upham listed politicized judges, structural irrationality, and lack of legal uniformity. *Id.* at 83–88. From 1995 to 1997, this author consulted with the Commercial Law Project for Ukraine (Kyiv) and attempted to explain the central differences for law reform between a civil law and common law country.

[237] USAID, "FROM RULE OF MEN TO RULE OF LAW IN EUROPE AND EURASIA": A SYNTHESIS OF EIGHT COUNTRY IMPACT ASSESSMENTS 1–5, 7, 13–14, 15–19, 21, 23, 26, 39, 46 (2004) [hereinafter USAID SYNTHESIS], https://pdf.usaid.gov/pdf_docs/PNADC210.pdf; *see* Keith A. Rosten, *The Scaffolding for Legal Infrastructure: Developing Sustainable Approaches*, 16 TUL. J. INT'L & COMP. L. 395–418 (2008). The ABA's CEELI program fared somewhat better in the assessment. USAID SYNTHESIS, *supra*, at 13, 16, 18, 24, 27.

[238] ABA, *Rule of Law Initiative*, https://www.americanbar.org/advocacy.

[239] RULE OF LAW ANNUAL REPORT, *supra* note 235, at 25–33, 62–65, 72–73; Hammerslev, *supra* note 234, at 149–50.

development experts, and social scientists argued for measurement indicators to capture the implications of varying legal institutions, processes, and norms that could constitute a useable rule of law theory. This would need to be cross-national (thus comparative) and over time (historical) to understand the causes and consequences of different components.[240]

The rise of legal indicators was a consequence of wider acceptance of evidence-based governance. With reliance on statistical data beyond economic sectors and its synthesis into scales, ranks, and composite indices, officials could use indicators for policy formation and decision making. Scholars could use them for historical or comparative analysis; however, they tended to control how scholars conceptualized issues and presented evaluation as knowledge.[241]

There were two measurement strategies typically used: surveys or objective data. The former could be questionnaires for experts or lay persons on rule of law dimensions. The sponsoring agency might be interested in rule of law itself or something broader such as governance that included rule of law as an element. The major data problems were reliability, validity, and bias associated with aggregation. Rule of law definitions had multiple factors. Since a researcher would need to aggregate those to form a numeric index, weighing components such as judicial independence one way or another permitted bias to affect the index. Independence was not an absolute good since accountability should balance it for optimal judicial performance. In addition, for national comparison, context was necessary to determine if in a country a substitute factor compensated for a component's low score (comparability issue). These problems made a thin rule of law definition easier to defend against ethnocentricity than a thick rule of law.[242]

From the early twenty-first century, one could find comparative quantified constituent elements for a rule of law concept among various published or internet sources. For example, using Transparency International's Corruption Perceptions Index, the World Bank's Ease of Doing Business Index for regulatory efficiency in protecting property rights and enforcing contracts, its Worldwide Governance Indicators (WGI) for government accountability and political stability, and Freedom House for democratic governance and political and civil

---

[240] Tom Ginsburg, *Difficulties with Measuring the Rule of Law* [hereinafter Ginsburg, *Measuring*], in RULE OF LAW HANDBOOK, *supra* note 196, at 48, 55–56; *see* Jørgen Møller & Svend-Erik Skaaning, *Systematizing Thin and Thick Conceptions of the Rule of Law*, 33 JUST. SYS. J. 136–50 (2012). Ginsburg discussed the challenges of conceptualization and measurement. Ginsburg, *Measuring*, *supra*, at 49–55.
[241] Kevin E. Davis, Benedict Kingsbury, & Sally Engle Merry, *Introduction: The Local-Global Life of Indicators: Law, Power, and Resistance*, in QUIET POWER, *supra* note 197, at 1–4.
[242] Ginsburg, *Measuring*, *supra* note 240, at 51–53, 56; May & Winchester, *supra* note 196, at 11; *see* Debora Valentina Malito, *The Creative Disorder of Measuring Governance and Stateness*, in PALGRAVE HANDBOOK, *supra* note 222, at 97, 124–28 (reliability, validity, and comparability).

rights, one could construct her own rule of law index for synchronic and diachronic comparison.[243]

Alternatively, since 1996, the World Bank's WGI included an aggregate rule of law indicator tailored toward its mission. At that time, it had estimated scores for 167 nations, which increased to 195 nations in 2002. For 2002, based on polls of experts and surveys of business and laypeople—and thus perceptions—the meta-indicator had answers to questions about crime, police, property rights, contract enforcement, judicial independence and process, tax evasion, and government legitimacy. There was an average of seven data sources per country. Methodological issues existed for both time series and cross-national comparison, which the bank's statisticians confronted. Nevertheless, they felt the quality of its governance indicators was improving with more experience.[244]

An ambitious endeavor to focus solely on rule of law was the World Justice Project (WJP), which began under the umbrella of the ABA during the presidency of William Neukom, who had served as Microsoft Corporation's chief lawyer for 25 years, where he managed the company's legal, governmental, and philanthropic activities. In 2008, with support from the Bill & Melinda Gates Foundation and others, WJP held its first world justice forum in Vienna, issued a report on the initial Rule of Law Index, and established itself as an NGO, with Neukom as CEO and offices in Washington. D.C., and Seattle.[245]

WJP is best known for its Rule of Law Index, but it also sponsored interdisciplinary research and conferences to promote rule of law. Since 2008, WJP has refined its definition and operationalization of rule of law and expanded the index's coverage to more than 139 jurisdictions in 2021. The definition consisted of the aggregate of four universal principles: accountability for government and private persons under law; just law (clear, publicized, stable, and evenly applied)

---

[243] May & Winchester, *supra* note 196, at 11–12; *see* Christopher G. Bradley, *International Organizations and the Production of Indicators: The Case of Freedom House*, in QUIET POWER, *supra* note 197, at 27, 32–65; FREEDOM HOUSE, FREEDOM IN THE WORLD 2021: DEMOCRACY UNDER SIEGE (2021), at www.freedomhouse.org/reports; René Urueña, *Activism through Numbers? The Corruption Perceptions Index and the Use of Indicators by Civil Society Organizations*, in PALGRAVE HANDBOOK, *supra* note 222, at 371–87. Since 2021, the bank closed the Doing Business Index. *See supra* text accompanying note 220–222 (index irregularities).

[244] DANIEL KAUFMANN, AART KRAAY, & MASSIMO MASTRUZZI, GOVERNANCE MATTERS III: GOVERNANCE INDICATORS FOR 1996–2002, at 5–6, 11–22, 43–44, 96 (2003); Ginsburg, *Measuring*, *supra* 240, at 53–54. By 2008, GOVERNANCE MATTERS VIII had data for 212 countries annually between 2002 and 2008. KAUFMANN ET AL., GOVERNANCE MATTERS VIII: AGGREGATE AND INDIVIDUAL GOVERNANCE INDICATORS, 1996–2008 2 (2009).

[245] May & Winchester, *supra* note 196, at 11, 13; James Podgers, *A Vienna Convergence: World Justice Forum Raises Rule of Law Issues*, 94 A.B.A. J. 63 (no. 8, Aug. 2008); World Justice Project, Home, https://worldjusticeproject.org (select About Us/Who We Are/Officers) [hereinafter WJP]; *see* MARK DAVID AGRAST ET AL., THE WORLD JUSTICE PROJECT RULE OF LAW INDEX: MEASURING ADHERENCE TO THE RULE OF LAW AROUND THE WORLD i, 24 (2008); Urueña, *Indicators*, *supra* note 197, at 80–97. Neukom was ABA president from 2007 to 2008 and made rule of law his central issue. James Podgers, *It's a Small World: Rule of Law Will Be the ABA's Focus over the Next Year*, 93 A.B.A. J. 62 (no. 10, Oct. 2007).

ensuring property, contract, and procedural rights as well as human rights; open government so that processes by which law is adopted, administered, and adjudicated are accessible, fair, and efficient; and accessible and impartial justice delivered by competent, ethical, and independent representatives who have adequate resources and reflect the makeup of their communities. The principles orient the surveys, which in 2021 included almost 140,000 households and more than 4,000 legal practitioners and experts to measure how they experience and perceive elements that make up rule of law.[246]

WJP organized the scores and rankings of the index around eight primary factors: constraints on government powers, absence of corruption, open government, fundamental rights, order and security, regulatory enforcement, civil justice, and criminal justice. Each of these factors had multiple indicators, so that a researcher could compare nations on specific legal dimensions. The fundamental rights factor was the one that most directly would take the overall index from a thin to a thicker rule of law, undercutting its universality but making it more interesting to social scientists and legal comparatists. Thus, its first indicator, equal treatment and absence of discrimination, preferred individuals to be free of public discrimination based on categories many nations did not recognize in law, or if they did, tended to ignore, such as religion, ethnicity, sexual orientation, or gender identity. Interestingly, WJP omitted democracy as an indicator of rule of law; the closest it came was under the factor open government and its third indicator, civic participation, which included freedoms of expression, assembly, and association, plus the right to petition government, but not a right to vote or participate in elections.[247]

A study of several rule of law measures, including those of the WGI and WJP, found that although they varied in their thickness, there was a high correlation among them as well as with a measure of corruption. This suggested that an underlying broader variable was responsible, such as impartial administration or degree of government corruption. It might well be that something distinctive in the historical evolution of Western constitutionalism gave rise to modern rule of law. Despite this historical and cultural connection, and consequent ethnocentric bias, Ginsburg argued that it was worthwhile to measure rule of law cross-nationally and longitudinally to ascertain its spread or regression.[248]

---

[246] WORLD JUSTICE PROJECT, RULE OF LAW INDEX 2021, at 9, 14–19 (2021); WJP, *supra* note 245 (select Our Work); *id.*, (select About Us/What Is the Rule of Law?). See Alyssa Dougherty, Amy Gryskiewicz, & Alejandro Ponce, *Measuring the Rule of Law: The World Justice Project's Rule of Law Index*, *in* PALGRAVE HANDBOOK, *supra* note 222, at 255–73; May & Winchester, *supra* note 196, at 14.

[247] WJP, *supra* note 245 (select About Us/What Is the Rule of Law?); *see* May & Winchester, *supra* note 196, at 12–15; Christopher May, *The Centrality of Predictability to the Rule of Law*, *in* RULE OF LAW HANDBOOK, *supra* note 196, at 96, 103–06.

[248] Ginsburg, *Measuring*, *supra* note 240, at 55; *see* Migai Akech, *Evaluating the Impact of Corruption Indicators on Governance Discourses in Kenya*, *in* QUIET POWER, *supra* note 197, at 248–54, 258–67;

More comparatists have recognized the importance of incorporating legal indicators into their work notwithstanding the World Bank's Ease of Doing Business Index debacle. The bank continues publishing its Worldwide Governance Indicators, which include information on government effectiveness, regulatory quality, rule of law, and degree of corruption, and many NGOs also publish reliable legal and social indicators.[249]

E. Challenges in the Twenty-First Century

1. Reassessment of Globalization and the Return to Nationalism

In 2018, Fukuyama published a revision of his *End of History* volume to reflect developments in the twenty-first century. He no longer thought of liberal democratic capitalism as inevitable; rather he saw a decline in the number of democracies, the rise of populist nationalism, and a shift from economic issues associated with improved equality or liberty toward identity politics and resentment.[250] Instead of aiming for universal recognition of human dignity, there were now partial forms of recognition based on nation, religion, race, ethnicity, or gender. "The rise of identity politics in modern liberal democracies is one of the chief threats that they face, and unless we can work our way back to more universal understandings of human dignity, we will doom ourselves to continuing conflict."[251]

By 2005, the number of democracies in all regions fell; income inequality increased in developed countries and social change disrupted many developing nations. At the same time, authoritarian countries, particularly China and Russia,

---

Mila Versteeg & Tom Ginsburg, *Measuring the Rule of Law: A Comparison of Indicators*, 42 LAW & SOCIAL INQUIRY 100–37 (2017); Robert P. Beschel, Jr., *Measuring Governance: Revisiting the Uses of Corruption and Transparency Indicators*, in PALGRAVE HANDBOOK, supra note 222, at 161–77. It was also possible that the usual measurement strategy relying on surveys and expert perceptions caused convergence among the indicators. Versteeg & Ginsburg, *supra*.

[249] See Ralf Michaels, *Comparative Law by Numbers? Legal Origins Thesis, Doing Business Reports, and the Silence of Traditional Comparative Law*, 57 AM. J. COMP. L. 765–96 (2009); Holger Spamann, *Large-Sample, Quantitative Research Designs for Comparative Law*, id. at 797–810; Curtis J. Milhaupt, *Beyond Legal Origin: Rethinking Law's Relationship to the Economy—Implications for Policy*, id. at 831–46; John Reitz, *Legal Origins, Comparative Law, and Political Economy*, id. at 847–62; see supra text accompanying note 220–222 (index irregularities).

[250] FRANCIS FUKUYAMA, IDENTITY: THE DEMAND FOR DIGNITY AND THE POLITICS OF RESENTMENT x–xiii, xv–xvi, 5–6 (2018) [hereinafter FUKUYAMA, IDENTITY]; see FUKUYAMA, LAST MAN, supra note 1. In 1970, there were 35 electoral democracies, which increased rapidly in the 1990s to more than 110 in 2005. FUKUYAMA, IDENTITY, supra, at xi, 3; see SAMUEL P. HUNTINGTON, THE THIRD WAVE: DEMOCRATIZATION IN THE LATE TWENTIETH CENTURY (1991).

[251] FUKUYAMA, IDENTITY, supra note 250, at xvi.

became more assertive. China began to promote its development model abroad while Russia attacked liberal decadence in the European Union (E.U.) and the United States. In 2016, elections in the United Kingdom to leave the European Union (Brexit) and in the United States for the populist Donald Trump as president confirmed the reality of spreading inward-focused nationalism. In both cases, voters were mainly concerned with economic inequality issues, principally affecting the working class subjected to years of job losses, stagnant wages, and deindustrialization. In addition, opposition to immigration took on a cultural dimension as supportive politicians accused migrants of taking jobs from native-born workers.[252]

The emergence of identity politics in the 1980s was a feature of cultural politics, where identity referred to social categories or groups based on nation, religion, race, ethnicity, gender, or sexual orientation. "Identity grows . . . out of a distinction between one's true inner self and an outer world of social rules and norms that does not adequately recognize that inner self's worth or dignity." With identity politics, society needed to change to conform with the inner self. The inner self of dignity sought public recognition. The economic inequalities worsening during the recent decades of globalization generated grievance, which then attached to feelings of disrespect and demands on the legal system to recognize marginalized groups as special.[253]

Another way to frame these developments was through the concept of multiculturalism, which recognized de facto cultural diversity in certain societies and was popular among some in the E.U. and North America.[254] As Fukuyama explained, multiculturalism also became a political label that sought to value each separate culture equally, especially those previously undervalued. Classical liberalism had protected the autonomy of equal individuals, while this new ideology promoted equal respect for cultures, even those that abridged the autonomy of its individual members. After 1990, progressive politicians tended to lose their interest in large-scale socioeconomic reforms to achieve equality and gradually shifted to identity politics. They left the working class and its trade unions

---

[252] *Id.* at 4–8, 74–90; KRASTEV & HOLMES, *supra* note 6, at 1–3; Nye, *American Hegemony, supra* note 206, at 67–68, 70–71, 76–78. For Eastern Europe, one could add the election of Viktor Orbán (prime minister, Hungary) in 2010 and the success of Jarosław Kaczyński's Law and Justice Party (Poland) in 2015 to illustrate citizen disappointment with Western democracy and rule of law and support for communitarian populism. KRASTEV & HOLMES, *supra*, at 13–14, 22, 40–47, 62–76.

[253] FUKUYAMA, IDENTITY, *supra* note 250, at 9–11, 59–73, 105–23 (quotation at 9–10). The German Basic Law prioritized human dignity. "(1) Human dignity shall be inviolable. To respect and protect it shall be the duty of all state authority. (2) The German people therefore acknowledge inviolable and inalienable human rights as the basis of every community, of peace and of justice in the world." Grundgesetz art. 1, at https://www.gesetze-im-internet.de (select Titelsuche, enter Basic Law).

[254] *See* Steven Dijkstra, Karin Geuijen, & Arie de Ruijter, *Multiculturalism and Social Integration in Europe*, 22 INT'L POL. SCI. REV. 55–83 (2001).

behind and embraced the psychological demands of marginalized groups such as immigrants, racial minorities, or women that they felt were worse off than workers and should have group rights. Finally, the preoccupation with identity clashed with a democracy's need for free speech and rational discourse. The focus on a group's so-called lived experience of their members' opinions of perceived authentic selves trumped reasoned deliberation. An argument offensive to someone's sense of self-worth was enough to delegitimize that argument.[255]

Within the E.U., populists in Eastern Europe directed their illiberalism less at multiculturalism than at supranational individualism, constitutional rights for all, and cosmopolitanism. Their supporters favored national identity, traditional values, and communitarianism so that the E.U. could not defeat populism by simply abandoning identity politics in the name of liberal individualism. The E.U.'s endorsement of global migration, especially from Africa and the Middle East, was a threat to white Christian populations. Leaders in Hungary and Poland demanded to control their own immigration policy, which they argued was necessary for the future for Europe.[256]

U.S. politics of multiculturalism and identity politics did not affect mainstream American comparative law as much as it influenced other fields of law. Most American comparatists continued to investigate foreign legal systems that they usually characterized as national in scope. Occasionally, someone wrote about legal pluralism, normally defined by ethnicity, linguistics, or religion, especially as such diversity existed in the nations of Africa or Latin America.[257] In addition, some comparatists called for attention to identity groups within a country, their differences rather than similarities, and in general, an approach of cultural immersion. A group's attitudes and values relevant to law and the legal system were significant.[258]

---

[255] FUKUYAMA, IDENTITY, *supra* note 250, at 111–17. Fukuyama believed the solution to this problem was not to abandon the idea of identity, but to define it as a larger and more integrative national identity that accommodated existing diversity in democracies and other regimes. *Id.* at 122–23; *see id.* at 124–62 (function of national identity and relationship to law in various countries). For the United States, Fukuyama suggested a national identity founded on substantive ideas such as constitutionalism, rule of law, and human equality. He rejected the victimization theme that racism, gender discrimination, and other systematic exclusion had been the dominant ideas in American history. *Id.* at 170–71, 182–83.

[256] KRASTEV & HOLMES, *supra* note 6, at 13–14, 40, 43–47; *see supra* note 252 (Hungary and Poland).

[257] *See, e.g.*, Jill E. Hickson, *Using Law to Create National Identity: The Course to Democracy in Tajikistan*, 38 TEX. INT'L L.J. 347–80 (2003); Natsu Taylor Saito, *Model Minority, Yellow Peril: Functions of Foreignness in the Construction of Asian American Legal Identity*, 4 Asian L.J. 71–96 (1997); Alemante G. Selassie, *Ethnic Identity and Constitutional Design for Africa*, 29 STAN. J. INT'L L. 1–56 (1992); Siems, *New Directions*, *supra* note 195, at 264–66; Walter O. Weyrauch, *Romaniya: An Introduction to Gypsy Law*, 45 AM. J. COMP. L. 225 (1997) (symposium with nine essays); *id.*, *The Romani People: A Long Surviving and Distinguished Culture at Risk*, 51 AM. J. COMP. L. 679–89 (2003).

[258] See text accompanying notes 66–68 (identity and cultural immersion). Identity groups formed their own law organizations. For instance, The Coalition of Bar Associations of Color (created in 1992) was comprised of the Hispanic National Bar Association, the National Bar Association

We earlier surveyed the tenacity of legal traditions, cultures, and pluralism.[259] Most legal comparatists in the United States looked outward and rejected nativism as destructive of the knowledge necessary to understand and appreciate the diversity of traditions, cultures, and legal systems that existed among the world's societies. Globalization promoted elements of universalism that advances in trade, technology, and information dissemination facilitated throughout societies, including in their legal systems. But globalization had its limits as people accessed its consequences on their own and their group's interests and values. Overreaching by one nation or alliance to coerce others to adopt the dominant system's institutions, rules, and values inevitably led to resentment that would undercut the former's mission.

2. Resistance from Islam

The Al Qaeda terrorist attack on the New York World Trade Center and the U.S. Pentagon building in Washington, D.C., on September 11, 2001 in the first year of George W. Bush's presidency set the stage for a broad policy retreat from globalization although the United States continued to aid nations amenable to democratic reform. Rather than treat the attack as a criminal matter, Bush declared it to be an act of war requiring a response, not against another nation, but against terrorism. To Muslims it appeared to be war with Afghanistan and its dominant political force. Like the Korean War and the Cold War, which were wars against communism, the United States and its allies portrayed the war against terrorism as a fight for the survival of civilization. Bush asserted greater executive war power and Congress passed legislation that granted the government broad authority to detain and deport non-citizens and expanded investigatory power for national officials and police. Faced with criticism for official abuse against its enemies and those who might thwart its mission, the United States retreated from asserted international regulation of its action. Domestically, the debate concerned the nature of constitutional limits on presidential authority.[260]

(predominantly African American), the National Native American Bar Association, and the National Asian Pacific American Bar Association.

[259] *See supra* pt. A.3 (traditions and cultures). *See also* WERNER MENSKI, COMPARATIVE LAW IN A GLOBAL CONTEXT: THE LEGAL SYSTEMS OF ASIA AND AFRICA (2d ed. 2006).

[260] Mary L. Dudziak, *Making Law, Making War, Making America*, in 3 THE CAMBRIDGE HISTORY OF LAW IN AMERICA: THE TWENTIETH CENTURY AND AFTER (1920-) 680, 713-17 (Michael Grossberg & Christopher Tomlins eds., 2008). In 2000, President Bill Clinton signed the 1998 Rome Statute that created the International Criminal Court to prosecute persons accused of serious international crimes, but declined to submit the treaty to the Senate for ratification. In 2002, Bush formally withdrew the U.S. signature to the statute and stated the government did not intend to ratify the treaty. Similarly, Clinton signed the Kyoto Protocol to reduce greenhouse gas emissions in 1998, but

If this action by the United States was not enough to provoke a sustained response from Muslim countries, the U.S. war with Iraq in 2003 over its supposed possession of weapons of mass destruction and the replacement of Saddam Hussein with a government dependent on the United States confirmed a continuing hostility from Islamic peoples. These incursions by the United States (and a few Western allies) into Afghanistan and Iraq and the continued presence of U.S. troops there in 2020 violated the first of three rules Huntington devised in 1996 to avoid global civilizational war. The "*abstention rule* that core states abstain from intervention in conflicts in other civilizations is the first requirement of peace in a multicivilizational, multipolar war." The other two requirements were the *joint mediation rule* that core states negotiate with each other and the *commonalities rule* supporting the search for common values and institutions among civilizations.[261]

The inattention to Huntington's rules allowed terrorism to mutate into the Islamic State (ISIS), which served as a magnet for illiberal and violent Islamists around the world.[262] From its rebranding in 2014, when it declared itself a worldwide caliphate, it asserted religious, political, and military authority over all Muslims. After occupying substantial territory in Iraq and Syria, the United States led a coalition to defeat ISIS as did Russia. By 2019, ISIS lost its last foothold in the Middle East.[263]

Was ISIS an inevitable unfolding of events in response to historical and renewed Western imperialism or perhaps due to political and cultural disruption associated with the forces of globalization? The election of Barack Obama as U.S. president (served 2009–2017) suggested not. In 2009, he called for an approach of mutual interest and respect for relations between the Muslim world and America and discontinued using the term War on Terror.[264] There followed from early 2011 through 2012 a series of protests and uprisings labeled the Arab Spring expressing discontent with political leaders, deposing four of them. Social media provided a means of communication among protesters, but authorities

---

Bush refused to submit the treaty to the Senate in 2001, a presidential position maintained through 2020. *Id.* at 690.

[261] HUNTINGTON, CLASH AND REMAKING, *supra* note 2, at 316, 320 (quotation at 316 with italics in original); *see supra* text accompanying notes 21–23 (commonalities and core nations). The United States withdrew its last troops from Afghanistan in 2021.

[262] FUKUYAMA, IDENTITY, *supra* note 250, at 5–6. The Islamic State was also known as the Islamic State of Iraq and Syria (ISIS), Islamic State of Iraq and the Levant (ISIL) and Daesh (its Arabic acronym).

[263] *See* HARORO J. INGRAM, CRAIG WHITESIDE, CHARLIE WINTER, THE ISIS READER: MILESTONE TEXTS OF THE ISLAMIC STATE MOVEMENT 1–3, 149–98, 279–302 (2020).

[264] John L. Esposito, *The Future of Islam and U.S.-Muslim Relations*, 126 POL. SCI. Q. 365–401 (2011).

and counter-demonstrators responded with violence and ultimately the hope for political and economic liberalization including rule of law ended with re-establishment of authoritarian governments.[265]

An alternative explanation looked to internal dynamics within Islam itself that formed the Umayyad rulers' quest for caliphate dating from the seventh century. Their empire favored Arabic-speaking peoples; they expected others to pay taxes and did not encourage them to become Muslims. This view considered the Middle East's millenarian imperial tradition to be the result of indigenous passions and behavior. External influences exerted only a secondary role in the region's volatility and political development. Consequently, contemporary Arab anti-Americanism was not primarily due to U.S. Middle Eastern policy, but rather to the dominant position of the United States that would thwart the millenarian *jihad* for a universal Islamic empire (*umma*).[266]

Traditionally, the sacred law of *shari'a* occupied a central role in the Islamic world, more important than theology. However, after World War I, Western-style legislation largely displaced Islamic law except for family and inheritance matters. That Western influence changed with the Iranian Revolution in 1979, when rebels called for rule of Islamic jurists. Islamic law and government experienced a renaissance across Shi'a countries for constitutional, banking, and economic law and by the early twenty-first century, *shari'a* was central in Muslim-majority countries, both Shi'a and Sunni. Consequently, comparative law now served the function of examining legislation for its compliance with *shari'a* for all fields of law. Considering the history of Islamic civilization, this comparison required a cultural lens including religion, literature, and science.[267]

The reality has been that most Islamic countries, especially in North Africa and the Middle East, have not been democratic, adopted constitutional rule of law, or protected minority rights. Courts in general were not independent of political authority and constitutional review tended to be meaningless. Even if a significant percentage of citizens admired some Western democratic values, they also believed their own religion and values were essential to progress. *Shari'a* should serve as a source of law and moral compass, although most would not want it to be the sole source of law in a theocracy. Women's rights have been quite limited while some elements support honor killings and death to apostates.

---

[265] *See* NIMER SULTANY, LAW AND REVOLUTION: LEGITIMACY AND CONSTITUTIONALISM AFTER THE ARAB SPRING 97–128 (2017).

[266] EFRAIM KARSH, ISLAMIC IMPERIALISM: A HISTORY 2–8 (2006); *see id.* at 21–39, 207–28; MENSKI, supra note 259, at 303–09. Karsh compared the Islamic experience with that of Christianity. "If Christendom was slower than Islam in marrying religious universalism with political imperialism, it was faster in shedding both notions. By the eighteenth century the West had lost its religious messianism. . . . [I]t had lost its imperial ambitions by the mid-twentieth century. Islam has retained its imperialist ambition to this day." KARSH, supra, at 6.

[267] Chibli Mallat, *Comparative Law and Islamic (Middle Eastern) Legal Culture, in* OXFORD HANDBOOK, *supra* note 27, at 624–27.

Many Muslims resent Western interference in their countries' internal affairs and frequent support for authoritarian rulers.[268]

Islam prescribes rules for the organization of political society as well as rules for religious practice and social interaction. This characteristic is unique among major legal traditions; furthermore, some Muslim nations have constitutions that make *shari'a* the main source for legislation, while other legal rules should not violate *shari'a*. *Shari'a* law is public, prospective, stable over time, and binds rulers as well as the ruled. Although these formal elements for rule of law exist, *shari'a* does not treat all persons equally, particularly women or non-believers. Because *shari'a* is God's immutable divine law, contrasted with *fiqh* or scholarly interpretations, the incompatibility of Islam with all but the thinnest formal version of rule of law appears inevitable.[269]

In addition, there are certain cultural features in Islam, not central to rule of law, that would make its implementation difficult. First, *umma* requires Muslims to partake in a homogeneous union in which community interests can take precedence over individual rights. The state might need to sacrifice certain persons to benefit the larger group. The *Qur'an* condemns separation from *umma* as an apostasy, sanctionable by death. Second, *hakimiyyatu* makes God sovereign, so that rule of God is superior to rule by human law. Third, the premise of nation states in which the rule of law occurs is contrary to the issuance of *fatwas*. Declared by Islamic experts, some Muslims believe it is their duty to privately enforce such judgments wherever an offender is located, regardless of geographical borders, based on religious brotherhood.[270]

Resistance to the rule of law varied depending on the degree of authority from Islam in politics. One could create an index of influence and measure it based on the share of Muslims in a national population, whether Islam was the official state religion, and whether the country was a member of the Organisation of Islamic Cooperation. Using these factors, nations such as Afghanistan, Algeria, Iran, Pakistan, and Saudi Arabia ranked high while Uzbekistan and Turkey ranked lower. Using this approach, and disaggregating rule of law into its components, one study found that the degree of Islamic influence correlated significantly with fewer rights for women and less independent judges. Alternatively, there was no significant correlation with protection of property rights or the extent of parliamentary power.[271]

---

[268] Esposito, *supra* note 264, at 371–75, 380–81, 393–97; Jerg Gutmann & Stefan Voigt, *The Rule of Law and Islam*, in RULE OF LAW HANDBOOK, *supra* note 196, at 345; Mallat, *supra* note 267, at 632–36, 645–50.

[269] Gutmann & Voigt, *supra* note 268, at 348–50.

[270] *Id.* at 350–53, 355.

[271] *Id.* at 353–55; *see id.*, *The Rule of Law and Constitutionalism in Muslim Countries*, 162 PUBLIC CHOICE 351–80 (2015); MENSKI, *supra* note 259, at 354–64 (Turkey), 364–79 (Pakistan).

Ultimately, a more liberal Islam would need to accept the reality of a secular state and religious tolerance as the better path forward for economic welfare and peaceful coexistence. State nationalism, not pan-Islamic imperialist dreams, would make Islam a matter of private faith rather than an instrument of political ambition.[272] For Islamic law, which jurists consider a personal rather than territorial system, this represents a substantial challenge.[273]

3. The Importance of China

China reintroduced legality as a core governance tool in the late 1970s. Its interest in rule of law extended to commercial matters—sending a signal to investors that legal rules and institutions would protect them—but not to political affairs. Some reformers hoped that this would create a virtuous circle of legal reform in other private law areas and perhaps in some public law such as criminal justice. This in fact occurred, but when Xi Jinping became general secretary of the Chinese Communist Party (CCP) in 2012, it was clear that the policy had shifted away from Western legal transplants and authoritarian legality and was accelerating toward nationalism, anti-corruption, and mediation all directed toward CCP control and social stability.[274]

Comparative law study was part of the transplantation of foreign legal rules and institutions after Mao Zedong's death in 1976 as a feature of the return to legality. Most law professors who survived the Cultural Revolution had specialized in German and Japanese law; once they renewed their contacts abroad, they regained influence and promoted a civil law system. Nevertheless, the prestige of American business and culture fostered interest in U.S. legal rules for commercial and financial law as well as for intellectual property and environmental law and made American legal transplants dominant. This led Chinese graduate students to choose U.S. universities for all academic disciplines including law, although Germany was second in desirability. Those in law who returned to China could parlay the institutional prestige of their degrees into high-level positions at academic centers and in the legal profession.[275]

---

[272] Karsh, *supra* note 266, at 234.
[273] Mallat, *supra* note 267, at 627–28, 638–42.
[274] Thomas E. Kellogg, *Rule of Law in Asia: The Case of China*, in RULE OF LAW HANDBOOK, *supra* note 196, at 490–94, 508; Carl F. Minzner, *China's Turn against Law*, 59 AM. J. COMP. L. 935–40 (2011). In 2012, the CCP Central Committee also selected Xi chairman of the Central Military Commission and the next year, the National People's Congress elected him PRC president. Elizabeth C. Economy, *China's New Revolution: The Reign of Xi Jinping*, 97 FOREIGN AFF. 60–62 (no. 3, 2018).
[275] Taisu Zhang, *The Development of Comparative Law in Modern China*, in OXFORD HANDBOOK, *supra* note 27, at 228–29, 244–46; *see* MENSKI, *supra* note 259, at 493–95, 564–66, 579–81, 584–85. German legal doctrine and rules and its emphasis on consistency were dominant for criminal law,

For most jurists, meaningful rule of law required a legal profession autonomous from the state and a judiciary independent from political authorities for decision of individual cases. Since the revival of a Chinese legal profession in 1979, lawyers have faced harassment and intimidation from the state, typically from the police, the procuracy, or the courts. By 2000, the Chinese bar transitioned from a public profession to a nearly private profession. To succeed in this new status, lawyers needed connections (*guanxi*) with public officials and state organizations, a situation of political embeddedness. Although this situation existed in other countries, *guanxi* was more important in China since the judiciary remained subordinate to the government bureaucracy and lawyers faced institutional discrimination that relegated them to a marginal status as outsiders.[276]

The swing away from foreign legal transplants and toward the idea that China needed to find its own path using local resources embedded in Chinese culture occurred prior to 2010. Those Chinese jurists trained in the United States had some exposure to law and society scholarship and to legal realism, which supported this shift. They emphasized national sovereignty and rejected the universality of human rights. Peking University led the way toward acceptance of Chinese cultural and political exceptionalism. The CCP found this development and the weakening of rule of law efforts attractive.[277]

China was important to the theme of rule of law and its purported universality fostered by globalization precisely because it succeeded economically without compliance to the rule's norms.[278] In 2017, Xi called on other nations to draw on Chinese wisdom for their own economic and political development. As the world's second largest economy and largest exporter, it had the financial ability to influence developing countries as a counterweight to Europe and North America, illustrated by the Belt and Road Initiative. Xi's approach has been to strengthen state-owned enterprises for economic development campaigns and to empower the CCP within each firm. Furthermore, the CCP applied similar oversight in joint ventures with multinational corporations and even such private companies such as Alibaba and Tencent.[279]

---

contracts, and torts. For business and financial law, American social science and normative methods held sway. Zhang, *supra*, at 246–47.

[276] Ethan Michelson, *Lawyers, Political Embeddedness, and Institutional Continuity in China's Transition from Socialism*, in LAWYERS AND GLOBALIZATION, *supra* note 161, at 39–46, 50–58; *see supra* notes 202–203 and accompanying text (lawyers in China).

[277] MENSKI, *supra* note 259, at 589–93; Zhang, *supra* note 275, at 246–50.

[278] Kwai Hang Ng, *Is China a Rule-by-Law Regime?*, 67 BUFFALO L. REV. 793–821 (2019); Randall Peerenboom, *Law and Development of Constitutional Democracy in China: Problem or Paradigm*, 19 COLUM. J. ASIAN L. 185–89, 229–34 (2005).

[279] Economy, *supra* note 274, at 60, 64–65, 68–69, 74; Nye, *American Hegemony*, *supra* note 206, at 73.

Under Xi's direction, the CCP has used constitutionalist rhetoric to strengthen political legitimacy rather than as a guide to bolster independent legal institutions needed for rule of law. In general, constitutions in authoritarian states, rather than guarantee rule of law, served to aid rulers with one or more functions beyond legitimacy: operating manual, billboard, blueprint, or window dressing. In China, the CCP made generous use of the billboard function from the 1954 Constitution forward. The PRC's 1982 Constitution and subsequent amendments allowed market reforms with rule of law rhetoric that signaled both the Chinese public and the international community that post-Mao leadership was serious about economic and legal reform. The Constitution's chapter II—fundamental rights and duties of citizens—illustrated window dressing since the rights were not legally enforceable and were in practice commonly violated. Finally, Chinese leaders have used their constitutions to legitimize CCP rule with the fiction that the state was transitioning toward constitutional governance.[280]

Unlike the United States and European Union countries, China has not been interested in the export of legal transplants. The PRC expanded its global influence without programs to transform other societies, including their legal systems, in which it operated. Chinese leaders wanted foreign countries to admire and respect China; they used Confucius Institutes as education centers to promote Chinese language and culture, an approach earlier initiated by several European countries. Xi apparently saw global competition with the United States through military and strategic measures, without regard to ideology or a vision of mankind's shared future. There has been resentment of Chinese assertiveness, such as building islands in disputed seas or onerous lending practices, but the PRC did not further inflame animosity with American-style moralistic lecturing. Chinese loans came with no ideological strings; there were no lessons on human rights, transparency, or rule of law; China did not seek converts to Chinese civilization.[281]

---

[280] Kellogg, *supra* note 274, at 494–500; KRASTEV & HOLMES, supra note 6, at 193–97; Han Liu, *Regime-Centered and Court-Centered Understandings: The Reception of American Constitutional Law in Contemporary China*, 68 AM. J. COMP. L. 95, 141–42, 148–50 (2020); *see* CONSTITUTIONS IN AUTHORITARIAN REGIMES (Tom Ginsburg & Alberto Simpser eds., 2014). Article 51 of the 1982 Constitution, as amended in 2004, states: "Citizens of the People's Republic of China, in exercising their freedoms and rights, may not infringe upon the interests of the State, of society or of the collective." National People's Congress of the PRC, *Home*, http://www.npc.gov.cn (select English, then Constitution). Some comparatists have argued that the PRC Constitution served an increasingly significant role through legislative interpretation within a party-state. Kellogg, *supra*, at 503–07; *see* Yan Lin & Tom Ginsburg, *Constitutional Interpretation in Lawmaking: China's Invisible Constitutional Enforcement Mechanism*, 63 AM. J. COMP. L. 467–92 (2015).

[281] KRASTEV & HOLMES, *supra* note 6, at 202–04. The United States military financed several Amerika Häuser in Germany and Austria after World War II to educate their citizens about American culture and politics. The U.S. Information Agency took over control after the end of military occupation until the U.S. government terminated the Houses beginning in the 1990s. Amerikahaus, *Our History*, https://www.amerikahaus.de/en/about-us/history.

F. An Interdisciplinary Empirical Comparative Law

Since 1990, there has been a growing use of quantitative methods and interdisciplinarity in comparative law, both in the United States and abroad. Teams have worked to integrate the methods of economics, political science, sociology, or anthropology into comparative studies of legal rules, professionals, their education and roles, institutions, and processes that earlier jurists would have carried out alone.[282] Could this improve the possibility of accumulating knowledge about legal systems? Here, I do not suggest simply more information about diverse legal systems and cultures. There has been an immense generation of information about the world's legal systems since World War II.[283] Rather I refer to building a set of propositions about parts of legal systems, their internal relationships, and their connection to social variables that scholars have identified, defined, operationalized, tested with hypotheses, and found to be valid and reliable.[284]

Quantitative comparative law faced issues avoided by other comparative law methods since, unlike economics that had money as a measurement tool, most law was qualitative and legal rules generally were normative. Nevertheless, one could define and count many legal processes such as legislative acts, executive orders, police arrests, or court cases. In addition, legal professionals exist for a variety of roles and one could count their number and interrelationship. Organizing these types of data over time and across jurisdictions provided another dimension to comparative law.[285]

Mathias Siems identified three types of what he called numerical comparative law. First, *counting facts about law* included, to illustrate, studies of how often one court cites another, the number of statutes in a jurisdiction or field of law, or the duration of court cases. Second, *coding law* translated the form and substance of legal rules into numbers. For instance, one might code countries that had the death penalty as 1 and those that did not as 0. Or one might use interval numbers

---

[282] Siems, *New Directions, supra* note 195, at 853–55, 858, 860; *see* Annelise Riles, *From Comparison to Collaboration: Experiments with a New Scholarly and Political Reform*, 78 LAW & CONTEMP. PROBS. 147–83 (2015); Francesco Parisi & Barbara Luppi, *Comparative Law and Economics: Accounting for Social Norms, in* COMPARATIVE LAW AND SOCIETY 92–104 (David S. Clark ed., 2012).

[283] Mathias Reimann, *The Progress or Failure of Comparative Law in the Second Half of the Twentieth Century*, 50 AM. J. COMP. L. 671, 673–85 (2002).

[284] *Id.* at 685–90, 695–99; *see, e.g.*, Katherine Y. Barnes, *Prediction Studies, in* 3 ENCYCLOPEDIA OF LAW AND SOCIETY: AMERICAN AND GLOBAL PERSPECTIVES 1171–72 (David S. Clark ed., 2007); *id.*, *Databases, in* 1 *id.* at 387–88; Günther Chaloupek, *Reliability and Validity, in* 3 *id.* at 1295–96; Jonathan Klick, *Empirical Research Strategies, in* 1 *id.*, at 478–80; *id.*, *Multivariate Analysis, in* 2 *id.* at 1047–48.

[285] *See, e.g.*, Christopher Slobogin, *Comparative Empiricism and Police Investigative Practices*, 37 N.C.J. INT'L L. & COM. REG. 321–48 (2011); *supra* notes 248–249 and accompanying text (quantitative methods); ch. 7, text accompanying note 330 (SLADE project).

such as 0 to 5 assigned by the extent of the punishment's use. One could then use such categorical information to investigate the death penalty's effectiveness on crime deterrence. Ginsburg and colleagues employed coding for the study of constitutions worldwide going back to 1789.[286] Third, *conducting surveys about law* allowed researchers to count responses to questionnaires yielding a numeric value. A common ordinal variable was a five-point scale from strongly agree to strongly disagree, resulting in an average score for that question. For example, one might ask a category of persons whether they believed their country's law was business friendly.[287]

There was also much more interdisciplinary research in comparative law during this period.[288] This involved broadening the scope of comparative law and utilizing the power of comparative methods in fields such as legal history, sociology, cultural studies, and literature.[289] As we earlier saw, comparative constitutional law and constitutionalism was possibly the most vibrant comparative law subject for the twenty-first century. Much of it was interdisciplinary—law and political science—and some was quantitative. Many of the books, symposia published in journals, and projects had multinational teams. The results could be descriptive, explanatory, or normative.[290]

As already discussed, another characteristic feature of comparative law since 1990 had been the use of legal indicators in research involving many countries. This combined interdisciplinarity with empirical methods typically involving quantification.[291] These large-N studies often drew upon multivariate statistical analyses to ascertain correlations among selected variables; they could be cross-national or longitudinal. Scholars were interested in assessing variation and change and sometimes explaining legal cause and social effect or vice versa. For many issues in comparative constitutional law, the concept of legal traditions or families was not helpful; more useful was the idea of cross-jurisdictional pollination or transplant for matters such as constitutional structure, interpretive techniques, or citation practice.[292]

---

[286] Siems, *New Directions, supra* note 195, at 859–60; *see* MATHIAS SIEMS, COMPARATIVE LAW 180–228 (2d ed. 2018); *supra* note 194 and accompanying text (Comparative Constitutions Project).

[287] Siems, *New Directions, supra* note 195, at 860; *see supra* text accompanying notes 220–22 (World Bank's *Doing Business* reports).

[288] Siems, *New Directions, supra* note 195, at 860–63, 870–72; *see* COMPARATIVE LAW AND SOCIETY, *supra* note 282.

[289] Mathias Siems, *The Power of Comparative Law: What Types of Units Can Comparative Law Compare?*, 67 AM. J. COMP. L. 861–63, 866–71 (2019).

[290] Ran Hirschl, *Comparative Methodologies, in* CAMBRIDGE COMPANION, *supra* note 189, at 11–39 [hereinafter Hirschl, *Methodologies*]; *see* Hirschl, COMPARATIVE MATTERS, *supra* note 190, at 224–81; *supra* pt. C.3 (comparative constitutional law).

[291] Siems, *New Directions, supra* note 195, at 872–73; *see* supra pt. D.3 and text accompanying notes 163, 168, 220–22, 233 (legal indicators).

[292] Hirschl, *Methodologies, supra* note 290, at 19–22.

For causal inference, explanation, and theory testing in comparative constitutional law, methodology and research design were central to success and case selection might be single case, small-N, or large-N depending on a study's aim and the availability of reliable data. Comparative political scientists have had the most experience with this type of research and comparative lawyers either have a background in that specialty or team up with political scientists. While comparatists have published only a small number of large-N constitutional studies, the availability of comprehensive databases and useful information technology promises to expand them in future decades. Ginsburg, Mila Versteeg, and others conducted large-N research to assess the global decline of American constitutional influence, determine why countries adopt constitutional review, and explain various patterns in judicial activity such as foreign case citation, the spread of economic and social rights, and the effectiveness of constitutional amendment. Of course, there are limits to this type of research, which single case and small-N cultural and contextual examination of constitutions and their processes could remedy.[293]

Marcelo Bergman, who received support from the Ford and Hewlett Foundations, illustrated small-N comparative research that used indicators from law and political science to test empirically the issue of citizen compliance as an aspect of rule of law.[294] By selecting Argentina and Chile to compare within the same Latin American civilization (in Huntington's sense), he avoided confounding variables present in multi-civilizational studies. Bergman considered the impact of institutional tax structures and enforcement processes on compliance in the two countries versus the cultural effect of peer social pressure or sharing information about fairness, which increased the collective level of obedience. For the former, he employed a natural longitudinal experiment with tax return data measuring taxpayer response in the face of tax auditing and punishment on subsequent behavior. For the latter, he utilized taxpayer surveys to assess attitudes toward compliance. In Argentina, with a culture of noncompliance, there were more cheaters who wanted to avoid being suckers compared to the more generalized compliance environment in Chile. For tax law, both enforcement and perceived fairness were important to achieving a positive equilibrium for revenue that would permit a state to continue economic and political development.[295]

The Bergman study demonstrated the role of culture—the effect of peer social pressure—in understanding differences between national legal systems.

---

[293] *Id.* at 26–37; *see supra* notes 187–94, 248 (research in comparative constitutional law).
[294] MARCELO BERGMAN, TAX EVASION AND THE RULE OF LAW IN LATIN AMERICA: THE POLITICAL CULTURE OF CHEATING AND COMPLIANCE IN ARGENTINA AND CHILE xii (2009).
[295] *Id.* at 1–49, 202–09; *see id.* at 238–45 (the state, law, and the rule of law in Latin America).

Interdisciplinarity comes naturally to this perspective, but beyond thick description of values and attitudes, legal culture is also susceptible to quantification with surveys and indirect measurements associated with content analysis or other methods. Although some globalists saw culture as an impediment to their normative aims—universal human rights or uniform trade law—comparatists in general understood that culture was the construct that humans use to derive meaning out of their circumstances. Culture might change slowly as circumstances dictate and it can vary among and within societies according to groupings such as ethnicity, religion, race, gender, age, social class, and geography. However, one cannot disentangle culture from law. Consequently, comparatists should be amenable to accept and analyze legal culture at different levels of generality—social, local, or national.[296]

Some anthropologists, such as Lawrence Rosen, with an interest in comparison argued that it was possible to identify common conceptual problems across cultures. Separate cultures address certain problems or situations differently, but the similarity of the problems can allow generalization. For instance, law usually encompasses a continuum of formal and informal structures such that one cannot understand the former without considering a range of social control practices. Culture represents a certain balance between the order law requires and the flexibility that life needs to fashion an acceptable society. Furthermore, law creates legal concepts and facts differently in distinct cultures so that their definition varies. Dispute resolution systems and evidentiary rules, for example, reflect and reinforce cultural assumptions.[297]

Legal culture remains a contested concept that has many meanings. Comparatists have used it for a single country (Japan), often implicitly comparing the situation in the author's country, for regional studies (Latin America), or for comparing a small number of countries.[298] Culture is the variable between belief and reality or action. Reform actors such as the World Bank accept that they should adapt their legal projects to a specific target culture or they will fail. Alternatively, an actor may attempt to change a prevailing legal culture, which then would be the object of reform. Since causality typically runs in both directions, measurement is very difficult. For instance, are legal rules and

---

[296] Paul Schiff Berman, *Book Review*, 57 AM. J. COMP. L. 249–52 (2009) (reviewing LAWRENCE ROSEN, LAW AS CULTURE: AN INVITATION (2006) and OSCAR G. CHASE, LAW, CULTURE, AND RITUAL: DISPUTING SYSTEMS IN CROSS-CULTURAL CONTEXT (2005)); *see* COMPARATIVE LAW AND ANTHROPOLOGY (James A.R. Nafziger ed., 2017); *supra* pt. A.3 (cultures and legal pluralism).

[297] Berman, *supra* note 296, at 252–55.

[298] *See, e.g.,* Tom Ginsburg & Glenn Hoetker, *The Unreluctant Litigant? An Empirical Analysis of Japan's Turn to Litigation, in* EMERGING CONCEPTS OF RIGHTS IN JAPANESE LAW 93–118 (Harry N. Scheiber & Laurent Mayali eds., 2007); Rogelio Pérez-Perdomo & Lawrence Friedman, *Latin Legal Cultures in the Age of Globalization, in* AGE OF GLOBALIZATION, *supra* note 57, at 1–19. *See also* COMPARING LEGAL CULTURES (David Nelken ed., 1997).

institutions ineffective because people distrust the courts, or do people distrust the courts because the rules and institutions are defective?[299]

Anthropology, political science, and sociology have dealt with culture in different ways that have informed comparative investigation of the role for beliefs, values, and attitudes about law and legal institutions in different societies. The latter two disciplines more often treat legal culture as a variable to explain how and why legal systems change or whether they might accept a legal transplant. This explanatory approach can be amenable to quantification. Alternatively, an interpretative approach to culture often is holistic, a thick description aimed at understanding difference. Using the two approaches to complement each other would be ideal.[300]

Although psychologists have investigated culture comparatively, few legal scholars have utilized their results. Beginning in the late 1960s, Geert Hofstede conducted an ambitious attitude survey of IBM employee values in 72 countries involving 116,000 respondents. After subsequent cross-national studies added to his database, he chose factor analysis to conclude that national societies differed on four cultural dimensions. In 1991, he supplemented those dimensions with a fifth one, and a colleague later brought in a sixth dimension.[301]

Hofstede's first dimension was *power distance*, examining how institutions in a society deal with inequality among its members. Institutions could include the family, schools, the workplace, religion, and politics. For each dimension, Hofstede calculated an index based on answers to survey questions that yielded a ranking from high to low.

Where the strength of social hierarchies was high, less powerful persons—in terms of status, wealth, or education—accepted authority, their place in society, and inequality. Where low, institutions shared power and were relatively egalitarian.[302]

The second dimension was *uncertainty avoidance*. Where high, people valued the authority of legal and informal rules, religion, ritual, and security over conflict. Structure and predictability were important. Where the index was low, people tolerated ambiguity and unorthodox behavior and ideas. The

---

[299] David Nelken, *Legal Cultures*, in COMPARATIVE LAW AND SOCIETY, *supra* note 282, at 310–14, 318–19. Another illustration about causality: Will the introduction of a new contract law fail to achieve its purpose because the business community prefers informal deals with family and friends, or does the preference for informal deals exist only because the legislature has not enacted an efficient contract law? *Id.* at 310.

[300] *Id.* at 312, 314, 317–23.

[301] Dave van Toor, *Case Selection in Comparative Law Based on Hofstede's Cultural Psychology Theory*, LAW AND METHOD n.p. (Oct. 2017), http://www.lawandmethod.nl (search van Toor); *see* Ruth Horry et al., *Comparative Legal Psychology: Eyewitness Identification*, *in* COMPARATIVE LAW AND SOCIETY, *supra* note 282, at 133–35, 153.

[302] GEERT HOFSTEDE, CULTURE'S CONSEQUENCES: COMPARING VALUES, BEHAVIORS, INSTITUTIONS, AND ORGANIZATIONS ACROSS NATIONS 79–143 (2d ed. 2001).

third dimension was *individualism versus collectivism*. It measured the degree to which people integrated into groups such that "we" was more relevant than "I." High, in this case, referred to individualism in the context where social groups were transitory and society expected people primarily to take care of themselves and their immediate families. Where the index was low, collectivism anticipated that people depended on their extended family and stable groups to which they owed loyalty and support, especially in conflict with other groups.[303]

The fourth dimension, today politically incorrect in the United States, was *masculinity versus femininity*. Societies that emphasized competition, assertiveness, and material rewards scored high and belonged in the first category—here renamed *competition*—and societies that favored consensus, cooperation, modesty, and care for the weak scored low and were in the second category, here *cooperation*. The fifth dimension reflected the degree to which people focused on the future compared to the present or past. With *long-term versus short-term orientation*, future-looking cultures valued persistence, thrift, and adaptability. Alternatively, cultures at the other end of the spectrum valued traditions and distrusted social change. Finally, the sixth dimension was *indulgence versus restraint*, with the former societies allowing liberal gratification of human desires while the latter suppressed gratification with social and legal norms.[304]

For comparative law, Hofstede's cultural dimensions provided a viable method to select countries in which to examine differences or similarities in their legal rules and institutions. For this case selection, countries' cultures would be the independent variable and might be similar or dissimilar along one dimension or another. The researcher would formulate a hypothesis about some legal element, the dependent variable, conceptually common among the nations to investigate. For instance, one might expect legal rules protecting privacy to be stronger in countries high on the individualism index than in collectivist countries. If this were not so, or if one found an outlier case, the data would challenge the comparatist to explain her findings. Was privacy as liberty or privacy as dignity dominant? Or, one might expect a high rule of law index to be inversely related to power distance ranks. Or, a high consensus rank should be correlated with greater parental leave laws.[305]

Hofstede's team demonstrated this approach with World Bank legal system data from 67 countries. The bank collected information about the average time required to collect on a bounced check or to evict a tenant for nonpayment of rent, which varied for the jurisdictions from 40 days to three years. These data

---

[303] *Id.* at 145–278.

[304] *Id.* at 279–372; Geert Hofstede, Gert Jan Hofstede, & Michael Minkov, Cultures and Organizations: Software of the Mind, Intercultural Cooperation and Its Importance for Survival 277-98 (3d ed. 2010).

[305] Van Toor, *supra* note 301.

were significantly correlated with the uncertainty avoidance index, but not with any other cultural index or with per capita GDP. Those countries high on the uncertainty avoidance index had more explicit legal rules on these issues, but it was harder for citizens to enforce the rules, which lengthened average duration.[306]

Taking cultural dimension data for 50 countries, Israeli researchers generated testable hypotheses about three elements of good governance: rule of law, low level of corruption, and democratic accountability. Social scientists other than Hofstede have developed dichotomies for describing national cultures. Selecting three opposites, the scholars tested their general hypothesis that political modes of wielding power were consistent with prevailing cultural orientations in a society. Consequently, cultures that emphasized individualism were more likely to develop norms that promoted societal transparency as a means for social coordination thereby facilitating independent action. Alternatively, cultures in which hierarchically organized groups embedded individuals within the community discouraged such action as inconsistent with social values. Leaders exercised power from the top for social coordination that compromised legal entitlements such as property and contract rights. Naturally, the former cultures were more likely to generate the rule of law, as were those that demonstrated egalitarianism and mastery (assertiveness).[307] These findings would not surprise comparatists who have worked in diverse cultural regions. However, the recommendation that rule of law, anti-corruption, and democracy advocates should in general focus on gradually changing a nation's culture rather than directly promoting reforms in legal institutions and norms might surprise some.[308]

A refinement in the cultural approach to examine legal diversity and change in numerous target countries involved combining a longitudinal component to the cross-national one. This might yield an improved theory of modernization and should lead to greater understanding of cultural variety as well as the way legal elements function in society over time. One study found that economic development and generational replacement could affect cultural change, for instance, by increased individualism, which might alter a nation's receptibility to importing certain legal rules and institutions.[309] It made extensive use of the World Values Survey, a project that Ronald Inglehart at the University of Michigan led from

---

[306] HOFSTEDE ET AL., *supra* note 304, at 216–17.

[307] Amir N. Licht, Chanan Goldschmidt, & Shalom H. Schwartz, *Culture Rules: The Foundations of the Rule of Law and Other Norms of Governance*, 35 J. COMP. ECON. 659–64, 669–72 (2007); *see* SUSAN ROSE-ACKERMAN, CORRUPTION AND GOVERNMENT: CAUSES, CONSEQUENCES, AND REFORM (1999). The researchers, using the World Bank's governance indicators, also demonstrated the relevance of their three cultural poles for degree of corruption and democratic accountability. They recognized that economic factors, history, and legal institutions influenced governance as well. Licht et al., *supra*, at 662, 664–68.

[308] Licht et al., *supra* note 307, at 681–82; *see* HOFSTEDE ET AL., *supra* note 304, at 221–23.

[309] *See* Sjoerd Beugelsdijk & Chris Welzel, *Dimensions and Dynamics of National Culture: Synthesizing Hofstede with Inglehart*, 49 J. CROSS-CULTURAL PSYCHOL. 1469–1505 (2018).

the early 1980s to test hypotheses that socioeconomic and technological change transformed a society's values, including those concerning rule of law and individual autonomy.[310]

Improved information technology and electronic data processing offer future legal comparatists opportunities to vastly expand the comparative law discipline both in membership and in research methods. Comparative law activity has always been significant in the United States, a consequence of the diversity of its citizenry; the country's decentralized political and legal system; the emphasis placed on lawyers, legal rules, institutions, and processes; and the role for the nation in the world. American jurists from the eighteenth century looked to Europe for ideas about law, in the latter nineteenth century turned inward toward its own legal history, and in the twentieth century began also to export their own notions of law and legal institutions. The history of American comparative law has seen periods of shared ideas about law and periods of nativism and perceived exceptionalism in law. Comparatists can put the ebb and flow of legal history in perspective.

---

[310] World Values Survey Association, *Home*, https://www.worldvaluessurvey.org; see JAMES MICHEL, THE RULE OF LAW AND SUSTAINABLE DEVELOPMENT (2020); RONALD INGLEHART & CHRISTIAN WELZEL, MODERNIZATION, CULTURAL CHANGE, AND DEMOCRACY: THE HUMAN DEVELOPMENT SEQUENCE (2005).

Index

For the benefit of digital users, indexed terms that span two pages (e.g., 52–53) may, on occasion, appear on only one of those pages.
Tables and figures are indicated by t and f following the page number.

AACSL. *See* American Association for the Comparative Study of Law; American Society of Comparative Law
AALL (American Association of Law Libraries), 429–30
AALS. *See* Association of American Law Schools
AASS (American Anti-Slavery Society), 218–19
ABA. *See* American Bar Association; Comparative Law Bureau
ABA Journal, 286, 297
Abbott, Nathan, 238, 289
Abortion and Divorce in Western Law (Glendon), 448–49
abstention rule, 512
academic comparative law, 9–10. *See also* American Association for the Comparative Study of Law; American Society of Comparative Law; legal science
 comparative law courses and institutes, 402–4
 comparative law journals and projects, 415–17
 constitutional and judicial globalization, 489–94
 degree programs for foreign students, 417–18
 in early twentieth century, 284–86
 general comparative law coursebooks, 404–8
 global law schools, 479–84
 initial reaction to accelerated globalization, 456–61
 interdisciplinary empirical comparative law, 518–25
 law and development programs, 484–89
 re-establishing in postwar twentieth century, 379–84
 specialized comparative law coursebooks, 408–15
 teaching Roman law as substitute for, 251–54
 themes in postwar twentieth century research, 428–49

academic law libraries, 186, 244, 316–20, 318t, 319t
Académie des Sciences Morales et Politiques (France), 181–82, 201n.293
Academy and College of Philadelphia, 115n.147
ACC (Allied Control Council), 364
Acheson, Dean, 351–52, 367–68n.74
ACLS (American Council of Learned Societies), 391n.172, 400, 469
ACLU (American Civil Liberties Union), 396
Act concerning Religion (colonial Maryland), 61
actions, law of, 167
activist state ideology, 447–48
Act of Toleration (Britain), 62
Adams, Charles Kendall, 239
Adams, Henry, 223, 226, 261
Adams, John, 7, 13n.36, 45, 46–47, 49–50n.27, 52, 72–83, 86n.5, 90, 91n.35, 93, 96–98, 99–100, 104, 104n.95, 107–8, 109–10n.126, 110, 111–15, 119, 121, 132n.225, 133–34, 144, 186
Adams, John Quincy, 87n.12, 208–9
Adams, Samuel, 78
Adams-Onís Treaty (1819), 150–51
Adenauer, Konrad, 357n.30, 374–75, 374n.99, 376–77, 379
Adicionado (Febrero), 206–7
administrative law, transplant to Philippines, 279. *See also* constitutional law
admiralty courts, 75–77, 184
adversarial legal culture, 213–14
Afghanistan
 rule of law programs in, 497–98, 502–3
 war against terrorism, 511–12
Afghanistan Legal Education Project (Stanford), 502–3
AFLA. *See* American Foreign Law Association
Africa, American legal transplants to, 422–23
African Law Association in America (ALAA), 422–23

African Law Center (Columbia), 422–23
Akademischer Austauschdienst (Germany), 354
Albert, Richard, 477
Alexander VI (Pope), 81
ALI (American Law Institute), 303, 306–10, 345, 345n.336, 433n.362
Alliance for Progress, 421
Allied Control Council (ACC), 364
American Anti-Slavery Society (AASS), 218–19
American Association for the Comparative Study of Law (AACSL), 9–10, 302, 323, 347, 419. *See also* American Society of Comparative Law
American Journal of Comparative Law, 392–96
and International Academy of Comparative Law, 398
international unification efforts, 434–35
in late twentieth century, 467–68
participation in International Congresses, 396–402
structure and membership, 384–92
American Association of Law Libraries (AALL), 429–30
American Bar Association (ABA), 9, 245, 267, 419. *See also* Comparative Law Bureau
ABA Journal, 286, 297
academic law libraries, 317n.208
Central and East European Law Initiative, 503–4, 504n.237
codification debate, 247–51
Committee on Jurisprudence and Law Reform, 248, 250
Committee on Legal Education and Admissions to the Bar, 235–37, 240–43
Committee on the Arrangement of the Law, 248
in early twentieth century, 286–87, 310–11
establishment of, 234–38
international unification efforts, 434–35
Legal Education Committee, 242–43
rule of law programs, 503–4, 504n.237
Section of International and Comparative Law, 286–87, 310–11, 339–40, 380–81, 394
Section of International Law, 482n.135
Section of Legal Education, 236–38, 244
Special Committee on Delay and Uncertainty in the Administration of Justice, 247
Special Committee on Uniformity of Procedure and Comparative Law, 243–44
Special Committee on Uniform State Laws, 250

Universal Congress of Lawyers and Jurists, 287–89
Wilson's association with, 275–77
American Civil Liberties Union (ACLU), 396
American Council of Learned Societies (ACLS), 391n.172, 400, 469
American Enlightenments (Winterer), 214n.360
American Foreign Law Association (AFLA), 9, 379
and American Association for the Comparative Study of Law, 384, 385–86
early twentieth century, 286, 302
international unification efforts, 435
in postwar twentieth century, 382–83
American Institute of Criminal Law and Criminology, 293, 324n.236
American institutionalist literature, 166–71
Americanization of the Common Law (Nelson), 33, 36
American Journal of Comparative Law, 323, 419–20, 426, 435, 436
early history of, 392–96
in late twentieth century, 468, 469, 470
in postwar twentieth century, 389
in twenty-first century, 472, 473–76, 477, 478–79
American Jurist and Law Magazine, 178–81, 203
American Law Institute (ALI), 303, 306–10, 345, 345n.336, 433n.362
American Law Journal and Miscellaneous Repertory, 176–77
American Law Review, 254–55
"American Lawyer's Pilgrimage on the Continent, An" (Wigmore), 341
American legal history, rise as distinct discipline, 36–39
American legal science, beginning of, 156–61
American Military Government (AMG) in Germany, 354–57, 364–67
American Participation in the Development of the International Academy of Comparative Law and Its First Two Hague Congresses (Clark), 298n.116
American republic, legal foundation for. *See* republic, legal foundation for American
American Revolutionary Era, 5–6, 69–70, 129–30. *See also* colonial period; republic, legal foundation for American
American Social Science Association (ASSA), 234n.46, 266–67
American Society of Comparative Law (ASCL), 11, 456, 468–79

American Society of International Law
  (ASIL), 299
American system of legal rules, establishment
  of, 12–16
American zone (Germany), 351, 364–65n.61
Amerika Häuser, 517n.281
Ames, James Barr, 233, 238, 239, 249–50,
  289, 291
AMG (American Military Government) in
  Germany, 354–57, 364–67
AMGK (Army Military Government in
  Korea), 361–64
Amnesty International, 426
analytical jurisprudence, 226–27, 228
Ancel, Marc, 416n.294
Angell, James, 330
Anglicans (Church of England), 60–62, 64
Anglicization of colonial legal system, 64–66
Anglo-American Legal Heritage, The
  (Coquillette), 42–43
Anniversary Discourse (Sampson), 208–9, 210
Annual Bulletin (Comparative Law Bureau),
  285, 286–87, 290, 291–92, 311
Anti-Federalists, 103, 104–5, 106–7, 116–
  17, 133–34
anti-Semitism at American universities, 326–31
antitrust reform
  in postwar Germany, 365–66, 367
  in postwar Japan, 371
  for postwar Western Europe, 373–79
apologists, slavery, 217–18
Appleton, Richard B., 372n.90
apprenticeship, legal, 45–46, 51–53, 161–62, 164
Aquinas, Thomas, 333–35
Arab Spring, 512–13
Argentina, interdisciplinary research on, 520
aristocratic republics, 105, 106, 113–15
Aristotle, 128
arms, right to bear, 140n.263
Army Military Government in Korea
  (AMGK), 361–64
Articles of Confederation, 104, 124, 125–
  26, 130
ASCL (American Society of Comparative Law),
  11, 456, 468–79
Ashmum, John, 162–63
ASIL (American Society of International
  Law), 299
ASSA (American Social Science Association),
  234n.46, 266–67
assembly, of European Coal and Steel
  Community, 377
Assheton, Ralph, 47n.14

*Association Internationale pour le Progrès des
  Sciences Sociales*, 265–66
Association of American Law Schools (AALS),
  22–23, 239, 273, 303n.139
  Continental Legal History Series, 323–24
  creation of, 237–38
  degree programs for foreign students, 417
  law libraries, 317
  Modern Legal Philosophy Series, 293, 324
  in postwar twentieth century, 383–84
atomic bombs, 352
attorneys. *See* lawyers
Auburn prison model, 200–1
Austin, John, 18–19
authoritarian economic development,
  488, 508–9

Baade, Hans, 403n.225, 405n.239, 435
Bacon, Francis, 43n.230, 48, 161n.72,
  242, 333–34
Bailyn, Bernard, 30–31, 99, 107, 116–17n.152
Baker, John, 45–46
Baker & McKenzie law firm, 317n.205, 481
Baldwin, Roger, 368n.77
Baldwin, Simeon, 234–35, 236–37, 238n.60,
  240, 242, 248, 266, 285–86n.58, 287–88,
  291–92, 460n.39
Balogh, Élemér, 298, 300n.125, 311–12, 341–42,
  343, 398
Baptist religion, 63
bar associations. *See also* American Bar
  Association
  in colonial period, 58–59
  libraries of, 316–17
  re-emergence in 1870s, 234
Barnes, William, 388, 389–90n.166
Barradall, Edward, 87–88n.14
Barthélemy, Jean-Jacques, 128
Bartolus, 189n.236, 289n.71
Barton, William, 104
Basedow, Jürgen, 475, 477
Basic Law (German), 357, 509n.253
Bates, Henry, 320
Batiza, Rodolfo, 155n.47, 205
Beale, Joseph, 239, 289, 426–27, 460n.39
bear arms, right to, 140n.263
Beaumont, Gustave de, 192, 203–4
Beccaria, Cesare, 100–1, 140n.263, 142, 158,
  197, 198–99, 204
Becker, Carl, 98–99
Bederman, David, 89–90, 91–92n.36, 108–9,
  143, 144
behavior, connection between ideology and, 5

Bell, Robert, 71n.134, 167–68n.100
Bentham, Jeremy, 43n.230, 48, 159–60, 178–79, 198–99, 204–5, 208–9, 259, 333–34
Bergman, Marcelo, 520–21
Berman, Harold, 400, 403–4
Bermann, George, 469, 470–72, 473, 474–75, 476n.112, 477
Bernstein, Herbert, 403n.225, 476n.110
Bibliography on Foreign and Comparative Law (Szladits), 429–30
Bilateral Studies in Private International Law (Parker School), 332–33, 416–17
Bill for Establishing Religious Freedom (Virginia), 86–87, 123–24
Bill for Proportioning Crimes and Punishments in Cases heretofore Capital (Virginia), 101n.86
Bill of Rights, 117, 133–42
binational law firms, 268–69
Bishop, William, 380
Blackstone, William, 12–13, 28n.129, 45–46, 71, 71n.134, 87, 88, 92n.39, 97–98, 107, 120–21, 155–56, 161n.72, 162, 166–69, 199, 257
Blackstone's Commentaries (Tucker), 162, 169, 171
Blakemore, Thomas, 368, 369–70, 371n.87
Blondel, Georges, 289
Blume, Fred, 296–97
Blume, William, 281–82
Bluntschli, Johann, 230
Bodenheimer, Edgar, 344
Body of Liberties (Massachusetts General Court), 55–56
Bolgár, Vera, 392n.175
Bonaparte, Napoléon, 149–50, 181n.196
Book of the General Lawes and Libertyes concerning the Inhabitants of the Massachusetts, The (Massachusetts General Court), 12n.32, 55–56
Borchard, Edwin, 292, 293–94, 311, 314, 327, 340–41, 342–43, 432–33
Bosch, Robert, 374–75
Boston Book Company, 292–93
Boston Declaration (1772), 78–79
Boston Gazette newspaper, 74–75, 79
Boston Public Library, 81
Boston Social Law Library, 186
Boudinot, Elias, 129
Bracton, Henry de, 43n.230, 45–46, 47–48, 73–74
Bracton treatise, 43n.230
Braintree Town Instructions (Massachusetts), 77

Brandeis, Louis, 277, 277n.21, 315
Breslau University (Germany), 230n.28
Brewer, David, 288
Brewster, James, 289n.72
Brexit, 508–9
Breyer, Stephen, 490
Briand, Aristide, 374–75
British colonial period
 Anglicization thesis, 64–66
 comparative law in England, 45–49
 Declaration of Independence, 94–101
 education in foreign law and political theory, 88–93
 establishment of American system of legal rules, 12–13
 immigrants in, 66–70
 John Adams as American comparatist, 72–83
 lawyers and courts, 57–60
 overview, 7
 regionalism and legal diversity, 71–72
 religious and cultural variation, 60–72
 Roman and civil law in, 49–53
 slavery in, 214–16
 social factors affecting law, 53–57
British law. *See* English law
Brockhaus, Friedrich, 191–92
Brophy, Alfred L., 65n.104
Brown, James, 153–56
Bruce, Andrew, 291n.76
Brutus, Lucius Junius, 103
Brutus, Marcus Junius, 103
Bruzelius, Anders, 395
Bryce, James, 274n.8
Bucerius Law School, 472–73
Buckland, William, 295, 312
Buergenthal, Thomas, 426–27
Bulletin (AFLA), 384, 392–93
Bundy, George, 426
Burgess, John, 195n.264, 267, 268, 271–72
Burlamaqui, Jean-Jacques, 49–50, 98–99, 333–34
Bush, George W., 497–98, 511
Bussani, Mauro, 486
Bustamante, Antonio de, 295n.102, 298, 299, 300, 300n.125, 311–12
Butler, Nicholas, 330
Butler, William E., 406n.244
Buxbaum, Hannah, 471–72, 479
Buxbaum, Richard, 396, 467–68, 473, 477n.116
Byrnes, James, 351, 352

Cairns, John, 155–56
Cairo Declaration (1943), 361

California, civil code of, 212, 245–46, 251
Calvert, Cecilius (Lord Baltimore), 61–62
Calvin's Case, 79–80n.179
Calvinus, Johannes, 76–77
Canada-United States Law Journal, 415
canon law
  in colonial British America, 49–51, 76–77, 81
  in England, 45–46, 47–49
capitalism, 452–54, 487. *See also* globalization
capital punishment, 101n.86, 199
Cappelletti, Mauro, 403n.225, 412–13, 447
Carleton, Henry, 154–55
Carnegie, Andrew, 300–1
Carnegie Endowment for International Peace, 280–81, 300–1
Carnegie Foundation, 300–1, 309, 341–42
Carrington, Paul D., 257n.150
carry arms, right to, 140n.263
cartel law, in postwar Europe, 365–66, 367, 378–79
Carter, James, 8, 18, 23, 26, 28–29, 226, 228, 245, 246–47, 249–50
Carter, Jimmy, 357n.33, 396n.195, 409
casebook method of instruction, 232, 240, 241n.73, 324–25
Cases and Material on Selected Topics in the Law of Trademarks and Unfair Competition in the United States, France and Germany (Deák, Schiller, & Handler), 346
Cases and Materials on the Development of Legal Institutions (Smith), 32
Cato, Marcus Porcius, 103, 104
causation, issue of, 4–6, 30
Cavers, David, 385n.141, 386–87, 388n.157
CCP (Chinese Communist Party), 515, 516–17
CCP (Comparative Constitutions Project), University of Illinois, 494
Centennial International Exhibition (1876), 269
Centennial World Congress on Comparative Law (2000), 461
Center of Latin American Legal Studies, 315, 381
Center on Democracy, Development and the Rule of Law (Stanford University), 489
Center on Globalization, Law, and Society (California-Irvine), 484
Central and East European Law Initiative (CEELI), ABA, 503–4, 504n.237
Central Intelligence Agency (CIA), 420n.311
Chamberlain, J.P., 308n.164
Charles I (King of England), 60, 61
Chase, Anthony, 41–42
chattel, view of slaves as, 216

Chayes, Abram, 434–35
checks and balances, of republican governments, 102n.90, 108, 113–14, 127, 143
Chesapeake region, colonial period, 54–55, 64, 71–72
Chiang Kai-shek, 330
Chicago Law Institute, 319–20
Chile
  authoritarian economic development in, 488
  interdisciplinary research on, 520
China
  and academic law and development programs, 486–87
  American legal transplant to, 280–84, 285–86, 418–19
  authoritarian economic development in, 488
  Corruption Perceptions Index, 501n.222
  coursebooks on, 408–9
  coursebooks on PRC, 408–9
  importance in twenty-first century, 515–17
  Pound's travels in, 329–30
  rule of law programs, 496
  World Bank *Doing Business* indicators, 500–1
China Guiding Cases Project (Stanford University), 488–89n.167
China Law Reporter journal, 415
Chinese Communist Party (CCP), 515, 516–17
Chinese Law and Government journal, 415
Chinese Law journal, 415
choice of law, 438–41. *See also* conflict of laws
Chroust, Anton, 329, 336, 394n.185
Churchill, Winston, 374–75, 375n.103
Church of England (Anglicans), 60–62, 64
CIA (Central Intelligence Agency), 420n.311
Cicero, Marcus Tullius, 74n.154, 94, 102, 103, 104, 109–10, 114–15, 121
Cincinnati Law School, 164
Cincinnatus, Lucius Quinctius, 103
CISG (Convention on Contracts for the International Sale of Goods), 436
Cist, Carl, 70n.127
civic humanism, 88–89, 98, 99–100
Civil Code of 1804 (France), 154, 167–68n.100, 212–13, 245–46, 251
Civil Code of 1825 (Louisiana), 204–5, 212–13, 220–21
civil code of California, 212, 245–46, 251
Civil Code of the German Empire, The, 292
civilian institutionalist writing, 167
Civilian Writers of Doctors' Commons, London, The (Coquillette), 47–48
civilizational war, rules to avoid, 512

532 INDEX

civilizations, and globalization, 453–56, 461–62, 464
civil law
  and American institutionalist literature, 166–71
  American jurists embracing in late nineteenth century, 256–59, 260–64
  and codification debate, 245–51
  in colonial British America, 49–53, 66–70
  coursebooks on, 409–10
  early twentieth century interest in, 285–86, 294–97
  in England, 46–49
  in formative era, 146–47, 158–59, 165–66, 173n.143, 174–87, 188, 195–97
  in John Adams' practice and writing, 72–74, 75–77, 80, 82
  in Korea, 372–73
  law journal literature on comparative law, 254–56
  in legal education, ABA approval of, 236
  and Louisiana Code of Practice, 206–7
  and New York Code of Civil Procedure, 212–14
  in nineteenth-century legal history books, 16–18, 21–22
  rise of American legal history as distinct discipline, 38–39
  and slavery in America, 217, 219–21
  teaching in late nineteenth century, 251–54
  and territorial expansion, 151–56
  translation of legal materials, 183–85
  in writings of Roscoe Pound, 24–25, 27
Civil Law (Scott), 295
Civil Law, The (Domat), 52–53, 76–77
Civil Law of Spain and Mexico, The (Schmidt), 190
Civil Law System, The (Von Mehren), 406–7
Civil Liberties Bureau (CLB) of Japan, 368
civil procedure, international, 441
Civil Procedure in Sweden (Ginsburg & Bruzelius), 395n.192
civil rights, in Bill of Rights, 134–35
Civil Rights Section, U.S. Department of Justice, 368n.77
Civil Service Law of 1933 (Germany), 326–27
Clagett, Helen, 293–94, 315, 428–29
Claiborne, William, 151–52, 153–54
Clap, William, 77
Clark, Charles, 213n.355, 327
Clark, David, 212–13, 298n.116, 391–92, 407, 421n.315, 425n.329, 465n.61, 467–68, 469, 469n.80, 473–75, 475n.109, 477n.116, 480n.125, 492–93

Clark, William, 150
Clash of Civilizations and the Remaking of World Order, The (Huntington), 451, 453–56
classical legal models, 114. *See also* Roman law
  Barthélemy's *Voyage*, 128
  and Bill of Rights, 137
  and Declaration of Independence, 98, 99–100
  decline in interest in, 145–46
  education about in eighteenth century, 88–93
  The Federalist essays, 122
  influence on American republicanism, 107, 108–9
  natural law, 94
  overview, 86
  sets of values provided by, 143–44
  temporal relation between liberalism and republicanism, 5–6
classification of law, 248
Clay, Lucius, 351, 354, 355–56, 357, 358n.34, 364n.60, 365
CLB (Civil Liberties Bureau) of Japan, 368
Clerke, Francis, 184n.213
Clinton, Bill, 396n.195, 511–12n.260
Coalition of Bar Associations of Color, 510–11n.258
Code civil of 1804 (French), 154, 167–68n.100, 212–13, 245–46, 251
Code of Practice of 1825 (Louisiana), 153, 206–7
Codex of Justinian, The (Blume), 296–97
codification
  of common law of Massachusetts, 159, 209
  of criminal law, 199–200
  in formative era, 159–60, 161, 204–14
  historical jurisprudence against, 245–51
  mentions in *American Jurist*, 178–79
  overview, 16–22
  restatements and, 309–10
  of South Carolina law, 195
  Timothy Walker's support of, 16
coding law, 518–19
Coffey, Hobart, 320
Cohen, Jerome, 408–9
Cohen, Morris, 293
Cohen, William, 412–13
Coke, Edward, 71, 74n.154, 75–76, 130n.212
Cold War, 350–52, 358n.34, 372n.92, 375–77, 419, 444, 452, 484–85
collectivism, individualism versus, 522–23
college law schools, 161–66. *See also* law schools
College of William and Mary, 190–91
colleges, in early republic, 89–90. *See also* universities

Colombia, World Bank loan to, 499–500
colonial period
   Anglicization thesis, 64–66
   comparative law in England, 45–49
   Declaration of Independence, 94–101
   education in foreign law and political theory, 88–93
   establishment of American system of legal rules, 12–13
   immigrants in, 66–70
   John Adams as American comparatist, 72–83
   lawyers and courts, 57–60
   overview, 7
   regionalism and legal diversity, 71–72
   religious and cultural variation, 60–72
   Roman and civil law in, 49–53
   slavery in, 214–16
   social factors affecting law, 53–57
Columbia College/University/Law School, 484. *See also* Parker School of Foreign and Comparative Law
   African Law Center, 422–23
   anti-Semitism at, 330
   curriculum reform, 304–5
   degree programs for foreign students, 417
   in early twentieth century, 346
   establishment of, 165
   first law professorship at, 162
   Japanese law at, 409–10
   Project on International Procedure, 395
   reinstitution of, 195
Commager, Henry Steele, 29–30, 40
commentaries, institutionalist, 166–71
Commentaries on American Law (Kent), 166–67, 169–71, 195–96
Commentaries on the Constitution of the United States (Story), 15
Commentaries on the Law of Bailments (Story), 171–72
Commentaries on the Laws of England (Blackstone), 12–13, 71n.134, 88, 97–98, 107, 155–56, 162, 166–69, 199, 251, 257
commercial law
   in colonial British America, 53–54
   translation of legal materials, 184, 185
   unification of, 433–36
   U.S. reforms to postwar Japanese, 371
Commercial Laws of the World, 292
Committee of Detail (Constitutional Convention), 115–16
Committee on Comparative Law (AALS), 383–84

Committee on Jurisprudence and Law Reform (ABA), 248, 250
Committee on Legal Education and Admissions to the Bar (ABA), 235–37, 240–43
Committee on the Arrangement of the Law (ABA), 248
commonalities rule, 512
common core concept, 436–37
common law
   and American institutionalist literature, 166–69
   codification of, 208–9
   in colonial British America, 57–58, 65, 71–72
   conversion of crimes into statutory form, 199–200
   in England, 46–47
   in formative era, 157, 159–60, 161, 170, 174–75, 196–97
   influence on Louisiana law, 155–56
   lack of attention to in American comparative law, xv–xvi
   and Louisiana Code of Practice, 206–7
   in nineteenth-century legal history books, 16–20
   skepticism toward in early republic, 121
   slavery in, 216
   Timothy Walker's separation of equity from, 16
   in writings of Max Radin, 27–28
   in writings of Roscoe Pound, 24–26
Common Law, The (Holmes), 18–19, 260, 261–62
Common Law in Colonial America, The (Nelson), 54–55, 82n.194
Commonwealth of the Philippines, 279–80
communism, 350–51, 419, 452. *See also* Cold War
communities, relationship between humans and, 337
Comparative Approach to American History, The (Woodward), 2n.6
Comparative Constitutionalism (Dorsen, Rosenfeld, & colleagues), 492
Comparative Constitutional Law (Tushnet & Jackson), 492
Comparative Constitutions Project (CCP), University of Illinois, 494
Comparative Criminal Law Project (NYU), 416
Comparative Judicial Review (Delaney & Dixon), 493
Comparative Law (Merryman & Clark), 407
Comparative Law (Schlesinger), 404–6

Comparative Law Bureau, 295, 299, 322–23
    and American Foreign Law Association, 302
    Annual Bulletin, 285, 286–87, 290, 291–92, 311
    creation of, 9, 285
    general discussion, 290–94
    merger with ABA International Law Section, 286–87, 339
    Tulane Law Review, 286, 310–12, 339, 341–42
Comparative Law Division (ABA Section), 381
comparative law libraries. *See* law libraries
Comparative Law School of China (Soochow Law School), 280, 281–84, 329
comparative legal history, 1–3
comparative legal sociology, 441–47
Comparative Legal Traditions (Glendon, Gordon & Osakwe), 407–8
Comparative Readings of Roscoe Pound's Jurisprudence (Lasser), 321n.222
competition, versus cooperation, 523
Conant, James, 327, 328, 330n.270
Conard, Alfred, 394n.184, 400, 402
Concerning the Historic Importance of Edward Livingston (Franklin), 201n.292
conditionality approach, World Bank, 500n.219
Confederation Congress, 132
confederations, 106–7, 117, 124–26, 131
conflict of laws, 14–15, 159n.64, 184, 189–90, 437–41
Conflict of Laws (Nadelmann), 440
Conflict of Laws (Symeonides, Perdue, & von Mehren), 458n.28
Conflict of Laws, The (Rabel), 333, 345, 436
conflict-solving processes, 447–48
congregate prison model, 200–1
Congregationalists (Puritans), 55–56, 57, 60–62, 63, 72n.137
Congressional Research Service (CRS), 315n.199
Congress on Jurisprudence and Law Reform (World's Fair, Columbian Exposition), 269–70
Conklin, Carl N., 97n.64
Conner, Alison, 477
consent theory of government, 100–1
Constitute website, 494
Constitution, U.S., 86–87, 113
    Bill of Rights, 117, 133–42
    classical legal models, 143–44
    versus constitutions of European nations, 491
    and debate about foreign law influence, 5–6
    The Federalist and ratification efforts, 122, 131
    ideological approach to, 88–89
    James Madison's views on, 124, 126–27
    principle of liberty, 109
    ratification of, 116–18, 122, 131, 133–34
    republican form of government, 101–9
    and tension related to slavery, 217–19
    Tiedeman's views on, 263–64
Constitutional Convention, 103, 104, 115–16
constitutional criminal procedure, 446
constitutional history, 6
constitutionalism, 350n.5, 491, 492, 517
constitutional law
    American legal transplant to Philippines, 279
    coursebooks related to, 411–13
    earliest comparative publications on, 267–68
    globalization of, 489–94
    interdisciplinary research, 519–20
Constitution of American Foreign Law Association, 302
Constitution of China
    of 1914, 280–81
    of 1947, 282–83
    of 1982, 517
Constitution of Georgia, 156–57
Constitution of Germany, 354–57
Constitution of Japan, 358–60, 363
Constitution of Korea, 361–64
Constitution of Massachusetts, 111–12, 114n.144
Constitution of New York, 132, 211–12
Constitution of Pennsylvania, 118–20
Constitution of Virginia, 97n.60, 97n.61, 123, 137
Consulate of the Sea, 176–77
Contemporary Civil Law Tradition, The (Merryman, Clark, & Haley), 492–93
Continental Congress, 96–97, 132
Continentalist, The (Hamilton), 130–31
Continental Legal History Series (AALS), 323–24
contract formation rules, 436–37
Convention on Contracts for the International Sale of Goods (CISG), 436
Conversations-Lexikon (Brockhaus), 191–92
Cooper, Thomas, 158, 167, 183–84, 208–9
cooperation, versus competition, 523
Cooperative Acquisitions Program (LC), 432n.354
coordinate states, 447–48
Coquillette, Daniel, 3n.14, 42–43, 47–48, 72, 76, 79–80, 82, 173n.143, 328n.259
corporate law, 371, 378–79
Corps of Discovery, 150

INDEX 535

Corpus juris civilis (Justinian), 92–93, 121, 295, 296–97
Corruption Perceptions Index (Transparency International), 501n.222, 505–6
Coudenhove-Kalergi, Richard, 374–75
Coudert, Alexis, 382–83, 383n.133, 385n.141, 386–87, 416–17
Coudert, Frederic, Jr., 268–69, 339–40
Coudert Brothers firm, 268–69
Council of Ministers (ECSC), 377
county law libraries, 316–17
Course of Legal Study, A (Hoffman), 14, 164–65, 174–75
courses, comparative law, 402–4
Court and the World, The (Breyer), 490
Court of Justice (ECSC), 377–78
courts
  in colonial British America, 53–54, 57–60, 66
  Japanese system, 360
Cowell, John, 73–74
Crane, William, 267–68
Creation of the American Republic, The (Wood), 5
crime, punishment for, 142. *See also* penal reform
criminal law, Japanese, 359–60n.39, 370, 371–72
criminal procedure, constitutional, 446
Criminal Process in the People's Republic of China, The (Cohen), 408
critical legal studies, 458n.31
CRS (Congressional Research Service), 315n.199
cultural hermeneutics, 448–49, 467
cultural immersion approach, 466
cultural legal history, 40
cultures, 451
  interdisciplinary research related to, 520–25
  legal, 463, 464–67, 520–22
  obstacles to globalization, 453
  tenacity of, 453–54, 461–67
  varied, in colonial British America, 60–72
Curia Philípica (Hevia Bolaños), 206–7
Curran, Vivian, 466, 473, 478–79
curriculum, law school, 240–44, 303–6
Currie, Brainerd, 439
Curtis, Michael Kent, 216–17n.369
Curtis, William, 289n.72
Cushing, Caleb, 182–83
Cushing, Luther, xivn.2, 17, 47, 159, 178–79, 180–82, 183–84, 185, 187–88, 193n.256, 203, 209n.336, 225–26
custom, evolution of and development of law, 23
cyclical theory of history, 452–53, 525

Daggett, Harriet, 342–43
Dainow, Joseph, 385n.141, 400
Damaška, Mirjan, 403n.225, 405n.239, 447–48
Dana Foundation, 391
Dane, Nathan, 14, 162–63
Darby, Joseph, 477n.116
Dargo, George, 145–46, 154–55
Dart, Henry Plauché, 207n.324
Darwin, Charles, 262
Das Obligationenrecht (Savigny), 224n.5
Das Recht des Besitzes (Savigny), 180–81
David, René, 383
Davies, D.J. Llewelyn, 184n.210
Davis, John, 178n.170
Dawson, John, 380n.121
Deák, Francis, 346, 432–33
Dean Pound and the Immutable Natural Law (Kreilkamp), 334n.285
death penalty, 101n.86, 199
decade of development (1960s), 421–25
De Capriles, Miguel, 385n.141, 387, 388, 410
decartelization, in postwar Europe, 365–66, 367, 378–79
Declaration of Independence, 78, 86–87, 94–101, 109, 112n.137, 139n.260
Declaration of Rights (England), 136, 137n.244, 139
Declaration of Rights (Massachusetts), 112, 114n.144
Declaration of Rights (Pennsylvania), 140n.263
Declaration of Rights (Virginia), 123, 137, 138–41
De Conflictu Legum (Huber), 184
Dedek, Helge, 477–78
deductive science, law as, 160–61
Defence of the Constitutions of Government of the United States of America, A (Adams), 93, 104, 108, 109–10n.126, 113–15
Defense of the Common Law against Postbellum American Codification (Masferrer), 245n.92
De Gasperi, Alcide, 374n.99
Dei Delitti e delle Pene (Beccaria), 198
De iure belli ac pacis (Grotius), 49–50, 52–53, 76, 80
De jure maritimo et navali (Molloy), 73–74
De jure naturae et gentium (Pufendorf), 49–50, 52–53, 80
Delaney, Erin, 493
Del Vecchio, Giorgio, 311–12
Demleitner, Nora, 466

democracy
　and academic law and development programs, 485–86
　focus on enhancing values of in 1950s, 419–20
　and globalization, 452–53
　in John Adams' *Defence*, 113–15
　liberal, 451
　versus republicanism, 104–5
Democratic People's Republic of Korea, 353–54. *See also* Korea
democratic republics, 105–7, 108. *See also* republic, legal foundation for American
denazification of Germany, 356, 364–65
Deng Xiaoping, 409
De officio hominis et civis (Pufendorf), 52–53
Derbigny, Pierre, 204–5
Derenberg, Walter, 385n.141, 392n.174
Der Hoch-Deutsch Pennsylvanischer Geschichts-Schreiber newspaper, 68n.121
Der Kampf um's Recht (Ihering), 19, 259–60, 262
Der Wöchentliche Philadelphische Staatsbote/ Der Wöchentliche Pennsylvanische Staatsbote newspaper, 69–70
Der Zweck im Recht (Ihering), 259–60
Descartes, René, 333–34
Destutt de Tracy, Antoine Louis Claude, 101n.85
Detroit Mercy Law School, 483–84
Deutsche Hochschule für Politik, 362n.51
Deutscher Akademischer Austauschdienst (DAAD), 354n.19
Deutschlandvertrag (1952), 351–52
development
　decade of (1960s), 421–25
　law and development approach, 410, 425, 444–47, 484–89
　rule of law programs, 497–98
　shift into investigation on, 425–26
De Vries, Henry, 438
Dewey, Thomas, 350n.6
Dezalay, Yves, 487
Dialogus de fundamentis legum Angliæ et de conscientia (St. German), 46, 73–74
dichotomies, 448
Dickinson, Edwin, 339–40
Dickinson, John, 51–52, 98, 115, 119
Die Rechtstatsachenforschung (Nussbaum), 332–33
Difficulties with Measuring the Rule of Law (Ginsburg), 505n.240
Digest (Justinian), 76–77, 176, 207

Digest of the Civil Laws Now in Force in the Territory of Orleans (Louisiana Digest), 153–56, 204–5, 219–21
Dillon, John, 20, 247
Dippel, Horst, 107
Discourses concerning Government (Sidney), 80
Dissertation on the Canon and Feudal Law, A (Adams), 74–75, 76n.160, 82, 91n.35
Dissertations on the Questions which Arise from the Contrariety of the Positive Laws of Different States and Nations (Livermore), 189–90
divergence principle, in colonial charters, 66
Dixon, Rosalind, 492–93
Dixon, S.F., 179n.179
Doane v. Gage (1766– 1769), 76
doctoral degrees, 229
Doctor and Student (St. German), 52–53
Doctors' Commons, 45–46, 77
Doing Business series (World Bank), 500–1
Domat, Jean, 47, 52–53, 76–77, 155–56, 172n.128, 185, 206–7, 220n.388
Domke, Martin, 438
Donahue, Charles, 47–48
Dorsen, Norman, 491, 492
Dower, John, 370–71, 372n.92
Drago, Roland, 401–2, 475
Dragon St. George Could Not Slay, The (Finkelman), 216–17n.369
Drake, Joseph, 293
Dubber, Markus, 203
Duke's Laws (colonial New York), 53–54, 56n.62
Dulles, Allen, 420
Dulles, John Foster, 420n.311
Dupin, André, 177, 181–82
Du Ponceau, Peter, 184
Durham, Cole, 391–92, 467–68, 469
Dutch law
　in colonial period, 53–54, 58, 62, 71–72
　influence on American law, 34–36, 38–39
Dutch Reformed Church, 62, 63n.98
Dutch West India Company, 62, 63n.98
Duve, Thomas, 44
Dwight, Theodore, 165, 195, 261n.171, 266

early American republic, legal foundation for
　Alexander Hamilton, 129–31
　Bill of Rights, 133–42
　classical legal models, 143–44
　Declaration of Independence, 98, 99–100
　education in foreign law and political theory, 88–93
　The Federalist essays, 122

golden age of comparative law, 85-88
James Madison, 122-28
James Wilson, 115-21
John Adams, 111-15
John Jay, 131-33
overview, 7-8
principle of liberty, 109-11
republican form of government in Constitution, 101-9
Thomas Jefferson, 94-101
early twentieth century
achievement during 1930s and 1940s, 339-47
American Foreign Law Association, 302
American Law Institute and unification of law, 306-10
attempts to transplant American law abroad, 277-84
Comparative Law Bureau, 290-94
German-American relations, 326-38
historiography, 22-29
International Academy of Comparative Law, 298-302
John Wigmore, 320, 323-26
law libraries, 312-20, 318t, 319t
overview, 9, 273
persistence of Roman law interest, 294-97
Roscoe Pound, 320-23
social science, 303-6
timeline through world wars, 284-87
Tulane University Law School, 310-12
Universal Congress of Lawyers and Jurists, 287-89
Woodrow Wilson, 274-77
Ease of Doing Business Index (World Bank), 505-6
Eason Weinmann Center for International and Comparative Law (Tulane), 404, 484
East Asia Legal Studies Program (Harvard), 404, 408, 409n.256
Eastern State Penitentiary of Pennsylvania, 192, 200
Economic Cooperation Act of 1948 (Marshall Plan), 351-52, 375-76
Economic Cooperation Administration (ECA), 375-76
economics. *See also* globalization
federalism and antitrust reform for Western Europe, 378-79
law and development, 425, 484-89
and legal reform in postwar Germany, 365-66, 367
liberalism, 452-54

ECSC (European Coal and Steel Community), 375, 376-78, 379
Eder, Phanor, 302, 339-40, 340n.308, 342-43, 380, 382-83, 384n.138, 385n.141, 386-87, 388, 410, 438
education. *See* legal education
EEC (European Economic Community), 378, 413-14
Ehrenzweig, Albert, 385n.141, 387, 400, 437, 438, 439-40
eighteenth century. *See also* colonial period; early American republic, legal foundation for; formative era
historiography, 12-13
immigrants in, 66-70
Einführung in die Rechtswissenschaft (Kohler), 242n.77
Eisenhower, Dwight, 351n.8, 378, 419
Elementa iuris naturae et gentium (Heineccius), 49-50
Elements of Law (Hilliard), 160n.71
Eliot, Charles, 226, 231-32, 233, 239, 260-61, 266, 280-81, 323
Eliot, T.S., xiii
Elkins, Zachary, 494
Ellinger, Werner, 431
Ely, James W., Jr., 38-39
emancipation, 216, 221
Emergency Committee in Aid of Displaced German Scholars, 327, 332, 356
Emérigon, Balthazard-Marie, 176-77, 185
empirical comparative law, interdisciplinary, 518-25
Encyclopædia Americana (Lieber), 172-73, 191-93
end of history concept, 452-53
Endurance of National Constitutions, The (Elkins, Ginsburg, & Melton), 494
England. *See* British colonial period; Great Britain
English Declaration of Rights, 136, 137n.244, 139
English law
and desirability of republicanism, 107
emphasis on, xv-xvi, 32-33
in formative era, 156-61, 170
Friedman's conclusions on, 35-36
John Adams' first writings on, 75
legal diversity in colonial period, 71-72
legal foundation for early American republic, 85-86, 88, 95-96
skepticism toward in early American republic, 121

English law (*cont.*)
  slavery in, 214–16
  as source for Digest of Orleans, 155–56
  in writings of Max Radin, 27–28
English Navigation Act (1696), 76n.160
Enlightenment political philosophy, 88–89, 98–101, 137, 138–39, 141–43
Enumeration Clause (U.S. Constitution), 217–18
equality
  and frugality, 106n.105
  Locke's idea of, 100–1
equity
  and New York Code of Civil Procedure, 212, 213–14
  Timothy Walker's separation of common law from, 16
Erhard, Ludwig, 379
Ernst, C.W., 255
Essays in Anglo-Saxon Law (Adams), 226
essentialism, 335, 336
ethics and law, 333–38
ethnocentrism, 466
Europe
  commonality among continental legal systems, 49
  federalism and antitrust reform for Western, 373–79
  political philosophy of, in legal foundation for republic, 86, 88–93
  Single European Act, 446–47
  slavery laws, 214–15
  supranational integration through law, 446–47
  U.S. Constitution versus that of nations in, 491
European Coal and Steel Community (ECSC), 375, 376–78, 379
European Economic Community (EEC), 378, 413–14
European Union (E.U.), 2, 510
European University Institute, 446–47
Evans, William, 185
evidence-based governance, 505
evolutionary theory of history, 452–53
Evolution of Law (Wigmore & Kocourek), 324–25
Ewald, William, 116
exceptionalism, American, 29–30, 40
exportation of American law. *See* legal transplantation
expositions, international, 269–72
externalist approach to legal history, 30–31

Faces of Justice and State Authority (Damaška), 447–48
family law
  comparative study of, 448–49
  U.S. reforms to postwar Japanese, 370–71
Farmer Refuted, The (Hamilton), 129
Farmington Plan, 313n.192
Farrar, Edgar, 291n.76
fatwas (in Islam), 514
Febrero, José, 206–7
federalism
  American Federalists, 102–3, 104, 116–17, 133–34
  German, 357
  for postwar Western Europe, 373–79
Federalism and Supranational Organizations (Hay), 414–15
Federalist, The (Madison, Hamilton, & Jay), 93, 106, 122, 125, 126–27, 132–33, 143
Federal Republic of Germany, 351–52
federal veto, 126
Feilchenfeld, Ernst, 310–11
Feinerman, James, 477–78
femininity, masculinity versus, 523
Fernandez, Mark, 155–56
Fernández Arroyo, Diego, 475
feudalism, 75, 214–15
Feuerbach, Paul von, 203, 204, 264–65
Field, David Dudley, 8, 17–18, 32, 145, 211–14, 226, 234n.46, 245–49, 251
Field, Emilia, 288
Field, Stephen, 212, 245–46
Field Code (New York), 17–18, 212–14, 245–47, 251
Finkelman, Paul, 38–39, 216–17n.369
First Part of the Institutes of the Lawes of England, The (Coke), 75–76
Fisch, William, 477–78
Fitch, Samuel, 74
Fleming, John, 390, 394–95, 396, 401n.213, 402n.221
Fletcher, Richard, 178n.170
Fletcher School of Law and Diplomacy (Tufts University), 389–90n.166
Florida, transfer of ownership of, 148–49, 150–51
Foelix, Jean-Jacques, 180n.189
Follen, Charles, 191
Fong Yue Ting v. United States (1893), 288
Ford, Edsel, 312–13n.187
Ford Foundation, 312, 387, 403–4, 417n.301, 421, 423–24, 426, 428, 430–31, 436n.379, 444, 447n.429

foreign development
  concern with in 1950s, 419
  rule of law programs, 497–98
foreign law
  in colonial British America, 53–57
  influence on American law, 4–51
  Law Library of Congress guides to, 314
  legal foundation for early republic, 88–93
  reliance on or citation of in American courts, 490
foreign policy
  in early twentieth century, 9, 277–84
  in postwar twentieth century, 420, 426
foreign students, programs for, 417–18, 482–84
formalism, 4, 19, 28–30, 39, 226–27, 228
formative era, 7n.31
  beginning of American legal science, 156–61
  codification, 204–14
  establishment of American system of legal rules, 13–16
  legal education and law books, 161–75
  locus for comparative law activity, 187–97, 188t
  other legal literature depicting Roman and civil law, 176–87
  overview, 8
  penal reform, 197–204
  resistance to English law, 156–61
  shift from public to private law, 145–47
  slavery, 214–21
  territorial expansion, 147–56, 148f
Formative Era of American Law, The (Pound), 27, 28–29, 321
Foster, Frances, 469n.80
Foucher, Victor, 181–82
Fraenkel, Ernst, 362–63, 373
France/French law
  Americans at universities in, 229n.22
  Civil Code of 1804, 154, 167–68n.100, 212–13, 245–46, 251
  Code of Civil Procedure of 1806, 206
  emergence of comparative law as discipline, 264–65
  federalism and antitrust reform for Western Europe, 375, 376–77
  influence on American law, 34–36, 154, 155
  and Louisiana Civil Code of 1825, 205
  and Louisiana Code of Practice, 206–7
  Louisiana Purchase, 148–50
  physiocrats, 100–1
  Society of Comparative Legislation, 265, 270, 271–72, 290–91, 302

translation of legal materials in formative era, 183–84
Frankfurter, Felix, 327, 328
Franklin, Benjamin, 34–35, 51–52, 68–70, 89–90n.25, 90, 93n.47, 96–97, 101n.85, 104n.95, 115n.147, 186n.223
Franklin, Mitchell, 201n.292, 309–10, 311, 342–43, 356n.27
Freedom House, 505–6
freedom of religion, 86–87, 123–24
French and Indian War (Seven Years War), 75–76, 148–49
French Penal Code, The (Moreau & Mueller), 416n.294
Freund, Ernst, 22n.94, 239, 255–56, 293, 309, 311n.180
Friedman, Lawrence, 12n.32, 30, 33–36, 58–59, 71, 200–1, 260n.169, 443
Friedmann, Wolfgang, 365, 366–67, 379
Friedrich, Carl, 350n.5, 354, 355–56, 357, 368–69, 411, 412
"Friend of America, A" (Hamilton), 129
frugality, and equality, 106n.105
Fugitive Slave Act (1793), 219
Fugitive Slave Clause (U.S. Constitution), 217–18
Fukuyama, Francis, 451, 452–53, 489, 508, 509–10
Fulbecke, William, 46
Fulbright fellowship program, 421
Fuller, Lon, 324
Fulton, Robert, 145–46n.2
functionalism, 4, 29–30, 34, 39. *See also* sociological jurisprudence
fundamental rights factor, Rule of Law Index, 507

Gaius, 167
Galanter, Marc, 422n.321, 423, 426, 445
Gans, Eduard, 264–65
Garth, Bryant, 486, 487
Geertz, Clifford, 448–49
general comparative law coursebooks, 404–8
General Headquarters (GHQ), in Japan. *See* Supreme Commander for the Allied Powers
General Theory of Law (Korkunov), 292
geníxaros, 214–15
George, B. James, 394n.184
Georgia, revision of judicial system in, 156–57
Georgia Constitution, 156–57
Georgieva, Kristalina, 500–1

Gerber, David, 459, 461n.43, 468, 469n.80, 477–79, 477n.116
Germanist branch of historical jurisprudence, 225n.7, 227
Germantown, Pennsylvania, 67–68
Germantowner Zeitung newspaper, 69n.123
Germany/German law
    American legal transplants, 210–11n.343, 350–52, 419
    Amerika Häuser, 517n.281
    Basic Law, 357, 509n.253
    Civil Code, 292
    Civil Service Law of 1933, 326–27
    denazification, 356, 364–65
    eighteenth-century immigrants and, 66–70, 72
    emergence of comparative law as discipline, 264–65
    federalism and antitrust reform for, 375, 376–77, 379
    first comparative law international congress in, 285n.56
    German-American relations during 1930s, 9, 326–38
    historical jurisprudence, 8, 19, 180–81, 223–27, 274–75
    influence on American law between world wars, 308–9
    Institute for Foreign and International Private Law in, 307
    legal history and comparative law, 41–42
    legal science, 227–28
    mentions in *American Jurist*, 180–81
    new constitution in postwar period, 354–57, 358n.34
    other legal reforms in postwar period, 364–67
    sociological jurisprudence in, 259–60
    university law faculties, 166, 229–31, 240–44
Geschichte des römischen Rechts im Mittelalter (Savigny), 224
Getman, Julius, 423–24
Gevurtz, Franklin, 477–78
GHQ (General Headquarters), in Japan. *See* Supreme Commander for the Allied Powers
Gilbert, Mark, 378
Gilman, Daniel C., 192n.247
Gilmore, Eugene, 289, 460n.39
Gilmore, Grant, 159
Gilson, Ronald, 488
Ginsburg, Ruth Bader, 388–89, 394–96, 400, 404, 476n.113

Ginsburg, Tom, 492–93, 494, 505n.240, 507, 518–19, 520
Glanvill, Ranulf de, 43n.230, 47–48
Glanvill book of royal court procedure, 43n.230
Glendon, Mary Ann, 389, 407–8, 442n.410, 447, 448–49, 477n.116
Glenn, Patrick, 462–64, 471–72, 477–79
global civilizational war, rules to avoid, 512
global governance, 11–12, 494–95. *See also* rule of law
globalization
    of American legal institutions, 479–94
    constitutional and judicial, 489–94
    initial comparative law reaction to accelerated, 456–61
    overview, 11–12
    reassessment of in twenty-first century, 508–11
    triumph of in late twentieth century, 452–56
    waves of, 461n.45
global law schools and law firms, 479–84
Global Legal Monitor online publication, 484
Gneist, Rudolf von, 230
Godefroy, Denis, 74
Goebel, Julius, 32
Goldberg, Jolande, 431
Goldschmidt, Chanan, 524n.307
Goldschmidt, Levin, 433–34
Goodnow, Frank, 267, 280–81
Gorbachev, Mikhail, 452
Gordley, James, 1n.2, 406–7, 473, 476n.112, 477n.116
Gordon, Michael, 407–8, 469n.80
Gordon, Robert, 30–31, 39, 41–42
Gothofredus, Dionysius, 167–68
Gould, James, 161–62
governance, evidence-based, 505. *See also* rule of law
Governance Project (Center on Democracy, Development and the Rule of Law), 489
governmental organizations, role in legal transplantation, 418–28
government law libraries, 316–17
government supervision of American legal transplants
    early postwar period, 349–54
    federalism and antitrust reform for Western Europe, 373–79
    new constitutions in Germany, Japan, and Korea, 354–64
    other legal reforms in Germany, Japan, and Korea, 364–73
    overview, 349

graduate education, 229, 231–33, 417–18
grammar schools, in early republic, 90
Grant, David E., 339n.303
Gray, John Chipman, 255–56
Great Britain. *See also* British colonial period;
   English law
   Americans at universities in, 229n.22
   comparative law in, 45–49
   legal education and literature, 45–47
   ownership of Louisiana and Florida, 148–49, 150–51
   Roman and canon law influence in, 47–49
   treaties with in formative era, 150
Great Exhibition of the Works of Industry of All Nations (1851), 269
Great Seal of the United States, 103–4, 144
Greece, ancient. *See* classical legal models
Green, Leon, 327
Greene, Jack, 96n.58
Greenleaf, Simon, 159
Gregory, Charles, 239
Gridley, Jeremiah, 52, 73, 74, 111
Grimké, Thomas, 208
Grotius, Hugo (Hugo de Groot), 49–50, 52–53, 54n.53, 54n.56, 76, 80, 333–34
Groves, Harry, 411–12
Growth of American Law, The (Hurst), 31
Guarantee Clause, U.S. Constitution, 143–44n.284
Guide to Foreign Legal Materials (Szladits), 429–30
Guide to the Law and Legal Literature series, 293–94
Gummere, Richard, 89–90, 91–92n.36, 96n.57, 99–100, 102n.88
Gunther, Gerald, 395n.189

Hadden, Sally, 216n.367
Hadley, James, 251–52
Hague Academy of International Law, 300–1, 438
Hague Conference of Private International Law, 434–35, 438, 440
hakimiyyatu (in Islam), 514
Hale, Matthew, 167–68
Haley, John, 407, 409–10, 492–93
Hall, Jerome, 199, 202, 290n.73, 324, 339, 342–43, 344n.332, 385n.141
Hall, John, 176–77, 184
Hall, Kermit, 38–39
Hallstein, Walter, 378
Hamilton, Alexander, 12–13, 93, 103n.94, 105n.100, 121, 122, 129–31, 132–33, 133n.232, 141, 143, 144

Hammond, William, 8, 193n.256, 234n.46, 236–37, 240–41, 241n.72, 252, 254, 256–58, 266
Hancock, John, 76–77
Handbook of Anglo-American Legal History (Radin), 27–28
Handbook of the Law of Code Pleading (Clark et al.), 213n.355
Handbuch des öffentlichen Rechts der Gegenwart in Monographien (Marquardsen), 274–75
Handler, Milton, 346
Hanfstaengl, Ernst, 327–28n.255
harmonization of law. *See* unification of law
Harper, William, 239
Harrington, James, 80, 107
Harris, George, 167
Hart, James, 231
Harvard College (colonial), 73n.141, 81–82n.192
Harvard Law Review, 255–56
Harvard Law School, 8, 183–84, 187–88, 228, 260–61
   comparative law courses in postwar twentieth century, 403–4
   degree programs for foreign students, 417–18
   and development of graduate education, 231–33
   in early nineteenth century, 162–63, 165n.89
   East Asia Legal Studies Program, 404, 408, 409n.256
   German-American relations during 1930s, 327–28, 329
   influence on American legal education, 238–40
   Japanese law at, 409–10
   library of, 81, 186, 244, 317–19, 318*t*, 319*t*
Harvey, William, 422n.317
Haskell, John, 478–79
Haskins, George, 53–54, 55–56n.60
Hastings, William, 291–92
Hay, Peter, 413–15, 435, 437, 440–41, 447, 477n.116
Hazard, John, 380–81, 382, 382n.129, 383–84, 383n.133, 385n.141, 386, 387, 388, 392n.174, 398, 398n.201, 399–400, 399n.208, 406, 408, 408–9n.254, 437, 438, 441–42
Hegel, Georg Wilhelm Friedrich, 453n.7
Heineccius, Johann, 49–50
Helmholz, R.H., 3n.14, 146, 157n.58, 158–59, 174n.146
Henderson, Dan, 409–10, 476n.110
Henretta, James, 65
Herget, James, 248, 305–6, 335

Herodotus, 114
Herz, Michael, 193n.256
Herzog, Peter, 405n.239, 471–72
Hessel Yntema Prize, 468
Hevia Bolaños, Juan de, 206–7
hierarchical states, 447–48
High Authority (ECSC), 377
Higher Education Act (1965), 431
Hillard, George, 178
Hilliard, Francis, 160n.71
Hirohito (Emperor of Japan), 352–53, 358–59
Hiroshima, Japan, 352
Hirschl, Ran, 493
historical comparative law, 1–3. *See also* legal history
Historical Introduction to the Legal System (Kimball), 32–33
historical jurisprudence
   American Bar Association, 234–38
   Christopher Tiedeman, 263–64
   against codification, 245–51
   emergence of comparative law as discipline, 264–72
   emulating Germany's law curriculum, 240–44
   German, 8, 19, 180–81, 223–27, 274–75
   and German legal science, 227–28
   Harvard model of education, 231–33, 238–40
   law journal literature on comparative law, 254–56
   law libraries, 244–45
   Oliver Wendell Holmes, 260–62
   overview, 8, 16–22
   Roscoe Pound on, 26
   and sociological jurisprudence in Germany, 259–60
   teaching Roman law in late nineteenth century, 251–54
   and transformation of American legal education, 228–45
   William Hammond, 256–58
   William Howe, 258–59
   Woodrow Wilson, 274–75
History and Harvard Law School (Kimball & Coquillette), 328n.259
History of American Law, A (Friedman), 12n.32, 33–36
History of the Common Law (Langbein et al.), 44
Hitler, Adolf, 306, 326–27, 327–28n.255, 337
Ho, Virginia Harper, 479
Hoadly, George, 247n.104
Hodge, John, 353, 361

Hoeflich, Michael H., 3n.14, 4n.16, 16–17n.62, 17, 146–47, 157–58, 160–61, 169, 173n.140, 173n.143, 184, 185, 191, 226n.10, 252, 255–56, 321
Hoffman, David, 14, 160–61, 164–65, 174–75, 208–9
Hoffman, Richard J., 146n.4
Hofstede, Geert, 522–24
Hohfeld, Wesley, 303
Hollis, Thomas, 74–75
Holmes, Oliver Wendell, Jr., 1, 8, 18–19, 26, 169–70, 252, 260–62
Holst, Hermann von, 229
Honnold, John, 435, 436
Hope, Anthony, 405n.240
Horwitz, Morton, 33, 36–37, 262
household system (*ie*), Japan, 370–71
Howe, Mark, 32
Howe, William, 8, 21–22, 243, 244, 258–59
Huber, Eugen, 291–92
Huber, Ulrich, 158, 184, 189–90, 189n.237
Huberich, Charles, 289, 292, 293, 324n.236
Hudson, Manley, 302, 426–27
Hug, Walther, 310–11, 325n.245
Hugo, Gustav von, 180–81
Hull, N.E.H., 321n.222
human rights, 419–20, 425–28, 495–96
Human Rights Watch, 428
Hume, David, 98–99, 127n.200, 333–34
Hunt, Carleton, 234n.46, 235
Huntington, Henry E., 55–56n.60
Huntington, Samuel, 451, 453–56, 461–62, 463–64, 512
Hurst, Willard, 31–32
Hussey, Alfred, 359n.37
Hutcheson, Francis, 50–51, 98–99
Hutchinson, Thomas, 78

IACL. *See* International Academy of Comparative Law; International Congress of Comparative Law
IALS (International Association of Legal Science), 388, 396–97, 419
Ibbetson, David, 2–3, 3n.14, 48–49
IBRD (International Bank for Reconstruction and Development). *See* World Bank
ICCL (International Committee for Comparative Law), 382–83, 388, 397n.197
ICJ (International Commission of Jurists), 420, 426, 427
IDA (International Development Association), 498
idealism, 426–28

identity politics, 453–54, 508–10
Ideological Origins of the American Revolution, The (Bailyn), 99
ideology, connection between behavior and, 5
ie (household system), Japan, 370–71
Ihering, Rudolf von, 19, 25, 28–29, 259–60, 262, 263–64, 321
ILC (International Legal Center), 421, 422n.317
immersion approach, 466
immigration in colonial British America, 35n.179, 35n.180, 61–62, 66–70
Impact of American Constitutionalism Abroad, The (Friedrich), 350n.5
imperial tradition, Islamic, 513
Importation Clause (U.S. Constitution), 217–18
importing, in legal transplantation, 3–4. *See also* legal transplantation
incommensurability across legal traditions, 462–63
Index to Foreign Legal Periodicals (Stern), 430–31
India, American legal transplants to, 423–24
Indian Law Institute, 423
individualism, versus collectivism, 522–23
indulgence, versus restraint, 523
influence, issue of, 4–6
Ingersoll, Joseph, 184
Inglehart, Ronald, 524–25
inheritance law, U.S. reforms to postwar Japanese, 370–71
Inleiding tot de Hollandsche rechts-geleertheyd (Grotius), 54n.53, 54n.56
Institute for Foreign and International Private Law, 307, 386
Institute of Comparative Law (Tulane), 312, 385, 404, 484
Institute of International Education, 327
Institute of Law at Johns Hopkins University, 304–5
Institutes (Justinian), 73–74, 76–77, 158, 167–69, 183–84, 207, 257
Institutes of the Laws of England (Coke), 74n.154
Institut international pour l'unification du droit privé, 308–9
institutionalist literature, American, 166–71
Institutiones iuris Anglicani (Cowell), 73–74
Institutions of the Law of Scotland, The (Stair), 70
Insular Cases, 268–69, 277–78
Integration Through Law Project (European University Institute), 446–47
intellectual legal history, 6, 28–31, 37, 38–39, 40–41
Inter caetera (Pope Alexander VI), 81

interdisciplinary empirical comparative law, 518–25
internalist approach to legal history, 29–31
International Academy of Comparative Law (IACL), 308n.161, 322–23, 341–42, 468. *See also* International Congress of Comparative Law
  in 1920s, 340–41
  American initiative for reform, 473, 474–75
  formation of, 9, 298–302
  restructuring of in twenty-first century, 477
International Association for Comparative Legal Science and Economics, 265
International Association of Constitutional Law, 494
International Association of Law Libraries (IALL), 430
International Association of Legal Science (IALS), 388, 396–97, 419
International Bank for Reconstruction and Development (IBRD). *See* World Bank
international civil procedure, 441
International Commission of Jurists (ICJ), 420, 426, 427
International Committee for Comparative Law (ICCL), 382–83, 388, 397n.197
International Congress of Comparative Law
  of 1900, 269–72, 290–91, 298
  of 1932, 312, 340–42
  of 1937, 312, 342–43
  of 1950, 312, 343, 382n.129
  of 1954, 398
  of 1958, 398–99
  of 1962, 399
  of 1966, 399
  of 1970, 391, 400
  of 1974, 400–1
  of 1978, 401
  of 1982, 391, 401
  of 1986, 402
  of 1990, 402
  of 1994, 468
  of 1998, 470–71
  of 2000, 470–71
  of 2002, 473
  of 2006, 474–75
  of 2010, 475, 476–77
  of 2014, 478
  AACSL participation in, 396–402
  growth of American attendance in twenty-first century, 472
International Congress of Jurists in New Delhi, 420–21n.312

544 INDEX

International Development Association (IDA), 498
International Encyclopedia of Comparative Law, 428
international expositions, 269–72
International Institute for the Unification of Private Law (UNIDROIT), 432–35
International Journal of Constitutional Law, 491
international law, private, 416–17, 437–41
International Lawyer quarterly, 394
International Legal Center (ILC), 421, 422n.317
international legal unification, 432–37. *See also* unification of law
International Protection of Human Rights (Sohn & Buergenthal), 427n.334
International Third World Legal Studies Association, 422–23
intraregional religious differences, colonial, 63–64
Introduction to American Law (Walker), 15–16, 164
Introduction to Roman Law (Hadley), 251–52
Introduction to the Study of the Roman Law, An (Cushing), 17, 188
Introductory Readings and Materials to the Study of Comparative Law (Deák & Schiller), 346
Iowa Law School, 256–57
Iraq
 rule of law programs in, 497–98, 502–3
 war against terrorism, 512
Ireland, Gordon, 310, 311, 325n.245
Islam, resistance from, 511–15
Islamic law (*shari'a*), 490, 513–14
Islamic State (ISIS), 512–13
Italian Penal Code, The (Wise), 416
Italian Styles (Clark), 464–65

Jackson, John, 424n.325
Jackson, Vicki, 492
James, Duke of York, 56n.62
James II (King of England), 137n.244
James Madison, David Hume, and Modern Political Parties (Moore), 127n.200
Japan
 American legal transplants to, 323, 350, 352–53, 419
 coursebooks on, 409–10
 Meiji Constitution, 358–59
 new constitution in postwar period, 358–60, 363
 occupation of Korea, 361, 372–73
 other legal reforms in postwar period, 367–72
Japan Civil Liberties Union (JCLU), 368

Japanese American Society for Legal Studies, 410n.259, 415n.288
Jay, John, 47, 93, 103n.94, 122, 131–33, 170n.115
Jayne, Allen, 98, 100, 101n.84
Jefferson, Thomas, 47, 50–51, 79n.178, 86–87, 86n.5, 90, 92, 93n.44, 94–101, 104n.95, 108, 112n.137, 115n.148, 121, 121n.172, 123–24, 123n.182, 128, 133–34, 135, 138n.251, 139n.260, 141, 144, 149–50, 152, 153–54, 186, 214n.360, 244, 432
Jensen, Erik, 503n.230
Jitta, Josephus, 289
John Adams Library, 81
Johns Hopkins Institute of Law, 304–5
Johnson, William, 184
joint mediation rule, 512
Jones, Harry, 424n.325
Jones, William, 171n.127
Josephs, Hilary, 469n.80
Jouffroy, Théodore Simon, 181n.194
Journal of Legal Pluralism, 422–23
journals, student-run, 415, 479
judicial globalization, 489–94
judicialization of politics, 496
judicial processes
 and codification, 205, 209–10, 246, 249–50
 Damaška's model for, 447–48
 use of civil law in, 158–59
judicial review of legislation
 in Japanese Constitution, 360
 in postwar Germany, 357
judicial system of Georgia, revision of, 156–57
judicial territorial jurisdiction, 438
Juenger, Friedrich, 388–89, 391–92, 403n.225, 440–41, 467–68, 472n.92, 476n.110
Jurisprudence of Holland, The (Grotius), 54n.53, 54n.56
Justinian, 73–74, 76–77, 92–93, 121, 158, 167–69, 176, 183–84, 207, 257, 295, 296–97

Kaal, Wulf, 477–78
Kaczyński, Jarosław, 509n.252
Kades, Charles, 358–59, 369n.79
Kahn-Freund, Otto, 436–37
Kaleidoscope of Justice, A (Wigmore), 326
Kant, Immanuel, 225n.6, 333–34
Kantorowicz, Hermann, 305n.146
Karsh, Efraim, 513n.266
Karst, Kenneth, 410, 424
Karsten, Peter, 38–39
Katz, Stanley, 7n.31, 30–31
Kaufmann, Philip, 166

Kauper, Paul, 411
Kay, Richard, 474n.101, 474n.104, 477, 479
Kearley, Timothy, 294–95, 297n.110
Keener, William, 21, 24–25, 238, 239, 260–61
Kelsen, Hans, 357
Kennedy, George, 122
Kennedy, John F., 421
Kent, James, 8, 13, 14–15, 152–53, 157, 158, 159–60, 161, 162, 166–67, 169–71, 195–96, 213–14
Kessler, Amalia, 213–14
Kessler, Friedrich, 308, 344–45
Keysor, William, 289n.72
Kilbourne, Richard Holcombe, 205n.316
Kim, Jim Yong, 500–1
Kimball, Bruce A., 328n.259
Kimball, Spencer, 32–33
Kim Il-sung, 353–54
Kirchwey, George, 291, 460n.39
Kirkwood, Marion, 327
Klaus, Sam, 328–29
KMT (Kuomintang) of China, 281, 282–83, 330
Knapp, Aaron, 120
Knox, Hugh, 129
Kocourek, Albert, 278n.27, 293, 296n.105, 324–25, 342–43, 346
Kohl, Helmut, 452n.4
Kohler, Josef, 242n.77, 265, 271, 323
Kommers, Donald, 412, 447
Konefsky, Alfred, 166
Konig, David, 71–72, 95–96, 157–58
Koons, Jack, 422n.317
Korea
  American legal transplants to, 350, 353–54, 419
  authoritarian economic development in, 488
  new constitution in postwar period, 361–64
  other legal reforms in postwar period, 372–73
Korkunov, N.M., 292
Kostal, Rande, 370n.85
Kozyris, John, 441n.403
Kreilkamp, Karl, 334n.285, 335
Kristallnacht, 331
Kritische Zeitschrift für Rechtswissenschaft und Gesetzgebung des Auslandes journal, 180
Kroncke, Jedidiah, 486–87
Kronstein, Heinrich, 344, 365–66, 378, 385n.141, 387
Krüger, Paul, 296–97, 315n.201
Kuhn, Arthur, 291–92, 302
Kühnemann, Eugen, 233
Kuomintang (KMT or Nationalist Party) of China, 281, 282–83, 330
Kyoto Protocol (1998), 511–12n.260

labor policy, reforms to postwar Japanese, 372
Lambert, Edouard, 173n.140, 306–7, 311–12, 341
Land Ordinance (1784), 147–48
Langbein, John, 44, 287–88
Langdell, Christopher, 19, 21, 32, 231–33, 238, 242, 261
Langer, Máximo, 479
Lansing, John, 152–53
large-N research, 519–20
Lasser, Mitchel, 321n.222
late twentieth century
  1990s as decade of opportunities, 452
  American Society of Comparative Law, 468–71
  globalization of American legal institutions, 479–94
  historiography, 29–39
  initial comparative law reaction to globalization, 456–61
  interdisciplinary empirical comparative law, 518–25
  overview, 10
  rule of law programs, 494–508
  tenacity of traditions, cultures, and legal pluralism, 461–67
  triumph of globalization, 452–56
Latin America
  American legal transplants in postwar twentieth century, 424
  Center of Latin American Legal Studies, 315
  Clagett's focus on, 429
  coursebooks on, 409–10
  Guide to the Law and Legal Literature series, 293–94
Laun, Rudolf von, 332
Law (Carter), 23
"Law, Legislation, Codes" (Story), 209
Law and Contemporary Problems journal, 435
law and development, 410, 425, 444–47, 484–89
Law and Development in Latin America (Karst & Rosenn), 410n.264
Law and History (Chase), 41–42
Law and Institutions of the Atlantic Area (Stein & Hay), 413–14
Law and Modernization Program (Yale), 417–18
"Law and Morals" (Chroust), 336
Law and Social Change in the U.S.S.R. (Hazard), 442n.407
law and society approach, 441–44. *See also* legal sociology; sociological jurisprudence
Law and Society Association, 443

Law and the Behavioral Sciences (Friedman & Macaulay), 443
Law and the Conditions of Freedom in the Nineteenth-Century United States (Hurst), 31
law books. *See* legal literature
law education. *See* legal education
law firm libraries, 317n.205
law firms, global, 479–84
Law for the Restoration of the Professional Civil Service of 1933 (Germany), 326–27
Law in Japan: An Annual journal, 410n.259
Law in Japan journal, 415
law libraries
   in colonial British America, 73n.145, 74n.154
   in early twentieth century, 312–20, 318t, 319t
   in formative era, 186–87
   in late nineteenth century, 244–45
   in postwar twentieth century, 428–32
Law Library of Congress
   Center of Latin American Legal Studies, 315, 381
   creation of, 186–87
   in early twentieth century, 313–16, 317–18, 318t, 319t
   in late nineteenth century, 244–45
   in postwar twentieth century, 428–29, 431–32
   in twenty-first century, 484
law office-type schools, 161–62
law of nations, 49–51, 121n.173
Law of Torts, The (Fleming), 394
Laws (Plato), 448–49
Laws and Jurisprudence of England and America, The (Dillon), 20
Laws and Liberties of Massachusetts, The (Massachusetts General Court), 12n.32, 55–56
law schools. *See* legal education
Lawyer of the Americas journal, 415
lawyers
   American assistance to foreign, in 1960s, 421
   in American revolutionary period, 89–90
   in China, 516
   in colonial British America, 57–60
   and rule of law, 496
   training for in formative era, 161–66
LC. *See* Law Library of Congress; Library of Congress
Learned, Marion, 67–68
learned law, 160n.68
   American Bar Association, 234–38
   Christopher Tiedeman, 263–64
   emergence of comparative law as discipline, 264–72
   emulating Germany's law curriculum, 240–44
   German historical jurisprudence, 223–27
   German legal science, 227–28
   Harvard model of education, 231–33, 238–40
   law journal literature on comparative law, 254–56
   law libraries, 244–45
   Oliver Wendell Holmes, 260–62
   overview, 8
   sociological jurisprudence in Germany, 259–60
   teaching Roman law in late nineteenth century, 251–54
   transformation of American legal education, 228–45
   William Hammond, 256–58
   William Howe, 258–59
Lectures on Law (Wilson), 118–19, 120–21
Le Droit Public (Domat), 185
Lee, R.W., 54n.53
Legal and Political Hermeneutics (Lieber), 193, 257
legal apprenticeship, 45–46, 51–53, 161–62, 164
legal cultures, 463, 464–67, 520–22
legal diversity, in colonial period, 71–72, 95
legal education
   academic law and development programs, 484–89
   American Bar Association and, 234–38
   in American revolutionary period, 89–90
   American Society of Comparative Law goals, 469–70
   in colonial British America, 51–53
   comparative law courses and institutes, 402–4
   comparative law journals and projects, 415–17
   David Hoffman's plan for, 174–75
   degree programs for foreign students, 417–18
   early twentieth century interest in Roman and civil law, 285–86
   emulating Germany's law curriculum, 240–44
   in England, 45–47
   in formative era, 146–47, 161–75, 190–91
   general comparative law coursebooks, 404–8
   German émigré legal scholars in U.S., 331–33
   global law schools, 479–84
   Harvard model, 231–33, 238–40
   initial reaction to globalization, 456–61
   in postwar twentieth century, 402–18

INDEX 547

social science in early twentieth
    century, 303–6
specialized comparative law
    coursebooks, 408–15
teaching Roman law in late nineteenth
    century, 251–54
transformation based on legal
    science, 228–45
legal foundation for new republic. *See* early
    American republic, legal foundation for
legal history
    comparative, historical comparative law
        and, 1–3
    and comparative law, 41–44
    historiography: 1771 to 1900, 12–22
    historiography: 1900 to 1950, 22–29
    historiography: 1950 to 2000, 29–39
    historiography: twenty-first century, 40–44
    methodological issues, 3–6
    scope of book, 7–12
legal indicators, 504–8, 519–20
legal institutions, globalization of
    American, 479–94
legal literature
    American institutionalist, 166–71
    in colonial British America, 52–53
    depicting Roman and civil law in formative
        era, 176–87
    and education in formative era, 161–75
    in England, 45–47
    in formative era, 191
    legal foundation for early republic, 87–88
legal missionaries, 421–25, 466, 484–85
Legal Outlines (Hoffman), 175
legal philosophy, 321. *See also* Enlightenment
    political philosophy; sociological
    jurisprudence
legal pluralism, 461–67, 510
legal realism, 39, 303–6, 334, 380–81, 382n.128,
    See also sociological jurisprudence
legal reform, foreign, 364–73, 421–25
Legal Research Institute, 484
legal rules, establishment of American system
    of, 12–16
legal science
    American Bar Association, 234–38
    American institutionalist literature, 166–71
    Christopher Tiedeman, 263–64
    emergence of comparative law as
        discipline, 264–72
    emulating Germany's law
        curriculum, 240–44
    in formative era, 159–61

German, 227–28
and German historical jurisprudence, 223–27
Harvard model of education, 231–33, 238–40
law journal literature on comparative
    law, 254–56
law libraries, 244–45
Oliver Wendell Holmes, 260–62
sociological jurisprudence in
    Germany, 259–60
teaching Roman law in late nineteenth
    century, 251–54
and transformation of American legal
    education, 228–45
and university legal education, 164–65
William Hammond, 256–58
William Howe, 258–59
legal services, global, 479–84
legal sociology, 259–60, 441–47, 464–65. *See
    also* sociological jurisprudence
legal systems, colonial, 54–55
*Legal Thought in the United States of America
    under Contemporary Pressures* (Hazard &
    Wagner), 399n.208
legal traditions, 462–64
Legal Traditions of the World (Glenn), 463–64
legal transplantation
    and academic law and development
        programs, 486–87, 488–89
    to China, 280–84, 285–86, 515
    from China, 517
    early attempts at American, 277–84, 285–86
    in early postwar twentieth century, 349–54
    federalism and antitrust reform for Western
        Europe, 373–79
    from Germany in 1930s and 1940s, 331–
        33, 343–47
    government supervision of
        American, 349–79
    and intellectual legal history, 41
    to Japan, 323, 350, 352–53, 419
    to Korea, 350, 353–54, 419
    legal foundation for early republic, 88
    new constitutions in Germany, Japan, and
        Korea, 354–64
    other legal reforms in Germany, Japan, and
        Korea, 364–73
    overview, 3–4
    role of governmental and nongovernmental
        organizations, 418–28
    rule of law programs, 502
legal treatises, American, 171–74
legal uniformity. *See* codification;
    unification of law

Legaré, Hugh, 160–61, 182–83, 191, 195–96, 225–26
legislative codification. *See* codification
Legislative Reference Service (LRS), 315
Lehrbuch des gemeinen in Deutschland geltenden peinlichen Rechts (Feuerbach), 203
Leonard, Daniel, 79
Leonhard, Rudolf, 294
Lerner, Renée, 44
Les Lois Civiles dans Leur Ordre Naturel (Domat), 47, 155–56, 185
Leval, Gaston de, 291–92
Levy, Ernst, 297
Lévy-Ullmann, Henri, 290–91, 298, 300n.125
Lewis, Meriwether, 150
Lewis, William Draper, 289, 291, 309, 345, 345n.336, 460n.39
Lexicon (Calvinus), 76–77
Lex Mundi, 481
lex-ratio tradition, 338
lex-voluntas tradition, 338
liberal democracy, 451
liberalism. *See also* globalization
  economic, 452–54
  temporal relation between republicanism and, 5–6
liberty, republican, 109–11
Liberty of Contract (Pound), 321n.222
libraries. *See* law libraries
Library Company of Philadelphia, 186n.223
Library of Congress (LC), 244–45. *See also* Law Library of Congress
  and comparative law movement, 293–94
  in early twentieth century, 312–13
  establishment of, 186
  in postwar twentieth century, 431–32
Licht, Amir N., 524n.307
Lieber, Francis, 172–73, 180n.185, 191–95, 203–4, 225–26, 257, 266
Life of the Mind in America, The (Miller), 29–30
lifetime achievement awards (ASCL), 473–74
Li Keqiang, 500–1
Litchfield Law School, 161–62
Little, Brown & Company, 293
Littlefield, Charles, 291n.76
Livermore, Samuel, 163n.80, 189–90
Lives (Plutarch), 130n.213
Livingston, Edward, 151–53, 170, 176n.159, 177, 192, 201–2, 204–5, 206, 208–9
Livingston, Robert, 96–97, 145–46n.2, 149–50, 152–53, 158
Livingston, William, 52n.44, 129
Livy (Titus Livius), 102, 109–10

Llewellyn, Karl, 305–6, 327, 328–29, 332–33, 433–34, 441–42
Lobingier, Charles, 278–79, 281–82, 283–84, 286n.60, 292, 295, 302, 310, 342–43, 373
Locke, John, 79n.176, 80, 94–95, 98–101, 107, 118n.160, 141–42, 333–34
Loewenstein, Karl, 342–43, 356, 364, 365
Loewy, Walter, 292
Logan, James, 46–47
London Conference (1948), 354–55
long-term orientation, 523
Lorenzen, Ernest, 184n.210, 291–92, 293, 311
Los Angeles County Law Library, 428–29, 430
Louisiana
  Civil Code of 1825, 204–5, 212–13, 220–21
  Code of Practice of 1825, 153, 206–7
  Digest of 1808, 153–56, 204–5, 219–21
  Hoffman's *Course* attraction in, 175
  Practice Act of 1805, 152n.32, 153, 204–5, 206–7
  slave law in, 219–21
Louisiana Law Journal, 182
Louisiana Purchase, 148–56
Louisiana Purchase Exposition Company, 287
Louisiana Remonstrance, 151–52
Lowell, Lawrence, 277n.22, 327
Lower Louisiana, 148n.13, 149–50, 152n.32, 152n.33
LRS (Legislative Reference Service), 315
Luther, Hans, 330
Lynch, Dennis, 424n.326

MacArthur, Douglas, 352–53, 358–59, 358n.34, 372
Macaulay, Stewart, 443
MacBride, Seán, 420n.311
Macias, Steven, 160–61, 208–9, 210
Mackeldey, Ferdinand, 188
Macmillan Company, 293
Macneil, Ian, 422n.317
Madison, James, 51, 86–87, 87n.12, 93, 100–1, 103, 103n.94, 105n.100, 106, 109n.121, 111, 116, 122–28, 133–34, 135–39, 141, 144, 149n.18, 151n.30
Maggs, Peter B., 406n.244
Magic Mirror, The (Hall), 38–39
Maier, Pauline, 96n.58
Maine, Henry, 261
Malcolm, George A., 278–79, 278n.26
Mamlyuk, Boris, 479
Mann, Bruce, 40
Mansfield, Lord, 47–48
Manual of Political Ethics (Lieber), 193

manumission, 216, 221
Marcus Aurelius (Roman Emperor), 109n.122
Maritain, Jacques, 334–35, 338
maritime law, 176–77, 184, 185
Markesinis, Basil, 458, 461n.44
market capitalism, 452–54, 487. *See also* globalization
Markovits, Inga, 448
Marquardsen, Heinrich, 274–75
Marriage and Divorce Laws in Europe (Coudert), 268
Marshall, George, 351–52, 375–76
Marshall, John, 92, 217n.370
Marshall Plan (Economic Cooperation Act of 1948), 351–52, 375–76
Martin, François, 175, 183–84
Marx, Karl, 453n.7
Mary II (Queen of England), 137n.244, 139
Maryland, colonial, 57–58, 61–62
masculinity, versus femininity, 523
Masferrer, Aniceto, 245n.92
Mason, George, 96–97, 112n.137, 123, 133–34, 137, 138–41
Massachusetts, 36
   codification of common law of, 159, 209
   colonial period, 55–56, 57n.71, 59, 62, 63, 77–78
   contingent ratification of Constitution, 133–34
Massachusetts Constitution, 111–12, 114n.144
Massachusetts Declaration of Rights, 112, 114n.144
Massachusetts Government Act (1774), 79n.177
Masterson, William E., 339n.303
Mayor's Court (colonial New York), 53–54
McCloy, John, 350, 352, 354n.19, 375, 420
McCullough, David, 81n.190
McDougal, Myres, 385n.141, 419–20
McGarvie, Mark, 63
McKinley, William, 278n.25
Means, Robert, 417–18
Mechem, Floyd, 293
Medina, Rubens, 431
Meiji Constitution (Japan), 358–59
Meili, Friedrich, 289
Melton, James, 494
Mensch, Elizabeth, 63
mercantile law, 189
Merryman, John, 388–89, 401–2, 407–8, 425, 445–46, 473–74, 492–93
methodology, 3–6
Michigan Law School, 403–4, 415–16, 417
Middle Colonies, 63, 71–72

Mikell, William, 22n.94, 289
Milhaupt, Curtis, 488
Mill, John Stuart, 259n.164
Millar, Robert, 343n.325
Miller, Henrich, 69–70
Miller, Perry, 29–30
Miller Center of Public Affairs (University of Virginia), 412
missionary lawyers, 421–25, 466, 484–85
Missouri Compromise, 219n.382
Mitchell, William, 341, 385n.140
Mittermaier, Carl, 180–81, 191, 192, 203, 211, 264–65
mixed laws, 189n.236
Miyakawa, Masuji, 291–92
Modern Criminal Science Series (AALS), 293
modernization, concern with in 1950s, 419
Modern Legal Philosophy Series (AALS), 293, 323–24
Molloy, Charles, 73–74
Mommsen, Theodor, 296–97
monarchical republics, 113–14
Money in the Law (Nussbaum), 332–33
Monnet, Jean, 376–77
Monroe, James, 123–24, 149–50
Montesquieu, Charles-Louis de Secondat de, 25, 73–74, 85, 87, 94–95, 104, 105–7, 105n.100, 109–10, 117–18, 126, 127, 128, 131, 133, 138–39, 141–42, 197–98, 214n.360, 227
Montesquieu and Constitution of Liberty (Rahe), 105n.102
Moore, Elon H., 202n.295
Moore, John Allphin, Jr., 127n.200
Moore, John Bassett, 298–99, 300
morality and law, 333–38
moral philosophy, in colonial British America, 49–51
Moreau, Jean F., 416n.294
Moreau-Lislet, Louis, 153–56, 204–5, 220
Morgenthau, Henry, 350
Morris, Richard, 412
Morris, Thomas, 216n.366
Morrison, James, 311–12
Moses, Bernard, 267–68
Mueller, Gerhard, 199n.284, 416
Muldoon, James, 49–50n.27, 81
multiculturalism, 455–56, 466, 509–10
multinational law firms, 479–84
Mumford, Quincy, 431
Murphy, Frank, 368n.77
Murphy, Walter, 412–13

Mutual Educational and Cultural Exchange Act (1961), 421n.315
Myers, Gustavus, 87–88n.14

Nadelmann, Kurt, 384, 385n.141, 387, 388, 392–93, 392n.174, 398–99, 434–35, 437, 439, 440
Nafziger, James, 470–71, 471n.87, 473n.96
Nagasaki, Japan, 352
Napoleonic Code of 1804 (French), 154, 167–68n.100, 212–13, 245–46, 251
nation, legal foundation for. *See* republic, legal foundation for American
National Assembly (South Korea), 353–54
national character of law, 225, 226, 275
National Conference of Commissioners on Uniform State Laws, 250–51
nationalism
  and globalization, 453, 456
  twenty-first century return to, 508–11
Nationalist Party (Kuomintang) of China, 281, 282–83, 330
National Program for Acquisitions and Cataloging (NPAC), 431, 432n.354
National Socialist Workers' Party (Nazis), Germany, 326–32, 337, 356, 364
nation building policies, 497–98, 502n.228
Native American law, 36
natural law
  Calvin's Case, 79–80n.179
  in colonial British America, 49–51, 82
  contrast with legal science, 227
  and Declaration of Independence, 94–101
  in eighteenth century Germany, 225
  in formative era, 146, 157–58, 173–74
  James Wilson's views on, 121
  Jean Domat's writings on, 47
  in John Adams' practice and writing, 79–80
  legal foundation for early republic, 86–87, 91–92
  revival of Thomistic in 1930s, 333–38
  and slavery, 218–19
  statutes against, English ideas on, 46
Natural Law, The (Rommen), 337, 338
natural rights, in Bill of Rights, 134–35, 136–37n.241, 138–39, 141
natural sciences, drawing from, 160–61
Nazis (National Socialist Workers' Party), Germany, 326–32, 337, 356, 364
Needham, Charles, 243, 271–72
negotiable instruments, comparative law projects centered on, 415–16

Negotiable Instruments Law (NIL) of 1896, 250–51
Nelson, William, 3n.12, 33, 36, 54–55, 65–66, 82n.194
neo-Romanticism, 466–67
Neukom, William, 506
New Amsterdam, 62, 63n.98
New Delhi Congress, 420–21n.312
New England, colonial, 54–55, 63, 71–72
New Institute of the Imperial or Civil Law, A (Wood), 46–47, 52–53, 73, 76–77
new nation, legal foundation for. *See* republic, legal foundation for American
New Netherland, 38–39, 58, 62, 63n.98
new property, 449
New York
  Code of Civil Procedure, 210, 211–14
  codification debate in, 245–47
  colonial period, 53–54, 56n.62, 58, 63
  Field Code, 17–18, 245–47, 251
  penal reform in formative era, 200–1
  slavery in, 215
New York Constitution, 132, 211–12
New York Law Institute, 318*t*
New York Supreme Court of Judicature, 132n.223
New York University (NYU) School of Law, 374, 416, 417n.301, 457, 480
NGOs. *See* nongovernmental organizations
Nicholas II (Tsar of Russia), 315n.201
Nicolls, Matthias, 56n.62
Nicolls, Richard, 53–54, 56n.62
NIL (Uniform Negotiable Instruments Law) of 1896, 250–51
nineteenth century historiography, 13–22. *See also* formative era; historical jurisprudence
Nollkaemper, André, 488–89n.167
nongovernmental organizations (NGOs)
  law and development approach, 444
  role in legal transplantation, 418–28
  rule of law programs, 494–95, 496, 498–501, 506–7
  supporting comparative law, 403–4
North, Douglass, 485
North American Review, 182–83
North Korea, 353–54, 361
Northwestern University, 319–20
Northwest Ordinance (1787), 147–48, 217–18
notaries, in New Netherland, 58
"Notes on Ancient and Modern Confederacies" (Madison), 124–25
"Notes on Government" (Madison), 127–28
Novanglus letters (Adams), 79–81

Nova Scotia, 35n.181
NPAC (National Program for Acquisitions and Cataloging), 431, 432n.354
Nugent, Thomas, 50n.32, 105n.102
numerical comparative law, 518–19
Nussbaum, Arthur, 332–33, 416–17, 438
NYU (New York University) School of Law, 374, 416, 417n.301, 457, 480

Obama, Barack, 497–98, 512–13
Oceana, The (Harrington), 80
OECD (Organisation for Economic Co-operation and Development), 376n.108
OEEC (Organisation for European Economic Cooperation), 375–76
Okudaira, Yasuhiro, 360
On Civil Liberty and Self Government (Lieber), 194
On Crimes and Punishments (Beccaria), 142
Open Society Foundations, 428
Oppenheimer, Fritz, 365n.62
Oppler, Alfred, 362, 367–68n.74, 368–71
Orbán, Viktor, 509n.252
Ordonnance Civile (France), 206
Oregon Treaty (1846), 150
O'Reilly, Alejandro, 153n.39
organicism, 232n.35
Organisation for Economic Co-operation and Development (OECD), 376n.108
Organisation for European Economic Cooperation (OEEC), 375–76
Origin, Growth and Function of Law, The (Carter), 249–50
Origin of Species (Darwin), 262
Orleans Territory, 150n.19, 151–56
Osakwe, Christopher, 407–8
Outlines of the History of English and American Law (Walsh), 29
Outline Study of Law (Russell), 21
Oxford Companion to American Law (Hall et al.), 43
Oxford Handbook of Comparative Law (Reimann & Zimmermann), 460
Oxford University Press (OUP), 475, 478–79

Palmer, Vernon, 155, 205, 219, 220, 477n.116
Palmieri, Edmund, 395n.189
Pan-Europa (Coudenhove-Kalergi), 374–75
Pan European Union (PEU), 374–75
Panorama of the World's Legal Systems, A (Wigmore), 325, 326
Parallele or Conference of the Civill Law, the Canon Law, and the Common Law of this Realme of England, A (Fulbecke), 46

Parise, Agustín, 190n.241
Parisi, Francesco, 473n.98
Paris World Exposition (1900), 270
Parker, Edwin, 385n.140
Parker School of Foreign and Comparative Law (Columbia), 332–33, 341n.318, 385, 404, 416–17, 429–30, 438, 484
Pastorius, Francis, 67–68
path dependence theory, 499n.215
"Path of the Law, The" (Holmes), 262
Patterson, Edwin, 24, 324
Paul, James, 422
Peace Corps, 421
Peace Palace (The Hague), 300–1
Pearson, Ellen, 161, 216–17n.369
Pechota, Vratislav, 430n.347
Peerenboom, Randall, 488–89
Peiyang University, 280n.35
penal reform, 100–1
 by Field, 245–46
 in formative era, 152–53, 192, 197–204
penitentiary system, 192, 200–1
Penn, William, 67–68, 72
Pennsylvania
 in colonial period, 63, 72
 eighteenth-century German immigrants in, 67–70
 penal reform in formative era, 200
Pennsylvania Constitution, 118–20, 197n.275
Pennsylvania Declaration of Rights, 140n.263
Pennsylvania State Bar Association, 290
Pensylvanischer Berichte newspaper, 69n.123
People's Republic of China (PRC). *See* China
Perdue, Wendy Collins, 458n.28
Permanent Court of Arbitration, 300–1
Permanent Court of International Justice, 300–1
personal law libraries, 186–87
personal laws, 189n.236
persons, law of, 167
Peterson, Courtland, 388–89, 389–90n.166, 390–92, 469
PEU (Pan European Union), 374–75
Pharr, Clyde, 296–97
Philadelphia Convention, 124, 125, 126
Philippine Assembly, 277n.24
Philippine Commission, 279–80
Philippine Law Review, 278–79
Philippine Organic Act, 277n.24
Philippines, American legal transplants to, 9, 277–80, 284, 418–19
Phillips, Willard, 178n.170, 183n.202
physiocrats, French, 100–1
Picker, Colin, 473–74

Pickering, John, 191
Pihlajamäki, Heikki, 44
Pincoffs, Adolphe, 252
Plato, 448–49
pluralism
    legal foundation for early republic, 86
    religious, in colonial British America, 60–72
    tenacity of, 461–67
Plutarch, 130n.213
Pocock, J.G.A., 99–100
policy-implementing processes, 447–48
political philosophy, 86, 88–93. *See also* Enlightenment political philosophy; republic, legal foundation for American
political science, 267–68
Political Science and Comparative Constitutional Law (Burgess), 268
politics
    of identity, 453–54, 508–10
    judicialization of, 496
    in writing and practice of John Adams, 74–77
Politics (Crane & Moses), 267–68
Pollock, Frederick, 271
Pollock, James, 355–56
Polybius, 85, 91–92n.36, 99–100, 102n.90
Pomeroy, John, 252, 258, 261
Pompidou, Georges, 374–75
Pope Alexander VI, 81
popular sovereignty, 116, 117–18, 120–21
populist nationalism, 508–11
positive law
    science of, 225, 227
    and slave laws, 219
postmodernism, 458
postwar twentieth century
    American Association for the Comparative Study of Law, 384–402
    American legal transplants, 349–79, 418–28
    developments in American law schools, 402–18
    historiography, 29–39
    overview, 9–10
    re-establishing comparative law as academic discipline, 379–84
    themes in comparative law research, 428–49
Pothier, Robert, 158, 172n.128, 183–84, 185, 206–7
Potsdam Agreement (1945), 354–55, 378
Potsdam Conference (1945), 350–51
Potsdam Declaration (1945), 352–53, 361
Pound, Roscoe, 7n.31, 8, 9, 24–27, 28–29, 156, 157–58, 171n.127, 226–27, 248n.107, 259n.164, 260, 262n.176, 273, 282–83, 284n.53, 291–92, 293, 298–99, 303, 305–6, 307n.154, 309, 311, 320–23, 324n.236, 328, 329, 334, 336, 339–41, 342–43, 346n.339, 392–93, 398n.201, 442n.409, 460n.39
power distance, 522
powers, separation of, 104–5, 106, 111, 127, 136n.240, 141
Practice Act (1805), 152n.32, 153, 204–5, 206–7
PRC (People's Republic of China). *See* China
precedent, 49, 194, 303
pre-revolutionary period. *See* colonial period; republic, legal foundation for American
presentism, 328n.259
Presser, Stephen, 37–39, 321n.223
Principes du droit naturel (Burlamaqui), 49–50, 98
Principes du droit politique (Burlamaqui), 98
Prisoner of Zenda, The (Hope), 405n.240
prison reform, 192, 200–1, 203–4
private international law, 416–17, 437–41
private law. *See also* codification; formative era
    coursebooks related to, 411
    shift from public law to, 145–47
private law libraries, 316–17
private notaries, in New Netherland, 58
Privy Council (England), 56
probate proceedings, 77
procedural systems, Damaška's model for, 447–48
procedure codes, civil, 211–14
Proceedings of the Section of International and Comparative Law journal, 310–11, 339, 380n.120
Progressive movement, 276, 277–78
Progress of Comparative Law, The (Hug & Ireland), 325n.245
Project in Intercultural Studies (University of Chicago), 403n.226
Project on International Procedure (Columbia), 395
property, view of slaves as, 216
property rights, 141, 142
proportionality principle, in criminal law, 142, 198n.279, 199
proprietary law schools, 161–63
Protestants, in colonial British America, 60–64
public law. *See also* republic, legal foundation for American
    American legal transplants to Philippines, 279
    coursebooks related to, 411
    shift to private law from, 145–47
    on slavery in formative era, 214–21

Publius (Valerius Publicola), 103, 122n.176
Pufendorf, Samuel von, 49–50, 52–53, 80, 333–34
punishment, 142, 197–204
Puritans (Congregationalists), 55–56, 57, 60–62, 63, 72n.137
Putnam, Herbert, 312–13
Pye, Kenneth, 424n.325

Quakers, 56, 57, 67, 68–69
quantitative comparative law, 518–19

Rabban, David, 2–3, 26n.118, 29n.131, 261, 262
Rabel, Ernst, 307, 308, 311–12, 333, 345, 366, 382, 386, 433–34, 435, 436, 437, 442
Radin, Max, 27–28, 250, 294, 332
Rahe, Paul A., 105n.102
Rakove, Jack, 137–38
Randolph, Edmund, 103
Rankin, Charles, 281–82, 283–84
Rasco, Russell, 385n.141
ratification of Constitution, 116–18, 122, 131, 133–34
Raynolds, Edward, 285–86
Re, Edward, 347, 386, 388, 389, 391–92, 394, 402–3
reactive state ideology, 447–48
Readings in American Legal History (Howe), 32
Readings in Roman Law and the Civil Law and Modern Codes as Developments Thereof (Pound), 322
Readings on the History and System of the Common Law (Pound), 24–25
Reagan, Ronald, 452n.4
realism, 39, 303–6, 334, 380–81, 382n.128. *See also* sociological jurisprudence
real laws, 189n.236
Recopilación de las Indias, 206–7
Rediscovering Francis Lieber (Herz), 193n.256
Redlich, Josef, 240
Reed v. Reed (1971), 396n.195
Rees, Peter, 329n.265
Reese, Willis, 386, 387n.149, 388, 389, 404, 438–39
Reeve, Tapping, 161–62, 171n.127
regionalism, in colonial period, 63–64, 71–72
Reid, John, 78, 96n.58
Reimann, Mathias, 3n.14, 224n.3, 224n.5, 261, 262, 387n.151, 437, 439–40, 457–58, 459–60, 461n.43, 469n.80, 473, 474–76, 477n.116, 481n.128
Reinhold, Meyer, 90–92, 93, 99–100, 122n.178, 145–46

Reitz, John, 459, 469n.80, 474n.104, 475, 477–78, 502
religion
  colonial religious establishment, 60–62, 63
  diversity of, and legal foundation for early republic, 86–87
  freedom of, 86–87, 123–24
  and globalization, 453–54, 453n.10, 453n.11, 454n.15
  and peace between civilizations, 464
  toleration of by state, 141–42
  variation in colonial British America, 60–72
Reports (Coke), 130n.212
republic, legal foundation for American
  Alexander Hamilton, 129–31
  Bill of Rights, 133–42
  classical legal models, 88–93, 143–44
  Declaration of Independence, 98, 99–100
  education in foreign law and political theory, 88–93
  The Federalist essays, 122
  golden age of comparative law, 85–88
  James Madison, 122–28
  James Wilson, 115–21
  John Adams, 111–15
  John Jay, 131–33
  overview, 7–8
  principle of liberty, 109–11
  republican form of government in Constitution, 101–9
  Thomas Jefferson, 94–101
republicanism, temporal relation between liberalism and, 5–6
republican liberty, 109–11
Republican Party, 128n.204
repugnancy principle, in colonial charters, 66
restatements, by American Law Institute, 309–10, 345, 438–39
restraint, indulgence versus, 523
Revised Uniform Sales Act, 433n.362
Revolutionary Era, 5–6, 69–70, 129–30. *See also* colonial period; republic, legal foundation for American
Revue Étrangère de Législation et d'Économie Politique, 180–81
Reynolds, Thomas, 430–31
Rhee, Syngman, 353–54, 362, 364
Rheinstein, Max, 309n.169, 324, 345, 364, 365, 385n.141, 387, 392n.175, 393–94, 399–400, 404–5, 406, 437, 442–43, 448–49
Rhode Island, colonial, 63
Richard, Carl J., 100, 107, 121, 144
Richardson, Sally, 479

Riesenfeld, Stefan, 332, 476n.110
rights
   emergence of human rights law, 425–28
   of Korean people, ordinance on, 363
   in rule of law programs, 495–96
   as theme in comparative constitutional law, 491
Robert R. Livingston (Scott), 149n.17
Robertson, Donald, 122–23
Robertson, Robbie, 461n.45, 462n.47
Rockefeller, John, 312–13n.187
Rockefeller Foundation, 312, 327, 332, 404
Roeber, A.G., 64n.101
Rogers, Henry, 236–37, 238n.60, 269–70
Roman Catholicism, 60, 61–62
Romanist branch of historical jurisprudence, 225n.7, 227
Roman law, 42–43. *See also* classical legal models
   and American institutionalist literature, 166–71
   American jurists embracing in late nineteenth century, 256–59, 260–64
   and codification of American law, 211
   in colonial British America, 49–53, 82
   and Declaration of Independence, 99–100
   early twentieth century interest in, 285–86, 294–97
   in England, 47–49
   expanded interest in nineteenth century, 146–47
   in formative era legal education, 165–66, 174–87
   Hugh Legaré's erudition in, 195–97
   in John Adams' practice and writing, 76–77, 80–81
   law journal literature on comparative law, 254–56
   legal foundation for early republic, 86, 88–93, 94, 138–39, 143
   Luther Cushing's introduction to, 188
   in nineteenth-century legal history books, 16–17, 21–22
   rise of American legal history as distinct discipline, 38–39
   Roscoe Pound's scholarship in, 27, 321
   on slavery, 214–15
   and slavery in America, 217, 219–21
   teaching in late nineteenth century, 8, 251–54
   translation of legal materials, 183–85
   use by formative era American judges, 158
Roman Law in the Modern World (Sherman), 295–96

Roman Principate, 102–3, 110
Roman Republic
   debate about republics and democracies, 104–5
   influence on U.S. Constitution, 101–4
   in John Adams' *Defence*, 114–15
   legal foundation for early republic, 143
   republican liberty, 109–10
   as resource for building American republic, 86, 91–92
Rome Reborn on Western Shores (Shalev), 87n.11
Rome Statute (1998), 511–12n.260
Rommen, Heinrich, 336–38
Roosevelt, Franklin D., 327–28n.255, 331, 350–51, 350n.6
Root, Elihu, 277n.22
Roscoe Pound and Karl Llewellyn (Hull), 321n.222
Rosen, Lawrence, 521
Rosenfeld, Michel, 491, 492, 494
Rosenn, Keith, 388–89, 410, 424
Ross, Edward, 306n.151
Ross, Jacqueline, 476n.111
Ross, Richard, 40
Rowe, Leo, 291–92
Rowell, Milo, 359n.37
rule of law
   in academic law and development programs, 485–86, 487, 488–89
   in China, 515, 516–17
   and constitutionalism, 492
   emergence of legal indicators, 504–8
   interdisciplinary research on, 520, 524
   and Islam, 514–15
   law and development approach, 444–45
   overview, 11–12
   programs related to from 1990 to 2020, 494–508
Rule of Law Index (WJP), 506–7
Rule of Law Initiative (ABA), 504
Rule of Law Program (Stanford), 502–3
Rush, Benjamin, 104, 119
Russell, Isaac, 21
Russia. *See* Soviet Union
Rutland, Robert Allen, 126n.195, 139n.260

Sadat, Leila, 473–74, 475
St. George Tucker and the Legacy of Slavery (Curtis), 216–17n.369
St. German, Christopher, 46, 52–53, 73–74
St. Louis Law School, 257
St. Louis Universal Congress of Lawyers and Jurists (1904), 284–85, 287–89, 298

INDEX 555

Saleilles, Raymond, 270–71, 306–7
Sampson, William, 208–9, 210
Sanford, H.S., 202n.299
Sauer, Christoph, 68–70
Savigny, Friedrich Carl von, 18, 23, 25, 28–29, 180–81, 196, 224, 225, 227, 228, 233, 241, 256–57, 259, 261, 263–64, 289n.71
Sayre, Paul, 342–43
Scalise, Ronald, 479
SCAP (Supreme Commander for the Allied Powers), 352–53, 358–60, 367–72
Scheppele, Kim, 476n.111
Schiller, Arthur, 346, 422
Schlesinger, Arthur, Jr., 452–53
Schlesinger, Arthur M., Sr., 453n.8
Schlesinger, Rudolf, 385n.141, 387, 400, 404–6, 407n.247, 436–37, 476n.110
Schmidt, Gustavus, 182, 190
Schoenrich, Otto, 302
Scholasticism and Politics (Maritain), 334n.286
Schuman, Robert, 374n.99, 376–77
Schwartz, Shalom H., 524n.307
Scialoja, Vittorio, 298, 300n.125, 308
science, legal. *See* legal science
science of comparative law, 181–82
Scotland, eighteenth-century immigrants from, 66–70
Scott, George, 314n.194
Scott, James Brown, 149n.17, 280–81, 289, 298–99, 300–1, 341–42
Scott, Samuel, 286n.60, 291–92, 294–95, 296–97
Scottish Enlightenment, 94, 115n.147, 120, 121
Seavey, Warren, 280n.35
Second Continental Congress, 96–97
Second Treatise of Government (Locke), 80, 100, 141
Section of International and Comparative Law (ABA), 286–87, 310–11, 339–40, 380–81, 394
Section of International and Comparative Law: Proceedings journal, 380n.120
Section of International Law (ABA), 482n.135
Section of Legal Education (ABA), 236–38, 244
secular natural law, 333–34
Select Essays in Anglo-American Legal History (Committee of the AALS), 22–23
Selections on the Elements of Jurisprudence (Keener), 21
self-study, 45–46, 51–53
Sellers, Mortimer, 1, 3n.14, 88–89, 101–3, 108, 109–10, 477–78
Semmes, Thomas, 247–48
Senate, 143

separate prison system, 200
separation of powers, 104–5, 106, 111, 127, 136n.240, 141
serfdom, 214–15
Seven Years War (French and Indian War), 75–76, 148–49
Sewall, Samuel, 178n.170
Shalev, Eran, 87n.11
shari'a, 490, 513–14
Sheehan, Colleen A., 128
Sheng, Robert, 282–83
Sherman, Charles, 285–86n.58, 295–96, 310n.174
Sherman, Gordon, 291–92
Sherman, Roger, 96–97
Shick, Robert, 291–92
Short Introduction to Moral Philosophy, A (Hutcheson), 50–51
short-term orientation, 523
Sidney, Algernon, 80, 94–95, 107
Siems, Mathias, 518–19
Siete Partidas, Las, 206–7, 220, 286n.60, 295
Simitis, Spiros, 401n.213
Simpson, A.W.B., 171–72, 171n.127
Simpson, Sidney, 441–42
Singapore, cultural identity in, 456n.22
Single European Act (European Community), 446–47
Sing Sing prison, 200–1
SLADE project (Stanford), 425
slavery, 64, 68, 138n.251, 214–21
Small, Albion, 239n.64
Small, William, 51, 94
small-N research, 520
Smit, Hans, 395, 404
Smith, Adam, 101n.85, 333–34
Smith, Bruce, 44
Smith, Joseph, 32
Smith, Munroe, 253–54, 274n.8, 289, 294, 295n.101, 298–99, 299n.118
Smith, William, Jr., 52–53
Smithers, William, 291–92, 293, 302
social engineering model, 424–25, 444, 484–85
socialist legal systems, 437
social legal history, 6, 31–36, 38–40, 53–57
social libraries, 186n.223
social relations, relation between law and, 487
social science
  associations to comparative law in nineteenth century, 265–69
  and early twentieth century legal education, 303–6
  expositions, 269–72
  in postwar legal education, 441–47

Social Science Research Council, 31
Social Science Research Network (SSRN) eLibrary: Comparative Law, 473n.98
Society of Comparative Legislation (France), 265, 270, 271–72, 290–91, 302
Society of Comparative Legislation (London), 243
sociological jurisprudence, 262
  comparative legal sociology, 441–47
  in Germany, 259–60
  Roscoe Pound and, 26, 28–29, 305–6, 321n.222
Socratic method in law instruction, 232
Sodalitas law club, 74–75
Sohn, Louis (Ludwig), 426–27
Soochow Law School (Comparative Law School of China), 280, 281–84, 329
Source Books of Louisiana Law (Tucker), 153n.39
South Carolina
  codification of law, 195, 208
  colonial period, 57–58
Southern Law Quarterly, 310
Southern Law Review, 254
Southern Review, 182–83, 195–96
South Korea
  American legal transplants to, 350, 353–54, 419
  authoritarian economic development in, 488
  constitution of, 361–64
  other legal reforms in postwar period, 372–73
sovereignty
  popular, 116, 117–18, 120–21
  Wilson's views on, 275
Soviet Legal System, The (Hazard, Butler & Maggs), 406n.244
Soviet Union
  American hard line against, 351–52
  collapse of, 452
  commencement of Cold War, 350–51, 375–77
  in Korea, 353–54, 361
  law in, 381n.124, 406, 408, 442n.407
Spain
  Louisiana Purchase, 148–50
  transfer of Florida to United States, 150–51
Spanish-American War, 277–78, 418–19
Spanish law
  influence on American law, 34–36, 151, 153, 154–55
  and Louisiana Code of Practice, 206–7
  and slave laws in Louisiana, 220

Special Committee on Delay and Uncertainty in the Administration of Justice (ABA), 247
Special Committee on Uniformity of Procedure and Comparative Law (ABA), 243
Special Committee on Uniform State Laws (ABA), 250
specialized comparative law coursebooks, 408–15
Spekack, Edmund, 357n.31
Spirit of the Common Law, The (Pound), 25–26
Spirit of the Laws, The (Montesquieu), 105–7, 131n.220, 141–42
Spofford, Ainsworth, 244–45, 432
SSRN (Social Science Research Network) eLibrary: Comparative Law, 473n.98
Stair, James Dalrymple of (Lord Stair), 70
Stalin, Joseph, 350–51
Stammler, Rudolf, 282n.43
Stamp Act (1765), 74–75, 76n.160, 77, 131–32
Stanford Law School, 425, 488–89n.167, 489, 502–3
State, Law and Family (Glendon), 449
State, The (Wilson), 274–75
State House Yard Speech (Wilson), 116–17
State in Catholic Thought, The (Rommen), 337
state law libraries, 316–17
statist economics, 452
statutory form, common law crimes in, 199–200. *See also* codification
Stein, Eric, 413–15, 447, 473–74
Stein, Peter, 3n.14, 49–50
Steiner, Kurt, 368, 369
Steiner, Melchior, 70n.127
Stern, David, 385n.141, 392n.174
Stern, William, 428–29, 430–31
Stevens, Robert, 303
Stimson, Henry, 350–51, 352, 385n.140
Stocquart, Émile, 255
Stoicism, 94, 100
Stone, Ferdinand, 312, 404
Stone, Harlan, 298–99, 315, 341n.318, 385n.140, 460n.39
Stone, Julius, 441–42
Story, Joseph, 8, 13, 14–15, 145, 158, 159–60, 162–63, 164–65, 171–74, 178, 180, 182–83, 187–88, 189–90, 191–92, 208, 209–10, 440
Strahan, William, 47, 185
Strauss, Leo, 338
structural constitution, 108–9, 143
Studies in the Civil Law (Howe), 21–22, 258–59
study abroad programs, 482
Stuyvesant, Petrus, 58, 62

Suggested Post-Surrender Program for Germany, 350
Sumner, Charles, 178
Sun Yat-sen, 282–83
supranational cooperation in Western Europe, 373–79
supranational European law, 413–14
supranational integration through law, 446–47
Supreme Commander for the Allied Powers (SCAP), 352–53, 358–60, 367–72
Supreme Court, Japanese, 359–60n.39, 360
Supreme Court building, U.S., 297
surveys about law, 518–19
Suzuki, Yoshio, 368
Swedish Code of Judicial Procedure (Bruzelius & Ginsburg), 395n.192
Swift, Zephaniah, 171n.127
Swift v. Tyson (1842), 173–74
Swiss Civil Code, The (Shick), 292
Symeonides, Symeon, 441, 458n.28, 469, 470–72, 472n.92, 473, 475, 477
System des heutigen römischen Rechts (Savigny), 224
Szladits, Charles, 393, 401, 416–17, 428–30, 438

Tacitus, Cornelius, 102, 104–5, 114–15, 118, 138–39
Taft, William Howard, 238, 276–77, 277n.22, 279–80n.33
Tanenhaus, Joseph, 412–13
Tarde, Gabriel de, 323
Taylor, Hannis, 181n.196
Tellkampf, Louis, 210–11
territorial expansion
  in early twentieth century, 277–84
  in formative era, 146–56, 148f
terrorism, war against, 511–13
Terry, Henry, 248
Thaman, Stephen, 446
Thatcher, Margaret, 452n.4
Thayer, James, 266, 310, 343n.325
Theories of Law (Pound), 321n.222
Theory of Legislation (Bentham), 204–5
Theory of the Common Law, The (Walker), 16–17, 196–97
Thibaut, Anton, 264–65
thick rule of law, 496–97, 505
things, law of, 167
thin rule of law, 485, 495–97, 505
Third World Legal Studies journal, 422–23
Thomistic natural law, 333–38
Thompson, Seymour, 254

Thoughts on Government (Adams), 83n.196, 110, 111–12, 119
Three-Fifths Compromise (U.S. Constitution), 217–18
TI (Transparency International), 501n.222, 505–6
Tiedeman, Christopher, 8, 263–64
Tocqueville, Alexis de, 192, 203–4
tolerance, in colonial America, 60–62
Tomlins, Christopher, 40
Toshiba Library for Legal Research (Columbia), 409n.256
totalitarianism, 337–38
trade law unification efforts, 433–36
traditions, tenacity of, 461–67
Traité de la Volonté et de ses Effets (Destutt de Tracy), 101n.85
Transformation of American Law, 1780-1860, The (Horwitz), 33, 36–37
Transformation of American Law, 1870-1960, The (Horwitz), 36–37
Transformation of Family Law, The (Glendon), 449n.437
Transition to Modernity, The (Whitman), 198n.279
translation of legal materials
  in formative era, 179–82, 183–85
  in postwar twentieth century, 416
transnational constitutionalism, 492
transnational law firms, 268–69
transnational legal services, 479–84
transnational litigation, 441
Transparency International (TI), 501n.222, 505–6
Transylvania University Law Department, 165
Trautman, Donald T., 438n.387
Treatise on Obligations, A (Pothier), 183–84, 185
Treatise on Political Economy, A (Destutt de Tracy), 101n.85
Treatise on the Contract of Sale (Pothier), 185
Treatise on the Limitation of Police Power in the United States, A (Tiedeman), 263
treatises
  institutionalist, 166–71
  by Joseph Story, 171–74
Treaty of Fontainebleau (1762), 148–49
Treaty of Ghent (1815), 147n.7, 150
Treaty of Paris (1763), 35, 75–76, 148–49
Treaty of Paris (1783), 45–46, 147–48, 150–51
Treaty of Paris (1898), 277–78
Treaty of San Francisco (1951), 352–53
Trott, Nicholas, 56

Trott's Laws (colonial province of Carolina), 56
Trubek, David, 424n.326, 426
Truman, Harry, 350–54, 375–76
Truman Doctrine, 351–52
Trump, Donald, 508–9
Tucker, Henry St. George, 13
Tucker, John H., Jr., 153n.39, 381
Tucker, Nathan Beverly, 160–61
Tucker, St. George, 72n.137, 92, 162, 166–67, 169, 171, 190–91, 216, 218n.374
Tufts University Fletcher School of Law and Diplomacy, 389–90n.166
Tulane, Paul, 165–66
Tulane Law Review, 286, 310–12, 339, 341–42
Tulane University Law School
　early twentieth century, 310–12
　Eason Weinmann Center for International and Comparative Law, 404, 484
　establishment of university, 165–66
　Institute of Comparative Law, 312, 385, 404, 484
　2000 International Congress of Comparative Law, 470–71
Tunc, André, 387
Tunc, Suzanne, 387
Turnbull, George, 50n.31
Tushnet, Mark, 491, 492
twentieth century historiography, 22–39. *See also* early twentieth century; late twentieth century; postwar twentieth century
twenty-first century
　American Society of Comparative Law, 471–79
　challenges in, 508–17
　globalization of American legal institutions, 479–94
　historiography, 40–44
　initial comparative law reaction to globalization, 460–61
　interdisciplinary empirical comparative law, 518–25
　overview, 11–12, 40–44
　rule of law programs, 494–508
Tydings-McDuffie Act (1934), 279–80

UCLA Pacific Basin Law Journal, 415
umma (in Islam), 513, 514
U.N. *See* United Nations
uncertainty avoidance, 522–24
unification of law. *See also* codification
　American Law Institute and, 306–10
　early efforts related to, 250–51
　in postwar twentieth century, 432–37

Uniform Commercial Code (UCC), 433–34
Uniform Law Commission (ULC), 250–51, 306–7, 308, 433n.362, 434, 434n.368
Uniform Negotiable Instruments Law (NIL) of 1896, 250–51
Uniform Sales Act (1906), 434
United Kingdom. *See* British colonial period; English law; Great Britain
United Nations (U.N.)
　decade of development, 421
　Treaty of San Francisco, 352–53
　U.N. Charter, 444n.418
　war in Korea, 353–54
United Nations Commission on International Trade Law (UNCITRAL), 435, 436
United Nations Educational, Scientific, and Cultural Organization (UNESCO), 334n.286, 382, 397, 419
United States Court for China, 283–84
United States Law Journal and Civilian's Magazine, 177, 201n.293
United States v. Hudson and Goodwin (1812), 200n.287
Universal Congress of Lawyers and Jurists, 284–85, 287–89
universalism
　in constitutionalism, 491
　Huntington's critiques of, 454–56, 462
　as unacceptable domination, 464
universal law, 275. *See also* human rights; natural law
universities. *See also* academic comparative law; law schools
　academic law libraries, 186, 244, 316–20, 318t, 319t
　German, 229–31
　German teachers at American, 229
　law schools at, 161–66
　Nazis and anti-Semitism at American, 326–31
　teaching Roman law in late nineteenth century, 251–54
University of California-Irvine, 484
University of Chicago Law School, 239, 403n.226
University of Illinois, 494
University of Louisiana law department, 165–66
University of Michigan Law School, 320
University of the Philippines, 278–79, 289n.71
University of Virginia, 412
University of Washington, 257, 409–10
University of Windsor Law Faculty, 483–84
University of Wisconsin Law School, 239

unwritten law, 16. *See also* common law; equity
Upham, Frank, 504n.236
U.S. Agency for International Development (USAID), 376n.107, 417–18, 444
  decade of development, 421
  rule of law programs, 501–2, 503, 504
  SLADE, 425
U.S. Constitution. *See* Constitution, U.S.
U.S. Department of Commerce, 297–98
U.S. Information Agency, 517n.281
U.S. Supreme Court building, 297
utilitarians, 259

Vance, John, 286n.60, 295, 315, 339–40, 343n.325
Vandenburg, Arthur, 351–52
Van Schaack, Peter, 53n.48
Vattel, Emer de, 94–95
Versailles Treaty (1919), 307
Versteeg, Mila, 520
veto, federal, 126
vice-admiralty courts, 75–77
"Vices of the Political System of the United States" (Madison), 125–26
Vinogradoff, Paul, 295n.101
Virgil (Vergilius Maro), 103–4
Virginia
  Bill for Establishing Religious Freedom, 86–87, 123–24
  Bill for Proportioning Crimes and Punishments in Cases heretofore Capital, 101n.86
  colonial period, 57–58, 64
  in early republic, 123–24
Virginia Constitution, 97n.60, 97n.61, 123, 137
Virginia Declaration of Rights, 96–97, 137, 138–41
Virginia Plan, 103, 115–16, 126
Visigothic Code, The (Scott), 292, 294–95
Vögelin, Eric, 338
Volksverein für das katholische Deutschland (Germany), 336–37
Von Mehren, Arthur, 364–65n.61, 382, 383–84, 385n.141, 387, 391–92, 392n.174, 399–400, 403–4, 406–7, 409–10, 417–18, 423, 424n.325, 434–35, 437, 438, 458n.28, 467–68, 469, 473–74
Voyage du Jeune Anacharsis en Grèce (Barthélemy), 128

Waelbroeck, Michel, 414
Wagner, Wenceslas, 388–89, 399–400, 399n.208
Walker, James, 16–17, 191, 196–97

Walker, Timothy, 15–16, 164, 208–9
Walnut Street jail (Philadelphia), 200
Walsh, William, 29
Walton, Clifford, 291n.76
Walz, William, 289
Wambaugh, Eugene, 238
Wang Chung-hui, 285–86
Ward, Nathaniel, 55n.59
Warner, Michael, 89–90
Warnkönig, L.A., 181n.193
War of 1812, 146–47
War on Terror, 511–13
Warren, Charles, 81–82n.192
Warren, Earl, 349, 446
Washington, George, 50n.29, 87n.12, 109n.121, 132
Washington Consensus, 452
Washington University Law Department, 257, 409–10
Watson, Alan, 41, 167–68, 217, 464–65
Webb, James, 289n.72
Weber, Max, 344–45, 442–43, 448–49
Webster, Timothy, 486–87
Weisberg, Morris, 406
Weiss, André, 298, 300n.125
Welke, Barbara, 40
Werro, Franz, 477–78
West, John, 303
Western Europe, federalism and antitrust reform for, 373–79
Western Jurist periodical, 257
Western Law Journal, 164
Western Penitentiary (Pittsburgh), 200
West Germany, 351–52, 375, 376–77. *See also* Germany/German law
West Publishing Company, 303
Wetherill, Charles, 291–92
Weyrauch, Walter, 403n.225
WGI (Worldwide Governance Indicators), World Bank, 505–6, 508
Wheeler, Albert, 252
Whig history, xvn.3
White, G. Edward, 37n.192, 40, 66
White, Morton, 97n.63, 98–99
Whitman, James, 86n.6, 198n.279, 467, 476n.111
Whitney, Courtney, 358–59, 369n.79
Why Did the Revolutionary Lawyers Confuse Custom and Reason? (Whitman), 86n.5
Wiecek, William, 38, 216, 218–19
Wigmore, John H., 9, 22n.94, 236–37, 238, 255–56, 286–87, 289, 291, 293, 298n.116, 301–2, 307n.154, 309, 310–11, 319–20, 323–26, 339–40, 341–42, 346

William III (King of England), 137n.244, 139
Williams, Roger, 63
Williston, Samuel, 236–37, 250–51, 252, 255–56, 292, 307n.154, 309, 434
Wills, Garry, 98–99
Wilson, Bird, 119n.162
Wilson, James, 13, 51–52, 93, 98, 115–21, 141, 143, 144, 162n.78, 217–18
Wilson, Woodrow, 9, 243, 274–78, 279–80, 307n.154
Winterer, Caroline, 214n.360
Wise, Edward, 416, 476n.110
Witherspoon, John, 51, 122–23
Witt, John, 306n.151, 321n.221
WJP (World Justice Project), 506–7
Wolff, Christian, 225
women and law, 394–95
Women's Rights Project (ACLU), 396n.195
Wood, Gordon, 5–6, 30–31, 107–8
Wood, Stephen, 391, 469n.78
Wood, Thomas, 46–47, 48, 52–53, 73, 76–77
Woodward, C. Vann, 2n.6
Woolsey, Theodore, 194n.258, 231–32, 234–35, 266
Workman, James, 177
World Bank, 497, 498–501, 505–6, 508, 523–24
World Justice Project (WJP), 506–7
World's Fair, Centennial Exposition (1904), 287–89
World's Fair, Columbian Exposition (1893), 269–70
World Values Survey, 524–25
Worldwide Governance Indicators (WGI), World Bank, 505–6, 508
Wu, John (Wu Jingxiong), 282–83, 329
Wyman, David S., 331n.273
Wythe, George, 83n.196, 92–93, 94, 100–1, 121, 144, 162, 169, 190–91

Xi Jinping, 515, 516, 517

Yale College/University/Law School, 231–32, 234–35, 327, 330
  degree programs for foreign students, 417–18
  doctoral degrees, 229n.23
  early law education at, 162–63
  in early twentieth century, 304
  law and development approach, 444
  Roman law at, 251–52
Yale Law Journal, 255–56
Yeates, Jasper, 46–47
Yiannopoulos, A.N., 403n.225, 438n.386, 471n.84
Yirush, Craig, 64–65
Yntema, Hessel, 9, 294n.96, 304–6, 308, 310, 333, 342–43, 345, 382–83, 383n.133, 384, 385n.141, 386–87, 388, 392, 393–94, 398n.201, 406, 415–16, 418, 419–20, 433n.359, 434–35
Young Country Clerk's Collection (Pastorius), 67–68
Younger Comparativists Committee (YCC), ASCL, 473–74, 477–78, 478n.119
Yuan Shikai, 281
Yu Chin-o, 363

Zachariae, Heinrich, 230
Zachariae, Karl, 180n.184, 264–65
Zainaldin, Jamil, 37–39
Zeitschrift für ausländisches und internationales Privatrecht journal, 307–8
Zeitschrift für geschichtliche Rechtswissenschaft journal, 224
Zekoll, Joachim, 469n.80
Zhou Enlai, 409
Zimmermann, Reinhard, 3n.14
Zürn, Michael, 488–89n.167
Zweiben, Beverly, 98n.67